studysync®

Reading & Writing Companion

Everyone Loves a Mystery

What attracts us to the mysterious?

studysync.com

Send all inquiries to:
BookheadEd Learning, LLC
610 Daniel Young Drive
Sonoma, CA 95476

ISBN 978-1-94-469585-9

4 5 6 LMN 24 23 22 21 20

B

Student Guide

Getting Started

Welcome to the **StudySync** Reading & Writing Companion! In this book, you will find a collection of readings based on the theme of the unit you are studying. As you work through the readings, you will be asked to answer questions and perform a variety of tasks designed to help you closely analyze and understand each text selection. Read on for an explanation of each section of this book.

Close Reading and Writing Routine

In each unit, you will read texts that share a common theme, despite their different genres, time periods, and authors. Each reading encourages a closer look through questions and a short writing assignment.

1 Introduction

An Introduction to each text provides historical context for your reading as well as information about the author. You will also learn about the genre of the text and the year in which it was written.

2 Notes

Many times, while working through the activities after each text, you will be asked to **annotate** or **make annotations** about what you are reading. This means that you should highlight or underline words in the text and use the "Notes" column to make comments or jot down any questions you have. You may also want to note any unfamiliar vocabulary words here.

You will also see sample student annotations to go along with the Skill lesson for that text.

First Read

During your first reading of each selection, you should just try to get a general idea of the content and message of the reading. Don't worry if there are parts you don't understand or words that are unfamiliar to you. You'll have an opportunity later to dive deeper into the text.

Think Questions

These questions will ask you to start thinking critically about the text, asking specific questions about its purpose, and making connections to your prior knowledge and reading experiences. To answer these questions, you should go back to the text and draw upon specific evidence to support your responses. You will also begin to explore some of the more challenging vocabulary words in the selection.

Skills

Each Skill includes two parts: Checklist and Your Turn. In the Checklist, you will learn the process for analyzing the text. The model student annotations in the text provide examples of how you might make your own notes following the instructions in the Checklist. In the Your Turn, you will use those same instructions to practice the skill.

First Read

Read "The Tell-Tale Heart." After you read, complete the Think Questions below.

THINK QUESTIONS

1. Write two or three sentences explaining how the narrator feels about the old man and why he decides to murder him.

2. Does the narrator seem trustworthy as he gives his account of the events in the story? Cite evidence from the text to explain your opinions.

3. What sound does the narrator hear at the end of the story that causes him to confess to the murder? Provide evidence to support your inference.

4. Find the word **sufficient** in paragraph 3 of "The Tell-Tale Heart." Use context clues in the surrounding sentences, as well as the sentence in which the word appears, to determine the word's meaning. Write your definition here and identify clues that helped you figure out its meaning.

5. Use context clues to determine the meaning of **sagacity** as it is used in paragraph 4 of "The Tell-Tale Heart." Write your definition here and identify clues that helped you figure out its meaning. Then check the meaning in a dictionary.

Skill: Language, Style, and Audience

Use the Checklist to analyze Language, Style, and Audience in "The Tell-Tale Heart." Refer to the sample student annotations about Language, Style, and Audience in the text.

CHECKLIST FOR LANGUAGE, STYLE, AND AUDIENCE

In order to determine an author's style, do the following:

✓ identify and define any unfamiliar words or phrases

✓ use context, including the meanings of surrounding words and phrases

✓ note possible reactions to the author's word choice

✓ examine your reaction to the author's word choice

✓ identify any analogies, or comparisons in which one part of the comparison helps explain the other

To analyze the impact of specific word choice on meaning and tone, ask the following questions:

✓ How did your understanding of the language change during your analysis?

✓ How do the writer's word choices impact or create meaning in the text?

✓ How do the writer's word choices impact or create a specific tone in the text?

✓ How could various audiences interpret this language? What different possible emotional responses can you list?

✓ What analogies do you see? Where might an analogy have clarified meaning or created a specific tone?

YOUR TURN

1. What effect do the punctuation choices in paragraphs 9 and 10 have on the tone?

   ○ A. The dashes and exclamation marks reveal that the narrator is losing control.
   ○ B. The italics make it clear that the narrator's words aren't to be trusted.
   ○ C. The semicolons introduce a formal tone into an informal speech.
   ○ D. The frequent questions reveal the narrator's attempt to engage the reader.

2. Which phrase from the passage most clearly suggests the narrator's disturbed mental state at the end of the story?

   ○ A. "but I talked more fluently"
   ○ B. "Why would they not be gone?"
   ○ C. "It grew louder—louder—louder!"
   ○ D. "And still the men chatted pleasantly"

The Tell-Tale HEART studysync●

Close Read

⑥

Reread "The Tell-Tale Heart." As you reread, complete the Skills Focus questions below. Then use your answers and annotations from the questions to help you complete the Write activity.

◎ SKILLS FOCUS

1. What inferences can you draw about the narrator's mental state based on the author's word choices?

2. What does the author imply about the narrator's mental state through the descriptions of the narrator's feelings about how the old man looks at him with the "eye of a vulture"?

3. Identify word choices the author uses to indicate that the narrator might be losing his mind. How do the word choices and tone indicate the narrator's troubled mental state?

4. What language does the author use to make the narrator seem untrustworthy? How does this language reveal the narrator's dishonest nature?

5. Explain how the author uses the narrator's personality to create a feeling of mystery for the reader.

✎ WRITE

⑦ LITERARY ANALYSIS: Can the narrator of "The Tell-Tale Heart" be trusted? Consider the author's word choice, tone, and description of events as you draw conclusions about the narrator's state of mind. Be sure to support your ideas with evidence from the text.

12 ▭ Reading & Writing Companion

Inside the House

DRAMA

Introduction

❝ "Inside the House" tells the story of two teenage siblings who spend a stormy night alone telling scary stories. In this scene from the play, Cristina and Fernando learn just how scary a story can be when their real life starts to match a tale they've told. The author uses dialogue, sound effects, and foreshadowing to build suspense.

⊽ VOCABULARY

⑧

predictable
easily guessed or expected

anxious
nervous or afraid

sarcastic
meaning the opposite of what is said to express humor, irritation, or meanness

embarrassed
feeling foolish or ashamed

---

⑥ Close Read & Skills Focus

After you have completed the First Read, you will be asked to go back and read the text more closely and critically. Before you begin your Close Read, you should read through the Skills Focus to get an idea of the concepts you will want to focus on during your second reading. You should work through the Skills Focus by making annotations, highlighting important concepts, and writing notes or questions in the "Notes" column. Depending on instructions from your teacher, you may need to respond online or use a separate piece of paper to start expanding on your thoughts and ideas.

⑦ Write

Your study of each selection will end with a writing assignment. For this assignment, you should use your notes, annotations, personal ideas, and answers to both the Think and Skills Focus Questions. Be sure to read the prompt carefully and address each part of it in your writing.

⑧ English Language Learner

The English Language Learner texts focus on improving language proficiency. You will practice learning strategies and skills in individual and group activities to become better readers, writers, and speakers.

Extended Writing Project and Grammar

This is your opportunity to use genre characteristics and craft to compose meaningful, longer written works exploring the theme of each unit. You will draw information from your readings, research, and own life experiences to complete the assignment.

1 Writing Project

After you have read all of the unit text selections, you will move on to a writing project. Each project will guide you through the process of writing your essay. Student models will provide guidance and help you organize your thoughts. One unit ends with an **Extended Oral Project** which will give you an opportunity to develop your oral language and communication skills.

2 Writing Process Steps

There are four steps in the writing process: Plan, Draft, Revise, and Edit and Publish. During each step, you will form and shape your writing project, and each lesson's peer review will give you the chance to receive feedback from your peers and teacher.

3 Writing Skills

Each Skill lesson focuses on a specific strategy or technique that you will use during your writing project. Each lesson presents a process for applying the skill to your own work and gives you the opportunity to practice it to improve your writing.

Everyone Loves a Mystery

What attracts us to the mysterious?

Genre Focus: FICTION

Texts

 Paired Reading

Extended Writing Project and Grammar

English Language Learner Resources

Unit 1: Everyone Loves a Mystery

What attracts us to the mysterious?

NELLIE BLY

Reporter Nellie Bly (1864–1922) feigned insanity to gain admittance to the Blackwell's Island Insane Asylum in New York City, the subject of her 1886 exposé, which began as a series of newspaper articles and was eventually published as a book, *Ten Days in a Mad-House* (1887). Her report on the inhuman conditions she encountered there—from mandatory ice baths to confinement in small, damp, vermin-infested rooms—resulted in increased government oversight and improved overall conditions. Bly's pioneering tactic developed into modern investigative journalism.

PAUL LAURENCE DUNBAR

In his lifetime, Paul Laurence Dunbar (1872–1906) achieved national recognition for his writing reflecting black life in turn-of-the-century America. Known for his innovative use of dialect in his poems, his first collection of poems, *Oak and Ivy* (1893), was written in dialect and in standard English. It includes "Sympathy," one of his most popular poems addressing the plight of black people in American society, which contains the famous line "I know why the caged bird sings," the inspiration for the title of Maya Angelou's autobiography.

RUDOLPH FISHER

Considered one of the central literary figures of the Harlem Renaissance, Rudolph Fisher (1897–1934) was also a practicing physician and esteemed orator. Much of his work dealt with the adjustment of Southern black migrants to the urban enclave of Harlem. His second novel, *The Conjure-Man Dies* (1932), is regarded as the first detective novel by an African American author. Fisher published at least two novels and two short stories before his untimely death at the age of thirty-seven.

NEIL GAIMAN

A self-described "feral child who was raised in libraries," Neil Gaiman (b. 1960) devoured fantasy and science-fiction books from a young age. Best known for his novella *Coraline* (2002), he is credited with being one of the first creators of modern comics and an author of genre works that refuse to stay true to their genres. Gaiman's *The Graveyard Book* (2008), conceived of as a take on Kipling's Mowgli stories, involves an orphaned toddler finding a safe haven in the local graveyard.

ALFRED HITCHCOCK

British film director Alfred Hitchcock (1899–1980) earned the nickname "The Master of Suspense" over the course of his long and prolific career. His distinct directorial style in films like *Rear Window* (1954), *Psycho* (1960), and *The Birds* (1963) had a lasting impact on cinema. Film critic Peter Conrad wrote that in his work, "Hitchcock diagnosed the discontents that chafe and rankle beneath the decorum of civilization."

SHIRLEY JACKSON

Called the master of the creepy story, Shirley Jackson (1916–1965) was interested in witchcraft, she writes, as "a way of embracing and channeling female power at a time when women in America often had little control over their lives." Her stories and novels of the supernatural included the well-known short story "The Lottery" and the best-selling novel *The Haunting of Hill House* (1959). When the former was first published in The New Yorker in 1948, it generated the largest volume of mail ever received by the magazine, most of it hateful.

W.W. JACOBS

English short-story writer and novelist W. W. Jacobs (1863–1943) grew up in a house on a River Thames wharf. His is best known for his horror story, "The Monkey's Paw," published in his 1902 collection, *The Lady of the Barge*. In the story, a couple is presented with a magical monkey's paw from India. Set in Victorian England, the ensuing tale of superstition and terror unfolds in a domestic setting. Jacobs's first collection had immediate success and he published more than a dozen volumes in his lifetime.

WALTER DEAN MYERS

American children's book author Walter Dean Myers (1937–2014) wrote books that reflected the lives of young people he met visiting schools and prisons around the country, whose life experiences often resonated with his own. Although he wrote over a hundred books in his lifetime, he is best known for *Monster*, his 1999 drama about a teenager who writes a movie script while incarcerated. This stylistically innovative work alternates between suspenseful courtroom scenes and introspective journal entries.

EDGAR ALLEN POE

Widely regarded as one of the foremost progenitors of modern Gothic literature, Edgar Allan Poe (1809–1849) was born the son of two actors in Boston, but grew up in foster care in Richmond, Virginia. Much of his work, especially his best-known horror tales, achieve a psychological intensity through the use of a first-person narrator. Poe had written numerous short stories, poems, and works of criticism by the time he died at the age of forty from suspected alcohol poisoning.

JOHN FLEISCHMAN

John Fleischman (b. 1948) began writing non-fiction for young adults when he noticed how engrossed a group of adolescents was looking at a scientific display of the skull of Phineas Gage. The subject of Fleischman's first book, Gage was a construction foreman who became an important case study in the field of neurology when he miraculously survived a freak accident. Fleischman has also published three non-fiction books about the history of his adopted city, Cincinnati, Ohio, and has written articles for numerous science magazines.

The Tell-Tale Heart

FICTION
Edgar Allan Poe
1843

Introduction

The works of Edgar Allan Poe (1809–1849) set the standard for Gothic fiction. "The Tell-Tale Heart" is one of his most famous and widely read stories. Convinced that officers at his house can hear the dead man's heart beating through the floorboard, Poe's narrator confesses to killing an old man in his care, despite the fact he bore the man no grudge. In a dramatic monologue of increasing volume and intensity—as well as mental disintegration—the "perfectly sane" murderer painstakingly describes how the "vulture eye" of his victim drove him to commit the horrible act.

"You fancy me mad. Madmen know nothing. But you should have seen me."

NOTES

1   True!—nervous—very, very dreadfully nervous I had been and am; but why will you say that I am mad? The disease had sharpened my senses—not destroyed—not dulled them. Above all was the sense of hearing **acute.** I heard all things in the heaven and in the earth. I heard many things in hell. How, then, am I mad? Hearken! and observe how healthily—how calmly I can tell you the whole story.

2   It is impossible to say how first the idea entered my brain; but once conceived, it haunted me day and night. Object there was none. Passion there was none. I loved the old man. He had never wronged me. He had never given me insult. For his gold I had no desire. I think it was his eye! yes, it was this! He had the eye of a vulture—a pale blue eye, with a film over it. Whenever it fell upon me, my blood ran cold; and so by degrees—very gradually—I made up my mind to take the life of the old man, and thus rid myself of the eye forever.

Hooded vulture

3   Now this is the point. You fancy me mad. Madmen know nothing. But you should have seen me. You should have seen how wisely I proceeded—with what caution—with what foresight—with what dissimulation I went to work! I was never kinder to the old man than during the whole week before I killed him. And every night, about midnight, I turned the latch of his door and opened it—oh so gently! And then, when I had made an opening **sufficient** for my head, I put in a dark lantern, all closed, closed, that no light shone out, and then I thrust in my head. Oh, you would have laughed to see how cunningly I thrust it in! I moved it slowly—very, very slowly, so that I might not disturb the old man's sleep. It took me an hour to place my whole head within the opening so far that I could see him as he lay upon his bed. Ha! would a madman have been so wise as this, And then, when my head was well in the room, I undid the lantern cautiously-oh, so cautiously—cautiously (for the hinges creaked)—I undid it just so much that a single thin ray fell upon the vulture eye. And this I did for seven long nights—every night just at

Skill:
Text-Dependent
Responses

The narrator claims to love the old man. So why does he want to kill him because of his eye? That's crazy. The narrator is obsessed!

Skill:
Textual Evidence

The last line does not make sense, since he says in the previous paragraph that he liked the old man. How can the narrator be a sane, kind person like he claims to be? If someone kills a person that they like, it usually means they are neither kind nor sane.

NOTES

midnight—but I found the eye always closed; and so it was impossible to do the work; for it was not the old man who vexed me, but his Evil Eye. And every morning, when the day broke, I went boldly into the chamber, and spoke courageously to him, calling him by name in a hearty tone, and inquiring how he has passed the night. So you see he would have been a very **profound** old man, indeed, to suspect that every night, just at twelve, I looked in upon him while he slept.

4   Upon the eighth night I was more than usually cautious in opening the door. A watch's minute hand moves more quickly than did mine. Never before that night had I felt the extent of my own powers—of my **sagacity.** I could scarcely contain my feelings of triumph. To think that there I was, opening the door, little by little, and he not even to dream of my secret deeds or thoughts. I fairly chuckled at the idea; and perhaps he heard me; for he moved on the bed suddenly, as if startled. Now you may think that I drew back—but no. His room was as black as pitch with the thick darkness, (for the shutters were close fastened, through fear of robbers,) and so I knew that he could not see the opening of the door, and I kept pushing it on steadily, steadily. I had my head in, and was about to open the lantern, when my thumb slipped upon the tin fastening, and the old man sprang up in bed, crying out—"Who's there?" I kept quite still and said nothing. For a whole hour I did not move a muscle, and in the meantime I did not hear him lie down. He was still sitting up in the bed listening;—just as I have done, night after night, hearkening to the death watches in the wall.

5   Presently I heard a slight groan, and I knew it was the groan of mortal terror. It was not a groan of pain or of grief—oh, no!—it was the low stifled sound that arises from the bottom of the soul when overcharged with awe. I knew the sound well. Many a night, just at midnight, when all the world slept, it has welled up from my own bosom, deepening, with its dreadful echo, the terrors that distracted me. I say I knew it well. I knew what the old man felt, and pitied him, although I chuckled at heart. I knew that he had been lying awake ever since the first slight noise, when he had turned in the bed. His fears had been ever since growing upon him. He had been trying to fancy them causeless, but could not. He had been saying to himself—"It is nothing but the wind in the chimney—it is only a mouse crossing the floor," or "It is merely a cricket which has made a single chirp." Yes, he had been trying to comfort himself with these suppositions: but he had found all in vain. All in vain; because Death, in approaching him had stalked with his black shadow before him, and enveloped the victim. And it was the mournful influence of the unperceived shadow that caused him to feel—although he neither saw nor heard—to feel the presence of my head within the room.

6   When I had waited a long time, very patiently, without hearing him lie down, I resolved to open a little—a very, very little crevice in the lantern. So I opened

it—you cannot imagine how stealthily, stealthily—until, at length a simple dim ray, like the thread of the spider, shot from out the crevice and fell full upon the vulture eye. It was open—wide, wide open—and I grew furious as I gazed upon it. I saw it with perfect distinctness—all a dull blue, with a hideous veil over it that chilled the very marrow in my bones; but I could see nothing else of the old man's face or person: for I had directed the ray as if by instinct, precisely upon the damned spot. And have I not told you that what you mistake for madness is but over-acuteness of the sense?—now, I say, there came to my ears a low, dull, quick sound, such as a watch makes when enveloped in cotton. I knew that sound well, too. It was the beating of the old man's heart. It increased my fury, as the beating of a drum stimulates the soldier into courage.

7 But even yet I refrained and kept still. I scarcely breathed. I held the lantern motionless. I tried how steadily I could maintain the ray upon the eye. Meantime the hellish tattoo of the heart increased. It grew quicker and quicker, and louder and louder every instant. The old man's terror must have been extreme! It grew louder, I say, louder every moment!—do you mark me well I have told you that I am nervous: so I am. And now at the dead hour of the night, amid the dreadful silence of that old house, so strange a noise as this excited me to uncontrollable terror. Yet, for some minutes longer I refrained and stood still. But the beating grew louder, louder! I thought the heart must burst. And now a new anxiety seized me—the sound would be heard by a neighbour! The old man's hour had come! With a loud yell, I threw open the lantern and leaped into the room. He shrieked once—once only. In an instant I dragged him to the floor, and pulled the heavy bed over him. I then smiled gaily, to find the deed so far done. But, for many minutes, the heart beat on with a muffled sound. This, however, did not vex me; it would not be heard through the wall. At length it ceased. The old man was dead. I removed the bed and examined the corpse. Yes, he was stone, stone dead. I placed my hand upon the heart and held it there many minutes. There was no pulsation. He was stone dead. His eye would trouble me no more.

8 If still you think me mad, you will think so no longer when I describe the wise precautions I took for the concealment of the body. The night waned, and I worked hastily, but in silence. First of all I dismembered the corpse. I cut off the head and the arms and the legs. I then took up three planks from the flooring of the chamber, and deposited all between the scantlings. I then replaced the boards so cleverly, so cunningly, that no human eye—not even his—could have detected any thing wrong. There was nothing to wash out—no stain of any kind—no blood-spot whatever. I had been too wary for that. A tub had caught all—ha! ha! When I had made an end of these labors, it was four o'clock—still dark as midnight. As the bell sounded the hour, there came a knocking at the street door. I went down to open it with a light heart,—for what had I now to fear? There entered three men, who introduced themselves,

Skill:
Language, Style, and Audience

The narrator is still trying to convince us he's sane. The author uses words like "wise," "cleverly," and "cunningly" to describe the narrator's actions. But he's talking about hiding the body of a person he just murdered! We can't trust him. When he laughs at his own cleverness in hiding the body, he seems mad, like a killer in a scary movie.

with perfect suavity, as officers of the police. A shriek had been heard by a neighbour during the night; suspicion of foul play had been aroused; information had been lodged at the police office, and they (the officers) had been deputed to search the premises. I smiled,—for what had I to fear? I bade the gentlemen welcome. The shriek, I said, was my own in a dream. The old man, I mentioned, was absent in the country. I took my visitors all over the house. I bade them search—search well. I led them, at length, to his chamber. I showed them his treasures, secure, undisturbed. In the enthusiasm of my confidence, I brought chairs into the room, and desired them here to rest from their fatigues, while I myself, in the wild **audacity** of my perfect triumph, placed my own seat upon the very spot beneath which reposed the corpse of the victim.

9   The officers were satisfied. My manner had convinced them. I was singularly at ease. They sat, and while I answered cheerily, they chatted of familiar things. But, ere long, I felt myself getting pale and wished them gone. My head ached, and I fancied a ringing in my ears: but still they sat and still chatted. The ringing became more distinct:—It continued and became more distinct: I talked more freely to get rid of the feeling: but it continued and gained definiteness—until, at length, I found that the noise was not within my ears. No doubt I now grew very pale;—but I talked more fluently, and with a heightened voice. Yet the sound increased—and what could I do? It was a low, dull, quick sound—much such a sound as a watch makes when enveloped in cotton. I gasped for breath—and yet the officers heard it not. I talked more quickly—more **vehemently;** but the noise steadily increased. I arose and argued about trifles, in a high key and with violent gesticulations; but the noise steadily increased. Why would they not be gone? I paced the floor to and fro with heavy strides, as if excited to fury by the observations of the men—but the noise steadily increased. Oh God! what could I do? I foamed—I raved—I swore! I swung the chair upon which I had been sitting, and grated it upon the boards, but the noise arose over all and continually increased. It grew louder—louder—louder! And still the men chatted pleasantly, and smiled. Was it possible they heard not? Almighty God!—no, no! They heard!—they suspected!—they knew!—they were making a mockery of my horror!-this I thought, and this I think. But anything was better than this agony! Anything was more tolerable than this derision! I could bear those hypocritical smiles no longer! I felt that I must scream or die! and now—again!—hark! louder! louder! louder! louder!

10   "Villains!" I shrieked, "dissemble no more! I admit the deed!—tear up the planks! here, here!—It is the beating of his hideous heart!"

Skill:
Text Dependent Responses

Use the Checklist to analyze Text Dependent Responses in "The Tell-Tale Heart." Refer to the sample student annotations about Text-Dependent Responses in the text.

••• CHECKLIST FOR TEXT DEPENDENT RESPONSES

In order to cite textual evidence that most strongly supports an analysis, consider the following:

✓ details from the text to make a strong inference or draw a strong conclusion

✓ read carefully and consider why an author gives particular details and information

- think about what you already know, and use your own knowledge and experiences to help you figure out what the author does not state directly

- cite textual evidence, or the specific words, phrases, sentences, or paragraphs that led you to make an inference

✓ details to support your ideas and opinions about a text

✓ explicit evidence of a character's feelings or motivations, or the reasons behind an historical event in a nonfiction text

- explicit evidence is stated directly in the text and must be cited accurately to strongly support a text-dependent answer or analysis

To cite the textual evidence that most strongly supports an analysis, consider the following questions:

✓ What types of textual evidence can I use to support an analysis of a text?

✓ What explicit evidence can I use to support my analysis?

✓ If I infer things in the text that the author does not state directly, what evidence from the text, along with my own knowledge, can I use to support my analysis?

✓ How do I know that I've used textual evidence that offers the strongest support for my analysis?

Please note that excerpts and passages in the StudySync® library and this workbook are intended as touchstones to generate interest in an author's work. The excerpts and passages do not substitute for the reading of entire texts, and StudySync® strongly recommends that students seek out and purchase the whole literary or informational work in order to experience it as the author intended. Links to online resellers are available in our digital library. In addition, complete works may be ordered through an authorized reseller by filling out and returning to StudySync® the order form enclosed in this workbook.

Reading & Writing
Companion

5

Skill:
Text Dependent Responses

Read the second Think question from the First Read lesson for "The Tell-Tale Heart" and answer the follow-up question below. Then, complete the chart by deciding which evidence from the text reveals when the narrator is trustworthy or untrustworthy.

⟳ YOUR TURN

Follow-Up Question

Does the narrator seem trustworthy as he gives his account of the events in the story? Cite textual evidence to explain your opinions.

	Textual Evidence Options
A	"Yet, for some minutes longer I refrained and stood still."
B	"You should have seen how wisely I proceeded—with what caution—with what foresight—with what dissimulation I went to work!"
C	"Never before that night had I felt the extent of my own powers—of my sagacity."
D	"I moved it slowly—very, very slowly, so that I might not disturb the old man's sleep."
E	". . . because Death, in approaching him, had stalked with his black shadow before him and enveloped the victim."
F	"Above all was the sense of hearing acute. I heard all things in the heaven and in the earth."

Trustworthy	Untrustworthy

First Read

Read "The Tell-Tale Heart." After you read, complete the Think Questions below.

 THINK QUESTIONS

1. Write two or three sentences explaining how the narrator feels about the old man and why he decides to murder him.

2. Does the narrator seem trustworthy as he gives his account of the events in the story? Cite evidence from the text to explain your opinions.

3. What sound does the narrator hear at the end of the story that causes him to confess to the murder? Provide evidence to support your inference.

4. Find the word **sufficient** in paragraph 3 of "The Tell-Tale Heart." Use context clues in the surrounding sentences, as well as the sentence in which the word appears, to determine the word's meaning. Write your definition here and identify clues that helped you figure out its meaning.

5. Use context clues to determine the meaning of **sagacity** as it is used in paragraph 4 of "The Tell-Tale Heart." Write your definition here and identify clues that helped you figure out its meaning. Then check the meaning in a dictionary.

Please note that excerpts and passages in the StudySync® library and this workbook are intended as touchstones to generate interest in an author's work. The excerpts and passages do not substitute for the reading of entire texts, and StudySync® strongly recommends that students seek out and purchase the whole literary or informational work in order to experience it as the author intended. Links to online resellers are available in our digital library. In addition, complete works may be ordered through an authorized reseller by filling out and returning to StudySync® the order form enclosed in this workbook.

Reading & Writing Companion   **7**

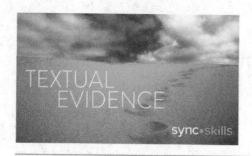

Skill:
Textual Evidence

Use the Checklist to analyze Textual Evidence in "The Tell-Tale Heart." Refer to the sample student annotations about Textual Evidence in the text.

••• CHECKLIST FOR TEXTUAL EVIDENCE

In order to support an analysis by citing textual evidence that is explicitly stated in the text, do the following:

- ✓ read the text closely and critically

- ✓ identify what the text says explicitly

- ✓ find the most relevant textual evidence that supports your analysis

- ✓ consider why an author explicitly states specific details and information

- ✓ cite the specific words, phrases, sentences, or paragraphs from the text that support your analysis

- ✓ cite evidence from the text that most strongly supports your analysis

In order to interpret implicit meanings in a text by making inferences, do the following:

- ✓ combine information directly stated in the text with your own knowledge, experiences, and observations

- ✓ cite the specific words, phrases, sentences, or paragraphs from the text that support this inference

In order to cite textual evidence to support an analysis of what the text says explicitly, as well as inferences drawn from the text, consider the following questions:

- ✓ Have I read the text closely and critically?

- ✓ What inferences am I making about the text? What textual evidence am I using to support these inferences?

- ✓ Am I quoting the evidence from the text correctly?

- ✓ Does my textual evidence logically relate to my analysis?

- ✓ What textual evidence most strongly supports your analysis?

Copyright © BookheadEd Learning, LLC

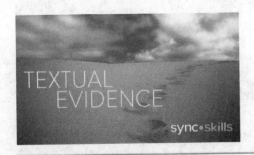

Skill:
Textual Evidence

Reread paragraphs 3, 8, and 9 of "The Tell-Tale Heart." Then, using the Checklist instructions on the previous page, complete the chart below by writing the explicit and implicit meaning of each paragraph. The first one is done for you.

🔄 YOUR TURN

Text	Explicit Meaning	Implicit Meaning
And every morning, when the day broke, I went boldly into the chamber, and spoke courageously to him, calling him by name in a hearty tone, and inquiring how he has passed the night.	The narrator speaks to the old man every morning, asking him how he slept the previous night.	The narrator is trying to figure out whether or not the old man heard the narrator spying on him the previous night.
There was nothing to wash out—no stain of any kind—no blood-spot whatever. I had been too wary for that. A tub had caught all—ha! ha!		
The officers were satisfied. My manner had convinced them. I was singularly at ease. They sat, and while I answered cheerily, they chatted of familiar things. But, ere long, I felt myself getting pale and wished them gone.		

Please note that excerpts and passages in the StudySync® library and this workbook are intended as touchstones to generate interest in an author's work. The excerpts and passages do not substitute for the reading of entire texts, and StudySync® strongly recommends that students seek out and purchase the whole literary or informational work in order to experience it as the author intended. Links to online resellers are available in our digital library. In addition, complete works may be ordered through an authorized reseller by filling out and returning to StudySync® the order form enclosed in this workbook.

Reading & Writing Companion   9

Skill:
Language, Style, and Audience

Use the Checklist to analyze Language, Style, and Audience in "The Tell-Tale Heart." Refer to the sample student annotations about Language, Style, and Audience in the text.

••• CHECKLIST FOR LANGUAGE, STYLE, AND AUDIENCE

In order to determine an author's style, do the following:

- ✓ identify and define any unfamiliar words or phrases

- ✓ use context, including the meanings of surrounding words and phrases

- ✓ note possible reactions to the author's word choice

- ✓ examine your reaction to the author's word choice

- ✓ identify any analogies, or comparisons in which one part of the comparison helps explain the other

To analyze the impact of specific word choice on meaning and tone, ask the following questions:

- ✓ How did your understanding of the language change during your analysis?

- ✓ How do the writer's word choices impact or create meaning in the text?

- ✓ How do the writer's word choices impact or create a specific tone in the text?

- ✓ How could various audiences interpret this language? What different possible emotional responses can you list?

- ✓ What analogies do you see? Where might an analogy have clarified meaning or created a specific tone?

Skill:
Language, Style, and Audience

Reread paragraphs 9 and 10 of "The Tell-Tale Heart." Then, using the Checklist on the previous page, answer the multiple-choice questions below.

↻ YOUR TURN

1. What effect do the punctuation choices in paragraphs 9 and 10 have on the tone?

   ○ A. The dashes and exclamation marks reveal that the narrator is losing control.
   ○ B. The italics make it clear that the narrator's words aren't to be trusted.
   ○ C. The semicolons introduce a formal tone into an informal speech.
   ○ D. The frequent questions reveal the narrator's attempt to engage the reader.

2. Which phrase from the passage most clearly suggests the narrator's disturbed mental state at the end of the story?

   ○ A. "but I talked more fluently"
   ○ B. "Why would they not be gone?"
   ○ C. "It grew louder—louder—louder!"
   ○ D. "And still the men chatted pleasantly"

Please note that excerpts and passages in the StudySync® library and this workbook are intended as touchstones to generate interest in an author's work. The excerpts and passages do not substitute for the reading of entire texts, and StudySync® strongly recommends that students seek out and purchase the whole literary or informational work in order to experience it as the author intended. Links to online resellers are available in our digital library. In addition, complete works may be ordered through an authorized reseller by filling out and returning to StudySync® the order form enclosed in this workbook.

Reading & Writing
Companion

11

Close Read

Reread "The Tell-Tale Heart." As you reread, complete the Skills Focus questions below. Then use your answers and annotations from the questions to help you complete the Write activity.

◎ SKILLS FOCUS

1. What inferences can you draw about the narrator's mental state based on the author's word choices?

2. What does the author imply about the narrator's mental state through the descriptions of the narrator's feelings about how the old man looks at him with the "eye of a vulture"?

3. Identify word choices the author uses to indicate that the narrator might be losing his mind. How do the word choices and tone indicate the narrator's troubled mental state?

4. What language does the author use to make the narrator seem untrustworthy? How does this language reveal the narrator's dishonest nature?

5. Explain how the author uses the narrator's personality to create a feeling of mystery for the reader.

✏ WRITE

LITERARY ANALYSIS: Can the narrator of "The Tell-Tale Heart" be trusted? Consider the author's word choice, tone, and description of events as you draw conclusions about the narrator's state of mind. Be sure to support your ideas with evidence from the text.

Monster

FICTION
Walter Dean Myers
1999

Introduction

Monster is one of the most unique and unforgettable works by American author Walter Dean Myers (1937–2014). Myers's prolific body of work features more than one hundred books for young readers, including both young adult literature and nonfiction. *Monster* is about a teenager named Steve Harmon, age 16, who decides to write a movie script about his current predicament. He's in jail and on trial, accused of acting as lookout in a drugstore robbery in which a man was shot and killed. This excerpt introduces Steve's screenplay as a way of introducing Steve to the reader.

"I'll call it what the lady who is the prosecutor called me."

1 They say you get used to being in jail, but I don't see how. Every morning I wake up and I am surprised to be here. If your life outside was real, then everything in here is just the opposite. We sleep with strangers, wake up with strangers, and go to the bathroom in front of strangers. They're strangers but they still find reasons to hurt each other.

2 Sometimes I feel like I have walked into the middle of a movie. It is a strange movie with no plot and no beginning. The movie is in black and white, and grainy. Sometimes the camera moves in so close that you can't tell what is going on and you just listen to the sounds and guess. I have seen movies of prisons but never one like this. This is not a movie about bars and locked doors. It is about being alone when you are not really alone and about being scared all the time.

3 I think to get used to this I will have to give up what I think is real and take up something else. I wish I could make sense of it.

4 Maybe I could make my own movie. I could write it out and play it in my head. I could **block** out the scenes like we did in school. The film will be the story of my life. No, not my life, but of this experience. I'll write it down in the notebook they let me keep. I'll call it what the lady who is the **prosecutor** called me.

MONSTER   **Monday, July 6th**

Monster!

5 **FADE IN: INTERIOR: Early** morning in **CELL BLOCK D, MANHATTAN DETENTION CENTER. Camera goes slowly down grim, gray corridor. There are sounds of inmates yelling from cell to cell; much of it is obscene. Most of the voices are clearly Black or Hispanic. Camera stops and slowly turns toward a cell.**

6 **INTERIOR: CELL. Sixteen-year-old STEVE HARMON** is sitting on the edge of a metal cot, head in hands. He is thin, brown skinned. On the cot next to him are the suit and tie he is to wear to court for the start of his trial.

7 **CUT TO: ERNIE, another prisoner, sitting on john, pants down.**

Skill:
Character

Steve is the protagonist. He's been arrested and thrown in jail, and now he feels alone and scared. His decision to write a screenplay about what's happening to him shows me Steve is someone who tries to deal with a bad situation by removing himself from it emotionally.

8   **CUT TO: SUNSET**, another prisoner, pulling on T-shirt.

9   **CUT TO: STEVE** pulling blanket over his head as screen goes dark.

VOICE-OVER (VO)

10   Ain't no use putting the blanket over your head, man. You can't cut this out; this is reality. This is the real deal.

11   **VO continues with anonymous PRISONER explaining how the Detention Center is the real thing. As he does, words appear on the screen, just like the opening credits of the movie *Star Wars*, rolling from the bottom of the screen and shrinking until they are a blur on the top of the screen before rolling off into space.**

12

**Monster!
The Story of
My
Miserable
Life**

13

**Starring
Steve Harmon**

14

**Produced by
Steve Harmon**

15

**Directed by
Steve Harmon**

16

(Credits continue to roll.)
**The incredible story
of how one guy's life
was turned around
by a few events
and how he might
spend the rest of his life
behind bars.
Told as it
actually
happened!**

17

Written and directed by Steve Harmon
Featuring. . .

18

Sandra Petrocelli
as the Dedicated Prosecutor

19

Kathy O'Brien
as the Defense Attorney with Doubts

NOTES

20   **James King**
            as the Thug

21   **Richard "Bobo" Evans**
            as the Rat

22 **Osvaldo Cruz, member of the Diablos,**
            as the Tough Guy Wannabe

23   **Lorelle Henry**
            as the Witness
            Jose Delgado. . .
            he found the body

24   *And Starring*
        16-year-old Steve Harmon
        As the Boy on Trial for Murder!

25 **Filmed at the Manhattan Detention Center**

26 **Set design, handcuffs, and prison outfits by**
            The State of New York

VO

27 Yo, Harmon, you gonna eat something? Come on and get your breakfast, man. I'll take your eggs if you don't want them. You want them?

STEVE (subdued)

28 I'm not hungry.

SUNSET

29 His trial starts today. He up for the big one. I know how that feels.

30 **CUT TO: INTERIOR: CORRECTIONS DEPT. VAN.** Through the bars at the rear of the van, we see people going about the business of their lives in downtown New York. There are men collecting garbage, a female traffic officer motioning for a taxi to make a turn, students on the way to school. Few people notice the van as it makes its way from the DETENTION CENTER to the COURTHOUSE.

31 **CUT TO: PRISONERS,** handcuffed, coming from back of van. STEVE is carrying a notebook. He is dressed in the suit and tie we saw on the cot. He is seen only briefly as he is herded through the heavy doors of the courthouse.

32 **FADE OUT** as last prisoner from the van enters rear of courthouse.

33 **FADE IN: INTERIOR COURTHOUSE.** We are in a small room used for prisoner-lawyer interviews. A guard sits at a desk behind STEVE.

34 **KATHY O'BRIEN, STEVE's lawyer, is petite, red-haired, and freckled. She is all business as she talks to STEVE.**

O'BRIEN

35 Let me make sure you understand what's going on. Both you and this King character are on trial for felony murder. **Felony** murder is as serious as it gets. Sandra Petrocelli is the prosecutor, and she's good. They're pushing for the death penalty, which is really bad. The jury might think they're doing you a big favor by giving you life in prison. So you'd better take this trial very, very seriously.

36 When you're in court, you sit there and you pay attention. You let the jury know that you think the case is as serious as they do. You don't turn and wave to any of your friends. It's all right to **acknowledge** your mother.

37 I have to go and talk to the judge. The trial will begin in a few minutes. Is there anything you want to ask me before it starts?

STEVE

38 You think we're going to win?

O'BRIEN (seriously)

39 It probably depends on what you mean by "win."

40 **CUT TO: INTERIOR: HOLDING ROOM. We see STEVE sitting at one end of bench. Against the opposite wall, dressed in a sloppy-looking suit, is 23-year-old JAMES KING, the other man on trial. King looks older than 23. He looks over at STEVE with a hard look and we see STEVE look away. Two GUARDS sit at a table away from the prisoners who are handcuffed. The camera finds the GUARDS in a MEDIUM SHOT (MS). They have their breakfast in aluminum take-out trays that contain eggs, sausages, and potatoes. A Black female STENOGRAPHER[1] pours coffee for herself and the GUARDS.**

STENOGRAPHER

41 I hope this case lasts two weeks. I can sure use the money.

GUARD 1

42 Six days—maybe seven. It's a motion[2] case. They go through the motions; then they lock them up.

43 **(Turns and looks off camera toward STEVE.)**

44 Ain't that right, bright eyes?

---

1. **stenographer** a person whose job is to transcribe spoken or recorded speech
2. **motion** a formal proposal for an action in a meeting or court proceeding

Skill:
Character

O'Brien talks to Steve very directly and doesn't mince words. This tells me she's very businesslike and probably knows what she's doing. And she's maybe a little sarcastic with "what you mean by win," but she's trying to show Steve how serious his situation is.

45 **CUT TO: STEVE, who is seated on a low bench. He is handcuffed to a U-bolt put in the bench for that purpose. STEVE looks away from the GUARD.**

46 **CUT TO: DOOR. It opens, and COURT CLERK looks in.**

COURT CLERK

47 Two minutes!

48 **CUT TO: GUARDS, who hurriedly finish breakfast. STENOGRAPHER takes machine into COURTROOM. They unshackle STEVE and take him toward door.**

49 **CUT TO: STEVE is made to sit down at one table. At another table we see KING and two attorneys. STEVE sits alone. A guard stands behind him. There are one or two spectators in the court. Then four more enter.**

50 **CLOSE-UP (CU) OF STEVE HARMON. The fear is evident on his face.**

51 **MS: People are getting ready for the trial to begin. KATHY O'BRIEN sits next to STEVE.**

O'BRIEN

52 How are you doing?

STEVE

53 I'm scared.

O'BRIEN

54 Good; you should be. Anyway, just remember what we've been talking about. The judge is going to rule on a motion that King's lawyer made to suppress Cruz's **testimony**, and a few other things. Steve, let me tell you what my job is here. My job is to make sure the law works for you as well as against you, and to make you a human being in the eyes of the jury. Your job is to help me. Any questions you have, write them down and I'll try to answer them. What are you doing there?

STEVE

55 I'm writing this whole thing down as a movie.

O'BRIEN

56 Whatever. Make sure you pay attention. Close attention.

Excerpted from *Monster* by Walter Dean Myers, published by HarperCollins Publishers.

First Read

Read *Monster*. After you read, complete the Think Questions below.

☁ THINK QUESTIONS

1. How does Steve Harmon introduce himself in the opening credits of the screenplay?

2. What advice does Kathy O'Brien, Steve's lawyer, have for Steve?

3. What do the stenographer and the guard say about Steve's case?

4. Find the word **anonymous** in paragraph 11 of *Monster*. Use context clues in the surrounding sentences, as well as the sentence in which the word appears, to determine the word's meaning. Write your definition here and identify clues that helped you figure out its meaning.

5. Use context clues to determine the meaning of **subdued** as it is used to describe Steve's dialogue for paragraph 28. Write your definition of *subdued* here and and identify clues that helped you figure out its meaning. Then check the meaning in a dictionary.

Please note that excerpts and passages in the StudySync® library and this workbook are intended as touchstones to generate interest in an author's work. The excerpts and passages do not substitute for the reading of entire texts, and StudySync® strongly recommends that students seek out and purchase the whole literary or informational work in order to experience it as the author intended. Links to online resellers are available in our digital library. In addition, complete works may be ordered through an authorized reseller by filling out and returning to StudySync® the order form enclosed in this workbook.

Reading & Writing Companion

19

Skill: Character

Use the Checklist to analyze Character in *Monster*. Refer to the sample student annotations about Character in the text.

••• CHECKLIST FOR CHARACTER

In order to determine how dialogue or incidents in a story propel the action, reveal aspects of a character, or provoke a decision, note the following:

✓ the characters in the story, including the protagonist and antagonist

✓ key dialogue and how it reveals character traits and moves the action, or the events of the plot, forward

✓ characters' responses and reactions to other characters or events, and what this reveals about them

✓ when an event or another character's actions or dialogue provokes a character to make a decision

✓ the resolution and how it affects the characters

To analyze how particular lines of dialogue or incidents in a story or drama propel the action, reveal aspects of a character, or provoke a decision, consider the following questions:

✓ How does the dialogue propel, or move forward, the action in the story?

✓ How does the dialogue reveal different aspects or traits of each character?

✓ Did an event or a character provoke another character to make a decision? What was it, and how did it affect the events of the plot?

✓ How does the resolution affect the characters?

Skill:
Character

Reread paragraphs 52–56 from *Monster*. Then, using the Checklist on the previous page, answer the multiple-choice questions below.

YOUR TURN

1. This question has two parts. First, answer Part A. Then, answer Part B.

   Part A: Which of the following is one character trait that O'Brien shows in this passage?

   ○ A. honesty
   ○ B. fearfulness
   ○ C. optimism
   ○ D. pessimism

   Part B: Which of the following lines of dialogue BEST reveals the character trait selected in Part A?

   ○ A. "How are you doing?"
   ○ B. "Anyway, just remember what we've been talking about."
   ○ C. "My job is to make sure the law works for you as well as against you, and to make you a human being in the eyes of the jury."
   ○ D. "Any questions you have, write them down and I'll try to answer them."

2. Which line shows that O'Brien is not overly concerned with Steve's feelings?

   ○ A. "Steve, let me tell you what my job is here."
   ○ B. "Your job is to help me."
   ○ C. "What are you doing there?"
   ○ D. "Whatever."

Please note that excerpts and passages in the StudySync® library and this workbook are intended as touchstones to generate interest in an author's work. The excerpts and passages do not substitute for the reading of entire texts, and StudySync® strongly recommends that students seek out and purchase the whole literary or informational work in order to experience it as the author intended. Links to online resellers are available in our digital library. In addition, complete works may be ordered through an authorized reseller by filling out and returning to StudySync® the order form enclosed in this workbook.

Reading & Writing Companion 21

Close Read

Reread *Monster*. As you reread, complete the Skills Focus questions below. Then use your answers and annotations from the questions to help you complete the Write activity.

⊚ SKILLS FOCUS

1. What do Steve's responses to other characters or events in the story reveal about him?

2. Minor characters in a story may support the protagonist or antagonist. How does the dialogue reveal character traits of some of the minor characters in *Monster*? Do they support Steve?

3. Identify ways in which suspense is created through incidents, the characters, and their dialogue. How does the use of suspense help to attract the reader to the novel's mysteriousness?

✏ WRITE

NARRATIVE: Choose a section from the screenplay in *Monster*, and rewrite it as a story rather than a screenplay. Include lines of dialogue, but also add descriptions about the characters' feelings and responses to one another.

Let 'Em Play God

INFORMATIONAL TEXT
Alfred Hitchcock
1948

Introduction

With films that consistently put viewers on the edge of their seats, British film director Alfred Hitchcock earned the nickname "The Master of Suspense." In the following excerpt from a 1948 essay, Hitchcock describes how he creates suspense by letting the audience "play God"—by providing them with certain information not known to characters in a movie—and illustrates how he used the technique to create dramatic tension in his 1948 thriller, *Rope*.

"As far as I'm concerned, you have suspense when you let the audience play God."

Skill: Author's
Purpose and
Point of View

Hitchcock is answering
a question, but is he
writing to inform or
explain?

He starts to answer
the question by
describing how
suspense is created, so
he must be writing to
explain. I'm just not sure
what he means yet.

From "Let 'Em Play God"

1   Every maker of mystery movies aims at getting the audience on the edge of their seats. The **ingredient** to keep them there is called "suspense." Producers[1] cry for it, writers cry in agony to get it, and actors cry for joy when they do get it. I've often been asked what it is.

2   As far as I'm concerned, you have suspense when you let the audience play God.

3   Suppose, for instance, you have six characters involved in a mystery. A man has been murdered and all six are possible **suspects** but no one is sure including the audience.

4   One of the characters, a young man, is standing in a shadowy room with his back to the door when an unidentified character in a cloak and black hat sneaks in and slugs him into **insensibility.** It's a brutal act, but if the audience does not know whether the young man is a killer or a hero they will not know whether to cheer or weep.

5   If the audience does know, if they have been told all the secrets that the characters do not know, they'll work like the devil for you because they know what fate is facing the poor actors. That is what is known as "playing God." That is suspense.

6   For 17 years I have been making pictures described alternately as thrillers, dark mysteries, and chillers, yet I have never actually directed a whodunit[2] or a puzzler. Offhand this may sound like **debunking,** but I do not believe that puzzling the audience is the essence of suspense.

7   Take, for instance, the drama I recently filmed at Warner Bros. called *Rope*. It stars James Stewart with Joan Chandler, our new discovery, in the feminine lead.

---

1. **Producers** the people who oversee the production of a film
2. **whodunit** a story about a murder in which the murderer's identity is concealed until the conclusion of the narrative

8   John Dall and Farley Granger strangle a young man in the opening shot. They put his body in a chest, cover the chest with a damask cloth and silver service, then serve *hors d'oeuvres* and drinks from it at a party for the victim's father, mother, sweetheart, and assorted friends. Everyone is gay and charming. When Stewart begins to suspect foul play late in the film John Dall puts a gun in his pocket in case things get too hot.

9   The audience knows everything from the start, the players know nothing. There is not a single detail to puzzle the audience. It is certainly not a whodunit for the simple reason that everyone out front knows who did it. No one on the screen knows except the two murderers. The fact that the audience watches actors go blithely through an atmosphere that is loaded with evil makes for real suspense.

10   These are the questions, now, that constantly pop up. Will the murderers break and give themselves away? When the victim does not show up for the party will his father suspect? Will Jimmy get killed before he discovers the actual crime? How long will that body lie in its wooden grave at a champagne party without being discovered? If we are successful we'll have the audience at such a pitch that they want to shout every time one of the players goes near that chest.

11   In order to achieve this, one of the necessary ingredients of the formula is a series of **plausible** situations with people that are real. When characters are unbelievable you never get suspense, only surprise.

12   Just because there is a touch of murder and an air of mystery about a story it is not necessary to see transoms opening, clutching fingers, hooded creatures, and asps on the Chinese rug.

13   *Spellbound* was based on complete psychiatric truth. *Foreign Correspondent* was simply the story of a man hammering away at events with a woman who was not much help. *Notorious* concerned a woman caught in a web of world events from which she could not extricate herself and *The Paradine Case* was a love story embedded in the emotional quicksand of a murder trial.

14   In none of these was the house filled with shadows, the weather dull and stormy throughout, the moor windswept, and the doors creaky. In fact, it is important in a story with sinister implications to use counterpoint, great contrast between situation and background, as we did in *Rope*.

15   John Dall is guilty of a bestial crime which the audience sees him perform with young Granger. But throughout the film he is grace and charm itself and his apartment is gay and beautifully appointed. And when Granger plays the piano he picks a light and childish piece, a minuet. Suspense involves contrast.

Copyrighted 2015. Prometheus Global Media. 120724:1215AT

First Read

Read "Let 'Em Play God." After you read, complete the Think Questions below.

☁ **THINK QUESTIONS**

1. What does the imaginary movie that Hitchcock describes in paragraphs 3 and 5 tell you about the kinds of movies he makes? Use evidence from the text to explain your answer.

2. Hitchcock says, "I do not believe that puzzling the audience is the essence of suspense." What kinds of examples does he use to help him support that statement?

3. What kinds of questions does Hitchcock hope his audience will ask while they watch the movie *Rope*? How do they build suspense? Refer to one or more details from the text to support your answer.

4. Find the word **suspects** in paragraph 3 of "Let 'Em Play God." Use context clues in the surrounding sentences, as well as the sentence in which the word appears, to determine the word's meaning. Write your definition here and identify clues that helped you figure out its meaning.

5. Use context clues to determine the meaning of **plausible** as it is used in paragraph 11 of "Let 'Em Play God." Write your definition here and identify clues that helped you figure out its meaning. Then check the meaning in a dictionary.

Skill: Author's Purpose and Point of View

Use the Checklist to analyze Author's Purpose and Point of View in "Let 'Em Play God." Refer to the sample student annotations about Author's Purpose and Point of View in the text.

••• CHECKLIST FOR AUTHOR'S PURPOSE AND POINT OF VIEW

In order to identify author's purpose and point of view, note the following:

- ✓ descriptions that present a complicated process in plain language, which may indicate that an author is writing to explain

- ✓ facts, statistics, and graphic aids, as these indicate that an author is writing to inform

- ✓ the author's use of emotional or figurative language, which may indicate the author is trying to persuade readers or stress an opinion

- ✓ the language the author uses, as figurative and emotional language can be clues to the author's point of view on a subject or topic

- ✓ whether the author acknowledges and responds to conflicting evidence or points of view that contradict his or her own

To determine the author's purpose and point of view in a text, consider the following questions:

- ✓ How does the author convey, or communicate, information in the text?

- ✓ Does the author use figurative or emotional language? What does this indicate?

- ✓ Are charts, graphs, maps, and other graphic aids included in the text? For what purpose?

- ✓ Does the author acknowledge contradictory or conflicting evidence or other points of view? How does the author respond to or address them?

Please note that excerpts and passages in the StudySync® library and this workbook are intended as touchstones to generate interest in an author's work. The excerpts and passages do not substitute for the reading of entire texts, and StudySync® strongly recommends that students seek out and purchase the whole literary or informational work in order to experience it as the author intended. Links to online resellers are available in our digital library. In addition, complete works may be ordered through an authorized reseller by filling out and returning to StudySync® the order form enclosed in this workbook.

Reading & Writing Companion   27

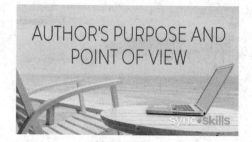

Skill: Author's Purpose and Point of View

Reread paragraphs 9 and 10 of "Let 'Em Play God." Then, using the Checklist on the previous page, answer the multiple-choice questions below.

⟳ YOUR TURN

1. Based on Hitchcock's explanation of suspense in paragraph 9, the reader can conclude that—

   ○ A. The author thinks that suspense is stronger when the characters know everything.
   ○ B. The author believes that whodunit films are not as suspenseful as thrillers.
   ○ C. The author prefers to keep suspenseful details from his audiences.
   ○ D. The author likes building suspense by telling the audience when characters are in danger.

2. The questions Hitchcock includes in paragraph 10 reveal his point of view. He believes that suspense builds when the audience—

   ○ A. knows how the film will end.
   ○ B. tries to guess what will happen.
   ○ C. is confused about the movie.
   ○ D. makes noise during the movie.

3. Based on the details Hitchcock gives in paragraphs 9 and 10, the reader can conclude that his purpose in writing these paragraphs is—

   ○ A. to explain.
   ○ B. to entertain and persuade.
   ○ C. to persuade only.
   ○ D. to entertain and inform.

4. How does the author achieve his purpose in paragraphs 9 and 10?

○ A. The author achieves his purpose by explaining how he shares information with the audience instead of the players.

○ B. The author achieves his purpose by explaining how he has built suspense in a film that he is making.

○ C. The author achieves his purpose by sharing an example of a film that interested audiences by puzzling them.

○ D. The author achieves his purpose by sharing an example of a film in which audiences always know what will happen next.

5. Which of the following best describes the supporting details that the author includes in paragraphs 9 and 10?

○ A. facts, statistics, and graphic aids

○ B. questions from audience members with conflicting reviews of his film

○ C. clear details about how and why an audience experiences suspense

○ D. conflicting evidence and the author's response to it

Please note that excerpts and passages in the StudySync® library and this workbook are intended as touchstones to generate interest in an author's work. The excerpts and passages do not substitute for the reading of entire texts, and StudySync® strongly recommends that students seek out and purchase the whole literary or informational work in order to experience it as the author intended. Links to online resellers are available in our digital library. In addition, complete works may be ordered through an authorized reseller by filling out and returning to StudySync® the order form enclosed in this workbook.

Reading & Writing
Companion

29

Close Read

Reread "Let 'Em Play God." As you reread, complete the Skills Focus questions below. Then use your answers and annotations from the questions to help you complete the Write activity.

◎ SKILLS FOCUS

1. Identify textual evidence that reveals Hitchcock's purpose for writing "Let 'Em Play God." Explain why you think Hitchcock is willing to expose his personal style for making films.

2. Identify textual evidence that reveals Hitchcock's point of view on creating suspense in a movie. Explain the effect his advice may have on future filmmakers.

3. Hitchcock gives clear recommendations for how to craft a successful mystery or suspense film. Identify examples of audiences' viewpoints that he acknowledges in his argument. Explain what these examples suggest about how Hitchcock attracts audiences to the mysterious.

✎ WRITE

LITERARY ANALYSIS: What is Hitchcock's purpose and point of view in "Let 'Em Play God"? How does his point of view emerge throughout the essay? Write a response of at least 300 words. Support your writing with evidence from the text.

Sympathy

POETRY
Paul Laurence Dunbar
1899

Introduction

Paul Laurence Dunbar (1872–1906) was one of the first nationally acclaimed African American poets. The son of people who were formerly enslaved, Dunbar was born after the Civil War and the abolition of slavery but at a time when African Americans continued to face the horrors of racism and discrimination. Dunbar was a gifted writer from a young age and published his first poems when he was only 16-years-old. His poem "Sympathy" includes the famous line "I know why the caged bird sings," the inspiration for the title of Maya Angelou's autobiography

"I know what the caged bird feels!"

1 I know what the caged bird feels, **alas**!
2 When the sun is bright on the upland slopes;
3 When the wind stirs soft through the springing grass,
4 And the river flows like a stream of glass;
5 When the first bird sings and the first bud opes[1],
6 And the faint perfume from its **chalice** steals—
7 I know what the caged bird feels!

8 I know why the caged bird beats his wing
9 Till its blood is red on the cruel bars;
10 For he must fly back to his perch and cling
11 When he fain[2] would be on the **bough** a-swing;
12 And a pain still throbs in the old, old scars
13 And they pulse again with a **keener** sting—
14 I know why he beats his wing!

15 I know why the caged bird sings, ah me,
16 When his wing is bruised and his bosom sore,—
17 When he beats his bars and he would be free;
18 It is not a carol of joy or glee,
19 But a prayer that he sends from his heart's deep core,
20 But a plea, that upward to Heaven he flings—
21 I know why the caged bird sings!

From SYMPATHY by Paul Laurence Dunbar, Copyright © 2014 by Poetry Foundation.

---

1. **opes** an archaic way of saying "opens"
2. **fain** gladly

WRITE

PERSONAL RESPONSE: Paul Laurence Dunbar uses the imagery of a caged bird to communicate feelings of oppression and a lack of freedom. What images from the poem were effective in communicating these feelings? How does it make you feel? Can you sympathize with someone who feels trapped like this? Choose several moments in the poem that you felt were effective and explain your reaction. Make sure to include details from the poem and your own thoughts and feelings in your response.

Ten Days in a Mad-House

INFORMATIONAL TEXT
Nellie Bly
1887

Introduction

n 1887, reporter Nellie Bly (1864–1922) went on an undercover assignment for a New York newspaper, the *World*, for which she feigned insanity in order to get committed to the Blackwell's Island Insane Asylum. Her exposé of the conditions inside the Women's Lunatic Asylum launched a criminal investigation that later led to an $850,000 budget increase from the Department of Public Charities and Corrections. *Ten Days in a Mad-House* began as a series of newspaper articles and

"At last the question of my sanity or insanity was to be decided."

Chapter IV: Judge Duffy and the Police

1 "Are you Nellie Brown?" asked the officer. I said I supposed I was. "Where do you come from?" he asked. I told him I did not know, and then Mrs. Stanard gave him a lot of information about me—told him how strangely I had acted at her home; how I had not slept a wink all night, and that in her opinion I was a poor unfortunate who had been driven crazy by inhuman treatment. There was some discussion between Mrs. Stanard and the two officers, and Tom Bockert was told to take us down to the court in a car.

2 "Come along," Bockert said, "I will find your trunk[1] for you." We all went together, Mrs. Stanard, Tom Bockert, and myself. I said it was very kind of them to go with me, and I should not soon forget them. As we walked along I kept up my refrain about my trunks, injecting occasionally some remark about the dirty condition of the streets and the curious character of the people we met on the way. "I don't think I have ever seen such people before," I said. "Who are they?" I asked, and my companions looked upon me with expressions of pity, evidently believing I was a foreigner, an emigrant or something of the sort. They told me that the people around me were working people. I remarked once more that I thought there were too many working people in the world for the amount of work to be done, at which remark Policeman P. T. Bockert eyed me closely, evidently thinking that my mind was gone for good. We passed several other policemen, who generally asked my sturdy guardians what was the matter with me. By this time quite a number of ragged children were following us too, and they passed remarks about me that were to me original as well as amusing.

3 "What's she up for?" "Say, kop, where did ye get her?" "Where did yer pull 'er?" "She's a daisy!"

4 Poor Mrs. Stanard was more frightened than I was. The whole situation grew interesting, but I still had fears for my fate before the judge.

---

1. **trunk** (archaic) luggage consisting of a large strong case used when traveling or for storage

5   At last we came to a low building, and Tom Bockert kindly volunteered the information: "Here's the express office. We shall soon find those trunks of yours."

6   The entrance to the building was surrounded by a curious crowd and I did not think my case was bad enough to permit me passing them without some remark, so I asked if all those people had lost their trunks.

7   "Yes," he said, "nearly all these people are looking for trunks."

8   I said, "They all seem to be foreigners, too." "Yes," said Tom, "they are all foreigners just landed. They have all lost their trunks, and it takes most of our time to help find them for them."

9   We entered the courtroom. It was the Essex Market Police Courtroom. At last the question of my sanity or insanity was to be decided. Judge Duffy sat behind the high desk, wearing a look which seemed to indicate that he was dealing out the milk of human kindness by wholesale. I rather feared I would not get the fate I sought, because of the kindness I saw on every line of his face, and it was with rather a sinking heart that I followed Mrs. Stanard as she answered the summons to go up to the desk, where Tom Bockert had just given an account of the affair.

The Essex Market Police Court, Essex Street, Lower East Side, New York City, circa 1857

10   "Come here," said an officer. "What is your name?"

11   "Nellie Brown," I replied, with a little accent. "I have lost my trunks, and would like if you could find them."

12   "When did you come to New York?" he asked.

13   "I did not come to New York," I replied (while I added, mentally, "because I have been here for some time.").

14   "But you are in New York now," said the man.

15   "No," I said, looking as **incredulous** as I thought a crazy person could, "I did not come to New York."

16   "That girl is from the west," he said, in a tone that made me tremble. "She has a western accent."

17   Someone else who had been listening to the brief dialogue here asserted that he had lived south and that my accent was southern, while another officer was positive it was eastern. I felt much relieved when the first spokesman turned to the judge and said:

18   "Judge, here is a peculiar case of a young woman who doesn't know who she is or where she came from. You had better attend to it at once."

19   I **commenced** to shake with more than the cold, and I looked around at the strange crowd about me, composed of poorly dressed men and women with stories printed on their faces of hard lives, abuse and poverty. Some were consulting eagerly with friends, while others sat still with a look of utter hopelessness. Everywhere was a sprinkling of well-dressed, well-fed officers watching the scene passively and almost **indifferently.** It was only an old story with them. One more unfortunate added to a long list which had long since ceased to be of any interest or concern to them.

20   "Come here, girl, and lift your veil," called out Judge Duffy, in tones which surprised me by a harshness which I did not think from the kindly face he possessed.

21   "Who are you speaking to?" I inquired, in my stateliest manner.

22   "Come here, my dear, and lift your veil. You know the Queen of England, if she were here, would have to lift her veil," he said, very kindly.

23   "That is much better," I replied. "I am not the Queen of England, but I'll lift my veil."

24   As I did so the little judge looked at me, and then, in a very kind and gentle tone, he said: "My dear child, what is wrong?"

25   "Nothing is wrong except that I have lost my trunks, and this man," indicating Policeman Bockert, "promised to bring me where they could be found."

26   "What do you know about this child?" asked the judge, sternly, of Mrs. Stanard, who stood, pale and trembling, by my side.

27   "I know nothing of her except that she came to the home yesterday and asked to remain overnight."

28   "The home! What do you mean by the home?" asked Judge Duffy, quickly.

NOTES

Skill: Author's Purpose and Point of View

The hopeless people are at the courthouse because they need help, but it looks like the officers are not willing to help them. I think the author's point of view here is that not enough is being done to help people in need.

Please note that excerpts and passages in the StudySync® library and this workbook are intended as touchstones to generate interest in an author's work. The excerpts and passages do not substitute for the reading of entire texts, and StudySync® strongly recommends that students seek out and purchase the whole literary or informational work in order to experience it as the author intended. Links to online resellers are available in our digital library. In addition, complete works may be ordered through an authorized reseller by filling out and returning to StudySync® the order form enclosed in this workbook.

Reading & Writing Companion   37

29 "It is a temporary home kept for working women at No. 84 Second Avenue."

30 "What is your position there?"

31 "I am assistant matron[2]."

32 "Well, tell us all you know of the case."

33 "When I was going into the home yesterday I noticed her coming down the avenue. She was all alone. I had just got into the house when the bell rang and she came in. When I talked with her she wanted to know if she could stay all night, and I said she could. After awhile she said all the people in the house looked crazy, and she was afraid of them. Then she would not go to bed, but sat up all the night."

34 "Had she any money?"

35 "Yes," I replied, answering for her, "I paid her for everything, and the eating was the worst I ever tried."

36 There was a general smile at this, and some murmurs of "She's not so crazy on the food question."

37 "Poor child," said Judge Duffy, "she is well dressed, and a lady. Her English is perfect, and I would stake everything on her being a good girl. I am positive she is somebody's darling."

38 At this announcement everybody laughed, and I put my handkerchief over my face and endeavored to choke the laughter that threatened to spoil my plans, in despite of my **resolutions.**

39 "I mean she is some woman's darling," hastily amended the judge. "I am sure someone is searching for her. Poor girl, I will be good to her, for she looks like my sister, who is dead."

40 There was a hush for a moment after this announcement, and the officers glanced at me more kindly, while I silently blessed the kind-hearted judge, and hoped that any poor creatures who might be afflicted as I pretended to be should have as kindly a man to deal with as Judge Duffy.

41 "I wish the reporters were here," he said at last. "They would be able to find out something about her."

---

2. **matron** a woman in charge of managing students at a school or residents of a boarding house

NOTES

42   I got very much frightened at this, for if there is anyone who can ferret out a mystery it is a reporter. I felt that I would rather face a mass of expert doctors, policemen, and detectives than two bright specimens of my craft, so I said:

43   "I don't see why all this is needed to help me find my trunks. These men are **impudent,** and I do not want to be stared at. I will go away. I don't want to stay here."

44   So saying, I pulled down my veil and secretly hoped the reporters would be detained elsewhere until I was sent to the asylum.

45   "I don't know what to do with the poor child," said the worried judge. "She must be taken care of."

46   "Send her to the Island," suggested one of the officers.

47   "Oh, don't!" said Mrs. Stanard, in evident alarm. "Don't! She is a lady and it would kill her to be put on the Island."

48   For once I felt like shaking the good woman. To think the Island was just the place I wanted to reach and here she was trying to keep me from going there! It was very kind of her, but rather provoking under the circumstances.

Please note that excerpts and passages in the StudySync® library and this workbook are intended as touchstones to generate interest in an author's work. The excerpts and passages do not substitute for the reading of entire texts, and StudySync® strongly recommends that students seek out and purchase the whole literary or informational work in order to experience it as the author intended. Links to online resellers are available in our digital library. In addition, complete works may be ordered through an authorized reseller by filling out and returning to StudySync® the order form enclosed in this workbook.

Reading & Writing Companion   39

First Read

Read *Ten Days in a Mad-House*. After you read, complete the Think Questions below.

 THINK QUESTIONS

1. Nellie Bly is a reporter. Who does she pretend to be, and why? Cite textual evidence from the selection to support your answer.

2. How does Bly alter her behavior to convince Mrs. Stanard, Tom Bockert, and the officers that she is mentally ill? Cite textual evidence from the selection to support your answer.

3. Write two to three sentences describing how Bly reacts to the judge's questions and comments.

4. Use context clues to determine the meaning of **indifferently** as it is used in paragraph 19 of the excerpt from *Ten Days in a Mad-House*. Write your definition here, and identify clues that help you figure out its meaning.

5. Use context clues to determine the meaning of **impudent** as it is used in paragraph 43 of the excerpt from *Ten Days in a Mad-House*. Write your definition here, and identify clues that helped you figure out the word's meaning.

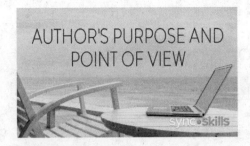

Skill: Author's Purpose and Point of View

Use the Checklist to analyze Author's Purpose and Point of View in *Ten Days in a Mad-House*. Refer to the sample student annotations about Author's Purpose and Point of View in the text.

••• CHECKLIST FOR AUTHOR'S PURPOSE AND POINT OF VIEW

In order to identify author's purpose and point of view, note the following:

- ✓ facts, statistics, and graphic aids, as these indicate that an author is writing to inform

- ✓ the author's use of emotional or figurative language, which may indicate the author is trying to persuade readers or stress an opinion

- ✓ descriptions that present a complicated process in plain language, which may indicate that an author is writing to explain

- ✓ the language the author uses, such as figurative and emotional language, can be clues to the author's point of view on a subject or topic

- ✓ whether the author acknowledges and responds to conflicting evidence or points of view that contradict his or her own

To determine the author's purpose and point of view in a text, consider the following questions:

- ✓ How does the author convey, or communicate, information in the text?

- ✓ Does the author use figurative or emotional language? What does this indicate?

- ✓ Are charts, graphs, maps, and other graphic aids included in the text? For what purpose?

- ✓ Does the author acknowledge contradictory or conflicting evidence or other points of view? How does the author respond to or address them?

Please note that excerpts and passages in the StudySync® library and this workbook are intended as touchstones to generate interest in an author's work. The excerpts and passages do not substitute for the reading of entire texts, and StudySync® strongly recommends that students seek out and purchase the whole literary or informational work in order to experience it as the author intended. Links to online resellers are available in our digital library. In addition, complete works may be ordered through an authorized reseller by filling out and returning to StudySync® the order form enclosed in this workbook.

Reading & Writing Companion   41

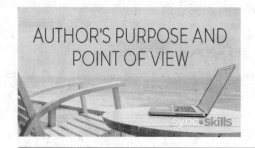

Skill: Author's Purpose and Point of View

Reread paragraphs 43–48 of *Ten Days in a Mad-House*. Then, using the Checklist on the previous page, answer the multiple-choice questions below.

YOUR TURN

1. Which paragraph best shows Bly's point of view to be that mentally ill people receive poor treatment?

   ○ A. 43
   ○ B. 44
   ○ C. 47
   ○ D. 48

2. Based on details in paragraph 48, the reader can infer that Bly's purpose in writing is—

   ○ A. to describe how to fool people to get what you want.
   ○ B. to entertain readers with a funny story from her real life.
   ○ C. to persuade readers that Mrs. Stanard is a very kind lady.
   ○ D. to inform readers about the treatment of mentally ill people.

Skill:
Compare and Contrast

Use the Checklist to analyze Compare and Contrast in *Ten Days in a Mad-House*. Refer to the sample student annotations about Compare and Contrast in the text.

••• CHECKLIST FOR COMPARE AND CONTRAST

In order to determine how to compare and contrast information in two or more texts that provide conflicting information on the same topic, use the following steps:

- ✓ first, choose two or more texts that present information on the same topic or subject

- ✓ next, identify the information each text offers

- ✓ after, identify the main ideas in each text, as well as the details that support these ideas

- ✓ then, identify the conflicting information each text offers on the same topic

- ✓ finally, explain where the texts disagree, both in their presentation of facts or their interpretation of events

To analyze a case in which two or more texts provide conflicting information on the same topic, consider the following questions:

- ✓ What kind of information does each text offer?

- ✓ How do the main ideas and supporting details differ? How are they the same? How does it result in conflicting information?

- ✓ In what ways do the authors of each text disagree? How does this contribute to the conflicting information that they provide?

Skill:
Compare and Contrast

Reread paragraphs 41–48 from *Ten Days in a Mad-House* and lines 15–21 from "Sympathy." Then, using the Checklist on the previous page, complete the chart below to compare and contrast the passages.

⟳ YOUR TURN

	Observation Options
A	When people try to prevent the narrator from being sent away, she feels upset, thinking her plans will be ruined.
B	The narrator has to adjust what she says and does, such as putting on a veil, because people react in ways she can't predict.
C	The narrator understands the feelings of frustration that one would experience if they were trapped.
D	Both the narrators are affected emotionally because other people are in control of their circumstances
E	The narrator understands that desperation can lead people to act wildly.
F	Both the narrators are hoping for their situations to change.

Ten Days in a Mad-House	Both	"Sympathy"

Close Read

Reread *Ten Days in a Mad-House* (Chapter IV). As you reread, complete the Skills Focus questions below. Then use your answers and annotations from the questions to help you complete the Write activity.

◎ SKILLS FOCUS

1. Reread the first eight paragraphs of *Ten Days in a Mad-House* (Chapter IV). Identify details in the text that show people's reactions to Nellie Bly being brought into the courthouse. Explain how these details reveal the author's point of view about how people taken into custody by the police are treated.

2. Identify details in the excerpt from *Ten Days in a Mad-House* (Chapter IV) that describe the officials in the courthouse. Explain how these details reveal the author's point of view about the treatment mentally ill people receive from these officials.

3. Identify evidence in the text that shows what Bly is trying to accomplish in her conversation with

the judge. Explain what her actions reveal about her purpose for writing *Ten Days in a Mad-House* (Chapter IV).

4. Identify examples of emotional responses to imprisonment in the excerpt from *Ten Days in a Mad-House* (Chapter IV). Then compare and contrast these examples with those in the poem "Sympathy."

5. Identify evidence in the text that shows what motivates Bly to occupy herself with the mystery of the conditions inside the asylum. Explain what Bly's curiosity suggests about why people are attracted to the mysterious.

✏ WRITE

COMPARE AND CONTRAST: Nellie Bly wants to access a "mad-house" from which other people would want to escape. Imagine that the speaker of "Sympathy" is an inmate being wrongly held there and that Bly conducts an interview with the inmate. Write a brief account of the interview, similar to what Bly might write for her newspaper. Be sure to show the contrasts between the two situations, relying on evidence from both texts.

Please note that excerpts and passages in the StudySync® library and this workbook are intended as touchstones to generate interest in an author's work. The excerpts and passages do not substitute for the reading of entire texts, and StudySync® strongly recommends that students seek out and purchase the whole literary or informational work in order to experience it as the author intended. Links to online resellers are available in our digital library. In addition, complete works may be ordered through an authorized reseller by filling out and returning to StudySync® the order form enclosed in this workbook.

Reading & Writing Companion   45

The Lottery

FICTION
Shirley Jackson
1948

Introduction

When this story appeared in *The New Yorker* in 1948, the response was loud, but divided: many distressed readers wrote in to cancel their subscriptions. Others asked which town it was modeled after so they could be spectators of such an event. Called "an icon in the history of the American short story," Shirley Jackson's piece may be controversial, but once read, it engraves

"I tell you it wasn't fair. You didn't give him time enough to choose."

1 The morning of June 27th was clear and sunny, with the fresh warmth of a full-summer day; the flowers were blossoming profusely and the grass was richly green. The people of the village began to gather in the square, between the post office and the bank, around ten o'clock; in some towns there were so many people that the lottery took two days and had to be started on June 26th, but in this village, where there were only about three hundred people, the whole **lottery** took less than two hours, so it could begin at ten o'clock in the morning and still be through in time to allow the villagers to get home for noon dinner.

2 The children assembled first, of course. School was recently over for the summer, and the feeling of liberty sat uneasily on most of them; they tended to gather together quietly for a while before they broke into boisterous play, and their talk was still of the classroom and the teacher, of books and reprimands. Bobby Martin had already stuffed his pockets full of stones, and the other boys soon followed his example, selecting the smoothest and roundest stones; Bobby and Harry Jones and Dickie Delacroix—the villagers pronounced this name "Dellacroy"—eventually made a great pile of stones in one corner of the square and guarded it against the raids of the other boys. The girls stood aside, talking among themselves, looking over their shoulders at the boys, and the very small children rolled in the dust or clung to the hands of their older brothers or sisters.

3 Soon the men began to gather, surveying their own children, speaking of planting and rain, tractors and taxes. They stood together, away from the pile of stones in the corner, and their jokes were quiet and they smiled rather than laughed. The women, wearing faded house dresses and sweaters, came shortly after their menfolk. They greeted one another and exchanged bits of gossip as they went to join their husbands. Soon the women, standing by their husbands, began to call to their children, and the children came reluctantly, having to be called four or five times. Bobby Martin ducked under his mother's grasping hand and ran, laughing, back to the pile of stones. His father spoke up sharply, and Bobby came quickly and took his place between his father and his oldest brother.

Skill:
Allusion

Why are the boys playing with stones in this scene? Since they're saving ones that are smooth and round, it seems like they're searching for stones that are good for throwing. I wonder what they'll use them for?

Skill:
Theme

The fact that villagers are talking about simple things like the weather or gossip shows that the setting of the village is at first presented as a very ordinary place, but later events in the story are anything but!

4　The lottery was conducted—as were the square dances, the teen club, the Halloween program—by Mr. Summers, who had time and energy to devote to civic activities. He was a round-faced, jovial man and he ran the coal business, and people were sorry for him because he had no children and his wife was a scold. When he arrived in the square, carrying the black wooden box, there was a murmur of conversation among the villagers, and he waved and called, "Little late today, folks." The postmaster, Mr. Graves, followed him, carrying a three-legged stool, and the stool was put in the center of the square and Mr. Summers set the black box down on it. The villagers kept their distance, leaving a space between themselves and the stool, and when Mr. Summers said, "Some of you fellows want to give me a hand?" there was a hesitation before two men, Mr. Martin and his oldest son, Baxter, came forward to hold the box steady on the stool while Mr. Summers stirred up the papers inside it.

5　The original **paraphernalia** for the lottery had been lost long ago, and the black box now resting on the stool had been put into use even before Old Man Warner, the oldest man in town, was born. Mr. Summers spoke frequently to the villagers about making a new box, but no one liked to upset even as much **tradition** as was represented by the black box. There was a story that the present box had been made with some pieces of the box that had preceded it, the one that had been constructed when the first people settled down to make a village here. Every year, after the lottery, Mr. Summers began talking again about a new box, but every year the subject was allowed to fade off without anything's being done. The black box grew shabbier each year: by now it was no longer completely black but splintered badly along one side to show the original wood color, and in some places faded or stained.

6　Mr. Martin and his oldest son, Baxter, held the black box securely on the stool until Mr. Summers had stirred the papers thoroughly with his hand. Because so much of the ritual had been forgotten or discarded, Mr. Summers had been successful in having slips of paper substituted for the chips of wood that had been used for generations. Chips of wood, Mr. Summers had argued, had been all very well when the village was tiny, but now that the population was more than three hundred and likely to keep on growing, it was necessary to use something that would fit more easily into the black box. The night before the lottery, Mr. Summers and Mr. Graves made up the slips of paper and put them in the box, and it was then taken to the safe of Mr. Summers' coal company and locked up until Mr. Summers was ready to take it to the square next morning. The rest of the year, the box was put way, sometimes one place, sometimes another; it had spent one year in Mr. Graves's barn and another year underfoot in the post office; and sometimes it was set on a shelf in the Martin grocery and left there.

Copyright © BookheadEd Learning, LLC

7　There was a great deal of fussing to be done before Mr. Summers declared the lottery open. There were the lists to make up—of heads of families, heads of households in each family, members of each household in each family. There was the proper swearing-in of Mr. Summers by the postmaster, as the official of the lottery; at one time, some people remembered, there had been a recital of some sort, performed by the official of the lottery, a **perfunctory,** tuneless chant that had been rattled off duly each year; some people believed that the official of the lottery used to stand just so when he said or sang it, others believed that he was supposed to walk among the people, but years and years ago this part of the ritual had been allowed to **lapse.** There had been, also, a ritual salute, which the official of the lottery had had to use in addressing each person who came up to draw from the box, but this also had changed with time, until now it was felt necessary only for the official to speak to each person approaching. Mr. Summers was very good at all this; in his clean white shirt and blue jeans, with one hand resting carelessly on the black box, he seemed very proper and important as he talked interminably to Mr. Graves and the Martins.

8　Just as Mr. Summers finally left off talking and turned to the **assembled** villagers, Mrs. Hutchinson came hurriedly along the path to the square, her sweater thrown over her shoulders, and slid into place in the back of the crowd. "Clean forgot what day it was," she said to Mrs. Delacroix, who stood next to her, and they both laughed softly. "Thought my old man was out back stacking wood," Mrs. Hutchinson went on, "and then I looked out the window and the kids was gone, and then I remembered it was the twenty-seventh and came a-running." She dried her hands on her apron, and Mrs. Delacroix said, "You're in time, though. They're still talking away up there."

9　Mrs. Hutchinson craned her neck to see through the crowd and found her husband and children standing near the front. She tapped Mrs. Delacroix on the arm as a farewell and began to make her way through the crowd. The people separated good-humoredly to let her through; two or three people said, in voices just loud enough to be heard across the crowd, "Here comes your Missus, Hutchinson," and "Bill, she made it after all." Mrs. Hutchinson reached her husband, and Mr. Summers, who had been waiting, said cheerfully, "Thought we were going to have to get on without you, Tessie." Mrs. Hutchinson said, grinning, "Wouldn't have me leave m'dishes in the sink, now, would you, Joe?" and soft laughter ran through the crowd as the people stirred back into position after Mrs. Hutchinson's arrival.

10　"Well, now," Mr. Summers said soberly, "guess we better get started, get this over with, so's we can go back to work. Anybody ain't here?"

11　"Dunbar," several people said. "Dunbar, Dunbar."

12   Mr. Summers consulted his list. "Clyde Dunbar," he said. "That's right. He's broke his leg, hasn't he? Who's drawing for him?"

13   "Me, I guess," a woman said, and Mr. Summers turned to look at her. "Wife draws for her husband," Mr. Summers said. "Don't you have a grown boy to do it for you, Janey?" Although Mr. Summers and everyone else in the village knew the answer perfectly well, it was the business of the official of the lottery to ask such questions formally. Mr. Summers waited with an expression of polite interest while Mrs. Dunbar answered.

14   "Horace's not but sixteen yet," Mrs. Dunbar said regretfully. "Guess I gotta fill in for the old man this year."

15   "Right," Mr. Summers said. He made a note on the list he was holding. Then he asked, "Watson boy drawing this year?"

16   A tall boy in the crowd raised his hand. "Here," he said. "I'm drawing for m'mother and me." He blinked his eyes nervously and ducked his head as several voices in the crowd said things like "Good fellow, Jack," and "Glad to see your mother's got a man to do it."

17   "Well," Mr. Summers said, "guess that's everyone. Old Man Warner make it?"

18   "Here," a voice said, and Mr. Summers nodded.

19   A sudden hush fell on the crowd as Mr. Summers cleared his throat and looked at the list. "All ready?" he called. "Now, I'll read the names—heads of families first—and the men come up and take a paper out of the box. Keep the paper folded in your hand without looking at it until everyone has had a turn. Everything clear?"

20   The people had done it so many times that they only half listened to the directions; most of them were quiet, wetting their lips, not looking around. Then Mr. Summers raised one hand high and said, "Adams." A man disengaged himself from the crowd and came forward. "Hi, Steve," Mr. Summers said, and Mr. Adams said, "Hi, Joe." They grinned at one another humorlessly and nervously. Then Mr. Adams reached into the black box and took out a folded paper. He held it firmly by one corner as he turned and went hastily back to his place in the crowd, where he stood a little apart from his family, not looking down at his hand.

21   "Allen," Mr. Summers said. "Anderson. . . . Bentham."

22   "Seems like there's no time at all between lotteries any more," Mrs. Delacroix said to Mrs. Graves in the back row. "Seems like we got through with the last one only last week."

23   "Time sure goes fast," Mrs. Graves said.

24   "Clark. . . . Delacroix."

25   "There goes my old man," Mrs. Delacroix said. She held her breath while her husband went forward.

26   "Dunbar," Mr. Summers said, and Mrs. Dunbar went steadily to the box while one of the women said, "Go on, Janey," and another said, "There she goes."

27   "We're next," Mrs. Graves said. She watched while Mr. Graves came around from the side of the box, greeted Mr. Summers gravely and selected a slip of paper from the box. By now, all through the crowd there were men holding the small folded papers in their large hands, turning them over and over nervously. Mrs. Dunbar and her two sons stood together, Mrs. Dunbar holding the slip of paper.

28   "Harburt. . . . Hutchinson."

29   "Get up there, Bill," Mrs. Hutchinson said, and the people near her laughed.

30   "Jones."

31   "They do say," Mr. Adams said to Old Man Warner, who stood next to him, "that over in the north village they're talking of giving up the lottery."

32   Old Man Warner snorted, "Pack of crazy fools," he said. "Listening to the young folks, nothing's good enough for them. Next thing you know, they'll be wanting to go back to living in caves, nobody work any more, live that way for a while. Used to be a saying about 'Lottery in June, corn be heavy soon.' First thing you know, we'd all be eating stewed chickweed and acorns. There's always been a lottery," he added petulantly. "Bad enough to see young Joe Summers up there joking with everybody."

33   "Some places have already quit lotteries," Mrs. Adams said.

34   "Nothing but trouble in that," Old Man Warner said stoutly. "Pack of young fools."

35   "Martin." And Bobby Martin watched his father go forward. "Overdyke. . . . Percy."

36 "I wish they'd hurry," Mrs. Dunbar said to her older son. "I wish they'd hurry."

37 "They're almost through," her son said.

38 "You get ready to run tell Dad," Mrs. Dunbar said.

39 Mr. Summers called his own name and then stepped forward precisely and selected a slip from the box. Then he called, "Warner."

40 "Seventy-seventh year I been in the lottery," Old Man Warner said as he went through the crowd. "Seventy-seventh time."

41 "Watson." The tall boy came awkwardly through the crowd. Someone said, "Don't be nervous, Jack," and Mr. Summers said, "Take your time, son."

42 "Zanini."

43 After that, there was a long pause, a breathless pause, until Mr. Summers, holding his slip of paper in the air, said, "All right, fellows." For a minute, no one moved, and then all the slips of paper were opened. Suddenly, all the women began to speak at once, saying, "Who is it?" "Who's got it?" "Is it the Dunbars?" "Is it the Watsons?" Then the voices began to say, "It's Hutchinson. It's Bill," "Bill Hutchinson's got it."

44 "Go tell your father," Mrs. Dunbar said to her older son.

45 People began to look around to see the Hutchinsons. Bill Hutchinson was standing quiet, staring down at the paper in his hand. Suddenly, Tessie Hutchinson shouted to Mr. Summers, "You didn't give him time enough to take any paper he wanted. I saw you. It wasn't fair!"

46 "Be a good sport, Tessie, " Mrs. Delacroix called, and Mrs. Graves said, "All of us took the same chance."

47 "Shut up, Tessie," Bill Hutchinson said.

48 "Well, everyone," Mr. Summers said, "that was done pretty fast, and now we've got to be hurrying a little more to get done in time." He consulted his next list. "Bill," he said, "you draw for the Hutchinson family. You got any other households in the Hutchinsons?"

49 "There's Don and Eva," Mrs. Hutchinson yelled. "Make them take their chance!"

50 "Daughters draw with their husbands' families, Tessie," Mr. Summers said gently. "You know that as well as anyone else."

51 "It wasn't fair," Tessie said.

52 "I guess not, Joe," Bill Hutchinson said regretfully. "My daughter draws with her husband's family, that's only fair. And I've got no other family except the kids."

53 "Then, as far as drawing for families is concerned, it's you," Mr. Summers said in explanation, "and as far as drawing for households is concerned, that's you, too. Right?"

54 "Right," Bill Hutchinson said.

55 "How many kids, Bill?" Mr. Summers asked formally.

56 "Three," Bill Hutchinson said. "There's Bill, Jr., and Nancy, and little Dave. And Tessie and me."

57 "All right, then," Mr. Summers said. "Harry, you got their tickets back?"

58 Mr. Graves nodded and held up the slips of paper. "Put them in the box, then," Mr. Summers directed. "Take Bill's and put it in."

59 "I think we ought to start over," Mrs. Hutchinson said, as quietly as she could. "I tell you it wasn't fair. You didn't give him time enough to choose. Everybody saw that."

60 Mr. Graves had selected the five slips and put them in the box, and he dropped all the papers but those onto the ground, where the breeze caught them and lifted them off.

61 "Listen, everybody," Mrs. Hutchinson was saying to the people around her.

62 "Ready, Bill?" Mr. Summers asked, and Bill Hutchinson, with one quick glance around at his wife and children, nodded.

63 "Remember," Mr. Summers said, "take the slips and keep them folded until each person has taken one. Harry, you help little Dave." Mr. Graves took the hand of the little boy, who came willingly with him up to the box. "Take a paper out of the box, Davy," Mr. Summers said. Davy put his hand into the box and laughed. "Take just one paper," Mr. Summers said. "Harry, you hold it for him." Mr. Graves took the child's hand and removed the folded paper from the tight fist and held it while little Dave stood next to him and looked up at him wonderingly.

64 "Nancy next," Mr. Summers said. Nancy was twelve, and her school friends breathed heavily as she went forward, switching her skirt, and took a slip

Please note that excerpts and passages in the StudySync® library and this workbook are intended as touchstones to generate interest in an author's work. The excerpts and passages do not substitute for the reading of entire texts, and StudySync® strongly recommends that students seek out and purchase the whole literary or informational work in order to experience it as the author intended. Links to online resellers are available in our digital library. In addition, complete works may be ordered through an authorized reseller by filling out and returning to StudySync® the order form enclosed in this workbook.

Reading & Writing
Companion

53

daintily from the box. "Bill, Jr.," Mr. Summers said, and Billy, his face red and his feet overlarge, nearly knocked the box over as he got a paper out. "Tessie," Mr. Summers said. She hesitated for a minute, looking around defiantly, and then set her lips and went up to the box. She snatched a paper out and held it behind her.

65 "Bill," Mr. Summers said, and Bill Hutchinson reached into the box and felt around, bringing his hand out at last with the slip of paper in it.

66 The crowd was quiet. A girl whispered, "I hope it's not Nancy," and the sound of the whisper reached the edges of the crowd.

67 "It's not the way it used to be," Old Man Warner said clearly. "People ain't the way they used to be."

68 "All right," Mr. Summers said. "Open the papers. Harry, you open little Dave's."

69 Mr. Graves opened the slip of paper and there was a general sigh through the crowd as he held it up and everyone could see that it was blank. Nancy and Bill. Jr., opened theirs at the same time, and both beamed and laughed, turning around to the crowd and holding their slips of paper above their heads.

70 "Tessie," Mr. Summers said. There was a pause, and then Mr. Summers looked at Bill Hutchinson, and Bill unfolded his paper and showed it. It was blank.

71 "It's Tessie," Mr. Summers said, and his voice was hushed. "Show us her paper, Bill."

**Skill:
Allusion**

The villagers will use the stones to throw at Mrs. Hutchinson, and this changes the tone of the story from a civil to horrific one. They might use stones because they're following an old tradition. In the Bible, people threw stones at a person as punishment, but Mrs. Hutchinson didn't commit a crime.

72 Bill Hutchinson went over to his wife and forced the slip of paper out of her hand. It had a black spot on it, the black spot Mr. Summers had made the night before with the heavy pencil in the coal company office. Bill Hutchinson held it up, and there was a stir in the crowd.

73 "All right, folks," Mr. Summers said. "Let's finish quickly."

74 Although the villagers had forgotten the ritual and lost the original black box, they still remembered to use stones. The pile of stones the boys had made earlier was ready; there were stones on the ground with the blowing scraps of paper that had come out of the box. Mrs. Delacroix selected a stone so large she had to pick it up with both hands and turned to Mrs. Dunbar. "Come on," she said. "Hurry up."

75 Mrs. Dunbar had small stones in both hands, and she said, gasping for breath, "I can't run at all. You'll have to go ahead and I'll catch up with you."

NOTES

76 The children had stones already, and someone gave little Davy Hutchinson a few pebbles.

77 Tessie Hutchinson was in the center of a cleared space by now, and she held her hands out desperately as the villagers moved in on her. "It isn't fair," she said. A stone hit her on the side of the head.

78 Old Man Warner was saying, "Come on, come on, everyone." Steve Adams was in the front of the crowd of villagers, with Mrs. Graves beside him.

79 "It isn't fair, it isn't right," Mrs. Hutchinson screamed and then they were upon her.

"The Lottery" from THE LOTTERY by Shirley Jackson. Copyright © 1948, 1949 by Shirley Jackson. Copyright renewed 1976, 1977 by Laurence Hyman, Barry Hyman, Mrs. Sarah Webster and Mrs. Joanne Schnurer. Reprinted by permission of Farrar, Straus and Giroux, LLC.

First Read

Read "The Lottery." After you read, complete the Think Questions below.

 THINK QUESTIONS

1. Describe the day on which the lottery takes place. How does the description of this day contrast with the events that take place later on? Cite textual evidence from the selection to support your answer.

2. What saying does Old Man Warner recite about the lottery in paragraph 32? What does this tell you about the original reason for holding the lottery? Cite specific textual evidence to support your statements.

3. How does the lottery affect Tessie and Bill Hutchinson at the end of the story? Cite specific textual evidence to support your statements.

4. Find the word **tradition** in paragraph 5 of "The Lottery." Use context clues in the surrounding sentences, as well as the sentence in which the word appears, to determine the word's meaning. Write your definition here and identify clues that helped you figure out its meaning.

5. Use context clues to determine the meaning of **perfunctory** as it is used in paragraph 7 of "The Lottery." Write your definition here and identify clues that helped you figure out its meaning. Then check the meaning in a dictionary.

Skill: Theme

Use the Checklist to analyze Theme in "The Lottery." Refer to the sample student annotations about Theme in the text.

••• CHECKLIST FOR THEME

In order to identify a theme, or central idea, of a text, note the following:

✓ the subject of the text and a theme that might be stated directly in the text

✓ details in the text that help to reveal theme

- the title and chapter headings
- details about the setting
- a narrator's or speaker's tone
- characters' thoughts, actions, and dialogue
- the central conflict in a story's plot
- the climax, or turning point, in the story
- the resolution of the conflict
- shifts in characters, setting, or plot events

✓ analyze the development of the theme and its relationship to the characters, setting, and plot

- a setting, such as a rugged wilderness or a boat lost at sea, can prevent characters from accomplishing something and affect them in some way
- the time and place, such as a narrative set in the past or future, can affect how a character responds to events

To determine a theme, or central idea, of a text and analyze its development over the course of the text, including its relationship to the characters, setting, and plot, use the following questions as a guide:

✓ What is a theme, or central idea, of the text? When did you become aware of that theme?

✓ How does the theme relate to the characters, setting, and plot?

✓ How does the theme develop over the course of the text?

Reading & Writing Companion

Skill:
Theme

Reread paragraphs 6 and 7 of "The Lottery." Then, using the Checklist on the previous page, answer the multiple-choice questions below.

↻ YOUR TURN

1. This question has two parts. First, answer Part A. Then, answer Part B.

   Part A: Which of the following describes most villagers' view of the lottery?

   ○ A. One should not follow or change any routines that have not been done in the past.

   ○ B. The current version of the tradition should be practiced even though parts of it have been let go or lost.

   ○ C. A routine should be changed when the villagers no longer understand the meaning behind it.

   ○ D. Most villagers think that the lottery should be stopped, but they do not have the power to stop it.

   Part B: Which of the following details BEST supports the conclusion drawn in Part A?

   ○ A. ". . . some people believed that the official of the lottery used to stand just so when he said or sang it, others believed that he was supposed to walk among the people, but years and years ago this part of the ritual had been allowed to lapse."

   ○ B. "There was a great deal of fussing to be done before Mr. Summers declared the lottery open. There were the lists to make up—of heads of families, heads of households in each family, members of each household in each family."

   ○ C. "The night before the lottery, Mr. Summers and Mr. Graves made up the slips of paper and put them in the box, and it was then taken to the safe of Mr. Summers' coal company and locked up until Mr. Summers was ready to take it to the square next morning."

   ○ D. "Mr. Summers was very good at all this; in his clean white shirt and blue jeans, with one hand resting carelessly on the black box, he seemed very proper and important as he talked interminably to Mr. Graves and the Martins."

2. Paragraph 6 describes where the villagers keep the black box during the lottery and where they have kept it throughout the rest of the year. What does that description imply about this tradition?

○ A. Historic objects are an essential part of practicing traditions, so they need to be carefully preserved.

○ B. As part of the tradition, the box needs to be stored in a different place each year so that everyone shares the responsibility for taking care of it.

○ C. No one wants to be in charge of the black box during the year because it is used to determine who will be sacrificed in the lottery.

○ D. The object associated with the lottery is an accepted part of village life, as much as the post office or grocery store is.

3. Based on the interactions between characters and the setting details in paragraphs 6 and 7, the reader can conclude that a possible theme is—

○ A. Small changes can make old traditions seem new and exciting.

○ B. Traditions can become less meaningful over time.

○ C. Failing to pass down a tradition can be hurtful to a community.

○ D. It can be dangerous to blindly stick to traditions.

Skill:
Allusion

Use the Checklist to analyze Allusion in "The Lottery." Refer to the sample student annotations about Allusion in the text.

••• CHECKLIST FOR ALLUSION

In order to identify an allusion, note the following:

✓ references or clues that suggest a reference to a myth, religious works such as The Bible, a story, person, historical event, object, idea, or other work of art with which readers may be familiar

✓ the theme, event, character, or situation in a text to which the references or clues add information

✓ patterns of events or character types that are used in other familiar texts

To better understand the allusion in a work of literature, do the following:

✓ use a print or digital resource to look up what you think might be an allusion

✓ list details about the allusion that relate to themes, events, or character types

To analyze how a modern work of fiction draws on themes, events, patterns of events, or character types from myths, traditional stories, or religious works, consider the following questions:

✓ What theme/event/character is referenced in the fiction I am reading? How do I know?

✓ How does that theme/event/character relate to what is happening in this new text?

To describe how the material is rendered new, consider the following questions:

✓ What does the modern version of the story add to the previous story?

✓ How does the inclusion of allusions impact the meaning or tone of the story?

✓ How does the theme/event/character change from its origin or source text?

Skill:
Allusion

Reread paragraphs 4 and 5 of "The Lottery." Then, using the Checklist on the previous page, answer the multiple-choice questions below.

⟳ YOUR TURN

1. In paragraph 4, which of the following could be a theme or event that the black box is referencing?

   ○ A. The black box is most likely an allusion to one year when crops did not grow.

   ○ B. The black box is most likely an allusion to a theme about fear because all of the villagers want to stay away from it.

   ○ C. The black box is most likely an allusion to a ceremonial object, so it could be a reference to a theme about tradition.

   ○ D. The black box is most likely an allusion to a theme about preserving natural resources because Mr. Summers also runs a coal business, and the box is made out of wood.

2. The condition of the black box is described in paragraph 5. What does its condition reveal to readers about the state of this village tradition?

   ○ A. The black box has lost many of its original qualities, and this village tradition has also lost many of the original practices.

   ○ B. The black box has been carefully preserved since it was first used, and this village tradition has also been carefully preserved over time.

   ○ C. In this village, each generation adds new material to this black box, and each generation adds a new practice to this village tradition.

   ○ D. The black box is fading, and it is evident that the yearly observance of this tradition will fade over time as well.

Please note that excerpts and passages in the StudySync® library and this workbook are intended as touchstones to generate interest in an author's work. The excerpts and passages do not substitute for the reading of entire texts, and StudySync® strongly recommends that students seek out and purchase the whole literary or informational work in order to experience it as the author intended. Links to online resellers are available in our digital library. In addition, complete works may be ordered through an authorized reseller by filling out and returning to StudySync® the order form enclosed in this workbook.

Reading & Writing Companion   61

Close Read

Reread "The Lottery." As you reread, complete the Skills Focus questions below. Then use your answers and annotations from the questions to help you complete the Write activity.

◎ SKILLS FOCUS

1. Identify clues about the village where "The Lottery" is set. Consider why the author may have decided to leave the village's exact location ambiguous, or unclear. Explain why an ambiguous setting connects to the story's theme about traditions.

2. Identify evidence of Old Man Warner's feelings about the lottery and what he thinks about stopping the tradition. Explain how his character's dialogue helps develop the story's theme.

3. Some of the last names in "The Lottery" make allusions to important characters, events, and themes, and "Mr. Graves" is an example of one of those names. What connections can you make to

this character's name? How might the name be an allusion? Use evidence from the text to explain your answer.

4. Identify setting details and examples of surprising behavior in the story's conclusion. Explain how living in the village has influenced the characters' beliefs and values.

5. Identify mysterious elements in "The Lottery" related to the story's setting, events, characters, and theme. Explain how these examples work together to create reader interest in the story.

✏ WRITE

LITERARY ANALYSIS: Sometimes terrible things happen in places that seem safe and pleasant on the surface. How did your knowledge about the setting of "The Lottery" expand or change as you read the story? What is one theme that the setting helped to develop as a result? Write a response of at least 300 words. Monitor details from the story to show how Shirley Jackson uses the setting not only to surprise readers, but also to develop the theme.

The Graveyard Book

FICTION

Neil Gaiman and
P. Craig Russell

2014

Introduction

Children's author Neil Gaiman (b. 1960) is best known for his novella *Coraline*, which won international praise and was adapted into a graphic novel as well as a high-budget feature film. Like *Coraline*, the British author's graphic novel version of *The Graveyard Book* was a critically acclaimed bestseller, with P. Craig Russell's award-winning illustrations bringing this Newbery Medal-winning book alive. In this excerpt, we meet a young boy (Nobody "Bod" Owens) immediately after his family is murdered by the man Jack. Wandering into a nearby graveyard, the orphan boy is adopted and raised by an elderly couple, Mister and Mistress Owens, and the tall, mysterious Silas — none of whom belong to the world of the living.

"Are you . . . is that . . . a ghost?!"

NOTES

6

7

Please note that excerpts and passages in the StudySync® library and this workbook are intended as touchstones to generate interest in an author's work. The excerpts and passages do not substitute for the reading of entire texts, and StudySync® strongly recommends that students seek out and purchase the whole literary or informational work in order to experience it as the author intended. Links to online resellers are available in our digital library. In addition, complete works may be ordered through an authorized reseller by filling out and returning to StudySync® the order form enclosed in this workbook.

Reading & Writing Companion

65

8

10

Please note that excerpts and passages in the StudySync® library and this workbook are intended as touchstones to generate interest in an author's work. The excerpts and passages do not substitute for the reading of entire texts, and StudySync® strongly recommends that students seek out and purchase the whole literary or informational work in order to experience it as the author intended. Links to online resellers are available in our digital library. In addition, complete works may be ordered through an authorized reseller by filling out and returning to StudySync® the order form enclosed in this workbook.

Reading & Writing Companion   69

13

Please note that excerpts and passages in the StudySync® library and this workbook are intended as touchstones to generate interest in an author's work. The excerpts and passages do not substitute for the reading of entire texts, and StudySync® strongly recommends that students seek out and purchase the whole literary or informational work in order to experience it as the author intended. Links to online resellers are available in our digital library. In addition, complete works may be ordered through an authorized reseller by filling out and returning to StudySync® the order form enclosed in this workbook.

Reading & Writing
Companion

71

FROM THE SHADOWS, THE STRANGER WATCHED JACK UNTIL HE WAS OUT OF SIGHT.

THEN HE MOVED THROUGH THE NIGHT, UP AND UP, TO A PLACE DOMINATED BY AN OBELISK DEDICATED TO THE MEMORY OF JOSIAH WORTHINGTON, BART., WHO HAD, THREE HUNDRED YEARS BEFORE, BOUGHT THE OLD CEMETERY AND THE LAND AROUND IT, AND GIVEN IT TO THE CITY IN PERPETUITY.

THERE WERE, ALL TOLD, SOME TEN THOUSAND SOULS IN THE GRAVEYARD, BUT MOST OF THEM SLEPT DEEP, AND THERE WERE LESS THAN THREE HUNDRED OF THEM UP THERE, IN THE MOONLIGHT.

THE STRANGER REACHED THEM AS SILENTLY AS THE FOG ITSELF, AND HE WATCHED THE PROCEEDINGS UNFOLD FROM THE SHADOWS.

AND HE SAID NOTHING.

MY DEAR MADAM, YOUR OBDURACY IS QUITE, IS...WELL, CAN'T YOU SEE HOW RIDICULOUS THIS IS?

NO, I CAN'T.

17

Please note that excerpts and passages in the StudySync® library and this workbook are intended as touchstones to generate interest in an author's work. The excerpts and passages do not substitute for the reading of entire texts, and StudySync® strongly recommends that students seek out and purchase the whole literary or informational work in order to experience it as the author intended. Links to online resellers are available in our digital library. In addition, complete works may be ordered through an authorized reseller by filling out and returning to StudySync® the order form enclosed in this workbook.

Reading & Writing Companion

75

18

19

Please note that excerpts and passages in the StudySync® library and this workbook are intended as touchstones to generate interest in an author's work. The excerpts and passages do not substitute for the reading of entire texts, and StudySync® strongly recommends that students seek out and purchase the whole literary or informational work in order to experience it as the author intended. Links to online resellers are available in our digital library. In addition, complete works may be ordered through an authorized reseller by filling out and returning to StudySync® the order form enclosed in this workbook.

Reading & Writing Companion **79**

Reading & Writing Companion

Please note that excerpts and passages in the StudySync® library and this workbook are intended as touchstones to generate interest in an author's work. The excerpts and passages do not substitute for the reading of entire texts, and StudySync® strongly recommends that students seek out and purchase the whole literary or informational work in order to experience it as the author intended. Links to online resellers are available in our digital library. In addition, complete works may be ordered through an authorized reseller by filling out and returning to StudySync® the order form enclosed in this workbook.

Reading & Writing
Companion

81

Text copyright © 2008 by Neil Gaiman. Illustrations copyright © 2014 by P. Craig Russell. Used by permission of HarperCollins Publishers.

WRITE

PERSONAL RESPONSE: Think about the title of this book and the excerpt that follows. What kind of story did you expect to read based on the title? Why? Did your expectations change after you read the excerpt? Use quotations and descriptions from the excerpt to explain whether or not the book matched what you expected from the title.

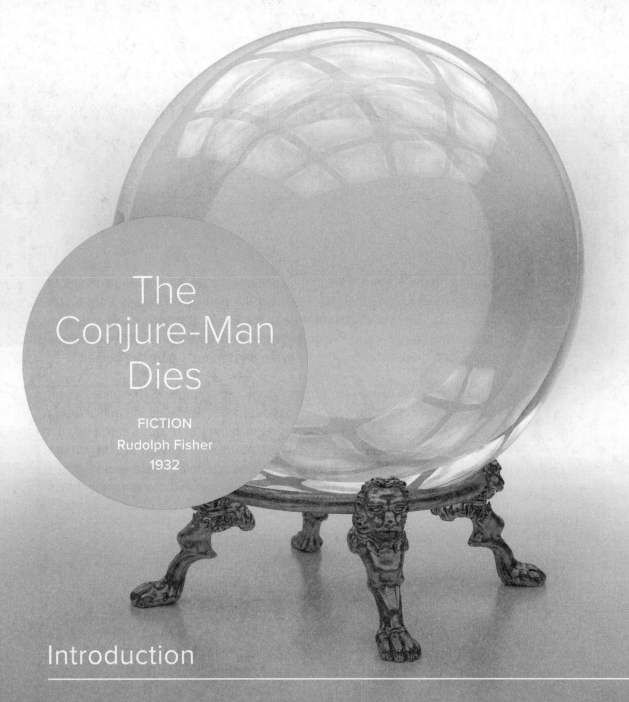

The Conjure-Man Dies

FICTION
Rudolph Fisher
1932

Introduction

Originally published in 1932, *The Conjure-Man Dies: A Mystery Tale of Dark Harlem* is widely considered the first detective novel by an African American author. Though writer Rudolph Fisher (1897–1934) published only two short stories and two novels before his untimely death at 37 years of age, he is still considered one of the central literary figures of the Harlem Renaissance. In this passage from the novel, Harlem physician Dr. Archer casts his keen analytical eye and medical expertise on the mysterious circumstances surrounding the sudden death of a local conjure-man, or fortune teller.

"But all of black Harlem was not thus gay and bright."

1.

1   Encountering the bright-lighted gaiety of Harlem's Seventh Avenue, the frigid midwinter night seemed to relent a little. She had given Battery Park a chill stare and she would undoubtedly freeze the Bronx. But here in this midrealm of rhythm and laughter she seemed to grow warmer and friendlier, observing, perhaps, that those who dwelt here were mysteriously dark like herself.

2   Of this favor the Avenue promptly took advantage. Sidewalks barren throughout the cold white day now sprouted life like fields in spring. Along swung boys in camels' hair beside girls in bunny and muskrat; broad, flat heels clacked, high narrow ones clicked, reluctantly leaving the disgorging theaters or eagerly seeking the **voracious** dance halls. There was loud jest and louder laughter and the frequent uplifting of merry voices in the moment's most popular song:

3   *"I'll be glad when you're dead, you rascal you,*
I'll be glad when you're dead, you rascal you.
What is it that you've got
Makes my wife think you so hot?
Oh you dog—I'll be glad when you're gone!"

4   But all of black Harlem was not thus gay and bright. Any number of dark, chill, silent side streets declined the relenting night's favor. 130th Street, for example, east of Lenox Avenue, was at this moment cold, still, and narrowly forbidding; one glanced down this block and was glad one's destination lay elsewhere. Its **concentrated** gloom was only intensified by an occasional spangle of electric light, splashed ineffectually against the blackness, or by the unearthly pallor of the sky, into which a wall of dwellings rose to hide the moon.

5   Among the houses in this looming row, one reared a little taller and gaunter than its fellows, so that the others appeared to shrink from it and huddle together in the shadow on either side. The basement of this house was quite black; its first floor, high above the sidewalk and approached by a long

graystone stoop, was only dimly lighted; its second floor was lighted more dimly still, while the third, which was the top, was vacantly dark again like the basement. About the place hovered an oppressive silence, as if those who entered here were warned beforehand not to speak above a whisper. There was, like a footnote, in one of the two first-floor windows to the left of the entrance a black-on-white sign reading:

6 "Samuel Crouch, Undertaker."

7 On the narrow panel to the right of the doorway the silver letters of another sign obscurely glittered on an onyx background:

8 "N. Frimbo, Psychist."

9 Between the two signs receded the high, narrow vestibule, terminating in a pair of tall glass-paneled doors. Glass curtains, tightly stretched in vertical folds, dimmed the already too subdued illumination beyond.

2.

10 It was about an hour before midnight that one of the doors rattled and flew open, revealing the bare headed, short, round figure of a young man who manifestly was **profoundly** agitated and in a great hurry. Without closing the door behind him, he rushed down the stairs, sped straight across the street, and in a moment was frantically pushing the bell of the dwelling directly opposite. A tall, slender, light-skinned man of obviously habitual composure answered the excited summons.

11 "Is—is you him?" stammered the agitated one, pointing to a shingle labeled "John Archer, M.D."

12 "Yes—I'm Dr. Archer."

13 "Well, arch on over here, will you, doc?" urged the caller. "Sump'm done happened to Frimbo."

14 "Frimbo? The fortune teller?"

15 "Step on it, will you, doc?"

16 Shortly, the physician, bag in hand, was hurrying up the graystone stoop behind his guide. They passed through the still open door into a hallway and mounted a flight of thickly carpeted stairs.

17 At the head of the staircase a tall, lank, angular figure awaited them. To this person the short, round, black, and by now quite breathless guide panted, "I

got one, boy! This here's the doc from 'cross the street. Come on, doc. Right in here."

18   Dr. Archer, in passing, had an impression of a young man as long and lean as himself, of a similarly light complexion except for a **profusion** of dark brown freckles, and of a curiously scowling countenance that glowered from either ill humor or apprehension. The doctor rounded the banister head and strode behind his pilot toward the front of the house along the upper hallway, midway of which, still following the excited short one, he turned and swung into a room that opened into the hall at that point. The tall fellow brought up the rear.

19   Within the room the physician stopped, looking about in surprise. The chamber was almost entirely in darkness. The walls appeared to be hung from ceiling to floor with black velvet drapes. Even the ceiling was covered, the heavy folds of cloth converging from the four corners to gather at a central point above, from which dropped a chain suspending the single strange source of light, a device which hung low over a chair behind a large desk-like table, yet left these things and indeed most of the room unlighted. This was because, instead of shedding its radiance downward and outward as would an ordinary shaded droplight, this mechanism focused a horizontal beam upon a second chair on the opposite side of the table. Clearly the person who used the chair beneath the odd spotlight could remain in relative darkness while the occupant of the other chair was brightly illuminated.

20   "There he is—jes' like Jinx found him."

21   And now in the dark chair beneath the odd lamp the doctor made out a huddled, shadowy form. Quickly he stepped forward.

22   "Is this the only light?"

23   "Only one I've seen."

24   Dr. Archer procured a flashlight from his bag and swept its faint beam over the walls and ceiling. Finding no sign of another lighting fixture, he directed the instrument in his hand toward the figure in the chair and saw a bare black head **inclined** limply sidewise, a flaccid countenance with open mouth and fixed eyes staring from under drooping lids.

25   "Can't do much in here. Anybody up front?"

26   "Yes, suh. Two ladies."

27   "Have to get him outside. Let's see. I know. Downstairs. Down in Crouch's. There's a sofa. You men take hold and get him down there. This way."

28   There was some hesitancy. "Mean us, doc?"

29   "Of course. Hurry. He doesn't look so hot now."

30   "I ain't none too warm, myself," murmured the short one. But he and his friend obeyed, carrying out their task with a dispatch born of distaste. Down the stairs they followed Dr. Archer, and into the undertaker's dimly lighted front room.

31   "Oh, Crouch!" called the doctor. "Mr. Crouch!"

32   "That 'mister' ought to get him."

33   But there was no answer. "Guess he's out. That's right—put him on the sofa. Push that other switch by the door. Good."

34   Dr. Archer inspected the supine figure as he reached into his bag. "Not so good," he commented. Beneath his black satin robe the patient wore ordinary clothing—trousers, vest, shirt, collar and tie. Deftly the physician bared the chest; with one hand he palpated the heart area while with the other he adjusted the ear-pieces of his stethoscope. He bent over, placed the bell of his instrument on the motionless dark chest, and listened a long time. He removed the instrument, disconnected first one, then the other, rubber tube at their junction with the bell, blew **vigorously** through them in turn, replaced them, and repeated the operation of listening. At last he stood erect.

35   "Not a twitch," he said.

36   "Long gone, huh?"

37   "Not so long. Still warm. But gone."

38   The short young man looked at his scowling freckled companion. "What'd I tell you?" he whispered.

39   "Was I right or wasn't I?"

40   The tall one did not answer but watched the doctor. The doctor put aside his stethoscope and inspected the patient's head more closely, the parted lips and half-open eyes. He extended a hand and with his extremely long fingers gently palpated the scalp. "Hello," he said. He turned the far side of the head toward him and looked first at that side, then at his fingers.

41   "Wh-what?"

42   "Blood in his hair," announced the physician. He procured a gauze dressing from his bag, wiped his moist fingers, thoroughly sponged and reinspected the wound. Abruptly he turned to the two men, whom until now he had treated

Please note that excerpts and passages in the StudySync® library and this workbook are intended as touchstones to generate interest in an author's work. The excerpts and passages do not substitute for the reading of entire texts, and StudySync® strongly recommends that students seek out and purchase the whole literary or informational work in order to experience it as the author intended. Links to online resellers are available in our digital library. In addition, complete works may be ordered through an authorized reseller by filling out and returning to StudySync® the order form enclosed in this workbook.

Reading & Writing Companion

91

quite impersonally. Still imperturbably, but incisively, in the manner of lancing an abscess, he asked, "Who are you two gentlemen?"

43   "Why—uh—this here's Jinx Jenkins, doc. He's my buddy, see? Him and me—"

44   "And you—if I don't presume?"

45   "Me? I'm Bubber Brown—"

46   "Well, how did this happen, Mr. Brown?"

47   "'Deed I don' know, doc. What you mean—is somebody killed him?"

48   "You don't know?" Dr. Archer regarded the pair curiously a moment, then turned back to examine further. From an instrument case he took a probe and proceeded to explore the wound in the dead man's scalp. "Well—what do you know about it, then?" he asked, still probing. "Who found him?" "Jinx," answered the one who called himself Bubber. "We jes' come here to get this Frimbo's advice 'bout a little business project we thought up."

49   "Jinx went in to see him. I waited in the waitin' room. Presently Jinx come bustin' out pop-eyed and beckoned to me. I went back with him—and there was Frimbo, jes' like you found him. We didn't even know he was over the river."

50   "Did he fall against anything and strike his head?"

51   "No, suh, doc." Jinx became **articulate.** "He didn't do nothin' the whole time I was in there. Nothin' but talk. He tol' me who I was and what I wanted befo' I could open my mouth. Well, I said that I knowed that much already and that I come to find out sump'm I didn't know. Then he went on talkin', tellin' me plenty. He knowed his stuff all right. But all of a sudden he stopped talkin' and mumbled sump'm 'bout not bein' able to see. Seem like he got scared, and he say, 'Frimbo, why don't you see?' Then he didn't say no more. He sound' so funny I got scared myself and jumped up and grabbed that light and turned it on him—and there he was."

© 1932 by Rudolph Fisher, The Conjure-Man Dies. Published by The University of Michigan Press, 1992. Used by permission of The University of Michigan Press.

✏️ **WRITE**

PERSONAL RESPONSE: In the first section of *The Conjure-Man Dies*, the author describes Harlem in great detail. Reread this section and note your reaction. What can you see or hear? What phrases are particularly effective, and why? How does the author use this description to gradually create a sense of mystery? Be sure to cite textual evidence.

Please note that excerpts and passages in the StudySync® library and this workbook are intended as touchstones to generate interest in an author's work. The excerpts and passages do not substitute for the reading of entire texts, and StudySync® strongly recommends that students seek out and purchase the whole literary or informational work in order to experience it as the author intended. Links to online resellers are available in our digital library. In addition, complete works may be ordered through an authorized reseller by filling out and returning to StudySync® the order form enclosed in this workbook.

Reading & Writing
Companion   **93**

The Monkey's Paw

FICTION
W. W. Jacobs
1902

Introduction

studysync tv

W. W. Jacobs (1863–1943) wrote numerous humorous short stories, but it is for his works of horror that he is mainly remembered. In "The Monkey's Paw," his cautionary tale from 1902, a well-to-do family in Victorian England is presented with a dubious opportunity to increase their fortunes. A magical monkey's paw from India has the power to make three wishes come true—but what will be the price?

"Hold it up in your right hand and wish aloud," said the sergeant-major, "but I warn you of the consequences."

NOTES

I.

1   Without, the night was cold and wet, but in the small parlour of Laburnam Villa the blinds were drawn and the fire burned brightly. Father and son were at chess, the former, who possessed ideas about the game involving **radical** changes, putting his king into such sharp and unnecessary perils that it even provoked comment from the white-haired old lady knitting placidly by the fire.

2   "Hark at the wind," said Mr. White, who, having seen a fatal mistake after it was too late, was amiably desirous of preventing his son from seeing it.

3   "I'm listening," said the latter, grimly surveying the board as he stretched out his hand. "Check."

4   "I should hardly think that he'd come to-night," said his father, with his hand poised over the board.

5   "Mate," replied the son.

6   "That's the worst of living so far out," bawled Mr. White, with sudden and unlooked-for violence; "of all the beastly, slushy, out-of-the-way places to live in, this is the worst. Pathway's a bog, and the road's a torrent. I don't know what people are thinking about. I suppose because only two houses in the road are let, they think it doesn't matter."

7   "Never mind, dear," said his wife, soothingly; "perhaps you'll win the next one."

8   Mr. White looked up sharply, just in time to intercept a knowing glance between mother and son. The words died away on his lips, and he hid a guilty grin in his thin grey beard.

9   "There he is," said Herbert White, as the gate banged to loudly and heavy footsteps came toward the door.

Please note that excerpts and passages in the StudySync® library and this workbook are intended as touchstones to generate interest in an author's work. The excerpts and passages do not substitute for the reading of entire texts, and StudySync® strongly recommends that students seek out and purchase the whole literary or informational work in order to experience it as the author intended. Links to online resellers are available in our digital library. In addition, complete works may be ordered through an authorized reseller by filling out and returning to StudySync® the order form enclosed in this workbook.

Reading & Writing Companion   95

10 The old man rose with hospitable haste, and opening the door, was heard condoling with the new arrival. The new arrival also condoled with himself, so that Mrs. White said, "Tut, tut!" and coughed gently as her husband entered the room, followed by a tall, burly man, beady of eye and rubicund of visage.

11 "Sergeant-Major Morris," he said, introducing him.

12 The sergeant-major shook hands, and taking the proffered seat by the fire, watched contentedly while his host got out whiskey and tumblers and stood a small copper kettle on the fire.

13 At the third glass his eyes got brighter, and he began to talk, the little family circle regarding with eager interest this visitor from distant parts, as he squared his broad shoulders in the chair and spoke of wild scenes and doughty deeds; of wars and plagues and strange peoples.

14 "Twenty-one years of it," said Mr. White, nodding at his wife and son. "When he went away he was a slip of a youth in the warehouse. Now look at him."

15 "He don't look to have taken much harm," said Mrs. White, politely.

16 "I'd like to go to India myself," said the old man, "just to look round a bit, you know."

17 "Better where you are," said the sergeant-major, shaking his head. He put down the empty glass, and sighing softly, shook it again.

18 "I should like to see those old temples and fakirs and jugglers," said the old man. "What was that you started telling me the other day about a monkey's paw or something, Morris?"

19 "Nothing," said the soldier, hastily. "Leastways nothing worth hearing."

20 "Monkey's paw?" said Mrs. White, curiously.

A fakir rests on a bed of nails in a display of public penance in Calcutta, India, circa 1930.

21 "Well, it's just a bit of what you might call magic, perhaps," said the sergeant-major, offhandedly.

22 His three listeners leaned forward eagerly. The visitor absent-mindedly put his empty glass to his lips and then set it down again. His host filled it for him.

NOTES

23　"To look at," said the sergeant-major, fumbling in his pocket, "it's just an ordinary little paw, dried to a mummy."

24　He took something out of his pocket and proffered it. Mrs. White drew back with a grimace, but her son, taking it, examined it curiously.

25　"And what is there special about it?" inquired Mr. White as he took it from his son, and having examined it, placed it upon the table.

26　"It had a spell put on it by an old fakir," said the sergeant-major, "a very holy man. He wanted to show that fate ruled people's lives, and that those who interfered with it did so to their sorrow. He put a spell on it so that three separate men could each have three wishes from it."

27　His manner was so impressive that his hearers were conscious that their light laughter jarred somewhat.

28　"Well, why don't you have three, sir?" said Herbert White, cleverly.

29　The soldier regarded him in the way that middle age is wont to regard **presumptuous** youth. "I have," he said, quietly, and his blotchy face whitened.

30　"And did you really have the three wishes granted?" asked Mrs. White.

31　"I did," said the sergeant-major, and his glass tapped against his strong teeth.

32　"And has anybody else wished?" persisted the old lady.

33　"The first man had his three wishes. Yes," was the reply; "I don't know what the first two were, but the third was for death. That's how I got the paw."

34　His tones were so grave that a hush fell upon the group.

35　"If you've had your three wishes, it's no good to you now, then, Morris," said the old man at last. "What do you keep it for?"

36　The soldier shook his head. "Fancy, I suppose," he said, slowly. "I did have some idea of selling it, but I don't think I will. It has caused enough mischief already. Besides, people won't buy. They think it's a fairy tale; some of them, and those who do think anything of it want to try it first and pay me afterward."

37　"If you could have another three wishes," said the old man, eyeing him keenly, "would you have them?"

38　"I don't know," said the other. "I don't know."

Skill:
Plot

When the sergeant-major says that the first man's final wish was for death, Mr. and Mrs. White never question why. These lines of dialogue build tension. I want to find out what happens when a wish is made with the monkey's paw.

Skill:
Story Structure

The inciting incident creates a feeling that something bad will happen.

39 He took the paw, and dangling it between his forefinger and thumb, suddenly threw it upon the fire. White, with a slight cry, stooped down and snatched it off.

40 "Better let it burn," said the soldier, solemnly.

41 "If you don't want it, Morris," said the other, "give it to me."

42 "I won't," said his friend, doggedly. "I threw it on the fire. If you keep it, don't blame me for what happens. Pitch it on the fire again like a sensible man."

43 The other shook his head and examined his new possession closely. "How do you do it?" he inquired.

44 "Hold it up in your right hand and wish aloud," said the sergeant-major, "but I warn you of the **consequences**."

45 "Sounds like the Arabian Nights[1]," said Mrs. White, as she rose and began to set the supper. "Don't you think you might wish for four pairs of hands for me?"

46 Her husband drew the talisman from pocket, and then all three burst into laughter as the sergeant-major, with a look of alarm on his face, caught him by the arm.

47 "If you must wish," he said, gruffly, "wish for something sensible."

48 Mr. White dropped it back in his pocket, and placing chairs, motioned his friend to the table. In the business of supper the talisman was partly forgotten, and afterward the three sat listening in an enthralled fashion to a second installment of the soldier's adventures in India.

49 "If the tale about the monkey's paw is not more truthful than those he has been telling us," said Herbert, as the door closed behind their guest, just in time for him to catch the last train, "we sha'nt make much out of it."

50 "Did you give him anything for it, father?" inquired Mrs. White, regarding her husband closely.

51 "A trifle," said he, colouring slightly. "He didn't want it, but I made him take it. And he pressed me again to throw it away."

52 "Likely," said Herbert, with pretended horror. "Why, we're going to be rich, and famous and happy. Wish to be an emperor, father, to begin with; then you can't be henpecked."

1. **Arabian Nights** a collection of Middle Eastern folktales told by the legendary Scheherazade, also frequently called *One Thousand and One Nights*

 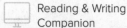

NOTES

53 He darted round the table, pursued by the maligned Mrs. White armed with an antimacassar[2].

54 Mr. White took the paw from his pocket and eyed it dubiously. "I don't know what to wish for, and that's a fact," he said, slowly. "It seems to me I've got all I want."

55 "If you only cleared the house, you'd be quite happy, wouldn't you?" said Herbert, with his hand on his shoulder. "Well, wish for two hundred pounds[3], then; that 'll just do it."

56 His father, smiling shamefacedly at his own **credulity,** held up the talisman, as his son, with a solemn face, somewhat marred by a wink at his mother, sat down at the piano and struck a few impressive chords.

57 "I wish for two hundred pounds," said the old man distinctly.

58 A fine crash from the piano greeted the words, interrupted by a shuddering cry from the old man. His wife and son ran toward him.

59 "It moved," he cried, with a glance of disgust at the object as it lay on the floor.

60 "As I wished, it twisted in my hand like a snake."

61 "Well, I don't see the money," said his son as he picked it up and placed it on the table, "and I bet I never shall."

62 "It must have been your fancy, father," said his wife, regarding him anxiously.

63 He shook his head. "Never mind, though; there's no harm done, but it gave me a shock all the same."

64 They sat down by the fire again while the two men finished their pipes. Outside, the wind was higher than ever, and the old man started nervously at the sound of a door banging upstairs. A silence unusual and depressing settled upon all three, which lasted until the old couple rose to retire for the night.

65 "I expect you'll find the cash tied up in a big bag in the middle of your bed," said Herbert, as he bade them good-night, "and something horrible squatting up on top of the wardrobe watching you as you pocket your ill-gotten gains."

---

2. **antimacassar** an ornamental cloth placed over the back of a chair to protect it
3. **pounds** the basic unit of currency in the United Kingdom

66 He sat alone in the darkness, gazing at the dying fire, and seeing faces in it. The last face was so horrible and so simian that he gazed at it in amazement. It got so vivid that, with a little uneasy laugh, he felt on the table for a glass containing a little water to throw over it. His hand grasped the monkey's paw, and with a little shiver he wiped his hand on his coat and went up to bed.

II.

67 In the brightness of the wintry sun next morning as it streamed over the breakfast table he laughed at his fears. There was an air of prosaic wholesomeness about the room which it had lacked on the previous night, and the dirty, shrivelled little paw was pitched on the sideboard with a carelessness which betokened no great belief in its virtues.

68 "I suppose all old soldiers are the same," said Mrs. White. "The idea of our listening to such nonsense! How could wishes be granted in these days? And if they could, how could two hundred pounds hurt you, father?"

69 "Might drop on his head from the sky," said the frivolous Herbert.

70 "Morris said the things happened so naturally," said his father, "that you might if you so wished attribute it to coincidence."

71 "Well, don't break into the money before I come back," said Herbert as he rose from the table. "I'm afraid it'll turn you into a mean, avaricious man, and we shall have to disown you."

72 His mother laughed, and following him to the door, watched him down the road; and returning to the breakfast table, was very happy at the expense of her husband's credulity. All of which did not prevent her from scurrying to the door at the postman's knock, nor prevent her from referring somewhat shortly to retired sergeant-majors of bibulous habits when she found that the post brought a tailor's bill.

73 "Herbert will have some more of his funny remarks, I expect, when he comes home," she said, as they sat at dinner.

74 "I dare say," said Mr. White, pouring himself out some beer; "but for all that, the thing moved in my hand; that I'll swear to."

75 "You thought it did," said the old lady soothingly.

76 "I say it did," replied the other. "There was no thought about it; I had just— What's the matter?"

77   His wife made no reply. She was watching the mysterious movements of a man outside, who, peering in an undecided fashion at the house, appeared to be trying to make up his mind to enter. In mental connection with the two hundred pounds, she noticed that the stranger was well dressed, and wore a silk hat of glossy newness. Three times he paused at the gate, and then walked on again. The fourth time he stood with his hand upon it, and then with sudden resolution flung it open and walked up the path. Mrs. White at the same moment placed her hands behind her, and hurriedly unfastening the strings of her apron, put that useful article of apparel beneath the cushion of her chair.

78   She brought the stranger, who seemed ill at ease, into the room. He gazed at her furtively, and listened in a preoccupied fashion as the old lady apologized for the appearance of the room, and her husband's coat, a garment which he usually reserved for the garden. She then waited as patiently as her sex would permit, for him to broach his business, but he was at first strangely silent.

79   "I—was asked to call," he said at last, and stooped and picked a piece of cotton from his trousers. "I come from 'Maw and Meggins.'"

80   The old lady started. "Is anything the matter?" she asked, breathlessly. "Has anything happened to Herbert? What is it? What is it?"

81   Her husband interposed. "There, there, mother," he said, hastily. "Sit down, and don't jump to conclusions. You've not brought bad news, I'm sure, sir;" and he eyed the other wistfully.

82   "I'm sorry—" began the visitor.

83   "Is he hurt?" demanded the mother, wildly.

84   The visitor bowed in assent. "Badly hurt," he said, quietly, "but he is not in any pain."

85   "Oh, thank God!" said the old woman, clasping her hands. "Thank God for that! Thank—"

86   She broke off suddenly as the sinister meaning of the assurance dawned upon her and she saw the awful confirmation of her fears in the other's averted face. She caught her breath, and turning to her slower-witted husband, laid her trembling old hand upon his. There was a long silence.

87   "He was caught in the machinery," said the visitor at length in a low voice.

88   "Caught in the machinery," repeated Mr. White, in a dazed fashion, "yes."

Please note that excerpts and passages in the StudySync® library and this workbook are intended as touchstones to generate interest in an author's work. The excerpts and passages do not substitute for the reading of entire texts, and StudySync® strongly recommends that students seek out and purchase the whole literary or informational work in order to experience it as the author intended. Links to online resellers are available in our digital library. In addition, complete works may be ordered through an authorized reseller by filling out and returning to StudySync® the order form enclosed in this workbook.

Reading & Writing
Companion   101

NOTES

89 He sat staring blankly out at the window, and taking his wife's hand between his own, pressed it as he had been wont to do in their old courting-days nearly forty years before.

90 "He was the only one left to us," he said, turning gently to the visitor. "It is hard."

91 The other coughed, and rising, walked slowly to the window. "The firm wished me to convey their sincere sympathy with you in your great loss," he said, without looking round. "I beg that you will understand I am only their servant and merely obeying orders."

92 There was no reply; the old woman's face was white, her eyes staring, and her breath inaudible; on the husband's face was a look such as his friend the sergeant might have carried into his first action.

93 "I was to say that 'Maw and Meggins' disclaim all responsibility," continued the other. "They admit no liability at all, but in consideration of your son's services, they wish to present you with a certain sum as **compensation."**

94 Mr. White dropped his wife's hand, and rising to his feet, gazed with a look of horror at his visitor. His dry lips shaped the words, "How much?"

95 "Two hundred pounds," was the answer.

96 Unconscious of his wife's shriek, the old man smiled faintly, put out his hands like a sightless man, and dropped, a senseless heap, to the floor.

III.

97 In the huge new cemetery, some two miles distant, the old people buried their dead, and came back to a house steeped in shadow and silence. It was all over so quickly that at first they could hardly realize it, and remained in a state of expectation as though of something else to happen —something else which was to lighten this load, too heavy for old hearts to bear.

98 But the days passed, and expectation gave place to resignation—the hopeless resignation of the old, sometimes miscalled, **apathy.** Sometimes they hardly exchanged a word, for now they had nothing to talk about, and their days were long to weariness.

99 It was about a week after that the old man, waking suddenly in the night, stretched out his hand and found himself alone. The room was in darkness, and the sound of subdued weeping came from the window. He raised himself in bed and listened.

100 "Come back," he said, tenderly. "You will be cold."

101 "It is colder for my son," said the old woman, and wept afresh.

102 The sound of her sobs died away on his ears. The bed was warm, and his eyes heavy with sleep. He dozed fitfully, and then slept until a sudden wild cry from his wife awoke him with a start.

103 "The paw!" she cried wildly. "The monkey's paw!"

104 He started up in alarm. "Where? Where is it? What's the matter?"

105 She came stumbling across the room toward him. "I want it," she said, quietly. "You've not destroyed it?"

106 "It's in the parlour, on the bracket," he replied, marvelling. "Why?"

107 She cried and laughed together, and bending over, kissed his cheek.

108 "I only just thought of it," she said, hysterically. "Why didn't I think of it before? Why didn't you think of it?"

109 "Think of what?" he questioned.

110 "The other two wishes," she replied, rapidly. "We've only had one."

111 "Was not that enough?" he demanded, fiercely.

112 "No," she cried, triumphantly; "we'll have one more. Go down and get it quickly, and wish our boy alive again."

113 The man sat up in bed and flung the bedclothes from his quaking limbs. "Good God, you are mad!" he cried, aghast.

114 "Get it," she panted; "get it quickly, and wish—Oh, my boy, my boy!"

115 Her husband struck a match and lit the candle. "Get back to bed," he said, unsteadily. "You don't know what you are saying."

116 "We had the first wish granted," said the old woman, feverishly; "why not the second?"

117 "A coincidence," stammered the old man.

118 "Go and get it and wish," cried his wife, quivering with excitement.

119 The old man turned and regarded her, and his voice shook. "He has been dead ten days, and besides he—I would not tell you else, but—I could only recognize him by his clothing. If he was too terrible for you to see then, how now?"

Copyright © BookheadEd Learning, LLC

120 "Bring him back," cried the old woman, and dragged him toward the door. "Do you think I fear the child I have nursed?"

121 He went down in the darkness, and felt his way to the parlour, and then to the mantelpiece. The talisman was in its place, and a horrible fear that the unspoken wish might bring his mutilated son before him ere he could escape from the room seized upon him, and he caught his breath as he found that he had lost the direction of the door. His brow cold with sweat, he felt his way round the table, and groped along the wall until he found himself in the small passage with the unwholesome thing in his hand.

122 Even his wife's face seemed changed as he entered the room. It was white and expectant, and to his fears seemed to have an unnatural look upon it. He was afraid of her.

123 "Wish!" she cried, in a strong voice.

124 "It is foolish and wicked," he faltered.

125 "Wish!" repeated his wife.

126 He raised his hand. "I wish my son alive again."

127 The talisman fell to the floor, and he regarded it fearfully. Then he sank trembling into a chair as the old woman, with burning eyes, walked to the window and raised the blind.

128 He sat until he was chilled with the cold, glancing occasionally at the figure of the old woman peering through the window. The candle-end, which had burned below the rim of the china candlestick, was throwing pulsating shadows on the ceiling and walls, until, with a flicker larger than the rest, it expired. The old man, with an unspeakable sense of relief at the failure of the talisman, crept back to his bed, and a minute or two afterward the old woman came silently and apathetically beside him.

129 Neither spoke, but lay silently listening to the ticking of the clock. A stair creaked, and a squeaky mouse scurried noisily through the wall. The darkness was oppressive, and after lying for some time screwing up his courage, he took the box of matches, and striking one, went downstairs for a candle.

130 At the foot of the stairs the match went out, and he paused to strike another; and at the same moment a knock, so quiet and stealthy as to be scarcely audible, sounded on the front door.

**Skill:
Plot**

Mr. White gives in to his wife and wishes again. This decision in the lines of dialogue is a turning point that moves the plot forward because the wish will bring their son back.

131   The matches fell from his hand and spilled in the passage. He stood motionless, his breath suspended until the knock was repeated. Then he turned and fled swiftly back to his room, and closed the door behind him. A third knock sounded through the house.

132   "What's that?" cried the old woman, starting up.

133   "A rat," said the old man in shaking tones—"a rat. It passed me on the stairs."

134   His wife sat up in bed listening. A loud knock resounded through the house.

135   "It's Herbert!" she screamed. "It's Herbert!"

136   She ran to the door, but her husband was before her, and catching her by the arm, held her tightly.

137   "What are you going to do?" he whispered hoarsely.

138   "It's my boy; it's Herbert!" she cried, struggling mechanically. "I forgot it was two miles away. What are you holding me for? Let go. I must open the door."

139   "For God's sake don't let it in," cried the old man, trembling.

140   "You're afraid of your own son," she cried, struggling. "Let me go. I'm coming, Herbert; I'm coming."

141   There was another knock, and another. The old woman with a sudden wrench broke free and ran from the room. Her husband followed to the landing, and called after her appealingly as she hurried downstairs. He heard the chain rattle back and the bottom bolt drawn slowly and stiffly from the socket. Then the old woman's voice, strained and panting.

142   "The bolt," she cried, loudly. "Come down. I can't reach it."

143   But her husband was on his hands and knees groping wildly on the floor in search of the paw. If he could only find it before the thing outside got in. A perfect fusillade of knocks reverberated through the house, and he heard the scraping of a chair as his wife put it down in the passage against the door. He heard the creaking of the bolt as it came slowly back, and at the same moment he found the monkey's paw, and frantically breathed his third and last wish.

144   The knocking ceased suddenly, although the echoes of it were still in the house. He heard the chair drawn back, and the door opened. A cold wind rushed up the staircase, and a long loud wail of disappointment and misery from his wife gave him courage to run down to her side, and then to the gate beyond. The street lamp flickering opposite shone on a quiet and deserted road.

First Read

Read "The Monkey's Paw." After you read, complete the Think Questions below.

☁ THINK QUESTIONS

1. What is "the monkey's paw"? What is Herbert's attitude toward the monkey's paw? Cite textual evidence from the selection to support your answer.

2. Write two to three sentences describing how Mr. White's feelings change about the monkey's paw after he makes his first wish and second wish.

3. Foreshadowing is a literary device in which a writer gives a subtle hint of what is to come later in the story. Can you identify an example of foreshadowing from the beginning of "The Monkey's Paw" that suggests making wishes on the paw will lead to tragedy? Cite textual evidence from the selection to support your answer.

4. Find the word **consequence** in paragraph 44 of "The Monkey's Paw." Use context clues in the surrounding sentences, as well as the sentence in which the word appears, to determine the word's meaning. Write your definition here and identify clues that helped you figure out its meaning.

5. Use context clues to determine the meaning of **compensation** as it is used in paragraph 93 of "The Monkey's Paw." Write your definition here and identify clues that helped you figure out its meaning. Then check the meaning in a dictionary.

PLOT

Skill:
Plot

Use the Checklist to analyze Plot in "The Monkey's Paw." Refer to the sample student annotations about Plot in the text.

••• CHECKLIST FOR PLOT

In order to identify plot elements in a story or drama, note the following:

✓ dialogue or conversations between two or more characters

✓ incidents or notable events throughout the story's plot

✓ central conflict

✓ characters' responses or decisions to incidents

✓ the ways in which the characters affect the resolution of the conflict

To analyze how particular lines of dialogue or incidents in a story or drama propel the action or provoke a decision, consider the following questions:

✓ What happens as a result of a dialogue between two characters?

✓ How does the plot unfold in the story?

✓ Do characters respond or change as the plot advances? How?

✓ What causes a character to act or make a decision? What events occur as a result of their actions or decisions?

PLOT

Skill:
Plot

Reread paragraphs 67–80 of "The Monkey's Paw." Then, using the Checklist on the previous page, answer the multiple-choice questions below.

♻ YOUR TURN

1. The author uses the dialogue between Mr. White, Mrs. White, and Herbert in paragraphs 68–70 to—

   ○ A. reveal that the sergeant-major is not credible.
   ○ B. provoke Herbert to ask for a raise at work.
   ○ C. build suspense about how the wish will be granted.
   ○ D. reveal that Mr. White, Mrs. White, and Herbert no longer care about the monkey's paw.

2. Which of the following is an example of an inciting incident?

   ○ A. In the brightness of the wintry sun next morning as it streamed over the breakfast table he laughed at his fears.
   ○ B. "Herbert will have some more of his funny remarks, I expect, when he comes home," she said, as they sat at dinner.
   ○ C. His mother laughed, and following him to the door, watched him down the road; and returning to the breakfast table, was very happy at the expense of her husband's credulity.
   ○ D. His wife made no reply. She was watching the mysterious movements of a man outside, who, peering in an undecided fashion at the house, appeared to be trying to make up his mind to enter.

3. The author builds tension at the end of the excerpt by—

   ○ A. hinting that the Whites will soon receive the 200 pounds.
   ○ B. indicating Mrs. White is unaware of what is happening.
   ○ C. suggesting that Mrs. White suspects there is something wrong.
   ○ D. implying that Mrs. White is uncomfortable talking to the man.

Skill:
Story Structure

Use the Checklist to analyze Story Structure in "The Monkey's Paw." Refer to the sample student annotations about Story Structure in the text.

••• CHECKLIST FOR STORY STRUCTURE

In order to determine how to compare and contrast the structure of two or more texts, note the following:

- ✓ the order of events, including the exposition, inciting incident, rising action, climax, falling action, and resolution in each text

- ✓ when the conflict is introduced in each text

- ✓ the use of flashback or foreshadowing in each text

- ✓ how the structure of each text contributes to its meaning and style

- ✓ the similarities and differences between the structures in each text

To compare and contrast the structure of two or more texts and analyze how the structure of each text contributes to its meaning and style, ask the following questions:

- ✓ How is each text structured?

- ✓ How are the structures of each text the same? How are they different?

- ✓ How does the structure of each text contribute to its meaning and style?

Please note that excerpts and passages in the StudySync® library and this workbook are intended as touchstones to generate interest in an author's work. The excerpts and passages do not substitute for the reading of entire texts, and StudySync® strongly recommends that students seek out and purchase the whole literary or informational work in order to experience it as the author intended. Links to online resellers are available in our digital library. In addition, complete works may be ordered through an authorized reseller by filling out and returning to StudySync® the order form enclosed in this workbook.

Reading & Writing Companion   109

Skill:
Story Structure

Reread paragraphs 54–59 of "The Monkey's Paw" and paragraphs 40–42 of *The Conjure-Man Dies*. Then, using the Checklist on the previous page, complete the chart below to compare and contrast the passages.

⟳ YOUR TURN

	Observation Options
A	The scene helps the reader understand the meaning and style of the story.
B	A character is in an unfamiliar room with two strangers and a dead body.
C	The scene shows rising action in the plot.
D	The scene suggests the style of a mystery novel.
E	A character makes a decision, and a supernatural event occurs.
F	The scene suggests the style of a spooky, horror story.

The Conjure-Man Dies	Both	"The Monkey's Paw"

Close Read

Reread "The Monkey's Paw." As you reread, complete the Skills Focus questions below. Then use your answers and annotations from the questions to help you complete the Write activity.

◎ SKILLS FOCUS

1. Identify evidence of Herbert's behavior in the story and explain how it influences events. Be sure to cite textual evidence to support your claims.

2. To wish or not to wish on the monkey's paw: this is the central conflict of W. W. Jacobs's story. Identify evidence of Mr. and Mrs. White's motivations in the story, and explain how their actions influence the resolution of the conflict. Be sure to cite evidence from the text to support your claims.

3. How do specific incidents or lines of dialogue in "The Monkey's Paw" propel the action of the plot? Be sure to use examples from the text to explain how the incident or dialogue drives action in the plot forward.

4. In *The Conjure-Man Dies*, something mysterious happens to Frimbo the conjure-man, leading Bubber Brown to hurriedly run to get help from Dr. Archer. Identify incidents in "The Monkey's Paw" that similarly provoke characters' decisions. How do these incidents drive the plot forward? How does the story structure contribute to the meaning of the texts?

5. Ghosts from the distant past and a figure cloaked in black help to create the mystery of the graveyard in *The Graveyard Book*. In "The Monkey's Paw," the mystery lies in the reader's interpretation of events. Identify one event from "The Monkey's Paw" and explain what makes it mysterious.

✎ WRITE

COMPARE AND CONTRAST: "The Monkey's Paw" (a short story), *The Conjure-Man Dies* (an excerpt from a novel), and *The Graveyard Book* (a graphic novel excerpt) have different story structures. How do these different structures contribute to the meanings of the texts? How do they impact the development of the plots? Compare and contrast how structure helps reveal the meaning of "The Monkey's Paw" against the *The Conjure-Man Dies* or *The Graveyard Book*. Remember to support your ideas with evidence from the texts.

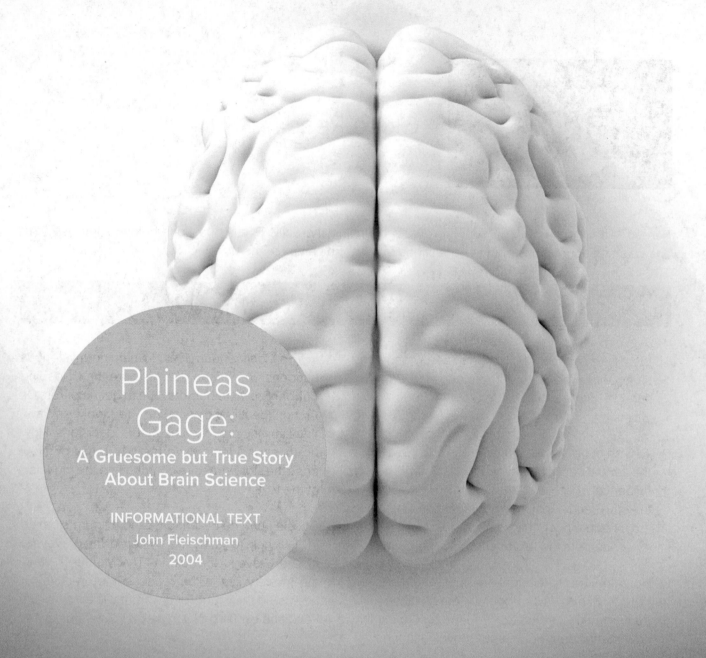

Phineas Gage:
A Gruesome but True Story About Brain Science

INFORMATIONAL TEXT
John Fleischman
2004

Introduction

After surviving a horrific accident that should have killed him instantly, Phineas Gage went on to live for 11 more years. What became of him after this accident—and why—would forever impact what scientists know about the human brain and how it functions. In the first chapter of *Phineas Gage: A Gruesome but True Story About Brain Science*, author John Fleischman draws readers into Phineas's shocking and fascinating story with a lively and engrossing account of the freak accident.

"Phineas will never be his old self again."

"Horrible Accident in Vermont"

• • •

Copyright © BookheadEd Learning, LLC

1   Phineas is the foreman of a track construction gang that is in the process of blasting a railroad right-of-way through granite bedrock near the small town of Cavendish, Vermont. Phineas is twenty-six years old, unmarried, and five feet, six inches tall, short for our time but about average for his. He is good with his hands and good with his men, "possessing an iron **will** as well as an iron frame," according to his doctor. In a moment, Phineas will have a horrible accident.

2   It will kill him, but it will take another eleven years, six months, and nineteen days to do so. In the short run, Phineas will make a full recovery, or so it will seem to those who didn't know him before. Old friends and family will know the truth. Phineas will never be his old self again. His "character" will change. The ways in which he deals with others, **conducts** himself, and makes plans will all change. Long after the accident, his doctor will sum up his case for a medical journal. "Gage," his doctor will write, "was no longer Gage." Phineas Gage's accident will make him world famous, but fame will do him little good. Yet for many others—psychologists, medical researchers, doctors, and especially those who suffer brain injuries—Phineas Gage will become someone worth knowing.

3   That's why we know so much about Phineas. It's been 150 years since his accident, yet we are still learning more about him. There's also a lot about Phineas we don't know and probably never will. The biggest question is the simplest one and the hardest to answer: Was Phineas lucky or unlucky? Once you hear his story, you can decide for yourself. But right now, Phineas is working on the railroad and his time has nearly come.

4   Building a railroad in 1848 is muscle work. There are no bulldozers or power shovels to open a way through Vermont's Green Mountains for the Rutland & Burlington Railroad. Phineas's men work with picks, shovels, and rock drills. Phineas's special skill is blasting. With well-placed charges of black

NOTES

Skill:
Central or
Main Idea

The author notes that Gage's accident changed his behavior. Gage also became the subject of medical research. These supporting ideas and details tell me that the author's central or main idea relates to how the accident affected Gage's brain.

gunpowder, he shatters rock. To set those charges, he carries the special tool of the blasting trade, his "tamping iron." Some people confuse a tamping iron with a crowbar, but they are different tools for different jobs. A crowbar is for lifting up or prying apart something heavy. A tamping iron is for the delicate job of setting explosives. Phineas had his tamping iron made to order by a neighborhood blacksmith. It's a tapering iron rod that is three feet, seven inches long and weighs thirteen and a half pounds. It looks like an iron spear. At the base, it's fat and round, an inch and three quarters in diameter. The fat end is for tamping—packing down—loose powder. The other end comes to a sharp, narrow point and is for poking holes through the gunpowder to set the **fuse.** Phineas's tamping iron is very smooth to the touch, smooth from the blacksmith's **forge** as well as from constant use.

5   His task is to blast the solid rock into pieces small enough for his crew to dig loose with hand tools and haul away in ox carts. The first step is to drill a hole in the bedrock at exactly the right angle and depth, or the explosion will be wasted. All day, Phineas must keep an eye on his drillers to make sure they stay ahead. All day, Phineas must keep an eye on his diggers to make sure they keep up. All the time between, Phineas and his assistant are working with touchy explosives.

6   They follow a strict **routine.** His assistant "charges" each new hole by filling the bottom with coarse-grained gunpowder. Phineas uses the narrow end of his iron to carefully press the ropelike fuse down into the powder. The assistant then fills up the rest of the hole with loose sand to act as a plug. Phineas will tamp the sand tight to bottle up the explosion, channeling the blast downward into the rock to shatter it. While his assistant is pouring the sand, Phineas flips his tamping iron around from the pointy end to the round end for tamping. Black powder is ticklish stuff. When it's damp, nothing will set it off. When it's too dry or mixed in the wrong formula, almost anything can set it off, without warning. But Phineas and his assistant have done this a thousand times—pour the powder, set the fuse, pour the sand, tamp the sand plug, shout a warning, light the fuse, and run like mad.

7   But something goes wrong this time. The sand is never poured down the hole; the black powder and fuse sit exposed at the bottom. Does his assistant forget, or does Phineas forget to look? Witnesses disagree. A few yards behind Phineas, a group of his men are using a hand-cranked derrick crane to hoist a large piece of rock. Some of the men remember seeing Phineas standing over the blast hole, leaning lightly on the tamping iron. Others say Phineas was sitting on a rock ledge above the hole, holding the iron loosely between his knees.

Skill:
Textual
Evidence

Gage has a dangerous job working with explosives. He also manages a crew. It must have been hard to keep track of so many things. These details show that Gage must have been a very hard worker to do such a difficult job.

NOTES

8   There is no argument about what happens next. Something or someone distracts Phineas. Does he hear his name called? Does he spot someone goofing off? Whatever the reason, Phineas turns his head to glance over his right shoulder. The fat end of his tamping iron slips down into the hole and strikes the granite. A spark flies onto the exposed blasting powder. Blam! The drill hole acts as a gun barrel. Instead of a bullet, it fires Phineas's rod straight upward. The iron shrieks through the air and comes down with a loud clang about thirty feet away.

9   This is what happens. Imagine you are inside Phineas's head, watching in extreme slow motion: See the pointy end of the rod enter under his left cheekbone, pass behind his left eye, through the front of his brain, and out the middle of his forehead just above the hairline. It takes a fraction of a fraction of a second for the iron rod to pass from cheekbone to forehead, through and through.

10   Amazingly, Phineas is still alive. The iron throws him flat on his back, but as his men come running through the gunpowder smoke, he sits up. A minute later, he speaks. Blood is pouring down his face from his forehead, but Phineas is talking about the explosion. His men insist on carrying him to an ox cart for the short ride into town. They gently lift him into the back of the cart so he can sit up with his legs out before him on the floor. An Irish workman grabs a horse and races ahead for the doctor while the ox cart ambulance rumbles slowly down the half-mile to Cavendish. Phineas's excited men crowd alongside, walking next to their injured boss. Still acting as a foreman, Phineas calls out for his time book and makes an entry as he rolls toward town.

 Skill:
Textual
Evidence

After the accident, Gage is talking and working. I'd expect him to be in pain. It seems he has no pain and doesn't know how badly he's hurt. This shows that the brain can trick a person into thinking that he's fine when he is not.

11   Something terrible has happened, yet Phineas gets down from the cart without help. He climbs the steps of the Cavendish hotel, where he has been living, and takes a seat on the porch beside his landlord, Joseph Adams. A few minutes earlier, Adams had seen the Irishman ride past shouting for Dr. Harlow, the town physician. Dr. Harlow was not to be found, so the rider was sent on to the next village to fetch Dr. Williams. Now Phineas takes a neighborly seat on the porch and tells his landlord what happened to him.

12   That's how Dr. Edward Williams finds Phineas nearly thirty minutes after the accident. Dr. Williams pulls up in his buggy at the hotel porch, and there is Phineas, talking away. Friends, workmates, and the curious crowd around as Dr. Williams climbs down from his carriage. "Well, here's work enough for you, Doctor," Phineas says to him quite cheerfully.

13   Dr. Williams examines Phineas's head. He can't believe that this man is still alive. His skull is cracked open, as if something has popped out from the inside. Accident victims are often too shaken to know what happened, so Dr. Williams turns to Phineas's workmen for the story, but Phineas insists on speaking for himself. He tells Dr. Williams that the iron went right through his head.

14   Dr. Williams does not believe him.

Excerpted from *Phineas Gage: A Gruesome but True Story About Brain Science* by John Fleischman, published by HMH Books for Young Readers.

First Read

Read *Phineas Gage: A Gruesome but True Story About Brain Science*. After you read, complete the Think Questions below.

 THINK QUESTIONS

1. How is Phineas Gage described by the author in the beginning of the excerpt? How might the accident affect or change his behavior? Explain, citing specific textual evidence.

2. Using textual evidence, summarize in three sentences what happens to Phineas Gage on this fateful day and why it is remembered centuries later.

3. Why doesn't Dr. Edward Williams believe Phineas's account of what happened? Explain, citing specific textual evidence.

4. Read the following dictionary entry:

   conduct
   con•duct \kən ˈdəkt\ *verb*

   1. organize or direct something
   2. transmit energy
   3. behave in a specified way or manner

   Which definition most closely matches the meaning of **conduct** as it is used in paragraph 2? Write the correct definition of *conduct* here and explain how you figured out the correct meaning.

5. Find the word **routine** in paragraph 6 of *Phineas Gage: A Gruesome but True Story About Brain Science*. Use context clues in the surrounding sentences, as well as the sentence in which the word appears, to determine the word's meaning. Write your definition here and identify clues that helped you figure out its meaning.

Please note that excerpts and passages in the StudySync® library and this workbook are intended as touchstones to generate interest in an author's work. The excerpts and passages do not substitute for the reading of entire texts, and StudySync® strongly recommends that students seek out and purchase the whole literary or informational work in order to experience it as the author intended. Links to online resellers are available in our digital library. In addition, complete works may be ordered through an authorized reseller by filling out and returning to StudySync® the order form enclosed in this workbook.

Reading & Writing Companion   **117**

Skill:
Central or Main Idea

Use the Checklist to analyze Central or Main Idea in *Phineas Gage: A Gruesome but True Story About Brain Science*. Refer to the sample student annotations about Central or Main Idea in the text.

••• CHECKLIST FOR CENTRAL OR MAIN IDEA

In order to identify a central idea of a text, note the following:

- ✓ the central or main idea, if it is explicitly stated
- ✓ when the central idea emerges
- ✓ ways in which supporting ideas relate to the central idea
- ✓ key details and supporting ideas that connect to the author's point or message

To determine a central idea of a text and analyze its development over the course of the text, including its relationship to supporting ideas, consider the following questions:

- ✓ What main idea(s) do the details in each paragraph explain or describe?
- ✓ What bigger idea do all the paragraphs support?
- ✓ What is the best way to state the central idea?
- ✓ How do the supporting ideas and details help develop the central idea over the course of the text?
- ✓ How might you objectively summarize the text and message? What details would you include?

Skill:
Central or Main Idea

Reread paragraphs 11–14 of *Phineas Gage: A Gruesome but True Story About Brain Science*. Then, using the Checklist on the previous page, answer the multiple-choice questions below.

↻ YOUR TURN

1. Based on how Gage behaves in paragraph 11, the reader can conclude that a central or main idea is —

   ○ A. The landlord and Gage know each other very well.
   ○ B. Gage is behaving very strangely for an accident victim.
   ○ C. The author is exaggerating how bad the accident really was.
   ○ D. Doctors in the 1800s were not as skillful as they are today.

2. The description of the "curious crowd" in paragraph 12 supports the central or main idea that—

   ○ A. Gage is well-liked.
   ○ B. Life in the town is dull.
   ○ C. What is happening is very unusual.
   ○ D. People in Vermont tend to be curious.

3. Details in paragraphs 13 and 14 build the central or main idea that—

   ○ A. Gage needed to receive medical attention sooner.
   ○ B. The town would benefit from more experienced doctors.
   ○ C. This is likely the first time someone survived such an accident.
   ○ D. Dr. Williams thinks Gage is not telling the truth about what happened.

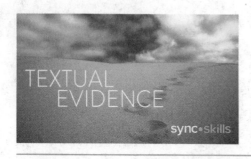

Skill:
Textual Evidence

Use the Checklist to analyze Textual Evidence in *Phineas Gage: A Gruesome but True Story About Brain Science*. Refer to the sample student annotations about Textual Evidence in the text.

••• CHECKLIST FOR TEXTUAL EVIDENCE

In order to support an analysis by citing textual evidence that is explicitly stated in the text, do the following:

- ✓ read the text closely and critically

- ✓ identify what the text says explicitly

- ✓ find the most relevant textual evidence that supports your analysis

- ✓ consider why an author explicitly states specific details and information

- ✓ cite the specific words, phrases, sentences, or paragraphs from the text that support your analysis

- ✓ cite evidence from the text that most strongly supports your analysis

In order to interpret implicit meanings in a text by making inferences, do the following:

- ✓ combine information directly stated in the text with your own knowledge, experiences, and observations

- ✓ cite the specific words, phrases, sentences, or paragraphs from the text that support this inference

In order to cite textual evidence to support an analysis of what the text says explicitly, as well as to support inferences drawn from the text, consider the following questions:

- ✓ Have I read the text closely and critically?

- ✓ What inferences am I making about the text? What textual evidence am I using to support these inferences?

- ✓ Am I quoting the evidence from the text correctly?

- ✓ Does my textual evidence logically relate to my analysis?

- ✓ What textual evidence from the text most strongly supports your analysis?

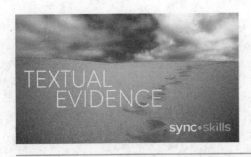

Skill:
Textual Evidence

Reread paragraphs 6–9 of *Phineas Gage: A Gruesome but True Story About Brain Science*. Then, using the Checklist on the previous page, answer the multiple-choice questions below.

⟳ YOUR TURN

1. Which response best shows an understanding of the text that is supported by textual evidence?

   ○ A. The accident shows that gunpowder was too dangerous to be used safely.

   ○ B. The incident proves that accidents can happen to even the most experienced experts.

   ○ C. The confusion after the accident suggests that witnesses are unreliable.

   ○ D. Gage deserved what happened because it was his fault.

2. Which paragraph best supports the inference that the cause of the accident is unknown?

   ○ A. 6

   ○ B. 7

   ○ C. 8

   ○ D. 9

3. Which textual evidence best supports the inference that the accident happens too quickly to be fully observed?

   ○ A. "When it's too dry or mixed in the wrong formula, almost anything can set it off, without warning."

   ○ B. "A few yards behind Phineas, a group of his men are using a hand-cranked derrick crane to hoist a large piece of rock."

   ○ C. "A spark flies onto the exposed blasting powder. Blam!"

   ○ D. "It takes a fraction of a fraction of a second for the iron rod to pass from cheekbone to forehead, through and through."

Close Read

Reread *Phineas Gage: A Gruesome but True Story About Brain Science*. As you reread, complete the Skills Focus questions below. Then use your answers and annotations from the questions to help you complete the Write activity.

◎ SKILLS FOCUS

1. Reread the first three paragraphs of *Phineas Gage: A Gruesome but True Story About Brain Science*. Identify a key detail in paragraph 3, and explain the central or main idea that is revealed by the beginning of the excerpt.

2. Reread paragraphs 4–6. Does the author think people who work on the railroad have a difficult job or an easy job? Describe the author's point of view about railroad workers, citing textual evidence.

3. An important idea in paragraph 6 is that working with gunpowder is risky. Identify textual evidence that supports this idea, and explain what makes working with gunpowder so risky.

4. Reread paragraphs 7–9. Identify a detail that reveals a central or main idea in this section of *Phineas Gage: A Gruesome but True Story About Brain Science*. Explain the central or main idea and how the textual evidence supports it.

5. In paragraph 3, the author states that 150 years after Phineas Gage's accident there is still a lot we don't know. Why are people still interested in Gage's story? Identify a detail that makes Gage's story still intriguing 150 years later.

✏ WRITE

INFORMATIVE: Explain how Gage's reaction to his serious injury impacts Dr. Williams. How do the details about the interaction between Phineas Gage and Dr. Williams connect to the central or main idea of the overall text? Be sure to cite specific textual evidence to support your claim.

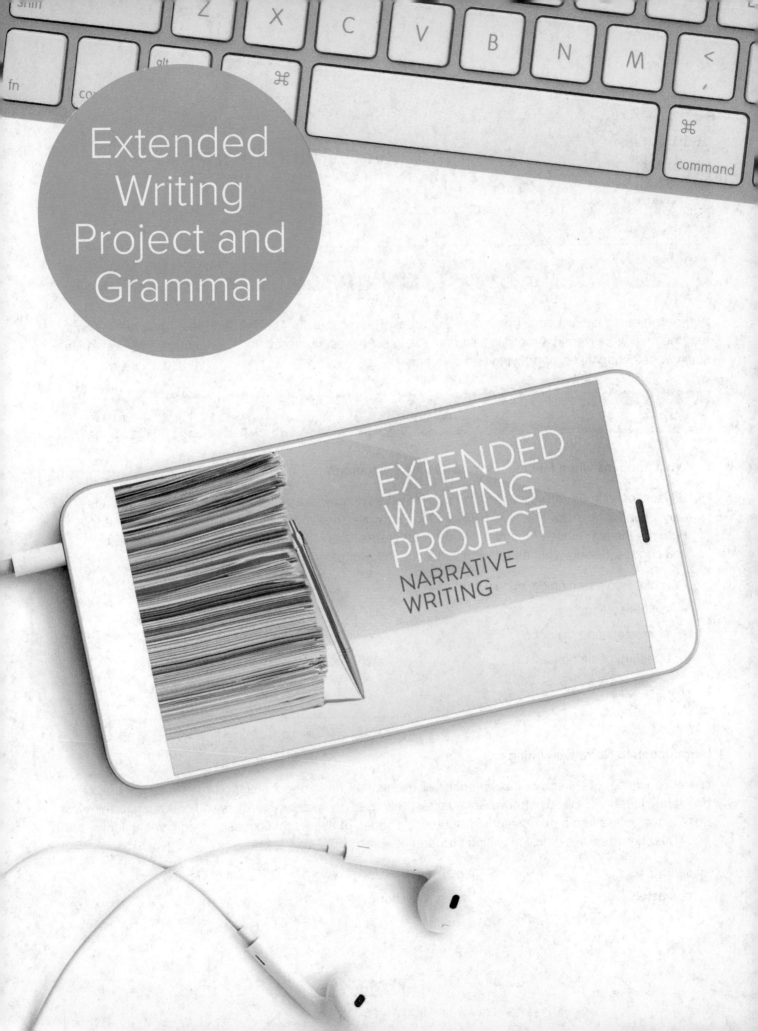

Extended Writing Project and Grammar

EXTENDED WRITING PROJECT

NARRATIVE WRITING

Narrative Writing Process: Plan

| PLAN | DRAFT | REVISE | EDIT AND PUBLISH |

Authors often create suspense from unlikely sources. The old man in "The Tell-Tale Heart" had no reason to fear the man who lived in a room in his home . . . until he was murdered. In "The Lottery," a town's annual summer gathering takes a horrifying turn of events.

WRITING PROMPT

What happens when fear comes from an unlikely source?

Use the techniques you've learned in this unit to write your own suspenseful narrative. Your characters may experience suspense in a familiar place or while they're with people they know and trust. Perhaps the fear comes from an everyday object or situation. Regardless of which unlikely source you choose, be sure your narrative includes the following:

- a plot with a beginning, middle, and end
- a clear setting
- characters and dialogue
- a feeling of suspense
- a clear theme

Introduction to Narrative Writing

Narrative writing tells a story of experiences or events that have been imagined by a writer or that have happened in real life. Good narrative writing effectively uses genre characteristics and craft such as relevant descriptive details and a purposeful structure with a series of events that contain a beginning, middle, and end. The characteristics of fiction writing include:

- setting
- characters
- plot
- theme/reflection
- point of view

Copyright © BookheadEd Learning, LLC

In addition to these characteristics, narrative writers also carefully craft their work through their use of dialogue, details, word choice, and figurative language. These choices help to shape the tone, mood, and overall style of the text. Effective narratives combine these genre characteristics and craft to engage the reader.

As you continue with this Extended Writing Project, you'll receive more instruction and practice at crafting each of the characteristics of fiction writing to create your own suspenseful narrative.

Before you get started on your suspenseful narrative, read a narrative that one student, Lucia, wrote in response to the writing prompt. As you read the Model, highlight and annotate the features of narrative writing that Lucia included in her narrative.

☰ STUDENT MODEL

1. The microwave timer chimes and I push the button to release the door. A wave of butter-scented popcorn hits my face, and my taste buds long to try it. I pour it eagerly into a big wooden bowl and shake on some salt, humming to myself. My cell phone rings. It's Mom.

2. "Just checking in!" Mom chirps.

3. "I'm fine. I promise," I say, rolling my eyes, which of course she can't see.

4. "Okay, okay. I'll let you go. But Ella—" Mom trails off. I can tell she wants to say something.

5. "Yes?" I ask.

6. "Not too much ZeldaZee, okay?"

7. "Sure, Mom. I promise." She also couldn't see my fingers, which are crossed.

8. While carrying the bowl of popcorn under one arm and a tall glass of fizzy water in one hand, I shuffle in my slippered feet down the hallway to my bedroom in record-breaking time. The house hums contentedly around me. It is Friday night, and I have the whole place to myself. Mom is at a work dinner, and my younger brother, Tom the Slob, is at a sleepover. The quiet feels like a rare treat, but most exciting of all is the promise of uninterrupted time with my favorite YouTube star, ZeldaZee.

9 Once I make it to my bedroom without spilling a thing, I climb up onto my neatly made bed—Mom's a stickler for asking me to make it. My open laptop has already fallen asleep there, but I awaken the screen with one click. ZeldaZee's channel is queued up and ready to go. So I toss a kernel of popcorn into my mouth and hit play.

10 Here's what I can tell you about ZeldaZee: She's sixteen. She has a little brother (just like me!) whom she calls Stinker, but I'm pretty sure that's not his real name. She has two Siamese cats, who often show up in her videos, dressed in different outfits or draped in some of her jewelry. She lives in the suburbs but I'm not sure where—she keeps it vague. ZeldaZee covers a lot of different topics—school life, fashion, family, beauty—but the thing I love about her is her personality; I swear it feels like she's talking right to me. When she looks into the camera and tells a story about her day, I laugh as though one of my friends were talking to me. Sometimes, I find myself responding to her out loud. I have to remind myself she can't hear me.

11 The title of this video is "How Not to Get Lost in Your Own Neighborhood." It shows ZeldaZee walking through her neighborhood on a sunny afternoon, pointing at familiar landmarks. "Look for street names!" she instructs, and the camera swings up to hold on the names of the cross streets: Magnolia and Pine. *Hey, wait a second*, I think. *We have an intersection of Magnolia and Pine not too far from here!* I take a sip of fizzy water, thinking a wonderful thought: What if ZeldaZee lives in my neighborhood? I've wondered it before. I swear she drove by a nearby mini mall in her episode "How to Shop Like a Boss." However, ZeldaZee has over twelve million followers. She's a star! If she lived in my neighborhood, wouldn't I have heard about it?

12 On screen, meanwhile, ZeldaZee continues down the list. "Ask a friendly-looking neighbor!" ZeldaZee instructs. She waves to an old woman in gardening gloves, repotting some tulips. "Hey!" calls ZeldaZee. "Do I look familiar to you?"

13 I squint at the screen. I'm almost positive I've seen that old lady before. Didn't she used to give me piano lessons? Miss Gomez, wasn't it? A feeling of unease creeps down my spine and it takes me

a second to realize why: Last week, Mom had told me that Miss Gomez died.

14   Suddenly, ZeldaZee whirls around to face the screen. In a low voice she says, "Ella, I have something to tell you."

15   The popcorn kernel in my fingers is frozen halfway to my open mouth. Ella. That's me.

16   "Don't freak out," says ZeldaZee, still in that same low voice. "But there's someone in your house."

17   My blood turns to ice in my veins. Then I shake it off. She can't possibly be talking to me. I look to the door of my room, force myself to laugh. "Whatever," I say aloud.

18   "You still have time," ZeldaZee continues. I search her face for the usual glint of mischief, but her eyes are oddly blank. "Ella, you need to act fast. Pick up your phone."

19   I scan the room, searching for my cell phone, but I am filled with a sense of dread once I realize that I left it in the kitchen.

20   "He's coming down the hallway," ZeldaZee tells me, her voice almost a whisper. "Now's your chance."

21   This can't be right. I snap the laptop shut. "Weird," I say. But the word sounds more casual than I feel. I'm just swinging my legs over the side of the bed when I hear it: the creak of floorboards just outside my door.

22   "Hello?" My voice makes a tiny scratchy sound as it leaves my throat.

23   To my horror, the doorknob begins to twist.

24   I run for the window. I'm on the second floor, but that hardly matters. As I scramble onto the roof, I see the door to my room swing open. "Ella! Ella!"

25   It's ZeldaZee. She's calling to me. But where is she? I peer over the ledge of the roof. My familiar front lawn looms in front of me, a map of shadows. *I'll climb down the trellis*, I tell myself. Once on the ground, I can run to a neighbor's house for help.

26   As I twist my body to try and catch hold of the trellis with my feet, I see through my bedroom window. Inside, someone rushes through the room. "Ella!"

27   My foot slips. I start to fall. I open my mouth to scream, but no sound comes out.

28   "Ella! Wake up!"

29   I jolt upright. I'm sitting in my room, blinking up into . . . Mom's face.

30   She looks concerned. "You were having a nightmare."

31   "Was I?" I look around. The bowl of popcorn has capsized on the bed, kernels dusting over the open laptop's keyboard as a result. "I must've fallen asleep."

32   "Watching ZeldaZee, I presume," says Mom. She doesn't try to conceal the disapproval in her voice.

33   Was it really all a dream? I click the keyboard and watch as my computer lurches to life. According to the screen, I've watched eleven episodes of ZeldaZee. That's funny, I can only remember the first.

34   "I had the weirdest dream," I say.

35   Mom is shaking her head. "And what have I told you about food in your room?"

36   "I'm sorry," I say.

37   "Just don't do it again."

38   "Oh, believe me," I say, meaning it this time. "I won't!" One look at ZeldaZee's face on my screen and my stomach clenches up. Now that the feelings of fear and confusion are wearing off, there's one consolation, though: I think I'm finally cured of my obsession with ZeldaZee!

✏️ WRITE

Writers often take notes about story ideas before they sit down to write. Think about what you've learned so far about narrative writing to help you begin prewriting.

- **Purpose:** What issue do you want to write about, and why is it a problem?

- **Audience:** Who is your audience and what message do you want to express to your audience?

- **Setting:** Where and when will your story be set? What kinds of problems might these characters face? How might the setting of your story affect the characters and problem?

- **Characters:** What types of characters would you like to write about in your narrative?

- **Plot:** What events will lead to the resolution of the conflict while keeping a reader engaged?

- **Theme/Reflection:** If you are writing an imagined narrative, what general message about life do you want to express? If you are writing a real narrative, what careful thoughts about the significance of your experience will you include?

- **Point of View:** From which point of view should your story be told, and why?

Response Instructions

Use the questions in the bulleted list to write a one-paragraph summary. Your summary should describe what will happen in your narrative.

Don't worry about including all of the details now; focus only on the most essential and important elements. You will refer to this short summary as you continue through the steps of the writing process.

Please note that excerpts and passages in the StudySync® library and this workbook are intended as touchstones to generate interest in an author's work. The excerpts and passages do not substitute for the reading of entire texts, and StudySync® strongly recommends that students seek out and purchase the whole literary or informational work in order to experience it as the author intended. Links to online resellers are available in our digital library. In addition, complete works may be ordered through an authorized reseller by filling out and returning to StudySync® the order form enclosed in this workbook.

Reading & Writing Companion **129**

Skill:
Organizing Narrative Writing

••• CHECKLIST FOR ORGANIZING NARRATIVE WRITING

As you consider how to organize your narrative, use the following questions as a guide:

- Who is the narrator and who are the characters in the story?

- From what point of view will the story be told?

- Where will the story take place?

- What conflict or problem will the characters have to resolve?

- Does my plot flow logically and naturally from one event to the next?

Here are some strategies to help you organize your narrative:

- Introduce a narrator and/or characters.

  > Characters can be introduced all at once or throughout the narrative.

  > Choose the role each character will play.

  > Choose a point of view.

    ○ A first-person narrator can be a participant or character in the story.

    ○ A third-person narrator tells the story as an outside observer.

- Establish a context.

  > Begin with your exposition—decide what background information your readers need to know about the characters, setting, and conflict.

  > List the events of the rising action—be sure that these events build toward the climax.

  > Describe what will happen during the climax of the story—make sure that this is the point of highest interest, conflict, or suspense in your story.

  > List the events of the falling action—make sure that these events show what happens to the characters as a result of the climax.

  > Explain the resolution of the main conflict in your story.

YOUR TURN

Complete the chart below by matching each event to its correct place in the narrative sequence.

Event Options	
A	He doesn't see anything familiar, but he decides to walk around and figure out where he is.
B	The main character wakes up in a world he doesn't recognize.
C	He figures out he has to stay in the new world.
D	He tries to find a way home but is unable to.
E	He realizes the new world is similar to his old one, and he can be happy there.

Narrative Sequence	Event
Exposition	
Rising Action	
Climax	
Falling Action	
Resolution	

YOUR TURN

Complete the chart below by writing a short summary of what will happen in each section of your narrative.

Narrative Sequence	Summary
Exposition	
Rising Action	
Climax	
Falling Action	
Resolution	

Narrative Writing Process: Draft

| PLAN | DRAFT | REVISE | EDIT AND PUBLISH |

You have already made progress toward writing your suspenseful short story. Now it is time to draft your suspenseful short story.

✏ WRITE

Use your plan and other responses in your Binder to draft your narrative. You may also have new ideas as you begin drafting. Feel free to explore those new ideas as you have them. You can also ask yourself these questions:

- Have I included specifics about my setting, characters, plot, theme, and point of view?
- Have I made my conflict clear to the reader?
- Does the sequence of events in my story make sense?

Before you submit your draft, read it over carefully. You want to be sure that you've responded to all aspects of the prompt.

Please note that excerpts and passages in the StudySync® library and this workbook are intended as touchstones to generate interest in an author's work. The excerpts and passages do not substitute for the reading of entire texts, and StudySync® strongly recommends that students seek out and purchase the whole literary or informational work in order to experience it as the author intended. Links to online resellers are available in our digital library. In addition, complete works may be ordered through an authorized reseller by filling out and returning to StudySync® the order form enclosed in this workbook.

Reading & Writing Companion **133**

Here is Lucia's short story draft. As you read, identify details that Lucia includes in her exposition. As she continues to revise and edit her narrative, she will find and improve weak spots in her writing, as well as correct any language or punctuation mistakes.

 NOTES

☰ STUDENT MODEL: FIRST DRAFT

A Quiet Friday Night

~~I am standing in my kitchen when my cell phone rings. The screen tells me that it's my Mom.~~

~~"Just checking in!"~~

~~"I'm fine. I promise," I say.~~

~~"Okay, okay. I'll let you go. But . . ." Mom trails off.~~

~~"Yes?"~~

~~"Not too much ZeldaZee, okay?"~~

~~"Sure, Mom. I promise."~~

The microwave timer chimes and I push the button to release the door. A wave of butter-scented popcorn hits my face, and my taste buds long to try it. I pour it eagerly into a big wooden bowl and shake on some salt, humming to myself. My cell phone rings. It's Mom.

"Just checking in!" Mom chirps.

"I'm fine. I promise," I say, rolling my eyes, which of course she can't see.

"Okay, okay. I'll let you go. But Ella—" Mom trails off. I can tell she wants to say something.

"Yes?" I ask.

"Not too much ZeldaZee, okay?"

"Sure, Mom. I promise." She also couldn't see my fingers, which are crossed.

 Skill:
Story Beginnings

Lucia adds action and description to help readers better imagine the opening scene. She describes what her character is doing as she talks to her mom, and these actions reveal parts of the main character's personality.

While carrying the bowl of popcorn under one arm and a tall glass of fizzy water in one hand I shuffle in my slippered feet down the hallway to my bedroom in record-breaking time. The house was queit around me. It is Friday night, and I have the whole place to myself. Mom is at a work dinner, and my younger brother, Tom the Slob, is at a sleepover. I'm excited, but most exciteing of all is the promise of unterrupted time with my favorite YouTube star, ZeldaZee.

I climb up onto my neatly made bed, and my open laptop has fallen asleep there. With one click, I awaken the screen. ZeldaZee's channel is queued up and ready to go. I toss a kernel of popcorn into my mouth and hit play.

Here's what I can tell you about ZeldaZee: She's sixteen. She has a little brother and two Siamese cats.They lives in a suburb. I don't know which one. ZeldaZee covers a lot of different topics-- school life, fashion, family, beauty-- but the thing I love about her is her personality; I swear it feels like she's talking right to me. When she looks into the camera and tells a story from her day, I laugh as though one of my friends is talking to me. Sometimes, I find myself responding to her out loud. I have to remind myself she can't hear me.

I watched "How Not to Get Lost in Your Own Neighborhood." It shows ZeldaZee walking through her nieghborhood on a sunny afternoon, pointing at familiar landmarks. "Look for street names!" she instructs, and the camera shows the name of the cross-street: Magnolia and Pine. *Hey wait a second*, I think. *We have an intersection of Magnolia and Pine not too far from here!* I think: ~~What if ZeldaZee lives in my neighborhood? I've wondered it before. I swear she drove by a nearby mini mall in one episode—. ZeldaZee has over twelve million followers. She's a star! If she lived in my nieghborhood, I think I would know?~~

~~On screen ZeldaZee continues down the list. "Ask a friendely-looking neighbor!" ZeldaZee instructs. She waves to an old woman. "Hey!" calls ZeldaZee. "Do I look familiar to you?"~~

~~I squint at the screen because I'm almost positive that I've seen that old lady before. A feeling of unease creeps down my spine.~~

Skill:
Transitions

Lucia adds transition words to signal important shifts in the plot of her story and show a relationship between events that are happening at the same time. She uses the word "however" to show how Ella's thoughts shift from supporting her idea about where ZeldaZee could live to doubting it.

What if ZeldaZee lives in my neighborhood? I've wondered it before. I swear she drove by a nearby mini mall in her episode "How to Shop Like a Boss." However, ZeldaZee has over twelve million followers. She's a star! If she lived in my neighborhood, wouldn't I have heard about it?

On screen, meanwhile, ZeldaZee continues down the list. "Ask a friendly-looking neighbor!" ZeldaZee instructs. She waves to an old woman in gardening gloves, repotting some tulips. "Hey!" calls ZeldaZee. "Do I look familiar to you?"

I squint at the screen. I'm almost positive I've seen that old lady before. Didn't she used to give me piano lessons? Miss Gomez, wasn't it? A feeling of unease creeps down my spine and it takes me a second to realize why: Last week, Mom had told me that Miss Gomez died.

Suddenly, ZeldaZee whirls around to face the screen. In a low voice she says "Ella."

The popcorn kernel in my fingers are frozen, halfway to my open mouth. Ella. That's me.

~~"Don't freak out, said ZeldaZee, still in that same low voice. "But there's someone in your house."~~

~~I'm scared. Then I shake it off. She can't possibly be talking to me. I look to the door of my room. "Whatever," I say aloud.~~

~~"You still have time." I search her face for the usual glint of mischief, but her eyes are oddly blank.~~

~~I scan the room, searching for my cellphone, but I realize that I left it in the kitchen. It must be near the microwave!~~

~~He's coming down the hallway," ZeldaZee tells me, her voice almost a whisper.~~

"Don't freak out," says ZeldaZee, still in that same low voice. "But there's someone in your house."

NOTES

My blood turns to ice in my veins. Then I shake it off. She can't possibly be talking to me. I look to the door of my room, force myself to laugh. "Whatever," I say aloud.

"You still have time," ZeldaZee continues. I search her face for the usual glint of mischief, but her eyes are oddly blank. "Ella, you need to act fast. Pick up your phone."

I scan the room, searching for my cell phone, but I am filled with a sense of dread once I realize that I left it in the kitchen.

"He's coming down the hallway," ZeldaZee tells me, her voice almost a whisper. "Now's your chance."

This can't be right. There's no way she's right as she's talking to me through my computer. I decide to ignore her words as I fold the screen on my laptop shut. "Weird," I say. But the word sounds more casual than I feel. I'm just swinging my legs over the side of the bed when I hear it: the creak of floorboards just outside my door.

"Hello?" My voice makes a tiny scratchy sound as it leaves my throat.

To my horror, the doorknob begins to twist.

~~I run for the window. I'm on the second floor, but that hardly matters. I climb onto the roof. The door to my room opens. "Ella! Ella!"~~

~~ZeldaZee is calling to me. But where is she? I peer over the ledge of the roof. *I'll climb down the trellis*, I tell myself. Once on the ground, I can run to a neighbor's house for help.~~

~~As I try and catch hold of the trellis with my feet, I see through my bedroom window. Inside, someone is moving around. "Ella!"~~

~~My foot slips. I start to fall. I open my mouth to scream, but I can't.~~

I run for the window. I'm on the second floor, but that hardly matters. As I scramble onto the roof, I see the door to my room swing open. "Ella! Ella!"

It's ZeldaZee. She's calling to me. But where is she? I peer over the ledge of the roof. My familiar front lawn looms in front of me, a map

---

Skill:
Narrative Techniques

Lucia improves her use of dialogue, including more description, and building more suspense in this part of her story. She adds an identifying name to a line of dialogue to make sure that readers know who is saying it. She also builds suspense by speeding up the pacing, removing unnecessary details, and breaking long sentences into short, simple ones.

Skill:
Descriptive Details

Lucia adds more descriptive details to her draft so readers can better imagine what is happening during the climax of the story. She wants to show readers what Ella is experiencing at this tense moment, so she adds sensory language.

of shadows. *I'll climb down the trellis*, I tell myself. Once on the ground, I can run to a neighbor's house for help.

As I twist my body to try and catch hold of the trellis with my feet, I see through my bedroom window. Inside, someone rushes through the room. "Ella!"

My foot slips. I start to fall. I open my mouth to scream, but no sound comes out.

"Ella! Wake up!"

I jolt upright. I'm sitting in my room, blinking up into . . . Mom's face.

She looks concerned. "You were having a nightmare."

"Was I?" I look around. "Watching ZeldaZee, I presume." says Mom.

She knows me too well. The bowl of popcorn is spilled all over my bed and laptop. "I must've fallen asleep."

~~Was it really all a dream? I click the keyboard and watch as my computer lurched to life. According to the screen, I've watched eleven episodes of ZeldaZee. That's funny. I can only remember the first.~~

~~Mom is shakeing her head. "And what have I told you about food in your room."~~

~~"I'm sorry," I say.~~

~~"Just don't do it again."~~

~~"Oh beleive me, I won't!"~~

Was it really all a dream? I click the keyboard and watch as my computer lurches to life. According to the screen, I've watched eleven episodes of ZeldaZee. That's funny, I can only remember the first.

"I had the weirdest dream," I say.

Mom is shaking her head. "And what have I told you about food in your room?"

Skill:
Conclusions

To improve her conclusion, Lucia adds important details that briefly summarize what has happened to Ella and show both characters' thoughts and feelings about the events.

"I'm sorry," I say.

"Just don't do it again."

"Oh, believe me," I say, meaning it this time. "I won't!" One look at ZeldaZee's face on my screen and my stomach clenches up. Now that the feelings of fear and confusion are wearing off, there's one consolation, though: I think I'm finally cured of my obsession with ZeldaZee!

Skill:
Story Beginnings

••• CHECKLIST FOR STORY BEGINNINGS

Before you write the beginning of your narrative, ask yourself the following questions:

- What information does my reader need to know at the beginning of the story about the narrator, main character, setting, and the character's conflict?

- What will happen to my character in the story?

- Who is the narrator of my story?

There are many ways you can engage and orient your reader. Here are some strategies to help you establish a context, show a point of view, and introduce the narrator and/or characters:

- Action

  > Instead of beginning with a description of a character, have the character doing something that will reveal his or her personality.

  > Opening a story with an immediate conflict, either between characters or due to an event in the plot, can help grab a reader's attention.

- Description

  > Use description to quickly establish the setting and establish a context for the story.

  > If the story is science or historical fiction, provide specific details about where and when the story takes place.

- Dialogue

  > Dialogue can immediately establish the point of view in a story.

    ◆ first person: narrator is a character in the story

    ◆ third person: narrator is outside the story

    ◆ third-person omniscient: narrator knows the thoughts and actions of all the characters

    ◆ third-person limited: narrator knows the thoughts and actions of only one character

  > A character's internal thoughts can provide information that only the reader knows.

↻ YOUR TURN

Choose the best answer for each question.

1. Below is a section from a previous draft of Lucia's story. The meaning of the underlined sentence is unclear. What changes should Lucia make to improve the clarity of the sentence?

> It is Friday night, and I have the whole house to myself. Mom is at a work dinner, and my younger brother, Tom the Slob, is at a sleepover. <u>The quiet feels cool.</u> However, the most exciting of all is the promise of uninterrupted time with my favorite YouTube star, ZeldaZee.

   ○ A. Change "cool" to "awesome."
   ○ B. Change "cool" to "soothing."
   ○ C. Change "quiet" to "absolute silence."
   ○ D. Change "quiet" to "quietly."

2. Lucia wants to improve the beginning of a previous draft of her story. How can she rewrite the underlined sentence to provide more detail and imagery?

> I haven't been home alone for months. Thankfully, tonight, my brother is at a sleepover and Mom is at a work dinner, so I have the place to myself for the next three hours. <u>The house feels so great right now.</u>

   ○ A. It feels exciting to have the house all to myself.
   ○ B. The house has not felt this empty since Halloween, when the rest of the family was out in their costumes trick-or-treating and I got to stay home all alone—my first time without our normal babysitter.
   ○ C. I love the house when it is this quiet and empty.
   ○ D. For once, I can actually hear the calming buzz of the air-conditioning and the quiet purr of my cat, without the nagging reminders of my mom and the loud laughter of my brother to drown them out.

✐ WRITE

Use the questions and techniques in the checklist to revise the beginning of your suspenseful narrative.

Skill:
Narrative Techniques

••• CHECKLIST FOR NARRATIVE TECHNIQUES

As you begin to develop the techniques you will use in your narrative, ask yourself the following questions:

- Is it clear which character is talking in a dialogue?

- How quickly or slowly do I want the plot to move?

- Which literary devices can I add to strengthen my characters or plot? How can I better engage my reader?

- What insight or personal reflection could I add to the overall message of my narrative?

Here are some methods that can help you write dialogue, pacing, description, and reflection to develop experiences, events, and/or characters in your narrative:

- Use dialogue to explain events or move the action forward.

  > Use quotation marks correctly.

  > Include identifying names as needed before or after quotation marks.

- Include description to help the reader visualize the characters, setting, and other elements.

  > Include only those descriptions relevant to the reader's understanding of the element being described.

- Use pacing effectively to convey a sense of urgency or calm.

  > To speed up the pace, try using limited description, short paragraphs, brief dialogue, and simpler sentences.

  > To slow down the pace, try using detailed description, longer paragraphs, and more complex sentence structures.

- Add reflection, if appropriate, to comment on the overall message.

  > Include characters' inner thoughts or your own insight.

- Use any combination of the above techniques.

↻ YOUR TURN

Read each quote below. Then, complete the chart by matching each quote with the narrative technique that it best illustrates.

	Quote Options
A	Now that the feelings of fear and confusion are wearing off, there's one consolation, though: I think I'm finally cured of my obsession with ZeldaZee!
B	"I had the weirdest dream," I say.
C	It's ZeldaZee. She's calling to me. But where is she?
D	My blood turns to ice in my veins.

Narrative Technique	Quote
Dialogue	
Pacing	
Description	
Reflection	

YOUR TURN

Complete the chart below by rewriting part of your narrative using each narrative technique.

Narrative Technique	Rewrite
Dialogue	
Pacing	
Description	
Reflection	

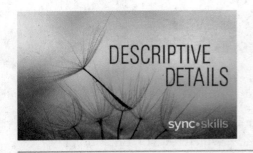

Skill:
Descriptive Details

••• CHECKLIST FOR DESCRIPTIVE DETAILS

First, reread the draft of your narrative and identify the following:

- where descriptive details are needed to convey experiences and events

- vague, general, or overused words and phrases

- places where you want to tell how something looks, sounds, feels, smells, or tastes, such as:

    > experiences

    > events

    > action

Use precise words and phrases, relevant descriptive details, and sensory language to capture the action and convey experiences and events, using the following questions as a guide:

- What experiences and events do I want to convey in my writing?

- Have I included relevant and descriptive details?

- Where can I add descriptive details to describe the characters and the events of the plot?

- How can I use sensory language, or words that describe sights, sounds, feelings, smells, or tastes, to help my reader create a picture of the action, experiences, and events?

- What can I refine or revise in my word choice to make sure that the reader can picture what is taking place?

↻ YOUR TURN

Choose the best answer to each question.

1. Below is a sentence from one of Lucia's previous drafts. Lucia wants to use sensory language to show readers how comfortable she felt just before she watched ZeldaZee. Which revision BEST helps readers imagine how she felt?

> Before I started to watch ZeldaZee, I sat on my bed with my popcorn, and my back was against some pillows.

- ○ A. I now had everything I needed to start the show—popcorn, water, pillows, and my laptop.
- ○ B. I kept my bowl of puffy popcorn beside me and sat with my back against a mound of fluffed pillows. I was now ready to click play.
- ○ C. After enjoying a handful of salty, buttery popcorn and a sip of the refreshing fizzy water, I clicked play on the latest ZeldaZee video.
- ○ D. I sat on my bed with my back against a pillow, allowing the silence of my house to be filled with the sound of ZeldaZee's voice and perfectly timed background music.

2. Below is a section of one of Lucia's previous drafts. In the underlined sentence, Lucia did not use the most appropriate word to describe the main character, Ella's, actions. Which of the following is the best replacement for the word *see*?

> I hear her. ZeldaZee is calling to me. But I can't see her. Where is she? <u>I see over the ledge of the roof.</u> *I'll climb down the trellis*, I tell myself. Once I am on the ground, I can run to a neighbor's house for help.

- ○ A. fall
- ○ B. shrink
- ○ C. gaze
- ○ D. hear

↻ YOUR TURN

Complete the chart by writing a descriptive detail that appeals to each sense for your narrative.

Sense	Descriptive Detail
Sight	
Smell	
Touch	
Taste	
Sound	

Please note that excerpts and passages in the StudySync® library and this workbook are intended as touchstones to generate interest in an author's work. The excerpts and passages do not substitute for the reading of entire texts, and StudySync® strongly recommends that students seek out and purchase the whole literary or informational work in order to experience it as the author intended. Links to online resellers are available in our digital library. In addition, complete works may be ordered through an authorized reseller by filling out and returning to StudySync® the order form enclosed in this workbook.

Reading & Writing
Companion

147

Skill:
Transitions

••• CHECKLIST FOR TRANSITIONS

Before you revise your current draft to include transitions, think about:

- the order of events, including the rising action, climax, falling action, and resolution

- moments where the time or setting changes

- relationships between characters and plot events

Next, reread your current draft and note areas in your narrative where:

- the order of events is unclear or illogical

- changes in time or setting are confusing or unclear. Look for:

  > sudden jumps

  > missing or illogical plot events or character experiences

  > places where you could add more context or exposition, such as important background information about the narrator, setting, characters, and conflict

Revise your draft to use a variety of transition words, phrases, and clauses to convey sequence, signal shifts from one time frame or setting to another, and show the relationships among experiences and events, using the following questions as a guide:

- Do the events of the rising action, climax, falling action, and resolution flow naturally and logically?

- Are there better transition words I can use to show shifts in time, setting, and relationships between experiences and events?

  > Transitions such as "moreover," "likewise," and "by the same token" show relationships between experiences and events.

  > Transitions such as "simultaneously" or "afterward" signal shifts in time and settings.

- Do the characters' experiences logically and naturally relate to the plot events?

 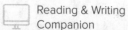

↻ YOUR TURN

Choose the best answer to each question.

1. Below is a section from a previous draft of Lucia's story. The connection between the first sentence and the underlined sentence is unclear. What transition word, phrase, or clause can be added to the underlined sentence to make the connection clear?

> I start to open up the bag of popcorn. <u>ZeldaZee made the perfect bowl of popcorn.</u> There were no unpopped kernels in it! Could mine be as good? Steam fogs up my glasses while I open the bag and begin to pour out the popcorn. It is hard to see, but I hear the jangle of unpopped kernels hit the bowl. They needed more time.

- ○ A. As a result,
- ○ B. In the last episode of the show,
- ○ C. With masterful microwaving skills,
- ○ D. Similarly,

2. Below is a section of one of Lucia's previous drafts. The transition from the second sentence to the underlined sentence is not clear. Which transition word, phrase, or clause can Lucia use to connect the two ideas?

> What if ZeldaZee lives in my neighborhood? I've wondered it before, and I swear that she drove by a nearby mini mall in one episode. <u>She is a celebrity with twelve million followers.</u> If she lived down the street, I would have to know about it!

- ○ A. Although
- ○ B. On the other hand,
- ○ C. In fact,
- ○ D. In contrast,

Please note that excerpts and passages in the StudySync® library and this workbook are intended as touchstones to generate interest in an author's work. The excerpts and passages do not substitute for the reading of entire texts, and StudySync® strongly recommends that students seek out and purchase the whole literary or informational work in order to experience it as the author intended. Links to online resellers are available in our digital library. In addition, complete works may be ordered through an authorized reseller by filling out and returning to StudySync® the order form enclosed in this workbook.

Reading & Writing
Companion

149

YOUR TURN

Complete the chart below by writing a sentence for each listed purpose using transition words, phrases, and clauses.

Purpose	Sentence
Convey sequence	
Signal shifts from one time frame or setting to another	
Show a relationship among experiences and events	

Skill:
Conclusions

••• CHECKLIST FOR CONCLUSIONS

Before you write your conclusion, ask yourself the following questions:

- What important details should I include in my conclusion?

- What other thoughts and feelings could characters share with readers in the conclusion?

- Should I use dialogue or characters' actions to show readers the importance of the events in my narrative?

Below are two strategies to help you provide a conclusion that follows from and reflects on the narrated experiences or events:

- Peer discussion

  > After you have written your introduction and body paragraphs, talk with a partner about possible endings for your narrative, writing notes about your discussion.

  > Review your notes and think about how you want to end your story.

  > Briefly summarize the events in the narrative through the narrator or one of the characters.

  > Describe how the narrator feels about the events he or she experienced.

  > Reveal to readers why the experiences in the narrative matter through a character's reflections or dialogue.

  > Write your conclusion.

- Freewriting

  > Freewrite for ten minutes about what you might include in your conclusion. Don't worry about grammar, punctuation, or writing down fully formed ideas.

  > Review your notes and think about how you want to end your story.

  > Briefly summarize the events in the narrative through the narrator or one of the characters.

  > Describe how the narrator feels about the events he or she experienced.

  > Reveal to readers why the experiences in the narrative matter through a character's reflections or dialogue.

  > Write your conclusion.

YOUR TURN

Choose the best answer to each question.

1. Lucia wants to revise the dialogue in her conclusion from a previous draft to reveal how Ella felt during the dialogue. How can she use descriptive language to show how Ella's feelings changed when she heard the underlined line?

> I call out the window to my neighbor, "Ms. Barton! Can you hear me? Can you help?!" Her dog barks repeatedly as she runs onto the front yard beneath my window.
>
> "Ella! How can I help? Would you like me to get your mom?" Ms. Barton asks and points toward the front door.
>
> "There's no time for that now!" I shouted. "Can you help me climb—"
>
> <u>"Oh! But she just got home a minute ago," Ms. Barton said.</u>

- ○ A. "What?!" I asked and shouted at the same time.
- ○ B. "Wow. How did it get that late?" I wondered.
- ○ C. My look of terror dissolved, and I breathed a sigh of relief.
- ○ D. I was speechless.

2. In a previous draft, Lucia had left out an important detail. She wants to add that detail after the underlined line below. Which sentence uses dialogue to add an important detail to the conclusion?

> "Ella! Ella! I'm home. Are you okay?" My mom rushes over and hugs me.
>
> I look around the room. The bowl of popcorn has spilled all over my bed and laptop.
>
> "Oh, no! Mom, I'm sorry." I run to my laptop to clear off the kernels, and it wakes up again. <u>According to the screen, I've watched eleven episodes of ZeldaZee, but I can only remember the first.</u>
>
> "Watching ZeldaZee, I presume." She shakes her head and begins to help me pick up the popcorn.

- ○ A. "I must have had a nightmare," I tell her as I stare at the floor.
- ○ B. "What a Friday night," I say as I gather up the kernels.
- ○ C. "Do you want to watch a different show after we pick all this up?" I ask her.
- ○ D. "How was your work dinner?" I ask her to try to change the subject.

WRITE

Use the questions in the checklist section to revise the conclusion of your suspenseful narrative.

NARRATIVE
WRITING
PROCESS
REVISE

Narrative Writing Process: Revise

PLAN	DRAFT	REVISE	EDIT AND PUBLISH

You have written a draft of your suspenseful narrative. You have also received input from your peers about how to improve it. Now you are going to revise your draft.

⬅ REVISION GUIDE

Examine your draft to find areas for revision. Keep in mind your purpose and audience as you revise for clarity, development, organization, and style. Use the guide below to help you review:

Review	Revise	Example
Clarity		
Annotate any places where important information about an experience, event, or character seems unclear.	Use narrative techniques like dialogue, pacing, description, and reflection to develop those parts of your story.	"Just checking in!" Mom chirps. "I'm fine. I promise," I say, rolling my eyes, which of course she can't see. "Okay, okay. I'll let you go. But Ella—" Mom trails off. I can tell she wants to say something. "Yes?" I ask.

Review	Revise	Example
Development		
Identify suspenseful moments leading up to the climax. Annotate places where you don't feel anxious about what's going to happen next.	Focus on a single event and add descriptive details such as sounds, sights, smells, touch, taste, or characters' thoughts and feelings to build suspense.	I squint at the screen. I'm almost positive I've seen that old lady before. Didn't she used to give me piano lessons? Miss Gomez, wasn't it? A feeling of unease creeps down my spine and it takes me a second to realize why: Last week, Mom had told me that Miss Gomez died.
Organization		
Identify shifts between times, settings, experiences, and events in your draft. Annotate places where those changes seem illogical or need transitions to make them clear.	Revise any events that seem illogical and use transitions to show readers clear relationships between different times, settings, experiences, and events in your story.	"You still have time," ZeldaZee continues. I search her face for the usual glint of mischief, but her eyes are oddly blank. "Ella, you need to act fast. Pick up your phone." I scan the room, searching for my cell phone, but I am filled with a sense of dread once I realize that I left it in the kitchen.
Style: Word Choice		
Identify every form of the verb *to be* (*am, is, are, was, were, be, being, been*).	Select sentences to rewrite using action verbs.	Inside, someone ~~is moving around~~ rushes through the room.

Review	Revise	Example
Style: Sentence Variety		
Think about a key event where you want your reader to feel a specific emotion. Long sentences can draw out a moment and make a reader think; short sentences can show urgent actions or danger.	Rewrite a key event making your sentences longer or shorter to achieve the emotion you want your reader to feel.	This can't be right. ~~There's no way she's right as she's talking to me through my computer. I decide to ignore her words as I fold the screen on~~ snap the laptop shut.

✏ WRITE

Use the guide above, as well as your peer reviews, to help you evaluate your suspenseful narrative to determine areas that should be revised.

Grammar:
Basic Spelling Rules I

Suffixes and the Silent *e*

Spelling Patterns	Base Words	Correct Spelling	Incorrect Spelling
When adding a suffix that begins with a consonant to a word that ends with a silent *e*, keep the *e*.	atone displace	atonement displacement	atonment displacment
When adding a suffix that begins with a vowel to a word that ends with a silent *e*, usually drop the *e*.	console admire adore	consolation admirable adoring	consoleation admireable adoreing
When adding a suffix that begins with *a* or *o* to a word that ends with *ce* or *ge*, usually keep the *e*.	replace courage	irreplaceable courageous	irreplacable couragous
When adding *-ly* to a word that ends in *l* plus the silent *e*, drop the *le*.	forcible prickle	forcibly prickly	forciblely pricklely

Suffixes and the Final *y*

Spelling Conventions	Base Words	Correct Spelling	Incorrect Spelling
When a word ends in a consonant + *y*, change the *y* to *i* before adding a suffix.	clarify witty	clarification witticism	clarifycation wittycism
When a word ends in a vowel + *y*, keep the *y* when adding a suffix.	deploy relay	deployment relaying	deploiment relaing

⟳ YOUR TURN

1. How should the spelling error in this sentence be corrected?

> Alfred Hitchcock wrote about how he achieved a suspenseful atmosphere without mysteryous special effects.

- ○ A. Change **achieved** to **acheived**.
- ○ B. Change **suspenseful** to **suspensful**.
- ○ C. Change **mysteryous** to **mysterious**.
- ○ D. No change needs to be made to this sentence.

2. How should the spelling error in this sentence be corrected?

> As Hitler rose to power there was a noticable surge in the mistreatment of Jews, with the perpetrators seemingly immunized from punishment.

- ○ A. Change **noticable** to **noticeable**.
- ○ B. Change **perpetrators** to **perpetraters**.
- ○ C. Change **immunized** to **immuneized**.
- ○ D. No change needs to be made to this sentence.

3. How should the spelling error in this sentence be corrected?

> In the story *Home*, a father who tries to discipline his young son wonders about the complexity and responsibility of being both self-indulgent and a parent.

- ○ A. Change **complexity** to **complexty**.
- ○ B. Change **responsibility** to **responsability**.
- ○ C. Change **self-indulgent** to **self-indulgeant**.
- ○ D. No change needs to be made to this sentence.

Grammar: Dashes and Hyphens—Dashes

A dash (—) looks like a long hyphen. When you are writing a sentence, use a dash or dashes to show a sudden break or a change of thought or speech. Using a dash or dashes is also an effective way of emphasizing a thought or giving new information.

Rule	Text
Use a pair of dashes if the new thought or emphasized information is in the middle of a sentence.	The creek he knew was frozen clear to the bottom—**no creek could contain water in that arctic winter**—but he knew also that there were springs that bubbled out from the hillsides and ran along under the snow and on top the ice of the creek. To Build a Fire
Use one dash if the new thought or emphasized information is at the end of a sentence.	But when Mami says, "Connie, please be nice to Abuela. She doesn't have too many years left. Do you promise me, Constancia?"—**when she uses my full name, I know she means business.** Abuela Invents the Zero
Do not use dashes if the additional or emphasized information is not a sudden break in the text.	Due to a shortage of wood, barracks were built with green pine that shrank and left cracks between the boards, **allowing sand and insects to seep and creep inside**. Dear Miss Breed

Please note that excerpts and passages in the StudySync® library and this workbook are intended as touchstones to generate interest in an author's work. The excerpts and passages do not substitute for the reading of entire texts, and StudySync® strongly recommends that students seek out and purchase the whole literary or informational work in order to experience it as the author intended. Links to online resellers are available in our digital library. In addition, complete works may be ordered through an authorized reseller by filling out and returning to StudySync® the order form enclosed in this workbook.

Reading & Writing
Companion

159

↻ YOUR TURN

1. How should this sentence be changed?

> That new restaurant—it's only been open two months is always swamped with eager diners.

○ A. Remove the dash after **restaurant**.
○ B. Put a dash after **months**.
○ C. Put a dash after **swamped**.
○ D. No change needs to be made to this sentence.

2. How should this sentence be changed?

> The contest—it's been advertised as "You could be a millionaire!"—starts next week.

○ A. Remove the dash after **millionaire!"**
○ B. Remove the dash after **contest**.
○ C. Insert a dash after **starts**.
○ D. No change needs to be made to this sentence.

3. How should this sentence be changed?

> The movie the star's breakout hit was a huge success at the box office.

○ A. Put dashes after **movie** and **hit**.
○ B. Put a dash after **movie**.
○ C. Put a dash after **success**.
○ D. No change needs to be made to this sentence.

4. How should this sentence be changed?

> The instructions for the machine—"Push button to start" were printed in large red letters.

○ A. Remove the dash after **machine**.
○ B. Insert a dash after **start."**
○ C. Insert a dash after **printed**.
○ D. No change needs to be made to this sentence.

Grammar: Commas After Transitions

Transition words and phrases help connect ideas in a text. Transitions can improve the flow in a piece of writing, and they can help readers better understand the ideas presented in the text. Examples of transition words and phrases include *for instance*, *however*, *as a result*, *therefore*, *first*, *on the other hand*, and *in addition*. Use a comma after transition words or phrases at the beginning of a sentence.

Correct	Incorrect
Therefore, Grace decided to change her study habits last semester.	**Therefore** Grace decided to change her study habits last semester.
In fact, Miguel surprised his mom by baking her favorite cake.	**In fact** Miguel surprised his mom by baking her favorite cake.

Follow this additional rule when using commas with transitions:

Rule	Text
Use a pair of commas to set off a transition that interrupts the flow of thought in the middle of a sentence.	He thought he was lazy and, **worse**, spoiled by the trappings of being middle class. Born Worker

⟳ YOUR TURN

1. How should this sentence be changed?

> For example Daniel plans to play a Mozart piece at his next piano recital.

- ○ A. Insert a comma after **example**.
- ○ B. Insert a comma after **Daniel**.
- ○ C. Insert a comma after **next**.
- ○ D. No change needs to be made to this sentence.

2. How should this sentence be changed?

> Mozart, after all is his favorite classical composer.

- ○ A. Delete the comma after **Mozart**.
- ○ B. Insert a comma after **all**.
- ○ C. Insert a comma after **favorite**.
- ○ D. No change needs to be made to this sentence.

3. How should this sentence be changed?

> In addition, Daniel loves the music of Beethoven, Chopin, and Debussy.

- ○ A. Insert a comma after **In**.
- ○ B. Delete the comma after **addition**.
- ○ C. Delete the comma after **Beethoven**.
- ○ D. No change needs to be made to this sentence.

4. How should this sentence be changed?

> Daniel in fact, wants to continue studying music in high school and beyond.

- ○ A. Insert a comma after **Daniel**.
- ○ B. Delete the comma after **fact**.
- ○ C. Insert a comma after **music**.
- ○ D. No change needs to be made to this sentence.

Narrative Writing Process: Edit and Publish

| PLAN | DRAFT | REVISE | EDIT AND PUBLISH |

You have revised your suspenseful narrative based on your peer feedback and your own examination.

Now, it is time to edit your narrative. When you revised, you focused on the content of your narrative. You probably looked at your story's beginning, descriptive details, and transitions. When you edit, you focus on the mechanics of your story, paying close attention to things like grammar and punctuation.

Use the checklist below to guide you as you edit:

☐ Have I followed spelling rules?

☐ Have I followed the guidelines for using dashes?

☐ Have I used commas to set off transitions when needed?

☐ Do I have any sentence fragments or run-on sentences?

☐ Have I punctuated everything correctly?

Notice some edits Lucia has made:

- followed spelling rules for words that contain *ie* and *ei*

- followed spelling rules for adding a suffix to a word that ends in a silent *e*

- followed spelling rules for adding prefixes to words

- followed the guidelines for using dashes

- followed the rules for using commas after transitions

Please note that excerpts and passages in the StudySync® library and this workbook are intended as touchstones to generate interest in an author's work. The excerpts and passages do not substitute for the reading of entire texts, and StudySync® strongly recommends that students seek out and purchase the whole literary or informational work in order to experience it as the author intended. Links to online resellers are available in our digital library. In addition, complete works may be ordered through an authorized reseller by filling out and returning to StudySync® the order form enclosed in this workbook.

Reading & Writing Companion

163

While carrying the bowl of popcorn under one arm and a tall glass of fizzy water in one hand, I shuffle in my slippered feet down the hallway to my bedroom in ~~record breaking time~~ record-breaking time. The house hums contentedly around me. It is Friday night, and I have the whole place to myself. Mom is at a work dinner, and my younger brother, Tom the Slob, is at a sleepover. The ~~queit~~ quiet feels like a rare treat, but most ~~exciteing~~ exciting of all is the promise of ~~unterrupted~~ uninterrupted time with my favorite YouTube star, ZeldaZee.

Once I make it to my bedroom without spilling a thing, I climb up onto my neatly made bed~~and my open laptop has fallen asleep there.~~—Mom's a stickler for asking me to make it. My open laptop has already fallen asleep there, but I awaken the screen with one click. ~~With one click, I awaken the screen.~~ ZeldaZee's channel is queued up and ready to go. So I toss a kernel of popcorn into my mouth and hit play.

✏ WRITE

Use the questions on the previous page, as well as your peer reviews, to help you evaluate your suspenseful narrative to determine areas that need editing. Then edit your narrative to correct those errors.

Once you have made all your corrections, you are ready to publish your work. You can distribute your writing to family and friends, hang it on a bulletin board, or post it on your blog. If you publish online, share the link with your family, friends, and classmates.

Inside the House

DRAMA

Introduction

" Inside the House" tells the story of two teenage siblings who spend a stormy night alone telling scary stories. In this scene from the play, Cristina and Fernando learn just how scary a story can be when their real life starts to match a tale they've told. The author uses dialogue, sound effects, and foreshadowing to build suspense.

V VOCABULARY

predictable

easily guessed or expected

anxious

nervous or afraid

sarcastic

meaning the opposite of what is said to express humor, irritation, or meanness

embarrassed

feeling foolish or ashamed

scratching

rubbing against something with a rough or sharp object

NOTES

≡ READ

1 [SCENE: *A teenager's bedroom on a stormy night. Thunder rumbles. Lightning flashes outside the window. Fifteen-year-old twins* CRISTINA *and* FERNANDO *sit together on the floor. Their only light is a flashlight. They are home alone. The power is out. They are telling scary stories.* CRISTINA *finishes her story as the scene begins.*]

2 CRISTINA [*speaking quickly*]: Suddenly, the knocking stopped. The bedroom door flew open. They reached for the phone, but it was too late. The killer was already inside the house! [*She smiles proudly.*]

3 FERNANDO [*coldly*]: That was not scary. Of course the killer was already inside the house. The killer is always already inside the house! Nice try, Tina. But that ending was so **predictable**.

4 CRISTINA: Can you do better?

5 FERNANDO: Yes! [*Eager to tell a scarier tale.*] This guy was camping alone in the woods. . .

6   CRISTINA [*looks at her watch*]: You will have to finish that story another night. It's bedtime. Mom and Dad will be home from their party soon. I promised we would be asleep by 10:00. School tomorrow.

7   FERNANDO: Whatever. You're just too scared to hear my story.

8   CRISTINA [*sarcastic*]: Yeah, that's it. I am just too scared—and too tired. [*stands*] Go to bed, Fernando.

9   [CRISTINA *leaves the room. She closes the door.* FERNANDO *gets into bed. The rain gets louder. We hear a persistent* **scratching** *on the window.*]

10 FERNANDO [*jumping up*]: Cristina!

11 CRISTINA [*rushing in*]: What's wrong?

12 FERNANDO [*anxious and embarrassed*]: I don't know. I heard something. A scratching. By the window.

13 CRISTINA [*doubtful*]: You did not. You are trying to scare me. We're twins. I know how you think. Go to bed. We have a big test in the morning.

14 [CRISTINA *leaves again. She slams the door. There are three loud knocks against the window.*]

15 FERNANDO: Tina!

16 CRISTINA [*opening the door, annoyed*]: What?

17 FERNANDO [*terrified*]: Tell me you heard that.

18 CRISTINA: Heard what?

19 FERNANDO: That knocking! On the window!

20 CRISTINA: There is nobody knocking on the window. You are not going to scare me. [*turns to go*]

21 FERNANDO: Wait. I heard it when you closed my door. Close the door again.

22 CRISTINA: Fine. But this isn't funny.

23 FERNANDO: You're right. It's not. There is somebody out there.

24 [CRISTINA *closes the door. She turns toward her brother.* FERNANDO *waits to hear another noise.* CRISTINA *stays quiet. Someone knocks three times against the bedroom door. The doorknob begins to turn.*]

First Read

Read the story. After you read, answer the Think Questions below.

☁ THINK QUESTIONS

1. Who are the main characters in the story? What is their relationship?

   The main characters are _____ and _____.

   They are _____.

2. Where does the story take place? What kind of night is it?

   The story takes place _____.

   It is a _____.

3. At the end of the story, why do the characters get scared?

   The characters get scared because _____

   _____.

4. Use context to confirm the meaning of the word *annoy* as it is used in "Inside the House." Write your definition of *annoy* here.

   Annoy means _____.

   A context clue is _____.

5. What is another way to say that someone is *anxious*?

   Someone is _____.

Skill:
Analyzing Expressions

★ DEFINE

When you read, you may find English expressions that you do not know. An **expression** is a group of words that communicates an idea. Three types of expressions are idioms, sayings, and figurative language. They can be difficult to understand because the meanings of the words are different from their **literal**, or usual, meanings.

An **idiom** is an expression that is commonly known among a group of people. For example: "It's raining cats and dogs" means it is raining heavily. **Sayings** are short expressions that contain advice or wisdom. For instance: "Don't count your chickens before they hatch" means do not plan on something good happening before it happens. **Figurative** language is when you describe something by comparing it with something else, either directly (using the words *like* or *as*) or indirectly. For example, "I'm as hungry as a horse" means I'm very hungry. None of the expressions are about actual animals.

••• CHECKLIST FOR ANALYZING EXPRESSIONS

To determine the meaning of an expression, remember the following:

✓ If you find a confusing group of words, it may be an expression. The meaning of words in expressions may not be their literal meaning.

- Ask yourself: Is this confusing because the words are new? Or because the words do not make sense together?

✓ Determining the overall meaning may require that you use one or more of the following:

- context clues

- a dictionary or other resource

- teacher or peer support

✓ Highlight important information before and after the expression to look for clues.

YOUR TURN

Read the following excerpt from "Inside the House". Then, complete the multiple-choice questions below.

---

from **"Inside the House"**

FERNANDO [*jumping up*]: Cristina!

CRISTINA [*rushing in*]: What's wrong?

FERNANDO [*anxious and embarrassed*]: I don't know. I heard something. A scratching. By the window.

CRISTINA [*doubtful*]: You did not. You are trying to scare me. We're twins. I know how you think. Go to bed. We have a big test in the morning.

---

1. What does Cristina mean when she says "I know how you think?"

   ○ A. She can read Fernando's mind.

   ○ B. Fernando told Cristina he wanted to scare her.

   ○ C. Cristina and Fernando think alike.

   ○ D. Cristina tells Fernando what to think.

2. Which context clue helped you determine the meaning of the expression?

   ○ A. "What's wrong?"

   ○ B. "I don't know. I heard something."

   ○ C. "You are trying to scare me. We're twins."

   ○ D. "Go to bed. We have a big test in the morning."

Skill:
Conveying Ideas

★ DEFINE

Conveying ideas means communicating a **message** to another person. When speaking, you might not know what word to use to convey your ideas. When you do not know the exact English word, you can try different strategies. For example, you can ask for help from classmates or your teacher. You may use gestures and physical movements to act out the word. You can also try using **synonyms** or **defining** and describing the meaning you are trying to express.

••• CHECKLIST FOR CONVEYING IDEAS

To convey ideas for words you do not know when speaking, use the following learning strategies:

- ✓ Request help.

- ✓ Use gestures or physical movements.

- ✓ Use a synonym for the word.

- ✓ Describe what the word means using other words.

- ✓ Give an example of the word you want to use.

Please note that excerpts and passages in the StudySync® library and this workbook are intended as touchstones to generate interest in an author's work. The excerpts and passages do not substitute for the reading of entire texts, and StudySync® strongly recommends that students seek out and purchase the whole literary or informational work in order to experience it as the author intended. Links to online resellers are available in our digital library. In addition, complete works may be ordered through an authorized reseller by filling out and returning to StudySync® the order form enclosed in this workbook.

Reading & Writing Companion   171

↻ YOUR TURN

Imagine that someone is trying to convey the meaning of the word *knocking*. Find the correct example for each strategy to complete the chart below.

	Examples
A	The person says, "It is like when you go to someone's house and you want them to let you inside."
B	The person uses the similar word *tapping*.
C	The person mimes hitting the door with her first.
D	The person explains that the word means making a noise on a door or wall to get someone's attention.

Strategies	Examples
Use gestures or physical movements.	
Use a synonym for the word.	
Describe what the word means using other words.	
Give examples of the word you want to use.	

Close Read

✏ WRITE

PERSONAL NARRATIVE: In "Inside the House," Cristina and Fernando are home alone when something scary happens. Tell about a time something scary happened to you, using specific details. How did you feel? How did you react? Pay attention to spelling patterns as you write.

Use the checklist below to guide you as you write:

☐ What is a scary experience that you've had?

☐ How did you feel while it was happening?

☐ How did you react? What did you do?

Use the sentence frames to organize and write your personal narrative.

A scary experience that I had is _____.

It happened when _____.

I felt very _____.

I thought _____.

I reacted by _____.

It helped me _____.

The Lucky Coin

FICTION

Introduction

Maggie is a hard-working teen who doesn't believe in magic. At least, she doesn't until her grandfather gives her a lucky coin that makes her every wish come true. But when she accidentally loses the coin, Maggie also loses her confidence in herself. "The Lucky Coin" tells the story of Maggie's journey from skeptic to believer and back again.

V VOCABULARY

ridiculous
absurd; very silly

undefeated
having no losses; never beaten

miracle
an extremely amazing or unlikely event, thing, or accomplishment

confidence
a feeling of certainty in one's own abilities

captain
a person who leads a team or group

≡ READ

NOTES

1   Maggie did not believe in magic. She worked hard to make her dreams come true. When she wanted to make the basketball team, she practiced for a month. So when her grandpa gave her a lucky coin, Maggie thought it was a joke.

2   "Your future will be bright," Grandpa said. "But if you need some luck, hold this coin and make a wish. The coin will do the rest."

3   Maggie laughed, "I don't believe in magic."

4   Grandpa winked. "The coin is very powerful. Promise me you will use it responsibly."

5   Maggie put the coin in her pocket. She thought, *A lucky coin. How **ridiculous!***

NOTES

6   The next day Maggie's teacher surprised the class with a quiz. Maggie was nervous. She forgot to do the reading assignment. *What am I going to do?* Maggie realized that the coin was in her pocket. *This is silly, but what have I got to lose? I wish for a* **miracle**.

7   Maggie took a deep breath and looked down at the quiz. It was about a story she read last week! *It's a miracle! The coin worked!*

8   The bell rang for lunch. Maggie's stomach grumbled. *I know exactly what to wish for next: pizza.* She made her wish. Maggie cheered when she saw the menu in the cafeteria. As she bit into her second slice of pizza she thought, *I could get used to this.*

9   Maggie wished to be chosen as **captain** of the basketball team. Then she wished that the team would win all their games. Soon she was leading the **undefeated** team into the championship.

10 Then one day, Maggie led the team on an outdoor run. The coin bounced out of her pocket somewhere along the trail. It was gone.

11 On the morning of the championship game, Maggie couldn't do anything right. She didn't sink a basket during the first half of the game. Her teammates struggled without Maggie's **confidence** to guide them. It looked like the team would lose. The referee blew his whistle, announcing a time-out. Maggie ignored her coach's pep talk. *I didn't used to believe in magic. Now I can't do anything without it. I wish I'd never heard of that lucky coin!*

12 "Hey, Maggie! Are you listening?"

13 Maggie snapped to attention.

14 Her coach said, "We need some of your usual magic, or we don't have a chance. Can we count on you?"

15 A second whistle called the team back. Within seconds, the ball was in Maggie's hands. She took a deep breath and took a shot.

First Read

Read the story. After you read, answer the Think Questions below.

☁ THINK QUESTIONS

1. Who are the main characters in the story? What is their relationship?

   The main characters are _____.

   They are _____.

2. What happens at the beginning of the story?

   At the beginning of the story _____.

3. At the end of the story, why is Maggie upset?

   Maggie is upset because _____.

4. Use context to confirm the meaning of the word *miracle* as it is used in "The Lucky Coin." Write your definition of *miracle* here.

   Miracle means _____.

   A context clue is _____.

5. What is another way to say that a lucky coin is *ridiculous*?

   A lucky coin is _____.

Please note that excerpts and passages in the StudySync® library and this workbook are intended as touchstones to generate interest in an author's work. The excerpts and passages do not substitute for the reading of entire texts, and StudySync® strongly recommends that students seek out and purchase the whole literary or informational work in order to experience it as the author intended. Links to online resellers are available in our digital library. In addition, complete works may be ordered through an authorized reseller by filling out and returning to StudySync® the order form enclosed in this workbook.

Reading & Writing
Companion

177

Skill:
Language Structures

★ DEFINE

In every language, there are rules that tell how to **structure** sentences. These rules define the correct order of words. In the English language, for example, a **basic** structure for sentences is subject, verb, and object. Some sentences have more **complicated** structures.

You will encounter both basic and complicated **language structures** in the classroom materials you read. Being familiar with language structures will help you better understand the text.

••• CHECKLIST FOR LANGUAGE STRUCTURES

To improve your comprehension of language structures, do the following:

✓ Monitor your understanding.

- Ask yourself: Why do I not understand this sentence? Is it because I do not understand some of the words? Or is it because I do not understand the way the words are ordered in the sentence?

✓ Break down the sentence into its parts.

- In English, most sentences share the same pattern: subject + verb + object.
  > The **subject** names who or what is doing the action.
  > The **verb** names the action or state of being.
  > The **object** answers questions such as Who?, What?, Where?, and When?
- Ask yourself: What is the action? Who or what is doing the action? What details do the other words provide?

✓ Confirm your understanding with a peer or teacher.

YOUR TURN

Read the following excerpt from "The Lucky Coin." Then, complete the chart by writing the words and phrases into the "Subject," "Verb," and "Object" columns. The first row has been done as an example.

---

from **"The Lucky Coin"**

Maggie wished to be chosen as captain of the basketball team. Then she wished that the team would win all their games. Soon she was leading the undefeated team into the championship.

Then one day, Maggie led the team on an outdoor run. The coin bounced out of her pocket somewhere along the trail. It was gone.

Sentence	Subject	Verb	Object
Maggie wished to be chosen as captain of the basketball team.	Maggie	wished	to be chosen
Then she wished that the team would win all their games.			
Soon she was leading the undefeated team into the championship.			
Then one day, Maggie led the team on an outdoor run.			
The coin bounced out of her pocket somewhere along the trail.			

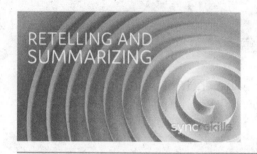

Skill: Retelling and Summarizing

★ DEFINE

You can retell and summarize a text after reading to show your understanding. **Retelling** is telling a story again in your own words. **Summarizing** is giving a short explanation of the most important ideas in a text.

Keep your retelling or summary **concise**. Only include important information and keywords from the text. By summarizing and retelling a text, you can improve your comprehension of the text's ideas.

••• CHECKLIST FOR RETELLING AND SUMMARIZING

In order to retell a story or summarize text, note the following:

✓ Identify the main events of the story.

- Ask yourself: What happens in this text? What are the main events that happen at the beginning, the middle, and the end of the text?

✓ Identify the main ideas in a text.

- Ask yourself: What are the most important ideas in the text?

✓ Determine the answers to the six WH questions.

- Ask yourself: After reading this text, can I answer Who?, What?, Where?, When?, Why?, and How? questions.

YOUR TURN

Read the following excerpt from "The Lucky Coin." Then, write each event in the beginning, middle, or end of the chart to retell what happened in the story.

---

from **"The Lucky Coin"**

On the morning of the championship game, Maggie couldn't do anything right. She didn't sink a basket during the first half of the game. Her teammates struggled without Maggie's confidence to guide them. It looked like the team would lose. The referee blew his whistle, announcing a time-out. Maggie ignored her coach's pep talk. *I didn't used to believe in magic. Now I can't do anything without it. I wish I'd never heard of that lucky coin!*

Event Options		
Maggie thinks it is because of the coin	The team was probably going to lose.	Maggie didn't sink a basket in the first half.

Beginning	
Middle	
End	

THE
LUCKY
COIN

Close Read

 WRITE

ARGUMENTATIVE--LITERARY ANALYSIS: How do the descriptions and events help readers understand why Maggie makes the choices she does? Write a response to this question. Support your writing with evidence from the text. Pay attention to subject-verb agreement as you write.

Use the checklist below to guide you as you write.

☐ Which details tell how Maggie feels about magic?

☐ Which event first leads Maggie to believe that magic is real?

☐ What does Maggie start doing after this event?

☐ What is one negative decision Maggie makes because of her belief in magic?

Use the sentence frames to organize and write your literary analysis.

At first, Maggie does not believe in _____.

She thinks the lucky coin is silly.

Then, Maggie forgets to read her homework. The teacher gives her a_____

_____.

Maggie is nervous. She makes a wish with the lucky coin. The quiz is about something she already read.

Other events like this start happening.

For example, _____.

Then, _____.

These examples show why Maggie starts to _____.

Text Fulfillment
Through StudySync

If you are interested in specific titles, please fill out the form below and we will check availability through our partners.

ORDER DETAILS

Date:

TITLE	AUTHOR	Paperback/ Hardcover	Specific Edition *If Applicable*	Quantity

SHIPPING INFORMATION

Contact:

Title:

School/District:

Address Line 1:

Address Line 2:

Zip or Postal Code:

Phone:

Mobile:

Email:

BILLING INFORMATION ☐ *SAME AS SHIPPING*

Contact:

Title:

School/District:

Address Line 1:

Address Line 2:

Zip or Postal Code:

Phone:

Mobile:

Email:

PAYMENT INFORMATION

☐ CREDIT CARD

Name on Card:

Card Number:

Expiration Date:

Security Code:

☐ PO

Purchase Order Number:

StudySync Text Fulfillment, BookheadEd Learning, LLC
610 Daniel Young Drive I Sonoma, CA 95476

Drugs and Society

Glen R. Hanson

Professor, Department of Pharmacology and Toxicology
University of Utah
Salt Lake City, UT
Director, Utah Addiction Center
Senior Advisor
National Institute on Drug Abuse, NIH

Peter J. Venturelli

Chair and Associate Professor of Sociology and Criminology
Department of Sociology
Valparaiso University
Valparaiso, IN

Annette E. Fleckenstein

Professor, Department of Pharmacology and Toxicology
University of Utah
Salt Lake City, UT

JONES AND BARTLETT PUBLISHERS

Sudbury, Massachusetts

BOSTON   TORONTO   LONDON   SINGAPORE

World Headquarters
Jones and Bartlett Publishers
40 Tall Pine Drive
Sudbury, MA 01776
978-443-5000
info@jbpub.com
www.jbpub.com

Jones and Bartlett Publishers Canada
6339 Ormindale Way
Mississauga, Ontario L5V 1J2
Canada

Jones and Bartlett Publishers International
Barb House, Barb Mews
London W6 7PA
United Kingdom

Jones and Bartlett's books and products are available through most bookstores and online booksellers. To contact Jones and Bartlett Publishers directly, call 800-832-0034, fax 978-443-8000, or visit our website www.jbpub.com.

Substantial discounts on bulk quantities of Jones and Bartlett's publications are available to corporations, professional associations, and other qualified organizations. For details and specific discount information, contact the special sales department at Jones and Bartlett via the above contact information or send an email to specialsales@jbpub.com.

Production Credits
Acquisitions Editor: Jacqueline Ann Geraci
Production Director: Amy Rose
Associate Editor: Amy L. Flagg
Editorial Assistant: Kyle Hoover
Production Editor: Tracey Chapman
Marketing Manager: Jessica Faucher
Manufacturing Buyer: Therese Connell
Composition: Arlene Apone
Cover Design: Kristin E. Ohlin
Photo Research Manager and Photographer: Kimberly Potvin
Associate Photo Researcher and Photographer: Christine McKeen
Photo Researcher: Lee Michelsen
Cover Image: © stock shots by itani/Alamy Images
Printing and Binding: Courier Kendallville
Cover Printing: Courier Kendallville

Library of Congress Cataloging-in-Publication Data
Hanson, Glen (Glen R.)
  Drugs and society / Glen R. Hanson, Peter J. Venturelli, Annette E. Fleckenstein. — 10th ed.
    p. ; cm.
  Includes bibliographical references and index.
  ISBN-13: 978-0-7637-5642-0 (pbk.)
  ISBN-10: 0-7637-5642-3 (pbk.)
  1. Drugs. 2. Drugs—Toxicology. 3. Drug abuse. I. Venturelli, Peter J., 1949- II. Fleckenstein, Annette E. III. Title.
  [DNLM: 1. Substance-Related Disorders. WM 270 H2505d 2009]
  RM301.W58 2009
  362.29—dc22
                        2008020466
6048

Printed in the United States of America
14 13 12 11 10   10 9 8 7 6 5 4

BRIEF CONTENTS

CONTENTS

FEATURE CONTENTS

Preface

THE TENTH EDITION of *Drugs and Society* is intended to convey to students the impact of drug use and/or abuse on the lives of ordinary people. The authors have combined their expertise in the fields of drug abuse, pharmacology, and sociology with their extensive experiences in research, treatment, teaching, drug policy-making, and drug policy implementation to create an edition that reflects the most current information and understanding relative to drug abuse issues available in a textbook.

We made the tenth edition of *Drugs and Society* an exceptionally comprehensive text on drug use and drug-related problems. This book is written on a personal level and directly addresses the college student by incorporating individual drug use and abuse experiences, as well as personal and institutional perspectives. For example, many chapters include excerpts from personal experiences with recreational drug users, habitual (often addicted) drug users, and former drug users. Students will find these personal accounts both insightful and interesting. This approach makes *Drugs and Society* truly unique. This was implemented in response to suggestions from readers, students, and instructors to further stimulate students' interest.

Drugs and Society was written to instruct university students from a wide range of disciplines to gain a realistic perspective of drug-related problems in our society. Students in nursing, physical education and other health sciences, psychology, social work, and sociology will find that our text provides useful current information and perspectives to help them understand these critical issues:

- Social, psychological, and biological reasons why drug use and abuse occurs
- The results of drug use and abuse
- How to prevent and treat drug use and abuse
- How drugs/medications can be used effectively for therapeutic purposes

To achieve this goal, we have presented the most current and authoritative views on drug abuse in an objective and easily understood manner. To help students appreciate the multifaceted nature of drug-related problems, the *Tenth Edition* exposes the issues from pharmacological, neurobiological, psychological, and sociological perspectives. Besides including the most current information concerning drug use and abuse topics,

each chapter includes updated and helpful learning aids for students:

- **Holding the Line:** Vignettes intended to help readers assess governmental efforts to deal with drug-related problems.
- **Case in Point:** Examples of relevant clinical issues that arise from the use of each major group of drugs discussed.
- **Here and Now:** Current events that illustrate the personal and social consequences of drug abuse.
- **Point/Counterpoint:** Features that expose students to different perspectives on drug-related issues and encourage them to draw their own conclusions.
- **Highlighted definitions:** Definitions of new terminology are conveniently located on the same page of their discussion in the text.
- **Learning objectives:** Goals for learning are listed at the beginning of each chapter to help students identify the principal concepts being taught.
- **Summary statements:** Concise summaries found at the end of each chapter correlate with the learning objectives.
- **Chapter questions:** Provocative questions at the end of each chapter encourage students to discuss, ponder, and critically analyze their own feelings and biases about the information presented in the book.
- **Concise and well-organized tables and figures:** Updated features found throughout the book present the latest information to students in an easily understood format.
- **Color photographs and drawings:** These additions graphically illustrate important concepts and facilitate comprehension as well as retention of information.

Because of these updated features, we believe that this edition of *Drugs and Society* continues to be much more "user friendly" than the previous editions and will encourage student motivation and learning.

The *Tenth Edition* of *Drugs and Society* includes updated statistics and current examples of the key principles being taught in this text. The new topical coverage includes discussion of:

- The abuse of prescription and performance-enhancing drugs
- Details on public advertising of prescription products and the resulting consumer controversy

xiv

- The most recent information on the methamphetamine epidemic and the personal and social consequences
- The latest status of over-the-counter (OTC) stimulants and decongestants, as well as abuse of other OTC products
- Updated data on abuse levels in young people
- Current topics such as steroids in baseball, OxyContin, restrictions on pain pills, and heroin potency
- The latest information on HIV/AIDS impact, especially in drug abusers
- Risk factors and protective factors for drug abuse
- The most recent information on alcohol problems in young people and college students
- "National Household Survey" (National Survey on Drug Use and Health) and "Monitoring the Future" survey data

The material in the text encompasses biomedical, sociological, and social-psychological views. Chapter 1 provides a helpful overview: the current dimensions of drug use (statistics and trends) and the most common currently abused drugs. Chapter 2 comprehensively explains addiction and drug use and abuse from multidisciplinary and theoretical standpoints. The latest biological, psychological, social-psychological, and sociological perspectives are explained. Chapter 3 discusses how the law deals with drug use and abuse of both licit (alcohol, OTC, and prescription) and illicit (marijuana, hallucinogens, and cocaine) drugs.

Chapter 4 helps the student understand the basic biochemical operations of the nervous and endocrine systems and explains how psychoactive drugs and anabolic steroids alter such functions. Chapter 5 instructs students about the factors that determine how drugs affect the body. This chapter details the physiological and psychological variables that determine how and why people respond to drugs used for therapeutic and recreational purposes.

Chapters 6 through 14 deal with specific drug groups that are commonly abused in this country. Those drugs that depress brain activity are discussed in Chapters 6 (sedative-hypnotic agents), 7 and 8 (alcohol), and 9 (opioid narcotics). The drugs that stimulate brain activity are covered in Chapters 10 (amphetamines, cocaine, and caffeine) and 11 (tobacco and nicotine). The last major category of substances of abuse is hallucinogens. Such drugs alter the senses and create hallucinatory and/or distorted experiences. These substances are discussed in Chapters 12 (hallucinogens such as LSD, mescaline, Ecstasy, and PCP) and 13 (marijuana). Chapter 14 discusses inhalants, substances that are particularly popular among youth.

Although most drugs that are abused cause more than one effect (for example, cocaine can be a stimulant and have some hallucinatory properties), the classification we have chosen for this text is frequently used by experts and pharmacologists in the drug abuse field and is based on the most likely drug effect. All of the chapters in this section are similarly organized. They discuss:

- The historical origins and evolution of the agents so students can better understand society's attitudes toward, and regulation of, these drugs
- Previous and current clinical uses of these drugs to help students appreciate distinctions between therapeutic use and abuse
- Patterns of abuse and distinctive features that contribute to each drug's abuse potential
- Nonmedicinal and medicinal therapies for drug-related dependence, withdrawal, and abstinence

Chapter 15 explores the topic of drugs and therapy. Like illicit drugs, nonprescription, prescription, and herbal drugs can be misused if not understood. This chapter helps the student to appreciate the uses and benefits of proper drug use as well as to recognize that licit (legalized) drugs can also be problematic.

Chapter 16 explores drug use in several major subcultures: sports/athletics, women, adolescents, college students, HIV-positive people, and entertainment. Included in this chapter is a discussion of new media "electronic" drug subcultures that have recently arisen.

Chapter 17 acquaints students with drug abuse prevention. This chapter focuses on the following topics: (1) the most prominent factors affecting an individual's use of drugs, (2) major types of drug prevention programs, (3) major types of drug users that must be recognized before creating a prevention program, (4) the four levels of comprehensive drug prevention programs for drug use and abuse, (5) major family factors that can affect the use of drugs, (6) primary prevention programs in higher education, (7) four recent large-scale prevention programs, and (8) two additional prevention measures that may substitute for the attraction to drug use.

Chapter 18 focuses on treating drug dependence.

The Appendix in this *Tenth Edition* includes a detailed presentation of schedules for drugs of abuse.

Instructor's Aids

The ancillary package for the *Tenth Edition* includes the most contemporary technology. For instructors who adopt the *Tenth Edition*, an Instructor's ToolKit CD-ROM is available. Designed for classroom use, this CD contains PowerPoint presentations, a TestBank, an Image Bank, and lecture outlines. Other instructor resources such as answers to the Student Study Guide can be found on http://health.jbpub.com/drugsandsociety/10e. For distance learning options or additional information, call your Jones and Bartlett Publishers Representative at 800-832-0034.

Student's Aids

For students using the *Tenth Edition*, a study guide is available packaged with the text or available for purchase separately. This study guide helps students to master key concepts, new terms, and critical issues. The companion web site, available at http://health.jbpub.com/drugsandsociety/10e, offers students practical learning and studying tools including Web links, practice quizzes, animated flashcards, crossword puzzles, and an online glossary.

About the Authors

Dr. Glen R. Hanson, a professor in the Department of Pharmacology and Toxicology at the University of Utah and the director of the Utah Addiction Center, has researched the neurobiology of drug abuse for over 25 years and authored more than 200 scientific papers and book chapters on the subject. Dr. Hanson has lectured on drug abuse topics throughout the world. He served as the Director of the Division of Neuroscience and Behavioral Research at the National Institute on Drug Abuse (NIDA) after which he became NIDA's acting director from 2001 to 2003. He continues to serve as a NIDA senior advisor. As a component of the National Institutes of Health (NIH), NIDA is the federal agency recognized as the world's premier science organization dealing with drug abuse issues and funds 85% of the drug abuse–related research in the world. Dr. Hanson is also the Director of the Utah Addiction Center and works with scientists, public officials, policy makers, and the general public to more effectively deal with problems of drug abuse addiction.

Dr. Peter J. Venturelli has been the coauthor of this text since the second edition of *Drugs and Society* in 1988. In addition to revising this text every three years, Dr. Venturelli's experiences and qualifications in academia and professional life include publishing research in drug and ethnic anthologies, other drug texts, and scholarly journals; authoring more than 43 conference papers at national professional sociological meetings; serving in elected and administrative positions in professional drug research associations; receiving several research grants involving drug use and ethnicity; authoring the latest drug research in sociological encyclopedias; and teaching of undergraduate and graduate students full-time for the past 20 years.

Dr. Annette E. Fleckenstein is a professor in the Department of Pharmacology and Toxicology at the University of Utah. She has researched the neurobiology of substance abuse for over 10 years, lectured on drug abuse topics throughout the United States and abroad, and authored more than 75 scientific papers and book chapters on the subject. She continues to lecture to undergraduate, graduate, and professional students.

Acknowledgments

The many improvements that have made this the best edition yet of the *Drugs and Society* series could not have occurred without the hard work and dedication of numerous people.

We are indebted to the many reviewers who evaluated the manuscript at different stages of development. Much of the manuscript was reviewed and greatly improved by comments from:

Zuzana Bic, DrPH, MUDr
University of California, Irvine

Jewel C. Carter, DHSc, MPH, CHES
William Paterson University

Deborah A. Danzis, PhD
High Point University

Mary Jo Desprez, MA
Eastern Michigan University

Ethel A. Elkins, MA, MHA, LCSW, LMFT, LMHC, SAP
University of Southern Indiana

Jeanne Freeman, PhD, CHES
California University of Pennsylvania

Melissa L. Grim, PhD, CHES
Radford University

Joan Hart, MS
John A. Logan College

John Janowiak, PhD
Appalachian State University

John P. Kowalczyk, PhD, MPH, RS, CHES
University of Minnesota Duluth

Alan J. Lipps, PhD, LMSW, LPC
South Texas College

Thomas R. Liszewski, MA, LLP
Ferris State University

Paul Mazeroff, EdD
McDaniel College

Bill Meil, PhD
Indiana University of Pennsylvania

Dawn R. Rager, PhD
Chair, St. John Fisher College

Frank M. Scalzo, PhD
Bard College

Diane Sevening, EdD, CCDC III
University of South Dakota

Victoria Rae Smith, BS, MS
North Hennepin Community College

David S. Soriano, PhD
University of Pittsburgh-Bradford

Sherman K. Sowby, PhD, CHES
California State University, Fresno

Dr. Toni Terling Watt, PhD
Texas State University

Glyn Young, PhD, MSW
East Carolina University

The authors would like to express, once again, their gratitude for the comments and suggestions of users and reviewers of previous editions of *Drugs and Society*.

At their respective institutions, each of the authors would like to thank a multitude of people too numerous to list individually but who have given them invaluable assistance.

Dr. Fleckenstein acknowledges the support of her family in her participation in the preparation of this revised text. She also thanks Dr. Barbara Sullivan, University of Utah, for her expert and thoughtful suggestions for this revision.

At Valparaiso University, Professor Venturelli is very grateful to two staff members at the university. Very special mention and thanks go to Nancy Young, Associate Administrator, School of Law, who created many of the figures, provided data for the tables, continuously surfed the web for invaluable data and other drug information, and continuously helped with many other "chores" necessary for updating his chapters. To be without Nancy Young's help is unthinkable! Special thanks goes to Linda Matera, administrative associate in the college of arts and sciences, who continuously helped with filing the multitude of articles that made the information in his chapters current and "crisp." In addition, her vigilant warnings about deadline dates kept him on his toes. Professor Venturelli would also like to gratefully acknowledge the countless other students and working people who were interviewed for hours on end regarding their observations, knowledge, and personal use and/or past experiences with drugs. Last and certainly not least, a special thank you goes to Jason Kresich for all the times he had to include last minute proofreading, Web site searches, and assistance with testbank questions and answers from a student's perspective, while maintaining his dedication to his studies at Valparaiso University. His conscientiousness, hard work, patience, and infectious humor was not only appreciated but also needed, especially when deadlines loomed. While the final copy of his chapters remains his responsibility, this edition has been *substantially* enhanced by all their efforts, loyalties, and dedicated assistance.

Dr. Hanson is particularly indebted to his wife, Margaret, for her loving encouragement. Without her patience and support this endeavor would not have been possible. She reminds him that what is truly important in this world is service to our family and to each other. Also appreciated is the support of his children.

CHAPTER 1

Introduction to Drugs and Society

Did You Know?

- O The popular use of legal drugs, particularly alcohol and tobacco, has caused far more deaths, sickness, violent crimes, economic loss, and other social problems than the use of all illegal drugs combined.

- O The effect a drug has depends on multiple factors: (1) the ingredients of the drug and its effect on the body, (2) the traditional use of the drug, (3) individual motivation, and (4) the social and physical surroundings in which the drug is taken.

- O Attempts to regulate drug use were made as long ago as 2240 B.C.

- O In the past, the penalty for cigarette smoking was having the nose cut off in Russia, the lips sliced off in Hindustan (India), and the head chopped off in China (Thio 1983, 1995, 2000).

- O Drug use — both licit and illicit drugs — is an "equal-opportunity affliction." This means that drug consumption is found across all income levels, social classes, genders, races, ethnicities, lifestyles, and age groups.

- O Approximately 76% of drug users in the United States are employed either full- or part-time.

- O Approximately 41% of convicted inmates had been drinking alcohol, and 36% were using drugs at the time they committed their offense (Harlow 1998).

Drugs and Society Online is a great source for additional drugs and society information for both students and instructors.
Visit **http://drugsandsociety.jbpub.com** to find a variety of useful tools for learning, thinking, and teaching.

Learning ◎bjectives

On completing this chapter you will be able to:

- ◎ Explain how drug use is affected by pharmacological, cultural, social, and contextual factors.

- ◎ Recognize the key terms for initially understanding drug use.

- ◎ Explain when drugs were first used and under what circumstances.

- ◎ Indicate how widespread drug use is and who the potential drug abusers are.

- ◎ List four reasons why drugs are used.

- ◎ Rank in descending order, from most common to least, the most commonly used licit and illicit drugs.

- ◎ Name three types of drug users, and explain how they differ.

- ◎ Describe how the mass media promote drug use.

- ◎ Explain when drug use leads to abuse.

- ◎ List and explain the phases of drug addiction.

- ◎ List the major findings regarding drugs and crime.

- ◎ Define employee assistance programs and explain their role in resolving productivity problems.

- ◎ Explain the holistic self-awareness approach.

Introduction

Each year, at an accelerating rate, as technology brings about new changes, our family, community, city, and nation, as well as the entire world, experience social change. These technological changes affect our everyday lives. It is no exaggeration to say that today, more than ever before, technology drives social change. More importantly, this change affects our lives. As an example, let us look at the cellular phone as a recent innovation. Your great-grandparents may have been fortunate to have a black stationary and wired telephone at home to communicate with friends and neighbors living at a distance. Likewise, your grandparents had newer versions of the same telephone with an extension telephone used in other parts of their homes. Your parent(s) had the same type of telephone, but it was more stylized with several extension phones in their homes. Today, your technological reality includes home-based telephones, facsimile machines, pagers, and mobile (cellular) telephones, with Internet capability, instant messaging, speaker capability, caller identification, alarm clock, games, and other software that were never imagined 20 years ago. Further, we now have another generation of mobile phones with which you can have a live, visual conversation with a friend living practically anywhere in the world.

Consider another example. More than likely, your great-grandparents wrote letters on manual typewriters. Your grandparents wrote letters on electric typewriters, whereas your parents started writing letters on electric typewriters and then had to change to computers. Today, you often communicate with family members and friends by email and instant messaging. Although the electronic "gadgets" that surround your life are perceived as normal, a visit to a museum displaying science and technology offers many surprises and, more than likely, an appreciation for how "things were and how much they have changed." These examples illustrate how the way we do things is in a continuous state of development. Life is changing so rapidly that there is constant demand to keep pace and remain current with newly developing gadgets.

What does this have to do with drug use and/or abuse? Just as electronics continually evolve, drugs follow similar paths of evolution. Today, there are thousands of new drugs available that are used either legally or illegally. These drugs are used for medicinal purposes, recreational purposes, or to achieve effects that do not include maintaining health. Other people in society use drugs to cope with pressures emanating from social change. Some people use and eventually abuse drugs to cope with, delay, or even avoid social change.

Despite the wealth of knowledge regarding the dangers of unnecessary drug use, together with the recent laws prohibiting drug manufacture and consumption, and the ensuing stiff penalties for violating such drug laws, many more people today than in the past use legal and illegal types of drugs without any medically approved reason.

Drug Use

Anyone can become dependent and addicted to a drug. For example, the desire to use a drug before drug dependence (addiction) sets in is both seductive and nondiscriminating of its users. Most people do not realize that drug use causes at least three major simultaneous changes:

1. The social and psychological basis of the attraction to a particular drug can be explained as feeling rewarded or satisfied from social pressures that have become postponed, momentarily rectified, or neutralized and defined as nonproblematic.
2. Pharmacologically, the use of such a drug alters body chemistry largely by interfering with (affecting) its proper (homeostatic) functioning. Drugs enhance, slow down, or distort the reception *and* transmission of reality.
3. The desire may satisfy an inborn or genetically programmed need or desire.

(Much more detail regarding this example is presented later in this chapter and in Chapter 2.)

Many argue that our "reality" would become perilous and unpredictable if people were legally free to dabble in their drugs of choice. Many do not realize, however, that if abused, even legal drugs can alter our perception of reality, become severely addicting, and destroy our social relationships with loved ones. Before delving into more detailed information, which is the basis of the other chapters in this book, we begin by examining and answering some key questions related to drug use:

1. What constitutes a drug?
2. What are the most commonly abused drugs?
3. What are designer drugs?

4. How widespread is drug abuse?
5. What is the extent and frequency of drug use in our society?
6. What are the current statistics on and trends in drug use?
7. What types of drug users exist?
8. How does the media influence drug use?
9. What attracts people to drug use?
10. When does drug use lead to drug dependence?
11. When does drug addiction occur?
12. What are the costs of drug addiction to society?
13. What can be gained by learning about the complexity of drug use and abuse?

Dimensions of Drug Use

To determine the perception of drug use in our country, we asked several of our many interviewees presented in this book, "What do you think of drug use in our society?" The following are three of the more typical responses:

I think it is a huge problem, especially when you think about the fact that there are so many people doing drugs. Even in my own family, my sister's kids have had drug problems. My niece became addicted to cocaine, nearly died one night from overdosing, had to leave college for a year and go into rehab. I cannot emphasize enough how this was one of the most beautiful (physically and mentally sharp) and polite nieces I ever had. The rest of the family had no idea why she left school last year. Then, just last week, my sister tearfully announced during a Christmas gathering that Cindee was heavily into drugs while attending her second year of college. We were all shocked by this information. Now, just think how many other kids are addicted to such junk while the people who really care and love them do not have a clue. If the kids are having to deal with this, just stop and think how many other people in other jobs and professions are battling or have caved into their drugs of choice.

How many workers are there on a daily basis doing jobs that require safety and are "high" on drugs? This is a scary thought. Just think of a surgeon on drugs, or an airline pilot. Yes, we have big monster problems with controlling drug use. *(From Venturelli's research files, 43-year-old female dietician, in Chicago, Illinois, February 9, 2003.)*

A second response to the same question:

Every effort by the government to stop illegal drug use has failed miserably. Even legal drug use, like alcohol and cigarettes, continues despite what the governmental public health media say. People should be left alone about their drug use unless such drug use is potentially harmful to others. I know that if I ever quit using both legal and illegal drugs it will be my own decision, not because the law can punish me. Yes, drug use is a problem for the addicted, but all throughout our history, drug use has been there. So why worry about it now? *(From Venturelli's research files, 24-year-old male graduate student in a Midwestern city, October 3, 1996.)*

A third response to the same question:

My drug use? Whose business is it anyway? As long as I don't affect your life when I do drugs, what business is it but my own? We come into the world alone and leave this world alone. I don't bother anyone else about whether or not so and so uses drugs, unless of course, their drug use puts me in jeopardy (like a bus driver or pilot high on drugs). On certain days when things are slow, I even get a little high on cocaine while trading stocks. These are the same clients who I have had for years and who really trust my advice. Ask my clients whether they are happy with my investment advice. I handle accounts with millions of dollars for corporations and even the board of education! Never was my judgment impaired or adversely affected because of too much coke. In fact, I know that I work even better under a little buzz. Now, I know this stuff has the potential to become addictive, but I don't let it. I know how to use it and when to lay off for a few weeks. *(From Venturelli's research files, 48-year-old male investment broker working in a major metropolitan city in California, June 2, 2000.)*

These three interviews reflect vastly contrasting views and attitudes about drug use. The first and second interviews show the most contrast, whereas the third interview, from an insider's perspective, shows the strong determination and belief that this man maintains about his drug use. Overall, this individual perceives his drug use as being under control. Although much about these viewpoints can be debated, an interesting finding is that such vastly different views about drug use often divide drug users and non-drug users. Drug users and/or sympathizers of drug use are often considered "**insiders**" with regard to their drug use, whereas nonusers and/or those who are against drug use are "**outsiders**." These two classifications result in very different sets of values and attitudes about drug usage. Such great differences of opinion and views about drugs and drug use often result from the following sources: (1) prior socialization experiences, such as family upbringing, relations with siblings, and types of peer group association, (2) the amount of exposure to drug use and drug users, (3) the age of initial exposure to drug use, and (4) whether an attitude change has occurred with regard to the acceptance or rejection of using drugs. (Most of these factors are discussed further in Chapter 2.) Keep in mind that in its entirety, this book views four principal factors as affecting how a drug user experiences a drug: pharmacological, cultural, social, and contextual.

Pharmacological factors. The ingredients of a particular drug affect the functions of the body and the nervous system, which in turn affect social behavior.

Cultural factors. Society's views of drug use, as determined by custom and tradition, affect our initial approach to and use of a particular drug.

Social factors. The motivation for taking a particular drug is affected by needs such as diminishing physical pain; curing an illness; providing relaxation; relieving stress or anxiety; trying to escape reality; self-medicating; heightening awareness; wanting to distort and change visual, auditory, or sensory inputs; or

strengthening confidence. Included in the category of social factors is the belief that attitudes about drug use develop from the values and attitudes of other drug users; the norms in their communities, subcultures, peer groups, and families; and the drug user's personal experiences with using drugs. These are also known as *influencing social factors.*

Contextual factors. Specific contexts define and determine personal dispositions toward drug use, as demonstrated by moods and attitudes about such activity. Specifically, these factors encompass the drug-taking social behavior that develops from the physical surroundings where the drug is used. For example, drugs may be taken at fraternity parties, outdoors in a secluded area with other drug users, in private homes, secretly at work, or at rock concerts.

Paying attention to the cultural, social, and contextual factors of drug use leads us to explore the sociology and psychology of drug use. Equally important are the pharmacological factors and consequences that directly focus on how the drugs taken affect the body — primarily the central nervous system (CNS) and the mind.

Although substances that affect both mind and body functioning are commonly called **drugs**, researchers in the field of drug or substance abuse use a more precise term: **psychoactive drugs (substances)**. Why the preference for using this term as opposed to *drugs?* Because the term *psychoactive drugs* is more precise in referring to *how* drugs affect the body. This term focuses on the particular effects these substances have on the CNS and emphasizes how they alter consciousness and perception. Because of their effects on the brain, psychoactive drugs can be used to treat physical or mental illness. Because the body can tolerate increasingly larger doses of them, many psychoactive drugs are used in progressively greater and more uncontrollable amounts to achieve the same level of effect. For many substances, a user is at risk of moving from occasional to regular use or from moderate use to heavy to chronic use. Whenever the drug is not supplied, a chronic user may then risk **addiction** (mostly psychological attachment) and experience **withdrawal symptoms** that are physical and/or psychological in nature whenever the drug is not supplied.

Generally speaking, any substance that modifies the nervous system and states of conscious-

KEY TERMS

insiders
people on the inside; those who approve of and/or use drugs

outsiders
people on the outside; those who do not approve of and/or use drugs

drug(s)
any substances that modify (either by enhancing, inhibiting, or distorting) mind and/or body functioning

psychoactive drugs (substances)
drug compounds (substances) that affect the central nervous system and alter consciousness and/or perceptions

Examples of licit drugs that can easily be abused.

Examples of illicit drugs that can become costly once drug dependence occurs.

ness is a drug. Such modification enhances, inhibits, or distorts the functioning of the body, thereby affecting patterns of behavior and social functioning. Psychoactive drugs are classified as either **licit** (legal) or **illicit** (illegal). (See Table 1.1 for a list of slang terms used by drug users.) For example, coffee, tea, cocoa, alcohol, tobacco, and **over-the-counter (OTC)** drugs are licit. When licit drugs are used in moderation, they often are socially acceptable. Marijuana, cocaine, and lysergic acid diethylamide (LSD) are examples of illicit drugs. Any use of these drugs is not generally socially acceptable by larger society or legally allowed.

Researchers have made some interesting findings about legal and illegal drug use:

1. The use of such legal substances as alcohol and tobacco is much more common than the use of illegal drugs such as marijuana, heroin, and LSD. Other legal drugs, such as depressants and stimulants, although less popular than alcohol and tobacco, are still more widely used than heroin and LSD.
2. The popular use of licit drugs, particularly alcohol and tobacco, has caused far more deaths, sickness, violent crimes, economic loss, and other social problems than the combined use of all illicit drugs.
3. Societal reaction to various drugs changes with time and place. Today, opium is an illegal drug and widely condemned as a *pan-pathogen* (a cause of all ills). In the 18th and 19th centuries, however, it was a legal drug and was popularly praised as a *panacea* (a cure for all ills). Alcohol use was widespread in the United States in the early 1800s, became illegal during the 1920s, and then was legalized a

second time and has been widely used since the 1930s. Cigarette smoking is legal in all countries today. In the 17th century, it was illegal in most countries, and smokers were sometimes harshly punished. For example, in Russia, smokers could lose their noses; in Hindustan (India), they could lose their lips; and in China, they could lose their heads (Thio 1983, 1995, 2000). Today, new emphasis in the United States on the public health hazards from cigarettes again is leading some people to consider new measures to restrict or even outlaw tobacco smoking.

KEY TERMS

addiction
generally refers to the psychological attachment to a drug(s); addiction to "harder" drugs such as heroin results in both psychological and physical attachment to the chemical properties of the drug, with the resulting satisfaction (reward) derived from using the drug in question

withdrawal symptoms
psychological and physical symptoms that result when a drug is absent from the body; physical symptoms are generally present in cases of drug dependence to more addictive drugs such as heroin; physical and psychological symptoms of withdrawal include perspiration, nausea, boredom, anxiety, and muscle spasms

licit drugs
legalized drugs such as coffee, alcohol, and tobacco

illicit drugs
illegal drugs such as marijuana, cocaine, and LSD

over-the-counter (OTC)
drugs sold without a prescription

Table 1.1 **Slang Terms Relating to Drugs and Drug Use**

SLANG TERM	WHAT IT MEANS	SLANG TERM	WHAT IT MEANS
24-7	Crack cocaine	Black beauties	Amphetamines, depressants
3750	Marijuana and crack rolled in a joint	Blasted	Under the influence
40, 40-bar	Oxycontin pill	Blow your mind	High on hallucinogens
51	Crack and marijuana or tobacco	Blunt	Marijuana inside a cigar
A-bomb	Marijuana cigarette with heroin or opium	Boost and shoot	To steal to support a drug habit
Abolic	Veterinary steroids	Brain ticklers	Amphetamines
AC/DC	Codeine cough syrup	Brown bombers	LSD
Acid, acid cube	LSD, sugar cube with LSD	Buda	Marijuana joint and crack
Acid freak, head	Heavy user of LSD	Buddha	Potent marijuana spiked with opium
Adam	Methylenedioxymethamphetamine (MDMA)	Bundle	Heroin
Air blast	Inhalants	Ditch weed	Inferior marijuana
All star	User of multiple drugs	Dr. Feelgood	Heroin
Amped	High on amphetamines	Easy lay	Gamma-hydroxybutyric acid (GHB)
Angel dust	PCP	Embalming fluid	PCP
Author	Doctor who writes illegal prescriptions	Flower tippling	Ecstacy (MDMA) mixed with mushrooms
Babysit	To guide someone through his first drug experience	Forget-me-drug	Rohypnol
Balloon	A penny balloon with heroin	Garbage rock	Crack cocaine
Banano	Cigarette laced with cocaine	Gluey	One who sniffs or inhales glue
Barbies	Depressants	Graduate	To progress to stronger drugs
Battery acid	LSD	Hippie crack	Inhalants
Batu	Smokable methamphetamine	Hot ice	Smokable methamphetamine
Beam me up Scotty	PCP and crack	Huff, huffing	Inhalants, to sniff an inhalant
Beanies	Methamphetamine	Ice cream habit	Occasional use of drugs
Beast	Heroin plus LSD	Idiot pills	Depressants
Belladonna	PCP	Kiddie dope	Prescription drugs
Bender	Drug party	Lemonade	Poor quality drugs
Biker's coffee	Methamphetamine in coffee	Lunch money drug	Rohypnol
Bin Laden	Heroin (after Sept. 11, 2001)	Magic mushroom	Psilocybin

(continued)

Table 1.1 (continued)

SLANG TERM	WHAT IT MEANS	SLANG TERM	WHAT IT MEANS
Monkey dust	PCP	Stacking	Use of steroids without a prescription
Moon gas	Inhalants	Toilet water	Inhalants
Mother's little helper	Depressants	Totally spent	Hangover after MDMA
Nose candy	Cocaine	Tragic magic	Crack dipped in PCP
Parachute	Smokable crack and heroin	Waffle dust	MDMA and amphetamines
Pepsi habit	Occasional use of drugs	Water-water	Marijuana cigarettes dipped in embalming fluid
Poor man's coke	Methamphetamine	West Coast	Ritalin (ADHD drug)
Quarter moon	Hashish	Zig Zag man	Marijuana rolling papers
Shoot	To inject a drug	Zombie	PCP, heavy user of drugs
Special K	Ketamine	Zoom	Marijuana laced with PCP

Source: Office of the National Drug Control Policy. "Drug Facts: Street Terms: Drugs and the Drug Trade." 2006. Available at www.whitehousedrugpolicy.gov/streetterms/byalpha.asp.

Table 1.2 introduces some of the terminology that you will encounter throughout this text. It is important that you understand how the definitions vary.

Major Types of Commonly Abused Drugs

In looking at drug use, this book examines the following topics: (1) OTC drugs (the drugs most subject to abuse); (2) prescription drugs; (3) other drugs and compounds not taken for a medical need or necessity but for pleasure or relief from boredom, stress, or anxiety; and (4) some of the most important information regarding drug use (for example, theories of why drugs are used, legality of drugs, addiction, bodily effects of drug use, lifestyles of drug users, and drug abuse treatment and prevention).

To begin, we now briefly examine the major drugs of use and often abuse. The drugs examined next are stimulants, hallucinogens and other similar compounds, depressants, alcohol, nicotine, cannabis (marijuana and hashish), anabolic steroids, inhalants/organic solvents, narcotics/opiates, and designer drugs. A brief overview is provided here, and these same drugs are discussed in much more detail in separate chapters throughout this book.

Stimulants

Although some of these drugs can be considered to be **gateway drugs** (see definition in Table 1.2), these substances act on the CNS by increasing alertness, excitation, euphoria, pulse rate, and blood pressure. Insomnia and loss of appetite are common outcomes. The user initially experiences pleasant effects, such as a sense of increased energy and a state of euphoria, or "high." In addition, users feel restless and talkative and have trouble sleeping. High doses used over the long term can produce personality changes. Some of the psychological risks associated with chronic stimulant use include violent, erratic, or paranoid behavior. Other effects can include confusion, anxiety and depression, and loss of interest in sex or food. Major stimulants include amphetamines,

KEY TERMS

gateway drugs
alcohol, tobacco, and marijuana—types of drugs that when used excessively may lead to using other and often more addictive drugs such as cocaine, heroin, or "crack."

Table 1.2 **Commonly Used Terms**

TERM	DESCRIPTION
Gateway drugs	The word *gateway* suggests a path leading to something else. Alcohol, tobacco, and marijuana are the most commonly used drugs. Almost all abusers of more powerfully addictive drugs have first experimented with these three substances.
Medicines	Generally, these drugs are prescribed by a physician to prevent or treat the symptoms of an illness.
Prescription medicines	These drugs are prescribed by a physician. Common examples include antibiotics, antidepressants, and drugs prescribed to relieve pain, induce stimulation, or induce relaxation. These drugs are taken under a physician's recommendation because they are more potent than OTC drugs. The amount spent on prescription medicines is approximately $94 billion per year. "In 2001 ... $3.1 billion prescriptions were written in the United States ...." (Goode 2005, p. 17).
Over-the-counter (OTC)	These drugs are sold without a prescription. "In 2001, the pharmaceutical drug industry sold about $60 billion worth of drugs each year at the retail level" (Goode 2005, p. 17). OTC drugs can be purchased at will without first seeking medical advice. Examples include aspirin, laxatives, diet pills, cough suppressants, and sore throat medicines. Often, these drugs are misused or abused (overused).
Drug misuse	The unintentional or inappropriate use of prescribed or OTC drugs. Misuse includes, but is not limited to, (1) taking more drugs than prescribed; (2) using OTC or psychoactive drugs in excess without medical supervision; (3) mixing drugs with alcohol or other drugs, often to accentuate euphoric effects; (4) using old medicines to self-treat new symptoms of an illness or ailment; (5) discontinuing certain prescribed drugs at will or against a physician's recommendation; and (6) administering prescription drugs to family members or friends without medical consultation and supervision.
Drug abuse	Also known as *chemical or substance abuse.* The willful misuse of either licit or illicit drugs for recreation, perceived necessity, or convenience. Drug abuse differs from drug use in that *drug use* is taking or using drugs, whereas *drug abuse* is a more intense and often willful misuse of drugs, often to the point of addiction.
Drug addiction	Drug addiction involves noncasual or nonrecreational drug use. A frequent symptom is intense psychological preoccupation with obtaining and consuming drugs. Most often psychological and — in some cases, depending on the drug — physiological symptoms of withdrawal are manifested when the craving for the drug is not satisfied. Today, more emphasis is placed on the psychological craving (mental attachment) to the drug than on the more physiological-based withdrawal symptoms of addiction. (See Chapter 4 for more detailed information regarding addiction and the addiction process.)

Source: Goode, E. *Drugs in American Society,* 6th ed. Boston, MA: McGraw-Hill College, 2005.

cocaine and crack, methamphetamine ("meth"), and methylphenidate. Minor stimulants include caffeine, tea, chocolate, and nicotine (the most addictive minor stimulant).

Hallucinogens/Psychedelics and Other Similar Drugs

Either synthetic or grown naturally, these drugs produce very intense alteration of perceptions, thoughts, and feelings. They most certainly influence the complex inner workings of the human mind, causing users to refer to these drugs as *psychedelics* (because they cause hallucinations or distortion of reality and thinking). For example, while under their influence, these drugs can affect the sense of taste, smell, hearing, and vision. Tolerance to hallucinogens builds very rapidly, which means that increasing amounts of this drug are needed for similar effects. Hallucinogens include LSD, mescaline, phencyclidine (PCP), psilocybin or "magic mushrooms," and the more potent (hybrid) varieties of marijuana, hashish, and opium that are smoked as well as a newer type known as ketamine.

Depressants

These drugs depress the CNS. If taken in a high enough quantity, they produce insensibility or stupor. Depressants are also taken for some of the same reasons as hallucinogens, such as to relieve boredom, stress, and anxiety. In addition, the effects of both opioids (drugs that are derived from opium) and morphine derivatives appeal to many people who are struggling with emotional problems and looking for physical and emotional relief, and in some cases to induce sleep. Depressants include alcohol (ethanol), barbiturates, benzodiazepines (such as diazepam [Valium]), and methaqualone (Quaaludes).

Alcohol

Known as a gateway drug, **ethanol** is a colorless, volatile, and pungent liquid resulting from fermented grains, berries, and other fruits and vegetables. Alcohol is a depressant that mainly affects the CNS. Excessive amounts of alcohol often cause a progressive loss of inhibitions, flushing and dizziness, loss of coordination, impaired motor skills, blurred vision, slurred speech, sudden mood swings, vomiting, irregular pulse, and memory impairment. Chronic heavy use may lead to high blood pressure, arrhythmia (irregular heartbeat), and cirrhosis (severe liver deterioration).

Nicotine

Nicotine is also considered a gateway drug. It is a very addictive, colorless, highly volatile liquid alkaloid found in all tobacco products, including cigarettes, chewing tobacco, pipe tobacco, and cigars. Because nicotine is highly addictive and tobacco use is still socially acceptable under certain circumstances, smokers often start young and have a very difficult time quitting. Long-term use of tobacco products can lead to several different chronic respiratory ailments and cancers.

KEY TERMS

ethanol
the pharmacological term for alcohol; consumable type of alcohol that is the psychoactive ingredient in alcoholic beverages; often called grain alcohol

Cannabis (Marijuana and Hashish)

Cannabis is the most widely used illicit drug in the United States. Marijuana consists of the dried and crushed leaves, flowers, stems, and seeds of the *Cannabis sativa* plant, which readily grows in many parts of the world. Delta 9-tetrahydrocannabinol (THC) is the primary psychoactive, mind-altering ingredient in marijuana that produces euphoria ("a high"). Plant parts are usually dried, crushed, and smoked much like tobacco products. Other ways of ingesting marijuana include crushing and mixing the leaves into cookie or brownie batter and baking the batter. Hashish is another cannabis derivative that contains the purest form of resin and contains the highest amount of THC.

Anabolic Steroids

Steroids are a synthetic form of the male hormone testosterone. They are often used to increase muscle size and strength. Medically, steroids are used to increase body tissue or to treat allergies. Steroids are available in either liquid or pill form. Athletes have a tendency to use and abuse these drugs because dramatic results can occur with regard to increased body mass and muscle tissue. Some side effects include heart disease, liver cancer, high blood pressure, septic shock, impotence, genital atrophy, manic episodes, depression, violence, and mood swings.

Inhalants. These volatile chemicals, which include many common household substances, are often the most dangerous drugs, per dose, that a person can take. In addition, inhalants are most often used by preteens and younger teenagers.

Inhalants/Organic Solvents

Inhalants and organic solvents are also often considered gateway drugs and are very attractive to and popular among preteens and younger teenagers. Products used include gasoline, model airplane glue, and paint thinner. When inhaled, the vapors from these solvents can produce euphoric effects. Organic solvents can also refer to certain foods, herbs, and vitamins, such as "herbal Ecstasy."

Narcotics/Opiates

These drugs also depress the CNS and, if taken in a high enough quantity, produce insensibility or stupor. Narcotics include opium, morphine, codeine, and meperidine (Demerol).

Designer Drugs/Synthetic Drugs or Synthetic Opioids

In addition to the most commonly abused illicit drug categories just described, innovations in technology have produced new categories known as **designer drugs/synthetic drugs or synthetic opioids**. These relatively new types of drugs are developed by people who seek to circumvent the illegality of a drug by modifying the drug into a new compound. Ecstasy is an example of a designer drug/synthetic drug or synthetic opioid. Such drugs are created as **structural analogs** of substances already scheduled and forbidden under the Controlled Substances Act (CSA). Structural analogs are the drugs that result from altered chemical structures of already existing illicit drugs. Generally, these drugs are created by underground chemists whose goal is to make a profit by creating compounds that mimic, change, or intensify the psychoactive effects of controlled substances. The number of designer drugs that are created and sold illegally is very large.

Anyone with knowledge of college-level chemistry can alter the chemical ingredients and produce new designer drugs, although it may be nearly impossible to predict their properties or effects except by trial and error. Currently, three major types of synthetic analog drugs are available through the illicit drug market: analogs of PCP; analogs of fentanyl and meperidine (both synthetic narcotic analgesics) such as Demerol or MPPP (also called MPTP or PEPAP); and analogs of amphetamine and methamphetamine (which have stimulant and hallucinogenic properties) such as **MDMA**, known as "Ecstasy" or "Adam," which is widely used on college campuses as a euphoriant.

The production of these high-technology psychoactive substances is a sign of the new levels of risk and additional challenge to the criminal justice system. As the production and risk associated with the use of such substances increase, the need for a broader, better-informed view of drug use becomes even more important than in the past. (Appendix B lists, among other information, (1) the most commonly abused drugs in society, (2) their more common street names/terms, (3) medical uses, (4) routes of administration, (5) Controlled Substances Act [CSA] schedules, and (6) duration of detection in the body.)

Designer pills containing the illicit drug Ecstasy. This drug has some stimulant properties like amphetamines as well as hallucinogenic properties like LSD.

KEY TERMS

designer drugs/synthetic drugs or synthetic opioids
new drugs that are developed by people intending to circumvent the illegality of a drug by modifying a drug into a new compound; Ecstasy is an example

structural analogs
modifying the basic molecular skeleton of a compound to form a new molecular species; structural analogs are structurally related to the parent compound

MDMA
a type of illicit drug known as "Ecstasy" or "Adam" and having stimulant and hallucinogenic properties

Here and Now

Recent Abuse of Prescription and Performance-Enhancing Drugs

In the United States, young people frequently abuse prescription drugs; the only illicit drug that is abused more frequently is marijuana (U.S. Department of Justice [USDOJ] 2004). In 2006, nearly 7 million persons were current users of psychotherapeutic drugs taken nonmedically (see Table 1.4). For example, according to the National Survey on Drug Use and Health (NSDUH), published in 2007, from 2002 through 2005, 6.7% of 12- to 17-year-olds reported past year nonmedical prescription pain reliever use while abuse of marijuana was also 6.7%).

Three categories of prescription drugs that are currently abused are narcotics, depressants, and stimulants. *Narcotics* (e.g., OxyContin, Vicodin, and Percocet) include analgesics or opioids that are generally prescribed for physical pain. Abuse occurs when they are used nonmedically because of their euphoric and numbing effects. *Depressants* (e.g., Xanax, Valium, and Librium) are generally used to treat anxiety and sleep disorders. These drugs are abused because of their sedating properties. *Stimulants* (e.g., Ritalin, Dexedrine, and Meridia) are used to treat attention deficit disorder (ADD), attention deficit hyperactivity disorder (ADHD), and asthma. These drugs are abused because of their euphoric effects and energizing potential (Publishers Group 2004).

The two drugs in the stimulants category that are most often abused are Ritalin (methylphenidate hydrochloride) and Adderall (amphetamine). These prescription drugs are legitimately prescribed for ADHD, ADD, and narcolepsy (a sleep disorder) (Center for Strategic Abuse Research [CESAR] 2003). When used nonmedically, they are taken orally as tablets or the tablets are crushed into a powder and snorted (a far more popular method). Students often illegally purchase these tablets for $5 each from other students who have a legal prescription for the medication.

> I feel like Dr. Pill. All these brothers [fraternity brothers] are always looking for me at parties so that I can sell them a few tabs. What the heck, I make extra money selling Ritalin, enough to buy essentials like beer and cigarettes. *(From Venturelli's research files, 20-year-old male undergraduate student at a Midwestern university, December 9, 2004.)*

These drugs are often used in conjunction with alcohol or marijuana to enhance the "high" or for staying awake so as to increase comprehension and remain focused while reading or studying for an exam (CESAR 2003). Both prescription drugs are readily available and can be easily obtained by teenagers, who may abuse these drugs to experience a variety of desired effects. Increasingly, younger adolescents are obtaining prescription drugs from classmates, friends, and family members, or are stealing the drugs from school medicine dispensaries and from family members or other people for whom the drug has been legitimately prescribed.

Ritalin and Adderall abusers tend to be high school and college students. "A 2006 national survey found that 3% to 5% of students in grades 8, 10, and 12 reported using Ritalin without medical supervision at least in the past year" (National Survey on Drug Use and Health [NSDUH] 2007). Further, in a 2002 study conducted at the University of Wisconsin at Madison, one out of five students reported taking such drugs nonmedically (Nichols 2004).

An Overview of Drugs in Society

Many people think that problems with drugs are unique to this era. In reality, drug use and abuse have always been part of nearly all — past and present — human societies. For example, the Grecian oracles of Delphi used drugs, Homer's Cup of Helen induced sleep and provided freedom from care, and the mandrake root mentioned in the first book of the Bible, Genesis, produced a hallucinogenic effect. In Genesis 30:14–16, the mandrake is mentioned in association with bartering for lovemaking:

In the time of wheat harvest Reuben went out, found some mandrakes in the open country, and brought them to his mother Leah. Then Rachel asked Leah for some of her son's mandrakes, but Leah said, "Is it so small a thing to have taken away my husband, that you should take my son's mandrakes as well?" However, Rachel said, "Very well, let him sleep with you tonight in exchange for your son's mandrakes." So when Jacob came in from the country in the evening, Leah went out to meet him and said, "You are to sleep with me tonight; I have hired you with my son's mandrakes." That night he slept with her.

Ancient literature is filled with references to the use of mushrooms, *datura,* hemp, marijuana, opium poppies, and so on. Under the influence of some of these drugs, many people experienced extreme ecstasy or sheer terror. Some old pictures of demons and devils look very much like those described by modern drug users during so-called bummers, or bad trips. The belief that witches could fly may also have been drug-induced because many natural preparations used in so-called witches' brews induced the sensation of disassociation from the body, as in flying or floating.

As far back as 2240 B.C., attempts were made to regulate drug use. For instance, in that year, problem drinking was addressed in the Code of Hammurabi, where it was described as "a problem of men with too much leisure time and lazy dispositions." Nearly every culture has experienced drug abuse, and as found in the historical record, laws were enacted to control the use of certain types of drugs.

How Widespread Is Drug Abuse?

As mentioned earlier, drug abuse today is more acute and widespread than in any previous age. The evidence for this development is how often large quantities of illicit drugs are seized in the United States as well as throughout the world (see "Here and Now," Current Global Status of Illicit Drug Use in Selected Countries). Media exposure about illicit drug use is more likely to occur today than in the past. On any given day, you can scan most major national and international newspapers and run across stories about illegal drug manufacture, storage and distribution, use and/or abuse, and convictions. Drug use is an "**equal-opportunity affliction.**" This means that no one is immune from the use and/or abuse of both licit and illicit drugs. Research shows that drug consumption is found across the many different income, education, social class, occupation, race and ethnic, lifestyle, and age groups. To date, no one has proved to be

immune from drug use and/or abuse. (See "Here and Now," How Widespread Is the Use of Drugs?, on page 18.)

Many of us, for example, are dismayed or surprised when we discover that certain individuals we admire — our family members, close friends, workmates, celebrities, politicians, athletes, clergy, law enforcement personnel, physicians, academics, and even the seemingly upstanding man or woman next door — either admit to, are accused of, or are arrested for either licit and/or illicit drug use.

We are also taken aback when we hear that cigarettes, alcohol, and marijuana abuse are commonplace in many public and private junior high schools. Furthermore, most of us know of at least one (and many times more than one) close friend or family member who appears to secretly or not so secretly use drugs.

Extent and Frequency of Drug Use in Society

Erich Goode (2005), a much-respected sociologist, lists four types of drug use:

1. *Legal instrumental use.* Taking prescribed drugs and OTC drugs to relieve or treat mental or physical symptoms.
2. *Legal recreational use.* Using such licit drugs as tobacco, alcohol, and caffeine to achieve a certain mental or psychic state.
3. *Illegal instrumental use.* Taking drugs without a prescription to accomplish a task or goal, such

An example of a situation that requires clear thinking without the use of mind-altering drugs.

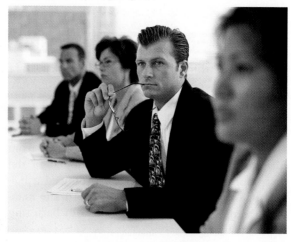

KEY TERMS

equal-opportunity affliction
refers to the use of drugs, stressing that drug use cuts across all members of society regardless of income, education, occupation, social class, and age

Here and Now

Current Global Status of Illicit Drug Use in Selected Countries

Afghanistan	World's largest producer of opium; cultivation dropped 48% to 107,400 hectares in 2005; better weather and lack of widespread disease returned opium yields to normal levels, meaning potential opium production declined by only 10% to 4475 metric tons; if the entire poppy crop were processed, it is estimated that 526 metric tons of heroin could be processed; many narcotics-processing labs throughout the country; drug trade is a source of instability and some antigovernment groups profit from the trade; significant domestic use of opiates; 80–90% of the heroin consumed in Europe comes from Afghan opium; vulnerable to narcotics money laundering through informal financial networks; source of hashish.
Albania	Increasingly active transshipment point for Southwest Asian opiates, hashish, and cannabis transiting the Balkan route and — to a lesser extent — cocaine from South America destined for Western Europe; limited opium and growing cannabis production; ethnic Albanian narcotrafficking organizations active and expanding in Europe; vulnerable to money laundering associated with regional trafficking in narcotics, arms, contraband, and illegal aliens.
Aruba	Transit point for U.S.- and Europe-bound narcotics with some accompanying money-laundering activity; relatively high percentage of population consumes cocaine.
Australia	Tasmania is one of the world's major suppliers of licit opiate products; government maintains strict controls over areas of opium poppy cultivation and output of poppy straw concentrate; major consumer of cocaine and amphetamines.
Bahamas	Transshipment point for cocaine and marijuana bound for U.S. and Europe; offshore financial center.
Belgium	Growing producer of synthetic drugs and cannabis; transit point for U.S.-bound Ecstasy; source of precursor chemicals for South American cocaine processors; transshipment point for cocaine, heroin, hashish, and marijuana entering Western Europe; despite a strengthening of legislation, the country remains vulnerable to money laundering related to narcotics, automobiles, alcohol, and tobacco; significant domestic consumption of Ecstasy.
Bolivia	World's third-largest cultivator of coca (after Colombia and Peru) with an estimated 26,500 hectares under cultivation in August 2005, an 8% increase from 2004; transit country for Peruvian and Colombian cocaine destined for Brazil, Argentina, Chile, Paraguay, and Europe; cultivation steadily increasing despite eradication and alternative crop programs; money-laundering activity related to narcotics trade, especially along the borders with Brazil and Paraguay; major cocaine consumption.
Brazil	Illicit producer of cannabis; trace amounts of coca cultivation in the Amazon region, used for domestic consumption; government has a large-scale eradication program to control cannabis; important transshipment country for Bolivian, Colombian, and Peruvian cocaine headed for Europe; also used by traffickers as a way station for narcotics air transshipments between Peru and Colombia; upsurge in drug-related violence and weapons smuggling; important market for Colombian, Bolivian, and Peruvian cocaine; illicit narcotics proceeds earned in Brazil are often laundered through the financial system; significant illicit financial activity in the Tri-Border Area.
Burma	Remains world's second largest producer of illicit opium with an estimated production in 2005 of 380 metric tons, up 13% from 2004, and cultivation in 2005 was 40,000 hectares, a 10% increase from 2004; the decline in opium production in areas of greatest control was more than offset by increases in south and east Shan state; lack of government will to take on major narcotrafficking groups and lack of serious commitment against money laundering continues to hinder the overall antidrug effort; major source of methamphetamine and heroin for regional consumption; in 2005, under Financial Action Task Force countermeasures due to continued failure to address its inadequate money-laundering controls.

(continued)

Current Global Status of Illicit Drug Use in Selected Countries (*continued*)

Canada	Illicit producer of cannabis for the domestic drug market and export to the United States; use of hydroponics technology permits growers to plant large quantities of high-quality marijuana indoors; increasing Ecstasy production, some of which is destined for the United States; vulnerable to narcotics money laundering because of its mature financial services sector.
China	Major transshipment point for heroin produced in the Golden Triangle region of Southeast Asia; growing domestic drug abuse problem; source country for chemical precursors, despite new regulations on its large chemical industry.
Colombia	Illicit producer of coca, opium poppy, and cannabis; world's leading coca cultivator with 144,000 hectares in coca cultivation in 2005, a 26% increase over 2004, producing a potential of 545 metric tons of pure cocaine; the world's largest producer of coca derivatives; supplies cocaine to most of the U.S. market and the great majority of other international drug markets; in 2005, aerial eradication dispensed herbicide to treat over 130,000 hectares, but aggressive replanting on the part of coca growers means Colombia remains a key producer; a significant portion of non-U.S. narcotics proceeds are either laundered or invested in Colombia through the black market peso exchange; important supplier of heroin to the U.S. market; opium poppy cultivation fell 50% between 2003 and 2004 to 2100 hectares, yielding a potential 3.8 metric tons of pure heroin, mostly for the U.S. market; no poppy estimate was conducted in 2005.
Germany	Source of precursor chemicals for South American cocaine processors; transshipment point for and consumer of Southwest Asian heroin, Latin American cocaine, and European-produced synthetic drugs; major financial center.
Haiti	Caribbean transshipment point for cocaine en route to the United States and Europe; substantial bulk cash smuggling activity; Colombian narcotics traffickers favor Haiti for illicit financial transactions; pervasive corruption; significant consumer of cannabis.
Iran	Despite substantial interdiction efforts, Iran remains a key transshipment point for Southwest Asian heroin to Europe; highest percentage of the population in the world using opiates; lacks anti-money-laundering laws.
Italy	Important gateway for and consumer of Latin American cocaine and Southwest Asian heroin entering the European market; money laundering by organized crime and from smuggling.
Korea, North	For years, from the 1970s into the 2000s, citizens of the Democratic People's Republic of (North) Korea (DPRK), many of them diplomatic employees of the government, were apprehended abroad while trafficking in narcotics, including two in Turkey in December 2004; police investigations in Taiwan and Japan in recent years have linked North Korea to large illicit shipments of heroin and methamphetamine, including an attempt by the North Korean merchant ship *Pong Su* to deliver 150 kg of heroin to Australia in April 2003.
Mexico	Major drug-producing nation; cultivation of opium poppy in 2005 amounted to 3300 hectares, yielding a potential production of 8 metric tons of pure heroin, or 17 metric tons of "black tar" heroin, the dominant form of Mexican heroin in the western United States; marijuana cultivation decreased 3% to 5600 hectares in 2005 — just 2 years after a decade-high cultivation peak in 2003 — and yielded a potential production of 10,100 metric tons; government conducts the largest independent illicit-crop eradication program in the world; continues as the primary transshipment country for U.S.-bound cocaine from South America, with an estimated 90% of annual cocaine movements towards the United States stopping in Mexico; major drug syndicates control majority of drug trafficking throughout the country; producer and distributor of Ecstasy; significant money-laundering center; major supplier of heroin and largest foreign supplier of marijuana and methamphetamine to the U.S. market.

(continued)

Current Global Status of Illicit Drug Use in Selected Countries (*continued*)

Morocco	One of the world's largest producers of illicit hashish; shipments of hashish mostly directed to Western Europe; transit point for cocaine from South America destined for Western Europe; significant consumer of cannabis.
Netherlands	Major European producer of synthetic drugs, including Ecstasy, and cannabis cultivator; important gateway for cocaine, heroin, and hashish entering Europe; major source of U.S.-bound Ecstasy; large financial sector vulnerable to money laundering; significant consumer of Ecstasy.
Nigeria	A transit point for heroin and cocaine intended for European, East Asian, and North American markets; consumer of amphetamines; safe haven for Nigerian narcotraffickers operating worldwide; major money-laundering center; massive corruption and criminal activity. Nigeria has improved some anti-money-laundering controls, resulting in its removal from the Financial Action Task Force's (FATF's) Noncooperative Countries and Territories List in June 2006; Nigeria's anti-money-laundering regime continues to be monitored by FATF.
Pakistan	Opium poppy cultivation estimated to be 800 hectares in 2005 yielding a potential production of 4 metric tons of pure heroin; federal and provincial authorities continue to conduct anti-poppy campaigns that force eradication — fines and arrests will take place if the ban on poppy cultivation is not observed; key transit point for Afghan drugs, including heroin, opium, morphine, and hashish, bound for Western markets, the Gulf States, and Africa; financial crimes related to drug trafficking, terrorism, corruption, and smuggling remain problems.
Panama	Major cocaine transshipment point and primary money-laundering center for narcotics revenue; money-laundering activity is especially heavy in the Colon Free Zone; offshore financial center; negligible signs of coca cultivation; monitoring of financial transactions is improving; official corruption remains a major problem.
Peru	Until 1996 the world's largest coca leaf producer, Peru is now the world's second largest producer of coca leaf, though it lags far behind Colombia; cultivation of coca in Peru rose 25% to 34,000 hectares in 2005; much of the cocaine base is shipped to neighboring Colombia for processing into cocaine, while finished cocaine is shipped out from Pacific ports to the international drug market; increasing amounts of base and finished cocaine, however, are being moved to Brazil and Bolivia for use in the Southern Cone or transshipped to Europe and Africa.
Poland	Despite diligent counternarcotics measures and international information sharing on cross-border crimes, a major illicit producer of synthetic drugs for the international market; minor transshipment point for Southwest Asian heroin and Latin American cocaine to Western Europe.
South Africa	Transshipment center for heroin, hashish, and cocaine, as well as a major cultivator of marijuana in its own right; cocaine and heroin consumption on the rise; world's largest market for illicit methaqualone, usually imported illegally from India through various east African countries, but increasingly producing its own synthetic drugs for domestic consumption; attractive venue for money launderers given the increasing level of organized criminal and narcotics activity in the region and the size of the South African economy.
United States	World's largest consumer of cocaine, shipped from Colombia through Mexico and the Caribbean; consumer of Ecstasy and of Mexican heroin, marijuana, and methamphetamine; minor consumer of high-quality Southeast Asian heroin; illicit producer of cannabis (marijuana), depressants, stimulants, hallucinogens, and methamphetamine; money-laundering center.
World	*Cocaine:* worldwide coca leaf cultivation in 2005 amounted to 208,500 hectares; Colombia produced slightly more than two thirds of the worldwide crop, followed by Peru and Bolivia; potential

(*continued*)

Current Global Status of Illicit Drug Use in Selected Countries (*continued*)

pure cocaine production rose to 900 from 645 metric tons in 2005 — partially due to improved methodologies used to calculate levels of production; Colombia conducts an aggressive coca erad- ication campaign, but both Peruvian and Bolivian governments are hesitant to eradicate coca in key growing areas; 551 metric tons of export-quality cocaine (85% pure) is documented to have been seized or destroyed in 2005; U.S. consumption of export-quality cocaine is estimated to have been in excess of 380 metric tons. *Opiates:* worldwide illicit opium poppy cultivation reached 208,500 hectares in 2005; potential opium production of 4990 metric tons was only a 9% decrease over 2004's highest total recorded since estimates began in the mid-1980s; Afghanistan is the world's primary opium producer, accounting for 90% of the global supply; Southeast Asia — responsible for 9% of global opium — saw marginal increases in production; Latin America pro- duced 1% of global opium, but most was refined into heroin destined for the U.S. market; if all potential opium was processed into pure heroin, the potential global production would be 577 metric tons of heroin in 2005.

Source: CIA — The World Factbook. Washington, DC: U.S. Government Printing Office, 2007. Available https://www.cia.gov/library/publications/ the-world-factbook/fields/2086.html.

---

as taking nonprescription amphetamines to drive through the night or relying excessively on barbiturates to get through the day.

4. *Illegal recreational use.* Taking illicit drugs for fun or pleasure to experience euphoria, such as abusing prescribed methylphenidate (Ritalin) as a substitute for cocaine.

Why has the prevalence of licit and illicit drug use remained consistent since 1988? Why has this trend occurred, when expenditures for fighting the drug war by the federal, state, and local govern- ments have been increasing at the same time? There are several possible answers, none of which, by itself, offers a satisfactory response. One perspec- tive notes that practically all of us use drugs in some form, with what constitutes "drug use" being merely a matter of degree. A second explanation is that more varieties of both licit and illicit drugs are avail- able today. One source estimated that approxi- mately 80% of all currently marketed drugs were either unknown or unavailable 30 years ago (Critser 1996). Regarding prescriptions, Critser (2005) states that "the average number of prescriptions per person, annually, in 1993 was seven, and in 2005 it was twelve." Another source stated, "The retail sales of OTC drugs (aspirin, Tylenol, No-Doz, and so on) totaled $15 billion in 1995"; "$111.1 billion worth of pharmaceutical prescription drugs were sold in 1999" (Pear 2000, A16); "In 2002, 3.34 billion pre-

scriptions were written for Schedule II through Schedule V drugs" (see Chapter 3 for information about drug schedules) (Goode 2005, p. 227).

Pharmacists' records show that in the United States, about $102 billion is spent annually on psy- choactive drug prescriptions (Ananth et al. 2000). In 2002 total worldwide sales for prescription pharmaceuticals were $430 billion (*Pharmacy Times* 2003). In the United States alone, the rate of yearly prescription growth is estimated at approxi- mately 9–12% and from May 2006 through May 2007, all retail drug sales (which includes prescrip- tion as well as over-the-counter drugs at pharma- cies) were $202.8 billion in the United States (World Pharmaceutical Market Summary 2007). Such figures indicate that it may be more difficult to find people who do *not* use psychoactive drugs compared to individuals who do.

Further, in recent years, a third category of drug sales has joined OTC and prescription drugs: herbal medicines, vitamins, minerals, enzymes, and other natural potions. These drugs were purchased by 123.5 million Americans in 2000 — totaling $16 billion (Spake 2002).

Drug use is so common that the average house- hold in the United States owns about five drugs, of which two are prescription drugs and the other three are OTC drugs. Of the many prescriptions written by physicians, approximately one third mod- ify moods and behaviors in one way or another. A

National Institute on Drug Abuse (NIDA) study and other research indicates that more than 60% of adults in the United States have, at some time in their lives, taken a *psychoactive drug* (one that affects mood or consciousness). More than one third of adults have used or are using depressants or sedatives. A third explanation is that ". . . in the modern age, increased sophistication has brought with it techniques of drug production and distribution that have resulted in a worldwide epidemic of drug use" (Kusinitz 1988, p. 149). In the 1980s and 1990s, for example, illicit drug cartels proliferated, and varieties of marijuana with ever-increasing potency infiltrated all urban and rural areas as well as the world. Many of these varieties are crossbred with ultrasophisticated techniques and equipment available everywhere.

Finally, even coffee (as discussed in Chapter 10, "Here and Now") has undergone a technological revolution. Higher caffeine content has become available worldwide. This trend has led to the phenomenal growth of the following: (1) franchise duplication of gourmet coffee bars in the United States (such as Starbucks and Three Brothers Coffee); (2) sales of espresso and cappuccino coffee makers for home use, with accompanying coffee grinders; and (3) sales of specialized coffees and teas through a multitude of email coffee/tea clubs.

Approximately 25 years ago, it was difficult to purchase a cup of espresso or cappuccino in a typical restaurant; today, availability of such types of coffees is commonplace. Even at airports, shopping malls, and inner-city coffee shops, it is not unusual to see people lined up waiting to order and purchase their specially made and specially flavored coffee or tea. This is just one example of how caffeine (often seen as a benign drug) has evolved, with many new varieties of coffee beans from exotic islands and countries coming together with

Often the consumption of drugs (such as caffeine) complements social interaction.

more sophisticated electronic equipment, with the result that the idea of simple brewing has been relegated to the past. The standard American "cup of coffee in the morning" has spilled into including coffee during the afternoon and evening. This is a small example of a much-tolerated drug maintaining its own impressive history of development, increased use, complexity in developing many more varieties, and added sophistication.

Drug Use: Statistics, Trends, and Demographics

An incredible amount of money is spent each year for licit (legal) and illicit (illegal) chemicals that alter consciousness, awareness, or mood. Five classes of these legal chemicals exist:

1. *Social drugs.* Approximately $104 billion is spent on alcohol each year. Another $51.9 billion goes toward tobacco products, of which 95% comes from cigarette sales. The other 5% accounts for the $2 billion or so spent on cigars, chewing tobacco, pipe tobacco, roll-your-own tobacco, and snuff tobacco. In addition, $5.7 billion is spent on coffee, tea, and cocoa.

2. *Prescription drugs.* Worldwide, $430 billion in sales was racked up for prescription pharmaceuticals in 2002 (*Pharmacy Times* 2003). The United States is the world's largest pharmaceutical market. Annually, Americans spend $176 billion on prescription drugs (*Pharmacy Times* 2005). Recent figures "[f]rom 1997 to 2004 indicate that total purchases of outpatient Rx medicines increased approximately 2 billion to nearly 3 billion scripts" (*Pharmacy Times* 2007, 2).

3. *Over-the-counter (patent) drugs.* These products account for $23.5 billion in sales, including cough and cold items, external and internal analgesics, antacids, laxatives, antidiarrhea products, sleep aids, sedatives, and so on.

4. *Nonmedical use of prescription-type drugs.* In recent years, another alarming statistic related to abuse is the growth of the nonmedical use of prescription-type drugs. In 2001, 36 million Americans (16% of persons age 12 or older) had used prescription-type drugs nonmedically at least once in their lifetime. This included 9.6 million persons (18%) ages 12 to 25. In 2001, almost 3 million youths ages 12 to 17 (12%) and almost 7 million young adults ages 18 to 25 (23%) had used prescription-type drugs nonmedically at least once in their lifetime. See Here and Now "Pain Relievers" (page 19). The most common category of prescription-type

Here and Now

How Widespread Is the Use of Drugs?

In the 1990s, a variety of factors came together in the United States to extend drug abuse beyond just the very rich or the urban poor. The ease of brewing cheaper, more potent strains of speed (methamphetamine, or "meth") and heroin, coupled with the fact that enforcement officials tended to focus on drug abuse and traffic in urban areas on the East and West Coasts, left middle-class and rural populations throughout the country largely overlooked. (See "Youth Drug Use" illustration in the next column.) Suddenly, the illicit drug market was booming where no one had been looking.

By the late 1990s, speed — which had gained popularity in the 1970s among outlaw bikers, college students facing exams, all-night party-goers, and long-haul truckers — was more sought after than ever. Teenagers, middle-class workers, and suburbanites joined the ranks of methamphetamine users. "We've been fighting it really strongly for nearly seven years," Edward Synicky, a special agent with California's Bureau of Narcotics Enforcement, told *Time* magazine in early 1996. "But cocaine gets all the publicity because it's glamorous. And law enforcement in general doesn't put the resources into meth that it should."

Increasingly, the illegal substance was produced in clandestine labs set up by both major drug dealers and individual users. By January 1996, John Coonce, head of the U.S. Drug Enforcement Administration's (DEA's) meth-lab task force, said methamphetamine use was "absolutely epidemic." The surge was attributed largely to powerful Mexican drug syndicates and motorcycle gangs that sold their goods on street corners. Speed acquired the nickname "crank" because it was frequently concealed in motorcycle crankcases.

Clandestine manufacture and use of speed were especially high in the West and Southwest. Speed kitchens flourished in California because it was relatively easy for the Mexican syndicates to smuggle in ephedrine, a key ingredient that is tightly controlled in the United States. From the mid-1980s to the mid-1990s, methamphetamine-related hospitalizations in California rose approximately 366%. In Arizona's Maricopa County, methamphetamine-linked crimes jumped nearly 400% over a 3-year period in the early 1990s. (See the sections The Costs of Drug Use to Society and Drugs, Crime, and Violence in this chapter.)

Soon this easy-access drug began spreading across the United States. In 1994, DEA field offices in Houston, Denver, Los Angeles, New Orleans, Phoenix, St. Louis, San Diego, and San Francisco were responsible for approximately 86% of the methamphetamine laboratory seizures in the country. By 1996, however, officials were seizing huge shipments of methamphetamine that originated in Mississippi and Tennessee.

Update: Recent information regarding this drug is very positive. In 2005, a relatively low number of U.S. residents — 4% or an estimated 212.8 million people — reported using methamphetamine at least once in their lifetime, compared to 46% for marijuana, 14% for cocaine, and 2% for heroin (Substance Abuse and Mental Health Services Administration [SAMHSA] 2006).

But speed was not the only drug barreling its way across the country. Use of heroin ran rampant as well. In a southeastern Massachusetts fishing community, at least 50 fishermen died of AIDS or other drug-related causes between 1991 and 1996. The captain of one scalloper told a local newspaper, "As a wild guess, I would say that if the fishing industry were to run a blood test and eliminate the people that had drug problems, there would be very few boats sailing with a full crew" (Associated Press 1996). Many skippers cited the ease with which drug users and dealers could find jobs on board ships as one reason for the alarming rise in drug abuse among their ranks.

Even crack cocaine, which was first seen primarily in New York and Los Angeles, infiltrated rural areas. Headlines reported that in many U.S. counties, 8th graders in rural areas were using more drugs than urban youth (Briske 2000). According to the DEA, a combination of factors forced some crack distributors to develop new markets in smaller towns and rural areas; Pike County, Mississippi, was hit especially hard. Enforcement officials believed most of the crack in Mississippi came from New Orleans, but some drug shipments originating in South America were flown to remote landing strips in the middle of Mississippi farmland.

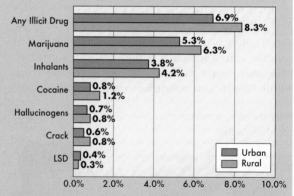

Youth Drug Use Rural teens are more likely to use drugs than their peers in large cities. Here are the results of a survey conducted of the percentage of 8th graders who used drugs during the previous month.

Source: Institute on Social Research at the University of Michigan, *Monitoring the Future,* National Survey Results on Drug Use 1975–2006: Vol I, Secondary Students, Ann Arbor, MI: University of MI, 2007.

How Widespread Is the Use of Drugs? (continued)

Whatever people's reasons for using these dangerous substances, it is clear that an important step toward stemming abuse is to dry up the supply lines to middle America. To accomplish that goal, the law enforcement community must look beyond traditional hotbeds of activity among the urban poor.

....

Sources: Associated Press. "Survey: Drug Use Pervading New Bedford Fleet." *Maine Sunday Telegram* (21 July 1996).
Briske, P. "Rural Eighth-Graders Using More Drugs Than Urban Kids." *The Times* (27 January 2000): 3. Available http://www.thetimesonline.com.
National Narcotics Intelligence Consumers Committee. *The NNICC Report, 1994.* Washington, DC: U.S. Drug Enforcement Agency, 1994: 70.
National Public Radio (NPR). "All Things Considered." *PM News* (18 September 1996).
Toufonio, A., et al. "There Is No Safe Speed." *Time* (8 January 1990).
Wilkie, C. "Crack Cocaine Moves South." *Boston Globe* (23 June 1996).

---

drugs used nonmedically by youths and young adults in the past year was pain relievers. Pain relievers include codeine, methadone, meperidine (Demerol), Percocet, hydrocodone (Vicodin), and oxycodone (OxyContin) (Substance Abuse and Mental Health Services Administration [SAMHSA] 2003).

5. *Others.* The amount spent on inhalants and other miscellaneous drugs, such as nutmeg and morning glory seeds, cannot be estimated.

How much money goes to purchase illicit drugs? The White House Office of National Drug Control Policy conducted a study to determine the amount Americans spent on illicit drugs. It found that in the 2000s, Americans spent $57.3 billion on drugs: $38 billion on cocaine, $9.6 billion on heroin, $7 billion on marijuana, and $2.7 billion on other illegal drugs and on legal drugs that were misused (NIDA 2006).

Further, regarding the extent of drug use, studies carried out by the Social Research Group of George Washington University, the Institute for Research in Social Behavior in Berkeley, California, and others provide detailed, in-depth data showing that drug use is universal. A major purpose of their studies was to determine the level of psychoactive drug use among people age 18 through 74, excluding those people hospitalized or in the armed forces. Data were collected to identify people who used specific categories of drugs (that is, caffeine, sleeping pills, nicotine, alcohol, and other psychoactive drugs). Other studies have shown that people in the 18- to 25-year-old age group are by far the heaviest users and experimenters in terms of past-month and past-year usage (see Table 1.3).

Here and Now

Pain Relievers

A recent bulletin alert highlights a new form of abuse involving pain relievers. It was found that in 2006 first-time users of pain relievers continue to surpass first-time users of all other drugs. More than 2.1 million persons ages 12 or older used prescription-type pain relievers* for the first time in 2006, according to recently released data from the National Survey on Drug Use and Health (NSDUH; SAMHSA 2007a). Although the number of new users of pain relievers has been decreasing since 2003, it continues to be the drug category with the largest number of new initiates since surpassing marijuana in 2002. The number of first-time marijuana users has declined significantly, from nearly 3 million in 2000 to slightly more than 2 million in 2006. Recent changes in the initiation of illicit drug use show increases in the number of first-time nonmedical users of prescription-type stimulants* (from 647,000 to 845,000). Previous research found that changes in initiation levels "are often leading indicators of emerging patterns of substance use" (CESAR 2007).

....

*Use of pain relievers and stimulants refers to the nonmedical use of prescription-type pain relievers and stimulants and does not include use of over-the-counter drugs.

Table 1.3 Trend Data on the Prevalence of Illicit Drug Use, 2000–2005

	2000	2001	2002	2003	2004	2005
Used in Past Month						
All ages 12+	6.3	7.1	8.3	8.2	7.9	8.1
12–17	9.8	10.8	11.6	11.2	10.6	9.9
18–25	15.6	18.5	20.2	20.3	19.4	20.1
26–34	7.9	9.2	10.8	11.1	11.3	11.3
35+	3.3	3.4	4.6	4.4	4.3	4.7
Used in Past Year						
All ages 12+	11	12.6	14.9	14.7	14.5	14.4
12–17	18.8	20.8	22.2	21.8	21	19.9
18–25	27.5	31.59	35.5	34.6	33.9	34.2
26–34	13.7	16.7	19.8	20.1	19.6	20.2
35+	5.5	6.2	8.2	8.1	8.2	8.2
Used in Lifetime (Ever Used)						
All ages 12+	38.9	41.2	46.6	46.4	45.8	46.1
12–17	27.1	28.3	30.9	30.5	30	27.7
18–25	51.2	55.6	59.8	60.5	59.3	59.3
26–34	51	53.5	58.2	57.4	57.3	57
35+	35.5	38.5	43.9	44.8	44.7	46.1

This table shows three major trends. First, for all three categories of drug users (used in past month, used in past year, and used in lifetime [ever used]) and within each age group category, there is a very steady and persistent growth in the percentage using illicit drugs from 2000 through 2005. Second, even though in 2002 and 2003 there appeared to be a higher increase (spike) over previous years in the percentage using illicit drugs, **the percentage increases in 2002 and 2003 are not comparable to data for prior years because beginning in 2002 and 2003 the survey questions changed, resulting in what appear to be increases in drug use. As a result, it is not possible to compare pre-2003 data with later years' data.** Third, for all three categories of drug users, the heaviest users of drugs are between 18 and 25 years of age.

Illicit drugs include marijuana/hashish, cocaine (including crack), heroin, hallucinogens, inhalants, or any prescription-type psychotherapeutic used nonmedically (sedatives, tranquilizers, stimulants, and analgesics). The figures presented here include use of marijuana, cocaine, hallucinogens, inhalants, heroin, and nonmedical use of sedatives, tranquilizers, stimulants, and analgesics.

2000 data: Substance Abuse and Mental Health Services Administration (SAMHSA). *National Household Survey on Drug Abuse, 1999 and 2000.* Rockville, MD: Office of Applied Studies and Substance Abuse and Mental Health Services Administration, 2000.

2001 data: Substance Abuse and Mental Health Services Administration (SAMHSA). *National Household Survey on Drug Abuse, 2000 and 2001.* Rockville, MD: Office of Applied Studies and Substance Abuse and Mental Health Services Administration, 2002.

2002 and 2003 data: Substance Abuse and Mental Health Services Administration (SAMHSA). *Results from the 2003 National Survey on Drug Use and Health: National Findings.* Rockville, MD: Office of Applied Studies, 2004.

2004 and 2005 data: Substance Abuse and Mental Health Services Administration (SAMHSA). *Results from the 2005 National Survey on Drug Use and Health: National Findings.* Rockville, MD: Office of Applied Studies, 2006.

Table 1.4 supports the findings of the Social Research Group of George Washington University. For example, in looking at past-month usage, an estimated 13.6 million Americans, or 50.9% of the total U.S. population age 12 and older, were drinkers. Statistics also reveal that with regard to past-month usage of cigarettes, approximately 61.5 million or 25% of Americans smoked cigarettes in 2006 (see Table 1.4).

■ Current Patterns of Licit and Illicit Drug Use

Table 1.4 shows that illicit drug use remains an alarming problem. In looking at the use of licit and illicit types of drugs, it is estimated that approximately 20.4 million Americans ages 12 years or older were current illicit drug users in 2006. This number represents 8.3% of the population age 22

Table 1.4 National Household Survey on Drug Abuse, 2006

Percentage of population and estimated number of alcohol, tobacco, and illicit drug users in the United States.

	LIFETIME*		PAST MONTH	
	PERCENTAGE	NUMBER OF USERS (IN THOUSANDS)	PERCENTAGE	NUMBER OF USERS (IN THOUSANDS)
Alcohol	82.7	203,368,000	50.9	125,309,000
Cigarettes	66.3	162,991,000	25.0	61,565,000
Marijuana/hashish	39.8	97,825,000	6.0	14,813,000
Nonmedical use of any psychotherapeutic+	19.8	49,842,000	2.8	6,991,000
Smokeless tobacco	18.6	45,832,000	3.3	8,231,000
Cocaine	14.3	35,298,000	1.0	2,421,000
Hallucinogens	14.3	35,281,000	0.4	1,006,000
Analgesics	13.6	33,472,000	4.9	5,220,000
Inhalants	9.3	22,879,000	0.3	761,000
Tranquilizers	8.7	21,303,000	0.7	1,766,000
Stimulants	8.2	20,118,000	0.5	1,191,000
Sedatives	3.6	8,822,000	0.2	385,000
Crack	3.5	8,554,000	0.3	702,000
PCP	2.7	6,618,000	0.0	30,000
Any illicit drug	45.4	111,774,000	8.3	20,357,000

Notes: Total population = 303,755,930.

* Lifetime refers to ever used.

+ Nonmedical use of any prescription stimulant, sedative, or tranquilizer, does not include over-the-counter drugs.

Source: Substance Abuse and Mental Health Services Administration (SAMHSA), Office of Applied Studies (OAS). *2006 National Survey on Drug Use & Health.* Rockville, MD: NIDA, 2007.

years and older (SAMHSA 2007a). The leading illicit types of drugs (see Figure 1.1) were marijuana (39.8%), hallucinogens (mainly LSD and Ecstasy, 14.3%), cocaine (14.3%), pain relievers (13.6%), and inhalants (8.8%).

Regarding the licit types of drugs used during the same year, from highest to lowest the most popular were alcohol (82.7%), tobacco (70.7%), and nonmedical use of psychotherapeutics (21.8%), which includes pain relievers (13.6%) and stimulants (8.2%); see Table 1.4.

Figure 1.2 shows the past-month use of illicit drugs among persons age 12 or older. Again the category "any illicit drug" shows the highest use, followed by use of marijuana, psychotherapeutics, cocaine, hallucinogens, and inhalants.

Nonmedical Use of Pain Relievers

Figure 1.3 shows the number of lifetime nonmedical users of selected pain relievers for 2002, 2003, and 2004. National surveys on drug use and health indicate that the nonmedical use of prescription pain relievers (analgesics) among persons age 12 or older did not differ significantly from 2002 to 2005. The number of persons who used prescription pain relievers nonmedically for the first time in the past year also did not differ significantly, with 2.3 million persons initiating use in 2002, 2.4 million in 2003, 2.4 million in 2004, and 2.2 million in 2005. An annual average of 4.8% of persons age 12 or older (11.4 million persons) used a prescription pain reliever nonmedically in the 12 months prior to the survey. Of the persons age 12 or older who first used pain relievers nonmedically in the past year, 57.7% used hydrocodone products* and 21.7% used oxycodone products†. Other noteworthy findings are:

- The percentage of persons age 12 or older who had used any product containing hydrocodone nonmedically in their lifetime increased from 5.9% to 7.4%. Among the drugs in this category are Vicodin, Lortab, or Lorcet, which as a

---

*This includes Vicodin, Lortab, Lorcet, generic hydrocodone, and other pain relievers containing hydrocodone that respondents specified.

†This includes Percocet, Percodan, Tylox, OxyContin, and other pain relievers containing oxycodone that respondents specified that they used nonmedically.

FIGURE 1.1

Percentage of U.S. residents (age 12 or older) reporting lifetime use of alcohol, tobacco, and illicit drugs, 2006.

*Nonmedical use only does not include over-the-counter drugs.

Source: Substance Abuse and Mental Health Services Administration (SAMHSA). *Overview of Findings from the 2003 National Survey on Drug Use and Health.* Office of Applied Studies, NSDUH Series H-24, DHHS Publication No. SMA 04-3963. Rockville, MD, 2004.

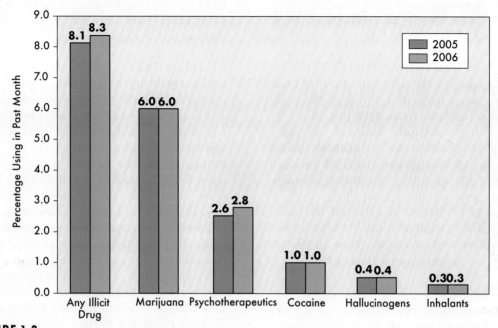

FIGURE 1.2

Past-month use of selected illicit drugs among persons aged 12 or older, 2005 and 2006.

Source: Substance Abuse and Mental Health Services Administration (SAMHSA). *Results from the 2006 National Household Survey on Drug Use and Health: National Findings.* Rockville, MD: Office of Applied Studies (OAS), 2006.

[a]Difference between this estimate and the 2004 estimate is statistically significant at the .05 level.
[b]Difference between this estimate and the 2004 estimate is statistically significant at the .01 level.

FIGURE 1.3

Number (in millions) of lifetime nonmedical users of selected pain relievers among persons aged 12 or older: 2003, 2004, and 2005.

Source: Substance Abuse and Mental Health Services Administration (SAMHSA). *Results from the 2006 National Household Survey on Drug Use and Health: National Findings.* Rockville, MD: Office of Applied Studies (OAS), 2006.

group increased from 5.6% to 6.9%, and generic hydrocodone, which increased from 1.9% to 2.5% (see Figure 1.3).

- The rate of lifetime misuse of any oxycodone product increased from 4.3% to 5.0%, reflecting increases in the nonmedical use of Oxycontin (from 0.8% to 1.3%) and Percocet, Percodan, or Tylox (from 4.5% to 4.6%).
- Modest but statistically significant increases also were observed for methadone (from 0.4% to 0.5%) and any tramadol product (from 0.4% to 0.5%). Tramadol products include generic tramadol and Ultram.
- Decreases in lifetime nonmedical use were observed for Demerol (from 1.2% to 1.0%), Phenaphen with codeine (from 0.4% to 0.2%) and Talwin (from 0.3% to 0.1%).

Age Patterns

Figure 1.4 shows the past-month use of illicit drugs by age in 2006. With regard to age patterns, the following trends are apparent:

- Rates of drug use showed substantial variation by age. For example, 3.9% of youths ages 12

or 13 reported current illicit drug use in 2006. As in other years, illicit drug use tended to increase with age among young persons.

- The 18–20 age category used the most types of illicit drugs. This report broke out the age categories slightly differently; in this figure, information on the 18- to 25-year-olds shows that 16.3% used marijuana, 6.4% used prescription-type drugs nonmedically, 2.2% used cocaine, and 1.7% used hallucinogens.
- Among youths, the types of drugs used differed by age in 2006, as was the case in prior years. Marijuana was the most commonly used drug among 12- to 17-year-olds (6.7%), followed by prescription-type drugs used nonmedically (3.3%), inhalants (1.3%), hallucinogens (0.7%), and cocaine (1.2%).
- An estimated 70% of all psychoactive prescription drugs used by people under 30 years old were obtained without the user having a prescription (SAMHSA 2004).

Racial and Ethnic Differences

Figure 1.5 shows average past-month illicit drug use among persons age 12 or older by racial and

FIGURE 1.4

Past-month illicit drug use, by age, 2006.

....

Source: Substance Abuse and Mental Health Services Administration (SAMHSA). *Results from the 2006 National Survey on Drug Use and Health: National Findings.* Rockville, MD: Office of Applied Studies (OAS), 2006.

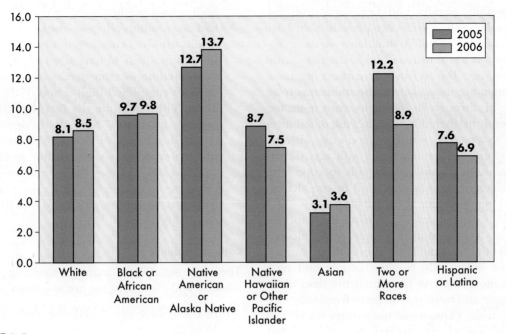

FIGURE 1.5

Past-month illicit drug use among persons aged 12 or older, by race/ethnicity, 2005 and 2006.

....

Source: Substance Abuse and Mental Health Services Administration (SAMHSA). Household Survey 2006. National Survey on Drug Use and Health: Detailed Tables. Rockville, MD: Office of Applied Studies, 2007.

ethnic differences in 2005 and 2006. The latest figures reveal the following trends:

- In 2006, from highest to lowest, racial ethnic groups had the following rates of illicit drug use: Native Americans or Alaska Natives (13.7%), blacks or African-Americans (9.8%), two or more races (8.9%), whites (8.5%), Native Hawaiians or other Pacific Islanders (7.5%), Hispanics or Latinos (6.9%), and Asians (3.6%).
- Asians continued to have the lowest percentage of current illicit drug use when this research was conducted, just as many other racial and ethnic group studies on drug use had found previously.
- Among youths ages 12 to 17 in 2006, the rate of current illicit drug use among American Indians or Alaska Natives was about twice the overall rate of all other ethnic youth groups among youths (18.7% vs. 9.8%, respectively). The rates were 11.8% among youths reporting two or more races, 10.2% among blacks, 10% among whites, 8.9% among Hispanics, and 6.7% among Asians.

- Among Hispanic groups, Puerto Ricans were the heaviest users of illicit drugs, followed by Mexican Americans and Cuban Americans. Central and South Americans had the lowest amount of current illicit drug use (SAMHSA 2007a).

Gender

In 2006 (SAMHSA 2007a), the following were major findings regarding illicit drug use by gender:

- As in prior years, in 2006 males were more likely than females among persons age 12 or older to be current illicit drug users (10.5% vs. 6.2%, respectively). The rate of past-month marijuana use for males was about twice as high for males as the rate for females (8.1% vs. 4.1%). However, males and females had similar rates of past-month use of stimulants (0.5% for both males and females), Ecstasy (0.2% for both), sedatives (0.1% and 0.2%, respectively), OxyContin (0.1% for both), LSD (0.1% and less than 0.1%), and PCP (less than 0.1% for both).

- Generally, gender and licit/illicit drug use correlate with specific age periods. Men have a tendency to prefer stimulants in their 30s, depressants in their 40s and 50s, and sedatives from age 60 on. In comparison to men, women are most likely to use stimulants from age 21 through 39 and depressants more frequently in their 30s. Women's use of sedatives shows a pattern similar to men's use, with the frequency of use increasing with age. Generally, women tend to take pills to cope with problems, whereas men tend to use alcohol and marijuana for the same purpose.

- People older than 35 are more likely to take pills, whereas younger people prefer alcohol and other licit and illicit types of drugs. Among those using pills, younger people and men are more likely to use stimulants than older people and women, who more frequently take sedatives. (The actual usage rates for all psychoactive drugs are probably 35% higher than the reported data.)

- Among younger people (ages 18 through 32 years), use of stimulants and depressants for nonmedical reasons often results from drug misuse or dependency. Methods for obtaining psychoactive drugs for nonmedical purposes include (1) getting drugs from friends and relatives who have legitimate prescriptions, (2) resorting to drug dealers, and (3) purchasing or shoplifting OTC medications.

Pregnant Women

In looking at this group, we find two major outcomes:

- In 2006 (SAMHSA 2007a), among pregnant women ages 15 to 44 years, 4.0% reported using illicit drugs in the month before their interviews during 2002 and 2003. This rate was significantly lower than the rate among women ages 15 to 44 who were not pregnant (10%).

- Pregnant women are less likely to use drugs than similar-age women who are not pregnant.

Education

Illicit drug use rates in 2006 were correlated with educational status (SAMHSA 2007a).

- Among adults age 18 or older, the rate of current illicit drug use was lower among college graduates (5.9%) compared with those who did not graduate from high school (9.2%),

high school graduates (8.6%), or those who had taken some college courses (9.1%).

- Adults who had completed 4 years of college were more likely to have tried illicit drugs in their lifetime as compared with adults who had not completed high school (50% versus 37%). This is despite the fact that although college graduates had used significantly more illicit types of drugs in their *lifetime*, their *current use* — usually after graduation and movement away from their respective campuses — was significantly less than that among their counterparts who had not completed high school.

College Students

The most significant findings regarding college students and illicit drug use are as follows:

- In the college-age population (persons ages 18 to 22 years), the rate of current illicit drug use was the same among full-time undergraduate college students (22.6%) as for other persons ages 18 to 22 years, including part-time students, students in other grades, and nonstudents (22.6%).

- The rate of current illicit drug use among college students and other 18- to 22-year-olds did not change between 2005 and 2006 (SAMHSA 2007a).

Employment

With regard to current employment status, the following are significant findings related to illicit drug use:

- Current employment status was highly correlated with rates of illicit drug use in 2007b. An estimated 18.5% of unemployed adults ages 18 or older were current illicit drug users compared with 8.8% of those employed full-time and 9.4% of those employed part-time.

- Although the rate of drug use was higher among unemployed persons compared with those from other employment groups, most drug users were employed. Of the 17.9 million illicit drug users ages 18 or older in 2005, 13.4 million (74.9%) were employed either full- or part-time.

Geographic Area

Several of the more significant findings related to illicit drug use in specific geographic areas follow:

- The rate of illicit drug use in metropolitan areas is higher than the rate in nonmetropolitan counties. Rates were 8.3% in large metropolitan counties, 8.6% in small metropolitan counties, and 7% in nonmetropolitan counties.
- Within nonmetropolitan areas, counties that were urbanized had an illicit drug use rate of 7.9%, while completely rural counties had a significantly lower rate (3.1%).
- Among persons age 12 or older, the rates of current illicit drug use in the United States were: 9.5% in the West, 8.9% in the Northeast, 7.9% in the Midwest, and 7.4% in the South (SAMHSA 2007a).

Criminal Justice Populations/Arrestees

Certain significant findings and correlations are unique to criminal justice populations:

- In 2006, among the estimated 1.6 million adults age 18 or older who were on parole or other supervised release from prison during the past year, 29.7% were current illicit drug users, compared with 7.9% of adults not on parole or supervised release.
- Among the estimated 4.6 million adults on probation at some time in the past year, 31.9% reported current illicit drug use in 2006. This compares with a rate of 7.6% among adults not on probation in 2006 (SAMHSA 2007a).
- In 2004, an estimated 333,000 prisoners were arrested for drug law violations; 21% of state, 55% of federal inmates (Bureau of Justice Statistics [BJS] 2004).
- In 2004, nearly a third of state and a quarter of federal prisoners committed their offense under the influence of drugs, which was unchanged since 1997.
- Among federal inmates, men (50%) were slightly more likely than women (48%) to report drug use in the month before the offense in 2004.
- Among federal inmates in 2004, 58% of whites, 53% of blacks, and 38% of Hispanics reported using drugs in the month before the offense.
- One in three property offenders in state prisons report drug money as a motive in their crimes.
- Marijuana remained the most common drug used by state prisoners. Forty percent of state prisoners reported using marijuana in the month before their offense, and 15% said they had used marijuana at the time of the offense. (Very similar percentages were found in the 1997 estimates.) (BJS 2004).

■ Types of Drug Users

Just as a diverse set of personality traits (for example, introverts, extroverts, type A, obsessive-compulsive, and so on) exists, so drug users vary according to their general approach or orientation, frequency of use, and types and amounts of the drugs they consume. Some are occasional or moderate users, whereas others display much stronger attachment to drug use. In fact, some display such obsessive-compulsive behavior that they cannot let a morning, afternoon, or evening pass without using drugs. Some researchers have classified such variability in the frequency and extent of usage as fitting into three basic patterns: experimenters, compulsive users, and "floaters" or "chippers" (members of the last category drift between experimentation and compulsive use).

Experimenters begin using drugs largely because of peer pressure and curiosity, and they confine their use to recreational settings. Generally, they more often enjoy being with peers who also use drugs recreationally. Alcohol, tobacco, marijuana, hallucinogens, and many of the major stimulants are the drugs they are most likely to use. They are usually able to set limits on when these drugs are taken (often preferred in social settings), and they are more likely to know the difference between light, moderate, and chronic use.

Compulsive users, in contrast, ". . . devote considerable time and energy to getting high, talk incessantly (sometimes exclusively) about drug use . . . [and "funny" or "weird" experiences] . . . and become connoisseurs of street drugs" (Beschner 1986, 7). For compulsive users, recreational fun is impossible without getting high.

KEY TERMS

experimenters
first category of drug use, typified as being in the initial stages of drug use; these people often use drugs for recreational purposes

compulsive users
second category of drug use, typified by an insatiable attraction followed by a psychological dependence to drugs

Other characteristics of these users include the need to escape or postpone personal problems, to avoid stress and anxiety, and to enjoy the sensation of the drug's euphoric effects. Often, they have difficulty assuming personal responsibility and suffer from low self-esteem. Many compulsive users are from dysfunctional families, have persistent problems with the law and/or have serious psychological problems underlying their drug-taking behavior. Problems with personal and public identity, excessive confusion about their sexual orientation, boredom, family discord, childhood sexual and/or mental abuse, academic pressure, and chronic depression all contribute to the inability to cope with issues *without* drugs (see "Case in Point," Ignoring the Signs of Drug Abuse: A Hard Lesson Learned).

Floaters or **chippers** focus more on using other people's drugs without maintaining a steady supply of drugs. Nonetheless, chippers, like experimenters, are generally light to moderate consumers of drugs. Chippers vacillate between the need for pleasure seeking and the desire to relieve moderate to serious psychological problems. As a result, although most are on the path to drug dependence, at this stage they drift between experimental drug-taking peers and chronic drug-using peers. In a sense, these drug users are marginal individuals who do not strongly identify with experimenters or compulsive users. (An example of how the various types of drug users are often adversely affected by peers is discussed in more detail in Chapters 2 and 4.)

■ Drug Use: Mass Media and Family Influences

Studies continually show that the majority of young drug users come from homes in which drugs are

KEY TERMS

floaters or **chippers**
third category of drug users; these users vacillate between the need for pleasure seeking and the desire to relieve moderate to serious psychological problems. This category of drug use has two major characteristics: (1) a general focus mostly on using other people's drugs (often without maintaining a personal supply of the drug) and (2) vacillation between the characteristics of chronic drug users and experimenter types

liberally used (Goode 1999; SAMHSA 1996b). These children frequently witness drug use at home. For instance, parents may consume large quantities of coffee to wake up in the morning and other forms of medication throughout the day: cigarettes with morning coffee, antacid tablets for an upset stomach, vitamins for stress, or aspirin for a headache. Finally, before going to bed, the grown-ups may take a few "nightcaps" or a sleeping pill to relax. The following is an interview related to the overuse of drugs:

> Yeah, I always saw my mom smoking early in the morning while reading the newspaper and slowly sipping nearly a full pot of coffee. She took prescription drugs for asthma, used an inhaler, and took aspirin for headaches. When she accused me of using drugs at concerts, I would pick up her pack of cigarettes and several prescription bottles and while she was raging on me, I would quietly wave all her drugs close up in front of her face. She would stop nagging within seconds and actually one time I think she wanted to laugh but turned away toward the sink and just started washing cups and saucers. The way I figure it, she has her drugs, and I have mine. She may not agree with my use of my drugs but then she is not better either. It's great to have a drug-using family ain't it? *(From Venturelli's research files, male, age 20, college student, June 12, 2000.)*

Some social scientists believe that everyday consumption of legal drugs — caffeine, prescription and OTC drugs, and alcohol — is fueled by the pace of modern lifestyles and greatly accelerated by the influence of today's increasingly sophisticated mass media.

If you look around your classroom building, the dormitories at your college, or your own home, evidence of mass media and electronic equipment can be found everywhere. Cultural knowledge and information are transmitted via media through electronic gadgets we simply "can't live without," to the point that they help us define and shape our everyday reality.

In regard to drug advertising, television remains the most influential medium. Most homes today have more than one television in the home. Knowing this, "Drug firms increased their spending on television advertising to consumer seven-fold from 1996 to 2000, . . . (CBS News 2002). Overall advertising spending aimed at ordinary people tripled

►Case in Point   Ignoring the Signs of Drug Abuse: A Hard Lesson Learned

Michael Alig missed all of the warning signs of the dangers of drug abuse and addiction. He states, "There is no excuse for killing someone, no reason to justify being wholly or even partly responsible for the death of another human being. I have never been a violent person. I don't even like sports." Now in prison for the accidental death of a friend, Michael recalls the following warning signs he refused to note:

1. Michael was living without any real boundaries. Now that he looks back at his life, he says it was out of control, and his friends were out of control.

2. Michael overdosed many times on many different drugs and would often wake up unaware of where he was, where he had been, who he was with, what he was doing with whomever he was with, what took place while he was on drugs, and so on.

3. One time Michael regained consciousness and was in the presence of "... an entire dinner of cocaine on the floor!" which he admits was too tempting to pass up.

4. People around Michael were constantly warning him to stop using drugs, and these were the same people with whom he was annoyed.

5. Just before his arrest, Michael had overdosed numerous times with naloxone, barely escaping death several times.

6. Michael used heroin with the false sense of euphoric security that all was good.

Now Michael, who was called the King of the Club Kids, believes he has finally learned to accept responsibilities as an adult. After solitary confinement for several months to stop using heroin in prison, he says that his approach to life has completely changed. Michael says, "A smile or a laugh isn't just a reaction to the most extreme situations anymore, but to my average daily experiences like eating a piece of sour candy, or seeing a fat boy in the prison yard with the crack of his butt exposed for everyone to see." Michael believes it will take a lot of time for his brain to rewire itself toward enjoying the simple pleasures of life. He states, "Now it will be the small, subtle life experiences that will be my reinforcements ... [besides] parties in jail are dangerous." Today, Michael is approximately 43 years of age.

Reconstructed by author from source: Michiana Point of View/Michael Alig. "Alig Missed Signs Along the Road to Tragedy." *The South Bend Tribune* (10 January 1999): B-3.

---

between 1996 and 2000 to nearly $2.5 billion a year. Drug companies spent $1.6 billion in 2000 on television advertisements for Viagra, Claritin, Allegra, and other brand-name drugs that have become household names . . ." (CBS News 2002). As another example, the alcohol industry spends more than $1 billion on yearly advertising (Critser 1996; Kilbourne 1989; Robert Wood Johnson Foundation 2001). "The advertising budget for one beer — Budweiser — is more than the entire budget for research on alcoholism and alcohol abusers" (Kilbourne 1989, 13). More recent findings indicate that "Alcohol companies spent $4.9 billion on television advertising between 2001 and 2005. They spent 2.1% of this amount ($104 million) on 'responsibility advertisement'" (CAMY 2007).

Radio, newspapers, and magazines are also saturated with advertisements for OTC drugs that constantly offer relief from whatever illness you may have. There are pills for inducing sleep and those for staying awake, as well as others for treating indigestion, headache, backache, tension, constipation, and the like. Using these medicinal compounds can significantly alter mood, level of consciousness, and physical discomfort. Experts warn that such drug advertising is likely to increase.

In the early 1990s, the Food and Drug Administration (FDA) lifted a 2-year ban on consumer advertising of prescription drugs; since then, there has been an onslaught of new sales pitches. In their attempts to sell drugs, product advertisers use the authority of a physician or health expert or the seemingly sincere testimony of a product user. Adults are strongly affected by testimonial advertising because these drug commercials can appear authentic and convincing to large numbers of viewers, listeners, or readers.

The constant barrage of commercials, including many for OTC drugs, relays the message that, if

Amanda Geiger never saw the drunk driver.

Friends Don't Let Friends Drive Drunk.

Photo by Michael Mazzeo

U.S. Department of Transportation

Ad Council

Although the media are often blamed for glamorizing dangerous drug use, many successful prevention campaigns have used TV, radio, and print media as outlets. Since the Advertising Council began the campaign "Friends Don't Let Friends Drive Drunk," 79% of Americans have stopped an intoxicated friend from getting behind the wheel.

you are experiencing restlessness or uncomfortable symptoms, taking drugs is an acceptable and normal response. As a result, television viewers, newspaper and magazine readers, and radio listeners are led to believe or unconsciously select the particular brand advertised when confronted with dozens upon dozens of drug choices for a particular ailment. In effect, this advertising reaffirms the belief that drugs are necessary when taken for a real or an imagined symptom.

Drug Use and Drug Dependence

Why are so many people attracted to drugs and the effects of recreational drug use? Like the ancient Assyrians, who sucked on opium lozenges, and the Romans, who ate hashish sweets some 2000 years ago, many users claim to be bored, in pain, frustrated, unable to enjoy life, or alienated. Such people turn to drugs in the hope of finding oblivion, peace, inner connections, outer connections (togetherness), or euphoria. The fact that many OTC drugs never really cure the ailment,

especially if taken for social and psychological reasons, and the fact that frequent use of most drugs increases the risk of addiction do not seem to be deterrents. People continue to take drugs for many reasons, including the following:

1. Searching for pleasure and using drugs to heighten good feelings.
2. Taking drugs to temporarily relieve stress or tension or provide a temporary escape for people with anxiety.
3. Taking drugs to temporarily forget one's problems and avoid or postpone worries.
4. Viewing certain drugs (such as alcohol, marijuana, and tobacco) as necessary to relax after a tension-filled day at work.
5. Taking drugs to fit in with peers, especially when peer pressure is strong during early and late adolescence; seeing drugs as a *rite of passage.*
6. Taking drugs to enhance religious or mystical experiences. (Very few cultures teach children how to use specific drugs for this purpose.)
7. Taking drugs to relieve pain and some symptoms of illness.

It is important to understand why historically many people have been unsuccessful in eliminating the fascination with drugs. To reach such an understanding, we must address questions dealing with (1) why people are attracted to drugs, (2) how experiences with the different types of drugs vary (here, many attitudes are conveyed from the "inside" — the users themselves), (3) how each of the major drugs affects the body and the mind, (4) how patterns of use vary among different groups, and (5) what forms of treatment are available for the addicted. In Chapter 2, explanations and responses to such questions are addressed from a more theoretical (explanatory) level. In Chapters 8 through 16, each of the major types of drugs is separately examined.

■ When Does Use Lead to Abuse?

Views about the use of drugs depend on one's perspective. For example, from a pharmacological perspective, if a patient is suffering severe pain because of injuries sustained from an automobile accident, high doses of a narcotic such as morphine or Demerol should be given to control discomfort. While someone is in pain, no reason exists not to take the drug. From a medical standpoint, once healing has occurred and pain has been relieved, drug use should cease. If the patient continues using the narcotic because it provides a sense of well-being or he or she has become dependent to the point of addiction, the pattern of drug intake is then considered abuse. Thus, the *amount* of drug taken or the frequency of dosing does not necessarily determine abuse (even though individuals who abuse drugs usually consume increasingly higher doses). Most important is the *motive* for taking the drug, which is the principal factor in determining the presence of abuse.

Initial drug abuse symptoms include: (1) excessive use, (2) constant preoccupation about the availability and supply of the drug, (3) refusal to admit excessive use, and (4) reliance on the drug. All of these four factors frequently result in producing the initial symptoms of withdrawal whenever the user attempts to stop taking the drug. As a result, the user often begins to neglect other responsibilities or ambitions in favor of using the drug.

Even the legitimate use of a drug can be controversial. Often, physicians cannot decide even among themselves what constitutes legitimate use of a drug. For example, MDMA ("Ecstasy") is currently prohibited for therapeutic use, but in 1985, when the DEA was deciding MDMA's status, some 35 to 200 physicians (mostly psychiatrists) were using the drug in their practice. These clinicians claimed that MDMA relaxed inhibitions and enhanced communication and was useful as a psychotherapeutic adjunct to assist in dealing with psychiatric patients (Levinthal 1996; Schecter 1989). From the perspective of these physicians, Ecstasy was a useful medicinal tool. However, the DEA did not agree and made Ecstasy a Schedule I drug (see Chapter 3). In a legal sense, Schedule I excludes any legitimate use of the drug in therapeutics; consequently, according to this ruling, anyone taking Ecstasy is guilty of drug abuse (Goode 1999).

If the problem of drug abuse is to be understood and solutions are to be found, identifying the causes of the abuse is most important. When a drug is being abused, it is not legitimately therapeutic; that is, it does not improve the user's physical or mental health. If such drug use is not for therapeutic purposes, what is the motive for taking the drug?

There are many possible answers to this question. Initially, most drug abusers perceive some psychological advantage when using these compounds. For many, the psychological lift is significant enough that they are willing to risk social exclusion, health problems, dramatic changes in personality, arrest, incarceration, and fines to have their drug. The psychological effects that these drugs cause may entail an array of diverse feelings. Different types of drugs have different psychological effects. The type of drug an individual selects to abuse may ultimately reflect his or her own mental state.

For example, people who experience chronic depression, feel intense job pressures, are unable to focus on accomplishing goals, or have a sense of inferiority may find that a stimulant such as cocaine or amphetamines appears to provide a solution to such dilemmas. These drugs cause a spurt of energy, a feeling of euphoria, a sense of superiority, and imagined self-confidence. In contrast, people who experience nervousness and anxiety and want instant relief from the pressures of life may choose a depressant such as alcohol or barbiturates. These agents sedate, relax, provide relief, and even have some amnesiac properties, allowing users to suspend or forget their problems. People who perceive themselves as creative or who have artistic talents may select hallucinogenic types of drugs to "expand" their minds, heighten their senses, and distort the confining, often perceived monotonous nature of reality. As individuals come to rely more on drugs to inhibit, deny, accelerate, or distort their realities, they run the risk of becoming psychologically dependent on drugs — a process described in detail in Chapters 2, 4, and 6.

Some have argued that taking a particular drug to meet a psychological need, especially if a person is over 21 years of age, is not very different from taking a drug to cure an ailment. The belief here is that physical needs and psychological needs are really indistinguishable. In fact, several drug researchers and writers, including Szasz (1992) and Lenson (1995), believe that drug taking is a citizen's right and a personal matter involving individual decision making. They see drug taking as simply a departure from consciousness. Lenson states that taking drugs for recreational purposes is simply an additional form of diversity among many other acceptable forms of diversity, such as racial, religious, gender, and sexual orientation. (For additional elaboration on these views, see Venturelli 2000.) Obviously, within drug use research, this topic remains strongly debatable.

■ Drug Dependence

Although Chapters 2 and 18 discuss addiction and drug dependence in detail, here we introduce some underlying factors that lead to drug dependence. Our discussion emphasizes *drug dependence* instead of *addiction* because the term *addiction* is both controversial and relative (an issue that came to the forefront during the 1996 presidential election, for example). Even when drug dependence becomes full-fledged, addiction remains debatable, with many experts unable to agree on one set of characteristics that constitutes addiction. Furthermore, the term *addiction* is viewed by some as a pejorative that adds to the labeling process (see labeling theory in Chapter 2).

The main characteristics necessary for drug dependence are as follows:

- Both physical and psychological factors precipitate drug dependence. Recently, closer attention has been focused on the mental (psychological) attachments than on physical addiction to drug use as principally indicative of addiction — mostly, the craving aspect in wanting the drug for consumption.
- More specifically, *psychological dependence* refers to the need that a user may feel for continued use of a drug to experience its effects. *Physical dependence* refers to the need to continue taking the drug to avoid withdrawal symptoms, which often include feelings of discomfort and illness.
- There is a tendency to eventually become addicted with repeated use of most psychoactive drugs.
- Generally, *addiction* refers to mind and body dependence. In the process of dependence, addiction can be viewed as one stage within the dependence phase.

The process of addiction involves five separate phases (Figure 1.6): relief, increased use, preoccupation, dependency, and withdrawal. Initially, the **relief phase** refers to the relief experienced by using a drug, which allows a potential addict to escape one or more of the following feelings: boredom, loneliness, tension, fatigue, anger, and anxiety. The **increased use phase** involves taking greater quantities of the drug. The **preoccupation phase** consists of a constant concern with the substance — that is, taking the drug becomes "normal" behavior. The **dependency phase** is synonymous with addiction. In this phase, more of the drug is sought without regard for the presence of physical symptoms, such as coughing and/or shortness of breath in cases of cigarette and marijuana addiction, blackouts from advanced abuse, and moderate to severe soreness of nasal passages and inflammation from snorting cocaine. The **withdrawal phase** involves such symptoms as itching, chills, tension, stomach pain, or depression from the nonuse of the addictive drug and/or an entire set of psychological concerns mainly involving an insatiable craving for the drug (Monroe 1996).

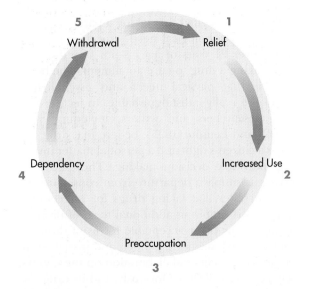

FIGURE 1.6

Stages of Drug Dependence

KEY TERMS

relief phase
satisfaction derived from escaping negative feelings in using the drug

increased use phase
taking increasing quantities of the drug

preoccupation phase
constant concern with the supply of the drug

dependency phase
synonym for addiction

withdrawal phase
physical and/or psychological effects derived from not using the drug

The Costs of Drug Use to Society

Society pays a high price for drug addiction. Many of the costs are immeasurable — for example, broken homes, illnesses, shortened lives, and loss of good minds from industries and professions. The dollar costs are also enormous. The National Institute on Drug Abuse (**NIDA**) has estimated that the typical narcotic habit costs the user $100 or more per day to maintain, depending on location, availability of narcotics, and other factors. If a heroin addict has a $100-a-day habit, he or she needs about $36,500 per year just to maintain the drug supply. It is impossible for most addicts to get this amount of money legally; therefore, many support their habits by resorting to criminal activity or working as or for drug dealers.

Most crimes related to drugs involve theft of personal property — primarily, burglary and shoplifting — and, less commonly, assault and robbery (often mugging). Estimates are that a heroin addict must steal three to five times the actual cost of the drugs to maintain the habit, or roughly $100,000 per year. Especially with crack and heroin use, a large number of addicts resort to pimping and prostitution. No accurate figures are available regarding the cost of drug-related prostitution, although some law enforcement officials have estimated that prostitutes take in a total of $10 to $20 billion per year. It has also been estimated that nearly three out of every four prostitutes in major cities have a serious drug dependency.

Another significant concern arises from the recent increase in clandestine laboratories throughout the country that are involved in synthesizing or processing illicit drugs. Such laboratories produce amphetamine-type drugs, heroin-type drugs, designer drugs, and LSD and process other drugs of abuse such as cocaine and crack. The **DEA** reported that 390 laboratories were seized in 1993, a figure that increased to 967 in 1995. Another example of the phenomenal growth of methamphetamine laboratories can be found in Missouri. From 1995 to 1997, seizures of such labs in Missouri increased by 535% (Steward and Sitarmiah 1997). "In Dawson County in western Nebraska . . . 'The percentage of meth-related crimes is through the roof' . . . as reiterated by an investigator with the county sheriff's office. . . . In the state as a whole, officials discovered 38 methamphetamine laboratories in 1999; last year [2001] they discovered 179" (Butterfield 2002, A23).

The reasons for such dramatic increases relate to the enormous profits and relatively low risk associated with these operations. As a rule, clandestine laboratories are fairly mobile and relatively crude (often operating in a kitchen, basement, or garage) and are run by individuals with only elementary chemical skills.

Another interesting discovery is that these laboratories are not always stationary in locations such as garages, barns, homes, apartments, and so on. Though these stationary "labs" predominate, especially in the production of methamphetamine, recently mobile labs have made an appearance:

Cooking in cars and trucks helps producers in two ways: It eludes identification by law enforcement; and motion helps the chemical reaction [of methamphetamine production]. Motels are a new production setting. . . . Clandestine labs are also set up in federal parklands, where toxic byproducts pose a danger to hikers and campers. (ONDCP 2002, 58)

In 2003, the following was reported:

With portable meth labs popping up everywhere from motel bathrooms to the back seat of a Chevy, it was only a matter of time before they made their way onto campus. Last November, a custodian notified campus police at . . . [university in Texas] . . . about what appeared to be a lab set up in a music practice room in the . . . [university's] . . . Fine Arts Center. "We found beakers of red liquid, papers and other residue, and the room had this horrible odor. . . ." Students were on vacation, so the practice room, which had its windows blackened out, would have afforded the occupant a few days to cook. [One campus police official] . . . speculates that this is just the beginning: "Labs are popping up on campuses all over the country. It's just too easy now. You can get the recipe on the Internet. Still, how could someone be so brazen as to set up an operation next to the French horn section?" (Jellinek 2003, 54)

Because of a lack of training, inexperience, and the danger of experiencing the effects of methamphetamine while making the drug, the chemical "cooking" procedures are performed crudely, sometimes resulting in adulterants and impure products. Such contaminants can be very toxic, causing severe harm or even death to the unsuspecting user as well as a greater likelihood of sudden explosion (Drug Strategies 1995). Fortunately, when looking at all the illicit drugs produced by such underground laboratories, such outbreaks of physically harmful drugs do not occur very often. Partial proof of this is found in the small number of news media stories of deaths or poisonings from illicit drugs. Nevertheless, because profit drives these clandestine labs, which obviously have no government supervision, impurities or "cheap fillers" are always possible so that greater profits can be made. Here, caution is very advisable in that drug purchasers do not have any guarantees when purchasing powerful illicit drugs.

Society continues paying a large sum even after users, addicts, and drug dealers are caught and sentenced because it takes from $75 to $1500 per day to keep one person incarcerated. Supporting programs such as methadone maintenance costs much less. New York officials estimate that methadone maintenance costs about $3000 per year per patient. Some outpatient programs, such as those in Washington, D.C., claim a cost as low as $8 to $12 per day (not counting cost of staff and facilities), which is much less than the cost of incarceration.

A more long-term effect of drug abuse that has substantial impact on society is the medical and psychological care often required by addicts due to disease resulting from their drug habit. Particularly noteworthy are the communicable diseases spread because of needle sharing within the drug-abusing population, such as hepatitis and HIV.

In the United States, in 2004, an estimated 1 million Americans were living with HIV — and one in four of them did not know it (NIDA 2007). HIV eventually causes AIDS. Worldwide, approximately 39 million are living with HIV. This number includes sub-Saharan Africa, Asia, Latin America and the Caribbean, Eastern Europe and Central Asia, North America, Western and Central Europe, North Africa and the Middle East, and Oceania (see Chapter 16 for more detailed information on HIV and AIDS) (Clinton 2006).

In the United States, HIV is spread primarily through unprotected sexual intercourse and sharing of previously used needles to inject drugs. HIV in the injecting-drug-user subpopulation is transmitted in the small (minuscule) amount of contaminated blood remaining in the used needles. The likelihood of a member of the drug-abusing population contracting HIV directly correlates with the frequency of injections and the extent of needle sharing. Care for AIDS patients lasts a lifetime, and many of these medical expenses come from federal- and state-funded programs. Many cities throughout the United States have publicly funded programs that distribute new, uncontaminated needles to drug addicts. The needles are free of charge in exchange for used injection needles in order to prevent the spread of HIV and hepatitis B and C from contaminated needles. These programs are often referred to as **needle-exchange programs**.

Also of great concern is drug abuse by women during pregnancy. Some psychoactive drugs can have profound, permanent effects on a developing fetus. The best documented is fetal alcohol syndrome (FAS), which can affect the offspring of alcoholic mothers (see Chapter 7). Cocaine and amphetamine-related drugs can also cause irreversible congenital changes when used during pregnancy (see Chapter 10). All too often, the affected offspring of addicted mothers become the responsibility of welfare organizations. In addition to the costs to society just mentioned, other costs of drug abuse include drug-related deaths, emergency room visits and hospital stays, and automobile fatalities.

KEY TERMS

needle-exchange programs
publically funded programs that distribute new, uncontaminated needles to drug addicts in exchange for used injection needles in order to prevent the spread of HIV and hepatitis B and C

■ Drugs, Crime, and Violence

There is a long-established close association between drug abuse and criminality. The beliefs (hypotheses) for this association range along a continuum between two opposing views: (1) criminal behavior develops as a means to support addiction, and (2) criminality is inherently linked to the user's personality and occurs independently of drug use (Drug Strategies 1995; McBride and McCoy 2003). In other words, does addiction to drugs cause a person to engage in criminal behavior such as burglary, theft, and larceny to pay for the drug habit? On the other hand, does criminal behavior stem from an already existing criminal personality such that drugs are used as an adjunct to commit such acts? In other words, are drugs used in conjunction with crime to sedate and give the added confidence needed to commit daring law violations?

The answers to these questions have never been clear because findings that contradict one view in favor of the other continue to mount on both sides. Part of the reason for the controversy about the relationship between criminal activity and drug abuse is that studies have been conducted in different settings and cultures, employing different research methods, and focusing on different addictive drugs. As a result, too many factors are involved to allow us to distinguish the cause from the result. We know that each type of drug has unique addictive potential and that interpretation of exactly when a deviant act is an offense (violation of law) varies. Furthermore, we know that people think differently while under the influence of drugs. Whether criminalistic behavior is *directly* caused by the drug use or whether prior socialization and peer influence work in concert to cause criminal behavior remains unclear. Certainly, we think it would be safe to view prior socialization, law-violating peers, and drugs as strong contributing factors for causing criminal behavior.

Although this controversy about the drugs and crime connection continues to challenge our thinking, the following findings are clear:

1. In 2002 more than two thirds of jail inmates were found to be dependent on or to abuse alcohol or drugs.
2. Two in five inmates were dependent on alcohol or drugs while nearly one in four abused alcohol or drugs, but were not dependent on them. Jail inmates who met the criteria for substance dependence or abuse (70%) were more likely than other inmates (46%) to have a criminal record.
3. Fifty-two percent of female jail inmates were found to be dependent on alcohol or drugs, compared to 44% of male inmates.

4. Half of all convicted jail inmates were under the influence of drugs or alcohol at the time of their offense.
5. Jail inmates between ages 25 and 44 had the highest rate of substance dependence or abuse (seven in ten inmates). Those age 55 or older had the lowest rate (nearly five in ten inmates).
6. More than 50% of drug or property offenders were dependent on or had abused a substance, compared to over 60% of violent and public-order offenders.
7. Women and white inmates are more likely to have used drugs at the time of their offense (Karberg and James 2002).
8. Thirty-two percent of state and 26.4% of federal prison inmates reported being under the influence of drugs at the time of their offense in 2004 (see Table 1.5). Approximately 44% were incarcerated for drug offenses in state prisons and 32% were incarcerated in federal prisons. Of these, 46% were arrested for possession in state prisons and 21% were arrested in federal prisons. Forty-two percent were serving time in state prisons and 34% were serving time in federal prisons for trafficking in drugs. One outcome of these findings is that one out of every four major crimes committed — violent offenses, property, and drug offenses — involves an offender who is under the influence of drugs.
9. Another study also shows a dramatic increase in the correlation between drug use and crime. This study by the Robert Wood Johnson Foundation (2001, 45) reported that with regard to homicide, theft, and assault, at least half of the adults arrested for such major crimes tested positive for drugs at the time of their arrest. "Among those convicted of violent crimes, approximately half of state prison inmates and 40 percent of federal prisoners had been drinking or taking drugs at the time of their offense."
10. Approximately one out of every six major crimes is committed because of the offender's need to obtain money for drugs.

In regard to the connection between drug use and crime, the following findings can be summarized: (1) drug users in comparison to non-drug users are more likely to commit crimes, (2) arrestees are often under the influence of a drug while committing crimes, and (3) drugs and violence (more than likely cocaine, crack, and other stimulant-type drugs) often go hand in hand.

Table 1.5 **Percentage of State and Federal Prison Inmates Who Reported Being Under the Influence of Drugs at the Time of Their Offense, 2004**

	STATE	FEDERAL
Total[a]	32.1%	26.4%
Violent Offenses	27.7%	24.0%
Homicide	27.3%	16.8%
Sexual Assault[b]	17.4%	13.8%
Robbery	40.7%	29.4%
Assault	24.1%	20.1%
Property Offenses	38.5%	13.6%
Burglary	41.1%	:
Larceny/theft	40.1%	:
Motor vehicle theft	38.7%	:
Fraud	34.1%	9.3%
Drug Offenses	43.6%	32.3%
Possession	46.0%	20.9%
Trafficking	42.3%	33.8%
Public Order Offenses	25.4%	18.7%
Weapons	27.6%	27.8%
Other public order offenses	24.6%	8.0%

[a] Includes offenses not shown
[b] Includes rape and other sexual assault
[c] Excluding DWI/DUI
: Not calculated; too few cases to permit calculation.

Source: Bureau of Justice Statistics. *Drug Use and Dependence, State and Federal Prisoners.* Washington, DC: U.S. Department of Justice, Office of Justice Programs, 2004.

Drug-related crimes are undoubtedly overwhelming the U.S. judicial system. Not long ago, it was discovered that "in the last few years, the number of gang-related web sites has grown to tens of thousands, with about 20% to 30% run by actual gang members,' said Detective Chuck Zeglin of the Los Angeles Police Department's career criminal apprehension section" (Associated Press 2001).

According to the U.S. Department of Justice, alcohol consumption is associated with 27% of all murders, almost 33% of all property offenses, and more than 37% of robberies committed by young people. In fact, nearly 40% of the young people (often younger than 21 years of age) in adult correctional facilities reported drinking before committing a crime.

Drug Cartels

Here are some reports of incidents in the world of drugs, violence, and crime:

Shortly before 10:00 p.m. on August 3, 1997, as fans gathered in the bars and eateries near the Plaza Monumental bullring in Ciudad Juarez [in Chihuahua, Mexico], four suspected drug traffickers strolled into the popular Max Fim restaurant, pulled out their guns, and squeezed off 130 rounds into the post-fight Sunday night crowd, killing three men and two women and wounding another four people. On their way out, the assailants paused long enough to claim another victim — an off-duty law enforcement officer who had run into the street from the bar next door, gun drawn, to check out the commotion. (Combs 1999, 1)

In another news report:

. . . one indication of the export of money laundering, more than $53 million in cash was seized by U.S. customs agents at Southwest border checkpoints between 1994 and 1996. The U.S. government suggested that drug profits of as much as $50 billion a year — $6 billion more than was appropriated in fiscal 1998 for Texas state government — flowed through Texas into Mexico. The estimate included electronic transfers, exchange house operation, and bulk cash. (Combs 1999, 3)

And in another news report:

The new dominance of Mexican cartels has caused a spike in violence along the 2,000-mile U.S.–Mexico border where rival cartels are warring against Mexican and U.S. authorities. Drugs are either flown from Columbia to Mexico in small planes, or, in the case of marijuana and methamphetamine, produced locally. Then, they're shipped into the U.S. by boat, private vehicles, or in commercial trucks crossing the border. (Worldpress Organization 2006).

And finally,

> The Tijuana-based Felix drug cartel and the Juarez-based Fuentes cartel began buying legitimate business in small towns in Los Angeles County in the early 1990s . . . They purchased restaurants, used-car lots, auto-body shops and other small businesses. One of their purposes was to use these businesses for money-laundering operations. Once established in their community, these cartel-financed business owners ran for city council and other local offices (Farah 2006 quoting an excerpt from *In Mortal Danger* by Tom Tancredo, U.S. Congressman, Colorado).

These news briefs are just a small sampling of the types of crimes and violence perpetrated by drug dealers. It is clear that production, merchandising, and distribution of illicit drugs have developed into a worldwide operation worth hundreds of billions of dollars (Goldstein 1994). These enormous profits have attracted organized crime, in both the United States and abroad, and all too frequently even corrupt law enforcement agencies (McShane 1994). For the participants in such operations, drugs can mean incredible wealth and power. For example, dating back to 1992, Pablo Escobar was recognized as a drug kingpin and leader of the cocaine cartel in Colombia, and he was acknowledged as one of the world's richest men and Colombia's most powerful man (Wire Services 1992). With his drug-related wealth, Escobar financed a private army to conduct a personal war against the government of Colombia (Associated Press 1992) and until his death in 1993, he was a serious threat to his country's stability.

In December 1999, the notorious Juarez drug cartel was believed to be responsible for burying more than 100 bodies (22 Americans) in a mass grave at a ranch in Mexico. All of the deaths were believed to be drug-related. According to a news story on this gruesome discovery, the alleged perpetrator, Vincente Carrillo Fuentes, is one among dozens of drug lords and lieutenants wanted by U.S. law enforcement agents (Associated Press 1999). This same news release indicated that the drug trade would not end until drug cartels are eliminated. Such occurrences, which are often reported by the mass media, indicate the existence of powerful and dangerous drug cartels that are responsible for the availability of illicit drugs around the world.

Drug-related violence takes its toll at all levels, as rival gangs fight to control their "turf" and associated drug operations. Innocent bystanders often become unsuspecting victims of the indiscriminate violence. For example, a Roman Catholic cardinal was killed on May 24, 1993, when a car he was a passenger in was inadvertently driven into the middle of a drug-related shoot-out between traffickers at the international airport in Guadalajara, Mexico. Five other innocent bystanders were killed in the incident (Associated Press 1993). In many other incidents, unsuspecting people have been injured or killed by drug users who, while under the influence of drugs, commit violent criminal acts.

▨ Drugs in the Workplace: A Costly Affliction

"He was a good, solid worker, always on the job — until he suddenly backed his truck over a 4-inch gas line." If the line had ruptured, there would have been a serious explosion, according to the driver's employer. The accident raised a red flag. ". . . under the company's standard policy, the employee was tested for drugs and alcohol. He was positive for both." (Edelson 2000, 3)

Most adults spend the majority of their hours each day in some type of family environment. For most adults employed full-time, the second greatest number of hours is spent in the workplace. Generally, once drug use becomes habitual, drug use often continues at work. The National Household Surveys, for example, found evidence of significant drug use in the workplace. In the surveys, 65.6% of full-time workers reported alcohol use within the past month. Some 6.4% of full-time workers reported marijuana use within the past month. Part-time employees did not differ much in their use of alcohol and marijuana (SAMHSA 2007b).

▨ Worker Substance Abuse in Industry Categories

Substance use in the workplace negatively affects U.S. industry through lost productivity, workplace accidents and injuries, employee absenteeism, low morale, and increased illness. The loss to U.S.

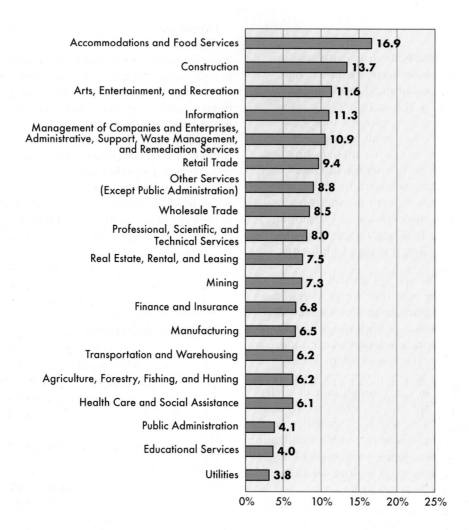

FIGURE 1.7

Substance Use, by Industry Category: Past Month Illicit Drug Use Among Full-Time Workers Ages 18 to 64, by Industry Categories: 2002–2004 Combined

....

Source: Substance Abuse and Mental Health Services Administration (SAMHSA), Office of Applied Studies (OAS), 2004. *The National Household Survey on Drug Use and Health (NSDUH) Report. Worker Substance Use, by Industry Category.* Rockville, MD, 23 August 2007.

companies due to employees' alcohol and drug use and related problems is estimated at billions of dollars a year. Research shows that the rate of substance use varies by occupation and industry (Larson et al. 2007). Studies also have indicated that employers vary in their treatment of substance use issues and that workplace-based employee assistance programs (EAPs) can be a valuable resource for obtaining help for substance-using workers (Delaney et al. 1998; Reynolds and Lehman 2003).

Highlights from SAMHSA (2007b) indicate the following (also see Figure 1.7):

1. Among the 19 major industry categories, the highest rates of past-month illicit drug use among full-time workers ages 18 to 64 were found in accommodations and food services (16.9%) and construction (13.7%).
2. The industry categories with the lowest rates of past-month illicit drug use were utilities

(3.8%), educational services (4%), and public administration (4.1%).

3. Combined data from 2002 to 2004 indicate that an annual average of 8.2% of full-time workers ages 18 to 64 used illicit drugs in the past month and 8.8% used alcohol heavily in the past month.

4. Combined data from 2002 to 2004 indicate that the prevalence of alcohol and illicit drug use among adults ages 18 to 64 was higher among unemployed persons than among persons in other employment groups.

5. Among adults ages 18 to 64, an estimated 18.6% of those who were unemployed used illicit drugs in the past month compared with 11.9% of those employed part time, 8.2% of those employed full time, and 8.3% of those in other employment statuses.

6. Approximately 13.6% of unemployed adults ages 18 to 64 drank alcohol heavily in the past month compared with 8.8% of those employed full time.

7. Reflecting the fact that almost two thirds of the adult population (64.3%) were employed full time, a majority of past-month illicit drug and heavy alcohol users were employed full time.

8. Among full-time workers ages 18 to 64, the highest rates of past-month heavy alcohol use were found in construction (15.9%); arts, entertainment, and recreation (13.6%); and mining (13.3%). The industry categories with the lowest rates of heavy alcohol use were educational services (4.0%) and health care and social assistance (4.3%).

9. From 2002 to 2004, over half of all past-month illicit drug users (57.5%) and past-month heavy alcohol users (67.3%) ages 18 to 64 were employed full time.

10. Approximately 70% of large companies test for drug use. Approximately 50% of medium companies and 22% of small companies perform such testing. Of those companies that drug test, more than 90% use urine analysis, less than 20% use blood analysis, and less than 3% use hair analysis.

11. Most companies that administer drug tests test for marijuana, cocaine, opiates, amphetamines, and PCP.

12. Age is the most significant predictor of marijuana and cocaine use. Younger employees (18 to 24 years old) are more likely to report drug use than older employees (25 years or older).

13. In general, unmarried workers report roughly twice as much illicit drug and heavy alcohol use as married workers. Among food preparation workers, transportation drivers, and mechanics, and in industries such as construction and machinery (not electrical), the discrepancy between married and unmarried workers is especially notable.

14. Workers who report having three or more jobs in the previous 5 years are twice as likely to be current or past-year illicit drug users as those who held two or fewer jobs over the same period.

15. Workers in occupations that affect public safety, including truck drivers, firefighters, and police officers, report the highest rate of participation in drug testing.

16. "Among full-time workers, heavy drinkers and illicit drug users are more likely than those who do not drink heavily or use illicit drugs to have skipped work in the past month or have worked for three or more employers in the past year" (Robert Wood Johnson Foundation 2001, 45).

17. Most youths do not cease drug use when they begin working.

In summarizing this research on employees who abuse alcohol or other drugs, five major findings emerge: (1) these workers are 3 times more likely than the average employee to be late to work; (2) they are 3 times more likely to receive sickness benefits; (3) they are 16 times more likely to be absent from work; (4) they are 5 times more likely to be involved in on-the-job accidents (note that many of these hurt others, not themselves); and (5) they are 5 times more likely to file compensation claims.

Employee Assistance Programs

Many industries have responded to drugs in the workplace by creating **drug testing** and **employee assistance programs (EAPs)**. Drug testing generally

KEY TERMS

drug testing
urine, blood screening, or hair analysis used to identify those who may be using drugs

employee assistance programs (EAPs)
drug assistance programs for drug-dependent employees

involves urine screening that is undertaken to identify which employees are using drugs and which employees may have current or potential drug problems. EAPs are employer-financed programs administered by a company or through an outside contractor. More than 400,000 EAPs have been established in the United States. The most recent findings regarding workplace substance use policies and programs among full-time workers are (SAMHSA 2007b):

- Of employees ages 18 to 64 who had used an illicit drug in the past month, 32.1% worked for an employer who offered educational information about alcohol and drug use, 71% were aware of a written policy about drug and alcohol use in the workplace, and 45.4% worked for an employer who maintained an EAP or other type of counseling program for employees who have an alcohol- or drug-related problem.
- Among full-time workers who used alcohol heavily in the past month, 37.2% worked for an employer who provided educational information about drug and alcohol use, 73.7% were aware of written policies about drug and alcohol use, and 51.1% had access to an EAP at their workplace.

These programs are designed to aid in identifying and resolving productivity problems associated with employees' emotional or physical concerns, such as those related to health, marital, family, financial, and substance abuse. EAPs have also expanded their focus to combat employee abuse of OTC and prescription drugs in addition to illicit psychoactive substances. Overall, the programs attempt to formally reduce problems associated with impaired job performance.

Recently, however, what has been occurring is that "as the economy falters and hiring slows, many employers have decided not to spend money on testing job applicants for drug use . . . [as reported by *Knight-Ridder Newspapers* on May 11, 2003]" (Join Together Online 2003). Part of the reason is the current state of the U.S. economy, especially when the bottom line continues to be cutting costs and increasing profits, and as is known, the cost of drug testing continues to escalate. The other reason cited for companies that are beginning to scale back on drug testing is "[younger-generation management personnel] . . . are moving into the upper echelons of corporate America now that take the stance that if it's not affecting the person's performance, it's not an issue" (Join Together Online 2003). These two reasons alone may have a profound impact on workplace drug testing in the near future.

Venturing to a Higher Form of Consciousness: The Holistic Self-Awareness Approach to Drug Use

Throughout this book, we continually approach drug use from a multidisciplinary perspective, blending pharmacological, psychological, and sociological perspectives and interpretations of the most commonly used licit and illicit drugs. Most chapters discuss the major drugs and their common usage and abuse patterns and emphasize this multiapproach in an effort to more fully comprehend how drugs affect both the mind and the body.

As you proceed through this book, it will become apparent that whenever drug use leads to abuse, it rarely results from a single, isolated cause. Instead, it is often caused or preceded by multiple factors, which may include combinations of the following:

- Hereditary (genetic) factors
- Psychological conditioning
- Peer group pressures
- Inability to cope with stress and anxiety of daily living
- Quality of role models
- Degree of attachment to a family structure
- Level of security with gender identity and sexual orientation
- Personality traits
- Perceived ethnic and racial compatibility with larger society and socioeconomic status (social class)

Gaining knowledge of the reasons for drug use, the effects of drugs, and their addictive potential is the purpose of this text. As authors, we strongly endorse and advocate a **holistic self-awareness approach** that emphasizes a healthy balance among

KEY TERMS

holistic self-awareness approach
emphasizes that nonmedical and often recreational drug use interferes with the healthy balance among the mind, the body, and the spirit

mind, body, and spirit. Health and wellness can be achieved only when these three domains of existence are free from any unnecessary use of psychoactive substances. The holistic philosophy is based on the idea that the mind has a powerful influence on maintaining health. All three — mind, body, and spirit — work as a unified whole to promote health and wellness. Similarly, we are in agreement with holistic health advocates who emphasize the following viewpoint:

> Holistic Health is based on the law of nature that a whole is made up of interdependent parts. The earth is made up of systems, such as air, land, water, plants and animals. If life is to be sustained, they cannot be separated, for what is happening to one is also felt by all the other systems. In the same way, an individual is a whole made up of interdependent parts, which are the physical, mental, emotional, and spiritual. While one part is not working at its best, it impacts all the other parts of that person. . . . A common explanation is to view wellness as a continuum along a line. The line represents all possible degrees of health. The far left end of the line represents premature death. On the far right end is the highest possible level of wellness or maximum well-being. The center point of the line represents a lack of apparent disease. This places all levels of illness on the left half of the wellness continuum. The right half shows that even when no illness seems to be present, there is still a lot of room for improvement. . . . Holistic Health is an ongoing process. As a lifestyle, it includes a personal commitment to be moving toward the right end of the wellness continuum. No matter what their current status of health, people can improve their level of well-being. Even when there are temporary setbacks, movement is always headed toward wellness. (Walter 1999, 1–2)[1]

This book works toward this direction by presenting a blend of different perspectives about drug information to more fully comprehend how drugs work and their effects on the mind, body, and spirit.

The different perspectives expand upon limited and narrow points of view so that drug information can be viewed and understood from pharmacological, psychological, and sociological perspectives. As mentioned earlier, understanding drug use is important not only for comprehending our own health, but also for understanding (1) why and how others are attracted to drugs; (2) how to detect drug use in others; (3) what to do (remedies and solutions) when family members and/or friends abuse drugs; (4) how to help and advise drug abusers about the pitfalls of substance use; (5) what the best educational, preventive, and treatment options available are for victims of drug abuse; and (6) what the danger signals are that can arise in yourself and others you care about when drug use exceeds normal and necessary use. Once knowledge is gained about drug use and/or abuse, holistic health awareness results in self-awareness, and self-awareness leads to self-understanding and assurance. Self-awareness initially begins by understanding your own drug use practices as well as those of close family and friends. By practicing this approach regarding the use of psychoactive substances, you will be better equipped to understand not only yourself, but also others who may be in need.

Discussion Questions

1. Give an example of a drug-using friend and describe how he or she may be affected by pharmacological, cultural, social, and contextual factors.

2. Discuss and debate whether the often considered "benign" drug known as marijuana *is* or *is not* addictive. In your discussion/debate, also consider the finding by the Substance Abuse and Mental Health Services Administration (SAMHSA) that in 2006, marijuana had the highest rates of past-year dependence or abuse, with 4.2 million dependent, and that this accounted for 59.4% of total drug abuse problems. (See Chapter 17, Drug Prevention,

---

1. From Walter, Susan. *The Illustrated Encyclopedia of Body-Mind Disciplines.* New York: Rosen Publishing Group, 1999. Used with permission.

subheading entitled, "How Serious Is the Problem of Drug Dependence.")

3. In reviewing the ancient historical uses of drugs, do you think drug use today is different from back then? Explain your answer.

4. Why do Americans use so many legal drugs (for example, alcohol, tobacco, and OTC drugs)? What aspects of our society promote extensive drug use?

5. Table 1.3 shows that drug use remained high from 2000 to 2005. Cite two reasons why you think this trend has occurred despite the media campaigns against drug use promoted by private organizations, state and nationally sponsored media campaigns, and the efforts of law enforcement organizations.

6. Because many experimental drug users do not gravitate toward excessive drug use, should experimenters be left alone or perhaps just given legal warnings or fines?

7. Do the mass media really promote drug use, or do they merely reflect our extensive use of drugs? Provide some evidence for your position.

8. At what point do you think drug use leads to abuse? When do you think drug use does not lead to abuse?

9. What do you believe is the relationship between excessive drug use and crime? Does drug use *cause* crime or is crime simply a manifestation of personality?

10. What principal factors are involved in the relationship between drugs and crime?

11. Should all employees be randomly tested for drug use? If not, which types of employees or occupations should be randomly tested?

12. Should all students be randomly drug tested at their schools and universities? Why or why not?

13. Do you think the approach advocated by the authors regarding a holistic self-awareness approach toward drug use is a viable approach and can be successfully used for stopping drug use? Why or why not? What improvements can be made to strengthen this approach?

Summary

1 Pharmacological, cultural, social, and contextual issues are the four principal factors responsible for determining how a drug user experiences drug use. Pharmacological factors take into account how a particular drug affects the body. Cultural factors examine how society's views, as determined by custom and tradition, affect use of a particular drug. Social factors include the specific reasons why a drug is taken and how drug use develops from social factors, such as family upbringing, peer group alliances, subcultures, and communities. Contextual factors account for how drug use behavior develops from the physical surroundings in which the drug is taken.

2 Initial understanding of drug use includes the following key terms: drug, gateway drugs, medicines and prescription medicines, over-the-counter (OTC), drug misuse, drug abuse, and drug addiction.

3 Mentions of drug use date back to biblical times and ancient literature that goes back to 2240 B.C. Under the influence of drugs, many people experienced feelings ranging from extreme ecstasy to sheer terror. At times, drugs were used to induce sleep and provide freedom from care.

4 Drug users are found in all occupations and professions, at all income and social class levels, and in all age groups. No one is immune to drug use. Thus, drug use is an equal-opportunity affliction.

5 According to sociologist Erich Goode (1999), drugs are used for four reasons: (1) legal instrumental use, (2) legal recreational use, (3) illegal instrumental use, and (4) illegal recreational use.

6 The most commonly used licit and illicit lifetime drug use (rated from highest to lowest in the frequency of use) are alcohol, cigarettes, marijuana/hashish, nonmedical use of any psychotherapeutic, smokeless tobacco, cocaine, hallucinogens, analgesics, inhalants, tranquilizers, stimulants, sedatives, crack, and PCP.

7 The three types of drug users are experimenters, compulsive users, and floaters. Experimenters try drugs because of curiosity and peer pressure. Compulsive users use drugs on a full-time basis and seriously desire to escape from or

alter reality. Floaters or chippers vacillate between experimental drug use and chronic drug use.

8 The mass media tend to promote drug use through advertising. The constant barrage of OTC drug commercials relays the message that, if you are experiencing some symptom, taking drugs is an acceptable option.

9 The following are the major findings of the connection between drugs and crime: (1) drug users are more likely to commit crimes, (2) arrestees are often under the influence of drugs while committing their crimes, and (3) drugs and violence often go hand in hand.

10 The five phases of drug addiction are relief, increased use, preoccupation, dependency, and withdrawal.

11 Employee assistance programs (EAPs) are employer-financed programs administered by a company or through an outside contractor. They are designed to aid in identifying and resolving productivity problems associated with employees' emotional or physical concerns, such as those related to health, marriage, family, finances, and substance abuse. Recently, EAPs have expanded their focus to combat employee abuse of OTC and prescription drugs as well as illicit psychoactive substances.

12 The holistic self-awareness philosophy is based on the idea that the mind has a powerful influence on maintaining health. The three domains — mind, body, and spirit — work best when unobstructed by unnecessary drug use, and all three domains work as a unified whole to promote health and wellness.

References

Ananth, P., C. Annis, C. Gonzalez, K. McRae, R. Longoria, and A. Medina. "Prescription Smoothies?" Stanford Learning Lab, *Web Journal,* Department of Human Biology, 2000. Stanford University, Stanford, CA.

Associated Press. "Program to Fight Drug Smuggling Costs U.S. a Lot, Produces Little." *Salt Lake Tribune* 244 (17 August 1992): A-1.

Associated Press. "Mexican Cardinal, Six Others Killed in Cross-Fire as Drug Battles Erupt in Guadalajara." *Salt Lake Tribune* 246 (25 May 1993): A-1.

Associated Press. "Discovery of Mexican Graves Unlikely to Slow Flow of Drugs." *The Times* (5 December 1999): A-13.

Associated Press. "Gang Members Go Online to Recruit, Discuss Crimes." *Fox News Channel: Top Stories* (5 September 2001): 1.

Associated Press. "Survey: Drug Use Pervading New Bedford Fleet." *Maine Sunday Telegram* (21 July 1996).

Associated Press. "Virus Spread, But There Is Hope." *The Post Tribune* (27 November 2002): A8.

Begley, S. "AIDS at 20." Special Report. *Newsweek* (11 June 2001): 35–37.

Beschner, G. "Understanding Teenage Drug Use." In *Teen Drug Use,* edited by G. Beschner and A. Friedman, 1–18. Lexington, MA: D.C. Heath, 1986.

Briske, P. "Rural Eighth-Graders Using More Drugs Than Urban Kids." *The Times* (27 January 2000): 3. Available http://www.thetimesonline.com.

Bureau of Justice Statistics (BJS). *Prisoners: Drugs and Crime Facts.* U.S. Department of Justice, Office of Justice Programs (OJP), 2004. Available http://www.ojp.usdoj.gov/bjs/dcf/duc.htm.

Bureau of Justice Statistics (BJS), *Drug Use and Dependence, State and Federal Prisoners.* U.S. Department of Justice (USDOJ), Office of Justice Programs (OJP), 2006. Available http//: www.ojp.usdoj.gov/bjs/pub/ascii/dudsfp04.txt.

CBS News. *Drug Advertising Skyrockets.* New York, NY: CBS Worldwide Inc, 13 February 2002. Available http://www.cbsnews.com/stories/2002/02/13/health/printable329293.shtml.

Center for Substance Abuse Research (CESAR). *First Time Users of Pain Relievers Continue to Surpass All Other Drugs; Number of New Ecstasy and Stimulant Users Increases.* 17 September 2007. Available http://www.cesar.umd.edu.

Clinton, Bill. My quest to Improve Care. *Newsweek.* Volume CXLVII: (15 May 2006):50-53.

Combs, S. (Texas Comptroller of Public Accounts). "Bordering the Future: Crime — Line of Fire." *Window on State Government* (7 April 1999). Available http://www.window.state.tx.us/border/c10/ch10.html.

Critser, G. "Oh, How Happy We Will Be: Pills, Paradise, and the Profits of the Drug Companies." *Harper's Magazine* (June 1996): 39–48.

Critser, G. *Generation RX: How Prescription Drugs Are Altering American Lives, Minds and Bodies.* Boston, MA: Houghton-Mifflin, 2005.

Delaney, W., J. W. Grube, and G. M. Ames. "Predicting Likelihood of Seeking Help Through the Employee Assistance Program Among Salaried and Union Hourly Employees." *Addiction,* 93 (1998): 399–410.

Drug Strategies. *Keeping Score: What We Are Getting for Our Federal Drug Control Dollars 1995.* Washington, DC: 1995.

Edelson, E. "Drug Use in the Workplace Plummets." *APB News, Inc.* (7 February 2000): 3. Available http://www.cannabisnews.com/news/4/thread4627.shtml.

Farah, J. Invasion USA: Mexican Drug Cartels Take Over U.S. Cities. *WorldNet Daily,* 18 June 2006. Available http://www.worldnetdaily.com/news/article.asp?article_id=50518.

Goldstein, A. *Addiction from Biology to Drug Policy.* New York: Oxford University Press, 2001.

Goode, E. *Drugs in American Society,* 5th ed. Boston, MA: McGraw-Hill College, 1999.

Goode, E. *Drugs in American Society,* 6th ed. New York: McGraw-Hill, 2005.

Harlow, C. W. "Profile of Jail Inmates." Bureau of Justice Statistics. NCJ-164620, April 1998, revised June 1998. Available http://www.ojp.usdoj.gov/bjs/pub/ascii/parip.txt.

IMS Health, "World Pharmaceutical Market Summary. Sales Through Retail Pharmacies." 2007. Available http://marketing.imshealth.com/mk/get/wpnnewsJuly07.

Johnston, L. D., P. M. O'Malley, J. G. Bachman, and J. E. Schulenberg. *Monitoring the Future: National Survey Results on Drug Use, 1975–2002, Volume I: Secondary School Students.* Bethesda, MD: National Institute on Drug Abuse, 2003.

Join Together Online. "Workplace Drug Testing Slows with Economy." *Join Together Online,* Boston University School of Public Health (22 May 2003): 1. Available http://www.jointogether.org/jtodirect.

Karberg, J. C. and D. J. James. *Bureau of Justice Statistics (BJS): Special Report, Substance Dependence, Abuse, and Treatment of Jail Inmates, 2002.* Washington, DC: U.S. Department of Justice, Office of Justice Programs, 2002.

Kilbourne, J. "Advertising Addiction: The Alcohol Industry's Hard Sell." *Multinational Monitor* (June 1989): 13–16.

Kusinitz, M. "Drug Use Around the World." In *Encyclopedia of Psychoactive Drugs,* edited by S. Snyder. Series 2. New York: Chelsea House, 1988.

Larson, S. L., J. Eyeman, M. S. Foster, and J. C. Gfoerer. *Worker Substance Use and Workplace Policies and Program* (DHHS Publication No. SMA 07-4273, Analytic Series A-29). Rockville, MD: Substance Abuse and Mental Health Services Administration, Office of Applied Studies, 2007.

Lenson, D. *On Drugs.* Minneapolis, MN: University of Minnesota Press, 1995.

Levinthal, C. F. *Drugs, Behavior, and Modern Society.* Boston, MA: Allyn and Bacon, 1996.

McBride, D. C., and C. B. McCoy. "The Drugs–Crime Relationship: An Analytical Framework." In *Drugs, Crime, and Justice,* edited by L. K. Gaines and B. Kraska, 100–119. Prospect Heights, IL: Waveland Press, 2003.

McShane, L. "Cops Are Crooks in N.Y.'s 30th Precinct." *Salt Lake Tribune* 238 (18 April 1994): A-5.

Monroe, J. "What Is Addiction?" *Current Health* 2 (January 1996): 16–19.

National Institute on Drug Abuse (NIDA). "NIDA Plays Key Role in Studying Links Between AIDS and Drug Abuse." *NIDA Notes* 10, no. 3 (May/June 1995): 1.

National Institute on Drug Abuse (NIDA). *Principles of Drug Addiction Treatment,* National Institutes of Health Publication No. 99-4180, October 1999.

National Institute on Drug Abuse (NIDA). *Drugs and HIV.* U.S. Department of Health and Human Services (USDHHS). Bethesda, MD: U.S. Government Printing Office, 2007.

National Survey on Drug Use and Health (NSDUH). *The NSDUH Report: Patterns and Trends in Nonmedical Prescription Pain Reliever Use: 2002 to 2005.* Rockville, MD: Substance Abuse and Mental Health Services Administration, Office of Applied Studies, 2007.

Nichols, K. "The Other Performance-Enhancing Drugs." *The Chronicle of Higher Education,* LI (17 December 2004): A11.

Nielsen Media Research. *1998 Report on Television.* Northbrook, IL: Nielsen, 1998.

Office of National Drug Control Policy (ONDCP). *Drug Data Summary.* Drug Policy Information Clearinghouse, Rockville, MD: March 2003. Available www.whitehousedrugpolicy.gov.

Office of National Drug Control Policy (ONDCP). *Pulse Check: Trends in Drug Abuse.* Washington, DC: Executive Office of the President, Office of National Drug Control Policy, 2002.

Pear, R. "Marketing Tied to Increase in Prescription Drug Sales." *New York Times* (20 September 2000): A16.

Pharmacy Times. Generic Pharmacy RX Report, a Supplement to *Pharmacy Times.* "Pharmaceutical Fraud." (December 2005): 5.

Pharmacy Times, Generic Rx Product Report. "Did You Know." (Spring 2003): 3.

Pharmacy Times. "Drug Spending Increases Dramatically in 8 Years." 73 (July 2007): 2.

Publishers Group. *Prescription Drugs.* Plymouth, MN: 2004. Available http://www.streetdrugs.org/prescription.htm.

Reynolds, G. S. and W. E. Lehman. "Levels of Substance Use and Willingness to Use the Employee Assistance Program." *Journal of Behavioral Health Services & Research,* 30 (2003): 238–248.

Robert Wood Johnson Foundation. *Substance Abuse: The Nation's Number One Health Problem.* Prepared by the Schneider Institute for Health Policy for the Robert Wood Johnson Foundation, Brandeis University. Princeton, NJ: Robert Wood Johnson Foundation, February 2001.

Rylander, C. K. (Texas Comptroller of Public Accounts). "Bordering the Future: Crime — Line of Fire." *Window on State Government* (7 April 1999). Available http://www.window.state.tx.us/border/ch10/ch10.html.

Schecter, M. "Serotonergic-Dopaminergic Mediation of 3, 4-Methylenedioxy-Methamphetamine (MDMA, Ecstasy)." *Pharmacology, Biochemistry and Behavior* 31 (1989): 817–824.

Spake, A. "Natural Hazards." In *Annual Editions: Drugs, Society, and Behavior 2002/2003,* edited by H. T. Wilson, 101–106. Guilford, CT: McGraw-Hill/Dushkin, 2002.

Steward, P., and G. Sitarmiah. "America's Heartland Grapples with Rise of Dangerous Drug." *The Christian Science Monitor* (13 November 1997): 1, 18.

Substance Abuse and Mental Health Services Administration (SAMHSA). *Overview of Findings from the 2003 National Survey on Drug Use and Health.* Rockville, MD: Office of Applied Studies, NSDUH Series H-24, DHHS Publication No. SMA 04-3963, 2004.

Substance Abuse and Mental Health Services Administration (SAMHSA), Office of Applied Studies (OAS). *The Relationship Between Family Structure and Adolescent Substance Use.* Rockville, MD: U.S. Department of Health and Human Services, July 1996.

Substance Abuse and Mental Health Services Administration (SAMHSA). *National Survey on Drug Use and Health (NSDUH) Report. Substance Use Disorder and Serious Psychological Distress by Employment Status.* Rockville, MD: Substance Abuse and Mental Health Services Administration, Office of Applied Studies, 2006.

Substance Abuse and Mental Health Services Administration (SAMHSA). *Results from the 2006 National Survey on Drug Use and Health: National Findings.* Rockville, MD: Substance Abuse and Mental Health Services Administration, 2007a.

Substance Abuse and Mental Health Services Administration (SAMHSA), Office of Applied Studies. *The National Survey on Drug Use and Health (NSDUH) Report. Worker Substance Use, by Industry Category.* Rockville, MD: Substance Abuse and Mental Health Services Administration, 2007b.

Szasz, T. *Our Right to Drugs: The Case for a Free Market.* Westport, CT: Praeger, 1992.

Thio, A. *Deviant Behavior,* 2nd ed. Boston: Houghton Mifflin, 1983: 332–333.

Thio, A. *Deviant Behavior,* 4th ed. New York: Harper-Collins College, 1995.

Thio, A. *Deviant Behavior,* 6th ed., New York: Pearson Education, 2000.

U.S. Department of Justice (USDOJ). *Information Brief: Prescription Drug Abuse and Youth.* Johnstown, PA: National Drug Intelligence Center, 2004. Available http://www.usdoj.gov/ndic/pubs/1765/.

Venturelli, P. J. "Drugs in Schools: Myths and Reality." In *Annals of the American Academy of Political and Social Science 567,* edited by W. Hinkle and S. Henry, Thousand Oaks, CA: Sage, 2000.

Walter, S. "Holistic Health." *The Illustrated Encyclopedia of Body–Mind Disciplines,* edited by N. Alison, 1–2. New York: The Rosen Publishing Group, Inc., 1999. Available http://ahha.org/rosen.htm.

Wire Services. "Cocaine Kingpin Escapes After Bloody Shootout." *Salt Lake Tribune* 244 (23 July 1992): A-1.

Worldpress.org. *Viewpoints: Mexico: Drug Cartels a Growing Threat,* 2 November 2006. Available http://www.worldpress.org/pring_article.cfm?article_id=2i669%dont=yes.

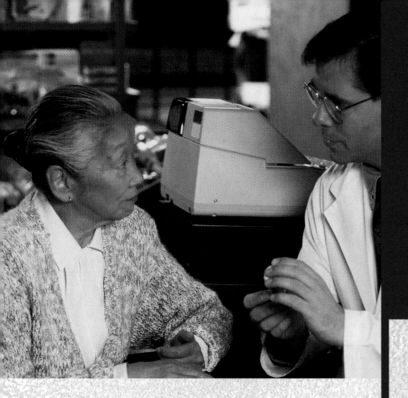

CHAPTER 2

Explaining Drug Use and Abuse

Did You Know?

- O Contrary to public perception, addiction is a complex disease.
- O Most drugs of abuse include both physical and psychological addictions.
- O Every culture has experienced problems with drug use or abuse. As far back as 2240 B.C., Hammurabi, the Babylonian king and lawgiver, addressed the problems associated with excessive use of alcohol.
- O Today, drugs are more potent than they were years ago.
- O According to biological theories, drug abuse has an innate physical beginning stemming from physical characteristics that cause certain individuals either to experiment with or to crave drugs to the point of abuse.
- O Abuse of drugs by some people may represent an attempt to relieve underlying psychiatric disorders.
- O No single theory can explain why most people use drugs.
- O People who perceive themselves as drug users are more likely to develop serious drug abuse problems.

 Drugs and Society Online is a great source for additional drugs and society information for both students and instructors.
Visit **http://drugsandsociety.jbpub.com** to find a variety of useful tools for learning, thinking, and teaching.

Learning Objectives

On completing this chapter you will be able to:

- ◎ List three to five major contributing factors responsible for addiction.
- ◎ List and briefly explain three models used to describe addiction.
- ◎ List six reasons why drug use or abuse is a more serious problem today than it was in the past.
- ◎ List and briefly describe the genetic and biophysical theories that biologically explain how drug use often leads to abuse.
- ◎ Explain how drugs of abuse act as positive reinforcers.
- ◎ Explain the relationships between some mental disorders and possible effects of certain drugs.
- ◎ Briefly define and explain reinforcement or learning theory and some of its applications to drug use and abuse.
- ◎ List and briefly describe the four sociological theories broadly known as social influence theories.
- ◎ Describe symptoms and indicators of possible drug use or abuse in childhood behavior patterns.
- ◎ List and describe three factors in the learning process that Howard Becker believes first-time users go through before they become attached to using illicit, psychoactive drugs.
- ◎ Define the following concepts as they relate to drug use: primary and secondary deviance, master status, and retrospective interpretation.
- ◎ Explain how Reckless's containment theory accounts for the roles of both internal and external controls regarding the attraction to drug use.
- ◎ Understand how making low-risk and high-risk drug choices directly affects drug use.

Introduction

Chapter 1 provided an overview of drug use. In this chapter, we focus on the major explanations of drug use and/or abuse. The questions we explore are these: Why would anyone voluntarily consume drugs when they are not medically needed or required? Why are some people attracted to altering their minds? Why are others uneasy and uncomfortable with the euphoric effects of recreational drug use? Why do people subject their bodies and minds to the harmful effects of repetitive drug use, eventual addiction, and relapse back into drug use? What logical reasons could explain such apparently irrational behavior?

Following are three perspectives regarding drug use.

First perspective:

Yes, I use a lot of drugs. I like the high from weed [marijuana], the buzz from coke [cocaine], and liquor also. I like psychedelic drugs but can't do them often because one, they are harder to get, and two, I work all the time and go to school at night. Psychedelics require big-time commitment and I just don't have that amount of time anymore to play around with intense mind trips. I think I am biologically attracted to drugs. What else would explain the desire to get high all the time? Some of my friends are worse than me. They don't just hang with the desire to continually want to get high, they just do it. One friend of mine does not accomplish much; my other two friends are coke addicts but they say they are not addicted, they claim to just like it. I don't think a day goes by, unless I am sick with the flu or something, that I don't get at least a little buzzed on some drug. My wife does not do any drugs, but hey, she's cool with my drug use as long as I keep working every day. *(From Venturelli's research files, graduate student and full-time insurance claims adjuster, age 28, July 12, 2000.)*

Second perspective:

When you ask about drug use, I literally draw a blank. This topic is really unknown to me. In my family, my grandparents on my dad's side were big-time drinkers. I think . . . my dad's experiences and especially . . . the car crash that killed my grandparents when they were in their 50s while coming home from a wedding after drinking heavily, affected my dad very much. My mom comes from a Mormon family, so, obviously she also does not drink any alcohol. My parents raised me and my three brothers without any examples or experiences regarding drug use. In my family, my wife and I hardly ever use any types of drugs — not even much of over-the-counter drugs. Occasionally, I will have a half a glass of wine several times a year, but I have to admit, I would rather be drinking water or freshly made fruit juice. I just do not like the taste and the mild effect that such a small amount of alcohol has on me. As you can imagine, I am very much against the use of any types of drugs, especially the illicit types of drugs. Drugs are addictive and people should not be doing or taking drugs. Taking drugs for fun does not have any real positive outcomes, and in the end, causes a lot of misery to families, and medical problems. I am quite certain that all of our family friends are nondrinkers and I know for certain that our best friends do not use any of the recreational types of drugs. You could say our lives are really drug free. Everything we do as a family is in the absence of drug use. *(From Venturelli's research files, male graduate university student, age 36, May 19, 2007.)*

Third perspective:

Yes, I have friends who try to tell me to slow down when we are smoking weed and drinking. I just like to get high until I am about to pass out. If I could, I would be high all day without any time out. Never think about quitting or slowing down when it comes to drugs. The only time I am happy is when I am completely zonked out. I guess I am a little attached to these drugs — I am addicted to them! *(From Venturelli's research files, male public high school student in a small Midwestern city, age 15, September 9, 1996.)*

The preceding excerpts show extensive variations in values and attitudes regarding drug use. The perspective of the first interviewee represents a type of drug user who is powerfully attracted to drug use. He appears to believe that his attraction to drugs has a biological basis and he wants to feel the effects of drugs on a daily basis. The perspective of the second interviewee represents a type of user who shuns any alteration of his reality. Finally, the perspective of the third interviewee represents a type of drug user who is unaware of the pitfalls of drug addiction and is recklessly involved with substance abuse. These three views represent only a small fraction of the reasons and motivations that push people to either use or not use drugs.

Why the differences in drug use? In this chapter, we offer answers to this question by examining the motivations underlying drug use. We offer different major theoretical explanations about what causes people to initially use and often eventually abuse drugs.

To accomplish these goals, this chapter frames these and literally dozens of other perspectives *within* the major biological, psychological, and sociological perspectives. Similar to the United States, nearly all other countries are experiencing increasing amounts of drug use within certain subcultures. Moreover, as we attempt to offer major scientific and theoretical explanations for drug use, we should be able to develop a much more comprehensive understanding of why drugs are so seductive, and why so many people succumb, become addicted, and inflict damage to themselves and others as they become hijacked by the nonmedical use of drugs. Not only does this hold true for members of U.S. society, but also for countless numbers of others throughout the world.

Drug Use: A Timeless Affliction

Historical records document drug use as far back as 2240 B.C., when Hammurabi, the Babylonian king and lawgiver, addressed the problems associated with drinking alcohol. Even before then, the Sumerian people of Asia Minor, who created the cuneiform (wedge-shaped) alphabet, included references to a "joy plant" that dates from about 5000 B.C. Experts indicate that the plant was an opium poppy used as a sedative (O'Brien et al. 1992).

As noted in Chapter 1, virtually every culture has experienced problems with drug use or abuse. Today's drug use problems are part of a very long and rich tradition.

> These [intoxicating] substances have formed a bond of union between men of opposite hemispheres, the uncivilized and the civilized; they have forced passages which, once open, proved of use for other purposes; they produced in ancient races characteristics which have endured to the present day, evidencing the marvelous degree of intercourse that existed between different peoples just as certainly and

exactly as a chemist can judge the relations of two substances by their reactions. (Louis Lewin, *Phantasica,* in Rudgley 1993, 3)

The quest for explaining drug use is more important than ever as the problem continues to evolve. There are many reasons why drug use and abuse are even more serious issues now than they were in the past:

1. From 1960 to the present, drug use has become a widespread phenomenon.

2. Today, drugs are much more potent than they were years ago. The drug content of marijuana in 1960 was 1% to 2%; today, due to new cultivation techniques, it varies from 4% to 6%.

3. Whether they are legal or not, drugs are extremely popular. Their sale is a multibillion dollar a year business, with a major influence on many national economies.

4. More so today than years ago, both licit and illicit drugs are introduced and experimented with by youth at a younger age. These drugs are often supplied by older siblings, friends, and acquaintances.

5. Through the media, people in today's society are more affected by direct television and radio advertising, especially by drug companies that are "pushing" their newest drugs. Similarly, advertisements and sales promotions (coupons) for alcohol, coffee, tea, and vitamins are targeted to receptive consumer audiences, as identified through sophisticated market research.

6. Today, there is greater availability and wider dissemination of drug information. Literally thousands of web sites provide information on drug usage, chat rooms devoted to drug enthusiasts, and instructions on how to make or purchase drugs on the Internet. On a daily basis, hundreds of thousands of "spam" emails are automatically sent regarding information on purchasing OTC drugs and prescription drugs without medical authorization (medical prescription).

7. Crack and other manufactured drugs offer potent effects at low cost, vastly multiplying the damage potential of drug abuse (Clatts et al. 2008; Inciardi et al. 1993; Office of National Drug Control Policy [ONDCP] 2003).

8. Drug use endangers the future of a society by harming its youth and potentially destroying the lives of many young men and women. When gateway drugs, such as alcohol and

tobacco, are used at an early age, a strong probability exists that the use will progress to other drugs, such as marijuana, cocaine, and amphetamines. Early drug use will likely lead to a lifelong habit, which usually has serious implications for the future.

9. Drug use and especially drug dealing are becoming major factors in the growth of crime rates among the young. Membership in violent delinquent gangs is growing at an alarming rate. Violent shootings, drive-by killings, carjacking, and "wilding" occur frequently in cities (and increasingly in small towns).

10. Seven in 10 drug users work full time (*USA Today* 1999). More recent findings also indicate that of 2.9 million adults ages 18 to 64 employed full time who had co-occurring substance use disorder and serious psychological distress, nearly 60% were not treated for either problem, and less than 5% were treated for both problems (Substance Abuse and Mental Health Services Administration [SAMHSA] 2006). Such startling findings regarding employment and drug use lead to not only decreased productivity, absenteeism, job turnover, and medical costs, but also near or serious accidents and mistakes caused by workers.

11. Another related problem is that drug use is especially serious today because we have become highly dependent on the expertise of others and highly dependent on technology. For example, the operation of sophisticated machines and electronic equipment requires that workers and professionals be free of the intoxicating effects of mind-altering drugs. Imagine the chilling fact that on a daily basis, a certain percentage of pilots, surgeons, and heavy-equipment operators are under the influence of mind-altering drugs while working, or that a certain percentage of school-bus drivers are under the effects of, say, marijuana and/or cocaine.

With remarkable and unsurpassed excellence in scientific, technological, and electronic accomplishments, one might think that in the United States, drug use and abuse would be considered irrational behavior. One might also think that the allure of drugs would diminish on the basis of the statistically high proportions of accidents, crimes, domestic violence and other relationship problems, and early deaths that result from the use and abuse of both licit and illicit drugs. Yet, as the latest drug use figures show (see Chapter 1), knowledge of these effects is often not a deterrent to drug use.

Considering these costs, what explains the continuing use and abuse of drugs? What could possibly sustain and feed the attraction to use mind-altering drugs? Why are drugs used when the consequences are so well documented and predictable?

In answering these questions, we need to recall from Chapter 1 some basic reasons why people take drugs:

1. People may be searching for pleasure.
2. Drugs may relieve stress or tension or provide a temporary escape for people with excessive anxieties or severe depression.
3. Peer pressure is a strong influence, especially for young people.
4. In some cases, drugs may enhance religious or mystical experiences.
5. Drugs are used for enhancing recreational pursuits such as the popular use of Ecstasy at raves and music festivals.
6. Some believe that illicit use of drugs can enhance work performance, such as the use of cocaine by stockbrokers, office workers, and lawyers.
7. Drugs can relieve pain and the symptoms of an illness.

Although these reasons may indicate some underlying causes of excessive or abusive drug use, they also suggest that the variety and complexity of explanations and motivations are almost infinite. For any one individual, it is seldom clear when the drug use shifts from nondestructive use to abuse and addiction. When we consider the wide use of such licit drugs as alcohol, nicotine, and caffeine, we make the following discoveries: (1) More than 88% of the U.S. population use different types of drugs on a daily basis (National Institute on Drug Abuse [NIDA] 2007; SAMHSA 1998); (2) more than half (54%) have tried an illicit drug by the time they finish high school; and (3) three out of four students (75%) have consumed alcohol (more than just a few sips) by the end of high school, and nearly half (47%) had done so by 8th grade (Johnston, O'Malley, Bachman, and Schulenberg 2003).

Further, as we will see in later chapters, some drugs can mimic many of the hundreds of moods people can experience. We can, therefore, begin to understand why the explanations for drug use and abuse are multiple and depend on both socialization experiences and biological differences. As a result of these two factors, which imply hundreds of variations, explanations for drug use cannot be forced into one or two theories.

Researchers have tackled the drug use and abuse question from three major theoretical positions: biological, psychological, and sociological perspectives. Although the remainder of this chapter discusses these three major types of theoretical explanations, before delving into them, we begin with a discussion of the motivation or "engine" responsible for the consistent attraction to recreational and/or nonmedical use of drugs — namely, addiction.

The Origin and Nature of Addiction

Humans can develop a very intense relationship with chemicals. Most people have chemically altered their mood at some point in their lives, if only by consuming a cup of coffee or a glass of white wine, and a majority do so occasionally. Yet for some individuals, chemicals become the center of their lives, driving their behavior and determining their priorities, even to the point at which catastrophic consequences to their health and social well-being ensue. Although the word *addiction* is an agreed-upon term referring to such behavior, little agreement exists as to the origin, nature, or boundaries of the concept of addiction. It has been classified as a very bad habit, a failure of will or morality, a symptom of other problems, or a chronic disease in its own right.

Although public perception of drug abuse and addiction as a major social problem has waxed and waned over the past 20 years, the social costs of addiction have not: The total criminal justice, health, insurance, and other costs in the United States are roughly estimated at $90 to $185 billion annually, depending on the source. Despite numerous prevention efforts, the "War on Drugs," and a falloff in the heavy drug use of the 1960s and 1970s, lessons learned in one decade seem to quickly pass out of awareness.

For example, the rate of lifetime use of marijuana among 12th graders in 1991 was approximately 36%; in 2005, it had increased to approximately 45% (Johnston et al. 2006). For marijuana, the highest initiation rates are now seen in grades 7 through 11, although in 2003 6.1% of 8th graders reported that they had tried marijuana by the end of 6th grade (Johnston, O'Malley, Bachman, and Schulenberg 2003). Alcohol use also remains very widespread among today's teenagers. Three out of every four (75%) have consumed alcohol (more than just a few sips) by the end of high school; about two fifths (41%) have done so by 8th grade. In fact, more than half (58%) of the 12th graders and a fifth (20%) of the 8th graders in 2005 reported having been drunk at least once in their life (Johnston et al. 2006). Another study found that more than one fourth (28%) of high school students had consumed more than a few sips of alcohol before age 13, compared to 18% who had smoked a whole cigarette and 10% who had tried marijuana before that age (Centers for Disease Control and Prevention [CDCP] 2004). Finally, very recent findings indicate that the percentage of U.S. 8th graders who perceive the harmfulness of Ecstasy, LSD, and inhalant use continues to decrease from 43% in 2004 to 33% in 2006 (Center for Substance Abuse Research [CESAR] 2007). Government officials and researchers believe that decreases in perceived harmfulness of using a drug are often leading indicators of future increases in actual use of that drug. "The authors of this study suggest that these trends may reflect "generational forgetting" of the dangers of these drugs, leaving the newer cohorts vulnerable to a resurgence of use" (CESAR 2007, 7). From these major studies, it is apparent that both licit and illicit types of drugs continue to penetrate into increasingly younger age groups.

■ Defining Addiction

Addiction can be described as a complex disease. In 1964, the World Health Organization (WHO) of the United Nations defined it as "a state of periodic or chronic intoxication detrimental to the individual and society, which is characterized by an overwhelming desire to continue taking the drug and to obtain it by any means" (pp. 9–10). Accordingly, addiction is characterized as compulsive, at times uncontrollable, drug craving, seeking, and use that persist even in the face of extremely negative consequences (NIDA 1999). This relentless pursuit of a drug of choice occurs despite the fact that the drug is usually harmful and injurious to bodily and mental functions.

The word *addiction*, derived from the Latin verb *addicere*, refers to the process of binding to things. Today, the word largely refers to a chronic adherence to drugs. This can include both physical and psychological dependence. *Physical dependence* is the body's need to constantly have the drug or drugs, and *psychological dependence* is the mental inability to stop using the drug or drugs.

The *Diagnostic and Statistical Manual of Mental Disorders*, 4th edition, text revision *(DSM-IV-TR)*, published by the American Psychiatric Association (2000), differentiates among intoxication by, abuse of, and addiction to drugs. Although *substance abuse* is considered maladaptive, leading to recurrent adverse consequences or impairment, it is carefully differentiated from true addiction, called *substance dependence*, the essential feature of which is continued use despite significant substance-related problems known to the user. Many of the following features are usually present:

- *Tolerance.* The need for increased amounts or diminished effect of same amount.
- *Withdrawal.* The experience of a characteristic withdrawal syndrome for the specific substance, which can be avoided by taking closely related substances. Unsuccessful attempts to cut down.
- *Compulsive.* An increasing amount of time spent in substance-related activities, such as obtaining, using, and recovering from its effects.

Models of Addiction

Various models attempt to describe the essential nature of drug addiction. Newspaper accounts of "inebriety" in the 19th and early 20th centuries contain an editorializing undertone that looks askance at the poor morals and lifestyle choices followed by the inebriate. This view has been termed the **moral model**, and although it may seem outdated from a modern scientific standpoint, it still characterizes an attitude among many traditional North Americans and members of many ethnic groups.

The prevailing concept or model of addiction in America is the **disease model**. Most proponents of this concept specify addiction to be a chronic and progressive disease, over which the sufferer has no control. This model originated in part from research performed by Jellinek, one of the founders of addiction studies (1960), among members of Alcoholics Anonymous (AA). He observed a seemingly inevitable progression in his subjects, which they made many failed attempts to arrest. This philosophy is currently espoused by the recovery fellowships of AA and Narcotics Anonymous (NA) and the treatment field in general. It has even permeated the psychiatric and medical establishments' standard definitions of addiction. There are many variations within the broad rubric of the disease model.

This model has been bitterly debated: viewpoints range from fierce adherence to equally fierce opposition, with intermediate views casting the disease concept as a convenient myth (Smith et al. 1985).

Those who view addiction as another manifestation of something gone awry with the personality system adhere to the **characterological or personality predisposition model**. Every school of psychoanalytic, neopsychoanalytic, and psychodynamic psychotherapy has its specific "take" on the subject of addiction (Frosch 1985). Tangentially, many addicts are also diagnosed with **personality disorders** (formerly known as "character disorders"), such as impulse control disorders and sociopathy. Although few addicts are treated by **psychoanalysis** or psychoanalytic psychotherapy, a characterological type of model was a formative influence on the drug-free, addict-run, "therapeutic community" model, which uses harsh confrontation and time-extended, sleep-depriving group encounters. People who follow the therapeutic community model conclude that addicts must have withdrawn behind a **"double wall" of encapsulation**, where they failed to grow, making such techniques necessary.

KEY TERMS

moral model
the belief that people abuse alcohol because they choose to do so

disease model
the belief that people abuse alcohol because of some biologically caused condition

characterological or personality predisposition model
the view of chemical dependency as a symptom of problems in the development or operation of the system of needs, motives, and attitudes within the individual

personality disorders
a broad category of psychiatric disorders, formerly called "character disorders," that includes the antisocial personality disorder, borderline personality disorder, schizoid personality disorder, and others; these serious, ongoing impairments are difficult to treat

psychoanalysis
a theory of personality and method of psychotherapy originated by Sigmund Freud, focused on unconscious forces and conflicts and a series of psychosexual stages

"double wall" of encapsulation
an adaptation to pain and avoidance of reality, in which the individual withdraws emotionally and further anesthetizes himself or herself by chemical means

Others view addiction as a "career," a series of steps or phases with distinguishable characteristics. One career pattern of addiction includes six phases (Clinard and Meier 1992; Waldorf 1983):

1. Experimentation or initiation
2. Escalation (increasing use)
3. Maintenance or "taking care of business" (optimistic use of drugs coupled with successful job performance)
4. Dysfunction or "going through changes" (problems with constant use and unsuccessful attempts to quit)
5. Recovery or "getting out of the life" (arriving at a successful view about quitting and receiving drug treatment)
6. Ex-addict (having successfully quit)

■ Factors Contributing to Addiction

Many, perhaps millions, of individuals use or even occasionally abuse drugs without compromising their basic health, legal, and occupational status and social relationships. Why do a significant minority become caught up in abuse and addictive behavior? The answer stems from the fact that many (i.e., not a single) factors generally contribute to an individual becoming addicted (Syvertsen 2008). Table 2.1 represents a compilation of factors identified as complicit in the origin or "etiology" of addiction, taken from the fields of psychology, sociology, and addiction studies.

In addition to the social and cultural factors listed in Table 2.1, other "cultural" risk factors for development of abuse include the following:

- Drinking at times other than at meals
- Drinking alone
- Drinking defined as an antistress and antianxiety potion
- Patterns of solitary drinking
- Drinking defined as a rite of passage into an adult role
- Recent introduction of a chemical into a social group with insufficient time to develop informal social control over its use (Marshall 1979)

It is important to recall that the "mix" of risk factors differs for each person. It varies according to social, cultural, and age groups and individual and family idiosyncrasies. Most addiction treatment professionals believe that it is difficult, if not impossible, to tease out these factors before treatment, when the user is still "talking to a chemical," or during early treatment, when the brain and body are still recuperating from the effects of long-term abuse. Once a stable sobriety is established, one can begin to address any underlying problems. An exception is the mentally ill chemical abuser, whose treatment requires special considerations from the outset.

In addition to the factors just listed, a number of age-dependent stressors and conflicts sometimes promote drug misuse. Risk factors that apply especially to adolescents include the following:

- Peer norms favoring use
- Misperception of peer norms (users set the tone)
- Power of age group (peer norms versus other social influences)
- Conflicts that generate anxiety or guilt, such as dependence versus independence, adult maturational tasks versus fear, new types of roles versus familiar safe roles
- Teenage risk taking, sense of omnipotence or invulnerability
- Use defined as a rite of passage into adulthood
- Use perceived as glamorous, sexy, facilitating intimacy, fun, and so on

Risk factors that apply especially to middle-aged individuals include the following:

- Loss of meaningful role or occupational identity due to retirement
- Loss, grief, or isolation due to loss of parents, divorce, or departure of children ("empty nest syndrome")
- Loss of positive body image
- Disappointment when life expectations are not met

Even in each of these age groups, a mix of factors is at play. The adolescent abuser might have risk factors that were primarily neurological vulnerabilities, such as undiagnosed attention deficit hyperactivity disorder. Alternatively, he or she may experience failure and rejection at school, disappoint his or her parents, or be labeled odd, lazy, or unintelligent (Kelly and Ramundo 2006).

In response to the information presented in Table 2.1, a student who was a recovering alcoholic commented: "You're an alcoholic because you drink!" He had a good point: The mere presence of one, two, or more risk factors does not create addiction. Drugs must be available, they must be used, and they must become a pattern of adaptation to any of the many painful, threatening, uncomfortable, or unwanted sensations or stimuli that occur in the presence of genetic, psychosocial, or environmental risk factors. Prevention workers

Table 2.1 Risk Factors for Addiction

RISK FACTOR	LEADING TO THIS EFFECT
Biologically Based Factors (genetic, neurological, biochemical, and so on)	
• A less subjective feeling of intoxication	• More use to achieve intoxication (warning signs of abuse absent)
• Easier development of tolerance; liver enzymes adapt to increased use	• Easier to reach the addictive level
• Lack of resilience or fragility of higher (cerebral) brain functions	• Easy deterioration of cerebral functioning, impaired judgment, and social deterioration
• Difficulty in screening out unwanted or bothersome outside stimuli (low stimulus barrier)	• Feeling overwhelmed or stressed
• Tendency to amplify outside or internal stimuli (stimulus augmentation)	• Feeling attacked or panicked; need to avoid emotion
• Attention deficit hyperactivity disorder and other learning disabilities	• Failure, low self-esteem, or isolation
• Biologically based mood disorders (depression and bipolar disorders)	• Need to self-medicate against loss of control or pain of depression; inability to calm down when manic or to sleep when agitated
Psychosocial/Developmental "Personality" Factors	
• Low self-esteem	• Need to block out pain; gravitation to outsider groups
• Depression rooted in learned helplessness and passivity	• Use of a stimulant as an antidepressant
• Conflicts	• Anxiety and guilt
• Repressed and unresolved grief and rage	• Chronic depression, anxiety, or pain
• Post-traumatic stress syndrome (as in veterans and abuse victims)	• Nightmares or panic attacks
Social and Cultural Environment	
• Availability of drugs	• Easy frequent use
• Chemical-abusing parental model	• Sanction; no conflict over use
• Abusive, neglectful parents; other dysfunctional family patterns	• Pervasive sense of abandonment, distrust, and pain; difficulty in maintaining attachments
• Group norms favoring heavy use and abuse	• Reinforced, hidden abusive behavior that can progress without interference
• Misperception of peer norms	• Belief that most people use or favor use or think it's "cool" to use
• Severe or chronic stressors, as from noise, poverty, racism, or occupational stress	• Need to alleviate or escape from stress via chemical means
• "Alienation" factors: isolation, emptiness	• Painful sense of aloneness, normlessness, rootlessness, boredom, monotony, or hopelessness
• Difficult migration/acculturation with social disorganization, gender/generation gaps, or loss of role	• Stress without buffering support system

often note the presence of multiple messages encouraging use: the medical use of minor tranquilizers to offset any type of psychic discomfort; the marketing of alcohol as sexy, glamorous, adult, and facilitative of social interaction; and so forth.

The Vicious Cycle of Addiction

First, the man takes a drink, then the drink takes a drink, then the drink takes the man.
(Traditional Chinese proverb)

Drug addiction develops as a process, and it is not a sudden occurrence. The body makes simple physiological adaptations to the presence of alcohol and other drugs. For instance, brain cell tolerance and increased metabolic efficiency of the liver can develop, necessitating consumption of more of the chemical to achieve the desired effect. Physical dependence can also develop, in which cell adaptations cause withdrawal syndromes to occur in the absence of the chemical.

Other factors can promote the cycle of addiction. For instance, abuse impairs cerebral functioning, including memory, judgment, behavioral organization, ability to plan, ability to solve problems, and motor coordination. Thus, poor decision making, impaired and deviant behavior, and overall dysfunction result in adverse social consequences, such as accidents, loss of earning power and relationships, and impaired health. Such adverse social and health consequences cause pain, depression, and lowered self-esteem, which may result in further use of the drug as an emotional and physical anesthetic. The addict often adapts to this chronically painful situation by erecting a defense system of denial, minimization, and rationalization; the chemical blunting of reality may exacerbate this denial of reality. It is unlikely, at this point, that the addict or developing addict will feel compelled to cease or cut back on drug use on his or her own (Tarter et al. 1983).

Family, friends, and colleagues often unwittingly "enable" the maintenance and progression of addiction by making excuses for addicts, literally and figuratively bailing them out, taking up the slack, denying and minimizing their problems, and otherwise making it possible for addicts to avoid facing the reality and consequences of what they are doing to themselves and others. Although these friends may be motivated by simple naïveté, embarrassment, or misguided protectiveness, there are often hidden gains in taking up this role, known pop-

ularly as "codependency" (Beattie 1987). Varieties of cultural and organizational factors also operate in the workplace or school that allow denial of the existence or severity of abuse or dependency. This triad of personal denial, peer and kin denial and codependency, and institutional denial represents a formidable impediment to successful intervention and recovery (Miller 1995; Myers 1990).

■ Nondrug Addictions?

The addictive disease model and the 12-step recovery model followed by AA and NA have seemed so successful for both addicts and their families and friends that other unwanted syndromes have been added to the list of "addictions." The degree to which the concept of addiction fits these syndromes varies. Gambling, for example, shows progressive worsening, loss of control, relief of tension from the activity, and continuance despite negative (often disastrous) consequences experienced by the addicted gambler. Some recovering gamblers even claim to have experienced a form of withdrawal. Gamblers Anonymous is a fellowship that has formed to assist its members. Clearly, gambling

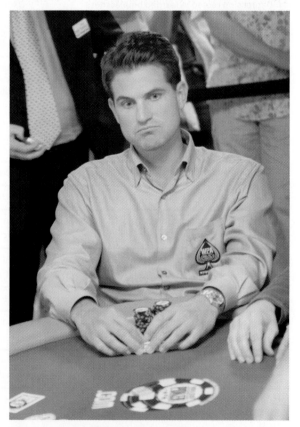

Like drug use, gambling can become addictive.

as an activity has much in common with chemical addictions, but it is debatable whether it belongs in the category of addiction (the *DSM-IV-TR* does not include it, for example).

Many other groups have followed in the footsteps of Gamblers Anonymous, including those related to eating (Overeaters Anonymous) and sexual relationships (The Augustine Fellowship, Sex and Love Addicts Anonymous). In recent years, any excessive or unwanted behaviors, including excess shopping, chocolate consumption, and even Internet use, have been labeled "addictions," which has led to satirical reporting in the press. Addiction professionals lament the overdefinition, which they believe trivializes the seriousness and suffering of rigorously defined addictions.

Major Theoretical Explanations: Biological

As noted in Chapter 1, biological explanations have tended to use genetic theories and the disease model to explain drug addiction. The view that alcoholism is a sickness dates back approximately 200 years (Conrad and Schneider 1980; Heitzeg 1996). The disease perspective is upheld by Jellinek's (1960) view that alcoholism largely involves a loss of control over drinking and that the drinker experiences clearly distinguishable phases in his or her drinking patterns. For example, concerning alcoholism, the illness affects the abuser to the point of loss of control. Thus, the disease model views drug abuse as an illness in need of treatment or therapy.

According to biological theories, drug abuse has a beginning stemming from physical characteristics that cause certain individuals either to experiment with or to crave drugs to the point of abusive use. **Genetic and biophysiological theories** explain addiction in terms of genetics, brain dysfunction, and biochemical patterns.

Biological explanations emphasize that the **central nervous system** (CNS) reward sensors in some people are more sensitive to drugs, making the drug experience more pleasant and more rewarding for these individuals (Khantzian 1998; Mathias 1995). In contrast, others find the effects of drugs of abuse very unpleasant; such people are not likely to be attracted to these drugs (Farrar and Kearns 1989).

Most experts acknowledge that biological factors play an essential role in drug abuse. These factors likely determine how the brain responds to these drugs and why such substances prove addic-

tive. It is thought that by identifying the nature of the biological systems that contribute to drug abuse problems, improved prevention and treatment methods can be developed (Koob 2000).

All the major biological explanations related to drug abuse assume that these substances exert their **psychoactive effects** by altering brain chemistry or neuronal (basic functional cell of the brain) activity. Specifically, the drugs of abuse interfere with the functioning of **neurotransmitters**, chemical messengers used for communication between brain regions (see Chapter 4 for details). The following sections detail three principal biological theories that help explain why some drugs are abused and why certain people are more likely to become addicted when using these substances.

■ Abused Drugs as Positive Reinforcers

Biological research has shown that stimulating some brain regions with an electrode causes very pleasurable sensations. In fact, laboratory animals would rather self-administer stimulation to these brain areas than eat or engage in sex. It has been demonstrated that drugs of abuse also activate these same pleasure centers of the brain (Weiss 1999).

It is generally believed that most drugs with abuse potential enhance pleasure centers by causing the release of specific brain neurotransmitters such as **dopamine** (Bespalov et al. 1999). Brain cells become accustomed to the presence of these neurotransmitters and crave them when they are absent, leading the person to seek more drugs (Spanagel and

KEY TERMS

genetic and biophysiological theories
explanations of addiction in terms of genetic brain dysfunction and biochemical patterns

central nervous system
one of the major divisions of the nervous system, composed of the brain and the spinal cord

psychoactive effects
how drug substances alter and affect the brain's mental functions

neurotransmitters
the chemical messengers released by nervous (nerve) cells for communication with other cells

dopamine
the brain transmitter believed to mediate the rewarding aspects of most drugs of abuse

Weiss 1999). In addition, it has been proposed that overstimulation of these brain regions by continual drug use "exhausts" these dopamine systems and leads to depression and an inability to experience normal pleasure (Volkow 1999).

Drug Abuse and Psychiatric Disorders

Biological explanations are thought to be responsible for the substantial overlap that exists between drug addiction and mental illness (NIDA 2007). Because of the similarities, severe drug dependence itself is classified as a form of psychiatric disorder by the American Psychiatric Association (see the discussion of the *DSM-IV-TR* classifications later in this chapter). For example, abuse of drugs can, in and of itself, cause mental conditions that mimic major psychiatric illness, such as schizophrenia, severe anxiety disorders, and suicidal depression (APA 2000). It is believed that these similarities occur as a result of common chemical factors that are altered both by drugs of abuse and during episodes of psychiatric illness (NIDA 1993). Several important potential consequences of this relationship may help us understand the nature of drug abuse problems.

1. *Psychiatric disorders and drug addiction sometimes occur simultaneously.* This conclusion is supported by the fact that substance abuse-related problems often coexist with other mental diseases such as conduct disorder, schizophrenia, and mood disorders (APA 2000). Due to the common mechanisms, drug abuse is likely to expose or worsen psychiatric illnesses, making management of these problems considerably more difficult (APA 2000).

2. *Therapies that are successful in treating psychiatric disorders may be useful in treating mental problems caused by drugs of abuse.* It is likely that many of the therapeutic lessons we learn about dealing with psychiatric illnesses can be useful in drug abuse treatment, and vice versa.

3. *Abuse of drugs by some people may represent an attempt to relieve underlying psychiatric disorders.* Such people commonly use CNS depressants such as alcohol to relieve anxiety, whereas CNS stimulants such as cocaine are frequently used by patients with depression disorders (Grinspoon 1993). In such cases, if the underlying psychiatric problem is relieved, the like-

lihood of successfully treating the drug abuse disorder improves substantially.

Genetic Explanations

One biological theory receiving scrutiny suggests that inherited traits can predispose some individuals to drug addiction (Lemonick with Park 2007). Such theories have been supported by the observation that increased frequency of alcoholism and drug abuse exists among children of alcoholics and drug abusers (APA 2000; Uhl et al. 1993). Using adoption records of some 3000 individuals from Sweden, researchers Cloninger, Gohman, and Sigvardsson conducted one of the most extensive research studies examining genetics and alcoholism. They found that ". . . children of alcoholic parents were likely to grow up to be alcoholics themselves, even in cases where the children were reared by nonalcoholic adoptive parents almost from birth" (Doweiko 2002). Such studies estimate that drug vulnerability due to genetic influences accounts for approximately 38% of all cases, whereas environmental and social factors account for the balance (Uhl et al. 1993).

Other studies attempting to identify the specific genes that may predispose the carrier to drug abuse problems have suggested that a brain target site (called a receptor — see Chapter 4 for details) for dopamine is altered in a manner that increases the drug abuse vulnerability (Radowitz 2003; Wyman 1997). Studies that test for genetic factors in complex behaviors such as drug abuse are very difficult to conduct and interpret. It is sometimes impossible to design experiments that distinguish among genetic, social, environmental, and psychological influences in human populations. For example, inherited traits are known to be major contributors to psychiatric disorders, such as schizophrenia and depression. Many people with one of these illnesses also have a substance abuse disorder (APA 2000). A high incidence of an abnormal gene in a cocaine-abusing population, for example, not only may be linked to drug abuse behavior but also may be associated with depression or another psychiatric disorder (Uhl et al. 1992).

Theoretically, genetic factors can directly or indirectly contribute to drug abuse vulnerability in several ways:

1. Psychiatric disorders that are genetically determined may be relieved by taking drugs of abuse, thus encouraging their use.

2. In some people, reward centers of the brain may be genetically determined to be especially sensitive to addictive drugs; thus, the use of drugs by these people would be particularly pleasurable and would lead to a high rate of addiction.

3. Volkow states that "addiction is a medical condition" and that "[i]n the brains of addicts, there is reduced activity in the prefrontal cortex where rational thought can override impulsive behavior." (Lemonick with Park 2007).

4. Character traits, such as insecurity and vulnerability, that often lead to drug abuse behavior may be genetically determined, causing a high rate of addiction in people with those traits.

5. Factors that determine how difficult it is to break away from drug addiction may be genetically determined, causing severe craving or very unpleasant withdrawal effects in some individuals. People with this predisposition are less likely to abandon their drug of abuse.

The genetic theories for explaining drug abuse may help us to understand the reasons that drug addiction occurs in some individuals but not in others. In addition, if genetic factors play a major role in drug abuse, it might be possible to use genetic screening to identify those people who are especially vulnerable to drug abuse problems and to help such individuals avoid exposure to these substances.

Major Theoretical Explanations: Psychological

Psychological theories mostly deal with mental or emotional states, which are often associated with or exacerbated by social and environmental factors. Psychological explanations of addiction include one or more of the following: escape from reality, boredom (Burns 1997), inability to cope with anxiety, destructive self-indulgence to the point of constantly desiring intoxicants, blind compliance with drug-abusing peers, self-destructiveness, and conscious and unconscious ignorance regarding the harmful effects of abusing drugs. Freud established early psychological theories. He linked "primal addictions" with masturbation and postulated that all later addictions, including those involving alcohol and other drugs, were caused by ego impairments.

Freud said that drugs compensate for insecurities that stem from parental inadequacies, which

themselves may cause difficulty in adequately forming bonds of friendships. He claimed that alcoholism (see Chapter 8) is an expression of the death instinct, as are self-destruction, narcissism, and oral fixations. Although Freud's views represent interesting intuitive insights often not depicted in other theories, his theoretical concerns are difficult to observe and test, and they do not generate enough concrete data for verification.

■ Distinguishing Between Substance Abuse and Mental Disorders

The American Psychiatric Association has established widely accepted categories of diagnosis for behavioral disorders, including substance abuse. As standardized diagnostic categories, the characteristics of mental disorders have been analyzed by professional committees over many years and today are summarized in the *DSM-IV-TR.* In addition to categories for severe psychotic disorders and more common neurotic disorders, experts in the field of psychiatry have established specific diagnostic criteria for various forms of substance abuse. All patterns of drug abuse that are described in this text have a counterpart description in the *DSM-IV-TR* for medical professionals. For example, the *DSM-IV-TR* discusses the mental disorders resulting from the use or abuse of sedatives, hypnotics, or antianxiety drugs; alcohol; narcotics; amphetamine-like drugs; cocaine; caffeine; nicotine (tobacco); hallucinogens; phencyclidine (PCP); inhalants; and cannabis (marijuana). This manual of psychiatric diagnoses discusses in detail the mental disorders related to the drug use, the side effects of medications, and the consequences of toxic exposure to these substances (APA 2000).

Because of the similarities between, and the coexistence of, substance-related mental disorders and primary psychiatric disorders, it is sometimes difficult to distinguish between the two problems. However, for proper treatment to be rendered, the cause of psychological symptoms must be determined. According to *DSM-IV-TR* criteria, substance use (or abuse) disorders can be identified by the occurrence and consequence of dependence, abuse, intoxication, and withdrawal. These important distinguishing features of substance abuse disorders are discussed in detail in Chapter 5 and in conjunction with each drug group.

According to the *DSM-IV-TR,* the following information can also help distinguish between substance-induced and primary mental disorders: (1) personal and family medical, psychiatric, and drug histories; (2) physical examinations; and (3) laboratory tests to assess physiological functions and determine the presence or absence of drugs. However, the possibility of a primary mental disorder should not be excluded just because the patient is using drugs — remember, many drug users use drugs to self-medicate their primary psychiatric problems. The coexistence of underlying psychiatric problems in a drug user is suggested by the following circumstances: (1) The psychiatric problems do not match the usual drug effects (e.g., use of marijuana usually does not cause severe psychotic behavior); (2) the psychiatric disorder was present before the patient began abusing substances; and (3) the mental disorder persists for more than 4 weeks after substance use ends. The *DSM-IV-TR* makes it clear that elucidating the relationship between mental disorders and substances of abuse is important for proper diagnosis, treatment, and understanding (APA 2000).

The Relationship Between Personality and Drug Use

Since medieval times, personality theories of increasing sophistication have been used to classify long-term behavioral tendencies or traits that appear in individuals, and these traits have long been considered to be influenced by biological or chemical factors. Although such classification systems have varied widely, nearly all have shared two commonly observed dimensions of personality: introversion and extroversion. Individuals who show a predominant tendency to turn their thoughts and feelings inward rather than to direct attention outward have been considered to show the trait of *introversion*. At the opposite extreme, a tendency to seek outward activity and share feelings with others has been called *extroversion*. Of course, every individual shows a mix of such traits in varying degrees and circumstances.

In some research studies, introversion and extroversion patterns have been associated with levels of neural arousal in brainstem circuits (Apostolides 1996; Carlson 1990; Gray 1987) and these forms of arousal are closely associated with effects caused by drug stimulants or depressants. Such research hypothesizes that people whose systems produce high levels of sensitivity to neural arousal may find high-intensity external stimuli to be painful and may react by turning inward. With these extremely high levels of sensitivity, such people may experience neurotic levels of anxiety or panic disorders. At the other extreme, individuals whose systems provide them with very low levels of sensitivity to neural arousal may find that moderate stimuli are inadequate to produce responses. To reach moderate levels of arousal, they may turn outward to seek high-intensity external sources of stimulation (Eysenck and Eysenck 1985; Gray 1987; Rousar et al. 1995).

Because high- and low-arousal symptoms are easy to create by using stimulants, depressants, or hallucinogens, it is possible that these personality patterns of introversion or extroversion affect how a person reacts to substances. For people whose experience is predominantly introverted or extroverted, extremes of high or low sensitivity may lead them to seek counteracting substances that become important methods of bringing experience to a level that seems bearable.

Theories Based on Learning Processes

How are drug use patterns learned? Research on learning and conditioning explains how human beings acquire new patterns of behavior by the close association or pairing of one significant reinforcing stimulus with another less significant or neutral stimulus. Also known as **social learning theory** (Bandura 1977; explained more fully in the "Social Learning Theory" section later in this chapter), this theory emphasizes that learned associations occur in the presence of other people using drugs coupled with other, often preconceived associations with the attitudes of society and friends about drug use (Gray 1999). In this method of learning, people form expectations and become used to certain behavior patterns. This specific process of learning is known as conditioning, and it explains why pleasurable activities may become intimately connected with other

KEY TERMS

social learning theory
the theory that places emphasis on how an individual learns patterns of behavior from the attitudes of others, society, and peers

activities that are also pleasurable, neutral, or even unpleasant. In addition, people can turn any new behavior into a recurrent and permanent one by the process of **habituation** — repeating certain patterns of behavior until they become established or habitual.

The basic process by which learning mechanisms can lead a person into drug use is also described in Bejerot's **"addiction to pleasure" theory** (Bejerot 1965, 1972, 1975; NIDA 1980). This theory assumes that it is biologically normal to continue a pleasure stimulus once started. Several research findings support this theory, indicating that "a strong, biologically based need for stimulation appears to make sensation-seeking young adults more vulnerable to drug abuse" (Mathias 1995, p. 1; also supporting this view is Khantzian n.d.). A second research finding complementing this theory states, "Certain areas of the brain, when stimulated, produce pleasurable feelings. Psychoactive substances are capable of acting on these brain mechanisms to produce these sensations. These pleasurable feelings become reinforcers that drive the continued use of the substances" (Gardner 1992, p. 43). People at highest risk for drug use and addiction are those who maintain a constant preoccupation with getting high, seek new or novel thrills in their experiences, and are known to have a relentless desire to pursue physical stimulation or dangerous behaviors and are classified as **sensation-seeking individuals**.

Drug use may also be reinforced when it is associated with receiving affection or approval in a social setting, such as within a peer group relationship. Initially, the use of drugs may not be very important or pleasurable to the individual. However, eventually the affection and social rewards experienced when drugs are used become associated with the drug. Drug use and intimacy may then become perceived as very worthwhile.

> I don't know how to explain why but an attractive part of cocaine use is the instant feeling of intimacy with others who are also snorting this drug. You just don't want to leave the scene when the lines are cut on the glass surface and people are taking turns snorting coke. Even after I have had four or five lines and the conversation is very friendly and engaging, leaving the scene because someone is waiting for you at home or even if you have to meet with someone that night does not matter. Usually, everyone is feeling high, a lot of feelings of togetherness, and open to intimate conversation. I never saw anyone getting violent or anything like that, but I hear that it can happen especially if you have a grudge against someone before doing the coke. I think that coke just makes you more open and if you are an angry person then it will just bring it out in you. My experiences have been that everyone is just so friendly and everyone just pretends not to be overly anxious to do the next line. Actually, everyone is kind of pretending, because what they really want is more powder up their nose and an unending amount of time for talking the night away. *(From Venturelli's research files, 26-year-old male graduate student, residing in Chicago, Illinois, May 18, 2000.)*

It is important to keep in mind that the *amount* of a drug taken can affect the extent of sociability, as the interview below indicates:

> Yes, I did read that quote [referring to the preceding quote] about how friendly everyone is while snorting lines. Well, I bet that person does not do too much coke — maybe it is like a weekend thing. What I am trying to say is that everyone is friendly at the beginning when snorting lines, but after doing a lot of snorting, people get real quiet — they sort of geek out. You see, too much of it at any one time makes you feel overloaded. It's like an amphetamine bombardment. In the beginning, it is like a "dusting" and people can become real friendly and talkative, but after doing it for an hour or so, it gets to you. Whenever I overdo it, and it is easy to do so, I become real quiet and several times even when I tried to change my mood by having sex, I could not even "get it up" so-to-speak. I usually

KEY TERMS

habituation
repeating certain patterns of behavior until they become established or habitual

"addiction to pleasure" theory
the theory assuming that it is biologically normal to continue a pleasure stimulus once begun

sensation-seeking individuals
types of people who characteristically are continually seeking new or novel thrills in their experiences

do very well when I just have a little, but too much certainly can cause the sexual desire to peak, but the follow through is an entirely different matter. Too much just geeks you out after awhile. (*From Venturelli's research files, male, 28 years of age, construction worker, Hobart, Indiana, June 9, 2007.*)

By the conditioning process, a pleasurable experience such as drug taking may become associated with a comforting or soothing environment. When this happens, two different outcomes may result. First, the user may feel uncomfortable taking the drug in any other environment. Second, the user may become very accustomed or habituated to the familiar environment as part of the drug experience. The user may not experience the same level of rush or high in this environment and in response may take more drugs or seek a different environment.

Finally, through this process of conditioning and habituation, a drug user becomes accustomed to unpleasant effects of drug use such as withdrawal symptoms. Such unpleasant effects and experiences may become habituated — neutralized or less severe in their impact — so that the user can continue taking drugs without feeling or experiencing the negative effects of the drug.

■ Social Psychological Learning Theories

Other extensions of reinforcement or learning theory focus on how positive social influences by drug-using peers reinforce the attraction to drugs. Social interaction, peer camaraderie, social approval, and drug use work together as positive reinforcers to sustain drug use (Akers 1992). Thus, if the effects of drug use become personally rewarding "or become reinforcing through conditioning, the chances of continuing to use are greater than for stopping" (Akers 1992, p. 86). It is through learned expectations or association with others who reinforce drug use that individuals learn the pleasures of drug taking (Becker 1963, 1967). Similarly, if drug use leads to poor and disruptive social interactions, drug use may cease.

Note that positive reinforcers, such as peers, other friends and acquaintances, family members, and drug advertisements, do not act alone in inciting and sustaining drug use. Learning theory as defined here also relies on some variable amounts of imitation and trial-and-error learning methods.

Finally, **differential reinforcement** — defined as the ratio between reinforcers favorable and disfavorable for sustaining drug use behavior — must be considered. The use and eventual abuse of drugs can vary with certain favorable or unfavorable reinforcing experiences. The primary determining conditions are listed here:

1. The amount of exposure to drug-using peers versus non-drug-using peers
2. The general preference for drug use in a particular neighborhood or community
3. The age of initial use (younger adolescents are more greatly affected than older adolescents)
4. The frequency of drug use among peers

Major Theoretical Explanations: Sociological

Sociological explanations for drug use share important commonalities with psychological explanations under social learning theories. The main features distinguishing psychological and sociological explanations are that psychological explanations focus more on how the internal states of the drug user are affected by social relationships within families, peers, and other close and more distant relationships, whereas sociological explanations focus on how factors external to the drug user affect drug use. Such outside forces include the types of families, adopted lifestyles of peer groups, and types of neighborhoods and communities in which avid drug users reside. The sociological perspective views the motivation for drug use as largely determined by the types and quality of bonds (attachment versus detachment) that the drug user or potential drug user has with significant others and with the social environment in general. The degree of influence and involvement with external factors affecting the individual compared with the influence exerted by internal states distinguishes sociological from psychological analyses.

As previously stated, no one biological and psychological theory can adequately explain why most people use drugs. People differ from one another

KEY TERMS

differential reinforcement
ratio between reinforcers, both favorable and disfavorable, for sustaining drug use behavior

in terms of personality, motivational factors, upbringing, learned priority of values and attitudes, and problems faced. Because of these differences, many responses and reasons exist why people take drugs, which results in a plurality of theoretical explanations. Furthermore, the diverse perspectives of biology, psychology, and sociology offer their own explanations for drug use and abuse.

There are two sets of sociological theories: social influence and social structural. **Social influence theories** focus on microscopic explanations that concentrate on the roles played by significant others and their impact on an individual. **Structural influence theories** focus on macroscopic explanations of drug use and the assumption that the organizational structure of society has a major independent impact on an individual's use of drugs. The next sections examine these theories.

■ Social Influence Theories

The theories presented in this section are (1) social learning, (2) role of significant others in socialization, (3) labeling, and (4) subculture theories. These theories share a common theme: An individual's motivation to seek drugs is caused by social influences or social pressures.

Social Learning Theory

Social learning theory explains drug use as learned behavior. Conventional learning occurs through imitation, trial and error, improvisation, rewarded behavior, and cognitive mental associations and processes (Liska and Messner 1999). Social learning theory focuses directly on how drug use and abuse are learned through interaction with other drug users.

This theory emphasizes the pervasive influence of *primary groups* — that is, groups that share a high amount of intimacy and spontaneity and whose members are emotionally bonded. Families and long-term friends are examples of primary groups. In contrast, *secondary groups* share segmented relationships in which interaction is based on prescribed role patterns. An example of a secondary group is the relationship between you and a salesclerk in a grocery store or relationships between employees scattered throughout a corporation. Social learning theory addresses a type of interaction that is highly specific. This type of interaction involves learning specific motives, techniques, and appropriate meanings that are commonly attached to a particular type of drug.

The following are examples of first-time users learning drug-using techniques from their social circles:

The first time I tried smoking weed, nothing much happened. I always thought it was like smoking a cigarette. When the joint came around the first time, I refused it. The next time it came around, I noticed everyone was looking at me. So, I took the joint and started to inhale, then exhale. My friend sitting next to me said something to the effect, "Dude, hold it in; don't waste it. This is good weed and we don't have that much between us." Right after that, we did some "shotguns." This is where someone exhales directly into your mouth — lips to lips. My friend filled my lungs with his exhaled weed breath. After the first comment about holding it in, I started to watch how everyone was inhaling and realized that you really don't smoke weed like an ordinary cigarette; you have to hold in the smoke. *(From Venturelli's research files, male, age 16, second-year high school student in a small Midwestern town, February 15, 1997.)*

I first started using drugs, mostly alcohol and pot, because my best friend in high school was using drugs. My best friend Tim [a pseudonym] learned from his older sister. Before I actually tried pot, Tim kept telling me how great it was to be high on dope; he said it was much better than beer. I was really nervous the first time I tried pot with Tim and another friend, even though I heard so much detail about it from Tim. The first time I tried it, it was a complete letdown. The second time (the next day, I think it was), I remember I was talking about a teacher we had and in the middle of the conversation, I remember how everything appeared different. I started feeling happy and while listening to Tim as he poked jokes about the teacher, I started to hear the background music more clearly than ever before. By the time the music ended and a new CD started, I knew I was high. *(From Venturelli's research files, 22-year-old male student at a private liberal arts college in the Midwest, February 15, 1997.)*

First time I tried acid [LSD], I didn't know what to expect. Schwa [a pseudonym] told me it was a very different high from grass [marijuana]. After munching on one "square" [one dose of LSD] — after about 20 minutes — I looked at Schwa and he started laughing and said, "Feelin' the effects, Ki-ki?" I said, "Is this it? Is this what it feels like? I feel weird." With a devious grin . . . Schwa said, "Yep. We are now on the runway, ready to take off. Just wait a little while longer, it's going to get better and better. Fasten your seat belts!" *(From Venturelli's research files, male, age 33, May 6, 1996.)*

Learning to perceive the effects of the drug is the second major outcome in the process of becoming a regular user. Here, the ability to feel the authentic effects of the drug is being learned. The more experienced drug users in the group impart their knowledge to naive first-time users. The coaching information they provide describes how to recognize the euphoric effects of the drug.

I just sat there waiting for something to happen, but I really didn't know what to expect. After the fifth "hit," I was just about ready to give up ever getting high. Then suddenly, my best buddy looked deeply into my eyes and said, "Aren't you high yet?" Instead of just answering the question, I immediately repeated the same words the exact way he asked me. In a flash, we both simultaneously burst out laughing. This uncontrollable laughter went on for what appeared to be over 5 minutes. Then he said, "You silly ass, it's not like an alcohol high, it's a 'high high.' Don't you feel it? It's a totally different kind of high." At that very moment, I knew I was definitely high on the stuff. If this friend would not have said this to me, I probably would have continued thinking that getting high on the hash was impossible for me. *(From Venturelli's research files, 17-year-old male attending a small, private liberal arts college in the Southeast, May 15, 1984.)*

Once drug use has begun, continuing the behavior involves learning the following sequence: (1) identifying where and from whom the drug can be purchased, (2) maintaining steady contact with drug dealers, (3) developing a preoccupation with maintaining the secrecy of use from authority figures and casual non–drug-using acquaintances, (4) reassuring yourself that the drug use is pleasurable, (5) using with more frequency, and (6) replacing non–drug-using friends with drug-using friends.

Role of Significant Others

After a pattern of drug use has been established, the learning process plays a role in sustaining drug-taking behavior. Edwin Sutherland (1947; Liska and Messner 1999), a pioneering criminologist in sociology, believed that the mastery of criminal behavior depended on the frequency, duration, priority, and intensity of contact with others who are involved in similar behavior (Heitzeg 1996). This theory can also be applied to drug-taking behavior.

In applying Sutherland's principles of social learning to drug use, which he called differential association theory, the focus is on how other members of social groups reward criminal behavior and

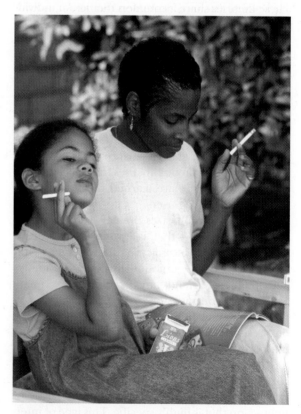

This child is role-playing largely by imitating the habits of a significant other.

under what conditions this deviance is perceived as important and pleasurable.

Becker's and Sutherland's theories explain why adolescents may use psychoactive drugs. Essentially, both theories say that the use of drugs is learned during intimate interaction with others who serve as a primary group. (See "Here and Now," Symptoms of Drug and Alcohol Abuse, for information on how the role of significant others can determine a child's disposition toward or away from illicit drug use.)

Learning theory also explains how adults and the elderly are taught the motivation for using a particular type of drug. This learning occurs through influences such as drug advertising, with its emphasis on testimonials by avid users, by medical experts, and by actors and actresses portraying physicians or nurses. Listeners, viewers, and readers who experience such commercials promoting a particular brand name of over-the-counter drugs are bombarded with the necessary motives, preferred techniques, and appropriate attitudes for consuming drugs. When drug advertisements and medical experts recommend a particular drug for specific ailments, in effect they are authoritatively persuading viewers, listeners, or readers that taking a drug will soothe or cure the medical problem presented.

Are Drug Users More Likely to Be Devious?

Social scientists — primarily sociologists and social psychologists — believe that many social development patterns are closely linked to drug use. Based on the age when an adolescent starts to consume alcohol and other drugs, predictions can be made about his or her sexual behavior, academic performance, and other behaviors, such as lying, cheating, fighting, and using marijuana. Similar predictions can be made when the adolescent begins using marijuana. A more detailed study (SAMHSA 2000) shows that there is a strong relationship between adolescent behavior problems and alcohol use.

Figure 2.1 shows that past-month adolescent heavy drinking and emotional/behavioral problems often arise concurrently. Adolescents who drink heavily between the ages of 12 to 17 are more likely to report behavior problems, such as aggressiveness and delinquent and criminal behaviors (SAMHSA 2000).

Figure 2.2 shows that children who began drinking or experimenting with alcohol at or before the 7th grade were more likely at 23 years of age to report smoking (data not shown), marijuana use, and involvement with criminal activities, such as

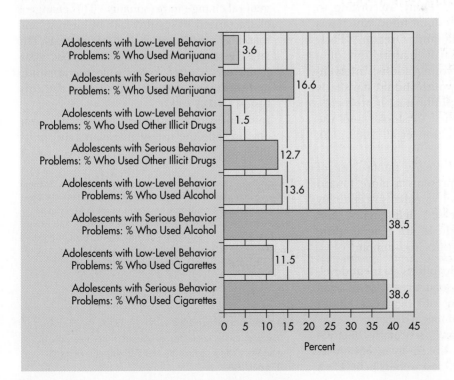

FIGURE 2.1

Adolescent behavior problems and substance use in past month.

....

Source: SAMHSA. "Study Shows Strong Relationship Between Adolescent Behavior Problems and Alcohol Use." (1 March 2000). Also see a related study, "Patterns of Alcohol Use Among Adolescents and Associations with Emotional and Behavioral Problems" by Janet C. Greenblatt. Available http://www.oas.samhsa.gov/NHSDA/Teenalc/teenalc.pdf.

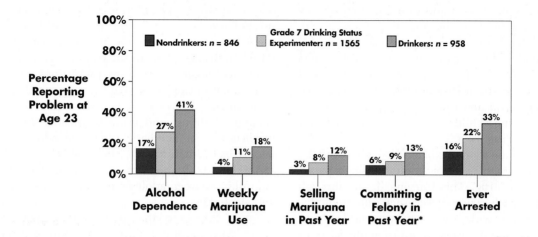

FIGURE 2.2

Percentage of grade 7 nondrinkers, experimenters, and drinkers exhibiting problem behaviors at age 23.

---

*Felonies were defined as buying/selling/holding stolen goods, taking a joy ride without the vehicle owner's permission, breaking into property, arson, or attempted arson.

Note: Nondrinkers never had a drink, not even a few sips. Experimenters drank less than three times in the past year, and not in the past month. Drinkers drank three or more times in the past year or drank in the past month. Subjects were assessed in grade 7, again at grade 12, and again at age 23.

Source: Adapted by CESAR (Center for Substance Abuse Research) from P. L. Ellickson, J. S. Tucker, and D. J. Klein, "Ten-Year Prospective Study of Public Health Problems Associated with Early Drinking," *Pediatrics* 111, 5(2003):949–955.

arrest and committing a felony. According to the authors of this longitudinal study, which was conducted in California and Oregon, "Early drinkers do not necessarily mature out of a problematic lifestyle as young adults. Interventions for these high-risk youth should start early and address their other public health problems, particularly their tendency to smoke and use other illicit drugs" (Ellickson et al. 2003, 949; CESAR 2003).

Other studies show that early intense use of alcohol or marijuana represents a move toward less conventional behavior, greater susceptibility to peer influence, increased delinquency, and lower achievement in school. In general, drug abusers have 14 characteristics in common:

1. Their drug use usually follows clear-cut developmental steps and sequences. Use of legal drugs, such as alcohol and cigarettes, almost always precedes use of illegal drugs.
2. Use of certain drugs, particularly habitual use of marijuana, is linked to **amotivational syndrome**, which some researchers believe is a

general change in personality.[1] This change is characterized by apathy, lack of interest, and inability or difficulty accomplishing goals. The latest research also clearly shows that marijuana use is often responsible for attention and short-term memory impairment and confusion (NIDA 1996).

3. Immaturity, maladjustment, or insecurity usually precede the use of marijuana and other illicit drugs.

[1] Some argue that perhaps a general lack of ambition (*lethargic behavior*) may *precede* rather than *result from* marijuana use or that amotivational syndrome is present in some heavy marijuana users even before the initial use of this drug, and when the drug is used, the syndrome becomes more pronounced. In any case, some researchers believe that the steady use of marijuana and amotivational syndrome occur together.

KEY TERMS

amotivational syndrome
the assertion by some drug researchers that heavy use of marijuana causes a lack of motivation in achieving goal-directed behavior

Here and Now

Symptoms of Drug and Alcohol Abuse

Following are profiles of children who are less likely and more likely, respectively, to use and abuse drugs.

Less Likely to Use Drugs

- Child comes from a strong family.
- Family has a clearly stated policy toward drug use.
- Child has strong religious convictions.
- Child is an independent thinker, not easily swayed by peer pressure.
- Parents know the child's friends and the friends' parents.
- Child often invites friends into the house and their behavior is open, not secretive.
- Child is busy and productive and pursues many interests.
- Child has a good, secure feeling of self.
- Parents are comfortable with their own use of alcohol, drugs, and pills; set a good example in using these substances; and are comfortable in discussing their use.
- Parents set a good example in handling crisis situations.
- Child maintains at least average grades and good working relationships with teachers.

Symptoms Exhibited by the Child Who May Be Using Drugs

EDITOR'S NOTE: A child will usually display more than one of the symptoms below when experimenting with drugs. Please remember that any number of the symptoms could also be the result of a physical impairment or disorder.

More Likely to Use Drugs

- Abrupt change in behavior (for example, from very active to passive, loss of interest in previously pursued activities such as sports or hobbies).

- Diminished drive and ambition.
- Moodiness.
- Shortened attention span.
- Impaired communication such as slurred speech or jumbled thinking.
- Significant change in quality of school work.
- Deteriorating judgment and loss of short-term memory.
- Distinct lessening of family closeness and warmth.
- Suddenly popular with new friends who are older and unknown to family members.
- Isolation from family members (hiding in bedroom or locking bedroom door).
- Sneaking out of the house.
- Sudden carelessness regarding appearance.
- Inappropriate overreaction to even mild criticism.
- Secretiveness about whereabouts and personal possessions.
- Friends who avoid introduction or appearance in the child's home.
- Use of words that are odd and unfamiliar.
- Secretiveness or desperation for money.
- Rapid weight loss or appetite loss.
- "Drifting off" beyond normal daydreaming.
- Extreme behavioral changes such as hallucination, violence, unconsciousness, and so on that could indicate a dangerous situation close at hand and needing fast medical attention.
- Unprescribed or unidentifiable pills.
- Strange "contraptions" (for example, smoking paraphernalia) or hidden articles.
- Articles missing from the house. Child could be stealing to receive money to pay for drugs.

Sources: L.A.W. Publications, *Let's All Work to Fight Drug Abuse* (Addison, TX: C & L Printing Company, 1985), 38. Used with permission of the publisher. Santa Barbara Alcohol and Drug Program, 1996.
Liddle, H., *AAMFT Consumer Update: Adolescent Substance Abuse.* American Association for Marriage and Family Therapy (AAMFT). Available http://www.aamft.org/families/Consumer_Updates/AdolescentSubstanceAbuse.asp.

Here and Now

Does Divorce Affect Adolescent Drug Use?

As an example of how drug users may be affected by socialization, a study conducted by Needle (Needle et al. 1990; NIDA 1990; Siegel and Senna 1994) found higher drug use among adolescents whose parents divorce. According to the study, children who are adolescents when their parents divorce exhibit more extensive drug use and experience more drug-related health, legal, and other problems than their peers. This study linked the extent of teens' drug use to their age at the time of their parents' divorce. Teenagers whose parents divorce were found to use more drugs and experience more drug-related problems than two other groups of adolescents: those who were age 10 or younger when their parents divorced, and those whose parents remained married.

This study has important implications for drug abuse prevention efforts. Basically, it says that not everyone is at the same risk for drug use. People at greater risk can be identified, and programs should be developed to meet their special needs.

In this research project, drug use among all adolescents increased over time. However, drug use was higher among adolescents whose parents had divorced when their children were either preteens or teenagers.

Drug use was highest for those teens whose parents divorced during their children's adolescent years. Such families also reported more physical problems, family disputes, and arrests.

The research results showed that distinct gender differences existed in the way that divorce affected adolescent drug use, whether the divorce occurred during the offspring's childhood or adolescent years. Males whose parents divorced reported more drug use and drug-related problems than females. Females whose caretaking parents remarried experienced increased drug use after the remarriage. By contrast, males whose caretaking parents remarried reported a decrease in drug-related problems following the remarriage.

The researchers caution that these findings may have limited applicability, as most of the families studied were white and had middle to high income levels. Needle also notes that the results should not be interpreted as an argument in favor of the nuclear family. Overall, divorce affects adolescents in complex ways and remarriage can influence drug-using behavior, particularly when disruptions occur during adolescence; such turmoil can "trigger" a desire for extensive recreational licit and illicit drug use, often leading to drug abuse.

4. Those more likely to try illicit drugs, especially before age 12, usually have a history of poor school performance and classroom disobedience.

5. Delinquent or repetitive deviant activities usually precede involvement with illicit drugs.

6. A set of values and attitudes that facilitates the development of deviant behavior exists before the person tries illicit drugs.

7. A social setting in which drug use is common, such as communities and neighborhoods in which peers use drugs indiscriminately, is likely to reinforce and increase the predisposition to drug use.

8. Drug-induced behaviors and drug-related attitudes of peers are usually among the strongest predictors of subsequent drug involvement.

9. Children who feel their parents are distant from their emotional needs are more likely to become drug addicted (see "Here and Now," Does Divorce Affect Adolescent Drug Use?).

10. The younger people are when they begin using drugs, the higher the probability of continued and accelerated drug use. Likewise, the older people are when they start using drugs, the lower the probability of accelerated use and addiction. The period of greatest risk of initiation and habitual use of illicit drugs is usually over by the early twenties.

11. The family structure has changed, with substantially more than half of all women in the United States now working outside the home. A higher divorce rate has led to many children being raised in single-parent households. How the lack of a stay-at-home parent or how membership in a single-family household affects the quality of child care and nurturing is difficult to assess.

12. Mobility obstructs a sense of permanency, and it contributes to a lack of self-esteem. Often, when children are repeatedly moved from one location to another, their community becomes nothing more than a group of strangers. They may have little pride in their home or community and have no commitment to society.

13. Among minority members, a major factor involved in drug dependence is a feeling of powerlessness due to discrimination based on race, social standing, or other attributes. Groups subject to discrimination have a disproportionately high rate of unemployment and below-average incomes. In the United States, approximately 14 million children are reared in poverty (Henslin 2003). The adults they have as role models may be unemployed and experience feelings of powerlessness. Higher rates of delinquency and drug addiction occur in such settings.

14. Abusers who become highly involved in selling drugs begin by witnessing that drug trafficking is a lucrative business, especially in rundown neighborhoods. In some communities, selling drugs seems to be the only available route to real economic success (Jones 1996; Shelden et al. 2001).

Labeling Theory

Although controversy continues over whether labeling is a theory or a perspective (Akers 1968, 1992; Heitzeg 1996; Plummer 1979), this text takes the position that labeling is a theory (Cheron 2001; Hewitt 1994; Liska and Messner 1999), because it explains something very important with respect to drug use. Although labeling theory does not fully explain why initial drug use occurs, it does detail the processes by which many people come to view themselves as socially deviant from others. Note that the terms *deviant* (in cases of individuals) and *deviance* (in cases of behavior) are sociologically defined as involving the violation of significant social norms held by conventional society. The terms are not used in a judgmental manner, nor are the individuals judged to be immoral or "sick"; instead, the terms refer to an absence of the patterns of behavior expected by conventional society.

Labeling theory says that other people whose opinions we value have a determining influence over our self-image (Best and Luckenbill 1994; Goode 1997; Liska and Messner 1999). (For an example of how labeling theory applies to real-life situations, see "Case in Point.")

Implied in this theory is the idea that we exert only a small amount of control over the image we portray. In contrast, members of society, especially those we consider to be significant others, have much greater influence and power in defining or redefining our self-image. The image we have of ourselves is vested in the people we

admire and look to for guidance and advice. If these people come to define our actions as deviant, then their definition becomes incorporated as a "fact" of our reality.

We can summarize labeling theory by saying that the labels we use to describe people have a profound influence on their self-perceptions. For example, imagine a fictitious individual named Billy. Initially, Billy does not see himself as a compulsive drug user but as an occasional recreational drug user. Let us also assume that Billy is very humorous, unpretentious, and very outspoken about his drug use and likes to exaggerate the amount of marijuana he smokes on a daily basis. Slowly, Billy's friends begin to perceive him as a "real stoner." According to labeling theory, what happens to Billy? Because of being noticed when "high," his self-presentation, and the comments he makes about the pleasures of drug use, his friends may begin to reinforce the exaggerated drug use image. At first, Billy may enjoy the reflected image of a "big-time" drug user, but after nearly all of his peers maintain a constant exaggerated image, his projected image may turn negative, especially when his friends show disrespect for his opinions. In this example, labeling theory predicts that Billy's perception of himself will begin to mirror the consistent perception expressed by his accusers. If he is unsuccessful in eradicating the addict image or, in this example, the "stoner" image, Billy will reluctantly concur with the label that has been thrust on him. Or, to strive for a self-image as an occasional marijuana user, Billy may abandon his peers so that he can become acceptable once more in the eyes of other people.

An important originator of labeling theory is Edwin Lemert (Lemert 1951; Liska and Messner 1999; Williams and McShane 1999), who distinguished between two types of deviance: primary and secondary deviance. **Primary deviance** is inconsequential deviance, which occurs without having a lasting impression on the perpetrator. Generally,

KEY TERMS

labeling theory
the theory emphasizing that other people's perceptions directly influence one's self-image

primary deviance
any type of initial deviant behavior in which the perpetrator does not identify with the deviance

►Case in Point   Specific Signs of Marijuana Use

This excerpt, from the author's files, illustrates labeling theory.

After my mom found out, she never brought it up again. I thought the incident was over — dead, gone, and buried. Well, . . . it wasn't over at all. My mom and dad must have agreed that I couldn't be trusted anymore. I'm sure she was regularly going through my stuff in my room to see if I was still smoking dope. Even my grandparents acted strangely whenever the news on television would report about the latest drug bust in Chicago. Several times that I can't ever forget were when we were together and I could hear the news broadcast on TV from my room about some drug bust. There they all were whispering about me. My grandma asking if I "quitta the dope." One night, I overheard my mother reassure my dad and grandmother that I no longer was using dope. You can't believe how embarrassed I was that my own family was still thinking that I was a dope fiend. They thought I was addicted to pot like a junkie is addicted to heroin! I can tell you that I would never lay such a guilt trip on my kids if I ever have kids. I remember that for 2 years after the time I was honest enough to tell my mom that I had tried pot, they would always whisper about me, give me the third degree whenever I returned late from a date, and go through my room looking for dope. They acted as if I was hooked on drugs. I remember that for a while back then I would always think that if they think of me as a drug addict, I might as well get high whenever my friends "toke up." They should have taken me at my word instead of sneaking around my personal belongings. I should have left syringes laying around my room!

Source: Interview with a 20-year-old male college student at a private university in the Midwest, conducted by Peter Venturelli on November 19, 1993.

most first-time violations of law, for example, are primary deviations. Whether the suspected or accused individual has committed the deviant act does not matter. What matters is whether the individual identifies with the deviant behavior.

Secondary deviance develops when the individual begins to identify and perceive himself or herself as deviant. The moment this transition occurs, deviance shifts from being primary to secondary. Many adolescents casually experiment with drugs. If, however, they begin to perceive themselves as drug users, then this behavior is virtually impossible to eradicate. The same holds true with OTC drug abuse. The moment an individual believes that he or she feels better after using a particular drug, the greater the likelihood that he or she will consistently use the drug.

Howard Becker (1963) believed that certain negative status positions (such as alcoholic, mental patient, ex-felon, criminal, drug addict, and so on) are so powerful that they dominate others (Pontell 1996; Williams and McShane 1999). In the earlier example, if people who are important to Billy call him a "druggie," this name becomes a powerful label that takes precedence over any other status positions Billy may occupy. This label becomes Billy's **master status** — that he is a mindless "stoner." Even if Billy is also an above-average biology major, an excellent musician, and a de-

pendable and caring person, such factors become secondary because his primary status has been recast as a "druggie." Furthermore, once a powerful label is attached, it becomes much easier for the individual to uphold the image dictated by members of society and simply to act out the role expected by significant others. Master status labels distort an individual's public image because other people expect consistency in role performance.

Once a negative master status has been attached to an individual's public image, labeling theorist Edwin Schur asserted that retrospective interpretation occurs. **Retrospective interpretation** is a form of "reconstitution of individual charac-

KEY TERMS

secondary deviance
any type of deviant behavior in which the perpetrator identifies with the deviance

master status
major status position in the eyes of others that clearly identifies an individual — for example, doctor, professor, alcoholic, heroin addict

retrospective interpretation
social psychological process of redefining a person in light of a major status position — for example, homosexual, physician, professor, alcoholic, convicted felon, or mental patient

ter or identity" (Schur 1971, 52). It largely involves *redefining* a person's image within a particular social stereotype, category, or group (see cartoon as an illustration). In the eyes of his peers, Billy is now an emotional, intelligent, yet weird or "freaky" stoner.

Finally, William I. Thomas's (1923) contribution to labeling theory can be summarized in the following theorem: "If men define situations as real, they are real in their consequences" (p. 19). Thus, according to this dictum, when someone is perceived as a drug user, the perception functions as the reality of that person's character and in turn shapes his or her self-perception.

Subculture Theory

Subculture theory speaks to the role of peer pressure and the behavior resulting from peer group influences. In all groups, there are certain members who are more popular and respected and, as a result, exert more social influence than other peer members. Often, these more socially endowed members are group leaders, task leaders, or emotional leaders who possess greater ability to influence others. Drug use that results from peer pressure demonstrates the extent to which these more popular and respected leaders can influence and pressure others to initially use or abuse drugs. These three excerpts from interviews illustrate subculture theory:

> When I was 9 or 10, three of my best friends would all take turns sneaking alcohol out of our parents' houses. Then in one of our garages, we would drink the liquor and smoke cigarettes. It was like a street corner thing but it was in a garage. In high school, we would look for the "party-people" and hang out with them. Usually on a Friday or some other school day, we would cut classes and drink and get high at someone's house that would be available. We were a tight-ass group — the goal would be to find a party somewhere. In high school we just hung out together and were known on campus as "the party animals." *(From Venturelli's research files, 21-year-old male college student in a small town in the Midwest, November 23, 2000.)*

> I first started messing around with alcohol in high school. In order to be part of the crowd, we would sneak out during lunchtime at school and get "high." About 6 months after we started drinking, we moved on to other drugs. . . . Everyone in high school belongs to a clique,

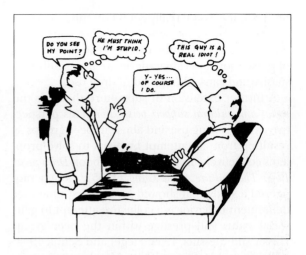

This cartoon illustrates the reflective process in retrospective interpretation that often occurs in daily conversations when we think that our unspoken thoughts are undetectable and hidden. In reality, however, these innermost thoughts are clearly conveyed through body language and nonverbal gestures.

Source: Reproduced with permission of Alex Silvestri.

and my clique was heavy into drugs. We had a lot of fun being "high" throughout the day. We would party constantly. Basically, in college, it's the same thing. *(From Venturelli's research files, 19-year-old male student at a small, religiously affiliated private liberal arts college in the Southeast, February 9, 1985.)*

The third interview illustrates how friendship, coupled with subtle and not-so-subtle peer pressure, influences the novice drug enthusiast:

> There I was on the couch with three of my friends, and as the joint was being passed around, everyone was staring at me. I felt they were saying, "Are you going to smoke with us or will you be a holdout again?" *(From Venturelli's research files, 20-year-old male university student, April 10, 1996.)*

In sociology, charismatic leaders are viewed as possessing status and power, defined as distinction in the eyes of others. In drug-using peer groups, such leaders have power over inexperienced drug users. Members of peer groups are often persuaded to experiment with drugs if the more popular members say, "Come on, try some, it's great"

KEY TERMS

subculture theory
explains drug use as a peer-generated activity

or "Trust me, you'll really get off on this, come on, just try it." In groups where drugs are consumed, the extent of peer influence coupled with the art of persuasion and camaraderie are powerfully persuasive and cause the spread of drug use.

A further extension of subculture theory is the *social and cultural support perspective.* This perspective explains drug use and abuse in peer groups as resulting from an attempt by peers to solve problems collectively. In the neoclassic book *Delinquent Boys: The Culture of the Gang* (1955), Cohen pioneered a study that showed for the first time that delinquent behavior is a collective attempt to gain social status and prestige within the peer group (Liska and Messner 1999; Siegel and Senna 1994; Williams and McShane 1999). Members of certain peer groups are unable to achieve respect within the larger society. Such status-conscious youths find that being able to commit delinquent acts and yet evade law enforcement officials is admirable in the eyes of their delinquent peers. In effect, Cohen believed, delinquent behavior is a subcultural solution for overcoming feelings of status frustration and low self-esteem largely determined by lower class status.

Although the emphasis of Cohen's perspective is on explaining juvenile delinquency, his notion that delinquent behavior is a subcultural solution can easily be applied to drug use and abuse primarily in members of lower-class peer groups. Underlying drug use and abuse in delinquent gangs, for example, results from sharing common feelings of alienation and escape from a society that appears noncaring, noninclusive, distant, and hostile.

Consider the current upsurge in violent gang memberships (see Chapter 16 for more details on adolescents and gangs). In such groups, not only is drug dealing a profitable venture, but drug use also serves as a collective response to alienation and estrangement from conventional middle-class society. In cases of violent minority gang members, the alienation results from racism, poverty, effects of migration and acculturation, and effects of minority status in a white, male-dominated society such as the United States (Glick and Moore 1990; Moore 1978, 1993; Sanders 1994; Thornberry 2001).

■ Structural Influence Theories

Structural influence theories focus on how elements in the *organization* of a society, group, or subculture affect the motivation and resulting drug use behavior that is for nonmedical — most often recreational — use. The belief is that no single factor in the society, the group, or the subculture produces the attraction to drug use, but rather that the organization itself or the lack of organization largely causes this behavior to occur.

Social disorganization and social strain theories (Liska and Messner 1999; Werner and Henry 1995) identify the different kinds of social change that are disruptive and explain how, in a general sense, people are adversely affected by the change. Social disorganization theory asks, What in the structure and organization of the social order (the larger social structure) causes people to deviate? Social strain theory attempts to answer the question, What in the structure and organization of the family, the peer, and employee social structure causes someone to deviate? This theory suggests that frustration results from being unable to secure the means to achieve sought-after goals, such as the goal of securing good income without much education, a well-paying job without prior training, and so on. Such perceived shortcomings compel an individual to deviate to achieve desired goals.

An example of feeling stressed and experiencing strain from an overly demanding society.

Overall, social disorganization theory describes a situation in which, because of rapid social change, previously affiliated individuals no longer find themselves integrated into a community's social, commercial, religious, and economic institutions. When this type of alienation occurs, community members whose parents were perhaps more affiliated find themselves more disconnected and feel a lack of effective attachment to the social order. As a result, these disconnected or "disaffiliated" people find deviant behavior to be an attractive alternative.

Developing trusting relationships, stability, and continuity are essential for proper socialization. As is discussed later in this chapter, when major identity development and transformation occur in the teen years, some stability in the immediate environment is very important. Yet, especially today, in our postindustrial and technological society, as well as in most other Westernized types of societies, there are more destabilizing and disorienting factors affecting us as a result of rapid technological development and social change (Gergen 2000; Ritzer 1999, 2000).

Although on the surface most people appear to have little or no difficulty adapting to rapid technological social change, many people find themselves forced to maintain a frantic pace merely to "keep up" on a daily basis. The drive to keep up with social and technological innovation is more demanding today than ever before (Gergen 2000). The constant need to keep pace with change and the increasing multiplicity of realities, and ever more contradictory realities, produced by such change often appears barely controllable and somewhat chaotic. Some individuals who are unable to cope with the constant demand for change and the required adjustment to all this change have difficulty securing a stable self-identity. For example, consider the large number of people who need psychological counseling and therapy because they find themselves unable to cope with personal, family, and work-related problems and conflicts. In a recent study, "an estimated 26.2% of Americans ages 18 and older — about one in four adults — suffer from a diagnosable mental disorder in a given year" (Kessler 2005, p. 617). The following interview shows how such confusion and lack of control can easily lead to drug use.

Interviewee: The world is all messed up.

Interviewer: Why? In what way?

Interviewee: Nobody gives a damn anymore about anyone else.

Interviewer: Why do you think this is so?

Interviewee: It seems like life just seems to go on and on. . . . I know that when I am under the influence, life is more mellow. I feel great! When I am high, I feel relaxed and can take things in better. Before I came to Chalmers College [a pseudonym], I felt home life was one great big mess; now that I am here, this college is also a big pile of crap. I guess this is why I like smoking dope. When I am high, I can forget my problems. My surroundings are friendlier; I am even more pleasant! Do you know what I mean? *(From Venturelli's research files, interview with a 19-year-old male marijuana user attending a small, private, liberal arts college in the Southeast, February 12, 1984.)*

Similarly, an interview illustrates how a work environment can affect drug use:

I had one summer job once where it was so busy and crazy that a group of us workers would go out on breaks just to get high. We worked the night shift and our "high breaks" were between 2:00 and 5:00 in the morning. *(From Venturelli's research files, first-year female college student, age 20, July 28, 1996.)*

Current Social Change in Most Societies

Does social change per se cause people to use and abuse drugs? In response to this question, social change — defined as any measurable change caused by technological advancement that disrupts cultural values and attitudes about everyday life — does not by itself cause widespread drug use. In most cases, social change materialistically advances a culture by profoundly affecting the manner of how things are accomplished. At the same time, *rapid* social change disrupts day-to-day behavior anchored by tradition, which has a tendency to fragment such conventional social groups as families, neighborhoods, and communities. By **conventional behavior**, we mean behavior that is largely dictated by custom and tradition and that evaporates or goes into a state of flux because of the speed of social change.

KEY TERMS

conventional behavior
behavior largely dictated by custom and tradition, which is often disrupted by the forces of rapid technological change

Examples include the number of youth subcultures that proliferated during the 1960s (Yinger 1982) and other more recent lifestyles and subcultures, such as pro-life groups, pro-choice groups, Mothers Against Drunk Driving (MADD), gay rights groups, rappers, punk rockers, metalheads, grunge rockers, taggers, skinheads, satanists, new wavers, and rave enthusiasts (Wooden 1995). Furthermore, two other subcultures, teenagers and the elderly, both have become increasingly independent and, in some subgroups, alienated from other age groups in society (see Figure 2.3).

Simply stated, today's social institutions no longer embrace, influence, and lead people as they did in the past. Consequently, people are free to explore different means of expression and types of recreation. For many, this liberating experience leads to new and exciting outcomes; for others, this freedom from conventional societal norms and attitudes creates an attraction to drug use and abuse.

The following two excerpts, gathered from interviews, illustrate social disorganization and strain theory:

Honest to God, I know things occur much faster than they did 20 years ago. Change is happening faster and occurs more often. What helps is doing some drugs at night at home. I either drink alcohol or do lines of coke. Two different highs but I like them both. This is about the only recreation I have except for the TV at night, after working all darn day nonstop writing letters, answering phone calls, attending meetings, having to go on-site for inspections, and many other things I do each day. *(From Venturelli's research files, interview with a 29-year-old male home security systems manager, Chicago, Illinois, June 23, 2000.)*

I am into my own life because everyone is doing this. I see nearly everyone doing well around here. It's only those who are too stupid to succeed who are poor. I have had a rough time making it lately. Cocaine and speed help, but I know it's not the answer to all my problems. For now, drugs help me to put up with all the shit going on in my life. *(From Venturelli's research files, interview with a 25-year-old male residing in the Southeast and receiving various forms of welfare, March 10, 1985.)*

There is no direct link between social change and drug use. However, plenty of proof exists that certain dramatic changes occur in the organization of society, and many eventually lead certain groups to use and abuse drugs. Figure 2.3 illustrates how the number of life-cycle stages increases depending on a society's level of technological development. Overall, it implies that, as societies advance from preindustrial to industrial to our current postindustrial type of society, new subcultures emerge at an increasing rate of development. (See Fischer 1976, for similar thinking.) In contrast to industrial and postindustrial societies, preindustrial societies do not have as many sepa-

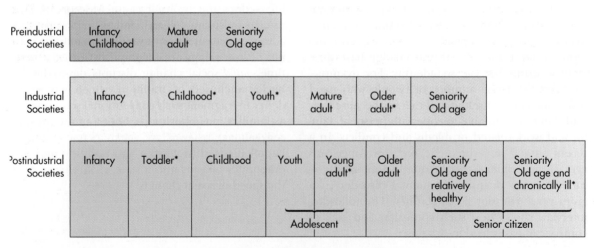

*Represents a newly developed and separate stage of identification and expression from the prior era.

FIGURE 2.3

Levels of technological development and resulting subcultures.

rate and distinct periods and cycles of social development. What is shown in Figure 2.3 and implied here is that the greater the number of distinct life cycles, the greater the fragmentation between the members of different stages of development. Generation gaps (conflicting sets of values and attitudes between age cohorts) cause much ignorance and lack of insight between age-group subcultures. This often leads to separation and fragmentation across age groups who develop distinct lifestyle patterns that can easily conflict.

Control Theory

The final major structural influence theory, control theory, emphasizes influences outside the self as the primary cause for deviating to drug use and/or abuse. **Control theory** places importance on positive socialization. **Socialization** is the process by which individuals learn to internalize the attitudes, values, and behaviors needed to become participating members of conventional society. Generally, control theorists believe that human beings can easily become deviant if left without the social controls provided by groups and organizations. Thus, theorists who specialize in control theory emphasize the necessity of maintaining bonds to family, school, peer groups, and other social, political, and religious organizations (Liska and Messner 1999; Thio 1998).

In the 1950s and 1960s, criminologist Walter C. Reckless (1961; Liska and Messner 1999; Siegel and Senna 1994) developed the containment theory. According to this theory, the socialization process results in the creation of strong or weak internal and external control systems. The degree of self-control, high or low frustration tolerance, positive or negative self-perception, successful or unsuccessful goal achievement, and either resistance or adherence to deviant behavior determine internal control. Environmental pressures, such as social conditions, may limit the accomplishment of goal-striving behavior; such conditions include poverty, minority group status, inferior education, and lack of employment.

The external, or outer, control system consists of effective or ineffective supervision and discipline, consistent or inconsistent moral training, and positive or negative acceptance, identity, and self-worth. Many believe that latchkey children have a higher risk of becoming delinquent due to their sporadic supervision and the uneven levels of attention they receive. Alcoholic parents, as well as parents or guardians who are dependent on other types of drugs, are often at risk for raising children with delinquent tendencies because these parents are more apt to be inconsistent with discipline as a result of their drug addiction(s).

In applying this theory to the use or abuse of drugs, we could say that if an individual has a weak external control system, the internal control system must take over to handle external pressure. Similarly, if an individual's external control system is strong, his or her internal control system will not be seriously challenged. If, however, either the internal or external control system is contradictory (weak internal versus strong external), or in the worst-case scenario in which both internal and external controls are weak, drug abuse is much more likely to occur.

Table 2.2 shows the likelihood of drug use resulting from either strong or weak internal and external control systems. It indicates that if both internal and external controls are strong, the use and abuse of drugs are much less likely to occur.

Travis Hirschi (1971; Liska and Messner 1999), a much-respected sociologist and social control theorist, believes that delinquent behavior tends to occur when people lack (1) attachment to others,

KEY TERMS

control theory
theory that emphasizes when people are left without bonds to other groups (peers, family, social groups), they generally have a tendency to deviate from upheld values and attitudes

socialization
the growth and development process responsible for learning how to become a responsible, functioning human being

Table 2.2 Likelihood of Drug Use

INDIVIDUAL INTERNAL CONTROL	EXTERNAL SOCIAL CONTROL	
	Strong	**Weak or Nonexistent**
Strong	Least likely (almost never)	Less likely (probably never)
Weak	More likely (probably will)	Most likely (almost certain)

Source: Reproduced with permission of Peter J. Venturelli.

(2) commitment to goals, (3) involvement in conventional activity, and (4) belief in a common value system. If a child or adolescent is unable to become circumscribed within the family setting, school, and nondelinquent peers, then the drift to delinquent behavior is most likely inevitable.

We can apply Hirschi's theories to drug use as follows:

1. Drug users are less likely than nonusers to be closely tied to their parents.
2. Good students are less likely to use drugs.
3. Drug users are less likely to participate in social clubs and organizations and engage in team sport activities.
4. Drug users are very likely to have friends whose activities are congruent with their own attitudes (drug users "hang with" other drug users and delinquents "hang with" other delinquents).

The following excerpt illustrates how control theory works:

I was 15 when my mother confronted me with drug use. I nearly died. We have always been very close and she really cried when she found my "dug out" [paraphernalia that holds a quantity of marijuana] and a "one hitter" [a tubular device for smoking very small quantities of this drug] in her car. My fear was that she would inquire about my drug use with our next-door neighbors, whose children were my best friends. The neighbor residing on the left of our house was one of my high school teachers who knew me from the day I was born. The neighbor on the right side of our house was our church pastor. For a while after she confronted me, I just sneaked around more whenever I wanted to get high. After a few months, I became so paranoid of how my mother kept looking at me when I would come in at night that I eventually stopped smoking weed. Our family is very close and the town I live in (at that time the population was 400) was filled with gossip. I could not handle the pressure, so I quit. *(From Venturelli's research files, female postal worker, age 22, residing in a small Midwestern town, February 9, 1997.)*

In conclusion, control theory depicts how conformity with supportive groups may prevent deviance. It suggests that control is either internally or externally enforced by family, school, and peer group expectations. In addition, individuals who are not equipped with an internal system of self-control reflecting the values and beliefs of conventional society or who feel personally alienated from major social institutions may deviate without feeling guilty for their actions, often because peer pressure results in a suspension or modification of internal beliefs.

Danger Signals of Drug Abuse

How does one know when the use of drugs moves beyond normal use? Many people are prescribed drugs that affect their moods. Using these drugs wisely can be important for both physical and emotional health. Sometimes, however, it may be difficult to decide when use of drugs to handle stress or anxiety becomes inappropriate. It is important that your use of drugs does not result in addiction. The following are some danger signals that can help you evaluate your drug use behavior:

1. Do people who are close to you often ask about your drug use? Have they noticed any changes in your moods or behavior?
2. Do you become defensive when a friend or relative mentions your drug or alcohol use?
3. Do you believe you cannot have fun without alcohol or other drugs?
4. Do you frequently get into trouble with the law, school officials, family, friends, or significant others because of your alcohol or other drug use?
5. Are you sometimes embarrassed or frightened by your behavior under the influence of drugs or alcohol?
6. Have you ever switched to a new doctor because your regular physician would not prescribe the drug you wanted?
7. When you are under pressure or feel anxious, do you automatically take a sedative, a drink, or both?
8. Do you turn to drugs after becoming upset, after confrontations or arguments, or to relieve uncomfortable feelings?
9. Do you take drugs more often or for purposes other than those recommended by your doctor?
10. Do you often mix drugs and alcohol?
11. Do you drink or take drugs regularly to help you sleep or even to relax?
12. Do you take a drug to get going in the morning?
13. Do you find it necessary or nearly impossible to not use alcohol and/or other drugs to have sex?

14. Do you find yourself not wanting to be around friends who do not use drugs or drink on a regular basis?
15. Have you ever seriously thought that you may have a drug addiction problem?
16. Do you make promises to yourself or others that you will stop getting drunk or using drugs?
17. Do you drink and/or use drugs alone, often secretly?

A higher number of "yes" answers indicates a greater likelihood that you are abusing alcohol and/or drugs. Many places offer help at the local level, such as programs in your community listed in the phone book under "Drug Abuse." Other resources include community crisis centers, telephone hotlines, and the National Mental Health Association.

■ Low-Risk and High-Risk Drug Choices

As will become readily apparent throughout this text, some very real risks are associated with recreational drug use. Low-risk and high-risk drug choices refer to two major levels of alcohol and other drug use. **Low-risk drug choices** refer to values and attitudes that keep the use of alcohol and other drugs in control. **High-risk drug choices** refer to values and attitudes that lead to using drugs habitually and addictively, resulting in emotional, psychological, and physical health problems. Low-risk choices include abstinence from all drugs or remaining in true control of the quantity and frequency of drugs taken.

Low-risk choices require self-monitoring your consumption of alcohol and other drugs to reduce your risk of an alcohol and other drug-related problem. Both "low-risk" and "high-risk" are appropriate descriptive concepts that allow us to focus on the health and safety issues involved in drug use and refer to developing and maintaining completely different values and attitudes in your approach to alcohol and other drugs.

This chapter described numerous factors influencing drug use and reasons why people start using or abusing drugs. There are also numerous theories that attempt to explain initial and habitual use. Some people can easily become addicted to alcohol and other drugs because of inherited characteristics, personality, mental instability or illness, and vulnerability to present situations. Others who have more resistance to alcohol and drug addiction may have stronger convictions and abilities to cope with different situations.

Maintaining a Low-Risk Approach

To minimize the risk of alcohol and drug-related problems, we suggest you remain aware of the following:

1. Investigate your family drug history. Does anyone in your family have a history of alcohol or drug abuse? How many members of your family who have alcohol or drug problems are blood relatives? In other words, are you more likely to become dependent on alcohol or drugs because of inherited genes or because of the values and attitudes to which you are exposed?
2. Do you particularly enjoy the effects of alcohol and other drugs? Do you spend a lot of time thinking about how "good" it feels to be high?
3. Does it seem as if the only time you really have fun is when you are using alcohol and other drugs?
4. Keep in mind the following, which is covered throughout this text:
   - *Body size.* A small person typically becomes more impaired by drug use than a larger person.
   - *Gender.* Women typically become more impaired than men of the same size, especially with regard to alcohol use.
   - *Other drugs.* Taking a combination of drugs generally increases the risk of impairment and, in some combinations, accidental death.
   - *Fatigue or illness.* Fatigue increases impairment from alcohol and increases the risk for impairment.
   - *Mind-set.* As you set out to drink or use other drugs, are you expecting heavy use of alcohol or heavy involvement with drugs to the point of inebriation or severe distortion of reality as the evening's outcome? More importantly, what view do you hold

KEY TERMS

low-risk drug choices
developing values and attitudes that lead to controlling the use of alcohol and drugs

high-risk drug choices
developing values and attitudes that lead to using drugs both habitually and addictively

regarding moderate use of drugs versus heavy use of drugs?

- *Empty stomach*. Taking drugs on an empty stomach increases impairment from most drugs.

Also keep in mind that most excessive drug use comes with the following risks:

1. It is against all school policies.
2. It is unlawful behavior (risky with the law).
3. Excessive alcohol and other drug use usually leads not only to public attention, but also to criminal justice attention (police and the courts). Jail time or prison, fines, costly forced rehabilitation programs, and community service work are possible outcomes.
4. The defense costs involved in even simple drug possession charges are often $3000 to $8000 (often beyond an individual's ability to pay for such legal services).
5. A criminal record is a public record and can be acquired or suddenly come to the attention of school officials (especially loan officers and/or government loan personnel), credit bureaus, as well as any other community members.

We leave you with this question: *Are excessive drug use and the resulting drug dependence still worth such risks?* This question is critical, especially when we know that the more often drugs are consumed, the greater the potential not only for drug dependence and addiction, but also for damage to health, personal well-being, family and interpersonal relationships, and community respect.

Discussion Questions

1. Define the terms *addiction, tolerance, dependence*, and *withdrawal*.

2. Describe and contrast the disease and characterological (personality predisposition) models of addiction.

3. List several biological, social, and cultural factors that may be responsible for addiction to drugs.

4. In addition to better cultivation techniques, cite several other possible reasons why the potency of the average marijuana joint has increased since 1960.

5. Given that more than 88% of the U.S. population members are daily drug users of some

form, do you think we need to reexamine our strict drug laws, which may be punishing a sizable number of drug users in our society who simply want to use illicit drugs?

6. Is there any way to combine the biological and sociological explanations for why people use drugs so that the two perspectives do not conflict? (Sketch out a synthesis between these two sets of theoretical explanations.)

7. What is the relationship between mental illness and drug abuse? Why is this relationship important?

8. Do you accept the "rats in a maze" concept that psychology offers for explaining why people come to abuse drugs? (This view primarily states that people are like automatons or robots and that reinforcement explains why certain people become addicted to drugs.) Explain your answer.

9. In reviewing the psychological and sociological theories, which best explain drug use? Defend your answer.

10. Does differential association theory take into account non–drug-using individuals whose socialization environment was drug-infested?

11. Do you believe drug users are socialized differently and that these alleged differences account for drug use? Defend your answer.

12. Can divorce be blamed for adolescent drug use? Why or why not? If so, to what extent?

13. Do the current and alarming drug abuse statistics reflect the failure of social change in our society? Why do you think they do or don't?

14. Is making low-risk choices regarding drug use a more realistic approach for drug moderation than advocating "Just say no" to drug use? Why or why not?

Summary

1 Chemical dependence has been considered a major social problem throughout U.S. history.

2 People define chemical addiction in many ways. The essential feature is a chronic adherence to drugs despite significant negative consequences.

3 The major models of addiction are the moral model, the disease model, and the characterological or personality predisposition model.

4 Transitional periods, such as adolescence and middle age, are associated with unique sets of risk factors.

5 Addiction is a gradual process during which a minority of drug users become caught up in vicious cycles that worsen their situation, cause psychological and biological abnormalities, and increase their drug use. Addiction tends to progress, although this step is not inevitable.

6 Drug use is more serious today than in the past because (1) drug use and abuse have increased dramatically since 1960; (2) today's illicit drugs are more potent than in the past; (3) the media present drug use as rewarding; (4) drug use physically harms members of society; and (5) drug use and dealing by violent gangs are increasing at alarming rates.

7 Genetic and biophysiological theories explain addiction in terms of genes, brain dysfunction, and biochemical patterns.

8 Drugs of abuse interfere with the functioning of neurotransmitters, chemical messengers used for communication between brain regions. Drugs with abuse potential enhance the pleasure centers by causing the release of a specific brain neurotransmitter such as dopamine, which acts as a positive reinforcer.

9 The American Psychiatric Association classifies severe drug dependence as a form of psychiatric disorder. Drug abuse can cause mental conditions that mimic major psychiatric illnesses, such as schizophrenia, severe anxiety disorders, and suicidal depression.

10 Four genetic factors can contribute to drug abuse: (1) Many genetically determined psychiatric disorders are relieved by drugs of abuse, which in turn encourages their use; (2) high rates of addiction result from people who are genetically sensitive to addictive drugs; (3) such character traits as insecurity and vulnerability, which are often genetically determined, can lead to drug abuse behavior; and (4) the inability to break from a particular type of drug addiction may be genetically determined, especially when severe craving or very unpleasant withdrawal effects dominate.

11 Introversion and extroversion patterns have been associated with levels of neural arousal in brain stem circuits. These forms of arousal are closely associated with effects caused by drug stimulants or depressants.

12 Reinforcement or learning theory says that the motivation to use or abuse drugs stems from how the "highs" from alcohol and other drugs reduce anxiety, tension, and stress. Positive social influences by drug-using peers also promote drug use.

13 Social influence theories include social learning, the role of significant others, labeling, and subculture theories. Social learning theory explains drug use as a form of learned behavior. Significant others play a role in the learning process involved in drug use and/or abuse. Labeling theory says that other people we consider important can influence whether drug use becomes an option for us. If key people we admire or fear come to define our actions as deviant, then the definition becomes the "fact" of our reality. Subculture theories trace original drug experimentation, use, and/or abuse to peer pressure.

14 There are a number of consistencies in socialization patterns found among drug abusers, which range from immaturity, maladjustment, and insecurity to exposure and belief that selling drugs is a very lucrative business.

15 Sociologist Howard Becker believes that first-time drug users become attached to drugs because of three factors: (1) They learn the techniques of drug use; (2) they learn to perceive the pleasurable effects of drugs; and (3) they learn to enjoy the drug experience.

16 Primary deviance is deviant behavior that the perpetrator does not identify with; hence, it is inconsequential deviant behavior. Secondary deviance is deviance with which one readily identifies.

17 Both internal and external social control should prevail concerning drug use. Internal control deals with internal psychic and internalized social attitudes. External control is exemplified by living in a neighborhood and community in which drug use and abuse are severely criticized or not tolerated as a means to seek pleasure or avoid stress and anxiety.

18 Low-risk and high-risk drug use choices refer to the process of developing values and attitudes toward alcohol and other drugs. Low-risk drug choices encompass values and attitudes leading to a controlled use of alcohol and drugs — from total abstinence to very moderate use. High-risk choices encompass values and attitudes leading to using drugs both habitually and addictively.

References

Akers, R. L. "Problems in the Sociology of Deviance: Social Definition and Behavior." *Social Forces* 6 (June 1968): 455–465.

Akers, R. L. *Drugs, Alcohol, and Society: Social Structure, Process, and Policy.* Belmont, CA: Wadsworth, 1992.

American Psychiatric Association (APA). "Substance-Related Disorders." *Diagnostic and Statistical Manual of Mental Disorders (DSM-IV-TR)* 4th ed. Revised. A. Francis, Chair. Washington, DC: American Psychiatric Association, 2000: 191–295.

Apostolides, M. "Special Report: The Addiction Revolution: Old Habits Get New Choices." *Psychology Today* 29 (September/October 1996): 33–43, 75–76.

Bandura, A. *Social Learning Theory.* Englewood Cliffs, NJ: Prentice Hall, 1977.

Beattie, M. *Codependent No More.* San Francisco: Harper, 1987.

Becker, H. S. *Outsiders: Studies in the Sociology of Deviance.* New York: Free Press, 1963.

Becker, H. S. "History, Culture, and Subjective Experience: An Exploration of the Social Basis of Drug-Induced Experiences." *Journal of Health and Social Behavior* 8 (1967): 163–176.

Bejerot, N. "Current Problems of Drug Addiction." *Lakartidingen* (Sweden) 62, 50 (1965): 4231–4238.

Bejerot, N. *Addiction: An Artificially Induced Drive.* Springfield, IL: Thomas, 1972.

Bejerot, N. "The Biological and Social Character of Drug Dependence." In *Psychiatrie der Gegenwart, Forschung und Praxis,* 2nd ed., edited by K. P. Kisker, J. E. Meyer, C. Muller, and E. Stromogrew, Vol. 3: 488P518. Berlin: Springer-Verlag, 1975.

Bespalov, A., A. Lebedev, G. Panchenko, and E. Zvartau. "Effects of Abused Drugs on Thresholds and Breaking Points of Intracranial Self-Stimulation in Rats." *European Neuropsychopharmacology: The Journal of the European College of Neuropharmacology* 9 (1999): 377–383.

Best, J., and D. F. Luckenbill. *Organizing Deviance,* 2nd ed. Englewood Cliffs, NJ: Prentice-Hall, 1994.

Burns, D. B. "The Web of Caring: An Approach to Accountability in Alcohol Policy." In *Designing Alcohol and Other Drug Prevention Programs in Higher Education.* U.S. Department of Education. Newton, MA: Higher Education Center for Alcohol and Other Drug Prevention, 1997. Available http://www.edc.org/hec/pubs/theorybook/burns.html.

Carlson, N. *Psychology: The Science of Behavior,* 3rd ed. Boston: Allyn and Bacon, 1990.

Center for Substance Abuse Research (CESAR). "Early Alcohol Users More Likely to Report Substance Use and Criminal Activity as Young Adults" (September 2003). Available http://www.cesar.umd.edu.

Center for Substance Abuse Research (CESAR). "Eighth Graders' Perceived Harmfulness of Ecstasy, LSD, and Inhalant Use Continues to Decrease; Suggests 'Vulnerability to Resurgence of Use." 23 April 2007. Available http://www.cesar.umd.edu.

Centers for Disease Control and Prevention (CDCP). "Youth Risk Behavior Surveillance — United States, 2003." *Morbidity and Mortality Weekly Report* 53, SS-2 (2004): 1–96.

Cheron, J. M. *Symbolic Interactionism: An Introduction, an Interpretation, an Integration,* 7th ed. Englewood Cliffs, NJ: Prentice-Hall, 2001.

Clatts, M., D. L. Welle, L. A. Goldsamt, and S. E. Lankenau. "An Ethno-Epidemiological Model for the Study of Trends in Illicit Drug Use." In *The American Drug Scene: An Anthology,* edited by J. A. Inciardi and K. McElrath, 225–249. New York: Oxford University Press, 2008.

Clinard, M. B., and R. F. Meier. *Sociology of Deviant Behavior,* 8th ed. Fort Worth, TX: Harcourt Brace Jovanovich, 1992.

Cohen, A. K. *Delinquent Boys: The Culture of the Gang.* Glencoe, IL: Free Press, 1955.

Cohen, G. D. "No Job for a Grown-Up." *Utne Reader* (January/February 1997): 47.

Conrad, P., and J. W. Schneider. *Deviance and Medicalization.* St. Louis, MO: Mosby, 1980.

Doweiko, H. E. *Concepts of Chemical Dependency,* 5th ed. Pacific Grove, CA: Brooks/Cole, 2002.

Ellickson, P. L., J. S. Tucker, and D. J. Klein. "Ten-Year Prospective Study of Public Health Problems Associated with Early Drinking." *Pediatrics* 111, 5 (2003): 949–955.

Eysenck, H. J., and M. W. Eysenck. *Personality and Individual Differences: A Natural Science Approach.* New York: Plenum Press, 1985.

Farrar, H., and G. Kearns. "Cocaine: Clinical Pharmacology and Toxicology." *Journal of Pediatrics* 115 (1989): 665–675.

Fischer, C. S. *The Urban Experience.* New York: Harcourt Brace Jovanovich, 1976.

Frosch, W. A. "An Analytic Overview of the Addictions." In *The Addictions: Multidisciplinary Perspectives and Treatments,* edited by H. Milman and H. Shaffer. Lexington, MA: Lexington Books/D.C. Heath, 1985.

Gardner, E. L. "Brain Reward Mechanisms." In *Substance Abuse: A Comprehensive Textbook,* 2nd ed., edited by J. H. Lowinson, P. Ruiz, R. B. Millman, and J. G. Langrod, pp. 60–69. Baltimore: Williams & Wilkins, 1992.

Gergen, K. *The Saturated Self: Dilemmas of Identity in Contemporary Life.* New York: Basic Books, Inc., 2000.

Glick, R., and J. Moore, eds. *Drugs in Hispanic Communities.* New Brunswick, NJ: Rutgers University Press, 1990.

Goode, E. *Deviant Behavior,* 5th ed. Upper Saddle River, NJ: Prentice Hall, 1997.

Gray, J. A. *The Psychology of Fear and Stress,* 2nd ed. Cambridge, UK: Cambridge University Press, 1987.

Gray, P. *Psychology,* 3rd ed. New York: Worth, 1999.

Grinspoon, L. "Update on Cocaine." *Harvard Mental Health Letter* 10 (September 1993): 1–4.

Heitzeg, N. A. *Deviance: Rulemakers and Rulebreakers*. Minneapolis, MN: West Publishing, 1996.

Henslin, J. M. *Essentials of Sociology: A Down-to-Earth Approach*, 5th edition. Boston: Pearson/Allyn and Bacon, 2003.

Hewitt, J. P. *Self and Society: A Symbolic Interactionist Social Psychology*, 6th ed. Boston: Allyn and Bacon, 1994.

Hirschi, T. *Causes of Delinquency*, 2nd ed. Los Angeles: University of California Press, 1971.

Inciardi, J. A., D. Lockwood, and A. E. Pottieger. *Women and Crack Cocaine*. New York: Macmillan, 1993.

Jellinek, E. M. *The Disease Concept of Alcoholism*. Highland Park, NJ: Hillhouse Press, 1960.

Johnston, L. D., P. M. O'Malley, and J. G. Bachman. *Monitoring the Future National Results on Adolescent Drug Use: Overview of Key Findings, 2002*. Rockville, MD: National Institute on Drug Abuse, 2003.

Johnston, L. D., P. M. O'Malley, and J. G. Bachman. *Monitoring the Future: National Results on Adolescent Drug Use, Overview of Key Findings, 2005*. Bethesda, MD: National Institute on Drug Abuse, 2006.

Johnston, L. D., P. M. O'Malley, J. G. Bachman, and J. E. Schulenberg. *Monitoring the Future: National Survey Results on Drug Use, 1975–2003, Vol. 1: Secondary School Students 2003*. Bethesda, MD: National Institute on Drug Abuse, 2003.

Johnston, L. D., P. M. O'Malley, J. G. Bachman, and J. E. Schulenberg. *Monitoring the Future: National Results on Adolescent Drug Use: Overview of Key Findings*. Bethesda, MD: National Institute on Drug Abuse, 2004.

Jones, J. *Hep-Cats, Narcs, and Pipe Dreams: A History of America's Romance with Illegal Drugs*. Baltimore, MD: Johns Hopkins University Press, 1996.

Kelly, K. and P. Ramundo. *You Mean I'm Not Lazy, Stupid, and Crazy?!* New York: Scribner, Trade Paperback, 2006.

Kessler, R. C., W. T. Chiu, O Demler, E. E. Walters. "Prevalence, Severity, and Comorbidity of Twelve-Month DSM-IV Disorders in the National Comorbidity Survey Replication (NCS-R)." *Archives of General Psychiatry* 62 (2005): 617–627.

Khantzian, E. J. "Addiction as a Brain Disease." *American Journal of Psychiatry* 155 (June 1998): 711–713.

Koob, G. "Drug Addiction." *Neurobiology of Disease* 7, 5 (October 2000): 543–545.

Lemert, E. M. *Social Psychology: A Systematic Approach to the Theory of Sociopathic Behavior*. New York: McGraw-Hill, 1951.

Lemonick, M. D. with A. Park. "The Science of Addiction." *Time* (14 July 2007): 42–48.

Liska, A. E., and S. F. Messner. *Perspectives on Crime and Deviance*. Upper Saddle River, NJ: Prentice Hall, 1999.

Marshall, M. "Conclusions." In *Beliefs, Behavior, and Alcoholic Beverages: A Cross-Cultural Survey*, edited by M. Marshall, 451–457. Ann Arbor, MI: University of Michigan Press, 1979.

Mathias, R. "Novelty Seekers and Drug Abusers Tap Same Brain Reward System, Animal Studies Show." *NIDA Notes* 10, 4 (July/August 1995): 1–5.

Miller, N. S. *Addiction Psychiatry: Current Diagnosis and Treatment*. New York: Wiley, 1995.

Moore, J. *Homeboys: Gangs, Drugs and Prison in the Barrios of Los Angeles*. Philadelphia: Temple University Press, 1978.

Moore, J. "Gangs, Drugs, and Violence." In *Gangs: The Origins and Impact of Contemporary Youth Gangs in the United States*, edited by S. Cummings and D. J. Monti, 27–46. Albany: State University of New York Press, 1993.

Myers, P. L. "Sources and Configurations of Institutional Denial." *Employee Assistance Quarterly* 5(B) (1990): 43–54.

National Institute on Drug Abuse (NIDA). *Theories on Drug Abuse: Selected Contemporary Perspectives*. NIDA Research Monograph Series. U.S. Department of Health and Human Services. Rockville, MD: U.S. Government Printing Office, 1980.

National Institute on Drug Abuse (NIDA). "Study Finds Higher Use Among Adolescents Whose Parents Divorce." *NIDA Notes* 5 (Summer 1990): 10.

National Institute on Drug Abuse (NIDA). "Double Trouble: Substance Abuse and Psychiatric Disorders." *NIDA Notes* 8 (November/December 1993): 20.

National Institute on Drug Abuse (NIDA). "Attention and Memory Impaired in Heavy Users of Marijuana." Rockville, MD: Office of the National Institute on Drug Abuse, 20 February 1996.

National Institute on Drug Abuse (NIDA). *Principles of Drug Addiction Treatment*. New York: The Lindesmith Center, 1996.

National Institute on Drug Abuse (NIDA). *Principles of Drug Addiction Treatment*, National Institutes of Health Publication No. 99-4180, October 1999.

National Institute on Drug Abuse (NIDA). "Addiction and Co-Occurring Mental Disorders." *NIDA Notes* 21 (February 2007): 3.

Needle, R. H., S. S. Su, and W. J. Doherty. "Divorce, Remarriage, and Adolescent Substance Use: A Prospective Longitudinal Study." *Journal of Marriage and the Family* 52 (1990): 157–159.

O'Brien, R., S. Cohen, G. Evans, and J. Fine. *The Encyclopedia of Drug Abuse*, 2nd ed. New York: Facts on File, 1992.

Office of National Drug Control Policy (ONDCP). *Drug Facts: Cocaine*. White House Drug Policy. Clearing House: Rockville, MD: November 2003.

Plummer, K. "Misunderstanding Labelling Perspectives." In *Deviant Interpretations*, edited by D. Downes and P. Rock, 85–121. London: Robertson, 1979.

Pontell, H. N. *Social Deviance*, 2nd ed. Upper Saddle River, NJ: Prentice Hall, 1996.

Radowitz, J. V. "Smoking and Drug Abuse Traits Linked to Genes." *The Independent*, 18 June 2003, Independent Digital (UK) Ltd.

Reckless, W. C. "A New Theory of Delinquency." *Federal Probation* 25 (1961): 42–46.

Ritzer, G. *Enchanting a Disenchanted World: Revolutionizing the Means of Consumption*. Thousand Oaks, CA: Pine Forge Press, 1999.

Ritzer, G. *The McDonaldization of Society*, 3rd ed. Thousand Oaks, CA: Pine Forge Press, 2000.

Rousar, E., K. Brooner, M. W. Regier, and G. E. Bigelow. "Psychiatric Distress in Antisocial Drug Abusers: Relation to Other Personality Disorders." *Drug and Alcohol Dependence* 34 (1995): 149–154.

Rudgley, R. *Essential Substances: A Cultural History of Intoxicants in Society*. New York: Kodansha International, 1993.

Sanders, W. B. *Gangbangs and Drive-bys: Grounded Culture and Juvenile Gang Violence*. New York: Aldine De Gruyter, 1994.

Schur, E. M. *Labeling Deviant Behavior*. New York: Harper & Row, 1971.

Shelden, R. G., S. K. Tracy, and W. B. Brown. *Youth Gangs in American Society*, 2nd ed. Belmont, CA: Wadsworth/Thomson Learning, 2001.

Siegel, L. J., and J. J. Senna. *Juvenile Delinquency: Theory, Practice and Law*. St. Paul, MN: West Publishing, 1994.

Smith, D., E. Milkman, and S. Sunderwirth. "Addictive Disease: Concept and Controversy." In *Addictions: Multidisciplinary Perspectives and Treatments*, edited by H. Milkman and H. J. Shaffer. Lexington, MA: Lexington Books/ D.C. Heath, 1985.

Spanagel, R., and F. Weiss. "The Dopamine Hypothesis of Reward: Past and Current Status." *Trends in Neuroscience* 22 (1999): 521–527.

Substance Abuse and Mental Health Services Administration (SAMHSA). *National Household Survey on Drug Abuse: Fact Sheet*. Rockville, MD: U.S. Department of Health and Human Services, August 1998.

Substance Abuse and Mental Health Services (SAMHSA). *Study Shows Strong Relationship Between Adolescent Behavior Problems and Alcohol Use*. Rockville, MD: U.S. Department of Health and Human Services Press Release, 1 March 2000.

Substance Abuse and Mental Health Services Administration (SAMHSA). *National Survey on Drug Use and Health (NSDUH) Report. Substance Use Disorder and Serious Psychological Distress by Employment Status*. Rockville, MD: Substance Abuse and Mental Health Services Administration, Office of Applied Studies, 2006.

Sutherland, E. *Principles of Criminology*, 4th ed. Philadelphia: Lippincott, 1947.

Syvertsen, J. L. "Some Considerations on the Disease Concept of Addiction." In *The American Drug Scene: An Anthology*, edited by J. A. Inciardi and K. McElrath, 16–26. New York: Oxford University Press, 2008.

Tarter, R. E., A. Alterman, and K. L. Edwards. "Alcoholic Denial: A Biopsychosociological Interpretation." *Journal of Studies on Alcohol* 45 (1983): 214–218.

Thio, A. *Deviant Behavior*, 5th ed. New York: Addison Wesley Longman, 1998.

Thomas, W. I., with D. S. Thomas. *The Child in America*. New York: Knopf, 1923.

Thornberry, T. P. "Risk Factors for Gang Membership." In *The Modern Gang Reader*, 2nd ed., edited by J. Miller, C. L. Maxson, and M. W. Klein, 32–42. Los Angeles: Roxbury, 2001.

Uhl, G., K. Blum, E. Noble, and S. Smith. "Substance Abuse Vulnerability and D-2 Receptor Genes." *Trends in Neurological Sciences* 16 (1993): 83–88.

Uhl, G., A. Persico, and S. Smith. "Current Excitement with D-2 Dopamine Receptor Gene Alleles in Substance Abuse." *Archives of General Psychiatry* 49 (February 1992): 157–160.

USA Today. "Seven in 10 Drug Users Work Full-Time" (1999). Available http://www.mapinc.org/drugnews/ v99/n983/a01.html.

Volkow, N. *Cocaine and the Changing Brain: Changes in Human Brain Systems After Longterm Cocaine Use* (1 February 1999). Available http://www.drugabuse.gov/meetsum/ccb/ volkow.html.

Waldorf, D. "Natural Recovery from Opiate Addiction: Some Social-Psychological Processes of Untreated Recovery." *Journal of Drug Issues* 13 (1983): 237–280.

Weiss, F. *Cocaine and the Changing Brain: Cocaine Dependence and Withdrawal: Neuroadaptive Changes in Brain Reward and Stress Systems* (1999). Available http://www.nida. nih.gov/meetsum/ccb/weiss.html.

Werner, E., and S. Henry. *Criminological Theory: An Analysis of Its Underlying Assumptions*. Fort Worth, TX: Harcourt Brace College Publishers, 1995.

Williams III, F. P., and M. D. McShane. *Criminological Theory*, 3rd ed. Upper Saddle River, NJ: Prentice Hall, 1999.

Wooden, W. S. *Renegade Kids, Suburban Outlaws: From Youth Culture to Delinquency*. Belmont, CA: Wadsworth/Thomson Learning, 1995.

World Health Organization Expert Committee on Addiction-Producing Drugs. *World Health Organization Technical Report* 273 (1964): 9–10.

Wyman, J. "Promising Advances Toward Understanding the Genetic Roots of Addiction." *NIDA Notes* 12 (July/ August 1997): 1–5.

Yinger, M. J. *Countercultures: The Promise and the Peril of a World Turned Upside Down*. New York: Free Press, 1982.

Learning ◎bjectives

On completing this chapter you will be able to:

- ◎ Identify the major criteria that determine how society regulates drugs.

- ◎ Explain the significance of the Pure Food and Drug Act of 1906 and why it was important in regulating drugs of abuse.

- ◎ Describe the changes in drug regulation that occurred because of the Kefauver-Harris Amendment of 1962.

- ◎ Identify and explain the stages of testing for an investigational new drug.

- ◎ Discuss the special provisions (exceptions) made by the Food and Drug Administration (FDA) for drug marketing.

- ◎ Outline the procedures used by the FDA to regulate nonprescription drugs.

- ◎ List the three principal factors that influence the formation of laws regulating drug abuse.

- ◎ Outline the major approaches used to reduce substance abuse.

- ◎ Describe the three major strategies for combating drug use and abuse.

- ◎ Explain the main arguments for and against legalizing drugs.

- ◎ List the most common types of drug testing.

- ◎ Describe four major factors required for workable drug policies (pragmatic drug policies).

Did You Know?

- O Some patent medicines sold at the turn of the twentieth century contained opium and cocaine and were highly addictive.

- O Before World War II, all drugs, except those classified as narcotics, were available without prescription.

- O Enforcement of drug use policies and drug laws differs across different countries.

- O In 2005, an estimated 19.7 million Americans age 12 or older were current illicit drug users.

- O The United States spends approximately $3.4 billion per year on drug interdiction.

Drugs and Society Online is a great source for additional drugs and society information for both students and instructors.
Visit **http://drugsandsociety.jbpub.com** to find a variety of useful tools for learning, thinking, and teaching.

Introduction

Society mandates that it maintains control over which drugs are permissible and which drugs are prohibited. Through legislation, we decide which drugs are licit and illicit. We decide which licit drugs are readily available "over-the-counter" (OTC) and which can be obtained by prescription only. Thus, drug laws prohibit indiscriminate use of what society defines as a drug. As we saw in Chapter 1, licit and illicit drugs can produce vastly different effects on both mental and bodily functions. Chapters 4 and 5 focus on how and why different types of drugs affect our bodies. In this chapter, you will come to better understand how society attempts to control drug use and abuse.

Drug regulation brings to mind numerous questions. For example, why are the laws against drug use so controversial? When were these laws first created? In regulating and prohibiting the free marketing of either licit or illicit drug use, how does U.S. society compare with other societies? Do these other societies have fewer drug users as a result of being more lenient or restrictive toward drug abusers? Do our drug laws coincide with the opinions of most U.S. citizens? Are nonpunitive approaches toward drug use feasible? Do drug laws realistically diminish drug use? What common attitudes prevail regarding the enactment and enforcement of drug laws?

This chapter attempts to respond to many of these questions by delving into the relationship between drug use and the law. It examines the development of drug regulations in the United States that apply to both the manufacture of drugs and the control of their use. Although many think that the regulation of drug manufacturing and drug abuse lie at the opposite ends of the spectrum, regulation of drug manufacturing and abuse of drugs actually evolved from the same process.

Cultural Attitudes About Drug Use

Currently, cultural attitudes in the United States regarding the use of drugs blend beliefs in individuals' rights to live their lives as they desire with society's obligation to protect its members from the burdens imposed by uncontrolled behavior. The history of drug regulation consists of regulatory swings in response to attempts by government to balance these two factors while responding to public pressures and perceived public needs. For example, 100 years ago, most people expected the government to protect citizens' rights to produce and market new foods and substances; they did not expect or desire the government to regulate product quality or claims. Instead, the public relied on private morals and common sense to obtain quality and protection in an era of simple technology. Unfortunately, U.S. society had to learn by tragic experience that its trust was not well placed; many unscrupulous entrepreneurs were willing to risk the safety and welfare of the public in an effort to maximize profits and acquire wealth. In fact, many medicines of these earlier times were not merely ineffective but often dangerous.

Because of the advent of high technology and the rapid advancements society has made, we now rely on highly trained experts and government "watchdog" agencies for consumer information and protection. Out of this changing environment have evolved two major guidelines for controlling drug development and marketing:

1. Society has the right to protect itself from the damaging effects of drug use. This concept not only is closely aligned with the emotional and highly visible issues of drug abuse, but also includes protection from other drug side effects. Thus, although we expect the government to protect society from drugs that can cause addiction, we also expect it to protect us from drugs that cause cancer, cardiovascular disease, or other threatening medical conditions.
2. Society has the right to demand that drugs approved for marketing be safe and effective to the general public. If drug manufacturers promise that their products will relieve pain, those drugs should be analgesics; if they promise that their products will relieve depression, those drugs should be antidepressants; if they promise that their products will relieve stuffy noses, those drugs should be decongestants.

The public, through the activities of regulatory agencies and statutory enactments, has attempted to require that drug manufacturers produce safe and effective pharmaceutical products. Closely linked to these efforts is the fact that society uses similar strategies to protect itself from the problems associated with the specific drug side effect of dependence or addiction, which is associated with drug abuse.

The Road to Regulation and the FDA

In the late 1800s and early 1900s, sales of uncontrolled medicines flourished and became widespread. Many of these products were called patent medicines, which signified that the ingredients were secret, not that they were patented. The decline of patent medicines began with the 1906 Pure Food and Drug Act, which required manufacturers to indicate the amounts of alcohol, morphine, opium, cocaine, heroin, and marijuana extract on the label of each product. It became obvious at this time that many medicinal products on the market labeled "nonaddictive" were, in fact, potent drugs "in sheep's labeling" and could cause severe dependence. However, most government interest at the time centered on regulation of the food industry, not drugs.

Even though federal drug regulation was based on the free-market philosophy that consumers could make choices for themselves, it was decided that the public should have information about possible dependence-producing drugs to ensure that they understood the risks associated with using these products. The Pure Food and Drug Act made misrepresentation illegal, so that a potentially addicting patent drug could not be advertised as "non–habit forming." This step marked the beginning of new involvement by governmental agencies in drug manufacturing.

Shortcomings in the Pure Food and Drug Act quickly became obvious. For example, the law did not allow the government to stop the distribution of dangerous preparations designed to reduce weight. One such product contained dinitrophenol, a compound that purportedly increased metabolic rate and was responsible for many deaths (FDA History Office 1997).

The Pure Food and Drug Act was modified, albeit not in a consumer-protective manner, by the Sherley Amendment in 1912. The distributor of a cancer "remedy" was indicted for falsely claiming on the label that the contents were effective. The case was decided in the U.S. Supreme Court in 1911. Justice Holmes, writing for the majority opinion, said that, based on the 1906 act, the company had not violated any law because legally all it was required to do was accurately state the contents and their strength and quality. The accuracy of the therapeutic claims made by drug manufacturers was not controlled. Congress took the hint and passed the Sherley Amendment to add to the existing law the requirement that labels should not contain "any statement . . . regarding the curative or therapeutic effect . . . which is false and fraudulent." However, the law required that the government prove fraud, which turned out to be difficult (and is still problematic). This amendment did not improve drug products but merely encouraged pharmaceutical companies to be more vague in their advertisements (Temin 1980).

Prescription Versus OTC Drugs

The distinction between prescription and OTC drugs is relatively new to the pharmaceutical industry. All nonnarcotic drugs were available OTC before World War II. It was not until a drug company unwittingly produced a toxic product that killed 107 people that the FDA was given control over drug safety in the 1938 Federal Food, Drug, and Cosmetic Act (Hunter et al. 1993). The bill had been debated for several years in Congress and showed no promise of passage. Then, a pharmaceutical company decided to sell a liquid form of a sulfa drug (one of the first antibiotics) and found that the drug would dissolve well in a chemical solvent, diethylene glycol (presently used in antifreeze products). The company marketed the antibiotic as Elixir Sulfanilamide without testing the solvent for toxicity. Under the 1906 Pure Food and Drug Act, the company could not be prosecuted for the toxicity of this form of drug or for not testing the formulation of the drug on animals first. It could only be prosecuted for mislabeling the product on the technicality that *elixir* refers to a solution in alcohol, not a solution in diethylene glycol. Again, it was apparent that the laws in place provided woefully inadequate protection for the public.

The 1938 act differed from the 1906 law in several ways. It defined *drugs* to include products that affected bodily structure or function even in the absence of disease. Companies had to file applications with the government for all new drugs showing that they were safe (not effective — just safe) for use as described. The drug label had to list all ingredients and include the quantity of each, as well as provide instructions regarding correct use of the drug and warnings about its dangers. In addition, the act eliminated a Sherley Amendment requirement to prove intent to defraud in drug misbranding cases (FDA Backgrounder 2005).

Before passage of the 1938 act, you could go to a doctor and obtain a prescription for any nonnarcotic drug or go to the pharmacy directly if you had already decided what was needed. The labeling requirement in the 1938 act allowed drug companies to create a class of drugs that could not be sold legally without a prescription. It has been suggested that the actions by the FDA were motivated by the frequent public misuse of two classes of drugs developed before passage of the 1938 law: sulfa antibiotics and barbiturates. People often took too little of the antibiotics to cure an infection and too much of the barbiturates and became addicted.

The 1938 Food, Drug, and Cosmetic Act allowed the manufacturer to determine whether a drug was to be labeled *prescription* or *nonprescription*. The same product could be sold as prescription by one company and as OTC by another. After the Durham-Humphrey Amendment was passed in 1951, almost all new drugs were placed in the prescription-only class. The drugs that were patented and marketed after World War II included potent new antibiotics and phenothiazine tranquilizers such as Thorazine. Both the FDA and the drug firms thought these products were potentially too dangerous to sell OTC. The Durham-Humphrey Amendment established the criteria, which are still used today, for determining whether a drug should be classified as prescription or nonprescription. Basically, if a drug does not fall into one of the following three categories, it is considered nonprescription:

1. The drug is habit-forming.
2. The drug is not safe for self-medication because of its toxicity.
3. The drug is a new compound that has not been shown to be completely safe.

In 1959, Senator Estes Kefauver initiated hearings concerned with the enormous profit margins earned by drug companies due to the lack of competition in the market for new, patented drugs. Testimony by physicians revealed that an average doctor in clinical practice often was not able to evaluate accurately the efficacy of the drugs he or she prescribed. The 1938 law did not give the FDA authority to supervise clinical testing of drugs; consequently, the effectiveness of drugs being sold to the public was not being determined. Both the Kefauver and Harris Amendments put forth in Congress were intended to deal with this problem but showed no likely signs of becoming law until the thalidomide tragedy occurred.

During the Kefauver hearings, the FDA received an approval request for Kevadon, a brand of thalidomide that the William Merrell Company hoped to market in the United States. **Thalidomide** had been used in Europe as a sedative for pregnant women. Despite ongoing pressure, medical officer Frances Kelsey refused to allow the request to be approved because of insufficient safety data (FDA History Office 1997). By 1962, the horrifying effects of thalidomide on developing fetuses became known. There are two approximately 24-hour intervals early in pregnancy when thalidomide can alter the development of the arms and legs of an embryo. If a woman takes thalidomide on one or both of these days, the infant could be born with abnormally developed arms and/or legs (called **phocomelia**, from the Greek words for flippers, or "seal-shaped limbs"). Even though Kevadon was never approved for marketing in this country, Merrell had distributed more than 2 million tablets in the United States for investigational use — use that the law and regulations left mostly unchecked. Once thalidomide's deleterious effects became known, the FDA moved quickly to recover the supply from physicians, pharmacists, and patients. For her efforts, Kelsey received the President's Distinguished Federal Civilian Service Award in 1962, the highest civilian honor available to government employees (FDA History Office 1997).

Although standard testing probably would not have detected the congenital effect of thalidomide and the tragedy would likely have occurred anyway, these debilitated infants stimulated passage of the 1962 Kefauver and Harris Amendments. They strengthened the government's regulation of both the introduction of new drugs and the production and sale of existing drugs. The amendments required, for the first time, that drug manufacturers demonstrate the efficacy as well as the safety of their drug products. The FDA was empowered to retract approval of a drug that was already being marketed. In addition, the agency was permitted to regulate and evaluate drug testing by pharmaceutical companies and mandate standards of good drug-manufacturing policy.

KEY TERMS

thalidomide
a sedative drug that, when used during pregnancy, can cause severe developmental damage to a fetus

phocomelia
a birth defect; impaired development of the arms, legs, or both

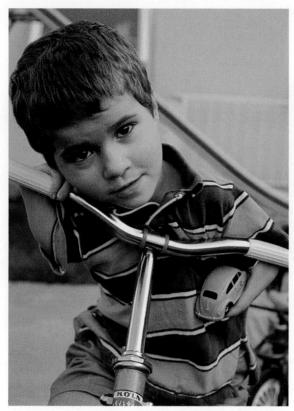

Characteristic limb deformities caused by thalidomide.

The Rising Demand for Effectiveness in Medicinal Drugs

To evaluate the effectiveness of the more than 4000 drug products that were introduced between 1938 and 1962, the FDA contracted with the National Research Council to perform the Drug Efficacy Study. This investigation started in 1966 and ran for 3 years. The council was asked to rate drugs as either effective or ineffective. Although the study was supposed to be based on scientific evidence, this information often was not available, which meant that conclusions sometimes relied on the clinical experience of the physicians on each panel; these judgments were not always based on reliable information.

A legal challenge resulted when the FDA took an "ineffective" drug off the market and the manufacturer sued. This action finally forced the FDA to define what constituted an adequate and well-controlled investigation. Adequate, documented clinical experience was no longer satisfactory proof that a drug was safe and effective. Each new drug application now had to include information about the drug's performance in patients compared with the experiences of a carefully defined control group. The drug could be compared with (1) a placebo, (2) another drug known to be active based on previous studies, (3) the established results of no treatment, or (4) historical data about the course of the illness without the use of the drug in question. In addition, a drug marketed before 1962 could no longer be grandfathered in. If the company could not prove the drug had the qualifications to pass the post-1962 tests for a new drug, it was considered a new, unapproved drug and could not legally be sold.

Regulating the Development of New Drugs

The amended Federal Food, Drug, and Cosmetic Act in force today requires that all new drugs be registered with and approved by the FDA. The FDA is mandated by Congress to (1) ensure the rights and safety of human subjects during clinical testing of experimental drugs; (2) evaluate the safety and efficacy of new treatments based on test results and information from the sponsors (often health-related companies); and (3) compare potential benefits and risks to determine whether a new drug should be approved and marketed. Because of FDA regulations, all pharmaceutical companies must follow a series of steps when seeking permission to market a new drug (see Figure 3.1).

Regulatory Steps for New Prescription Drugs

Step 1: Preclinical Research and Development A chemical must be identified as having potential value in the treatment of a particular condition or disease. The company interested in marketing the chemical as a drug must run a series of tests on at least two or more animal species. Careful records must be kept of side effects, absorption, distribution, metabolism, excretion, and the dosages of the drug necessary to produce the various effects. Carcinogenic, mutagenic, and teratogenic variables are tested. The dose-response curve must be determined along with potency, and then the risk and benefit of the substance must be calculated (see Chapter 5). If the company still believes there is a market for the substance, it forwards the data to the FDA to obtain an investigational new drug (IND) number for further tests. No more than 5 in 5000 tested compounds pass these preclinical trials and are proposed for clinical studies (FDA 2002).

FIGURE 3.1
Steps required by the FDA for reviewing a new drug.

Step 2: Clinical Research and Development Animal tests provide some information, but ultimately tests must be done on the species for which the potential drug is intended — that is, humans. These tests usually follow three phases.

Phase 1 is called the *initial clinical stage.* Small numbers of volunteers (usually 20–100), typically healthy people but sometimes patients, are recruited to establish drug safety and dosage ranges for effective treatment and to examine side effects. Formerly, much of this research was done on prison inmates, but because of bad publicity and the possibility of coercion, fewer prisoners are used today. Medical students, paid college student volunteers, and volunteers being treated at free clinics are more often used after obtaining informed consent. The data from Phase 1 clinical trials are collected, analyzed, and sent to the FDA for approval before beginning the next phase of human subject testing.

Phase 2 testing is called the *clinical pharmacological evaluation stage.* The effects of the drug are tested to eliminate investigator bias and to determine side effects and the effectiveness of the treatment. Because the safety of the new drug has not been thoroughly established, a few patients (perhaps 100–300 volunteers) with the medical problem the drug is intended to treat participate in these studies. Statistical evaluation of this information is carried out before proceeding with Phase 3 testing.

Phase 3 is the *extended clinical evaluation stage.* By this time, the pharmaceutical company has a good idea of both drug effectiveness and dangers. The drug can be offered safely to a wider group of participating clinics and physicians, who cooperate in the administration of the potential drug — when medically appropriate — to thousands of volunteer patients who have given informed consent.

This stage makes the drug available on a wide experimental basis. Sometimes, by this point, there has been publicity about the new drug, and people with the particular disease for which the drug was developed may actively seek out physicians licensed to experiment with it.

During Phase 3 testing, safety checks are made and any side effects that might show up as more people are exposed to the drug are noted. After the testing program concludes, careful analysis is made of the effectiveness, side effects, and recommended dosage. If there are sufficient data to demonstrate that the drug is safe and effective, the company submits a new drug application (NDA) as a formal request that the FDA consider approving the drug for marketing. The application usually comprises many thousands of pages of data and analysis, and the FDA must sift through it and decide whether the risks of using the drug justify its potential benefits. The FDA usually calls for additional tests before the drug is determined to be safe and effective and before granting permission to market it.

Step 3: Permission to Market At this point, the FDA can allow the drug to be marketed under its patented name. In 2001, the average cost of developing a new drug was $802 million (Tufts Center for the Study of Drug Development 2005). It takes an average of 8.5 years to develop a new drug in the United States (FDA 2002). The situation is similar elsewhere, although in some countries the clinical evaluations are less stringent and require less time.

Once the drug is marketed, it continues to be closely scrutinized for adverse effects. This post-marketing surveillance is often referred to as *Phase 4* and is important because, in some cases, negative effects may not show up for a long time. For example, it was determined in 1970 that diethylstilbestrol (DES), when given to pregnant women to prevent miscarriage, causes an increased risk of a rare type of vaginal cancer in their daughters when these children enter their teens and young adult years. The FDA subsequently removed from the market the form of DES that had been used to treat pregnant women.

Exceptions: Special Drug-Marketing Laws There is continual concern that the process used by the FDA to evaluate prospective drugs is laborious and excessively lengthy. Hence, an amendment was passed to accelerate the evaluation of urgently needed drugs. The so-called fast-track rule has been applied to the testing of certain drugs used for the treatment of rare cancers, AIDS, and some other diseases. For example, Herceptin (trastuzumab), a drug used to treat breast cancer, received fast-track approval by the FDA in less than 5 months (FDA 1999). As a result, these drugs have reached the market after a much reduced testing program.

A second amendment, the Orphan Drug Law, allows drug companies to receive tax advantages if they develop drugs that are not very profitable because they are useful in treating only small numbers of patients, such as those who suffer from rare diseases. A *rare disease* is defined as one that affects fewer than 200,000 people in the United States or one for which the cost of development is not likely to be recovered by marketing.

The federal government and the FDA are continually refining the system for evaluating new drugs to ensure that new effective therapeutic substances can be made available for clinical use as soon as it is safely possible. Some of these modifications reflect the fact that patients with life-threatening diseases are willing to accept greater drug risks to gain faster access to potentially useful medications. Attempts to accelerate the drug review are exemplified by the Prescription Drug User Fee Act of 1992. This law required drug manufacturers to pay fees to the FDA for the evaluation of NDAs. Congress required the FDA to use these fees to hire more reviewers so as to expedite the reviews. Since passage of this act, the number of new drug approvals increased from 63 in 1991 to 131 in 1996 (FDA History Office 1997).

The Regulation of Nonprescription Drugs

The Durham-Humphrey Amendment to the Food, Drug, and Cosmetic Act made a distinction between prescription and nonprescription (OTC) drugs and required the FDA to regulate OTC drug marketing. In 1972, the FDA initiated a program to evaluate the effectiveness and safety of the nonprescription drugs on the market and to ensure that they included appropriate labeling (for more details, see Chapter 15). Each so-called active ingredient in the OTC medications was reviewed by a panel of drug experts including physicians, pharmacologists, and pharmacists. Based on the recommendations of these panels, the ingredients were placed in one of the following three categories:

I. Generally recognized as safe and effective for the claimed therapeutic indication
II. Not generally recognized as safe and effective or unacceptable indications
III. Insufficient data available to permit final classification

By 1981, the panels had made initial determinations about over 700 ingredients in more than 300,000 OTC drug products and submitted more than 60 reports to the FDA.

In the second phase of the OTC drug review, the FDA evaluated the panels' findings and submitted a tentative adoption of the panels' recommendations (after revision, if necessary), following public comment and scrutiny. After some time and careful consideration of new information, the agency issued a final ruling and classification of the ingredients under consideration.

The Effects of the OTC Review on Today's Medications

The review process for OTC ingredients has had a significant impact on the public's attitude about OTC products and their use (both good and bad) in self-medication. It was apparent from the review process that many OTC drug ingredients did not satisfy the requirements for safety and effectiveness. Consequently, it is almost certain that, in the future, there will be fewer active ingredients in OTC medicines, but these drugs will be safer and more effective than ever before.

In addition, with heightened public awareness, greater demand has been brought to bear on the FDA to make better drugs available to the public for self-medication. In response to these pressures, the FDA has adopted a **switching policy**, which allows the agency to review prescription drugs and evaluate their suitability as OTC products. The following criteria must be satisfied if a drug is to be switched to OTC status:

1. The drug must have been marketed by prescription for at least 3 years.
2. Use of the drug must have been relatively high during the time it was available as a prescription drug.
3. Adverse drug reactions must not be alarming, and the frequency of side effects must not have increased during the time the drug was available to the public.

In general, this switching policy has been well received by the public. The medical community and the FDA are generally positive about OTC switches as well. There are some concerns, however, that the wider access to more effective drug products will lead to increased abuse or misuse of OTC products. Hence, emphasis is placed on adequate labeling and education to ensure that consumers have sufficient information to use OTC products safely and effectively.

The Regulation of Drug Advertising

Much of the public's knowledge and impressions about drugs come from advertisements. It is difficult to ascertain the amount of money currently spent by the pharmaceutical industry to promote its products. One study estimated that total spending on promotion increased from $11.4 billion in 1996 to $29.9 billion in 2005. The same study reported that the percentage of sales spent on promotion grew from 14.2% to 18.2% during that same period (Donahue et al. 2007).

There is no doubt that these promotional efforts by pharmaceutical manufacturers have a tremendous impact on the drug-purchasing habits of the general public and health professionals.

The economics of prescription drugs are unique because a second party, the health professional, dictates what the consumer, the patient, will purchase. As a general rule, the FDA oversees most issues related to advertising of prescription drugs. In contrast, the Federal Trade Commission (FTC) regulates OTC and dietary supplement advertising. (Note that the FDA generally oversees decisions regarding the labeling of each of these three product classes; FTC 2007).

Direct to consumer advertising has both advantages and disadvantages. Advocates believe that it provides useful information to consumers that results in better health outcomes. Patients become more aware of potential treatments. They are encouraged to talk with healthcare professionals about health problems, particularly undertreated conditions such as high blood pressure and high cholesterol. This advertising also can help remove the stigma that accompanies diseases that in the past were rarely openly discussed, such as depression. Finally, direct to consumer advertising can remind patients to get their prescriptions refilled and help them adhere to their medication regimens. On the other hand, critics argue that this advertising encourages overuse of prescription drugs and use of the most costly treatments, instead of less expensive treatments that would be just as satisfactory (Rados 2004).

A significant amount of prescription drug promotion is directed at health professionals. The approaches employed by manufacturers to encourage health professionals to prescribe their products include advertising in prestigious medical journals, direct mail advertising, and some radio and television advertising. All printed and audio materials distributed by drug salespeople are controlled by government advertising regulations. Perhaps the most effective sales approach is for drug representatives to personally visit health professionals; this tactic is harder to regulate.

Many health professionals rely on drug company salespeople for the so-called latest scientific information concerning drugs and their effects. Although these representatives of the drug indus-

KEY TERMS

switching policy
an FDA policy allowing the change of suitable prescription drugs to over-the-counter status

try can provide an important informational service, it is essential that health professionals remember that these people make a living by selling these products, and often their information may be biased accordingly.

Many people in and out of the medical community have questioned the ethics of drug advertising and marketing in the United States and are concerned about the negative impact that deceptive promotion has on target populations. One of the biggest problems in dealing with misleading or false advertising is defining such deception. Probably the best guideline for such a definition is summarized in the Wheeler-Lea Amendment to the FTC Act:

> The term *false advertisement* means an advertisement, other than labeling, which is misleading in a material respect; and in determining whether any advertisement is misleading, there shall be taken into account not only representations . . . but the extent to which the advertisement fails to reveal facts.

Tough questions are being asked as to how much control should be exerted over the pharmaceutical industry to protect the public without excessively infringing on the rights of these companies to promote their goods. The solutions to these problems will not be simple. Nevertheless, efforts to keep drug advertisements accurate, in good taste, and informative are worthwhile and are necessary if the public is expected to make rational decisions about drug use (see "Here and Now," What's in an Ad?).

■ Federal Regulation and Quality Assurance

No matter what policy is adopted by the FDA and other drug-regulating agencies, there will always be those who criticize their efforts and complain that they do not do enough or that they do too much. On the one hand, the FDA has been blamed for being excessively careful and requiring too much testing before new drugs are approved for marketing. On the other hand, when new drugs are released and cause serious side effects, the FDA is condemned for being sloppy in its control of drug marketing.

What is the proper balance, and what do we, as consumers, have the right to expect from the government? These are questions each of us should ask, and we have a right to share our answers with government representatives.

Regardless of our individual feelings, it is important to understand that the current (and likely future) federal regulations do not ensure drug safety or effectiveness for everyone. Too many individual variables alter the way each of us responds to drugs, making such universal assurances impossible. Federal agencies can only deal with general policies and make general decisions. For example, what if the FDA determines that a given drug is reasonably safe in 95% of the population and effective in 70%? Are these acceptable figures, or should a drug be safe in 99% and effective in 90% before it is deemed suitable for general marketing? What of

Here and Now

What's in an Ad?

The Federal Food, Drug, and Cosmetic Act requires that all drug advertisements contain information in brief summary relating to side effects, contraindications, and effectiveness. The current advertising regulations specify that this information disclosure needs to include all the risk information in a product's approved labeling. Typically, print advertisements include a reprinting of the risk-related sections of the approved labeling (also called full prescribing information or the package insert). Sponsors, however, can write this risk information in language appropriate for the targeted audience. The FDA encourages this approach.

In addition to the specific disclosure requirements, advertisements cannot be false or misleading or omit material facts. They also must present a fair balance between effectiveness and risk information.

In addition, all prescription drug broadcast advertisements must abide by two specific requirements. First, broadcast advertisements must include the product's most important risk-related information in the audio or audio and visual parts of the advertisement. Second, broadcast advertisements must contain either a brief summary of the advertised product's risk information or, alternatively, make adequate provision for disseminating the product's approved labeling in connection with the ad. Thus, the regulations for broadcast advertisements recognize this medium's inherent limitations by providing an alternative mechanism for meeting the act's information disclosure requirement (FDA, Division of Drug Marketing, Advertising and Communications 2007).

the 5% or 1% of the population who will be adversely affected by this drug? What rights do they have to be protected?

There are no simple answers to these questions. Federal policies are inevitably compromises that assume that the clinician who prescribes the drug and/or the patient who buys and consumes it will be able to identify when use of that drug is inappropriate or threatening. Unfortunately, sometimes drug prescribing and drug consuming are done carelessly and unnecessary side effects occur or the drug does not work. Then the questions surface again: Are federal drug agencies doing all they can to protect the public? Should the laws be changed?

It is always difficult to predict the future, especially when it depends on sometimes fickle politicians and erratic public opinion. Nevertheless, with the dramatic increase in new and better drugs becoming available to the public, it is not likely that federal or state agencies will diminish their role in regulating drug use. Now more than ever, the public demands safer and more effective drugs. This public attitude will likely translate into even greater involvement by regulatory agencies in issues of drug development, assessment, and marketing.

Another reason for increased regulation in the future is that many of the larger pharmaceutical companies have become incredibly wealthy. Several of the most profitable companies have become subsidiaries of large corporations, and there is concern that some may be driven more by profit margins than by philanthropic interests. In such an environment, governmental agencies are essential to ensure that the rights of the public are protected.

Drug Abuse and the Law

The laws that govern the development, distribution, and use of drugs in general and drugs of abuse in particular are interrelated. There are, however, some unique features concerning the manner in which federal agencies deal with the drugs of abuse that warrant special consideration. A summary of drug abuse laws in the United States is shown in Table 3.1.

Coffee, tea, tobacco, alcohol, marijuana, hallucinogens, depressants (such as barbiturates), and narcotics have been subject to a wide range of controls, varying from none to rigid restrictions. A few countries historically have instituted severe penalties, such as strangulation for smoking tobacco or

Table 3.1 Federal Laws Associated with the Control of Narcotics and Other Abused Drugs

DATE	NAME OF LEGISLATION	SUMMARY OF COVERAGE AND INTENT OF LEGISLATION
1914	Harrison Act	First federal legislation to regulate and control the production, importation, sale, purchase, and free distribution of opium or drugs derived from opium.
1924	Heroin Act	Made it illegal to manufacture heroin.
1956	Narcotics Control Act	Intended to impose very severe penalties for those convicted of narcotics or marijuana charges.
1965	Drug Abuse Control Amendments (DACA)	Adopted strict controls over amphetamines, barbiturates, LSD, and similar substances, with provisions to add new substances as the need arises.
1970	Comprehensive Drug Abuse Prevention and Control Act	Replaced previous laws and categorized drugs based on abuse and addiction potential as well as therapeutic value.
1973	Methadone Control Act	Placed controls on methadone licensing.
1973	Drug Enforcement Administration (DEA)	Remodeled the Bureau of Narcotics and Dangerous Drugs to become the DEA.
1986	Analogue (Designer Drug) Act	Made illegal the use of substances similar in effects and structure to substances already scheduled.
2000	Drug Addiction Treatment Act	Allowed qualified physicians to dispense or prescribe specially approved Schedule III, IV, and V narcotics for the treatment of opioid addiction in medical treatment settings, rather than limiting it to specialized drug treatment clinics.

opium, and strict bans on alcohol. In other countries, these substances have been deemed either legal or prohibited, depending on the political situation and the desires of the population. Historically, laws have been changed when so many people demanded access to a specific drug of abuse that it would have been impossible to enforce a ban (as in the revocation of Prohibition) or when the government needed tax revenues that could be raised by selling the drug (one argument for legalizing drugs of abuse today). A current example is the controversy over decriminalization or legalization of marijuana (see Chapter 13).

The negative experiences that Americans had at the turn of the 20th century with addicting substances such as opium led to the **Harrison Act of 1914**. It marked the first legitimate effort by the federal government to regulate and control the production, importation, sale, purchase, and distribution of addicting substances. The Harrison Act served as the foundation and reference for subsequent laws directed at regulating drug abuse issues.

Today, the ways in which law enforcement agencies deal with substance abuse are largely determined by the Comprehensive Drug Abuse Prevention and Control Act of 1970. This act divided substances with abuse potential into categories based on the degree of their abuse potential and their clinical usefulness. The classifications, which are referred to as *schedules*, range from I to V. *Schedule I* substances have high abuse potential and no currently approved medicinal use; they cannot be prescribed by health professionals. *Schedule II* drugs also have high abuse potential but are approved for medical purposes and can be prescribed with restrictions. The distinctions between *Schedule II* through *V* substances reflect the likelihood of abuse occurring and the degree to which the drugs are controlled by governmental agencies. The least addictive and least regulated of the substances of abuse are classified as Schedule V drugs (see "Here and Now," Controlled Substance Schedules). Penalties for illegal use and/or trafficking of these agents vary according to the agent's schedule, amount possessed, and number of previous drug-associated offenses (see Table 3.2, page 92).

very likely they will continue to do so despite stricter laws and greater support for law enforcement.

As the amount of addiction increased during the mid-1960s, many ill-conceived programs and laws were instituted as knee-jerk reactions, with little understanding about the underlying reasons for the rise in drug abuse. Unpopular, restrictive laws rarely work to reduce the use of illicit drugs. Even as laws become more restrictive, they usually have little impact on the level of addiction; in fact, in some cases addiction problems actually have increased. For example, during the restrictive years of the 1960s and 1980s, drugs were sold everywhere to everyone — in high schools, colleges, and probably every community. In the 1980s especially, increasingly large volumes of drugs were sold throughout the United States. Billions of dollars were paid for those drugs. Although no one knows precisely how much was exchanged, the amount likely approached $80 to $100 billion per year for all illegal drugs, of which the two biggest subcategories were an estimated $30 billion for cocaine and $24 billion for marijuana.

Because of the large sums of money involved, drugs have brought corruption to all levels of society. Other problems associated with the implementation of drug laws are an insufficient number of law enforcement personnel and inadequate detention facilities; consequently, much drug traffic goes unchecked. In addition, the judiciary system sometimes gets so backlogged that many cases never reach court. Plea bargaining is often used to clear the court docket. Many dealers and traffickers are back in business on the same day they are arrested. This apparent lack of punishment seriously damages the morale of law enforcers, legislators, and average citizens.

It is estimated that in 2005, over 1.6 million adults and over 191,000 juveniles were arrested in the United States for drug-abuse violations (U.S. Department of Justice [USDOJ], Bureau of Justice Statistics [BJS] 2006). This problem represents a tremendous cost to society in terms of damaged lives and family relationships; being arrested for a drug-related crime seriously jeopardizes a person's opportunity to pursue a normal life. Drug taking is closely

Drug Laws and Deterrence

As previously indicated, drug laws often do not serve as a satisfactory deterrent against the use of illicit drugs. People have used and abused drugs for thousands of years despite governmental restrictions. It is

Table 3.2 Federal Trafficking Penalties

DRUG/SCHEDULE	QUANTITY	PENALTIES	QUANTITY	PENALTIES
Cocaine (Schedule II)	500–4999 g mixture	**First Offense:** Not less than 5 years, and not more than 40 years. If death or serious injury, not less than 20 years or more than life. Fine of not more than $2 million if an individual, $5 million if not an individual. **Second Offense:** Not less than 10 years, and not more than life. If death or serious injury, life imprisonment. Fine of not more than $4 million if an individual, $10 million if not an individual.	5 kg or more mixture	**First Offense:** Not less than 10 years, and not more than life. If death or serious injury, not less than 20 years or more than life. Fine of not more than $4 million if an individual, $10 million if not an individual. **Second Offense:** Not less than 20 years, and not more than life. If death or serious injury, life imprisonment. Fine of not more than $8 million if an individual, $20 million if not an individual. **Two or More Prior Offenses:** Life imprisonment.
Cocaine base (Schedule II)	5–49 g mixture		50 g or more mixture	
Fentanyl (Schedule II)	40–399 g mixture		400 g or more mixture	
Fentanyl analog (Schedule I)	10–99 g mixture		100 g or more mixture	
Heroin (Schedule I)	100–999 g mixture		1 kg or more mixture	
LSD (Schedule I)	1–9 g mixture		10 g or more mixture	
Methamphetamine (Schedule II)	5–49 g pure or 50–499 g mixture		50 g or more pure or 500 g or more mixture	
PCP (Schedule II)	10–99 g pure or 100–999 g mixture		100 g or more pure or 1 kg or more mixture	

		PENALTIES
Other Schedule I and II drugs	Any amount	**First Offense:** Not more than 20 years. If death or serious injury, not less than 20 years, or more than life. Fine $1 million if an individual, $5 million if not an individual.
Flunitrazepam (Schedule IV)	1 g or more	**Second Offense:** Not more than 30 years. If death or serious injury, not less than life. Fine $2 million if an individual, $10 million if not an individual.
Other Schedule III drugs	Any amount	**First Offense:** Not more than 5 years. Fine $250,000 if an individual, $1 million if not an individual.
Flunitrazepam (Schedule IV)	30–999 mg	**Second Offense:** Not more than 10 years. Fine $500,000 if an individual, $2 million if not an individual.
All other Schedule IV drugs	Any amount	**First Offense:** Not more than 3 years. Fine $250,000 if an individual, $1 million if not an individual.
Flunitrazepam (Schedule IV)	Less than 30 mg	**Second Offense:** Not more than 6 years. Fine $500,000 if an individual, $2 million if not an individual.
All Schedule V drugs	Any amount	**First Offense:** Not more than 1 year. Fine $100,000 if an individual, $250,000 if not an individual. **Second Offense:** Not more than 2 years. Fine $200,000 if an individual, $500,000 if not an individual.

(continued)

Table 3.2 (*continued*)

DRUG	QUANTITY	FIRST OFFENSE	SECOND OFFENSE
Marijuana	1000 kg or more mixture; or 1000 or more plants	• Not less than 10 years, not more than life • If death or serious injury, not less than 20 years, not more than life • Fine of not more than $4 million if an individual, $10 million if other than an individual	• Not less than 20 years, not more than life • If death or serious injury, mandatory life • Fine of not more than $8 million if an individual, $20 million if other than an individual
Marijuana	100–999 kg mixture; or 100–999 plants	• Not less than 5 years, not more than 40 years • If death or serious injury, not less than 20 years, not more than life • Fine of not more than $2 million if an individual, $5 million if other than an individual	• Not less than 10 years, not more than life • If death or serious injury, mandatory life • Fine of not more than $4 million if an individual, $10 million if other than an individual
Marijuana	More than 10 kg hashish; 50–99 kg mixture More than 1 kg of hashish oil; 50–99 plants	• Not more than 20 years • If death or serious injury, not less than 20 years, not more than life • Fine of $1 million if an individual, $5 million if other than an individual	• Not more than 30 years • If death or serious injury, mandatory life • Fine of $2 million if an individual, $10 million if other than an individual
Marijuana	1–49 plants; less than 50 kg mixture	• Not more than 5 years • Fine of not more than $250,000 if an individual, $1 million if other than an individual	• Not more than 10 years • Fine of $500,000 if an individual, $2 million if other than an individual
Hashish	10 kg or less		
Hashish oil	1 kg or less		

Source: U.S. Drug Enforcement Administration. http://www.usdoj.gov/dea/agency/penalties.htm. Accessed 8/23/07.

tied to societal problems, and it will remain a problem unless society provides more meaningful experiences to those who are most susceptible to drug abuse. Improved education and increased support should be given to preteens because that is the age when deviant behavior starts. In cases in which drug education programs have been successful in involving students, the amount of drug taking and illegal activity seems to have decreased (see Chapter 17).

■ Factors in Controlling Drug Abuse

Three principal issues influence laws regarding drug abuse:

1. If a person abuses a drug, should he or she be treated as a criminal or as a sick person afflicted with a disease?

2. How is the user (supposedly the victim) distinguished from the pusher (supposedly the criminal) of an illicit drug, and who should be more harshly punished — the person who creates the demand for the drug or the person who satisfies the demand?

3. Are the laws and associated penalties effective deterrents against drug use or abuse, and how is effectiveness determined?

In regard to the first issue, drug abuse may be considered both an illness and a crime. It can be a psychiatric disorder, an abnormal functional state, in which a person is compelled (either physically or psychologically) to continue using the drug. It becomes a crime when the law, reflecting social opinion, makes abuse of the drug illegal. Health issues are clearly involved because uncontrolled abuse of almost any drug can lead to physical and

Here and Now

Controlled Substance Schedules

Controlled substances classified as Schedule I, II, III, IV, or V drugs are described below.

Schedule I

- The drug or other substance has a high potential for abuse.
- The drug or other substance has no currently accepted medical use in treatment in the United States.
- There is a lack of accepted safety for use of the drug or other substance under medical supervision.

Schedule II

- The drug or other substance has a high potential for abuse.
- The drug or other substance has a currently accepted medical use in treatment in the United States or a currently accepted medical use with severe restrictions.
- Abuse of the drug or other substance may lead to severe psychological or physical dependence.

Schedule III

- The drug or other substance has less of a potential for abuse than the drugs or other substances in Schedules I and II.
- The drug or other substance has a currently accepted medical use in treatment in the United States.

- Abuse of the drug or other substance may lead to moderate or low physical dependence or high psychological dependence.

Schedule IV

- The drug or other substance has a low potential for abuse relative to the drugs or other substances in Schedule III.
- The drug or other substance has a currently accepted medical use in treatment in the United States.
- Abuse of the drug or other substance may lead to limited physical dependence or psychological dependence relative to the drugs or other substances in Schedule III.

Schedule V

- The drug or other substance has a low potential for abuse relative to the drugs or other substances in Schedule IV.
- The drug or other substance has a currently accepted medical use in treatment in the United States.
- Abuse of the drug or other substance may lead to limited physical dependence or psychological dependence relative to the drugs or other substances in Schedule IV.

Source: U.S. Code, January 24, 1995.

psychological damage. Because the public must pay for healthcare costs or societal damage, laws are created and penalties are implemented to prevent or correct drug abuse problems (see Table 3.2 on federal trafficking penalties).

Concerning the second issue, drug laws have always been more lenient on the user than the seller of a drug of abuse. Actually, it is often hard to separate user from pusher, as many drug abusers engage in both activities. Because huge profits are often involved, some people may not use the drugs they peddle and are only pushers; the law tries to deter use of drugs by concentrating on these persons but has questionable success. Organized crime is involved in major drug sales, and these "drug rings" have proven hard to destroy.

In regard to the third issue, considerable evidence indicates that, in the United States, criminal law has only limited success in deterring drug abuse. During 2006, approximately 36% of 12th graders used an illicit drug during the prior 12 months; marijuana was used by 32%, LSD by 2%, and cocaine by 6% (Johnston et al. 2007). The total number of Americans ages 12 and older currently using illegal drugs in 2005 has been estimated by the National Survey on Drug Use and Health to be 19.7 million. This estimate represents 8.1% of the population ages 12 years and older (Substance Abuse and Mental Health Services Administration [SAMHSA], 2006). It is clear that the drug abuse problem is far from being resolved, and many feel that some changes should be made in how we deal with this problem.

Strategies for Preventing Drug Abuse

The U.S. government and the public became concerned about the increasing prevalence of drug use during the 1960s, when demonstrations and nationwide protests against the Vietnam War proliferated as youth (mostly college students) rebelled against what they viewed as an unnecessary and unjust war. During the 1960s and early 1970s, for the first time, large numbers of middle- and upper-middle-class youth began using licit and illicit gateway drugs on a massive scale. In response, the government developed strategies for combating drug use and abuse. Important strategies it employed were **supply reduction**, **demand reduction**, and **inoculation**. More recently, the use of **drug courts** has become a major strategy.

Supply Reduction Strategy

Early attempts at drug abuse prevention included both the Harrison Narcotic Act of 1914 and the 18th Amendment (Prohibition) to the U.S. Constitution. Both laws were intended to control the manufacture and distribution of classified drugs, with legislators anticipating that these restrictions would compel people to stop using drugs. The laws enforced supply reduction, which involves a lessening, restriction, or elimination of available drugs.

Supply reduction drug prevention policy attempts to curtail the supply of illegal drugs or their precursors and exert greater control over other, more therapeutic drugs. Part of the supply reduction policy includes **interdiction**, which is defined as decreasing the amounts of these agents that are carried across U.S. borders by using foreign crop eradication measures and agreements, by imposing stiff penalties for drug trafficking, and by controlling alcoholic beverages through licensing.

The United States dedicates enormous resources to interdiction programs. For fiscal year 2007, the federal drug control budget for interdiction was $3.37 billion (USDOJ Bureau of Justice Statistics 2007). Although seizures of large caches of illicit drugs are reported routinely in the national press, there is relatively little indication that the availability of drugs has diminished substantially. For example, according to the National Threat Assessment 2007 (USDOJ 2006), cocaine availability has not changed despite "record interdictions and seizures." One can argue that as long as a strong demand for these psychoactive agents exists, demand will be satisfied if the price is right. Even if interdiction successfully reduces the supply of one drug of abuse, if demand persists, that drug is usually replaced by another drug with similar abuse potential (for example, substitution of amphetamines for cocaine; see Chapter 10).

Demand Reduction Strategy

The demand reduction approach attempts to minimize the actual demand for drugs. Through programs and activities often aimed at youth, emphasis is placed on reformulating values, attitudes, skills, and behaviors conducive to resisting drug use. (Chapter 17 provides extensive information about methods and techniques for reducing drug use.) As part of this strategy, support for medical and group drug treatment programs for abusers is encouraged. Although this approach does not address drug supply, it does attempt to curb and eventually eliminate the need to purchase drugs by reducing the buyer's demand.

Drug abuse is a complex and very individual problem, with many causes and aggravating factors. Even so, experience has shown that prevention and demand reduction are better strategies and, in the long run, less costly than interdiction or penalties administered via the criminal justice system (Goldstein 1994).

KEY TERMS

supply reduction
a drug reduction policy aimed at reducing the supply of illegal drugs and controlling other therapeutic drugs

demand reduction
attempts to decrease individuals' tendencies to use drugs, often aimed at youth, with emphasis on reformulating values and behaviors

inoculation
a method of abuse prevention that protects drug users by teaching them responsibility

drug courts
a process that integrates substance abuse treatment, incentives, and sanctions and places nonviolent, drug-involved defendants in judicially supervised rehabilitation programs

interdiction
the policy of cutting off or destroying supplies of illicit drugs

The following are some suggestions and strategies for how to reduce demand for drugs:

1. The top priority of any prevention program, if it is to provide a long-term solution, must be reduction of drug demand by youth. Children must be the primary focus in any substance abuse program. Achieving success requires stabilizing defective family structures, implementing school programs that create an antidrug attitude, establishing a drug-free environment, and promoting resistance training to help youth avoid drug involvement. In addition, children should be encouraged to become involved in alternative activities that can substitute for drug-abusing activity. Potential drug abusers need to be convinced that substance abuse is personally and socially damaging and unacceptable.

2. Education about drug abuse must be carefully designed and customized for the target population or group. For example, education based on scare tactics is not likely to dissuade adolescents from experimenting with drugs. Adolescents are at a point in their lives when they feel invincible, and graphically depicting the potential health consequences of drug and alcohol abuse has little impact. A discussion about the nature of addiction and the addiction process is more likely to influence their attitudes. Adolescents need to understand why people use drugs to appreciate the behavior patterns in themselves. Other important topics that should be discussed are how drug abuse works and why it leads to dependence. To complement drug education, adolescents also should be taught coping strategies that include effective decision-making and problem-solving skills.

3. Attitudes toward drug abuse and its consequence must be changed. The drug use patterns of many people, both young and old, are strongly influenced by their peers. If individuals believe that drug abuse is glamorous and contributes to acceptance by friends and associates, the incidence of drug abuse will remain high. In contrast, if the prevailing message in society is that drug abuse is unhealthy and not socially acceptable, the incidence will be much lower.

4. Replacement therapy has been shown to be a useful approach to weaning the individual off of drugs of abuse. A common example of this strategy is the use of the narcotic methadone to treat the heroin addict (see Chapter 9).

Use of methadone prevents the cravings and severe effects of withdrawal routinely associated with breaking the heroin habit. Unfortunately, many heroin addicts must be maintained on methadone indefinitely. Even though methadone is easier to control and is less disruptive than heroin, one drug addiction has been substituted for another, which draws criticism. Replacement therapy certainly is not the entire answer to all drug abuse problems, but it often can provide a window of opportunity for behavioral modification so that a long-term solution to the abuse problem is possible.

Inoculation Strategy

The inoculation method of abuse prevention aims to protect drug users by teaching them responsibility. The emphasis is on being accountable, rational, and responsible about drug use, and informing users about the effects of drugs on both mind and bodily function. Nonalcohol parties and responsible drinkers who use designated drivers are outcomes of applying inoculation strategy.

Drug Courts

Drug courts are designed to deal with nonviolent, drug-abusing offenders. Since 1989, when the first drug courts were established, nearly 1700 jurisdictions across the country have implemented a drug court program. As of April 2007, another 349 were in the planning stages (USDOJ, National Criminal Justice Reference Service 2007). Drug courts integrate mandatory drug testing, substance abuse treatment, sanctions, and incentives in a judicially supervised setting. These courts hold offenders accountable for their actions and provide them with the support and tools necessary to rebuild their lives and become productive members of the community.

Current and Future Drug Use

During the administrations of former Presidents Ronald Reagan and George H. W. Bush (1980–1992), the official policy of the U.S. federal government included a "get tough" attitude about drug abuse. Slogans such as "Just Say No" and "War on Drugs" reflected the frustration of a public that had been victimized by escalating crime (many incidents were drug related); personally touched by drug tragedies in families, at work, or with associates and friends; and economically strained by dealing with the cost of the problem.

Much remains to be accomplished in the fight against substance abuse. For example:

- The economic cost to society of drug abuse remains staggering. In 2002, it was estimated at $180.9 billion, and reflects costs necessary to address health and crime consequences, as well as loss of productivity from death, disability, and withdrawal from the workforce (Office of National Drug Control Policy [ONDCP] 2004).
- The costs of drug abuse increased an average of 5.3% per year from 1992–2002. The most rapid increases were in criminal justice efforts, especially increased spending on law enforcement, adjudication, and incarceration (ONDCP 2004).
- The number of first-time users is staggering. For example, in 2005, an estimated 2.9 million persons in the United States age 12 or older used an illicit drug for the first time within the 12 months preceding collection of these data. This represented nearly 8000 initiates each day (SAMHSA 2006).
- Millions of dollars have been spent in an attempt to educate young people regarding the dangers of substance abuse. Despite the introduction of "Drug-Free School Zones" throughout the country, in 2005 approximately 16% of youths ages 12–17 reported that they had been approached by someone selling drugs in the past month (SAMHSA 2006).

Fighting the "War on Drugs" is clearly difficult and complex. Despite substantial efforts, significant problems still exist and require the attention of politicians, clinicians, law enforcement agencies, families, counselors, and all concerned citizens.

Drug Legalization Debate

The persistence of the drug abuse problem and the high cost in dollars and frustration of waging the "War on Drugs" have energized the ongoing debate regarding legalizing the use of drugs of abuse. Proponents of legalization are no longer limited to libertarians and so-called academic intellectuals. Increasingly, this group includes representatives of a distressed law enforcement system. For example, some discontented judges whose courts are swamped with drug cases and police officers who spend much of their on-duty time trying to trap and arrest every drug dealer and user on the street are publicly declaring that the drug laws are wasteful and futile.

Several arguments are commonly cited by individuals and groups promoting the legalization of all substances of abuse. For instance, proponents often contend that if drugs were legalized, violence and crime would become less frequent. These individuals point out that users often commit crimes to pay for illicit drugs. If these drugs were legal, then the tremendous profits associated with drugs because of their illegal status would disappear and, once gone, the black market and criminal activity associated with drugs would be eliminated. Furthermore, legalization would decrease law enforcement costs by

An example of the many public awareness advertisement cautions against drinking and driving.

Substance abuse can lead to serious legal problems.

eliminating the backlog of drug-related court cases and reduce populations in overcrowded prisons.

Conversely, opponents of drug legalization believe that legalization would lead to increased availability of drugs, which would in turn lead to increased use. They point out that the use of drugs, especially methamphetamine, phenylcyclidine (PCP), and cocaine, is often associated with violent criminal behavior. Numerous studies demonstrate the links among drugs, violence, and crime; the link between alcohol, a legal substance, and crime is also well documented. According to legalization opponents, drug use would merely increase the incidence of crime, even if the drugs were legally purchased. Accordingly, the economic (as well as social) cost to society would increase.

Legalization proponents claim that making illicit drugs licit would not cause more of these substances to be consumed, nor would addiction increase. They note correctly that many people use drugs in moderation. Furthermore, many would choose not to use drugs, just as many abstain currently from tobacco and alcohol. Opponents contend that if drugs were made licit and more widely available, usage and addiction rates would increase. These individuals contend that legalizing drugs

sends a message that drug use (like tobacco and alcohol) is acceptable and encourages drug use among people who currently do not use drugs.

Proponents claim that drug legalization would allow users the right to practice a diversity of consciousness. Just as diversity of race, ethnicity, sexual orientation, religion, and other varied lifestyles are allowed, legalization of drugs would permit citizens in our society to alter their consciousness without legal repercussions as long as they do not harm or threaten the safety and security of others. Moreover, proponents argue that education, health care, road building, and a wide array of other worthwhile causes would benefit from the taxes that could be raised by legalizing and then taxing drugs. They argue that the United States has spent billions of dollars to control drug production, trafficking, and use with few, if any, positive results. They contend that the money spent on drug control should be shifted to other, more productive endeavors.

Opponents believe that health and societal costs would increase with drug legalization. It has been predicted that drug treatment costs; hospitalization for long-term, drug-related diseases; and treatment of the consequences of drug-associated family violence would further burden our already strapped healthcare system. Such a policy would increase costs to society due to greater medical and social problems resulting from greater availability and increased use of drugs. Two of the most frequently abused substances, alcohol and tobacco, are both legal and readily available today. These two substances cause more medical, social, and personal problems than all the illicit drugs of abuse combined. Many question whether society really wants to legalize additional drugs with abuse potential.

Although arguments for both sides warrant consideration, extreme policies are not likely to be implemented; instead, a compromise will most probably be adopted. For example, areas potentially ripe for compromise include the following (Kalant 1992):

> *Selective legalization.* Eliminate harsh penalties for those drugs of abuse that are the safest and least likely to cause addiction, such as marijuana.

> *Control of substances of abuse by prescription or through specially approved outlets.* Have the availability of the illegal drugs controlled by physicians and trained clinicians, rather than by law enforcement agencies.

Discretionary enforcement of drug laws. Allow greater discretion by judicial systems for prosecution and sentencing of those who violate drug laws. Such decisions would be based on perceived criminal intent.

In conclusion, drug legalization remains a highly divisive issue in the United States. Although legalization would lessen the number of drug violators involved in the criminal justice system, the problems associated with legalizing current illicit drugs cause many members in our society to view this idea with disfavor. As stated earlier, opponents of legalization argue that we already have massive problems with licit drugs such as tobacco and alcohol. According to them, legalizing additional types of drugs would produce a substantial increase in the rate of addiction and in the social and psychological problems associated with drug use. Proponents favoring legalization assert that, despite the current drug laws and severe penalties for drug use, people continue to use illicit drugs.

■ Drug Testing

In response to the demand by society to stop the spread of drug abuse and its adverse consequences, drug testing has been implemented in some situations to detect drug users. The most common types of drug testing use Breathalyzers and laboratory studies of urine, blood, and hair specimens. Urine and blood testing are preferred for detecting drug use. Hair specimen testing must overcome technical problems before hair can be used as a definitive proof of drug use, including complications from hair treatment (e.g., hair coloring) and environmental absorption.

The drugs of abuse most frequently tested for are marijuana, cocaine, amphetamines, narcotics, sedatives, and anabolic steroids. Drug testing is often mandatory in some professions in which public safety is a concern (such as airline pilots, railroad workers, law enforcement employees, and medical personnel) and for employees of some organizations and companies as part of general policy (such as the military, many federal agencies, and some private companies). Drug testing is also often mandatory for participants in sports at all levels — whether in high school, college, international, or professional competition — to prevent unfair advantages that might result from the pharmacological effects of these drugs and to discourage the spread of drug abuse among athletes.

Likewise, drug testing is used routinely by law enforcement agencies to assist in the prosecution of those believed to violate drug abuse laws. Finally, drug testing is used by health professionals to assess the success of drug abuse treatment — that is, to determine whether a dependent patient is diminishing his or her drug use or has experienced a relapse in drug abuse habits.

Drug testing to identify drug offenders is usually accomplished by analyzing body fluids (in particular urine), although other approaches (such as analysis of expired air for alcohol) are also used. To understand the accuracy of these tests, several factors should be considered.

1. *Testing must be standardized and conducted efficiently.* To interpret testing results reliably, it is essential that fluid samples be collected, processed, and tested using standard procedures. Guidelines for proper testing procedures have been established by federal regulatory agencies as well as scientific organizations. Deviations from established protocols can result in false positives (tests that indicate a drug is present when none was used), false negatives (tests that are unable to detect a drug that is present), or inaccurate assessments of drug levels.

2. *Sample collection and processing must be done accurately and confidentially.* In many cases, drug testing can have punitive consequences (for example, athletes cannot compete or employees are fired if results are positive). Consequently, drug users often attempt to outsmart the system. Some individuals have attempted to avoid submitting their own drug-containing urine for testing by filling specimen bottles with "clean" urine from artificial bladders hidden under clothing or in the vagina or by introducing "clean" urine into their own bladders just before collection. To confirm the legitimacy of the specimen, it often is necessary to have the urine collection witnessed directly by a trustworthy observer. To ensure that the fluid specimens are not tampered with and that confidentiality is maintained, samples should be immediately coded and movement of each sample from site to site during analysis should be documented and confirmed.

Just as it is important that testing identify individuals who are using drugs, it is also important that those who have not used drugs not be wrongfully accused. To avoid false positives, all samples that test positive in screening (usually via fast and inexpensive procedures) should be analyzed again using more accurate, sensitive, and sophisticated analytical procedures to confirm the results.

3. *Confounding factors that interfere with the accuracy of the testing can be inadvertently or deliberately present.* For example, normal dietary consumption of pastries containing poppy seeds is sufficient to cause a positive urine test for the narcotic morphine. Excessive intake of fluid or use of diuretics increases the volume of urine formed and decreases the concentration of drugs, making them more difficult to detect.

The dramatic increase in drug testing since 1985 has caused experts to question its value in dealing with drug abuse problems. Unfortunately, drug testing often is linked exclusively to punitive consequences, such as disqualification from athletic competition, loss of job, or even fines and imprisonment. Use of drug testing in such negative ways does little to diminish the number of drug abusers or deal with their personal problems.

However, drug testing programs can have positive consequences by identifying drug users who require professional care. After being referred for drug rehabilitation, the offender can be monitored using drug testing to confirm the desired response to therapy. In addition, tests can identify individuals who put others in jeopardy because of their drug abuse habits when they perform tasks that are dangerously impaired by the effects of these drugs (for example, airline pilots, train engineers, and truck drivers).

The widespread application of drug testing to control the illicit use of drugs in the general population would be extremely expensive, difficult to enforce, and almost certainly ineffective. In addition, such indiscriminate testing would likely be viewed as an unwarranted infringement on individual privacy and declared unconstitutional. However, the use of drug testing to discourage inappropriate drug use in selected crucial professions that directly impact public welfare appears to be publicly tolerated. Even so, it is probably worthwhile to periodically revisit the issue of drug testing and analyze its benefits and liabilities relative to "public safety" and "individual privacy" issues.

■ Pragmatic Drug Policies

Several principles for a pragmatic drug policy emerge from a review of past drug policies and an understanding of the drug-related frustrations of

today. To create drug policies that work, the following suggestions are offered:

1. It is important that the government develop programs that are consistent with the desires of the majority of the population.

2. Given the difficulties and high cost of efforts to prevent illicit drugs from reaching the market, it is logical to deemphasize interdiction and instead stress programs that reduce demand. To reduce demand, drug education and drug treatment must be top priorities.

3. Government and society need to better understand the role played by law in their efforts to reduce drug addiction. Antidrug laws by themselves do not eliminate drug problems; indeed, they may even create significant social difficulties (for example, as did the Prohibition laws banning all alcohol use). Used properly and selectively, however, laws can reinforce and communicate expected social behavior and values (for example, laws against public drunkenness or against driving a vehicle under the influence of alcohol).

4. Programs that employ "public consensus" should be implemented more effectively to campaign against drug abuse. For example, antismoking campaigns demonstrate the potential success that could be achieved by programs that alter drug abuse behavior. Similar approaches can be used to change public attitudes about drugs through education without making moral judgments and employing crusading tactics. Our society needs to engage in more collaborative programs in which drug-using individuals and their families, communities, and helping agencies work together.

Discussion Questions

1. Describe the FDA approval process for assessing the safety and efficacy of a newly developed drug. What are its advantages and disadvantages?

2. Name the principal legislative initiatives that mandate that drugs be proven safe or effective.

3. What are the principal advantages and disadvantages of switching products from prescription to OTC status?

4. What could account for the vast differences in attitudes and opinions regarding drug use

and the law voiced by drug users/abusers and nonusers of drugs?

5. Would decriminalization of illicit drug use increase or decrease drug-related social problems? Justify your answer.

6. Compare and contrast supply reduction, demand reduction, and inoculation strategies for dealing with drug abuse.

7. List the principal arguments for and against legalizing drugs of abuse such as marijuana and cocaine.

Summary

1 Societies have evolved to believe that they have the right to protect themselves from the damaging impact of drug use and abuse. Consequently, governments, including that of the United States, have passed laws and implemented programs to prevent social damage from inappropriate drug use. In addition, such societies have come to expect that drugs be effective.

2 The 1906 Pure Food and Drug Act was not a strong law, but it required manufacturers to include on labels the amounts of alcohol, morphine, opium, cocaine, heroin, and marijuana extract in each product. It represented the first real attempt to make consumers aware of the active contents in the drug products they were consuming.

3 The 1938 Federal Food, Drug, and Cosmetic Act gave the FDA control over drug safety.

4 The 1951 Durham-Humphrey Amendment to the Food, Drug, and Cosmetic Act made a formal distinction between prescription and nonprescription drugs.

5 The Kefauver-Harris Amendment of 1962 required manufacturers to demonstrate both the efficacy and the safety of their products.

6 All drugs to be considered for marketing must first be tested for safety in animals. Following these initial tests, if the drug is favorably reviewed by the FDA, it is given IND status. It then generally undergoes three phases of human clinical testing before receiving final FDA approval.

7 In 1972, the FDA initiated a program to ensure that all OTC drugs were safe and effective. Specific panels were selected to evaluate the safety and effectiveness of OTC drug ingredients. Each of the ingredients was classified into a particular category: I, II, or III.

8 The switching policy of the FDA allows the agency to review prescription drugs and evaluate their suitability as OTC products.

9 Three of the principal questions that influence laws on drug abuse address the following issues: Should drug abusers be treated as criminals or patients? How can drug users and drug pushers be distinguished from one another? What types of laws and programs are effective deterrents against drug abuse?

10 Controversy exists as to how to best reduce substance abuse. A principal strategy used by governmental agencies to achieve this objective is interdiction; the majority of money used to fight drug abuse is spent on trying to stop and confiscate drug supplies. Experience has proved that interdiction is often ineffective. To reduce drug abuse, demand for these substances must be diminished. Youth must be a top priority in any substance abuse program. Treatment that enables drug addicts to stop their habits with minimal discomfort should be provided. Finally, education should be used to change attitudes toward drug abuse and its consequences. Potential drug abusers need to be convinced that substance abuse is personally and socially damaging and is unacceptable.

11 Major strategies for combating drug use and abuse are supply reduction, demand reduction, and inoculation. Supply reduction involves using drug laws to control the manufacturing and distribution of classified drugs. Demand reduction aims to reduce the actual demand for drugs by working mainly with youth and teaching them to resist drugs. Inoculation aims to protect potential drug users by teaching them responsibility and explaining the effects of drugs on bodily and mental functioning.

12 Drug courts are designed to deal with nonviolent, drug-abusing offenders. They require substance abuse treatment and implement sanctions in a judicially supervised program. This emerging strategy has had positive social and economic impacts.

13 In response to the demand by society to stop the spread of drug abuse and its adverse consequences, drug testing has been implemented in some situations to detect drug users. Common drug testing uses Breathalyzers and analysis of urine, blood, and hair specimens. Urine and blood testing are the preferred methods of testing for drug use. Hair specimen testing must overcome a number of technical problems before it can be used as a definitive proof of drug use, including complications caused by hair treatment and environmental absorption.

References

Donahue, J. M., M. Cevasco, and M. B. Rosenthal. "A Decade of Direct to Consumer Advertising of Prescription Drugs." *New England Journal of Medicine* 357 (2007): 673–681.

Federal Trade Commission (FTC). "Facts for Business." 2007. Available www.ftc.gov/bcp/conline/pubs/buspubs/ad_faqs.shtm.

Food and Drug Administration (FDA), History Office. "A Brief History of the Center for Drug Evaluation and Research." 1997. Available www.fda.gov/cder/about/history/Histext.htm.

Food and Drug Administration (FDA). "Updates." *FDA Consumer Magazine* January–February 1999. Available www.fda.gov/fdac/departs/1999/199_upd.html.

Food and Drug Administration (FDA). "FDA and the Drug Development Process: How the Agency Ensures That Drugs Are Safe and Effective" 2002. Available http://www.fda.gov/opacom/factsheets/justthefacts/17drgdev.html.

Food and Drug Administration (FDA). "Milestones in the U.S. Food and Drug Law History." 2005. Available www.fda.gov/opacom/backgrounders/miles.html.

Food and Drug Administration (FDA), Division of Drug Marketing, Advertising and Communications (2007). "Frequently Asked Questions." Available http://www.fda.gov/cder/ddmac/FAQS.HTM.

Goldstein, A. "Lessons from the Street." In *Addiction from Biology to Drug Policy.* New York: Freeman, 1994.

Hunter, J. R., D. L. Rosen, and R. DeChristoforo. "How FDA Expedites Evaluation of Drugs." *Welcome Trends in Pharmacy* (January 1993): 2–9.

Johnston, L. D., P. M. O'Malley, J. G. Bachman, and J. E. Schulenberg. *Monitoring the Future, National Survey of Results on Drug Use 1975–2006.* (Volume I, Secondary School Students), NIH Publication No. 07-6205. Bethesda, MD: National Institute on Drug Abuse, 2007.

Kalant, H. "Formulating Policies on the Non-medical Use of Cocaine." In *Cocaine: Scientific and Social Dimensions.* Ciba Foundation Symposium 166, 261–276. New York: Wiley, 1992.

Office of National Drug Control Policy (ONDCP). *The Economic Costs of Drug Abuse in the United States 1992–2002.* Publication No. 207303. Washington DC: The Executive Office of the President. December 2004.

Rados, C. *FDA Consumer Magazine, 2004.* "Truth in Advertising: Rx Drug Ads Come of Age." Available http://www.fda.gov/fdac/features/2004/404_ads.html.

Substance Abuse and Mental Health Services Administration (SAMHSA). *Results from the 2005 National Household Survey on Drug Abuse and Health: National Findings.* NSDUH Series H30. DHHS Publication No. SMA 06-4194. Rockville, MD: Office of Applied Studies, 2006.

Temin, P. *Taking Your Medicine: Drug Regulation in the United States.* Cambridge, MA: Harvard University Press, 1980.

Tufts Center for the Study of Drug Development. *Outlook 2005.* Boston, MA: Author. 2005.

U.S. Department of Justice (USDOJ). *National Drug Threat Assessment 2007.* Document ID 2006-Q0317-003 October 2006.

U.S. Department of Justice (USDOJ), Bureau of Justice Statistics. "Key Facts at a Glance." September 2006. Available www.ojp.gov/bjs/glance/tables/drugtab.htm.

U.S. Department of Justice (USDOJ), Bureau of Justice Statistics. "Drugs and Crime Facts: Drug Control Budget." 2007. Available www.ojp.usdoj.gov/bjs/dcf/dcb.htm.

U.S. Department of Justice (USDOJ), National Criminal Justice Reference Service. "Drug Courts — Facts and Figures." 2007. Available www.ncjrs.gov/spotlight/drug_courts/facts.html.

Introduction

Why is your body susceptible to the influence of drugs and other substances? Part of the answer is that your body is constantly adjusting and responding to its environment in an effort to maintain internal stability and balance. This delicate process of dynamic adjustments — **homeostasis** — is necessary to optimize bodily functions and is essential for survival. These continual compensations help to maintain physiological and psychological balances and are mediated by the release of endogenous regulatory chemicals (such as **neurotransmitters** from neurons and **hormones** from glands). Many drugs exert intended or unintended effects by altering the activity of these regulatory substances, which changes the status and function of the nervous or **endocrine system**. For example, all drugs of abuse profoundly influence mental states by altering the chemical messages of the neurotransmitters in the brain, and some alter endocrine function by affecting the release and activity of hormones. By understanding the mechanisms of how drugs alter these body processes, we are able to distinguish drug benefits and risks and devise therapeutic strategies to deal with related biomedical problems.

This chapter is divided into two sections. The first is a brief overview that introduces the basic concept of how the body is controlled by nervous systems and explains why drugs influence the elements of these systems. The second section is intended for readers who desire a more in-depth understanding of the anatomical, physiological, and biochemical basis of homeostatic functions. In this second section, the elements of the nervous system are discussed in greater detail, followed by an examination of its major divisions: the central, peripheral, and autonomic nervous systems (CNS, PNS, and ANS). The components and operation of the endocrine system are also discussed in specific relation to drugs. The use of anabolic steroids is given as an example.

1: Overview of Homeostasis and Drug Actions

The body continuously adjusts to both internal and external changes in the environment. To cope with these adjustments, the body systems include elaborate self-regulating mechanisms. The name given to this compensatory action is *homeostasis*, which refers to the maintenance of internal stability or equilibrium of the body and its functions. For example, homeostatic mechanisms control the response of the brain to changes in the physical, social, and psychological environments, as well as regulate physiological factors such as body temperature, metabolism, nutrient utilization, and organ functions. The two principal systems that help human beings maintain homeostasis are the nervous system and the endocrine system (described in Section 2). They are independent yet work together in a coordinated manner.

Introduction to Nervous Systems

All nervous systems consist of specialized nerve cells called **neurons**. The neurons are responsible for conducting the homeostatic functions of the brain and other parts of the nervous system by receiving and sending information. The transfer of messages by neurons includes electrochemical processes that consist of the following steps (see Figure 4.1):

1. The *receiving region* of the neuron (B) is affected by a chemical message (A) that either excites (causes the neuron to send its own message) or inhibits (prevents the neuron from sending a message) it.
2. If the message is excitatory, a chemical impulse (much like electricity) moves from the receiving region of the neuron, down its wire-

KEY TERMS

homeostasis
maintenance of internal stability; often biochemical in nature

neurotransmitters
chemical messengers released by neurons

hormones
chemical messengers released into the blood by glands

endocrine system
relating to hormones, their functions, and sources

neurons
specialized nerve cells that make up the nervous system and release neurotransmitters

CHAPTER 4

Homeostatic Systems and Drugs

Did You Know?

- ○ The brain is composed of 100 billion neurons that communicate with one another by releasing chemical messengers called *neurotransmitters*.

- ○ Many drugs exert their effects by interacting with specialized protein regions in cell membranes called *receptors*.

- ○ Some natural chemicals produced by the body have the same effect as narcotic drugs; these chemicals are called *endorphins*.

- ○ The body likely produces natural substances that have effects similar to those produced by marijuana and diazepam (Valium).

- ○ Drugs that affect the neurotransmitter dopamine usually alter mental state, motor activity, and can cause addiction behavior.

- ○ The hypothalamus is the principal brain region for control of endocrine systems.

Drugs and Society Online is a great source for additional drugs and society information for both students and instructors.
Visit **http://drugsandsociety.jbpub.com** to find a variety of useful tools for learning, thinking, and teaching.

Learning ◎bjectives

On completing this chapter you will be able to:

- ◎ Explain the similarities and differences between the nervous and endocrine systems.
- ◎ Describe how a neuron functions.
- ◎ Describe the role of receptors in mediating the effects of hormones, neurotransmitters, and drugs.
- ◎ Distinguish between receptor agonists and antagonists, and describe how their effects relate to those of neurotransmitters.
- ◎ Describe the different features of the principal neurotransmitters associated with drug addiction.
- ◎ Outline the principal components of the central nervous system, and explain their general functions.
- ◎ Identify which brain areas are most likely to be affected by drugs of abuse.
- ◎ Distinguish between the sympathetic and parasympathetic nervous systems.
- ◎ Identify the principal components of the endocrine system.
- ◎ Explain how and why anabolic steroids are abused and the health impact attributed to abuse.

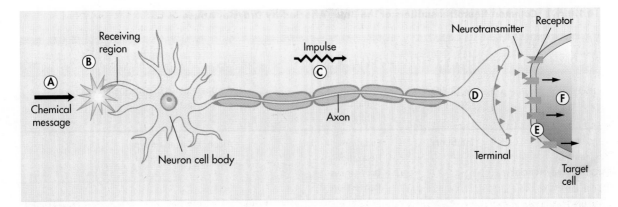

FIGURE 4.1

The process of sending messages by neurons. The receiving region (B) of the neuron is activated by an incoming message (A) near the neuronal cell body. The neuron sends an electricity-like chemical impulse down the axon to its terminal (C). The impulse causes the release of neurotransmitters from the terminal to transmit the message to the target (D). This is done when the neurotransmitter molecules activate the receptors on the membranes of the target cell (E). The activated receptors then cause a change in intracellular functions to occur (F).

like processes (called **axons**) to the sending region (called the terminal) (C). When the electrochemical impulse reaches the terminal, chemical messengers called neurotransmitters are released (D) (for examples see Table 4.1, page 106).

3. The neurotransmitters travel very short distances and bind to specialized and specific receiving proteins called **receptors** on the outer membranes of their target cells (E).

4. Activation of receptors by their associated neurotransmitters causes a change in the activity of the target cell (F). The target cells can be other neurons or cells that make up organs (such as the heart, lungs, kidneys, and so on), muscles, or glands.

Neurons are highly versatile and, depending on their functions, can send discrete excitatory or inhibitory messages to their target cells. Neurons are distinguished by the types of chemical substances they release as neurotransmitters to send their messages. The neurotransmitters represent a wide variety of molecules that are classified according to their functional association as well as their ability to stimulate or inhibit the activity of target neurons, organs, muscles, and glands. They are discussed in greater detail in Section 2.

An example of a common neurotransmitter used by neurons in the brain to send messages is the substance dopamine. When released from neurons associated with the pleasure center in the brain, dopamine causes substantial euphoria by activating its receptor on target neurons (O'Brien 2006). This effect is relevant to drugs of abuse because the addictive properties of these substances relate to their ability to stimulate dopamine release from these neurons (for example, amphetamine or cocaine) and thus cause pleasant euphoric effects in the user (O'Brien 2006).

It is important to understand that many of the desired and undesired effects of **psychoactive** drugs (which alter the mental functions of the brain), such as the drugs of abuse, are due to their ability to alter the neurotransmitters associated with neurons. Some of the transmitter messenger systems most likely to be affected by drugs of abuse are listed in Table 4.1 and are discussed in greater detail in Section 2.

KEY TERMS

axons
an extension of the neuronal cell body along which electrochemical signals travel

receptors
special proteins in a membrane that are activated by natural substances or drugs to alter cell function

psychoactive
drugs that affect mood or alter the state of consciousness

Table 4.1 Common Neurotransmitters of the Brain Affected by Drugs of Abuse

NEUROTRANSMITTER	TYPE OF EFFECT	MAJOR CENTRAL NERVOUS SYSTEM CHANGES	DRUGS OF ABUSE THAT INFLUENCE THE NEUROTRANSMITTER (DRUG ACTION)
Dopamine	Inhibitory– excitatory	Euphoria Agitation Paranoia	Amphetamines (e.g., methamphetamine), cocaine (activate)
GABA (gamma- aminobutyric acid)	Inhibitory	Sedation Relaxation Drowsiness Depression	Alcohol, diazepam-type, barbiturates (activate)
Serotonin	Inhibitory	Sleep Relaxation Sedation	LSD (activate), Ecstasy (MDMA)
Acetylcholine	Excitatory– inhibitory	Mild euphoria Excitation Insomnia	Tobacco, nicotine (stimulate)
Endorphins	Inhibitory	Mild euphoria Blockage of pain Slow respiration	Narcotics (activate)

2: Comprehensive Explanation of Homeostatic Systems

For those desiring a more complete understanding of the consequences of drug effects on the homeostatic systems of the body, this section provides an in-depth discussion of the anatomical and physiological nature and biological arrangements of the nervous and endocrine systems. Because drugs of abuse are most likely to exert their psychoactive effects on neurons and their receptor targets, the nervous system is presented first and in greater depth, followed by a briefer description of endocrine function.

The Building Blocks of the Nervous System

The nervous system is composed of the brain, spinal cord, and all the neurons that connect to other organs and tissues of the body (see Figure 4.7 later in the chapter). Nervous systems enable an organism to receive information about the internal and external environment and to make the appropriate responses essential to survival. Considerable money and scientific effort are cur-

rently being dedicated to explore the mechanisms whereby the nervous system functions and processes information, resulting in frequent new and exciting discoveries.

■ The Neuron: The Basic Structural Unit of the Nervous System

The building block of the nervous system is the nerve cell, or *neuron*. Each neuron in the CNS (brain and spinal cord) is in close proximity with other neurons, forming a complex network. The human brain contains 100 billion neurons, each of which is composed of similar components but with different shapes, sizes, and distinguishing neurochemistry. Neurons do not form a continuous network. They always remain separate, never actually touching, although they are in close proximity. The typical point of communication between one neuron and another is called a **synapse**. The gap

KEY TERMS

synapse
site of communication between a message-sending neuron and its message-receiving target cell

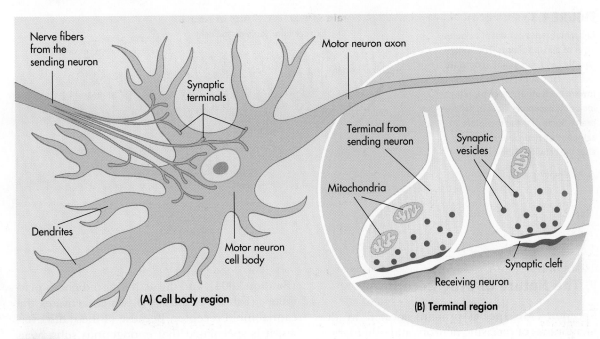

Nerve fibers from the sending neuron

Synaptic terminals

Dendrites

Motor neuron cell body

(A) Cell body region

Motor neuron axon

Terminal from sending neuron

Synaptic vesicles

Mitochondria

Synaptic cleft

Receiving neuron

(B) Terminal region

FIGURE 4.2

(A) Each neuron may have many synaptic connections. They are designed to deliver short bursts of a chemical transmitter substance into the synaptic cleft, where the substance can act on the surface of the receiving nerve cell membrane. Before release, molecules of the chemical neurotransmitter are stored in numerous vesicles, or sacs. (B) A close-up of the synaptic terminals, showing the synaptic vesicles and mitochondria. *Mitochondria* are specialized structures that help supply the cell with energy. The gap between the synaptic terminal and the target membrane is the *synaptic cleft.*

(called the **synaptic cleft**) between neurons at a synapse may be only 0.00002 millimeter wide, but it is essential for proper functioning of the nervous system (see Figure 4.2).

The neuron has a cell body with a nucleus and receiving regions called **dendrites**, which are short, treelike branches that are influenced by information from the environment and surrounding neurons such as released neurotransmitters.

The axon of a neuron is a threadlike extension that receives information from the dendrites near the cell body, in the form of an electrochemical impulse; then, like an electrical wire, it transmits the impulse to the cell's terminal. Although most axons are less than 1 inch in length, some may be quite long; for example, some axons extend from the spinal cord to the toes.

At the synapse, information is transmitted chemically to the next neuron, as shown in Figure 4.1. A similar synaptic arrangement also exists at sites of communication between neurons and target cells in organs, muscles, and glands; that is, neurotransmitters are released from the message-sending neurons and activate

receptors located in the membranes of message-receiving target cells.

There are two types of synapses: excitatory and inhibitory. The *excitatory synapse* initiates an impulse in the receiving neuron when stimulated, thereby causing release of neurotransmitters or increasing activity in the target cell. The *inhibitory synapse* diminishes the likelihood of an impulse in the receiving neuron or reduces the activity in other target cells. A receiving neuron or target cell may have thousands of synapses connecting it to other neurons and their excitatory or inhibitory information (see Figure 4.2, part A). The final cellular activity is a summation of these many excitatory and inhibitory synaptic signals.

KEY TERMS

synaptic cleft
a minute gap between the neuron and target cell, across which neurotransmitters travel

dendrites
short branches of neurons that receive transmitter signals

FIGURE 4.3

Cell membranes consist of a double layer of phospholipids. The water-soluble layers are pointed outward and the fat-soluble layers are pointed toward each other. Large proteins, including receptors, float in the membrane. Some of these receptors are activated by neurotransmitters to alter the activity of the cell.

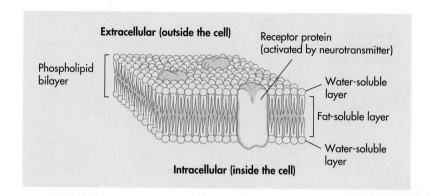

■ The Nature of Drug Receptors

Receptors are special proteins located in the membranes of receiving neurons and other target cells (see Figure 4.3). They help regulate the activity of cells in the nervous system and throughout the body. These selective protein sites on specific cells act as transducers to communicate the messages caused by *endogenous messenger substances* (chemicals produced and released within the body), such as neurotransmitters and hormones. The receptors process the complex information each cell receives as it attempts to maintain metabolic stability, or *homeostasis*, and fulfill its functional role (Kandel et al. 2000). Many drugs used therapeutically and almost all drugs of abuse exert their effects on the body by directly or indirectly interacting (either to activate or antagonize) with these receptors.

Understanding how receptors interact with specific drugs has led to some interesting results. For example, **opiate receptors** (sites of action by narcotic drugs, such as heroin and morphine) are naturally present in animal and human brains (Fattore et al. 2004). Why would human and animal brains have receptors for opiate narcotics, which are plant chemicals? Discovery of the opiate receptors suggested the existence of internal (endogenous) neurotransmitter substances in the body that normally act at these receptor sites and have effects like narcotic drugs, such as codeine and morphine. This finding led to the identification of the body's own opiates, the **endorphins** (Sabatowski et al. 2004). Specific receptors have also been found for other drugs such as the CNS depressant diazepam (Valium), which activates benzodiazepine receptors

(Bateson 2004), and the active ingredient in marijuana (Fattore et al. 2004), which activates the cannabinoid receptor. Because of these discoveries, it is speculated that endogenous substances that mimic the effects of Valium and marijuana and help provide natural sedation and relaxation for the body exist. These are discussed in greater detail in Chapters 6 and 13.

Much remains unknown about how receptors respond to or interact with drugs. Using molecular biology techniques, many of these receptors have been found to initiate a cascade of linked chemical reactions, which can change intracellular environments to produce either activation or inactivation of cellular functions and metabolism (Ferguson 2007).

Receptors that have been isolated and identified are protein molecules; it is believed that the shape of the protein is essential in regulating a drug's interaction with a cell. If the drug is the proper shape and size and has a compatible electrical charge, it may substitute for the endogenous messenger substance and activate the receptor protein by causing it to change its shape, or conform.

KEY TERMS

opiate receptors
receptors activated by opioid narcotic drugs such as heroin and morphine

endorphins
neurotransmitters that have narcotic-like effects

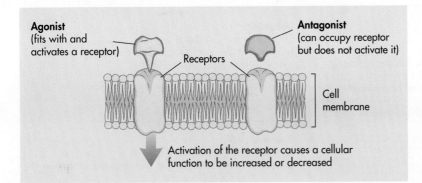

Agonist
(fits with and
activates a receptor)

Antagonist
(can occupy receptor
but does not activate it)

Receptors

Cell
membrane

Activation of the receptor causes a cellular
function to be increased or decreased

FIGURE 4.4

Interaction of agonist and antagonist
with membrane receptor. When this
receptor is occupied and activated by an
agonist, it can cause cellular changes.

Agonistic and Antagonistic Effects on Drug Receptors

A drug may have two different effects on a receptor when interaction occurs: **agonistic** or **antagonistic**. As shown in Figure 4.4, an agonistic drug interacts with the receptor and produces some type of cellular response, whereas an antagonistic drug interacts with the receptor but prevents that response.

An agonistic drug mimics the effect of a messenger substance (such as a neurotransmitter) that is naturally produced by the body and interacts with the receptor to cause some cellular change. For example, narcotic drugs are agonists that mimic the naturally occurring endorphins and activate opiate receptors. An antagonist has the opposite effect: It inhibits the sequence of metabolic events that a natural substance or an agonist drug can stimulate, usually without initiating an effect itself. Thus, the drug naloxone (created to treat heroin overdoses) is an antagonist at the opiate receptors and blocks the effects of narcotic drugs, such as heroin, as well as the effects of the naturally occurring endorphins.

Neurotransmitters: The Messengers

Many drugs affect the activity of neurotransmitters by altering their synthesis, storage, release, or deactivation (e.g., metabolism). By changing these processes, a drug may modify or block information transmitted by these neurochemical messengers. Thus, by altering the amount of neurotransmitters, such drugs can act indirectly, like agonists and antagonists, even though they do not directly change neurotransmitter receptors. They do influence the activity of these receptors by altering the amount of neurotransmitters available to naturally influence receptor function.

Experimental evidence shows that many different neurotransmitters exist, although much remains to be learned about their specific functions. These biochemical messengers are selectively released from specific neurons. Transmitters frequently altered by drugs of abuse include acetylcholine (ACh), norepinephrine, epinephrine, dopamine, serotonin, gamma-aminobutyric acid (GABA), and the endorphins (peptides). Because of the unique shapes and chemical features, each neurotransmitter affects only its specific receptors (Bloom 1995). Drugs can also affect these receptors if they are sufficiently similar in shape to the neurotransmitters. Figure 4.5 summarizes some of the important features about the common neurotransmitters.

Neurotransmitters are inactivated after they have done their job by diffusion or metabolism (by enzymes), or they are taken back up into the neuron by selective transporter proteins. If a deactivating enzyme or the reuptake is blocked by a drug, the effect of the transmitter may be prolonged or intensified.

Acetylcholine

Large quantities of acetylcholine (ACh) are found in the brain. ACh is one of the major neurotransmitters in the autonomic portion of the PNS, which is discussed later in the chapter.

Neurons that respond to ACh are distributed throughout the brain. Depending on the region, ACh can have either excitatory or inhibitory effects.

KEY TERMS

agonistic
a type of substance that activates a receptor

antagonistic
a type of substance that blocks a receptor

Acetylcholine
Chemical type: Choline product
Location: CNS—Basal ganglia, cortex, reticular activating
                system
              PNS—Neuromuscular junction, parasympathetic
                system
Action: Excitatory (nicotine receptor) and inhibitory
              (muscarinic receptor)

Norepinephrine
Chemical type: Catecholamine
Location: CNS—Limbic system, cortex, hypothalamus,
                reticular activating system, brain stem, spinal cord
              PNS—Sympathetic nervous system
Action: Usually inhibitory; some excitation

Epinephrine
Chemical type: Catecholamine
Location: CNS—Minor
              PNS—Adrenal glands
Action: Usually excitatory

Dopamine
Chemical type: Catecholamine
Location: CNS—Basal ganglia, limbic system,
                hypothalamus
Action: Usually inhibitory

Serotonin (5HT)
Chemical type: Tryptophan-derivative
Location: CNS—Basal ganglia, limbic system, brain stem,
                spinal cord, cortex
              Other—Gut, platelets, cardiovascular
Action: Usually inhibitory

GABA
Chemical type: Amino acid
Location: CNS—Basal ganglia, limbic system, cortex
Action: Usually inhibitory

Endorphins
Chemical type: Peptide (small protein)
Location: CNS—Basal ganglia, hypothalamus, brain stem,
                spinal cord
              Other—Gut, cardiovascular system
Action: Inhibitory (narcotic-like effects)

Key: CNS—Central nervous system
         PNS—Peripheral nervous system

FIGURE 4.5

Features of common neurotransmitters.

The receptors activated by ACh have been divided into two main subtypes based on the response to two drugs derived from plants: muscarine and nicotine. Muscarine (a substance in mushrooms that causes mushroom poisoning) and similarly acting drugs activate **muscarinic** receptors. Nicotine, whether experimentally administered or inhaled by smoking tobacco, stimulates **nicotinic** receptors.

Catecholamines

Catecholamines include the neurotransmitter compounds norepinephrine, epinephrine, and dopamine, all of which have similar chemical structures. Neurons that synthesize catecholamines convert the amino acids phenylalanine or tyrosine to dopamine. In some neurons, dopamine is further converted to norepinephrine, and finally to epinephrine.

After release, most of the catecholamines are taken back up into the neurons that released them, to be used over again; this process is called *reuptake.* An enzymatic breakdown system also metabolizes the catecholamines to inactive compounds. The reuptake process and the activity of metabolizing enzymes, especially monoamine oxidase (MAO), can be greatly affected by some of the drugs of abuse. If these deactivating enzymes or reuptake systems are blocked, the concentration of norepinephrine and dopamine may build up in the brain, significantly increasing the effect. Cocaine, for example, prevents the reuptake of norepinephrine and dopamine in the brain, resulting in continual stimulation of neuron catecholamine receptors.

Norepinephrine and Epinephrine Although norepinephrine and epinephrine are structurally very similar, their receptors are selective and do not respond with the same intensity to either transmitter or to **sympathomimetic** drugs. Just as the receptors to ACh can be separated into muscarinic and nicotinic types, the norepinephrine and epinephrine receptors are classified into alpha and beta categories. Receiving cells may have alpha- or beta-type receptors, or both. Norepinephrine acts predominantly on alpha receptors and with less action on beta receptors.

The antagonistic (blocking) action of many drugs that act on these catecholamine receptors can be selective for alpha receptors, whereas others block only beta receptors. This distinction can be therapeutically useful. For example, beta receptors tend to stimulate the heart, whereas alpha receptors constrict blood vessels; thus, a drug that selectively affects beta receptors can be used to treat heart ailments without directly altering the state of the blood vessels.

Dopamine Dopamine is a catecholamine transmitter that is particularly influenced by drugs of abuse (O'Brien 2006). Most, if not all, drugs that elevate mood, have abuse potential, or cause psychotic behavior alter the activity of dopamine in some way, particularly in brain regions associated with regulating mental states. In addition, dopamine is an important transmitter in controlling movement and fine muscle activity, as well as endocrine functions. Thus, because many drugs of abuse affect dopamine neurons, they can also alter all of these functions.

Serotonin

Serotonin (5-hydroxytryptamine, or 5HT) is synthesized in neurons and elsewhere (for example, in the gastrointestinal tract and platelet-type blood cells) from the dietary source of tryptophan. Tryptophan is an essential amino acid, meaning that human beings do not have the ability to synthesize it and must obtain it through diet. Like the catecholamines, serotonin is degraded by the enzyme MAO; thus, drugs that alter this enzyme affect levels of not only catecholamines but also serotonin.

Serotonin is also found in the upper brain stem, which connects the brain and the spinal cord (see Figure 4.6). Axons from serotonergic neurons are distributed throughout the entire CNS. Serotonin generally inhibits action on its target neurons. One important role of the serotonergic neurons is to prevent overreaction to various stimuli, which can cause aggressiveness, excessive motor activity,

exaggerated mood swings, insomnia, and abnormal sexual behavior. Serotonergic neurons also help regulate the release of hormones from the hypothalamus. Because many drugs of abuse affect serotonin systems, use of these drugs can interfere with these systems.

Alterations in serotonergic neurons, serotonin synthesis, and degradation have been proposed to be factors in mental illness and to contribute to the side effects of many drugs of abuse. In support of this hypothesis is the fact that drugs such as psilocybin and lysergic acid diethylamide (LSD), which have serotonin-like chemical structures, are frequently abused because of their hallucinogenic properties and can cause psychotic effects (see Chapter 12).

Major Divisions of the Nervous System

The nervous system can be divided into two major components: the central (**CNS**) and peripheral (**PNS**) nervous systems. The CNS consists of the brain and spinal cord (see Figure 4.6), which receive information through the input nerves of the PNS. This sensory information allows the CNS to evaluate the specific status of all organs and the general status of the body. After receiving and processing this information, the CNS reacts by regulating muscle and organ activity through the output nerves of the PNS (Lefkowitz et al. 1995).

The PNS is composed of neurons whose cell bodies or axons are located outside the brain or spinal cord. It consists of input and output nerves to the CNS. The PNS input to the brain and spinal cord conveys sensory information such as pain, pressure, and temperature, whereas its output activities are separated into somatic types (control of voluntary muscles) and autonomic types (control

KEY TERMS

sympathomimetic
agents that mimic the effects of norepinephrine or epinephrine

CNS
the central nervous system, including the brain and spinal cord

PNS
the peripheral nervous system, including neurons outside the CNS

FIGURE 4.6

Functional components of the central nervous system. The caudate nucleus is part of the basal ganglia and important for behavior selection and motor activity. Limbic structures include the hypothalamus, thalamus, medial forebrain bundle, and frontal lobe of the cerebrum and are important for controlling emotions and other mental states. The insula has been identified as important for motivation.

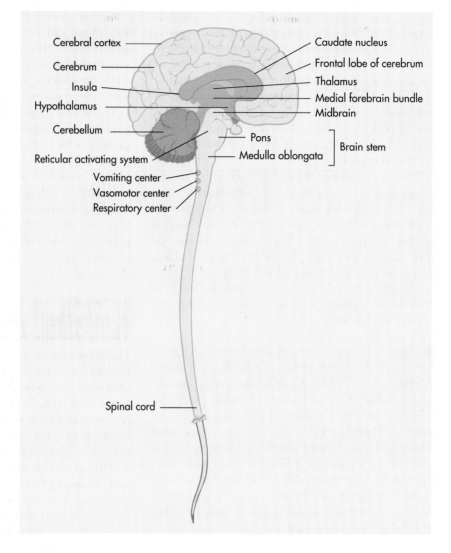

Cerebral cortex
Cerebrum
Insula
Hypothalamus
Cerebellum
Reticular activating system
Vomiting center
Vasomotor center
Respiratory center

Caudate nucleus
Frontal lobe of cerebrum
Thalamus
Medial forebrain bundle
Midbrain
Pons
Medulla oblongata
Brain stem

Spinal cord

of unconscious functions, such as essential organ and gland activity).

The Central Nervous System

The human brain is an integrating (information processing) and storage device whose abilities are unequaled by the most complex computers. It can not only handle a great deal of information simultaneously from the senses, but can also evaluate and modify the response to the information rapidly. Although the brain weighs only 3 pounds, its 100 billion neurons give it the potential to perform a multitude of functions. The following are some important brain regions influenced by drugs of abuse.

The Reticular Activating System

The reticular activating system (RAS) is an area of the brain that receives input from all of the sensory systems as well as from the cerebral cortex. The RAS is found at the junction of the spinal cord and the brain (see Figure 4.6). One of its major functions is to control the brain's state of arousal (sleep versus awake).

Because of its complex, diffuse network structure, the RAS is very susceptible to the effects of drugs. It is sensitive to the effects of LSD, potent stimulants such as cocaine and amphetamines, and CNS depressants such as alcohol and barbiturates.

Norepinephrine and ACh are important neurotransmitters in the RAS. High levels of epinephrine, norepinephrine, or stimulant drugs, such as amphetamines, activate the RAS. In contrast, drugs

ANIMALS VS. HUMANS (ABILITY TO REASON)
OR LOSS OF = ADDICTION.

that block the actions of another transmitter, ACh, called **anticholinergic** drugs (for example, antihistamines), suppress RAS activity, causing sleepiness.

The Basal Ganglia

The basal ganglia include the caudate nucleus and are the primary centers for involuntary and finely tuned motor functions involving, for example, posture and muscle tone. In addition, these structures are involved in establishing and maintaining behaviors. Two important neurotransmitters in the basal ganglia are dopamine and ACh. Damage to neurons in this area may cause *Parkinson's disease*, the progressive yet selective degeneration of the main dopaminergic neurons in the basal ganglia. The structures of the basal ganglia are especially important for developing addictions.

A close association exists between control of motor abilities and control of mental states. Both functions rely heavily on the activity of dopamine-releasing neurons. Consequently, drugs that affect dopamine activity usually alter both systems, resulting in undesired side effects. For example, heavy use of tranquilizers (such as chlorpromazine [Thorazine]) in the treatment of psychotic patients can produce Parkinson-like symptoms. If such drugs are administered daily over several years, problems with motor functioning may become permanent. Drugs of abuse, such as stimulants, increase dopamine activity, causing enhanced motor activity as well as psychotic behavior.

The Limbic System

The limbic system includes an assortment of linked brain regions located near to and including the hypothalamus (see Figure 4.6). Besides the hypothalamus, the limbic structures include the thalamus, medial forebrain bundle, and front portion of the cerebral cortex. Functions of the limbic and basal ganglia structures are inseparably linked; drugs that affect one system often affect the other as well.

The primary roles of limbic brain regions include regulating emotional activities (such as fear, rage, and anxiety), memory, modulation of basic hypothalamic functions (such as endocrine activity), and activities such as mating, procreation, and caring for the young. In addition, reward centers are also believed to be associated with limbic structures. For this reason, it is almost certain that the mood-elevating effects of drugs of abuse are mediated by the limbic systems of the brain.

For example, studies have shown that, when given the option, laboratory animals will self-administer most stimulant drugs of abuse (such as amphetamines and cocaine) through a cannula surgically placed into limbic structures (such as the medial forebrain bundle and frontal cerebral cortex). This self-administration is achieved by linking injection of the drug into the cannula with a lever press or other activity by the animal (Porrino 2004). It is thought that the euphoria or intense "highs" associated with these drugs result from their effects on these brain regions. Some of the limbic system's principal transmitters include dopamine, norepinephrine, and serotonin; dopamine activation appears to be the primary reinforcement that accounts for the abuse liability of most drugs (DiChiara et al. 2004).

The Cerebral Cortex

The unique features of the human cerebral cortex give human beings a special place among animals. The cortex is a layer of gray matter made up of nerves and supporting cells that almost completely surrounds the rest of the brain and lies immediately under the skull (see Figure 4.6). It is responsible for receiving sensory input, interpreting incoming information, and initiating voluntary motor behavior. Many psychoactive drugs, such as psychedelics, dramatically alter the perception of sensory information by the cortex and cause hallucinations that result in strange behavior.

The most developed part of the cortex is called the *associative cortex*. The associative areas of the brain do not directly receive input from the environment, nor do they directly initiate output to the muscles or the glands. Instead, these cortical areas may store memories, control complex behaviors, help process information, and help make decisions. Some psychoactive drugs disrupt the normal functioning of these areas, thereby interfering with an individual's ability to deal effectively and rationally with complex issues.

Insula

The insula is a structure recently implicated in drug addiction. It is located deep in the brain, connected with the pleasure pathways, and appears to

KEY TERMS

anticholinergic
agents that antagonize the effects of acetylcholine

BRAIN SURGERY FOR ADDICTION!

be important for motivation. A recent finding determined that smokers who have injury to their insula lose interest in using tobacco (Vorel et al. 2007).

The Hypothalamus

The hypothalamus (see Figures 4.6 and 4.7) is located near the base of the brain. It integrates information from many sources and serves as the CNS control center for the ANS and many vital support functions. It also serves as the primary point of contact between the nervous and endocrine systems. Because the hypothalamus controls the ANS, it is responsible for maintaining homeostasis in the body; thus, drugs that alter its function can have a major impact on systems that control homeostasis. The catecholamine transmitters are particularly important in regulating the function of the hypothalamus, and most drugs of abuse that alter the activity of norepinephrine and dopamine are likely to alter the activity of this brain structure.

FIGURE 4.7

Autonomic pathways of the parasympathetic and sympathetic nervous systems and the organs affected.

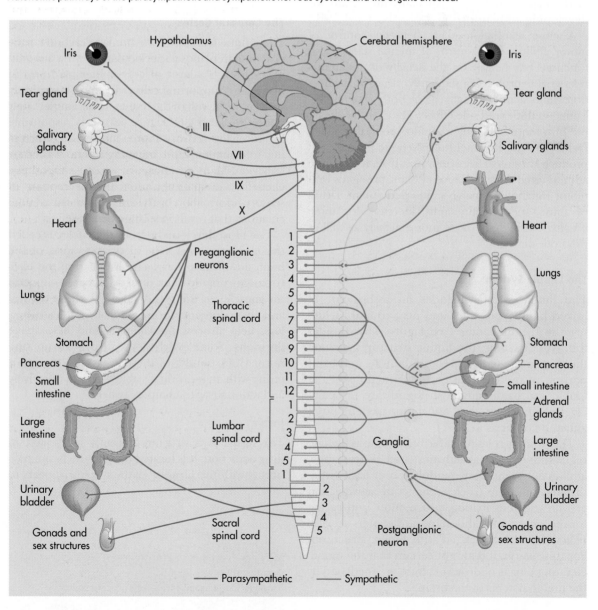

Table 4.2 **Sympathetic and Parasympathetic Control**

STRUCTURE OR FUNCTION	SYMPATHETIC	PARASYMPATHETIC
Heart rate	Speeds up	Slows
Breathing rate	Speeds up	Slows
Stomach wall	Slows motility	Increases motility
Skin blood vessels (vasomotor function)	Constricts	Dilates
Iris of eye	Constricts (pupil enlarges)	Dilates
Vomiting center	Stimulates	—

The Autonomic Nervous System

Although the cell bodies of the neurons of the **ANS** are located within the brain or spinal cord, their axons project outside of the CNS to involuntary muscles, organs, and glands; thus, the ANS is considered part of the PNS. The ANS is an integrative, or regulatory, system that does not require conscious control (that is, you do not have to think about it to make it function). It is usually considered primarily a motor or output system. A number of drugs that cannot enter the CNS because of the blood–brain barrier are able to affect the ANS only. The ANS is divided into two functional components: the sympathetic and the parasympathetic nervous systems (Westfall and Westfall 2006). Both systems include neurons that project to most visceral organs and to smooth muscles, glands, and blood vessels (see Figure 4.7).

The two components of the ANS generally have opposite effects on an organ or its function. The working of the heart is a good example of sympathetic and parasympathetic control. Stimulation of the parasympathetic nervous system slows the heart rate, whereas stimulation of the sympathetic nerves accelerates it. These actions constitute a constant biological check-and-balance, or regulatory system. Because the two parts of the ANS work in opposite ways much of the time, they are considered physiological antagonists. These two systems control most of the internal organs, the circulatory system, and the secretory (glandular) system. The sympathetic system is normally active at all times; the degree of activity varies from moment to moment and from organ to organ. The parasympathetic nervous system is organized mainly for lim-ited, focused activity and usually conserves and restores energy rather than expends it. For example, it slows the heart rate, lowers blood pressure, aids in absorption of nutrients, and is involved in emptying the urinary bladder. Table 4.2 lists the structures and/or functions of the sympathetic and parasympathetic nervous systems and their effects on one another.

The two branches of the ANS use two different neurotransmitters. The parasympathetic branch releases ACh at its synapses, whereas the sympathetic neurons release norepinephrine. An increase in epinephrine in the blood released from the adrenal glands (see the next section) or the administration of drugs that enhance norepinephrine activity causes the body to respond as if the sympathetic nervous system had been activated. As previously mentioned, such drugs are referred to as *sympathomimetics*. Thus, taking amphetamines (which enhance the sympathetic nervous system by releasing norepinephrine and epinephrine) raises blood pressure, speeds up heart rate, slows down motility of the stomach walls, and may cause the pupils of the eyes to enlarge; other so-called "uppers," such as cocaine, have similar effects.

Drugs that affect ACh release, metabolism, or interaction with its respective receptor are referred to as *cholinergic* drugs. They can either mimic or antagonize the parasympathetic nervous system, according to their pharmacological action.

KEY TERMS

ANS
the autonomic nervous system, which controls the unconscious functions of the body

The Endocrine System

The endocrine system consists of glands, which are ductless (meaning that they secrete directly into the bloodstream) and release chemical substances called **hormones** (see Figure 4.8). These hormones are essential in regulating many vital functions, including metabolism, growth, tissue repair, and sexual behavior, to mention just a few. In contrast to neurotransmitters, hormones tend to have a slower onset, a longer duration of action, and a more generalized target. Although a number of tissues are capable of producing and releasing hormones, three of the principal sources of these chemical messengers are the pituitary gland, the adrenal glands, and the sex glands.

Endocrine Glands and Regulation

The pituitary gland is often referred to as the *master gland*. It controls many of the other glands that make up the endocrine system by releasing regulating factors and growth hormone. Besides controlling the brain functions already mentioned, the hypothalamus helps control the activity of the pituitary gland and thereby has a very prominent effect on the endocrine system.

The adrenal glands are located near the kidneys and are divided into two parts: the outer surface, called the *cortex*, and the inner part, called the *medulla*. The adrenal medulla is actually a component of the sympathetic nervous system and releases adrenaline (another name for *epinephrine*) during sympathetic stimulation. Other important hormones released by the adrenal cortex are called *corticosteroids* or just **steroids**. Steroids help the body respond appropriately to crises and stress. In addition, small amounts of male sex hormones (chemically related to the steroids), called **androgens**, are released by the adrenal cortex. The androgens produce anabolic effects that increase the reten-

tion and synthesis of proteins, causing growth in the mass of tissues such as muscles and bones (Snyder 2006).

Sex glands are responsible for the secretion of male and female sex hormones that help regulate the development and activity of the respective reproductive systems. The organs known as *gonads* include the female ovaries and the male testes. The activity of the gonads is regulated by hormones released from the pituitary gland (see Figure 4.8) and, for the most part, remains suppressed until puberty. After activation, estrogens and progesterones are released from the ovaries, and androgens (principally testosterone) are released from the testes. These hormones are responsible for the development and maintenance of the secondary sex characteristics. They influence not only sex-related body features but also emotional states, suggesting that these sex hormones enter the brain and significantly affect the functioning of the limbic systems.

For the most part, drugs prescribed to treat endocrine problems are intended as replacement therapy. For example, diabetic patients suffer from a shortage of insulin produced by the pancreas, so therapy consists of insulin injections. Patients who suffer from dwarfism receive insufficient growth hormone from the pituitary gland; thus, growth hormone is administered to stimulate normal growth. Because some hormones can affect growth, muscle development, and behavior, they are sometimes abused to enhance athletic performance or body building.

The Abuse of Hormones: Anabolic Steroids

Androgens are the hormones most likely to be abused in the United States. In 2006, these drugs were self-administered by 2.5% of high school seniors in this country (Johnston 2007). Testosterone, the primary natural androgen, is produced by the testes. Naturally produced androgens are essential for normal growth and development of male sex organs as well as secondary sex characteristics such as male hair patterns, voice changes, muscular development, and fat distribution. The androgens are also necessary for appropriate growth spurts during adolescence (Snyder 2006). Accepted therapeutic use of the androgens is usually for replacement in males with abnormally functioning testes.

Androgens clearly have an impressive effect on development of tissue (Kolata 2002). In particular,

KEY TERMS

hormones
regulatory chemicals released by the endocrine system

steroids
hormones related to the corticosteroids released from the adrenal cortex

androgens
male sex hormones

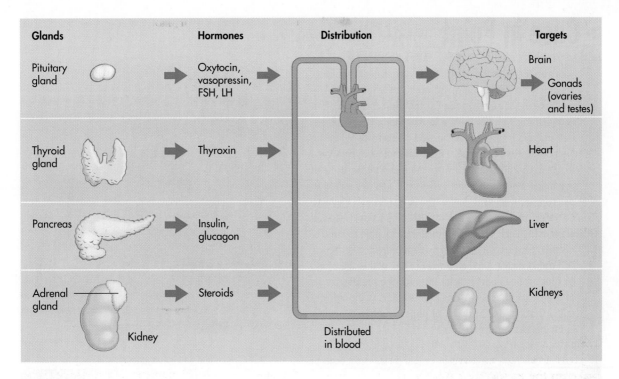

FIGURE 4.8

Examples of some glands in the endocrine system.

they cause pronounced growth of muscle mass and a substantial increase in body weight in young men with deficient testes function. Because of these effects, androgens are classified as **anabolic** (able to stimulate the conversion of nutrients into tissue mass) **steroids** (they are chemically similar to the steroids).

In addition, many athletes and trainers have assumed that, when taken in very high doses, androgens can enhance muscle growth and increase strength above that achieved by normal testicular function, thereby improving athletic performance (Snyder 2006). Because of this effect, male and female athletes, as well as nonathletes who are into body building and sports, have been attracted to these drugs in hopes of enlarging muscle size, improving their athletic performances, and enhancing their physiques (see Chapter 16) despite their negative side effects (see "Case in Point").

Several studies have suggested that anabolic hormones can have especially substantial negative effects. Athletic trainers and managers claim to be seeing an increase in severe injuries such as tears of muscles and ligaments due to aggravated trauma created by overmuscled bodies (Verducci 2002).

Anabolic steroids can cause pronounced growth of muscle mass.

KEY TERMS

anabolic steroids
compounds chemically like the steroids that stimulate production of tissue mass

►Case in Point Winning — But at What Cost?

Steroids' ability to make athletes run faster, be stronger, and endure longer are no longer disputed. What is disputed is the question of "at what cost?" The message being sent by today's star athletes all too often is unsettling. Ken Caminiti, a former Major League Baseball player, admitted that he was on steroids when he won the National League's Most Valuable Player Award in 1996. In 2003, Caminiti proclaimed that he did not regret his steroid use and believed it was necessary to be competitive and make the big money. He also declared that at least half of the players in baseball were using such drugs. Caminiti was not able to control his own drug use and as late as September 2004 he was still doing drugs. On October 11, 2004, at the age of 41, he died from a heart attack. Although the precise cause of the heart attack was not identified, it is thought by many that his use of drugs of abuse, such as steroids, led to his premature demise.

Sources: CNNsi.com. "Caminiti Comes Clean" (28 May 2003); MSNBC News. "Caminiti, 41, Dies of Heart Attack." Available msnbc.msn.com/id/6222790/.

These drugs can also affect the limbic structures of the brain. Consequently, they may cause excitation and a sense of superior strength and performance in some users. These effects, coupled with increased aggressiveness, could encourage continual use of these drugs. Other CNS effects, however, may be disturbing to the user. Symptoms that may occur with very high doses include uncontrolled rage (referred to as "roid rage"), headaches, anxiety, insomnia, and perhaps paranoia (*Drug Facts and Comparisons* 2005; Talih et al. 2007). Because of concern about the abuse potential and side effect profile of the anabolic steroids, these drugs are controlled as Schedule III substances.

Designer Steroids

In an attempt to circumvent the restriction on steroid use, some athletes have used the "designer" steroid known as tetrahydrogestrinone (THG). THG was banned by the FDA in products classified as nutritional supplements. Because of concerns that athletes were using THG to enhance performance, professional athletic organizations and the International Olympic Committee have tested athletes for this drug (Gardner 2003) and disqualify them from competition if THG is detected.

Conclusion

All psychoactive drugs affect brain activity by altering the ability of neurons to send and receive messages. Consequently, drugs of abuse exert their addicting effects by stimulating or blocking the activity of CNS neurotransmitters or their receptors. Thus, to understand why these drugs are abused and the nature of their dependence, how neurons and their neurotransmitter systems function must be studied. In addition, many scientists believe that elucidating how substances of abuse affect nervous systems will lead to new and more effective methods for treating drug addiction.

Discussion Questions

1. What are the similarities and differences between neurotransmitters and hormones?

2. Why is it important for the body to have chemical messengers that can be quickly released and rapidly inactivated?

3. Why are receptors so important in understanding the effects of drugs of abuse?

4. Why is it not surprising that drugs that affect the catecholamine transmitters also affect the endocrine system?

5. What are some mechanisms whereby a drug of abuse can increase the activity of dopamine transmitter systems in the brain?

6. How can knowing that the insula of the brain is important for motivation be used to treat tobacco addiction?

7. Why might a drug of abuse that damages the associative cortex make the user especially vulnerable to addiction?

8. Was classifying anabolic steroids as Schedule III drugs justified? What do you think will be the long-term consequence of this action?

Summary

1 The nervous and endocrine systems help mediate internal and external responses to the body's surroundings. Both systems release chemical messengers to achieve their homeostatic functions. These messenger substances are called neurotransmitters and hormones, and they carry out their functions by binding to specific receptors. Many drugs exert their effects by influencing these chemical messengers.

2 The neuron is the principal cell type in the nervous system. This specialized cell consists of dendrites, a cell body, and an axon. It communicates with other neurons and organs by releasing neurotransmitters, which can cause either excitation or inhibition at their target sites.

3 The chemical messengers from glands and neurons exert their effects by interacting with special protein regions in membranes called receptors. Because of their unique construction, receptors interact only with molecules that have specific shapes. Activation of receptors can alter the functions of the target system.

4 Agonists are substances or drugs that stimulate receptors. Antagonists are substances or drugs that bind to receptors and prevent them from being activated.

5 A variety of substances are used as neurotransmitters by neurons in the body. The classes of transmitters include the catecholamines, serotonin, acetylcholine, GABA, and peptides. These transmitters are excitatory, inhibitory, or sometimes both, depending on which receptor is being activated. Many drugs selectively act to either enhance or antagonize these neurotransmitters and their activities.

6 The central nervous system consists of the brain and spinal cord. Regions within the brain help to regulate specific functions. The hypothalamus controls endocrine and basic body functions. The basal ganglia include the caudate nucleus and are primarily responsible for controlling motor activity. The limbic system regulates mood and mental states and establishing behaviors. The cerebral cortex helps interpret, process information, make decisions, and respond to input information.

7 The limbic system and its associated transmitters, especially dopamine and serotonin, are major sites of action for the drugs of abuse. Substances that increase the activity of dopamine cause a sense of well-being and euphoria, which encourages psychological dependence.

8 The autonomic nervous system is composed of the sympathetic and parasympathetic systems; neurons associated with these systems release noradrenalin and acetylcholine as their transmitters, respectively. These systems work in an antagonistic fashion to control unconscious, visceral functions such as breathing and cardiovascular activity. The parasympathetic nervous system usually helps conserve and restore energy in the body, whereas the sympathetic nervous system is continually active.

9 The endocrine system consists of glands that synthesize and release hormones into the blood. Distribution via blood circulation carries these chemical messengers throughout the body, where they act on specific receptors. Some of the principal structures include the pituitary, adrenals, and gonads (testes and ovaries).

10 Anabolic steroids are structurally related to the male hormone testosterone. They are often abused by both male and female athletes trying to build muscle mass and enhance performance. The continual use of high doses of anabolic steroids can cause annoying and dangerous side effects. The long-term effects of low, intermittent doses of these drugs have not been determined. Because of concerns voiced by most medical authorities, anabolic steroids are controlled substances and have been classified as Schedule III substances.

References

Bateson, A. "The Benzodiazepine Site of the GABA A Receptor: An Old Target with a New Potential." *Sleep Medicine* 5 (2004): S9–S59.

Bloom, F. "Neurotransmission and the Central Nervous System." In *The Pharmacological Basis of Therapeutics*, 9th ed., edited by J. Harman and T. Limbird, 267–293. New York: McGraw-Hill, 1995.

DiChiara, G., V. Bassareo, S. Fenu, M. DeLuca, et al. "Dopamine and Drug Addiction: The Nucleus Accumbens Shell Connections." *Neuropharmacology* 47 Supplement 1 (2004): 227–241.

Drug Facts and Comparisons. 59th ed. St. Louis: Walters Kluwar Health, 2005: 322–336.

Fattore, L., G. Cossu, M. Spano, S. Deiana, P. Fadda, M. Scherma, and W. Fratta. "Cannabinoids and Rewards: Interactions with Opioid Systems." *Critical Reviews in Neurobiology* 16 (2004): 147–158.

Ferguson, S. "Phosphorylation-Independent Attenuation of BPCR-Signalling." *Trends in Pharmacological Science* 28 (2007): 173–179.

Gardner, A. "Controversy Grows Over Designer Steroid. Feds Ban THG: Grand Jury Subpoenas Top Athletes." *Healthscout* (30 October 2003): 10F2.

Johnston, L. "Monitoring the Future 2006." 2007. Available www.monitoringthefuture.org/07data.html#2007data-drugs.

Kandel, E., J. Schwartz, and T. Jessell. "Overview of Synaptic Transmission." In *Principles of Neural Science*, 4th ed., 175–186. New York: McGraw-Hill, 2000.

Kolata, G. "With No Answers on Risks: Steroid Users Still Say 'Yes'." *The New York Times* (2 December 2002). Available nytimes.com.

Lefkowitz, R., B. Hoffman, and P. Taylor. "Neurotransmission, the Autonomic and Somatic Motor Nervous Systems." In *The Pharmacological Basis of Therapeutics*, 9th ed., edited by J. Hardman and T. Limbird, 361–396. New York: McGraw-Hill, 1995.

O'Brien, C. "Drug Addiction and Drug Abuse." In *The Pharmacological Basis of Therapeutics*, 11th ed., edited by L. Brunton, J. Lazo, and K. Parker, 607–627. New York: McGraw-Hill, 2006.

Porrino, L., J. Daunais, H. Smith, and M. Nadar. "The Expanding Effects of Cocaine: Studies in Nonhuman Primate Model of Cocaine Self-Administration." *Neuroscience Biobehavioral Reviews* 27 (2004): 893–920.

Sabatowski, R., D. Shafer, S. Kasper, H. Brunsch, and L. Radbruh. "Pain Treatment: A Historical Overview." *Current Pharmaceutical Design* 10 (2004): 701–716.

Snyder, P. "Androgens." In *The Pharmacological Basis of Therapeutics*, 11th ed., edited by L. Brunton, J. Lazo, and K. Parker, 1573–1585. New York: McGraw-Hill, 2006.

Talih, F., O. Fattal, and D. Malone. "Anabolic Steroid Abuse: Psychiatric and Physical Costs." *Cleveland Clinical Journal of Medicine* 74 (2007): 341–344.

Verducci, T. "The Injury Toll." (May 28, 2002). Available CNNSI.com.

Vorel, S., A. Bisaga, G. McKhann, and H. Kleber. "Insula Damage and Quitting Smoking." *Science* 317 (2007): 318–319.

Westfall, T. and D. Westfall. "Neurotransmission. The Autonomic and Somatic Motor Nervous Systems." In *The Pharmacological Basis of Therapeutics*, 11th ed., edited by L. Brunton, J. Lazo, and K. Parker, 137–181. New York: McGraw-Hill, 2006.

CHAPTER 5

How and Why Drugs Work

Learning ◎bjectives

On completing this chapter you will be able to:

◎ Describe some of the common unintended drug effects.

◎ Explain why the same dose of a drug may affect individuals differently.

◎ Explain the difference between potency and toxicity.

◎ Describe the concept of a drug's "margin of safety."

◎ Identify and give examples of additive, antagonistic, and potentiative (synergistic) drug interactions.

◎ Identify the pharmacokinetic factors that can influence the effects caused by drugs.

◎ Cite the physiological and pathological factors that influence drug effects.

◎ Explain the significance of the blood–brain barrier to psychoactive drugs.

◎ Define *threshold dose, plateau effect,* and *cumulative effect.*

◎ Discuss the role of the liver in drug metabolism and the consequences of this process.

◎ Define *biotransformation*.

◎ Describe the relationships among tolerance, withdrawal, rebound, physical dependence, and psychological dependence.

◎ Discuss the significance of placebos in drug therapy and drug abuse.

◎ Describe drug craving, and explain how it can cause relapse to a drug addiction.

Did You Know?

- o Twenty percent of the total hospital costs in the United States are due to medical care for health damage caused by substances of abuse. *O.D. ACCIDENTS E-ROOM*

- o The same dose of a drug does not have the same effect on everyone.

- o In excessive doses, almost any drug or substance can be toxic.

- o Sixty-five percent of the strokes among young Americans are related to cigarette, cocaine, or amphetamine use.

- o Many people who abuse cocaine also abuse alcohol to counter unpleasant side effects.

- o Many drugs are unable to pass from the blood into the brain. *AND ?*

- o Gender affects responses to alcohol and tobacco.

- o Hereditary factors may predispose some individuals to becoming psychologically dependent on drugs with abuse potential.

Drugs and Society Online is a great source for additional drugs and society information for both students and instructors.
Visit **http://drugsandsociety.jbpub.com** to find a variety of useful tools for learning, thinking, and teaching.

Introduction

A common belief is that drugs can solve most of life's serious physical, emotional, and medical problems. Although medications are essential to treatment for many diseases, excessive reliance on drugs causes unrealistic expectations that may lead to dangerous — even fatal — consequences. For example, drug addiction and dependence often follow from such unrealistic drug expectations. Obviously, not every person who uses drugs inappropriately becomes a drug addict, nor are patients who use drugs as prescribed by the doctor immune from becoming physically and mentally dependent on their prescribed medications. In fact, because of individual variability, it is difficult to predict accurately which drug users will or will not have drug problems such as addiction and dependence.

In this chapter, we consider the factors that account for the variability of drug responses — that is, what determines how the body responds to drugs and why some drugs work while others do not. First, we review the general effects of drugs, both intended and unintended. The correlation between the dose and response to a drug is addressed next, followed by a discussion of how drugs interact with one another. The section on *pharmacokinetic* factors considers how drugs are introduced into, distributed throughout, and eliminated from the body, along with physiological and pathological variables that modify how drugs affect the body. The final sections in the chapter consider concepts important to understanding drug abuse, such as tolerance, physical versus psychological dependence, and addiction.

The Intended and Unintended Effects of Drugs

When physicians prescribe drugs, their objective is usually to cure or relieve symptoms of a disease. Frequently, however, drugs cause unintended effects that neither the physician nor the patient expected. These are called **side effects**.

KEY TERMS

side effects
unintended drug responses

withdrawal
unpleasant effects that occur when use of a drug is stopped

A response that is considered a side effect in one situation may, in fact, be the therapeutic objective in another. For example, the antihistamines found in many over-the-counter (OTC) drugs have an intended main effect of relieving allergy symptoms, but they often cause annoying drowsiness as a side effect; in fact, for this reason their labels include warnings that they should not be used while driving a car. These antihistamines are also included in OTC sleep aids, in which their sedating action is the desired main effect.

Side effects can influence many body functions and occur in any organ (see Figure 5.1), and they send more than 700,000 people to U.S. hospitals every year according to the Centers for Disease Control and the Food and Drug Administration (FDA) (Hitti 2007). The following are basic kinds of side effects that can result from drug use:

Nausea or vomiting.

Changes in mental alertness such as sedation or nervousness.

Dependence, which compels people to continue using a drug because they want to achieve a desired effect or because they fear unpleasant reactions, called **withdrawal**, that occur when use of the drug is discontinued.

Allergic reactions (hypersensitive reactions or sensitization) often experienced as rashes or breathing difficulty.

Changes in cardiovascular activity altering the activity of the heart or blood pressure.

This partial list of side effects demonstrates the types of risks involved whenever any drug (prescription, nonprescription, illicit, and even some herbal products) is used. Consequently, before taking a drug, whether for therapeutic or recreational use, you should understand its potential problems and determine whether the benefits justify the risks. For example, it is important to know that morphine is effective for relieving severe pain, but it also depresses breathing and retards intestinal activity, causing constipation. Likewise, amphetamines can be used to suppress appetite for losing weight, but they also increase blood pressure and stimulate the heart. Cocaine is a good local anesthetic, but it can be extremely addicting and can cause tremors or even seizures. The greater the danger associated with using a drug, the less likely that the benefits will warrant its use.

Adverse effects of drugs of abuse are particularly troublesome in the United States. Studies have

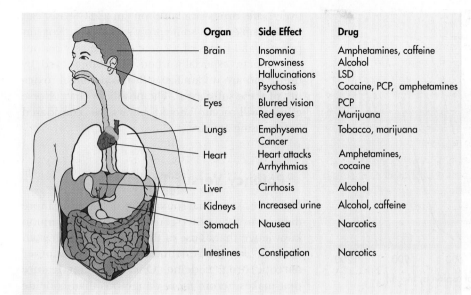

Organ	Side Effect	Drug
Brain	Insomnia	Amphetamines, caffeine
	Drowsiness	Alcohol
	Hallucinations	LSD
	Psychosis	Cocaine, PCP, amphetamines
Eyes	Blurred vision	PCP
	Red eyes	Marijuana
Lungs	Emphysema	Tobacco, marijuana
	Cancer	
Heart	Heart attacks	Amphetamines,
	Arrhythmias	cocaine
Liver	Cirrhosis	Alcohol
Kidneys	Increased urine	Alcohol, caffeine
Stomach	Nausea	Narcotics
Intestines	Constipation	Narcotics

FIGURE 5.1

Common side effects with drugs of abuse. Almost every organ or system in the body can be negatively affected by the substances of abuse.

suggested that tens of billions of dollars are spent each year in the United States on medical care and premature deaths due to the use of addicting substances (Cartwright 2007; Rice 1999).

The Dose-Response Relationship of Therapeutics and Toxicity

All effects — both desired and unwanted — are related to the amount of drug administered. A small concentration of drug may have one effect, whereas a larger dose may create a greater effect or a different effect entirely. Because some correlation exists between the response to a drug and the quantity of the drug dose, it is possible to calculate **dose-response** curves (see Figure 5.2).

Once a dose-response curve for a drug has been determined in an individual, it can be used to predict how that person will respond to different doses of the drug. For example, the dose-response curve for user B in Figure 5.2 shows that 600 mg of aspirin will relieve only 50% of his or her headache. It is important to understand that not everyone responds the same way to a given dose of drug. Thus, in Figure 5.2, although 600 mg of aspirin gives 50% relief from a headache for user B, it relieves 100% of the headache for user A and none of the headache for user C. This variability in response makes it difficult to predict the precise drug effect from a given dose.

Many factors can contribute to the variability in drug responses (Buxton 2006). One of the most important is **tolerance**, or reduced response over

time to the same dosage, an effect that is examined carefully in a later section of this chapter. Other factors include the size of the individual, stomach contents if the drug is taken by mouth, different levels of enzymatic activity in the liver (which changes the drug via metabolic action), acidity of the urine (which affects the rate of drug elimination), time of day, and state of the person's health. Such multiple interacting factors make it difficult to calculate accurately the final drug effect for any given individual at any given time.

Margin of Safety

An important concept for developing new drugs for therapy, as well as for assessing the probability of serious side effects for drugs of abuse, is called the **margin of safety**. The margin of safety is determined by the difference between the doses

KEY TERMS

dose-response
correlation between the amount of a drug given and its effects

tolerance
changes in the body that decrease response to a drug even though the dose remains the same

margin of safety
range in dose between the amount of drug necessary to cause a therapeutic effect and that needed to create a toxic effect

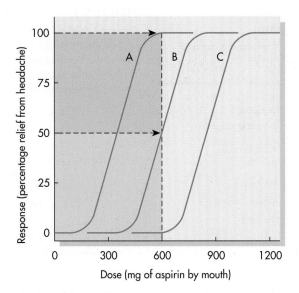

FIGURE 5.2

Dose-response curve for relieving a headache with aspirin in three users. User A is the most sensitive and has 100% headache relief at a dose of 600 mg. User B is the next most sensitive and experiences 50% headache relief with a 600-mg dose. The least sensitive is user C; with a 600-mg dose, user C has no relief from a headache.

necessary to cause the intended (therapeutic or recreational) effects and the toxic unintended effects. The larger the margin of safety, the less likely that serious adverse side effects will occur when using the drug to treat medical problems or even when abusing it. Drugs with relatively narrow margins of safety, such as phencyclidine (PCP) or cocaine, have a very high rate of serious reactions in populations who abuse these substances.

There is no such thing as the perfect drug that goes right to the target in the body, has no toxicity, produces no side effects, and can be removed or neutralized when not needed. Unfortunately, most effective drugs are potentially dangerous if the doses are high enough, if they are used recklessly, or if they are used by persons who are especially vulnerable to their adverse effects. Pharmacologists refer to the perfect drug as a "magic bullet"; so far, no magic bullets have been discovered. Even rela-

tively safe drugs available on an OTC basis can cause problems for some prospective users. Not surprisingly, all drugs of abuse can cause very serious side effects, especially when self-administered by users who are unfamiliar with the potential toxicities of these substances. The possibility that adverse effects will occur should always be considered before using any drug.

Potency Versus Toxicity

Most of us know that some drugs of abuse are more dangerous than others. For example, it is common knowledge that abuse of the narcotic drug heroin is more likely to be lethal than abuse of another narcotic drug, codeine. One important feature that makes heroin more dangerous than codeine is its high potency. **Potency** is a way of expressing how much of a drug is necessary to cause an effect, whether it be desired or toxic. The smaller the dose required to achieve a drug action, the greater the drug potency.

The concept of potency can also be used to describe a drug's ability to create a therapeutic effect. More potent medications require lower doses to be effective. Knowledge of a drug's potency is essential if it is to be used properly and safely.

Toxicity is the capacity of a drug to upset or even destroy normal body functions. Toxic compounds are often called *poisons*, although almost any compound — including sugar, table salt, aspirin, and vitamin A — can be toxic at sufficiently high doses. If a foreign chemical is introduced into the body, it may disrupt the body's normal functions. In many instances, the body can compensate for this disruption, perhaps by metabolizing and rapidly eliminating the chemical, and little effect is noted. Sometimes, however, the delicate balance is altered and the person becomes sick or even dies. If the body's functional balance is already under stress from disease, the introduction of a drug may have a much more serious effect than its use in a healthy person who can adjust to its toxicity.

A drug with high potency often is toxic even at low doses; therefore, the amount given must be carefully measured and the user closely monitored. If caution is not taken, serious damage to the body or death can occur. Very potent drugs that are abused, such as heroin-related drugs, are particularly dangerous because they are often consumed by unsuspecting users who are ignorant of the drug's extreme toxicity (see "Here and Now," Deadly Drug Mix Resurfaces, page 125). Potency depends on many factors, such as the drug's

Here and Now

Deadly Drug Mix Resurfaces

In 2006 more than 17 people in New York City and hundreds across the country died because they used heroin or cocaine laced with an extremely potent narcotic pain killer. The deadly additive is a narcotic drug called fentanyl that can be up to 80 times more potent and more deadly than morphine if abused. It is thought that most of the victims were unaware that they were consuming this powerful drug. Although fentanyl is available legally by prescription, authorities concluded that the fentanyl in these cocktails likely was manufactured illicitly. It is suspected that drug dealers added fentanyl to the mix in order to increase their supply while strengthening the effect of the drug mixture. In some ways this most recent outbreak of fentanyl deaths is a replay of a similar occurrence in 1990 when a deadly fentanyl product called Tango and Cash hit the streets.

Source: Santora, M. "Deadly Mix Resurfaces." *The New York Times* (30 August 2006): A19.

absorption, its distribution in the body, individual metabolism, the form of excretion, the rate of elimination, and its activity at the site of action (Buxton 2006).

Drug Interaction

A drug's effects can be dramatically altered when other drugs are also present in the body; this effect is known as **drug interaction** (Oates 2006). A typical example of multiple drug use occurs when you treat your common cold. Because of your many cold-related symptoms, you may consume an assortment of pain relievers, antihistamines, decongestants, and anticough medications all at the same time.

Multiple drug use can create a serious medical problem because many drugs influence the actions of other drugs (Oates 2006). Even physicians may be baffled by unusual effects when multiple drugs are consumed. Frequently, drug interactions are misdiagnosed as symptoms of a disease. Such errors in diagnosis can lead to inappropriate treatment and serious health consequences. Complications can arise that are dangerous, even fatal. The interacting substance may be another drug, or it may be some substance in the diet or in the environment, such as a pesticide. Because of the increasing popularity of herbal products, we are also observing that herbs can interact with both prescription and nonprescription drugs. These interactions are not surprising because some of the herbs themselves contain drugs that occur naturally. Consequently, an herb that causes sedation almost certainly will enhance the depressing effects of either prescription or nonprescription sleep aids. Drug interac-

tion is an area in which more research and public education are required.

Depending on the effect on the body, drug interaction may be categorized into three types: *additive, antagonistic (inhibitory),* and *potentiative (synergistic).*

■ Additive Effects

Additive interactions are the summation of effects of drugs taken concurrently. An example of an additive interaction results from using aspirin and acetaminophen (Tylenol) at the same time. The pain relief provided is equal to the sum of the two analgesics, which could be achieved by a comparable dose of either drug alone. Thus, if a 300-mg tablet of Bayer aspirin were taken with a 300-mg tablet of Tylenol, the relief would be the same as if two tablets of either Bayer aspirin or Tylenol were taken instead.

■ Antagonistic (Inhibitory) Effects

Antagonistic interactions occur when one drug cancels or blocks the effect of another drug. For

KEY TERMS

drug interaction
presence of one drug alters the action of another drug

additive interactions
effects created when drugs are similar and actions are added together

antagonistic interactions
effects created when drugs cancel one another

ELDERLY / MULTIPLE DRs

example, if you take antihistamines to reduce nasal congestion, you may be able to antagonize some of the drowsiness often caused by these drugs by using a central nervous system (CNS) stimulant such as caffeine.

Often, drug abusers who use two drugs at the same time are trying to antagonize the unpleasant side effects of the first drug by administering the second. It has been reported that many of those currently abusing cocaine also use alcohol (Fillmore and Rush 2006). The combined use of these two drugs may be a major factor in drug-related problems and death in emergency rooms (Coffin et al. 2003). Nevertheless, it appears that some users may coadminister these drugs in an attempt to antagonize the disruptive effects of alcohol with the stimulant action of the cocaine (O'Brien 2001).

■ Potentiative (Synergistic) Effects

The third type of drug interaction is known as *potentiation,* or **synergism.** Synergism occurs when the effect of a drug is enhanced by the presence of another drug or substance. A common example is the combination of alcohol and diazepam (Valium) (see Table 5.1). It has been estimated that as many as 3000 people die each year from mixing alcohol with CNS depressants such as Valium. Alcohol, like Valium, is a CNS depressant. When depressants are taken together, CNS functions become impaired and the person becomes groggy. A person in this state may forget that he or she has taken the pills and repeat the dose. The combination of these two depressants (or other depressants, such as antihistamines) can interfere with the CNS to the point where vital functions such as breathing and heartbeat are severely impaired.

Although the mechanisms of interaction among CNS depressants are not entirely clear, these drugs likely enhance one another's direct effects on inhibitory chemical messengers in the brain (see Chapter 4). In addition, interference by alcohol with liver-metabolizing enzymes contributes to the synergism that arises with the combination of alcohol and some depressants, such as barbiturates (Fleming et al. 2006; Hobbs et al. 1995).

■ Dealing with Drug Interactions

Although many drug effects and interactions are not very well understood, it is important to be aware of them. A growing body of evidence indicates that many of the drugs and substances we deliberately consume will interact and produce unexpected and sometimes dangerous effects (see Table 5.1). It is alarming to know that many of the foods we eat and some chemical pollutants also interfere with and modify drug actions. Pesticides, traces of hormones in meat and poultry, traces of metals in fish, nitrites and nitrates from fertilizers, and a wide range of chemicals — some of which are used as food additives — have been shown, under certain conditions, to interact with some drugs (Meekling 2006).

It is essential that the public be educated about the interactions most likely to occur with drugs that are prescribed, self-administered legitimately (for example, OTC drugs and herbal products), or taken recreationally (for example, drugs of abuse). People need to be aware that OTC and herbal drugs are as likely to cause interaction problems as prescription drugs. For example, an OTC or herbal decongestant that contains mild CNS stimulants (e.g., pseudoephedrine) taken with potent CNS stimulants, such as cocaine and amphetamines, can cause interactions that fatally affect the heart and brain. If any question arises concerning the possibility of drug interaction, individuals should talk to their physicians, pharmacists, or other healthcare providers.

Most drug abusers are multiple drug (polydrug) users with little concern for the dangerous interactions that might occur. It is common, for example, for drug abusers to combine multiple CNS depressants to enhance their effects, to combine a depressant with a stimulant to *titrate* a CNS effect (to determine the smallest amount that can be taken to achieve the desired "high"), or to experiment with a combination of stimulants, depressants, and hallucinogens just to see what happens. The effects of such haphazard drug mixing are impossible to predict, difficult to treat in emergency situations, and all too frequently fatal.

Pharmacokinetic Factors That Influence Drug Effects

Although it is difficult to predict precisely how any single individual will be affected by drug use, the following major factors represent different aspects of the body's response that should be considered

Table 5.1 **Common Interactions with Substances of Abuse**

DRUG	COMBINED WITH	CONSEQUENCE OF INTERACTION
Sedatives		
Diazepam (Valium), triazolam (Halcion)	Alcohol, barbiturates	Increase sedation
Stimulants		
Amphetamines, cocaine	Insulin Antidepressants	Decrease insulin effect Cause hypertension
Narcotics		
Heroin, morphine	Barbiturates, Valium Anticoagulant Antidepressants Amphetamines	Increase sedation Increase bleeding Cause sedation Increase euphoria
Tobacco		
Nicotine	Blood pressure medication Amphetamines, cocaine	Elevate blood pressure Increase cardiovascular effects
Alcohol	Cocaine	Produces cocaethylene, which enhances euphoria and toxicity

when attempting to anticipate a drug's effects (Buxton 2006).

1. How does the drug enter the body? (administration)
2. How does the drug move from the site of administration into the body's system? (absorption)
3. How does the drug move to various areas in the body? (distribution)
4. How and where does the drug produce its effects? (activation)
5. How is the drug inactivated, metabolized, and/or excreted from the body? (biotransformation and elimination)

These issues relate to the **pharmacokinetics** of a drug and are important considerations when predicting the body's response.

■ Forms and Methods of Taking Drugs

Drugs come in many forms. How a drug is formulated — solution, powder, capsule, or pill — influences the rate of passage into the bloodstream and consequently its efficacy.

The means of introducing the drug into the body will also affect how quickly the drug enters the bloodstream and how it is distributed to the site of action, as well as how much will ultimately reach its target and exert an effect (Buxton 2006) (see Figure 5.3). The principal forms of drug administration are *oral ingestion, inhalation, injection,* and *topical application.*

Oral Ingestion

One of the most common and convenient ways of taking a drug is orally. This type of administration usually introduces the drug into the body by way of the stomach or intestines.

Following oral administration, it is difficult to control the amount of drug that reaches the site of action, for three reasons:

1. The drug must enter the bloodstream after passing through the wall of the stomach or intestines without being destroyed or changed to an inactive form. From the blood, the drug must diffuse to the target area and remain there in sufficient concentration to have an effect.
2. Materials in the stomach or intestines, such as food, may interfere with the passage of some

KEY TERMS

pharmacokinetics
the study of factors that influence the distribution and concentration of drugs in the body

Method of Administration	Onset	Duration	Effect
Smoking			
cocaine	fast (~15 sec)	brief (10–15 min)	potent and strong
heroin	fast (~20 sec)	short (1–2 hr)	potent and strong
Intravenous			
cocaine	fast (20 sec)	short (30 min)	potent and strong
heroin	fast (1–2 min)	short (1–2 hr)	potent and strong
Snorting			
cocaine	moderate (~10 min)	short (45 min)	less potent
heroin	moderate (~15 min)	short (1–2 hr)	less potent
Oral			
cocaine (coca leaf)	slow (30 min)	moderate (~2–4 hr)	minor
methadone	slow (30–60 min)	long (24 hr)	less euphoria/ used for treatment

FIGURE 5.3

Relationship between the method of drug administration and drug effects.

drugs through the gut lining and thus prevent drug action. For example, food in your stomach will diminish the effects of alcohol by altering its absorption.

3. The liver might metabolize orally ingested drugs too rapidly, before they are able to exert an effect. The liver is the major detoxifying organ in the body, which means it removes chemicals and toxins from the blood and usually changes them into an inactive form that is easy for the body to excrete. This function is essential to survival, but it creates a problem for the pharmacologist in developing effective drugs or the physician prescribing the correct dose of a drug to treat a serious disease. The liver is especially problematic to oral administration because the substances absorbed from the digestive tract usually go to the liver before being distributed to other parts of the body and their site of action. For this reason, cocaine taken orally is not very effective.

Inhalation

Some drugs are administered by inhalation into the lungs through the mouth or nose. The lungs include large beds of capillaries, so chemicals capable of crossing membranes can enter the blood as rapidly as they can via intravenous (IV) injection and can be equally as dangerous (Meng et al.

1999). Ether, chloroform, and nitrous oxide anesthetics are examples of drugs that are therapeutically administered by inhalation. Nicotine, cocaine, methamphetamine, and heroin are drugs of abuse that can be inhaled as smoke (Mathias 1997). One serious problem with inhalation is the potential for irritation to the mucous membrane lining of the lungs; another is that the drug may have to be continually inhaled to maintain the concentration necessary for an effect. Inhalation

Drugs can be introduced into the body using various mechanisms such as pills, capsules, oral liquids, topicals, or injections.

of illicit drugs of abuse is common to prevent contracting AIDS, which can be transmitted by IV injection with contaminated needles (Meng et al. 1999; *NIDA Notes* 1999).

Injection

Some drugs are given by **intravenous (IV)**, **intramuscular (IM)**, or **subcutaneous (SC)** injection. A major advantage of administering drugs by IV is the speed of action; the dosage is delivered rapidly and directly, and often less drug is needed because it reaches the site of action quickly. This method can be very dangerous if the dosage is calculated incorrectly, the drug effects are unknown, or the user is especially sensitive to the drug's adverse effects. In addition, impurities in injected materials may irritate the vein; this issue is a particular problem in the drug-abusing population, in which needle sharing frequently occurs. The injection itself injures the vein by leaving a tiny point of scar tissue where the vein is punctured. If repeated injections are administered into the same area, the elasticity of the vein is gradually reduced, causing the vessel to collapse.

Intramuscular injection can damage the muscle directly if the drug preparation irritates the tissue or indirectly if the nerve controlling the muscle is damaged. If the nerve is destroyed, the muscle will degenerate (atrophy). A subcutaneous injection may damage the skin at the point of injection if a particularly irritating drug is administered. Another danger of drug injections arises when contaminated needles are shared by drug users. This danger has become a serious problem in the spread of infectious diseases such as AIDS and hepatitis (National Institute on Drug Abuse [NIDA], 2007).

Topical Application

Those drugs that readily pass through surface tissue such as the skin, the lining of the nose, and under the tongue can be applied topically, for systemic (whole-body) effects. Although many drugs do not appreciably diffuse across these tissue barriers into the circulation, there are notable exceptions. For example, a product to help quit smoking, a nicotine transdermal patch (Nicoderm), is placed on the skin; the drug passes through the skin and enters the body to prevent tobacco craving and withdrawal. In addition, several drugs of abuse, such as heroin and cocaine, can be "snorted" into the nose and rapidly absorbed into the body through the nasal lining.

■ Distribution of Drugs in the Body and Time-Response Relationships

Following administration (regardless of the mode), most drugs are distributed throughout the body in the blood. The circulatory system consists of many miles of arteries, veins, and capillaries and includes 5 to 6 liters of blood. Once a drug enters the bloodstream by passing through thin capillary walls, it is rapidly diluted and carried to organs and other body structures. It requires approximately 1 minute for the blood, and consequently the drugs it contains, to circulate completely throughout the body.

Factors Affecting Distribution

Drugs have different patterns of distribution depending on the following chemical properties (Buxton 2006):

- Their ability to pass across membranes and through tissues
- Their molecular size (large versus small molecules)

Transdermal nicotine patches are popular smoking cessation aids.

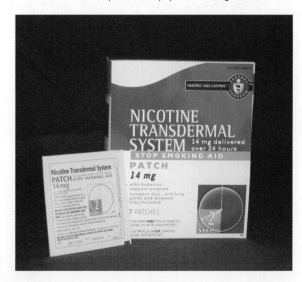

KEY TERMS

intravenous (IV)
drug injection into a vein

intramuscular (IM)
drug injection into a muscle

subcutaneous (SC)
drug injection beneath the skin

- Their solubility properties (do they dissolve in water or in fatty [oily] solutions?)
- Their tendency to attach to proteins and tissues throughout the body

These distribution-related factors are very important because they determine whether a drug can pass across tissue barriers in the body and reach its site of action. By preventing the movement of drugs into organs or across tissues, these barriers may interfere with drug activity and limit the therapeutic usefulness of a drug if they do not allow it to reach its site of action. Such barriers may also offer protection by preventing entry of a drug into a body structure where it can cause problems.

Blood is carried to the nerve cells of the brain in a vast network of thin-walled capillaries. Drugs that are soluble in fatty (oily) solutions are most likely to pass across these capillary membranes (known as the **blood–brain barrier**) into the brain tissue. Most psychoactive drugs, such as the drugs of abuse, are able to pass across the blood–brain barrier with little difficulty. However, many water-soluble drugs cannot pass through the fatty capillary wall; such drugs are not likely to cross this biological barrier and affect the brain.

A second biological barrier, the placenta, prevents the transfer of certain molecules from the mother to the fetus. A principal factor that determines passage of substances across the placental barrier is molecule size. Large molecules do not usually cross the placental barrier, whereas small molecules do. Because most drugs are relatively small molecules, they usually cross from the maternal circulation into the fetal circulation; thus, most drugs (including drugs of abuse) taken by a woman during pregnancy enter and affect the fetus.

KEY TERMS

blood–brain barrier
selective filtering between the cerebral blood vessels and the brain

threshold dose
minimum drug dose necessary to cause an effect

plateau effect
maximum drug effect, regardless of dose

acute
immediate or short-term effects after taking a single drug dose

chronic
long-term effects, usually after taking multiple drug doses

Required Doses for Effects

Most drugs do not take effect until a certain amount has been administered and a crucial concentration has reached the site of action in the body. The smallest amount of a drug needed to elicit a response is called its **threshold dose**.

The effectiveness of some drugs may be calculated in a *linear* (straight-line) fashion — that is, the more drug that is taken, the more drug that is distributed throughout the body and the greater the effect. However, many drugs have a maximum possible effect, regardless of dose; this is called the **plateau effect**. OTC medications, in particular, have a limit on their effects. For example, use of the nonprescription analgesic aspirin can effectively relieve your mild to moderate pain, but aspirin will not effectively treat your severe pains, regardless of the dose taken. Other drugs may cause distinct or opposite effects, depending on the dose. For example, low doses of alcohol may appear to act like a stimulant, whereas high doses usually cause sedation.

Time-Response Factors

An important factor that determines responses is the time that has elapsed between when a drug was administered and the onset of its effects. The delay in effect after administering a drug often relates to the time required for the drug to disseminate from the site of administration to the site of action. Consequently, the closer a drug is placed to the target area, the faster the onset of action.

The drug response is often classified as immediate, short-term, or **acute**, referring to the response after a single dose. The response can also be **chronic**, or long-term — a characteristic usually associated with repeated doses. The intensity and quality of a drug's acute effect may change considerably within a short period of time. For example, the main intoxicating effects of a large dose of alcohol generally peak in less than 1 hour and then gradually taper off. In addition, an initial stimulating effect by alcohol may later change to sedation and depression.

The effects of long-term, or chronic, use of some drugs can differ dramatically from the effects noted with their short-term, or acute, use. The administration of small doses may not produce any immediately apparent detrimental effect, but chronic use of the same drug (frequent use over a long time) may yield prolonged effects that do not become apparent until years later. Although for most people there is little evidence to show any immediate damage or detrimental response to short-term use of small doses of tobacco, its chronic use has damaging effects on heart and lung functions (Westmaas and Brandon 2004). Because of these long-term consequences, research on tobacco and its effects often continues for years, making it difficult to unequivocally prove a correlation between specific diseases or health problems and use of this substance. Thus, the results of tobacco research are often disputed by tobacco manufacturers with vested financial interests in the substance and its public acceptance.

Another important time factor that influences drug responses is the interval between multiple administrations. If sufficient time for drug metabolism and elimination does not separate doses, a drug can accumulate within the body. This drug buildup due to relatively short dosing intervals is referred to as a **cumulative effect**. Because of the resulting high concentrations of drug in the body, unexpected prolonged drug effects or toxicity can occur when multiple doses are given within short intervals. This situation occurs with cocaine or methamphetamine addicts who repeatedly administer these stimulants during "binges" or "runs," increasing the likelihood of dangerous effects.

■ Inactivation and Elimination of Drugs from the Body

Immediately after drug administration, the body begins to eliminate the substance in various ways. The time required to remove half of the original amount of drug administered is called the **half-life** of the drug. The body eliminates the drug either

directly without altering it chemically or (in most instances) after it has been metabolized (chemically altered) or modified. The process of changing the chemical or pharmacological properties of a drug by metabolism is called **biotransformation** (Buxton 2006). **Metabolism** usually makes it possible for the body to inactivate, detoxify, and excrete drugs and other chemicals, although metabolism can sometimes actually cause a drug such as heroin to become *more* active.

The liver is the primary organ that metabolizes drugs in the body. This complex biochemical laboratory contains hundreds of enzymes that continuously synthesize, modify, and deactivate biochemical substances such as drugs. The healthy liver is also capable of metabolizing many of the chemicals that occur naturally in the body (such as hormones). After the liver enzymes metabolize a drug (the resulting chemicals are called **metabolites**), the products usually pass into the urine or feces for final elimination. Drugs and their metabolites can appear in other places as well, such as sweat, saliva, or expired air (Buxton 2006).

The kidneys are probably the next most important organ for drug elimination because they remove metabolites and foreign substances from the body. The kidneys constantly eliminate substances from the blood. The rate of excretion of some drugs by the kidneys can be altered by making the urine more acidic or more alkaline. For example, nicotine and amphetamines can be cleared faster from the body by making the urine slightly more acidic, and salicylates and barbiturates can be cleared more rapidly by making it more alkaline. Such techniques are used in emergency rooms and can be useful in the treatment of drug overdosing.

KEY TERMS

cumulative effect
buildup of a drug in the body after multiple doses taken at short intervals

half-life
time required for the body to eliminate and/or metabolize half of a drug dose

biotransformation
process of changing the chemical properties of a drug, usually by metabolism

metabolism
chemical alteration of drugs by body processes

metabolites
chemical products of metabolism

The Breathalyzer takes advantage of the fact that alcohol is partially eliminated from the body in the breath.

The body may eliminate small portions of drugs through perspiration and exhalation. Approximately 1% of consumed alcohol is eliminated in the breath and thus may be measured with a Breathalyzer; this apparatus is used by police officers in evaluating suspected drunk drivers. Most people are aware that consumption of garlic will change body odor because garlic is excreted through perspiration. Some drugs are handled in the same way. The mammary glands are modified sweat glands, so it is not surprising that many drugs are concentrated and excreted in milk during lactation, including antibiotics, nicotine, barbiturates, caffeine, and alcohol. Excretion of drugs in a mother's milk can pose a particular concern during nursing, as the excreted drugs can be consumed by and affect the infant.

Physiological Variables That Modify Drug Effects

As previously mentioned, individuals' responses to drugs vary greatly, even when the same doses are administered in the same manner. This variability can be especially troublesome when dealing with drugs that have a narrow margin of safety. Many of these variables reflect differences in the pharmacokinetic factors just discussed and are associated with diversity in body size, composition, or functions. They include the following factors (Buxton 2006).

Age Changes in body size and makeup occur throughout the aging process, from infancy to old age. Changes in the rates of drug absorption, biotransformation, and elimination also arise as a consequence of aging. As a general rule, young children and elderly people should be administered smaller drug doses (calculated as drug quantity per unit of body weight) due to their immature or compromised body processes.

Gender Variations in drug responses due to gender usually relate to differences in body size, composition, or hormones (male versus female types — for example, androgens versus estrogens). Most clinicians find many more similarities than differences between males and females relative to their responses to drugs, although there are clinically

relevant differences in the effects of alcohol and tobacco on males and females.

Pregnancy During the course of pregnancy, unique factors must be considered when administering drugs. For example, the physiology of the mother changes as the fetus develops and puts additional stress on organ systems, such as the heart, liver, and kidneys. This increased demand can make the woman more susceptible to the toxicity of some drugs. In addition, as the fetus develops, it can be very vulnerable to drugs with **teratogenic** (causing abnormal development) properties. Consequently, it is usually advisable to avoid taking any drugs during pregnancy, if possible.

Pathological Variables That Modify Drug Effects

Individuals with diseases or compromised organ systems need to be particularly careful when taking drugs. Some diseases can damage or impair organs that are vital for appropriate and safe responses to drugs. For example, hepatitis (inflammation and damage to the liver caused by a viral infection) interferes with the metabolism and disposal of many drugs, resulting in a longer duration of drug action and increased likelihood of side effects. Similar concerns are associated with kidney disease, which causes compromised renal activity and diminished excretion capacity. Because many drugs affect the cardiovascular system (especially drugs of abuse, such as stimulants, tobacco, and alcohol), patients with a history of cardiovascular disease (heart attack, stroke, hypertension, or abnormal heart rhythm) should be particularly cautious when using drugs. They should be aware of medicines that stimulate the cardiovascular system, especially those that are self-medicated, such as OTC decongestants and diet aids. These drugs should be either avoided or used only under the supervision of a physician.

Adaptive Processes and Drug Abuse

Your body systems are constantly changing so that they can establish and maintain balance in their physiological and mental functions; such balance is necessary for optimal functioning of all organ systems, including the brain, heart, lungs, gastrointestinal tract, liver, and kidneys. Sometimes, drugs

KEY TERMS

teratogenic
something that causes physical defects in the fetus

Here and Now

The Death Toll of Substance Abuse

Deaths resulting from using substances of abuse are increasing throughout the world. It is estimated that approximately 7 million people are killed each year by the drugs they abuse. Tobacco heads the list, causing almost 5 million deaths annually. Next is alcohol, causing almost 2 million deaths worldwide each year. Use of the illicit drugs results in approximately 223,000 annual deaths. It is expected that these grim numbers will become worse as there is increased use of these substances around the world.

Source: Alcoholism and Drug Abuse Weekly. "Deaths from Substance Use Are Increasing Worldwide." 15 (2003): 8.

interfere with the activity of the body's systems and compromise their normal workings. These drug-induced disruptions can be so severe that they can even cause death (see "Here and Now," The Death Toll of Substance Abuse). For example, stimulants can dangerously increase the heart rate and blood pressure and cause heart attacks, whereas CNS depressants can diminish brain activity, resulting in unconsciousness and a loss of breathing reflexes.

To protect against potential harm, the organ systems of the body can adjust to disruption. Of particular relevance to drugs of abuse are the adaptive processes known as *tolerance* and **dependence** (both psychological and physical types) and the related phenomenon of *withdrawal* (see Figure 5.4).

Tolerance and dependence are closely linked, most likely to result from multiple drug exposures, and thought to be caused by similar mechanisms. Tolerance occurs when the response to the same dose of a drug decreases with repeated use (O'Brien 2006). Increasing the dose can sometimes compensate for tolerance to a drug of abuse. For the most part, the adaptations that cause the tolerance phenomenon are also associated with altered physical and psychological states that lead to dependence. The user develops dependence in the sense that if the drug is no longer taken, the systems of the body become overcompensated and unbalanced, causing withdrawal. In general, withdrawal symptoms are opposite in nature to the direct effects of the drug that caused the dependence (O'Brien 2006).

Although tolerance, dependence, and withdrawal are all consequences of adaptation by the body and its systems, they are not inseparable processes. It is possible to become tolerant to a drug without developing dependence, and vice versa (see Table 5.2). The following sections provide greater detail about these adaptive drug responses, which are very important for many therapeutic drugs and almost all drugs of abuse (O'Brien 2006).

■ Tolerance to Drugs

The extent of tolerance and the rate at which it is acquired depend on the drug, the person using the drug, the dosage, and the frequency of administration. Some drug effects may be reduced more rapidly than others when drugs are used frequently. Tolerance to effects that are rewarding or reinforcing often causes users to increase the dosage. Sometimes, abstinence from a drug can reduce tolerance, but with renewed use, the tolerance often returns quickly. It is important to remember that the body does not necessarily develop tolerance to all effects of a drug equally.

The exact mechanisms by which the body becomes tolerant to different drug effects are not completely understood, but may be related to those mechanisms that cause dependence (American Psychiatric Association 2000). Several processes have been suggested as candidates. Drugs such as barbiturates stimulate the body's production of metabolic enzymes, primarily in the liver, and cause drugs to be inactivated and eliminated faster. In addition, evidence suggests that a considerable degree of CNS tolerance to some drugs develops independent of changes in the rate of metabolism or excretion. This process reflects the adaptation of drug target sites in nervous tissue, such as neurotransmitter receptors, so that the effect produced by the same concentration of drug decreases over time.

Another type of drug response that can appear to be tolerance, but is actually a learned adjustment,

KEY TERMS

dependence
physiological and psychological changes or adaptations that occur in response to the frequent administration of a drug

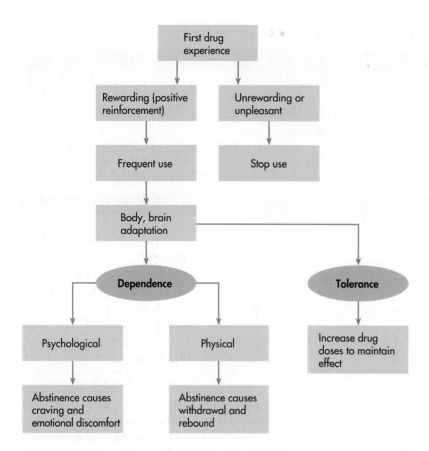

FIGURE 5.4
The relationship and consequences of adaptive processes to drug use. The processes discussed in the text are highlighted in the figure.

is called *behavioral compensation.* Drug effects that are troubling may be compensated for or hidden by the drug user. Thus, alcoholics learn to speak and walk slowly to compensate for the slurred speech and stumbling gait they usually experience. To an observer, it might appear as though the pharmacological effects of the drug are diminished, but they are actually unchanged. Consequently, this type of adaptation is not a true form of tolerance.

Other Tolerance-Related Factors

The tolerance process can affect drug responses in several ways. We have discussed the effect of tolerance that diminishes the action of drugs and causes the user to compensate by increasing the dose. The following are examples of two other ways that processes related to tolerance can influence drug responses.

Reverse Tolerance (Sensitization) Under some conditions, a response to a drug that is the opposite of tolerance is elicited. This effect is known as **reverse tolerance**, or sensitization. If you were sensitized, you would have the same response to a lower dose

of a drug as you initially did to the original, higher dose. This condition seems to occur in users of morphine as well as amphetamines and cocaine (McDaid et al. 2005).

Although the causes of reverse tolerance are still unclear, some researchers believe that its development depends on how often, how much, and in which setting the drug is consumed. It has been speculated that this heightened response to drugs of abuse may reflect adaptive changes in the nervous tissues (target site of these drugs). The reverse tolerance that occurs with cocaine use may be responsible for the psychotic effects or the seizures caused by chronic use of this drug (O'Brien 2006).

Cross-Tolerance Development of tolerance to a drug sometimes can produce tolerance to other

Table 5.2 Tolerance, Dependence, and Withdrawal Properties of Common Drugs of Abuse

DRUG	TOLERANCE	PSYCHOLOGICAL DEPENDENCE	PHYSICAL DEPENDENCE	WITHDRAWAL SYMPTOMS (INCLUDE REBOUND EFFECTS)
Barbiturates	▪▪	▪▪	▪▪▪	Restlessness, anxiety, vomiting, tremors, seizures
Alcohol	▪▪	▪▪	▪▪▪	Cramps, delirium, vomiting, sweating, hallucinations, seizures
Benzodiazepines	▪	▪▪	▪▪	Insomnia, restlessness, nausea, fatigue, twitching, seizures (rare)
Narcotics (heroin)	▪▪▪	▪▪	▪▪▪	Vomiting, sweating, cramps, diarrhea, depression, irritability, gooseflesh
Cocaine, amphetamines	▪*	▪▪▪	▪▪	Depression, anxiety, drug craving, need for sleep ("crash"), anhedonia
Nicotine	▪	▪▪	▪▪	Highly variable; craving, irritability, headache, increased appetite, abnormal sleep
Caffeine	▪	▪	▪	Anxiety, lethargy, headache, fatigue
Marijuana	▪	▪	▪	Irritability, restlessness, decreased appetite, weight loss, abnormal sleep
LSD (lysergic acid diethylamide)	▪▪	▪	—	Minimal
PCP (phencyclidine)	▪	▪	▪	Fear, tremors, some craving, problems with short-term memory

▪▪▪ Intense   ▪▪ Moderate   ▪ Some   — Not significant
*Can sensitize.

similar drugs. This phenomenon, known as **cross-tolerance**, may be due to altered metabolism resulting from chronic drug use. For example, a heavy drinker will usually exhibit tolerance to barbiturates, other depressants, and anesthetics because the alcohol has induced (stimulated) his or her liver metabolic enzymes to inactivate these other drugs more rapidly. Cross-tolerance might also occur among drugs that cause similar pharmacological actions. For example, if adaptations have occurred in nervous tissue that cause tolerance to one drug, such changes might produce tolerance to other similar drugs that exert their effects by interacting with that same nervous tissue site.

◼ Drug Dependence

Drug dependence can be associated with either physiological or psychological adaptations. Physical dependence reflects changes in the way organs and systems in the body respond to a drug, whereas psychological dependence is caused by changes in attitudes and expectations. In both types of dependence, the individual experiences a

KEY TERMS

cross-tolerance
development of tolerance to one drug causes tolerance to related drugs

need (either physical or emotional) for the drug to be present for the body or the mind to function normally.

Physical Dependence

In general, the drugs that cause physical dependence also cause a drug withdrawal phenomenon called the rebound effect. This condition is sometimes known as the *paradoxical effect* because the symptoms associated with rebound are nearly opposite to the direct effects of the drug. For example, a person taking barbiturates or benzodiazepines will be greatly depressed physically but during withdrawal may become irritable, hyperexcited, and nervous and generally show symptoms of extreme stimulation of the nervous system, and perhaps even life-threatening seizures. These reactions constitute the rebound effect.

Physical dependence may develop with high-intensity use of such common drugs as alcohol, barbiturates, narcotics, and other CNS depressants. However, with moderate, intermittent use of these drugs, most people do not become physically dependent. Those who do become physically dependent experience damaged social and personal skills and relationships and impaired brain and motor functions.

Withdrawal symptoms resulting from physical dependency can be prevented by administering a sufficient quantity of the original drug or one with similar pharmacological activity. The latter case, in which different drugs can be used interchangeably to prevent withdrawal symptoms, is called **cross-dependence**. For example, barbiturates and other CNS depressants can be used to treat the abstinence syndrome experienced by the chronic alcoholic. Another example is the use of methadone, a long-acting narcotic, to treat withdrawal from heroin (O'Brien 2006). Such therapeutic strategies allow the substitution of safer and more easily managed drugs for dangerous drugs of abuse and play a major role in treatment of drug dependency.

Psychological Dependence

The World Health Organization states that **psychological dependence** instills a feeling of satisfaction and psychic drive that requires periodic or continuous administration of the drug to produce a desired effect or to avoid psychological discomfort. This sense of dependence usually leads to repeated self-administration of the drug in a fashion described as abuse. Such dependence may be found either independent of or associated with

physical dependence. Psychological dependence does not produce the physical discomfort, rebound effects, or life-threatening consequences that can be associated with physical dependence. Even so, it does produce intense cravings and strong urges that frequently lure former drug abusers back to their habits of drug self-administration. In many instances, psychological aspects may be more significant than physical dependence in maintaining chronic drug use. Thus, the major problem with cocaine or nicotine dependence is not so much the physical aspect, because withdrawal can be successfully achieved in a few weeks; rather, strong urges often cause a return to chronic use of these substances because of psychological dependence.

How does psychological dependence develop? If the first drug trial is rewarding, a few more rewarding trials will follow until drug use becomes a conditioned pattern of behavior. Continued positive psychological reinforcement with the drug leads, in time, to primary psychological dependence. Primary psychological dependence, in turn, may produce uncontrollable compulsive abuse of any psychoactive drug in certain susceptible people and cause physical dependence. The degree of drug dependence is contingent on the nature of the psychoactive substance, the quantity used, the duration of use, and the characteristics of the person and his or her environment.

Even strong psychological dependence on some psychoactive substances does not necessarily result in injury or social harm. For example, typical dosages of mild stimulants such as coffee usually do not induce serious physical, social, or emotional harm. Even though the effects on the CNS are barely detectable by a casual observer, strong psychological dependence on stimulants like tobacco and caffeine-containing beverages may develop; however, the fact that their dependence does not typically induce antisocial and destruc-

---

KEY TERMS

rebound effect
form of withdrawal; paradoxical effects that occur when a drug has been eliminated from the body

cross-dependence
dependence on a drug can be relieved by other similar drugs

psychological dependence
dependence that results because a drug produces pleasant mental effects

tive behavior distinguishes them from most forms of dependence-producing drugs.

Psychological Factors

The general effect of most drugs is greatly influenced by a variety of psychological and environmental factors. Unique qualities of an individual's personality, his or her past history of drug and social experience, attitudes toward the drug, expectations of its effects, and motivation for use are extremely influential. These factors are often referred to collectively as the person's **mental set**. The setting, or total environment, in which a drug is taken may profoundly modify its effect.

The mental set and setting are particularly important in influencing the responses to psychoactive drugs (drugs that alter the functions of the brain). For example, ingestion of LSD, a commonly abused hallucinogen, can cause pleasant, even spiritual-like experiences in comfortable, congenial surroundings. In contrast, when the same amount of LSD is consumed in hostile, threatening surroundings, the effect can be frightening, taking on a nightmarish quality.

The Placebo Effect

The psychological factors that influence responses to drugs, independent of their pharmacological properties, are known as **placebo effects**. The word *placebo* is derived from Latin and means "I shall please." The placebo effect is most likely to occur when an individual's mental set is susceptible to suggestion. A placebo drug is a pharmacologically inactive compound that the user thinks causes some therapeutic or physiological change.

In some persons or in particular settings, a placebo substance may have surprisingly powerful consequences (Solomon 2002). For example, a substantial component of most pain is perception. Consequently, placebos administered as pain relievers and promoted properly can provide dramatic relief. Therefore, in spite of what appears to be a drug effect, the placebo is not considered a pharmacological agent because it does not directly alter any body functions by its chemical nature.

The bulk of medical history may actually be a history of confidence in the cure — a history of placebo medicine — because many effective cures of the past have been shown to be without relevant pharmacological action, suggesting that their ef-

fects were psychologically mediated. In fact, even today, some people argue that placebo effects are a significant component of most drug therapy, particularly when using OTC medications or herbal products. It is important when testing new drugs for effectiveness that drug experiments be conducted in a manner that allows a distinction to be drawn between pharmacological and placebo effects. Such studies can usually be done by treating one group with the real drug and another group with a placebo that looks like the drug, and then comparing the responses to both treatments.

Addiction and Abuse: The Significance of Dependence

The term *addiction* has many meanings (see Chapter 2). It is often used interchangeably with *dependence* or *drug abuse* (drug addiction).

The traditional model of the addiction-producing drug is based on opiate narcotics and requires the individual to develop tolerance and both physical and psychological dependence. This model often is not satisfactory because only a few commonly abused drugs fit all of these parameters. It is clearly inadequate for many drugs that can cause serious dependency problems but that produce little tolerance, even with extended use (see Table 5.2).

Because it is difficult to assess the contribution of physical and psychological factors to drug dependency, determining whether all psychoactive drugs truly cause drug addiction poses a challenge. To alleviate confusion, it has been suggested that the term *dependence* (either physical or psychological) be used instead of *addiction*. However, because of its acceptance by the public, the term *addiction* is not likely to disappear from general use.

Some have speculated that the only means by which drug dependence can be eliminated from society is to prevent exposure to those drugs that have the potential to be abused. Because some drugs

KEY TERMS

mental set
the collection of psychological and environmental factors that influence an individual's response to drugs

placebo effects
effects caused by suggestion and psychological factors independent of the pharmacological activity of a drug

Here and Now

Children of Addicted Parents

Substance abuse, alcoholism, and associated trauma seem to have both genetic and environmental components, the interaction of which can have serious consequences. For example, alcoholism tends to run in families. Thus, children of alcoholics are at high risk to become alcohol users themselves because of their genetic vulnerability as well as because of the traumatic environments to which they are often exposed. Levels of conflict in families characterized by alcoholism are much higher than in families with no alcoholism. The environment to which children with alcoholic parents are exposed may include a lack of communication, emotional and physical violence, isolation, and financial problems. At least half of all cases of child maltreatment are linked to a prevalence of substance abuse and alcoholism in the home. It has also been reported that children who receive prenatal exposure to drugs are two to three times more likely to be neglected or abused.

Source: "Children of Addicted Parents" (9 February 2005). Available Hopenetworks.org/addiction/children%20of%20Addicts.htm.

are such powerful, immediate reinforcers (i.e., they cause a rapid reward), it is feared that rapid dependence (psychological) will occur when anyone uses them. Although it may be true that most people, under certain conditions, could become dependent on some drug with abuse potential, in reality most people who have used psychoactive drugs do not develop significant psychological or physical dependence. For example, approximately 87% of those who use alcohol experience minimal personal injury and few negative social consequences. Of those who have used stimulants, depressants, or hallucinogens for illicit recreational purposes, only 10% to 20% become dependent (O'Brien 2006). The following sections discuss some possible reasons for the variability.

Hereditary Factors

The reasons why some people readily develop dependence on psychoactive drugs and others do not are not well understood. Of importance may be heredity, which predisposes some people to drug abuse (Kreek at al. 2004), and the interaction of genetic vulnerability with high-risk environments (see "Here and Now," Children of Addicted Parents). For example, studies of identical and fraternal twins have revealed that a greater similarity in the rate of alcoholism for identical twins than for fraternal twins occurs if alcohol abuse begins before the age of 20 years (McGue et al. 1992; Vanyukov and Tarter 2000). Because identical twins have 100% of their genes in common whereas fra-

ternal twins share significantly fewer of their genes, these results suggest that genetic factors can be important in determining the likelihood of alcohol dependence (O'Brien 2006). It is possible that similar genetic factors contribute to other types of drug dependence as well (Kreek et al. 2004).

Drug Craving

Frequently, a person who becomes dependent develops a powerful, uncontrollable desire for drugs during or after withdrawal from heroin, cocaine, alcohol, nicotine, or other addicting substances. This desire for drugs is known as *craving*. Because researchers do not agree as to the nature of craving, there does not exist a universally recognized scientific definition or an accepted method to measure this psychological phenomenon; however, it is thought to be distinct from the phenomenon of withdrawal. Some drug abuse experts claim that craving is the principal cause of drug abuse and relapse after treatment; others believe that it is not a cause but a side effect of drugs that produce dependence. Craving is often assessed by (1) questioning patients about the intensity of their drug urges; (2) measuring physiological changes such as increases in heart and breathing rates, sweating, and subtle changes in the tension of facial muscles; and (3) determining patients' tendency to relapse into drug-taking behavior (Hester and Garavan 2004).

Evidence indicates that at least two levels of craving can exist. For example, cocaine users experience an acute craving when using the drug itself, but the ex-cocaine abuser can have chronic cravings that are triggered by familiar environmental cues that elicit positive memories of cocaine's reinforcing effects.

Although it is not likely that craving itself causes drug addiction, it is generally believed that, if pharmacological or psychological therapies could be devised that reduced or eliminated drug craving, treatment of drug dependence would be more successful. Thus, many researchers are attempting to identify drugs or psychological strategies that interfere with the development and expression of the craving phenomenon.

■ Other Factors

If a drug causes a positive effect in the user's view, it is much more likely to be abused than if it causes an aversive experience (see Figure 5.4). Perhaps genetic factors influence the brain or personality so that some people find taking drugs an enjoyable experience (at least initially), whereas others find the effects very unpleasant and uncomfortable (**dysphoric**). Other factors that could contribute significantly to drug use patterns include (1) peer pressure (especially in the initial drug experimentation); (2) home, school, and work environments (Swadi 1999); (3) mental state; and (4) excessive stress. It is estimated that 30% to 60% of drug abusers have some underlying psychiatric illness, such as personality disorder, major depression, bipolar disorder, or schizophrenia (Buckley and Brown 2006). In some cases, the drug user may be attempting to relieve symptoms associated with the mental disorder by self-medicating with the substance of abuse (Buckley and Brown 2006).

It is difficult to identify all of the specific factors that influence the risk of drug abuse for each individual. (Some of the possible influences are discussed in Chapter 2.) If such factors could be identified, treatment would be improved and those at greatest risk for drug abuse could be determined and informed of their vulnerability.

KEY TERMS

dysphoric
characterized by unpleasant mental effects; the opposite of euphoric

Discussion Questions

1. What is the significance of drug "potency" in the therapeutic use and the abuse of drugs?

2. How can drug interactions be both detrimental and beneficial? Give examples of each.

3. Why would a drug with a relatively narrow "margin of safety" be approved by the Food and Drug Administration for clinical use? Give an example.

4. What are possible explanations for the fact that you (for example) may require twice as much of a drug to get an effect as does your friend?

5. Why might the blood–brain barrier prevent a drug from having abuse potential?

6. Contrary to your advice, a friend is going to spend $20 on methamphetamine. What significance will the pharmacokinetic concepts of threshold, half-life, cumulative effect, and biotransformation have on your friend's drug experience?

7. How would the factors of tolerance, physical dependence, rebound, and psychological dependence affect a chronic heroin user?

8. Why would the lack of physical dependence on LSD for some drug abusers make it less likely to cause addiction than cocaine, which does cause physical dependence?

Summary

1 All drugs have intended and unintended effects. The unintended actions of drugs can include effects such as nausea, altered mental states, dependence, a variety of allergic responses, and changes in the cardiovascular system.

2 Many factors can affect the way an individual responds to a drug: dose, inherent toxicity, potency, and pharmacokinetic properties such as the rate of absorption into the body, the way it is distributed throughout the body, and the manner in which and rate at which it is metabolized and eliminated. The form of the drug as well as the manner in which it is administered can also affect the response to a drug.

3 Potency is determined by the amount of a drug necessary to cause a given effect. Toxicity is the

ability of the drug to affect the body adversely. A drug that is very toxic is very potent in terms of causing a harmful effect.

4 A drug's margin of safety relates to the difference in the drug doses that cause a therapeutic or a toxic effect. The bigger the difference, the greater the margin of safety.

5 Additive interactions occur when the effects of two drugs are combined; for example, the analgesic effects of aspirin plus acetaminophen are additive. Antagonistic effects occur when the effects of two drugs cancel; for example, the stimulant effects of caffeine tend to antagonize the drowsiness caused by antihistamines. Synergism (potentiation) occurs when one drug enhances the effect of another; for example, alcohol enhances the CNS depression caused by Valium.

6 Pharmacokinetic factors include absorption, distribution, biotransformation, and elimination of drugs.

7 Many physiological and pathological factors can alter the response to drugs. For example, age, gender, and pregnancy are all factors that should be considered when making drug-related decisions. In addition, some diseases can alter the way in which the body responds to drugs. Medical conditions associated with the liver, kidneys, and cardiovascular system are of particular concern.

8 For psychoactive drugs to influence the brain and its actions, they must pass through the blood–brain barrier. Many of these drugs are fat-soluble and able to pass through capillary walls from the blood into the brain.

9 The threshold dose is the minimum amount of a drug necessary to have an effect. The plateau effect is the maximum effect a drug can have, regardless of dose. The cumulative effect is the buildup of the drug in the body due to multiple doses being taken within short intervals.

10 The liver is the primary organ for the metabolizing of drugs and many naturally occurring substances in the body, such as hormones. By altering the molecular structure of drugs, the metabolism usually inactivates drugs and makes them easier to eliminate through the kidneys.

11 Biotransformation is the process that alters the molecular structure of a drug. Metabolism contributes to biotransformation.

12 Drug tolerance causes a decreased response to a given dose of a drug. It can be caused by increasing metabolism and elimination of the drug by the body or by a change in the systems or targets that are affected by the drug.

13 Physical dependence is characterized by the adaptive changes that occur in the body due to the continual presence of a drug. These changes, which are often chemical in nature, reduce the response to the drugs and cause tolerance. If drug use is halted after physical dependence has occurred, the body is overcompensated, causing a rebound response. Rebound effects are similar to the withdrawal that occurs because drug use is stopped for an extended period. Psychological dependence occurs because drug use is rewarding, causing euphoria, increased energy, and relaxation, or because stopping drug use produces craving.

14 Suggestion can have a profound influence on a person's drug response. Health problems with significant psychological aspects are particularly susceptible to the effects of placebos. For example, because the intensity of pain is related to its perception, a placebo can substantially relieve pain discomfort. Other placebo responses may likewise be due to the release of endogenous factors in the body.

15 A powerful, uncontrollable desire (craving) for drugs can occur with chronic use of some drugs of abuse. Although craving by itself may not cause drug addiction, if it can be eliminated, treatment of substance abuse is more likely to be successful.

References

American Psychiatric Association. "Substance Related Disorders." In *Diagnostic and Statistical Manual of Mental Disorders*, 4th ed., text revision, 191–295. Washington, DC: APA, 2000.

Buckley, P., and E. Brown. "Prevalence and Consequences of Dual Diagnosis." *Journal of Clinical Psychiatry* 67 (2006): e01.

Buxton, I. "Pharmacokinetics and Pharmacodynamics." In *The Pharmacological Basis of Therapeutics*, 11th ed., edited by L. Brunton, J. Lazo, and K. Parker, 1–39. New York: McGraw-Hill, 2006.

Cartwright, W. "Economic Costs of Drug Abuse: Financial, Costs of Illness, and Services." *Journal of Substance Abuse Treatment* 25 (2007): ahead of print.

Coffin, P., S. Galea, J. Ahern, A. Leon, D. Vlahov, and K. Tardiff. "Opiates, Cocaine and Alcohol Combinations in Accidental Overdose Deaths in New York City, 1990–1998," *Addiction* 98 (2003): 739–747.

Fillmore, M., and C. Rush. "Polydrug Abusers Display Impaired Discrimination-Reversal Training Learning in a Model of Behavioral Control." *Journal of Psychopharmacology* 20 (2006): 24–32.

Fleming, M., S. Mihic, and A. Harris. "Ethanol." In *The Pharmacological Basis of Therapeutics,* 11th ed.. edited by L. Brunton, J. Lazo, and K. Parker, 591–606. New York: McGraw-Hill, 2006.

Goeders, N. "The Impact of Stress on Addiction." *European Neuropsychopharmacology* 13 (2003): 435–441.

Hester, R., and H. Garavan. "Executive Dysfunction in Cocaine Addiction: Evidence for Discordant Frontal, Cingulate, and Cerebellar Activity." *Journal of Neuroscience* 24 (2004): 11017–11022.

Hitti, M. "Bad Events from Drugs Are Common." Medicine Net.com (Sept. 17, 2007). Available www.medicinenet.com/script/main/art.asp?articlekey=76964.

Hobbs, W. R., T. Rall, and T. Verdoorn. "Hypnotics and Sedatives: Ethanol." In *The Pharmacological Basis of Therapeutics,* 9th ed., edited by J. Hardman and L. Limbird, 386–396. New York: McGraw-Hill, 1995.

Kreek, M., S. Schlussman, G. Bart, K. Laforge, and E. Butelman. "Evolving Perspectives on Neurobiological Research on the Addictions: Celebration of the 30th Anniversary of NIDA." *Neuropharmacology* 47 Supplement 1 (2004): 324–344.

Mathias, R. "Rate and Duration of Drug Activity Play Major Roles in Drug Abuse, Addiction and Treatment." *NIDA Notes* 12 (March/April 1997): 8–11.

McDaid, J., J. Dallimore, A. Mackie, A. Mickiewicz, and T. Napier. "Cross-Sensitization to Morphine in Cocaine-Sensitized Rats: Rats' Behavioral Assessments Correlate with Enhanced Responding of Ventral Pallidal Neurons to Morphine and Glutamate, with Diminished Effects of GABA." *Journal of Pharmacology and Experimental Therapeutics* 313 (2005): 1182–1193.

McGue, M., R. Pickens, and D. Svikis. "Sex and Age Effects on the Inheritance of Alcohol Problems: A Twin Study." *Journal of Abnormal Psychology* 101 (January 1992): 3–17.

Meckling, K. *Nutrient-Drug Interactions.* Boca Raton, FL: CRC Press, 2006.

Meng, Y., M. Dukat, D. Bridgen, B. R. Martin, and A. H. Lichtman. "Pharmacological Effects of Methamphetamine and Other Stimulants via Inhalation Exposure." *Drugs and Alcohol Dependence* 53 (1999): 111–120.

National Institute on Drug Abuse (NIDA). "What Are HIV and AIDS?" *NIDA for Teens* (2007). Available http://teens.drugabuse.gov/facts/facts_hiv1.asp.

NIDA Notes. "Infectious Diseases and Drug Addiction." 14 (1999): 15.

Oates, J. "The Science of Drug Therapy." In *The Pharmacological Basis of Therapeutics.* 11th ed., edited by L. Brunton, J. Lazo, and K. Parker, 117–136. New York: McGraw-Hill, 2006.

O'Brien, C. "Drug Addiction and Drug Abuse." In *The Pharmacological Basis of Therapeutics*, 9th ed., edited by J. Hardman and L. Limbird, 557–577. New York: McGraw-Hill, 1995.

O'Brien, C. "Drug Addiction and Drug Abuse." In *The Pharmacological Basis of Therapeutics*, 10th ed., edited by J. Hardman and L. Limbird, 621–644. New York: McGraw-Hill, 2001.

O'Brien, C. "Drug Addiction and Drug Abuse." In *The Pharmacological Basis of Therapeutics*, 11th ed., edited by L. Brunton, J. Lazo, and K. Parker, 607–627. New York; McGraw-Hill, 2006.

Rice, D. P. "Economic Costs of Substances of Abuse, 1995." *Proceedings of the Association of American Physicians* 111 (1999): 119–125.

Santora, M. "Deadly Drug Mix Resurfaces in New York." *The New York Times* (August 30, 2006): A19.

Solomon, S. "A Review of Mechanisms of Response to Pain Therapy: Why Voodoo Works." *Headache* 42 (2002): 656–662.

Swadi, H. "Individual Risk Factors for Adolescent Substance Use." *Drug and Alcohol Dependence* 55 (1999): 209–224.

Vanyukov, M. M., and R. E. Tarter. "Genetic Studies of Substance Abuse." *Drug and Alcohol Dependence* 59 (2000): 101–123.

Westmaas, J., and T. Brandon. "Reducing Risk in Smokers." *Current Opinions on Pulmonary Medicine* 10 (2004): 284–288.

CHAPTER 6

CNS Depressants: Sedative-Hypnotics

Did You Know?

- ○ Alcohol temporarily relieves anxiety and stress because of its central nervous system (CNS) depressant effects.

- ○ Benzodiazepines are by far the most frequently prescribed CNS depressants.

- ○ Most people who are dependent on benzodiazepines obtain their drugs legally by prescription.

- ○ Long-term users of Valium can experience severe withdrawal symptoms if drug use is stopped abruptly.

- ○ Our bodies probably produce a natural antianxiety substance that functions like drugs such as Valium, triazolam (Halcion), and alprazolam (Xanax).

- ○ The short-acting CNS depressants are the most likely to be abused.

- ○ GHB (gamma-hydroxybutyrate) is a Schedule I "club drug" that occurs naturally in the body and can be easily synthesized by using information available on the Internet.

Drugs and Society Online is a great source for additional drugs and society information for both students and instructors.
Visit **http://drugsandsociety.jbpub.com** to find a variety of useful tools for learning, thinking, and teaching.

Learning ◎bjectives

On completing this chapter you will be able to:

- ◎ Identify the primary drug groups used for CNS depressant effects.

- ◎ Explain the principal therapeutic uses of the CNS depressants and their relationship to drug dose.

- ◎ Explain why CNS depressant drugs are commonly abused.

- ◎ Identify the unique features of benzodiazepines.

- ◎ Relate how benzodiazepine dependence usually develops.

- ◎ Describe the differences in effects produced by short- versus long-acting CNS depressants.

- ◎ Describe the CNS depressant properties of antihistamines, and compare their therapeutic usefulness to that of benzodiazepines.

- ◎ List the four principal types of people who abuse CNS depressants.

- ◎ Identify the basic principles in treating dependence on CNS depressants.

- ◎ Explain why GHB is abused and how it relates to its analog compounds.

- ◎ Explain the role of detoxification in the treatment of dependency on CNS depressants.

Introduction

Central nervous system (CNS) depressants are some of the most widely used and abused drugs in the United States. Why? When taken at low doses, they all produce a qualitatively similar "high" by their disinhibitory effects on the brain. In addition, they relieve stress and anxiety and even induce sleep — effects that appeal to many people, particularly those who are struggling with emotional problems and looking for a break, physically and mentally. CNS depressants also can cause a host of serious side effects, including problems with tolerance and dependence. Ironically, many individuals who become dependent on depressants obtain them through legitimate means: a prescription given by a physician. Depressants are also available on the street, although this illicit source does not account for the bulk of the problem.

In this chapter, we briefly review the history of CNS depressants, in terms of both development and use, and then discuss the positive and negative effects these drugs can produce. Each of the major types of depressant drugs is then reviewed in detail: *benzodiazepines* (Valium-like drugs), *barbiturates*, and other minor categories. We conclude with an examination of abuse patterns related to depressant drugs, and discuss how drug dependence and withdrawal are treated.

An Introduction to CNS Depressants

Why are CNS depressants problematic? First, in contrast to most other substances of abuse, CNS depressants are usually not obtained illicitly and self-administered but rather are prescribed under the direction of a physician. Second, use of CNS depressants can cause very alarming — even dangerous — behavior if not monitored closely; most problems associated with these drugs occur due to inadequate professional supervision. Third, several seemingly unrelated drug groups have some

ability to cause CNS depression. When these drugs are combined, bizarre and dangerous interactions can result. (See Chapter 5 for a discussion on drug interactions.) Particularly problematic is the combination of alcohol with other CNS depressants. Finally, CNS depressants can cause disruptive personality changes that are unpredictable and sometimes very threatening.

This chapter will help you understand the nature of the CNS depressant effects. In addition, the similarities and differences among the commonly prescribed CNS depressant drugs are discussed.

■ The History of CNS Depressants

Before the era of modern drugs, the most common depressant used to ease tension, cause relaxation, and help forget problems was alcohol. These effects undoubtedly accounted for the immense popularity of alcohol and help explain why this traditional depressant is the most commonly abused drug of all time. (Alcohol is discussed in detail in Chapters 7 and 8.)

Attempts to find CNS depressants other than alcohol that could be used to treat nervousness and anxiety began in the 1800s with the introduction of bromides. These drugs were very popular until their toxicities became known. In the early 1900s, bromides were replaced by **barbiturates**. Like bromides, barbiturates were initially heralded as safe and effective depressants; however, problems with tolerance, dependence, and lethal overdoses soon became evident. It was learned that the doses of barbiturates required to treat anxiety also could cause CNS depression, affecting respiration and impairing mental functions (Charney et al. 2006). The margin of safety for barbiturates was too narrow, so research for safer CNS depressants began again.

It was not until the 1950s that the first **benzodiazepines** were marketed as substitutes for the dangerous barbiturates. Benzodiazepines were originally viewed as extremely safe and free from the problems of tolerance, dependence, and withdrawal that occurred with the other drugs in this category (Mondanaro 1988). Unfortunately, benzodiazepines have since been found to be less than ideal antianxiety drugs. Although relatively safe when used for short periods, long-term use can cause dependence and withdrawal problems much like those associated with their depressant predecessors (Charney et al. 2006). These problems have become a major concern of the medical

KEY TERMS

barbiturates
potent CNS depressants, usually not preferred because of their narrow margin of safety

benzodiazepines
the most popular and safest CNS depressants in use today

community, as is discussed in greater detail later in the chapter.

Many of the people who become dependent on CNS depressants such as benzodiazepines began using the drugs under the supervision of a physician. Some clinicians routinely prescribe CNS depressants for patients with stress, anxiety, or apprehension without trying nonpharmacological approaches, such as psychotherapy or counseling. This practice sends an undesirable and often detrimental message to patients — that is, CNS depressants are a simple solution to their complex, stressful problems. The following quote illustrates the danger of this practice:

> I am still, unfortunately, lost in "'script addiction." . . . I have gone on-line asking for pills. I could really identify with the one posting about doctors who continue to write the 'scripts to increase/continue the patient "flow." This is exactly what is happening with me and my doctor. (*From America Online Alcohol and Drug Dependency and Recovery message board.*)

During the 1970s and 1980s, there was an epidemic of prescriptions written for CNS depressants. For example, in 1973, 100 million prescriptions were written for benzodiazepines alone. Approximately twice as many women as men were taking these drugs at this time; a similar gender pattern continues today. During this period, many homemakers made CNS depressants a part of their household routine, as described in the lyrics of the song "Mother's Little Helper" on the Rolling Stones' album *Flowers:*

> Things are different today
> I hear every mother say
> "Mother needs something today to calm
>   her down"
> And though she's not really ill,
> There's a little yellow pill.
> She goes running for the shelter
> Of her "mother's little helper"
> And it helps her on her way,
> Gets her through her busy day.

As the medical community became more aware of the problem, the use of depressants declined (Latner 2000). Today, efforts are being made by pharmaceutical companies and scientists to find new classes of CNS depressants that can be used to relieve stress and anxiety without causing serious side effects such as dependence and withdrawal.

■ The Effects of CNS Depressants: Benefits and Risks

The CNS depressants are a diverse group of drugs that share an ability to reduce CNS activity and diminish the brain's level of awareness. Besides the benzodiazepines, barbiturate-like drugs, and alcohol, depressant drugs include **antihistamines** and opioid narcotics such as heroin (see Chapter 9).

Depressants are usually classified according to the degree of their medical effects on the body. For instance, **sedatives** cause mild depression of the CNS and relaxation. This drug effect is used to treat extreme anxiety and often is referred to as **anxiolytic**. Many sedatives also have muscle-relaxing properties that enhance their relaxing effects.

Depressants are also used to promote sleep and are frequently prescribed. Approximately 43 million sleeping pills were distributed in the United States in 2005. This represented a 32% increase over 2001 (Payne 2006). **Hypnotics** (from the Greek god of sleep, *Hypnos*) are CNS depressants that encourage sleep by inducing drowsiness. Often when depressants are used as hypnotics, they produce **amnesiac** effects as well. As already mentioned, the effects produced by depressants can be very enticing and encourage inappropriate use.

The effects of the CNS depressants tend to be dose dependent (see Figure 6.1). Thus, if you were to take a larger dose of a sedative, it might have a hypnotic effect. Often, the only difference between a sedative and a hypnotic effect is the dosage; consequently, the same drug may be used

KEY TERMS

antihistamines
drugs that often cause CNS depression, are used to treat allergies, and are often included in over-the-counter (OTC) sleep aids

sedatives
CNS depressants used to relieve anxiety, fear, and apprehension

anxiolytic
drug that relieves anxiety

hypnotics
CNS depressants used to induce drowsiness and encourage sleep

amnesiac
causing the loss of memory

FIGURE 6.1

Dose-dependent effects of CNS depressants.

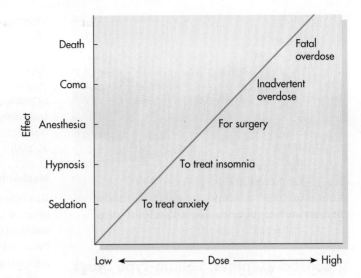

for both purposes by varying the dose. By increasing the dose still further, an anesthetic state can be reached. **Anesthesia**, a deep depression of the CNS, is used to achieve a controlled state of unconsciousness so that a patient can be treated, usually by surgery, in relative comfort and without memory of a traumatic experience. With the exception of benzodiazepines, if the dose of most of the depressants is increased much more, coma or death will ensue because the CNS becomes so depressed that vital centers controlling breathing and heart activity cease to function properly (*Drug Facts and Comparison* 2007).

As a group, CNS depressant drugs used in a persistent fashion cause tolerance. Because of the diminished effect due to the tolerance, users of these drugs continually escalate their doses. Under such conditions, the depressants alter physical and psychological states, resulting in dependence. The dependence can be so severe that abrupt drug abstinence results in severe withdrawals that include life-threatening seizures (*Drug Facts and Comparison* 2007). Because of these dangerous pharmacological features, treatment of dependence on CNS depressants must proceed very carefully (O'Brien 2006). This issue is dis-

cussed in greater detail at the end of this chapter and in Chapter 5.

Types of CNS Depressants

All CNS depressants are not created equal. Some have wider margins of safety; others have a greater potential for nonmedicinal abuse. These differences are important when considering the therapeutic advantages of each type of CNS depressant. In addition, unique features of the different types of depressants make them useful for treatment of other medical problems. For example, some barbiturates and benzodiazepines are used to treat forms of epilepsy or acute seizure activity, whereas opioid narcotics are used to treat many types of pain. Some of these unique features will be dealt with in greater detail when the individual drug groups are discussed. The benzodiazepines, barbiturate-like drugs, antihistamines, and the naturally occurring gamma-hydroxybutyrate (GHB) are discussed in this chapter. Other CNS depressants, such as alcohol and opiates, are covered in Chapters 7, 8, and 9.

The unique features of the CNS depressants help determine the likelihood of their abuse. For example, abuse is more likely to occur with the fast-acting depressant agents than with those agents that have long-lasting effects. Currently, nonmedicinal use of the sedatives occurs in approximately 2–4% of the population. This abuse is most likely to be caused by the benzodiazepines (Substance Abuse and Mental Health Services Administration [SAMHSA] 2007).

KEY TERMS

anesthesia

a state characterized by loss of sensation or consciousness

CNS depressants can be used as hypnotics to initiate sleep.

■ Benzodiazepines: Valium-Type Drugs

Benzodiazepines are by far the most frequently prescribed CNS depressants for anxiety and sleep. Because of their wide margin of safety (death from overdose is rare), benzodiazepines have replaced barbiturate-like drugs for use as sedatives and hypnotics (Landis and Bryant 1999). Benzodiazepines were originally referred to as *minor tranquilizers*, but this terminology erroneously implied that they had pharmacological properties similar to those of antipsychotic drugs (*major tranquilizers*), when they are actually very different. Consequently, the term *minor tranquilizer* is usually avoided by clinicians.

The first true benzodiazepine, chlordiazepoxide (Librium), was developed for medical use and marketed about 1960. The very popular drug Valium came on the market about the same time. In fact, Valium was so well received that from 1972 to 1978 it was the top-selling prescription drug in the United States. Its popularity has since declined considerably.

Because of dependence problems, the benzodiazepines are now classified as Schedule IV drugs (see Appendix B). In recent years, considerable concern has arisen that benzodiazepines are overprescribed because of their perceived safety; it has been said, somewhat facetiously, that the only way a person could die from using benzodiazepines would be to choke on them. Clinicians are concerned about this overconfident attitude toward benzodiazepines and warn patients against prolonged and unsupervised administration of these drugs (Charney et al. 2006).

Medical Uses

Benzodiazepines are used for an array of therapeutic objectives, including the relief of anxiety, treatment of neurosis, relaxation of muscles, alleviation of lower back pain, treatment of some convulsive disorders, induction of sleep (hypnotic), relief from withdrawal symptoms associated with narcotic and alcohol dependence, and induction of amnesia, usually for preoperative administration (administered just before or during surgery or very uncomfortable medical procedures) (Charney et al. 2006).

Mechanisms of Action

In contrast to barbiturate-type drugs, which cause general depression of most neuronal activity, benzodiazepines selectively affect those neurons that have receptors for the neurotransmitter gamma aminobutyric acid (GABA) (Charney et al. 2006). GABA is a very important inhibitory transmitter in several regions of the brain: the limbic system, the reticular activating system, and the motor cortex (see Chapter 4). In the presence of benzodiazepines, the inhibitory effects of GABA are increased. Depression of activity in these brain regions likely accounts for the ability of benzodiazepines to alter mood (a limbic function), cause drowsiness (a reticular activating system function), and relax muscles (a cortical function). The specific GABA-enhancing effect of these drugs explains the selective CNS depression caused by benzodiazepines.

Of considerable interest is the observation that these Valium-like drugs act on specific receptor sites that are linked to the GABA receptors in the CNS. As yet, no endogenous substance has been identified that naturally interacts with this so-called benzodiazepine site. It is very likely, however, that a natural benzodiazepine does exist that activates this same receptor population and serves to reduce stress and anxiety by natural means. Because benzodiazepines have specific target receptors, it has been possible to develop a highly selective antagonist drug, flumazenil (Romazicon). This drug is used to treat benzodiazepine overdoses, but must be used carefully because its administration can precipitate withdrawal in people taking benzodiazepines (Charney et al. 2006).

Types of Benzodiazepines

Because benzodiazepines are so popular and thus profitable, several of these drugs are available by prescription. Currently, approximately 14 benzodiazepine compounds are available in the United States.

Benzodiazepines are distinguished primarily by their duration of action (see Table 6.1). As a gen-

Table 6.1 Half-Lives of Various Benzodiazepines

DRUG	HALF-LIFE (HOURS)
Alprazolam (Xanax)	12–15
Chlordiazepoxide (Librium)	5–30
Clonazepam (Klonopin)	18–50
Diazepam (Valium)	20–50
Estazolam (ProSom)	10–24
Lorazepam (Ativan)	10–20
Midazolam (Versed)	1–12
Oxazepam (Serax)	5–21
Quazepam (Doral)	25–41
Temazepam (Restoril)	10–17
Triazolam (Halcion)	1.5–5.5
Zolpidem (Ambien; not a true benzodiazepine)	2–5

Source: Charney et al. 2006

eral rule, the short-acting drugs are used as hypnotics to treat insomnia, thus allowing the user to awake in the morning with few aftereffects (such as a hangover). The long-acting benzodiazepines tend to be prescribed as sedatives, giving prolonged relaxation and relief from persistent anxiety. Some of the long-acting drugs can exert a relaxing effect for as long as 2 to 3 days. One reason for the long action in some benzodiazepines is that they are converted by the liver into metabolites that are as active as the original drug (Charney et al. 2006). For example, Valium has a half-life of 20 to 80 hours and is converted by the liver into several active metabolites, including oxazepam (which itself is marketed as a therapeutic benzodiazepine; see Table 6.1).

Side Effects

Reported side effects of benzodiazepines include drowsiness, lightheadedness, lethargy, impairment of mental and physical activities, skin rashes, nausea, diminished libido, irregularities in the menstrual cycle, blood cell abnormalities, and increased sensitivity to alcohol and other CNS

depressants (Charney et al. 2006). In contrast to barbiturate-type drugs, only very high doses of benzodiazepines have a significant impact on respiration. There are few verified instances of death resulting from overdose of benzodiazepines alone (Longo and Johnson 2000). Almost always, serious suppression of vital functions occurs when these drugs are combined with other depressants, most often alcohol (Charney et al. 2006).

Although their long-term effectiveness has been challenged, benzodiazepines are often used to treat persistent disorders such as chronic insomnia (Gorman 2003). Benzodiazepines have less effect on **REM sleep** (rapid eye movement, the restive phase) than do barbiturates. Consequently, sleep under the influence of benzodiazepines is more likely to be restful and satisfying. However, prolonged use of hypnotic doses of benzodiazepines may cause rebound (see Chapter 5) increases in REM sleep and insomnia when the drug is stopped especially if used for long periods of time.

On rare occasions, benzodiazepines can have **paradoxical effects**, producing unusual responses, such as nightmares, anxiety, irritability, sweating, and restlessness (*Drug Facts and Comparisons* 2007). Bizarre, uninhibited behavior — extreme agitation with hostility, paranoia, and rage — may occur as well. One such case was reported in 1988 in Utah. A 63-year-old patient who was taking Halcion (a relatively short-acting benzodiazepine) murdered her 87-year-old mother. The suspect claimed that the murder occurred because of the effects of the drug and that she was innocent of committing a crime. Her defense was successful, and she was acquitted of murder. After her acquittal, the woman initiated a $21 million lawsuit against Upjohn Pharmaceuticals for marketing Halcion, which she claimed was a dangerous drug. The lawsuit was settled out of court for an undisclosed amount. This tragic episode came to a surprising conclusion in 1994 when the daughter committed suicide (Associated Press 1994).

Critics' complaints that Halcion causes unacceptable "amnesia, confusion, paranoia, hostility and

KEY TERMS

REM sleep
the restive phase of sleep associated with dreaming

paradoxical effects
unexpected effects

seizures" (Associated Press 1994, p. D-3) prompted the Food and Drug Administration (FDA) to closely evaluate this benzodiazepine. Despite the fact that several other countries have banned Halcion, the FDA concluded that its benefits outweigh the reported risks; however, the FDA also concluded that "In no way should this [the FDA's conclusion] suggest that Halcion is free of side effects. It has long been recognized and emphasized in Halcion's labeling that it is a potent drug that produces the same type of adverse effects as other CNS sedative hypnotic drugs" (*Drug Facts and Comparisons* 2007, pp. 1347–1350). Although the FDA did not require that Halcion be withdrawn, it did negotiate changes in the labeling and package inserts with Halcion's manufacturer, Upjohn Pharmaceuticals. These changes emphasize appropriate Halcion use in treatment of insomnia and additional information about side effects, warnings, and dosage. As a result of these concerns, sales of Halcion plummeted, causing it to fall from the 18th-largest-selling prescription drug in 1987 to not even being one of the top 200 most-prescribed drugs in 2006 (Drugs.com 2007).

There is no obvious explanation for the strange benzodiazepine-induced behaviors. It is possible that, in some people, the drugs mask inhibitory centers of the brain and allow expression of antisocial behavior that is normally suppressed and controlled.

Related concerns have also been made public about another very popular benzodiazepine, alprazolam (Xanax). In 1990, Xanax became the first drug approved for the treatment of *panic disorder*—repeated, intense attacks of anxiety that can make life unbearable (McEvoy 2003). Reports that long-term use of Xanax can cause severe withdrawal effects and a stubborn dependency on the drug raised public concerns about use of benzodiazepines in general. For example, how many people are severely dependent on these CNS depressants? What is the frequency of side effects such as memory impairment, serious mood swings, and cognitive problems? And how many patients using the benzodiazepines would be better served with nondrug psychotherapy? Clearly, use of the benzodiazepines to relieve acute stress or insomnia can be beneficial, but these drugs should be prescribed at the lowest dose possible and for the shortest time possible or withdrawal problems can result, as illustrated in the following quote:

I was put on alprazolam (Xanax) two and a half years ago by [my] doctor. Now told by another doctor that it is for short-term use

only and I am trying to get off slowly, but having difficulty. [I] have never used other drugs and do not have any information on the withdrawal process. (*From America Online Alcohol and Drug Dependency and Recovery message board.*)

Tolerance, Dependence, Withdrawal, and Abuse

As with most CNS depressants, frequent, chronic use of benzodiazepines can cause tolerance, dependence (both physical and psychological), and withdrawal (*Drug Facts and Comparisons* 2007). Such side effects are usually not as severe as those of most other depressants, and they occur only after using the drugs for prolonged periods (*Drug Facts and Comparisons* 2007). In addition, for most people, the effects of the benzodiazepines are not viewed as reinforcing; thus, compared with other depressants, such as barbiturates, benzodiazepines are not especially addicting (O'Brien 2006). However, these drugs should be prescribed with caution for patients with a history of drug abuse (O'Brien 2006).

Withdrawal can mimic the condition for which the benzodiazepine is given; for example, withdrawal symptoms can include anxiety or insomnia (Charney et al. 2006). In such cases, a clinician may be fooled into thinking that the underlying emotional disorder is still present and may resume drug therapy without realizing that the patient has become drug dependent. This can happen after as little as 1 month of treatment. In situations in which users have consumed high doses of benzodiazepine over the long term, more severe, even life-threatening withdrawal symptoms may occur (*Drug Facts and Comparisons* 2007); depression, panic, paranoia, and convulsions (Charney et al. 2006) have been reported (see Table 6.2). Severe withdrawal can often be avoided by gradually weaning the patient from the benzodiazepine (Charney et al. 2006). Long-term use of benzodiazepines (periods exceeding 3 to 4 months) to treat anxiety or sleep disorders has not been shown to be therapeutically useful for most patients (*Drug Facts and Comparisons* 2007). Even so, this approach is a common indiscriminate practice. As one user explains:

I went through a trauma 4 years ago, and the doctor prescribed a very high dose of Ativan. Well, I soon became addicted, both emotionally and physically . . . How do I get off? . . . This stuff is very addicting and my body can't really function without it. (*From America Online Alcohol and Drug Dependency and Recovery message board.*)

Table 6.2 Abstinence Symptoms That Occur When Long-Term Users of Benzodiazepines Abruptly Stop Taking the Drug

DURATION OF ABSTINENCE	SYMPTOMS
1–3 days	Often no noticeable symptoms
3–4 days	Restlessness, agitation, headaches, problems eating, and inability to sleep
4–6 days	The preceding symptoms plus twitching of facial and arm muscles and feeling of intense burning in the skin
6–7 days	The preceding symptoms plus seizures

Source: W. Hobbs, T. Rall, and T. Verdoorn. "Hypnotics and Sedatives." In *The Pharmacological Basis of Therapeutics,* 9th ed., edited by J. Hardman and L. Limbird, 361–396. New York: McGraw-Hill, 1995.

It is very unusual to find nontherapeutic drug-seeking behavior in a patient who has been properly removed from benzodiazepines, unless that individual already has a history of drug abuse (Longo and Johnson 2000). Research has shown that when benzodiazepines are the primary drug of abuse, these CNS depressants are usually self-administered to prevent unpleasant withdrawal symptoms in dependent users. If benzodiazepine-dependent users are properly weaned from the drugs and withdrawal has dissipated, there is no evidence that craving for the benzodiazepines occurs because people usually do not consider the benzodiazepines particularly reinforcing (Kosten and Hollister 1998). An exception to this conclusion appears to be former alcoholics. Many people with a history of alcoholism find the effects of benzodiazepines rewarding; consequently, almost one fourth of prior alcoholics use benzodiazepines chronically (Johansson et al. 2003).

Benzodiazepines are commonly used as a secondary drug of abuse and combined with illicit drugs. For example, it is very common to find heroin users who are dependent on benzodiazepines as well as narcotics (Backmund et al. 2005).

Another frequent combination is the use of benzodiazepines with stimulants such as cocaine (DeMaria et al. 2000). Some addicts claim that this combination enhances the pleasant effects of the stimulant and reduces the "crashing" that occurs after using high doses. (More is said about benzodiazepine abuse later in this chapter.)

It should also be mentioned that benzodiazepines are occasionally used to make people vulnerable to sexual assaults referred to as *date rapes* (Charney et al. 2006). The use of CNS depressants to commit these acts of violence is discussed in greater detail later in the chapter, but such assaults have sometimes involved the use of the **club drug** Rohypnol. Rohypnol (sometimes called *Rophie, Roche,* or *Forget Me*) is the proprietary name for flunitrazepam, a benzodiazepine. Rohypnol, which has been outlawed in the United States, comes as a tablet that can be dissolved in beverages without leaving an odor or taste and impairs short-term memory, making victims unable to recall details of the assault (*NIDA Notes* 2000; Publishers Group 2002). In 2006, 1.1% of high school seniors claimed to have used this drug (Johnston 2007).

Barbiturates

Barbiturates are barbituric acid derivatives that are used in medicine as sedatives and hypnotics. Barbituric acid was first synthesized by A. Bayer (of

Rohypnol is a benzodiazepine outlawed in the United States.

KEY TERMS

club drug
drug used at all-night raves, parties, dance clubs, and bars to enhance sensory experiences

aspirin fame) in Germany in 1864. The reason that he chose the name *barbituric acid* is not known. Some have speculated that the compound was named after a girl named Barbara whom Bayer knew. Others think that Bayer celebrated his discovery on the Day of St. Barbara in a tavern that artillery officers frequented. (St. Barbara is the patron saint of artillery soldiers.)

The first barbiturate, barbital (Veronal), was used medically in 1903. The names of the barbiturates traditionally end in *-al*, indicating a chemical relationship to barbital, the first one synthesized. Historically, barbiturates have played an important role in therapeutics because of their effectiveness as sedative-hypnotic agents, which allowed them to be routinely used in the treatment of anxiety, agitation, and insomnia. However, because of their narrow margin of safety and their abuse liability, barbiturates have been largely replaced by safer drugs, such as benzodiazepines. Despite the reduced therapeutic use of the barbiturates, in 2006, 6.6% of high school seniors recreationally used a barbiturate (Johnston 2007).

Uncontrolled use of barbiturates can cause a state of acute or chronic intoxication. Initially, there may be some loss of inhibition, euphoria, and behavioral stimulation — a pattern often seen with moderate consumption of alcohol. When taken to relieve extreme pain or mental stress, barbiturates may cause delirium and produce other side effects that can include nausea, nervousness, rash, and diarrhea. The person intoxicated with barbiturates may have difficulty thinking and making judgments, may be emotionally unstable, may be uncoordinated and unsteady when walking, and may slur speech (not unlike the drunken state caused by alcohol).

When used for their hypnotic properties, barbiturates cause an unnatural sleep. The user awakens feeling tired, edgy, and quite unsatisfied, most likely because barbiturates markedly suppress the REM phase of sleep. (REM sleep is necessary for the refreshing renewal that usually accompanies a good sleep experience.) Because benzodiazepines suppress REM sleep (as do all CNS depressants) less severely than barbiturates, use of these agents as sleep aids is generally better tolerated.

Continued misuse of barbiturate drugs has a cumulative toxic effect on the CNS that is more life threatening than misuse of opiates. When taken in large doses or in combination with other CNS depressants, barbiturates may cause death from respiratory or cardiovascular depression.

Because of this toxicity, barbiturates have been involved in many drug-related deaths, both accidental and suicidal. Repeated misuse induces severe tolerance of and physical dependence on these drugs. Discontinuing use of short-acting barbiturates in people who are using large doses can cause dangerous withdrawal effects such as life-threatening seizures. The Signs and Symptoms feature on page 151 summarizes the range of effects of barbiturates and other depressants on the mind and body.

Concern about the abuse potential of barbiturates caused the federal government to include some of these depressants in the Controlled Substances Act. Consequently, the short-acting barbiturates, such as pentobarbital and secobarbital, are classified as Schedule II drugs, whereas the long-acting barbiturates, such as phenobarbital, are less rigidly controlled as Schedule IV drugs (see Appendix B).

Effects and Medical Uses

Barbiturates have many pharmacological actions. They depress the activity of nerves and skeletal, smooth, and cardiac muscles and affect the CNS in several ways, ranging from mild sedation to coma, depending on the dose. At sedative or hypnotic dosage levels, only the CNS is significantly affected. Higher anesthetic doses cause slight decreases in blood pressure, heart rate, and flow of urine. The metabolizing enzyme systems in the liver are important in inactivating barbiturates; thus, liver damage may result in exaggerated responses to barbiturate use (Charney et al. 2006).

Low doses of barbiturates relieve tension and anxiety, effects that give several barbiturates substantial abuse potential. The drawbacks of barbiturates are extensive and severe:

- They lack selectivity and safety.
- They have a substantial tendency to create tolerance, dependence, withdrawal, and abuse.
- They cause problems with drug interaction.

As a result, barbiturates have been replaced by benzodiazepines in most treatments. Because of this decreased use, these drugs tend not to be readily available and are becoming less frequently abused in this country (U.S. Department of Justice [USDOJ] 2003). The long-acting phenobarbital is still frequently used for its CNS depressant activity to alleviate or prevent convulsions in some epileptic patients and seizures caused by strychnine, cocaine, and other stimulant drugs. Thiopental

Signs & Symptoms Effects of Barbiturates and Other Depressants

	BODY	MIND
Low dose	Drowsiness	Decreased anxiety, relaxation
	Trouble with coordination	Decreased ability to reason and solve problems
	Slurred speech	
	Dizziness	Difficulty in judging distance and time
	Staggering	
	Double vision	Amnesia
	Sleep	
	Depressed breathing	Brain damage
	Coma (unconscious and cannot be awakened)	
	Depressed blood pressure	
High dose	Death	

(Pentothal) and other ultrashort- and short-acting barbiturates are used as anesthesia for minor surgery and as preoperative anesthetics in preparation for major surgery.

Mechanism of Action and Elimination

The precise mechanism of action for barbiturates is unclear. Like benzodiazepines, they likely interfere with activity in the reticular activating system, the limbic system, and the motor cortex. However, in contrast to benzodiazepines, barbiturates do not seem to act at a specific receptor site; they probably have a general effect that enhances the activity of the inhibitory transmitter GABA (Charney et al. 2006). Because benzodiazepines also increase GABA activity (albeit in a more selective manner), these two types of drugs have overlapping effects. Because the mechanisms whereby they exert their effects are different, it is not surprising that these two types of depressants also have different pharmacological features.

The fat solubility of barbiturates is another important factor in the duration of their effects (Charney et al. 2006). Barbiturates that are the most fat soluble move in and out of body tissues (such as the brain) rapidly and are likely to be shorter acting. Fat-soluble barbiturates also are more likely to be stored in fatty tissue; conse-

quently, the fat content of the body can influence the effects on the user. Because women have a higher body-fat ratio than men, their reaction to barbiturates may be slightly different.

Withdrawal from barbiturates after dependence has developed causes hyperexcitability because of the rebound of depressed neural systems. Qualitatively (but not quantitatively), the withdrawal symptoms are similar for all sedative-hypnotics (Trevor and Lay 1998).

Table 6.3 gives details on the barbiturates that are abused most frequently.

Other CNS Depressants

Although benzodiazepines and barbiturates are by far used the most frequently to produce CNS depressant effects, many other agents, representing an array of distinct chemical groups, can similarly reduce brain activity. Although the mechanisms of action might be different for some of these drugs, if any CNS depressants (including alcohol) are combined, they will interact synergistically and can suppress respiration in a life-threatening manner. Thus, it is important to avoid such mixtures if possible. Even some over-the-counter (OTC) products, such as cold and allergy medications, contain drugs with CNS depressant actions.

Table 6.3 **Details on the Most Frequently Abused Barbiturates**

DRUG	NICKNAMES	EFFECTS
Amobarbital (Amytal Sodium)	Blues, blue heavens, blue devils	Moderately rapid action
Pentobarbital (Nembutal Sodium)	Nembies, yellow jackets, yellows	Short-acting
Phenobarbital (Luminal Sodium)	Purple hearts	Long-acting barbiturate particularly well suited for treatment of epilepsy
Secobarbital (Seconal Sodium)	Reds, red devils, red birds, Seccy	Short-acting with a prompt onset of action
50% amobarbital and 50% secobarbital (Tuinal)	Tooeys, double trouble, rainbows	Results in a rapidly effective, moderately long-acting sedative

Nonbarbiturate Drugs with Barbiturate-Like Properties

This category of depressants includes agents that are not barbiturates but have barbiturate-like effects (Charney et al. 2006). All of these drugs cause substantial tolerance, physical and psychological dependence, and withdrawal symptoms. The therapeutic safety of these CNS depressants more closely resembles that of barbiturates than benzodiazepines; consequently, like barbiturates, these agents have been replaced by the safer and easier-to-manage benzodiazepines (Charney et al. 2006).

Because these drugs have significant abuse potential, they are restricted much like other CNS depressants. In this group of depressants, methaqualone is a Schedule II drug; glutethimide and methyprylon are Schedule III drugs; and chloral hydrate is a Schedule IV drug. Each classification is based on the drug's relative potential for physical and psychological dependence. Abuse of Schedule II drugs may lead to severe or moderate physical dependence or high psychological dependence, and abuse of Schedule III drugs may cause moderate physical and psychological dependence. Schedule IV drugs are considered much less likely to cause either type of dependence.

Chloral Hydrate Chloral hydrate (Noctec), or "knock-out drops," has the unsavory reputation of being a drug that is slipped into a person's drink to cause unconsciousness. In the late 1800s, the combination of chloral hydrate and alcohol was given the name *Mickey Finn* on the waterfront of the Barbary Coast of San Francisco when sailors were in short supply. An unsuspecting man would have a friendly drink and wake up as a crew member on an outbound freighter to China.

Chloral hydrate is a good hypnotic, but it has a narrow margin of safety. This compound is a stomach irritant, especially if given repeatedly and in fairly large doses. Addicts may take enormous doses of the drug; as with most CNS depressants, chronic, long-term use of high doses will cause tolerance and physical dependence (Charney et al. 2006).

Glutethimide Glutethimide (Doriden) is another example of a barbiturate-like drug that can be abused and that causes severe withdrawal symptoms. It also induces blood abnormalities in sensitive individuals, such as a type of anemia and abnormally low white cell counts. Nausea, fever, increased heart rate, and convulsions occasionally occur in patients who have been taking this sedative regularly in moderate doses.

Methyprylon Methyprylon (Noludar) is a short-acting nonbarbiturate that is used as a sedative and hypnotic. Its effects are similar to those of Doriden, and it is capable of causing tolerance, physical dependence, and addiction, much like barbiturates.

Methaqualone Few drugs have become so popular so quickly as methaqualone. This barbiturate-like sedative-hypnotic was introduced in India in the 1950s as an antimalarial agent. Its sedative properties, however, were soon discovered. It then became available in the United States as Quaalude, Mequin, and Parest.

After several years of street abuse, methaqualone was classified as a Schedule II drug. Since 1985, methaqualone has not been manufactured in the United States because of adverse publicity, although in 2006 almost 1% of high school seniors in the United States claimed to have used it (Johnston 2007).

Common side effects of methaqualone include fatigue, dizziness, anorexia, nausea, vomiting, diarrhea, sweating, dryness of the mouth, depersonalization, headache, and paresthesia of the extremities (a pins-and-needles feeling in the fingers and toes). Hangover is frequently reported.

Antihistamines

Antihistamines are drugs used in both nonprescription and prescription medicinal products. The most common uses for antihistamines are to relieve the symptoms associated with the common cold, allergies, and motion sickness (see Chapter 15). Although frequently overlooked, many antihistamines cause significant CNS depression and are used as both sedatives and hypnotics (*Drug Facts and Comparisons* 2007). For example, the agents hydroxyzine (Visteril) and promethazine (Phenergan) are prescribed for their sedative effects, whereas diphenhydramine is commonly used as an OTC sleep aid.

The exact mechanism of CNS depression caused by these agents is not totally known but appears to relate to their blockage of acetylcholine receptors in the brain (they antagonize the muscarinic receptor types). This anticholinergic activity (see Chapter 4) helps cause relaxation and sedation and can be viewed as a very annoying side effect when these drugs are being used to treat allergies or other problems.

Therapeutic Usefulness and Side Effects Antihistamines are viewed as relatively safe agents. Compared with other more powerful CNS depressants, antihistamines do not appear to cause significant physical or psychological dependence or addiction problems, although drugs with anticholinergic activity, such as the antihistamines, are sometimes abused, especially by children and teenagers (Sharman et al. 2006). However, tolerance to antihistamine-induced sedation occurs quite rapidly. Reports of significant cases of withdrawal problems when use of antihistamines is stopped are rare. This situation may reflect the fact that these agents are used as antianxiety drugs for only minor problems and for short periods of time (often only for a single dose).

One significant problem with antihistamines is the variability of responses they produce. Different antihistamines work differently on different people. Usually therapeutic doses cause decreased alertness, relaxation, slowed reaction time, and drowsi-

Antihistamines are found in OTC medicines used to relieve cold and allergy symptoms.

ness. But it is not uncommon for some individuals to be affected in the opposite manner — that is, an antihistamine sometimes causes restlessness, agitation, and insomnia. There are even cases of seizures caused by toxic doses of antihistamine, particularly in children (Sharman et al. 2006). Side effects of antihistamines related to their anticholinergic effects include dry mouth, constipation, and inability to urinate. These factors probably help to discourage high-dose abuse of these drugs. However, OTC antihistamines are still sometimes taken for recreational purposes despite the unpleasant side effects (Hughes et al. 1999).

Even though antihistamines are relatively safe in therapeutic doses, they can contribute to serious problems if combined with other CNS depressants. Many OTC cold, allergy, antimotion, and sleep aid products contain antihistamines and should be avoided by patients using the potent CNS depressants or alcohol.

In the past few years, several prescription products have been marketed for treating insomnia with the claim that they are less sedating and less likely to cause dependence than the traditional benzodiazepines and barbiturates. These heavily marketed medications include brand names such as Ambien, Lunesta, Rozerem, and Sonata. It is clear that although less sedating than the older sedative/hypnotics, this new generation of sleep aids can cause next-day sedation and have resulted in some dependency, especially when used with other CNS depressants such as alcohol (Payne 2006).

GHB (Gamma-Hydroxybutyrate): The Natural Depressant

GHB is a colorless, tasteless, and odorless substance found naturally in the body resulting from

GHB is often stored as a clear, colorless, odorless liquid.

the metabolism of the inhibitory neurotransmitter GABA (see Chapter 4; Drasbek et al. 2006; Lingenhoehl et al. 1999). It was first synthesized nearly 30 years ago by a French researcher who intended to study the CNS effects of GABA (Poldrugo and Addolorato 1999). It was initially believed that GHB exerted its effects by enhancing CNS GABA systems, although this mechanism has recently been questioned (Carter et al. 2003). There is some evidence that GHB is itself a neuromodulator with its own receptor targets in the brain (Carter et al. 2003). Because of its central depressant effects, GHB has been used in Europe as an adjunct for general anesthesia, a treatment for insomnia and narcolepsy (a daytime sleep disorder), and a treatment for alcoholism and alcohol withdrawal and narcotic dependence (Nava et al. 2007). During the 1980s, GHB became available without a prescription in health food stores and was used principally by body builders to stimulate the release of growth hormone with the intent to reduce fat and build muscle (Publishers Group 2002). More recently, this substance became popular for recreational use due to what has been described as a pleasant, alcohol-like, hangover-free high with aphrodisiac properties (Morgenthaler and Joy 1994). In 2006, 1.1% of high school seniors were reported to have used GHB (Johnston 2007). Because of its frequent use by young people at nightclubs and bars, GHB became known as a *club drug* (Sumnall et al. 2007).

GHB is generally taken orally after being mixed with a liquid or beverage. It has a rapid onset and, when large doses are consumed, can cause unconsciousness and coma in 15 to 40 minutes.

These dangerous effects typically require emergency room treatment. Often, the recovery is also rapid with persons regaining consciousness in 2 to 4 hours (Publishers Group 2002).

Due to concerns about GHB abuse and side effects, an advisory warning that this substance is unsafe was first issued by the FDA in 1990. In 1997, the FDA released another warning that GHB was not approved for clinical use in the United States and was a potentially dangerous substance. Finally, due to the rising illicit use of GHB and resultant problems, this drug was made a Schedule I Controlled Substance by the DEA in March 2000 ("Gamma Hydroxybutyric Acid" 2000).

Despite claims about its benign nature (Dean et al. 1997), evidence is mounting that in high doses, GHB can be dangerous and even deadly. There have been more than 70 documented deaths attributed to GHB overdoses as of 2001 (USDOJ 2003). It has been reported that GHB use can cause significant side effects, such as hormonal problems, sleep abnormalities, drowsiness, nausea, vomiting, and changes in blood pressure (Teter and Guthrie 2001). Both users and clinicians seem to agree that GHB is most dangerous when combined with other drugs, especially other CNS depressants such as alcohol ("Gamma Hydroxybutyric Acid" 2000).

Because GHB is illegal in the United States, it is currently available only through the underground "gray market" as a "bootleg" product manufactured by kitchen chemists and with suspicious quality and purity. The lack of reliability of these GHB-containing products and the highly variable responses of different people to this substance increase the likelihood of problems when using this depressant.

Instructions on how to make GHB are readily available on multiple Internet sites. It is typically portrayed as a relatively benign substance, but one for which proper dosing is critical for "safe" use.

There is some debate as to whether the use of GHB can cause dependence and withdrawal. Some evidence suggests that chronic high-dose use of GHB may lead to prolonged abuse and a withdrawal syndrome consisting of insomnia, anxiety, and tremors that typically resolves in 3 to 12 days (Craig et al. 2000; Galloway et al. 1997; Mioto and Roth 2001). Another major concern with this substance is its use in cases of date rape. Because GHB can be stored as a clear, colorless, odorless liquid, it is easily added undetected to a beverage such as an alcoholic drink (*NIDA Notes* 2000). Its amnesiac and sedative properties disable users and make them vulnerable to sexual assault (Lesh-ner 2000). Despite attempts to vigorously prose-cute these cases, because the victims frequently are unable to recall details of the attack and the drug disappears so quickly from the bloodstream (its half-life is 2 to 3 hours), rape under the influ-ence of GHB can be difficult to prove.

Other GHB-related drugs have become readily available as substitutes, although they are only legal if they are included in products technically not intended for human use. These products are supposedly promoted as chemical solvents and typically make a disclaimer that the products are not for human consumption even though the label often implies that the product may be ingested. For example, the label on one industrial solvent stated "Warning! Accidental ingestion . . . will produce GHB in your body. If you ingest some by mistake, don't take alcohol or any other drug" (USDOJ 2002b). The most commonly used of these GHB analogs are gamma-butyrolactone (GBL) and 1,4-butanediol (BD) (USDOJ 2002b). Because these compounds are converted into GBH in the body, they can cause serious side effects (see "Case in Point").

Patterns of Abuse with CNS Depressants

The American Psychiatric Association (APA) con-siders dependence on CNS depressants to be a psy-chiatric disorder. According to its widely used *Diagnostic and Statistical Manual of Mental Disorders*, fourth edition (DSM-IV-TR) (American Psychiatric Association 2000), a *substance dependence disorder* can be diagnosed when three of the following cri-teria are satisfied at any time in a 12-month period:

1. The person needs greatly increased amounts of the substance to achieve the desired effect

or experiences a markedly diminished effect with continued use of the substance.
2. Characteristic withdrawal occurs when drug use is stopped, which encourages continued use of the substance to avoid the unpleasant effects.
3. The substance is consumed in larger amounts over a longer period of time than originally intended.
4. The person shows persistent desire or repeated unsuccessful efforts to decrease or control sub-stance use.
5. A great deal of time is spent obtaining and using the substance or recovering from its effects.
6. All daily activities revolve around the sub-stance — important social, occupational, or recreational activities are given up or reduced because of substance use.
7. The person withdraws from family activities and hobbies to use the substance privately or spend more time with substance-using friends.
8. The person continues use of the substance despite recognizing that it causes social, occu-pational, legal, or medical problems (see "Case in Point: Representative Patrick Kennedy Pleads for Help.").

A review of the previous discussion about the properties of CNS depressants reveals that severe dependence on these drugs can satisfy all these *DSM-IV-TR* criteria; thus, according to the APA, dependence on CNS depressants is classified as a form of mental illness.

The principal types of people who are most inclined to abuse CNS depressants include the following:

1. Those who seek sedative effects to deal with emotional stress, to try to escape from prob-lems they are unable to face. Sometimes, these individuals are able to persuade clinicians to administer depressants for their problems; at

▶Case in Point BD in "Natural" Sleep Aid

On January 27, 2000, a Utah man died as a conse-quence of excessive consumption of a product called Zen. The man purchased the product from a local health food store but was unaware that it con-tained the GHB analog 1,4-butanediol (BD). After fre-quent use, he realized that he had become dependent on the product and was trying to wean himself off when he died. In April 2002, the man's widow reached an undisclosed settlement with the manufacturer claiming consumers were not warned that this active ingredient is converted into GHB in the body.

Source: U.S. Department of Justice, 2002.

►Case in Point   "Representative Patrick Kennedy Pleads for Help"

On May 4, 2006, representative Patrick Kennedy crashed his car into a Capitol barricade late at night. Fortunately, no one was seriously injured, but Kennedy agreed to plead guilty on a charge of driving under the influence of prescription drugs. The congressman has a history of having problems using CNS depressants such as sedative/hypnotics and alcohol. He admits he has difficulty managing his stress levels and sometimes inappropriately uses depressants to cope with the adverse emotions. Because of his experiences with these drugs, Congressman Kennedy has developed an appreciation for the problem of substance dependence in general and prescription abuse in particular. This awareness has motivated Kennedy to work for passage of a congressional bill that would require group health plans to offer benefits for mental health and drug dependence at the same level as for other medical conditions.

Source: Miga, A. "Kennedy Slowly Battles Drug Addiction." *Washington Post*, May 2, 2007. Available http://www.washingtonpost.com/wp-dyn/content/article/2007/05/02/AR2007050201758.html.

other times, they self-medicate with depressants that are obtained illegally.

2. Those who seek the excitation that occurs, especially after some tolerance has developed. Instead of depression, they feel exhilaration and euphoria.

3. Those who try to counteract the unpleasant effect or withdrawal associated with other drugs of abuse, such as some stimulants, lysergic acid diethylamide (LSD), and other hallucinogens.

4. Those who use sedatives in combination with other depressant drugs such as alcohol and heroin. Alcohol plus a sedative gives a faster high but can be dangerous because of the multiple depressant effects and synergistic interaction. Heroin users often resort to barbiturates if their heroin supply is compromised.

As mentioned earlier, depressants are commonly abused in combination with other drugs (*Drug Facts and Comparisons* 2007). In particular, opioid narcotic users take barbiturates, benzodiazepines, and other depressants to augment the effects of a weak batch of heroin or to counteract a rapidly shrinking supply. Chronic narcotic users also claim that depressants help to offset tolerance to opioids, thereby requiring less narcotic to achieve a satisfactory response by the user. It is not uncommon to see joint dependence on both narcotics and depressants.

Another common use of depressants is by alcoholics to soften the withdrawal from ethanol or to help create a state of intoxication without the telltale odor of alcohol. Interestingly, similar strategies are also used therapeutically to help detoxify the alcoholic. For example, long-acting barbiturates or benzodiazepines are often used to wean an alcohol-dependent person away from ethanol. Treatment with these depressants helps to reduce the severity of withdrawal symptoms, making it easier and safer for alcoholics to eliminate their drug dependence.

Finally, as already mentioned, CNS depressants are used in conjunction with alcohol to commit sexual assaults. Because these drugs are sedating, remove inhibitions, and can induce a temporary state of amnesia, they are sometimes secretly added to an alcoholic beverage to incapacitate the intended victim of a date rape. Some studies suggest that about 40% of women who are sexually assaulted have alcohol in their blood, 20% have cannabinoids (from marijuana use), 8% have cocaine, 8% have a benzodiazepine, 4% have amphetamines, 4% have GHB, less than 2% have opioid narcotics, and 1% have barbiturates (Elsohly and Salamone 1999).

In general, those who chronically abuse the CNS depressants prefer (1) the short-acting barbiturates, such as pentobarbital and secobarbital; (2) the barbiturate-like depressants, such as

Table 6.4 **Lifetime Prevalence of Abuse of CNS Depressants for 12th Graders**

	1992	1995	1998	1999	2002	2004	2006
Any illicit drug	40.7%	48.4%	54.1%	54.7%	53.0%	51.1%	48.2%
All depressants (including benzodiazepines)	6.1%	7.6%	9.2%	NA	11.4%	10.4%	10.2%

Source: L. Johnston. *Drug Abuse Survey.* Lansing, MI: University of Michigan, 2007. Available www.monitoringthefuture.org.

glutethimide, methyprylon, and methaqualone; or (3) the faster-acting benzodiazepines, such as diazepam (Valium), alprazolam (Xanax), or lorazepam (Ativan).

Dependence on sedative-hypnotic agents can develop insidiously. Often, a long-term patient is treated for persistent insomnia or anxiety with daily exposures to a CNS depressant. When an attempt to withdraw the drug is made, the patient becomes agitated, unable to sleep, and severely anxious; a state of panic may be experienced when deprived of the drug. These signs are frequently mistaken for a resurgence of the medical condition being treated and are not recognized as part of a withdrawal syndrome to the CNS depressant. Consequently, the patient frequently resumes use of the CNS depressant, and the symptoms of withdrawal subside. Such conditions generally lead to a gradual increase in dosage as tolerance to the sedative-hypnotic develops. The patient becomes severely dependent on the depressant, both physically and psychologically, and the drug habit becomes an essential feature in the user's daily routines. Only

after severe dependence has developed does the clinician often realize what has taken place. The next stage is the unpleasant task of trying to wean the patient from the drug (**detoxification**) with as little discomfort as possible.

The prevalence of abuse of illicit CNS depressants appeared to peak in the early 1980s for 12th graders. Illegal use of these drugs then decreased dramatically until 1992, at which time abuse appears to have rebounded (see Table 6.4).

■ Treatment for Withdrawal

All sedative-hypnotics, including alcohol and benzodiazepines, can produce physical dependence and a barbiturate-like withdrawal syndrome if taken in sufficient dosage over a long period. Withdrawal symptoms include anxiety, tremors, nightmares, insomnia, anorexia, nausea, vomiting, seizures, delirium, and maniacal activity.

The duration and severity of withdrawal depend on the particular drug taken. With short-acting depressants, such as pentobarbital, secobarbital, and methaqualone, withdrawal symptoms tend to have a faster onset of action and be more severe. They begin 12 to 24 hours after the last dose and peak in intensity between 24 and 72 hours later. Withdrawal from longer-acting depressants, such as phenobarbital and diazepam, develops more slowly and is less intense; symptoms peak on the fifth to eighth day (Trevor and Lay 1998).

Not surprisingly, the approach to detoxifying a person who is dependent on a sedative-hypnotic depends on the nature of the drug itself (that is,

Detoxification of patients is often done in groups to help provide support during this difficult time.

KEY TERMS

detoxification
elimination of a toxic substance, such as a drug, and its effects from the body

to which category of depressants it belongs), the severity of the dependence, and the duration of action of the drug. The general objectives of detoxification are to eliminate drug dependence (both physical and psychological) in a safe manner while minimizing discomfort. Having achieved these objectives, it is hoped that the patient will be able to remain free of dependence on all CNS depressants. However, in reality detoxification is rarely sufficient by itself to assure long-term abstinence from the drug.

Often, the basic approach for treating severe dependence on sedative-hypnotics is substitution with either pentobarbital or the longer-acting phenobarbital for the offending, usually shorter-acting, CNS depressant. Once substitution has occurred, the long-acting barbiturate dose is gradually reduced. Using a substitute is necessary because abrupt withdrawal for a person who is physically dependent can be dangerous, causing life-threatening seizures. This substitution treatment uses the same rationale as the treatment of heroin withdrawal by methadone replacement. Detoxification also includes supportive measures such as vitamins, restoration of electrolyte balance, and prevention of dehydration. The patient must be watched closely during this time because he or she will be apprehensive, confused, and unable to make logical decisions (O'Brien 2006).

If the person is addicted to both alcohol and barbiturates, the phenobarbital dosage must be increased to compensate for the double withdrawal. Many barbiturate addicts who enter a hospital to be treated for withdrawal are also dependent on heroin. In such cases, the barbiturate dependence should be addressed first because the associated withdrawal can be life-threatening. Detoxification from any sedative-hypnotic should take place under close medical supervision, typically in a hospital (O'Brien 2006).

It is important to remember that elimination of physical dependence is not a cure. The problem of psychological dependence can be much more difficult to handle. If an individual is abusing a CNS depressant because of emotional instability, personal problems, or a very stressful environment, eliminating physical dependence alone will not solve the problem and drug dependence is likely to recur. These types of patients require intense psychological counseling and must be trained to deal with their difficulties in a more constructive and positive fashion. Without such psychological support, benefits from detoxification will only be temporary, and therapy will ultimately fail.

■ DEPRESSANTS

Natural Substances

Some plants that contain naturally occurring CNS depressants are included in herbal products or made into herbal teas for relaxation or as treatment for sleep problems (McQueen and Hume 2006). Probably the best known of this group is the kava kava plant (*Piper methysticum*). Drinks and bars containing extracts from kava kava root are legally available in many health food stores, are especially popular in Polynesian populations, and are sometimes used in religious ceremonies. The extract is prepared from the part of the kava kava plant beneath the surface of the ground. Small amounts of kava kava can produce euphoria and increased sociability, whereas larger doses cause substantial relaxation, lethargy, relaxed lower limbs, and eventually sleep (Boerner et al. 2003). Some users may experience visual and auditory hallucinations that can last 1 to 2 hours. Some users report that kava kava drinks can make the mouth numb much like topical local anesthetics used by dentists.

A second type of common herb that contains CNS depressants belong to the *Datura* family of plants. Although these botanicals are typically associated with hallucinogenic effects, in smaller amounts they sometimes can cause sedation and even induce sleep. Examples of these plants include *Datura inoxia* (Devil's weed) and *Datura strammonium* (jimson weed or thornapple). The active ingredients in these plants are typically anticholinergic drugs such as atropine or scopolamine. In lower doses, these herbs, especially if they contain scopolamine, have been used to encourage sleep. In fact, the actions of the herbs are somewhat similar to the OTC antihistamine-containing sleep aids, which also work due to their anticholinergic actions. In higher doses, both atropine and scopolamine can cause hallucinogenic effects. The anticholinergic actions of these herbs can be quite annoying and include constipation, dry mouth, and blurred vision, just to mention a few.

Discussion Questions

1. Why have benzodiazepine drugs replaced the barbiturates as the sedative-hypnotic drugs most prescribed by physicians?

2. Which features of CNS depressants give them abuse potential?

3. Why is long-term use of the benzodiazepines more likely to cause dependence than short-term use?

4. Why are some physicians careless when prescribing benzodiazepines for patients suffering from severe anxiety?

5. Currently, sleep aid products are available OTC. Should the FDA also allow sedatives to be sold without a prescription? Support your answer.

6. Are there any real advantages to using barbiturates as sedatives or hypnotics? Should the FDA remove them from the market?

7. What types of people are most likely to abuse CNS depressants? Suggest ways to help these people avoid abusing these drugs.

8. What is the appeal for using GHB? Why is it used to commit sexual assaults?

9. What dangers are associated with treating individuals who are severely dependent on CNS depressants?

10. Why are CNS depressants often combined with alcohol, and what is the consequence?

11. Why is detoxification by itself usually insufficient to achieve long-term therapeutic success when dealing with severe CNS depressant dependence?

Summary

1 Several unrelated drug groups cause CNS depression, but only a few are actually used clinically for their depressant properties. The most frequently prescribed CNS depressants are benzodiazepines, which include drugs such as Valium, Ambien, and Xanax. Barbiturates once were popular, but, because of their severe side effects, they are no longer prescribed by most clinicians. Much like barbiturates, drugs such as chloral hydrate, glu-tethimide, and methaqualone are little used today. Finally, some OTC and prescription antihistamines, such as diphenhydramine, hydroxyzine, and promethazine, are used for their CNS depressant effects.

2 The clinical value of CNS depressants is dose dependent. When used at low doses, these drugs relieve anxiety and promote relaxation (*sedatives*). When prescribed at higher doses, they can cause drowsiness and promote sleep (*hypnotics*). When administered at even higher doses, some of the depressants cause anesthesia and are used for patient management during surgery.

3 Because CNS depressants can relieve anxiety and reduce stress, they are viewed as desirable by many people. If used frequently over long periods, however, they can cause tolerance that leads to dependence.

4 The principal reason that benzodiazepines have replaced barbiturates in the treatment of stress and insomnia is that benzodiazepines have a greater margin of safety and are less likely to alter sleep patterns. Benzodiazepines enhance the GABA transmitter system in the brain through a specific receptor, whereas the effects of barbiturates are less selective. Even though benzodiazepines are safer than barbiturates, dependence and significant withdrawal problems can result if the former drugs are used indiscriminately.

5 Often, benzodiazepine dependence occurs in patients who suffer stress or anxiety disorders and are under a physician's care. If the physician is not careful and the cause of the stress is not resolved, drug treatment can drag on for weeks or months. After prolonged benzodiazepine therapy, tolerance to the drug develops; when benzodiazepine use is stopped, withdrawal occurs, which itself causes agitation. A rebound response to the drug might resemble the effects of emotional stress (agitation), so use of benzodiazepine is continued. In this way, the patient becomes severely dependent.

6 The short-acting CNS depressants are preferred for treatment of insomnia. These drugs help the patient get to sleep and then are inactivated by the body; when the user awakens the next day, he or she is less likely to experience residual effects than with long-acting drugs. The short-acting depressants are also more likely to be abused because of their relatively rapid onset and intense effects. In contrast, the long-acting depressants are better suited to treating persistent problems such as anxiety and stress. The long-acting depressants are also used to help wean dependent people from their use of short-acting compounds such as alcohol.

7 Many antihistamines cause sedation and drowsiness due to their anticholinergic effects. Several of these agents are useful for short-term relief of anxiety and are available in OTC sleep aids. The effectiveness of these CNS depressants is usually less than that of benzodiazepines. Because of their anticholinergic actions, antihistamines can cause some annoying side effects. These agents are not likely to be used for long periods; thus, dependence or serious abuse usually does not develop.

8 The people most likely to abuse CNS depressants include individuals who (1) use drugs to relieve continual stress; (2) paradoxically feel euphoria and stimulation from depressants; (3) use depressants to counteract the unpleasant effects of other drugs of abuse, such as stimulants; and (4) combine depressants with alcohol and heroin to potentiate the effects.

9 The basic approach for treating dependence on CNS depressants is to detoxify the individual in a safe manner while minimizing his or her discomfort. This state is achieved by substituting a long-acting barbiturate or benzodiazepine, such as phenobarbital or Valium, for the offending CNS depressant. The long-acting drug causes less severe withdrawal symptoms over a longer period of time. The dependent person is gradually weaned from the substitute drug until he or she is depressant-free.

10 GHB is a naturally occurring substance related to the neurotransmitter GABA that has been used for its sedating, euphorigenic, and muscle-building properties. It has also been used to debilitate victims of date rape during sexual assaults. Because of concerns that this substance is frequently abused, GHB was classified as a Schedule I drug in 2000.

11 Some plants such as kava kava that contain naturally occurring CNS depressants are included in herbal teas for relaxation or treatment of insomnia.

References

American Psychiatric Association. "Substance Related Disorders." In *Diagnostic and Statistical Manual of Mental Disorders Text Revision*, 4th ed., 191–295. Washington, DC: APA, 2000.

Associated Press. "Woman Who Used Halcion Defense Hangs Self." *Salt Lake Tribune* 248 (1994): D-3.

Backmund, M., K. Meyer, C. Henkel, M. Soyka, J. Reimer, and C. Schutz. "Co-consumption of Benzodiazepines in Heroin Users, Methadone-Substituted and Codeine-Substituted Patients." *Journal of Addiction Disorder* 24 (2005): 17–29.

Boerner, R., H. Sommer, W. Berger, U. Kuhn, U. Schmidt, and M. Manner. "Kava Kava Extract LI 150 Is as Effective as Opipramol and Buspirone in Generalized Anxiety Disorder." *Phytomedicine* 10 Supplement 4 (2003): 38–49.

Carter, L., L. Flores, H. Wu, C. Weibin, A. Unzeitig, A. Coop, and C. France. "The Role of GABA-B Receptors in the Discriminative Stimulus Effects of GHB in Rats: Time Course and Antagonism Studies." *Journal of Pharmacology and Experimental Therapeutics* 305 (2003): 668–674.

Charney, D., S. Mihic, and R. Harris. "Hypnotics and Sedatives." In *The Pharmacological Basis of Therapeutics,* 11th ed. Edited by L. Brunton, J. Lazo, and K. Parker, 401–427. New York: McGraw-Hill, 2006.

Craig, K., H. Gomez, J. McMannus, and T. Bania. "Severe Gamma-Hydroxybutyrate Withdrawal: A Case Report and Literature Review." *Journal of Emergency Medicine* 18 (2000): 65–70.

Dean, W., J. Morgenthaler, and S. Fowkes. *GHB: The Natural Mood Enhancer: The Authoritative Guide to Its Responsible Use.* Petaluma, CA: Smart Publications, 1997.

DeMaria, P., R. Sterling, and S. Weinstein. "The Effect of Stimulant and Sedative Use on Treatment Outcome of Patients Admitted to Methadone Maintenance Treatment." *American Journal of Addiction* 9 (2000): 145–153.

Drasbek, K., J. Christenen, and K. Jensen. "Gamma-hydroxybutyrate — A Drug of Abuse." *Acta Neurologica Scandinavia* 115 (2006): 368.

Drug Facts and Comparisons, 2007 Edition. St. Louis, MO: Wolters Kluwar Health, 2007: 1339–1365.

Drugs.com. Top 200 Drugs for 2006. Available www.drugs.com/top200.html.

Elsohly, M., and S. Salamone. "Prevalence of Drugs Used in Cases of Alleged Sexual Assault." *Journal of Analytical Toxicology* 23 (1999): 141–146.

Galloway, G., S. Frederick, F. Staggers, M. Gonzales, S. Stalcup, and D. Smith. "Gamma-Hydroxybutyrate: An Emerging Drug of Abuse That Causes Physical Dependence." *Addiction* 92 (1997): 89–96.

"Gamma Hydroxybutyric Acid (GHB, Liquid X, Goop, Georgia Home Boy)." *DEA Bulletin* DEA/ODE #000612 (12 June 2000).

Gorman, J. "Treating Generalized Anxiety Disorder." *Journal of Clinical Psychiatry* 64 (2003): 24–29.

Hobbs, W., T. Rall, and T. Verdoorn. "Hypnotics and Sedatives." In *The Pharmacological Basis of Therapeutics,* 9th ed., edited by J. Hardman and L. Limbird, 361–396. New York: McGraw-Hill, 1995.

Hughes, G., J. McElnay, C. Hughes, and P. McKenna. "Abuse/Misuse of Non-prescription Drugs." *Pharmacy World Science* 21 (1999): 251–255.

Johansson, B., M. Berglund, M. Hanson, C. Pohlen, and I. Persson. "Dependence on Legal Psychotropic Drugs Among Alcoholics." *Alcohol, Alcoholism* 38 (2003): 613–618.

Johnston, L. "Monitoring the Future 2006." (2007). Available www.monitoringthefuture.org/pubs/monographs/vol1_2006.pdf.

Kosten, T., and L. Hollister. "Drugs of Abuse." In *Basic and Clinical Pharmacology*, 7th ed., edited by B. Katzung, 516–531. Stamford, CT: Appleton & Lange, 1998.

Landis, B., and S. Bryant. "Mental Health Disorders." In *Pharmacotherapeutics, a Primary Care Clinical Guide*, edited by E. Youngkin, 747–799. Stamford, CT: Appleton & Lange, 1999.

Latner, A. "The Top 200 Drugs of 1999." *Pharmacy Times* 66 (2000): 16–32.

Leshner, A. E. "Club Drug Alert." *NIDA Notes* 14 (2000): 3 (posted 22 May 2000). Available http://www.drugabuse.gov/NIDA_notes/NNVol14N6/DirRepVol14N6.html.

Lingenhoehl, K., R. Brom, J. Heid, P. Beck, W. Froestl, K. Kaupman, B. Bettler, and J. Mosbacher. "Gamma-Hydroxybutyrate Is a Weak Agonist Against Recombinant GABA (B) Receptors." *Neuropharmacology* 38 (1999): 1667–1673.

Longo, L., and B. Johnson. "Addiction: Part I. Benzodiazepines, Side Effects, Abuse Risks and Alternatives." *American Family Physician* 61 (2000): 2121–2128.

McEvoy, G., ed. *American Hospital Formulary Service Drug Information*. Bethesda, MD: American Society of Hospital Pharmacists, 2003.

McQueen, C., and A. Hume. "Introduction to Botanical and Nonbotanical Natural Medicines." In *Handbook of Nonprescription Drugs*, 15th ed. Edited by R. Berardi, 1095–1136. Washington, DC: American Pharmacists Association, 2006.

Miga, A. "Kennedy Slowly Battles Drug Addiction." *Washington Post* (May 2, 2007). Available http://www.washingtonpost.com/wp-dyn/content/article/2007/05/02/AR2007050201758.html.

Mioto, K., and B. Roth. "GHB Withdrawal." Austin, TX: Texas Commission on Alcohol and Drug Abuse, March 2001.

Mondanaro, J. *Chemically Dependent Women*. Lexington, MA: Lexington Books/D. C. Heath, 1988.

Morgenthaler, J., and D. Joy. *Special Report on GHB*. Petaluma, CA: Smart Publication, 1994.

Nava, F. S. Premi, E. Manzato, W. Campagnola, W. Luccini, and L. Gessa. "Gamma-hydroxybutyrate Reduces Both Withdrawal Symptoms and Hypercortisolism in Severe Abstinent Alcoholics: An Open Study vs. Diazepam." *American Journal of Drug and Alcohol Abuse.* 33 (2007): 379–392.

NIDA Notes. "What Are Club Drugs?" 14 (22 May 2000). Available http://www.drugabuse.gov/NIDA_Notes/NNVol14N6/WhatAre.html.

O'Brien, C. "Drug Addiction and Drug Abuse." In *The Pharmacological Basis of Therapeutics*, 11th ed. Edited by L. Brunton, J. Lazo, and K. Parker, 607–627. New York: McGraw-Hill, 2006.

Payne, J. "Report: Go Easy on Sleeping Pills." *Washington Post* (August 15, 2006). Available http://www.washingtonpost.com/wp-dyn/content/article/2006/08/14/AR2006081400875.html.

Poldrugo, F., and G. Addolorato. "The Role of Gamma-Hydroxybutyrate Acid in the Treatment of Alcoholism: From Animal to Clinical Studies." *Alcohol, Alcoholism* 34 (1999): 15–34.

Publishers Group. "Street Drugs." Plymouth, MN: 2002. Available www.Streetdrugs.org.

Scharman, E., A. Erdman, P. Wax, P. Chyka, E. Caravati, et al. "Diphenhydramine and Dimenhydrinate Poisoning: An Evidence-Based Consensus Guideline for Out-of-Hospital Management." *Clinical Toxicology (Philadelphia)* 44 (2006): 205–233.

Substance Abuse and Mental Health Services Administration (SAMHSA). "2006 National Survey on Drug Use and Health." Office of Applied Studies. Available www.oas.samhsa.gov/nsduhlatest.htm.

Sumnall, H., K. Woolfall, S. Edwards, J. Cole, and C. Beynon. "Use, Function, and Subjective Experiences of Gamma-hydroxybutyrate (GHB)." *Drugs and Alcohol Dependency* (Aug. 31, 2007).

Teter, C., and S. Guthrie. "A Comprehensive Review of MDMA and GHB: Two Common Club Drugs." *Pharmacotherapy* 21 (2001): 1486–1513.

Trevor, A., and W. Lay. "Sedative-Hypnotic Drugs." In *Basic and Clinical Pharmacology*, 7th ed., edited by B. Katzung, 354–371. Stamford, CT: Appleton & Lange, 1998.

U.S. Department of Justice (USDOJ). "National Drug Threat Assessment 2003." National Drug Intelligence Center, Product No. 2003-Q0317-001, January 2003.

U.S. Department of Justice (USDOJ). "Information Bulletin. GHB Analogs." Product No. 2002-L0424-0034, 2002.

CHAPTER 7

Alcohol: Pharmacological Effects

Learning Objectives

On completing this chapter you will be able to:

◎ Explain how common alcohol (ethanol) is a drug.

◎ Explain the pharmacokinetic properties of alcohol and describe how they influence the effects of the drug.

◎ Explain the role of alcohol in "polydrug" abuse.

◎ Identify the possible physical effects of prolonged heavy ethanol consumption.

◎ Explain the potential cardiovascular benefits of moderate alcohol use.

◎ Describe FAS and its effects.

◎ Explain how prolonged consumption of alcohol affects the brain and nervous system, liver, digestive system, blood, cardiovascular system, sexual organs, endocrine systems, and kidneys, and how it leads to mental disorders and damage to fetuses.

◎ Explain why malnutrition is so common among alcoholics.

Did You Know?

○ Ethanol leads all other substances of abuse in treatment admissions.

○ Ethanol is the only alcohol used for human consumption; most of the other common alcohols are poisonous.

○ Some wild animals and insects become drunk after seeking out and consuming alcohol-containing fermented fruit.

○ Alcohol-related deaths outnumber deaths related to other drugs of abuse (except tobacco) by a four to one margin.

○ Women who abuse alcohol are more likely to suffer depression than male abusers.

○ The lethal level of alcohol is between 0.4% and 0.6% by volume in the blood.

○ Among alcoholics, liver disorders account for approximately 10–15% of deaths.

○ Fetal alcohol syndrome (FAS) is characterized by facial deformities, growth deficiencies, and mental retardation.

Drugs and Society Online is a great source for additional drugs and society information for both students and instructors.
Visit **http://drugsandsociety.jbpub.com** to find a variety of useful tools for learning, thinking, and teaching.

Introduction

In Chapters 7 and 8, we examine several aspects of alcohol use. This chapter focuses on how alcohol affects the body from a pharmacological perspective. Chapter 8 discusses the social effects of this drug — mainly the effects and consequences of alcohol on an individual's personal and social life.

As a licit drug, alcohol is extensively promoted socially through advertising. Alcoholic beverage companies spent almost $5 billion on television advertising of their products from 2001 to 2005 (Center on Alcohol Marketing and Youth at Georgetown University 2007; see "Here and Now," Alcohol Ads Are for Kids). But more important, drinking is perceived as acceptable. The popularity of this drug is clear; in 2006, 56.4% of high school seniors said they had been drunk sometime during their life (Johnston 2007). Binge drinking among teens is thought to be at epidemic levels with about 25% of the teenagers in this country participating in episodes of very heavy alcohol use (CBS News 2007). College youth also consume large quantities of alcohol, and many authorities believe alcohol is the leading drug problem among this population (National Center on Addiction and Substance Abuse at Columbia University 2007).

This chapter focuses on the many adverse effects of alcohol on the human body. Overall, it provides you with a foundation to understand the pharmacological nature of alcohol. We hope that such an understanding of how this drug affects the various organ systems of the body will lead to more responsible use and less abuse of alcohol. Because of its widespread consumption, alcohol leads all other addicting substances as a reason for treatment admissions. In 2006, of the 4 million people treated for substance dependence, 2.8 mil-

Because of frequent advertising, use of alcohol is perceived as normal and acceptable.

lion received treatment for alcoholism (Office of Applied Studies 2007).

The Nature and History of Alcohol

Alcohol has been part of human culture since the beginning of recorded history. The technology for alcohol production is ancient. Several basic ingredients and conditions are needed to

Here and Now

Alcohol Ads Are for Kids

A report from the Center on Alcohol Marketing and Youth at Georgetown University revealed that in 2001 and 2002 underage youth were more likely to hear radio ads promoting beer and other alcoholic beverages than people of legal drinking age. This is partially due to the fact that the alcohol radio advertising most often was placed on radio stations with "youth" music formats that routinely have a disproportionately large listening audience of 12- to 20-year-olds. These data suggest that the alcohol industry targets the underage population for its alcoholic products.

Source: Center on Alcohol Marketing and Youth. "Radio Daze: Alcohol Ads Tune in Underage Youth." Georgetown University (2 April 2003): 1, 2.

produce this substance: sugar, water, yeast, and warm temperatures.

The process of making alcohol, called **fermentation**, is a natural one. It occurs in ripe fruit and berries and even in honey that bees leave in trees. These substances contain sugar and water and are found in warm climates, where yeast spores are transported through the air. Animals such as elephants, baboons, birds, wild pigs, and bees will seek out and eat fermented fruit. Elephants under the influence of alcohol have been observed bumping into one another and stumbling around. Intoxicated bees fly an unsteady beeline toward their hives. Birds eating fermented fruit become so uncoordinated that they cannot fly or, if they do, crash into windows or branches. In fact, fermented honey, called **mead**, may have been the first alcoholic beverage.

The Egyptians had breweries 6000 years ago; they credited the god Osiris with introducing wine to humans. The ancient Greeks used large quantities of wine and credited a god, Bacchus (Dionysus), with introducing the drink. Today, we use the words *bacchanalia* and *dionysian* to refer to revelry and drunken events. The Hebrews were also heavy users of wine. The Bible mentions that Noah, just nine generations removed from Adam, made wine and became drunk.

Alcohol is produced by a single-celled microscopic organism, one of the yeasts, that breaks down sugar by a metabolic form of combustion, thereby releasing carbon dioxide and forming water and ethyl alcohol as waste products. Carbon dioxide creates the foam on a glass of beer and the fizz in champagne. Fermentation continues until the sugar supply is exhausted or the concentration of alcohol reaches the point at which it kills the yeast (12–14%). Thus, 12–14% is the natural limit of alcohol found in fermented wines or beers.

The **distillation** device, or *still*, was developed by the Arabs around A.D. 800 and was introduced into medieval Europe around A.D. 1250. By boiling the fermented drink and gathering the condensed vapor in a pipe, a still increases the concentration of alcohol, potentially to 50% or higher. Because distillation made it easier for people to get drunk, it greatly intensified the problem of alcohol abuse. However, even before the invention of the still, alcoholic beverages had been known to cause problems in heavy users that resulted in severe physical and psychological dependence. But not until the past century did the concept of alcoholism as a disease develop

(Mann et al. 2000). (See "Here and Now," A Century of Alcohol.)

Alcohol as a Drug

Alcohol (more precisely designated as **ethanol**), as a natural product of fermentation, is an extremely popular social beverage, the second most widely used and abused psychoactive drug (after caffeine), and widely misunderstood (Pociluyko 2003). Its impact on college students has been particularly disturbing, with reports stating that binge drinking among such individuals is commonplace; alcohol use has resulted in assaults (approximately 600,000/year), injuries (500,000/year), and even deaths (1400/year; National Institute on Alcohol Abuse and Alcoholism [NIAAA] 2002). This psychoactive substance depresses the central nervous system (CNS) while influencing almost all major organ systems of the body. Alcohol is also an addictive drug in that it may produce a physical and behavioral dependence (American Psychiatric Association [APA] 2000). Although tradition and attitude are important factors in determining the use patterns of this substance, the typical consumer rarely appreciates the diversity of pharmacological effects caused by alcohol, the drug. The pharmacological action of alcohol accounts for both its pleasurable and CNS effects as well as its hazards to health and public safety.

■ Alcohol as a Social Drug

Why is alcohol often perceived as an acceptable adjunct to such celebrations as parties, birthdays,

KEY TERMS

fermentation
biochemical process through which yeast converts sugar to alcohol

mead
fermented honey often made into an alcoholic beverage

distillation
heating fermented mixtures of cereal grains or fruits in a still to evaporate and be trapped as purified alcohol

ethanol
consumable type of alcohol that is the psychoactive ingredient in alcoholic beverages; often called *grain alcohol*

Here and Now

A Century of Alcohol

An overwhelming need to consume alcohol (known today as alcoholism) was first described in the literature by Benjamin Rush in 1784, but the concept that excessive use of alcohol is a disease didn't really evolve until the past 100 years. This perspective was encouraged by the "temperance movement" of the late 19th century. Because of the ill effects of alcohol, temperance legally became "Prohibition" in 1919. *Prohibition* (alcohol made illegal) was initially successful in reducing consumption, but consumption began to rebound in the late 1920s. However, it has been suggested that Prohibition was repealed in 1933 not because it failed to reduce alcohol use but because of shift-ing policy during the Great Depression that argued liquor manufacturing would create jobs and provide taxes on alcoholic beverages that could fund government programs.

The second half of the 20th century saw the emergence of the belief that genetics plays a major role in alcoholism. This concept suggests that because of inherited traits, some families and individuals are more vulnerable to alcohol addiction than others. Researchers today are energetically moving forward to identify which genes might contribute to the development and expression of the addiction in an effort to improve prevention and treatment for alcoholism.

Source: Quindien, A. "America's Most Pervasive Drug Problem Is the Drug That Pretends It Isn't." *Salt Lake Tribune* (20 April 2000): A-11.

weddings, and anniversaries, and as a way of relieving stress and anxiety? Social psychologists refer to the perception of alcohol as a **social lubricant**. This term implies that drinking is misconceived as safely promoting conviviality and social interaction, and as an activity that bolsters confidence by repressing inhibitions and strengthening extroversion. Why do many people have to be reminded that alcohol is a drug like marijuana or cocaine and may have serious consequences for some people? Four reasons explain this misconception:

1. The use of alcohol is legal.
2. Through widespread advertising, the media promote the notion that alcohol consumption is as normal and safe as drinking fruit juices and soft drinks.
3. The distribution, advertisement, and sale of alcoholic beverages are widely practiced.
4. Alcohol use has a long tradition, dating back to 3000 B.C. (Royce 1989).

KEY TERMS

social lubricant
belief that drinking (misconceived as safe) represses inhibitions, strengthens extroversion, and leads to increased sociability

▪ Impact of Alcohol

Although many consider the effects of alcohol enjoyable and reassuring, the adverse pharmacological impacts of this drug are extensive, its use causes approximately 14 million cases of alcoholism (severe alcohol dependence), and its effects are associated with more than 100,000 deaths each year in the United States (Fleming et al. 2006). It is estimated that at some time during their lives, almost 50% of all Americans will be involved in an alcohol-related traffic accident. The pharmacological effects of alcohol abuse cause severe dependence, which is classified as a psychiatric disorder according to the *Diagnostic and Statistical Manual of Mental Disorders,* fourth edition, revised (APA 2000) criteria. These effects also disrupt personal, family, social, and professional functioning and frequently result in multiple illnesses and accidents, violence, and crime (Hanson and Li 2003). Alcohol consumed during pregnancy can lead to devastating damage to offspring and is a principal cause of mental retardation in newborns (Hanson and Li 2003). After tobacco, alcohol is the leading cause of premature death in America. In the United States, approximately $176 billion is spent annually dealing with the social and health problems resulting from the pharmacological effects of alcohol (Marin Institute 2007). Of course, such estimates fall short in assessing the emotional upheaval and human suffering caused by this drug.

Despite all of the problems that alcohol causes, our free society has demanded access to this drug. At the same time, it is unthinkable to ignore the tremendous negative social impact of this drug. There are no simple answers to this dichotomy, yet clearly governmental and educational institutions could do more to protect members of society from the dangers associated with alcohol. The best weapons we have against the problems caused by alcohol are education, prevention, and treatment (see Chapter 17).

Different alcoholic beverages have a wide range of alcohol content.

The Properties of Alcohol

Technically, alcohol is a chemical structure that has a hydroxyl group (OH, for one oxygen and one hydrogen atom) attached to a carbon atom (Pociluyko 2003). Of the many types of alcohol, several are important in this context. The first is **methyl alcohol** (*methanol* or *wood alcohol*), which is made from wood products. Its metabolites are poisonous. Small amounts (4 mL) cause blindness by affecting the retina, and larger amounts (80–150 mL) are usually fatal. Methyl alcohol is added to ethyl alcohol (*ethanol* or *grain alcohol*, the drinking type) intended for industrial use so that people will not drink it. A similar mixture is also sometimes added to illegally manufactured ("bootleg") liquor.

Another type of poisonous alcohol, **ethylene glycol**, is used in antifreeze. A third type, **isopropyl alcohol**, is commonly used as rubbing alcohol and as an *antiseptic* (a solution for preventing the growth of microorganisms). These two types of alcohol are also poisonous if consumed. Pure ethyl alcohol (ethanol) is recognized as an official drug in the U.S. Pharmacopoeia, although the various alcoholic beverages are not listed for medical use.

Alcohol can be used as a solvent for other drugs or as a preservative. It is used to cleanse, disin-

fect, and harden the skin and to reduce sweating. A 70% alcohol solution is an effective bactericide (Pociluyko 2003). However, it should not be used on open wounds because it will dehydrate the injured tissue and worsen the damage. Alcohol may be deliberately injected in or near nerves to treat severe pain; it causes local anesthesia and deterioration of the nerve.

In all alcoholic beverages — beer, wine, liqueurs or cordials, and distilled spirits — the psychoactive agent is the same, but the amount of ethanol varies (see Table 7.1). The amount of alcohol is expressed either as a percentage by volume or, in the older proof system, as a measurement based on the military assay method. To make certain that they were getting a high alcohol content in the liquor, the British military would place a sample on gunpowder and touch a spark to it. If the alcohol content exceeded 50%, it would burn and ignite the gunpowder. This test was "proof" that the sample was at least 50% alcohol. If the distilled spirits were "under proof," the water content would

KEY TERMS

methyl alcohol
wood alcohol

ethylene glycol
alcohol used as antifreeze

isopropyl alcohol
rubbing alcohol, sometimes used as an antiseptic

Table 7.1 The Concentration of Ethanol in Common Alcoholic Beverages

TYPE OF BEVERAGE	CONCENTRATION OF ETHANOL
U.S. beers	4–6%
Wine coolers	10–12%
Cocktail and dessert wines	17–20%
Liqueurs	22–50%
Distilled spirits	40–50%

prevent the gunpowder from igniting. The percentage of alcohol volume is one-half the proof number. For example, 100-proof whiskey has a 50% alcohol content.

The Physical Effects of Alcohol

How does alcohol affect the body? Figure 7.1 illustrates how alcohol is absorbed into the body. After a drink, alcohol has direct contact with the mouth, esophagus, stomach, and intestines, acting as an irritant and an **anesthetic** (blocking sensitivity to pain). In addition, alcohol influences almost every organ system in the body after entering the bloodstream. Alcohol diffuses into the blood rapidly after consumption by passing (absorption process) through gastric and intestinal walls. Once the alcohol is in the small intestine, its absorption is largely independent of the presence of food, unlike in the stomach, where food retards absorption.

The effects of alcohol on the human body depend on the amount of alcohol in the blood, known as the **blood alcohol concentration (BAC)**. This concentration largely determines behavioral and physical responses to alcoholic beverages. Relative to behavior, circumstances in which the drinking occurs, the drinker's mood, and his or her attitude and previous experience with alcohol all contribute to the reaction to drinking. People demonstrate individual patterns of psychological functioning that may affect their reactions to alcohol as well. For instance, the time it takes to empty the stomach may be either reduced or accelerated as a result of anger, fear, stress, nausea, and the condition of the stomach tissues.

The blood alcohol level produced depends on the presence of food in the stomach, the rate of alcohol consumption, the concentration of the alcohol, and the drinker's body composition. Fatty foods, meat, and milk slow the absorption of alcohol, allowing more time for its metabolism and reducing the peak concentration in the blood. When alcoholic beverages are taken with a substantial meal, peak BACs may be as much as 50% lower than they would have been had the alcohol been consumed by itself. When large amounts of alcohol are consumed in a short period, the brain and other organs are exposed to higher peak concentrations. Generally, the more alcohol in the stomach, the greater the absorption rate. There is, however, a modifying effect of very strong drinks on the absorption rate. The absorption of drinks stronger than 100 proof is inhibited. This effect may be due to blocked passage into the small intestine or irritation of the lining of the stomach, causing mucus secretion, or both. (See "Here and Now," Half-Truths About Alcohol.)

Diluting an alcoholic beverage with water helps to slow down absorption, but mixing with carbonated beverages increases the absorption rate. The carbonation causes the stomach to empty its contents into the small intestine more rapidly, causing a more rapid "high." The carbonation in champagne has the same effect.

Once in the blood, distribution occurs as the alcohol uniformly diffuses throughout all tissues and fluids, including fetal circulation in pregnant women. Because the brain has a large blood supply, its activity is quickly affected by a high alcohol concentration in the blood. Body composition — the amount of water available for the alcohol to be dissolved in — is a key factor in BAC and distribution. The greater the muscle mass, the lower the BAC that will result from a given amount of alcohol. This relationship arises because muscle has more fluid volume than does fat. For example, if two men each weigh 180 pounds but one man has substantially more lean mass than the other man, the former will have a lower blood alcohol level after consuming 4 ounces of whiskey. The leaner man will show fewer effects. A woman of a weight equivalent to a man will have a higher blood alcohol level because women generally have a higher percentage of fat. Thus, they are affected more by identical drinks.

Alcoholic beverages contain almost no vitamins, minerals, protein, or fat — just large amounts of carbohydrates (Pociluyko 2003). Alcohol cannot be used by most cells; it must be metabolized by an enzyme, **alcohol dehydrogenase**, which is found almost exclusively in the liver. Alcohol provides more calories per gram than does carbohydrate or protein and only slightly less than does pure fat. Because it can provide many calories, the

KEY TERMS

anesthetic
a drug that blocks sensitivity to pain

blood alcohol concentration (BAC)
concentration of alcohol found in the blood, often expressed as a percentage

alcohol dehydrogenase
principal enzyme that metabolizes ethanol

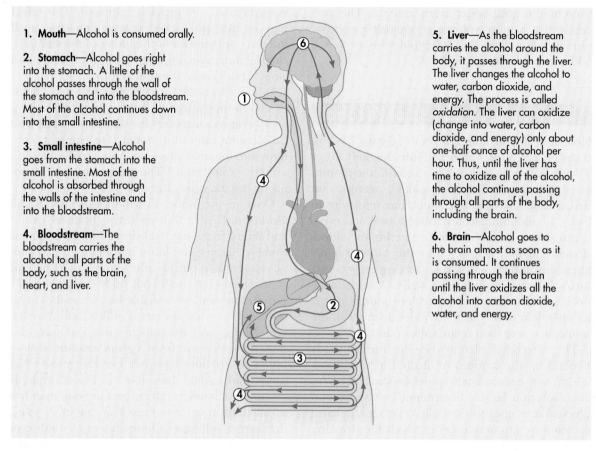

1. **Mouth**—Alcohol is consumed orally.

2. **Stomach**—Alcohol goes right into the stomach. A little of the alcohol passes through the wall of the stomach and into the bloodstream. Most of the alcohol continues down into the small intestine.

3. **Small intestine**—Alcohol goes from the stomach into the small intestine. Most of the alcohol is absorbed through the walls of the intestine and into the bloodstream.

4. **Bloodstream**—The bloodstream carries the alcohol to all parts of the body, such as the brain, heart, and liver.

5. **Liver**—As the bloodstream carries the alcohol around the body, it passes through the liver. The liver changes the alcohol to water, carbon dioxide, and energy. The process is called *oxidation*. The liver can oxidize (change into water, carbon dioxide, and energy) only about one-half ounce of alcohol per hour. Thus, until the liver has time to oxidize all of the alcohol, the alcohol continues passing through all parts of the body, including the brain.

6. **Brain**—Alcohol goes to the brain almost as soon as it is consumed. It continues passing through the brain until the liver oxidizes all the alcohol into carbon dioxide, water, and energy.

FIGURE 7.1

How alcohol is absorbed in the body.

Source: National Institute on Alcohol Abuse and Alcoholism. *Alcohol Health and Research World. Washington,* DC: U.S. Department of Health and Human Services, 1988.

drinker's appetite may be satisfied; as a result, he or she may not eat properly, causing malnutrition (Achord 1995). The tolerance that develops to alcohol is comparable to that observed with barbiturates (see Chapter 6). Some people have a higher tolerance for alcohol and can more easily disguise intoxication.

■ Alcohol and Tolerance

Repeated use of alcohol results in tolerance and in reduction in many of alcohol's pharmacological effects. As with other psychoactive drugs, tolerance to alcohol encourages increased consumption to regain its effects and can lead to severe physical and psychological dependence (Fleming et al. 2006). Tolerance to alcohol is similar to that seen with CNS depressants, such as the barbiturates and benzodiazepines. It consists of both an increase in the rate of alcohol metabolism (due to stimulation of metabolizing enzymes in the liver; see Chapter 5) and a reduced response by neurons and transmitter systems (particularly by increasing the activity of the inhibitory neurotransmitter, gamma-aminobutyric acid [GABA]) to this drug. Development of tolerance to alcohol is extremely variable; some users can consume large quantities of this drug with minor pharmacological effects. The tolerance-inducing changes caused by alcohol can also alter the body's response to other drugs (referred to as *cross-tolerance*; see Chapter 5) and can specifically reduce the effects of some other CNS depressants (Fleming et al. 2006; NIAAA 2007).

Many chronic alcohol users learn to compensate for the motor impairments of this drug by modifying their patterns of behavior. These adjustments

Here and Now

Half-Truths About Alcohol

Much is known about alcohol, but much more needs to be learned to effectively and safely manage its use. There are several half-truths that are commonly believed by the general public that should be clarified:

Belief: Alcohol, if used in moderation, is healthy for everyone.

Fact: Moderate drinking benefits only men older than 50 years of age and women who are post-menopausal. Even for these populations, the benefits appear to be minimal in persons who already have healthy lifestyles.

Belief: Pound for pound, women hold their liquor as well as men.

Fact: Because women have proportionally less body water and tend to metabolize alcohol more slowly than men, women become more intoxicated with comparable dose consumption per body weight.

Belief: A drink before bed induces sleep.

Fact: After moderate drinking, onset of sleep may be faster, but the sleep itself becomes restless, marked by frequent wakings and inability to get back to sleep.

Belief: If you don't feel drunk, it is okay to drive.

Fact: People are typically unable to determine accurately how much alcohol is in their system. For most states in the United States, 0.08–0.1% alcohol in the blood is the legal threshold for driving (i.e., it is against the law to drive with this blood alcohol content or higher), but studies have shown that driving performance is significantly impaired at half this concentration.

Sources: "Your Health: Alcohol: The Whole Truth, Seven Half-Truths About Drinking, Exposed." *Consumer Reports* 64 (December 1999): 60–61; "FAQs on Alcohol Abuse and Alcoholism." NIAAA (2000). Available http://silk.nih.gov/silk/niaaa1/questions/q-a.htm#questions2; Greenfield 2002.

---

are referred to as **behavioral tolerance**. Examples of this adjustment include individuals altering and slowing their speech, walking more deliberately, or moving more cautiously to hide the fact that they have consumed debilitating quantities of alcohol.

Alcohol Metabolism

Alcohol is principally inactivated by liver metabolism (Fleming et al. 2007). The liver metabolizes alcohol at a slow and constant rate and is unaffected by the amount ingested. Thus, if one can of beer is consumed each hour, the BAC will remain constant without resulting in intoxication. If more alcohol is consumed per hour, the BAC will rise proportionately because large amounts of alcohol that cannot be metabolized spill over into the bloodstream.

Polydrug Use

It is a common practice to take alcohol with other drugs, such as tobacco (Hitti 2006) and even illegal substances (Hanson and Li 2003); this mode of consumption is known as **polydrug use**. Mixing alcohol with other types of drugs can intensify intoxication. This probably helps explain why marijuana users are more likely to combine their marijuana use with alcohol than with other drugs (Liquori et al. 2002). In a recent report, almost one half of those seeking treatment for alcoholism also were treated for abuse of other drugs (Office of Applied Studies 2007).

The reasons why individuals combine alcohol with other drugs of abuse are not always apparent. The following explanations have been proposed (Hettema et al. 1999):

1. Alcohol enhances the reinforcing properties of other CNS depressants.
2. It decreases the amount of an expensive and difficult-to-get drug required to achieve the desired effect.

KEY TERMS

behavioral tolerance
compensation for motor impairments through behavioral pattern modification by chronic alcohol users

polydrug use
the concurrent use of multiple drugs

3. It helps to diminish unpleasant side effects of other drugs of abuse, such as the withdrawal caused by CNS stimulants (NIAAA 1993).

4. There is a common predisposition to use alcohol and other substances of abuse.

Clearly, coadministration of alcohol with other substances of abuse is a common practice that can be very problematic and result in dangerous interactions.

Short-Term Effects

The impact of alcohol on the CNS is most similar to that of sedative-hypnotic agents such as barbiturates. Alcohol depresses CNS activity at all doses (Pociluyko 2003), producing definable results.

At low to moderate doses, **disinhibition** occurs; this loss of conditioned reflexes reflects a depression of inhibitory centers of the brain. The effects on behavior are variable and somewhat unpredictable. To a large extent, the social setting and mental state determine the individual's response to such alcohol consumption. For example, alcohol can cause one person to become euphoric, friendly, and talkative but can prompt another to become aggressive and hostile. Low to moderate doses also interfere with motor activity, reflexes, and coordination. Often this impairment is not apparent to the affected person ("Your Health" 1999).

In moderate quantities, alcohol slightly increases the heart rate; slightly dilates blood vessels in the arms, legs, and skin; and moderately lowers blood pressure. It stimulates appetite, increases production of gastric secretions, and markedly stimulates urine output.

At higher doses, the social setting has little influence on the expression of depressive actions of the alcohol. The CNS depression incapacitates the individual, causing difficulty in walking, talking, and thinking. These doses tend to induce drowsiness and cause sleep. If large amounts of alcohol are consumed rapidly, severe depression of the brain system and motor control area of the brain occurs, producing incoordination, confusion, disorientation, stupor, anesthesia, coma, and even death.

The lethal level of alcohol is between 0.4% and 0.6% by volume in the blood (Fleming et al. 2006). Death is caused by severe depression of the respiration center in the brain stem, although the person usually passes out before drinking an amount capable of producing this effect. Although an alcoholic may metabolize the drug more rapidly than a light drinker, the toxicity level of alcohol stays about the same. In other words, it takes approximately the same concentration of alcohol in the body to kill a nondrinker as to kill someone who drinks on a regular basis. The amount of alcohol required for anesthesia is very close to the toxic level, which is why it would not be a useful anesthetic. See Signs and Symptoms: Psychological and Physical Effects of Various Blood Alcohol Concentration Levels for a summary of the psychological and physical effects of various BAC levels.

As a general rule, it takes as many hours as the number of drinks consumed to sober up completely. Despite widely held beliefs, drinking black coffee, taking a cold shower, breathing pure oxygen, and so forth will not hasten the sobering process. Stimulants such as coffee may help keep the drunk person awake but will not improve judgment or motor reflexes to any significant extent.

The Hangover

A familiar consequence of overindulgence is fatigue combined with nausea, upset stomach, headache, sensitivity to sounds, and ill temper — the *hangover* (Wiese et al. 2000). These symptoms are usually most severe many hours after drinking, when little or no alcohol remains in the body. No simple explanation exists for what causes the hangover. Theories include accumulation of acetaldehyde (a metabolite of ethanol), dehydration of the tissues, poisoning due to tissue deterioration, depletion of important enzyme systems needed to maintain routine functioning, an acute withdrawal (or rebound) response, and metabolism of the impurities in alcoholic beverages.

The body loses fluid in two ways through alcohol's **diuretic** action, which sometimes results in dehydration: (1) the water content, such as in beer, increases the volume of urine, and (2) the alcohol depresses the center in the hypothalamus of the brain that controls release of a water conservation hormone (*antidiuretic hormone*). With less of this hormone, urine volume is further increased. Thus, after drinking heavily, especially the highly concentrated forms of alcohol, the person is thirsty. However, this effect by itself does not explain the symptoms of hangover.

KEY TERMS

disinhibition
loss of conditioned reflexes due to depression of inhibitory centers of the brain

diuretic
a drug or substance that increases the production of urine

Signs & Symptoms
Psychological and Physical Effects of Various Blood Alcohol Concentration Levels

NUMBER OF DRINKS*	BLOOD ALCOHOL CONCENTRATION	PSYCHOLOGICAL AND PHYSICAL EFFECTS
1	0.02–0.03%	No overt effects, slight mood elevation
2	0.05–0.06%	Feeling of relaxation, warmth; slight decrease in reaction time and in fine muscle coordination
3	0.08–0.09%	Balance, speech, vision, hearing slightly impaired; feelings of euphoria, increased confidence; loss of motor coordination
3–4	0.10%	Legal intoxication in all states; driving is illegal with this level (however, many states are changing or have changed the legal limit to 0.08%)
4	0.11–0.12%	Coordination and balance becoming difficult; distinct impairment of mental faculties, judgment
5	0.14–0.15%	Major impairment of mental and physical control; slurred speech, blurred vision, lack of motor skills
7	0.20%	Loss of motor control — must have assistance in moving about; mental confusion
10	0.30%	Severe intoxication; minimum conscious control of mind and body
14	0.40%	Unconsciousness, threshold of coma
17	0.50%	Deep coma
20	0.60%	Death from respiratory failure

Note: For each hour elapsed since the last drink, subtract 0.015% blood alcohol concentration, or approximately one drink.

*One drink = one beer (4% alcohol, 12 oz) or one highball (1 oz whiskey).

Source: Modified from data given in Ohio State Police Driver Information Seminars and the National Clearinghouse for Alcohol and Alcoholism Information, 5600 Fishers Lane, Rockville, MD 85206.

The type of alcoholic beverage one drinks may influence the hangover that results. Some people are more sensitive to particular alcohol impurities than others. For example, some drinkers have no problem with white wine but an equal amount of some red wines gives them a hangover. Whiskey, scotch, and rum may cause worse hangovers than vodka or gin, given equal amounts of alcohol, because vodka and gin have fewer impurities. There is little evidence that mixing different types of drinks per se produces a more severe hangover. It is more likely that more than the usual amount of alcohol is consumed when various drinks are sampled.

A common treatment for a hangover is to take a drink of the same alcoholic beverage that caused the hangover. This practice is called "taking the hair of the dog that bit you" (from the old notion that the burnt hair of a dog is an antidote to its bite). This treatment might help the person who is physically dependent, in the same way that giving heroin to a heroin addict eases the withdrawal symptoms. The "hair of the dog" method may work by depressing the centers of the brain that interpret pain or by relieving a withdrawal response. In addition, it may affect the psychological factors involved in having a hangover; distraction or focusing attention on something else may ease the effects.

Another remedy is to take an analgesic compound such as an aspirin–caffeine combination after drinking. This treatment is based on the belief that aspirin helps control headache; the caffeine may help counteract the depressant effect of the alcohol. In reality, these ingredients have no effect on the actual sobering-up process. In fact, products such as aspirin, caffeine, and Alka-Seltzer can irritate the stomach lining to the point where the person feels worse.

■ Dependence

Because of the disinhibition, relaxation, and sense of well-being mediated by alcohol, some degree of psychological dependence often develops, and the use of alcoholic beverages at social gatherings may become routine. It is estimated that in the United States, more than 8 million persons meet the criteria for alcohol dependence and an additional 5.6 million meet the diagnostic criteria for alcohol abuse (Hanson and Li 2003). In 2006, 30% of high school seniors drank enough alcohol to get drunk (Johnston 2007). Unfortunately, many people become so dependent on the psychological influences of alcohol that they become compulsive, continually consuming it. These individuals can be severely handicapped because of their alcohol dependence and often become unable to function normally in society. People who have become addicted to this drug are called alcoholics.

Because of the physiological effects, physical dependence also results from the regular consumption of large quantities of alcohol. This consequence becomes apparent when ethanol use is abruptly interrupted and withdrawal symptoms result. The severity of the withdrawal can vary according to the length and intensity of the alcohol habit. The prototypic withdrawal patterns are as follows (Fleming et al. 2006):

Stage 1 (minor): Restlessness, anxiousness, sleeping problems, agitation, tremors, and rapid heartbeat

Stage 2 (major): "Minor" symptoms plus hallucinations, whole-body tremors, increased blood pressure, and vomiting

Stage 3 (delirium tremens): Fever, disorientation, confusion, seizures, and fatality in 3% to 5% of cases

Recovery from alcohol dependence is a long-term process. Because of the severe withdrawal and the need for behavioral adjustments, most people relapse several times before long-term abstinence is achieved. Even people who have not used alcohol for years may relapse under very stressful circumstances (NIDA 2000). The behavioral treatment of alcoholism is discussed in more detail in Chapter 8. Three medications have been approved by the FDA for adjunctive intervention (i.e., they should be used in combination with behavioral therapy). These medications are (Williams 2005):

1. Disulfinam, which causes severe nausea and aversion when the user consumes alcohol
2. Naltrexone (an opiate antagonist; see Chapter 9), which helps to relieve alcohol craving
3. Acamprosate, which resembles the neurotransmitter GABA and delays relapse in abstinent alcoholics

The Effects of Alcohol on Organ Systems and Bodily Functions

As mentioned earlier, BAC depends on the size of the person, presence of food in the stomach, rate of drinking, amount of carbonation, and ratio of muscle mass to body fat. Furthermore, alcohol has pervasive effects on the major organs and fluids of the body (Worman 2000). In fact, the effects of this substance on body functions potentially can be so profound and destructive that alcoholism (*severe dependence*) is now considered a disease (Mann et al. 2000). The pervasive effects of alcohol on bodily organs are discussed in greater detail in the next section.

■ Brain and Nervous System

Every part of the brain and nervous system is affected — and in extreme cases can be damaged — by alcohol (Figure 7.2). A recent study demonstrated that even moderate consumption of alcohol can cause shrinkage of brain size. People who routinely drink more than 14 drinks per week experience a loss of approximately 1.6% compared to nondrinkers. The greatest effect was observed in female heavy drinkers over 70 years of age (Reinberg 2007). Alcohol suppresses subcortical inhibitions of the cortical control centers, resulting in disinhibition. In higher doses, it depresses the cerebellum, causing slurred speech and staggering gait. Very high doses depress the respiratory centers of the medulla, resulting in death (Fleming et al. 2001). Furthermore, alcohol alters the production and functioning of transmitters such as dopamine, serotonin, GABA, and brain endorphins (Ratsma et al. 2002). A recent report suggests that even cannabinoid receptors (see Chapter 13) — the targets of the active ingredients in marijuana — are affected by alcohol (Basavarajappa 2007). These neurochemical effects contribute to the fact that alcohol consumption can aggravate underlying psychiatric disorders such as depression and schizophrenia (Bertolote et al. 2004) and may suggest novel ways to develop more effective therapies (Basavarajappa 2007).

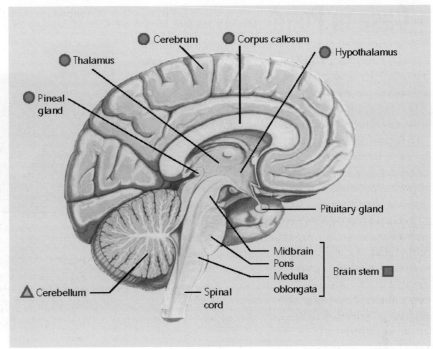

● Brain regions influenced by moderate doses of alcohol

▲ Brain region suppressed by moderately high doses of alcohol

■ Brain regions suppressed by very high doses of alcohol

FIGURE 7.2

The principal control centers of the brain affected by alcohol consumption. Note that all areas of the brain are interconnected.

Heavy drinking over many years may result in serious mental disorders and irreversible damage to the brain and peripheral nervous system, leading to permanently compromised mental function and memory and alterations in other brain systems (Preidt 2003).

Liver

Among alcoholics, liver disorders are responsible for 10% to 15% of deaths (Worman 2000). There are three stages of alcohol-induced liver disease (Worman 2000). In the first stage, known as *alcoholic fatty liver*, liver cells increase the production of fat, resulting in an enlarged liver. This direct toxic effect on liver tissue is known as the **hepatotoxic effect**. This effect is reversible and can disappear if alcohol use is stopped. Several days of drinking five or six alcoholic beverages each day produces fatty liver in

KEY TERMS

hepatotoxic effect
a situation in which liver cells increase the production of fat, resulting in an enlarged liver

A normal liver (*top*) as it would be found in a healthy human body. An abnormal liver (*bottom*) that exhibits the effects of moderate to heavy alcohol consumption.

▶Case in Point   Mickey Mantle Dies from Complications of Alcoholism

Mickey Mantle, the legendary center fielder for the New York Yankees, died August 14, 1995, at the age of 63, from complications of alcoholism. During his heyday as a baseball star, his heavy drinking was discreetly hidden from adoring fans. It wasn't until well after his retirement from baseball that Mantle checked himself into a treatment clinic and admitted publicly that he had been severely dependent on alcohol for most of his life. He sought professional treatment only after doctors warned Mantle that his drinking habits had almost destroyed his liver. Despite heroic attempts to save Mantle's life with a liver transplant in June of the same year, a cancer from the diseased liver spread rapidly, resulting in death only 2 months later.

Mickey Mantle

Sources: Knight-Ridder/Tribune News Service, 14 August 1995, p. 814K6829; "Mickey Mantle" (24 April 2004). Available fixedreference.org/en/20040424/wikipedia/Mickey_Mantle.

males. For females, as few as two drinks of hard liquor per day several days in a row can produce the same condition. After several days of abstaining from alcohol, the liver returns to normal.

The second stage develops as the fat cells continue to multiply. Generally, irritation and swelling that result from continued alcohol intake cause **alcoholic hepatitis**. At this stage, chronic inflammation sets in and can be fatal. This second stage is also reversible if the intake of alcohol ceases.

Unlike stages 1 and 2, stage 3 is not reversible. Scars begin to form on the liver tissue during this stage. These scars are fibrous, and they cause hardening of the liver as functional tissue shrinks and deteriorates. This condition of the liver is known as **cirrhosis** and often is fatal. (See "Case in Point," Mickey Mantle Dies from Complications of Alcoholism.)

The liver damage caused by heavy alcohol consumption can cause problems when taking drugs that affect liver function. For example, the over-the-counter analgesic acetaminophen (Tylenol) can have a deleterious effect on the liver, especially when the function of this organ has already been compromised by alcohol (Ramack 2004).

■ Digestive System

The digestive system consists of gastrointestinal structures involved in processing and digesting food and liquids; it includes the mouth, pharynx, esophagus, stomach, and small and large intestines. As alcohol travels through the digestive system, it irritates tissue and can even damage the tissue lining as it causes acid imbalances, inflammation, and acute gastric distress. Often, the result is *gastritis* (an inflamed stomach) and heartburn. The more frequently consumption takes place, the greater the irritation. One out of three heavy drinkers suffers from chronic gastritis. Furthermore, the heavy drinker has double the probability of developing cancer of the mouth and esophagus because alcohol passes these two organs on the way to the stomach.

Prolonged heavy use of alcohol may cause ulcers, hiatal hernia, and cancers throughout the digestive tract. The likelihood of cancers in the mouth, throat, and stomach dramatically increases (15 times) if the person is also a heavy smoker (Lee et al. 2005). The pancreas is another organ associated with the digestive system that can be

KEY TERMS

alcoholic hepatitis
the second stage of alcohol-induced liver disease in which chronic inflammation occurs; reversible if alcoholic consumption ceases

cirrhosis
scarring of the liver and formation of fibrous tissues; results from alcohol abuse; irreversible

damaged by heavy alcohol consumption. Alcohol can cause pancreatitis, pancreatic cirrhosis, and alcoholic diabetes (Fleming et al. 2006).

■ Blood

High concentrations of alcohol diminish the effective functioning of the *hematopoietic* (blood-building) system. They decrease production of red blood cells, white blood cells, and platelets. Problems with clotting and immunity to infection are not uncommon among alcohol abusers. Often, the result is lowered resistance to disease. Heavy drinking appears to affect the bone marrow, where various blood cells are formed. The suppression of the bone marrow can contribute to anemia, in which red blood cell production cannot keep pace with the need for those cells. Heavy drinkers are also likely to develop alcoholic bleeding disorders because they have too few platelets to form clots (Fleming et al. 2006).

■ Cardiovascular System

The effects of ethanol on the cardiovascular system have been extensively studied, but much remains unknown. Ethanol causes dilation of blood vessels, especially in the skin. This effect accounts for the flushing and sensation of warmth associated with alcohol consumption.

The long-term effects of alcohol on the cardiovascular system are dose dependent. Some studies have suggested that regular light to moderate drinking (two or fewer glasses of wine per day) actually reduces the incidence of heart diseases such as heart attacks, strokes, and high blood pressure by 20% to 40% in some populations. The type of alcoholic beverage consumed does not appear to be important as long as the quantity of alcohol consumed is moderate (1–2.5 ounces per day; "Your Health" 1999). Although the precise explanation for this coronary benefit is not known, it appears to be related to the effects of moderate alcohol doses in relieving stress and increasing the blood concentration of high-density lipoproteins (HDL) (Bakalar 2006). HDL is a molecular complex used to transport fat through the bloodstream, and its levels are negatively correlated with cardiovascular disease. In addition, moderate levels of alcohol decrease the formation of blood clots that can plug arteries and deprive tissues of essential oxygen and nutrients. The populations most likely to benefit from the protective properties of moderate levels of alcohol are men older than 50 years of age and postmenopausal women. Moderate drinking on a daily average is approximately one drink (e.g., a glass of wine) for women and two drinks for men. Drinking more than this amount can result in increased health risks that more than offset the benefits (Biotech Week 2004).

The cardiovascular protective effect of moderate drinking may be at least partially race specific. A recent report suggests that alcohol use that prevents cardiovascular disease in white men may actually increase heart disease in black men (Fuchs 2004).

Because of the potential for developing addiction to alcohol and the increased health risk with heavy drinking, most doctors would not encourage a nondrinker to start to consume alcohol in an attempt to gain a health benefit. In addition, even in those populations most likely to benefit from moderate alcohol consumption, the benefit is likely to disappear in persons who already have healthy lifestyles that include low-fat diets, stress and weight management techniques, and regular exercise ("Your Health" 1999). In general, most clinicians believe that alcohol use kills more people (approximately 100,000/year) than it saves, and those it kills tend to be younger (Hanson and Li 2003; Special Report 1997).

Chronic intense use of alcohol changes the composition of heart muscle by replacing it with fat and fiber, resulting in a heart muscle that becomes enlarged and flabby. Congestive heart failure from **alcoholic cardiomyopathy** often occurs when heart muscle is replaced by fat and fiber. Other results of alcohol abuse that affect the heart are irregular heartbeat or *arrhythmia*, high blood pressure, and stroke. A common example of damage is "holiday heart," so called because people drinking heavily over a weekend turn up in the emergency room with a dangerously irregular heartbeat. Chronic excessive use of alcohol by people with arrhythmia causes congestive heart failure. Malnutrition and vitamin deficiencies associated with prolonged heavy drinking also contribute to cardiac abnormalities (Fairfield and Fletcher 2002; Mozes 2007).

KEY TERMS

alcoholic cardiomyopathy
congestive heart failure due to the replacement of heart muscle with fat and fiber

■ Sexual Organs

Although alcohol lowers social inhibition, its use interferes with sexual functioning. As Shakespeare said in *Macbeth*, alcohol "provokes desire, but it takes away the performance." Continued alcohol use causes *prostatitis*, which is an inflammation of the prostate gland. This condition directly interferes with a man's ability to maintain an adequate erection during sexual stimulation. Another frequent symptom of alcohol abuse is atrophy of the testicles, which results in lowered sperm count and diminished hormones in the blood (Dhawan and Sharma 2002).

■ Endocrine System

As mentioned in Chapter 4, endocrine glands release hormones into the bloodstream. The hormones function as messengers that directly affect cell and tissue function throughout the body. Alcohol abuse alters endocrine functions by influencing the production and release of hormones, and affects endocrine regulating systems in the hypothalamus, pituitary, and gonads. Because of alcohol abuse, levels of *testosterone* (the male sex hormone) may decline, resulting in sexual impotence, breast enlargement, and loss of body hair in men. Women experience menstrual delays, ovarian abnormalities, and infertility (Fleming et al. 2006).

■ Kidneys

Frequent abuse of alcohol can severely damage the kidneys. The resulting decrease in kidney function diminishes this organ's ability to process blood and properly form urine and can result in serious metabolic problems. Another consequence of impaired kidney function in alcoholics is that they tend to experience more urinary tract infections than do nondrinkers or moderate drinkers (Fleming et al. 2006; NIAAA 1997).

■ Mental Disorders and Damage to the Brain

Long-term heavy drinking can severely affect memory, judgment, and learning ability (Fleming et al. 2006). **Wernicke-Korsakoff's syndrome** is a characteristic psychotic condition caused by alcohol use and the associated nutritional and vitamin deficiencies. Patients who are brain-damaged cannot remember recent events and compensate for their memory loss with *confabulation* (making up fictitious events that even the patient accepts as fact).

■ The Fetus

In pregnant women, alcohol easily crosses the placenta and often damages the fetus in cases of moderate to excessive drinking. It can also cause spontaneous abortion due to its toxic actions. Another tragic consequence of high alcohol consumption during pregnancy is **fetal alcohol syndrome (FAS)**, which is characterized by facial deformities, growth deficiency, mental retarda-

Fetal alcohol syndrome is characterized by facial deformities, as well as growth deficiency and mental retardation.

KEY TERMS

Wernicke-Korsakoff's syndrome
psychotic condition connected with heavy alcohol use and associated vitamin deficiencies

fetal alcohol syndrome (FAS)
a condition affecting children born to alcohol-consuming mothers that is characterized by facial deformities, growth deficiency, and mental retardation

tion, and joint and limb abnormalities (Fleming et al. 2006). The growth deficiency occurs in embryonic development, and the child usually does not catch up after birth. The mild to moderate mental retardation does not appear to lessen with time, apparently because the growth impairment affects the functional development of the brain as well.

The severity of FAS appears to be dose related: The more the mother drinks, the more severe the fetal damage. A safe lower level of alcohol consumption has not been established for pregnant women (Larroque and Kaminski 1998). Birthweight decrements have been found at levels corresponding to about two drinks per day, on average. Clinical studies have established that alcohol itself clearly causes the syndrome; it is not related to the effects of smoking, maternal age, parity (number of children a woman has borne), social class, or poor nutrition. One study reports that 30–45% of women who are moderate to heavy alcohol consumers will give birth to a child with FAS (*Life Science Weekly* 2004). In addition, a recent study demonstrated that just a few episodes of heavy drinking by a pregnant woman increases the likelihood that the offspring will also abuse alcohol later in life (*Psychology Today* 2007).

Gender Differences

Research has demonstrated that there are important pharmacological differences in how males and females respond to the consumption of alcohol. For example, in women heavy alcohol use will cause accelerated damage to the brain, liver, heart, and muscles compared to male users (Leigh, 2007). These differences persist even after adjusting for the quantity of alcohol according to the differences in gender size. It is thought that at least part of the greater sensitivity of women to the effects of this drug is due to their tendency to metabolize alcohol more slowly than their male counterparts (Baraona et al. 2001) or may be due to a higher percentage of body fat in females leading to greater retention of the drug (Leigh 2007). In addition, problems associated with alcohol abuse might express differently in men and women, with females more likely to experience depression, while men are more likely to binge drink and engage in fighting (Norton 2007). Other differences relate to their response to treatment. Gender differences in treatment outcomes likely reflect factors such as women's tendency to

have a later onset of alcohol use and associated problems, a more positive family history, more marital disruption (Gomberg 2003), and more associated psychiatric disorders, such as depression, anxiety, and stress (*Women's Health Weekly* 2003). Although the reasons for these differences are unclear, they must be considered as researchers and clinicians try to elucidate the causes, consequences, and most effective treatments for alcoholism.

Malnutrition

As previously mentioned, malnutrition is a frequent and extremely serious consequence of severe alcoholism that tends to occur most often in less affluent alcoholics. It has been suggested that malnutrition exaggerates the damage that alcohol causes to the body's organs, especially the liver (Lieberman 2003). Malnutrition apparently arises so frequently in this population because many alcoholics find it difficult to eat a balanced diet with adequate caloric intake. Many alcoholics consume between 300 and 1000 kilocalories per day (2000 kilocalories per day is considered normal for an average man). In addition, most of the calories consumed by alcoholics come from alcohol, which contains 7 kilocalories/gram (less than fat, which contains 9 kilocalories/gram). The malnutrition problem is aggravated because alcohol's calories are empty — that is, alcohol does not contain other nutrients such as vitamins, minerals, protein, or fat (Pociluyko 2003). Because alcoholics may be deriving 50% or more of their usual caloric intake from alcoholic beverages, profound deficiencies in important nutrients result, leading to serious degeneration of health.

Discussion Questions

1. What evidence indicates that alcohol is a drug like marijuana, cocaine, or heroin?

2. Explain how alcohol is manufactured.

3. In the Western world, alcohol use has a long history. List and discuss some of these historical events, and describe how they affect present attitudes.

4. Explain how the effect of alcohol on brain function compares to that caused by other CNS depressants.

5. Explain how alcohol affects the mouth, stomach, small intestine, brain, liver, and bloodstream.

6. List at least five factors that affect the absorption rate of alcohol in the bloodstream.

7. Explain why alcohol is commonly consumed together with other drugs.

8. List three short-term effects of alcohol abuse.

9. Explain why moderate use of ethanol may prevent heart attacks.

10. Describe the symptoms and causes of a hangover.

11. What characterizes FAS?

12. How does gender affect responses to alcohol?

13. Why is malnutrition a common occurrence in alcoholics, and what are its consequences?

Summary

1 Alcohol is considered a drug because it is a CNS depressant, and it affects both mental and physiological functioning.

2 Three types of poisonous alcohols are methyl alcohol, made from wood products; ethylene glycol, used as antifreeze; and isopropyl alcohol, used as an antiseptic. A fourth type, ethanol, is the alcohol used for drinking purposes.

3 The blood alcohol level produced depends on the presence of food in the stomach, the rate of alcohol consumption, the concentration of alcohol, and the drinker's body composition.

4 Alcohol depresses CNS activity at all doses. Low to moderate doses of alcohol interfere with motor activities, reflexes, and coordination. In moderate quantities, alcohol slightly increases heart rate; slightly dilates blood vessels in the arms, legs, and skin; and moderately lowers blood pressure. It stimulates appetite, increases production of gastric secretions, and at higher doses markedly stimulates urine output. The CNS depression incapacitates the individual, causing difficulty in walking, talking, and thinking.

5 Alcohol is commonly used in combination with other drugs (1) to enhance reinforcing properties; (2) to reduce the amount of expensive or hard-to-get drug required for an effect; (3) to reduce unpleasant side effects; or (4) because a predisposition for use of alcohol and other drugs exists.

6 Moderate daily alcohol use can reduce cardiovascular diseases in men older than 50 years of age and in postmenopausal women.

7 Long-term heavy alcohol use directly causes serious damage to nearly every organ and function of the body.

8 Prolonged heavy drinking causes various types of muscle disease and tremors. Heavy alcohol consumption causes irregular heartbeat. Heavy drinking over many years results in serious mental disorders and permanent, irreversible damage to the brain and peripheral nervous system. Memory, judgment, and learning ability can deteriorate severely.

9 Women who are alcoholics or who drink heavily during pregnancy have a higher rate of spontaneous abortions. Infants born to drinking mothers have a high probability of being afflicted with FAS. These children have characteristic patterns of facial deformities, growth deficiency, joint and limb irregularities, and mental retardation.

10 Alcohol has pervasive effects on the major organs and fluids of the body. Every part of the brain and nervous system is affected and can be damaged by alcohol. Among alcoholics, liver disorders include alcoholic fatty liver, alcoholic hepatitis, and cirrhosis. Alcohol also irritates tissue and damages the digestive system. Heavy use of alcohol seriously affects the blood, heart, sexual organs, endocrine system, and kidneys.

11 Malnutrition is a common occurrence in severe alcoholism. It is the result of decreased caloric intake by alcoholics and the diminished consumption of essential nutrients due to the nutritional deficiency of alcoholic beverages.

References

Achord, J. L. "Alcohol and the Liver." *Scientific American and Medicine* 2 (1995): 16–25.

American Psychiatric Association (APA). *Diagnostic and Statistical Manual of Mental Disorders,* 4th ed., revised (*DSM-IV-TR*). Washington, DC: American Psychiatric Association, 2000.

Bakalar, N. "For Heart Health, Liquor Is Quicker for Women and Slower for Men." *The New York Times* (June 6, 2006): D-5.

Baraona, E., C. Abittan, K. Dohmen, M. Moretti, G. Pazzote, Z. Chayes, C. Schaefer, and C. Lieber. "Gender Differences in Pharmacokinetics of Alcohol." *Alcohol Clinical Experimental Research* 25 (2001): 502–507.

Basavarajappa, B. "The Endocannabinoid Signaling System: A Potential Target for Next Generation Therapeutics for Alcoholism." *Minireview of Medicinal Chemistry* 7 (2007): 769–779.

Bertolote, J., A. Fleishmann, D. DeLeo, and D. Wasserman. "Psychiatric Diagnoses and Suicide: Revisiting the Evidence." *Crisis* 25 (2004): 147–155.

Biotech Week. "Excess Drinking Shortens Life by 30 Years." *Morbidity and Mortality Weekly Report.* 53 (20 October 2004): 866–870.

CBS News. "More Teens Are Binge Drinking." *CBS Evening News* (January 2, 2007). Available http://www.cbsnews.com/stories/2007/01/02/eveningnews/main2324726.shtml.

Center on Alcohol Marketing and Youth. "Drops in the Bucket: Alcohol Industry 'Responsibility' Advertising on Television in 2001." *Georgetown University* (February 3, 2003): 1, 2.

Center on Alcohol Marketing and Youth at Georgetown University. "Drowned Out." (September 25, 2007). Available http://camy.org/research/responsibility2007/.

"Centerpiece: Alcohol in Perspective." *Wellness Letter* 9 (February 1993): 4–6.

Dhawan, K., and A. Sharma. "Prevention of Chronic Alcohol and Nicotine-Induced Azospermia, Sterility and Decreased Libido, by a Novel Tri-substituted Benzoflavone Moiety." *Life Science* 71 (2002): 3059–3069.

Fairfield, K., and R. Fletcher. "Vitamins for Chronic Disease Prevention in Adults: Scientific Review." *Journal of the American Medical Association* 288 (2002): 1720.

Fleming, M., S. Mihic, and R. Harris. "Ethanol." In *The Pharmacological Basis of Therapeutics,* 10th ed., edited by J. Hardman and L. Limbird, 429–446. New York: McGraw-Hill, 2001.

Fleming, M., S. Mihic, and R. Harris. "Ethanol." In *The Pharmacological Basis of Therapeutics,* 11th ed., edited by L. Brunton, J. Lazo, and K. Parker, 591–606. New York: McGraw-Hill, 2006.

Fuchs, F. "Association Between Alcoholic Beverage Consumption and Incidence of Coronary Heart Disease in Whites and Blacks — The Atherosclerosis Risk in Communities Studies." *American Journal of Epidemiology* 160 (2004): 466–474.

Gomberg, E. "Treatment for Alcohol-Related Problems: Special Populations: Research Opportunities." *Recent Developments in Alcoholism* 16 (2003): 313–333.

Greenfield, S. "Women and Alcohol Use Disorders." *Harvard Review Psychiatry* 10 (2002): 76–85.

Hanson, G. R., and T. K. Li. "Public Health Implications of Excessive Alcohol Consumption." *Journal of the American Medical Association* 289 (2003): 1031, 1032.

Hettema, J., L. Corey, and K. Kendler. "A Multivariate Genetic Analysis of the Use of Tobacco, Alcohol and Caffeine in a Population Sample of Male and Female Twins." *Drug and Alcohol Dependency* 57 (1999): 9–78.

Hitti, M. "Does Smoking Make You Drink More?" *WebMD* (July 24, 2006). Available http://www.medscape.com/viewarticle/541445.

Johnston, L. "Monitoring the Future 2006." (2007). Available www.monitoringthefuture.org/pubs/monographs/vol1_2006.pdf.

Knight-Ridder/Tribune News Service, 14 August 1995, p. 814K6829.

Larroque, B., and M. Kaminski. "Prenatal Alcohol Exposure and Development at Preschool Age: Main Results of a French Study." *Alcoholism: Clinical and Experimental Research* 22 (1998): 295–303.

Lee, C., J. Lee, D. Wu, H. Hsu, E. Kao, H. Huang, et al. "Independent and Combined Effects of Alcohol Intake, Tobacco Smoking and Betel Quid Chewing on the Risk of Esophageal Cancer in Taiwan." *International Journal of Cancer* 113 (2005): 475–482.

Leigh, S. "A Woman's Brain Hit Harder by Alcohol Abuse; Damage Occurs Faster and with Fewer Drinks, Study Finds." *Health Day* (April 27, 2007). Available http://www.washingtonpost.com/wp-dyn/content/article/2007/04/27/AR2007042701345.html.

Lieberman, C. "Relationship Between Nutrition, Alcohol Use, and Liver Disease." *Alcohol Research and Health* 27 (2003): 220–231.

Life Science Weekly. "Fetal Alcohol Syndrome Is Still a Threat, Says Publication." (28 September 2004). Available http://www.newsrx.com/article.php?articleID=88877.

Liquori, A., C. Gatto, and D. Jarrett. "Separate and Combined Effects of Marijuana and Alcohol on Mood, Equilibrium and Simulated Driving." *Psychopharmacology* 163 (2002): 399–405.

Mann, K., D. Herman, and A. Heinz. "One Hundred Years of Alcoholism: The Twentieth Century." *Alcohol and Alcoholism* 35 (2000): 10–15.

Marin Institute Alcohol Policy. "Health Care Costs of Alcohol." (2007). Available http://www.marininstitute.org/alcohol_policy/health_care_costs.htm.

Mozes, A. "Heavy Drinking in College May Harm Heart; But Moderate Amounts of Alcohol Could Be Healthy, Study Shows." *HealthScout* (April 19, 2007). Available http://www.healthcentral.com/heart-disease/news-37232-31.htm.

National Center on Addiction and Substance Abuse at Columbia University. "Wasting the Best and the Brightest." *CASA Press Release* (March 15, 2007). Available www.casacolumbia.org/absolutenm/templates/PressReleases.aspx?articleid=477&zoneid=65.

National Institute on Alcohol Abuse and Alcoholism (NIAAA). "Changing the Culture of Campus." *Alcohol Alert* 58 (October 2002): 1.

National Institute on Alcohol Abuse and Alcoholism (NIAAA). Publication 21 (1997). Available http://pubs.niaaa.nih.gov/publications/arh21-1/toc21-1.htm.

National Institute on Alcohol Abuse and Alcoholism (NIAAA). *8th Special Report to Congress on Alcohol and Health.* (September 1993): 121.

National Institute on Alcohol Abuse and Alcoholism (NIAAA). "Harmful Interactions: Mixing Alcohol with Medicines." (2007). Available http://pubs.niaaa.nih.gov/publications/medicine/medicine.htm.

National Institute on Alcohol Abuse and Alcoholism (NIAAA). (2007). "FAQs on Alcohol Abuse and Alcoholism." Available http://www.niaaa.nih.gov/FAQs/General-English/.

Norton, A. "Men and Women Show Alcohol Problems Differently." *Reuters Health* (April 24, 2007). Available http://www.reuters.com/article/healthNews/idUSLAU376770 20070423.

Office of Applied Studies. "2006 National Survey on Drug Use & Health: National Results." SAMHSA (2007). Available http://www.oas.samhsa.gov/p0000016.htm.

Preidt, R. "Alcohol Damage Continues After Drinking Stops." *Health Scout* (April 17, 2003). Available http://thestressoflife.com/alcohol_damage_continues_after_d.htm.

Psychology Today. "Pregnant and Under the Influence." (May 1, 2007). Available http://psychologytoday.com/articles/pto-2691.html.

Quindien, A. "America's Most Pervasive Drug Problem Is the Drug That Pretends It Isn't." *Salt Lake Tribune* (20 April 2000): A11.

Ramack, B. "Acetaminophen Misconceptions." *Hepatology* 40 (2004): 10–15.

Ratsma, J., O. van der Stelt, and W. Gunning. "Neurochemical Markers of Alcoholism Vulnerability." *Alcohol and Alcoholism* 37 (2002): 522–533.

Reinberg, S. "Drinking Shrinks the Brain." *HealthScout* (May 2, 2007). Available http://www.healthscout.com/template.asp?page=newsdetail&ap=1&id=604213.

Royce, J. E. *Alcohol Problems and Alcoholism: A Comprehensive Survey.* New York: Free Press, 1989.

Special Report. "Alcohol: Weighing the Benefits and Risks for You." *U.C. Berkeley Wellness Letter* 13 (August 1997): 4–5.

Wiese, J., M. Shlipak, and W. Browner. "The Alcohol Hangover," *Annals of Internal Medicine* 134 (2000): 533, 534.

Williams, S. "Medications for Treating Alcohol Dependence." *American Family Physician* 72 (2005): 1775–1780.

Women's Health Weekly. "Female Drinkers and Drug Users Tend to Have More Depressive Disorders." (March 20, 2003): 1.

Worman, H. "Alcoholic Liver Disease." Columbia University (2000). Available http://cpmcnet.columbia.edu/dept/gi/alcohol.html.

"Your Health: Alcohol: The Whole Truth, Seven Half-Truths About Drinking, Exposed." *Consumer Reports* 64 (December 1999): 60–61.

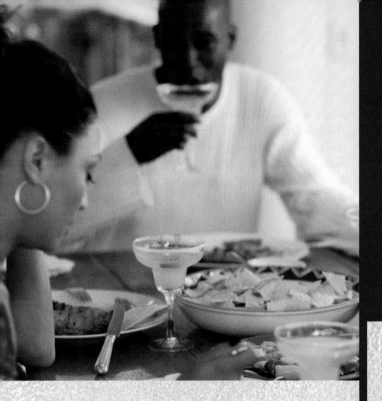

CHAPTER 8

Alcohol: Behavioral Effects

Learning Objectives

On completing this chapter you will be able to:

◎ Cite some of the latest statistics on the use of alcohol.

◎ Cite the countries with the highest and lowest rates of alcohol consumption.

◎ Discuss major ways alcohol is costly to our society.

◎ Discuss the main events of the temperance movement and the Prohibition era.

◎ Define alcoholism and identify the general characteristics of an alcoholic.

◎ Cite some of the cultural differences for defining problem drinkers.

◎ Explain how culture influences the views about alcohol.

◎ List four cultural factors that affect our views about consuming alcohol.

◎ List four findings about alcohol consumption and college students.

◎ Provide at least three reasons why the effects of alcohol consumption differ in women and men.

◎ Understand the differences between codependency and enabling behaviors.

◎ List two major factors that alcohol treatment must consider.

Did You Know?

○ Seventy-seven percent of the U.S. population believe that alcohol creates the most problems in our society.

○ Americans consumed twice as much alcohol in 1830 as they do now.

○ Of all U.S. adult minority groups, Asian Americans have the highest rate of abstinence, the lowest rate of heavy drinking, and the lowest level of drinking-related problems.

○ People have complained about fraternity drinking since 1840.

○ Most of the economic costs of alcohol and drug problems fall on taxpayers, most of whom do not abuse alcohol and drugs.

○ From 8th to 12th grades, the percentage of students using alcohol doubles to approximately 60%.

○ On most weekend nights throughout the United States, 70% of all fatal single-vehicle crashes involve a driver who is legally intoxicated.

○ Less affluent people drink less than more affluent individuals.

 Drugs and Society Online is a great source for additional drugs and society information for both students and instructors.
Visit **http://drugsandsociety.jbpub.com** to find a variety of useful tools for learning, thinking, and teaching.

Introduction

As a clerk here at this store, I see all kinds of people buying alcohol. Sometimes, you can tell who more than likely have big problems with alcohol by just looking at them. One man comes in about three times a week, usually at night. He buys fifths, half gallons, and pints of vodka. He is usually well dressed and works at some office job somewhere here in town. I know someone who knows him, and a lady friend of his says that if you call him up after 10 at night, his speech is slurred, and she knows for a fact that he keeps pints under his car seat while driving during the day. This lady friend lives right next door to him and she sees him going to and from work and taking swigs from his stash so-to-speak. *(From Venturelli's research files, interview with a 50-year-old female liquor store clerk in a small Midwestern town, August 9, 1999.)*

I even knew a professor who would buy pints of whiskey as soon as we would open in the morning. He would drive off and go to your university [referring to the author's university] to teach. He was a heck of a nice fella, always ready with a joke and very pleasant to talk to, but I knew he had a problem with this stuff. *(From Venturelli's research files, interview with a 50-year-old female liquor store clerk in a small Midwestern town, August 9, 1999.)* [Update: This professor with an alleged drinking problem has changed jobs and is no longer at this university.]

I vividly recall at age 10 seeing at least three or four middle-aged men arrive at my father's tavern as soon as the doors were opened at 8:00 A.M. on most mornings, desperately looking for the morning's first drink of alcohol. I recall my dad would crack a raw egg into an 8-ounce glass. Draft beer and the raw egg filled the glass half full. The reason for the raw egg was to get some breakfast protein and the reason for the half full glass of beer was because their hands were very shaky and they had to steady the drink to their mouths. Immediately following what my dad referred to as a "full" breakfast were at least several double shots of Jim Beam whiskey. These alcoholic customers had to have the drinks so that they could feel "normal" for the rest of the day. Some would even be dressed in formal attire ready to go off to their office jobs. *(Venturelli, personal observation, May 18, 2000.)*

Alcohol Consumption in the United States

Similar to nearly all societies past and present, alcohol has always been a part of American society. The preceding quotes illustrate how an individual can consume an excessive amount of a psychoactive and addictive substance without necessarily coming to the attention of anyone except perhaps a neighbor, a lone liquor store employee, or even a bar owner and his young son. Furthermore, this same depressant chemical is often not perceived as a drug by many Americans. It is considered more of a social substance, something that is "always" found at social gatherings and is even expected at such gatherings.

Consider these findings from the National Household Survey on Drug Abuse in 2005 (Substance Abuse and Mental Health Services Administration [SAMHSA] 2006):

- Slightly more than half of American age 12 or older reported being **current drinkers** of alcohol in the 2005 survey (51.8%). This translates to an estimated 126 million people, which is higher than the 2004 estimate of 121 million people (50.3%).
- More than one fifth (22.7%) of persons age 12 or older participated in **binge drinking** at least once in the 30 days prior to the survey in 2005. This translates to about 55 million people, comparable with the estimates reported since 2002.
- In 2005, heavy drinking (**heavy use**) was reported by 6.6% of the population ages 12 or older, or 16 million people. This percentage is similar to the rates of heavy drinking in 2002 (6.7%), 2003 (6.8%), and 2004 (6.9%).

KEY TERMS

current alcohol use (current drinkers)
at least one drink in the past 30 days; can include binge and heavy use

binge use (binge drinking)
five or more drinks on the same occasion (i.e., at the same time or within a couple of hours of each other) on at least 1 day in the past 30 days; includes heavy use

heavy use (heavy drinkers)
five or more drinks on the same occasion on each of 5 or more days in the past 30 days

- In 2005, rates of current alcohol use were 4.2% among persons ages 12 or 13, 15.1% of persons ages 14 or 15, 30.1% of 16- or 17-year-olds, 51.1% of those ages 18 to 20, and 67.4% of 21- to 25-year-olds (Figure 8.1). Among older age groups, the prevalence of alcohol use decreased with increasing age, from 63.7% among 26- to 29-year-olds to 47.5% among 60- to 64-year-olds and 40% among people age 65 or older.
- The rates of binge alcohol use in 2005 peaked at ages 21 to 23 (49.9% at age 21, 46.6% at age 22, and 47.7% at age 23), then decreased beyond young adulthood from 32.9% of 26- to 34-year-olds to 18.3% of persons age 35 or older.
- The rate of binge drinking was 41.9% for young adults ages 18 to 25. Heavy alcohol use was reported by 15.3% of persons ages 18 to 25. These rates are similar to the rates in 2002, 2003, and 2004.

Encouraging findings also indicate that the rate of current alcohol use among youth ages 12 to 17 *declined* from 17.6% in 2004 to 16.5% in 2005. Youth binge drinking also *declined* during that period, from 11.1% to 9.9%, but heavy drinking *did not change significantly* (2.7% in 2004 and 2.4% in 2005).

Once again, these trends indicate that despite all the laws, increased campaigns and advertisements against drug and alcohol abuse, and continually increasing enforcement expenditures since 1994, the number of underage drinkers has not changed much (SAMHSA 2006).

Current Statistics and Trends in Alcohol Consumption

A recent Gallup Poll indicated that 64% of the adult population drinks alcohol, whereas 26% reported excessive alcohol consumption patterns (Gallup Poll 2007). In an earlier Gallup Poll, 35% of the population reported that drinking alcohol has caused family problems, and 77% of those questioned indicated that in comparison to all other drug problems, alcohol creates the most family problems in our society (Newport 2000).

In looking at more detailed figures about consumption patterns, we find the following (summarized largely from Newport 2000, unless otherwise designated):

- Among persons age 12 or older, whites in 2005 were more likely than other racial/ethnic

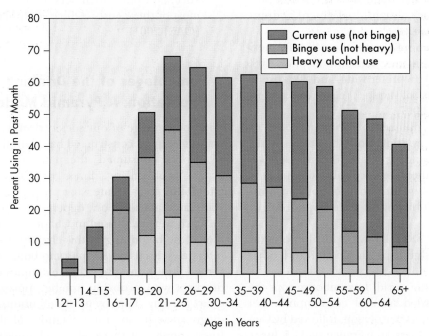

FIGURE 8.1

Current, binge, and heavy alcohol use among persons aged 12 or older, by age.

....

Source: Substance Abuse and Mental Health Services Administration (SAMHSA). *Results from the 2005 National Survey on Drug Use and Health: National Findings.* Rockville, MD: Office of Applied Studies, 2006.

groups to report current use of alcohol (56.5%). The rates were 47.3% for persons reporting two or more races, 42.6% for Hispanics, 42.4% for American Indians or Alaska Natives, 40.8% for blacks, 38.1% for Asians, and 37.3% for native Hawaiians or other Pacific Islanders (SAMHSA 2006).

- Gallup has not found much change in drinking patterns among the general public. Currently 64% report themselves as being current drinkers. (In 1939 the average was 63%.) In regard to regular drinking, it was reported to be 4.8 alcoholic beverages in the past week. In 2001, the average was below four drinks (Jones 2007).
- Sixty percent of men prefer to drink beer, whereas women prefer wine.
- As men age, their preference for beer steadily decreases.
- Overall, as both men and women age, they say wine is their favorite alcoholic beverage.
- Lower-income drinkers prefer beer, whereas higher-income drinkers prefer wine.
- The highest rate of family drinking problems is among 18- to 29-year-olds.
- Currently, 42% of the population report family disputes caused by excessive drinking; 17% reported this problem in 1996.
- Sixty-four percent claim they drink and 36% report that they abstain. In 1999, 61% drank and 39% abstained.
- Gallup also reports that of the 64% of Americans who claim they consume alcohol, 40% prefer beer, 34% prefer wine, and 22% prefer harder forms of liquor (e.g., vodka, gin, scotch; Jones 2007).
- Of the total number of drinkers, 24% reported that they drink more than they should.
- Estimated spending for healthcare services was $18.8 billion for alcohol problems and medical consequences of alcohol consumption and $9.9 billion for other types of drug problems.
- An estimated $82 billion was lost in potential productivity due to both alcohol and other drug abuse.
- Throughout the world, Luxembourg tops the list for recorded alcohol consumption per year, at 12.6 liters per person, followed by Germany at 12.1 liters and France at 11.5 liters. The lowest levels are found in Turkey, Krygyzstan, Turkmenistan, Israel, and Armenia, which all have levels below 3 liters per person.

- When illegal imports and illicit home production of alcohol are taken into account, several countries exceed the amount of alcohol consumed in Luxembourg, Germany, and France. Latvia leads at 16 to 20 liters per person, followed by Slovenia at 18 liters per person, and in descending order Estonia, Russia, Lithuania, Macedonia, and Greece (Alcohol Concern 2000).
- In contrast to common assumptions, the higher the level of education attained, the higher the likelihood of current alcohol use. College graduates registered an average of 93% alcohol use, those with some college 91%, high school graduates 86%, and those with less than a high school degree 76% (SAMHSA 1999b).
- Drinking is commonly believed to be associated with poverty, yet according to a Gallup Poll, the people most likely to drink have higher incomes, are younger than age 65, do not attend church, live in regions of the United States other than the South, and are more likely to identify themselves as liberals.
- Research shows that much of the economic burden of alcohol and drug problems falls on the population of taxpayers who do not abuse alcohol and drugs. Government, private insurance, and other members of households bear most of these costs (Office of Applied Studies [OAS] 2001).

■ Percentages of the Drinking Population: A Pyramid Model

What percentage of our society drinks alcohol? A pyramid can be constructed based on the amount of alcohol consumed, the pattern of drinking, or the "problem" or "illness" dimension (e.g., by attempting to calculate what proportion of Americans are "abusers" or "dependent"; the criteria for each were discussed in Chapter 7). For example, at the beginning of this chapter, the first two interviews discussed people who bought and consumed liquor and are prime examples of alcohol drinkers who probably imbibe approximately 1 quart per day. This, by most definitions, is a clear diagnostic criterion for a diagnosis of alcoholism. Interestingly, all three of the chapter's opening examples indicate that the alcohol drinkers are apparently functional, or at least they manage to create this impression.

The pyramid shown in Figure 8.2 has a base of 35% who are **teetotalers**, then a layer of about 13% who occasionally drink, and a top 52% who drink fairly regularly. Some 11 million Americans, or 5.5% of Americans age 12 or older, had five or more drinks on the same occasion at least five different days in the past month, which is one possible definition of heavy drinking. Different definitions of what constitutes heavy drinking exist. Thus, if we define *heavy drinking* differently — for example, as more than two drinks per day — we come up with a much larger slice of the pyramid — three times as large.

Dual Problems: Underage and Adult Drinking

As we saw in Figure 8.1, concerning age, alcohol consumption does not have any boundaries. Although since 1988, all states have had a legal drinking age of 21, a high percentage of the underage population drinks alcohol.

Overall, we can see the larger picture regarding the percentages of persons age 12 or older reporting past-month alcohol use, by level of use and age group in 2005, by considering the following data:

Underage Alcohol Use (SAMHSA 2006)

1. In 2005, about 10.8 million persons ages 12 to 20 (28.2% of this age group) reported drinking alcohol in the past month. Nearly 7.2 million (18.8%) were binge drinkers, and 2.3 million (6.0%) were heavy drinkers. These figures have remained essentially the same since the 2002 survey.
2. More males than females ages 12 to 20 reported current alcohol use (28.9% vs. 27.5%, respectively), binge drinking (21.3% vs. 16.1%), and heavy drinking (7.6% vs 4.3%) in 2005.
3. Across geographic regions in 2005, underage current alcohol use rates were higher in the Northeast (31.4%) and Midwest (31%) than in the South (26.4%) and West (26%). This pattern has remained essentially the same since 2002.
4. Among persons ages 12 to 20, past-month alcohol use rates were 12% among Native Hawaiians or other Pacific Islanders, 15.5% among Asians, 19.0% among blacks, 21.7% among American Indians or Alaska Natives, 24% among those reporting two or more races, 25.9% among Hispanics, and 32.3% among whites.

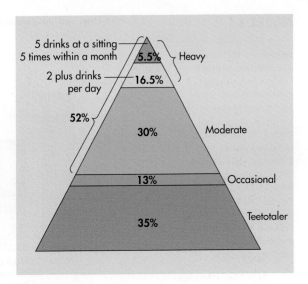

FIGURE 8.2
Broad distribution of drinking behaviors.

Alcohol Use: Age 12 or Older by Ethnicity and Race (SAMHSA 2006)

5. Among persons age 12 or older, whites in 2005 were more likely than other racial/ethnic groups to report current use of alcohol (56.5%); see Figure 8.3A. The rates were 47.3% for persons reporting two or more races, 42.6% for Hispanics, 42.4% for American Indians or Alaska Natives, 40.8% for blacks, 38.1% for Asians, and 37.3 percent for Native Hawaiians or other Pacific Islanders.
6. Figure 8.3A also shows that the rate of binge alcohol use was lowest among Asians (12.7%). Rates for other racial/ethnic groups were 20.3% for blacks, 20.8% for persons reporting two or more races, 23.4% for whites, 23.7% for Hispanics, 25.7% for Native Hawaiians or other Pacific Islanders, and 32.8% for American Indians or Alaska Natives.

Driving Under the Influence of Alcohol

7. Figure 8.3B shows that in 2005, an estimated 13% of persons age 12 or older drove under the influence of alcohol at least once in the

KEY TERMS

teetotalers
individuals who drink no alcoholic beverages whatsoever; a term in common usage in decades past

FIGURE 8.3

....

Sources: A and B: Substance
Abuse and Mental Health
Services Administration
(SAMHSA). *Results from the
2003 National Survey on Drug
Use and Health: National
Findings.* Rockville, MD: Office
of Applied Studies.
C: Office of Applied Studies
(OAS). "Driving Under the
Influence (DUI) Among Young
Persons." *National Survey on
Drug Use and Health (NSDUH).*
Rockville, MD: Substance Abuse
and Mental Health Services
Administration, 2006.

A. Current, binge, and heavy alcohol use among persons aged 12 or older, by race/ethnicity, 2005

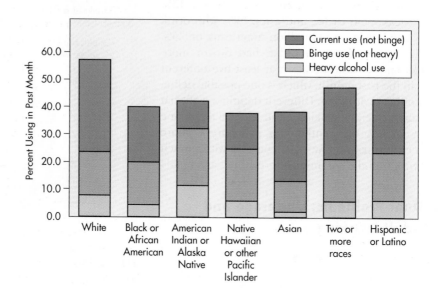

B. Driving under the influence of alcohol in the past year among persons ages 16 or older, by age, 2002–2005

C. Driving under the influence in the past year among persons aged 12 or older, 2002–2005

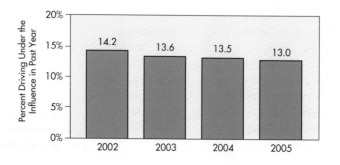

past year. This percentage has dropped since 2002, when it was 14.2%. The 2005 estimate corresponds to 31.7 million persons.

8. Figure 8.3C shows that driving under the influence of alcohol was associated with age in 2005. An estimated 8.3% of 16- to 17-year-olds, 19.8% of 18- to 20-year-olds, and 27.9% of 21- to 25-year-olds reported driving under the influence of alcohol in the past year. Beyond age 25, these rates showed a general decline with increasing age.

9. Though not shown in any of the three charts in Figure 8.3, among persons age 12 or older, males were nearly twice as likely as females (17.1% vs. 9.2%) to drive under the influence of alcohol in the past year.

Education and Alcohol Use

10. The rate of past-month alcohol use increased with increasing levels of education. Among adults age 18 or older with less than a high school education, 36.7% were current drinkers in 2005. By comparison, 69.4% of college graduates were current drinkers. Binge drinking and heavy drinking were least prevalent among college graduates, however (SAMHSA 2006).

College Students and Alcohol Use

11. Young adults ages 18 to 22 enrolled full time in college were more likely than their peers not enrolled full time (i.e., part-time college students and persons not enrolled in college) to use alcohol, binge drink, and drink heavily. Past-month alcohol use was reported by 64.4% of full-time college students compared with 53.2% of persons ages 18 to 22 who were not currently enrolled full time. Binge and heavy use rates for college students were 44.8% and 19.5%, respectively, compared with 38.3% and 13%, respectively, for other 18- to 22-year-olds enrolled full time in college.

Employment Status and Alcohol Use

12. Rates of current alcohol use were 63.2% for full-time employed adults age 18 or older in 2005 compared with 56.5% of their unemployed peers. The patterns were different for binge and heavy alcohol use; rates were higher for unemployed persons (10.4% and 8.4%, respectively, for binge and heavy use) than for full-time employed persons (8.4% and 8.6% respectively).

Alcohol and the Very Young

Use of either of the two major licit drugs, alcohol and cigarettes, remains more widespread than use of any of the illicit drugs. Alcohol has been tried by 41% of current 8th graders, 63% of 10th graders, 75% of 12th graders, and 87% of college students; active use is also widespread. Most important is the prevalence of occasions of heavy drinking — five or more drinks in a row at least once in the prior 2-week period — which was reported by 11% of 8th graders, 21% of 10th graders, 27% of 12th graders, and 40% of college students (Johnston et al. 2005).

Marijuana is by far the most widely used illicit drug. Nearly half of all 12th graders (45%) reported some marijuana use in their lifetime, 34% reported some use in the past year, and 20% reported some use in the past month. Among 10th graders, the corresponding rates are 34%, 27%, and 15%, respectively. Even among 8th-grade students, marijuana has been used at least once by one in six (17%), with 12% reporting use in the prior year and 7% use in the prior month (Johnston et al. 2005). Although much more is said in Chapter 13 about marijuana, the noteworthy finding here is that on a daily basis for this group of minors, marijuana usage now exceeds alcohol usage.

Of greater concern than just any use of alcohol is its use to the point of inebriation: 20% of 8th graders, 42% of 10th graders, and 58% of 12th graders said they have been drunk at least once in their lifetime. The prevalence rates of self-reported drunkenness during the 30 days immediately preceding the survey are strikingly high — 6%, 18%, and 30%, respectively, for grades 8, 10, and 12 (Johnston et al. 2005). (See "Point/Counterpoint," Lower the Legal Drinking Age?)

With regard to the three major types of alcohol (beer, wine coolers, and liquor) used by junior high and high school students, we find that from 9th through 12th grades, alcohol consumption increases dramatically (Johnston et al. 2005; *Pride USA Survey* 1998).

In looking at 12th graders' consumption of alcohol, white underage students are much more likely to binge drink (36%) compared with African American students (12%) and Hispanic students (28%). Finally, boys in 12th grade are more likely to drink alcohol on a daily basis compared with girls of the same grade and age; daily use among boys is reported at 6.4%, whereas the rate among girls is reported at 1.4%. Boys are more likely than girls to drink large quantities of alcohol in a single

▶Point/Counterpoint   Lower the Legal Drinking Age?

If we look around the world, we find that the United States appears to be the only country that sets the minimum legal drinking age at 21 (see Table 8.1). A number of countries, such as Ireland, Finland, and Sweden, specify a minimum age of 18, and other countries such as Germany, France, Italy, the Netherlands, Poland, and the United Kingdom specify a minimum age of 16. Still other countries, such as Belgium, Denmark, Greece, Spain, and Austria, do not specify any legal age for alcohol consumption (Harkin and Klinkenberg 1995).

Arguments *against* lowering the legal limit for consuming alcohol are as follows:

1. A higher minimum legal drinking age (MLDA) is effective in preventing alcohol-related deaths and injuries among youth. When the MLDA is lowered, injury and death rates increase, and when the MLDA is increased, death and injury rates decline (McCartt and Kirley 2006; Wagenaar 1993).

2. A higher MLDA results in fewer alcohol-related problems among youth, and the 21-year-old MLDA saves the lives of more than 1000 youths each year. Conversely, when the MLDA is lowered, motor vehicle crashes and deaths among youths increase. At least 50 studies have evaluated this correlation (McCartt and Kirley 2006; Wagenaar 1993).

3. Research shows that when the MLDA is 21, people younger than age 21 drink less overall and continue to do so through their early twenties (O'Malley and Wagenaar 1991).

4. Higher MLDAs reduce traffic fatalities involving drivers 18 to 20 years old by 13%. These laws have saved an estimated 18,220 lives since 1975 (National Highway Traffic Safety Administration [NHTSA] 1999).

5. "Young drivers are less likely than adults to drive after drinking alcohol, but their crash risk is substantially higher when they do" (McCartt and Kirley 2006).

6. ". . . a preponderance of evidence shows that MLDA is an effective deterrent to underage drinking and driving and has reduced alcohol-related crashes among young drivers" (McCartt and Kirley 2006).

Arguments *for* lowering the legal limit for consuming alcohol are as follows:

1. A study of a large sample of young people between the ages of 16 and 19 in Massachusetts and New York after Massachusetts raised its drinking age revealed that the average, self-reported daily alcohol consumption in Massachusetts did not decline in comparison with New York (Hanson 1999).

2. Comparison of college students attending schools in states that had maintained, for at least 10 years, a minimum drinking age of 21 with those in states that had similarly maintained minimum drinking ages below 21 revealed few differences in drinking problems (Hanson 1999).

3. A study of all 50 states and the District of Columbia found "a positive relationship between the purchase age and single-vehicle fatalities." Thus, single-vehicle fatalities were found to be more frequent in those states with high purchase ages (Hanson 1999).

4. Comparison of drinking before and after the passage of raised minimum age legislation has generally revealed little impact on behavior. For example, a study that examined college students' drinking behavior before and after an increase in the minimum legal drinking age from 18 to 19 in New York found the law had no impact on underage students' consumption rates, intoxication rates, drinking attitudes, or drinking problems. These studies were corroborated by other researchers at a different college in the same state (Hanson 1999).

5. An examination of East Carolina University students' intentions regarding their behavior following passage of the age-21 drinking law revealed that only 6% intended to stop drinking, 70% planned to change their drinking location, 21% expected to use a false or borrowed identification to obtain alcohol, and 22% intended to use other drugs. Anecdotal statements by students indicated the belief by some that it "might be easier to hide a little pot in my room than a six pack of beer" (Hanson 1999).

Research and the information from sources in this chapter indicate that with regard to under-21 alcohol violations, the United States continues to have serious problems. Thus, we are not any better than most

—continued on next page

countries regarding the percentage of minors consuming alcohol, despite our unique minimum age–21 requirement for alcohol consumption. What about the idea that instead of prohibiting alcohol consumption to those under age 21 (which to date continues to be ineffective), we need to teach moderation at an early age so that the percentage of youth who decide to consume alcohol can learn to do so responsibly?

Because the age-21 requirement has not deterred our nation's youth from consuming alcohol and in light of younger and younger age groups consuming alcohol, do you think it is time to reconsider lowering the age limit of alcohol consumption so that:

1. We are in alignment with the remainder of the world.

2. We can eliminate costly, burdensome, and unnecessary underage drinking violations. These infractions with the law include fines, legal costs, imprisonment, court time, legal expenses, and introducing our nation's youth into the criminal justice system (which many believe should remain "lean and mean" so that it can effectively prohibit and prosecute serious law violators).

3. We can teach responsible drinking and drinking in moderation, and alcohol consumption can be promoted and taught to be a "normal" part of behavior when eating or socializing with friends (like consuming coffee or fruit juice). Such prevention measures can clearly emphasize that excessive alcohol consumption is a sign of immaturity and lack of self-respect.

How successful do you think a campaign calling for lowering the legal drinking age would be with (1) family members, (2) your school, (3) your community, (4) your city/town, and (5) American society in general? Would it be successful? If yes, why? If no, why? Have you had any experiences in foreign countries where alcohol consumption was not severely restricted? If so, what did you observe?

In essence, do you think we should try to change the current drinking laws, in light of the fact that the current laws continue to be ineffective? Why are we not like other nations with regard to age limits on the use of alcohol? How important is it for the United States to be like other nations?

Table 8.1 World Minimum Drinking Ages

NO MINIMUM	AGE 16	AGE 18	AGE 19	AGE 20	AGE 21
Armenia	Antigua	Argentina	South Korea	Japan	(United States)
Azerbaijan	Austria	Australia		Iceland	
China	Belgium	Bahamas			
Fiji	France	Barbados			
Nigeria	Germany*	Bermuda			
Poland*	Greece*	Brazil			
Portugal	Italy	British Virgin Islands			
Soviet Georgia	Netherlands*	Canada (age 19 in			
Thailand	Norway*	some provinces)			
Viet Nam	Poland	Chile			
	Spain*	Colombia			
	Switzerland*	Czech Republic			
	Turkey*	Denmark			
		Estonia			
		Finland*			
		Hong Kong			
		Hungary			
		Indonesia			
		Ireland			
		Israel			
		Jamaica			
		Latvia			
		Lithuania			
		Luxembourg (age 17 with an adult)			

—continued on next page

Table 8.1   World Minimum Drinking Ages (continued)

NO MINIMUM	AGE 16	AGE 18	AGE 19	AGE 20	AGE 21
		Malaysia			
		Mexico			
		Moldova			
		Mongolia			
		New Zealand*			
		Peru			
		Philippines			
		Puerto Rico			
		Russia			
		Saint Martin			
		Slovak Republic			
		Slovenia			
		South Africa			
		Sweden*			
		Turkmenistan			
		Ukraine			
		United Kingdom (age 16 in restaurants)			
		Uruguay			
		Venezuela			

* with exceptions

Source: Hanson, David J. "Legal Drinking Age" Available http://www2.potsdam.edu/hansondj/LegalDrinkingAge.html.

Sources: Hanson, D. J. "The Legal Drinking Age: Science vs. Ideology" (1999). Available http://www2.potsdam.edu/hansondj/YouthIssues/1046348726.html.

Harkin, A. M., with assistance of L. Klinkenberg. *Profiles of Alcohol in the Member States of the European Region of the World Health Organization.* Copenhagen: WHO Regional Office for Europe, May 1995.

McCartt, A. T. and B. B. Kirley. *Minimum Purchase Age Laws: How Effective Are They in Reducing Alcohol-Impaired Driving?* Arlington, VA: Insurance Institute for Highway Safety, 2006. Available www.iihs.org.

National Highway Traffic Safety Administration (NHTSA), National Center for Statistics and Analysis. *Drunk Driving Facts.* Washington, DC: NHTSA, 1999.

O'Malley, P. M., and Wagenaar, A. C. "Effects of Minimum Drinking Age Laws on Alcohol Use, Related Behaviors and Traffic Crash Involvement Among American Youth: 1976–1987." *Journal of Studies on Alcohol* 52 (1991): 478–491.

Wagenaar, A. C. "Minimum Drinking Age and Alcohol Availability to Youth: Issues and Research Needs." In *Economics and the Prevention of Alcohol-Related Problems,* edited by M. E. Hilton and B. Bloss, 175–200. National Institute on Alcohol Abuse and Alcoholism (NIAAA) Research Monograph No. 25, NIH Pub. No. 93-3513. Bethesda, MD: NIAAA, 1993.

sitting; 39% of 12th-grade males reported drinking five or more drinks in a row 2 weeks prior to being surveyed, but only 24% of the 12th-grade females drank the same amount. When reviewing the statistics, keep in mind that females differ from males in terms of their alcohol drinking capacities (see Chapter 7 for more details).

■ Economic Costs of Alcohol Abuse

The economic costs of alcohol abuse to society are staggering. For example, from a global perspective, when including illness, accidents, and crimes connected to alcohol, the costs add up to more than $250 billion yearly (Reuters Limited 1999). The following are some of the current results of alcohol abuse shown in Figure 8.4 (National Institute on Alcohol Abuse and Alcoholism [NIAAA] 2000):

- The estimated cost of alcohol abuse and alcoholism (not including other drugs) to the United States was approximately $184.6 billion in 1998. (This cost rises approximately 12.5% yearly.)
- This 1998 estimate amounted to roughly $683 for every man, woman, and child living in the United States in 1998.
- More than 70% of the estimated costs of alcohol abuse were attributed to lost productivity ($134.2 billion), most of which resulted from alcohol-related illness or premature death.
- Most of the remaining estimated costs were expenditures for healthcare services to treat alcohol use disorder and the medical consequences of alcohol consumption ($26.3 billion, or 14.3% of total), property and administrative costs of

alcohol-related motor vehicle crashes ($15.7 billion, or 8.5%), and various criminal justice system costs of alcohol-related crime ($6.3 billion, or 3.4%).

Regarding how the burden of the costs of alcohol abuse is distributed across various segments of society, Figure 8.5 shows the following (published in NIAAA 2000, reference Harwood 2000; Harwood et al. 1998):

- Much of the economic burden of alcohol abuse falls on segments of the population *other than* the alcohol abusers themselves.
- Approximately 45% of the estimated total cost is borne by alcohol abusers and their families, almost all of which is due to lost or reduced earnings.
- Approximately 20% of the total estimated cost of alcohol abuse is borne by the federal government and 18% by state and local governments.

FIGURE 8.4

Economic costs of alcohol abuse, United States, 1998 (total estimated cost: $184.6 billion).

....

Source: Harwood, H., D. Fountain, and G. Livermore. *The Economic Costs of Alcohol and Drug Abuse in the United States, 1992.* Report prepared for the National Institute on Drug Abuse and the National Institute on Alcohol Abuse and Alcoholism, National Institutes of Health, U.S. Department of Health and Human Services. NIH Pub. No. 98-4327. Rockville, MD: National Institute on Drug Abuse, 1998.

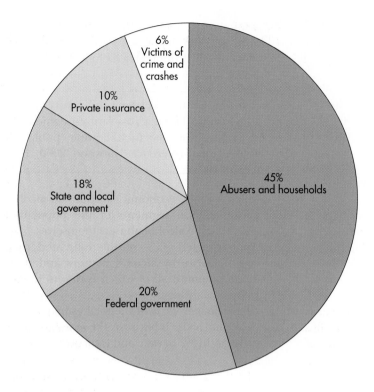

FIGURE 8.5

Distribution of the costs of alcohol abuse.

⋯⋯⋯⋯⋯⋯⋯⋯⋯⋯⋯⋯⋯⋯⋯⋯⋯⋯⋯

Source: Harwood, H., D. Fountain, and G. Livermore. *The Economic Costs of Alcohol and Drug Abuse in the United States, 1992.* Report prepared for the National Institute on Drug Abuse and the National Institute on Alcohol Abuse and Alcoholism, National Institutes of Health, U.S. Department of Health and Human Services. NIH Pub. No. 98-4327. Rockville, MD: National Institute on Drug Abuse, 1998.

- Nearly three fourths of the costs borne by the federal government take the form of reduced tax revenues resulting from alcohol-related productivity losses, and most of the remaining federal burden relates to healthcare costs. The burden on state and local governments (reductions in tax revenue) resulting from such productivity losses accounts for just over half, while 38% is for criminal justice and motor-vehicle–related costs. Private insurance arrangements (including life, health, auto, fire, and other kinds of insurance) shoulder the burden for 10% of the total estimated cost, primarily in the area of healthcare costs and motor vehicle crashes.
- Six percent of the total costs are borne by victims of alcohol-related crimes (including homicide) and by nondrinking victims of alcohol-related motor vehicle crashes.

Other findings include that the percentage of traffic fatalities that are alcohol related remains at around 40%, according to data from the National Highway Transportation Safety Administration's Fatality Analysis Reporting System (FARS) (Center for Substance Abuse Research [CESAR] 2005).

Another set of findings in a published report by the National Institute on Alcohol Abuse and Alcoholism (NIAAA 2000) discloses the following:

- Each year, more than 107,400 people die because of alcohol-related abuse.
- Productivity losses resulting from alcohol-related illness were estimated at $87.6 billion for 1998.
- Total costs attributed to alcohol-related motor vehicle crashes were estimated to be $24.7 billion.
- Expenditures for alcohol-related crime totaled $6.2 billion, and $17.4 billion for illicit drugs.
- Alcohol abuse is estimated to have contributed to 25% to 30% of violent crime.
- Alcohol is officially linked to at least half of all highway fatalities, and that figure includes only legal intoxication. In most states, the cutoff for the blood alcohol level ranges from 0.08% to 0.1%. In as many as 70% of all single-vehicle fatal crashes on weekend nights, the driver was legally intoxicated, and this proportion holds during most weekends throughout the United States. Interestingly, this single issue has been the only alcohol problem that

"All states have passed a .08 per se law. The final [state] took effect in August 2005." (Available at http://www.ou.edu/oupd/BAC.htm#BAC)

has inspired very vocal and effective groups to lobby for stricter enforcement of laws against alcohol-impaired automobile driving. Groups such as MADD (Mothers Against Drunk Driving) and SADD (Students Against Drunk Driving) are the largest prevention organizations in the nation (Alcoholism Kills 2000).

History of Alcohol in America

Drinking Patterns

From a peak in 1830, when the amount of alcohol ingested by the average American was 7.1 gallons per year, use declined continuously until 1871–1880, when the average was 1.72 gallons. Numbers then rose to a high in 1906–1910 to 2.6 gallons, then fell to 1.96 gallons just before Prohibition, 1916–1919. Under Prohibition, less than a gallon of absolute alcohol per person was consumed annually, on average. During the last half of the 20th century, alcohol consumption stayed constant, within the 2- to 3-gallon range. Wine and beer gained in popularity, while the popularity of "spirits" (hard liquor) declined (Lender 1985).

Historical Considerations

Alcoholic beverages have played an important role in the history of the United States as well as in most countries throughout the world. Most likely, fermentation was the first method for mak-

ing alcohol, dating to 4200 B.C. As early as A.D. 100, it appears that brandy was the first distilled beverage. In Ireland and Scotland, whiskey was first distilled in the 1400s, and gin began appearing in the 1600s, after being initially distilled by a Flemish physician. Other types of liquor also have distinct origins. For example, rum was first invented in Barbados in the 1650s. Bourbon was first made near Georgetown, Kentucky, in the late 1700s. In the United States, the first distillery was created in the 1600s in the area that is now New York City.

In colonial America, alcohol was viewed very favorably. From an economic standpoint, the manufacturing of rum became New England's largest and most profitable industry in the so-called triangle trade. It acquired this name because Yankee traders would sail with a cargo of rum to the West Coast of Africa, where they bargained the "demon" for slaves. From there, they sailed to the West Indies, where they bartered the slaves for molasses. Finally, they took the molasses back to New England, where it was made into rum, thus completing the triangle. For many years, New England distilleries flourished and the slave trade proved highly lucrative (see Figure 8.6). This process continued until 1807, when an act of Congress prohibited the importation of slaves.

From a social standpoint, the consumption of alcohol was seen as a part of life. The colonial tavern "was a key institution, the center of social and political life" (Levine 1983, p. 66). In the 17th and 18th centuries, alcohol flowed freely at weddings, baptisms, and funerals. Especially in the 18th century, people drank at home, at work, and while traveling. In the 19th century, largely because of the temperance movement, taverns became stigmatized and were viewed as dens where the lower classes, immigrants, and mostly men would congregate. "Any drinking, [Lyman Beecher] argued, was a step toward 'irreclaimable' slavery to liquor" (Lender and Martin 1987). People in the 19th century began to report that they were addicted to alcohol. Here is where the temperance movement had its effects in bringing about a change in attitudes regarding drinking.

From the Temperance Movement (1830–1850) to the Prohibition Era (1920–1933)

The time from the temperance movement to the Prohibition era was a very turbulent period in the history of alcohol in America. The period of

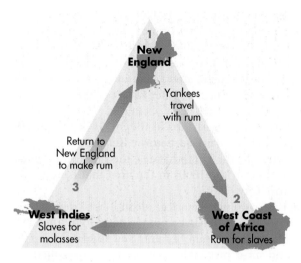

FIGURE 8.6
Slave trade triangle.

heaviest drinking in America began during Jefferson's term of office (1800–1808). The nation was going through uneasy times, trying to stay out of the war between Napoleon and the British allies. The transient population had increased, especially in the seaport cities, and the migration westward had begun. Heavy drinking had become a major form of recreation and a "social lubricant" at elections and public gatherings. The temperance movement never began with the intention of stopping alcohol consumption but with the goal of encouraging moderation. In fact, in the 1830s, at the peak of this early campaign, temperance leaders (many of whom drank beer and wine) recommended abstinence only from distilled spirits, not from the other forms of alcohol such as beer or wine. This movement developed from several very vocal spiritual leaders who preached that alcohol harms "the health and physical energies of a nation" and that alcohol interfered with the spreading of the gospel. Later, as is explained shortly in more detail, the temperance movement went against all other forms of alcohol.

Because the temperance movement was closely tied to the abolitionist movement as well as to the African American church, African Americans were preeminent promoters of temperance. Leaders such as Frederick Douglass stated that "it was as well to be a slave to master, as to whisky and rum. When a slave was drunk, the slaveholder had no fear that he would plan an insurrection; no fear

that he would escape to the north. It was the sober, thinking slave who was dangerous, and needed the vigilance of his master to keep him a slave" (Douglass 1892, p. 133).

Over the next decades, partly in connection with religious revivals, the meaning of *temperance* was gradually altered from "moderation" to "total abstinence." All alcoholic beverages were attacked as being unnecessary, harmful to health, and inherently poisonous. Over the course of the 19th century, the demand gradually arose for total prohibition (Austin 1978).

By the late 19th and early 20th centuries, a number of countries either passed legislation or created alcohol restrictions. Most of these laws and restrictions eventually failed. In the United States, attempts to control, restrict, or abolish alcohol were made, but they all met with abysmal failure. From 1907 to 1919, 34 states passed prohibition laws. Finally, on a national scale, the 18th Amendment to the Constitution was ratified in 1919 in an attempt to stop the rapid spread of alcohol addiction. In January 1920, alcohol was outlawed. As soon as such a widely used substance became illegal, criminal activity to satisfy the huge demand for alcohol flourished. Illegal outlets developed for purchasing liquor. Numerous not-so-secret **speakeasies** developed as illegal establishments where people could buy and consume alcoholic beverages, despite the laws of Prohibition. **Bootlegging** was a widely accepted activity. In effect, such "dens of sin" filled the vacuum for many drinkers during Prohibition.

During the temperance movement and Prohibition period, doctors and druggists prescribed whiskey and other alcohol known as **patent medicines** (see "Case in Point," The Great American Fraud: Patent Medicines).

KEY TERMS

speakeasies
places where alcoholic beverages were illegally sold during the Prohibition era

bootlegging
making, distributing, and selling alcoholic beverages during the Prohibition era

patent medicines
the ingredients in these uncontrolled "medicines" were secret, often consisting of large amounts of colored water, alcohol, cocaine, or opiates

By 1928, doctors made an estimated $40 million per year writing prescriptions for whiskey. Patent medicines flourished, with alcohol contents as high as 50%. Whisko, a "nonintoxicating stimulant," was 55 proof (or 27.5% alcohol). Another, Kaufman's Sulfur Bitters, was labeled "contains no alcohol" but was 40 proof (20% alcohol) and did not contain sulfur. There were dozens of others, many of which contained other types of drugs, such as opium.

Both Prohibitionists and critics of the law were shocked by the violent gang wars that broke out between rivals seeking to control the lucrative black market in liquor. More important, a general disregard for the law developed. Corruption among law enforcement agents was widespread and organized crime began and grew to be an enormous illegitimate business. In reaction to these developments, political support rallied against Prohibition, resulting in its repeal in 1933 by the 21st Amendment. Early in the 20th century, women suffragettes had been prominent temperance organizers; paradoxically, flappers organized against Prohibition and were vital in gathering the signatures for its repeal.

Three main developments occurred as a result of Prohibition. First, alcohol use continued to diminish for the first 2 or 3 years after Prohibition was in effect. This trend had begun several years before the law was passed. More importantly, after 3 years of steady decline, the use of distilled liquors rose every year afterward. Further, even minors were becoming addicted to alcohol during this period.

Second, enforcement of laws against alcohol use was thwarted by corrupt law enforcement officials, enforcement was uneven (in some areas of the United States, enforcement was lax, while in other areas very strict), and law enforcement experienced more than 50% turnover in its ranks. Corruption of law enforcement officials stands out as a paramount concern. Reportedly, 10% of law enforcement was "on the take" and had to be continually discharged.

Third, among the Western Europeans who immigrated to the United States *en masse* during this period, the consumption of alcohol was culturally prescribed. Prohibition against alcohol usage to the Italian, German, French, Polish, Irish, and other European-based immigrants was perceived as unnecessary and an infringement to the right to common existence. One 93-year-old Italian American émigré to Chicago exemplified some of these attitudes:

Al Capone ("Scarface") (*center*), the undisputed leader of Chicago's gang scene during Prohibition, made millions of dollars in his bootlegging operations until he was convicted of tax evasion in 1931 and eventually imprisoned in Alcatraz.

Well, when we were not allowed to drink because of the government, I thought it was a stupid law. Many of us here in the neighborhood [a fading Italian American community in Chicago's West Side and the original home of Venturelli] made lots of money as "alki cookers."

We would make the alcohol in our bathtubs and sell to other people or even to those mafia types. Oh, it was horrible cheap and crappy alcohol; if you drank too much the night before, it gave you headaches sometimes for days. On Sunday afternoons, if you walked through this neighborhood in the hot summer days, you could smell the alcohol oozing from people's windows. Nearly everyone my mother's and father's age and older at the time made extra money as alki cookers. It was actually a good law [referring to Prohibition] for making a few bucks to help out the family expenses. No one around here gave a damn about the law, because too many were "on the take" so-to-say . . . and it was not just us [referring to the local Italian Americans]. At least for us when we meet together and eat for fun, alcohol is like the air we breathe. Who the hell is going to change that, especially something so deep? (*From Venturelli's research files, interview with a 93-year-old male, May 26, 2000.*)

►Case in Point   The Great American Fraud: Patent Medicines

In the late 1800s and early 1900s, before the days of FDA legislation, the sales of uncontrolled medicines flourished and became widespread. Many of these products were called *patent medicines*, which signified that the ingredients were secret, not that they were patented. The law of the day seemed to be more concerned with someone's recipe being stolen than with preventing harm to the naive consumer. Some of these patent medicines included toxic ingredients such as acetanilide in Bromo-Seltzer and Orangeine and prussic (hydrocyanic) acid in Shiloh's Consumption Cure.

Most patent medicines appear to have been composed largely of either colored water or alcohol, with an occasional added ingredient such as opium or cocaine. Hostetter's Stomach Bitters with 44% alcohol could easily have been classified as liquor. Sale of Peruna (28% alcohol) was prohibited to Native Americans because of its high alcoholic content. Birney's Catarrh Cure contained 4% cocaine. Wistar's Balsam of Wild Cherry (see Figure 8.7), Dr. King's Discovery for Consumption, Mrs. Winslow's Soothing Syrup, and several others contained opiates as well as alcohol.

The medical profession of the mid- and late 19th century was ill prepared to do battle with the ever-present manufacturers and distributors of patent medicines. Qualified physicians during this time were rare. Much more common were medical practitioners with poor training and little scientific understanding. In fact, many of these early physicians practiced a brand of medicine that was generally useless and frequently more life-threatening than the patent medicines themselves.

In 1905, *Collier's Magazine* ran a series of articles called the "Great American Fraud," which warned of the abuse of patent medicines. This brought the problem to the public's attention (Adams 1905). *Collier's* coined the phrase "dope fiend" from "dope," an African word meaning "intoxicating substance." The American Medical Association (AMA) joined in and widely distributed reprints of the *Collier's* story to inform the public about the dangers of these medicines, even though the AMA itself accepted advertisements for patent medicines that physicians knew were addicting. The publicity created mounting pressure on Congress and President Theodore Roosevelt to do something about these fraudulent products. In 1905, Roosevelt proposed that a law be enacted to regulate interstate commerce of misbranded and adulterated foods, drinks, and drugs. This movement received further impetus when Upton Sinclair's book *The Jungle* was published in 1906 — this nauseatingly realistic exposé detailed how immigrant laborers worked under appalling conditions of filth, disease, putrefaction, and other extreme exploitations at Chicago's stockyards.

Two substances used in patent medicines helped shape attitudes that would form the basis of regulatory policies for years to come: the opium derivatives (narcotic drugs, such as heroin and morphine) and cocaine (see Chapter 3).

FIGURE 8.7

This poster advertises one of the patent medicines that contained liberal doses of opium and a high concentration of alcohol. This medicine was widely used to treat tuberculosis ("consumption") around the turn of the century, when more than 25% of all adult deaths were attributable to this disease. The U.S. government finally forced the remedy off the market by 1920.

Defining Alcoholics

As discussed in Chapter 7 and at the beginning of this chapter, creating absolute definitions or categories of behavior that represent an alcoholic *type* is very difficult because all behaviors vary enormously from one person to the next; thus most behaviors range along a continuum. Adding to this confusion is the fact that some disagreement exists among experts on what the exact criteria should be regarding the definition of an alcoholic. In other words, when is a person an alcoholic? Is it the daily drinker or the inebriated weekend drinker? What if the person is able to maintain a job and provide for his or her family? How does this type of alcoholic compare with an unemployed resident of skid row? In the minds of many Americans, an alcoholic is a derelict who frequents skid rows, train stations, and bus terminals; panders for money; and sleeps on a park bench at night. Yet, this stereotypical image of an alcoholic represents only a few percent of the millions of Americans who qualify as alcoholic by any of the accepted medical definitions. The more typical alcoholic, in fact, is the example of the professor or businessman purchasing alcohol at a liquor store (described at the opening of this chapter). In effect, most alcoholics are secret or hidden drinkers who look very much like everyday working people.

■ Cultural Differences

Although much more will be presented later in this chapter about the pervasive role that culture plays in drinking behavior, we begin with a quote highlighting cultural differences in interpreting alcohol consumption:

> Even definitions of a "problem drinker" differ from one culture to the next. In Poland, loss of productivity tends to demonstrate a drinking problem, while Californians emphasize drunk driving as an important and sometimes key indicator . . . [Among Italian Americans, an inability to provide for one's family because of heavy drinking qualifies a person as an alcoholic.] . . . Some methods of assessing problem-drinking look to behavior that leads to a brush with the law. However, drunkenness may or may not lead to disruptive behavior. In the Netherlands, alcoholic beverage consumption is similar to that in Finland and Poland, but there is much less disruptive or public drinking. In these nations, the actual amount of alcohol consumed is not indicated by the arrest figures, the actual amount consumed, and the number of physical ailments caused by excessive alcohol consumption. Secondly, the social response to drunkenness may not be arrest and conviction. Ireland, for example, has traditionally used psychiatric institutions to control drunkenness. (Osterberg 1986, p. 83)

Estimates vary, but it is believed that approximately three fourths of problem drinkers are men and one fourth are women. The proportion of women has risen in recent years. This increase occurred for two reasons: (1) Women as problem drinkers are more visible and numerous because they now make up about half of the workforce, and (2) women are more likely to acknowledge the problem and seek treatment, especially if they are in white-collar occupations. Thus, female problem drinkers may now be more visible and more self-assured as well as more numerous.

Next, in attempting to define alcoholism, we turn to models that speak of the state of addiction. **Alcoholism** is a state of physical and psychological addiction to ethanol, a psychoactive substance (see also Chapter 7). It was once viewed as a vice and dismissed as sinful, but over the years, there has been a shift from this perspective to one that views alcoholism as a disease. The sinfulness perspective failed to focus on the fact that alcoholism is an addiction — an illness — and not the result of a lack of personal discipline and morality.

Attempts to expand the basic definition of alcoholism to include symptoms of the condition and psychological and sociological factors have been difficult; no one definition satisfies everyone. The World Health Organization defines *alcohol dependence syndrome* as a syndrome characterized by a state, psychic and usually also physical, resulting from drinking alcohol. This state is characterized by behavioral and other responses that include a compulsion to drink alcohol (like an unquenchable thirst) on a continuous or periodic basis to experience its psychic effects and sometimes to avoid the discomfort of its absence; tolerance may or may not be present (NIAAA 1980).

Another more classic explanation of alcoholism that remains popular is, "Alcoholism is a chronic behavioral disorder manifested by repeated drinking of alcoholic beverages in excess of the dietary and social uses of the community, to an extent that interferes with the drinker's health or his social or economic functioning" (Keller 1958, p. 78). Another definition emphasizes, "Alcoholism is a chronic, primary, hereditary disease that progresses from an early, physiological susceptibility into an addiction characterized by tolerance changes,

KEY TERMS

alcoholism

a state of physical and psychological addiction to ethanol, a psychoactive substance physiological dependence, and loss of control over drinking. [In this definition], [P]sychological symptoms are secondary to the physiological disease and not relevant to its onset" (Gold 1991, p. 99).

In summary, the preceding definitions either list or hint at the following major components of *alcoholism* (NIAAA "Frequently Asked Questions"):

Craving: An overwhelming compulsion to drink even when not feasible, such as at work, driving a car, mowing a lawn, and so on.

Very impaired or loss of control: An inability to limit one's drinking once drinking has begun — for example, one drink only before going to bed is impossible to control.

Physical dependence: The presence of withdrawal symptoms when attempting to abstain from usage. Such symptoms as nausea, sweating, shakiness, and anxiety about the availability of alcohol are common.

Tolerance: A need to continually increase the amount of alcohol consumed to maintain its effects (or to maintain the "buzz").

■ Alcohol Abuse and Alcoholism

When attempting to understand the meaning of chronic drinking, one additional clarification that should be made is to distinguish between **alcohol abuse** and alcoholism. The two explanations of drinking behavior differ as a matter of degree. When speaking of *alcohol abuse*, the craving, loss of control, and physical dependence just listed as primary manifestations are less prominent and not as pronounced as in alcoholism. There is diminished ability to fulfill obligations and goals; more occasions of drinking at the wrong time, such as while driving; legal problems such as driving under the influence; and relationship problems. Note that many of these problems that result from alcohol abuse are also experienced by alcoholics, but not

all manifestations of alcoholics are experienced by alcohol abusers. For example, an alcoholic may repeatedly argue with family members two or three times per week, whereas an alcohol abuser may have fewer occurrences of the same type of alcohol-inspired arguments with a family member. Thus, even though the alcohol abuser has fewer occasions of uncontrollable drinking than the alcoholic, the drinking remains largely uncontrollable when it occurs. For many years, people with drinking problems were lumped together under the label *alcoholic,* and *alcohol abusers* were assumed to be suffering from the same illness. Today, because of greater understanding about addiction and addictive behaviors, the distinction between the two terms leads to a more precise understanding of excessive alcohol abuse (see "Here and Now," Are You "On the Road" to Alcoholism?).

■ Types of Alcoholics

Although written more than 3 decades ago, Jellinek's (1960) original personality-typology (characterizations) differentiating the types of alcoholics remains very important for adding more preciseness in understanding alcohol abuse and its outcomes. Jellinek's categories are as follows:

Alpha alcoholism. Mostly a psychological dependence on alcohol to bolster an inability to cope with life. The alpha type constantly needs alcohol and becomes irritable and anxious when it is not available.

Beta alcoholism. Mostly a social dependence on alcohol. Often, although not exclusively, this type is a heavy beer drinker who continues to meet social and economic obligations. Some nutritional deficiencies can occur, including organic damage such as gastritis and cirrhosis.

Gamma alcoholism. The most severe form of alcoholism. This type of alcoholic suffers from emotional and psychological impairment. Jellinek believed this type of alcoholic suffered from a true disease and progresses from a psychological dependence to physical dependence. Loss of control over when alcohol is consumed and how much is taken characterizes the latter phase of this type of alcoholism.

Delta alcoholic. Called the maintenance drinker (Royce 1989). The person loses control over drinking and cannot abstain for even a day or

KEY TERMS

alcohol abuse
uncontrollable drinking that leads to alcohol craving, loss of control, and physical dependence but with less prominent characteristics than found in alcoholism

Here and Now

Are You "On the Road" to Alcoholism?

Answer the following questions with either a simple "yes" or "no."

1. Do you frequently drink because you have problems or need to relax?

2. When out with friends, do you become irritated or bored when the evening does not lead to the use of alcohol and/or drugs?

3. Do you drink when you get mad at other people, such as your friends or parents?

4. Do you often prefer to drink alone?

5. Are your grades suffering because of the time you spend drinking?

6. Do you stop drinking "for good" and then start again?

7. Have you begun to drink in the morning, before school or work?

8. Do you often gulp your drinks?

9. Do you have loss of memory because of your drinking?

10. Do you lie about the amount you drink?

11. Do you ever get into trouble when you are drinking?

12. Do you get drunk when you drink, even when you do not plan to?

13. Do you think you are cool when you can hold your liquor?

If you answered more than one as "yes," you may have a drinking problem that will become increasingly problematic, moving in the direction of alcoholism.

Sources: Reformulated from The A.A. Grapevine, Inc., A.A. World Services, Inc., 2006. Available http://www.aagrapevine.org.

two. Many wine-drinking countries such as France and Italy contain delta-type alcoholics who sip wine throughout most of their waking hours. Being "tipsy" but never completely inebriated is typical of the delta alcoholic.

Epsilon alcoholic. This type of alcoholic is characterized as a binge drinker. The epsilon-type drinker drinks excessively for a certain period (for days and sometimes weeks) but then abstains completely from alcohol until the next binge period. The dependence on alcohol is both physical and psychological. Loss of control over the amount consumed is another characteristic of this type of alcoholic.

Zeta alcoholic. This category was added to Jellinek's types to describe the moderate drinker who becomes abusive and violent. Although this type is also referred to as a "pathological drinker" or "mad drunk," zeta types may not be addicted to alcohol.

Another, much more recent classification of alcoholism subtypes includes five alcohol-dependent subtypes created by Dr. Moss and colleagues

(National Institutes of Health [NIH] and NIAAA 2007). Quoted extensively, the five types are:

Young Adult subtype. 31.5% of U.S. alcoholics. Young adult drinkers, with relatively low rates of co-occurring substance abuse and other mental disorders, a low rate of family alcoholism, and who rarely seek any kind of help for their drinking.

Young antisocial subtype. 21% of U.S. alcoholics. Tend to be in their mid-twenties, had early onset of regular drinking, and alcohol problems. More than half come from families with alcoholism, and about half have a psychiatric diagnosis of antisocial personality disorder. Many have major depression, bipolar disorder, and anxiety problems. More than 75% smoke cigarettes and marijuana, and many also have cocaine and opiate addictions. More than one third of these alcoholics seek help for their drinking.

Functional subtype. 19.5% of U.S. alcoholics. Typically middle-aged, well-educated, with stable jobs and families. About one third have a multigenerational family history of alcoholism, about one quarter have major depressive illness sometime in their lives, and nearly 50% are smokers.

Intermediate familial subtype. 19% of U.S. alcoholics. Middle-aged, with about 50% from families with multigenerational alcoholism. Almost half have had clinical depression, and 20% have had bipolar disorder. Most of these individuals smoke cigarettes, and nearly one in five have had problems with cocaine and marijuana use. Only 25% ever seek treatment for their problem drinking.

Chronic severe subtype. 9% of U.S. alcoholics. Composed mostly of middle-aged individuals who had early onset of drinking and alcohol problems, with high rates of antisocial personality disorder and criminality. Almost 80% come from families with multigenerational alcoholism. They have the highest rates of other psychiatric disorders including depression, bipolar disorder, and anxiety disorders as well as high rates of smoking, and marijuana, cocaine, and opiate dependence. Two thirds of these alcoholics seek help for their drinking problems, making them the most prevalent type of alcoholic in treatment.

Other classifications differentiate alcoholics by their reaction to the drug as quiet, sullen, friendly, or angry types. Another method is to classify alcoholics according to drinking patterns: people with occupational, social, escape, and emotional disorders.

Cultural Influences

This section explains how views of alcohol are culturally determined — that is, how culture encodes the thoughts, attitudes, values, and beliefs about alcohol and how it influences our behavior regarding the use and abuse of alcohol.

I was just drinking beer a lot and hardly ever drank the hard stuff. I was drinking about a six-pack after work each night. My wife never said anything much about my drinking. Then as time went on, I remember that I would start drinking beer earlier and earlier after work. Then came the six-pack and an extra quart of beer each night while sitting home trying to relax after a pressure-filled day at the office. Well, little did I realize then, I was having a drinking problem and it was only beer! I could

Many cultural social interactions demand drinking together.

not believe that I was sort of a beer alcoholic. Back then, I never thought that silly ole' beer could get a person hooked. *(From Venturelli's research files, male, age 32, member of Alcoholics Anonymous, April 12, 2000.)*

Or,

Q: Do you consider yourself a heavy drinker?
A: No, I only drink beer.
Q: But, you are often drunk at night?
A: Yea, but it's only beer.

These two interviews illustrate a belief shared by many Americans, which is that the milder alcohols such as beer, wine, and wine coolers are often placed outside the domain of potentially addictive types of beverages. Some may even believe that the distilled spirits such as vodka, gin, and whiskey are the only types of addictive alcoholic beverages. Finally, the comment that "I don't use and never would use drugs; I only drink" can easily be heard being espoused by a large portion of Americans (probably a majority), who place alcohol in a completely separate category from drugs. However, each 12-ounce bottle of beer is equal to 1 ounce of liquor. Thus, two beers equal a double shot of bourbon or vodka.

Culture and Drinking Behavior

Another way of looking at how culture influences us is to stand outside of our culture and see how people behave when intoxicated in our culture and in a variety of other cultures in an effort to understand the real relationship among culture, alcohol, and human beings. A major contribution to our knowledge of intoxicated behavior from an outside perspective comes from the field of cultural anthropology.

How, or in what way, does culture affect the way we view alcohol? Why would our culture differ from other cultures in the use and abuse of alcoholic beverages? We focus on these two questions in this section.

Throughout the world, cultures create a climate for the development of attitudes toward most behaviors. Like other behaviors, the use of alcohol is embedded within our culture. Culture does more than contain the attitudes and feelings that people have toward alcohol use: It dictates the variety, the attachment, and the intensity of attitudes that are held toward other people's behavior. For example, in the 1930s, American college students acquired a "reverence for strong drink" (Room 1984, p. 8). Although for decades many people believed that college students "majored in drinking," during the 1930s, students grew to consider heavy use as romantic and adult, resonating with the romantic, heavy-drinking expatriate community of writers in Paris, such as Ernest Hemingway.

American culture in general views ethanol-containing beverages as sexy, mature, sophisticated, facilitating socializing, and enhancing status. Today, many of these beliefs are communicated through the mass media, and advertising is a key medium of communication. Advertising uses positive images to persuade observers to purchase a particular brand of alcohol. For example, what messages are found in newspapers and especially magazines about drinking certain types of wine, bourbon, gin, scotch, and the numerous types of domestic and imported beers? What attitudes are generally conveyed when a sexy, glamorous woman is dressed in formal evening attire standing next to her man in front of a perfectly glowing fireplace, smiling confidently as he stares into her eyes and sips his special-label cognac?

Culture and Disinhibited Behavior

The concept of **drunken comportment** was first formulated by MacAndrew and Edgerton (1969). Drunken comportment refers to the behavior demonstrated while under the influence of alcohol within the norms and expectations of a particular culture. Instead of simply labeling drinking behavior as "drunken behavior," this concept sensitizes us to how drinking behavior is influenced by cultural norms and expectations. For example, in the

United States, drinking is comported to mean time out away from duties and obligations. "The symbolism of alcohol in American culture contains this motif of release and remission, as in the emergence of TGIF [Thank God It's Friday]" (Gusfield 1986, p. 203). Another example is that in some cultures, drinking occurs during celebrations and festivities, and as part of religious ceremony.

In France and Italy, drinking alcohol occurs while eating with family members. Alcohol is a **disinhibitor**, which refers to depression of the cerebral cortex functions. When this occurs, it results in a suspension of rational or thoughtful constraints on impulsive behavior. *Inhibitions* (inner raw feelings and attitudes) are normally controlled through rationality and logical thought processes. The popular image of office Christmas parties at which too much alcohol is consumed and parties that get out of control because of overconsumption of alcohol are examples. People at such events can easily become uncontrollable, loud, impulsive, and just plain irrational. In such situations, outbreaks of arguing and physical and verbal abuse are more likely to occur. Such behavior is disinhibited behavior.

Although all of us know that the alcohol content that is usually measured in terms of alcohol proof (see Chapter 7 for more details) has an independent effect on the user, two additional factors contribute to the effects of alcohol: **set and setting** (Goode 1999; Zinberg 1984; Zinberg and Robertson 1972). *Set* is the individual's expectation of what a drug will do to his or her personality. *Setting* is both the physical environment and the social environment in which the drug is consumed. How important are these two distinctions? Some psychologists contend that both set and setting can overshadow the pharmacological effects

KEY TERMS

drunken comportment
behavior exhibited while under the direct influence of alcohol; determined by the norms and expectations of a particular culture

disinhibitor
a psychoactive chemical that depresses thought and judgment functions in the cerebral cortex, which has the effect of allowing relatively unrestrained behavior (as in alcohol inebriation)

set and setting
set refers to the individual's expectation of what a drug will do to his or her personality; *setting* is the physical and social environments where the drug is consumed

of most drugs. In fact, set and setting are far more influential in determining a drug user's experience even when the less immediately addictive drugs, such as alcohol and marijuana, are used, in contrast to more potent addictive drugs, such as cocaine and heroin. Good examples of this are when people who drink alcohol say "I felt that drink right away" or "I drank a lot last night but I had something on my mind and dude, I was just not in the partying mood."

A review of various ethnographic studies (Marshall 1983) reveals **pseudointoxicated** behavior among Tahitians, Rarotongans, Chippewa, Dakota, Pine Ridge and Teton Sioux, Aleuts, Baffin Island Inuits, and Potawatomi — that is, people *acting* drunk before or seconds after the bottle is opened, or as the drink is consumed. The frequency of use or the amount consumed has less effect on how drinkers comport themselves; instead, the cultural values, beliefs, mental maps, and norms cause a particular behavioral outcome. Using the terminology of psychology, we would say that it is not the biochemical effects on the brain alone that account for disinhibitory behavior but rather the belief that one has been drinking a substance that has a disinhibitory effect; that is, the mental (cognitive) appraisal of the physiological state allows disinhibited behavior. In using the terminology of sociology and revising a famous sociological axiom, we could say that "what we believe to be (or personally define as true) is true in its consequences or in the obtained results." Thus, if you believe you are drunk and you act drunk, then you are drunk.

Cultures vary in how they evaluate alcohol consumption. Some religions in the United States view drinking as evil, whereas other religions view alcohol as a gift from God and use it in religious ceremonies. In some subcultures, excessive use of alcohol is an indication of manhood, strength, and virility; in other subcultures, excessive alcohol use in public is disgusting and embarrassing. Even drug education has different perspectives. Do we emphasize total abstinence or teach people how to drink in moderation? Why such vastly different approaches? Because our culture includes contradictory practices on this front.

Similarly, the views we maintain about alcohol abuse and addiction vary. For example, is alcoholism a disease? Is it prescribed by certain customs within ethnic groups? Does it result from some type of personality flaw? The three concepts discussed in this section — drunken comportment, set and setting, and pseudointoxication — demonstrate that social and cultural contexts exert their influences independently of the effects of alcohol consumption.

■ Culture Provides Rules for Drinking Behavior

Many cultures, such as traditional Italian and Jewish cultures, permit moderate drinking within the family, especially at meals, but disapprove of drunken behaviors. Note that many differences separate these groups. For example, Italians use wine as a food item, whereas it has only ritual value among Orthodox Jews. In one study of Scandinavian nations, by contrast, drinking was considered absolutely separated from work. Where drinking at work was permitted, however, it was allowed to go on to the point of intoxication (Makela 1986). Finnish, Polish, and Russian cultures are associated with binge drinking, whereas French culture is linked with sipping. In the United States, we encounter a vast variety of subgroups; some heavy drinkers may live in a community in which it is not considered excessive to drink with their friends out of paper bags on the street in the morning. In other communities, all outdoor drinking is done in either parks, restaurants, bars, or outdoor cafes. Some people may belong to a "workplace culture of drinking" at a post office, construction site, or law firm where "three-martini lunches" are not unheard of. Perhaps this type of drinking is not much different from the habits of teenage peer groups. To be "treated" for this behavior might seem as strange as going into rehab for acting "normal."

■ Culture Provides Ceremonial Meaning for Alcohol Use

The first notable work on ceremonial use and ethnic drinking practices was undertaken by Bales (1946), who attempted to explain the different rates of drinking between Jews (low) and Irish (high) in terms of symbolic and ceremonial mean-

KEY TERMS

pseudointoxicated
acting drunk even before alcohol has had a chance to cause its effects

ings. For Jews, drinking had familial and sacramental significance, whereas for the Irish it represented male convivial bonding.

A high rate of heavy drinking was observed among the Irish in the 1800s. It was said that these individuals drank because they were Irish. Today, some descendants of the Irish continue to live the stereotype; for them, it represents Irishness — they drink because they are Irish. A button displayed on St. Patrick's Day proclaimed, "Today I'm Irish, Tomorrow I'm Hung Over," and a *New York Post* supplement declared this event to be "Three Days of Drinking and Revelry." Jews, on the other hand, think that Jews cannot be alcoholic. That is, they believe that if a person is Jewish, even though he or she drinks a lot, true alcoholism is impossible. If the individual gives up denial, however, and admits to alcoholism, then he or she cannot be Jewish (Blume et al. 1980).

Culture Provides Models of Alcoholism

Chapter 2 discussed models of addiction, such as the disease model. U.S. citizens define alcoholism as a disease far more often than French Canadians or French people (Babor et al. 1986). Some South Bronx Hispanics have ascribed alcoholism to "spells," spirits (Garrison and Podell 1981), the evil eye (*mal ojo*), or witchcraft (*brujeria*). The entire addiction may also be ignored or bypassed; ulcers, divorce, or car accidents that an alcohol counselor may recognize as alcoholism-based may instead be traced directly to supernatural influence. One way or another, if it is attributed to a supernatural cause, a supernatural solution may be called upon to cure this problem. Thus, many seek the help of a folk curer (*espiritista, santero,* and so on). Some African Americans interpret their problems as a punishment from God, and they may subscribe to a moral model that conflicts with a disease or other psychiatric or addictive model.

Cultural Stereotypes of Drinking May Be Misleading

African American drinking patterns run the gamut from middle-class cocktail lounges (as seen in liquor ads in *Ebony*), to blue-collar wakes and birthday parties, to the "bottle-gang" of homeless poor. By class, middle-class African American

women drinkers are not dramatically different from middle-class white women drinkers; they are typically moderate drinkers, with few nondrinkers and heavy drinkers. Poorer African American female groups have a larger proportion of nondrinkers; among those who do drink, more are heavy drinkers. Breaking it down further, being married, older, and church affiliated has also been associated with nonacceptance of heavy drinking (Gary and Gary 1985; Kinney 2000). At initially established black colleges and universities, blacks have lower levels of alcohol and other types of drug consumption than are observed at colleges and universities with a majority of white students. At all colleges and universities, white students drink significantly more than African American students (Kinney 2000).

Gordon, who studied a Connecticut city in 1981, examined three Hispanic groups, all new to the United States and all blue collar. In this group, Dominicans drank less after migration. They emphasized suave or sophisticated drinking, and they saw drunkenness as indecent (without respect). Alcoholics were seen as "sick," perhaps from some tragic experience. Guatemalans drank substantially more after migration: One third of males were often drunk and binged most weekends. Being drunk was considered glamorous and sentimentalized — like Humphrey Bogart under the hanging light bulb, alone in a hotel room. These individuals boasted of hangovers, even when they did not have one. The Guatemalan Alcoholics Anonymous (AA) group was alien to Puerto Ricans. Puerto Ricans broke down into middle-class American-style moderate drinkers, depressed and wife-abusing alcoholic welfare recipients, and various sorts of polydrug abusers, including those who entered into the mainland "druggie" youth culture (Gordon 1981). Among Hispanics in general, men were twice as likely to be involved in heavy drinking as both white and African American males (Kinney 2000). In fact, African American students have the lowest lifetime, annual, and 30-day prevalence rates for alcohol use; they also tend to have the lowest rates for daily drinking (NIDA 1999).

Even when looking at physiological responses to alcohol, ethnicity appears to matter. The long-term effects of alcohol dependence are reported to cause more damage to the immune systems of African Americans than other ethnic groups. The greater sensitivity to alcohol and its damaging effects puts this group at an increased risk for infection and, in many cases, at a greater likelihood of death (Rostler 2000).

In regard to the international frequency of drinking, Bloomfield et al. (2003) report the following:

- Spain had the highest frequency of drinking for men, Italy had the highest frequency for women, and Ireland had the lowest frequency for both genders.
- Among nine European countries, France had the highest and Finland had the lowest frequency of drinking (i.e., number of drinking occasions within a month).
- Wilsnack and colleagues (2000), with their sample of 10 countries, found the highest frequencies of drinking (i.e., number of drinking occasions in a month) among Dutch women and Czech men and the lowest frequencies among Estonian women and men.
- In two studies, Italy had the highest and Finland the lowest rates of daily drinking.
- In a two-country comparison of drinking and nondrinking respondents, Germany reported almost twice as many drinking days as did U.S. respondents.
- All of these studies suggest that the main wine-consuming (and wine-producing) countries of Europe have the highest frequencies of drinking.
- The frequency of consumption was highest in the United Kingdom, followed by the European countries and Canada, and the United States ranked third.

In a 2005 study of forty-five countries, another source listing total liters of pure alcohol consumed per drinking-age person (which includes beer, wine, and spirits), from highest to lowest, the top ten countries are: Luxemburg, Hungary, Czech Republic, Ireland, Germany, Spain, Portugal, United Kingdom, Denmark, and Austria, with the United States listed as 26th. Lowest ranking countries (bottom 10 countries, highest to lowest) were Sweden, South Africa, Venezuela, Norway, Thailand, Brazil, China, Columbia, Taiwan, and Mexico (World Advertising Research Center, 2005).

As information on cultural differences in alcohol use and abuse has become known throughout the alcohol abuse field, administrative agencies have attempted to incorporate these insights into professional standards of practice, under the rubric of "cultural competence." Prevention and treatment programs are to be evaluated from the standpoint of their competence in providing services to the cultural populations they serve. To avoid stereotyping, these considerations include understanding of such variables as ethnic acculturation and skills at eliciting information on the cultural background of clients (Office for Substance Abuse Prevention [OSAP] 1992). Prevention issues such as consumption of gateway drugs and media advocacy have been refined to target ethnic at-risk populations. For example, urban African American youths are bombarded with aggressive marketing of 40-ounce malt liquors, known as "40s." Consumption of 40s is celebrated in rap lyrics such as "Tap the Bottle." The alcohol content of malt liquors ranges from 5.6% to 8%, compared with 3.5% for regular beers. This large, inexpensive bottle of potent brew offers a cheap high, often leading to alcohol abuse. Moreover, in the mid-1990s, 40s drinking increasingly became associated with marijuana smoking, going together like cookies and milk, used before school or at "hooky parties."

■ Culture Provides Attitudes Regarding Alcohol Consumption

Although cultures often maintain generalized (normative) attitudes regarding alcohol use and abuse, significant differences in attitudes also exist within cultures (Arkin and Funkhouser 1992; Inciardi 1992). The United States is characterized as culturally ambivalent regarding alcohol use (Kinney 2000). That is, alcohol consumption enormously varies across our culture. Different geographic regions, diverse religious beliefs, and racial and ethnic differences result in confusing attitudes about drinking alcohol. Other factors that contribute to diversity in attitudes include social upbringing, peer group dynamics, social class, income, education, and occupational differences.

What specific impact do such attitudes have on drinking? As just mentioned, attitudes are responsible for making alcohol consumption acceptable or unacceptable — or even relished as a form of behavior. For example, in one segment of impoverished African American groups, alcohol use and abuse are so common that they have become accepted behavior. The following excerpt describes an accepted use of alcohol consumption:

A party without liquor or a street rap without a bottle is often perceived as unimaginable.

These attitudes about drinking are shaped as youth grow up seeing liquor stores in their communities next to schools, churches, and homes. Liquor stores and bootleg dealers frequently permeate the black residential community, where in traditionally white communities they are generally restricted to commercial or business zones. With liquor stores throughout the fabric of black residential life, black youth grow up seeing men drinking in the streets and relatives drinking at home. (Harper 1986)

Contrast this attitude with orthodox religious and fundamentalist communities in which the use of alcohol and other drugs is strictly prohibited:

I was raised in a very religious, Seventh-Day Adventist family. My father was a pretty strong figure in our little church of 18 members. My mother stayed home most of the time, living in a way like an Old Testament kind of biblical life, so-to-speak. We were strict vegetarians, and all of us in the family had to be very involved with church life. The first time I ever saw alcohol outside of always hearing how corrupting it was to the mind and the body, was when I was 7. One day the father of a friend of mine — the only non-Adventist family friend I was allowed to play with — was drinking a beer in the kitchen when we walked in. I asked, "What's that?" The father's reply was "This is beer, dear John." I looked strangely at him and pretended to be amused at the father's answer. Actually, inside I remember being very surprised and scared at the same time for I was always told that people who drink alcohol were not doing what God wanted them to do in life. *(From Venturelli's research files, 18-year-old male university student, May 21, 1993.)*

From these contrasting examples, we can see that the values expressed through group and family attitudes regarding drug use are very significant in determining the extent of alcohol consumption.

College and University Students and Alcohol Use

Over the years, alcohol use and consumption rates among college students have remained largely stable, although rates for other drugs show a lot more variance. For example, marijuana use has dramatically risen, fallen, and then risen again. There do exist some interesting findings about college students and alcohol consumption:

- College students drink an estimated 4 billion cans of beer annually.
- The total amount of alcohol consumed by college students each year is 430 million gallons, enough for every college and university in the United States to fill an Olympic-size swimming pool.
- As many as 360,000 of the nation's 12 million undergraduates will die from alcohol-related causes while in school. This is more than the number who will receive master's and doctorate degrees (Alcoholism Kills 2000).
- Nearly half of all college students are binge drinkers.
- The number of college women who drink to get drunk has more than tripled in the past 10 years, rising from 10% to 35%.
- On America's college campuses, alcohol is a factor in 40% of all academic problems and 28% of all dropouts.
- Seventy-five percent of male students and 55% of female students involved in acquaintance rape had been drinking or using drugs at the time.
- For college men, alcohol consumption is inversely related to the size of the institution; that is, male students at smaller institutions consume far more than those at larger institutions. (Lack of social activities could be a precipitating factor.)
- Nearly one quarter of students report failing a test or project because of the aftereffects of drinking or doing drugs.
- Although only 2 in 20 college students are arrested for driving under the influence, "...27% of students said they drove while under the influence of alcohol ... [and this] ... translates to 2.1 million students." (Hitt 2001, p. 1).
- A related consequence of alcohol abuse is motor vehicle accidents. For young people under the age of 25, motor vehicle accidents rate as the number one cause of death (Presley et al. 1996).
- Findings from the CORE Institute survey (see paragraph following this list) indicate that 300,000 of today's college students will die of alcohol-related causes, such as drunk driving accidents, liver disorders, sexually transmitted diseases from improper sexual protection

Alcohol consumption is routine at many social activities for college students.

(lack of condoms leading to HIV), cancers from alcohol abuse, and severely damaged organs from chronic drinking (see Chapter 7; Phoenix House 2000).

- Although the average cost for book purchases for classes is about $450 per year, the average student spends about $900 on alcohol each year (Phoenix House 2000).
- On the positive side, there is a small but very significant downward trend in alcohol use on America's campuses. In 1985, the percentage of college students who had consumed alcohol in the previous 30 days was approximately 80%. By 1990, that number had declined to 74.5% and it continues to decline each year. However, counterbalancing this positive trend, the use of other illegitimate-type drugs continues to increase. Further, the latest studies show that although overall alcohol consumption is slowly decreasing, binge drinking remains high on most campuses throughout the United States (Wechsler et al. 2000a).

The CORE Institute survey is a validated survey instrument that has been administered to more than 1 million students — by far the largest sample of college students surveyed. The available figures from this survey (Presley et al. 1996) indicate that on average, approximately 83% of college students consumed alcohol within the year this survey was given. The average number of drinks that students consumed was 5.1 per week (Presley et al. 1996). Approximately 42% engaged in binge drinking 2 weeks before the CORE survey was administered. Of all the drugs reported, alcohol was the most heavily abused on college campuses, followed by tobacco (44%) and marijuana (31%).

■ Binge Drinking

Binge drinking is defined as consumption of five or more drinks in one sitting or five or more drinks in short succession. The widely reported study by Wechsler and colleagues (1994 and 2000b) brought this issue to the public's attention. One report, which surveyed 17,592 students at 140 campuses, revealed that 44% engaged in binge drinking, which impacted on many areas of students' lives — both their own and those of others whose lives were disrupted by this behavior (giving rise to the term *secondhand drinking*).

As mentioned in the previous section, 42% to 50% of all college students often binge drink.[1] This type of alcohol consumption remains very worrisome to anyone supporting, nurturing, protecting, caring for, and responsible for the behavior of young people in this subculture. In addition, health professionals see this as a serious form of alcohol abuse.

One may question whether all five-drink episodes qualify as *binge drinking,* a term that calls to mind a weekend of drinking, or Jellinek's epsilon alcoholism. However, 11.1% of males and 7.4% of females reported three or more episodes of memory loss during the past year due to drug or alcohol use, of which the overwhelming majority were alcohol-related, both because alcohol is the major drug consumed by students and because it produces amnesiac episodes. Amnesiac episodes are accepted as symptoms of problem drinking behavior.

In one national survey of 17,600 students at 140 4-year colleges and universities, which is regularly conducted by the Harvard School of Public Health (Wechsler et al. 2000a, p. 1), the findings were as follows:

- "Overall, 44% of the students were binge drinkers. Among men, 50% were binge drinkers; among women, the figure was 39%."
- "The main reason given for binge drinking was 'to get drunk.'"
- "Being white, involved in athletics, or a resident of a fraternity or sorority made it more likely that a student would be a binge drinker."

---

1. The variation depends on the methodology of testing (self-report versus survey) and type of campuses (private versus public institutions, alcohol policies and extent of police enforcement, size of campuses, urban versus rural campuses, commuter versus dormitory, college versus university).

"White students were over twice as likely to be binge drinkers compared to other racial/ethnic groups."

"Students who said that religious participation is not very important to them were more than twice as likely to be binge drinkers compared to other students."

"Students who said that athletic participation was very important or important to them were also one-and-a-half times more likely to be binge drinkers."

"Residents of fraternities or sororities were four times as likely to be binge drinkers compared to other students."

Another study revealed the following:

- Community college students were less likely to engage in binge drinking; 29.9% had binged in the previous 2 weeks compared with 40.4% of their peers at 4-year schools.

- Approximately one fourth of all males enrolled at 4-year colleges reported three or more binge episodes during the previous 2 weeks.

- Students who lived on campus were more likely to binge drink than those who lived off campus. Furthermore, older, working, off-campus students were less likely to engage in such behavior, lowering their scores in this regard relative to the standard college student.

- Native American students had the highest frequency of drinking episodes, binge drinking, and memory loss, followed (in order) by white, Hispanic, African American, and Asian students.

It is not unusual for college students to overconsume alcohol when they are partying.

Gender and Collegiate Alcohol Use

The findings from the CORE survey consistently indicate greater frequency of male drinking, frequency of male binge drinking, and consequences of drinking. In a review of the literature addressing gender and student drinking patterns, Berkowitz and Perkins (1987) found a historical pattern of male-dominated college drinking patterns. The transition into college is associated with a doubling of the percentages of those who drink for both genders. Both men and women drink to enhance sociability or social interaction, to escape negative emotions or release otherwise unacceptable ones, and to simply get drunk. "Drinking to get drunk" is generally considered more of a male pursuit. Indeed, males are more frequently associated with binge drinking and negative public consequences than female drinkers. Severe drunkenness and a customary rowdiness or drunken comportment are normative for male drinkers who binge, with the results including fighting, property damage, and troubles with authorities. The latter were twice as likely to be male problems.

Unsurprisingly, drinking is inversely related to academic achievement. With heavier drinkers, grades suffered for both male and female students. According to the studies cited by Berkowitz and Perkins (1987) for binge drinkers, the impact on impaired academic performance is just as great for women drinkers. More recent information (De Jong 1995; Presley et al. 1996; Wechsler 2000a, 2000b) corroborates this finding and shows similar consequences among male and female binge drinkers in terms of health problems, personal injury, and unplanned sexual activity. Over the past few decades, however, drinking behaviors (amount and percentage of drinking) have been becoming more similar between males and females.

Alcohol Consumption Patterns of Women

Women are affected by alcohol differently than are men. Women possess greater sensitivity to alcohol, have a greater likelihood of addiction, and develop alcohol-related health problems sooner than men.[2] Why do women respond differently than men to

---

2. Even currently accepted definitions of binge drinking differ by gender. For men, binge drinking consists of *five* or more drinks; for women, binge drinking consists of *four* or more drinks in one sitting.

alcohol? Three reasons are (1) women have a smaller body size (men are generally larger than women); (2) women absorb alcohol sooner than men because on average they possess more body fat and body fat does not dilute alcohol as well as water (male bodies contain more water); and (3) women possess less of a metabolizing enzyme that functions to get rid of (process out) alcohol.

In Great Britain, for example, the proportion of women drinking has risen steadily since 1984. This increase in drinking still holds true for all age groups with the exception of women older than 65 (Alcohol Concern 2000). Other notable facts regarding women and drinking can be summarized as follows (*About.com* 1998):

- Although men begin drinking earlier in life, women are more likely than men to start drinking heavily later in life.
- Women are more easily affected by alcohol consumption, both its effects and diseases related to alcoholism — cirrhosis of the liver, stomach cancer, and so on.

- Women's alcohol consumption is often similar to that of people they are close to, such as a lover or husband.
- Full-time working, professionally oriented women drink at the end of their working day, whereas women who stay at home drink alcohol throughout the day.
- More women in alcohol treatment come from sexually abusive homes (70%), in comparison to men (12%).
- Today, women are more visible and their behavior, especially alcohol consumption, is more observable (e.g., drinking in bars, purchasing alcohol).

Figure 8.8 shows the prevalence of binge drinking among childbearing-aged women (18–44), by state (Centers for Disease Control and Prevention [CDC] 2004). While the U.S. average of all the states is 12.4% of women 18–44 years, the state of Wisconsin has the highest percentage (21.6%) and the state of Kentucky has the lowest percentage (5.4%). This figure also shows that:

FIGURE 8.8

Prevalence of reported frequent alcohol consumption* among childbearing-age women (18 to 44 years) — United States, Behavioral Risk Factor Surveillance System, 2002.

*Consumption of an average of seven or more drinks per week or five or more drinks on at least one occasion during the preceding month.

Source: Centers for Disease Control and Prevention (CDC). "Alcohol Consumption Among Women Who Are Pregnant or Might Become Pregnant–United States, 2002." *Morbidity and Mortality Weekly Report (MMWR), 53* (24 December 2004): 1178–1181.

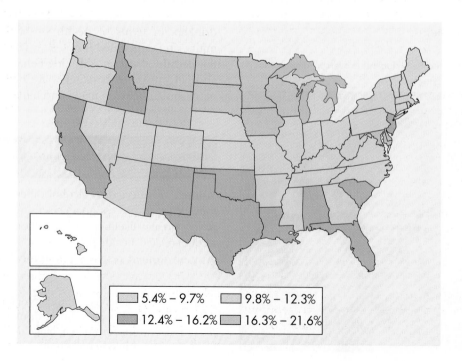

- The highest consumption (first tier of states) with 16.3–21.6% of childbearing women is in the following states: Delaware, Iowa, Minnesota, Montana, Nevada, New Jersey, North Dakota, South Dakota, Wisconsin, and Wyoming.
- The second highest states (second-tier states) with 12.4–16.2% are the following: Alaska, Arizona, Colorado, Hawaii, Illinois, Indiana, Kansas, Maine, Massachusetts, Michigan, Missouri, Nebraska, New Hampshire, New York, Ohio, Oregon, Pennsylvania, Rhode Island, Vermont, Virginia, and Washington.
- The third highest states (third-tier states) with 9.8–12.3% are the following: Alabama, California, Connecticut, Florida, Idaho, Louisiana, New Mexico, Oklahoma, South Carolina, and Texas.
- The fourth highest states (fourth-tier states) with 5.4–9.7% are the following: Arkansas, Georgia, Kentucky, Mississippi, North Carolina, Tennessee, Utah, and the Virgin Islands.

As a group, alcohol-abusing women are more likely to drink alone at home. A high incidence of alcohol abuse is found in women who are unemployed and looking for work, whereas less alcohol abuse is likely in women who are employed part-time. Divorced or separated women, women who never marry, and those who are unmarried and living with a partner are more likely to use and abuse alcohol than married women. Other high-risk groups are women in their twenties and early thirties and women with heavy-drinking husbands or partners. Other researchers (Williams et al. 1997; Wilsnack et al. 1986) found that women who experience depression or encounter problems with fertility or menopausal changes also demonstrate heavier drinking behavior.

Looking at specific age groups, the following conclusions were drawn by the National Institute on Alcohol Abuse and Alcoholism (1990), Register et al. (2002), and by Waters at Northern Arizona University (1999):

1. The course of alcohol addiction progresses at a faster rate among women than among men.
2. For many women, heavy drinking came after a health problem such as depression or reproductive difficulties.
3. Women in the 21- to 34-year-old age group were least likely to report alcohol-related problems if they had stable marriages and were working full time. In other words, young mothers with full-time occupations reported less reliance on alcohol in comparison to childless women without full-time work.
4. Women tend to marry men whose drinking habits match their own.
5. In the 35- to 49-year-old age group, the heaviest drinkers were divorced or separated women without children in the home.
6. In the 50- to 64-year-old age group, the heaviest drinkers were women whose husbands or partners drank heavily.
7. Women 65 years and older constitute less than 10% of drinkers with drinking problems.

More alcohol consumption is also found in women who closely work in traditionally so-called masculine occupations and levels of management, such as executives and traditional blue-collar occupations. In April 1995, former First Lady Betty Ford made the following statement:

Today, we know that when a woman abuses alcohol or other drugs, the risk to her health is much greater than it is for a man. Yet there is not enough prevention, intervention, and treatment targeting women. It is still much harder for women to get help. That needs to change. (SAMHSA 1995, p. 14)

In fact, women risk serious health consequences when they choose to use alcohol and other drugs. Alcohol, in particular, can often be devastating to women's health.

Not only does alcohol have a greater immediate effect on women, but its long-term risks are also more dangerous. Some surveys now show that more alcohol consumption occurs among girls 12 to 17 years old than among boys of the same age. This places young women at a risk of delaying the onset of puberty, a condition that can wreak havoc in terms of adolescent maturation.

Finally, women are more likely to combine alcohol with prescription drugs than men are. When the use of other drugs enters into the equation, ovulation may become inhibited and fertility may be adversely affected. Women also risk early menopause when they consume alcohol.

The Role of Alcohol in Domestic Violence

Much attention became focused on domestic violence in the mid-1990s through high-profile criminal cases such as those involving the Menendez brothers and O. J. Simpson. The increased emphasis on decreasing domestic violence has inspired much research into its causes and effects as well as into common traits of abusers. Recent studies have found a significant relationship between the incidence of battering and the abuse of alcohol; furthermore, the abuse of alcohol overwhelmingly emerges as a primary predictor of marital violence (De Jong 1995; Drug Strategies 1999). A study of 2000 American couples conducted in 1993 showed that rates of domestic violence were as much as 15 times higher in households in which the husband was described as "often" being drunk, as opposed to "never" drunk (Collins and Messerschmidt 1993). The same study found that alcohol was present in more than half of all reported incidences of domestic abuse.

Domestic violence also creates significant problems for its victims later in life. A study of 472 women by the Research Institute on Addictions found that 87% of female alcoholics had been physically or sexually abused as children (Drug Strategies 1999; Miller and Downs 1993). The insidiousness of domestic violence may exist because of the consistent abuse of alcohol that is associated with both abusers and victims. Given these disturbing statistics, more research and counseling programs focused on the prevention of alcoholism and subsequent domestic violence are necessary before the very foundations of identity, security, and happiness are forever destroyed. As one reformed alcoholic explains:

> I had gone too far. I had abused my family, I had beaten my wife. I had driven them off, all for a drink. (*From Venturelli's research files, 50-year-old male, October 1996.*)

■ Alcohol and Sex

Alcohol use is linked to an overwhelming proportion of unwanted sexual behaviors, including **acquaintance and date rape**, unplanned pregnancies, and sexually transmitted diseases, including HIV infections (Abbey 1990; World Health Organization [WHO] 1998). Factors that immediately come to mind include disinhibition concerning restraints on sexuality, poor judgment, and unconsciousness or helplessness on the part of victims. The links between unwanted sex and substance abuse are subtler than many imagine, however. Although disinhibition, impulsivity, and helplessness are certainly major considerations, other elements come into play, as illustrated in the following paragraphs.

Recall the drunken comportment thesis that was introduced in the section on culture and drinking behavior. Some nonreligious ceremonial drinking settings incorporate expectations of disinhibited behaviors, such as at holiday office parties. Drinking is a signal or cue that it is acceptable to be amorous, even sexually aggressive, and that the intoxicated object of one's affections will not object and is disinhibited.

Intoxicated people are not as capable of attending to multiple cues. When cues are ambiguous, drunken men are more likely to miss the ambiguity and to interpret cues as meaning that sex will occur and should be initiated (men are generally more likely to interpret friendly cues as sexual signals, but intoxication makes this misunderstanding more likely). In addition, possible dangers implicit in a private setting, on a date, with a drunken male will not be picked up as often or as easily by the intoxicated and potentially victimized female (Abbey 1990).

Alcohol and the Family: Destructive Types of Support and Organizations for Victims of Alcoholics

■ Codependency and Enabling

Codependency and enabling generally occur together. **Codependency** (which some call *co-alcoholism*) refers to a relationship pattern, and *enabling* refers to a set of specific behaviors (Doweiko 1999). Codependency is defined as the behavior displayed by either addicted or nonaddicted family members (codependents) who identify with the alcohol addict and *cover up* the excessive drinking behavior. An example of codependency is when a family member remains silent when empty bottles of vodka (for example) are discovered under a bed or in the garage.

KEY TERMS

acquaintance and date rape
unplanned and unwanted forced sexual attack from a friend or a date partner

codependency
behavior displayed by either addicted or nonaddicted family members (codependents) who identify with the alcohol addict and cover-up the excessive drinking behavior, allowing it to continue and letting it affect the codependent's life

Enablers are those close to the alcohol addict who deny or make excuses for enabling the excessive drinking. Often, both codependency and enabling are done by the same person. An example is the husband who calmly conspires and phones his wife's place of employment and reports that his wife has stomach flu when the reality is that she is too drunk or hung over to even realize it is time to go to work.

Such a husband is both codependent and an enabler. He lies to cover up his wife's addiction and enables her not to face her irresponsible drinking behavior. In this example, the husband is responsible for perpetuating the spouse's addiction. Even quiet toleration of the alcoholic's addiction enables the drinker to continue the drinking behavior.

Children of Alcoholics and Adult Children of Alcoholics

Alcoholism is a disease of the family. Not only is there a significant genetic component that is passed from generation to generation, but also the drinking problems of a single-family member affect all other family members. The family environment and genetics can perpetuate a vicious and destructive cycle. (George Washington University Medical Center 2002, pp. 1–2)

Children of alcoholics are at high risk for developing problems with alcohol and other drugs; they often do poorly at school, live with pervasive tension and stress, have high levels of anxiety and depression and experience coping problems. (George Washington University Medical Center 2002, pp. 1–2)

It is estimated that out of 260 million Americans, 14 million Americans — 7.4% of the population — meet the diagnostic criteria for alcohol abuse or alcoholism (Grant et al. 1997). There are 28.6 million children of alcoholics (COAs) in the United States, and 6.6 million are younger than the age of 18 (Alcoholism Kills 2000; National Clearinghouse for Alcohol and Drug Information [NCADI] 1992). Approximately 25% of American children are exposed before the age of 18 to at least one person in

the family who is either an alcoholic or an alcohol abuser (George Washington University Medical Center 2003). Children of alcoholics are at high risk of developing the same attachment to alcohol. Alcoholics are more likely than nonalcoholics to have an alcoholic parent, sibling, or other relative.

Within the last decade, both COAs and adult children of alcoholics (ACOAs) have been studied extensively. Here are some findings concerning these two groups:

1. COAs are two to four times more likely to develop alcoholism. In addition, both COAs and ACOAs are more likely to marry into families in which alcoholism is prevalent.
2. Approximately one third of alcoholics come from families in which one parent was or is an alcoholic.
3. Both physiological and environmental factors appear to place COAs and ACOAs at greater risk of becoming alcoholics.
4. COAs and ACOAs exhibit more symptoms of depression and anxiety than do children of nonalcoholic parents.
5. Young children of alcoholics exhibit an excessive amount of crying, bed-wetting, and sleep problems, such as nightmares.
6. Teenagers display excessive perfectionism, hoarding, staying by themselves (loners), and excessive self-consciousness.
7. Phobias develop, and difficulty with school performance is not uncommon.

Treatment of Alcoholism

Chapter 18 provides an overview of treatment and rehabilitation of addicts. Although treatment of alcoholism and treatment of other addictions have somewhat separate historical roots and consequently gave rise to separate therapy systems, governmental authorities, and counselor certifications, they have now merged in most states in the United States. In addition to recognizing that alcohol is a drug addiction, epidemiologically few "pure" alcoholics and drug addicts exist any more. Most addicts drink in addition to their other drug addictions (making them *polydrug users*); many alcoholics abuse other drugs; and some move through stages of heroin, methadone, and alcohol use, in that order. Alcoholism and its treatment have a few special features:

1. While addicts remain in denial, the socially acceptable nature of drinking, or even of heavy

drinking, makes it easier to maintain denial as a psychological defense. As an example, it is more difficult to remain in denial of crack addiction.

2. Although all addictions could result in **relapsing syndrome** and most addicts have a tendency to relapse, the social environment that permits or even encourages drinking and the ready availability of alcohol make it easy to relapse without a radical shift in lifestyle. Again, the alcoholic is buffered within a subcultural (social and cultural) cloud of use. Alcoholics Anonymous remains particularly vigilant in looking for signs of relapse, advising the alcoholic to "keep the memory regarding the misery of addiction green," to HALT (which stands for do not get too **h**ungry, **a**ngry, **l**onely, or **t**hirsty/**t**ired, as these are possible relapse triggers), and not to become isolated from others but to stay in the support system, making phone calls and attending "90 meetings in 90 days."

3. Alcohol rehabilitation differs from other addiction treatments mainly in its medical ramifications. Alcoholism is devastating to the liver, muscles, nutritional system, gastrointestinal system, and brain. Alcoholics who have become "dry" only recently may still suffer from pancreatitis, weakness, impaired cognitive capacities, and so forth. The fact that treatment is so structured, simplified, and made into a slogan ("Don't drink and go to meetings," "Keep coming: It works") makes it possible for the bleary and confused, recently dried-out alcoholic to follow (an AA term for this condition is *mokus*). Although the cognitive impairment tends to clear up somewhat over a period of 6 months (unless clear cortical wasting has occurred, a condition known as "wet brain"), the alcoholic is often physically ravaged to an extent that requires years

to mend the damage, if it is ever possible.

4. The alcoholic is typically more emotionally fragile than other addicts in treatment.

5. The other major medical ramification is withdrawal. Withdrawal from alcohol and withdrawal from barbiturates are the two most severe withdrawal syndromes. Before modern medical management techniques, many individuals succumbed to **acute alcohol withdrawal syndrome**.

Getting Through Withdrawal

An alcoholic who is well nourished and in good physical condition can go through withdrawal as an outpatient with reasonable safety. However, an acutely ill alcoholic needs medically supervised care. A general hospital ward is best for preliminary treatment.

The alcohol withdrawal syndrome is quite similar to that described in Chapter 6 for barbiturates and other sedative hypnotics. Symptoms typically appear within 12 to 72 hours after total cessation of drinking but can appear whenever the blood alcohol level drops below a certain point. The alcoholic experiences severe muscle tremors, nausea, and anxiety. In extremely acute alcohol syndromes, a condition known as **delirium tremens** occurs, in which the individual hallucinates, is delirious, and suffers from a high fever and rapid heartbeat. Delirium tremens, commonly called DTs, is an uncommon but life-threatening condition.

Alcohol withdrawal syndrome reaches its peak intensity within 24 to 48 hours. About 5% of the alcoholics in hospitals and perhaps 20% to 25% who suffer the DTs without treatment die. Phenobarbital, chlordiazepoxide (Librium), and diazepam (Valium) are commonly prescribed to prevent withdrawal symptoms. Simultaneously, the alcoholic may need treatment for malnutrition and vitamin deficiencies (especially the B vitamins). Pneumonia is also a frequent complication. After the alcoholic patient is over the acute stages of intoxication and withdrawal, administration of CNS depressants may be continued for a few weeks, with care taken not to transfer dependence on alcohol to dependence on the depressants. Long-term treatment with sedatives (such as Librium or Valium) does not prevent a relapse of drinking or assist with behavioral adaptation. A prescription of disulfiram (Antabuse) may be offered to encourage patients to abstain from alcohol; it blocks metabolism of acetaldehyde, so that

KEY TERMS

relapsing syndrome
returning to the use of alcohol after quitting

acute alcohol withdrawal syndrome
symptoms that occur when an individual who is addicted to alcohol does not maintain his or her usual blood alcohol level

delirium tremens
the DTs; the most severe, even life-threatening form of alcohol withdrawal, involving hallucinations, delirium, and fever

drinking any alcohol will result in a pounding headache, flushing, nausea, and other unpleasant symptoms. The patient must decide about 2 days in advance to stop taking Antabuse before he or she can drink. Antabuse is an aid to other supportive treatments, not the sole method of therapy.

■ Helping the Alcoholic Family Recover

Alcoholism is a pervasive family disease. The family is a system, not of planets or subatomic particles, but of people who affect one another and who play certain roles, all maintaining a balance in the system. We are all familiar with the stereotype of families in which the oldest child is the "hero," the middle child is "forgotten," and the youngest is the "baby." Whatever the roles of the individuals, when the family includes an alcoholic, it means that a member of the system is ill. The system adapts to dysfunction by rearranging itself around the problem. The family is like a mobile, a sculpture with interdependent parts that revolve around one another. We are not talking about adjusting to a person with a broken leg or diabetes, but someone who is in denial — manipulative, lying, and blaming other family members. By adjusting around the addiction, the family members enable the addict to progress further along the disease path. Roles become exaggerated and distorted. Persons may be blamed, scapegoated, or lost and forgotten. One major adaptation is related to the person who "takes up the slack" by assuming extra responsibilities and taking on the role of a parent or even spouse.

Early family therapy systems research described how the family often acts as a unit. It focused on the disturbed communication patterns within families and the process by which the family throws up a scapegoat, often in the form of a child who is presented as the "identified patient" (Kolevzon and Green 1985). The concept of the "super-responsible one" was first described by Virginia Satir in 1964. In modern, popular writing on addiction in the family and codependent roles of children that are carried into adulthood, all of these roles are depicted as especially characteristic of addicted families (Wegscheider 1991). Because such roles are so common, many individuals may identify with them and ascribe a variety of ills to their being addict offspring. Many individuals do suffer tremendously from the legacy of family addiction, and some have indeed been cast in one of these roles as a by-product of addiction in the

Even after the alcoholic is ready for rehabilitation, the other family members will also need treatment and support.

family. Acting as if only one kind of family or one kind of addicted family exists, which transcends cultural backgrounds, is not much better than saying that all languages or religions are the same, however. For example, "executive authority" over younger children can be the normal role of the eldest female child in African American families as part of a broader pattern of role flexibility (Brisbane 1985, 1986). When an older child plays a parental part in the family, it may represent culturally routine behavior or it may be indicative of a response to addiction in the family.

There is some gain or perceived benefit to the person playing a role, and to the system as a whole, in the individual's actions, although this gain may seem very indirect and, in fact, be injurious in the long run. Although the super-responsible person may be overburdened and resentful, he or she also feels important, heroic, and capable. Over a period, this role solidifies. Perhaps the hero becomes unable to remember or imagine it any other way. If the alcoholic enters or promises to enter into recovery, it may threaten the benefits to the family member. One of many examples is a wife in a subservient role who relishes, at some level, the power, control, and authority she enjoys with an alcoholic husband or the recognition she receives in martyrdom — perhaps her only recognition in life. Another example is the child who is given executive authority, prematurely, in the family. Without knowing it, the family members may resist change, not only for what they may have to give up but also because change is always feared. Thus, they may undermine recovery.

The role systems found in alcoholic families can be enmeshed so that everyone is hyperresponsive to and dependent on one another — disorganized, chaotic, or exploded into nothingness. The old-fashioned, middle-class alcoholic family is commonly enmeshed. If religion represents a barrier to divorce, and hence removal of the alcoholic, this situation is even more likely to arise.

A family counselor can help the family members understand the roles they are playing and start a process of change. This recognition allows family members to develop their own identities separate from the roles they have been playing. Two of the techniques used in understanding roles and relationships are **psychodrama** (or **role playing**) and the **genogram**, a kind of family tree in which behavioral relationships as well as biological relationships are explored.

The family counselor can help the family members figure out their patterns of thinking, which involves certain modes of information processing. In the alcoholic family, these patterns typically involve denial, minimization, rationalization, shame, blame, and projection. Counselors also rely on certain self statements (see "Here and Now," The "Top Tens" of Helping Alcoholics and Their Families).

In addition, the family counselor can help the family members understand their patterns of communication. Alcoholic family communication is almost certainly a type of abnormal communication, characterized by either simple absence of communication (chaotic, destructive, manipulative, blaming) or a combination of communication methods. What the family does in the public view, visible to the outside world ("front stage"), differs from what goes on when the family is alone ("back stage"). Some individuals may be cut off from communication or embroiled in endless argument and acrimony. Teaching people how to communicate their feelings and opinions in a direct, honest, and nonhurtful way begins the healing process.

The alcoholic family is injured, traumatized, often in debt, and collectively suffering from **posttraumatic stress disorder**. Impacted grief, loss, pain, and rage are present. Healing will not take place overnight and will not occur just because the alcoholic stops drinking. The child, in particular, may have been wounded by violence, neglect, and inconsistent parenting, and may have been witness to sex, violence, or depression.

KEY TERMS

psychodrama
a family therapy system developed by Jacques Moreno in which significant interpersonal and intrapersonal issues are enacted in a focused setting using dramatic techniques

role playing
a therapeutic technique in which group members play assigned parts to elicit emotional reactions

genogram
a family therapy technique that records information about behavior and relationships on a type of family tree to elucidate persistent patterns of dysfunctional behavior

posttraumatic stress disorder
a psychiatric syndrome in which an individual who has been exposed to a traumatic event or situation experiences persistent psychological stress that may manifest itself in a wide range of symptoms, including reexperiencing the trauma, numbing of general responsiveness, and hyperarousal

Discussion Questions

1. Why do you think alcohol has always been part of our existence as human beings?

2. Cite three positive and three negative outcomes of alcohol use. Do you think negatives outweigh the positives? If so, why? If not, why not?

3. Look at the pyramid of drinkers shown in Figure 8.2. How do you think the percentages will change 10 years, 20 years, and 30 years from now? Support your projections.

4. In light of having read Chapters 7 and 8, what are three positive and three negative outcomes regarding lowering the legal drinking age to 18?

5. Do you personally believe in the strong independent effects of set and setting and pseudo-intoxication? Can these psychological processes have more effects on the alcohol user than the alcohol itself? Wherever possible, give personal examples.

6. Why do you think the temperance movement and Prohibition failed? Cite three main reasons that also support the text material.

7. It is believed that gays and homeless people tend to abuse alcohol more than the straight (heterosexual) and nonhomeless populations. What are three reasons why you think each of the members of these two subcultures have a tendency to overconsume alcohol?

Here and Now

The "Top Tens" of Helping Alcoholics and Their Families

10 "Don'ts"

Don't "persecute" the addict. Confront lovingly.

Don't have the goal of "saving the family."

Don't start sentences with "you never" or "you always."

Don't live in the past or in the future.

Don't make excuses for the alcoholic.

Don't let the alcoholic be the center of your life.

Don't clean up after the alcoholic (literally or figuratively).

Don't protect the alcoholic from the consequences of his or her behavior.

Don't blame, excuse, justify, or rationalize.

Don't join in drinking.

10 "Dos"

Set limits, using "I" words (I need to stop).

Set limits empathetically (I know, you want me to _____, but I can't).

Detach, lovingly, from the addict's problems.

Teach parenting skills.

Concentrate on the here and now.

Talk about violence and abuse.

Remember that you didn't cause it, you can't cure it, and you can't control it.

Take life a day at a time.

Give "self" assignments, taking care of yourself.

Accept the right to have your feelings and for others to have their feelings.

10 Alcoholic Family Self-Statements

In an Actively Alcoholic Family

"Don't talk" (about how you feel, about what's going on).

"Don't trust."

"Don't feel."

"Alcoholism isn't the cause of our problems."

"Keep the status quo at all costs."

In a Family Having a Hard Time Becoming Used to Sobriety

"We liked you better drunk."

"You're always away at AA meetings."

"Who are these people you're always having coffee with?"

"I felt important feeding my brothers and sisters, Mom."

"I felt important going to the school on Open School Night, Dad."

10 Roles for Spouses of Alcoholics

Rescuer

Long-suffering martyr

Blamer, conscience

Fellow drinker

Placater

Overextended, superresponsible one

Composed computer

Sick hypochondriac

Scapegoat ("it's all your fault")

Avoider

10 Roles for Children of Alcoholics

Family hero*

Scapegoat*

Lost child*

Mascot*

Placater

Sick role

Parental child or pseudoparent to younger children

Pseudoparent to alcoholic parent

Pseudospouse to sober parent

Place of refuge (for younger children)

---

*Wegscheider, S. *Another Chance*. Palo Alto, CA: Science and Behavior Books, 1991.

Source: Inservice Training Program, Essex County, New Jersey, Professional Advisory Committee on Alcohol and Drug Abuse. November 1993. Prepared by Peter L. Myers, Ph.D. *Helping the Alcoholic Family Recover*.

8. Why do you think children desire to consume alcohol with their peers?

9. After reviewing the different definitions of what is an alcoholic, what definition do you believe suits you best? Write out a clear definition of what you think is a "real" alcoholic.

10. What specific criteria would you include when teaching college students to drink in moderation during freshman orientation?

11. Should alcohol be available on college campuses for those 21 years of age or over? Why or why not?

12. Recall and discuss the question of how you may have unknowingly acted as an enabler for a family member or a friend. Can you cite the reason why you acted like this?

Summary

1 Approximately 52% of Americans age 12 or older (121 million people) indicated that they were current drinkers of alcohol in 2005. Approximately 23% participated in binge drinking at least once in the 30 days before the 2005 National Survey on Drug Use and Health, and approximately 16 million (6%) were heavy drinkers.

2 Luxembourg ranks first in terms of consumption of alcohol, followed by Germany and France. The lowest levels of drinking are found in Turkey, Kyrgyzstan, Turkmenistan, Israel, and Armenia.

3 Globally, alcohol costs add up to more than $250 billion yearly when including illness, accidents, and crime connected to alcohol. Much of the economic burden of alcohol abuse falls on segments of the population *other than* the alcohol abusers themselves. Approximately 45% of the estimated total cost is borne by alcohol abusers and their families, almost all of which is due to lost or reduced earnings. Approximately 20% of the total estimated cost of alcohol abuse is borne by the federal government and 18% by state and local governments. Each year, more than 107,400 people die because of alcohol-related abuse. Productivity losses resulting from alcohol-related illness were estimated at $87.6 billion for 1998 (NIAAA 2000). Total costs attributed to alcohol-related motor vehicle crashes were estimated to be $24.7 billion. Expenditures for alcohol-related crime totaled $6.2 billion, and $17.4 billion for

illicit drugs. Alcohol abuse is estimated to have contributed to 25% to 30% of violent crime. Finally, alcohol is officially linked to at least half of all highway fatalities, and that figure includes only legal intoxication. In all states, the cutoff for the illegal blood alcohol level is 0.08%.

4 The temperance movement was a response to the heaviest drinking period in America during Jefferson's term in office (1800–1808). The original goal of this movement was to promote moderate use of alcohol. Largely because it was unsuccessful, the temperance movement began advocating total abstinence. Over the course of the 19th century, reformers sought to have complete prohibition enacted into law. Shortly after Prohibition laws were created making alcohol use illegal, organized crime monopolized the production and sale of alcohol as an illicit drug.

5 There are several accepted definitions of alcoholism. Alcohol addiction involves both a physical and psychological dependence on ethanol. Most definitions include chronic behavioral disorders, repeated drinking to the point of loss of control, health disorders, and difficulty functioning socially and economically.

6 The definition of who is a problem drinker varies from one culture to the next. In Poland, a person becomes a problem drinker when there is a loss of productivity. Californians find that drunken driving violations are a key indication. For Italian Americans, an inability to provide for one's family because of heavy drinking qualifies a person as a problem drinker.

7 Culture influences our view of alcohol and alcohol consumption. Culture dictates the self-definition, attachment, and intensity of our behavior. For example, with regard to drinking, much of how we feel after ingesting alcohol is determined by social and psychological experiences. In addition to the amount consumed, *drunken comportment* refers to society's expectations regarding drinking behavior. *Set and setting* refer to the expectation and the environment where alcohol is consumed. *Pseudointoxication* refers to the psychological belief regarding how one feels under the effects of alcohol — that is, how inebriated the drinker imagines the effect of the consumed alcohol.

8 The broader ways in which culture influences the consumption of alcohol are the following: (1) Culture provides rules for drinking behavior; (2) culture provides ceremonial meaning for alcohol use; (3) culture provides models of alcoholism; and (4) culture provides attitudes regarding alcohol consumption.

9 Regarding alcohol and college students, (1) college students consume an estimated 4 billion cans of beer annually; (2) nearly half of all college students are binge drinkers; (3) one consequence of alcohol abuse is motor vehicle accidents (the number one cause of death in people younger than age 25 is motor vehicle accidents); and (4) 75% of male students and 55% of female students involved in acquaintance rape had been drinking or using drugs at the time.

10 In comparison to men, women possess greater sensitivity to alcohol, are more likely to become addicted, and develop health problems earlier in life than men. Three main reasons why women are more sensitive and are more easily affected by alcohol use are (1) men have larger bodies than women; (2) women absorb alcohol sooner than men because women have more body fat (fat does not dilute alcohol) and men's bodies contain more water; and (3) women possess less of a metabolizing enzyme that functions to get rid of (process out) alcohol.

11 Codependency and enabling generally occur together. *Codependency* is the behavior that a family member or close friend displays to cover up the excessive drinking. *Enabling* refers to anyone who helps the excessive drinker deny or makes excuses for the excessive drinking.

12 Alcoholism treatment must take into consideration physical withdrawal *and* denial.

References

Abbey, A. "Sex and Substance Abuse: What Are the Links?" *Eta Sigma Gamman* 22 (Fall 1990): 16–18.

About.com. "Alcoholism: Greater Risks for Women" (4 November 1998). Available http://alcoholism.about.com/cs/women/a/aa981104.htm.

About.com. "Alcoholism: Are Women More Vulnerable to Alcohol's Effects?" *The New York Times Company,* 1998. Available http://alcoholism.about.com/cs/alerts/l/blnaa46.htm.

Adams, S. H. "The Great American Fraud." *Collier's* 36, 5 (1905): 17–18; 10 (1905): 16–18; 16 (1906): 18–20.

Alcohol Concern 2000. *Alcohol Concern Fact Sheet* 445, London (10 October 2000). Available www.alcoholconcern.org.uk/servlets/doc/445.

Alcoholismkills.com. "Alcoholism Statistics." (January 2008). Available http://www.alcoholismkills.com.

Arkin, E. B., and J. E. Funkhouser, eds. *Communicating About Alcohol and Other Drugs: Strategies for Reaching Populations at Risk,* OSAP Prevention Monograph No. 5. Rockville, MD: Office of Substance Abuse Prevention, U.S. Department of Health and Human Services, 1992.

Austin, G. A. "Perspectives on the History of Psychoactive Substance Use." *National Institute on Drug Abuse Research Issues* 23. Washington, DC: U.S. Department of Health, Education, and Welfare, 1978.

Babor, T. F., M. Hesselbrock, S. Radouce-Thomas, L. Feguer, J. P. Ferrant, and K. Choquette. "Concepts of Alcoholism Among American, French-Canadian, and French Alcoholics." In *Alcohol and Culture: Comparative Perspectives from Europe and America,* edited by T. F. Babor, 98–109. New York: Academy of Sciences, 1986.

Bales R. F. "Cultural Differences in Rates of Alcoholism." *Quarterly Journal of Studies on Alcohol* 6 (1946): 489–499.

Berkowitz, A. D., and H. W. Perkins. "Recent Research on Gender Differences in Collegiate Alcohol Use." *Journal of American College Health* 36 (September 1987): 12–15.

Bloomfield, K., T. Stockwell, G. Gmel, and N. Rehn. "International Comparisons of Alcohol Consumption." *Alcohol Res Health,* 2003; 27(11): 95–109.

Blume, S., D. Dropkin, and L. Sokolow. "The Jewish Alcoholic: A Descriptive Study." *Alcohol, Health, and Research World* 4 (1980): 21–26.

Brisbane, F. L. "A Self-Help Model for Working with Black Women of Alcoholic Parents." *Alcoholism Treatment Quarterly* 2 (Fall 1985b/Winter 1986): 47–53.

Brisbane, F. L. "Understanding the Female Child Role of Family Hero in Black Alcoholic Families." *Bulletin of the NY State Chapter of the National Black Alcoholism Council* 4 (April 1985a).

Center for Substance Abuse Research (CESAR). "Alcohol-Related Traffic Fatalities Remain Steady at Around 40%." (10 October 2005). Available http://www.cesar.umd.edu/cesar/cesarfax/vol14/14-41.pdf.

Centers for Disease Control and Prevention (CDC). "Alcohol Consumption among Women Who Are Pregnant or Who Might Become Pregnant — United States, 2002." *Morbidity and Mortality Weekly Report (MMWR),* 53 (24 December 2004): 1178–1181.

Collins, J. J., and M. A. Messerschmidt. "Epidemiology of Alcohol-Related Violence." *Alcohol, Health, and Research World* 17 (1993): 93–100.

De Jong, J. "Scope of the Problem: Gender and Drinking." *Catalyst (Higher Education Center for Alcohol and Other Drug Prevention)* 1 (Spring 1995): 1.

Douglass, F. *Life and Times of Frederick Douglass.* New York: Collier Books, 1892 (1967): 147–148.

Doweiko, H. E. *Concepts of Chemical Dependency,* 4th ed. Monterey, CA: Brooks/Cole, 1999.

Drug Strategies. "Alcohol and Crime." *Millennium Hangover: Keeping Score on Alcohol.* Washington, DC (1999): 5. Available http://www.drugstrategies.org/keepingscore1999/crime.html.

Gallup Poll. "Alcohol and Drinking." Princeton, NJ, 2007. Available www.galluppoll.com/poll/1582/alcohol-drinking.aspx.

Garrison, V., and J. Podell. "Community Support Systems Assessment for Use in Clinical Interviews." *Schizophrenia Bulletin* 7 (1981): 1.

Gary, L. E., and R. B. Gary. "Treatment Needs of Black Alcoholic Women." *Alcoholism Treatment Quarterly* 2 (1985): 97–113.

George Washington University Medical Center. "Resources: Fact Sheets." *Ensuring Solutions to Alcohol Problems.* Washington, DC: George Washington University Medical Center, 2002. Available http://www.ensuringsolutions.org/resources/resources_show.htm?doc_id=339037.

Gold, M. S. *The Good News About Drugs and Alcohol.* New York: Villard Books, 1991.

Goode, E. *Drugs in American Society.* Boston: McGraw-Hill College, 1999.

Gordon, A. J. "The Cultural Context of Drinking and Indigenous Therapy for Alcohol Problems in Three Migrant Hispanic Cultures." *Journal of Studies on Alcohol* supplement 9 (1981): 217–240.

Grant, B. F., T. C. Harford, P. Chou, R. Pickering, D. A. Dawson, E. S. Stinson, and J. Noble. "Prevalence of DSM-IV Alcohol Abuse and Dependence: United States." *Alcohol Health Research World* 18 (1997): 243–248.

Gusfield, J. R. *Symbolic Crusade: Status Politics and the American Temperance Movement,* 2nd ed. Chicago: University of Illinois, 1986.

Harper, F. D. *The Black Family and Substance Abuse.* Detroit, MI: Detroit Urban League, 1986.

Harwood, H. *Updating Estimates of the Economic Costs of Alcohol Abuse in the United States: Estimates, Update Methods and Data.* Report prepared by The Lewin Group for the National Institute on Alcohol Abuse and Alcoholism, 2000.

Harwood, H., D. Fountain, and G. Livermore. *The Economic Costs of Alcohol and Drug Abuse in the United States, 1992.* NIH Pub. No. 98-4327. Rockville, MD: National Institute on Drug Abuse, 1998.

Hitt, E. "Alcohol Abuse Takes Major Toll on College Students." *Yahoo! News,* Reuters Limited (24 October 2001).

Inciardi, J. A. *The War on Drugs II.* Mountain View, CA: Mayfield, 1992.

Jellinek, E. M. *The Disease Concept of Alcoholism.* New Haven, CT: College and University Press, 1960.

Johnston, L. D., P. M. O'Malley, and J. G. Bachman. *Monitoring the Future: National Results on Adolescent Drug Use: Overview of Key Findings* (NIH Publication No. 06-5882). Bethesda, MD: National Institute on Drug Abuse, 2005.

Jones, J. M. "Beer Again Edges Out Wine as Americans' Drink of Choice." *The Gallup Poll.* Princeton, NJ: The Gallup Organization, 12 July 2007. Available http://www.gallup.com/poll/28234/Beer-Again_Edges_Wine-Americans_Drink_Choice.aspx.

Keller, M. "Alcoholism: Nature and Extent of the Problem: Understanding Alcoholism." *Annals American Academy Political and Social Science* 315 (1958): 1–11.

Kinney, J. *Loosening the Grip,* 6th ed. Boston: McGraw-Hill, 2000.

Kolevzon, M. S., and R. G. Green. *Family Therapy Models.* New York: Springer, 1985.

Lender, M. E., and J. K. Martin. *Drinking in America,* rev. ed. New York: Free Press, 1987.

Levine, H. G. "The Good Creature of God and the Demon Rum." In *Research Monograph No. 12: Alcohol and Disinhibition: Nature and Meaning of the Link,* 111–161. Rockville, MD: National Institute on Alcohol Abuse and Alcoholism, 1983.

MacAndrew, C., and R. B. Edgerton. *Drunken Comportment: A Social Explanation.* Chicago, IL: Aldine, 1969.

Makela, K. "Attitudes Towards Drinking and Drunkenness in Four Scandinavian Countries." In *Alcohol and Culture: Comparative Perspectives from Europe and America. Annals of the New York Academy of Science* 472, edited by T. F. Babor. New York: New York Academy of Sciences, 1986.

Marshall, M. "Four Hundred Rabbits: An Anthropological View of Ethanol as a Disinhibitor." In *Alcohol and Disinhibition: Nature and Meaning of the Link.* Washington, DC: U.S. HHS, PHS, ADAMHA, NIAAA Research Monograph No. 12, 1983.

Miller, B. A., and W. R. Downs, "The Impact of Family Violence on the Use of Alcohol by Women." *Alcohol, Health, and Research World* 17 (1993): 137–143.

National Clearinghouse for Alcohol and Drug Information (NCADI). *The Fact Is . . . Alcoholism Tends to Run in Families.* OSAP Prevention Resource Guide. Rockville, MD: NCADI, 1992.

National Institute on Alcohol Abuse and Alcoholism (NIAAA). *10th Special Report to the U.S Congress on Alcohol and Health: Highlights from Current Research.* Washington, DC: US Government Printing Office, June 2000.

National Institute on Alcohol Abuse and Alcoholism (NIAAA). *Tenth Special Report to the U.S. Congress on Alcohol and Health.* NIH Publication No. 97-5017. Bethesda, MD: National Institute on Alcohol Abuse and Alcoholism, 1997.

National Institute on Alcohol Abuse and Alcoholism (NIAAA). *Seventh Special Report to the U.S. Congress on Alcohol and Health.* Washington, DC: U.S. Government Printing Office, 1990.

National Institute on Alcohol Abuse and Alcoholism (NIAAA). *Facts About Alcohol and Alcoholism.* Washington, DC: U.S. Government Printing Office, 1980.

National Institute on Alcohol Abuse and Alcoholism (NIAAA). "Frequently Asked Questions on Alcohol Abuse and Alcoholism." 2007. Available http://www.niaaa.nih.gov/faqs/general-english/.

National Institute on Drug Abuse (NIDA). *National Survey Results on Drug Use from the Monitoring the Future Study, 1975–1998. Volume 1: Secondary School Students.* Washington, DC: U.S. Government Printing Office, 1999.

National Institutes of Health (NIH) and the National Institute on Alcohol Abuse and Alcoholism (NIAAA), U.S. Department of Health and Human Services (USDHHS).

Researchers Identify Alcoholism Subtypes. Bethesda, MD: Government Printing Office, 2007. Available http://www.nih.gov/news/pr/jun2007/niaaa-28.htm.

Newport, F. "Alcohol and Drinking." Princeton, NJ: The Gallup Organization, November 13–15, 2000. Available http://www.gallup.com/poll/1582/alcohol-drinking.aspx.

Office for Substance Abuse Prevention (OSAP). *Cultural Competence for Evaluators.* Washington, DC: Office for Substance Abuse Prevention, U.S. HHS, PHS, ADAMHA, DHHS Publication No. (ADM) 92-1884, 1992.

Office of Applied Studies (OAS). Substance Abuse and Mental Health Services Administration (SAMHSA) "Driving Under the Influence (DUI) Among Young Persons." National Survey on Drug Use and Health (NSDUH). Rockville, MD: Substance Abuse and Mental Health Services Administration (SAMHSA), 2004.

Office of Applied Studies (OAS), Substance Abuse and Mental Health Services Administration (SAMHSA), "The NHSDA Report: Alcohol Use." Rockville, MD: Substance Abuse and Mental Health Services Administration, 2001. Available http://www.drugabusestatistics.samhsa.gov.

Osterberg, E. "Alcohol-Related Problems in Cross-National Perspective." *Alcohol and Culture: Comparative Perspectives from Europe and America. Annals of the New York Academy of Sciences,* 472 (1986): 10–21.

Phoenix House. School Daze? (2000). Available http://www.factsontap.org/factsontap/alcohol_student_life/school_daze.htm.

Presley, C., P. Meilman, and R. Lyerla. *Recent Statistics on Alcohol and Other Drug Use on American College Campuses: 1995–1996.* Carbondale, IL: CORE Institute, Southern Illinois University at Carbondale, 1996. Available http://www.siu.edu/department/coreinst/public_html/files/aggregate_data/1995-96_aggregate%20Data.doc.

Pride USA Survey, 1994–95, 1995–96, and 1996–97 (1998). Available http://www.marijuananews.com/marijuananews/cowan/family_research_council_issues_a.htm.

Register, T. C., J. M. Cline, and C. A. Shively. "Minority Women and Alcohol Use." *Alcohol Research and Health* (2002): 243–244.

Reuters Limited. "Global Costs of Alcohol Abuse Top $250 Billion." *Yahoo News. Health Headlines* (27 December 1999): 1–2.

Room, R. "A Reverence for Strong Drink: The Lost Generation and the Elevation of Alcohol in American Culture." *Journal of Studies on Alcohol* 43 (1984): 540–545.

Rostler, S. "Alcoholism Puts Blacks at Greater Risk of Infection." *Reuters Health Headlines* (28 April 2000).

Royce, James E. *Alcohol Problems and Alcoholism,* rev. ed. New York: Free Press, 1989.

Satir, V. *Conjoint Family Therapy.* Palo Alto, CA: Science and Behavior Books, 1964.

Substance Abuse and Mental Health Services Administration (SAMHSA). *1998 Fact Sheet, National Household Survey on Drug Abuse.* Rockville, MD: Office of Applied Studies, Department of Health and Human Services, August 1999a.

Substance Abuse and Mental Health Services Administration (SAMHSA). *National Household Survey on Drug Abuse: Main Findings, 1997.* Office of Applied Studies, Department of Health and Human Services, August 1999b.

Substance Abuse and Mental Health Services Administration (SAMHSA). *Overview of Findings from the 2003 National Survey on Drug Use and Health.* Rockville, MD: Office of Applied Studies, Department of Health and Human Services, 2004a.

Substance Abuse and Mental Health Services Administration (SAMHSA). *Results from the 2003 National Survey on Drug Use and Health: National Findings.* Rockville, MD: Office of Applied Studies, 2004b.

Substance Abuse and Mental Health Services Administration (SAMHSA). *Making the Link: Alcohol, Tobacco, and Other Drugs and Women's Health.* Rockville, MD: U.S. DHHS Publication No. ML011, Spring 1995.

Substance Abuse and Mental Health Services Administration (SAMHSA), Office of Applied Studies. *National Household Survey on Drug Abuse, The NHSDA Report. Alcohol Use by Persons Under the Legal Drinking Age of 21.* Rockville, MD: Office of Applied Studies, 9 May 2003.

Substance Abuse and Mental Health Services Administration (SAMHSA). *Results from the 2005 National Survey on Drug Use and Health: National Findings.* Rockville, MD: Office of Applied Studies, 2006.

Waters, T. "Women and Drugs." Criminal Justice course CJ-325. Drug Issues and the Law, Northern Arizona University (1999). Available http://jan.ucc.nau.edu/tfw/cj325/class/women/lesson11.html.

Wechsler, H., A. Davenport, G. Dowdall, B. Moeykens, and S. Castillo. "Health and Behavioral Consequences of Binge Drinking in College: A National Survey of Students at 140 Campuses." *Journal of the American Medical Association* 272 (7 December 1994).

Wechsler, H, G. W. Dowdall, A. Davenport, and W. De Jong. "Binge Drinking on Campus: Results of a National Study." Harvard School of Public Health, *Higher Education Center for Alcohol and Other Drug Prevention,* Washington, DC: U.S. Department of Education (2000a).

Wechsler, H., J. Eun Lee, M. Kuo, and H. Lee. "College Binge Drinking in the 1990s: A Continuing Problem: Results of the Harvard School of Public Health 1999 College Alcohol Study." 1999 College Alcohol Study (CAS) Binge Drinking Survey, Harvard School of Public Health (2000b).

Wegscheider, S. *Another Chance.* Palo Alto, CA: Science and Behavior Books, 1991.

Williams, G. D., F. S. Stinson, D. A. Parker, T. C. Harford, and V. Noble. "Demographic Trends, Alcohol Abuse and Alcoholism, 1985–1995." *Epidemiologic Bulletin No. 15. Alcohol, Health, and Research World* 11 (1997): 80–83.

Wilsnack, R. W., N. D. Vogeltanz, and S. C. Wilsnack. "Gender Differences in Alcohol Consumption and Adverse Drinking Consequences: Cross-cultural Patterns." *Addiction* 95 (2000): 251–265.

Wilsnack, S. C., R. W. Wilsnack, and A. D. Klassen. "Epidemiological Research on Women's Drinking,

1978–1984." In *Women and Alcohol: Health-Related Issues*. Research Monograph No. 16. DHHS Pub. No. (ADM). Washington, DC: U.S. Government Printing Office, 1986.

World Advertising Research Center (WARC). *World Drink Trends 2005*. Oxfordshire, UK: The Advertising Association, 2005. Available http://store.warc.com/displaysection.aspx?productid=843.

World Health Organization (WHO). "Trends in Substance Use and Associated Health Problems." *Trends in Substance Use*. Fact Sheet No. 127 (1998). Available http://www.who.int/inffs/en/fact127.html.

Zinberg, N. E. *Drug, Set, and Setting: The Basis for Controlled Intoxicant Use*. New Haven, CT: Yale University Press, 1984.

Zinberg, N. E., and J. A. Robertson. *Drugs and the Public*. New York: Simon & Schuster, 1972.

Learning ⊚bjectives

On completing this chapter you will be able to:

- ⊚ Describe the principal pharmacological effects of narcotics and their main therapeutic uses.
- ⊚ Identify the major side effects of narcotics.
- ⊚ Identify the abuse patterns for heroin.
- ⊚ Outline the stages of heroin dependence.
- ⊚ List the withdrawal symptoms that result from narcotic dependence, and discuss the significance of tolerance.
- ⊚ Describe and compare the use of methadone and buprenorphine in treating narcotic addiction.
- ⊚ Identify the unique features of fentanyl that make it appealing to illicit drug dealers but dangerous to narcotic addicts.
- ⊚ Describe how "designer" drugs have been associated with narcotics and Parkinson's disease.
- ⊚ Describe why dextromethorphan in cough medicines is abused.

Did You Know?

- ○ The release of natural substances called *endorphins* can mimic the effects of narcotics such as heroin.
- ○ By the end of the 19th century, almost 1 million Americans were addicted to opiates, primarily due to the use of patent medicines that contained opium products.
- ○ Narcotics are among the most potent analgesics available today.
- ○ There is evidence that acupuncture reduces pain by activating a natural opioid system.
- ○ Many heroin addicts have been exposed to the AIDS virus.
- ○ Heroin supplies today are more potent and cheaper than those available in the 1980s.
- ○ One designer drug, made from the narcotic fentanyl, is 6000 times more potent than heroin.
- ○ Some heroin addicts have to be treated with the narcotic methadone for the rest of their lives to keep them from abusing heroin.
- ○ Dextromethorphan (a common over-the-counter cough medicine chemically related to codeine), when taken in high doses, can cause phencyclidine (PCP)-like hallucinations.

Drugs and Society Online is a great source for additional drugs and society information for both students and instructors.
Visit **http://drugsandsociety.jbpub.com** to find a variety of useful tools for learning, thinking, and teaching.

Introduction

In 2005, it was estimated that about 50 million patients in the United States spent $12 billion for narcotic analgesics to relieve pain. Approximately 1.5 million of these users became seriously dependent on their medications (Meshberg 2006). What are these drugs, where do they come from, and how do they work?

The term *narcotic* in general means a central nervous system (CNS) depressant that produces insensibility or stupor. The term has also come to designate those drugs and substances with pharmacological properties related to opium and its drug derivatives. All opioid narcotics activate opioid receptors and have abuse potential. In addition, the narcotics are effective pain relievers (**analgesics**) and anticough medications and are effective in the treatment of diarrhea.

In this chapter, we introduce the opioid narcotics with a brief historical account. The pharmacological and therapeutic uses of these drugs are discussed, followed by a description of their side effects and problems with tolerance, withdrawal, and addiction. Narcotic abuse is presented in detail, with special emphasis on heroin. In addition, treatment approaches for narcotic addiction and dependence are included. This chapter concludes with descriptions of other commonly used opioid narcotics and related drugs.

What Are Narcotics?

The word *narcotic* has been used to label many substances, from opium to marijuana to cocaine. The translation of the Greek word *narkoticos* is "benumbing or deadening." The term *narcotic* is sometimes used to refer to a CNS depressant, producing insensibility or stupor, and at other times to refer to an addicting drug. Most people would not consider marijuana among the narcotics today, although for many years it was included in this category. Although pharmacologically cocaine

is not a narcotic either, it is still legally classified as such. Perhaps part of this confusion is due to the fact that cocaine, as a local anesthetic, can cause a numbing effect.

For purposes of the present discussion, the term *narcotic* is used to refer to those naturally occurring substances derived from the opium poppy and their synthetic substitutes. These drugs are referred to as the **opioid** (or opiate) narcotics because of their association with opium. They have similar pharmacological features, including abuse potential, pain-relieving effects (referred to as *analgesics*), cough suppression (**antitussive**), and reduction of intestinal movement, often causing constipation. Some of the most commonly used opioid narcotics are listed in Table 9.1.

The History of Narcotics

The opium poppy, *Papaver somniferum*, from which opium and its naturally occurring narcotic derivatives are obtained, has been cultivated for millennia. A 6000-year-old Sumerian tablet has an ideograph for the poppy shown as "joy" plus "plant," suggesting that the addicting properties of this substance have been appreciated for millenia. The Egyptians listed opium along with approximately 700 other medicinal compounds in the famous Ebers Papyrus (~1500 B.C.).

The Greek god of sleep, Hypnos, and the Roman god of sleep, Somnus, were portrayed as carrying containers of opium pods, and the Minoan goddess of sleep wore a crown of opium pods.

During the so-called Dark Ages that followed the collapse of the Roman Empire, Arab traders actively engaged in traveling the overland caravan routes to China and to India, where they introduced opium. Eventually, both China and India grew their own poppies.

■ Opium in China

The opium poppy had a dramatic impact in China, causing widespread addiction (Karch 1996). Initially, the seeds were used medically, as was opium later. However, by the late 1690s, opium was being smoked and used for diversion. The Chinese government, fearful of the weakening of national vitality by the potent opiate narcotic, outlawed the sale of opium in 1729. The penalty for disobedience was death by strangulation or decapitation.

Table 9.1 **Commonly Used Opioid Narcotic Drugs and Products**

NARCOTIC DRUGS	COMMON NAMES	MOST COMMON USES
Heroin	Horse, smack, junk (street names)	Abuse
Morphine	(Several)	Analgesia
Methadone	Dolophine	Treat narcotic dependence
Meperidine	Demerol	Analgesia
Oxycodone	Percodan, OxyContin	Analgesia
Propoxyphene	Darvon	Analgesia
Codeine	(Several)	Analgesia, antitussive
Loperamide	Imodium A-D	Antidiarrheal
Diphenoxylate	Lomotil	Antidiarrheal
Opium tincture	Paregoric	Antidiarrheal
Buprenorphine	Suboxone	Treat narcotic dependence

Despite these laws and threats, the habit of opium smoking became so widespread that the Chinese government went a step further and forbade its importation from India, where most of the opium poppy was grown. In contrast, the British East India Company (and later the British government in India) encouraged cultivation of opium. British companies were the principal shippers to the Chinese port of Canton, which was the only port open to Western merchants. During the next 120 years, a complex network of opium smuggling routes developed in China with the help of local merchants, who received substantial profits, and local officials, who pocketed bribes to ignore the smugglers.

Everyone involved in the opium trade, but particularly the British, continued to profit until the Chinese government ordered the strict enforcement of the edict against importation. Such actions by the Chinese caused conflict with the British government and helped trigger the Opium War of 1839 to 1842. Great Britain sent in an army, and by 1842, 10,000 British soldiers had won a victory over 350 million Chinese. Because of the war, the island of Hong Kong was ceded to the British, and an indemnity of $6 million was imposed on China to cover the value of the destroyed opium and the cost of the war. In 1856, a second Opium War broke out. Peking was occupied by British and French troops, and China was compelled to make further concessions to Britain. The importation of opium continued to increase until 1908, when Britain and China made an agreement to limit the importation of opium from India (Austin 1978).

American Opium Use

Meanwhile, in 1803, a young German named Frederick Serturner extracted and partially purified the

Famous cartoon, showing a British sailor shoving opium down the throat of a Chinese man, which dates back to the Opium War of 1839–1842.

active ingredients in opium. It was 10 times more potent than opium itself and was named *morphine* after Morpheus, the Greek god of dreams. This discovery increased worldwide interest in opium. By 1832, a second compound had been purified and named *codeine*, after the Greek word for "poppy capsule" (Maurer and Vogel 1967).

The opium problem was aggravated further in 1853, when Alexander Wood perfected the hypodermic syringe and introduced it first in Europe and then in America. Christopher Wren and others had worked with the idea of injecting drugs directly into the body by means of hollow quills and straws, but the approach was never successful or well received. Wood perfected the syringe technique with the intent of preventing morphine addiction by injecting the drug directly into the veins rather than by oral administration (Golding 1993). Unfortunately, just the opposite happened; injection of morphine increased the potency and the likelihood of dependence (Maurer and Vogel 1967).

The hypodermic syringe was used extensively during the Civil War to administer morphine to treat pain, dysentery, and fatigue (Kosten and Hollister 1998). A large percentage of the soldiers who returned home from the war were addicted to morphine. Opiate addiction became known as the "soldier's disease" or "army disease."

By 1900, an estimated 1 million Americans were dependent on opiates (Abel 1980). This drug problem was made worse because of (1) Chinese laborers, who brought with them to the United States opium to smoke (it was legal to smoke opium in the United States at that time); (2) the availability of purified morphine and the hypodermic syringe; and (3) the lack of controls on the large number of patent medicines that contained opium derivatives (Karch 1996). Until 1914, when the Harrison Narcotic Act was passed (regulating opium, coca leaves, and their products), the average opiate addict was a middle-aged, Southern, white woman who functioned well and was adjusted to her role as a wife and mother. She bought opium or morphine legally by mail order from Sears and Roebuck or at the local store, used it orally, and caused very few problems. A number of physicians were addicted as well. One of the best-known morphine addicts was William Holsted, a founder of Johns Hopkins Medical School. Holsted was a very productive surgeon and innovator, although secretly an addict for most of his career. He became dependent on morphine as a substitute for his cocaine dependence (Brecher 1972).

Looking for better medicines, chemists found that modification of the morphine molecule resulted in a more potent compound. In 1898, diacetylmorphine was placed on the market as a cough suppressant by Bayer. It was to be a "heroic" drug, without the addictive potential of morphine — it thus received the name *heroin*.

With the development of the hypodermic needle and its use during the Civil War, heroin addiction became more likely and more severe.

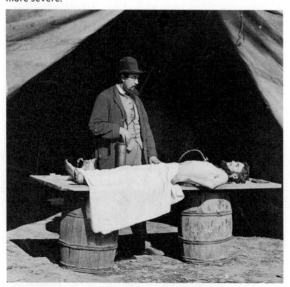

Chinese laborers often smoked heroin at the turn of the 20th century.

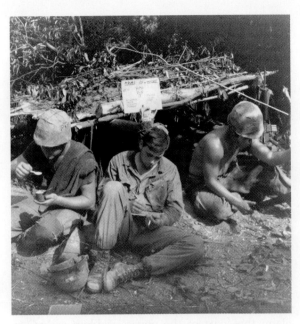

Heroin use was particularly high among soldiers fighting in Vietnam.

Heroin was first used in the United States as a cough suppressant and to combat addiction to other substances (Hubbard 1998). However, its inherent abuse potential was quickly discovered. When injected, heroin is more addictive than most of the other narcotics because of its ability to enter the brain rapidly and cause a euphoric surge (DiChiara and North 1992). Heroin was banned from U.S. medical practice in 1924, although it is still used legally as an analgesic in other countries (Wikipedia October 2007).

The Vietnam War was an important landmark for heroin use in the United States (Hubbard 1998). It has been estimated that as many as 40% of the U.S. soldiers serving in Southeast Asia at this time used heroin to combat the frustrations and stress associated with this unpopular military action. Although only 7% of the soldiers continued to use heroin after returning home, those who were addicted to this potent narcotic became a major component of the heroin-abusing population in this country (Golding 1993).

Heroin smoking became popular in the mid-1980s in response to the AIDS epidemic. This was due to a fear of HIV infection when using infected needles to administer the drug intravenously (Hubbard 1998). The effect resulting from inhalation is as intense as that caused by injection, although a very pure drug is required for smoking. Smoking continues to be a favorite form of heroin administration today.

Pharmacological Effects

Even though opioid narcotics have a history of being abused, they continue to be important therapeutic agents.

■ Narcotic Analgesics

The most common clinical use of the opioid narcotics is as analgesics to relieve pain. These drugs are effective against most varieties of pain, including *visceral* (associated with internal organs of the body) and *somatic* (associated with skeletal muscles, bones, skin, and teeth) types. Used in sufficiently high doses, narcotics can even relieve the intense pain associated with some types of cancer (Gutstein and Akil 2006).

The opioid narcotics relieve pain by activating the same group of receptors that are controlled by the endogenous substances called *endorphins* (Kreek et al. 2004). As discussed in Chapter 4, the endorphins are peptides (small proteins) that are released in the brain, in the spinal cord, and from the adrenal glands in response to stress and painful experiences. When released, the endorphins serve as transmitters and stimulate receptors designated as opioid types. Activation of opioid receptors by either the naturally released endorphins or administration of the narcotic analgesic drugs blocks the transmission of pain through the spinal cord or brain stem and alters the perception of pain in the "pain center" of the brain. Because the narcotics work at multiple levels of pain transmission, they are potent analgesics against almost all types of pain.

Interestingly, the endorphin system appears to be influenced by psychological factors as well. It is possible that pain relief caused by administration of placebos or nonmedicinal manipulation such as acupuncture is due in part to the natural release of endorphins (Eshkevaria and Heath 2005). This relationship suggests that physiological, psychological, and pharmacological factors are intertwined in pain management through the opioid system, which makes it impossible to deal with one without considering the others.

Although the narcotics are very effective analgesics, they do cause some side effects that are particularly alarming; thus, their clinical use usually is limited to the treatment of moderate to severe pain (*Drug Facts and Comparisons* 2005). Other, safer drugs, such as the aspirin-type analgesics (see Chapter 15), are preferred for pain management when possible. Often, the amount of narcotic required for pain relief can be reduced by combining a narcotic, such as codeine, with aspirin or acetaminophen (the active ingredient in Tylenol). Such combinations reduce the chance of significant narcotic side effects while providing adequate pain relief (McEvoy 2003).

Morphine is a particularly potent pain reliever and often is used as the analgesic standard by which other narcotics are compared (Gutstein and Akil 2006). With continual use, tolerance develops to the analgesic effects of morphine and other narcotics, sometimes requiring a dramatic escalation of doses to maintain adequate pain control (*Drug Facts and Comparisons* 2005).

Because pain is expressed in different forms with many different diseases, narcotic treatment can vary considerably. Usually, the convenience of oral narcotic therapy is preferred but often is inadequate for severe pain. For short-term relief from intense pain, narcotics are effective when injected subcutaneously or intramuscularly. Narcotics can also be given intravenously for persistent and potent analgesia or administered by transdermal patches for sustained chronic pain (Worrich et al. 2007). Despite the fact that most pain can be relieved if enough narcotic analgesic is properly administered, physicians frequently underprescribe narcotics or are not well trained in how to use the opioid narcotics properly (Young 2007). Because of fear of causing narcotic addiction or creating legal problems with federal agencies such as the Drug Enforcement Administration (DEA) (see "Here and Now," Are Restrictions on Pain Pills Too Painful?), cancer patients in the United States are often inadequately treated for their pain (Hall and Sykes 2004). An important rule of narcotic use is that adequate pain relief should not be denied because of concern about the abuse potential of these drugs (Hall and Sykes 2004). Indeed, addiction to narcotics is rare in patients receiving these drugs for therapy unless they have a history of drug abuse or have an underlying psychiatric disorder (Gutstein and Akil 2006; O'Brien 2006).

Occasionally, there are outbreaks of abuse of commonly prescribed narcotic products such as OxyContin. (Oxy Kids' Crisis 2007). This product includes the opiate oxycodone, which has the approximate narcotic potency of morphine and can be obtained with relative ease. Authorities claim that the illegal pills come from doctors' offices, from dealers who fake illness to get legal prescriptions or who are writing phony orders, and from others who steal the supplies from pharmacies. OxyContin has been called "oxys," "O.C.," and "killers" on the street and is popular with narcotic abusers because of its rapid and potent effect. On the street, the drug can cost 10 times its prescription price. Because of its potent ability to suppress respiration, OxyContin appears to have been involved in overdose deaths throughout the country, although there is some evidence that other drugs were also involved in many of these cases. Critics claim that part of the abuse problem with OxyContin stems from overuse in situations that should be managed by a less potent and less addicting opioid analgesic.

■ Other Therapeutic Uses

Opioid narcotics are also used to treat conditions not related to pain. For example, these drugs suppress the coughing center of the brain, so they are effective antitussives. Codeine, a natural opioid narcotic, is commonly included in cough medicine. In addition, opioid narcotics slow the movement of materials through the intestines, a property that can be used to relieve diarrhea or can cause the side effect of constipation (*Drug Facts and Comparisons* 2005). Paregoric contains an opioid narcotic substance and is commonly used to treat severe diarrhea.

When used carefully by the clinician, opioid narcotics are very effective therapeutic tools. Precautions for avoiding unnecessary problems with these drugs include the following (Way and Way 1992):

1. Before beginning treatment, therapeutic goals should be clearly established.
2. Doses and duration of use should be limited as much as possible while permitting adequate therapeutic care.
3. If other, safer drugs (for example, nonnarcotic analgesics such as ibuprofen or aspirin) adequately treat the medical condition, narcotics should be avoided.

Here and Now

Are Restrictions on Pain Pills Too Painful?

Because of a spiraling increase in the abuse of prescription "painkillers," the DEA has warned doctors who specialize in pain management that they risk special investigation if they do not comply with DEA guidelines. For example, the DEA recommends avoiding the use of opioid analgesics for the treatment of pain in patients who have a history of abusing these drugs. In addition, the DEA frowns upon the practice of doctors writing prescriptions for these pain drugs that can be filled on a future date. These and other restrictive DEA policies are viewed by some pain doctors as overregulation. Some are concerned that physicians will hesitate to prescribe even needed pain medication for fear of being investigated and charged with breaking the law. They worry that the DEA's actions are sending a chilling message that could result in withholding opioid narcotics from millions of patients who cannot be adequately treated by other drugs.

Source: Kaufman, M. "New DEA Statement Has Pain Doctors More Fearful." *The Washington Post* (30 November 2004): A-17.

■ Mechanisms of Action

As mentioned, the opioid receptors are the site of action of the naturally occurring endorphin peptide transmitters and are found throughout the nervous system, intestines, and other internal organs. Because narcotic drugs such as morphine and heroin enhance the endorphin system by directly stimulating opioid receptors, these drugs have widespread influences throughout the body.

For example, the opioid receptors are present in high concentration within the limbic structures of the brain. Stimulation of these receptors by narcotics causes release of the transmitter dopamine in limbic brain regions. This effect contributes to the rewarding actions of these drugs and leads to dependence and abuse (Zocchi et al. 2003).

■ Side Effects

One of the most common side effects of the opioid narcotics is constipation. Other side effects include drowsiness, mental clouding, respiratory depression (suppressed breathing is usually the cause of death from overdose), nausea and vomiting, itching, inability to urinate, a drop in blood pressure, and constricted pupils (*Drug Facts and Comparisons* 2005). This array of seemingly unrelated side effects is due to widespread distribution of the opioid receptors throughout the body and their involvement in many physiological functions (Gourlay 2004). With continual use, tolerance develops to some of these undesirable narcotic responses.

Drugs that selectively antagonize the opioid receptors can block the effects of natural opioid

Signs & Symptoms Narcotics

POSSIBLE SIGNS OF USE	POSSIBLE SIGNS OF OVERDOSE
Euphoria	Slow and shallow breathing
Drowsiness	Clammy skin
Respiratory depression	Convulsions
Constricted pupils	Coma
Nausea	Possible death

systems in the body and reverse the effects of narcotic opiate drugs (*Drug Facts and Comparisons* 2005). When an opioid antagonist such as the drug naloxone is administered alone, it has little noticeable effect. The antiopioid actions of naloxone become more apparent when the antagonist is injected into someone who has taken a narcotic opioid drug. For example, naloxone will cause (1) a recurrence of pain in the patient using a narcotic for pain relief, (2) the restoration of consciousness and normal breathing in the addict who has overdosed on heroin, and (3) severe withdrawal effects in the opioid abuser who has become dependent on narcotics (Szalavitz 2005).

An interesting recent use of opioid antagonists is to treat alcohol dependence. The Food and Drug Administration (FDA) has approved the use of naltrexone (a narcotic antagonist) to relieve the craving of alcoholics for excessive alcohol consumption (*Drug Facts and Comparisons* 2005). Early research suggests that this drug may have an important effect on the future therapeutic approach taken with alcoholism. Only time and experience will reveal whether the benefits are truly as dramatic as originally thought. The initial findings suggest that the natural opioid (endorphin) system likely contributes to the dependence seen in alcoholics.

Abuse, Tolerance, Dependence, and Withdrawal

All the opioid narcotic agents that activate opioid receptors have abuse potential and are classified as scheduled drugs (see Table 9.2). Their patterns of abuse are determined by the ability of these drugs to cause tolerance, dependence, and withdrawal effects.

The process of tolerance literally begins with the first dose of a narcotic, but tolerance does not become clinically evident until after 2 to 3 weeks of frequent use (either therapeutic- or abuse-related). Tolerance occurs most rapidly with high doses given in short intervals. Doses can be increased as much as 35 times so as to regain the narcotic effect. Physical dependence invariably accompanies severe tolerance (Reisine and Pasternak 1995). Psychological dependence can also develop with continual narcotic use because these drugs can cause euphoria and relieve stress. Such psychological dependence leads to compulsive use

(Gutstein and Akil 2006; O'Brien 2006). Because all narcotics affect the same opioid systems in the body, developing tolerance to one narcotic drug means the person has cross-tolerance to all drugs in this group.

The development of psychological and physical dependence makes breaking the narcotic habit very difficult. Abstinence from narcotic use by a long-term addict can cause severe withdrawal effects such as exaggerated pain responses, agitation, anxiety, stomach cramps and vomiting, joint and muscle aches, runny nose, and an overall flu-like feeling. Although these withdrawal symptoms are not fatal, they are extremely aversive and encourage continuation of the narcotic habit (McEvoy 2003). Overall, the narcotics have similar actions; there are differences, however, in their potencies, severity of side effects, likelihood of being abused, and clinical usefulness.

Although it is difficult to accurately predict which pain patients are most likely to develop addiction problems when using the opioid analgesics, re-

Table 9.2 **Schedule Classification of Some Common Narcotics**

NARCOTIC	SCHEDULE*
Heroin	I
Morphine	II, III
Methadone	II
Fentanyl	II
Hydromorphone	II
Meperidine	II
Codeine	II, III, V
Buprenorphine	III
Pentazocine	IV
Propoxyphene	IV
Narcotics combined with nonsteroidal anti-inflammatory drugs	III

*According to the Drug Enforcement Administration classification, Controlled Substances Act.

search suggests that persons with a previous history of substance dependence or with a history of mood disorders, psychological problems, or psychosocial stressors will be at greater risk for misuse of prescription narcotics (American Academy of Pain Medicine 2007).

Heroin Abuse

> This is the key to a heroin high: Nothing matters . . . when one is high on smack, one looks at the outside world and only has one thought: Who . . . (cares)? You feel as if you've been wrapped in the most pleasing, warm and comfortable blanket in the world. At high doses, you fall in and out of consciousness, and getting this "nod" is what the veteran user prays for every time he shoots up: to sleep the sleep of angels is the ultimate goal of the heroin addict. (Drugs, Youth and the Internet 2002, p. 23)

This quote illustrates the powerful attraction of heroin and helps explain why it is so frequently abused.

Heroin is currently classified as a Schedule I drug by the DEA (see Table 9.2). It is not approved for any clinical use in the United States, is one of the most widely abused illegal drugs in the world, and is reported to account for more than $120 billion in global sales each year (Chossudousky 2006). It is also thought to be associated with some of the highest mortality rates and most emergency room visits of any of the illegal drugs of abuse in the United States (National Institute on Drug Abuse [NIDA] 2005). Heroin was illicitly used more than any other drug of abuse in the United States (except for marijuana) until 20 years ago, when it was unseated by cocaine (DiChiara and North 1992). In 2006, 1.4% of high school seniors reported having used heroin (Johnston 2007).

From 1970 through 1976, most of the heroin reaching the United States originated from the Golden Triangle region of Southeast Asia, which includes parts of Burma, Thailand, and Laos. During that period, the United States and other nations purchased much of the legal opium crop from Turkey in an effort to stop opium from being converted into heroin. From 1975 until 1980, the major heroin supply came from opium poppies grown in Mexico. The U.S. government furnished the Mexican government with heli-

copters, herbicide sprays, and financial assistance to destroy the poppy crop. Changes in political climates have shifted the source of supply back to the Golden Triangle and Latin American countries (e.g., Colombia; Seper 2003) and more recently to Afghanistan, despite efforts by the U.S. military to eliminate the opium crops (Motlagh 2006). (See "Here and Now" Afghans' Drug War.)

Heroin Combinations

Heroin is typically smuggled into the United States from one of four foreign sources: Mexico, South America, Southeast Asia (e.g., Burma), or Southwest Asia (e.g., Afghanistan). It is carried into the United States hidden in commercial and private vehicles driven from Mexico or Canada or carried by couriers traveling on commercial flights (National Drug Threat Assessment 2003). Pure heroin is a white powder. Other colors, such as brown Mexican heroin, result from unsatisfactory processing of morphine or from adulterants (Drug Enforcement Agency [DEA] 2000). Heroin is usually "cut" (diluted) with lactose (milk sugar) to give it bulk and thus increase profits (DEA 2000). When heroin first enters the United States, it can be up to 95% pure; by the time it is sold to users, its purity can be as low as 3% or (recently) as high as 30–60% (Epstein and Gfroerer 1998; Stockman 2003). If users are unaware of the variance in purity and do not adjust doses accordingly, the results can be extremely dangerous and occasionally fatal (NIDA Infofax 2005).

Crude heroin is dark, whereas purified heroin is a white powder.

Here and Now

Heroin has a bitter taste, so sometimes it is cut with quinine, a bitter substance, to disguise the fact that the heroin content has been reduced. Quinine can be a deadly adulterant. Part of the "flash" from direct injection of heroin may be caused by this contaminant. Quinine is an irritant, and it causes vascular damage, acute and potentially lethal disturbances in heartbeat, depressed respiration, coma, and death from respiratory arrest. Opiate poisoning causes acute pulmonary edema as well as respiratory depression. To counteract the constipation caused by heroin, sometimes mannitol is added for its laxative effect.

Another potentially lethal combination emerges when heroin is laced with the much more potent artificial narcotic fentanyl. This adulterated heroin can be extremely dangerous due to its unexpected potency (NIDA Research Report Series 2004).

Frequently, heroin is deliberately combined with other drugs when self-administered by addicts (Hickman et al. 2007). According to the National Institute on Drug Abuse (NIDA)–sponsored Drug Abuse Warning Network (DAWN) survey of emergency rooms in the United States, 41% of the reported heroin abuse cases involved other drugs of abuse in combination with this narcotic. Heroin is most frequently used with alcohol, but it is often combined with CNS stimulants, such as cocaine (Hickman et al. 2007). Some crack cocaine smokers turn to heroin to ease the jitters caused by the CNS stimulant (Leland 1996). It also has been reported that heroin addicts use cocaine to withdraw or detoxify themselves from heroin by gradually decreasing amounts of heroin while increasing amounts of cocaine. This drug combination is called **speedballing**, and addicts claim the cocaine provides relief from the unpleasant withdrawal effects that accompany heroin abstinence in a dependent user (Wikipedia March 2007).

KEY TERMS

speedballing
combining heroin and cocaine

Profile of Heroin Addicts

An estimated 600,000–1 million active heroin addicts live in the United States, a figure that has remained relatively stable despite changes in the number of infrequent and moderate users. Heroin addicts often search for a better and purer drug; however, if they do find an unusually potent batch of heroin, there is a good chance they will get more than they bargained for. Addicts are sometimes found dead with the needle still in the vein after injecting heroin. In such cases, the unsuspecting addict may have died in reaction to an unusually concentrated dose of this potent narcotic. Thousands of deaths occur annually in the United States from heroin overdoses. Death associated with heroin injection is usually due to concurrent use of alcohol or barbiturates — not the heroin alone — and frequently occurs after an addict has gone weeks or months without the drug and injects the same amount of heroin he or she used before, not realizing that tolerance has worn off (Rombey 2003b).

Hard-core addicts often share a common place where they can stash supplies and equipment for their heroin encounters. These locations, called *shooting galleries*, serve as gathering places for addicts (Cowan and Carvel 2006). Shooting galleries can be set up in homes, but are usually located in less established locations such as abandoned cars, cardboard lean-tos, and weed-infested vacant lots. An entrance charge often is required of the patrons. Conditions in shooting galleries are notoriously filthy, and these places are frequented by intravenous heroin users with blood-borne infections that can cause AIDS or hepatitis. Because of needle sharing and other unsanitary practices, shooting galleries have become a place where serious communicable diseases are spread to a wide range of people of different ages, races, genders, and socioeconomic statuses (Bearak 1992; Bourgois 1999). Some addicts become resigned to their fate. One user, after testing positive for HIV, responded, "I've seen lots of guys die already. They turned into skeletons and their teeth fell out . . . I hope I die before I get that far. Maybe I'll be lucky and just die one night up in the gallery" (Bearak 1992, p. A4).

The heroin in shooting galleries is typically prepared by adding several drops of water to the white powder in an improvised container (such as a metal bottle cap), and lightly shaking the container while heating it over a small flame to dissolve the powder. The fluid is then drawn through a tiny wad of cotton to filter out the gross contaminants into an all-too-often used syringe where it is ready for injection (Bearak 1992).

Some addicts become fixated on the drug's paraphernalia, especially the needle. They can get a psychological "high" from playing with the needle and syringe. The injection process and syringe plunger action appear to have sexual overtones for them. As one reformed user explained, "I think what I miss more than heroin sometimes is just the ritual of shooting up." A current user concurred, explaining, "You get addicted to the needle . . . Just the process of sticking something into your vein, having such a direct involvement with your body . . . " ("Mary" 1996, p. 42).

Heroin and Crime

In 1971, the Select Committee on Crime in the United States released a report on methods used to combat the heroin crisis that arose in the 1950s and 1960s. This report was a turning point in setting up treatment programs for narcotic addicts. The report stated that drug arrests for heroin use had increased 700% since 1961, that there were as many as 4000 deaths per year from heroin, and that the cost of heroin-related crimes to U.S. society was estimated to exceed $3 billion per year. Other studies since that time have linked heroin addiction with crime (McMurran 2007).

Although many young heroin addicts come from affluent or middle-class families (Weiss 1995), research shows most heavy users are poorly educated with minimal social integration. Because

Heroin paraphernalia is usually simple and crude but effective: a spoon on which to dissolve the narcotic and a makeshift syringe with which to inject it.

of these disadvantages, heroin addicts often have a low level of employment, exist in unstable living conditions, and socialize with other illicit drug users. Clearly, such undesirable living conditions encourage criminal activity. However, three other factors also likely contribute to the association between heroin use and crime:

1. The use of heroin and its pharmacological effects encourage antisocial behavior that is crime related. Depressants such as heroin diminish inhibition and cause people to engage in activities they normally would not. The effects of heroin and its withdrawal make addicts self-centered, demanding, impulsive, and governed by their "need" for the drug.

2. Because heroin addiction is expensive, the user is forced to resort to crime to support the drug habit (McMurran 2007).

3. A similar personality is driven to engage in both criminal behavior and heroin use. Often, heroin addicts start heroin use about the same time they begin to become actively involved in criminal activity. In most cases, the heroin user has been taking other illicit drugs, especially marijuana, years before trying heroin (Reid et al. 2007).

These findings suggest that for many heroin addicts, the antisocial behavior causes the criminal behavior rather than the criminal behavior resulting from the heroin use. Thus, the more a drug such as heroin is perceived as being illegal, desirable, and addictive, the more likely it will be used by deviant criminal populations. However, typically heroin users are not violent, although they may participate in criminal activity to fund their drug habit. Violence is more likely associated with heroin trafficking and distribution because of the criminal groups involved in this activity (National Drug Threat Assessment 2003).

Patterns of Heroin Abuse

It has become apparent that problems with narcotics are no longer confined to the inner cities, but have infiltrated suburban areas and small towns and afflict both rich and poor (see "Here and Now," Heroin Use in a Small Town). The following are recent heroin trends (see Table 9.3):

- Heroin use among adolescents and young adults, after holding steady at high levels in the late 1990s, declined significantly by 2007 (Johnston 2007; see Table 9.3)
- Heroin has become purer (60–70% purity) and cheaper ($10/bag [~100 mg]) than ever before Community Epidemiology Workgroup [CEWG] 2002).
- Thanks to the greater purity, new users are able to administer heroin in less efficient ways, such as smoking and snorting, and avoid the dangers of intravenous use (National Trends in Drug Abuse 2000).

Here and Now

Heroin Use in a Small Town

Heroin is supposed to be a "big town" drug. Tell that to Sandi Daost, whose 19-year-old son Robby died from a heroin overdose after months of going in and out of rehab centers trying to stay clean. He grew up in the typical small town — Springville, Utah. The family believed that Robby finally had kicked the habit. He had been clean for 7 months and laughed and joked with the family again. He had a job and a cute girlfriend, and was attending church with his family. One Sunday, he told his mother he was going to play golf with a friend. Robby didn't go golfing, but made his last trip to meet his heroin connection. He was found in his bed the next morning, dead from a heroin overdose. The citizens of Springville were bewildered and shocked. Robby was only one of at least six heroin overdose deaths in this small town from 1999 to 2004. All were young men in their late teens or early 20s. We expect this type of thing in Los Angeles or New York, but no one seems to have an answer to "why in Springville?"

Sources: Rombey 2003a, 2003b.

Table 9.3 Prevalence of Heroin and Other Opioid Abuse Among High School Seniors

Year	ANNUAL USE		LIFETIME USE	
	Heroin	Other Opioids	Heroin	Other Opioids
1989	0.6%	4.4%	1.3%	8.3%
1992	0.6%	3.3%	1.2%	6.1%
1995	1.1%	4.7%	1.6%	7.2%
1999	1.1%	6.7%	2.0%	10.2%
2002	1.0%	7.0%	1.7%	10.1%
2007	0.9%	9.2%	1.5%	13.1%

Source: Johnston, L. "Monitoring the Future" (2007). Available www.monitoringthefuture.org/pubs/monographs/vol1_2006.pdf.

- Many youths believe that heroin can be used safely if it is not injected (Epstein and Gfroerer 1998).
- Because of its association with popular fashions and entertainment, heroin has been viewed as glamorous and chic, especially by many young people, despite its highly publicized lethal consequences ("Heroin '96" 1996). More recently, "heroin chic" has been falling out of fashion within the glamour business because of its very negative consequences (Quinion 2005).
- In 2005 there were 162,137 emergency room visits due to heroin overdoses (Substance Abuse and Mental Health Services Administration [SAMHSA] 2006a).

The reasons for these disturbing changes in heroin use patterns and attitude are not immediately apparent. It has been speculated that because antidrug efforts in the late 1980s and early 1990s targeted cocaine, they inadvertently encouraged drug users to replace cocaine with heroin. Another possible reason for increased heroin use in the late 1990s is that many drug dealers previously selling cocaine switched to heroin to make greater profits ("Heroin '96" 1996), making heroin even more readily available. Whatever the reasons, it has become imperative to educate all populations about the dangers of this potent drug.

Stages of Dependence

Initially, the early effects of heroin are often unpleasant, especially after the first injection (Gutstein and Akil 2006). It is not uncommon to experience nausea and vomiting after administration; gradually, however, the euphoria overwhelms the aversive effects (Quinion 2005). There are two major stages in the development of a psychological dependence on heroin or other opioid narcotics:

1. In the rewarding stage, euphoria and positive effects occur in at least 50% of users. These positive feelings and sensations increase with continued administration and encourage use.
2. Eventually, the heroin or narcotic user must take the drug to avoid withdrawal symptoms that start about 6 to 12 hours after the last dose. At this stage, it is said that "the monkey is on his back." This stage is psychological dependence. If one grain of heroin (about 65 milligrams) is taken over a 2-week period on a daily basis, the user becomes physically dependent on the drug.

Methods of Administration

Many heroin users start by sniffing the powder or injecting it into a muscle (intramuscular) or under the skin ("skin popping"). Because of the increased purity and decreased cost, many of today's heroin users are administering their drug by smoking and snorting (CEWG 2002).

Most established heroin addicts still prefer to **mainline** the drug (intravenous injection) (CEWG 2002). The injection device can be made from an eyedropper bulb, part of a syringe, and a hypodermic needle. Mainlining drugs causes the thin-walled veins to become scarred and, if done frequently, the veins will collapse. Once a vein is collapsed, it can no longer be used to introduce the drug into the blood. Addicts become expert in locating new veins to use: in the feet, the legs, the neck, even the temples. When addicts do not want "needle tracks" (scars) to show, they inject under the tongue or in the groin ("Opioids" 1996).

Heroin Addicts and AIDS

As noted previously, because needle sharing is common among heavy heroin users, the transmission of deadly communicable diseases such as AIDS is a major problem (see Chapter 17). More than 50% of intravenous heroin users have been exposed to the AIDS virus (Baglole 2003). Fear of contracting this deadly disease has contributed to the increase of administering this drug by smoking and snorting (Hubbard 1998). However, many heroin users who start by smoking and snorting eventually progress to intravenous administration due to its more intense effects (Leland 1996).

Heroin and Pregnancy

Many women use heroin during their pregnancy (SAMHSA 2006a, 2006b). In the United States, as many as 10,000 infants are born each year to women who chronically used either heroin or other opioid drugs during their pregnancies (Paule 1998). There is no evidence that prenatal exposure to opioid drugs causes overt structural damage, although incidents of smaller birthweights or even reduced head size have been reported in infants born to mothers using opioid drugs; these findings have not been universally confirmed (Bennett 1999; Paule 1998). The most devastating consequence of heroin or opioid use during pregnancy appears to be physical dependence in the newborn, resulting in withdrawal symptoms usually immediately after birth. These symptoms are characterized by high-pitched crying, inconsolability, tightened

A heroin addict "mainlining" his drug.

muscle tone, tremors, vomiting, and even seizures. Treatment for such withdrawal problems generally includes low doses of a long-lasting opioid narcotic to reduce the intensity of the symptoms and then a gradual tapering of the dose to eventually wean the infant from the drug. For heroin, this typically takes up to 2 weeks (Pain and Central Nervous System 2005). In addition, there is some evidence that the use of heroin during pregnancy increases the likelihood of sudden infant death syndrome (SIDS) in offspring (American SIDS Institute 2005).

Withdrawal Symptoms

After the effects of heroin wear off, the addict usually has only a few hours in which to find the next dose before severe withdrawal symptoms begin. A single "shot" of heroin lasts only 4 to 6 hours. It is enough to help addicts "get straight" or relieve the severe withdrawal symptoms called *dope sickness* but is not enough to give a desired "high" (Bearak 1992). Withdrawal symptoms start with a runny nose, tears, and minor stomach cramps. The addict may feel as if he or she is coming down with a bad cold (O'Brien 2006). Between 12 and 48 hours after the last dose, the addict loses all of his or her appetite, vomits, has diarrhea and abdominal cramps, feels alternating chills and fever, and develops goose pimples all over (going "cold turkey"). Between 2 and 4 days later, the addict continues to experience some of the symptoms just described, as well as aching bones and muscles and powerful muscle spasms that cause violent kicking motions ("kicking the habit"). After 4 to 5 days, symptoms start to subside, and the person may get his or her appetite back. However, attempts to move on in life will be challenging because compulsion to keep using the drug remains strong.

The severity of the withdrawal varies according to the purity and strength of the drug used and the personality of the user. The symptoms of withdrawal from heroin, morphine, and methadone are summarized in Table 9.4. Withdrawal symptoms from opioids such as morphine, codeine, meperidine, and others are similar, although the time frame and intensity vary (Gutstein and Akil 2006).

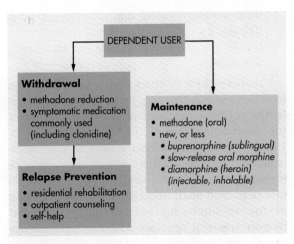

FIGURE 9.1
Treatment of Heroin Addiction
The principal aspects of treating heroin addiction include minimizing the very aversive withdrawal effect (usually with drug adjuncts); preventing relapse (usually with behavioral modification); and if necessary, providing maintenance support with other opioid-like drugs that have longer action than heroin.

Treatment of Heroin and Other Narcotic Dependence

The ideal result of treatment for dependency on heroin or other narcotics is to help the addict live a normal, productive, and satisfying life without drugs. Unfortunately, the minority of heroin addicts receive adequate treatment for their addiction. Of those who are treated, relatively few heroin users become absolutely "clean" from drug use; thus, therapeutic compromise is often neces-

sary (see Figure 9.1). In the real world, treatment of heroin dependency is considered successful if the addict does the following:

1. Stops using heroin
2. No longer associates with dealers or users of heroin
3. Avoids dangerous activities often associated with heroin use (such as needle sharing, injecting unknown drugs, and frequenting shooting galleries)

Table 9.4 Symptoms of Withdrawal from Heroin, Morphine, and Methadone

Symptoms	TIME IN HOURS		
	Heroin	Morphine	Methadone
Craving for drugs; anxiety	4	6	24–48
Yawning, perspiration, runny nose, tears	8	14	34–48
Pupil dilation, goose bumps, muscle twitches, aching bones and muscles, hot and cold flashes, loss of appetite	12	16	48–72
Increased intensity of preceding symptoms, insomnia, raised blood pressure, fever, faster pulse, nausea	18–24	24–36	≥ 72
Increased intensity of preceding symptoms, curled-up position, vomiting, diarrhea, increased blood sugar, foot kicking ("kicking the habit")	26–36	36–48	—

4. Improves employment status
5. Refrains from criminal activity
6. Is able to enjoy normal family and social relationships

For more than 30 years, many heroin addicts have achieved these goals by substituting a long-lasting synthetic narcotic, such as methadone, for the short-acting heroin (O'Brien 2006; Zickler 1999). The maintenance ("substitute") narcotic is made available to heroin-dependent people through drug treatment centers under the direction of trained medical personnel. The dispensing of the substitute narcotic is tightly regulated by governmental agencies. The rationale for the substitution is that a long-acting drug such as methadone can conveniently be taken once a day (O'Brien 2006) to prevent the unpleasant withdrawal symptoms that occur within 4 hours after each heroin use (see Table 9.4). Although the substitute narcotic may also have abuse potential and be scheduled by the DEA (see Table 9.2), it is given to the addict in its oral form; thus, its onset of action is too slow to cause a rush like that associated with heroin use, which means that its abuse potential is substantially less (*Medical Letter* 1998). In addition, the cost to society is dramatically reduced. According to one study, an untreated heroin addict costs the community $21,000 for 6 months, but the cost of methadone maintenance for a person dependent on heroin is only $1750 for the same period (Hubbard 1998).

Currently, methadone is approved by the FDA for "opiate maintenance therapy" in the treatment of heroin (or other narcotic) dependency (Hubbard 1998). Proper use of methadone has been shown to effectively decrease illicit use of narcotics and other undesirable behavior related to drug dependence (Lucky 1998).

Another drug called LAAM (*l*-alpha-acetylmethadol) has been clinically tested and also approved to treat narcotic addiction (Eissenberg et al. 1999). LAAM is a very long-acting narcotic and is more convenient because it requires only three administrations per week to block heroin withdrawal symptoms (Eissenberg et al. 1999). However, due to its potential for damaging the liver, LAAM treatment has decreased dramatically.

A third narcotic, buprenorphine, which is used as an analgesic, also has been approved for treatment of narcotic dependence (Hanson 2003). Because buprenorphine is both an opioid agonist and antagonist, it has minimal potential for dependence and is easy to manage, which makes this drug a desirable substitute for heroin (Robinson 2002). Efforts are being made to provide education and training to primary care physicians so they will be able to use buprenorphine to treat patients addicted to narcotics in their own offices (Landers 2003). This novel strategy opens the door to physicians heretofore not involved in the treatment of drug addiction to become familiar with substance abuse management and hopefully increase the opportunities to diagnose and treat these patients.

Table 9.5 compares the three major opioid drugs used for maintenance therapy. Other drugs used for similar maintenance therapy of heroin addicts include slow-release oral morphine and even heroin itself for addicts who do not respond to the other maintenance opioid drugs (Bammer 1999).

Some people, including some professionals involved in drug abuse therapy, view heroin or

Table 9.5 **Comparison of Narcotic Substitutes Used in Opiate Maintenance Therapy**

PROPERTIES	METHADONE	LAAM	BUPRENORPHINE
Administration	Oral	Oral	Oral or sublingual
Frequency of doses	Daily	Three times per week	Daily
Other uses	Analgesic	None	Analgesic
Physical dependence	Yes	Yes	Little
Causes positive subjective effects	Yes	Some	Yes
Abuse potential	Yes	Limited	Limited

Source: Swan, N. "Two NIDA-Tested Heroin Treatment Medications Move Toward FDA Approval." *NIDA Notes* (March/April 1993): 45.

▶Case in Point Death by Heroin Habit

Together, Theresa LaMarca, 22, and Damien Conners, 26, walked out onto the railroad tracks in their neighborhood and sat down in front of an oncoming Amtrak train. Both were killed instantly. Although papers sensationalized the story, calling the New Jersey couple a "real-life Romeo and Juliet," it soon became apparent that the real reason behind the double suicide was not doomed love, but a $300-a-day painkiller and heroin habit. The couple, after exhausting all of their financial resources and being evicted from their apartment, began cashing forged checks. A few days after the forgeries were discovered, the two committed suicide. Both LaMarca and Conners had managed to free themselves of drugs after treatment, but apparently only temporarily. In the end, they paid for their drug addiction with their lives.

Source: Johnson, J. "New Jersey Couple's Suicide Highlights Failure of US 'Drug War'" (3 June 2002). Available www.wsws.org/articles/2002/jun2002/nj-j03.shtml.

narcotic addiction as a "failure of the will" and see methadone treatment as substituting one addiction for another (Goldstein 1994). As a result, unrealistic treatment expectations are sometimes imposed on heroin addicts, leading to high failure rates. For example, many methadone treatment programs distribute inadequate methadone doses to maintain heroin or narcotic abstinence (Strain et al. 1999); alternatively, narcotic-dependent patients may be told their methadone will be terminated within 6 months regardless of their progress in the program. Such ill-advised policies often drive clients back to their heroin habits and demonstrate that many professionals who treat heroin and narcotic dependency do not understand that methadone is not a cure for heroin addiction but is a means to achieve a healthier, more normal lifestyle (Millstein 1992; Swan 1994).

It also is essential to understand that even proper treatment does not guarantee resolution of heroin or narcotic addiction (see "Case in Point," Death by Heroin Habit). To maximize the possibility of successful treatment, clients must also participate in regular counseling sessions to help modify the drug-seeking behavior and receive on-site care from professionals, including job training, career development, education, general medical care, and family counseling. These supplemental services dramatically improve the success rate of narcotic dependence treatment (Grinspoon 1995; McLellan et al. 1993).

Other Narcotics

A large number of nonheroin narcotics are used for medical purposes. However, many are also distributed in the streets, such as morphine, methadone, codeine, hydromorphone (Dilaudid), meperidine (Demerol), and other synthetics (hydrocodone [Vicodin] and oxycodone [OxyContin]). A few of the most commonly abused opioids are discussed briefly in the following sections. Except where noted, they are all Schedule II or III drugs.

▪ Morphine

As noted earlier, morphine is the standard by which other narcotic analgesic agents are measured (Way et al. 1998). It has been used to relieve pain since it was first isolated in 1803. Morphine has about half the analgesic potency of heroin but 12 times the potency of codeine. It is commonly used to relieve moderate to intense pain that cannot be controlled by less potent and less dangerous narcotics. Because of its potential for serious side effects, morphine is generally used in a hospital setting where emergency care can be rendered, if necessary. Most pain can be relieved by morphine if high enough doses are used (Reisine and Pasternak 1995; Way et al. 1998); however, morphine is most effective against continuous dull pain.

The side effects that occur when using therapeutic doses of morphine include drowsiness, changes in mood, and inability to think straight. In addition, therapeutic doses depress respiratory activity; thus, morphine decreases the rate and depth of breathing and produces irregular breathing patterns. Like the other narcotics, it can create an array of seemingly unrelated effects throughout the body, including nausea and vomiting, constipation, blurred vision, constricted pupils, and flushed skin (Way et al. 1998).

The initial response to morphine is varied. In normal people who are not suffering pain, the first exposure can be unpleasant, with nausea and vomiting being the prominent reactions. However, continual use often leads to a euphoric response and encourages dependence. When injected subcutaneously, the effects of heroin and morphine are almost identical; this situation occurs because heroin is rapidly metabolized in the body into morphine. After intravenous administration, the onset of heroin's effects is more rapid and more intense than that of morphine because heroin is more lipid-soluble and enters the brain faster. Because heroin is easier to manufacture and is more potent, it is more popular in illicit trade than morphine. Even so, morphine also has substantial abuse potential and is classified as a Schedule II substance (McEvoy 2003).

Tolerance to the effects of morphine can develop very quickly if the drug is used continuously. For example, an addict who is repeatedly administering the morphine to get a "kick" or maintain a "high" must constantly increase the dose. Such users can build up to incredible doses. One addict reported using 5 grams of morphine daily; the normal analgesic dose of morphine is 50 to 80 milligrams per day (Jaffe and Martin 1990). Such high doses are lethal in a person without tolerance to narcotics.

■ Methadone

Methadone was first synthesized in Germany in 1943, when natural opiate analgesics were not available because opium could not be obtained from the Far East during World War II. Methadone was first called *Dolophine*, after Adolph Hitler; one company still uses that trade name. (On the street, methadone pills have been called *dollies*.) As previously described, methadone is often substituted for heroin in the treatment of narcotic-dependent people (*Drug Facts and Comparisons* 2005). It is an effective analgesic, equal to morphine if injected and more potent if taken orally (Way et al. 1998).

The physiological effects of methadone are the same as those of morphine and heroin. As a narcotic, methadone produces psychological dependence, tolerance, and then physical dependence and addiction if repeated doses are taken (Belluck 2003). It is effective for about 24 to 36 hours; therefore, the addict must take methadone daily to avoid narcotic withdrawal. It is often considered

as addictive as heroin if injected; consequently, because methadone is soluble in water, it is formulated with insoluble, inert ingredients to prevent it from being injected by narcotic addicts.

Among methadone's most useful properties are cross-tolerance with other narcotic drugs and a less intense withdrawal response. If it reaches a sufficiently high level in the blood, methadone blocks heroin euphoria. In addition, withdrawal symptoms of patients physically dependent on heroin or morphine and the postaddiction craving can be suppressed by oral administration of methadone. The effective dose for methadone maintenance is 50 to 100 milligrams per day to treat severe withdrawal symptoms (Way et al. 1998; Zickler 1999).

The value of substituting methadone for heroin lies in its longer action. Because addicts no longer need heroin to prevent withdrawal, they often can be persuaded to leave their undesirable associates, drug sources, and dangerous lifestyles. The potential side effects from methadone are the same as those from morphine and heroin, including constipation and sedation; yet if properly used, methadone is a safe drug (Way et al. 1998).

When injecting methadone, some people feel the same kind of euphoria that can be obtained from heroin. Methadone addicts receiving maintenance treatment sometimes become euphoric if the dose is increased too rapidly. There are cases of people who injected crushed methadone pills and developed serious lung conditions from particles that lodged in the tissue, creating a condition somewhat like emphysema. The number of deaths from methadone overdose has approached those from heroin in some major cities like New York. Many of these deaths involved young children who took methadone that parents in maintenance programs had brought home or teenagers who tried to shoot up with street methadone or methadone in combination with other drugs (*Charleston Gazette* 2007). Like heroin, methadone overdoses can be reversed by the antagonist naloxone if the person is treated in time.

■ Fentanyls

The fentanyls belong to a family of very potent narcotic analgesics (>200 times the potency of morphine) that are often administered intravenously for general anesthesia. These synthetic opioid narcotics include drugs such as sufentanil and alfentanil (Gutstein and Akil 2007). Fentanyls are also used in transdermal systems (patches on the skin) in the treatment of chronic pain (Duragesic). Occasionally, reports surface of individuals abusing a fentanyl patch by licking, swallowing, or even smoking it (Hull et al. 2007).

It is estimated that some 100 different active forms of fentanyl could be synthesized; up to now, about 10 derivatives have appeared on the street. They are considered to be "designer" drugs (see Chapter 1). Because of their great potency, ease of production, and low costs, the fentanyls have sometimes been used to replace heroin (Fodale 2006). Fentanyl-type drugs can appear in the same forms and colors as heroin, so there is nothing to alert users that they have been sold a heroin substitute (NIDA 2007). Due to their powerful effects, these drugs are especially dangerous, and incredibly small doses can cause fatal respiratory depression in an unsuspecting heroin user (Fodale 2006). It is likely that hundreds have died from overdosing with heroin laced with fentanyl. Because of an enhanced "high," addicts are tempted to use these lethal combinations (Boddigger 2006). Because these drugs are sometimes very difficult to detect in the blood owing to the small quantities used, there is no reliable information regarding the extent of fentanyl abuse. Fentanyl is so potent that even abusing the patch has caused overdoses and even death (Douglas 2006).

Hydromorphone

Hydromorphone (Dilaudid) is prepared from morphine and used as an analgesic and cough suppressant. It is a stronger analgesic than morphine and is used to treat moderate to severe pain. Nausea, vomiting, constipation, and euphoria may be less marked with hydromorphone than with morphine (Karch 1996; Way et al. 1998). On the street, it is taken in tablet form or injected.

Oxycodone (OxyContin)

Oxycodone is a moderate narcotic analgesic that in the past few years has been increasingly abused as the proprietary product OxyContin and has created considerable controversy (see "Here and Now," OxyContin Controversy Rages). OxyContin is a long-lasting version of oxycodone and considered to be an important and effective therapy for the treatment of severe pain from cancer or other lingering diseases (*Medical Letter on the CDC and FDA* 2003). A dramatic rise in the abuse of OxyContin has been a considerable cause for alarm by officials. Street names for OxyContin include OC, Kicker, OxyCotton, and Hillbilly heroin (CBS News 2007). This is underscored by the report that in 2006, 4.3% of high school seniors used this drug (Johnston 2007). Interestingly, the abuse rate by this population for the less potent Vicodin was more than double that for OxyContin, likely due to easier access (Johnston 2007). Concern has been further heightened with reports of drug rings, including physicians illegally distributing OxyContin (DEA 2002); more than 100 deaths in 2002 linked to an overdose of this product (Marsa 2003); and a 352% increase in the visits to hospital emergency rooms associated with OxyContin use (Substance Abuse

Here and Now

OxyContin Controversy Rages

Controversy surrounds the drug OxyContin, with some hailing its painkilling abilities even as others emphasize its potentially deadly effects. At a 3-day conference on drug abuse prevention, protesters held up signs referring to friends and family members who they claimed had died as a result of OxyContin overdose, in the hopes of raising awareness about the potential problems associated with the drug. One protester described a young man who had gone through withdrawal and depression after being prescribed the drug as a painkiller, and who eventually died from an accidental overdose. Others recognized the beneficial effects of the drug, noting that OxyContin had relieved pain that other drugs could not alleviate in their loved ones. Most individuals attending the conference felt that the problem was not OxyContin or prescriptions, but rather persuading communities to work together to create solutions to the abuse of this drug.

Source: Bloodsworth, D. "Crowd Protests" (20 November 2003) Available www.oxyabusekills.com/crowdprotests.html.

Letter 2003). However, these reports of adverse events associated with OxyContin use must be put into perspective by the knowledge that the vast majority of these emergency events are associated with drug abuse or physical causes (e.g., cancer) other than the effects of OxyContin (*Biotech Week* 2003). As a result, the FDA and DEA control Oxy-Contin at the same level as morphine.

Meperidine

Meperidine (Demerol) is a synthetic drug that frequently is used as an analgesic for treatment of moderate pain; it can be taken in tablet form or injected. Meperidine is about one tenth as powerful as morphine, and its use can lead to dependence (Gutstein and Akil 2006). This drug is sometimes given too freely by some physicians because tolerance develops, requiring larger doses to maintain its therapeutic action. With continual use, it causes physical dependence. Meperidine addicts may use large daily doses (3–4 grams per day). Repeated use of high doses of meperidine can cause seizures (Gutstein and Akil 2006).

Buprenorphine

Buprenorphine, a mild-to-moderate narcotic analgesic, has been available as a Schedule V pain reliever for years. After extensive research, this drug was approved in 2002 as an effective medication for the treatment of narcotic abuse and dependence (Hanson 2003). Buprenorphine has been shown to be effective in relieving the cravings for narcotic pain relievers with minimal tendency to cause addiction itself (Landers 2003; *NIDA Notes* 2002). Although buprenorphine has been reported to have a minimal high (Leinweind 2006), when used properly, there have been isolated reports of occasional deaths, especially when combined with other CNS depressant drugs (Forensic Drug Abuse Advisor 2003). Despite its significant safety record and its minimal propensity for abuse, because its new FDA-approved indication would cause it to be dispensed to patients with drug abuse histories, the DEA revised its classification of buprenorphine to a Schedule III drug. Of particular importance is the fact that buprenorphine (Subutex and Suboxone, a combination of buprenorphine and naloxone) has been approved for the treatment of opiate dependence in an office setting. Due to a recent law, trained physicians are allowed to treat up to 100 narcotic-

dependent patients with buprenorphine in their medical offices (Curley 2007). This means for the first time a drug used to treat addiction can be prescribed by trained primary care physicians, in the offices of private doctors. This is an important step in what may become a revolution in addiction treatment, allowing patients to discreetly receive help from a family doctor for their substance abuse problem (Center for Substance Abuse Research [CESAR] FAX 2003; Landers 2003). Currently, more than 2000 physicians have been certified to prescribe it for treatment of opioid drug dependence (Curley 2007). However, there are still some bureaucratic problems that make reimbursement difficult and at times make use of this drug a hassle for doctors. But with time, it is likely that use of buprenorphine by primary care physicians will become more routine (Anderson 2007).

MPTP: A "Designer" Tragedy

Attempts to synthesize illicit designer versions of meperidine by street chemists have proved tragic for some unsuspecting drug addicts. In 1976, a young drug addict with elementary laboratory skills attempted to make a meperidine-like drug by using shortcuts in the chemical synthesis. Three days after self-administering his untested drug product, the drug user developed a severe case of tremors and motor problems identical to Parkinson's disease, a neurological disorder generally occurring in the elderly. Even more surprising to attending neurologists was that this young drug addict improved dramatically after treatment with levodopa, a drug that is very effective in treating the symptoms of traditional Parkinson's disease. After 18 months of treatment, the despondent addict committed suicide. An autopsy revealed he had severe brain damage that was almost identical to that occurring in classical parkinsonian patients (Schwarcz 2005). It was concluded that a by-product resulting from the sloppy synthesis of the meperidine-like designer narcotic was responsible for the irreversible brain damage.

This hypothesis was confirmed by a separate and independent event on the West Coast in 1981, when a cluster of relatively young heroin addicts (ages 22–42) in the San Francisco area also developed symptoms of Parkinson's disease. All of these patients had consumed a new "synthetic heroin" obtained on the streets, which was produced by attempting to synthesize meperidine-like drugs (Aminoff 1998; Langston et al. 1983). Common to both incidents was the presence of the compound

MPTP, which was a contaminant resulting from the careless synthesis. MPTP is metabolized to a very reactive molecule in the brain that selectively destroys neurons containing the transmitter dopamine in the motor regions of the basal ganglia (see Chapter 4). Similar neuronal damage occurs in classical Parkinson's disease over the course of 50 to 70 years, whereas ingestion of MPTP dramatically accelerates the degeneration to a matter of days (Goldstein 1994). As tragic as the MPTP incident was, it was heralded as an important scientific breakthrough; MPTP is now used by researchers as a tool to study why Parkinson's disease occurs and how to treat it effectively (Lane and Dunnett 2007).

Codeine

Codeine is a naturally occurring constituent of opium and the most frequently prescribed of the narcotic analgesics. It is used principally as a treatment for minor to moderate pain and as a cough suppressant. Maximum pain relief from codeine occurs with 30 to 50 milligrams. Usually, when prescribed for pain, codeine is combined with either a salicylate (such as aspirin) or acetaminophen (Tylenol). Aspirin-like drugs and opioid narcotics interact in a synergistic fashion to give an analgesic equivalence greater than what can be achieved by aspirin or codeine alone. Although not especially powerful, codeine may still be abused. Codeine-containing cough syrup is currently classified as a Schedule V drug. Because the abuse potential is considered minor, the FDA has ruled that codeine cough products can be sold without a prescription; however, the pharmacist is required to keep them behind the counter and must be asked in order to provide codeine-containing cough medications. Despite the FDA ruling, about 50% of the states have more restrictive regulations and require that codeine-containing cough products be available only by prescription (Way et al. 1998).

Although codeine dependence is possible, it is not very common; most people who abuse codeine developed narcotic dependence previously with one of the more potent opioids. In general, large quantities of codeine are needed to satisfy a narcotic addiction; therefore, it is not commonly marketed on the street.

Pentazocine

Pentazocine (Talwin) was first developed in the 1960s in an effort to create an effective analgesic with low abuse potential. When taken orally, its analgesic effect is slightly greater than that of codeine. Its effects on respiration and sedation are similar to those of the other opioids, but it does not prevent withdrawal symptoms in a narcotic addict. In fact, pentazocine will precipitate withdrawal symptoms if given to a person on methadone maintenance (Gutstein and Akil 2006). Pentazocine is not commonly abused because its effects can be unpleasant, resulting in dysphoria. It is classified as a Schedule IV drug.

Propoxyphene

Propoxyphene (Darvon, Dolene) is structurally related to methadone, but it is a much weaker analgesic, about half as potent as codeine (Gutstein and Akil 2006). Like codeine, propoxyphene is frequently given in combination with aspirin or acetaminophen. Although it was once an extremely popular analgesic, the use of propoxyphene has declined as its potency has been questioned. Some research suggests this narcotic is no more effective in relieving pain than aspirin (Gutstein and Akil 2006). To a large extent, new, more effective non-narcotic analgesics have replaced propoxyphene. In very high doses, it can cause delusions, hallucinations, and convulsions. Alone, propoxyphene causes little respiratory depression; however, when combined with alcohol or other CNS depressants, this drug can depress respiration.

Narcotic-Related Drugs

Although not classified as narcotics, the following drugs are either structurally similar to narcotics (dextromethorphan) or are used to treat narcotic withdrawal (clonidine) or overdose (naloxone).

Dextromethorphan

Dextromethorphan is a synthetic used in cough remedies since the 1960s and can be purchased without prescription. Although its molecular structure resembles that of codeine, this drug does not have analgesic action nor does it cause typical narcotic dependence (*Drug Facts and Comparisons* 2005).

Although dextromethorphan is not traditionally considered a major drug abuse problem, recent studies are cause for concern. They reveal that more than 3 million young people have used OTC products containing dextromethorphan to get high (Buddy 2008). Dextromethorphan-containing cough medicines has been reported in the United States and other countries sometimes resulting in deadly consequences (see "Here and Now," Dextromethorphan: No Coughing Matter). The abuse typically occurs among adolescents and young adults. The relatively few cases of addiction reveal a pattern of high-dose use for months to even years. The principal symptoms of abuse include altered perceptions, sense of floating, hallucinations, visual distortions, and even paranoia and psychotic reactions. Its effects have been described to be similar to those of phencyclidine (PCP) and the general anesthetic ketamine (Morgan et al. 2006). There is some suggestion that both physical and psychological dependence can occur with dextromethorphan, resulting in withdrawal when its use is discontinued (Cranston 1999). Dextromethorphan is sometimes mixed with drugs such as alcohol, amphetamines, and cocaine to give unusual psychoactive interactions. As of 2007, the DEA had taken no steps to restrict the use of dextromethorphan in over-the-counter (OTC) products.

Young people are becoming aware of dextromethorphan's abuse potential from web sites on the Internet. A growing number of these sites have promoted dextromethorphan as a powerful OTC mind-altering drug. Included on these sites are personal experiences of users as well as directions on how to use the drug, predictions about what to expect, warning signs of adverse reactions, and instructions as to how to extract dextromethorphan from OTC cough medicines (The Vaults of Erowid 2007).

Clonidine

Clonidine (Catapres) was created in the late 1970s. It is not a narcotic analgesic and has no direct effect on the opioid receptors; instead, it stimulates receptors for noradrenaline, and its principal use is as an oral antihypertensive (*Drug Facts and Comparisons* 2005). Clonidine is mentioned here because it is a nonaddictive, noneuphoriagenic prescription medication with demonstrated efficacy in relieving some of the physical effects of opiate withdrawal (such as vomiting and diarrhea). However, clonidine does not alter narcotic craving or the generalized aches associated with withdrawal (O'Brien 2006). The dosing regimen is typically a 7- to 14-day inpatient treatment for opiate withdrawal. Length

Here and Now

Dextromethorphan: No Coughing Matter

Dextromethorphan, a key active ingredient in cough suppressants, is the reason why many young people are using OTC cough medicines to get high. The substance — also known as robo, skittles, dxm, dex, and tussein — is found in at least 80 OTC products. Dextromethorphan usually produces a disassociative feeling (roboing, robo rolling, robo tripping) or a feeling of intoxication, but its abuse can also lead to psychotic behavior. When large amounts of dextromethorphan are taken, the drug attaches to receptors in the central nervous system — the same receptors to which PCP attaches. In the long term, this effect can cause depression, memory problems, and suicidal tendencies. Dextromethorphan abuse can also result in death: In 2003, 14 people younger than age 18 died as a result of dextromethorphan use, with many more overdoses reported nationwide.

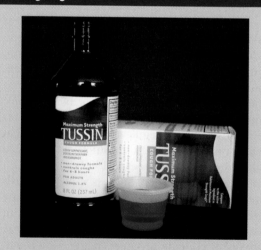

Source: Magnus, E. "Addicted to Cough Medicine?" *MSNBC News* (27 March 2004). Available www.msnbc.msn.com/id/4608341/.

of treatment can be reduced to 7 days for withdrawal from heroin and short-acting opiates; the 14-day treatment is needed for the longer-acting methadone-type opiates. Because tolerance to clonidine may develop, opiates are discontinued abruptly at the start of treatment. In this way, the peak intensity of withdrawal will occur while clonidine is still maximally effective (McEvoy 2003).

One of the most important advantages of clonidine over other treatments for opiate withdrawal detoxification is that it shortens the time for withdrawal to 14 days compared with several weeks or months using standard procedures, such as methadone treatment (Kleber 1998). The potential disadvantage of taking clonidine is that it can cause serious side effects of its own, the most serious being significantly lowered blood pressure, which can cause fainting and blacking out (*Drug Facts and Comparisons* 2005). Overall, its lack of abuse potential makes clonidine particularly useful in rapid treatment of narcotic dependence; however, the long-term benefit is controversial (Gowing et al. 2003).

Naloxone/Naltrexone

Naloxone and the related drug naltrexone are relatively pure narcotic antagonists. These drugs attach to opiate receptors in the brain and throughout the body. They do not activate but rather prevent narcotic drugs, such as heroin and morphine, from having an effect. By themselves, these antagonists do not cause much change, but potently block or reverse the effects of all narcotics. Because of its antagonistic properties, naloxone is a useful antidote in the treatment of narcotic overdoses; its administration reverses life-threatening, narcotic-induced effects on breathing and the cardiovascular system (Gutstein and Akil 2006; O'Brien 2006). However, if not used carefully, this antagonist will also block the analgesic action of the narcotics and initiate severe withdrawals in narcotic-dependent people (Way et al. 1998). Its use has been proposed to prevent addicts from experiencing the effects of heroin (Mathias 2003); however, most individuals dependent on heroin are not interested in using this drug because it can precipitate withdrawal symptoms. An interesting use of naloxone has been to combine it with buprenorphine in small quantities (Suboxone). As long as this product is taken as prescribed, the quantity of naloxone is too small

to have an antagonistic effect. However, if Suboxone is consumed in high doses, such as would occur if it were being abused, there would be sufficient naloxone to block the opioid effect (CESAR 2003). There has been interest in employing this drug to reduce the craving for alcohol in the treatment of chronic alcoholism. It has been approved by the FDA for this purpose (*Drug Facts and Comparisons* 2005).

■ NATURAL SUBSTANCES

Narcotics

Although many herbal preparations can cause drowsiness or have some analgesic properties, few of these actually contain opioid narcotic drugs. The naturally occurring opioid drugs include morphine, codeine, heroin, papaverine, and thebaine and are found only in the opium poppy,

Opium poppy containing natural narcotics such as morphine, codeine, and heroin.

Papaver somniferum. Although several varieties of opium-yielding poppies exist, they are typically winter crops in the Southern Hemisphere and do best in climates that have warm days and cool nights. All of the plants thrive in sandy soil. Most of the active drugs are found in the seepage from the seed heads located beneath the flower petals of the poppy flowers, although small amounts of these active ingredients are found in other parts of the plant such as the stem and leaves. The poppy flowers persist until the end of October in the Southern Hemisphere. Although this species of plant can survive in the United States if the environment is rigidly controlled, the vast majority of the supplies of the naturally occurring narcotic drugs are brought into the country, either legally and sold as legitimate pharmaceuticals or smuggled across borders and sold as illicit narcotics.

Discussion Questions

1. Why do narcotics have high abuse potential?

2. What are the principal clinical uses of the opioid narcotics?

3. What is the relationship between endorphin systems and the opioid narcotics?

4. Why was there a substantial increase in heroin abuse in the United States throughout the 1990s?

5. Why does heroin addiction contribute to criminal activity?

6. What are the principal withdrawal effects when heroin use is stopped in addicts?

7. How does "methadone maintenance" work for the treatment of narcotic dependence? Explain a possible drawback to this approach.

8. How does buprenorphine compare to methadone as treatment for narcotic addictions?

9. What is considered to be successful treatment for heroin addiction?

10. How does morphine compare with heroin?

11. Why is dextromethorphan potentially addicting, and what should the federal government do to stop its abuse?

12. What does the fact that naloxone is effective in the treatment of alcoholism suggest about the role of endogenous opioid systems in alcohol dependence?

Summary

1. The term *narcotic* refers to naturally occurring substances derived from the opium poppy and their synthetic substitutes. These drugs are referred to as the opioid (or opiate) narcotics because of their association with opium. For the most part, the opioid narcotics possess abuse potential, but they also have important clinical value and are used to relieve all kinds of pain (they are analgesic), suppress coughing (they are antitussive), and stop diarrhea.

2. The principal side effects of the opioid narcotics, besides their abuse potential, include drowsiness, respiratory depression, nausea and vomiting, constipation, inability to urinate, and sometimes a drop in blood pressure. These side effects can be annoying or even life-threatening, so caution is required when using these drugs.

3. Heroin is the most likely of the opioid narcotics to be severely abused; it is easily prepared from opium and has a rapid, intense effect.

4. When narcotics such as heroin are first used by people not experiencing pain, the drugs can cause unpleasant, dysphoric sensations. However, euphoria gradually overcomes the aversive effects. The positive feelings increase with narcotic use, leading to psychological dependence. After psychological dependence, physical dependence occurs with frequent daily use, which reinforces the narcotic abuse. If the user stops taking the drug after physical dependence has occurred, severe withdrawal symptoms result.

5. Tolerance to narcotics can occur rapidly with intense use of these drugs. This tolerance can result in the use of incredibly large doses of narcotics that would be fatal to a nontolerant person.

6. Methadone and buprenorphine are frequently used to help narcotic addicts stop using heroin or one of the other highly addicting drugs. Oral methadone relieves the withdrawal symptoms that would result from discontinuing narcotics. Methadone can also cause psychological and physical dependence, but it is less addicting than heroin

and easier to control. Buprenorphine is distinct from methadone in that it has been approved for use in primary care settings.

7 Fentanyls are very potent synthetic opioid narcotics. They can be easily synthesized and converted into drugs that are as much as 3000 to 6000 times more potent than heroin itself. Detection and regulation of these fentanyl derivatives by law enforcement agencies are very difficult. The fentanyl-type drugs are used as heroin substitutes and have killed narcotic addicts because of their unexpected potency.

8 Attempts to create designer narcotics have led to the synthesis of very potent fentanyl-like drugs that are responsible for a number of overdose deaths. In addition, attempts to synthesize a meperidine (Demerol) designer drug resulted in the inadvertent creation of MPTP, a very reactive compound that causes a dramatic onset of Parkinson's disease in its users.

9 Dextromethorphan is a codeine-related drug used as an antitussive in OTC cough medicines. In very high doses, dextromethorphan can cause PCP-like hallucinations and sensory distortions. The abuse of this drug has not been substantial enough to result in its removal or special control by federal agencies.

References

Abel, E. L. *Marijuana: The First Twelve Thousand Years.* New York: Plenum, 1980.

American Academy of Pain Medicine. "Psychiatric Factors Linked to Increased Risk for Misuse of Opioid Medications." 23rd Annual Meeting. Abstract 151. February 7 2007.

American SIDS Institute. "Reducing the Risk of SIDS" (2005). Available www.sids.org/prevent.htm.

Aminoff, M. "Pharmacologic Management of Parkinsonism and Other Movement Disorders." In *Basic and Clinical Pharmacology,* 7th ed., edited by Bertram Katzung, 450–463. Stamford, CT: Appleton and Lange, 1998.

Anderson, L. "A Drug-War Setback. Red Tape, Doctors Say, Cuts Buprenorphine Prescription." *Baltimore Sun* (20 June 2007). Available http://www.baltimoresun.com/news/local/bal-md.bupe20jun20,0,6881220.story?coll=bal-1...

Austin, G. A. *Perspective on the History of Psychoactive Substance Use.* NIDA Research Issues No. 24. Washington, DC: U.S. Department of Health, Education, and Welfare, 1978.

Baglole, J. "Vancouver's Heroin 'Fix.'" *The Wall Street Journal* (1 April 2003): D-8.

Bammer, G., A. Dobler-Mikola, M. Fleming, J. Strang, and A. Uchtenhagen. "The Heroin Prescribing Debate: Integrating Science and Politics." *Science* 284 (1999): 1277–1278.

Bearak, B. "Junkies Playing Roulette with Needles." *Salt Lake Tribune* (29 November 1992): A-4.

Belluck, P. "Methadone, Once the Way Out, Suddenly Grows as a Killer Drug." *The New York Times* (9 February 2003): 8.

Bennett, A. "Perinatal Substance Abuse and the Drug-exposed Neonate." *Advanced Nurse Practitioner* 7 (1999): 32–36.

Biotech Week. "Purdue Pharma: OxyContin Rarely the Sole Cause of Drug Abuse Deaths." (19 March 2003): 1.

Boddigger, D. "Fentanyl-Laced Street Drugs Kill Hundreds." *The Lancet* 368 (2006): 1237–1238.

Bourgois, P. "Participant Observation Study of Indirect Paraphernalia Sharing/HIV Risk in a Network of Heroin Injection." NIDA web site (17 November 1999). Available www.nida.nih.gov/about/organization/CEWG/Ethno.html.

Brecher, E. M. *Licit and Illicit Drugs.* Boston: Little, Brown, 1972.

Buddy, T. "Cough Syrup More Abused by Youth than Meth." About.com.: Alcoholism. 29 January, 2008. Available http://alcoholism.about.com/b/2008/01/29/cough-syrup-more-abused-by-youth-than-meth.htm.

CBS News. "OxyContin: Pain Relief vs. Abuse." (11 June 2007). Available www.cbsnews.com/stories/2007/06/19/health/webmd/main2953950.shtml.

Center for Substance Abuse and Research (CESAR). FAX. "Buprenorphine Now Available for Treating Heroin Dependence in U.S." *University of Maryland* 12 (31 March 2003): 1.

Charleston Gazette. "The Killer Cure" (2007). Available www.wvgazette.com/section/series/The+Killer+Cure.

Chossudovsky, M. "Who Benefits from the Afghan Opium Trade?" *Global Research* (21 September, 2006). Available www.globalresearch.ca/index.php?context=va&aid=3294.

Community Epidemiology Workgroup (CEWG). Vol. 1. "Highlights and Executive Summary." NIDA, NIH Publications No. 03-5109A, December 2002.

Constable, P. "A Poor Yield for Afghans' War on Drugs." *The Washington Post* (19 September 2006). 14A.

Cowan, R. and J. Carvel. "Heroin Addicts Could Inject Themselves at Supervised Centres in Police-Backed Plans" *Guardian Unlimited* (23 May 2006). Available www.guardian.co.uk/society/2006/may/23/drugsandalcohol.drugs.

Cranston, J. "Abuse of Dextromethorphan." *Archives of Family Medicine* 8 (1999): 99.

Curley, B. "New Law Expands Access to Buprenorphine." Join Together (2007). Available www.jointogether.org/news/features/2007/new-law-expands-access-to.html

Davies, G., A. Williams, S. Markey, M. Ebert, E. Caine, C. Reickert, and I. Kopin. "Chronic Parkinsonism Secondary to Intravenous Injection of Meperidine Analogues." *Psychiatry Research* 1 (1979): 249–254.

DiChiara, G., and A. North. "Neurobiology of Opiate Abuse." *Trends in Pharmacological Sciences* 13 (May 1992): 185–193.

Douglas, J. "Painkiller Patch Abuse Blamed for Deaths." *Los Angeles Times* (15 June 2006).

Drug and Alcohol Resource Center. "Drug Addiction Information" (January 2005). Available www.addict-help.com.

Drug Enforcement Agency (DEA). "Domestic Strategic June 2002 Highlights." *DEA 02047* (September 2002): 1.

Drug Enforcement Agency (DEA). "Heroin." Chapter from *Drugs of Abuse* (2000). Available http://www.dea.gov/pubs/abuse/4-narc.htm.

Drug Facts and Comparisons. St. Louis, MO: Wolters Kluwer, 2005: 488, 489, 616, 617, 942–977, 1424–1428.

Eissenberg, T., M. Stitzer, G. Bigelow, A. Buchalter, and S. Walsh. "Relative Potency of Levo-alpha-acetylmethadol and Methadone in Humans Under Acute Dosing Conditions." *Journal of Pharmacology and Experimental Therapeutics* 289 (1999): 936–945.

Epstein, J., and J. Gfroerer. "Data Point to Increase in Numbers of Young Heroin Users." *Connection* (a semiannual newsletter published by the Association for Health Services Research) (June 1998): 3.

Eshkevari, L., and J. Heath. "Use of Acupuncture for Chronic Pain: Optimizing Clinical Practice." *Holistic Nursing Practice* 19 (2005): 217–221.

Fodale, V. "Killer Fentanyl: A Lesson from Anesthesiology." *Lancet* 368 (2006): 1237–1238.

Forensic Drug Abuse Advisor. "Buprenorphine-Related Deaths." 15 (February 2, 2003): 1, 2.

Golding, A. "Two Hundred Years of Drug Abuse." *Journal of the Royal Society of Medicine* 86 (May 1993): 282–286.

Goldstein, A. *Addiction from Biology to Drug Policy.* New York: Freeman, 1994: 137–154.

Gourlay, G. "Advances in Opioid Pharmacology." *Supportive Care for Cancer* (21 December 2004).

Gowing, L., M. Farrell, R. Ali, and J. White. "Alpha 2 Adrenergic Agonists for the Management of Opioid Withdrawal." *Cochrane Database Systems Review* 2 (2003).

Grinspoon, L. "Psychotherapy for Methadone Patients — Part II." *Harvard Mental Health Letter* 12 (October 1995): 7.

Gutstein, H., and H. Akil. "Opioid Analgesics." In *The Pharmacological Basis of Therapeutics,* 11th ed. Edited by L. Brunton, J. Lazo, and K. Parker, 547–590. New York: McGraw-Hill, 2006.

Hall, E., and N. Sykes. "Analgesia for Patients with Advanced Disease." *Postgraduate Medical Journal* 80 (2004): 148–154.

Hanson, G. R. "Opening the Door to Mainstream Medical Treatment of Drug Addiction." *NIDA Notes* 17 (January 2003): 3, 4.

"Heroin '96: What Americans Need to Know." *Prevention Pipeline* 8 (November/December 1996): 20.

Hickman, M., S. Carrivick, S. Paterson, N. Hunt, D. Zador, L. Cusick, and J. Henry. "London Audit of Drug-Related Overdose Deaths: Characteristics and Typology, and Implications for Prevention and Monitoring." *Addiction* 102 (2007): 317–323.

Hubbard, R. "Focus on Heroin: Increase in Users and Changing Treatment System Present New Challenges for Services Researchers." *Connection* (a semiannual newsletter published by the Association for Health Services Research) (June 1998): 1–2.

Hull, M. et al. "Fatalities Associated with Fentanyl and Coadministered Cocaine on Opiates." *Journal of Forensic Science* 52 (2007): 1383–1388.

Jaffe, J., and M. Martin. "Opioid Analgesics and Antagonists." In *The Pharmacological Basis of Therapeutics,* 8th ed., edited by A. Gilman, T. Rall, A. Nies, and P. Taylor, 522–573. New York: Pergamon, 1990.

Johnston, L. "Monitoring the Future 2006" (2007). Available www.monitoringthefuture.org/pubs/monographs/vol1_2006.pdf.

Karch, S. "Narcotics." In *The Pathology of Drug Abuse,* 281–408. New York: CRC, 1996.

Kosten, T., and L. Hollister. "Drugs of Abuse." In *Basic and Clinical Pharmacology,* 7th ed., edited by B. Katzun, 516–531. Stamford, CT: Appleton & Lange, 1998.

Kreek, M., S. Schlussman, G. Bart, K. Laforge, and E. Butelman. "Evolving Perspectives on Neurobiological Research on the Addictions: Celebration of the 30th Anniversary of NIDA." *Neuropharmacology* 47, supplement 1 (2004): 324–344.

Landers, P. "Fighting Addiction with a Pill." *The Wall Street Journal* (20 February 2003): D-1.

Lane, E., and S. Dunnett. "Animal Models of Parkinson's Disease and L-dopa Induced Dyskinesia. How Close Are We to the Clinic?" *Psychopharmacology* (2007).

Langston, J., P. Ballard, J. Tetrud, and I. Irwin. "Chronic Parkinsonism in Humans Due to a Product of Meperidine-Analogue Synthesis." *Science* 219 (1983): 979–980.

Leinweind, D. "Baltimore Has New Way to Treat Addict." *USA Today* (5 October 2006): 5a.

Leland, J. "The Fear of Heroin Is Shooting Up." *Newsweek* (26 August 1996): 55–56.

Lucky, B. "MTQS Study Highlights Possibilities and Challenges for Performance Measurement." *Connection* (a semiannual newsletter published by the Association for Health Services Research) (June 1998): 4.

Marsa, L. "Drug Mix Proves Deadly." *Los Angeles Times* (3 March 2003): A-1.

"Mary." *Rolling Stone* 30 (1996): 42–43.

Mathias, R. "New Approaches Seek to Expand Naltrexone Use in Heroin Treatment." *NIDA Notes* 17 (January 2003): 8.

Maurer, D., and V. Vogel. *Narcotics and Narcotic Addiction,* 3rd ed. Springfield, IL: Thomas, 1967.

Maxwell, J. "Unmet Treatment Needs Among Heroin Addicts Raise Ethical Issues." *Connection* (a semiannual newsletter published by the Association for Health Services Research) (June 1998): 5.

McEvoy, G., ed. "Opiate Agonists and Antagonists." In *American Hospital Formulary Service Drug Information,* 2022–2097. Bethesda, MD: American Society of Hospital Pharmacists, 2003.

McLellen, T., O. Arndt, D. Metzger, G. Woody, and C. O'Brien. "The Effects of Psychosocial Services in Substance Abuse Treatment." *Journal of the American Medical Association* 269 (21 April 1993): 1953–1959.

McMurran, M. "What Works in Substance Misuse Treatments for Offenders." *Criminal Behavior and Mental Health* 17 (2007): 225–233.

Medical Letter. Opioid Analgesics. 40 (1998): 81–82.

Medical Letter on the CDC and FDA. "FDA Warns OxyContin Maker over Safety Statement in Ads." (16 February 2003).

Meshberg, R. "A Story of Addiction." *Hartford Courant (NE Magazine).* (1 October 2006): 8.

Millstein, R. "Methadone Revisited" *NIDA Notes* 7 (July/August 1992): 3–4.

Morgan, T., M. Porritt, and A. Poling. "Effects of Dextromethorphan on Rats' Acquisition of Responding with Delayed Reinforcement." *Pharmacology and Biochemical Behavior* 85 (2006): 637–642.

Motlagh, J. "Official Pushes Opium Alternative." *The Washington Times* (6 October 2006): 15a.

National Institute on Drug Abuse. "Heroin" (January 2005). Available www.drugabuse.gov/Infofax/heroin.html.

National Institute on Drug Abuse (NIDA). "Fentanyl" (2007). Available www.drugabuse.gov/drugpages/fentanyl.html.

National Institute on Drug Abuse. *NIDA Notes.* "Buprenorphine Approval Expands Options for Addiction Treatment." 17 (2002): 13.

National Institute on Drug Abuse. Research Report Series. "Heroin Abuse and Addiction" (December 2004). Available www.drugabuse.gov/ResearchReports/heroin/heroin5.html.

National Trends in Drug Abuse. "Information About Heroin from ONDCP Pulse Check." *Newsweek* (26 August 1996): 54.

O'Brien, C. "Drug Addiction and Drug Abuse." In *The Pharmacological Basis of Therapeutics,* 11th ed. Edited by L. Brunton, J. Lazo, and K. Parker, 607–627. New York: McGraw-Hill, 2006.

"Opioids." *Medical Letter* 38 (10 May 1996).

"'Oxy' Kids Crisis." *New York Post* (18 June 2007).

Pain & Central Nervous System. "Helping Opiate-Addicted Babies." *Pain & Central Nervous System Week* (5 September 2005).

Paule, M. G. "Maternal Drug Abuse and Adverse Effects on Neurobehavior of Offspring." In *Handbook of Developmental Neurotoxicology,* edited by W. Slikker and L. Chang, 617–629. New York: Academic Press, 1998.

Payte, J. T. "The Evolution of Methadone Treatment Programs." *Connection* (a semiannual newsletter published by the Association for Health Services Research) (June 1998): 1–2.

Quinion, M. "Heroin Chic." *World Wide Words* (January 2005). Available www.worldwidewords.org/turnsofphrase/tp-her1.htm.

Reid, L., K. Elifson, and C. Sterk. "Ecstasy and Gateway Drugs: Initiating the Use of Ecstasy and Other Drugs." *Annals of Epidemiology* 17 (2007): 74–80.

Reisine, T., and G. Pasternak. "Opioid Analgesics and Antagonists." In *The Pharmacological Basis of Therapeutics,* 9th ed., edited by J. Hardman and L. Limbird, 521–555. New York: McGraw-Hill, 1995.

Robinson, S. "Buprenorphine: An Analgesic with an Expanding Role in the Treatment of Opioid Addiction." *CNS Drug Review* 8 (Winter 2002): 377–390.

Rombey, D. "Heroin Is Silent Scourge of Sheltered Springville." *Deseret News* (9 June 2003a): A-1.

Rombey, D. "Heroin Takes Toll on Families." *Deseret News* (10 June 2003b): A-1.

Schwarcz, J. "Chemistry Students' Drug Abuse Was Fatal, But Good May Still Come of It." *The Gazette* (Montreal) (11 September 2005).

Seper, J. "Colombia Policy Cited for Rise in Heroin Use; Investigators Hit Focus on Cocaine." *Washington Times* (26 May 2003); A-1.

Stockman, F. "Heroin Is Surpassing Cocaine as Users' Choice." *Boston Globe* (26 May 2003): A-1.

Strain, E., G. Bigelow, I. Liebson, and M. Stitzer. "Moderate- vs. High-dose Methadone in the Treatment of Opioid Dependence: A Randomized Trial." *Journal of the American Medical Association* 281 (1999): 1000–1005.

Substance Abuse and Mental Health Services Administration (SAMHSA). "Data on Drug-Related Emergency Room Visits Released by SAMHSA." (10 May 2006a). Available http://dawninfo.samhsa.gov.

Substance Abuse and Mental Health Services Administration (SAMHSA). "Results from the 2005 National Survey on Drug Use and Health: National Findings." NSDUH Series H-30, DHHS Publications No. SMA 06-4194. Rockville, MD: Office of Applied Studies, 2006b.

Substance Abuse Letter. "Growing Painkiller Abuse Concerns Federal Officials." *Pace Publications* 8 (2003): 1.

Swan, N. "Research Demonstrates Long-Term Benefits of Methadone Treatment." *NIDA Notes* 9 (1994): 1, 4–5.

Szalavitz, M. "The Shot That Saves." *New York Times* (21 August 2005). Available www.nytimes.com/2005/08/21/opinion/nyregionopinions/21cslzalavitz.html.

The Vaults of Erowid. "Dextromethorphan" (6 January 2007). Available www.erowid.org/chemicals/dxm/dxm.shtml.

U.S. Department of Justice. Drugs, Youth and the Internet. "Heroin/Opiates." Product # 2002-R0430-002 (August 2002): 21–24.

U.S. Department of Justice. National Drug Threat Assessment 2003. "Heroin." Product No. 2003-Q0317-001 (January 2003): 41–50.

Way, W., H. Fields, and E. L. Way. "Opioid Analgesics and Antagonists." In *Basic and Clinical Pharmacology,* 7th ed., edited by B. Katzung, 496–515. Stamford, CT: Appleton & Lange, 1998.

Way, W., and E. Way. "Opioid Analgesics and Antagonists." In *Basic and Clinical Pharmacology,* 5th ed., edited by B. Katzung, 420–436. Norwalk, CT: Appleton & Lange, 1992.

Weiss, E. "Seattle Scene Represents Nation's Rising Heroin Use." *All Things Considered,* National Public Radio (2 January 1995).

Wikipedia. "Heroin" (1 October 2007). Available http://en.wikipedia.org/wiki/heroin.

Wikipedia. "Speedball (drug)" (March 2007). Available http://en.wikipedia.org/wiki/speedball-(drug).

Worrich, S., G. Schuler, and P. Janicki. "Effect of Local Administration of Transdermal Fentanyl on Peripheral Opioid Analgesia." *Pain Medication* 8 (2007): 41–47.

Young, D. "Scientists Examine Pain Relief and Addiction." *American Society of Health-System Pharmacists* 64 (2007): 796–798.

Zickler, P. "High-Dose Methadone Improves Treatment Outcomes." *NIDA Notes* 14 (1999): 81–82.

Zocchi, A., et al. "Dopamine Responsiveness to Drugs of Abuse: A Shell-Core Investigation in the Nucleus Accumbens of the Mouse." *Synapse* 50 (2003): 293–302.

Learning ⊚bjectives

On completing this chapter you will be able to:

◎ Explain how amphetamines work.

◎ Identify the FDA-approved uses for amphetamines.

◎ Recognize the major side effects of amphetamines on brain and cardiovascular functions.

◎ Identify the terms *speed, ice, run, high,* and *tweaking* as they relate to amphetamine use.

◎ Explain what "designer" amphetamines are and how Ecstasy compares to methamphetamine.

◎ Explain what "club drugs" are.

◎ Trace the changes in attitude toward cocaine abuse that occurred in the 1980s and explain why they occurred.

◎ Compare the effects of cocaine with those of amphetamines.

◎ Identify the different stages of cocaine withdrawal.

◎ Discuss the different approaches to treating cocaine dependence.

◎ Identify and compare the major sources of the caffeine-like xanthine drugs.

◎ List the principal physiological effects of caffeine.

◎ Compare caffeine dependence and withdrawal to that associated with the major stimulants.

◎ Understand the potential dangers of using herbal stimulants such as ephedra.

◎ Identify the role of the FDA in regulating herbal stimulants.

Did You Know?

○ The first therapeutic use of amphetamines was in inhalers to treat nasal congestion.

○ Methylphenidate (Ritalin) is a type of amphetamine used to treat hyperactive (attention deficit hyperactivity disorder) children.

○ Illegal methamphetamine can be easily made from drugs found in common over-the-counter (OTC) decongestants and some herbal products.

○ Smoking "freebased" or "crack" cocaine is more dangerous and more addicting than other forms of administration.

○ Using high doses of amphetamines or cocaine can cause behavior that resembles schizophrenia.

○ Caffeine is the most frequently used stimulant in the world.

○ Herbal stimulants promoted as "natural highs" contain CNS stimulants that can cause high blood pressure, seizures, and strokes.

○ Ephedrine found in natural herbal products has caused fatal cardiovascular problems in unsuspecting athletes and was recently removed from the list of FDA-approved OTC products.

Drugs and Society Online is a great source for additional drugs and society information for both students and instructors.
Visit **http://drugsandsociety.jbpub.com** to find a variety of useful tools for learning, thinking, and teaching.

Introduction

Stimulants are substances that cause the user to feel pleasant effects such as a sense of increased energy and a state of euphoria, or "high." This effect is likely due to the ability of these drugs to release dopamine (Deslandes et al. 2002). The user may also feel restless and talkative and have trouble sleeping. High doses administered over the long term can produce personality changes or even induce violent, dangerous, psychotic behavior. Methamphetamine addicts make notoriously bad decisions that hurt them and their loved ones. The following is a quote from a former methamphetamine user: "For 5 months I hung out with a crew who cooked meth. My job was to write bad checks to get ingredients to make it. This was my life. My house was a mess and I couldn't take care of anyone including myself. I weighed 100 pounds and stayed up for weeks at a time because I never ran out of gas. . . . I also picked my eye for no reason, until it would get so swollen and red it would stay shut for days. I had my first son when I was 26 and later gave up my second son for adoption because I was such a mess. . . . My mother called social services and made sure that I was not allowed to take care of my children" (Snider 2007).

Many users self-medicate psychological conditions (for example, depression) with stimulants. Because the initial effects of stimulants are so pleasant, these drugs are repeatedly abused, leading to dependence.

In this chapter, you will learn about two principal classifications of stimulant drugs. Major stimulants, including amphetamines and cocaine, are addressed first, given their prominent role in current drug abuse problems in the United States. The chapter concludes with a review of minor stimulants — in particular, caffeine. The stimulant properties of over-the-counter (OTC) sympathomimetics and "herbal highs" are also discussed. (Because nicotine has unique stimulant properties, it is covered separately in Chapter 11 on tobacco.)

Major Stimulants

All major stimulants increase alertness, excitation, and euphoria; thus, these drugs are referred to as **uppers**. The major stimulants are classified as either Schedule I ("designer" amphetamines) or Schedule II (amphetamine and cocaine) controlled substances because of their abuse potential. Although these drugs have properties in common, they also have unique features that distinguish them from one another. The similarities and differences of the major stimulants are discussed in the following sections.

■ Amphetamines

More than 12 million Americans have abused methamphetamine and 1.5 million of these users are addicted to this potent stimulant (Partnership 2007). Amphetamines are potent synthetic central nervous system (CNS) stimulants capable of causing dependence due to their euphorigenic properties and ability to eliminate fatigue. Despite their addicting effects, amphetamines can be legally prescribed by physicians. Consequently, amphetamine abuse occurs in people who acquire their drugs by both legitimate and illicit means (McCaffrey 1999).

The History of Amphetamines

The first amphetamine was synthesized by the German pharmacologist L. Edeleano in 1887, but it was not until 1910 that this and several related compounds were tested in laboratory animals. Another 17 years passed before Gordon Alles, a researcher looking for a more potent substitute for ephedrine (used as a decongestant at the time), self-administered amphetamine and gave a firsthand account of its effects. Alles found that when inhaled or taken orally, amphetamine dramatically reduced fatigue, increased alertness, and caused a sense of confident euphoria (Grinspoon and Bakalar 1978).

Because of Alles's impressive findings, the Benzedrine (amphetamine) inhaler became available in 1932 as a nonprescription medication in drugstores across America. The Benzedrine inhaler, marketed for nasal congestion, was widely abused for its stimulant action but continued to be available OTC until 1949. Because of a loophole in a law that was passed later, not until 1971 were all potent amphetamine-like compounds in nasal inhalers withdrawn from the market (Grinspoon and Bakalar 1978; McCaffrey 1999).

Owing to the lack of restrictions during this early period, amphetamines were sold to treat a

KEY TERMS

uppers
CNS stimulants

variety of ailments, including obesity, alcoholism, bed-wetting, depression, schizophrenia, morphine and codeine addiction, heart block, head injuries, seasickness, persistent hiccups, and caffeine mania. Today, most of these uses are no longer approved as legitimate therapeutics but would be considered forms of drug abuse.

World War II provided a setting in which both the legal and "black market" use of amphetamines flourished (Grinspoon and Bakalar 1978). Because of their stimulating effects, amphetamines were widely used by the Germans, Japanese, and British in World War II to counteract fatigue. By the end of World War II, large quantities of amphetamines were readily available without prescription in seven types of nasal inhalers.

In spite of warnings about these drugs' addicting properties and serious side effects, the U.S. armed forces issued amphetamines on a regular basis during the Korean War and, in fact, may still make it available to pilots in the Air Force to relieve fatigue. Amphetamine use became widespread among truck drivers making long hauls; it is believed that among the earliest distribution systems for illicit amphetamines were truck stops along major U.S. highways. High achievers under continuous pressure in the fields of entertainment, business, and industry often relied on amphetamines to counteract fatigue. Homemakers used them to control weight and to combat boredom from unfulfilled lives. At the height of the U.S. epidemic in 1967, some 31 million prescriptions were written for **anorexiants** (diet pills) alone.

Today, a variety of related drugs and mixtures exist, including amphetamine substances such as dextroamphetamine (Dexedrine), methamphetamine (Desoxyn), and amphetamine itself. Generally, if doses are adjusted, the psychological effects of these various drugs are similar, so they will be discussed as a group. Other drugs with some of the same pharmacological properties are phenmetrazine (Preludin) and methylphenidate (Ritalin). Common slang terms for amphetamines include *speed, crystal, meth, bennies, dexies, uppers, pep pills, diet pills, jolly beans, copilots, hearts, footballs, white crosses, crank,* and *ice.*

How Amphetamines Work

Amphetamines are synthetic chemicals that are similar to natural neurotransmitters such as norepinephrine (noradrenaline), dopamine, and the stress hormone epinephrine (adrenaline). The amphetamines exert their pharmacological effect by increasing the release and blocking the metabolism of these catecholamine substances as well as serotonin (see Chapter 4), both in the brain and in nerves associated with the sympathetic nervous system. Because amphetamines cause release of norepinephrine from sympathetic nerves, they are classified as sympathomimetic drugs. The amphetamines generally cause an arousal or activating response (also called the *fight-or-flight response*) that is similar to the normal reaction to emergency situations, stress, or crises.

Amphetamines also cause alertness so that the individual becomes aroused, hypersensitive to stimuli, and feels "turned on." These effects occur even without external sensory input. This activation may be a very pleasant experience in itself, but a continual high level of activation may convert to anxiety, severe apprehension, or panic.

Amphetamines have potent effects on dopamine in the reward (pleasure) center of the brain (see Chapter 4). This action probably causes the "flash" or sudden feeling of intense pleasure that occurs when amphetamine is taken intravenously. Some users describe the sensation as a "whole-body orgasm," and many associate intravenous methamphetamine use with sexual feelings. The actual effect of these drugs on sexual behavior is quite variable and dependent on dose (McCaffrey 1999).

What Amphetamines Can Do

A curious condition commonly reported with heavy amphetamine use is **behavioral stereotypy**, or getting *hung up.* This term refers to a simple activity that is done repeatedly. An individual who is "hung up" will get caught in a repetitious thought or act for hours. For example, he or she may take objects apart, like radios or clocks, and carefully categorize all the parts, or sit in a tub and bathe all day, persistently sing a note, repeat a phrase of music, or repeatedly clean the same object. This phenomenon seems to be peculiar to potent stimulants such as the amphetamines and cocaine. Similar patterns of repetitive behavior also occur in psychotic conditions, which suggests that the intense use of stimulants such as amphetamines or cocaine alters the brain in a manner like that causing psychotic mental disorders (American Psychiatric Association [APA] 2000) and can lead to violent behavior.

KEY TERMS

anorexiants
drugs that suppress appetite for food

behavioral stereotypy
meaningless repetition of a single activity

Chronic use of high doses of amphetamines causes dramatic decreases in the brain content of the neurotransmitters dopamine and serotonin that persist for months, even after drug use is stopped (Gehrke et al. 2003). These decreases have been shown to reflect damage to the CNS neurons that release these transmitters. It is not clear why this neuronal destruction occurs, although there is evidence that the amphetamines can stimulate production of very reactive molecules, called *free radicals,* which in turn damage brain cells (Riddle et al. 2006).

Approved Uses

Until 1970, amphetamines were prescribed for a large number of conditions, including depression, fatigue, and long-term weight reduction. In 1970, the Food and Drug Administration (FDA), acting on the recommendation of the National Academy of Sciences, restricted the legal use of amphetamines to three medical conditions: (1) narcolepsy, (2) attention deficit hyperactivity disorder (ADHD), and (3) short-term weight reduction programs (APA 2000).

Narcolepsy Amphetamine treatment of narcolepsy is not widespread because this condition is a relatively rare disorder. The term **narcolepsy** comes from the Greek words for numbness and seizure. A person who has narcolepsy falls asleep as frequently as 50 times a day if he or she stays in one position for very long. Taking low doses of amphetamines helps keep narcoleptic people alert.

Attention Deficit Hyperactivity Disorder This common behavioral problem in children and adolescents involves an abnormally high level of physical activity, an inability to focus attention, and frequent disruptive behavior. Four to six percent of children and adults have ADHD (Polanczyk and Rohole 2007) The drug commonly used to treat children with ADHD is the amphetamine-related methylphenidate or Ritalin (discussed later in this chapter).

Weight Reduction The most common use of amphetamines is for the treatment of obesity. Am-

phetamines and chemically similar compounds are used as anorexiants to help obese or severely overweight people control appetite. Amphetamines are thought to act by affecting the appetite center in the hypothalamus of the brain, which causes the user to decrease food intake. The FDA has approved short-term use of amphetamines for weight loss programs but has warned of their potential for abuse. Many experts believe that the euphoric effect of amphetamines is the primary motivation for their continued use in weight reduction programs. It is possible that many obese people have a need for gratification that can be satisfied by the euphoric feeling this drug produces (Wang et al. 2004). If the drug is taken away, these individuals return to food to satisfy their need and sometimes experience "rebound," causing them to gain back more weight than they lost. Some persons who become addicted to amphetamine-like substances begin illicit use of these drugs by trying to prevent weight gain or to lose weight on their own without the guidance of a physician (APA 2000).

Side Effects of Therapeutic Doses

The two principal side effects of therapeutic doses of amphetamines are (1) abuse, which has already been discussed at length, and (2) cardiovascular toxicities. Many of these effects derive from the amphetamine-induced release of epinephrine from the adrenal glands and norepinephrine from the nerves associated with the sympathetic nervous system. The effects include increased heart rate, elevated blood pressure, and damage to vessels, especially small veins and arteries (Drug War Facts 2004; Swan 1996). In users with a history of heart attack, coronary arrhythmia, or hypertension, amphetamine toxicity can be severe or even fatal.

Current Misuse

Because amphetamine drugs can be readily and inexpensively synthesized in makeshift laboratories for illicit sale, can be administered by several routes, and cause a more sustained effect, these drugs are more popular than cocaine in many parts of the United States (Johnston 2007). Surveys suggest that there was a decline in the abuse of amphetamines in the late 1980s and early 1990s in parallel with a similar trend in cocaine abuse (Johnston 1996). However, in 1993, the declines were replaced by a rise in the number of persons abusing amphetamines. By 2001, approximately 5.6% of high school seniors used amphetamines at least each month. Currently, approximately 5.7% of high school seniors in the United States are regularly using amphetamines (Johnston 2007). In general, 4–5% of the population has abused methamphetamine. Of those who become addicted, many end up in the criminal justice system, accounting for about 30% of the court cases in the United States (Leinwand 2007).

Because of the potential for serious side effects, U.S. medical associations have asked all physicians to be more careful about prescribing amphetamines. Presently, use is recommended only for narcolepsy and some cases of hyperactivity in children (*Drug Facts and Comparisons* 2005; Hoffman and Lefkowitz 1995). In spite of FDA approval, most medical associations do not recommend the use of amphetamines for weight loss. Probably less than 1% of all prescriptions now written are for amphetamines, compared with 8% in 1970.

Amphetamine abusers commonly administer a dose of 10 to 30 milligrams. Besides the positive effects of this dose — the "high" — it can cause hyperactive, nervous, or jittery feelings that encourage the use of a depressant such as a benzodiazepine, barbiturate, or alcohol to relieve the discomfort of being "wired" (Hoffman and Lefkowitz 1995).

A potent and commonly abused form of amphetamine is **speed**, an illegal methamphetamine available as a white, odorless, bitter-tasting crystalline powder for injection. Methamphetamine is a highly addictive stimulant that is often cheaper and much longer lasting than cocaine (American Council for Drug Education 2007). The profit for the speed manufacturer is substantial enough to make illicit production financially attractive. Because the cost ranges from $10 to $20 a dose, it is sometimes known as the "poor man's cocaine" (Leinwand 2007). Methamphetamine is relatively easy and inexpensive to make. The illicit manufacturers are usually individuals without expertise in chemistry. Such people, referred to as "cookers," produce methamphetamine batches by using cookbook-style recipes (often obtained in jail or over the Internet). The most popular recipe uses common OTC ingredients — ephedrine, pseudoephedrine, and phenylpropanolamine — as **precursor chemicals** for the methamphetamine. To discourage the illicit manufacture of this potent stimulant, the Comprehensive Methamphetamine Control Act was passed in October 1996. This law increases penalties for trafficking in methamphetamine and in the precursor chemicals used to create this drug and gives the government authority to regulate and seize these substances (Comprehensive Methamphetamine Control Act 2008).

Due to the ease of production and the ready availability of chemicals used to prepare methamphetamine, this drug has become particularly problematic in the United States and has been declared the number 1 drug problem in the majority of counties across the country (Rutledge 2006). Traditional methamphetamine users have been white, male, blue-collar workers over 26 years of age, although currently there also is a disturbingly high rate of use in adolescents (3–5% annual use; Johnston 2007) and use by young women is on the rise in some regions of the United States. There has been higher abuse of this drug in the western United States, illustrated by the fact that methamphetamine dependence dominates the treatment systems in this region (National Institute on Drug Abuse [NIDA] 2007d). In contrast, methamphetamine abuse is much less common on the East Coast. In general, production and trafficking are rampant throughout the West and Midwest areas, with the highest levels occurring in California, Arizona, and Utah. However, the methamphetamine problem is moving across the country, with Iowa, Missouri, and Tennessee being particularly affected, and there are increasing reports of its use in the South and some Northeast areas (Leinwand 2007; NIDA 2007d).

Today, so-called meth or speed labs are frequently raided by law enforcement agencies across the country as local drug entrepreneurs try to grab a share of the profits. In 2003, law enforcement agencies shut down more than 17,000 illegal methamphetamine labs, most of which were in the western United States. This number decreased to 7,347 in 2006 (Leinwand 2007). The laboratory operators are usually well armed, and the facilities are frequently booby-trapped with explosives. Not surprisingly, these operations pose a serious threat to their neighbors (U.S. Department of Justice 2003a) and to residents, especially children, in the structure that contains the lab (U.S. Department of Justice 2002; see "Here and Now" Innocent Victims of Meth). Law enforcement personnel and firefighters are also at risk when dealing with methamphetamine labs owing to ignitable, corrosive, reactive, and toxic chemicals that might explode, start a fire, emit toxic fumes, or cause serious injury

KEY TERMS

speed
an injectable methamphetamine used by drug addicts

precursor chemicals
chemicals used to produce a drug

Here and Now

Innocent Victims of Meth

In almost one quarter of meth labs seized, children are found who have been exposed to the toxins used to "cook" the drug as well as the emotional and physical abuse of parents more preoccupied with satisfying their addiction than caring for their children. Burners have been left on next to a baby's crib. Bottles filled with potent acids are stored in the refrigerator. Children have been starved and 3-year-olds left to care for themselves and also care for a baby brother or sister while their mom or dad binges on meth for days or even weeks and then crash into a sleeping stupor. Explosive ingredients are abundant with vaporized drugs, contaminating the food, drinking water, clothing, and even the air. Officials must decide what to do with children abused and injured both physically and emotionally by parents who ignore their children's basic needs because they are so preoccupied

with obtaining their next meth fix. Reports are that meth addiction has caused foster-care programs across the country to be swamped with young victims.

Source: Tseng, N. "Children Fall by Wayside in Meth-Addicted Homes." *Orlando Sentinel* (11 September 2005): B1.

at the site. The toxic chemicals can create fumes that contaminate neighboring buildings, the water supply, or soil. These labs are especially dangerous when they are set up in poorly ventilated rooms (Kennedy 1999; see "Here and Now," Chemical Toxins Associated with Meth Labs).

Although still a problem, the incidences of "mom and pop" neighborhood methamphetamine labs are decreasing dramatically across the nation. This is the result of federal and state laws that limit access to large quantities of precursor drugs found in OTC decongestants. The new statutes require these decongestant products be kept behind the pharmacy counter, and the quantity sold to a customer must be minimal in order to limit access (Leinwand 2007; see "Holding the Line," Cold Restrictions). While decreasing the number of

meth labs in the United States, this strategy unfortunately has had minimal effect on actual supplies of this drug for illegal sales. Methamphetamine is being smuggled across U.S. borders from Mexico (Berkes 2007) and is being manufactured by criminal organizations from chemicals diverted by the ton from Asian pharmaceutical companies (Haus 2006; Randolph 2007). It is estimated that currently 90% of meth is imported, keeping supplies abundant and cost low (Leinwood 2007).

Patterns of High-Dose Use Amphetamines can be taken orally, intravenously, or by smoking. The intensity and duration of effects vary according to the mode of administration. The "speed freak" uses chronic, high doses of amphetamines intravenously and is often infected with HIV (see Chapter 16) (NIDA, Research Report 2000). Another approach to administering amphetamines is smoking **ice**, which can cause effects as potent, but perhaps more prolonged and erratic, than intravenous doses. The initial effect (after 5 to 30 minutes) of these potent stimulants is called the **rush** and includes a racing heartbeat and elevated blood pressure, metabolism, and pulse. During this phase, the user has powerful impressions of

KEY TERMS

ice
a smokable form of methamphetamine

rush
initial pleasure after amphetamine use that includes racing heartbeat and elevated blood pressure

Here and Now

Chemical Toxins Associated with Meth Labs

Methamphetamine labs can be set up almost anywhere and pose a serious threat to occupants as well as to law officers and emergency personnel. The following are some of the chemicals often present and their toxic potentials.

Chemicals	Toxic Reactions
Sodium hydroxide	Irritant to skin and eyes
Ammonia	Induces vomiting and nausea
Ether, acetone, and alcohol	Flammable
Chloroform	Carcinogen and volatile
Mercuric chloride	Poisonous (used as insecticide)
Cyanide gas	Extremely poisonous if breathed
Acids	Potent irritants
Iodine	Irritant; causes nausea, headaches, and dizziness
Phosphene gas	Poison, flammable (used as nerve gas)

Source: Office of Drug Control Policy. 2006.

pleasure and enthusiasm. The next stage is the **high** (4 to 16 hours after drug use) when the person feels aggressively smarter, energetic, talkative, and powerful and may initiate and complete highly ambitious tasks. The amphetamine addict tries to maintain the high for as long as possible with continual drug use leading to extended mental and physical hyperactivity; this is referred to as a **run** or **binge** and can persist from 3 to 15 days. Persistent use of these drugs, such as methamphetamine, to maintain the high for long periods of time is called **tweaking**. The tweaker often has neither slept nor eaten much for 3 to 15 days and can be extremely irritable and paranoid and have an elevated body temperature, a condition known as **hyperpyrexia**. This is a potentially dangerous stage for medical personnel or law enforcement officers because if the tweaker becomes agitated, he or she can respond violently to the efforts of others to help. To relieve some of the side effects of the extensive use of methamphetamine, tweakers often use a depressant such as alcohol, barbiturates, benzodiazepines, or opioid narcotics. The consequences of such a drug combination are to intensify negative feelings and worsen the dangers of the drug. Tweakers are frequently involved in domestic violence and frequently injure their children and partners (Transitions 2007). Withdrawal follows for 30 to 90 days, including feelings of depression and lethargy. During this phase, crav-

ing can be intense and the abuser may even become suicidal. Because a dose of methamphetamine often relieves these symptoms, many addicts in treatment return to abusing this stimulant (Prevline 1999).

After the first day or so of a run, unpleasant symptoms become prominent as the dosage is increased. Symptoms commonly reported at this stage are teeth grinding, disorganized patterns of thought and behavior, stereotypy, irritability, self-consciousness, suspiciousness, and fear. Hallucinations and delusions that are similar to a paranoid psychosis and indistinguishable from schizophrenia

KEY TERMS

high
4 to 16 hours after drug use; includes feelings of energy and power

run
intense use of a stimulant, consisting of multiple administrations over a period of days

binge
similar to a run, but usually of shorter duration

tweaking
repeated administration of methamphetamine to maintain the high

hyperpyrexia
elevated body temperature

Holding the Line   Cold Restrictions

As of September 30, 2006, it became somewhat more difficult for a person with a cold, and a lot more difficult for persons desiring to make methamphetamine from decongestant ingredients, to obtain adequate OTC cold medicine for their needs. This is due to a federal law to stop the manufacture of methamphetamine in illegal meth labs found in homes, garages, or basements. To achieve this objective, the new restrictions require customers to show a picture ID to purchase cold medicine such as NyQuil Cold & Flu, Actifed Cold & Allergy, and Claritin-D. These and similar decongestant products that contain drugs that can be converted into methamphetamine must be kept behind the store counters. Customers must sign a logbook identifying what they purchased and where they live. The logbook remains on file for 2 years. This law restricts purchase to 3–6 grams of product/day and 9 grams/month.

Toxic chemicals are often found in meth labs.

can occur (APA 2000). The person is likely to show aggressive and antisocial behavior for no apparent reason, although recent brain imaging studies have revealed that addictions to the amphetamines can cause long-term damage to the brain's inhibitory control centers (Kuehn 2007). Severe chest pains, abdominal discomfort that mimics appendicitis, and fainting from overdosage are sometimes reported. "Cocaine bugs" represent one bizarre effect of high doses of potent stimulants such as amphetamines: The user experiences strange feelings, like insects crawling under the skin. The range of physical and mental symptoms experienced from low to high doses is summarized in "Signs and Symptoms" Summary of the Effects of Amphetamines on the Body and Mind.

Toward the end of the run, the adverse symptoms dominate. When the drug is discontinued because the supply is exhausted or the symptoms become too unpleasant, an extreme crash can occur, followed by prolonged sleep, sometimes lasting several days. On awakening, the person is lethargic, hungry, and often severely depressed. The amphetamine user may overcome these unpleasant effects by smoking ice or injecting speed, thereby initiating a new cycle (APA 2000).

Continued use of massive doses of amphetamine often leads to considerable weight loss, sores in the skin, poor oral hygiene and deterioration of the teeth (Rauscher 2006), nonhealing

ulcers, liver disease, hypertensive disorders, cerebral hemorrhage (stroke), heart attack, kidney damage, and seizures (Hall and Hando 1993; Kinkead and Romboy 2004). For some of these effects, it is impossible to tell whether they are caused by the drug, poor eating habits, or other factors associated with the lifestyle of people who inject methamphetamine.

Speed freaks are generally unpopular with the rest of the drug-taking community, especially "acid-heads" (addicts who use lysergic acid diethylamide [LSD]), because of the aggressive,

Devastation of oral structures called "METH Mouth" sometimes is associated with methamphetamine addiction.

Signs & Symptoms Summary of the Effects of Amphetamines on the Body and Mind

	BODY	MIND
Low dose	Increased heartbeat.	Decreased fatigue
	Increased blood pressure	Increased confidence
	Decreased appetite	Increased feeling of alertness
	Increased breathing rate	Restlessness, talkativeness
	Inability to sleep	Increased irritability
	Sweating	Fearfulness, apprehension
	Dry mouth	Distrust of people
	Muscle twitching	Behavioral stereotypy
	Convulsions	Hallucinations
	Fever	Psychosis
	Chest pain	
	Irregular heartbeat	
High dose	Death due to overdose	

unpredictable behavior associated with use of potent stimulants. In general, drug abusers who take high doses of these agents, such as amphetamines or cocaine, are more likely to be involved in violent crimes than those who abuse other drugs (Drug Enforcement Agency [DEA] 2007). Heavy users are generally unable to hold steady jobs because of their drug habits and often have a parasitic relationship with the rest of the illicit drug-using community.

Although claims have been made that amphetamines do not cause physical dependence, it is almost certain that depression (sometimes suicidal), lethargy, muscle pains, abnormal sleep patterns, and, in severe cases, suicide attempts occur after high chronic doses as part of withdrawal (Cantwell and McBride 1998; NIDA Diagnosis 2000). During withdrawal from amphetamine use, the dependent user often turns to other drugs for relief (Cantwell and McBride 1998). Rebound from the amphetamines is opposite to that experienced with withdrawal from CNS depressants (see Chapter 6).

Although the effects of amphetamines on the unborn fetus are not fully understood, some animal studies suggest that there is a possibility of long-term problems in the offspring. However, these findings remain to be verified in humans (Slamberova et al. 2007). There is evidence that repeated high-dose use of amphetamines, such as methamphetamine, by adolescents or adults causes long-term and perhaps permanent damage to both dopamine and serotonin systems of the brain (Cohen 2006; Hanson et al. 2004). This brain damage may result in persistent episodes of psychosis (Yui et al. 1999) as well as long-lasting memory, motor impairment, and cognitive deficits. (Hanson et al. 2004; Volkow et al. 2001). Abuse of amphetamines often seriously damages personal relationships with friends, associates, and even family members. Particularly disturbing is the increasing methamphetamine use by young mothers. Moms on meth have claimed that use of this stimulant makes them feel invincible, and like they can run around the world — and then do it again. They claim to lose weight, but they also can lose their instinct to mother their children as they become obsessed with the drug (Holt 2005). Consequently, children are being exposed to dangerous levels of this drug in many forms (see "Here and Now," Small Towns, Big Problems: The Female Methamphetamine Epidemic).

Here and Now

Small Towns, Big Problems: The Female Methamphetamine Epidemic

Methamphetamine is causing a drug-related epidemic never before experienced in this country. Its abuse and devastating social effects are popping up in communities across the country and greatly taxing public social services in unanticipated ways. For example, 10 years ago social workers in Missoula, Montana, rarely heard of people abusing methamphetamine — let alone had to deal with these addicts. That situation has now changed. Today local and state governments find themselves overrun by the methamphetamine plague.

One of the most striking aspects of this drug's abuse in Montana is its effect on, and appeal to, young adult women. Typically, state figures show that the number of women seeking treatment for drug addiction are considerably lower than the number of men in the same situation; in 2004, however, roughly equal numbers of men and women sought help for methamphetamine as their primary addiction. Clearly, the destructive influence of methamphetamine abuse is taking an enormous toll on homes and families. In Missoula alone, almost half of the 137 children placed in the care of Family Services were removed from their homes due to use of methamphetamine by their mothers. Likewise, Montana's criminal justice system for women offenders is being overwhelmed. In 2004, the Montana State Prison for Women was filled for the first time, principally due to the methamphetamine epidemic in this population.

Women who are addicted to methamphetamine often do not do well in conventional drug treatment. Because of the potent addicting properties of this drug, they typically struggle with the requirements of probation or parole and often end up back in prison. While it is not clear why this stimulant is so seducing to young women, it is apparent that "this drug is a massive black hole. It's swallowing these people alive. It takes a miracle to put these families back together again."

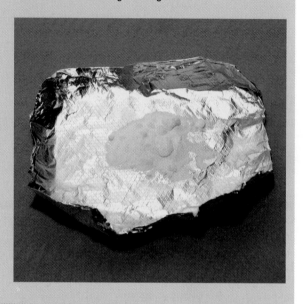

Source: "Escalation in Methamphetamine Use Also Leads to Escalation in Social Service." *Health & Medicine Week* (14 February 2005).

Treatment

Admissions for treatment of methamphetamine addiction have more than doubled since 2000 (Join Together 2006). The dependence disorder caused by the amphetamines is very hard, but not impossible, to treat successfully. Many of the methamphetamine addicts do not self-refer, but are forced into treatment by drug courts and other components of the criminal justice system (Newswise 2007). This has led to a dramatic rise in admissions to treatment for methamphetamine dependence in many parts of the country (Health and Medicine Week 2006). Presently, the most effective treatments for amphetamine addiction are behavioral interventions to help modify thinking patterns, improve cognitive skills, change expectations, and increase coping with life's stressors. Amphetamine support groups also appear to

be successful as adjuncts to behavioral therapies. There currently are no well-established pharmacological treatments for amphetamine dependency. Approaches used for cocaine have been tried with some success. Antidepressant medication may help relieve the depression that occurs during early stages of withdrawal (*Los Angeles Times* 2005; NIDA, Research Report 2000).

Amphetamine Combinations

As previously mentioned, amphetamines are frequently used in conjunction with a variety of other drugs such as barbiturates, benzodiazepines, alcohol, and heroin (Nuckols and Kane 2003). Amphetamines intensify, prolong, or otherwise alter the effects of LSD, and the two types of drugs are sometimes combined. The majority of speed users have also had experience with a variety of

Table 10.1 "Designer" Amphetamines

AMPHETAMINE DERIVATIVE	PROPERTIES
Methcathinone ("cat")	Properties like those of methamphetamine and cocaine
Methylenedioxy**methamphetamine** (MDMA, "Ecstasy")	Stimulant and hallucinogen
Methylenedioxy**amphetamine** (MDA)	More powerful stimulant and less powerful hallucinogen than MDMA
4-Methylaminorex	CNS stimulant like amphetamine
N,N-Dimethyl**amphetamine**	One-fifth potency of amphetamine
4-Thiomethyl-2, 5-dimethoxy**amphetamine**	Hallucinogen
Para-methoxymeth**amphetamine**	Weak stimulant

psychedelics or other drugs. In addition, people dependent on opiate narcotics frequently use amphetamines or cocaine. These combinations are called **speedballs** (Wikipedia 2007b).

"Designer" Amphetamines

Underground chemists can synthesize drugs that mimic the psychoactive effects of amphetamines. Although the production of such drugs diminished in the early 1990s, their use by American teens surged in the late 1990s and early 2000s, but decreased in 2003 and 2004 and remained low in 2006 (Johnston 2007). These substances have become known as "designer drugs" (Christophersen 2000).

Designer amphetamines sometimes differ from the parent compound by only a single element. These "synthetic spinoffs" pose a significant abuse problem because often several different designer amphetamines can be made from the parent compound and still retain the abuse potential of the original substance.

For many years, the production and distribution of designer amphetamines were not illegal, even though they were synthesized from controlled substances. In the mid-1980s, however, the DEA actively pursued policies to curb their production and sale. Consequently, many designer amphetamines were outlawed under the Substance Analogue Enforcement Act (1986), which makes illegal any substance that is similar in structure or psychological effect to any substance already scheduled, if it is manufactured, possessed, or sold with the intention that it be consumed by human beings (Beck 1990).

The principal types of designer amphetamines are:

- Derivatives from amphetamine and methamphetamine that retain the CNS stimulatory effects, such as methcathinone ("cat").
- Derivatives from amphetamine and methamphetamine that have prominent hallucinogenic effects in addition to their CNS stimulatory action, such as MDMA (Ecstasy).

Because the basic amphetamine molecule can be easily synthesized and readily modified, new amphetamine-like drugs occasionally appear on the streets. Although these designer amphetamines are thought of as new drugs when they first appear, in fact most were originally synthesized from the 1940s to the 1960s by pharmaceutical companies trying to find new decongestant and anorexiant drugs to compete with the other amphetamines. Some of these compounds were found to be too toxic to be marketed but have been rediscovered by "street chemists" and are sold to unsuspecting victims trying to experience a new sensation. Table 10.1 lists some of these designer amphetamines.

Some designer drugs of abuse that are chemically related to amphetamine include DOM (STP), methcathinone (called *cat* or *bathtub speed*), MDA, and MDMA (or methylenedioxymethamphetamine, called *Ecstasy, X, E, XTC,* or *Adam*). All of these drugs are currently classified as Schedule I agents.

KEY TERMS

speedballs
combinations of amphetamine or cocaine with an opioid narcotic, often heroin

MDMA (Ecstasy) Among the designer amphetamines, MDMA continues to be the most popular. It gained widespread popularity in the United States throughout the 1980s, and its use peaked in 1987 despite its classification as a Schedule I drug in 1985 by the DEA. At the height of its use, 39% of the undergraduates at Stanford University reported having used MDMA at least once (Randall 1992a). In the late 1980s and early 1990s, use of MDMA declined in this country, but about this time it was "reformulated": This reformulation was not in a pharmacological sense but in a cultural context.

The "rave" scene in England provided a new showcase for MDMA or Ecstasy (Randall 1992a). Partygoers attired in "Cat in the Hat" hats and psychedelic jumpsuits paid $20 to dance all night to heavy electronically generated sound mixed with computer-generated video and laser light shows. An Ecstasy tablet could be purchased for the sensory enhancement caused by the drug (Randall 1992b). At one time, it was estimated that as many as 31% of English youth from 16 to 25 years old had used Ecstasy (Grob et al. 1996). The British rave counterculture and its generous use of Ecstasy were exported to the United States in the early 1990s. High-tech music and video trappings were encouraged by low-tech laboratories that illegally manufactured the drug and shipped it into this country. Ecstasy rapidly became the drug of choice for many young people in the United States (Cloud 2000) looking for a novel "chemical" experience. The availability of Ecstasy tablets dramatically escalated in the United States, as demonstrated by the report that the DEA seized approximately 400,000 of these tablets in 1997, which increased to more than 9 million tablets seized in 2000 (Aarons 2000). Most of these illegal drugs originate in European countries such as the Netherlands and are smuggled into the United States (U.S. Department of Justice 2003b). The association of Ecstasy with raves has continued. Because of its frequent association with raves, clubs, and bars, MDMA has been referred to as a **club drug** (Leshner 2000). At its peak in 2000, Ecstasy was being used by 11% of all U.S. high school seniors. During the next few years, however, the popularity of this drug declined; in 2006, only 6% of high school seniors reported use (Johnston 2007).

Some have compared the rave culture of the past decade and its use of MDMA to the acid-test parties of the 1960s and the partygoers' use of LSD and amphetamines (Cloud 2000; Randall 1992a). This drug is said by some not to cause dependence, but intense use appears to be able to cause addiction. Incidents of medical emergencies caused by MDMA reported by hospitals from 1999 to 2001 almost doubled, suggesting that during this period more intense use of this drug caused severe dependence (U.S. Department of Justice 2003b). However, part of the explanation for the recent dramatic reduction in MDMA use by young populations appears to be a perceived increase in the "risk" of this drug (Johnston 2007).

MDMA was first inadvertently discovered in 1912 by chemists at E. Merck in Darmstadt, Germany (Grob et al. 1996). No pharmaceutical company has ever manufactured MDMA for public marketing, and the FDA has never approved it for therapy. MDMA was first found by the DEA on the streets in 1972 in a drug sample bought in Chicago (Beck 1990). The DEA earnestly began gathering data on MDMA abuse a decade later, which led to its classification as a Schedule I substance in 1985 despite the very vocal opposition by a number of psychiatrists who had been giving MDMA to patients since the late 1970s to facilitate communication, acceptance, and fear reduction (Beck 1990). Some health professionals believe that MDMA should be made available to clinicians for the treatment of some psychiatric disorders such as fear and anxiety (Benedetti 2002; Cloud 2000). In fact, with FDA approval, small trial stud-

Ecstasy tablets are often imprinted with cartoon figures.

Dancers at a "rave" often consume Ecstasy for sensory enhancement.

ies are being conducted to test the safety of this drug (Drug Monkey 2007). MDMA and related designer amphetamines are somewhat unique from other amphetamines in that, besides causing excitation, they have prominent hallucinogenic effects (Tancer and Johanson 2007; see Chapter 12). These drugs have been characterized as combining the properties of amphetamine and LSD (Schifano et al. 1998). The psychedelic effects of MDMA are likely caused by release of the neurotransmitter serotonin (Tancer and Johanson 2007). After using hallucinogenic amphetamines, the mind is often flooded with irrelevant and incoherent thoughts and exaggerated sensory experiences and is more receptive to suggestion.

MDMA is often viewed as a "smooth amphetamine" and does not appear to cause the severe depression, "crash," or violent behavior (U.S. Department of Justice 2003b) often associated with frequent high doses of the more traditional amphetamines. MDMA was originally thought to be nonaddictive; however, some reports suggest that addiction does occur when high doses of this drug are used (Jansen 1999). Many users tend to be predominantly positive when describing their initial MDMA experiences (Cloud 2000). They claim the drug causes them to dramatically drop their defense mechanisms or fear responses while they feel an increased empathy for others (Benedetti 2002). Combined with its stimulant effects, this action often increases intimate communication and association with others (Cloud 2000; Goldstein 1995). However, heavy users often experience adverse effects, such as loss of appetite, grinding of teeth, muscle aches and stiffness, sweating, rapid heartbeat, hostility, anxiety, and

altered sleep patterns (Gamma et al. 2000; Goodchild and Johnson 2005; Morland 2000; Parrott et al. 2000). In addition, fatigue can be experienced for hours or even days after use. In high doses, MDMA can cause panic attacks and severe anxiety (NIDA 2007c). There is evidence that these high doses can seriously damage serotonin neurons in the brain and cause long-term memory deficits and psychological disturbances in some people (Lyles and Cadet 2003; Parrott 2001).

Along with the increases in MDMA-related emergencies, there has been an increase in MDMA-related deaths. Although the 76 MDMA-linked deaths in the United States during 2001 are tragic, compared to other drugs of abuse such as cocaine and heroin, this number is relatively small (DEA 2003). The leading causes of deaths associated with MDMA use appear to be complications from either hyperthermia (related to heatstroke), metabolic problems, or underlying heart problems (DEA 2003).

Methylphenidate: A Special Amphetamine

Methylphenidate (Ritalin) is related to the amphetamines but is a relatively mild CNS stimulant that has been used to alleviate depression. Research now casts doubt on its effectiveness for treating depression, but it is effective in treating narcolepsy (a sleep disorder). As explained previously, Ritalin has also been found to help calm children suffering from attention deficit hyperactivity disorder (ADHD) and is currently the drug of choice for this indication. The stimulant potency of Ritalin lies between that of caffeine and amphetamine. Although it is not used much on the street by hardcore drug addicts, there are frequent reports of use by high school and college students because of claims that it helps them to "study better," "party harder," and experience a buzz (Hinkle and Winckler 1996; Khan 2003). However, there is no evidence when used properly and taken orally that this drug will cause serious dependence or addiction. Recent statistics from the Monitoring the Future Survey suggest that in 2006, 4.4% of high school seniors used this drug for nonmedical purposes (Johnston 2007). Because of its potential for abuse, some critics claim its medical use in the treatment of childhood ADHD may increase the likelihood that patients will later abuse drugs. However, this has not been found to be the case (Barkley et al. 2003). High doses of Ritalin can cause tremors, seizures, and strokes. Ritalin has been classified as a Schedule II drug, like the other prescribed amphetamines. Its principal mechanism of action is to block the reuptake of dopamine and noradrenaline into their respective neurons; thus, its pharmacological action is more like cocaine than methamphetamine.

■ Cocaine

In the so-called War on Drugs, cocaine eradication has been considered to be a top priority. The tremendous attention directed at cocaine reflects the fact that from 1978 to 1987 the United States experienced the largest cocaine epidemic in history. Antisocial and criminal activities related to the effects of this potent stimulant have been highly visible and widely publicized.

As recently as the early 1980s, cocaine use was not believed to cause dependency because it did not cause gross withdrawal effects, as do alcohol and narcotics (Goldstein 1994). In fact, a 1982 article in *Scientific American* stated that cocaine was "no more habit forming than potato chips" (Van Dyck and Byck 1982). This perception has clearly been proven false; cocaine is so highly addictive that it is readily self-administered not only by human beings but also by laboratory animals (personal observation). Surveys suggest that during 2000, 2.7 million chronic and 3.0 million casual cocaine users lived in the United States (Office of National Drug Control Policy [ONDCP] 2003).

There is no better substance than cocaine to illustrate the "love-hate" relationship that people can have with drugs. Many lessons can be learned by understanding the impact of cocaine and the social struggles that have ensued as people and societies have tried to determine their proper relationship with this substance.

The History of Cocaine Use

Cocaine has been used as a stimulant for thousands of years. Its history can be classified into three eras, based on geographic, social, and therapeutic considerations. Learning about these eras can help us understand current attitudes about cocaine.

The First Cocaine Era

The first cocaine era was characterized by an almost harmonious use of this stimulant by South American Indians living in the regions of the Andean Mountains and dates back to about 2500 B.C. in Peru. It is believed that the stimulant properties of cocaine played a major role in the advancement of this isolated civilization, providing its people with the energy and motivation to realize dramatic social and architectural achievements while being able to endure tremendous hardships in barren, inhospitable environments. The *Erythroxylon coca* shrub (cocaine found in the leaves) was held in religious reverence by these people until the time of the Spanish conquistadors (Golding 1993).

The first written description of coca chewing in the New World was by the explorer Amerigo Vespucci in 1499:

> They were very brutish in appearance and behavior, and their cheeks bulged with the leaves of a certain green herb which they chewed like cattle, so that they could hardly speak. Each had around his neck two dried gourds, one full of that herb in their mouth, the other filled with a white flour-like powdered chalk. . . . [This was lime, which was mixed with the coca to enhance its effects.] When I asked . . . why they carried these leaves in their mouth, which they did not eat, . . . they replied it prevents them from feeling hungry, and gives them great vigor and strength. (Aldrich and Barker 1976, p. 3)

It is ironic that there are no indications that these early South American civilizations had any significant social problems with cocaine, considering the difficulty it has caused contemporary civilizations. There are three possible explanations for their lack of negative experiences with coca:

1. The Andean Indians maintained control of the use of cocaine. For the Incas, coca could only be used by the conquering aristocracy, chiefs, royalty, and other designated honorables (Aldrich and Barker 1976).

2. These Indians used the unpurified, and less potent, form of cocaine in the coca plant.

3. Chewing the coca leaf was a slow, sustained form of oral drug administration; therefore, the effect was much less potent, and less likely to cause serious dependence, than snorting, intravenous injection, or smoking techniques most often used today.

The Second Cocaine Era

A second major cocaine era began in the 19th century. During this period, scientific techniques were used to determine the pharmacology of cocaine and identify its dangerous effects. It was also during this era that the threat of cocaine to society — both its members and institutions — was first recognized (DiChiara 1993; Musto 1998). At about this time, scientists in North America and Europe began experimenting with a purified, white, powdered extract made from the coca plant.

In the last half of the 19th century, Corsican chemist Angelo Mariani removed the active ingredients from the coca leaf and identified cocaine. This purified cocaine was added into cough drops and into a special Bordeaux wine called Vin Mariani (Musto 1998). The Pope gave Mariani a medal in appreciation for the fine work he had done developing this concoction. The cocaine extract was publicized as a magical drug that would free the body from fatigue, lift the spirits, and cause a sense of well-being, and the cocaine-laced wine became widely endorsed throughout the civilized world (Fischman and Johanson 1996). Included in a long list of luminaries who advocated this product for an array of ailments were the Czar and Czarina of Russia; the Prince and Princess of Wales;

An Andean chews coca leaves.

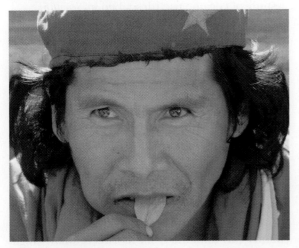

the Kings of Sweden, Norway, and Cambodia; commanders of the French and English armies; President McKinley of the United States; H. G. Wells; August Bartholdi (sculptor of the Statue of Liberty); and some 8000 physicians.

The astounding success of this wine attracted imitators, all making outlandish claims. One of these cocaine tonics was a nonalcoholic beverage named Coca-Cola, which was made from African kola nuts and advertised as the "intellectual beverage and temperance drink"; it contained 4 to 12 milligrams per bottle of the stimulant (DiChiara 1993). By 1906, Coca-Cola no longer contained detectable amounts of cocaine, but caffeine had been substituted in its place.

In 1884, the esteemed Sigmund Freud published his findings on cocaine in a report called "Uber Coca." Freud recommended this "magical drug" for an assortment of medical problems, including depression, hysteria, nervous exhaustion, digestive disorders, hypochondria, "all diseases which involve degeneration of tissue," and drug addiction.

In response to a request by Freud, a young Viennese physician, Karl Köller, studied the ability of cocaine to cause numbing effects. He discovered that it was an effective local anesthetic that could be applied to the surface of the eye and permit painless minor surgery to be conducted. This discovery of the first local anesthetic had tremendous worldwide impact. Orders for the new local anesthetic, cocaine, overwhelmed pharmaceutical companies.

Soon after the initial jubilation over the virtues of cocaine came the sober realization that with its benefits came severe disadvantages. As more people used cocaine, particularly in tonics and patent medicines, the CNS side effects and abuse liability became painfully evident. By the turn of the 20th century, cocaine was being processed from the coca plant and purified routinely by drug companies. People began to snort or inject the purified form of this popular powder, which increased both its effects and its dangers. The controversy over cocaine exploded before the American public in newspapers and magazines.

As medical and police reports of cocaine abuse and toxicities escalated, public opinion demanded that cocaine be banned. In 1914, the Harrison Act misleadingly classified both cocaine and coca as narcotic substances (cocaine is a stimulant) and outlawed their uncontrolled use.

Although prohibited in patent and nonprescription medicines, prescribed medicinal use of cocaine continued into the 1920s. Medicinal texts included descriptions of therapeutic uses for

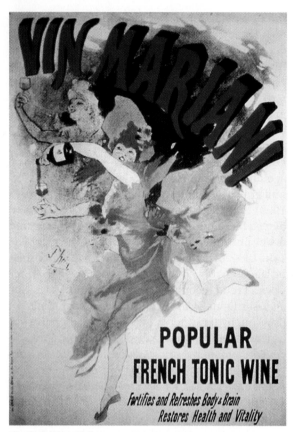

The "refreshing" element in Vin Mariani was coca extract.

Sigmund Freud was an early advocate of cocaine, which he referred to as a "cure-all."

cocaine to treat fatigue, vomiting, seasickness, melancholia, and gastritis. However, they also included lengthy warnings about excessive cocaine use, "the most insidious of all drug habits" (Aldrich and Barker 1976).

Little of medical or social significance occurred for the next few decades (Fischman and Johanson 1996). The medicinal use of cocaine was replaced mostly by the amphetamines during World War II because cocaine could not be supplied from South America. (Cocaine is not easily synthesized, so even today the supply of cocaine, both legal and illegal, continues to come from the Andean countries of South America.) During this period, cocaine continued to be employed for its local anesthetic action, was available on the "black market," and was used recreationally by musicians, entertainers, and the wealthy. Because of the limited supply, the cost of cocaine was prohibitive for most would-be consumers. Cocaine abuse problems continued as a minor concern until the 1980s.

The Third Cocaine Era

With the 1980s came the third major era of cocaine use. This era started much like the second in that the public and even the medical community were

naive and misinformed about the drug. Cocaine was viewed as a glamorous substance and portrayed by the media as the drug of celebrities. Its use by prominent actors, athletes, musicians, and other members of a fast-paced, elite society was common knowledge. By 1982, more than 20 million Americans had tried cocaine in one form or another, compared with only 5 million in 1974 (Green 1985).

The following is an example of a report from a Los Angeles television station in the early 1980s, which was typical of the misleading information being released to the public:

> Cocaine may actually be no more harmful to your health than smoking cigarettes or drinking alcohol; at least that's according to a 6-year study of cocaine use [described in *Scientific American*]. It concludes that the drug is relatively safe and, if not taken in large amounts, it is not addictive. (Byck 1987)

With such visibility, an association with prestige and glamour, and what amounted to an indirect endorsement by medical experts, the stage was set for another epidemic of cocaine use. Initially, the high cost of this imported substance limited its use. With increased demand came increased supply, and prices tumbled from an unaffordable $100 per "fix" to an affordable $10. The epidemic began.

By the mid-1980s, cocaine permeated all elements of society. No group of people or part of the country was immune from its effects. Many tragic stories were told of athletes, entertainers, corporate executives, politicians, fathers and mothers, high school students, and even children using and abusing cocaine. It was no longer the drug of the laborer or even the rich and famous. It was everybody's drug and everybody's problem (Golding 1993). As one user recounted:

> I think I was an addict. I immediately fell in love with cocaine. I noticed right away it was a drug that you had power with, and I wanted more and more. *(From Venturelli's research files, interview with a 22-year-old male, 1995.)*

Cocaine prices in the United States recently have been dropping again to about $135/gram of pure cocaine, a price similar to that of the early 1990s. Officials are concerned these low prices will result in increased abuse (CBS News 2007).

Cocaine Production

Because cocaine is derived from the coca plant, which is imported from the Andean countries, the United States' problems with this drug have had a profound effect on several South American countries. With the dramatic rise in U.S. cocaine demand in the early 1980s, coca production in South America increased in tandem. The coca crop is by far the most profitable agricultural venture in some of these countries. In addition, it is easily cultivated and maintained (the coca plant is a perennial and remains productive for decades) and can be harvested several times a year (on average, two to four). The coca harvest has brought many jobs and some prosperity to these struggling economies.

It has been claimed that the U.S. coca eradication program has seriously damaged the fragile economies of poor Latin American countries, such as Bolivia and Peru, causing anti-American

sentiment especially in poor rural communities that depend on money from their coca crops (Caesar 2002). In addition, the spraying of herbicides from U.S.-piloted aircraft to destroy coca harvests is suspected of posing health hazards to the native populations (DeYoung 2003). Because of these problems, there is evidence that the attempts by the U.S. government to control cocaine abuse by eliminating coca crops have not been as successful as hoped (Hall 2003). In fact, some of these countries have initiated a program to develop products that "legally" contain extract from the coca plant, an effort not likely to be endorsed by the United States (see "Here and Now" Entrepreneurs Promote Addition of Coca to Toothpaste, Shampoo, and Liquor).

Trafficking of illegal cocaine is very profitable and often very dangerous (see "Here and Now," Bloody "Drug War" Fought in Streets of Mexico). Because of the highly addictive nature of cocaine and the profits associated with the illegal purchasing and selling of this drug, criminal groups frequently engage in violent struggles for control of the cocaine market (Weiner 2003).

Cocaine Processing

Cocaine is one of several active ingredients from the leaves of *Erythroxylon coca* (its primary source). The leaves are harvested two or four times per year and used to produce coca paste, which contains as much as 80% cocaine. The paste is processed in clandestine laboratories to form a pure, white hydrochloride salt powder (Hatsukami and Fischman 1996). Often, purified cocaine is **adulterated** (or "cut") with substances such as powdered sugar, talc, arsenic, lidocaine, strychnine, and methamphetamine before it is sold on the streets. Adverse responses to street cocaine are sometimes caused by the additives, not the cocaine itself. The resultant purity of the cut material ranges from 10% to 85%.

Cocaine is often sold in the form of little pellets, called *rocks*, or as flakes or powder. If it is in pellet form, it must be crushed before use. Such exotic names as Peruvian rock and Bolivian flake are bandied about to convince the buyer that the "stash" is high grade. Other street names used for cocaine have included *blow, snow, flake, C, coke, toot, white lady, girl, cadillac, nose candy, gold dust,* and *stardust*.

Cocaine is often sold in a form that appears like small rocks.

Here and Now

Entrepreneurs Promote Addition of Coca to Toothpaste, Shampoo, and Liquor

The governments of Bolivia, Peru, and Columbia are attempting to give the coca leaf a new, more profitable and respectable life. The leaders of these countries want to profit from coca crops, but do it in a legal way. They are attempting to persuade the United Nations to lift a 45-year-old ban on trade in coca products and allow the use of coca extracts in products such as bread, pastes, toothpastes and shampoos, ointments, candies, and liquors. The argument being made is that the coca leaf is nutritious because it contains significant amounts of iron, phosphorous, calcium, vitamin A, and riboflavin. Currently, coca extract is permitted as a flavoring of Coca-Cola, a point being made by coca-producing governments to persuade the United Nations to rescind its ban on international trade of legal coca products. Although the U.N. is

considering the request, it is unlikely the United States will be supportive in light of the billions of dollars it has spent to eradicate coca crops in these countries as part of its war on drugs.

Source: Langman, J. "Andean Entrepreneurs Are Pushing Coca Beyond Cola, in New Teas, Toothpaste, Shampoo, Liquor and More." *Newsweek* (30 October 2006). Available www.newsweek.com/id/45077.

■ Current Attitudes and Patterns of Abuse

Given contemporary medical advances, we have greater understanding of the effects of cocaine and its toxicities and the dependence it produces. The reasons for abusing cocaine are better understood as well. For example, it has been suggested that some chronic cocaine users are self-medicating psychiatric disorders, such as depression, attention deficit disorders, or anxiety (Gunnarsdottir et al. 2000). Such knowledge helps in identifying and administering effective treatment. The hope is that society will never again be fooled into thinking that cocaine

abuse is glamorous or an acceptable form of entertainment.

Attempts are being made to use this understanding (either recently acquired or merely relearned) to educate people about the true nature of cocaine. Such education was likely responsible for trends of declining cocaine use observed from 1987 to 1991 (see Figure 10.1). Decreases occurred in virtually every age group evaluated during this period. Surveys during this time revealed that, in general, cocaine use became less acceptable; these changes in attitude almost certainly contributed to the dramatic reduction in use. From 1992 to 1999 cocaine use rose, but since then it has leveled off (Johnston 2007).

Here and Now

Bloody "Drug War" Fought in Streets of Mexico

Drug cartels ship hundreds of tons of cocaine to the United States. Because of the billions of dollars that can be made from this illegal market, gangs fight each other for control of the production and merchandising of this substance. This competition frequently turns violent,

as appeared to be the case in the small Mexican border city of Nuevo Laredo, where nine people were found tortured and killed in April 2003. These assassinations were thought to be the result of a power struggle within the cartels.

Source: Weiner, T. "9 Linked to Drug War Found Slain Outside Mexican Border City." *The New York Times* (3 April 2003): A5.

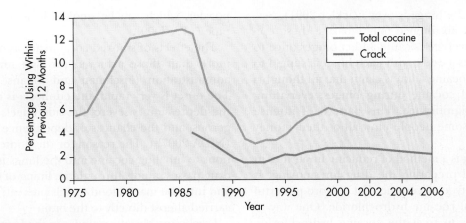

FIGURE 10.1

Trends in cocaine and crack use by high school seniors, 1975–2006. These data represent the percentages of high school seniors surveyed who reported using cocaine during the year.

⋯⋯⋯

Note: Crack cocaine did not become widely available until 1986.

Source: Johnston, L. "Monitoring the Future" 2007. Available www.monitoringthefuture.org/pubs/monographs/vol1_2006.pdf.

Cocaine Administration

Cocaine can be administered orally, inhaled into the nasal passages, injected intravenously, or smoked. The form of administration is important in determining the intensity of cocaine's effects, its abuse liability, and the likelihood of toxicity (Nathan et al. 1998).

Oral administration of cocaine produces the least potent effects; most of the drug is destroyed in the gut or liver before it reaches the brain. The result is a slower onset of action with a milder, more sustained stimulation. This form is least likely to cause health problems and dependence (Grinspoon 1993). South American Indians still take cocaine orally to increase their strength and for relief from fatigue. Administration usually involves prolonged chewing of the coca leaf, resulting in the consumption of about 20 to 400 milligrams of the drug (DiChiara 1993). Oral use of cocaine is not common in the United States.

"Snorting" involves inhaling cocaine hydrochloride powder into the nostrils, where deposits form on the lining of the nasal chambers and approximately 100 milligrams of the drug passes through the mucosal tissues into the bloodstream (DiChiara 1993). Substantial CNS stimulation occurs in several minutes, persists for 30 to 40 minutes, and then subsides. The effects occur more rapidly and are shorter-lasting and more intense than those achieved with oral administration, because more of the drug enters the brain more quickly. Because concentrations of cocaine in the body are higher after snorting than after oral ingestion, the side effects are more severe. One of the most common consequences of snorting cocaine is rebound depression, or "crash," which is of little consequence after oral consumption. As a general rule, the intensity of the depression correlates with the intensity of the euphoria (Goldstein 1995).

According to studies performed by the National Institute on Drug Abuse, 10% to 15% of those who try intranasal (snorting) cocaine go on to heavier forms of dosing, such as intravenous administration. Intravenous administration of cocaine is a relatively recent phenomenon because the hypodermic needle was not widely available until the late 1800s. This form of administration has contributed to many of the cocaine problems that appeared at the turn of the 20th century. Intravenous administration allows large amounts of cocaine to be introduced very rapidly into the body and causes severe side effects and dependence. Within seconds after injection, cocaine users experience an incredible state of euphoria. The "high" is intense but short-lived; within 15 to 20 minutes, the user experiences dysphoria and is heading for a "crash." To prevent these unpleasant rebound effects, cocaine is readministered every 10 to 30 minutes. Readministration continues as long as there is drug available (NIDA 1998).

This binge activity resembles that seen in the methamphetamine "run," except it is usually shorter in duration. When the cocaine supply is exhausted, the binge is over (Zickler 2001). Several days of abstinence may separate these episodes; the average cocaine addict binges once to several times a week, with each binge lasting 4 to 24 hours. Cocaine addicts claim that all thoughts turn toward cocaine during binges; everything else loses significance. This pattern of intense use is how some people blow all of their money on cocaine.

Freebasing is a method of reducing impurities in cocaine and preparing the drug for smoking. It produces a type of cocaine that is more powerful than normal cocaine hydrochloride. One way to "freebase" is to treat the cocaine hydrochloride with a liquid base such as sodium carbonate or ammonium hydroxide. The cocaine dissolves, along with many of the impurities commonly found in it (such as amphetamines, lidocaine, sugars, and others). A solvent, such as petroleum or ethyl ether, is added to the liquid to extract the cocaine. The solvent containing the cocaine floats to the top and is drawn off with an eyedropper; it is placed in an evaporation dish to dry, and crystalized cocaine residue is then crushed into a fine

powder, which can be smoked in a special glass pipe (APA 2000).

The effects of smoked cocaine are as intense or more than those achieved through intravenous administration (Fischman and Johanson 1996). The onset is very rapid, the euphoria is dramatic, the depression is severe, the side effects are dangerous, and the chances of dependence are high (NIDA 2007b). The reason for these intense reactions to inhaling cocaine into the lungs is that the drug passes rapidly through the lining of the lungs and into the many blood vessels present; it is then carried almost directly to the brain.

Freebasing became popular in the United States in the 1980s due to the fear of diseases such as AIDS and hepatitis, which are transmitted by sharing contaminated hypodermic needles. But freebasing involves other dangers. Because the volatile solvents required for freebasing are very explosive, careless people have been seriously burned or killed during processing (Seigel 1985). Street synonyms used for freebased cocaine include *baseball, bumping, white tornado, world series,* and *snowtoke.*

"Crack"

Between 1985 and 1986, a special type of freebased cocaine known as **crack** or "rock" appeared on the streets (Hatsukami and Fischman 1996). By 1988, approximately 5% of high school students had tried crack. As of 1992 this number had fallen to 2.6%, by 1999 it rose to 4.6%, but by 2006 it declined again to 2.1% (Johnston 2007). Crack is inexpensive and can be smoked without the dangerous explosive solvents mentioned earlier in the discussion of freebasing. It is made by taking powdered cocaine hydrochloride and adding sodium bicarbonate (baking soda) and water. The paste that forms removes impurities as well as the hydrochloride from the cocaine. The substance is then dried into hard pieces called rocks, which may contain as much as 90% pure cocaine. Other slang terms for crack include *base, black rock, gravel, Roxanne,* and *space basing.*

Like freebased cocaine, crack is usually smoked in a glass water pipe. When the fumes are absorbed

"Freebasing" paraphernalia. A water pipe is often used to smoke freebased cocaine, or "crack." Cocaine administered by smoking is very potent and fast-acting; the effect lasts for 10 to 15 minutes, after which depression occurs. This is the most addicting form of cocaine.

KEY TERMS

freebasing
conversion of cocaine into its alkaline form for smoking

crack
already processed and inexpensive "freebased" cocaine, ready for smoking

into the lungs, they act rapidly, reaching the brain within 8 to 10 seconds. An intense "rush" or "high" results, and later a powerful state of depression, or "crash," occurs. The high may last only 3 to 5 minutes, and the depression may persist from 10 to 40 minutes or longer in some cases. As soon as crack is smoked, the nervous system is greatly stimulated by the release of dopamine, which seems to be involved in the rush. Cocaine prevents resupply of this neurotransmitter, which may trigger the crash.

Because of the abrupt and intense release of dopamine, smoked crack is viewed as a drug with tremendous potential for addiction (APA 2000) and is considered by users to be more enjoyable than cocaine administered intravenously (Fischman and Johanson 1996). In fact, some people with serious cardiovascular disease continue using crack despite knowing their serious risk for heart attacks and strokes (Fischman and Foltin 1992).

Crack and cocaine marketing and use are often associated with criminal activity (APA 2000) such as robberies and homicides (Swan 1995).

In general, crack use has been more common among African American and Hispanic populations than among white Americans. Of special concern is the use of crack among women during pregnancy. Children born under these circumstances have been referred to as **crack babies**. Even though the effects of crack on fetal development are not fully understood, many clinicians and researchers have predicted that these crack babies will impose an enormous social burden as they grow up. However, other experts have expressed concern that the impact of cocaine on the fetus is grossly overstated and have suggested that behavioral problems seen in these children are more a consequence of social environment than direct pharmacological effects (Vidaeff and Mastrobattista 2003). This issue is discussed in greater detail later in this section.

It is not coincidental that the popularity of crack use paralleled the AIDS epidemic in the mid-1980s. Because crack administration does not require injection, theoretically the risk of contracting HIV from contaminated needles is avoided. Even so, incidence of HIV infection in crack users is still very high because many crack smokers also use cocaine intravenously, thereby increasing the chances of their becoming HIV infected (see Chapter 16). Another reason for the high incidence of HIV infection (as well as other sexually transmitted diseases, such as syphilis and gonorrhea) among crack users is the dangerous sexual behavior in which these people engage (Castilla et al. 1999). Not only is crack commonly used as payment for sex, but its users are also much less inclined to be cautious about their sexual activities while under the influence of this drug (Ladd and Petry 2003).

Major Pharmacological Effects of Cocaine

Cocaine can have profound effects on several vital systems in the body (*Drug Facts and Comparisons* 2005). With the assistance of modern technology, the mechanisms whereby cocaine alters body functions have become better understood today. Such knowledge may eventually lead to better treatment of cocaine dependence.

Most of the pharmacological effects of cocaine use stem from enhanced activity of catecholamine (dopamine, noradrenaline, adrenaline) and serotonin transmitters. It is believed that the principal action of the drug is to block the reuptake and inactivation of these substances following their release from neurons. Such action prolongs the activity of these transmitter substances at their receptors and substantially increases their effects. The summation of cocaine's effects on these four transmitters causes CNS stimulation (Woolverton and Johnston 1992). The increase of noradrenaline activity following cocaine administration increases the effects of the sympathetic nervous system and alters cardiovascular activity.

CNS Effects Because cocaine has stimulant properties, it has antidepressant effects as well. Some users self-administer cocaine to relieve severe depression or the negative symptoms of schizophrenia (Markou and Kenny 2002), but in general its short-term action and abuse liability make cocaine unsatisfactory for the treatment of depression disorders. The effects of stimulation appear to increase both physical and mental performance while masking fatigue. High doses of cocaine cause euphoria (based on the form of administration) and enhance the sense of strength, energy, and performance. Because of these positive effects, cocaine has intense reinforcing properties, which encourage continual use and dependence (Nathan et al. 1998).

KEY TERMS

crack babies
infants born to women who use crack cocaine during pregnancy

Cocaine addicts can often distinguish between the two phenomena of the rush and the high associated with cocaine administration. Both the rush and the high peak about 3 minutes after use. The rush seems to be associated with elevated heart rate, sweating, and feelings of "speeding" or "being out of control"; the high includes feelings of euphoria, self-confidence, well-being, and sociability. Drug craving also occurs rapidly and is evident as soon as 12 minutes after administration. Interestingly, brain scans of cocaine users have demonstrated that specific brain regions are associated with these drug effects; thus, the rush and craving are linked with different regions of the limbic system in the brain (see Figure 4.6; Stocker 1999).

The feeling of exhilaration and confidence caused by cocaine can easily become transformed into irritable restlessness and confused hyperactivity (APA 2000). In addition, high chronic doses alter personality, frequently causing psychotic behavior that resembles paranoid schizophrenia (APA 2000; Nathan et al. 1998). For example, in an interview with Peter Venturelli, a 17-year-old female explained that a cocaine-abusing friend ". . . was so coked up that he carved the word 'pain' in his arm and poured coke on it. He thought it symbolized something." In addition, cocaine use heightens the risk of suicide, major trauma, and violent crimes (APA 2000). In many ways, the CNS effects of cocaine resemble those of amphetamines, although perhaps with a more rapid onset, a more intense high (due partially to the manner in which the drugs are administered), and a shorter duration of action (APA 2000).

Besides dependence, other notable CNS toxicities that can be caused by cocaine use include headaches, temporary loss of consciousness, seizures, and death (*Drug Facts and Comparisons* 2005).

Cardiovascular System Effects   Cocaine can initiate pronounced changes in the cardiovascular system by enhancing the sympathetic nervous system, increasing the levels of adrenaline, and causing vasoconstriction (Zickler 2002). The initial effects of cocaine are to increase heart rate and elevate blood pressure. While the heart is being stimulated and working harder, the vasoconstriction effects deprive the cardiac muscle of needed blood (Fischman and Johanson 1996). Such a combination can cause severe heart arrhythmia (an irregular contraction pattern) or heart attack. Other degenerative processes have also been described in the hearts and blood vessels of chronic

cocaine users (Kloner and Rezkalla 2003). In addition, the vasoconstrictive action of this sympathomimetic can damage other tissues, leading to stroke, lung damage in those who smoke cocaine, destruction of nasal cartilage in those who snort the drug, and injury to the gastrointestinal tract (Goodger et al. 2005).

Local Anesthetic Effects   Cocaine was the first local anesthetic used routinely in modern-day medicine (Musto 1998). There is speculation that in ancient times, Andes Indians of South America used cocaine-filled saliva from chewing coca leaves as a local anesthetic for surgical procedures (Aldrich and Barker 1976). However, this assumption is contested by others (Byck 1987). Even so, cocaine is still a preferred local anesthetic for minor pharyngeal (back part of the mouth and upper throat area) surgery due to its good vasoconstriction (reduces bleeding) and topical, local numbing effects. Although relatively safe when applied topically, significant amounts of cocaine can enter the bloodstream and, in sensitive people, cause CNS stimulation, toxic psychosis, or, on rare occasions, death (Harris and Batki 2000; *Medical Letter* 1996).

Cocaine Withdrawal

Considerable debate has arisen as to whether cocaine withdrawal actually happens and, if so, what it involves. With the most recent cocaine epidemic and the high incidence of intense, chronic use, it has become apparent that nervous systems do become tolerant to cocaine and that, during abstinence, withdrawal symptoms occur (APA 2000). In fact, because of CNS dependence, the use of cocaine is less likely to be stopped voluntarily than is the use of many other illicit drugs (Sofuoglu et al. 2003). Certainly, if the withdrawal experience is adverse enough, a user will be encouraged to resume the cocaine habit.

The extent of cocaine withdrawal is proportional to the duration and intensity of use. The physical withdrawal symptoms are relatively minor compared with those caused by long-term use of CNS depressants and by themselves are not considered to be life-threatening (MedlinePlus 2007). Short-term withdrawal symptoms include depression (chronic cocaine users are 60 times more likely to commit suicide than nonusers), sleep abnormalities, craving for the drug, agitation, and *anhedonia* (inability to experience pleasure). Long-term withdrawal effects include a return to normal pleasures, accompanied by mood swings and occasional craving triggered by cues in the surroundings (APA 2000; Mendelson and Mello 1996).

Of particular importance to treatment of chronic cocaine users is that abstinence after bingeing appears to follow three unique stages, each of which must be dealt with in a different manner if relapse is to be prevented. These phases are classified as phase 1, or "crash" (occurs 9 hours to 4 days after drug use is stopped); phase 2, or withdrawal (1 to 10 weeks); and phase 3, or extinction (indefinite). The basic features of these phases are outlined in Table 10.2 (APA 2000).

Treatment of Cocaine Dependence

Cocaine dependency is classified as a psychiatric disorder by the American Psychiatric Association (APA 2000) and is resulting in a growing number of persons seeking treatment for drug addiction (Platt et al. 2002). Treatment of this condition has improved as experience working with these patients has increased. Even so, success rates vary for different programs (Nathan et al. 1998). The problem with program assessments is that they often do not take into account patients who drop out. Also, no clear-cut criteria for qualifying success have been established. For example, is success considered to be abstaining from cocaine for 1 year, 2 years, 5 years, or forever?

No one treatment technique has been found to be significantly superior to others or universally effective (Mendelson and Mello 1996; NIDA 2007; Substance Abuse and Mental Health Services Administration [SAMHSA] 1999), nor is there a particularly effective medication to treat cocaine addiction (Platt et al. 2002). Consequently, substantial disagreement exists as to what is the best strategy for treating cocaine dependency. There is a major ongoing effort by federal agencies and scientists to find effective therapy for cocaine addiction. Most treatments are directed at relieving craving. Major differences in treatment approaches include (1) whether outpatient or inpatient status is deemed appropriate, (2) which drugs and what dosages are used to treat patients during the various stages of abstinence, and (3) what length of time the patient is isolated from cocaine-accessible environments.

It is important to treat each individual patient according to his or her unique needs. Some questions that need to be considered when formulating a therapeutic approach include the following:

Why did the patient begin using cocaine, and why has dependency occurred?

What is the severity of abuse?

How has the cocaine been administered?

What is the psychiatric status of the patient; are there underlying or coexisting mental disorders, such as depression or attention deficit disorder?

What other drugs are being abused along with the cocaine?

Table 10.2 Cocaine Abstinence Phases

	PHASE 1: "CRASH"	PHASE 2: WITHDRAWAL	PHASE 3: EXTINCTION
Time since last binge	24–48 hours	1–10 weeks	Indefinite
Features	*Initial*	*Initial*	
	Agitation, depression, anorexia, suicidal thoughts	Mood swings, sleep returns, some craving, little anxiety	Normal pleasure, mood swings, occasional craving, cues trigger craving
	Middle Fatigue, no craving, insomnia	*Middle and late* Anhedonia, anxiety, intense craving, obsessed with drug seeking	
	Late Extreme fatigue, no craving, exhaustion		

Source: Gawin, F. "Cocaine Addiction: Psychology and Neurophysiology." *Science* 251 (1991): 1580–1586.

What is the patient's motivation for eliminating cocaine dependence?

What sort of support system (family, friends, coworkers, and so on) will sustain the patient in the abstinence effort?

Outpatient Versus Inpatient Approaches The decision as to whether to treat a patient who is dependent on cocaine as an outpatient or an inpatient is based on a number of factors. For example, inpatient techniques allow greater control than outpatient treatment; thus, the environment can be better regulated, the training of the patient can be more closely supervised, and the patient's responses to treatment can be more closely monitored. In contrast, the advantages of the outpatient approach are that supportive family and friends are better able to encourage the patient, the surroundings are more comfortable and natural, and potential problems that might occur when the patient returns to a normal lifestyle are more likely to be identified. In addition, outpatient treatment is less expensive.

Cocaine-dependent patients should be matched to the most appropriate strategy based on their personalities, psychiatric status, and the conditions of their addiction (Mendelson and Mello 1996). For instance, a cocaine addict who lives in the inner city, comes from a home with other drug-dependent family members, and has little support probably would do better in the tightly controlled inpatient environment. However, a highly motivated cocaine addict who comes from a supportive home and a neighborhood that is relatively free of drug problems would probably do better on an outpatient basis.

Therapeutic Drug Treatment Several drugs have been used to treat cocaine abstinence, some of which are themselves active on dopamine systems, but none has been found to be universally effective (Smith et al. 1999). Table 10.3 lists some drugs that have been used in each of the three principal phases of cocaine abstinence. Besides relieving acute problems of anxiety, agitation, and psychosis, drugs can diminish cocaine craving; this effect is achieved by giving drugs such as bromocriptine or levodopa that stimulate the dopamine transmitter system or the narcotic buprenorphine. As mentioned, the pleasant aspects of cocaine likely relate to its ability to increase the activity of dopamine in the limbic system. When cocaine is no longer available, the dopamine system becomes less active, causing depression and anhedonia, which result in a tremendous craving for cocaine. The intent of these cocaine substitutes is to stimulate dopamine activity and relieve the cravings. Although this approach sometimes works initially, it is temporary. In the third phase of cocaine abstinence, antidepressants such as desipramine are effective for many cocaine-dependent patients in relieving underlying mood problems and occasional cravings.

The beneficial effects of these drugs are variable and not well studied. There is some debate over their use. Drugs are, at best, only adjuncts in the treatment of cocaine dependence (Carroll et al. 1994). Successful treatment of cocaine abuse requires intensive counseling; strong support from family, friends, and coworkers; and a highly motivated patient. It is important to realize that a complete "cure" from cocaine dependence is not likely; ex-addicts cannot return to cocaine and control its use (Kleber 1992).

Recovery from Cocaine Dependence Although numerous therapeutic approaches exist for treating cocaine addiction, successful recovery is not likely

Table 10.3 Medications Used in Treatment of Cocaine Abstinence at Various Phases

PHASE	DRUG	DRUG GROUP (RATIONALE)
1. Crash	Benzodiazepines	Depressants (relieve anxiety)
2. Withdrawal	Bromocriptine, levodopa	Dopamine agonists (relieve craving)
3. Extinction	Desipramine, imipramine	Antidepressants (relieve depression and craving)

Source: Mendelson, J., and N. Mello. "Management of Cocaine Abuse and Dependence." *New England Journal of Medicine* 334 (1996): 965–972.

unless the individual will substantially benefit by giving up the drug. Research has shown that treatment is most likely to succeed in patients who are middle-class, employed, and married; for example, 85% of addicted medical professionals recover from cocaine addiction. These people can usually be convinced that they have too much to lose in their personal and professional lives by continuing their cocaine habit. In contrast, a severely dependent crack addict who has no job, family, home, or hope for the future is not likely to be persuaded that abstinence from cocaine would be advantageous, so therapy is rarely successful (Grinspoon 1993). Unfortunately, there currently is no uniformly effective pharmacological treatment available to deal with long-term cocaine addiction, although intensive research to identify such therapeutic agents is under way (SAMHSA 1999).

Polydrug Use by Cocaine Abusers Treatment of most cocaine abusers is complicated by the fact that they are *polydrug* (multiple drug) users. It is unusual to find a person who abuses only cocaine. For example, many cocaine abusers also use alcohol (Pennings et al. 2002). In general, the more severe the alcoholism, the greater the severity of the cocaine dependence. Alcohol is used to relieve some of the unpleasant cocaine effects, such as anxiety, insomnia, and mood disturbances (Pennings et al. 2002). This drug combination can be dangerous for several reasons:

1. The presence of both cocaine and alcohol (ethanol) in the liver results in the formation of a unique chemical product called cocaeth-ylene, which is created in the reaction of ethanol with a cocaine metabolite. Cocaethylene is often found in high levels in the blood of victims of fatal drug overdoses and appears to enhance the euphoria as well as the cardiovascular toxicity of cocaine (Pennings et al. 2002).

2. Both cocaine and alcohol can damage the liver; thus, their toxic effects on the liver are likely to add together when the drugs are used in combination (Pennings et al. 2002).

3. The likelihood of damaging a fetus is enhanced when both drugs are used together during pregnancy (Pennings et al. 2002).

4. Cardiovascular stress is increased in the presence of both drugs (Pennings et al. 2002).

Like users of amphetamines, cocaine abusers frequently coadminister narcotics, such as heroin; this combination is called a *speedball* and has been associated with a high risk for HIV infection (NIDA 2007b). Cocaine users sometimes combine their drug with other depressants, such as benzodiazepines, or marijuana to help reduce the severity of the crash after their cocaine binges. Codependence on cocaine and a CNS depressant can complicate treatment but must be considered.

Cocaine and Pregnancy

One of the consequences of widespread cocaine abuse is that since the mid-1980s approximately 1 million babies in the United States have been born to mothers who used cocaine during pregnancy (March of Dimes 2003). Cocaine use during pregnancy is highest in poor, inner-city regions. In the United States, more than $1 billion is spent

Infants born to crack-using mothers are often premature.

Here and Now

Cocaine and Pregnancy

Public health concerns have recently been raised about the long-term cognitive development of cocaine babies. A research study published by Case Western Reserve University School of Medicine and local Cleveland-area hospitals reported that children who were exposed to cocaine prenatally experienced effects on their cognitive development but not on their motor development.

The study also found that prenatal exposure to cocaine was linked to lower birthweight and younger gestational age at delivery. Children exposed to cocaine prenatally were found to have a mental retardation rate almost five times higher than the general population, and they were twice as likely to have mild delays in brain function.

Source: Cocaine.org. "At 2 Years, Cocaine Babies Suffer Cognitive Development Effects" (16 April 2002).

annually for care of cocaine-using women during their pregnancies. Many of these **cocaine babies** are abandoned by their mothers and left to the welfare system for care.

It is still not clear exactly what types of direct effects cocaine has on the developing fetus (Vidaeff and Mastrobattista 2003). Some early studies have been criticized because (1) the pregnant populations examined were not well defined and properly matched, (2) use of other drugs (such as alcohol) with cocaine during pregnancy was often ignored, and (3) the effects of poor nutrition, poor living conditions, and a traumatic lifestyle were not considered when analyzing the results. Due to these problems, much of the earlier work examining prenatal effects of cocaine is flawed and the conclusions are questionable (Vidaeff and Mastrobattista 2003; *Women's Health Week* 2006).

It is known that cocaine use during pregnancy can cause vasoconstriction of placental vessels, thereby interfering with oxygen and nutrient exchange between mother and child, or contraction of the uterine muscles, resulting in trauma or premature birth. Current data also suggest that infants exposed to cocaine during pregnancy are more likely to suffer a small head (microencephaly), reduced birthweight, increased irritability, and subtle learning and cognitive deficits (March of Dimes 2003; Singer et al. 2004). Recent findings also suggest that children who had experienced prenatal cocaine exposure have problems with some motor skills, subtle deficits in I.Q., and some minor problems with language development,

attention span, and ability to gather and use information (March of Dimes 2003). Clearly, individuals exposed to cocaine during fetal development can function in society, but they frequently require special help. It remains to be seen how these individuals will cope as adults (Schiller and Allen 2005).

Minor Stimulants

Minor stimulants enjoy widespread use in the United States because of the mild lift in mood provided by their consumption. The most popular of these routinely consumed agents are methylxanthines (commonly called *xanthines*), such as caffeine, which are consumed in beverages made from plants and herbs. Other minor stimulants are contained in OTC medications, such as cold and hay fever products; these will be mentioned briefly in this chapter but discussed at greater length in Chapter 15. Because of their frequent use, some dependence on these drugs can occur; however, serious dysfunction due to dependence is infrequent. Consequently, abuse of xanthines such as caffeine is not viewed as a major health problem by most health experts (Daly and Fredholm 1998). However, there has been recent concern that many people, especially adolescents and young adults, do not appreciate that caffeine is a drug and consume it like a food group resulting in side effects and even trips to the emergency room (Hitti 2006).

■ Caffeinelike Drugs (Xanthines)

Caffeine is the world's most frequently used stimulant and perhaps its most popular drug (Demos 2001). Beverages and foods containing caffeine are consumed by almost all adults and children living in the United States today (see Table 10.4). In this country, the average daily intake of caffeine is approximately 200 mg (the equivalent of approximately 2 cups of coffee), with as many as 30% of Americans consuming 500 mg or more per day (APA 2000). The most common sources of caffeine include coffee beans, tea plants, kola nuts, maté leaves, guaraná paste, and yoco bark.

Although the consumption of caffeine-containing drinks can be found throughout history, the active stimulant caffeine was identified by German and French scientists in the early 1820s. Caffeine was described as a substance with alkaloid (basic) properties that was extracted from green coffee beans and referred to as *kaffebase* by Ferdinand Runge in 1820 (Gilbert 1984). In the course of the next 40 to 60 years, caffeine was identified in several other genera of plants, which were used as sources for common beverages. These included tea leaves (originally the drug was called *thein*); guaraná paste (originally the drug was called *guaranin*); Paraguay tea, or maté; and kola nuts. Certainly, the popularity of these beverages over the centuries attests to the fact that most consumers find the stimulant effects of this drug desirable.

The Chemical Nature of Caffeine

Caffeine belongs to a group of drugs that have similar chemical structures and are known as the **xanthines**. Besides caffeine, other xanthines are *theobromine* (means "divine leaf"), discovered in cacao beans (used to make chocolate) in 1842, and *theophylline* (means "divine food"), isolated from tea leaves in 1888. These three agents have unique pharmacological properties (which are discussed later), with caffeine being the most potent CNS stimulant.

Beverages Containing Caffeine

To understand the unique role that caffeine plays in U.S. society, it is useful to gain perspective on its most common sources: unfermented beverages.

Coffee Coffee is derived from the beans of several species of coffea plants. The *Coffea arabica* plant grows as a shrub or small tree and reaches 4 to 6 meters in height when growing wild. Coffee beans are primarily cultivated in South America

and East Africa and constitute the major cash crop for exportation in several developing countries.

The name *coffee* was likely derived from the Arabian word *kahwa* or named after the Ethiopian prince Kaffa. From Ethiopia, the coffee tree was carried to Arabia and cultivated (Kihlman 1977); it became an important element in Arabian civilization and is mentioned in writings dating back to A.D. 900.

Coffee probably reached Europe through Turkey and was likely used initially as a medicine. By the middle of the 17th century, coffeehouses had sprung up in England and France — places to relax, talk, and learn the news. These coffeehouses turned into the famous "penny universities" of the early 18th century where, for a penny a cup, you could listen to some of the great literary and political figures of the day.

Coffee was originally consumed in the Americas by English colonists, although tea was initially preferred. Tea was replaced by coffee following the Revolutionary War. Because tea had become a symbol of English repression, the switch to coffee was more a political statement than a change in taste. The popularity of coffee grew as U.S. boundaries moved west. In fact, daily coffee intake continued to increase until it peaked in 1986, when annual coffee consumption averaged 10 pounds per person. Although concerns about the side effects associated with caffeine use have since caused some decline in coffee consumption, this beverage still plays a major role in the lifestyles of

Table 10.4 Caffeine Content of Beverages and Chocolate

BEVERAGE	CAFFEINE CONTENT (MG/CUP)	AMOUNT
Brewed coffee	90–125	5 oz
Instant coffee	35–164	5 oz
Decaffeinated coffee	1–6	5 oz
Tea	25–125	5 oz
Cocoa	5–25	5 oz
Coca-Cola	45	12 oz
Pepsi-Cola	38	12 oz
Mountain Dew	54	12 oz
Chocolate bar	1–35	1 oz

KEY TERMS

xanthines
the family of drugs that includes caffeine

most Americans (McMahon 2001), with approximately 56% of adults in the United States being coffee drinkers in 2006 (Painter 2006).

Tea Tea is made from the *Camellia sinensis* plant, which is native to China and parts of India, Burma, Thailand, Laos, and Vietnam. Tea contains two xanthines: caffeine and theophylline. As with coffee, the earliest use of tea is not known.

Although apocryphal versions of the origin of tea credit Emperor Shen Nung for its discovery in 2737 B.C., the first reliable account of the use of tea as a medicinal plant appears in an early Chinese manuscript written around A.D. 350. The popular use of tea slowly grew. The Dutch brought the first tea to Europe in 1610, where it was accepted rather slowly; with time, it was adopted by the British as a favorite beverage and became an integral part of their daily activities. In fact, the tea trade constituted one of the major elements of the English economy. Tea revenues made it possible for England to colonize India and helped to bring on the Opium Wars in the 1800s, which benefited British colonialism (see Chapter 9).

The British were constantly at odds with the Dutch as they attempted to monopolize the tea trade. Even so, the Dutch introduced the first tea into America at New Amsterdam around 1650. Later, the British gained exclusive rights to sell tea to the American colonies. Because of the high taxes levied by the British government on tea being shipped to America, tea became a symbol of British rule.

Soft Drinks The second most common source of caffeine is soft drinks. In general, the caffeine content per 12-ounce serving ranges from 30 to 60 milligrams (see Table 10.4). Soft drinks account for most of the caffeine consumed by U.S. children and teenagers; for many people, a can of cola has replaced the usual cup of coffee. Recently, caffeine has been added to juices and even water. These caffeine-containing products have names such as Buzz Water or Water Joe. Americans consumed 574 cans of soft drinks — 70% of which were caffeinated — for every man, woman, and child in 2003 (Kluger 2004).

Social Consequences of Consuming Caffeine-Based Beverages It is impossible to accurately assess the social impact of consuming beverages containing caffeine, but certainly the subtle (and sometimes not so subtle) stimulant effects of the caffeine present in these drinks have had some social influence.

These beverages have become integrated into social customs and ceremonies and recognized as traditional drinks.

Today, drinks containing caffeine are consumed by many people with ritualistic devotion first thing in the morning, following every meal, and at frequent interludes throughout the day known as "coffee breaks" or "tea times." The immense popularity of these products is certainly a consequence of the stimulant actions of caffeine. Both the dependence on the "jump-start" effect of caffeine and the avoidance of unpleasant withdrawal consequences in the frequent user ensure the continual popularity of these products.

Other Natural Caffeine Sources

Although coffee and tea are two of the most common sources of natural caffeine in the United States, other caffeine-containing beverages and food are popular in different parts of the world. Some of the most common include guaraná from Brazil; maté from Argentina, Southern Brazil, and Paraguay; and kola nuts from West Africa, West Indies, and South America (Kihlman 1977).

Chocolate

Although chocolate contains small amounts of caffeine (see Table 10.4), the principal stimulant in chocolate is the alkaloid theobromine, named after the cocoa tree, *Theobroma cacao*. (*Theobroma* is an Aztec word meaning "fruit of the gods.") The Aztecs thought very highly of the fruit and seed pods from the cacoa tree, and they used the beans as a medium of exchange in bartering. The Mayan Indians adopted the food and made a warm drink from the beans that they called *chocolatl* (meaning "warm drink"). The original chocolate drink was a very thick concoction that had to be eaten with a spoon. It was unsweetened because the Mayans apparently did not know about sugar cane.

Hernando Cortés, the conqueror of Mexico, took some chocolate cakes back to Spain with him in 1528, but the method of preparing them remained a secret for nearly 100 years. It was not until 1828 that the Dutch worked out a process to remove much of the fat from the kernels to make a chocolate powder that was the forerunner of the cocoa we know today. The cocoa fat, or cocoa butter as it is called, was later mixed with sugar and pressed into bars. In 1847, the first chocolate bars appeared on the market. By 1876, the Swiss had developed milk chocolate, which is highly popular in today's confectioneries.

OTC Drugs Containing Caffeine

Although the consumption of beverages is by far the most common source of xanthines, a number of popular OTC products contain significant quantities of caffeine. For example, many OTC analgesic products contain approximately 30 milligrams of caffeine per tablet (Anacin). Higher doses of 100 to 200 milligrams per tablet are included in stay-awake (NoDoz, Caffedrine) and "picker-upper" (Vivarin) products (Anderson and Nykamp 2004). The use of caffeine in these OTC drugs is highly controversial and has been criticized by clinicians who are unconvinced of caffeine's benefits. Some critics believe that the presence of caffeine in these OTC drugs is nothing more than a psychological gimmick to entice customers through mild euphoric effects provided by this stimulant. Caffeine is also included in so-called "energy drinks" sometimes advertised as a drug alternative, a dietary supplement, or a natural energy drink (Shute 2007). For example, such OTC products have been flagrantly marketed as "speed in a can," "Instant Rush," and "Liquid Cocaine" until the FDA declared the company involved was marketing its products illegally (Rubinsky 2007; see "Here and Now" Energized Profits).

Despite this criticism, it is likely that caffeine has some analgesic (pain-relieving) properties of its own (Dunwiddie and Masino 2001). Recent studies suggest that 130 milligrams, but not 65 milligrams, of caffeine is superior to a placebo in relieving nonmigraine headaches. In addition, the presence of caffeine has been shown to enhance aspirin-medicated relief from surgical pain (such as tooth extraction). Based on such findings, more clinicians are recommending the use of caffeine

OTC caffeine products frequently contain the equivalent of 2–3 cups of coffee and are used to stay awake.

in the management of some types of headaches and minor to moderate pains (Zhang 2001).

Physiological Effects of the Xanthines

The xanthines significantly influence several important body functions. Although the effects of these drugs are generally viewed as minor and short-term (Goldstein 1994), when used in high doses or by people who have severe medical problems, these drugs can be dangerous. The following sections summarize the responses of the major systems to xanthines.

CNS Effects Among the common xanthines, caffeine has the most potent effect on the CNS, followed by theophylline; for most people, theobromine has relatively little influence. Although the CNS responses of users can vary considerably,

Here and Now

Energized Profits

The increasingly popular energy drinks constitute a rapidly growing market, especially for young adults, that reached $3.4 billion in annual sales by 2005 and is expected to reach $10 billion by 2010. Some brands, such as Wired 344 (contains 344 mg caffeine/can) have more than three times the 100 mg/day that research suggests can cause a mild addiction. In addition, some companies are adding quantities of alcohol that are comparable to a can of beer to their energy products, advertising that the caffeine offsets the side effects of the alcohol ingestion — a notion not supported by clinical experience and research. There is some concern that consumption of these products by minors could cause a serious dependence problem.

Source: Twitchell, J. "Cheers? Alcohol Added to Some Energy Drinks." *Deseret News* (1 April 2007): B-1.

in general 100 to 200 milligrams of caffeine enhances alertness, causes arousal, and diminishes fatigue (Wikipedia 2007a). Caffeine is often used to block drowsiness and facilitate mental activity, such as when cramming for examinations into the early hours of the morning. In addition, caffeine stimulates the formation of thoughts but does not improve learning ability in the wide-awake student. The effects of caffeine are most pronounced in unstimulated, drowsy consumers (Goldstein 1994). The CNS effects of caffeine also diminish the sense of boredom (Wikipedia 2007a). Thus, people engaged in dull, repetitive tasks, such as assembly-line work, or nonstimulating and laborious exercises, such as listening to a boring professor, often consume caffeine beverages to help compensate for the tedium. Most certainly, xanthine drinks are popular because they cause these effects on brain activity.

Adverse CNS effects usually occur with doses greater than 300 milligrams per day. Some of these include insomnia, increased tension, anxiety, and initiation of muscle twitches. Doses over 500 milligrams can be dysphoric (unpleasant) and can cause panic sensations, chills, nausea, and clumsiness. Extremely high doses of caffeine, from 5 to 10 grams, frequently result in seizures, respiratory failure, and death (APA 2000).

Cardiovascular and Respiratory Effects Drugs that stimulate the brain usually stimulate the cardiovascular system as well. The response of the heart and blood vessels to xanthines is dependent on dose and previous experience with these mild stimulants. Tolerance to the cardiovascular effects occurs with frequent use (APA 2000). With low doses (100–200 milligrams), heart activity can either increase, decrease, or do nothing; at higher doses (more than 500 milligrams), the rate of contraction of the heart increases. Xanthines usually cause minor vasodilation in most of the body. In contrast, the cerebral blood vessels are vasoconstricted by the action of caffeine. In fact, cerebral vasoconstriction likely accounts for this drug's effectiveness in relieving some minor vascular headaches caused by vasodilation of the cerebral vessels.

Among the xanthines, theophylline has the greatest effect on the respiratory system, causing air passages to open and facilitate breathing. Because of this effect, tea has often been recommended to relieve breathing difficulties, and theophylline is frequently used to treat asthma-related respiratory problems.

Other Effects The methylxanthines have noteworthy — albeit mild — effects on other systems in the body. They cause a minor increase in the secretion of digestive juices in the stomach, which can be significant to individuals suffering from stomach ailments such as ulcers. These drugs also increase urine formation (as any heavy tea drinker undoubtedly knows).

Caffeine Intoxication

Consuming occasional low doses of the xanthines (equivalent of two to three cups of coffee per day) is relatively safe for most users (Kluger 2004). However, frequent use of high doses causes psychological as well as physical problems called **caffeinism**. This condition is found in about 10% of the adults who consume coffee (APA 2000; Heishman and Henningfield 1992).

The CNS components of caffeine intoxication are recognized as a "psychoactive substance-induced psychiatric disorder" in *DSM-IV-TR* criteria established by the American Psychiatric Association (2000). The essential features of this disorder are restlessness, nervousness, excitement, insomnia, flushed face, diuresis, muscle twitching, rambling thoughts and speech, and stomach complaints. These symptoms can occur in some sensitive people following a dose as low as 250 milligrams per day. Caffeine doses in excess of 1 gram per day may cause muscle twitching, rambling thoughts and speech, heart arrhythmias, and motor agitation. With higher doses, hearing ringing in the ears and seeing flashes of light can occur.

Some researchers suggest consuming large quantities of caffeine is associated with cancers of the bladder, ovaries, colon, and kidneys. These claims have not been reliably substantiated (Nawrot et al. 2003; Painter 2006).

One problem with many such studies is that they assess the effect of coffee consumption on cancers rather than the effect of caffeine itself. Because coffee contains so many different chemicals, it is impossible to determine specifically the effect of caffeine in such research (Gurin 1994). Other reports claim that caffeine promotes cyst formation in women's breasts. Although these conclusions have been challenged, many clinicians advise patients with breast cysts to avoid caffeine (Margen

KEY TERMS

caffeinism
symptoms caused by taking high chronic doses of caffeine

1994). Finally, some reports indicate that very high doses of caffeine given to pregnant laboratory animals can cause stillbirths or offspring with low birthweights or limb deformities. Studies found that moderate consumption of caffeine (less than 300 milligrams per day) did not significantly affect human fetal development (Mills et al. 1993); however, intake of more than 300 milligrams per day during pregnancy has been associated with an increase in spontaneous fetal loss (*Consumer Reports* 1997). Expectant mothers are usually advised to avoid or at least reduce caffeine use during pregnancy (Margen 1994).

Based on the information available, no strong evidence exists to suggest that moderate use of caffeine leads to disease (Nawrot et al. 2003; Painter 2006). In fact, some recent research has suggested that moderate caffeine consumption may even reduce the risk of degenerative diseases of the brain such as Parkinson's disease and Alzheimer's disease (Fackelmann 2006; Painter 2006). There are, however, implications that people with existing severe medical problems — psychiatric disorders (such as severe anxiety, panic attacks, and schizophrenia), cardiovascular disease, and possibly breast cysts — are at greater risk when consuming caffeine. Realistically, other elements, such as alcohol and fat consumption and smoking, are much more likely to cause serious health problems (Gurin 1994).

Caffeine Dependence

Caffeine causes limited dependence, which, for most people, is relatively minor compared with that of the potent stimulants; thus, the abuse potential of caffeine is much lower and depen-

dence is less likely to interfere with normal daily routines (Kluger 2004). Despite this, caffeine use is thought to be able to produce a significant addiction (*Biotech Week* 2004). Consequently, 50% of those consuming one to three cups of coffee each day develop headaches when withdrawing and 10% become significantly depressed, anxious, or fatigued without their coffee. Some people experience elements of withdrawal every morning before their first cup and claim caffeine gives them an edge at work or in school (Shute 2007). However, caffeine is so readily available and socially accepted (almost expected) that the high quantity of consumption has produced many modestly dependent users. In fact, we are seeing younger and younger persons consuming more and more caffeine; from 2004 to 2007 the percentage of 18–24-year-olds who consumed caffeine daily went from 16% to 31% (Shute 2007; see "Here and Now" Caffeine Emergencies).

The degree of physical dependence on caffeine is highly variable but related to dose. With typical caffeine withdrawal, adverse effects can persist for several days (see Table 10.5). Although these symptoms are unpleasant, they usually are not severe enough to prevent most people from giving up their coffee or cola drinks if motivated. It is noteworthy that two thirds of those patients who are treated for caffeinism relapse into their caffeine-consuming habits (Heishman and Henningfield 1992).

Variability in Responses

Caffeine is eventually absorbed entirely from the gastrointestinal tract after oral consumption. In most users, 90% of the drug reaches the bloodstream

Here and Now

Caffeine Emergencies

Because of the increased popularity of caffeine-containing products, especially with teenagers, poison control centers across the country are reporting increased numbers of people presenting at emergency rooms with rapid heart rates and nausea from caffeine overdose. Such was the case when a 14-year-old boy recently showed up at a Minneapolis emergency room having difficulty with breathing after washing down several caffeine pills with so-called "energy drinks" in order to continue playing video games all night. But instead of having a night of video recreation with friends, he spent the evening in an intensive care unit intubated until the caffeine cleared from his system and normal breathing was restored

Source: Shute, N. "Americans Young and Old Crave High-Octane Fuel, and Doctors Are Jittery." *U.S. News and World Report* (29 April 2007): 58–68.

Table 10.5 Caffeine Withdrawal Syndrome

SYMPTOM	DURATION
Headache	Several days to 1 week
Decreased alertness	2 days
Decreased vigor	2 days
Fatigue and lethargy	2 days
Nervousness	2 days

Source: Based on Holtzman, S. "Caffeine as a Model Drug of Abuse." *Trends in Pharmacological Sciences* 11 (1990): 355–356.

Table 10.6 Common OTC Sympathomimetics

DRUG	OTC PRODUCT (FORM)
Ephedrine	Before removed, was used as a decongestant (oral, nasal spray, or drops)
Naphazoline	Decongestant (nasal spray or drops)
Oxymetazoline	Decongestant (nasal spray or drops)
Phenylephrine	Decongestant (oral, nasal spray, or drops, eye drops)
Pseudoephedrine	Decongestant (oral)
Tetrahydrozoline	Decongestant (eye drops)

Source: Scolaro, K. "Disorders Related to Colds and Allergy." In *Handbook of Nonprescription Drugs*, 15th ed., 201–228. Washington, DC: American Pharmaceutical Association, 2004.

within 20 minutes and is distributed into the brain and throughout the body very quickly (Sawynok and Yaksh 1993). The rate of absorption of caffeine from the stomach and intestines differs from person to person by as much as sixfold. Such wide variations in the rate at which caffeine enters the blood from the stomach likely account for much of the variability in responses to this drug.

■ OTC Sympathomimetics

Although often overlooked, the sympathomimetic decongestant drugs included in OTC products such as cold, allergy, and diet aid medications have stimulant properties like those of caffeine (Appelt 1993). For most people, the CNS impact of these drugs is minor, but for those people who are very sensitive to these drugs, they can cause jitters and interfere with sleep. For such individuals, OTC products containing the sympathomimetics should be avoided before bedtime.

The common OTC sympathomimetics are shown in Table 10.6 and include ephedrine. In the past, OTC agents were packaged to look like amphetamines (called *look-alike drugs*) and legally sold on the street, usually to children or high school students. Although much less potent than amphetamines (even though they can be used as precursor chemicals to make methamphetamine), these minor stimulants can be abused and have caused deaths. Attempts to regulate look-alike drugs resulted in passage of the federal and state Imitation Controlled Substances Acts. These statutes prohibit the packaging of OTC sympathomimetics to look like amphetamines.

These laws have not resolved the problem, however. Other products containing the OTC sympathomimetics are promoted on the street as "harmless speed" and "OTC uppers." It is likely that use of such products can lead to the abuse of more potent stimulants.

As previously mentioned, some of the sympathomimetics that are included in cold medicines can be readily converted into methamphetamine. For this reason, as of 2006 federal statutes require these products be secured in a locked case behind the counter and sold in limited quantities (Baldauf 2006).

■ Herbal Stimulants

Some OTC sympathomimetics occur naturally and are also found in herbal stimulants or dietary supplements sold by mail and in novelty stores, beauty salons, health food stores, online, and sometimes by health professionals, including physicians (Fessenden and Drew 2003; Gugliotta 2000). These pills have been sold under names such as "Cloud 9," "Ultimate Xphoria," and "Herbal Ecstasy" and contained stimulants such as ephedrine, ephedra, or *ma huang* (Gugliotta 2000; *Pharmacy Times* 1996; Sprague et al. 1998). These products are promoted as natural highs to be used as diet aids, energy boosters, or performance enhancers for athletics (Legal Herbal Drugs 2007; Mihoces 2001). Excessive use of these products can cause seizures, heart attacks, and strokes (Gugliotta

Here and Now

Diet Pills Are Russian Roulette for Athletes

Steve Bechler, a 23-year-old pitcher for the Baltimore Orioles of the American League, died in 2003 after collapsing on the field during running drills due to "multiple organ failure resulting from heat stroke," says the autopsy report. Ephedrine was found in Bechler's body and likely contributed to his death. He was reported to be using an ephedrine supplement called Xenadrine RFA-1. Although advised not to use it by his trainer, Bechler was taking this ephedrine-containing product to get his weight down after being criticized by coaches for being too heavy and not performing well in preseason drills. A teammate explained that heavy athletes like Bechler are under a lot of pressure to control their weight to make big-league teams. Although at the time of Bechler's death use of ephedrine was not prohibited by Major League Baseball, it was prohibited by the National Football League in 2002. The NFL's ban came after Korey Stringer, a lineman for the Minnesota Vikings who was taking an ephedrine product, died after collapsing during a training camp workout in 2001.

Steve Bechler was a pitcher for the Baltimore Orioles.

Source: Shipley, A. "Bechler's Diet Pills Draw Scrutiny." *The Washington Post* (19 February 2003): D-1.

2000). In fact, several deaths and many cases of severe reactions have been reported in the United States from excessive use of these products (*Washington Times* 2003). The death of a major league baseball player (see "Here and Now," Diet Pills Are Russian Roulette for Athletes) resulted in particularly strong pressure to ban OTC products, including dietary supplements, containing either the herb ephedra or the active ingredient ephedrine (Shipley 2003). In response to these pressures, the FDA banned the use of ephedrine or ephedra in OTC products; however, it will be difficult to actually remove herbal stimulants from the marketplace because of a 1994 federal law that prohibits such action until the FDA conclusively proves the dangers of these substances (Rubin 2003). There have been numerous lawsuits filed against herbal companies that manufactured products containing *ma huang* and the drug ephedrine. These legal actions claim that such products have caused serious illness and even death. Several of these lawsuits have been settled out of court reportedly for millions of dollars (Ephedrine News 2007). Even before the FDA ban, because ephedrine can be converted into methamphetamine, the Comprehensive Methamphetamine Act passed in 1996 regulated the amount of ephedrine that could be purchased or sold at one time (Sprague et al. 1998).

Discussion Questions

1. Should the FDA continue to approve amphetamines for the treatment of obesity? Why?

2. How are methamphetamine and Ecstasy similar, and how do they differ?

3. Should children be taken from mothers who are addicted to methamphetamine?

4. What have past experiences taught us about cocaine? Do you think we have finally learned our lesson concerning this drug?

5. If clinical trials demonstrate that MDMA is effective in the treatment of stress and anxiety, should the FDA approve its use by prescription?

6. Why does the method of cocaine administration make a difference in how a user is affected by this drug? Use examples to substantiate your conclusions.

7. Why do people use crack cocaine, and what are the major toxicities caused by use of high doses of this stimulant?

8. How is cocaine dependence treated? What are the rationales for the treatments?

9. How does caffeine compare with cocaine and amphetamine as a CNS stimulant?

10. Because of caffeine's potential for abuse, do you think the FDA should control it more tightly? Defend your answer.

11. Do you feel that herbal stimulants, such as ephedra and *ma huang*, should have been removed from OTC products?

Summary

1 Amphetamines, originally developed as decongestants, are potent stimulants. Some amphetamines have been approved by the FDA as (1) diet aids to treat obesity; (2) treatment for narcolepsy; and (3) treatment for attention deficit hyperactivity disorder in children.

2 In therapeutic doses, amphetamines can cause agitation, anxiety, and panic owing to their effects on the brain; in addition, they can cause an irregular heartbeat, increased blood pressure, heart attack, or stroke. Intense, high-dose abuse of these drugs can cause severe psychotic behavior, stereotypy, and seizures as well as the severe cardiovascular side effects just mentioned.

3 Speed refers to the use of intravenous methamphetamine. Ice is smoked methamphetamine. A run is a pattern of intense, multiple dosing over a period of days that can cause serious neurological, psychiatric, and cardiovascular consequences.

4 Tweakers are individuals who repeatedly self-administer methamphetamine to maintain the high. They often have not slept or eaten for days, are very irritable, and sometimes are paranoid or even violent.

5 "Designer" amphetamines are chemical modifications of original amphetamines. Some designer amphetamines, such as Ecstasy, retain abuse potential and are marketed on the street under exotic and alluring names.

6 In the early 1980s, cocaine was commonly viewed by the U.S. public as a relatively safe drug with glamorous connotations. By the mid-1980s, it became apparent that cocaine was a very addicting drug with dangerous side effects.

7 The CNS and cardiovascular effects of both amphetamines and cocaine are similar. However, the effects of cocaine tend to occur more rapidly, be more intense, and wear off more quickly than those of amphetamines.

8 The intensity of the cocaine effect and the likelihood of dependence occurring are directly related to the means of administration. Going from least to most intense effect, the modes of cocaine administration include chewing, snorting, injecting, and smoking (or freebasing).

9 Crack is cocaine that has been converted into its "freebase" form and is intended for smoking.

10 Cocaine withdrawal goes through three main stages: (1) the "crash," the initial abstinence phase consisting of depression, agitation, suicidal thoughts, and fatigue; (2) withdrawal, including mood swings, craving, anhedonia, and obsession with drug seeking; and (3) extinction, when normal pleasure returns and cues trigger craving and mood swings.

11 Treatment of cocaine dependence is highly individualistic and has variable success. The principal strategies include both inpatient and outpatient programs. Drug therapy often is used to relieve short-term cocaine craving and to alleviate mood problems and long-term craving. Psychological counseling and support therapy are essential components of treatment.

12 Caffeine is the most frequently consumed stimulant in the world. It is classified as a xanthine (methylxanthine) and is added to a number of beverages, including water. It is also included in some OTC medicines such as analgesics and "stay-awake" products. Caffeine causes minor stimulation of cardiovascular activity, kidney function (it is a diuretic), and gastric secretion.

13 Dependence on caffeine can occur in people who regularly consume large doses. Withdrawal can cause headaches, agitation, and tremors. Although unpleasant, withdrawal from caffeine dependence is much less severe than that from amphetamine and cocaine dependence.

14 OTC sympathomimetics such as ephedrine have been consumed in high doses and used as "legal" highs. Although not as potent as the major stimulants, the recreational use of these drugs can be dangerous. Because of those potential dangers, the FDA has prohibited the use of ephedrine in OTC products.

References

Aarons, R. "Task Force Combats Ecstasy Smuggling." *U.S. Customs Today* (October 2000): 1.

Aldrich, M., and R. Barker. In *Cocaine: Chemical, Biological, Social and Treatment Aspects,* edited by S. J. Mule, 3–10. Cleveland, OH: CRC, 1976.

American Council for Drug Education. "Basic Facts About Drugs: Methamphetamine" (2007). Available http://www.acde.org/common/meth.pdf.

American Psychiatric Association. "Substance-Related Disorders." In *Diagnostic and Statistical Manual of Mental Disorders,* 4th ed., text revision, 223–250. Washington, DC: American Psychiatric Association, 2000.

Anderson, R., and D. Nykamp. "Drowsiness and Fatigue." In *Handbook of Nonprescription Drugs,* 15th ed., edited by R. Berardi. 1009–1020. Washington, DC: American Pharmacists Association, 2004.

Appelt, G. "Weight Control Products." In *Handbook of Nonprescription Drugs,* 10th ed., edited by T. Covington, 339–349. Washington, DC: American Pharmaceutical Association, 1993.

Baldauf, S. "Vanished Behind the Counter." *US News and World Report.* (2 October 2006). Available http://health.usnews.com/usnews/health/articles/060924/2cold.htm.

Barkley, R., M. Fischer, L. Smallish, and K. Fletcher. "Does the Treatment of ADHD with Stimulants Contribute to Drug Use/Abuse? A 13-Year Prospective Study." *Pediatrics* 111 (2003): 97–109.

Beck, J. "The Public Health Implications of MDMA Use." In *Ecstasy,* edited by S. Peroutka, 77–103. Norwell, MA: Kluwer, 1990.

Benedetti, W. "Ecstasy Supporters Hope FDA-Approved Study Will Vindicate Drug." *Seattle Post-Intelligencer* (9 May 2002). Available http://seattlepi.nwsource.com/lifestyle/69629_ecstasystudy.shtml.

Berkes, H. "Mexican 'Ice' Replaces Home-Cooked Meth in U.S." *National Public Radio* (3 April 2007).

Biotech Week. "Caffeine Withdrawal Recognized as a Disorder" (20 October 2004). Available www.newsrx.com/newsletters/Biotech-Week/2004-10-20.html.

Byck, R. "Cocaine Use and Research: Three Histories." In *Cocaine: Chemical and Behavioral Aspects,* edited by S. Fisher, 3–17. London: Oxford University Press, 1987.

Caesar, M. "US Finds Anger in South America." *Toronto Globe and Mail* (31 August 2002).

Cantwell, B., and A. McBride. "Self Detoxification by Amphetamine-Dependent Patients: A Pilot Study." *Drug and Alcohol Dependence* 49 (1998): 157–163.

Carroll, K., B. Rounsaville, L. Gordon, C. Nich, P. Jatlow, R. Bisighini, and F. Gawin. "Psychotherapy and Pharmacotherapy for Ambulatory Cocaine Abusers." *Archives of General Psychiatry* 51 (1994): 177–187.

Castilla, J., G. Barrio, M. Belza, and L. de la Fuente. "Drug and Alcohol Consumption and Sexual Risk Behaviour Among Young Adults: Results from a National Survey." *Drug, Alcohol and Dependence* 56 (1999): 47–53.

CBS News. Despite Drug War, Cocaine Purer, Cheaper. (19 June, 2007).

Christophersen, A. "Amphetamine Designer Drugs — An Overview and Epidemiology." *Toxicology Letters* 112–113 (2000): 127–131.

Cloud, J. "The Lure of Ecstasy." *Time* 155 (5 June 2000): 60.

Cohen, G. "A Front-Line Physicians' Perspective on the Crystal Meth Epidemic." *Counselor* 7 (October 2006): 51, 52.

Comprehensive Methamphetamine Control Act (MCA). (2008). Available http://designer-drug.com/ptc/12.162.180.114/dcd/chemistry/dojmeth1.txt.

Consumer Reports. "Coffee Clutch: Should You Worry About All That Caffeine?" 62 (1997): 52–53.

Daly, J., and B. Fredholm. "Caffeine — An Atypical Drug of Dependence." *Drug and Alcohol Dependence* 51 (1998): 199–206.

Deslandes, P., D. Pache, and R. Sewell. "Drug Dependence: Neuropharmacology and Management." *Journal of Pharmacy and Pharmacology* 54 (2002): 885–895.

DeYoung, K. "U.S.: Coca Cultivation Drops in Colombia." *Washington Post* (28 February 2003): A-19.

DiChiara, G. "Cocaine: Scientific and Social Dimensions." *Trends in Neurological Sciences* 16 (1993): 39.

Drug Enforcement Agency (DEA). "Drug Intelligence Brief." (October 2002): Publication DEA-02046.

Drug Enforcement Agency (DEA). "Ecstasy Statistics" (19 July 2003). Available http://theDEA.org/statistics.html.

Drug Enforcement Agency (DEA). "Maps of Methamphetamine Lab Seizures" (2005). Available www.dea.gov/concern/map_lab_seizures.html.

Drug Enforcement Agency (DEA). "Chapter 5 Stimulants" (2007). Available www.usdoj.gov/dea/pubs/abuse/5-stim.htm.

Drug Facts and Comparisons. St. Louis, MO: Walters Kluwars, 2005: 917–941, 2081.

Drug Monkey. "Slate on MDMA Clinical Trials." *Drug Monkey Biomedical Research* (February 8, 2007). Available http://drugmonkey.wordpress.com/2007/02/08/slate-on-mdma-clinical-trials/.

Drug War Facts. "Methamphetamine" (2004). Available www.drugwarfacts.org/methamph.htm.

Dunwiddie, T., and S. Masino. "The Role and Regulation of Adenosine in the Central Nervous System." *Annual Review of Neuroscience* 24 (2001): 31–55.

Ephedrine News. "Ephedra Side Effects News" (2 October 2007). Available www.ephedrine-news.com.

Fackelmann, K. "Can Caffeine Protect Against Alzheimer's?" *USA Today* (6 November 2006): 4D.

Fessenden, F., and C. Drew. "Bottom Line in Mind, Doctors Sell Ephedra." *The New York Times* (31 March 2003).

Fischman, M., and R. Foltin. "Self-Administration of Cocaine by Humans: A Laboratory Perspective." In *Cocaine:*

Scientific and Social Dimensions, edited by Ciba, 165–180. New York: Wiley, 1992.

Fischman, M., and C. Johanson. "Cocaine." In *Pharmacological Aspects of Drug Dependence: Towards an Integrated Neurobehavior Approach Handbook of Experimental Pharmacology,* edited by C. Schuster and M. Kuhar, 159–195. New York: Springer-Verlag, 1996.

Gamma, A., E. Lehman, R. Pasqual-Marqui, D. Hell, and F. Vollenweider. "Mood State and Brain Electric Activity in Ecstasy Users." *Clinical Neuroscience and Neuropsychology* 11 (January 2000): 157–162.

Gehrke, B., S. Harrod, W. Cass, and M. Bardo. "The Effect of Neurotoxic Doses of Methamphetamine on Methamphetamine-Conditioned Place Preference in Rats." *Psychopharmacology (Berlin)* 166 (2003): 249–257.

Gilbert, R. "Caffeine Consumption." In *The Methylxanthine Beverages and Foods: Chemistry, Consumption, and Health Effects,* edited by G. Spiller. New York: Liss, 1984.

Golding, A. "Two Hundred Years of Drug Abuse." *Journal of the Royal Society of Medicine* 86 (May 1993): 282–286.

Goldstein, A. *Addiction from Biology to Drug Abuse.* New York: Freeman, 1994.

Goldstein, F. "Pharmacological Aspects of Substance Abuse." In *Remington's Pharmaceutical Sciences,* 19th ed., edited by A. R. Genaro, 780–794. Easton, PA: Mack, 1995.

Goodchild, S., and A. Johnson. "Ecstasy Moves Out of the Nightclubs and into the Hands of 10-Year-Olds." *The Independent on Sunday* (11 September 2005). Available http://findarticles.com/p/articles/mi_qn4159/is_20050911/ai_n15367629.

Goodger, N., J. Wang. and M. Pogrel. "Palatal and Nasal Necrosis Resulting from Cocaine Misuse." *British Dental Journal* 198 (2005): 333–334.

Grant, K. "Methamphetamine Use in Rural Midwesterners." *American Journal of Addiction* 16 (2007): 79–84.

Green, E. "Cocaine, Glamorous Status Symbol of the 'Jet Set,' Is Fast Becoming Many Students' Drug of Choice." *Chronicle of Higher Education* 13 (November 1985): 1, 34.

Grinspoon, L. "Update on Cocaine, Parts 1 and 2." *Harvard Mental Health Letter* 10 (August-September 1993): 1–4.

Grinspoon, L., and J. Bakalar. "The Amphetamines: Medical Use and Health Hazards." In *Amphetamines: Use, Misuse and Abuse,* edited by D. Smith, 18–33. Boston: Hall, 1978.

Grob, C., R. Poland, L. Chang, and T. Ernst. "Psychobiological Effects of 3.4-Methylenedioxymethamphetamine in Humans: Methodological Considerations and Preliminary Observations." *Behavioral Brain Research* 73 (1996): 103–107.

Gugliotta, G. "Ephedra Lawsuits Show Big Increase." *The Washington Post* (23 July 2000): A-1.

Gunnarsdottir, E., R. Pingitore, B. Spring, L. Konopka, J. Crayton, T. Milo, and P. Shirazi. "Individual Differences Among Cocaine Users." *Addiction Behavior* 25 (2000): 641–652.

Gurin, J. "Coffee and Health." *Consumer Reports* (October 1994): 650–651.

Hall, K. "Peru: Peru's Coca Farmers Hoping to Boost Crops' Market." *Macon Telegraph (GA)* (23 July 2003).

Hall, W., and J. Hando. "Illicit Amphetamine Use Is a Public Health Problem in Australia." *Medical Journal of Australia* 159 (1993): 643–644.

Hanson, G. R., K. Rau, and A. Fleckenstein. "The Methamphetamine Experience: A NIDA Partnership." *Neuropharmacology* 47 (2004): 92–100.

Harris, D., and S. Batki. "Stimulant Psychosis: Symptom Profile and Acute Clinical Course." *American Journal of Addiction* 9 (2000): 28–37.

Hatsukami, D., and M. Fischman. "Crack Cocaine and Cocaine Hydrochloride." *Journal of the American Medical Association* 276 (1996): 1580–1588.

Haus, K. "Crystal Cartels Alter Face of U.S. Meth Epidemic." *MSN.com* (2007). Available www.msnbc.msn.com/id/14817871/.

Health & Medicine Week. "Admission to Treatment for Methamphetamine Abuse Rise Sharply." *Health & Medicine Week* (3 April 2006). Available http://www.newsrx.com/newsletters/Health-and-Medicine-Week/2006-04-03.html.

Heishman, S., and J. Henningfield. "Stimulus Functions of Caffeine in Humans: Relation to Dependence Potential." *Neuroscience and Behavior Review* 16 (1992): 273–287.

Hinkle, J., and S. Winckler. "Vitamin R: The Expansion of Ritalin Abuse." *PRN (Pharmacy Recovery Network)* 4 (April/June 1996): 1.

Hitti, M. "Caffeine Abuse: Buzz Gone Wrong." *WebMD* (16 October 2006). Available www.webmd.com/content/article/128/117124.

Hoffman, B., and R. Lefkowitz. "Catecholamines, Sympathomimetics Drugs, and Adrenergic Receptor Antagonists." In *The Pharmacological Basis of Therapeutics,* 9th ed., edited by J. Hardman and L. Limbird, 199–248. New York: McGraw-Hill, 1995.

Holt, L. "Former Meth Addicts Jenny Madonecky and Faye Benner Speak About Crystal Meth Addiction." *Saturday Today Show, NBC* (8 October 2005).

Jansen, K. "Ecstasy (MDMA)." *Drug and Alcohol Dependence* 53 (1999): 121–124.

Johnston, L. *University of Michigan Annual National Surveys of Secondary Students.* Lansing, MI: University of Michigan, 1996. Available from author at 412 Maynard, Ann Arbor, MI.

Johnston, L. "Monitoring the Future 2006" (2007). Available www.monitoringthefuture.org/new.html.

Join Together. "Study Says More Seeking Meth Treatment." (6 March 2006). Available www.jointogether.org/news/headlines/inthenews/2006/study-says-more-seeking-meth.html.

Kennedy, K. "Meth Mania: Even Cops Duck for Cover." *Salt Lake Tribune* (28 June 1999): B-1.

Khan, M. "Drugs Used to Enhance Studying Draw Concern." *Miami Herald* (8 July 2003).

Kihlman, B. *Caffeine and Chromosomes.* Amsterdam: Elsevier, 1977.

Kinkead, L., and Romboy, D. "Meth Emergency." *Deseret Morning News* 153 (14 November 2004): A1, A15–A17.

Kleber, H. "Treatment of Cocaine Abuse: Pharmacotherapy." In *Cocaine Scientific and Social Dimensions*, edited by Ciba, 195–206. Ciba Foundation Symposium 166. New York: Wiley, 1992.

Kloner, R., and S. Rezkalla. "Cocaine and the Heart." *New England Journal of Medicine* 348 (2003): 487–488.

Kluger, J. "The Buzz on Caffeine." *Time* (20 December 2004): 62.

Kuehn, B. "Brain Scans, Genes Provide Addiction Clues." *Journal of the American Medical Association* 297 (2007): 1419–1421.

Ladd, G., and N. Petry. "Antisocial Personality in Treatment-Seeking Cocaine Abusers: Psychosocial Functioning and HIV Risk." *Journal of Substance Abuse Treatment* 24 (2003): 323–330.

Langman, J. "Andean Entrepreneurs Are Pushing Coca Beyond Cola, in New Teas, Toothpaste, Shampoo, Liquor and More." *Newsweek* (30 October 2006). Available www.newsweek.com/id/45077.

Legal Herbal Drugs. "Aphrodisiacs, Stimulants, Hallucinogens . . ." (2007). Available www.herbalhighs.co.uk/stimulants.htm.

Leinwand, D. "Feds Score Against Homegrown Meth." *USA Today* (2 July 2007): A3.

Los Angeles Times. "Study Suggests Antidepressant May Help Treat Meth Addiction." (23 November 2005).

Lyles, J., and J. Cadet. "MDMA Neurotoxicity: Cellular and Molecular Mechanisms." *Brain Research Review* 42 (2003): 155–168.

March of Dimes. "Illicit Drug Use During Pregnancy." (July 2003). Available www.marchofdimes.com/professionals/14332_1169.asp.

Margen, S. "Caffeine: Grounds for Concern." *U.C. Berkeley Wellness Letter* 10 (March 1994): 4.

Markou, A., and P. Kenny. "Neuroadaptations to Chronic Exposure to Drugs of Abuse: Relevance to Depression Symptomology Even Across Psychiatric Diagnostic Categories." *Neurotoxicology Research* 4 (2002): 297–313.

McCaffrey, B. "Methamphetamine." *ONDCP, Drug Policy Information Clearinghouse*. NCJ-1756677 (May 1999): 1–3.

McMahon, P. "Cause Coffee's Produce a Cup with an Agenda." *USA Today* (26 July 2001): A-1.

Medical Letter. "Acute Reaction to Drugs of Abuse." (1996): 43.

MedlinePlus. "Cocaine Withdrawal." *MedlinePlus, U.S. National Library of Medicine* (2007). Available www.nlm.nih.gov/medlineplus/ency/article/000947.htm.

Mendelson, J., and N. Mello. "Management of Cocaine Abuse and Dependence." *New England Journal of Medicine* 334 (1996): 965–972.

Mihoces, G. "Ephedra: Is It Safe or Lethal." *USA Today* (8 November 2001): C1–2.

Mills, J., L. Holmes, J. Aarons, J. Simpson, Z. Brown, L. Peterson, M. Conley, B. Graubard, and R. Knopp. "Moderate Caffeine Use and the Risk of Spontaneous Abortion and Intrauterine Growth Retardation." *Journal of the American Medical Association* 269 (1993): 593–602.

Morland, J. "Toxicity of Drug Abuse — Amphetamine Designer Drugs (Ecstasy): Mental Effects and Consequences of Single Dose Use." *Toxicology Letters* 112–113 (2000): 147–152.

Musto, D. "International Traffic in Coca Through the Early 20th Century." *Drug and Alcohol Dependence* 49 (1998): 145–156.

Nash, M. "How We Get Addicted." *Time* (5 May 1997): 69–76.

Nathan, K., W. Bresnick, and S. Battei. "Cocaine Abuse and Dependence." *CNS Drugs* 10 (1998): 43–59.

National Institute on Drug Abuse (NIDA). "NIDA Info-Facts: Methamphetamine." Available www.drugabuse.gov/infofax/methamphetamine.html.

National Institute on Drug Abuse (NIDA). Diagnosis. "Diagnosis and Treatment of Drug Abuse in Family Practice" (May 2000). Available www.nida.nih.gov/Diagnosis-Treatment/Diagnosis.html.

National Institute on Drug Abuse (NIDA). Research Report. "Methamphetamine Abuse and Addiction" (22 May 2000). Available 165.112.78.61/ ResearchReports/Methamph/methamp5.html.

National Institute on Drug Abuse (NIDA). "An Individual Drug Counseling Approach to Treat Cocaine Addiction" (2007a). Available www.nida.nih.gov/TXManuals/IDCA/IDCA3.html.

National Institute on Drug Abuse (NIDA). "NIDA Info-Facts. Crack and Cocaine" (2007b). Available www.nida.nih.gov/infofacts/cocaine.html.

National Institute on Drug Abuse (NIDA). "NIDA Info-Facts: MDMA (Ecstasy)" (2007c). Available www.nida.nih.gov/infofacts/ecstasy.html.

National Institute on Drug Abuse (NIDA). Community Epidemiology Work Group (NIDA CEWG). "Proceedings of the Epidemiology Work Group on Drug Abuse" (January 2007d). Available www.drugabuse.gov/about/organization/cewg/Reports.html.

Nawrot, P., S. Jordan, J. Eastwood, J. Rotstein, A. Hugenholtz, and M. Feeley. "Effects of Caffeine on Human Health." *Food Additives and Contaminants* 20 (2003): 1–30.

Newswise. "Researchers See Trends in Synthetic Stimulant Misuse" (March 27, 2007). Available http://www.newswise.com/articles/view/528426/?sc=mwtn.

Nuckols, C., and J. Kane. "Methamphetamine Addiction: 'Speed' Still Kills." *Counselor* 4 (2003): 14–18.

Office of National Drug Control Policy (ONDCP). "Cocaine." ONDCP Drug Policy Information Clearinghouse (2003). Available www.whitehousedrugpolicy.gov/drugfact/cocaine/index.html.

Office of National Drug Control Policy. Synthetic Drug Control Strategy. "'Aftermeth': Following the Aftermath of Methamphetamine Production." (June 2006).

Office of National Drug Control Policy. Synthetic Drug Control Strategy. "A Focus on Methamphetamine and Prescription Drug Abuse." (June 2006). Available www.whitehousedrugpolicy.gov/publications/synthetic_drg_control_strat/synth_strat.pdf.

Painter, K. "Good News, Coffee Lovers." *USA Today* (6 November 2006): 4D.

Parrott, A. "Human Psychopharmacology of Ecstasy (MDMA)." *Human Psychopharmacology* 16 (2001): 557.

Parrott, A., E. Sisk, and J. Turner. "Psychobiological Problems in Heavy 'Ecstasy' (MDMA) Polydrug Users." *Drug and Alcohol Dependence* 60 (2000): 105–110.

Partnership for a Drug Free America. "What's Being Said About METH" (13 June 2007). Available www.drugfree.org/portal/drugissue/methresources/default.html.

Pennings, E., A. Leccese, and F. Wolff. "Effects of Concurrent Use of Alcohol and Cocaine." *Addiction* 97 (2002): 773–783.

Pharmacy Times. "New York County Bans Herbal Stimulants." 62 (1996): 8.

Platt, D., J. Rowlett, and R. Spealman. "Behavioral Effects of Cocaine and Dopaminergic Strategies for Preclinical Medication Development." *Psychopharmacology* 163 (2002): 265–282.

Polanczyk, G., and L. Rohde. "Epidemiology of Attention-Deficit/Hyperactivity Disorder Across the Lifespan." *Current Opinions of Psychiatry* 20 (2007): 386–392.

Prevline. "Methamphetamine." (1999). Available http://ncadistore.samhsa.gov/catalog/facts.aspx?topic=6.

Randall, T. "Ecstasy-Fueled 'Rave' Parties Become Dances of Death for English Youths." *Journal of the American Medical Association* 268 (1992a): 1505–1506.

Randall, T. "'Rave' Scene, Ecstasy Use, Leap Atlantic." *Journal of the American Medical Association* 268 (1992b): 1506.

Randolph, T. "Hazelden Study Suggests Drop in Meth Use." *Minnesota Public Radio* (19 June 2007). Available minnesota.publicradio.org/display/web/2007/06/19/methdecline/?dssource=1.

Rauscher, M. "Methamphetamine Hard on the Teeth." *Reuters Health* (October 5, 2006). Available http://www.medicineonline.com/news/12/6307/methamphetamine-hard-on-the-teeth.html.

Riddle, E., A. E. Fleckenstein, and G. R. Hanson. "Mechanisms of Methamphetamine-Induced Dopaminergic Neurotoxicity." *American Association of Pharmaceutical Scientists Journal* 9 (2006): E413–E418.

Rubin, R. "For FDA, Banning Ephedra Is Not as Easy as It Sounds." *USA Today* (3 March 2003): D-7.

Rubinsky, C. "'Cocaine' Drink Is Pulled from the Shelves." ABC News (8 May 2007). Available http://www.foxnews.com/wires/2007May08/0,4670,EnergyDrink,60.html.

Rutledge, J. "Counties Call Meth Top Drug Problem." *Washington Times* (19 July 2006).

Sawynok, J., and T. Yaksh. "Caffeine as an Analgesic Adjuvant: A Review of Pharmacology and Mechanisms of Action." *Pharmacological Reviews* 45 (1993): 43–85.

Schifano, F., L. Furia, G. Forza, N. Minicuci, and R. Bricolo. "MDMA ('Ecstasy') Consumption in the Context of Polydrug Abuse: A Report on 50 Patients." *Drug and Alcohol Dependence* 52 (1998): 85–90.

Schiller, C., and P. Allen. "Follow-up of Infants Prenatally Exposed to Cocaine." *Pediatric Nursing* 31 (2005): 427–436.

Scolaro, K. "Disorders Related to Colds and Allergy." In *Handbook of Nonprescription Drugs,* 15th ed., edited by R. Berardi. 201–228. Washington, DC: American Pharmacists Association, 2004.

Seigel, R. K. "Treatment of Cocaine Abuse." *Journal of Psychoactive Drugs* 17 (1985): 52.

Shipley, A. "Bechler's Diet Pills Draw Scrutiny." *The Washington Post* (19 February 2003): D-1.

Shute, N. "Americans Young and Old Crave High-Octane Fuel, and Doctors Are Jittery." *U.S. News and World Report* (29 April 2007): 58–68.

Singer, L., et al. "Cognitive Outcomes of Preschool Children with Prenatal Cocaine Exposure." *Journal of the American Medical Association* 291 (2004): 2448–2456.

Slamberova, R., M. Pomethlova, and R. Rokyta. "Effect of Methamphetamine Exposure During Prenatal and Preweaning Periods Lasts for Generations in Rats." *Developmental Psychobiology* 49 (2007): 312–322.

Smith, M., A. Hoeping, K. Johnson, M. Trzcinska, and A. Kozikovski. "Dopaminergic Agents for the Treatment of Cocaine Abuse." *Drug Discovery Technology* 4 (1999): 322–332.

Snider, G. "I Thought This Was My Destiny." *Partnership for a Drug-Free America.* (2006). Available www.askninanow.com/articleofthemonth1.html.

Sofuoglu, M., S. Dudish-Poulsen, S. Brown, and D. Hatsukami. "Association of Cocaine Withdrawal Symptoms with More Severe Dependence and Enhanced Subjective Response to Cocaine." *Drug and Alcohol Dependence* 69 (2003): 273–282.

Sprague, J., A. Harrod, and A. Teconchuk. "The Pharmacology and Abuse Potential of Ephedrine." *Pharmacy Times* (May 1998): 72–80.

Stocker, S. "Cocaine Activates Different Brain Regions for Rush Versus Craving." *NIDA Notes* 13 (1999): 7–10.

Substance Abuse and Mental Health Services Administration (SAMHSA). "Abuse Treatment Guidelines Released." *SAMHSA News.* 17 (Summer 1999): 17.

Swan, N. "31% of New York Murder Victims Had Cocaine in Their Bodies." *NIDA Notes* 10 (March/April 1995): 4.

Swan, N. "Response to Escalating Methamphetamine Abuse Build on NIDA-Funded Research." *NIDA Notes* 11 (November/December 1996): 1–12.

Tancer, M., and C. Johanson. "The Effects of Fluoxetine on the Subjective and Physiological Effects of 3,4-methylenedioxymethamphetamine (MDMA) in Humans." *Psychopharmacology (Berlin)* 189 (2007): 565–573.

Transitions Recovery Program. "Methamphetamine" (2007). Available www.drug-rehabcenter.com/methamphetamine.htm.

Tseng, N. "Children Fall By Wayside in Meth-Addicted Homes." *Orlando Sentinel* (11 September 2005): B1.

Twitchell, J. "Cheers? Alcohol Added to Some Energy Drinks." *Deseret News* (1 April 2007): B-1.

U.S. Department of Justice. "Children at Risk." *Information Bulletin* (July 2002). Product Number 2002-L0424-001.

U.S. Department of Justice. "Methamphetamine." *National Drug Threat Assessment* (April 2003a). Product Number 2003-Q0317-001: 13–25.

U.S. Department of Justice. "National Drug Threat Assessment 2003." *National Drug Intelligence Center* (January 2003b). Product No. 2003-Q0317-001: 51–58.

Van Dyck, C., and R. Byck. "Cocaine." *Scientific American* 246 (1982): 128–141.

Vidaeff, A., and J. Mastrobattista. "In Utero Cocaine Exposure: A Thorny Mix of Science and Mythology." *American Journal of Perinatology* 20 (2003): 165–172.

Volkow, N., L. Chang, G. Wong, J. Fowler, and D. Francesch. "Loss of Dopamine Transporters in Methamphetamine Abusers Recovers with Protracted Abstinence." *Journal of Neuroscience* 21 (2001): 9414–9418.

Wang, G., N. Volkow, P. Thanos, and J. Fowler. "Similarity Between Obesity and Drug Addiction As Assessed by Neurofunctional Imaging: A Concept Review." *Journal of Addiction Disease.* 23 (2004): 39–53.

Washington Times. "Yet Another Warning Against Ephedra." (5 February 2003): A-5.

Weiner, T. "9 Linked to Drug War Found Slain Outside Mexican Border City." *The New York Times* (3 April 2003): A-5.

Wikipedia. "Caffeine." (2007a). Available http://en.wikipedia.org/wiki/caffeine.

Wikipedia. "Speedball (Drug) (2007b). Available http://en.wikipedia.org/wiki/speedball_(drug).

Women's Health Weekly. "Bad Behavior in Kids Is Not Linked to Prenatal Cocaine Exposure" (22 May 2006). Available www.newsrx.com/newsletters/Women's-Health-Weekly12006-05-221/05222006333122ww.html.

Woolverton, W., and K. Johnston. "Neurobiology of Cocaine Abuse." *Trends in Pharmacological Sciences* 13 (1992): 193–200.

Yui, K., et al. "Methamphetamine Psychosis: Spontaneous Recurrence of Paranoid-Hallucinating States and Monoamine Neurotransmitter Function." *Journal of Clinical Psychopharmacology* 17 (1999): 34–43.

Zhang, W. "A Benefit–Risk Assessment of Caffeine as an Analgesic Adjuvant." *Drug Safety* 24 (2001): 1127–1142.

Zickler, P. "Cocaine's Effect on Blood Components May Be Linked to Heart Attack and Stroke." *NIDA Notes* 17 (2002): 5.

Zickler, P. "Methamphetamine, Cocaine Abusers Have Different Patterns of Drug Use, Suffer Different Cognitive Impairments." *NIDA Notes* 16 (December 2001): 11.

CHAPTER 11

Tobacco

Learning ◎bjectives

On completing this chapter you will be able to:

◎ Describe the social and economic costs of smoking in the United States.

◎ Describe the history of tobacco use.

◎ Explain how the quality of leaf tobacco has changed since the mid-1950s.

◎ Describe the pharmacological effects of nicotine.

◎ List several disease states caused by cigarette smoking.

◎ Explain the consequences of environmental tobacco smoke on nonsmokers.

◎ List several reasons individuals smoke.

◎ List several strategies that aid in smoking cessation.

◎ List the four primary aspects of tobacco control laws at the state level.

Did You Know?

O Approximately 29.4% of the U.S. population age 12 or older reports current use of a tobacco product.

O Tobacco use is the leading preventable cause of death in the United States.

O Tobacco kills approximately 440,000 United States citizens each year.

O Tobacco farming is among the top 10 largest legal cash crops in the United States.

O Nicotine is one of thousands of chemicals found in cigarette smoke.

O Nearly 4000 young people in the United States will begin smoking today.

O Several smoking cessation aids are available, including nicotine gum, patches, nasal spray, and inhalers. In addition, antidepressants are now used to help with smoking cessation.

Drugs and Society Online is a great source for additional drugs and society information for both students and instructors.
Visit **http://drugsandsociety.jbpub.com** to find a variety of useful tools for learning, thinking, and teaching.

Tobacco Use: Scope of the Problem

Tobacco use is the leading preventable cause of death in the United States, accounting for approximately 440,000 deaths per year (Centers for Disease Control and Prevention [CDC] 2007g). Another 8.6 million have a serious illness caused by smoking (CDC 2007g). The impact of nicotine addiction in terms of morbidity, mortality, and economic costs to society is staggering. Nationally, smoking results in more than 5 million years of potential life lost each year (CDC 2007b). Approximately 80% of adult smokers started smoking before age 18 and almost 70% of adult smokers want to quit but need help to quit permanently (CDC 2004).

In addition to these enormous health consequences, there is a significant economic burden. Tobacco use results in an annual cost of $75 billion in medical expenditures and another $92 billion from lost productivity (CDC 2007g). These high costs will likely continue and increase in the future because it is estimated that each day, nearly 4000 people younger than age 18 start smoking, and an estimated 1140 become daily smokers (CDC 2007c).

Although much of this chapter deals with tobacco use in the United States, it is noteworthy that tobacco is used throughout the world and that markets for tobacco sales abroad have expanded in recent years. "Tobacco is the second major cause of death in the world" (World Health Organization [WHO] 2007). The World Health Organization (WHO) estimates that tobacco kills 5 million people each year. By about 2020, if current smoking trends continue, that number will rise to approximately 10 million per year. It is estimated that 50% of current smokers, or approximately 650 million individuals, will eventually die from tobacco-related illnesses (WHO 2007).

■ Current Tobacco Use in the United States

In 2005, 71.5 million Americans, or 29.4% of the population age 12 or older, reported current use of a tobacco product. Among these individuals, 2.2 million smoked tobacco in pipes, 7.7 million used smokeless tobacco, 13.6 million smoked cigars, and 60.5 million smoked cigarettes (Substance Abuse and Mental Health Services Administration [SAMHSA] 2006). Approximately 35.8 percent of males and 23.4% of females age 12 or older

The WHO estimates that by 2020, tobacco will kill 10 million people per year worldwide. Early exposure increases the chance that young people will become regular adult smokers.

were current users of any tobacco product (SAMHSA 2006).

In 2005, current cigarette smoking rates peaked at 41.2% among adults ages 21–25. Noteworthy, 2.4% of 12–13-year-olds, 9.2% of 14–15-year-olds, and 20.6% of 16–17-year-olds were current smokers. Approximately 22% of persons age 35 or older were current smokers (SAMHSA 2006).

Past-month tobacco use among individuals age 12 or older by U.S. region is as follows: approximately 33% of the population in the Midwest region, 30.9% in the South region, 24.4% in the West region, and 28.4% in the Northeast region. Level of educational attainment was also correlated with tobacco usage: 34.8% of adults aged 18 or older who did not complete high school smoked cigarettes, whereas only 13.8% of college graduates smoked.

In 1999, the Substance Abuse and Mental Health Services Administration (SAMHSA) began reporting information on the use of specific cigarette brands. According to the 2005 SAMHSA survey, among past-month cigarette smokers age 12 or older, the five most commonly smoked brands were Marlboro (42.4%), Newport (11.3%), Camel (7.5%), Basic (4.2%), and Doral (3.1%) (SAMHSA 2006).

Several investigators have suggested that tobacco can serve as a **gateway drug**. In other words, its use

KEY TERMS

gateway drug
drug whose use leads to the use of other drugs; alcohol, cigarettes, and marijuana are considered gateway drugs

may lead to the use of other drugs. Although this possibility remains controversial, it is noteworthy that research indicates that cigarette smokers are more likely to use illicit drugs than are nonsmokers (SAMHSA 2006). For example, in 2005, the rate of current illicit drug use was approximately eight times greater among youths ages 12–17 who smoked cigarettes in the past month (46.7%) than it was among youth who did not smoke cigarettes in the past month (5.5%). Among individuals age 12 or older, 20.2% of past-month cigarette smokers reported current use of an illicit drug compared with 4.1% of persons who were not current cigarette smokers. Past-month alcohol use was reported by 67.6% of current cigarette smokers compared with 46.6% of those who did not use cigarettes in the past month. The association also was found with binge drinking (43.8% of current cigarette users vs. 15.7% of current nonusers) and heavy drinking (16.1% vs. 3.5%, respectively).

■ The History of Tobacco Use

Like alcohol, tobacco has a long history of use in the Americas and is indigenous to the United States. In fact, tobacco was one of the New World's contributions to the rest of humanity. The word *tobacco* may have come from *tabaco,* which was a two-pronged tube used by the natives of Central America to take snuff. Columbus reported receiving tobacco leaves from the natives of San Salvador in 1492. However, the native peoples had been smoking the leaves for many centuries before Columbus arrived. Practically all native people, from Paraguay to Quebec, used tobacco. The Mayans regarded tobacco smoke as divine incense that would bring rain in the dry season. The oldest known representation of a smoker is a stone carving from a Mayan temple, which shows a priest puffing on a ceremonial pipe. The Aztecs used tobacco in folk medicine and religious ritual.

Indeed, Native Americans used tobacco in every manner known — smoked as cigars and cigarettes (wrapped in corn husks) and in pipes; as a syrup to be swallowed or applied to the gums; chewed and snuffed; and administered rectally as a ceremonial enema (O'Brien et al. 1992; Schultes 1978).

In the 1600s, Turkey, Russia, and China all imposed death penalties for smoking. In Turkey, smoking was introduced in the 1600s, spread in popularity, and instantly created two camps. On the one hand, poets praised tobacco as one of four elements of the world of pleasure which also included opium, coffee, and wine. On the other hand, priests were violently opposed to this substance. They created the legend that tobacco grew from Mohammed's spittle after he was bitten by a viper, sucked out the venom, and spat.

Murad (Amurath) IV, known as Murad the Cruel, who reigned during 1623–1640, executed many of his subjects caught smoking.

> Whenever the Sultan went on his travels or on a military expedition, his halting-laces were always distinguished by a terrible increase in the number of executions. Even on the battlefield, he was fond of surprising men in the act of smoking, . . . he would punish them by beheading, hanging, quartering, or crushing their hands and feet and leaving them helpless between the lines. . . . Nevertheless, in spite of all the horrors of this lust [smoking] that seemed to increase with age, the passion for smoking still persisted. . . . Even the fear of death was of no avail with the passionate devotees of the habit. (Corti 1931)

The Romanov tsars publicly tortured smokers and exiled them to Siberia. The Chinese decapitated anyone caught dealing in tobacco with the "outer barbarians." Yet smoking continued to grow to epidemic proportions. Despite their opposition to anything foreign, the Chinese became the heaviest smokers in Asia, thus facilitating the later spread of opium smoking. Thus, no nation whose population has learned to use tobacco products has been successful in outlawing use or getting people to stop.

Snuffing first became fashionable in France during the reign of Louis XIII and spread throughout the European aristocracy. Snuffing was regarded as daintier and more elegant than constantly exhaling smoke. King Louis XIV, however, detested all forms of tobacco and would not permit its use in his presence. (He would have banned it, but he needed the tax revenue that tobacco brought in.) His sister-in-law, Charlotte of Orleans, was one of the few at court who agreed with him. As she wrote to her sister, "It is better to take no snuff at all than a little; for it is certain that he who takes a little will soon take much, and that is why they call it 'the enchanted herb,' for those who take it are so taken by it that they cannot go without it." Napoleon is said to have used seven pounds of snuff per month (Corti 1931).

■ Popularity in the Western World

When tobacco reached Europe, it was at first merely a curiosity, but its use spread rapidly. Europeans had no name for the process of inhaling smoke, so they called this "drinking" smoke. Perhaps the first European to inhale tobacco smoke was Rodrig de Jerez, a member of Columbus's crew. He had seen people smoking in Cuba and brought the habit to Portugal. When he smoked in Portugal, his friends, seeing smoke coming from his mouth, believed he was possessed by the devil. As a result, he was placed in jail for several years (Heimann 1960; O'Brien et al. 1992).

In 1559, the French ambassador to Portugal, Jean Nicot, grew interested in this novel plant and sent one as a gift to Catherine de Medici, Queen of France. The plant was named *Nicotiana tabacum* after him.

The next several hundred years saw a remarkable increase in the use of tobacco. Portuguese sailors smoked it and left tobacco seeds scattered around the world. Over the next 150 years, the Portuguese introduced tobacco to trade with India, Brazil, Japan, China, Arabia, and Africa. Many large tobacco plantations around the world were started by the Portuguese at this time.

An early Christian religious leader, Bishop Bartolome de las Casas (1474–1566), reported that Spanish settlers in Hispaniola (Haiti) smoked rolled tobacco leaves in cigar form like the natives. When the bishop asked about this disgusting habit, the settlers replied that they found it impossible to give up.

As the use of tobacco spread, so did the controversy about whether it was bad or good. Tobacco use inspired the first major drug controversy of global dimensions. As a medicine, tobacco was at first almost universally accepted. Nicholas Monardes, in his description of New World plants (dated 1574), recommended tobacco as an infallible cure for 36 different maladies. It was described as a holy, healing herb — a special remedy sent by God to humans.

Opponents of tobacco use disputed its medical value. They pointed out that tobacco was used in the magic and religion of Native Americans. Tobacco was attacked as an evil plant, an invention of the devil. King James I of England was fanatically opposed to smoking. In an attempt to limit tobacco use, he raised the import tax on tobacco and also sold the right to collect the tax (Austin 1978; O'Brien et al. 1992).

Nevertheless, tobacco use increased. By 1614, the number of tobacco shops in London had mushroomed to more than 7000, and demand for tobacco usually outstripped supply. Tobacco was literally worth its weight in silver; to conserve it, users smoked it in pipes with very small bowls. Use of tobacco grew in other areas of the world as well.

In 1642, Pope Urban VIII issued a formal decree forbidding the use of tobacco in church under penalty of immediate excommunication. This decree was in response to the fact that priests and worshippers had been staining church floors with tobacco juice. One priest in Naples sneezed so hard after taking snuff that he vomited on the altar in full sight of the congregation. In response, Pope Innocent X issued another edict against tobacco use in 1650, but the clergy and the laity continued to take snuff and smoke. Finally, in 1725, Pope Benedict XIII, himself a smoker and "snuff-taker," annulled all previous edicts against tobacco (Austin 1978).

■ History of Tobacco Use in America

Tobacco played a significant role in the successful colonization of the United States (Langton 1991). In 1610, John Rolfe was sent to Virginia to set up a tobacco industry. At first, the tobacco planted in Virginia was a native species, *Nicotiana rustica*, that was harsh and did not sell well. But in 1612, Rolfe managed to obtain some seeds of the Spanish tobacco species *Nicotiana tabacum*, and by 1613, the success of the tobacco industry and the Virginia colony was ensured.

The history of tobacco smoking in the United States is rich in terms of the tremendous number of laws, rules, regulations, and customs that have arisen around the habit of smoking. Many states have had laws prohibiting the use of tobacco by young people as well as women of any age. In the 1860s, for instance, it was illegal in Florida for anyone younger than the age of 21 to smoke cigarettes. A 20-year-old caught smoking could be taken to court and compelled to reveal his source (the cigarette "pusher"). In Pennsylvania, as in South Carolina, any child not informing on his or her cigarette supplier was a criminal.

Up to the turn of the 20th century, chewing and snuffing were the most common ways of using tobacco in the United States. In 1897, half of all tobacco was prepared for chewing. Law required that spittoons be placed in all public buildings until 1945 (Encyclopedia Americana 1988).

Cigars became popular in the United States in the early 1800s. Cigar manufacturers fought the introduction of cigarettes for many years. They spread rumors that cigarettes contained opium, were made with tobacco from discarded cigar butts, were made with paper made by Chinese lepers, and so on. By about 1920, cigarette consumption started to exceed that of cigars. The introduction of the cigarette-rolling machine in 1883 spurred cigarette consumption because cigarettes became cheaper than cigars. By 1885, 1 billion cigarettes per year were being produced. Americans produced more than 709.7 billion cigarettes in 1990 (CDC 2007a). More recent estimates show that the number of cigarettes manufactured in the United States has fallen to 492.8 billion pieces in 2004 (CDC 2007a).

Tobacco Production

Tobacco is one of the top 10 cash crops in the United States (U.S. Department of Agriculture [USDA] 2007). The United States is fourth behind China, Brazil, and India in world production (USDA 2007). Although there are more than 60 species of plants, *Nicotiana tabacum* is the primary species of tobacco cultivated in the United States. Its mature leaves are 1 to 2.5 feet long. The nicotine content ranges from 0.3% to 7%, depending on the variety, leaf position on the stalk (the higher the position, the more nicotine), and growing conditions. The flavor of tobacco comes from nicotianin, also called *tobacco camphor.*

After harvesting and drying, tobacco leaves are shredded, blown clean of foreign matter and stems, remoisturized with glycerine or other chemical agents, and packed in huge wooden barrels called

Use of spittoons (on floor at ends of table) was considered a preferment in public conduct.

hogsheads. These barrels are placed in storehouses for 1 to 2 years to age, during which time the tobacco becomes darker and loses moisture, nicotine, and other volatile substances. When aging has been completed, moisture is again added and the tobacco is blended with other varieties.

There are many types of tobacco, with varying characteristics of harshness, mildness, and flavor. Bright, also called flue-cured or Virginia, has traditionally been among the most common type used in cigarettes. (Flue-cured tobacco is heated in curing sheds to speed the drying process.) Developed just before the Civil War, this technique made tobacco smoke more readily inhalable.

The amount of leaf tobacco in a cigarette has declined by roughly 25% since 1956. There are at least two reasons for this drop. The first reason is the use of reconstituted sheets of tobacco. Parts of the tobacco leaves and stems that were discarded in earlier years are now ground up, combined with many other ingredients to control factors such as moisture, flavor, and color, and then rolled out as a flat, homogenized sheet of reconstituted tobacco. This sheet is shredded and mixed with regular leaf tobacco, thus reducing production costs. Nearly one-fourth of the tobacco in a cigarette comes from tobacco scraps made into reconstituted sheets.

A second technological advance has further reduced the amount of tobacco needed. This process, called puffing, is based on freeze-drying the tobacco and then blowing air or an inert gas, such as carbon dioxide, into it. The gas expands, or puffs up, the plant cells so they take up more space, are lighter, and can absorb additives better.

Tobacco additives are not controlled by the Food and Drug Administration (FDA) or any other government agency. Additives may include extracts of tobacco, as well as nontobacco flavors such as licorice, cocoa, fruit, spices, and floral compositions. (Licorice was first used in tobacco as a preservative around 1830 and became appreciated only later as a sweetener.) Synthetic flavoring compounds also may be used.

In the 1870s, a "cigarette girl" could roll about four cigarettes per minute by hand. When James Duke leased and improved the first cigarette-rolling machine in 1883, he could make about 200 cigarettes per minute. This advance was the last link in the chain of development leading to the modern American blended cigarette. Today's machines make more than 3600 uniform cigarettes per minute.

Tar and nicotine levels in cigarettes have dropped considerably over the past 40 years (Bartecchi et al.

Here and Now

What Is in Tobacco Smoke?

Tobacco smoke contains chemicals that are harmful to both smokers and nonsmokers. At least 250 of the 4000 chemicals in tobacco smoke are known to be harmful. These chemicals include carbon monoxide (found in car exhaust), hydrogen cyanide (used in chemical weapons), ammonia (used in household cleaners), formaldehyde (used as an embalming fluid), and toluene (found in paint thinners).

More than 50 of the 250 known harmful chemicals in tobacco smoke have been found to cause cancer. These include nickel (a metallic element), benzene (a chemical found in gasoline), cadmium (a metal used in batteries), ethylene oxide (a chemical used to sterilize medical devices), polonium-210 (a chemical element that gives off radiation), arsenic (a heavy metal toxin), and vinyl chloride (a toxic substance used in plastics manufacture).

Source: NCI 2007. Available http://www.cancer.gov/cancertopics/factsheet/Tobacco/cessation#q4.

1995; Palfai and Jankiewicz 1991). Most cigarettes today are low-tar and low-nicotine types. The filter tip, in which the filter is made of cellulose or in some cases charcoal, has also become common; the vast majority of all cigarettes sold currently in the United States have filter tips. The filter does help remove some of the harmful substances in smoke, but most, such as carbon monoxide, pass through into the mouth and lungs. More than 50 cancer-causing substances have been identified out of the 4000 substances found in cigarette smoke (National

Cancer Institute [NCI] 2007). The health consequences of many more substances found in cigarettes have not been adequately analyzed.

In 2004, domestic cigarette consumption was 388 billion pieces, 12 billion less than the previous year (CDC 2007a). Declines in sales have been attributed to health concerns, aggressive antismoking campaigns, price increases, and decreased social acceptance of smoking. Figure 11.1 shows the relationship between smoking rates and major smoking and health events.

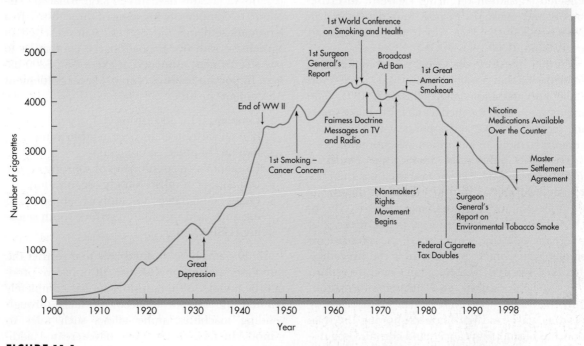

FIGURE 11.1

Annual adult per capita cigarette consumption and major smoking and health events, United States, 1900–1998.

Sources: United States Department of Agriculture; 1986 Surgeon General's Report.

Government Regulation

In the early 1960s, attitudes toward tobacco use began to change in the United States. Before this time, tobacco was perceived as being devoid of any negative consequences. After years of study and hundreds of research reports about the effects of smoking, the Advisory Committee to the U.S. Surgeon General reported in 1964 that cigarette smoking is a cause of lung cancer and laryngeal cancer in men, a probable cause of lung cancer in women, and the most important cause of chronic bronchitis. The committee stated that "cigarette smoking is a health hazard of sufficient importance in the United States to warrant appropriate remedial action." In 1965, Congress passed legislation setting up the National Clearinghouse for Smoking and Health. This organization has the responsibility of monitoring, compiling, and reviewing the world's medical literature on the health consequences of smoking.

Reports were published by this clearinghouse in 1967, 1968, and 1969. The statistical evidence presented in 1969 made it difficult for Congress to avoid warning the public that smoking was dangerous to their health. Since November 1, 1970, all cigarette packages and cartons have had to carry this label: "Warning: The Surgeon General Has Determined That Cigarette Smoking Is Dangerous to Your Health." In 1984, Congress enacted legislation requiring cigarette advertisements and packages to post four distinct warnings (see Figure 11.2), which are to be rotated every 3 months.

Further pressure on Congress prompted laws to be passed that prohibited advertising tobacco on radio and television after January 2, 1971. The intent was to limit the media's ability to make smoking seem glamorous and sophisticated. The loss in revenue to radio and television was enormous.

The 1979 publication *Smoking and Health: A Report of the Surgeon General* gave what was then up-to-date information on research about the effects of tobacco on cardiovascular disease, bronchopulmonary disease, cancer, peptic ulcer, and pregnancy. It also emphasized the increase in smoking by women and girls over the preceding 15 years. The 1981 U.S. Surgeon General's report, *The Changing Cigarette*, gave further information, and the 1985 report, *The Health Consequences of Smoking*, gave research findings showing the relationship of smoking, cancer, and chronic lung disease in the workplace.

Over the years, private insurance companies, as well as state and federal agencies, have paid bil-

SURGEON GENERAL'S WARNING: Quitting Smoking Now Greatly Reduces Serious Risks to Your Health.

SURGEON GENERAL'S WARNING: Smoking Causes Lung Cancer, Heart Disease, Emphysema, and May Complicate Pregnancy.

SURGEON GENERAL'S WARNING: Smoking by Pregnant Women May Result in Fetal Injury, Premature Birth, and Low Birth Weight.

SURGEON GENERAL'S WARNING: Cigarette Smoke Contains Carbon Monoxide.

FIGURE 11.2

Warnings on cigarette labels. Four warnings must be rotated on cigarette packages. The messages are based on the report of the U.S. Surgeon General, *The Health Consequences of Smoking* (1985), and went into effect on October 12, 1985.

lions of dollars to cover healthcare costs presumably resulting from diseases caused by tobacco use. A series of lawsuits have forced large tobacco companies to compensate for some of these losses. In a landmark settlement in 1998, 47 states reached an agreement with five major tobacco companies to pay a settlement estimated at exceeding $200 billion. Important features of this "Master Settlement Agreement" include:

1. Limitations on advertising
2. Ban on cartoon characters in advertising
3. Ban on "branded" merchandise
4. Limitations on sponsorship of sporting events
5. Disbanding of tobacco trade organizations
6. Funds designated to support antismoking measures and research to reduce youth smoking (USDA 2001)

All 50 states have enacted laws that restrict the purchase, possession, or use of tobacco products by minors. Although no state has completely banned the sale of tobacco products through vending machines, none allows such sales to minors. In fact, many states have created additional restrictions intended to reduce youth access to vending machines. Some have banned the placement of vending machines in areas accessible to young people and allow their placement only in bars, liquor stores, adult clubs, and other adult-oriented establishments.

All states tax cigarettes. In 2007, the federal excise tax was 39 cents per pack of cigarettes. The median state excise tax was 80 cents (CDC 2007d). Smokeless tobacco products are taxed in 42 states.

Since 1985, numerous other reports on smoking and health by the U.S. Surgeon General have been issued; they invariably repeat the assertions about the devastating effects of cigarette smoking. For a historical summation of the developments between cigarette consumption and efforts to diminish cigarette use, see Figure 11.1. A summary of federal policy and legislation regarding the regulation of tobacco sales, marketing, and use is provided in Table 11.1.

Pharmacology of Nicotine

Nicotine Administration

In 1828, **nicotine** was discovered to be one component of tobacco. This colorless, highly volatile liquid alkaloid is one of more than 4000 chemicals found in the smoke from tobacco products such as cigarettes (NCI 2007). When smoked, nicotine enters the lungs and is then absorbed into the bloodstream. When chewed (**tobacco chewing**) or dipped (**snuff dipping**), nicotine is absorbed through the mucous lining of the mouth.

The amount of nicotine absorbed into the body varies according to several factors:

1. The exact composition of the tobacco used
2. How densely the tobacco is packed in the cigarette and the length of the cigarette smoked
3. Whether a filter is used and the characteristics of the filter
4. The volume of smoke inhaled
5. The number of cigarettes smoked throughout the day

KEY TERMS

nicotine
a colorless, highly volatile liquid alkaloid

tobacco chewing
the absorption of nicotine through the mucous lining of the mouth

snuff dipping
placing a pinch of tobacco between the gums and the cheek

Depending on how tobacco is taken, the rate at which it enters the bloodstream varies widely. Cigarette smoking results in rapid distribution of nicotine throughout the body; it reaches the brain within 10 seconds of inhalation. A typical smoker will take 10 puffs on a cigarette during the 5 minutes that the cigarette is lit (NIDA 2006b). Thus, a person who smokes two packs (40 cigarettes) each day gets 400 "hits" of nicotine to the brain each day. In contrast, cigar and pipe smokers typically do not inhale the smoke; nicotine is absorbed more slowly through the lining of the mouth.

Effects on the Central Nervous System

Nicotine produces an intense effect on the central nervous system. Research has demonstrated that nicotine activates the brain circuitry in regions responsible for regulating feelings of pleasure. In particular, nicotine increases the release of the neurotransmitter dopamine in the so-called reward or pleasure pathways of the brain. This effect likely contributes to the abuse potential of the stimulant.

The pharmacokinetic properties of nicotine also enhance its abuse potential. Cigarette smoking allows nicotine to enter the brain rapidly, with drug levels peaking within 10 seconds of inhalation. The acute effects of this rapid increase in brain concentration dissipate within a few minutes, causing the smoker to continue to dose frequently throughout the day in an effort to maintain the pleasurable effects of the drug.

Other Effects of Nicotine

In addition to its direct effects in the brain, nicotine increases the respiration rate at low dose levels because it stimulates the receptors in the carotid artery (in the neck) that monitor the brain's need for oxygen. It also stimulates the cardiovascular system by releasing epinephrine, which increases coronary blood flow, heart rate, and blood pressure. The effect is to raise the oxygen requirements of the heart muscle. Initially, nicotine stimulates salivary and bronchial secretions; it then inhibits them. The excess saliva associated with smoking is typically caused by the irritating smoke, not the nicotine itself.

Nicotine and perhaps other substances in tobacco smoke tend to inhibit hunger contractions

TABLE 11.1   Federal Policy and Legislation: Selected Actions of the U.S. Government Regarding the Regulation of Tobacco Sales, Marketing, and Use (Excluding Laws Pertaining to Agriculture or Excise Tax)

1967	Federal Communications Commission rules that the Fairness Doctrine (an attempt to ensure that all coverage of controversial issues by a broadcast station be balanced and fair) applies to cigarette advertising. Stations broadcasting cigarette commercials must donate air time to antismoking messages.
1971	Fairness Doctrine antismoking messages end when cigarette advertising is prohibited on radio and television.
1973	Civil Aeronautics Board requires no-smoking sections on all commercial airline flights.
1975	Cigarettes are discontinued in K-rations and C-rations given to soldiers and sailors.
1987	Department of Health and Human Services establishes a smoke-free environment in its facilities.
1992	Federal Trade Commission takes first enforcement action under the Comprehensive Smokeless Tobacco Health Education Act, alleging that Pinkerton Tobacco Company's Red Man brand name appeared illegally during a televised event.
1993	Environmental Protection Agency releases final risk assessment on environmental tobacco smoke (ETS) and classifies ETS as a Group A (known human) carcinogen.
1994	Occupational Safety and Health Administration announces proposed regulation to prohibit smoking in the workplace, except in separately ventilated smoking rooms.
1994	Department of Defense (DOD) bans smoking in DOD workplaces.
1995	Department of Justice reaches a settlement with Philip Morris to remove tobacco advertisements from the line of sight of television cameras in sports stadiums.
	President Clinton announces the publication of the Food and Drug Administration's proposed regulations that would restrict the sale, distribution, and marketing of cigarettes and smokeless tobacco products to protect children and adolescents.
1996	On August 23, 1996, President Clinton announces the nation's first comprehensive program to prevent children and adolescents from smoking cigarettes or using smokeless tobacco and beginning a lifetime of nicotine addiction. With the August 1996 publication of a final rule on tobacco in the *Federal Register*, the Food and Drug Administration (FDA) will regulate the sale and distribution of cigarettes and smokeless tobacco to children and adolescents. The provisions of the FDA rule are aimed at reducing youth access to tobacco products and the appeal of tobacco advertising to young people. Additionally, the FDA will propose to require the major tobacco companies to educate young people about the real health dangers associated with tobacco use through a multimedia campaign.
1997	President Clinton announces an Executive Order to make all federal workplaces smoke free.
2000	The Supreme Court rules against the Food and Drug Administration, finding that the agency lacks the authority to regulate tobacco.

Source: CDC. Federal Policy and Legislation. Available http://www.cdc.gov/tobacco/data_statistics/by_topic/policy/regulation.htm.

Signs & Symptoms Tobacco

POSSIBLE SIGNS OF USE:
Smell of cigarette smoke
Increased use of breath freshener or gum to mask cigarette odor
Stained teeth and clothing (can also be signs of chewing tobacco use)
Bad breath
Coughing
Throat irritation
Hoarseness
Decreased athletic performance
Greater susceptibility to colds
Shortness of breath

in the stomach for as long as 1 hour. At the same time, this substance causes a slight increase in blood sugar and deadens the taste buds. These factors may explain the decreased feelings of hunger experienced by many smokers. Smokers have often reported that they gain weight after they stop smoking and that their appetite increases. In addition, when someone who smokes one or more packs per day quits, there may be a decrease in heart rate (two to three beats per minute) and as much as a 10% decrease in basal metabolic rate. The body is under less stress; therefore, it converts more food into fat.

Nicotine has been used as an insecticide, and at higher concentrations it can be extremely toxic. Symptoms of nicotine poisoning include sweating, vomiting, mental confusion, diarrhea, and breathing difficulty. Respiratory failure from the paralysis of muscles usually brings on death. The fatal dose for adults is 60 milligrams. Most cigarettes in the U.S. market today contain 10 milligrams or more of nicotine; through smoke, the average smoker takes in 1 to 2 milligrams of nicotine from every cigarette (NIDA 2006b). It is virtually impossible to overdose, in part because a smoker feels the effects before any lethal amount can accumulate in the body (Schelling 1992).

Nicotine and other products in smoke, such as carbon monoxide, produce several other effects. As much as 10% of all the hemoglobin in smokers may be in the form of carboxyhemoglobin. This type of hemoglobin cannot carry oxygen, so as much as 10% of the smoker's blood is effectively out of circulation as far as normal oxygen–carbon dioxide exchange is concerned. This situation could easily cause a smoker to become breathless following exertion. It is a factor in heart attacks and in the lower birthweights and survival rates of infants born to women who smoke during pregnancy (discussed later in this chapter).

Cigarette Smoking: A Costly Addiction

Mortality Rates

The past 25 years have been marked by a steady decline in cigarette consumption. Still, an estimated 60.5 million Americans age 12 or older smoke cigarettes (SAMHSA 2006), even though this single behavior will result in death or disability for many of its users.

As noted earlier, tobacco use is responsible for approximately 440,000 deaths each year in the United States. This includes approximately 86,800 deaths from heart disease, 123,800 deaths from lung cancer, 34,700 deaths from other forms of cancer, 90,600 deaths from chronic lung disease, 17,400 deaths from stroke, and approximately

Here and Now

Bidis and Kreteks

Bidis are small, thin, hand-rolled cigarettes consisting of tobacco wrapped in a tendu or temburni leaf. They can be flavored (e.g., cherry, chocolate, mango) or unflavored. They are imported into the United States primarily from India and other Southeast Asian countries. Bidis have higher concentrations of tar, nicotine, and carbon monoxide than conventional cigarettes sold in the United States.

Kreteks are sometimes referred to as clove cigarettes, and have historically been imported from Indonesia. They typically contain a mixture consisting of cloves, tobacco, and other additives. As with bidis, machine-smoking analyses indicate that kreteks deliver more tar, nicotine, and carbon monoxide than conventional cigarettes. There is no evidence to indicate that bidis or kreteks are safe alternatives to conventional cigarettes. In fact, although research studies on the health effects of bidis have not been conducted in the United States, studies conducted abroad indicate that bidi smoking is associated with an increased risk of a variety of cancers including oral and lung cancers. Similarly, research in Indonesia indicates that regular kretek smokers have a greater risk for abnormal lung function compared with nonsmokers.

There are no national estimates for bidi or kretek smoking among adults in the United States. However, an estimated 3% of high school and 2% of middle school students are current bidi smokers. Similar percentages smoke kreteks.

Source: Adapted CDC. Fact Sheet. Bidis and Kreteks (2007). http://www.cdc.gov/tobacco/data_statistics/Factsheets/bidis_kreteks.htm, and references cited therein.

84,600 deaths from other diagnoses (see Figure 11.3). In fact, tobacco use is the leading preventable cause of death in the United States (CDC 2007g). More deaths are caused each year by tobacco use than by HIV, illegal drug use, murders, alcohol use, suicides, and motor vehicle injuries combined (CDC 2007e).

FIGURE 11.3

Annual deaths attributable to cigarette smoking, 1997–2001.

Source: CDC, Targeting Tobacco Use, 2007g.

Overall mortality rates decline the longer ex-smokers abstain from smoking. The mortality rate for ex-smokers is related to the number of cigarettes they used to smoke per day and the age at which they started to smoke. People who stop smoking at approximately age 30 reduce their risk of dying from smoking-related diseases by more than 90%. Those who quit at approximately age 50 reduce their risk of dying prematurely by 50% (NCI 2007). Other benefits of quitting smoking are illustrated in Figure 11.4

■ Chronic Illnesses

Cigarette smokers not only tend to die at an earlier age than nonsmokers, but also have a higher probability of developing certain diseases, including cardiovascular disease, cancer, and bronchopulmonary disease.

Cardiovascular Disease

Overwhelming evidence shows that cigarette smoking increases the risk of cardiovascular disease. In fact, over the last 40 years, cigarette smoking has caused an estimated 5.5 million deaths from cardiovascular diseases (CDC 2007g). Data collected for the United States, the United Kingdom, Canada,

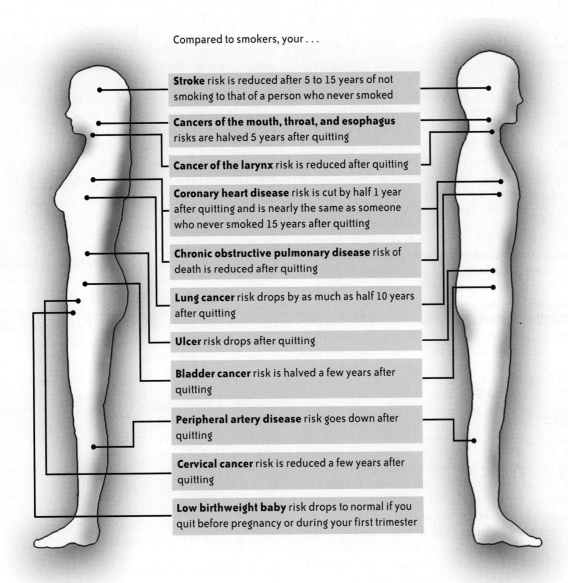

Compared to smokers, your . . .

Stroke risk is reduced after 5 to 15 years of not smoking to that of a person who never smoked

Cancers of the mouth, throat, and esophagus risks are halved 5 years after quitting

Cancer of the larynx risk is reduced after quitting

Coronary heart disease risk is cut by half 1 year after quitting and is nearly the same as someone who never smoked 15 years after quitting

Chronic obstructive pulmonary disease risk of death is reduced after quitting

Lung cancer risk drops by as much as half 10 years after quitting

Ulcer risk drops after quitting

Bladder cancer risk is halved a few years after quitting

Peripheral artery disease risk goes down after quitting

Cervical cancer risk is reduced a few years after quitting

Low birthweight baby risk drops to normal if you quit before pregnancy or during your first trimester

FIGURE 11.4
The Benefits of Quitting
After quitting smoking, a series of changes that continue for years affect the body.

Source: Centers for Disease Control and Prevention.

and other countries show that smoking is a major risk factor for heart attack. The probability of heart attack is related to the amount smoked, which has a synergistic relationship to other risk factors, such as obesity.

Smoking cigarettes is a major risk factor for arteriosclerotic disease and for death from arteriosclerotic aneurysm of the aorta (Palfai and Jankiewicz 1991). (An *aneurysm* is a weakened area in a blood vessel that forms a blood-filled sac and may rupture.) Smokers have a higher incidence of atherosclerosis of the coronary arteries that supply blood to the heart (the arteries become blocked with fat deposits), and the effect is dose related. Both the carbon monoxide and the nicotine in cigarette smoke can precipitate *angina attacks* (painful spasms in the chest when the heart muscle does not get the blood supply it needs). Women who smoke and use oral contraceptives have a significantly higher risk of death or disability from stroke, heart attack, and other cardiovascular diseases than nonsmokers.

Quitting smoking reduces the risk of cardiovascular disease. Immediate benefits can include decreases in heart rate and blood pressure. Improvements in circulation can occur weeks after cessation.

Cancer

Cigarette smoking is a major cause of cancers of the lung, bladder, pancreas, cervix, and kidney. The risk of cancer increases according to the number of cigarettes smoked each day, the number of years a person has smoked, and the age at which smoking began. For example, the risk of lung cancer in men who smoke two or more packs per day is twenty-two times greater than the risk for nonsmokers, while the risk for women is approximately twelve times greater (CDC 2007b).

There is no conclusive evidence of reduced health risks associated with low-tar cigarettes. Filtered cigarettes (i.e., those with small holes or perforations that dilute the smoke with air) reduce levels of tar, nicotine, and carbon monoxide at the mouth end of the filter and should be of some limited benefit. However, many smokers lose this benefit because they often smoke more cigarettes per day, increase puff number and volume, or block the filter holes with their fingers or lips (NCI 2004b). (See also "Here and Now," The Truth About Light Cigarettes.)

Pipe and cigar smokers are more likely to contract lung cancer than nonsmokers but less likely to do so than habitual cigarette smokers. Common types of cancers among cigar and pipe smokers include cancers of the mouth, larynx, and esophagus. The risk of cancer of the larynx is significantly higher in smokers compared with nonsmokers and is related to the amount smoked. A compounding effect has also been shown to exist between smoking and alcohol consumption and between exposure to asbestos and smoking, which increases a person's likelihood of developing cancer of the larynx. The risk of laryngeal cancer goes down if the person stops smoking; as with lung cancer, however, this form of cancer does not reach the level for nonsmokers until years following cessation.

Bronchopulmonary Disease

Cigarette smoking is the leading cause of bronchopulmonary disease, which includes a host of lung ailments. Cigarette smokers have higher death rates from pulmonary emphysema and chronic bronchitis and have impaired pulmonary function and other symptoms of pulmonary disease more frequently than nonsmokers.

Respiratory infections are more prevalent and more severe among cigarette smokers — particularly heavy smokers — than among nonsmokers. The risk of developing or dying from bronchopulmonary disease is higher among pipe or cigar smokers than nonsmokers but lower than for cigarette smokers. Ex-smokers have lower death rates from bronchopulmonary disease than do continuing smokers.

Cigarette smoking is the leading cause of bronchopulmonary disease.

Here and Now

The Truth About Light Cigarettes

Many smokers choose low-tar, mild, or light cigarettes because they believe that these cigarettes may be less harmful to their health than regular or full-flavor cigarettes. Unfortunately, light cigarettes do not reduce the health risks of smoking. The only way to reduce risk to oneself and others is to stop smoking completely.

Common questions and answers pertaining to low-tar, mild, or light cigarettes follow:

Q: What about the lower tar and nicotine numbers on light cigarette packs and in ads for lights?

A: These numbers are determined using smoking machines that smoke every brand of cigarettes exactly the same way. These numbers cannot absolutely predict the amount of tar and nicotine a particular smoker may get because people do not smoke cigarettes the same way the machines do, and because no two individuals smoke the same way.

Q: How do light cigarettes trick the smoking machines?

A: Tobacco companies design light cigarettes with tiny pinholes on the filters. These vents are uncovered when cigarettes are smoked on smoking machines. As a result, these vents dilute cigarette smoke with air when light cigarettes are puffed on by the machines, causing measurements of artificially low tar and nicotine levels. Many smokers do not know that vent holes are on their cigarette filters. Without realizing it and because it is difficult to avoid, many block the tiny vent holes with their fingers or lips — which basically turns the light cigarette into a regular cigarette. Some cigarette makers increased the length of the paper covering the cigarette filter, which decreases the number of puffs that occur during the machine test. The result is that the machine measures less tar and nicotine levels than is available to the smoker.

Because unlike machines, individuals crave nicotine, they may inhale more deeply; take larger, more rapid, or more frequent puffs; or smoke a few extra cigarettes each day to get enough nicotine to satisfy their craving. This is called compensating, and it results in smokers inhaling more tar, nicotine, and other harmful chemicals than the machine-based numbers suggest.

Q: What is the scientific evidence about the health effects of light cigarettes?

A: The National Cancer Institute (NCI) has concluded that light cigarettes provide no benefit to smokers' health. According to its report, those people who switch to light cigarettes from regular cigarettes are likely to inhale the same amount of hazardous chemicals and remain at high risk for developing smoking-related cancers and other diseases.

Q: Have the tobacco companies conducted research on the amount of nicotine and tar people actually inhale while smoking light cigarettes?

A: The tobacco industry's own documents show that companies were aware that smokers of light cigarettes compensate by taking bigger puffs. Industry documents also show that the companies were aware of the difference between machine-measured yields of tar and nicotine and the amount the smoker actually inhales.

Q: What is the bottom line for smokers who want to protect their health?

A: There is no such thing as a safe cigarette. The only proven way to reduce your risk of smoking-related disease is to quit smoking completely. Research has shown that people who quit before age 30 eliminate almost all of their risk of developing a tobacco-related disease. Even smokers who quit at age 50 reduce their risk of dying from a tobacco-related disease.

Source: NCI 2004. Available www.cancer.gov/cancertopics/factsheet/Tobacco/light-cigarettes

■ Effects Without Smoking

The harmful effects of tobacco are not restricted to smokers. For example, women who use tobacco during pregnancy are more likely to have adverse birth outcomes, including babies with low birth-weights, which is linked with an increased risk of infant death and with a variety of infant health disorders. Individuals who chew or dip tobacco run the risk of adverse consequences as well. Finally, the health of individuals who neither smoke nor

Heavy smoking can severely damage the lungs and cause emphysema. Left, a diseased lung due to smoking. Right, a healthy nonsmoker's lung.

chew is also adversely affected by tobacco — specifically, exposure to **environmental tobacco smoke** (ETS) that is inhaled by passive nonsmokers.

Effects on the Fetus

Smoking during pregnancy is the single most preventable cause of death and illness during pregnancy among mothers and infants (CDC 2007h). Still, a 2004 survey revealed that approximately 13% of women smoked during their last 3 months of pregnancy (CDC 2007h). Adverse effects on pregnancy range from increased risk for spontaneous abortion to impaired fetal growth, stillbirth, premature birth, and neonatal death. Babies born to mothers who smoke have a lower average body weight. Infants born to mothers who smoke have a reduced probability of survival. They are more likely to die from **sudden infant death syndrome (SIDS)** (CDC 2007h). If a smoking woman gives up smoking before or early in pregnancy, the risk of severe adverse outcomes is reduced significantly (CDC 2007h).

The below-average weight of babies born to smokers is caused by carbon monoxide and nicotine (Cook et al. 1990). Carbon monoxide reduces the oxygen-carrying capacity of the fetus's blood, just as it does the mother's. Fetal growth is retarded because the tissue becomes starved for oxygen. Inhaled nicotine enters the mother's blood from her lungs and rapidly constricts the blood flow to the placenta, reducing available oxygen and nutrients until the effect of the nicotine has worn off. In addition, nicotine crosses the

blood–placenta barrier to reach the fetal bloodstream. It has the same effects on the fetus's nervous system and blood circulation as on the mother's. However, the fetus cannot metabolize nicotine efficiently; therefore, the effects last longer for the child than for the mother.

One known carcinogen in tobacco smoke, benzo(a)pyrene, crosses the placenta and enters the fetal blood. Experiments with pregnant mice exposed to benzo(a)pyrene showed that their offspring had a markedly higher incidence of cancer. The impact of smoking during pregnancy on the incidence of cancer in infants is not known. In addition, if the father smokes but the mother does not, the infant may still be affected by secondhand smoke.

■ Tobacco Use Without Smoking

Although it is customary to associate the effects of tobacco use with smoking, in fact millions of nonsmokers experience tobacco effects through their use of smokeless tobacco products.

There are two main forms of smokeless tobacco in the United States. The first, **chewing tobacco**, comes in the form of loose leaf, a plug, or a twist. The second, **snuff**, is finely ground tobacco that can be moist, dry, or packaged in sachets. Although some forms of snuff can be inhaled, most smokeless tobacco users place the product in their cheek or between their cheek and gum. Users suck or chew the tobacco and then spit out the juices. Thus, smokeless tobacco is often called spitting tobacco (CDC 2007f).

Smokeless tobacco contains powerful chemicals — including nicotine, nitrosamines, polycyclic aromatic hydrocarbons, and dozens of other carcinogens — that can injure tissues in the mouth

KEY TERMS

environmental tobacco smoke
the mixture of predominantly sidestream smoke and exhaled mainstream smoke that is inhaled by the passive smoker

sudden infant death syndrome (SIDS)
unexpected and unexplainable death that occurs while infants are sleeping

chewing tobacco
tobacco leaves shredded and twisted into strands for chewing purposes

snuff
finely ground smokeless tobacco that can be moist or dry

and throat. The following findings have been made regarding smokeless tobacco:

- Approximately 7.7 million Americans age 12 or older used smokeless tobacco in 2005 (SAMHSA 2006).
- In 1986, the U.S. Surgeon General concluded that smokeless tobacco is not a safe substitute for smoking cigarettes for three reasons: (1) It can cause cancer, (2) it can produce a number of noncancerous oral conditions, and (3) it can lead to nicotine addiction and dependence.
- Oral cancer occurs several times more frequently among snuff dippers than among nontobacco users.
- Smokeless tobacco use is much higher among male (13.6%) than female (2.2%) high school students (CDC 2007f).
- An estimated 8% of high school students are current smokeless tobacco users; 3% of middle school users also use smokeless tobacco (CDC 2007f).

The popularity of snuff tobacco is largely due to more effective and persistent advertising campaigns depicting famous athletes using such products. During 2005, the five largest tobacco manufacturers spent a record $250.79 million on smokeless tobacco advertising and promotion (Federal Trade Commission [FTC] 2007). Some experts also believe that the increasing popularity of this tobacco product relates to its ability to satisfy the addiction to nicotine where smoking is prohibited. Thus, snuffing is perceived as an alternative to smoking in smoke-free environments.

How safe are smokeless tobacco products compared with cigarettes? Smokeless tobacco contains 28 carcinogens (NCI 1992). Use of smokeless products can cause cancer of the mouth, pharynx, and esophagus. The incidence of these cancers is related to the duration of use and the type of product used because "long-term snuff users have a 50% greater risk of developing oral cancer than nonusers" (American Dental Association [ADA] 1990). Other, less serious effects of using smokeless tobacco include severe inflammation of gum tissue, tooth decay, receding gums, and tooth loss (ADA 1990; Giovino et al. 1994).

In response to these developments, Congress enacted the Comprehensive Smokeless Tobacco Health Education Act of 1986. It requires rotation of three health warnings on smokeless tobacco packages and advertisements and bans smokeless tobacco advertising on broadcasting media.

■ Environmental Tobacco Smoke

Cigarette smoke drawn through the mouthpiece and inhaled directly from a cigarette is classified as **mainstream smoke**. **Secondhand smoke**, also known as environmental tobacco smoke (ETS), includes a mixture of smoke that comes directly from the lighted tip of a cigarette, cigar, or pipe tip (sidestream smoke) and exhaled mainstream smoke (CDC 2006). **Passive smoking** refers to nonsmokers' inhalation of tobacco smoke.

Studies of smoking and its effects have directed increased attention to secondhand smoke because the burning tobacco smoke that pollutes the air is breathed in by smokers and nonsmokers alike. This type of smoke contains at least 250 toxic chemicals, including over 50 carcinogens (CDC 2006).

Exposure to ETS causes an estimated 3000 nonsmoking Americans to die of lung cancer each year (CDC 2007b). If several people smoke in an enclosed area, the carbon monoxide level may exceed the safe limit recommended by the Environmental Protection Agency. Under conditions of heavy smoking and poor ventilation, high concentrations of carbon monoxide can occur from sidestream smoke. Carbon monoxide gas is not removed by most standard air filtration systems. It can be diluted only by increasing ventilation with fresh air containing low levels of carbon monoxide. Formation of carbon monoxide can be reduced by increasing the amount of oxygen available during the burning of the tobacco. This goal can be achieved by using perforated cigarette paper and perforated filter tips. Regular and small cigars produce more carbon monoxide than cigarettes because the tobacco leaf wrapper reduces the amount of oxygen available at the burning zone. The levels of carbon monoxide created by smokers may cause nonsmokers with coronary disease to have angina attacks.

KEY TERMS

mainstream smoke
smoke drawn directly through the mouthpiece of a cigarette

secondhand smoke
smoke released into the air from a lighted cigarette, cigar, or pipe tip and exhaled mainstream smoke

passive smoking
nonsmoker's inhalation of tobacco smoke

Reasons for Smoking and the Motivation to Quit

Reasons for Smoking

Nicotine dependency through cigarette smoking is not only one of the most common forms of drug addiction, but also one responsible for numerous deaths. As noted previously, more deaths each year are caused by tobacco use than by HIV, illegal drug use, murders, alcohol use, suicides, and motor vehicle injuries combined (CDC 2007e). Tobacco use continues despite the fact that, since the 1960s, medical research and government assessments have clearly proved that smoking leads to premature death.

If one asks tobacco users why they smoke, their answers are often quite similar:

1. It is relaxing.
2. It decreases the unpleasant effects of tension, anxiety, and anger.
3. It satisfies the craving.
4. It is a habit.
5. It provides stimulation, increased energy, and arousal.
6. It allows the manipulation of objects that have become satisfying habits (the cigarette, pipe, and so on).

In addition,

7. Parents and/or siblings smoke.
8. A close friend or boyfriend/girlfriend smokes.

Tobacco use fosters dependence for a number of reasons:

1. The habit can be rapidly and frequently reinforced by inhaling tobacco smoke.
2. The rapid metabolism and clearance of nicotine allows frequent and repeated use, which is encouraged by the rapid onset of withdrawal symptoms.
3. Smoking has complex pharmacological effects — both central and peripheral — that may satisfy a variety of the needs of the smoker.
4. Some groups offer psychological and social rewards for use, especially the peer groups of young people.
5. Smoking patterns can be generalized; that is, the smoker becomes conditioned to smoke with specific activities. For example, some smokers feel the need to smoke after a meal, when driving, and so on.

6. Smoking is reinforced by both pharmacological effects and ritual.
7. There is no marked performance impairment. In fact, smoking enhances performance in some cases. (Nicotine produces a state of alertness, prevents deterioration of reaction time, and improves learning.)

These reasons may not only explain why people continue to smoke, but also reveal why it is often difficult for them to stop.

Smokers appear to regulate their intake of nicotine. For example, the smoker of a low-nicotine cigarette is likely to smoke more and inhale more deeply. The average one-pack-a-day smoker is estimated to self-administer thousands of pulses (one pulse per inhalation) of nicotine to specific nicotinic receptors in the brain per year. This rate greatly surpasses the stimulation rate of any other known form of substance abuse. A habit that is reinforced as frequently and easily as smoking is very hard to break.

Other factors responsible for creating the addiction to nicotine follow:

1. Cigarettes are readily available.
2. No equipment other than a lighter or match is needed.
3. Cigarettes are portable and easy to store.
4. Cigarettes are legal for individuals over age 18.
5. Other rewarding behaviors can occur while smoking (for example, drinking, socializing, and eating).

The Motivation to Quit

Quitting smoking is easy. I've done it a thousand times.

— Mark Twain

Approximately 80% of adult smokers began smoking before age 18, and nearly 70% of adult smokers want to quit but need help to quit permanently (CDC 2004). When habitual smokers stop smoking on their own, without the use of smoking cessation aids, they may experience a variety of unpleasant withdrawal effects, including craving for tobacco, irritability, restlessness, sleep disturbances, gastrointestinal disturbances, anxiety, and impaired concentration, judgment, and psychomotor performance. The onset of nicotine withdrawal symptoms may occur within hours or days after quitting and may persist from a few days to several months. Frustration over these symptoms leads many people to start smoking again. The intensity of withdrawal effects may be mild, moderate, or severe; it is not always correlated with the amount smoked.

The National Cancer Institute (2004a) has several recommendations of alternative activities that ex-smokers might try as aids to handle the cravings associated with quitting and get through the withdrawal period. These include:

- Chewing on carrots, pickles, sunflower seeds, apples, celery, sugarless gum, or hard candy. Keeping the mouth busy may attenuate the psychological need to smoke.
- Avoiding situations and activities (like drinking alcohol) that one might normally associate with smoking.
- Using nicotine replacement products such as nicotine replacement patches, gum, lozenges, nasal spray, and inhalers.

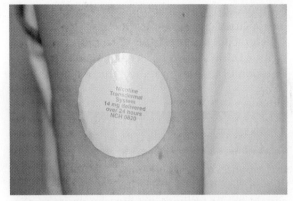

A transdermal patch, an example of a popular remedy for quitting smoking.

Nicotine Gum

Nicotine gum can be purchased over the counter without a prescription. Chewing the gum allows the rapid absorption of nicotine through the mucous membranes of the mouth. Users chew the gum until noting a peppery taste, and then hold it against the cheek to permit faster absorption. The user will chew on and off for about 20 to 30 minutes.

Significant advantages afforded by nicotine gum are that it is easy to use and allows the user to control the dose of nicotine by controlling the number of pieces chewed each day. Individuals gradually decrease the number of pieces chewed each day, with a goal of complete abstinence from the drug. Side effects of the gum can include a bad taste, throat irritation, nausea (if the gum is swallowed), jaw discomfort (if chewed too rapidly), and racing heartbeat.

Nicotine Patches

Nicotine patches, also known as *transdermal nicotine systems,* are available without a prescription. The patch, which is directly applied and worn on the skin, releases a continuous flow of small doses of nicotine to quell the desire for cigarette-provided nicotine. The method of delivering nicotine to the skin reduces the withdrawal symptoms as the smoker attempts to quit. As the nicotine doses are lowered over a course of weeks, the smoker is

weaned away from nicotine. The most common side effects are mild skin irritations such as redness and itching.

Nicotine Nasal Spray

Nicotine nasal sprays are available by prescription only. This form of administration rapidly delivers nicotine to the bloodstream as it is absorbed through the membranous lining of the nasal passages. It is easy to use and gives immediate relief of withdrawal symptoms. The most common side effects of using the spray include coughing, sinus irritation, runny nose, watery eyes, sneezing, and throat irritation. It is generally not recommended for individuals with asthma, allergies, or other pulmonary problems.

Nicotine Inhalers

Like nicotine nasal sprays, nicotine inhalers are only available by prescription. The nicotine inhaler is a small plastic tube that contains a nicotine plug. When the user puffs on the inhaler, the plug provides nicotine vapor into the mouth. One advantage to the inhaler is that the action of puffing it mimics some of the behaviors associated with smoking. Side effects associated with its use include coughing and throat irritation.

Bupropion and Varenicline

Bupropion is an antidepressant medication available only by prescription. In many individuals, this drug reduces symptoms of nicotine withdrawal. Bupropion can be used alone or in combination with nicotine replacement therapies as just described.

Varenicline is a prescription medicine approved by the FDA in 2006. This drug may aid in smoking cessation by helping to reduce the urge to smoke.

Smoking Prohibition Versus Smokers' Rights

In response to the percentage of the U.S. population that has effectively banned smoking from certain public facilities, people who desire to continue smoking have formed action groups to press their right to smoke. Through mailing lists, newsletters, and magazine promotions, the groups advocate and report on the following issues:

- How the rights of smokers have been eroded in public and private places
- How to write to members of Congress and other political leaders to urge them to uphold smokers' rights
- How to lobby effectively for smoking in the workplace
- How the harmful effects of secondhand smoke have been exaggerated or remain unproven
- How people who enjoy smoking have won major battles, preserving their right to smoke

Although some modest gains have been made by these groups, the trend toward restricting and banning cigarette smoking remains very strong. Antismoking groups have been highly successful in their own efforts, and restrictions on the sale of cigarettes and tobacco products remain very tight. As of 1999, 45 states and the District of Columbia required some variation of smoke-free indoor air. Forty-one states and the District of Columbia limit smoking in state government worksites. In contrast, only 20 states have laws that restrict smoking in private workplaces (CDC 2000). Many states have laws that regulate smoking in restaurants, and some have laws that regulate smoking in other locations, such as day-care centers, hospitals, public transportation facilities, grocery stores, and enclosed arenas.

Discussion Questions

1. If smoking is the most preventable cause of disease and premature death in the United States, why do people continue to smoke?

2. How effective are the health warning labels on cigarette packages? Interview two or three smokers about these warning labels.

3. List and define the diseases that cigarette smokers are most likely to contract.

4. What effects do cigarettes have on the fetus?

5. Why is smokeless tobacco perceived as safer than other forms of tobacco?

6. Who is most likely to smoke, and why?

7. Why do people who smoke become dependent on tobacco?

8. Assess the major methods for quitting smoking. Which methods are most likely to succeed?

9. Do you think smokers should have the right to smoke in public places? Explain.

Summary

1 Nicotine is a highly addictive substance.

2 Approximately 29.4% of the U.S. population age 12 and older reports current use of a tobacco product.

3 The quality of leaf tobacco has changed throughout the years of production. Since 1956, the amount of leaf tobacco in a cigarette has declined by approximately 25%. Most cigarettes today are low-tar and low-nicotine types.

4 Nicotine is the substance in tobacco that causes dependence. This drug initially stimulates and then depresses the nervous system.

5 The amount of tobacco absorbed varies according to five factors: (1) the exact composition of tobacco being used; (2) how densely the tobacco is packed in the cigarette and the length of the cigarette smoked; (3) whether a filter is used and the characteristics of the filter; (4) the volume of the smoke inhaled; and (5) the number of cigarettes smoked throughout the day.

6 Cigarette smoking is an addiction that is costly in several ways. For instance, each year approximately 440,000 deaths in the United States are attributed to cigarette smoking.

7 Chewing tobacco and snuff are types of smokeless tobacco products that are commonly referred to as "spit tobacco." Chewing tobacco consists of tobacco leaves that are shredded and twisted into strands and then either chewed or placed in the cheek between the lower lip and gum.

8 Research clearly shows that the tar and nicotine content of cigarettes affects mortality rates. Cigarette smokers tend to die at an earlier age than nonsmokers. They also have a greater probability of contracting various illnesses, including types of cancers, chronic bronchitis and emphysema, diseases of the cardiovascular system, and peptic ulcers. In addition, smoking has adverse effects on pregnancy and may harm the fetus.

9 Cigarette smoke is classified as either mainstream smoke (the smoke drawn directly through the mouthpiece of the cigarette) or secondhand smoke. Passive smoking refers to nonsmokers' inhalation of tobacco smoke.

References

American Dental Association (ADA). "Smokeless Tobacco, Think Before You Chew." (Leaflet) Chicago: American Dental Association, 1990.

Austin, G. A. *Perspectives on the History of Psychoactive Substance Use.* Washington DC: National Institute on Drug Abuse, 1978.

Bartecchi, C. E., T. D. MacKenzie, and R. W. Shrier. "The Global Tobacco Epidemic." *Scientific American* (May 1995): 49.

Centers for Disease Control and Prevention (CDC). Smoking and Tobacco Use, Cigarette Production, Exports and Domestic Consumption — United States, 1990–2004 (2007a). Available www.cdc.gov/tobacco/data_statistics/tables/economics/expdcom.htm.

Centers for Disease Control and Prevention (CDC). Smoking and Tobacco Use, Fact Sheet, Cigarette-Related Mortality (2007b). Available www.cdc.gov/tobacco/data_statistics/Factsheets/cig_smoking_mort.htm.

Centers for Disease Control and Prevention (CDC). Smoking and Tobacco Use, Fact Sheet, Youth and Tobacco Use: Current Estimates (2007c). Available www.cdc.gov/tobacco/data_statistics/Factsheets/youth_tobacco.htm.

Centers for Disease Control and Prevention (CDC). Smoking and Tobacco Use, Fact Sheet, Economic Facts about U.S. Tobacco Use and Tobacco Production (2007d). Available www.cdc.gov/tobacco/data_statistics/Factsheets/economic_facts.htm.

Centers for Disease Control and Prevention (CDC). Smoking and Tobacco Use, Fact Sheet, Health Effects of Cigarette Smoking (2007e). Available www.cdc.gov/tobacco/data_statistics/Factsheets/health_effects.htm.

Centers for Disease Control and Prevention (CDC). Smoking and Tobacco Use, Fact Sheet, SmokelessTobacco (2007f). Available www.cdc.gov/tobacco/data_statistics/Factsheets/smokeless_tobacco.htm.

Centers for Disease Control and Prevention (CDC). Targeting Tobacco Use, The Nation's Leading Cause of Preventable Death (2007g). Available www.cdc.gov/nccdphp/publications/aag/osh.htm.

Centers for Disease Control and Prevention (CDC). Tobacco Prevention and Control (2004). Available: www.cdc.gov/prc/pdf/PRC-tobacco-fact-sheet-Fall2004.pdf.

Centers for Disease Control and Prevention (CDC). Smoking and Tobacco Use, Fact Sheet, Secondhand Smoke (2006). Available www.cdc.gov/tobacco/data_statistics/Factsheets/SecondhandSmoke.htm.

Centers for Disease Control and Prevention (CDC). 2000 Surgeon General's Report — Reducing Tobacco Use (2000). Available www.cdc.gov/tobacco/data_statistics/sgr/sgr_2000/highlights/highlight_clean.htm.

Cook, P. S., R. C. Petersen, and D. T. Moore. *Alcohol, Tobacco, and Other Drugs May Harm the Unborn.* Rockville, MD: U.S. Department of Health and Human Services, 1990.

Corti, E. C. *A History of Smoking.* London: Harrap and Company, 1931.

Encyclopedia Americana. "Cigars." Danbury, CT: Grolier, 1988.

Federal Trade Commission (FTC). 2007 Smokeless Tobacco Report for the Years 2002–2005.

Giovino, G. A., M. W. Schooley, B. P. Zhu, J. H. Chrisman, S. L. Tambur, and J. P. Peddicord. "Trends and Recent Patterns in Selected Tobacco-Use Behaviors. Surveillance Summary." *Morbidity and Mortality Weekly Report* 43 (SS-3) (1994): 1–43.

Heimann, R. K. *Tobacco and Americans.* New York: McGraw-Hill, 1960.

Langton, P. A., *Drug Use and the Alcohol Dilemma.* Boston: Allyn and Bacon, 1991.

National Cancer Institute (NCI). Quitting Smoking: Why to Quit and How to Get Help (2007). Available www.cancer.gov/cancertopics/factsheet?Tobacco/cessation#q4.

National Cancer Institute (NCI). Quitting Tobacco, Handling Cravings . . . Without Smoking (2004a). Available www.cancer.gov/cancertopics/factsheet/Tobacco/cravings.

National Cancer Institute (NCI). The Truth About "Light" Cigarettes: Questions and Answers (2004b). Available www.cancer.gov/cancertopics/factsheet/Tobacco/light-cigarettes.

National Cancer Institute (NCI). Smokeless Tobacco and Health: An International Perspective (1992). Available http://cancercontrol.cancer.gov/TCRB/monographs/2/index.html.

National Institute on Drug Abuse (NIDA). Cigarettes and Other Tobacco Products, NIDAInfoFacts, 2006a.

National Institute on Drug Abuse (NIDA). NIDA Research Report — Tobacco Addiction, 2006b. NIH Publication No. 06-4342.

"Non-smoking Youth Better Resist Other Drugs." *Prevention Newsline* (Spring 1991): 5.

O'Brien, R. S. Cohen, G. Evans, and J. Fine. *The Encyclopedia of Drug Abuse,* 2nd ed. New York: Facts on File and Greenspring, 1992.

Palfai, T., and H. Jankiewicz. *Drugs and Human Behavior.* Dubuque, IA: William C. Brown, 1991.

Schelling, T. C. "Addictive Drugs: The Cigarette Experience." *Science* (24 January 1992): 430–433.

Schultes, R. E. "Ethnopharmacological Significance of Psychotropic Drugs of Vegetal Origin." In *Principles of Psychopharmacology,* 2nd ed., edited by W. G. Clark and J. del Guidice, 41–70. New York: Academic Press, 1978.

Substance Abuse and Mental Health Services Administration (SAMHSA). *Results from the 2005 National Household Survey on Drug Abuse and Health: National Findings.* NSDUH Series H30. DHHS Publication No. SMA 06-4194. Rockville, MD: Office of Applied Studies, 2006.

U.S. Department of Agriculture (USDA). Economic Research Service. Tobacco (2007). Available www.ers.usda.gov/Briefing/Tobacco.

U.S. Department of Agriculture (USDA). Economic Research Service. Trends in the Cigarette Industry After the Master Settlement Agreement (2001). Available www.ers.usda.gov/Publications/TBS/Oct01/TBS250-01/.

U.S. Department of Agriculture (USDA). Economic Research Service. Briefing Room: Tobacco (2001). Available www.ers.usda.gov/Briefing/Tobacco.

World Health Organization (WHO). Tobacco Free Initiative Why Is Tobacco a Public Health Priority? (2007). Available http://who.int/tobacco/health_priority/en/.

CHAPTER 12

Hallucinogens (Psychedelics)

Did You Know?

- ○ Hallucinogens were abused by relatively few people in the United States until the social upheaval of the 1960s.

- ○ Some hallucinogens — such as LSD, MDA, and Ecstasy — have been used by psychiatrists to assist in psychotherapy with certain patients.

- ○ Hallucinogens such as LSD do not tend to be physically addicting.

- ○ The senses are grossly exaggerated and distorted under the influence of hallucinogens.

- ○ Ecstasy abuse increased dramatically from 1996 to 2000 due to its popularity as a "club drug" and its use at "rave" parties, but recently its abuse has substantially diminished.

- ○ For some users, hallucinogens can cause frightening, nightmarish experiences called *bad trips*.

- ○ Phencyclidine (PCP) was originally developed as a general anesthetic, but because of its ability to cause psychosis it is no longer prescribed for use in humans.

- ○ High doses of OTC cough medicines that contain dextromethorphan can cause a PCP-like hallucinogenic effect.

Drugs and Society Online is a great source for additional drugs and society information for both students and instructors.
Visit **http://drugsandsociety.jbpub.com** to find a variety of useful tools for learning, thinking, and teaching.

Learning ◎bjectives

On completing this chapter you will be able to:

- ◎ Explain why hallucinogens became so popular during the 1960s.
- ◎ Describe how hallucinogens alter the senses.
- ◎ Outline how psychedelic, stimulant, and anticholinergic effects are expressed in the three principal types of hallucinogens.
- ◎ Describe why some psychotherapists believe that using MDMA for their patients may be beneficial.
- ◎ Explain the reason for Ecstasy's most recent popularity and the subsequent decline in its use.
- ◎ Explain how hallucinogens differ from other commonly abused drugs in terms of their addicting properties and their ability to cause dependence.
- ◎ Describe the effects that environment and personality have on the individual's response to hallucinogens.
- ◎ Explain the term *club drugs* and describe their particular problems.
- ◎ Characterize how PCP differs from other hallucinogens.
- ◎ Explain the similarities between PCP and ketamine.

Introduction

A person on LSD who becomes depressed, agitated, or confused may experience these feelings in an overwhelming manner that grows on itself. The best solution is to remove disturbing influences, get to a safe, comforting environment, and reassure the "tripper" that things are alright. It may comfort those who fear that they are losing their minds to be reminded that it will end in several hours. (from Erowid 2007)

This quote from an experienced user illustrates the sensory and emotional distortions that can be caused by using **hallucinogens** or **psychedelics**. The word *psychedelic* comes from the Greek root meaning "mind-revealing" (Harvard Mental Health Letter 2006). In this chapter, we begin with a brief historical review of the use of hallucinogens, tracing the trend in the United States from the 1960s to today. Next, the nature of hallucinogens and the effects they produce are examined. The rest of the chapter addresses the various types of psychedelic agents — LSD types, phenylethylamines (including Ecstasy), anticholinergics, and other miscellaneous substances.

The History of Hallucinogen Use

People have known and written about drug-related hallucinations for centuries. Throughout the ages, individuals who saw visions or experienced hallucinations were perceived as being holy or sacred, as receiving divine messages, or possibly as being bewitched and controlled by the devil. There are many indications that medicine men, shamans, witches, oracles, and perhaps mystics and priests of

Protests against the Vietnam War in the 1960s and 1970s often included the use of hallucinogens.

various groups were familiar with drugs and herbs that caused such experiences and today are known as hallucinogens (National Institute on Drug Abuse [NIDA] 2001).

Before the 1960s, several psychedelic substances, such as mescaline from the peyote cactus, could be obtained from chemical supply houses with no restriction in the United States. Abuse of hallucinogens did not become a major social problem in this country until this decade of racial struggles, the Vietnam War, and violent demonstrations. Many individuals frustrated with the hypocrisy of "the establishment" tried to "turn on and tune in" by using hallucinogens as pharmacological crutches.

Psychedelic drugs became especially popular when some medical professionals such as then-Harvard psychology professor, Timothy Leary, reported that these drugs allowed users to get in touch with themselves and achieve a peaceful inner serenity (Associated Press 1999). At the same time, it became well publicized that the natural psychedelics (such as mescaline and peyote) were and had been for many years used routinely by some religious organizations of Native Americans for enhancing spiritual experiences. This factor contributed to the mystical, supernatural aura associated with hallucinogenic agents and added to their enticement for the so-called dropout generation.

With widespread use of LSD, it was observed that this and similar drugs may induce a form of psychosis-like schizophrenia (American Psychiatric Association [APA] 2000). The term **psychotomimetic** was coined to describe these compounds; this term means "psychosis mimicking" and is still used in medicine today. The basis for the designation is the effects of these drugs that induce mental states that impair an individual's ability to recognize and respond appropriately to reality.

By the mid-1960s, federal regulatory agencies had become concerned with the misuse of hallucinogens and the potential emotional damage caused by these drugs. Access to hallucinogenic agents was restricted, and laws against their distribution were passed. Despite the problems associated with these psychedelics, some groups demanded that responsible use was possible and that they be allowed legal access to these substances.

The Native American Church

The hallucinogen peyote plays a central role in the ceremonies of Native Americans who follow a religion that is a combination of Christian doctrine and Native American religious rituals. Members of this church are found as far north as Canada. They believe that God made a special gift of this sacramental plant to them so that they might commune more directly with Him. The first organized peyote church was the First-Born Church of Christ, incorporated in 1914 in Oklahoma. The Native American Church of the United States was chartered in 1918 and is the largest such group at present (approximately 100,000–200,000 members).

Because of the religious beliefs of the members of the Native American Church concerning the powers of peyote, when Congress legislated against its use in 1965, it allowed room for religious use of this psychedelic plant. The American Indian Religious Freedom Act of 1978 was an attempt by Congress to allow the members of the Native American

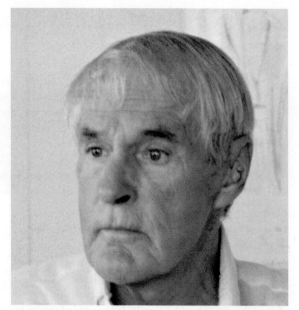
Timothy Leary advocated legalization of LSD in the 1960s.

Church access to peyote due to constitutional guarantees of religious freedom. Due to controversy inspired by the original piece of legislation, an amendment to the 1978 act was signed in 1994, which specifically protected the use of peyote in Native American Church ceremonies. This amendment also prohibits use of peyote for nonreligious purposes (Native American Church 2007). However, despite these efforts by Congress to resolve this issue, controversies continue to arise (see "Case in Point," Peyote and the Rights of Native Americans: How Far Should It Go?).

Timothy Leary and the League of Spiritual Discovery

In 1966, 3 years after being fired by Harvard because of his controversial involvement with hallucinogens (Associated Press 1999), Timothy Leary undertook a constitutional strategy intended to retain legitimate access to another hallucinogen, LSD. He began a religion called the League of Spiritual Discovery; LSD was the sacrament. This unorthodox religious orientation to the LSD experience was presented in a manual called *The Psychedelic Experience* (Leary et al. 1964), which was based on the *Tibetan Book of the Dead*. It became the "bible" of the psychedelic drug movement.

The movement grew, but most members used street LSD and did not follow Leary's directions.

Peyote is used as a sacramental plant by members of the Native American Church as part of their religious ceremonies.

►Case in Point   Peyote and the Rights of Native Americans: How Far Should It Go?

Jonathan Fowler, a member of the Grand Traverse Band of Ottawa and Chippewa Indians, requested a judge allow his 4-year-old son to ingest peyote with him, as part of a religious ritual at the Native American Church of the Morning Star. The boy's mother opposed the request, fearing potential neurological damage to the boy. Although the use of peyote in Native American rituals is legal in all 50 states, the judge ruled against Fowler, stating that the boy could use peyote when he becomes old enough to comprehend its effects and with permission from both parents. Several Native American congregations who use peyote already have age limitations indicating who can take the substance during religious rites.

Source: Center for Cognitive Liberty and Ethics. "Court Says No Peyote for Native American Boy" (22 April 2003). Available www.cognitiveliberty.org/dll/peyote_boy.html.

Leary believed that the hallucinogenic experience was only beneficial under proper control and guidance. But most members of this so-called religion merely used the organization as a front to gain access to an illegal drug. Federal authorities did not agree with Leary's freedom of religion interpretation and in 1969 convicted him for possession of marijuana and LSD and sentenced him to 20 years imprisonment (Stone 1991). Before being incarcerated, Leary escaped to Algeria and wandered for a couple of years before being extradited to the United States. He served several years in jail and was released in 1976.

Even in his later years, Leary continued to believe that U.S. citizens should be able to use hallucinogens without government regulation. He died in 1996 at the age of 75 years, revered by some but despised by others (Associated Press 1999; "Many Were Lost" 1996).

Hallucinogen Use Today

Today, the use of hallucinogens (excluding marijuana) is primarily a young-adult phenomenon (Johnston 2007). Although the use rate has not returned to that of the late 1960s and early 1970s (approximately 16%), in high school seniors lifetime use in 2006 was 8.3% (Johnston 2007). (See Table 12.1.) It has been speculated that this popularity reflects the ignorance of a new generation about the potential problems of the hallucinogens.

The Nature of Hallucinogens

Agreement has not been reached on what constitutes a hallucinogenic agent (O'Brien 2006), for several reasons. First, a variety of seemingly unrelated drug groups can produce hallucinations, delusions, or sensory disturbances under certain conditions. For example, besides the traditional hallucinogens (such as LSD), high doses of anticholinergics, cocaine, amphetamines, and steroids can cause hallucinations.

In addition, responses to even the traditional hallucinogens can vary tremendously from person to person and from experience to experience. Multiple mechanisms are involved in the actions of these drugs, which contribute to the array of responses that they can cause. These drugs most certainly influence the complex inner workings of the human mind and have been described as psychedelic, **psychotogenic**, or psychotomimetic. The features of hallucinogens that distinguish them from other drug groups are their ability to alter perception, thought, and feeling in such a manner that does not normally occur except in dreams or during experiences of extreme religious exaltation (NIDA 2001). We examine these characteristics throughout this chapter.

■ Sensory and Psychological Effects

In general, LSD is considered the prototype agent against which other hallucinogens are measured (NIDA 2001). Typical users experience several stages of sensory experiences; they can go through all stages during a single "trip" or, more likely, will pass through only some. These stages are as follows:

1. Heightened, exaggerated senses
2. Loss of control
3. Self-reflection
4. Loss of identity and a sense of cosmic merging

KEY TERMS

psychotogenic
substances that initiate psychotic behavior

Table 12.1 Trends (Shown in Percentages) in the Use of LSD and All Hallucinogens by 8th Graders Through Young Adults, 1994–2006

	USED DURING LIFETIME					USED DURING YEAR					USED DURING MONTH				
	1994	1996	1999	2004	2006	1994	1996	1999	2004	2006	1994	1996	1999	2004	2006
8th graders															
LSD	3.7	5.1	4.1	1.8	2.8	2.4	3.5	2.4	1.1	0.9	1.1	1.5	1.1	0.5	0.4
All hallucinogens	4.3	5.9	4.8	3.5	3.4	2.7	4.1	2.9	2.2	2.1	1.3	1.9	1.3	1.0	0.9
10th graders															
LSD	7.2	9.4	8.5	2.8	2.7	5.2	6.9	6.0	1.6	1.7	2.0	2.4	2.3	0.6	0.7
All hallucinogens	8.1	10.5	9.7	6.4	6.1	5.8	7.8	6.9	4.1	4.1	2.4	2.8	2.9	1.6	1.3
12th graders															
LSD	10.5	12.6	12.2	4.6	3.3	6.9	8.8	8.1	2.2	1.7	2.6	2.5	2.7	0.7	0.6
All hallucinogens	11.4	14.0	13.7	9.7	8.3	7.6	10.1	9.4	6.2	4.9	3.1	3.5	3.5	1.9	1.5
	1994	1996	2001	2006		1994	1996	2001	2006		1994	1996	2001	2006	
Young Adults															
LSD	13.8	15.0	16.0	6.8		4.0	4.5	3.4	2.5		1.1	0.7	0.7	—	
All hallucinogens	15.9	15.4	18.3	14.9		5.1	4.9	5.4	5.7		1.6	1.4	1.2	—	
Ecstasy	3.8	5.2	13.0	12.3		0.7	1.7	7.5	5.2		0.2	0.3	1.8	—	

*For this survey, inhalants and marijuana were not considered as hallucinogens.

Sources: Johnston, L., P. O'Malley, and J. Bachman. "Monitoring the Future National Results on Adolescents Drug Use. Overview of Key Findings, 2002." Lansing, MI: University of Michigan, 2003.

Johnston, L. "Monitoring the Future 2006." Available www.monitoringthefuture.org/new.html.

The following illustrations of the stages of the LSD experience are based primarily on an account by Solomon Snyder (1974), a highly regarded neuroscientist (one of the principal discoverers of endorphins; see Chapter 4), who personally experienced the effects of LSD as a young resident in psychiatry.

Altered Senses

In his encounter with LSD, Snyder used a moderate dose of 100 to 200 micrograms and observed few discernible effects for the first 30 minutes except some mild nausea. After this time had elapsed, objects took on a purplish tinge and appeared to be vaguely outlined. Colors, textures, and lines achieved an unexpected richness. Perception was so exaggerated that individual skin pores "stood out and clamored for recognition" (Snyder 1974, p. 42). Objects became distorted; when Snyder focused on his thumb, it began to swell, undulate, and then moved forward in a menacing fashion. Visions filled with distorted imagery occurred when his eyes were closed. The sense of

time and distance changed dramatically; "a minute was like an hour, a week was like an eternity, a foot became a mile" (Snyder 1974, p. 43). The present seemed to drag on forever, and the concept of future lost its meaning. The exaggeration of perceptions and feelings gave the sense of more events occurring in a time period, giving the impression of time slowing.

An associated sensation described by Snyder is called **synesthesia**, a crossover phenomenon between senses. For example, sound develops visual dimensions, and vice versa, enabling the user to see sounds and hear colors. These altered sensory experiences are described as a heightened sensory awareness and relate to the first component of the psychedelic state (NIDA 2001).

KEY TERMS

synesthesia
a subjective sensation or image of a sense other than the one being stimulated, such as an auditory sensation caused by a visual stimulus

Signs & Symptoms Hallucinogens

POSSIBLE SIGNS OF USE:	EXTREME REACTIONS:
Heightened senses	Increased body temperature (MDMA)
Loss of control	Electrolyte imbalance
Loss of identity	Cardiac arrest
Illusions and hallucinations	A nightmare-like trip (LSD)
Altered perception of time and distance	Unable to direct movement, feel pain, or remember

Loss of Control

The second feature of LSD also relates to altered sensory experiences and a loss of control (O'Brien 2006). The user cannot determine whether the psychedelic trip will be a pleasant, relaxing experience or a "bad trip," with recollections of hidden fears and suppressed anxieties that can precipitate neurotic or psychotic responses. The frightening reactions may persist for a few minutes or several hours and be mildly agitating or extremely disturbing. Some bad trips can include feelings of panic, confusion, suspicion, helplessness, and a total lack of control. The following example illustrates how terrifying a bad trip can be:

> I was having problems breathing [and] my throat was all screwed up. The things that entered my mind were that I was dead and people were saying good-bye, because they really meant it. I was witnessing my own funeral. I was thinking that I was going to wake either in the back seat of a cop car or in the hospital. *(From Venturelli's files, interview with a 19-year-old male, 1995.)*

Replays of these frightening experiences can occur at a later time, even though the drug has not been taken again; such recurrences are referred to as **flashbacks** (NIDA 2001) or hallucinogen persisting perception disorder (Halpern and Pope 2003).

It is not clear what determines the nature of the sensory response. Perhaps it relates to the state of anxiety and personality of the user or the nature of his or her surroundings. It is interesting that Timothy Leary tried to teach his "drug disciples" that "turning on correctly means to understand the many levels that are brought into focus; it takes years of discipline, training and discipleship" ("Celebration #1" 1966). He apparently felt that, with experience and training, you could control the sensory effects of the hallucinogens. This is an interesting possibility but has never been well demonstrated.

Self-Reflection

Snyder (1974) made reference to the third component of the psychedelic response in his LSD experience. During the period when sensory effects predominate, self-reflection also occurs. While in this state, Snyder explained, the user "becomes aware of thoughts and feelings long hidden beneath the surface, forgotten and/or repressed" (p. 44). As a psychiatrist, Snyder claimed that this new perspective can lead to valid insights that are useful psychotherapeutic exercises.

Some psychotherapists have used or advocated the use of psychedelics for this purpose since the 1950s, as described by Sigmund Freud, to "make conscious the unconscious" (Snyder 1974, p. 44). Although a case can be made for the psychotherapeutic use of this group of drugs, the Food and Drug Administration (FDA) has not approved any of these agents for psychiatric use. The psychedelics currently available are considered to be too unpredictable in their effects and possess substantial risks (Abraham et al. 1996). Not only is their administration not considered to be significantly therapeutic, but their use is also deemed a great enough risk that the principal hallucinogenic agents are classified (i.e., scheduled) as controlled substances (see Chapter 3 and Appendix B).

KEY TERMS

flashbacks
recurrences of earlier drug-induced sensory experiences in the absence of the drug

Loss of Identity and Cosmic Merging

The final features that set the psychedelics apart as unique drugs were described by Snyder (1974) as the "mystical-spiritual aspect of the drug experience." He claimed, "It is indescribable. For how can anyone verbalize a merging of his being with the totality of the universe? How do you put into words the feeling that 'all is one,' 'I am of the all,' 'I am no longer.' One's skin ceases to be a boundary between self and others" (p. 45). Because consumption of hallucinogen-containing plants has often been part of religious ceremonies, it is likely that this sense of cosmic merging and union with all humankind correlates to the exhilaratingly spiritual experiences described by many religious mystics.

The loss of identity and personal boundaries caused by hallucinogens is not viewed as being so spiritually enticing by all. In particular, for individuals who have rigid, highly ordered personalities, the dissolution of a well-organized and well-structured world is terrifying because the drug destroys the individual's emotional support. Such an individual finds that the loss of a separate identity can cause extreme panic and anxiety. During these drug-induced panic states, which in some ways are schizophrenic-like, people have committed suicide and homicide. These tragic reactions are part of the risk of using hallucinogenics and explain some of the FDA's hesitancy to legalize or authorize them for psychotherapeutic use.

Mechanisms of Action

As with most drugs, hallucinogens represent the proverbial "double-edged sword." These drugs may cause potentially useful psychiatric effects for many people. However, the variability in positive versus negative responses, coupled with lack of understanding as to what factors are responsible for the variables, have made these drugs dangerous and difficult to manage.

Some researchers have suggested that all hallucinogens act at a common central nervous system (CNS) site to exert their psychedelic effects. Although this hypothesis has not been totally disproven, there is little evidence to support it. The fact that so many different types of drugs can cause hallucinogenic effects suggests that multiple mechanisms are likely responsible for their actions.

The most predictable and typical psychedelic experiences are caused by LSD or similar agents. Consequently, these agents have been the primary focus of studies intended to elucidate the nature of hallucinogenic mechanisms. Although LSD has effects at several CNS sites, ranging from the spinal cord to the cortex of the brain, its effects on the neurotransmitter serotonin most likely account for its psychedelic properties (Nichols 2004). That LSD and similar drugs alter serotonin activity has been proven; how they affect this transmitter is not so readily apparent.

Although many experts believe changes in serotonin activity are the basis for the psychedelic properties of most hallucinogens, a case can be made for the involvement of norepinephrine, dopamine, acetylcholine, and perhaps other transmitter systems as well (see Chapter 4). Only additional research will be able to sort out this complex but important issue.

Types of Hallucinogenic Agents

Due to recent technological developments, understanding of hallucinogens has advanced; even so, the classification of these drugs remains somewhat arbitrary. Many agents produce some of the pharmacological effects of the traditional psychedelics, such as LSD and mescaline.

A second type of hallucinogen includes those agents that have amphetamine-like molecular structures (referred to as *phenylethylamines*) and possess some stimulant action; this group includes drugs such as DOM (dimethoxymethylamphetamine), MDA (methylenedioxyamphetamine), and MDMA (methylenedioxymethamphetamine or Ecstasy). These agents vary in their hallucinogen or stimulant properties. MDA is more like an amphetamine (stimulant), whereas MDMA is more like LSD (hallucinogen). In large doses, however, each of the phenylethylamines causes substantial CNS stimulation.

The third major group of hallucinogens comprises the anticholinergic drugs, which block some of the receptors for the neurotransmitter acetylcholine (see Chapter 4). Almost all drugs that antagonize these receptors cause hallucinations in high doses. Many of these potent anticholinergic hallucinogens are naturally occurring and have been known, used, and abused for millennia.

Traditional Hallucinogens: LSD Types

The LSD-like drugs are considered to be the prototypical hallucinogens and are used as the basis of comparison for other types of agents with psychedelic properties. Included in this group are LSD itself and some hallucinogens derived from plants, such as mescaline from the peyote cactus, psilocybin from mushrooms, dimethyltryptamine (DMT) from seeds, and myristicin from nutmeg. Because LSD is the principal hallucinogen, its origin, history, and properties are discussed in detail, providing a basis for understanding the other psychedelic drugs.

Lysergic Acid Diethylamide (LSD)

LSD is a relatively new drug, but similar compounds have existed for a long time. For example, accounts from the Middle Ages tell about a strange affliction that caused pregnant women to abort and others to develop strange burning sensations in their extremities. Today, we call this condition **ergotism** and know that it is caused by eating grain contaminated by the ergot fungus. This fungus produces compounds related to LSD called the *ergot alkaloids* (Goldstein 1994; NIDA 2007b). Besides the sensory effects, the ergot substances can cause hallucinations, delirium, and psychosis.

In 1938, Albert Hofmann, a scientist for Sandoz Pharmaceutical Laboratories of Basel, Switzerland, worked on a series of ergot compounds in a search for active chemicals that might be of medical value. Lysergic acid was similar in structure to a compound called *nikethamide*, a stimulant, and Hofmann tried to create slight chemical modifications that might merit further testing. The result of this effort was the production of lysergic acid diethylamide, or LSD. Hofmann's experience with this new compound gave insight into the effects of this drug (NIDA 2001).

Soon after LSD was discovered, the similarity of experiences with this agent to the symptoms of schizophrenia were noted, which prompted researchers to investigate correlations between the two (Weber 2006). The hope was to use LSD as a tool for producing an artificial psychosis to aid in understanding the biochemistry of psychosis (NIDA 2001). Interest in this use of LSD has declined because it is generally accepted that LSD effects differ from natural psychoses.

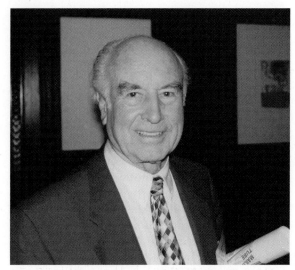

Albert Hofmann created LSD in 1938 while trying to synthesize a drug to study psychosis.

The use of LSD in psychotherapy has also been tried in connection with the treatment of alcoholism, autism, paranoia, schizophrenia, and various other mental and emotional disorders (Weber 2006). Therapeutic use of LSD has not increased to any great extent over the years because of its limited success, legal aspects, difficulty in obtaining the pure drug, adverse reactions to the drug ("bad trips" can occur under controlled as well as uncontrolled conditions), and rapid tolerance buildup in some patients.

Nonmedical interest in LSD and related drugs began to grow during the 1950s and peaked in the 1960s, when LSD was used by millions of young Americans for chemical escape. On rare occasions, a "bad trip" would cause a user to feel terror and panic; these experiences resulted in well-publicized accidental deaths due to jumping from building tops or running into the pathway of oncoming vehicles (U.S. Department of Justice 1991).

As with other hallucinogens, the use of LSD by teenagers declined somewhat over the 1970s and 1980s but began to rise again in the early 1990s. The reason for this rise was thought to relate to a decline in the perceived dangers of using LSD and an increase in peer approval (Johnston 1999). However, surveys have demonstrated a dramatic drop in LSD use in 2006 that has not been explained (Johnston 2007; Table 12.1). Of high school seniors sampled in 1975, 11.3% had used LSD sometime during their life; that number declined to 8.6% in

KEY TERMS

ergotism
poisoning by toxic substances from the ergot fungus
Claviceps purpurea

1992, rebounded to 12.2% in 1999, and tumbled to 4.6% in 2004 and further to 3.3% in 2006. LSD users are typically college or high school students, white, middle-class, and risk-takers (Johnston et al. 1996; Johnston 2007).

Synthesis and Administration LSD is a complex molecule that requires about 1 week to be synthesized. Because of the sophisticated chemistry necessary for its production, LSD is not manufactured by local illicit laboratories but requires the skills of a trained chemist (U.S. Department of Justice 2002, 2003). Because of LSD's potency, it has been difficult to locate illicit LSD labs; small quantities of LSD are sufficient to satisfy the demand and can be easily transported without detection. However, in 2000 a large lab was raided in Kansas resulting in a 95% decrease in LSD supplies in the United States by 2004, perhaps contributing to its decreased use in this country (*Philadelphia Inquirer* 2006).

The physical properties of LSD are not distinctive. In its purified form, LSD is colorless, odorless, and tasteless. It can be purchased in several forms, including tiny tablets (about one tenth the size of aspirins, called *microdots*), capsules, thin squares of gelatin called "window panes," or more commonly dissolved and applied to paper as "blotter acid" and cut up into 0.25-inch squares for individual dosing (Publishers Group 2002). Each square is swallowed or chewed and represents a single dose. One gram of LSD can provide 10,000 individual doses and be sold on the streets for $50,000. Although LSD usually is taken by mouth, it is sometimes injected. It costs about $1–10/dose (Schaffer Library 2007).

Small quantities of LSD are applied to squares of absorbent blotter paper to be chewed or swallowed.

Physiological Effects Like many hallucinogens, LSD is remarkably potent. The typical dose today is 20 to 30 micrograms, compared with a typical dose of 150 to 300 micrograms in the 1960s. This difference in dose likely explains why today fewer users of LSD are experiencing severe side effects (NIDA 2007b). In monkeys, the lethal dose has been determined to be about 5 milligrams per kilogram of body weight.

When taken orally, LSD is readily absorbed and diffused into all tissues. It passes through the placenta into the fetus and through the blood–brain barrier. The brain receives about 1% of the total dose.

Within the brain, LSD is particularly concentrated in the hypothalamus, the limbic system, and the auditory and visual reflex areas. Electrodes placed in the limbic system show an "electrical storm," or a massive increase in neural activity, which might correlate with the overwhelming flood of sensations and the phenomenon of synesthesia reported by the user (NIDA 2001). LSD also activates the sympathetic nervous system; shortly after the drug is taken, body temperature, heart rate, and blood pressure rise, the person sweats, and the pupils of the eyes dilate. Its effects on the parasympathetic nervous system increase salivation and nausea (NIDA 2007b). These systemic effects do not appear to be related to the hallucinogenic properties of the drug.

The effect of LSD begins within 30 to 90 minutes after ingestion and can last up to 12 hours. Tolerance to the effects of LSD develops more rapidly and lasts longer than tolerance to other hallucinogens (NIDA 2001). Tolerance develops very quickly to repeated doses, probably because of a change in sensitivity of the target cells in the brain rather than a change in its metabolism. Tolerance wears off within a few days after the drug is discontinued. Because there are no withdrawal symptoms, a person does not become physically dependent, but some psychological dependency on LSD can occur (NIDA 2007b).

Behavioral Effects Because LSD alters a number of systems in the brain, its behavioral effects are many and variable among individuals (Goldstein 1995). The following sections address common CNS responses to this drug.

Creativity and Insight. A question often raised by researchers interested in experimenting with LSD is this: Does LSD help expand the mind, increasing insight and creativity? This question is extremely difficult to answer because no one has ever determined the origin of insight and creativity. Moreover, each of us views these qualities differently.

Subjects under the influence of LSD often express the feeling of being more creative, but creative acts such as drawing and painting are hindered by the motor impairment caused by LSD. The products of artists under the influence of the drug usually prove to be inferior to those produced before the drug experience. Paintings done in LSD creativity studies have been described as reminiscent of "schizophrenic art."

In an often-cited study, creativity, attitude, and anxiety tests on 24 college students found that LSD had no objective effect on creativity, although many of the subjects said they felt they were more creative (McGlothin et al. 1967). This paradox is noted in several studies of LSD use. The subjects believe they have more insight and provide better answers to life's problems, but they do not or cannot demonstrate this increase objectively. Overt behavior is not modified, and these new insights are short-lived unless they are reinforced by modified behavior.

In spite of these results, some researchers still contend that LSD can enhance the creative process. For example, Oscar Janigar, a psychiatrist at the University of California, Los Angeles, claimed to have determined that LSD does not produce a tangible alteration in the way a painter paints; thus, it does not turn a poor painter into a good one. However, Janigar claimed that LSD does alter the way the painter appraises the world and allows the artist to "plunge into areas where access was restricted by confines of perceptions" and consequently becomes more creative (Tucker 1987, p. 16).

Adverse Psychedelic Effects. It is important to remember that there is no typical pattern of response to LSD. The experience varies for each user as a function of the person's *set*, or expectations, and *setting*, or environment, during the experience (Publishers Group 2002). Two of the major negative responses are described as follows (NIDA 2007b; Pahnke et al. 1970):

1. The psychotic adverse reaction, or "freakout," is an intense, nightmarish experience. The subject may have complete loss of emotional control and experience paranoid delusions, hallucinations, panic attacks, psychosis, and catatonic seizures. In rare instances, some of these reactions are prolonged, lasting days.

2. The nonpsychotic adverse reaction may involve varying degrees of tension, anxiety, fear, depression, and despair but not as intense a response as the "freakout."

A person with deep psychological problems or a strong need to be in conscious control or one who takes the drug in an unfavorable setting is more likely to have an adverse reaction than a person with a well-integrated personality.

Severe LSD behavioral toxicity can be treated with tranquilizers or a sedative like a benzodiazepine.

Perceptual Effects. Because the brain's sensory processing is altered by a hallucinogenic dose of LSD, many kinds of unusual illusions can occur. Some users report seeing shifting geometrical patterns mixed with intense color perception; others observe the movement of stationary objects, such that a speck on the wall appears as a large blinking eye or an unfolding flower. Interpretation of sounds can also be scrambled; a dropped ashtray may become a gun fired at the user, for instance. In some cases, LSD alters perceptions to the extent that people feel they can walk on water or fly through the air. The sensation that the body is distorted and even coming apart is another common effect, especially for novice users. Thoughts of suicide and sometimes actual attempts can be caused by use of LSD as well (NIDA 2007b; U.S. Department of Justice 1991).

Many LSD users find their sense of time distorted, such that hours may be perceived as years or an eternity. As discussed earlier, users may also have a distorted perception of their own knowledge or creativity; for instance, they may feel their ideas or work are especially unique, brilliant, or artistic. When analyzed by a person not on LSD or explained after the "trip" is over, however, these ideas or creations are almost always quite ordinary.

In sum, LSD alters perception such that any sensation can be perceived in the extreme. An experience can be incredibly beautiful and uplifting. However, sometimes the experience can be very unpleasant.

The flashback is an interesting but poorly understood phenomenon of LSD use. Although usually thought of as being adverse, sometimes flashbacks are pleasant and even referred to as "free trips." During a flashback, sensations caused by previous LSD use return, although the subject is not using the drug at the time.

This head was sculpted by a university student while under the influence of LSD.

There are three broad categories of negative LSD-related flashbacks:

1. *"Body trip"*: recurrence of an unpleasant physical sensation
2. *"Bad mind trip"*: recurrence of a distressing thought or emotion
3. *Altered visual perception:* the most frequent type of recurrence, consisting of seeing dots, flashes, trails of light, halos, false motion in the peripheral field, and other sensations

Flashbacks are most disturbing because they come on unexpectedly. Some have been reported years after use of LSD; for most people, however, flashbacks usually subside within weeks or months after taking LSD (NIDA 1999b). The duration of a flashback is variable, lasting from a few minutes to several hours (Fleckenstein 2000).

Although the precise mechanism of flashbacks is unknown, physical or psychological stresses and some drugs such as marijuana may trigger these experiences (Goldstein 1995). It has been proposed that flashbacks are an especially vivid form of memory that becomes seared into the subconscious mind due to the effects of LSD on the brain's transmitters.

Treatment consists of reassurance that the condition will go away and use of a sedative such as diazepam (Valium), if necessary, to treat the anxiety or panic that can accompany the flashback experience.

Genetic Damage and Birth Defects Experiments conducted in the mid-1960s suggested that LSD could cause birth defects, based on the observation that, when LSD was added to a suspension of human white blood cells in a test tube, the chromosomes of these cells were damaged. From this finding, it was proposed that when LSD was consumed by human beings, it could damage the chromosomes of the male sperm, female egg, or cells of the developing infant. Such damage theoretically could result in congenital defects in offspring (Dishotsky et al. 1971).

Carefully controlled studies conducted after news of LSD's chromosomal effects were made public have not supported this hypothesis. Experiments have revealed that, in contrast to the test tube findings, there is no chromosomal damage to white blood cells or any other cells when LSD is given to a human being (Dishotsky et al. 1971).

Studies have also shown that there are no carcinogenic or mutagenic effects from using LSD in experimental animals or human beings, with the exception of the fruit fly. (LSD is a mutagen in fruit flies if given in doses that are equivalent to 100,000 times the hallucinogenic dose for people.) Teratogenic effects occur in mice if LSD is given early in pregnancy. LSD may be teratogenic in rhesus monkeys if it is injected in doses (based on body weight) exceeding at least 100 times the usual hallucinogenic dose for humans. In other studies, women who took street LSD but not those given pure LSD had a higher rate of spontaneous abortions and births of malformed infants; this finding suggests that contaminants in adulterated LSD were responsible for the fetal effects and not the hallucinogen itself (Dishotsky et al. 1971).

Early Human Research In the 1950s, the U.S. government — specifically, the Central Intelligence Agency (CIA) and the army — became interested in reports of the effects of mind-altering drugs, including LSD. Unknown to the public at the time, these agencies conducted tests on human beings to learn more about such compounds and determine their usefulness in conducting military and clandestine missions. These activities became public when a biochemist, Frank Olson, killed himself in 1953 after being given a drink laced with LSD. Olson had a severe psychotic reaction and was being treated for the condition when he jumped out of a 10th-story window. His family was told only that he had committed suicide. The connection to LSD was not uncovered until 1975. The court awarded Olson's family $750,000 in damages in 1976.

In 1976, the extent of these studies was revealed; nearly 585 soldiers and 900 civilians had been given LSD in poorly organized experiments in which participants were coerced into taking this drug or not told that they were receiving it. Powerful hallucinogens such as LSD can cause serious psychological damage in some subjects, especially when they are unaware of what is happening.

The legal consequences of these LSD studies continued for years. As recently as 1987, a New York judge awarded $700,000 to the family of a mental patient who killed himself after having been given LSD without an explanation of the drug's nature. The judge said that there was a "conspiracy of silence" among the army, the Department of Justice, and the New York State Attorney General to conceal events surrounding the death of the subject, Harold Blauer.

Mescaline (Peyote)

Mescaline is one of approximately 30 psychoactive chemicals that have been isolated from the peyote cactus and used for centuries in the Americas (see "Here and Now," Peyote: An Ancient Indian Way). One of the first reports on the peyote plant was made by Francisco Hernandez to the court of King Philip II of Spain. King Philip was interested in reports from the earlier Cortés expedition about strange medicines the natives used and sent Hernandez to collect information about herbs and medicines. Hernandez worked on this project from

1570 to 1575 and reported on the use of more than 1200 plant remedies as well as the existence of many hallucinogenic plants. He was one of the first to record the eating of parts of the peyote cactus and the resulting visions and mental changes.

In the 17th century, Spanish Catholic priests asked their Indian converts to confess to the use of peyote, which they believed was used to conjure up demons. However, nothing stopped its use. By 1760, use of peyote had spread into what is now the United States.

Peyote has been confused with another plant, the mescal shrub, which produces dark red beans that contain an extremely toxic alkaloid called *cytisine.* This alkaloid may cause hallucinations, convulsions, and even death. In addition, a mescal liquor is made from the agave cactus. Partly because of misidentification with the toxic mescal beans, the U.S. government outlawed the use of both peyote and mescaline for everyone except members of the Native American Church (Mims 2000). Mescaline has been used for decades by this group as part of their religious sacrament. A recent study suggested that long-term religious use of peyote does not have significant psychological effects or cause problems with cognitive performance in Native Americans (Halpern et al. 2005).

Mescaline is the most active drug in peyote; it induces intensified perception of colors and euphoria in the user. However, as Aldous Huxley said in *The Doors of Perception* (1954), his book about his experimentation with mescaline, "Along with the happily transfigured majority of mescaline takers there is a minority that finds in the drug only hell and purgatory." After Huxley related his experiences with mescaline, it was used by an increasing number of people.

Physiological Effects The average dose of mescaline that will cause hallucinations and other physiological effects is from 300 to 600 milligrams. It may take up to 20 peyote (mescal) buttons (ingested orally) to get 600 milligrams of mescaline.

Based on animal studies, scientists estimate that a lethal dosage is 10 to 30 times greater than that which causes behavioral effects in human beings. (About 200 milligrams is the lowest mind-altering dose.) Death in animals results from convulsions and respiratory arrest. Mescaline is perhaps 1000 to 3000 times less potent than LSD and 30 times less potent than another common hallucinogen, psilocybin (Mathias 1993). Psilocybin is discussed later in this chapter.

The peyote cactus contains a number of drugs. The best known is mescaline.

Here and Now

Peyote: An Ancient Indian Way

Members of the Native American Church use the buttons of the hallucinogenic peyote cactus to brew a sacramental tea as sacred to them as the bread and wine of the Christian Eucharist. As described by one member, "Peyote is a gift given to the Indians, but its ways cannot be obtained overnight. It has to be done with sincerity. It becomes part of your way of life. One has to walk that walk." Those who accept this form of worship believe that respectful use of peyote can be a gateway to the realm of the spirit, visions, and guidance. The use of peyote as part of the latest New Age craze is very disturbing to members of this church and is viewed almost as a form of sacrilege.

Source: Mims, B. "Peyote: When the Ancient Indian Way Collides with a New Age Craze." *Salt Lake Tribune* 258 (1 July 1999): A-10. Native American Church. (2008). Available www.nativeamericanchurch.com/.

Mescaline's effects include dilation of the pupils (**mydriasis**), increase in body temperature, anxiety, visual hallucinations, and alteration of body image. The last effect is a type of hallucination in which parts of the body may seem to disappear or to become grossly distorted. Mescaline induces vomiting in many people and some muscular relaxation (sedation). Apparently, there are few aftereffects or drug hangover feelings at low doses. Higher doses of mescaline slow the heart and respiratory rhythm, contract the intestines and the uterus, and cause headache, difficulty in coordination, dry skin with itching, and hypertension (high blood pressure).

Mescaline users report that they lose all awareness of time. As with LSD, the setting for the "trip" influences the user's reactions. Most mescaline users prefer natural settings, most likely due to the historical association of this drug with Native Americans and their nature-related spiritual experiences (often under the influence of this drug). The visual hallucinations achieved depend on the individual. Colors are at first intensified and may be followed by hallucinations of shades, movements, forms, and events. The senses of smell and taste are enhanced. Some people claim (as with LSD) that they can "hear" colors and "see" sounds, such as the wind. Synesthesia occurs naturally in a small percentage of cases.

At low to medium doses, a state of euphoria is reported, often followed by a feeling of anxiety and less frequently by depression. Occasionally, users observe themselves as two people and experience the sensation that the mind and the body are separate entities. A number of people have had cosmic experiences that are profound — almost religious — and in which they discover a sense of unity with all creation. People who have this sensation often believe they have discovered the meaning of existence.

Mechanism of Action Within 30 to 120 minutes after ingestion, mescaline reaches a maximum concentration in the brain. The effects may persist for as long as 9 or 10 hours. Hallucinations may last up to 2 hours and are usually affected by the dose level. About half the dose is excreted unchanged after 6 hours and can be recovered in the urine for reuse (if peyote is in short supply). A slow tolerance builds up after repeated use, and there is cross-tolerance to LSD. As with LSD, mescaline intoxication can be alleviated or stopped by taking a dose of chlorpromazine (Thorazine), a tranquilizer, and to a lesser extent by taking diazepam (Valium). Like LSD, mescaline probably exerts much of its hallucinogenic effects by altering serotonin systems (Aghajanian and Marck 2000).

Analysis of street samples of mescaline obtained in a number of U.S. cities over the past decade shows that the chemical sold rarely is authentic. Regardless of color or appearance, these street drugs are usually other hallucinogens, such as LSD, 2,6-dimethoxy-4-methylamphetamine (DOM), or PCP. If a person decides to take hallucinogenic street drugs, "let the buyer beware." Not only is the actual content often different and potentially much more toxic than bargained for (they are frequently

KEY TERMS

mydriasis
pupil dilation

contaminated), but the dosage is usually unknown even if the drug is genuine.

Psilocybin

The drug psilocybin has a long and colorful history. Its principal source is the *Psilocybe mexicana* mushroom of the "magic" variety (Goldstein 1994; U.S. Department of Justice 2002). It was first used by some of the early natives of Central America more than 2000 years ago. In Guatemala, statues of mushrooms that date back to 100 B.C. have been found. The Aztecs later used the mushrooms for ceremonial rites. When the Spaniards came into Mexico in the 1500s, the natives were calling the *Psilocybe mexicana* mushroom "God's flesh" (Harvard Mental Health Letter 2006). Because of this seeming sacrilege, the natives were harshly treated by the Spanish priests.

Gordon Wasson identified the *Psilocybe mexicana* mushroom in 1955. The active ingredient was extracted in 1958 by Albert Hofmann, who also synthesized LSD. Doing research, Hofmann wanted to make certain he would feel the effects of the mushroom, so he ate 32 of them, weighing 2.4 grams (a medium dose by Native American standards) and then recorded his hallucinogenic reactions (Burger 1968).

Timothy Leary also tried some psilocybin mushrooms in Mexico in 1960; apparently, the experience influenced him greatly. On his return to Harvard, he carried out a series of experiments using psilocybin with student groups. Leary was careless in experimental procedures and did some work in uncontrolled situations. His actions caused a major administrative upheaval, ending in his departure from Harvard.

One of Leary's questionable studies was the "Good Friday" experiment in which 20 theological students were given either a placebo or psilocybin in a double-blind study (that is, neither the researcher nor the subjects know who gets the placebo or the drug), after which all attended the same 2.5-hour Good Friday service. The experimental group reported mystical experiences whereas the control group did not (Pahnke and Richards 1966). Leary believed that the experience was of value and that, under proper control and guidance, the hallucinatory experience could be beneficial.

Psilocybin is not very common on the street. Generally, it is administered orally and is eaten either fresh or dried. Accidental poisonings are common for those who mistakenly consume poiso-nous mushrooms rather than the hallucinogenic variety.

The dried form of these mushrooms contains from 0.2% to 0.5% psilocybin. The hallucinogenic effects produced are quite similar to those of LSD, and there is a cross-tolerance among psilocybin, LSD, and mescaline. The effects caused by psilocybin vary with the dosage taken. Up to 4 milligrams cause a pleasant experience, relaxation, and some body sensation. In some subjects, higher doses cause considerable perceptual and body image changes, accompanied by hallucinations, as illustrated in the following quote:

> The first time I 'shroomed, everything looked like it was made of plastic, like everything could be folded up or something. Whatever somebody told me, I would believe it to be true. Like if I was drinking a beer and someone told me it was tequila, I would taste tequila. *(From Venturelli's files, interview with a 20-year-old male, 1995.)*

In extreme cases, psilocybin can even induce the first stages of schizophrenia-like psychosis (Vollenwelder et al. 1998). Psilocybin stimulates the autonomic nervous system, dilates the pupils, and increases the body temperature. There is some evidence that psilocybin is metabolized into psilocin, which is more potent and may be the principal active ingredient. Psilocin is found in mushrooms, albeit in small amounts. Like the other hallucinogens, psilocybin apparently causes no physical dependence.

Tryptamines Some compounds related to the tryptamine class of drugs (molecules that resemble the

The *Psilocybe* mushroom is the source of the hallucinogens psilocybin and psilocin.

neurotransmitter serotonin) have hallucinogenic properties and can exist naturally in herbs, fungi, and animals or can be synthesized in the laboratory. Most of these compounds are Schedule I drugs and illegal (Drug Enforcement Agency [DEA] 2002b). Two examples are discussed in this section.

Dimethyltryptamine (DMT). DMT is a short-acting hallucinogen found in the seeds of certain leguminous trees native to the West Indies and parts of South America (Schultes 1978). It is also prepared synthetically in illicit laboratories. For centuries, the powdered seeds have been used as a snuff called *cohoba* in pipes and snuffing tubes. The Haitian natives claim that, under the influence of the drug, they can communicate with their gods. Its effects may last less than 1 hour, which has earned it the nickname "the businessman's lunch break" drug.

DMT has no effect when taken orally; it is inhaled either as smoke from the burning plant or in vaporized form. DMT is sometimes added to parsley leaves or flakes, tobacco, or marijuana to induce its hallucinogenic effect. The usual dose is 60 to 150 milligrams. In structure and action, it is similar to psilocybin although not as powerful. Like the other hallucinogens discussed, DMT does not cause physical dependence.

Foxy. The synthetic substance chemically named 5-methoxy-*N,N*-diisopropyltryptamine (Foxy) is a relatively new hallucinogen. This drug has been used at raves and clubs in Arizona, California, New York, and Florida. It was added to the DEA Schedule I category in 2004 (Wikipedia 2007). At lower doses, Foxy can cause euphoria; at higher doses, its effects are similar to LSD (DEA 2002b).

Nutmeg High doses of nutmeg can be quite intoxicating, causing symptoms such as drowsiness, stupor, delirium, and sleep. Prison inmates have known about this drug for years, so in most prisons use of spices such as nutmeg is restricted.

Nutmeg contains 5% to 15% myristica oil, which is responsible for the physical effects. Myristicin (about 4%), which is structurally similar to mescaline, and elemicin are probably the most potent psychoactive ingredients in nutmeg. Myristicin blocks release of serotonin from brain neurons. Some scientists believe that it can be converted in the body to MDMA (a close relative of MDA, discussed later), which also affects the CNS. Mace, the exterior covering of the nutmeg seed, also contains the hallucinogenic compound myristicin.

Two tablespoons of nutmeg (about 14 grams) taken orally cause a rather unpleasant "trip" with a dreamlike stage; rapid heartbeat, dry mouth, and thirst are experienced as well. Agitation, apprehension, and a sense of impending doom may last about 12 hours, with a sense of unreality persisting for several days (Claus et al. 1970).

■ Phenylethylamine Hallucinogens

The phenylethylamine drugs are chemically related to amphetamines. Phenylethylamines have varying degrees of hallucinogenic and CNS stimulant effects, which are likely related to their ability to release serotonin and dopamine, respectively. Consequently, the phenylethylamines that predominantly release serotonin are dominated by their hallucinogenic action and are LSD-like, whereas those more inclined to release dopamine are dominated by their stimulant effects and are amphetamine-like.

Dimethoxymethylamphetamine

The basic structure of dimethoxymethylamphetamine (DOM or STP) is amphetamine. Nonetheless, it is a fairly powerful hallucinogen that seems to work through mechanisms similar to those found with mescaline and LSD. In fact, the effects of DOM are similar to those caused by a combination of amphetamine and LSD, with the hallucinogenic effects of the drug overpowering the amphetamine-like physiological effects.

"Designer" Amphetamines

"Designer" amphetamines were discussed in Chapter 10 but are presented again here owing to their hallucinogenic effects. Their hybrid actions as psychedelic stimulants not only make them a particularly fascinating topic for research, but also provide a unique experience described by drug abusers as a "smooth amphetamine" or **entactogens** (implying that the pleasurable sensation of touch is enhanced). This characterization likely accounts for the popularity of the designer amphetamines (de la Torre et al. 2004).

KEY TERMS

entactogens
drugs that enhance the sensation and pleasure of touching

3,4-Methylenedioxyamphetamine (MDA) MDA, first synthesized in 1910, is structurally related to both mescaline and amphetamine. Early research found that MDA is an *anorexiant* (causing loss of appetite) as well as a mood elevator in some persons. Further research has shown that the mode of action of MDA is similar to that of amphetamines. It causes additional release of the neurotransmitters serotonin, dopamine, and norepinephrine.

MDA has been used as an adjunct to psychotherapy. In one study, eight volunteers who had previously experienced the effects of LSD under clinical conditions were given 150 milligrams of MDA. Effects of the drug were noted between 40 and 60 minutes following ingestion by all eight subjects. The subjective effects following administration peaked at the end of 90 minutes and persisted for approximately 8 hours. None of the subjects experienced hallucinations, perceptual distortion, or closed-eye imagery, but they reported that the feelings the drug induced had some relationship to those previously experienced with LSD. The subjects found that both drugs induced an intensification of feelings, increased perceptions of self-insight, and heightened empathy with others during the experience. Most of the subjects also felt an increased sense of aesthetic enjoyment at some point during the intoxication. Seven of the eight subjects said they perceived music as "three-dimensional" (Naranjo et al. 1967).

On the street, MDA has been called the *love drug* because of its effects on the sense of touch and the attitudes of the users. Users often report experiencing a sense of well-being (likely a stimulant effect) and heightened tactile sensations (like a hallucinogenic effect) and thus increased pleasure through sex and expressions of affection. Those under the influence of MDA frequently focus on interpersonal relationships and demonstrate an overwhelming desire or need to be with or talk to people. Some users say they have a very pleasant "body high" — more sensual than cerebral, and more emphatic than introverted. For these reasons, MDA is sometimes used by persons attending raves, much like MDMA or Ecstasy (Kalant 2001).

The unpleasant side effects most often reported are nausea, periodic tensing of muscles in the neck, tightening of the jaw and grinding of the teeth, and dilation of the pupils. Street doses of MDA range from 100 to 150 milligrams. Serious convulsions and death have resulted from larger doses, but in these cases the quantity of MDA was not accurately measured. Ingestion of 500 milligrams of pure MDA has been shown to cause death. The only adverse reaction to moderate doses reported is a marked physical exhaustion, lasting as long as 2 days (Marquardt et al. 1978).

An unpleasant MDA experience should be treated the same as a bad trip with any hallucinogen. The person should be "talked down" (reassured) in a friendly and supportive manner. The use of other drugs is rarely needed, although medical attention may be necessary. Under the Comprehensive Drug Abuse Prevention and Control Act of 1970, MDA is classified as a Schedule I substance; illegal possession is a serious offense.

Methylenedioxymethamphetamine (MDMA) MDMA is a modification of MDA but is thought to have more psychedelic and less stimulant activity (for example, euphoria) than its predecessor. MDMA is also structurally similar to mescaline. This drug has become known as *Ecstasy, XTC,* and *Adam* (Zickler 2000). (Ecstasy was also discussed in Chapter 10.)

MDMA was synthesized in 1912 to suppress appetite, but due to bizarre side effects it was withdrawn from development until it became widely used in the 1980s (Adam 2006). This designer amphetamine can be produced easily (DEA 2002a). Although the synthesis can be done by local illicit laboratories (Hyslop 2000), most of the MDMA supplies in this country are smuggled in from outlaw drug laboratories in European countries such as the Netherlands (Cool Nurse 2007). The unusual psychological effects it produces are part of the reason for its popularity. The drug causes euphoria, increased energy, increased sensitivity to touch, and lowered inhibitions. Many users claim it intensifies emotional feelings without sensory distortion and that it increases empathy and awareness both of the user's body and of the aesthetics of the surroundings (Farley 2000). Some consider MDMA to be an aphrodisiac. Because MDMA lowers defense mechanisms and reduces inhibitions, it has even been used during psychoanalysis (Cloud 2000). In fact, recently MDMA was approved by the FDA to be tested as a psychotherapeutic drug with the ultimate objective of determining its value in the treatment of patients suffering from posttraumatic stress disorder (PTSD) (Multidisciplinary Association for Psychedelic Studies [MAPS] 2007).

MDMA — popularized in the 1980s by articles in *Newsweek* (Adler 1985), *Time* (Toufexis 1985), and other magazines — recently was again touted on the national newsstands as a drug with euphoric effects, potential therapeutic value, and lack of serious side effects. MDMA is popular with college-age students and young adults (Office of National Drug Control Policy [ONDCP] 2008). Because of its effect of enhancing sensations, MDMA has been used as part of a countercultural rave scene, including high-tech music and laser light shows. Observers report that MDMA-linked rave parties are reminiscent of the acid parties of the 1960s and 1970s. The latest cycle of MDMA popularity peaked in 2001 and was being used by 10% of high school seniors (Johnston 2007). However, due to reports of MDMA neurotoxicity and persistent negative side effects, use of this drug has decreased dramatically and by 2006 was being used by only 4.1% of high school seniors (Johnston 2007).

Because of the widespread abuse of MDMA, the DEA prohibited its use by formally placing it on the Schedule I list in 1988 (Office of National Drug Control Policy [ONDCP] 2008). At the time of the ban, it was estimated that as many as 200 physicians were using the drug in psychotherapy (Greer and Tolbert 1990) and an estimated 30,000 doses per month were being taken for recreational purposes. Currently, MDMA is referred to as a "club drug" because of its frequent use at rave dances, clubs, and bars (Office of National Drug Control Policy [ONDCP] 2008). A dose of this drug is readily affordable at $10 to $20 (Hegadoran et al. 1999).

MDMA is usually taken orally, but it is sometimes snorted or even occasionally smoked. After the high starts, it may persist for minutes or even

Ecstasy is frequently used at raves to increase sensory stimulation and the pleasure of touching.

an hour, depending on the person, the purity of the drug, and the environment in which it is taken. When coming down from an MDMA-induced high, people often take small oral doses known as "boosters" to get high again. If they take too many boosters, they become very fatigued the next day. The average dose is about 75 to 150 milligrams; toxic effects have been reported at higher doses (Cami et al. 2000). Some statistics suggest that almost 50% of the tablets sold as MDMA actually contain other drugs such as aspirin, caffeine, cocaine, methamphetamine, or pseudoephedrine (Tanner-Smith 2006).

There is disagreement as to the possible harmful side effects of MDMA. Use of high doses can cause psychosis and paranoia (Parrott 2000a). Some negative physiological responses caused by recreational doses include dilated pupils, dry mouth and throat, clenching and grinding of teeth (resulting in the use of baby pacifiers), muscle aches and stiffness (in 28% of users), fatigue (in 80% of users), insomnia (in 38% of users), agitation, and anxiety. Some of these reactions can be intense and unpredictable. Under some conditions, death can be caused by hyperthermia (elevated body temperature), instability of the autonomic nervous system, and kidney failure (Burke 2001).

Several studies have demonstrated long-term damage to serotonin neurons in the brain following a single high dose of either MDMA or MDA, which may result in impaired memory, diminished ability to process information, and heightened impulsivity (Parrott 2000b; Williams 2002). Although the behavioral significance of this damage in people is not clear, at the present time caution using this drug is warranted (see "Here and Now," MDMA's Casual User).

There has been considerable debate as to the addictive properties of MDMA. Some claim this drug is like LSD with little likelihood of causing physical dependence, whereas others claim its properties are likely to be more amphetamine-like. Part of the difficulty in sorting out this controversy is that most moderate MDMA users also use other drugs, making it difficult to determine which effects are specifically attributable to the MDMA. The potential to cause addiction and dependence by MDMA is likely somewhere between that of amphetamine and LSD. Because of its ability to cause euphoria and release dopamine in the brain, it is very probable that use by smoking or injection can cause significant dependence.

Here and Now

MDMA's Casual User

A study examined fifteen regular Ecstasy users, fifteen novice (first-time) Ecstasy users, and fifteen control subjects who attended a Saturday night rave. The regular users consumed, on average, 1.8 MDMA tablets, the novice users took 1.4 MDMA tablets, and the control subjects had no drug except alcohol. All groups reported positive moods during the dance. However, 2 days later, the Ecstasy users felt significantly more depressed, unsociable, unpleasant, and less good-tempered than the control subjects. Verbal recall was also diminished in MDMA users, who remembered only 60% to 70% of the words remembered by the control subjects. Those who used Ecstasy regularly had the most difficulty remembering.

Source: Parrott, A., and J. Lasky. "Ecstasy (MDMA) Effects Upon Mood and Cognition: Before, During and After a Saturday Night Dance." *Psychopharmacology* 139 (1998): 261–268.

■ Anticholinergic Hallucinogens

The anticholinergic hallucinogens include naturally occurring alkaloid (bitter organic base) substances that are present in plants and herbs found around the world. These drugs are often mentioned in folklore and in early literature as being added to potions. They are thought to have killed the Roman Emperor Claudius and to have poisoned Hamlet's father. Historically, they have been the favorite drugs used to eliminate inconvenient people (Marken et al. 1996). Hallucinogens affecting the cholinergic neurons also have been used by South American Indians for religious ceremonies (Schultes and Hofmann 1980) and were probably used in witchcraft to give the illusion of flying, to prepare sacrificial victims, and even to give some types of marijuana ("superpot") its kick.

The potato family of plants (Solanaceae) contain most of these mind-altering drugs. The following three potent anticholinergic compounds are commonly found in these plants: (1) scopolamine, or hyoscine; (2) hyoscyamine; and (3) atropine. Scopolamine may produce excitement, hallucinations, and delirium even at therapeutic doses. With atropine, doses bordering on toxic levels are usually required to obtain these effects (Schultes and Hofmann 1973). All of these active alkaloid drugs block some acetylcholine receptors (see Chapter 4).

These alkaloid drugs can be used as ingredients in cold symptom remedies because they have a drying effect and block production of mucus in the nose and throat. They also prevent salivation; therefore, the mouth becomes uncommonly dry and perspiration may stop. Atropine may increase the heart rate by 100% and dilate the pupils markedly, causing inability to focus on nearby objects. Other annoying side effects of these anticholinergic drugs include constipation and difficulty in urinating. These inconveniences tend to discourage excessive abuse of these drugs for their hallucinogenic properties. Usually, people who abuse these anticholinergic compounds are receiving the drugs by prescription (Marken et al. 1996).

Anticholinergics can cause drowsiness by affecting the sleep centers of the brain. At large doses, a condition occurs that is similar to a psychosis, characterized by delirium, loss of attention, mental confusion, and sleepiness (Carlini 1993). Hallucinations may also occur at higher doses. At very high doses, paralysis of the respiratory system may cause death.

Although hundreds of plant species naturally contain anticholinergic substances and consequently can cause psychedelic experiences, only a few of the principal plants are mentioned here.

Atropa Belladonna:
The Deadly Nightshade Plant

Knowledge of *Atropa belladonna* is very old, and its use as a drug is reported in early folklore. The name of the genus, *Atropa,* is the origin for the drug name atropine and indicates the reverence the Greeks had for the plant. Atropos was one of the three Fates in Greek mythology, whose duty it was to cut the thread of life when the time came. This plant has been used for thousands of years by assassins and murderers. In *Tales of the Arabian Nights,* unsuspecting potentates were poisoned with atropine from the deadly nightshade or one of its relatives. Fourteen berries of the deadly nightshade contain enough drug to cause death.

The species name, *belladonna,* means "beautiful woman." In early Rome and Egypt, girls with large pupils were considered attractive and friendly. To create this condition, they would put a few drops of an extract of this plant into their eyes, causing the pupils to dilate (Marken et al. 1996). Belladonna has also enjoyed a reputation as a love potion.

Mandragora Officinarum: The Mandrake

The mandrake contains several active psychedelic alkaloids: hyoscyamine, scopolamine, atropine, and mandragorine. Mandrake has been used as a love potion for centuries but has also been known for its toxic properties. In ancient folk medicine, mandrake was used to treat many ailments in spite of its side effects. It was recommended as a sedative, to relieve nervous conditions, and to relieve pain (Schultes and Hofmann 1980), as portrayed in the 2007 movie, *Pan's Labyrinth.*

The root of the mandrake is forked and, viewed with a little imagination, may resemble the human body (as portrayed in the *Harry Potter and the Chamber of Secrets* movie in 2002). Because of this resemblance, it has been credited with human attributes, which gave rise to many superstitions in the Middle Ages about its magical powers. Shakespeare referred to this plant in *Romeo and Juliet.* In her farewell speech, Juliet says, "And shrieks like mandrakes torn out of the earth, that living mortals hearing them run mad."

Hyoscyamus Niger: Henbane

Henbane is a plant that contains both hyoscyamine and scopolamine. In A.D. 60, Pliny the Elder spoke of henbane: "For this is certainly known, that if one takes it in drink more than four leaves, it will put him beside himself" (Jones 1956). Henbane was also used in the orgies, or bacchanalias, of the ancient world.

Although rarely used today, henbane has been given medicinally since early times. It was frequently used to cause sleep, although hallucinations often occurred if given in excess. It was likely included in witches' brews and deadly concoctions during the Dark Ages (Schultes and Hofmann 1980).

Datura Stramonium: Jimsonweed

The *Datura* genus of the Solanaceae family includes a large number of related plants found worldwide. The principal active drug in this group is scopolamine; there are also several less active alkaloids.

Throughout history, these plants have been used as hallucinogens by many societies. They are mentioned in early Sanskrit and Chinese writings and were revered by the Buddhists. There is also some indication that the priestess (oracle) at the ancient Greek Temple of Apollo at Delphi was

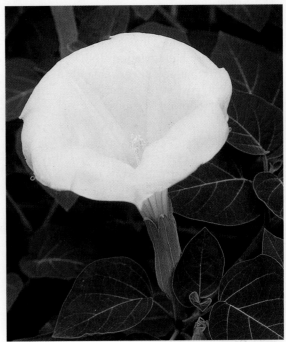

Datura stramonium, or jimsonweed, is a common plant that contains the hallucinogenic drug scopolamine.

under the influence of this type of plant when she made prophecies (Schultes 1970). Before the supposed divine possession, she appeared to have chewed leaves of the sacred laurel. A mystic vapor was also reported to have risen from a fissure in the ground. The sacred laurel may have been one of the *Datura* species, and the vapors may have come from burning these plants.

Jimsonweed gets its name from an incident that took place in 17th-century Jamestown. British soldiers ate this weed while trying to capture Nathaniel Bacon, who had made seditious remarks about the king. Although still abused occasionally by adventuresome young people, the anticholinergic side effects of jimsonweed are so unpleasant that it rarely becomes a long-term problem (Leinwand 2006; Tiongson and Salen 1998).

■ Other Hallucinogens

Technically, any drug that alters perceptions, thoughts, and feelings in a manner that is not normally experienced except in dreams can be

KEY TERMS

jimsonweed
a potent hallucinogenic plant

classified as a hallucinogen. Because the brain's sensory input is complex and involves several neurotransmitter systems, drugs with many diverse effects can cause hallucinations (NIDA 2001).

Four agents that do not conveniently fit into the principal categories of hallucinogens are discussed in the following sections.

Phencyclidine

Phencyclidine (PCP) is considered by many experts as the most dangerous of the hallucinogens (APA 2000; Maier 2003). PCP was developed in the late 1950s as an intravenous anesthetic. Although it was found to be effective, it had serious side effects that caused it to be discontinued for human use (NIDA 2001). Sometimes when people were recovering from PCP anesthesia, they experienced delirium and manic states of excitation lasting 18 hours (APA 2000). PCP is currently a Schedule II drug, legitimately available only as an anesthetic for animals but has even been banned from veterinary practice since 1985 because of its high theft rate. Most, if not all, PCP used in the United States today is produced illegally (National Drug Intelligence Center 2004).

Street PCP is mainly synthesized from readily available chemical precursors in clandestine laboratories. Within 24 hours, cooks (the makers of street PCP) can set up a lab, make several gallons of the drug, and destroy the lab before the police can locate them. Liquid PCP is then poured into containers and ready for shipment (Maier 2003).

PCP first appeared on the street drug scene in 1967 as the *PeaCe Pill*. In 1968, it reappeared in New York as a substance called *hog*. By 1969, PCP was found under a variety of guises. It was sold as *angel dust* and sprinkled on parsley for smoking. Today, it is sold on the streets under many different slang names, including *angel dust, supergrass, killerweed, embalming fluid, bobbies, dippies, hydro a,* and *purple haze,* to mention a few (Dewan 2003; Maier 2003).

In the late 1960s, PCP began to find its way into a variety of street drugs sold as psychedelics. By 1970, authorities observed that phencyclidine was used widely as a main ingredient in psychedelic preparations. It has been frequently substituted for and sold as LSD, mescaline, marijuana, and cocaine (Maier 2003; National Drug Intelligence Center 2004).

One difficulty in estimating the effects or use patterns of PCP is caused by variance in drug purity. Also, there are about 30 **analogs** of PCP,

some of which have appeared on the street. PCP has so many other street names that people may not know they are using it or they may have been deceived when buying what they thought was LSD or mescaline (Dewan 2003). Users may not question the identity of the substances unless they have a bad reaction.

PCP is available as a pure, white crystalline powder, as tablets, or as capsules. However, because it is usually manufactured in makeshift laboratories, it is frequently discolored by contaminants from a tan to brown with a consistency ranging from powder to a gummy mass (U.S. Department of Justice 1991). PCP can be taken orally, smoked, sniffed, or injected (NIDA 2007c). In the late 1960s through the early 1970s, PCP was mostly taken orally, but it is now commonly snorted or applied to dark brown cigarettes, leafy materials such as parsley, mint, oregano, marijuana, or tobacco, and smoked (U.S. Department of Justice 2003). By smoking PCP, the experienced user is better able to limit his or her dosage to a desired level. After smoking, the subjective effects appear within 1 to 5 minutes and peak within the next 5 to 30 minutes. The high lasts about 4 to 6 hours, followed by a 6- to 24-hour "comedown" (APA 2000).

In the 1979 national drug survey performed by the National Institute on Drug Abuse, about 7% of U.S. high school seniors had used PCP in a 12-month period; however, in 2004, that rate had declined to 0.7% (Johnston 2007).

Physiological Effects Although PCP may have hallucinogenic effects, it can cause a host of other physiological actions, including stimulation, depression, anesthesia, and analgesia. The effects of PCP on the CNS vary greatly. At low doses, the most prominent effect is similar to that of alcohol intoxication, with generalized numbness. As the dose of PCP increases, the person becomes even more insensitive and may become fully anesthetized. Large doses can cause coma, convulsions, and death (APA 2000).

The majority of peripheral effects are apparently related to activation of the sympathetic nervous system (see Chapter 5). Flushing, excess sweating, and a blank stare are common, although the size

KEY TERMS

analogs
drugs with similar structures

of the pupils is unaffected. The cardiovascular system reacts by increasing blood pressure and heart rate. Other effects include side-to-side eye movements (called *nystagmus*), muscular incoordination, double vision, dizziness, nausea, and vomiting (National Drug Intelligence Center 2004). These symptoms occur in many people taking medium to high doses.

Psychological Effects PCP has unpleasant effects most of the time it is used. Why, then, do people use it repeatedly as their drug of choice?

PCP has the ability to markedly alter the person's subjective feelings; this effect may be reinforcing, even though the alteration is not always positive. Some say use of PCP makes them feel godlike and powerful (Maier 2003). There is an element of risk, not knowing how the trip will turn out. PCP may give the user feelings of strength, power, and invulnerability (NIDA 2007c). Other positive effects include heightened sensitivity to outside stimuli, a sense of stimulation and mood elevation, and dissociation from surroundings. Also, PCP is a social drug; virtually all users report taking it in groups rather than during a solitary experience. PCP also causes serious perceptual distortions. Users cannot accurately interpret the environment and as a result may do what appear to be absurd things such as jump out of a window thinking they can fly (APA 2000).

Chronic users may take PCP in "runs" extending over 2 to 3 days, during which time they do not sleep or eat. In later stages of chronic administration, users may develop outright paranoia, unpredictable violent behavior, and auditory hallucinations (APA 2000). Law enforcement officers claim to be more fearful of suspects on PCP than of suspects on other drugs of abuse. Often such people seem to have superhuman strength and are totally irrational and very difficult — even dangerous — to manage (NIDA 2007a; 2007c).

PCP has no equal in its ability to produce brief psychoses similar to schizophrenia (Jentsch and Roth 1999). The psychoses — induced with moderate doses given to normal, healthy volunteers — last about 2 hours and are characterized by changes in body image, thought disorders, estrangement, autism, and occasionally rigid inability to move (**catatonia**, or catalepsy). Subjects report feeling numb, have great difficulty differentiating between themselves and their surroundings, and complain afterward of feeling extremely isolated and apathetic. They are often violently paranoid during the

psychosis (APA 2000; *Medical Letter* 1996). When PCP was given experimentally to hospitalized chronic schizophrenics, it made them much worse not for a few hours but for 6 weeks. PCP is not just another hallucinogen — many authorities view it as much more dangerous than other drugs of abuse (Dewan 2003; Maier 2003).

Medical Management The diagnosis of a PCP overdose is frequently missed because the symptoms often closely resemble those of an acute schizophrenic episode.

Simple, uncomplicated PCP intoxication can be managed with the same techniques used in other psychedelic drug cases. It is important to have a quiet environment, limited contact with an empathic person capable of determining any deterioration in the patient's physical state, protection from self-harm, and the availability of hospital facilities. Talking down is not helpful; the patient is better off isolated from external stimuli as much as possible.

Valium is often used for its sedating effect to prevent injury to self and to staff and also to reduce the chance for severe convulsions. An antipsychotic agent (for example, haloperidol [Haldol]) is frequently administered to make the patient manageable (Jaffe 1990).

The medical management of a comatose or convulsing patient is more difficult. The patient may need external respiratory assistance and external cooling to reduce fever. Blood pressure may have to be reduced to safe levels and convulsions controlled. Restraints and four to five strong hospital aides are often needed to prevent the patient from injuring himself or herself or the medical staff. After the coma lightens, the patient typically becomes delirious, paranoid, and violently assaultive.

Effects of Chronic Use Chronic PCP users may develop a tolerance to the drug; thus, a decrease in behavioral effects and toxicity can occur with frequent administration. Different forms of dependence may occur when tolerance develops. Users may complain of vague cravings after cessation of the drug. In addition, long-term difficulties

KEY TERMS

catatonia
a condition of physical rigidity, excitement, and stupor

in memory, speech, and thinking persist for 6 to 12 months in the chronic user (NIDA 2007c). These functional changes are accompanied by personality deficits such as social isolation and states of anxiety, nervousness, and extreme agitation (APA 2000).

Ketamine

Ketamine has received attention lately as a club drug. Its annual use in 2006 by high school seniors was 1.4% (Johnston 2007). Almost all persons who abuse ketamine have abused at least three other illicit drugs (Center for Substance Abuse Research [CESAR] 2006). Ketamine, like PCP, was originally developed for its general anesthetic properties (NIDA 2001). Its effects resemble those of PCP except they are more rapid and less potent (NIDA 2001). Depending on the dose, ketamine can have many effects, ranging from feelings of weightlessness to out-of-body or near-death experiences. Ketamine, often referred to as "Special K," has been abused as a "date rape" drug like other CNS depressants, such as Rohypnol or gamma-hydroxybutyrate (GHB) (see Chapter 6; NIDA 2001). Abuse of ketamine has been reported in many cities throughout the United States, and the drug is sometimes snorted as a substitute for cocaine. Several deaths have been linked to ketamine overdoses (NIDA 2007a).

Dextromethorphan

Dextromethorphan is the active ingredient used in many OTC cough medicines because of its ability to suppress the cough reflex (CESAR 2005). However, when consumed in high quantities (approximately ten times the recommended dose), it can cause some hallucinogenic effects much like PCP and ketamine do. These effects can vary and have been described as ranging from a mild stimulant effect to a complete dissociation from one's body. The effects can last for several hours. Abuse of dextromethorphan is typically done by teenagers and is sometimes referred to as "roboing" (CESAR 2005).

Marijuana

In high doses, marijuana use can result in image distortions and hallucinations (Nunez and Gurpegui 2002). Some users claim that marijuana can enhance hearing, vision, and skin sensitivity, although these claims have not been confirmed in controlled laboratory studies.

Although typical marijuana use does not appear to cause severe emotional disorders like the other hallucinogens, some experts suggest it can aggravate underlying mental illness such as depression. Each month, thousands of people seek professional treatment due to marijuana-related problems (Narconon 2007). In contrast to other hallucinogens that have a combination of stimulant and psychedelic effects, high doses of marijuana cause a combination of depression and hallucinations and enhance the appetite (Fleckenstein 2000). Marijuana is discussed thoroughly in Chapter 13.

■ NATURAL SUBSTANCES

Naturally Occurring Hallucinogens

Many plants contain naturally occurring hallucinogens. As already discussed, examples of such substances include mescaline from the peyote cactus, psilocybin from psilocybe mushrooms, and anticholinergic drugs such as atropine from the deadly nightshade plant, mandrake, or jimsonweed. Although some of these plants have been used for medicinal purposes for centuries, typically the therapeutic benefit has not been a consequence of the hallucinogenic effects of the substance. For example, anticholinergic drugs usually cause CNS depression and induce sleep; therefore, herbs that contain these drugs have been used as sleep potions. The hallucinogenic properties of some natural products, such as peyote, are viewed as positive by some cultures. As already mentioned, peyote is employed in a religious context as a sacrament for the Native American Church. In the United States today, the hallucinogen-containing natural substances are generally not viewed as ther-

Ketamine is frequently used as a general anesthetic for veterinarian procedures.

►Case in Point Jimsonweed Abuse in Idaho

Jimsonweed is a natural herb whose medicinal purposes include treatment for asthma, muscle spasms, and whooping cough. Its dangerous side effects include hallucinogenic actions and induction of a rapid heartbeat. Because of the effects jimsonweed has on the body, and because it is a legal, uncontrolled substance, adolescents have been known to take this herb for its psyche-

delic properties. For example, a new wave of jimsonweed abuse in eastern Idaho recently resulted in several teenagers entering the emergency room in drug-induced comas. Jimsonweed is a fairly accessible and somewhat inexpensive herb that is dangerous not only because of its biological effects, but also because of the variability of its side effects' intensity from batch to batch.

Source: "Jimson Weed Abuse in Idaho" (2003). Available www.drug-rehabs.org/content.php?cid=1097&state=Idaho.

apeutic and are more likely to be used for their mind-altering properties as recreational drugs by adolescents (see "Case in Point," Jimsonweed Abuse in Idaho). In 2006 there were almost 1,000 reported incidents of poisonings with these hallucinogenic plants, most frequently by kids trying to get high (Leinwand 2006). Some users claim because these are natural rather than synthetic sources of a hallucinogenic episode, that somehow it makes the experience more rewarding and desirable. There is no evidence that the natural-versus-synthetic features of a hallucinogen are

responsible for the quality of a drug-induced hallucination. Frequently, consumption of these seeds and weeds causes severe hallucinations, dry mouth, hyperthermia, seizures, and occasionally death (Leinwand 2006).

Salvia Divinorum

Occasionally, obscure hallucinogenic herbs make their way into the culture of hallucinogenic substance users. This migration has become easier because of the Internet and specialized web sites that provide information (some accurate and much

Here and Now

A Legal High, At Least for Now

One user described smoking *Salvia divinorum* he purchased legally at a local health shop near his home. He related an experience unlike any other that gave him a consciousness-expanding journey. His body felt disconnected, resulting in people and objects taking on a cartoonish, surreal, and marvelous appearance. Abruptly the visions ended and the user found himself back in his room with his "sitter" (a person designated to watch the drug user to prevent accidents or harm — this was recommended on the product's package). The user felt awkward and clumsy when talking or trying to stand. Within a couple of minutes his mind felt clear although his body was damp from sweating. The whole experience lasted approximately 5 minutes. The user admits little is known about the adverse effects of *Salvia* and acknowledges the need for additional study. But in the interim, products containing legal hallucinogenic herbs such as *Salvia* are

available in shops throughout the United States and around the world without regulation.

Source: Vince, G. "Legally High." *New Scientist.* (30 September 2006): 40–45.

anecdotal) and the means to acquire these typically natural substances. For example, a relatively recent hallucinogenic fad has been the use of the Mexican herb *Salvia divinorum,* a drug that did not reach the United States until the late 1980s (Allday 2007). This bright, leafy green plant can be smoked or chewed (Allday 2007). This relatively unknown plant is referred to as "diviner's mint" and is legal in most of the United States despite its ability to cause intense hallucinations, "out-of-body" experiences, and short-term memory loss (Jones 2001; Pienciak 2003). Promotions for these products include advertising claims such as "The Mazatec people have preserved *Salvia divinorum* and the knowledge surrounding its use for hundreds of years. We are privileged to have them share their sacred herb with us" (Jones 2001, p. A14). The dried herb can sell for as much as $15 to $50 a hit (Allday 2007). The drug typically makes the user introverted while "altering the conscious in unusual ways" (Vince 2006; see "Here and Now," A Legal High, At Least for Now). Although national drug information sources and law enforcement officers are not well informed about this hallucinogenic herb, the DEA has started to take notice and it has been outlawed in four states (Allday 2007). Law enforcement agencies claim to be watching carefully to see whether its use will cause significant health or social problems. This herb can have dramatic effects on perception similar to LSD (Allday 2007), causing hallucinations when chewed or smoked (Leinwand 2003). It typically is not used in social settings and often is used only once because the effects can be quite unpleasant, often triggering a lack of coordination and frightening perceptions (Simmie 2003). Because of its frequent negative consequences, this herb is not viewed as particularly addicting (Pienciak 2003).

Discussion Questions

1. Why were substances with hallucinogenic properties used by ancient religions and cults?

2. Would you expect natural hallucinogens such as peyote to have less adverse effects than other hallucinogens? Why or why not?

3. Why would a drug with both stimulant and hallucinogenic effects have peculiar abuse potential?

4. Why do some users find psychedelic experiences terrifying while others find them desirable?

5. Do you think the federal government is justified in lying to the public about the dangers of hallucinogens to convince people to stop using these drugs? Defend your answer.

6. How do the side effects of LSD compare with those of the CNS stimulants?

7. Why does MDMA have the potential to be popular?

8. Why is PCP more dangerous than LSD?

9. How do PCP and ketamine compare?

10. What is the best way to convince people that hallucinogenic drugs of abuse can be harmful?

11. What is a flashback, and how is it caused?

Summary

1 Many drugs can exert hallucinogenic effects. The principal hallucinogens include LSD types, phenylethylamines, and anticholinergic agents. The four major effects that occur from administering LSD are (1) heightened senses, (2) loss of sensory control, (3) self-reflection or introspection, and (4) loss of identity or sense of cosmic merging.

2 Hallucinogens exaggerate sensory input and cause vivid and unusual visual and auditory effects.

3 The classic hallucinogens, such as LSD, cause predominantly psychedelic effects. Phenylethylamines are related to amphetamines and cause varying combinations of psychedelic and stimulant effects. Anticholinergic drugs also produce psychedelic effects when taken in high doses.

4 One of the prominent effects of hallucinogens is self-reflection. The user becomes aware of thoughts and feelings that had been forgotten or repressed. It is claimed that some experiences help to clarify motives and relationships and cause periods of greater openness. These effects have been promoted by some psychiatrists as providing valid insights useful in psychotherapy.

5 The classic hallucinogens do not cause physical dependence. Although some tolerance can build up to the hallucinogenic effects of drugs such as LSD, withdrawal effects are usually minor.

6 The environment plays a major role in determining the sensory response to hallucinogens. Environments that are warm, comfortable, and hospitable tend to create a pleasant sensory response to the psychedelic effects of these drugs. Threatening, hostile environments are likely to lead to intimidating, frightening "bad trips."

7 In some users, high doses of LSD can cause a terrifying destruction of identity, resulting in panic and severe anxiety that resembles schizophrenia. Another psychological feature commonly associated with LSD is the flashback phenomenon. LSD use can cause recurring, unexpected visual and time distortions that last a few minutes to several hours. Flashbacks can occur months to years after use of the drug.

8 Designer amphetamines such as MDMA (Ecstasy) have been included in the "club drug" phenomenon. MDMA has been frequently used by young people to enhance the sensory experience of raves and the nightclub scene. Although viewed by some as harmless and even therapeutic, evidence of potentially serious negative consequences suggests that these drugs can be extremely dangerous in high doses and under some conditions.

9 Hallucinogens purchased on the street are often poorly prepared and contaminated with adulterant substances. This practice of cutting the pure drugs with other substances also makes use of street hallucinogens very dangerous.

10 PCP differs from the other traditional hallucinogens in several ways. (1) It is a general anesthetic in high doses. (2) It causes schizophrenia-like psychosis. PCP can produce incredible strength and extreme violent behavior, making users very difficult to manage. (3) Management of the severe psychological reactions to PCP requires drug therapy, whereas treatment of other hallucinogens often requires only reassurance, talking down, and supportive therapy. (4) Reactions to overdoses include fever, convulsions, and coma.

11 Other substances also abused for their hallucinogenic properties include ketamine, a veterinary general anesthetic; dextromethorphan, a common OTC anticough medication; and some natural herbs, such as *Salvia divinorum*, that are promoted over the Internet.

References

Abraham, H., A. Aldridge, and P. Gogia. "The Psychopharmacology of Hallucinogens." *Neuropharmacology* 14 (1996): 285–298.

Adam, D. "Truth About Ecstasy's Unlikely Trip from Lab to Dance Floor." *The Guardian* (18 August 2006). Available guardian.co.uk/uk/2006/aug/18/topstories3.drugsandalcohol.

Adler, J. "Getting High on Ecstasy." *Newsweek* (15 April 1985): 15.

Aghajanian, G., and G. Marck. "Serotonin Model of Schizophrenia Emerging Role of Glutamate Mechanisms." *Brain Research Review* 31 (2000): 302–312.

Allday, E. "Legal, Intense Hallucinogen Raises Alarms, *Salvia Divinorum* Produces Short Dreamlike Experience." *San Francisco Chronicle* (27 June 2007). Available sfgate.com/cgi-bin/article.cgi?f=/c/a/2007/06/27/MNGDPQMLU31.DTL.

American Psychiatric Association (APA). *Diagnostic and Statistical Manual of Mental Disorders.* 4th ed., Text Revision (*DSM-IV-TR*). Washington, DC: APA, 2000.

Associated Press. "60s Icon Timothy Leary Cooperated with the FBI." *Salt Lake Tribune* 258 (1 July 1999): A-10.

Burger, A., ed. "Quotes from Albert Hofmann." Drugs Affecting the Central Nervous System. *Psychotomimetic Agents,* vol. 2. New York: Dekker, 1968.

Burke, J. "Ecstasy Death Toll Set to Go on Rising." *Guardian Unlimited* (2001). Available http://society.guardian.co.uk.

Cami, J., M. Farre, M. Mas, and P. Roset. "Human Pharmacology of Ecstasy: Psychomotor Performance and Subjective Effects." *Journal of Clinical Psychopharmacology* 20 (2000): 455–466.

Carlini, E. "Preliminary Note: Dangerous Use of Anticholinergic Drugs in Brazil." *Drugs and Alcohol Dependence* 32 (1993): 1–7.

"Celebration #1." *New Yorker* 42 (1966): 43.

CESAR. "Dextromethorphan." *Center for Substance Abuse Research, University of Maryland* (2005). Available www.cesar.umd.edu/cesar/drugs/dxm.asp.

CESAR. *Majority of U.S. Youths and Young Adults Who Have Used Club Drugs Have Used 3 or More Types of Illicit Drugs.* [FAX] (22 May 2006).

Claus, E. P., V. E. Tyler, and L. R. Brady. *Pharmacognosy,* 6th ed. Philadelphia: Lea & Febiger, 1970.

Cloud, J. "The Lure of Ecstasy." *Time* 155 (5 June 2000): 62.

Cool Nurse. "Ecstasy-MDMA" (2007). Available www.coolnurse.com/ecstasy.htm.

Dewan, S. "A Drug Feared in the '70s Is Tied to Suspect in Killing." *The New York Times* (6 April 2003).

de la Torre, R., M. Farré, P. Roset, S. Abanade, M. Segura, and J. Cami. "Human Pharmacology of MDMA: Pharmacokinetics, Metabolism, and Disposition." *Therapeutic Drug Monitor* 26 (2004): 137–144.

Dishotsky, N. I., W. D. Loughman, R. E. Mogar, and W. R. Lipscomb. "LSD and Genetic Damage." *Science* 172 (1971): 431–440.

Drug Enforcement Agency (DEA). "September 2002 Highlight." *Domestic Strategy* (December 2002a): Publication # DEA-02060.

Drug Enforcement Agency (DEA). "Trippin on Tryptamine." *Intelligence Brief* (October 2002b): Document # DEA-02052.

Erowid. (2007). Available www.erowid.org/chemicals/lsd/lsd_faq.shtml#bad%20trips.

Farley, C. "Rave New World." *Time* 15 (5 June 2000): 69.

Fleckenstein, A. "Pharmacological Aspects of Substance Abuse." In *Remington: The Science and Practice of Pharmacy*, 20th edition, edited by A. Gennaro, 1175–1182. Baltimore, MD: Lippincott Williams & Wilkins, 2000.

Goldstein, A. *Addiction from Biology to Drug Policy*. New York: Freeman, 1994.

Goldstein, F. "Pharmacological Aspects of Substance Abuse." In *Remington's Pharmaceutical Sciences*, 19th ed., edited by A. R. Gennaro, 780–794. Easton, PA: Mack, 1995.

Greer, G., and R. Tolbert. "The Therapeutic Use of MDMA." In *Ecstasy: The Clinical, Pharmacological and Neurotoxicological Effects of the Drug MDMA*, edited by S. J. Peroutka, 28. Boston: Kluwer, 1990.

Halpern, J., and H. Pope. "Hallocinogen Persisting Perception Disorder: What Do We Know After 50 Years?" *Drug and Alcohol Dependence* 69 (2003): 109–119.

Halpern, J., A. Sherwood, J. Hudson, D. Yurgelun-Todd, and H. Pope. "Psychological and Cognitive Effects of Long-Term Peyote Use Among Native Americans." *Biological Psychiatry*, 58 (2005): 624–631.

Harvard Mental Health Letter. "Reviving the Study of Hallucinogens." (1 October 2006). Available http://read.health.harvard.edu/user/user.fas/s=784/fp=3/tp=76?T=open_summary,940482&P=summary.

Hegadoran, K., G. Baker, and M. Bourin. "3,4-Methylenedioxy Analogues of Amphetamine: Defining the Risks to Humans." *Neuroscience and Behavioral Review* 23 (1999): 539–553.

Huxley, A. *The Doors of Perception*. New York: Harper, 1954.

Hyslop, M. "Townsend Spearheads Campaign to Curb Rising Use of Ecstasy." *The Washington Times* (29 September 2000): C-1.

Jaffe, J. "Drug Addiction and Drug Abuse." In *The Pharmacological Basis of Therapeutics*, 8th ed., edited by A. Gilman, T. Rall, A. Nies, and P. Taylor, 522–573. New York: Pergamon, 1990.

Jentsch, J., and R. Roth. "The Neuropsychopharmacology of Phencyclidine: From NMDA Receptor Hypofunction to the Dopamine Hypothesis of Schizophrenia." *Neuropsychopharmacology* 20 (1999): 201–225.

Johnston, L. University of Michigan News Release (17 December 1999), citing the National Survey on Drug Abuse.

Johnston, L. "Monitoring the Future, 2006" (2007). Available www.monitoringthefuture.org/new.html.

Johnston, L., P. O'Malley, and J. Bachman. *National Survey Results on Drug Use from Monitoring the Future Study, 1975–1994*, vol. 2. University of Michigan, NIDA, NIH Publication No. 96-4027. Washington, DC: National Institute on Drug Abuse, 1996.

Jones, R. "New Cautions About an Herb That's Hip, Hallucinogenic and Legal." *The New York Times* (9 July 2001): A-14.

Jones, W. H. S. *Natural History*. Cambridge, MA: Harvard University Press, 1956.

Kalant, H. "The Pharmacology and Toxicology of 'Ecstasy' (MDMA) and the Related Drugs." *Canadian Medical Association Journal* 165 (2001): 917–928.

Leary, T., R. Metzner, and R. Alpert. *The Psychedelic Experience*. New Hyde Park, NY: University Books, 1964.

Leinwand, D. "Teens, and Now DEA, Are on Trail of Hallucinogenic Herb." *USA Today* (23 June 2003): 1.

Leinwand, D. "Jimson Weed Users Chase High All the Way to the Hospital." *USA Today* (1 November 2006). Available www.usatoday.com/news/nation/2006-11-01-jimson_x.htm.

Maier, T. "PCP Is Rearing Its Ugly Head Again." *Insight on the News* (17 February 2003): 4–6.

"Many Were Lost Because of Leary" Letters (to the editor). *USA Today* 14 (3 June 1996): 12-A.

Marken, P., S. Stoner, and M. Bunker. "Anticholinergic Drug Abuse and Misuse." *CNS Drugs* 5 (1996): 190–199.

Marquardt, G. M., V. DiStefano, and L. L. Ling. "Pharmacological Effects of (S)-, and (R)-MDA." In *The Psychopharmacology of Hallucinogens*, edited by R. C. Stillman and R. E. Willette. New York: Pergamon, 1978.

Mathias, R. "NIDA Research Takes a New Look at LSD and Other Hallucinogens." *NIDA Notes* 8 (March/April 1993): 6.

McGlothin, W., S. Cohen, and M. S. McGlothin. "Long-Lasting Effects of LSD on Normals." *Archives of General Psychiatry* 17 (1967): 521–532.

Medical Letter. "Phencyclidine (PCP)." 38 (10 May 1996): 45.

Mims, B. "Peyote: When the Ancient Indian Way Collides with a New Age Craze." *Salt Lake Tribune* 260 (12 August 2000): C-1.

Multidisciplinary Association for Psychedelic Studies (MAPS). "MDMA Research Information" (2007). Available www.maps.org/mdma/.

Naranjo, C., A. T. Shulgin, and T. Sargent. "Evaluation of 3,4-Methylenedioxyamphetamine (MDA) as an Adjunct to Psychotherapy." *Medicina et Pharmacologia Experimentalis* 17 (1967): 359–364.

Narconon. "FAQ About Marijuana." *Narconon of Southern California* (2007). Available www.addictionca.com/FAQ-marijuana.htm.

National Drug Intelligence Center. Intelligence Bulletin. "PCP, Increasing Availability and Abuse" (2004). DOJ Document ID: 2004-L0424-002.

National Institute on Drug Abuse [NIDA]. "Hallucinogens and Dissociative Drugs." *NIDA Research Report Series* (March 2001): NIH Publication # 01-4209.

National Institute on Drug Abuse [NIDA]. Infofax. Club Drugs (2007a). Available nida.nih.gov/Infofax/clubdrugs.html.

National Institute on Drug Abuse [NIDA]. Infofax. LSD (2007b). Available nida.nih.gov/Infofax/lsd.html.

National Institute on Drug Abuse [NIDA]. Infofax. PCP (Phencyclidine) (2007c). Available nida.nih.gov/Infofax/pcp.html.

Native American Church. (2008). Available www.nativeamericanchurch.com/.

Nichols, D. "Hallucinogens." *Pharmacological Therapeutics* 101 (2004): 131–181.

Nunez, L., and M. Gurpegui. "Cannabis-Induced Psychosis: A Cross-sectional Comparison with Acute Schizophrenia." *Acta Psychiatry Scandinavia* 105 (2002): 1173–1178.

O'Brien, C. "Drug Addiction and Drug Abuse." In *The Pharmacological Basis of Therapeutics*, 11th ed., edited by

L. Brunton, J. Lazo, and K. Parker, 607–627. New York: McGraw-Hill, 2006.

Office of National Drug Control Policy [ONDCP]. "Drug Facts: Club Drugs" (January 2008). Available whitehouse drugpolicy.gov/drugfact/club/index.html.

Pahnke, W. N., A. A. Kurland, S. Unger, C. Savage, and S. Grof. "The Experimental Use of Psychedelic (LSD) Psychotherapy." In *Hallucinogenic Drug Research: Impact on Science and Society,* edited by J. R. Gamage and E. L. Zerkin. Beloit, WI: Stash, 1970.

Pahnke, W. N., and W. A. Richards. "Implications of LSD and Experimental Mysticism." *Journal of Religion and Health* 5 (1966): 175–208.

Parrott, A. "Human Research on MDMA Neurotoxicity: Cognitive and Behavioral Indices of Changes." *Neuropsychobiology* 43 (2000a): 17–24.

Parrott, A. "Psychobiological Problems in Heavy 'Ecstasy' (MMA) Polydrug Users." *Drug and Alcohol Dependence* 60 (2000b): 105–110.

Philadelphia Inquirer. "We Are Winning the War on Drugs." (5 February 2006). Available www.mapinc.org/drugnews/v06/n150/a08.html.

Pienciak, R. "DEA Issues Warning for Legal Herb Stronger Than LSD." *Daily News (NY)* (25 July 2003).

Publishers Group. "Street Drugs." 2805 Alvarado Lane North, Plymouth, MN 55447 (2002).

Schaffer Library. "DEA LSD Field Division Assessments." *Schaffer Library of Drug Policy* (2007). Available www.druglibrary.org/schaffer/dea/pubs/lsd/LSD-8.htm.

Schultes, R. E. "Ethnopharmacological Significance of Psychotropic Drugs of Vegetal Origin." In *Principles of Psychopharmacology,* 2nd ed., edited by W. G. Clark and J. del Giudice. New York: Academic Press, 1978.

Schultes, R. E. "The Plant Kingdom and Hallucinogens (Part III)." *Bulletin on Narcotics* 22 (1970): 25–53.

Schultes, R. E., and A. Hofmann. *The Botany and Chemistry of Hallucinogens.* Springfield, IL: Thomas, 1973.

Schultes, R. E., and A. Hofmann. *The Botany and Chemistry of Hallucinogens,* 2nd ed. Springfield, IL: Thomas, 1980.

Simmie, S. "Herb Inspires High Expectations." *Toronto Star* (28 July 2003): F01.

Snyder, S. H. *Madness and the Brain.* New York: McGraw-Hill, 1974.

Stone, J. "Turn On, Tune In, Boot Up." *Discover* 12 (June 1991): 32–33.

Tanner-Smith, E. "Pharmacological Content of Tablets Sold as 'Ecstasy' Results from an Online Testing Service." *Drug and Alcohol Dependence* 83 (2006): 243–254.

Tiongson, J., and P. Salen. "Mass Ingestion of Jimsonweed by Eleven Teenagers." *Delaware Medical Journal* 70 (1998): 1–6.

Toufexis, A. "A Crackdown on Ecstasy." *Time* (10 June 1985): 64.

Tucker, R. "Acid Test." *Omni* (November 1987): 16.

U.S. Department of Justice. "Drugs, Youth, and the Internet." *Information Bulletin* (October 2002): Product #2002-L0424-006.

U.S. Department of Justice. "Let's All Work to Fight Drug Abuse." Pamphlet from DEA published by L.A.W. Publications and distributed with permission by International Drug Education Association, 1991.

U.S. Department of Justice. National Drug Threat Assessment 2003. "Other Dangerous Drugs, Hallucinogens." *National Drug Intelligence Center.* (2003): Product No. 2003-Q0317-001.

Vince, G. "Legally High." *New Scientist.* (30 September 2006): 40–45.

Vollenwelder, F., M. Vollenwelder-Scherpenhuyzen, A. Baber, N. Vogel, and D. Nell. "Psilocybin Induces Schizophrenia-like Psychosis in Human via a Serotonin-2 Agonist Action." *NeuroReport* 9 (1998): 3897–3902.

Weber, B. "Prairie LSD Studies Coined 'Psychedelic.'" *Toronto Star* (6 October 2006): A8.

Wikipedia. "5-Methoxy-diisopropyl-tryptamine" (2007). Available http://en.wikipedia.org/wiki/5-methoxy-diisopropyl tryptamine.

Williams, J. "Prenatal Exposure to Ecstasy May Impair Memory and Cognition." *NIDA Notes* 17 (October 2002): 8.

Zickler, P. "NIDA Launches Initiative to Control Club Drugs." *NIDA Notes* 14 (2000): 1.

CHAPTER 13

Marijuana

Learning ◎bjectives

On completing this chapter you will be able to:

◎ Explain what marijuana is and why it remains so controversial.

◎ Differentiate between the effects of low and high doses of marijuana.

◎ List and explain the potential effects marijuana use has on the body.

◎ Describe how tolerance and dependence affect the response to marijuana and its use.

◎ Explain the medical uses of marijuana.

◎ Explain what age groups are most likely to use marijuana.

◎ Explain the major characteristics of first-time marijuana users.

◎ Explain how the perceived danger of marijuana use has changed with regard to high school seniors and younger age groups.

◎ Differentiate between prior and current beliefs regarding the effects of chronic marijuana use.

Did You Know?

O George Washington grew marijuana plants at Mount Vernon for medicine and rope making.

O Out of 19.5 million illicit drug users in the United States, marijuana was used by approximately 75% of current illicit drug users, or approximately 14.6 million people.

O In some states, marijuana is one of the largest cash-producing crops.

O Marijuana still grows wild in many American states today.

O Research shows that many users have difficulty learning and remembering what they have learned when they are "high."

O "Although two-thirds of the U.S. population opposes legalizing marijuana, almost three-quarters think it should be made legally available to physicians to prescribe to patients for reducing pain and suffering" (Robert Wood Johnson Foundation 2001, p. 78).

O From 1975 to the present day, between 83% and 90% of every senior middle school class have said they could get marijuana fairly easily or very easily if they wanted some (Johnston et al. 2006).

Drugs and Society Online is a great source for additional drugs and society information for both students and instructors.
Visit **http://drugsandsociety.jbpub.com** to find a variety of useful tools for learning, thinking, and teaching.

Since I was in college and tried my first hit, I have always been a connoisseur of what we used to call grass, now it's weed or even "the ganja." I first went through a period of using it a lot — it was a different way to get a buzz. Then I got married and my wife did not like me smoking it, and we had kids, so except for a few occasional puffs from my neighbor, I just about gave it up. Then I got divorced [from my wife] and I married a woman who does not object to me smoking a little weed every now and then, even though she does not do it herself. So sometimes on weekends, I will roll a joint before going to bed and take a few puffs off of it. I know it is illegal, but big deal, who knows about it? I used to watch that program "Cops" and just found it silly when police officers would arrest someone (usually a young kid) for possession. Big bust, I would think. Isn't it silly to charge someone with possession of marijuana? I consider it to be like alcohol and cigarettes. I don't think it should be illegal anymore. I know so many people who do it and there are dozens of people who probably use this drug that I am not even aware of their using it. What happens if two-thirds of our population uses this drug? Are we going to charge and arrest all these people? The whole illegality of it is silly. *(From Venturelli's research files, interview with a 48-year-old male working as a restaurant owner, residing in Reno, Nevada, June 10, 2000.)*

We used to have one great big bong and fill it with dope [referring to marijuana], and all of us in someone's fraternity room would each take hits from the bong. Today, it's a different life altogether. I am working three different jobs, one teaching at a junior high school, [one] working at a film production studio, and my third claim to fame is my job as a part-time waiter. . . . I feel that I wasted many nights by just "smokin'," "dopin'," and "drinkin'" back during those college days. I sometimes think that I could have accomplished a lot more if I would not have inhaled so much dope. If I had to do it over again I would not have wasted so much time. *(From Venturelli's research files, interview with a 28-year-old male, August 9, 1996.)*

The preceding interviews illustrate two contrasting views regarding marijuana usage as a subcultural phenomenon. The first interview presents a "die-hard" user who refuses to relinquish his use of this drug. This individual has been using mari-

juana for many years and considers it an essential recreational drug. Conversely, the second interviewee expresses some regret over the time "wasted" while becoming intoxicated with marijuana when he could have been pursuing other, more career-oriented activities.

Introduction

Although marijuana is potentially less addictive than other drugs, such as cocaine, crack, heroin, and barbiturates (to name a few), it remains one of the few drugs that is controversial. It is difficult to wade through the emotion, politics, and rigidity found in the writings on marijuana to tease out the objective, clinical reality. In the United States, extreme views go back to the 1930s, when the film *Reefer Madness* portrayed an after-school marijuana "club" for high school students in suits and ties who became hallucinatory, homicidal, violent, and suicidal; such symptoms were highly exaggerated. As a complete contradiction, in the same decade, the Rastafarian religion spread among Jamaican agricultural workers, who named marijuana a *holy plant*.

[In] *Ganja in Jamaica* (Rubin and Comitas 1975) [the book] focused its findings to refute the claim that marijuana users damaged their productive capability. The study found that most rural Jamaicans who smoked ganja (marijuana) were extraordinarily diligent peasants who invested impressive amounts of time and energy in multiple income-bearing schemes every day of the year. Starting before sunrise, they tended livestock and poultry; farmed gardens; hired out their labor for wages; exchanged goods and services in an indigenous marketing system; maintained churches, self-help associations, political parties, guilds, schools, and households; and sometimes, at night, clandestinely cleared acres of forest to cultivate marijuana. They listened to the radio, watched television, and read newspapers to perform better as citizens in a modern democracy. These active, clear-sighted economic strategist and community builders depended on a heavy daily intake of ganja for nourishment as "brain food," and relied on it specifically to improve production. Adult Jamaican marijuana smokers consumed some six or more large "spliffs" (hand-rolled cigars) of ganja a day, or a few ounces. They also consumed it in teas, tisanes, and tonics. As employers, they preferred to pay their employees ganja rather than money and encouraged its use in the workplace. (Rubin and Comitas 1975, cited in Hamid 1998, p. 61)

Marijuana is simply the hemp plant, *Cannabis sativa*, which has been cultivated for thousands of years. When smoked, the dried and crushed leaves, stems, and seeds of cannabis produce sedative and mind-altering effects, which vary according to the potency of the variety of plant used. Usage in the United States began in the 1920s, rose during the 1960s and 1970s, and fell in every year from 1978 until 1991. From 1991 on, however, usage began to climb. In this chapter, we review the history, past and current usage trends, attitudes, and controversies surrounding marijuana (including the amotivational syndrome and the recent debate inspired by proposals for medical legalization), and its physiological and behavioral effects on the user.

History and Trends in Marijuana Use

In many societies, marijuana has historically been a valued crop. It is called *hemp* because the woody fibers of the stem yield a fiber that can be made into cloth and rope. The term *cannabis* comes from the Greek word for hemp. Initially, the Spaniards brought cannabis to the Western Hemisphere as a source of fiber and seeds. For thousands of years, the seeds have been pressed to extract red oil used for medicinal and euphorigenic purposes (Abood and Martin 1992; Iversen 1993). The plant (both male and female) also produces a resin with active ingredients that affect the central nervous system (CNS). Marijuana contains hundreds of chemical compounds, but only a few found in the resin are responsible for producing the euphoric high.

Even the original uses of marijuana remain controversial. Botanists have never been able to trace cannabis to its origins, although some think it originated in Asia. Ancient Chinese documents contain the earliest record name of hemp — *ma*, meaning fiber producing plant. In the late 1970s, during an archeological dig in Gansu, the seat of Chinese civilization, workers uncovered cannabis seed stored in an earthen jar.

Ayurvedic documents from 600 B.C. describe an intoxicating resin from the plant. The fifth-century B.C. Greek historian Herodotus recorded that the Scythians burned the tops of the plant, producing a narcotic smoke. And a first-century Greek physician wrote that hemp was made into intoxicating cakes, perhaps the forerunners of the marijuana brownies of 1960s fame. (Pollan 1998, p. 39)

Other sources report that the first known record of marijuana use is the *Book of Drugs* written about 2737 B.C. by the Chinese Emperor Shen Nung; he prescribed marijuana for treating gout, malaria, gas pains, and absentmindedness. The Chinese apparently had much respect for the plant. They obtained fiber for clothes and medicine from it for thousands of years. The Chinese named the plant *ma* (maw), which in the Chinese language can also mean "valuable" or "endearing." The term *ma* was still used as late as 1930.

Around 500 B.C., another Chinese book of treatments referred to the medical use of marijuana. Nonetheless, the plant got a bad name from the moralists of the day, who claimed that youngsters became wild and disrespectful from the recreational use of *ma*. They called it the "liberator of sin" because, under its influence, the youngsters refused to listen to their elders and did other scandalous things. Although the Chinese recognized *ma*'s medical usefulness, they eventually banned it because of its unpredictable intoxicating effects. Later, because of rampant use, it was legalized again.

India also has a long and varied history of marijuana use. It was an essential part of Indian religious ceremonies for thousands of years. The well-known Rig Veda and other chants describe the use of *soma*, which some believe was marijuana. Early writings describe a ritual in which resin was collected from the plants. After fasting and purification, certain men ran naked through the cannabis fields. The clinging resin was scraped off their bodies, and cakes were made from it and used in feasts. For centuries, missionaries in India tried to ban the use of marijuana, but they were never successful, because its use was too heavily ingrained in the culture. From India, the use of marijuana spread throughout Asia, Africa, Europe, and the Americas — English settlers brought it to the U.S. colonies.

Assyrian records dating back to 650 B.C. refer to a drug called *azulla* that was used for making rope and cloth and was consumed to experience euphoria. The ancient Greeks also knew about marijuana. Galen described the general use of hemp in cakes, which, when eaten in excess, produced narcotic effects. Herodotus described the Scythian custom of burning marijuana seeds and leaves to produce a narcotic smoke in steam baths. It was believed that breathing the smoke from the burning plants would cause frenzied activity. Groups of people stood in the smoke and laughed and danced as it took effect.

One legend about cannabis is based on the travels of Marco Polo in the 12th century. Marco Polo told of the legendary Hasan Ibn-Sabbah, who terrorized a part of Arabia in the early 1100s. His men were some of the earliest political murderers and he ordered them to kill under the influence of hashish, a strong, unadulterated cannabis derivative. The cult was called the *hashishiyya*, from which came the word *hashish*. (The word *assassin* may be derived from the name of Sheik Hasan, who was a political leader in the 10th century.)

It is unlikely, however, that using hashish can turn people into killers. Experience suggests that people tend to become sleepy and indolent rather than violent after eating or smoking hashish or another of the strong cannabis preparations available in Arabia (Abel 1989).

Napoleon's troops brought hashish to France after their campaign in Egypt at the beginning of the 19th century, despite Napoleon's strict orders to the contrary. By the 1840s, the use of hashish, as well as opium, was widespread in France, and efforts to curb its spread were unsuccessful.

In North America, hemp was planted near Jamestown in 1611 for use in making rope. By 1630, half of the winter clothing at this settlement was made from hemp fibers. There is no evidence that hemp was used medicinally at this time. Hemp was also valuable as a source of fiber for clothing and rope for the Pilgrims at Plymouth. To meet the demand for fiber, a law was passed in Massachusetts in 1639 requiring every household to plant hemp seed. However, it took much manual labor to work the hemp fiber into usable form, resulting in a chronic shortage of fiber for fishnets and the like (Abel 1989).

George Washington cultivated a field of hemp at Mount Vernon, and there is some indication that it was used for medicine as well as for making rope. In his writings, Washington once mentioned that he forgot to separate the male and female plants, a process usually done because the female plant gave more resin if not pollinated.

In the early 1800s, U.S. physicians used marijuana extracts to produce a tonic intended for both medicinal and recreational purposes. This practice changed in 1937 with passage of the Marijuana Tax Act. The Marijuana Tax Act was modeled after the Harrison Act of 1914 in that marijuana was considered a narcotic and subject to the same legal controls as cocaine and the opiates (see Chapter 3). Like these opiates, marijuana distributors had to register and pay a tax to legally import, buy, or sell this drug (Musto 1999). As a result, the Marijuana Tax Act prohibited the use of this drug as an intoxicant and regulated its use as a medicine.

Most of the abuse of marijuana in the United States during the early part of the 20th century took place near the Mexican border and in the ghetto areas of major cities. Cannabis was mistakenly considered a narcotic, like opium, and legal authorities treated it as such (Abood and Martin 1992). In 1931, Harry Anslinger, who was the first appointed head of the Bureau of Narcotics and later would become responsible for the enforcement of marijuana laws, believed that the problem was slight (Musto 1999). By 1936, however, he claimed that the increase in the use of marijuana was of great national concern (Anslinger and Cooper 1937; see Figure 13.1). Anslinger set up an informational program that ultimately led to the federal law that banned marijuana. The following sensationalized statement was part of Anslinger's campaign to outlaw the drug:

> What about the alleged connection between drugs and sexual pleasure? . . . What is the real relationship between drugs and sex? There isn't any question about marijuana being a sexual stimulant. It has been used throughout the ages for that: in Egypt, for instance. From what we have seen, it is an aphrodisiac, and I believe that the use in colleges today has sexual connotations. (Anslinger and Cooper 1937, p. 19)

FIGURE 13.1

This antimarijuana poster was distributed by the Federal Bureau of Narcotics in the late 1930s.

In addition, during this time, some usually accurate magazines reported that marijuana was partly responsible for crimes of violence. In 1936, *Scientific American* reported that "marijuana produces a wide variety of symptoms in the user, including hilarity, swooning, and sexual excitement. Combined with intoxicants, it often makes the smoker vicious, with a desire to fight and kill" ("Marijuana Menaces Youth" 1936, p. 151). A famous poster of the day, called "The Assassination of Youth," was effective in molding attitudes against drug use.

Largely because of the media's influence on public opinion, Congress passed the Marijuana Tax Act in 1937. However, as a result of the discussions and debates before the passage of the 1970 Comprehensive Drug Abuse Prevention and Control Act, which replaced or updated all other laws concerning narcotics and dangerous drugs, the Marijuana Tax Act of 1937 was declared unconstitutional in 1969 because it classified marijuana as a narcotic. (For further historical details, see Chapter 3.) Marijuana has not been classified as a narcotic since 1971.

In the early 1900s, marijuana was brought across the U.S. borders by Mexican laborers who entered the United States seeking jobs. From the border areas of the United States, recreational use of marijuana spread into mainly the southwestern region of the United States. Such use reached major cities in Texas and surrounding states as well as a number of African American communities in these cities. Heavy users of marijuana included a subpopulation of jazz musicians as well as other "bohemian types" who led more of an unstructured existence in unconventional jobs and occupations (artists, entertainers, poets, criminals, and so on). Thus, before the 1960s, marijuana use was largely confined to small segments of African American urban youth, jazz musicians, and particularly artists and writers who belonged to the 1950s Beat Generation. Use rose tremendously in the 1960s, when it was closely associated with the hippie counterculture, in which marijuana was categorized as a psychedelic (consciousness-expanding) sacrament. It spread into other youth categories during the 1970s, until approximately 1978. In each year from 1978 until 1991, marijuana use fell. After 1991, researchers and prevention specialists were astounded to see a rise in usage among youth.

Marijuana still grows wild in many American states today. Curiously, one reason for the survival of this supply is that, during World War II, the fiber used to make rope (sisal) was hard to import, so the government paid subsidies to farmers who grew hemp. Much of today's crop comes from these same plants. Another reason for the spread of the plants is that, until recently, the seeds were used in birdseed. Leftover seed was discarded in the garbage and thus spread to landfill dumps, where it sprouted. Birdseed containing marijuana seeds is still available, but the seeds are sterilized so that they cannot germinate.

The Indian Hemp Drug Commission Report in the 1890s and the 1930 Panama Canal Zone Report on marijuana stressed that available evidence did not prove marijuana to be as dangerous as it was popularly thought; these reports were given little publicity, however, and for the most part were disregarded. In 1944, a report was issued by the LaGuardia Committee on Marijuana, which consisted of 31 qualified physicians, psychiatrists, psychologists, pharmacologists, chemists, and sociologists appointed by the New York Academy of Medicine. They stated in one key summary that marijuana was not the killer many thought it to be:

> It was found that marijuana in an effective dose impairs intellectual functioning in general. . . . Marijuana does not change the basic personality structure of the individual. It lessens inhibition and this brings out what is latent in his thoughts and emotions but it does not evoke responses that would otherwise be totally alien to him. . . . Those who have been smoking marijuana for years showed no mental or physical deterioration that may be attributed to the drug. (Solomon 1966, p. 37)

Much of the early research conducted did not consider the potency of marijuana. As a result, findings from various studies are often conflicting and difficult to compare. Because the quality of marijuana varies so greatly, it is impossible to know the amount of drug taken without analyzing the original material and the leftover stub, or "roach." Conditions such as type of seed, soil moisture and fertility, amount of sunlight, and temperature all have an effect on the amounts of active ingredients found in the resulting marijuana plant.

Current Use of Marijuana

The National Survey on Drug Use and Health (NSDUH) in 2007 reported that among persons age 12 or older, the rate of past-month marijuana use was about the same in 2005 (6%) as it was in 2004 (6.1%), 2003 (6.2%), and 2002 (6.2%). Marijuana remains the most commonly used illicit drug with 4.6 million past-month users (SAMHSA 2006).

Figure 13.2 shows that in 2005, out of an estimated 19.7 million Americans age 12 or older who were current users of *any* type of illicit drugs, the percentage of past-month marijuana users was a staggering 74.1%* (54.5% + 19.6%). This leaves a minority (25.8%) of illicit drug users (approximately 5.1 million) who did *not* use marijuana. An estimated 54.5% of current illicit drug users used only marijuana, and 19.6% used marijuana and another illicit drug.

Other current findings regarding marijuana use are as follows (SAMHSA 2006):

- In 2005, 2.1 million persons had used marijuana for the first time within the past 12 months; this averages to approximately 6,000 initiates per day! Somewhat dampening this large number of new users is the fact that this estimate was not significantly different from the number in 2004 (2.1 million), 2003 (2.0 million), and 2002 (2.2 million) **(see Figure 13.3A).**

- Most (59.1%) of the 2.1 million recent marijuana initiates were younger than age 18 when they first used the drug.

- In 2005, the average age at first marijuana use among recent initiates ages 12 to 49 was 17.4 years. This average increased from 17.0 years in 2002, 16.8 years in 2003, and 17.1 years in 2004.

*Current drug use is defined as having used an illicit drug in the month before the NSDUH surveys were conducted.

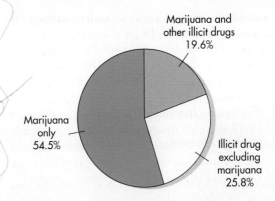

19.7 million past month illicit drug users

FIGURE 13.2

Types of drugs used in the past month, illicit drug users age 12 or older in 2005.

Source: Substance Abuse and Mental Health Services Administration (SAMHSA). *Results From the 2005 National Survey on Drug Use and Health: National Findings.* Rockville, MD: Office of Applied Studies, 2006.

- The rate of current marijuana use among youth ages 12 to 17 declined from 7.6% in 2004 to 6.8% in 2005. The rate of current marijuana use has declined significantly from 8.2% in 2002.

- Among 14- or 15-year-olds, marijuana was the dominant drug used (5.9%). Marijuana also

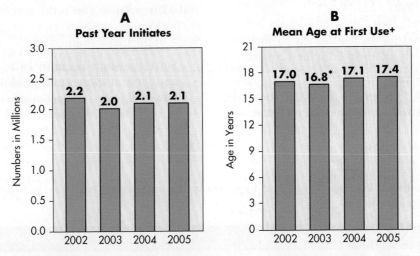

*Difference between estimate and the 2005 estimate is statistically significant at the .05 level.
+Mean age at first use estimates are among recent initiates ages 12 to 49.

FIGURE 13.3

Past-year marijuana initiates among persons age 12 or older and mean age at first use of marijuana among past-year initiates ages 12 to 49: 2002–2005.

Source: Substance Abuse and Mental Health Services Administration (SAMHSA). *Results from the 2005 National Survey on Drug Use and Health: National Findings.* Rockville, MD: Office of Applied Studies, 2006.

was the most commonly used drug among 16- or 17-year-olds (13.6%).

- In 2005, 9.9% of youth ages 12–17 were current illicit drug users and 6.8% used marijuana. Among young adults ages 18–25, 16.6% used marijuana.
- Past-month marijuana use among males ages 12–17 was 7.5% whereas for females it was 6.2%. (From 2002–2005 use has been slowly dropping for both males and females (ages 12–17).

As Table 13.1 shows (SAMHSA 2006), the frequency of marijuana use is strongly correlated with age. The age group reporting the highest lifetime (52.4%), past-year (28%), and past-month (16.6%) use was 18- to 25-year-olds. For the 26 and older age group, marijuana use sharply drops during the past year (6.9%) and past month (4.1%).

AGE OUT ?

■ Recent Trends in Use of Marijuana: 8th, 10th, and 12th Graders

Figure 13.4A (Johnston et al. 2006) shows the percentage who used marijuana in the last 12 months. Some of the major findings are:

- Since 1960 (not shown), annual percentages of marijuana use among 12th graders peaked in 1979 at approximately 51%.
- Use declined steadily for 13 years, bottoming at 22% in 1992.
- For 8th, 10th, and 12th grades, from 1993 to 1997, marijuana use continued to increase, declining very slowly to 38% for 12th graders in 2005.

Figure 13.4B (Johnston et al. 2006) shows the trends in perceived harmfulness of marijuana use

for 12th graders. The figure shows the percentage who say there is a "great risk" from using marijuana. Some of the major findings are:

- Over half (53%) of all 12th graders think that regular use of marijuana involves a great risk to the user; 47% do not.
- Approximately 28% of all 12th graders think that occasional use of marijuana is harmful; 72% do not.
- Approximately 19% of 12th graders believe that using marijuana once or twice is harmful; 81% do not.

Figure 13.4C (Johnston et al. 2006) shows the trends in disapproval of marijuana use for 12th graders. This is the percentage saying they "disapprove" of using marijuana. Some of the major findings are:

- Approximately 80% of 12th graders disapprove of using marijuana on a regular basis; 20% do not.
- In 2005, approximately 68% of 12th graders disapproved of using marijuana on an occasional basis; 32% did not.
- Approximately 54% of 12th graders disapprove of using marijuana one or twice; 46% do not.

Figure 13.4D (Johnston et al. 2006) shows the trends in availability of marijuana for 8th, 10th, and 12th graders. This is the percentage saying it is "fairly easy" or "very easy" to get marijuana. Some of the major findings are:

- Since the study begin in 1975, between 83% and 90% of every senior middle school class have said they could get marijuana fairly easily or very easily if they wanted some.

Table 13.1 Marijuana Use Reported in 2005 by Americans During Lifetime, Past Year, and Past Month, According to Age

AGE (YEARS)	LIFETIME (%)	PAST YEAR (%)	PAST MONTH (%)
12–17	17.4	13.3	6.8
18–25	52.4	28.0	16.6
26 and older	41.1	6.9	4.1

Source: SAMHSA. 2005. Results from the 2005 National Survey on Drug Use and Health: National Findings. Rockville, MD: Department of Health and Human Services, Substance Abuse and Mental Health Services Administration, Office of Applied Studies, 2006.

• Since 1991, when data were first available for 8th and 10th graders, marijuana was considerably less accessible to younger adolescents. Still, in 2005, two fifths of 8th graders (41%) and almost three quarters of 10th graders (73%) reported it as being accessible. This compares to 86% for 12th graders.

Finally, adding to what figures and percentages cannot capture, is an interview this author had:

What, weed? It's so easy to get. In fact, many times [referring to junior high school] I didn't even have to buy, it would be offered in the morning, at lunchtime, and whenever we get together, even after school it is there. Among the users (and we know each other real well), it's as common as sharing candy. *(From Venturelli's research files, 15-year-old male, first-year high school student residing in a medium-size town in the Midwest, June 19, 2000)*

Use
% who used in last 12 months

FIGURE 13.4a

Marijuana: trends in annual use, risk, disapproval, and availability, 8th, 10th, and 12th graders.

....

Source: Johnston, L. D., P. M. O'Malley, J. G. Bachman, and J. E. Schulenberg. *Monitoring the Future: National Results on Adolescent Drug Use.* Bethesda, MD: National Institutes of Health, National Institute on Drug Abuse, 2006.

Percent saying "great risk" from using marijuana. . . .

FIGURE 13.4b

Marijuana: trends in perceived harmfulness of use for 12th graders.

....

Source: Johnston, L. D., P. M. O'Malley, J. G. Bachman, and J. E. Schulenberg. *Monitoring the Future: National Results on Adolescent Drug Use.* Bethesda, MD: National Institutes of Health, National Institute on Drug Abuse, 2006.

Percent saying they "disapprove" of using marijuana. . . .

FIGURE 13.4c

Marijuana: trends in disapproval of use for 12th graders.

....

Source: Johnston, L. D., P. M. O'Malley, J. G. Bachman, and J. E. Schulenberg. *Monitoring the Future: National Results on Adolescent Drug Use.* Bethesda, MD: National Institutes of Health, National Institute on Drug Abuse, 2006.

Availability
% saying "fairly easy" or "very easy" to get

FIGURE 13.4d

Marijuana: trends in availability for 8th, 10th, and 12th graders.

....

Source: Johnston, L. D., P. M. O'Malley, J. G. Bachman, and J. E. Schulenberg. *Monitoring the Future: National Results on Adolescent Drug Use.* Bethesda, MD: National Institutes of Health, National Institute on Drug Abuse, 2006.

Marijuana: Is It the Assassin of Youth?

In the late 1930s, the poster "Marijuana: Assassin of Youth" made a clever play on words, bringing up reminders of the Middle Eastern "hashashin" cult, whose terrible exploits were attributed to their use of hashish (marijuana resin).

At the time, marijuana was even incorrectly classified as a narcotic, like opium and morphine. Amotivational syndrome, lassitude, poor driving skills the day after smoking, educational failure, and dependence may not quite add up to "assassination," as wildly exaggerated in *Reefer Madness*. The poster was right, however, in associating use of this drug with young people, among whom marijuana is popular in both local peer groups and broad youth cultures.

■ Major Factors Affecting Marijuana Use

As discussed in the beginning chapters of this text, the mass media, parental role models, perceived risk, availability, and peers have the most direct influence on the development of youths' attitudes regarding drug use. Just recently, parental use of marijuana has been found to be a significant influence on teens' use of this drug.

In a study by Kandel et al. (2001), when parents had used marijuana at some time in their lives, their teen children were 40% more likely to have used the drug in their lifetime than teens whose parents had never used marijuana. Moreover, when parents had used marijuana in the past year, their children were *twice* as likely to have used in the same time period than were teens whose parents had not used in the past year. This same study also found that when parents had used marijuana in the past year, their teen children were more likely to have used marijuana in the past year when compared with the children of parents who had used at some time in their life, but not in the last year. Similarly, parental use of other drugs, such as alcohol, nicotine, and cocaine, was also found to have an impact on their teen children's use of marijuana. More importantly, the perceived risk of use is the most important influence on teen marijuana use. In the Kandel et al. (2001) study, it was found to be *five* times more important than parental use.

As shown in Figure 13.4D, when comparisons are made among 8th, 10th, and 12th graders, the perceived availability of marijuana rises sharply with grade level. One main reason for this is because children in lower grades are less likely to have friends and access to friends who use marijuana (as well as access to other major drugs of abuse). Marijuana has been almost universally available to American high school seniors (from 83% to 90%) over at least the past 28 years (Johnston et al. 2006).

Beginning several years before age 13 (early adolescence), peers and peer groups begin to exert the most influence (Greenblatt 1999; Heitzeg 1996; Tudor et al. 1987; Venturelli 2000). In fact, even in acquiring the drug, a recent finding stated that "Marijuana distribution relies primarily on informal dealing though social networks . . ." (Center for Substance Abuse Research [CESAR] 2007). More than one half (58%) of household residents who had used marijuana in the past year reported that they most recently obtained their marijuana for free, compared to 39% who reported purchasing it. Nearly all (89%) marijuana users reported getting their most recent acquisition from a friend or relative. Unlike users of more expensive drugs such as cocaine and heroin, the majority of people who used marijuana in the past year (58%) gave away or shared some of their most recent acquisition (CESAR 2007).

Research shows that it is unlikely that an individual will use drugs when his or her peers do not use them. Marijuana use, in particular, is a group-motivated behavior that is strongly affected by peer pressure and influence. In effect, habitual drug users are likely to belong to drug-using groups. In contrast, people who do not use drugs belong to groups in which drug use is perceived as an unacceptable and devious form of social recreation. Learning theory (see Chapter 2) explains how peers can influence one another; drug-using peer members serve as role models, legitimizing use. Peers in

A common example of polydrug use (alcohol and marijuana).

such groups are saying, in essence, "It's perfectly normal to use drugs"; in turn, this justifies usage.

In addition to these major factors (the mass media, parental role models, perceived risk, availability, and peer influences), six other factors must be taken into account as influencing drug use:

1. Structural factors, such as age, gender, family background, and religious beliefs.
2. Social and interactional factors, such as the type of interpersonal relationships, friendship cliques, and drug use within the peer group setting.
3. Setting, such as the type of community and neighborhood (physical location of drug use).
4. Attitudinal factors, such as personal beliefs and attitudes regarding drug use, and personality factors, such as self-esteem, level of security versus insecurity, and maturation level.
5. Participation in after-school activities is associated with higher levels of academic achievement and self-esteem, as well as *lower* levels of substance use (SAMHSA 2007b). Regardless of family income, youth ages 12 to 17 who did not participate in any activities had higher rates of past-month cigarette and illicit drug use than those who participated in four, six, seven, or more activities (SAMHSA 2007b).
6. Finally, even the amount of religious involvement affects illicit drug use (which includes marijuana use). In regard to religious involvement and substance use, adults who reported that religious beliefs are a very important part of their lives were less likely to use illicit drugs in the past month than those who reported that religious beliefs are not a very important part of their lives (6.1% vs. 14.3%; SAMHSA 2007a). Thus, religiosity has been identified in other research as an important protective factor against substance use (Kendler et al. 1997; National Center on Addiction and Substance Abuse 2001; Wallace et al. 2004).

Keep in mind these factors can easily overlap; they are not separate and distinct.

Sociologists have long studied "youth cultures" (Coleman 1961). In the 1970s, sociologists began to examine different subcultures of youth in terms of the behaviors that symbolically represent the group, in which participation in drug use is a ritual that marks off entrance into the group and out of childhood — a rite of passage. Typically, American high school culture includes a leading clique, often associated with team sports, whose members might be called "jocks," "collegiates," or "rah-rahs," and a marginal, deviant, or rebellious group (Eckert 1989). In some cases, the latter group is associated with marijuana use. In the mid-1960s, hippies were perceived as a group whose members were part of a counterculture committed to unconventional values, pacifism, and communalism in addition to psychedelic drugs. By 1970, this name denoted broader segments of youth who adhered merely to hippie styles of clothing and drug use (Buff 1970). By the 1980s, marijuana use was identified with subgroups of youth often called "burnouts." In many communities that were studied by sociologists, burnouts came from all social levels, but were often overrepresented in upper-middle classes, and they were marginal and/or rebellious within the educational system, if not dropouts (Eckert 1989; Gaines 1992). Membership in such marijuana-using subcultures often bonds the youth to often ongoing and persistent drug use.

Is Marijuana Really a Gateway Drug?

Gateway drugs are drugs that serve as the gate or path that usually precedes the use of illicit drugs, such as marijuana, heroin, and LSD. Gateway drugs, or drugs of entry, serve to initiate a novice user into the drug-using world. Although the linkage is not biochemical, common gateway drugs include tobacco, inhalants, alcohol, and anabolic steroids.

The claim that marijuana use most often leads to the use of other more serious drugs, such as heroin, remains controversial (Gardner 1992). A Rand press release reported that the gateway theory does not explain the progression to other more addictive drugs; instead, "The people who are predisposed to use drugs and have the opportunity to use drugs are more likely than others to use both marijuana and harder drugs. . . . Marijuana typically comes first because it is more available" (Rand Drug Policy Research Center 2002). Thus, instead of assuming that marijuana, alcohol, and other, more commonly used drugs are simply gateway drugs responsible for leading to other, more serious drugs, it is more likely that

KEY TERMS

gateway drug
drug whose use leads to the use of other drugs; alcohol, cigarettes, and marijuana are considered gateway drugs

other factors such as (1) the age when teens have opportunities to use marijuana and other drugs, (2) associated opportunities, and (3) the willingness to use drugs are better predictors of the progression from less addictive to more addictive and powerful types of drugs.

For example, the gateway theory cannot explain the fact that although it is true many heroin addicts began drug use with marijuana, it is also true that many, if not most, also used coffee and cigarettes. Millions of marijuana users never go beyond the gateway drugs used. "There are only a few thousand opiate addicts in Great Britain, yet there are millions who have tried cannabis" (Gossop 1987, p. 9).

Nevertheless, some explanation is needed for the small percentage of marijuana users who do progress to hard drugs such as heroin. It is unlikely that the use of marijuana is the *principal* cause of moving to harder drugs.

As described in Chapter 16, youths who turn to drugs are usually slightly to seriously alienated individuals. Thus, progression from marijuana to other drugs is more likely to depend on peer group composition, family relationships, social class, and the age at which drug use begins (Indiana Prevention Resource Center 1996).

It is important to note, however, that many, if not most, young drug users do eventually leave drug-using groups and abandon their drug-using behavior, a process sometimes called *maturing out.* An example that often typifies maturing out is found in the following interview:

Sure, smoking dope and tripping on acid was a way of life when I was a teenager. But then I graduated college and had to join the real world — that everyday work world that my dull parents lived in. *(From Venturelli's research files, 28-year-old female, working for a national private security firm, August 12, 2000.)*

Other research further documents some young "burnouts" quitting marijuana smoking without sacrificing group membership (Eckert 1989).

Misperceptions of Marijuana Use

In a world in which marijuana can be considered either an assassin or a sacrament, and in which it is associated with membership in prized or despised peer groups, it is not surprising that estimates of its use vary widely and inaccurately. Parents, for example, tend to underestimate their children's use of drugs. Findings from one study indicated that, "only 14% of the parents interviewed thought their children had experimented with marijuana while 38% of the teenagers said they had tried it" (Wren 1996, p. 1). In the same survey, 52% of teenagers reported having been offered drugs, while 34% of the parents thought their children might have been offered drugs.

Interestingly, another report by the former president of the National Center on Addiction and Substance Abuse at Columbia University stated the following with regard to baby boomer parents (parents born between the late 1940s through late 1950s):

Almost half know someone who uses illegal drugs; a third have friends who use marijuana. Almost half expect their children to try illegal drugs, and 65 percent of those who smoked pot regularly when young believe their kids will try drugs . . . almost half of the parents don't think they can have much influence on whether their kids will use drugs. (Califano 1996, p. 19)

Even with regard to users' perceptions of other users, beliefs about marijuana remain distorted. College students tend to have exaggerated misperceptions of use, believing that their peers use marijuana much more than is true (Berkowitz 1991). For example, at one campus in northern New Jersey, two thirds of students reported never using marijuana, yet most students polled believed that the average student uses marijuana once per week. Thus, with regard to marijuana users, interest in using remains persistently strong for the time being. In the early years of this millennium, high usage of marijuana remains stubbornly persistent.

Characteristics of Cannabis

In 1753, Carolus Linnaeus, a Swedish botanist, classified marijuana as *Cannabis sativa* (see Figure 13.5). *Cannabis sativa* is a plant that grows readily in many parts of the world. Most botanists agree that there is only one species (*sativa*) and that all the variants (*indica, Americana,* and *africana*) be-

KEY TERMS

Cannabis sativa
biological species name for the variety of hemp plant known as *marijuana*

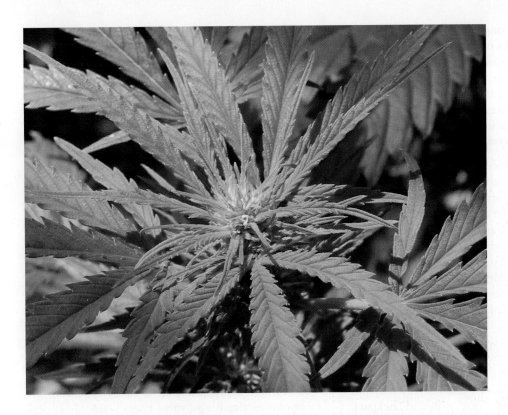

FIGURE 13.5
Marijuana plant.

long to that species, whereas others believe that the variants are three distinct species (Schultes 1978). *Indica* is considered to have the most potent resin, but climate, soil, and selective plant breeding all influence potency. The world's record marijuana plant was 39 feet tall, and its woody stem was nearly 3 inches in diameter.

Cannabis is *dioecious*, meaning that there are male and female plants. After the male plant releases its pollen, it usually dies. In any case, even before the male plant dies, cultivators of marijuana often eliminate or remove the male plants after the female plant has been pollinated.

There are more than 421 different chemicals in the cannabis plant, many of which have not yet been identified. Tetrahydrocannabinol, or THC, is the primary mind-altering (psychoactive) agent in marijuana (Abood and Martin 1996; Swan 1996) and appears to be important for the reinforcing properties of this substance (Kelly et al. 1994). THC is most highly concentrated in the flowering tops and upper leaves of the female plant. When crushed or beaten, these flowering tops produce a resin in which the psychoactive ingredient THC is found.

In cultivated marijuana crops, male plants are eradicated from the growing fields so that they cannot pollinate the female plants. The lack of pollination makes the potency of female plants increase dramatically. *Sinsemilla* (meaning "without seeds" in Spanish) is one of the most potent derivatives of the cannabis plant known in the United States, with an average of 7.5% and a range reaching as high as 24% THC. *Sinsemilla* is made from the buds of flowering tops of female plants (National Institute on Drug Abuse [NIDA] 1998). Other known types that have a much higher THC content include "hydro" (which means grown in water) and "kind bud."

In the United States, the amount of THC found in street-sold marijuana ranges broadly from 0.5% to 11%. Reports indicate that the amount of THC in marijuana has risen dramatically since the 1960s (Kaplan and Whitmire 1995; MSNBC 2007; NIDA 1998). "More efficient agriculture — new methods of harvesting and processing marijuana plants — has made pot about 20 times more potent than the marijuana on the street in the 1960s and 1970s, drug treatment experts and law

KEY TERMS

sinsemilla
meaning without seeds, this marijuana is made from the buds and flowering tops of female plants and is one of the most potent types

officials say" (Henneberger 1994, p. F-18). Further, the quantities of other, more potent types of marijuana such as sinsemilla as well as hydroponic types of marijuana (hydro) are more readily available in illegal drug markets. The actual potencies of the more generic types of marijuana have remained the same in the past 30 years.

The latest reports indicate the following:

Marijuana produced in Mexico remains the most widely available in the United States. High potency marijuana has also entered the U.S. drug market from Canada. Another source for marijuana in the United States is domestically grown marijuana, which includes both indoor and outdoor operations. Groups operating from Mexico employ a variety of transportations and concealment methods to smuggle marijuana into the United States. Most of the marijuana smuggled into the United States is concealed in vehicles — often in false compartments — or hidden in shipments of legitimate agricultural or industrial products. Marijuana is also smuggled across the border by rail, horse, raft, and backpack. Canada is becoming a source country for indoor-grown, high potency (15% to 25% THC) marijuana destined for the United States. Such indoor-grow operations have become an enormous and lucrative illicit industry, producing a potent form of marijuana that has come to be known as "BC Bud." (Office of National Drug Control Policy [ONDCP] 2003)

Native U.S. street-variety marijuana, often referred to as "ditch weed" *cannabis,* is sometimes considered inferior because of its low concentration of THC, usually less than 0.5%. THC levels in Jamaican, Colombian, and Mexican varieties range between 0.5% and 7%. This type of marijuana is made from parts of the cannabis plant that contain the least amount of THC. Some members of drug-using subcultures grind this type of marijuana (as well as more potent types of marijuana) into a powder and mix it into drinks, teas, and cookie and brownie batter.

Hashish (or hasheesh) is a second derivative of cannabis that contains the purest form of resin. This type of marijuana consists of the sticky resin from the female plant flowers and has an average THC level of 3.6%, but can have as much as 28% (NIDA 1998). Historically, hashish users have represented a somewhat small percentage of the cannabis user population in the United States,

whereas in Europe use is much more prevalent. Hashish is produced in Lebanon, Afghanistan, and Pakistan.

A third derivative of the cannabis plant is *ganja,* which is produced in India. This preparation consists of the dried tops of female plants. *Ganja* is also used as a slang term for marijuana (as are pot, Mary Jane, reefer).

The Behavioral Effects of Marijuana Use

■ The High

The then-widely held belief of the 1930s that marijuana is a destructive assassin of youth is no longer considered valid for casual or occasional users of this drug. In most individuals, low to moderate doses of cannabis produce euphoria and a pleasant state of relaxation (Goldstein 1994). What are the common effects experienced from marijuana use? After a few minutes of forcibly holding the smoke in the lungs, most users suddenly experience the high. In this state of euphoria, the user experiences a dry mouth, elevated heartbeat, and some loss of coordination and balance, coupled with slower reaction times and a feeling of euphoria (mild to elevated intoxication). Blood vessels in the eyes expand, which accounts for reddening of the eyes. Some people experience slightly elevated blood pressure, which can double the normal heart rate. These effects can become intensified when other drugs, such as LSD and/or psychedelic ("magic") mushrooms, are combined with the marijuana.

The state of euphoria that results from the high is usually mild and short-lived; a typical high from one joint may last from 2 to 3 hours. Subjectively, the user experiences altered perception of space and time, impaired memory of recent events, and impaired physical coordination (more of these subjective effects are discussed at length in the next section; Abood and Martin 1992). An occasional high is not usually hazardous unless the person

KEY TERMS

hashish
sticky resin from the female plant flowers, which has an average THC level of 3.6% but can contain as much as 28%

attempts to drive a car, operate heavy machinery, fly a plane, or function in similar ways requiring coordination, good reflexes, or quick judgment (Nahas and Latour 1992). Even low doses of marijuana adversely affect perception, such as being able to judge the speed of an approaching vehicle or how much to slow down on an exit ramp. One interview revealed the following:

> In trying to describe the high, it's not like an alcohol high. In an alcohol high, you are a lot more uncoordinated if drinking a lot. With weed, it's like reality changes — you add a lot more bass so-to-speak to what you see, hear, think, and feel. The reality is tempered with some distortion that to me and many others is pleasurable. You know how you feel after three or four very strong drinks [referring to alcoholic beverages]. Well take two more of those drinks and then look around the room you are in. Now, the difference between alcohol and weed is that you can walk to the bathroom quite well while under the influence of weed, while with alcohol you walk carefully so that no one notices that you are just about drunk. Weed is a mind high while alcohol is more of a body high. *(From Venturelli's research files, May 19, 2000, 23-year-old female, professionally employed and residing in San Francisco.)*

Two other interviews (same interviewee on two different occasions) also attempted to compare the high from marijuana with the effects of alcohol:

> The marijuana high is also not nearly as harsh on the body. Being high doesn't give you that painful hangover as alcohol does. The actual high is very functional; I tend to do some of my best work (after burning a "dubbie") in that state [of mind]. It is part of the lifestyle of marijuana. [In contrast], alcohol makes me (and most people I know) very unproductive when the "buzz" is reached. *(From Venturelli's research files, "Lectus Ferberger," 21-year-old male, undergraduate student at a Midwestern university, August 10, 2000.)*

> There seems to be a small misconception about the effects of marijuana and alcohol. For me, anyway, in looking at the physical "buzz" you get from alcohol, it is very physically disabling. You get drunk and stumble around, your lips loosen up, and you say things that you would not normally say. I find that marijuana has more of a calming effect. It makes you relaxed and a little more perceptive to some stimuli and obviously less perceptive to other stimuli. It is a light feeling, but not overwhelming to the equilibrium. *(From Venturelli's research files, same student as above, August 11, 2000.)*

An acute dose of cannabis can produce adverse reactions, ranging from mild anxiety to panic and paranoia in some users. These reactions occur most frequently in individuals who are under stress or who are anxious, depressed, or borderline schizophrenic (Nahas and Latour 1992). Such effects may also be seen in normal users who accidentally take much more than they feel they can handle.

Extreme reactions can also occur because of ingesting marijuana treated (or "laced") with such things as opium, PCP, or other additives. Based on limited evidence from survey studies, mild or often adverse reactions are experienced on one or more occasions by more than one-half of regular users; they are mainly self-treated and usually go unreported (see "Signs and Symptoms" Specific Indicators of Marijuana Use).

▉ Subjective Euphoric Effects

Subjective euphoric effects associated with marijuana use are the ongoing social and psychological experiences incurred while intoxicated by marijuana. These effects of intoxication include both the user's altered state of consciousness and his or her perceptions.

Subjective effects also include a general sense of relaxation and tranquility, coupled with heightened sensitivity to sound, taste, and emotionality. Some users report occasional similarities to the typical hallucinogenic high. How closely the marijuana high resembles a hallucinogenic high depends on the amount of THC absorbed from marijuana. For example, higher amounts of THC found in more potent plants of marijuana, like *sinsemilla*, hydro, and kind bud more clearly mimic a hallucinogenic high. These effects are especially evident when considering the extent to which the senses of hearing, vision, sound, and taste are distorted by use of highly potent forms of marijuana.

Some marijuana users become very attached to these euphoric effects (in search of reexperiencing

Signs & Symptoms Specific Indicators of Marijuana Use

BODY:	MIND:
• A sweet odor similar to burnt rope in room, on clothes, and so on.	• Eye drops: For disguising red eyes.
• Roach: The small butt end of a marijuana cigarette.	• Excessive use of incense, room deodorizers, or breath fresheners.
• Joint: Looks like a hand-rolled cigarette; usually the ends are twisted or crimped.	• Devices for keeping the substance such as film canisters, boxes, or cans.
• Roach clips: Holders for the roach could be any number of common items such as paper clips, bobby pins, or hemostats. They could also be of a store-bought variety in a number of shapes and disguises.	• Eating binges: An aftereffect for some marijuana users.
• Seeds or leaves in pockets or possession.	• Appearance of intoxication, yet no smell of alcohol.
• Rolling papers or pipes, usually hidden somewhere.	• Excessive laughter.
	• Initial use (first hour): Animated behavior (loud or excessive talking).
	• (Hours later): Fatigue or drowsiness.

these effects). Such users often pride themselves on their extensive knowledge of this drug and maintain interest in discussing past experiences of "when I was really high" or "let me tell you about that night we smoked hydro. . . ." Devotees stay current with developments in the marijuana field by avidly reading monthly issues of magazines devoted to marijuana (the art of marijuana use) and frequently scan the Internet for information and conversations in chat rooms about the best varieties of marijuana, best growing techniques, announcements of hemp festivals, advice, and information regarding current laws, fines, and other information.

Why is marijuana so attractive to many individuals? One quote from an interview illustrates the extensive psychological and social reinforcement experienced by marijuana users:

It's the high that I particularly like. Everything becomes mellower. Everyday tensions are released or submerged by more inner-like experiences. I can review the day and how happy or miserable I feel. Actually, when I am thinking and I am high on grass, I always feel that my thoughts are profound. You think from another perspective, one that numbs the more reality-based everyday strains. On the other hand, there are moments when this drug affects your mood and channels it [in] different ways. You have moments when you either feel sad, happy, angry (in a more contemplative way), or

worried. These moods are both good and bad. If for the moment you feel good, then your mood is positive. If you feel down, your mood is negative in a particular way. If I am with friends and we are all sharing the bong or joint or pipe, we laugh a lot together. It's a type of drug that makes you more jovial, more introspective, and friendly, gregarious. . . . *(From Venturelli's research files, 40-year-old male personnel manager, August 20, 1996.)*

Intense attachment to passionate feelings surrounding the use of marijuana is quite common. As explained in Chapter 2, largely through the reinforcement of pleasurable feelings, psychologists believe the drug user becomes attached and habituated to the drug. If these subjective euphoric experiences were to become largely negative, attachment to and repeated use of this drug would cease. Thus, the theory of differential association applies. This theory, developed by Edwin Sutherland in 1939 and revised in 1947, attempts to explain delinquent behavior. Sociologists define the term **differential association** as the process by which individuals become socialized

KEY TERMS

differential association
process by which individuals become socialized into the perceptions and values of a group

into the perceptions and values of a group. The application of this concept can be redefined as differential association with respect to drug use. In the case of marijuana, the drug-using group or even a fellow drug user rewards such behavior. It can include the perception that marijuana relieves boredom, stress, or is the perfect drug for just hanging out or partying and getting high. Specifically, the definition of differential association is the behavioral satisfaction derived from friends who use marijuana. Psychologically, the high with others is the positive reward that cements the user to his or her friends and the drug.

■ Driving Performance

Evidence shows that the ability to perform complex tasks, such as driving, can be strongly impaired while under the influence of marijuana (Goldstein 1994; Mathias 1996). Research indicates that "Cannabis consumption impairs motor coordination, reaction time, sensory perceptions and glare recovery" (Teen Challenge 2000, p. 1). This effect has been demonstrated in laboratory assessments of driving-related skills such as eye–hand coordination and reaction time, in driver simulator studies, in test course performance, and in actual street driving situations (Chait and Pierri 1992; Mathias 1996; Teen Challenge 2000). Another study tested the effects of known amounts of marijuana, alcohol, or both on driving. The subjects drove a course rigged with various traffic problems. There was a definite deterioration in driving skills among those who had used either drug, but the greatest deterioration was observed in subjects who had taken both. In another test, 59 subjects smoked marijuana until they were intoxicated and then were given sobriety tests on the roadside by highway patrol officers. Overall, 94% of the subjects did not pass the test 90 minutes after smoking, and 60% failed at 150 minutes, even though the blood THC was much lower at this time (Hollister 1986). Other studies on driving show this same inability to drive for as long as 12 to 24 hours after marijuana use.

In surveys, from 70% to 80% of marijuana users indicate that they sometimes drive while high. A study of drivers involved in fatal accidents in the greater Boston area showed that marijuana smokers were overrepresented in fatal highway accidents as compared with a control group of nonusers of similar age and gender. A 1998 study found that, of nearly 1800 blood samples taken from drivers arrested for driving while intoxicated, 19% tested positive for marijuana.

Recent research by the Drug Enforcement Administration (DEA) (DEA 2006) involving government surveys that ask young people about their drug use patterns indicate that about 600,000 high school seniors drive after smoking marijuana. Thirty-eight thousand seniors told surveyors that they had been involved in accidents while driving under the influence of marijuana. Other surveys conducted by MADD and the Liberty Mutual insurance company revealed that many teenagers (41%) were not concerned about driving after taking drugs. Medical data indicates a connection between drugged driving and accidents — a study of patients in a shock-trauma unit who had been in collisions revealed that 15% of those who had been driving a car or motorcycle had been smoking marijuana and another 17% had both THC and alcohol in their blood.

Recent research conducted by the University of Auckland, New Zealand, proves the link between marijuana use and car accidents. The research found that habitual cannabis users were 9.5 times more likely to be involved in crashes, with 5.6% of people who had crashed having taken the drug, compared to 0.5% of the control group.

A new study published by researchers at the University of Maryland Medical Center Shock Trauma Center indicates that during a 90-day study, about half of the drivers admitted to the Maryland Shock Trauma Center tested positive for drugs other than alcohol. Additionally, one in four drivers admitted to the shock trauma unit tested positive for marijuana. "This population-based case–control study indicates that habitual use of marijuana is strongly associated with car crash injury. The nature of the relationship between marijuana use and risk-taking is unclear and needs further research. The prevalence of marijuana use in this driving population was low, and acute use was associated with habitual marijuana use, suggesting that intervention strategies may be more effective if they are targeted towards high use groups (Blows et al. 2005, p. 2).

One notable interview presents us with a negative experience regarding use of marijuana and driving experiences:

One time I smoked some real strong dope at my friend's house, then had to drive back home, which was 2 miles in one direction. I remember wigging out (panicking) in trying to get home. There were moments when I did not know where I was until I would see the next marker of my neighborhood. I remember having seconds of panic because I did not know where I was; then suddenly, I would notice a neighborhood restaurant or some other marker that said I was right around my neighborhood. I took smaller streets on the way home and even took a longer way home because I was freaking out about the cops — what if one would spot me? This was bogus thinking because how the hell would anyone suddenly spot me while driving home? Well, that's an example of wigging out on weed. But, I still don't think that even that time I would be getting into an accident. I was so freaked out that I was extra careful not to speed, pass stop signs, or violate any law for fear of being seen. If anything, I drive slower when I am really high, not more dangerously. *(From Venturelli's research files, 20-year-old male college student in a Midwestern town, July 19, 2000.)*

In contrast, more scientific research indicates that some perceptual or other performance deficits resulting from marijuana use may persist for some time after the high, and users who attempt to drive, fly, operate heavy machinery, perform surgery, and so on may not recognize their impairment because they do not feel intoxicated. States such as California have established testing procedures to detect the presence of THC in urine or blood samples from apparently intoxicated drivers.

If the use of marijuana becomes more socially acceptable (or perhaps even legal) and penalties for simple possession become more lenient, it is likely that individuals will feel less inclined to hide their drug use. Unfortunately, it follows that these individuals may also be more inclined to drive while high, endangering themselves and others.

■ Critical Thinking Skills

Marijuana has been found to have a negative impact on critical thinking skills. Recent research by NIDA shows that heavy marijuana use impairs critical skills related to attention, memory, and learning. Another study showed that even alertness, coordination, and reaction time were impaired by marijuana usage (National Clearinghouse on Alcohol and Drug Information [NCADI] 1998). Impairment continues even after discontinuing this drug's use for at least 24 hours (Brown and Massaro 1996).

In the same study, researchers compared 65 *heavy users* (using approximately every other day) with *light users* (using once or twice per week).

Heavy users made more mistakes and had greater difficulty sustaining attention, shifting attention to meet demands of challenges in the environment, and registering, processing, and using information (Brown and Massaro 1996) compared with the light users. In addition, heavy users had greater difficulty completing the tests, which specifically measured aspects of attention, memory, and learning, such as intellectual functioning, abstraction ability, attention span, verbal fluency, and learning and recalling abilities (Brown and Massaro 1996; Teen Challenge 2000). One researcher stated, "If you could get heavy users to learn an item, then they could remember it; the problem was getting them to learn it in the first place" (Brown and Massaro 1996, p. 3). The researchers surmised that marijuana alters brain activity because residues of the drug persist in the brain or because a withdrawal syndrome follows the euphoric effects of the marijuana. In another study, researchers tested the cognitive functioning of 65 marijuana-using college students. Residual impairments were seen the day (24 hours) after use in terms of sustaining attention, shifting attention, and hence in registering, organizing, and using information (Pope and Yurgulen-Todd 1996). This study, which was undertaken during the 1990s, is significant because it was carefully controlled. The unresolved question is whether these memory impairments are short term or long term. These noteworthy findings complement many other similar findings that identified protracted cognitive impairment among heavy users of marijuana (NCADI 1998).

■ Amotivational Syndrome

The so-called **amotivational syndrome** (sometimes referred to as "antimotivational syndrome") is a flashpoint of controversy about marijuana, although not as newsworthy as that regarding medical legalization. *Amotivational syndrome* refers to a belief that heavy use of marijuana causes a lack of motivation and reduced productivity. Specifically, users show apathy, poor short-term memory, difficulty in concentration, and a linger-

KEY TERMS

amotivational syndrome
a belief that heavy use of marijuana causes a lack of motivation and reduced productivity

Typical effects of amotivational syndrome

ing disinterest in pursuing goals (Abood and Martin 1992).

In the past, this syndrome received considerable attention. People who are high, or stoned, lack the desire to perform hard work and are not interested in doing difficult tasks. There is some evidence of this behavior in regular marijuana users (Nahas and Latour 1992). Overall, although not solely the result of cannabis use, *chronic users* have lower grades in school, are more likely to be absent from classes, and are likely not to complete assignments and to drop out of school (Henneberger 1994; Liska 1997). In terms of age, the earlier someone begins smoking marijuana, coupled with heavier use, the more likely the amotivational characteristics will prevail and the more difficult it will be to cease using this drug.

Although the effects of marijuana per se are somewhat responsible for creating this syndrome, other factors contribute as well. For instance, is the lack of motivation caused by the drug itself or is it that poorly motivated people begin using marijuana, which then further exacerbates their lack of motivation? Surveys show that a sizable number of marijuana users and their peer groups tend to be alienated from society and are likely to be classified as nonconformists and/or rebellious youths. They may, in fact, select to emphasize pleasure and nonconformity rather than goal-directed behavior.

Advocates of marijuana legalization stress data that tend to debunk research on amotivational syndrome. One institute that supports legalization, the Lindesmith Center, published a study asserting that college students who are users have higher grades than nonusers (Zimmer and Morgan 1997). How can we account for the discrepancies between this study and others, not to mention the clinical experiences of students, who often report academic repercussions of heavy use? One factor in the explanation is sociocultural:

> In the New York–New Jersey metro region, there are "druggy" schools and "drinking" schools. The "druggy" schools are more upper-middle class, liberal arts schools, artsy types, latter-day hippies, etc. The boozer campuses are filled with blue-collar and lower-middle-class kids — sometimes big fraternity schools. Front-loading at basketball games, comas after pledge parties. . . . Not as good educational backgrounds as the artsy potheads, who went to better schools, private schools, read a lot, or heard a lot at dinner before college, so they get by with their profs. However, the potheads ratchet down into easier majors, and they get crummier grades as they get into regular use. *(Interview with Pearl Mott, prevention specialist, Drug Prevention Programs in Higher Education, Washington, D.C., October 1994, for a prevention newsletter.)*

A second methodological factor complicating drug research among such students is simply that academic failures stay in "F" categories for only one or two semesters. Many then disappear from statistics entirely, via academic attrition.

A more serious challenge to the notion of amotivational syndrome comes from the same ethnographic research that was mentioned at the beginning of this chapter. The most well known of these investigations was carried out by Vera Rubin and Labros Comitas, as reported in their book *Ganja in Jamaica* (1975). Follow-up studies were done in Jamaica (Dreher 1982; Hamid 1998) and Costa Rica (Carter 1980; Pollan 1998). None of these works found that chronic use impaired occupational or other functioning; in fact, the main point of the Jamaican studies was that users defined this drug as helpful and motivating for work — a "motivational syndrome." This work is often cited to counter amotivational syndrome claims. By this logic, dropping out of the rat race is a cultural posture, with marijuana being secondary to, or, at most, reinforcing the drift away from a mainstream lifestyle. The Jamaican and Costa Rican subjects, however, were not observed engaging in an academic, cognitively complex, or rapid reflex activity, nor were they found in occupations that are competitive and striving for mobility. Rather, these subjects were involved in repetitive, physical labor such as sugar-cane cutting. In such a context, marijuana drug use functions to provide a pleasant sedation that counters the monotony and physical discomfort of such

►Case in Point   Marijuana Use May Lead to a Life of Trouble

Dear Ann Landers: Twenty years ago, when I was in my early 20s, you printed a column about marijuana. You expressed concern that marijuana may have "taken a generation of doers and turned them into a generation of dreamers."

I used to smoke pot daily. I somehow managed to get through college and hold down a job, but I wasn't getting anywhere. Every night, I would get high and write down in a journal all the things I planned to do. After reading your column, I realized I had been doing the same thing year after year and was getting nowhere. I decided to quit smoking pot.

I can't begin to tell you how my life changed. I became bored with my party-animal boyfriend and later married a wonderful man. I went back to school, earned a master's degree and got an excellent position with a *Fortune* 500 company. I also developed much needed self-esteem. It was your column on marijuana that helped me turn my life around, and I want to write a belated "thank you." — *Margie in Tennessee*

Dear Tennessee: I very much appreciate your generous letter. Please keep reading for one that should be of special interest to you:

Dear Ann Landers: Last fall, my teen-age son began smoking marijuana and was soon out of control. I sent him away to a special program. He is much better now, but I could not understand how my son got into so much trouble. Two weeks ago, the truth came out.

Last summer, I sent my two teen-agers to visit their uncle and aunt across the country. I decided it would be a good way for my brother and his wife to get to know their niece and nephew. I was mistaken. He and his wife smoked pot in front of my kids and offered it to them.

I believe that my brother and his wife contributed to my son's problems, and I am considering suing them for the cost of the special program I put my son in. I am so angry about this that I am considering a break with the entire family. Please advise. — *A Canadian Mom*

Dear Mom: Be thankful the "special program" was a success, and forget about a lawsuit and becoming estranged from the entire family. Mass retaliation is never a good idea.

Next summer, see that your son has a local job, and keep your eye on the companions he hangs out with.

Source: Ann Landers/*The Times of Northwest Indiana*, c/o Times Mirror, Los Angeles, CA 90053. Reprinted with permission of Esther P. Lederer Trust and Creators Syndicate, Inc.

---

labor. When studies in other cultures contradict the largely American notion of amotivational syndrome, we are left to be cautious in making a direct assumption that marijuana use leads to such a syndrome. (For related information on how marijuana affects personality, see "Case in Point," Marijuana Use May Lead to a Life of Trouble.)

Therapeutic Uses and the Controversy over Medical Marijuana Use

In the last 7 years, new controversy about the medical uses of marijuana has begun to emerge. Basically, **medical marijuana use** involves using cannabis, primarily THC, as a drug to calm or to relieve symptoms of an illness. At the heart of this controversy is the use of an illicit drug for medical purposes. However, the desire to use cannabis in this fashion is nothing new. Between 1840 and 1900, European and American medical journals pub-

lished more than 100 articles on the therapeutic use of the drug known then as *Cannabis indica* (or Indian hemp) and now as marijuana. It was recommended as an appetite stimulant, muscle relaxant, analgesic, hypnotic, and anticonvulsant. As late as 1913, Sir William Osler recommended it as the most satisfactory remedy for migraines (Grinspoon and Bakalar 1995).

Marijuana was used to treat a variety of human ills in folk and formal medicine for thousands of years in South Africa, Turkey, South America, and Egypt as well as such Asian countries as India, Malaysia, Myanmar, and Siam. Thus, marijuana, known as *cannabis* back then, has a 5000-year medical history that came to an abrupt end by passage of the Marijuana Tax Act of 1937. When the Marijuana Tax Act became law, marijuana was legally

KEY TERMS

medical marijuana use
use of the THC in cannabis as a drug to calm or to relieve symptoms of an illness

▶ Holding the Line   Should Cannabis Buyers' Clubs Be Fully Legalized?

Should medically ill patients, those afflicted with AIDS, chronic pain, or those suffering the deleterious effects of chemotherapy and/or radiation, glaucoma, and other illnesses, be able to legally purchase marijuana if they find relief from the effects of their illnesses? The first cannabis buyers club began in 1996, when the voting citizens of Marin County, California passed " . . . Proposition 215, which authorized the use of medical marijuana . . . for those who have a doctor's recommendation" (*Cannabis News* 2002). The main problem this club in Marin County, as well as other cannabis buyers' clubs, is faced with is that, while the counties have legalized such enterprises, they violate federal drug laws. This conflict is between federal and state law. Usually, the clubs are ordered closed by a superior court judge, resulting in federal agents raiding the clubs, confiscating the marijuana, and arresting the owners and operators of these establishments. To date, this cyclical pattern of raids and arrests by federal officials is repetitive and ongoing because of this rift between state and federal laws. The clubs are for either profit or nonprofit organizations whose sole intent is to distribute marijuana for medicinal purposes when prescribed by a licensed physician. Many of the buyers (known as patients) report relief and satisfaction from their use of marijuana. For example, a man by the name of Clay Shinn, 46, was diagnosed with

AIDS in 1992. He's been going to the Marin Alliance's Cannabis Buyers Club for 5 years. "'It's made a major difference in my life,'" he said. After taking his [AIDS] medication morning, afternoon, and evening, he said, "I was always getting nauseated . . . I could set my watch by it. I hate it. God, it's awful. Now I don't barf anymore" (*Cannabis News* 2002). Another interviewee, who is an arthritic, HIV–positive cabaret performer, said, "After I leave here . . . I won't feel my pain" (Goldberg 1996). Another man, the club's director, reiterated that, "You have to be sick or dying" . . . If you are, with a doctor's note to prove that you have AIDS or cancer or another condition with symptoms that marijuana is known to alleviate, Mr. Peron (the club's director) is willing to sell some relief (Goldberg, 1996).

What are your views regarding the prescribed use of marijuana, especially when these clubs or cooperatives provide seriously ill patients with a safe and reliable source of medical cannabis information and patient support? Would you support a cannabis buyers club or cooperative in your community? What are your views regarding federal laws that prohibit such establishments? How do you think this current problem of the illegality on the federal level should be resolved? Finally, in your lifetime how do you think this dilemma will be resolved?

Sources: Cannabis News. "Medical Pot War Rages On." *Marin Independent Journal*, (1 July 2002). Available http://cannabisnews.com/news/13/thread13278.shtml

Goldberg, C. "Marijuana Club Helps Those in Pain." *The New York Times* (26 February 1996). Available http://query.nytimes.com/gst/fullpage.html?res=9C06E6DF1139F936A15751C0A960958260&sec=&spon=&pagewanted=all

classified as a narcotic, and at that time medical use of this substance effectively ceased. Only in the past decade has there been organized renewed interest in possible medical uses for cannabis. Because of potential clinical uses for marijuana, enforcement of laws prohibiting the use of this substance has been very controversial (see "Holding the Line," Cannabis Buyers' Club).

Marijuana has been shown to be effective in the treatment of certain types of medical conditions. However, because medicines are available that are at least as effective and without abuse potential, none of these applications is currently approved by the Food and Drug Administration (FDA). According to researchers (Abood and Martin 1992; Consroe and Sandyk 1992; Iversen 1993) and proponents for the medical uses of marijuana, the potential uses are as follows:

Reduction in intraocular (eye) pressure. Marijuana lowers glaucoma-associated intraocular pressure, even though it does not cure the condition or reverse blindness (Goldstein 1995). **Glaucoma** is the second leading cause of blindness, caused by uncontrollable eye pressure (Julian 1994).

Antiasthmatic effect. Some research indicates that short-term smoking of marijuana improves breathing for asthma patients. Marijuana smoke

KEY TERMS

glaucoma
potentially blinding eye disease causing continual and increasing intraocular pressure

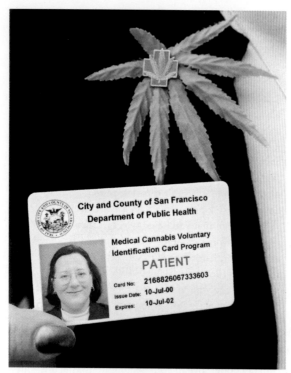

In July 2000, California began to issue cards that allow the users to purchase marijuana for medicinal purposes.

dilates the lungs' air passages (bronchodilation). Findings also show, however, that the lung-irritating properties of marijuana smoke seem to offset its benefits. Regardless, marijuana may still prove useful when other drugs are not effective because of a different mode of action in causing bronchodilation.

Muscle-relaxant effect. Some studies indicate that muscle spasms are relieved when patients with muscle disorders, such as multiple sclerosis, use marijuana.

Antiseizure effect. Marijuana has both convulsing and anticonvulsant properties and has been considered for use in preventing seizures associated with epilepsy. In animal experimentation, the cannabinoids reduced or increased seizure activities, depending on how the experiments were conducted. One or more of the marijuana components may be useful in combination with other standard antiseizure medication, although at present their value seems limited.

Antidepressant effect. Cannabis and the synthetic cannabinoid synhexyl have been used

successfully in Great Britain as specific euphoriants for the treatment of depression.

Analgesic effect. Published testimonials have reported that marijuana can relieve the intense pain associated with migraine and chronic headaches or inflammation (Grinspoon and Bakalar 1995). In South Africa, native women smoke cannabis to dull the pain of childbirth (Hamid 1998; Solomon 1966). The pain-relieving potency of marijuana has not been carefully studied and compared with other analgesics, such as narcotics or aspirin-type drugs.

Appetite stimulant. The stimulant effects on appetite are seen as useful for patients with HIV and some eating disorders (Sewester 1993; see Chapter 16).

Short-Term Dangers of Smoking Marijuana

According to Brown University, health education website (2007): Discomforts associated with smoking marijuana include dry mouth, dry eyes, increased heart rate and visible signs of intoxication such as bloodshot eyes and puffy eyelids. Other problems include:

- Impaired memory and ability to learn
- Difficulty thinking and problem solving
- Anxiety attacks or feelings of paranoia
- Impaired muscle coordination and judgment
- Increased susceptibility to infections
- Dangerous impairment of driving skills. Studies show that it impairs braking time, attention to traffic signals, and other driving behaviors.
- Cardiac problems for people with heart disease or high blood pressure, because marijuana increases the heart rate (Brown University, Health Education 2007).

Long-Term Consequences of Smoking Marijuana

- Respiratory problems — many of the same as cigarette smokers (persistent coughing, symptoms of bronchitis, and more frequent chest colds are possible symptoms from the 400-plus chemicals (some carcinogen) in marijuana smoke. "Researchers report that marijuana cigarettes release five times as much carbon monoxide into the bloodstream and three times as much tar into the lungs of smokers as tobacco cigarettes" (Marijuana Detox.com 2003).

- Memory and learning — regular marijuana use compromises the ability to learn and to remember information by impairing the ability to focus, sustain, and shift attention. One study also found that long-term use reduces the ability to organize and integrate complex information.
- Marijuana impairs short-term memory and decreases motivation to accomplish tasks, even after the high is over.
- Fertility — long-term marijuana use suppresses the production of hormones that help regulate the reproductive system. For men, this can cause decreased sperm counts and very heavy users can experience erectile dysfunction. Women may experience irregular periods from heavy marijuana use.
- Is marijuana addictive? — More studies are finding that marijuana has addictive properties. Both animal and human studies show physical and psychological withdrawal symptoms from marijuana, including irritability, restlessness, insomnia, nausea, and intense dreams. Tolerance to marijuana also builds up rapidly. Heavy users need eight times higher doses to get the same effects as infrequent users. For a small percentage of people who use it, marijuana can be highly addictive. It is estimated that 10% to 14% of users will become heavily dependent. More than 120,000 people in the United States seek treatment for marijuana addiction every year (Brown University, Health Education 2007). Why would abusers go to treatment centers if this drug is not addictive?

All of these reasons have either been disputed or shown to be exaggerated claims by proponents who are in favor of allowing marijuana to be medically used. Proponents for medical use argue that "its illegality (marijuana) . . . imposes much anxiety and expense on suffering people, forces them to bargain with illicit drug dealers, and exposes them to the threat of criminal prosecution" (Grinspoon and Bakalar 1995, p. 1876).

Though more fully discussed in this section, since 1996, the following twelve states have legalized medical marijuana use: Arkansas, California, Colorado, Hawaii, Maine, Montana, Nevada, New Mexico, Oregon, Rhode Island, Vermont, and Washington. Eight of the twelve did so through the initiative process. Hawaii's law was enacted by

the legislature and signed by the governor in 2000, Vermont's was enacted by the legislature and passed into law without the governor's signature in May 2004, Rhode Island's was passed into law over the governor's veto in January 2006, and New Mexico's legislation was signed into law by Governor Bill Richardson on April 2, 2007 (*Common Sense for Drug Policy*, 2008) Further, in 1996, Canada approved propositions permitting physicians to prescribe marijuana for medical problems, with the idea that terminally ill patients could be given the option of smokable marijuana as opposed to the already-approved **Marinol** (dronabinol). This event triggered a major response by the federal government. Former President Clinton, the Secretary of Health and Human Services, and the U.S. Attorney General all made pronouncements reiterating the negative effects of marijuana, its abuse potential, and the danger of sending a "pro-use message" or one that suggested use was not outside the realm of accepted behavior (U.S. Department of Health and Human Services [HHS] 1996). The government warned that physicians who availed themselves of the permission given in these new state regulations would be prosecuted, lose their privilege of writing prescriptions, and be excluded from Medicare and Medicaid reimbursement. The entire legislative initiative was cast as being a smokescreen for legalization, with the federal government purporting that those who supported it were "closet" marijuana advocates or, at best, legalization advocates.

Physicians responded indignantly to what they considered a heavy-handed attempt to overrule their medical judgments and to smear them unfairly, especially when most of them were neither pro-use nor even pro-legalization, except in this one medical situation. An editorial in the prestigious *New England Journal of Medicine*, titled "Federal Foolishness and Marijuana" (Kassirer 1997), claimed that it was hypocritical to allow physicians to prescribe the highly addicting opiates morphine or meperidine, which cause death at doses not much greater than those that relieve pain, but not marijuana, which is far less addictive and does not cause death. The purpose of the legislative initiative, the editorial pointed out, was to alleviate the suffering of terminally ill patients, for whom long-term abuse potential is irrelevant.

KEY TERMS

Marinol
FDA-approved THC in capsule form (dronabinol)

Many of these patients perceive the smokable form of THC as being more effective than Marinol, a factor that is difficult to measure in experimental procedures. As far as the governmental reasons for prohibiting the drug for medical purposes, a few joked, it was a rerun of *Reefer Madness*.

In June 2000, Hawaii became the first state to pass a medical marijuana bill that approved the possession and use of marijuana for medical purposes. Hawaii's governor, Benjamin J. Cayetano, "said it was one aspect of his effort to make Hawaii the health care center of the Pacific" (Associated Press 2000). Passage of this bill currently affects 500 to 1000 residents of Hawaii. The belief by the governor is that "Hawaii law will lead to similar legislation in other states" (Associated Press 2000). This means that anyone found in possession of marijuana would be exempt if he or she can verify medical usage. This same article mentioned that Alaska, Arizona, California, Maine, Nevada, Oregon, Washington, and the District of Columbia have approved medical marijuana laws even though the U.S. Justice Department is challenging those laws. In addition, in March 2000, London's conservative Tory party voted in favor of supporting an experiment in legalization by beginning to hold public debates on this matter (Hopps 2000). Members of the party were expecting to experiment with legalization. Interestingly, in England,

cannabis possession carries up to a 7-year jail sentence, although such long sentences are rare. Time will tell what the outcomes in the United States, Canada, and the United Kingdom (see "Case in Point," Six High Points: Forget Amsterdam. These Pot-Friendly Spots Are Closer to Home) will be. As mentioned previously, several states are at variance with federal law, under which medical and recreational use of marijuana remains illegal.

The Physiological Effects of Marijuana Use

Although the literature on marijuana use repeatedly states that "in 5,000 years of medical and nonmedical use, marijuana has not caused a single overdose death" (Grinspoon and Bakalar 1995, p. 1875), the effects of marijuana use should not be overlooked. We begin by examining the effects of marijuana on the lungs.

When marijuana smoke is inhaled into the lungs, THC, the psychoactive ingredient, leaves the blood rapidly through metabolism and efficient uptake into the tissues. THC and its metabolites tend to bind to proteins in the blood and remain stored for long periods in body fat. Five days after a single dosage of THC, 20% remains stored, whereas 20% of its metabolites remain in

▶**Case in Point** Six High Points: Forget Amsterdam. These Pot-Friendly Spots Are Closer to Home

California:
State Proposition 215 made medical marijuana legal 10 years ago. Los Angeles has the most dispensaries, although San Francisco has the most per capita.

Alaska:
Alaskan citizens have the right to possess up to 1 ounce of marijuana in their home for personal use.

Vancouver:
Known as "Vansterdam" for it leniency. Medical marijuana is legal, and possession of up to 15 grams is a minor offense. Tourists can even book pot-themed tours.

Mississippi:
The National Center for Natural Products Research in Oxford is the only U.S. facility federally licensed to cultivate ganja for scientific research.

Mexico:
Congress passed a law legalizing small amounts of drugs; however, the president never signed it into effect. But law enforcement tends to look the other way when it comes to small quantities of pot.

Ontario:
A 2003 ruling made possession legal, although it was overturned. But many people still believe possession is lawful and law enforcement is generally lax.

Source: Grigoriadis, V. "The Great California Weed Rush: How Medical Marijuana Is Turning L.A. Pot Dealers into Semilegit Businessmen — No Beeper Required." *Rolling Stone* 1020 (22 February 2007): 58–61, 82.

the blood (Indiana Prevention Resource Center 1996; Kryger 1995). Complete elimination of a single dose can take up to 30 days. Measurable levels of THC in blood from chronic users can often be detected for several days or even weeks after their last marijuana cigarette (joint).

In smokers, lung absorption and transport of THC to the brain are rapid; THC reaches the brain within as little as 14 seconds after inhalation. Marijuana is metabolized more efficiently through smoking than via intravenous injection or oral ingestion. Smoking is also three to five times more potent than these two methods (Jones 1980; Kaplan and Whitmire 1995; Kryger 1995). Other findings that compare the amounts of marijuana with tobacco conclude that "three to four joints a day is about as harmful to your lungs as smoking a pack of cigarettes a day" (Reaney 2000, p. 1).

Some effects of cannabis described in the following sections are unquestionably toxic in that they can either directly or indirectly produce adverse health effects. Other effects may be beneficial in treating some medical conditions. The use of marijuana, THC, and synthetic cannabinoids, either alone or in combination with other drugs, is currently being investigated for treating pain, inflammation, glaucoma, nausea, and muscle spasms (Iversen 1993).

Effects on the Central Nervous System

The primary effects of marijuana — specifically, of THC — are on CNS functions. The precise CNS effects of consuming marijuana or administering THC can vary according to the expectations of the user, the social setting, the route of administration, and previous experiences (Abood and Martin 1992; Jaffe 1990). Smoking a marijuana cigarette can alter mood, coordination, memory, and self-perception. Usually, such exposure causes some euphoria, a sense of well-being, and relaxation. Marijuana smokers often claim heightened sensory awareness and **altered perceptions** (particularly a slowing of time), associated with hunger (the **munchies**) and a dry mouth (Hubbard et al. 1999; Swan 1994).

High doses of THC or greater exposure to marijuana can cause hallucinations, delusions, and paranoia (American Psychiatric Association [APA] 1994; Goldstein 1995; Hubbard et al. 1999). Some

users describe anxiety after high-dose exposure. Due to the availability and widespread use of marijuana, psychiatric emergencies from marijuana overdose are becoming somewhat common. Long-term, chronic users often show decreased interest in personal appearance or goals (part of the amotivational syndrome discussed earlier in this chapter) as well as an inability to concentrate, make appropriate decisions, and recall information from short-term memory (Abood and Martin 1992; Block 1996).

The precise classification of THC is uncertain because the responses to marijuana are highly variable and appear to have elements of all three major groups of drugs of abuse. Consequently, marijuana use can cause euphoria and paranoia (like stimulants), drowsiness and sedation (like depressants), and hallucinations (like psychedelics). It is possible that THC alters several receptor or transmitter systems in the brain and this action would account for its diverse and somewhat unpredictable effects.

The recent dramatic discovery of a specific receptor site in the brain for THC, called the *cannabinoid* receptor, suggests that a selective endogenous marijuana system exists in the brain and is activated by THC when marijuana is consumed (Hudson 1990). Some researchers speculate that an endogenous fatty acid–like substance called **anandamide** naturally works at these marijuana sites; efforts are being made to characterize this substance, which perhaps is a neurotransmitter (Iversen 1993). It is possible that, from this discovery, a group of new therapeutic agents that can selectively interact with the marijuana receptors will be developed, resulting in medical benefits without the side effects that generally accompany marijuana use (Iversen 1993; Swan 1993).

KEY TERMS

altered perceptions
changes in the interpretation of stimuli resulting from marijuana

munchies
hunger experienced while under the effects of marijuana

anandamide
possible neurotransmitter acting at the marijuana (cannabinoid) receptor

■ Effects on the Respiratory System

Marijuana is often smoked like tobacco and, like tobacco, it can cause damage to the lungs (Adams and Martin 1996; Consroe and Sandyk 1992). When smoking tobacco, nearly 70% of the total suspended particles in the smoke are retained in the lungs. Because marijuana smoke is inhaled more deeply than tobacco smoke, even more tar residues may be retained with its use.

Smoke is a mixture of tiny particles suspended in gas, mostly carbon monoxide. These solid particles combine to form a residue called *tar*. Cannabis produces more tar (as much as 50% more) than an equivalent weight of tobacco and is smoked in a way that increases the accumulation of tar (Jones 1980).

More than 140 chemicals have been identified in marijuana smoke and tar. A few are proven carcinogens; many others have not yet been tested for carcinogenicity. The carcinogen benzopyrene, for example, is 70% more abundant in marijuana smoke than in tobacco smoke. When cannabis tar is applied to the skin of experimental animals, it causes precancerous lesions similar to those caused by tobacco tar. Similarly, whenever isolated lung tissue is exposed to these same tars, precancerous changes result (Hollister 1986; Jones 1980; Turner 1980).

Special white blood cells in living lung tissue — alveolar macrophages — play a role in removing debris from the lungs. When exposed to smoke from cannabis, these cells are less able to remove bacteria and other foreign debris.

Smoking only a few marijuana cigarettes a day for 6 to 8 weeks can significantly impair pulmonary function. Laboratory and clinical evidence often indicate that heavy use of marijuana causes cellular changes and that users have a higher incidence of such respiratory problems as laryngitis, pharyngitis, bronchitis, asthma-like conditions, cough, hoarseness, and dry throat (Goldstein 1995; Hollister 1986). Some reports emphasize the potential damage to pulmonary function that can occur from chronic marijuana use (NIDA 1991). Evidence suggests that many 20-year-old smokers of both hashish and tobacco have lung damage comparable to that found in heavy tobacco smokers older than 40 years of age. It is believed that the tar from tobacco and marijuana has damaging effects, but it is not known whether smokers who use both products suffer synergistic or additive effects (Hollister 1986; Jones 1980).

■ Effects on the Cardiovascular System

In human beings, cannabis causes both *vasodilation* (enlarged blood vessels) and an increase in heart rate related to the amount of THC consumed (Abood and Martin 1992; NIDA 2000). The vasodilation is responsible for the reddening of the eyes often seen in marijuana smokers. In physically healthy users, these effects, as well as slight changes in heart rhythm, are transitory and do not appear to be significant. In patients with heart disease, however, the increased oxygen requirement due to the accelerated heart rate may have serious consequences. The effect of cannabis on people with heart rhythm irregularities is not known. Because of vasodilation caused by marijuana use, abnormally low blood pressure can occur when standing. In addition, if a user stands up quickly after smoking, a feeling of lightheadedness or fainting may result. Chronic administration of large doses of THC to healthy volunteers shows that tolerance develops to the increase in heart rate and vasodilation.

People with cardiovascular problems seem to be at an increased risk when smoking marijuana (Hollister 1986). Marijuana products also bind hemoglobin, limiting the amount of oxygen that can be carried to the heart tissue. In a few cases, this deficiency could trigger heart attacks in susceptible people (Palfai and Jankiewicz 1991). The National Academy of Sciences' Institute of Medicine recommends that people with cardiovascular disease avoid marijuana use because there are still many unanswered questions about its effects on the cardiovascular system.

■ Effects on Sexual Performance and Reproduction

Drugs may interfere with sexual performance and reproduction in several ways. They may alter sexual behavior, affect fertility, damage the chromosomes of germ cells in the male or female, or adversely affect fetal growth and development.

KEY TERMS

aphrodisiac
a compound that is believed to be the cause of sexual arousal

The Indian Hemp Commission (Taylor 1963, 1966), which wrote the first scientific report on cannabis, commented that it had a sexually stimulating effect, like alcohol. However, the report also said that cannabis was used by Asian Indian ascetics to destroy the sexual appetite. This apparent discrepancy may be a dose-related effect. Used occasionally over the short term, marijuana may act as an **aphrodisiac** by decreasing CNS inhibitions. In addition, the altered perception of time under the influence of the drug could make the pleasurable sensations appear to last longer than they actually do.

Marijuana affects the sympathetic nervous system, increasing vasodilation in the genitals and delaying ejaculation. High doses over a period of time lead to depression of libido and impotence — possibly due to the decreased amount of testosterone, the male sex hormone.

Cannabis has several effects on semen. The total number of sperm cells and the concentration of sperm per unit volume are decreased during ejaculation. Moreover, there is an increase in the proportion of sperm with abnormal appearance and reduced motility. These qualities are usually associated with lower fertility and a higher probability of producing an abnormal embryo should fertilization take place.

Despite these effects, there are *no* documented reports of children with birth defects in which the abnormality was linked to the father's smoking marijuana. It is possible that damaged sperm cells are incapable of fertilization (so that only normal sperm cells reach the egg) or that the abnormal sperm appearance is meaningless in terms of predicting birth defects. When marijuana use stops, the quality of sperm gradually returns to normal over several months.

Less reliable data are available on the effects of cannabis on female libido, sexual response (ability to respond to sexual stimulation with vaginal lubrication and orgasm), and fertile reproductive (menstrual) cycles (Consroe and Sandyk 1992; Grinspoon 1987). Preliminary data from the Reproductive Biology Research Foundation show that chronic smoking of cannabis (at least three times per week for the preceding 6 months) adversely affects the female reproductive cycle. Results with women were correlated with work in rhesus monkeys; it was found that THC blocks ovulation (due to effects on female sex hormones).

Data on effects of marijuana use during pregnancy and lactation are inconclusive. Some evidence suggests that the use of this drug by pregnant women can result in intrauterine growth retardation, which is characterized by increased fetal mortality, prolonged labor, low-birthweight babies, and behavioral abnormalities in newborns (Fernandez-Ruiz et al. 1992; Nahas and Latour 1992; Roffman and George 1988). THC and other cannabinoids pass through the blood–placenta barrier and concentrate in the fetus's fatty tissue, including its brain. Ethical considerations prevent duplication of the experiment in humans.

Women who smoke marijuana during pregnancy also often use other drugs — such as alcohol, tobacco, and cocaine — that are known to have adverse effects on the developing fetus. Because multiple drugs are used, it is difficult to isolate the specific effects of marijuana during pregnancy. Like many other substances, THC is taken up by the mammary glands in lactating women and is excreted in the breast milk. Effects of marijuana in the breast milk on human infants have not been determined (Christina 1994; Murphy and Bartke 1992).

In studies on mice and rats (but not humans), the addition of THC to pregnant animals lowered litter size, increased fetal reabsorption, and increased the number of reproductive abnormalities in the surviving offspring (Dewey 1986). The offspring of the drug-treated animal mothers had reduced fertility and more testicular abnormalities. The dose of cannabinoids used in these studies was higher than that used by humans. Clearly, pregnant women should be advised against using marijuana, even though there are few direct data on its prenatal effects in humans (Dewey 1986; Murphy and Bartke 1992).

Tolerance and Dependence

It has been known for many years that tolerance to some effects of cannabis builds rapidly in animals — namely, the drug effect becomes less intense with repeated administration. Frequent use of high doses of marijuana or THC in humans produces similar tolerance. For example, increasingly higher doses must be given to obtain the same intensity of subjective effects and increased heart rate that occur initially with small doses (Abood and Martin 1992).

Frequent high doses of THC also can produce mild physical dependence. Healthy subjects who smoke several joints a day or who are given comparable amounts of THC orally experience irritability, sleep disturbances, weight loss, loss of appetite, sweating, and gastrointestinal upsets when drug use is stopped abruptly. However, not all subjects experience this mild form of withdrawal.

It is much easier to show psychological dependence in heavy users of marijuana (Abood and Martin 1992; Hollister 1986). Psychological dependence involves an attachment to the euphoric effects of the THC content in marijuana and may include craving for the drug. The subjective psychological effects of marijuana intoxication include a heightened sensitivity to and distortion of sight, smell, taste, and sound; mood alteration; and diminished reaction time.

Diagnosis: Cannabis Dependence

In general, outright cannabis addiction, with obsessive drug-seeking and compulsive drug-taking behavior, is relatively rare with low-THC cannabis. Contributing to this is the fact that the less potent forms of marijuana are most readily available in the United States, resulting in most chronic users in this country having little problem controlling or eliminating their cannabis habit if they so desired.

The Diagnostic and Statistical Manual of Mental Disorders, fourth edition (*DSM-IV*), recognizes a diagnosis of cannabis dependence. It is characterized by compulsive use and spending hours per day acquiring and using the substance. Compulsive users persist in their use despite knowledge of physical problems (for example, chronic cough related to smoking) or psychological problems (for example, excessive sedation resulting from repeated use of high doses) (APA 1994).

■ Chronic Use

Research on *chronic use of marijuana* (repeated daily use of this drug) in the 1970s indicated the possibility of three types of damage: (1) chromosomal damage (Stenchever et al. 1974); (2) *cerebral atrophy* (shrinking of the brain) (Campbell et al. 1971); and (3) lowered capacity of white blood cells to fight disease (Suciu-Foca et al. 1974). These findings have all been found to be contradicted or refuted by subsequent research. The only finding that appears very credible is that heavy use of this drug impairs lung capacity (Bloodworth 1987; Henneberger 1994; Kaplan and Whitmire 1995; Oliwenstein 1988; Swan 1994).

Other evidence indicates that chronic, heavy use of cannabis can lead to unforeseen calamities in some users (see "Case in Point," Chronic Marijuana Use). We have pointed out that marijuana produces a variety of psychoactive effects. One of those effects is sedation of unwanted emotional states such as anxiety, which are inevitable given the conflicts and turmoil of living in our fast-paced society today. As with the chronic use of any psychoactive drug that produces sedating effects, normal emotional and psychosocial development can be arrested by heavy marijuana consumption. For example, a youth who is usually high at a party avoids the anxieties and embarrassments of introspective and critical interpersonal interactions, but instead will be interested in thrill-seeking behavior, such as romantic and sexual involvements, experimentation with and heavy use of other drugs, and other types of more daring experiences.

From years of research with this drug, we find that heavy and chronic use of marijuana can very easily compromise cognitive functions, such as short-term memory, concentration, moderately taxing problem solving, and even spiritual growth and development. Often, the more serious costs in using this drug are that the individual acquires a poor record for development and advancement of learning, as is often expected in educational settings (schools, colleges, trade schools, and universities). Another cost that is more serious is the retardation in emotional development. Such types of development are often obscured by being high all the time. Further, in such chronic use cases, much time is wasted seeking the pleasures and sometimes the longed-for thrills derived from the habitual use of marijuana.

The amotivational syndrome, in fact, can be deconstructed into the sedation, depression, and cognitive impairment discussed throughout this chapter. The user who is experiencing a subjective euphoric effect, enjoying the presence and social reinforcement of peers, feeling no pain, and remaining cognitively unfocused finds it difficult to intellectually grasp the learned experiences from such developmental delays. Although many do mature out of use, this step may occur only after years of development have slipped away, never to be regained. Sometimes treatment interventions are necessary to get the subject into a drug-free state and reunited with non–drug-using peer groups.

►Case in Point   Chronic Marijuana Use

The following comments show how marijuana use can become a disturbing habit:

I guess you could say it was peer pressure. Back in 1969, I was a sophomore in college, and everyone was smoking "dope." The Vietnam War was in progress, and most students on college campuses were heavily involved in the drug scene. I first started smoking marijuana when my closest friends did. I was taught by other students who already knew how to enjoy the effects of "pot."

I recall that one of my fellow students used to supply me with "nickel bags," and many users nicknamed him "God." How did he get such a name? Because he sold some very potent marijuana that at times caused us to hallucinate.

I used pot nearly every day for about a year and a half, and hardly an evening would pass without smoking dope and listening to music. Smoking marijuana became as common as drinking alcohol. I used it in the same manner a person has a cocktail after a long day. At first, I liked the effects of being "high," but later I became so accustomed to the stuff that life appeared boring without it.

After graduating, my college friends went their separate ways, and I stopped using marijuana for a few years. A year later, in graduate school, a neighborhood friend reintroduced me to the pleasure of smoking pot. I began to use it again but not as often. Whenever I experienced some pressure, I would use a little to relax.

After finishing my degree, I found myself employed at an institution that at times was boring. Again, I started using pot at night to relax, and somehow it got out of control. I used to smoke a little before work and sometimes during lunch. I thought all was well until one day I got fired because someone accused me of being high on the job.

Soon afterward, I came to the realization that the use of marijuana can be very insidious. It has a way of becoming psychologically addictive, and you don't even realize it. When I was high, I thought that no one knew, and that I was even more effective with others. Little did I know, I was dead wrong and fooling no one.

Source: From Venturelli's files, interview with a 39-year-old male, May 1990.

In concluding this chapter, we note that the history of this drug indicates that usage and availability will remain widespread despite all the efforts to eradicate its existence. Despite all the prevention efforts to date, marijuana remains the most popular illicit drug, topped only by alcohol and tobacco, which are licit drugs.

Discussion Questions

1. What are the pharmacological, sociological, and psychological reasons why the very young continue to use marijuana at alarming rates despite the illegality of usage?

2. Do you believe that prosecution for marijuana possession should be more or less rigid than it currently is? Why?

3. Debate whether marijuana use adversely affects driving capabilities.

4. Either directly interview or imagine interviews of several users and nonusers of marijuana. How do you think they would answer the question of whether their critical thinking skills are adversely affected by this drug?

5. Among marijuana users, does the amotivational syndrome exist? Interview several users and try to either add to the characteristics of this syndrome from your interviews or modify the syndrome as explained in this chapter.

6. In light of the information in this chapter regarding medical marijuana use, do you believe in legalizing medical marijuana use? Why or why not?

7. What is your reaction to legalizing marijuana as a controlled substance like alcohol and tobacco products? Give reasons either for or against legalization.

8. Do you believe consistent use of marijuana changes personality? If so, how?

9. Summarize how marijuana affects the CNS, respiratory system, cardiovascular system, and sexual performance and reproduction.

10. Debate how much family upbringing and attachment to a religion contribute to later drug use.

11. From reading this chapter, try to explain why most heroin users have used marijuana, whereas the vast majority of marijuana users never advance to such highly addictive drugs.

12. Explain why a user of cannabis might develop psychological dependence.

13. Do you believe that use of marijuana is more or less harmful than use of tobacco products? Should they be regulated differently?

14. Why do you think such a high percentage of 12th graders *do not* disapprove of using marijuana? (The 2005 results were that 46% thought that using once or twice was acceptable and 32% thought that occasional use was acceptable.)

Summary

1 Marijuana consists of the dried and crushed leaves, flowers, stems, and seeds of the *Cannabis sativa* plant. THC (tetrahydrocannabinol) is the primary mind-altering (psychoactive) ingredient in marijuana.

2 Marijuana remains very controversial for the following reasons: (1) a high percentage of the U.S. population uses this drug; (2) it remains illegal; (3) several states, but not the federal government, have approved medical uses of marijuana; (4) marijuana accounts for a large number of arrests for simple possession; (5) it is one of the least addictive-type drugs; and (6) most marijuana users do not graduate to other more addictive illicit drugs.

3 Effects of marijuana can vary according to expectations and surroundings. At low doses, such as when smoked or ingested (eaten), marijuana often has a sedative effect. At higher doses, it can produce hallucinations and delusions.

4 As with tobacco, heavy use of marijuana can impair pulmonary function, cause chronic respiratory diseases (such as bronchitis and asthma), and promote lung cancer. Marijuana causes vasodilation and a compensatory increase in heart rate. The effects of marijuana on sexual performance and reproduction are controversial. Some studies have suggested this substance not only enhances sexual arousal but also promotes risky sexual behavior (unprotected sex).

5 Tolerance to the CNS and cardiovascular effects of marijuana develop rapidly with repeated use. Although physical dependence and associated withdrawal are minor, psychological dependence can be significant in chronic, heavy users.

6 The active ingredient in marijuana, THC, has been used for treating a variety of seemingly unrelated medical conditions. This drug is indicated for treatment of nausea and vomiting in cancer patients receiving chemotherapy and for treatment of anorexia (lack of appetite) in AIDS patients. Other potential therapeutic uses for THC include relief of intraocular pressure associated with glaucoma, as an antiasthmatic drug, for muscle relaxation, as prevention for some types of seizures, as an antidepressant, and as an analgesic to relieve migraines and other types of pain.

7 The age groups most likely to use marijuana are the following: (1) highest lifetime use, adults between 26 and 34 years of age (53.9%); (2) highest past-year and past-month use, 18- to 25-year-olds; and (3) sharp drop in use, 26 and older age group.

8 The frequency of marijuana use is strongly correlated with age. The age group reporting the highest lifetime (52.4%), past-year (28%), and past-month (16.6%) use was 18- to 25-year-olds. For the 26 and older age group, marijuana use sharply drops during the past year (6.9%) and past month (4.1%). From 1993 to 1997 marijuana use continued to increase, then declined very slowly to 38% for 12th graders in 2005.

9 Among 8th, 10th, and 12th graders, some of the major findings in 2005 were: (a) over half (53%) of all 12th graders think that regular use of marijuana involves a great risk to the user, whereas 47% do not; (b) approximately 19% of 12th graders believe that using mari-

juana once or twice is harmful, whereas 81% do not; (c) approximately 80% of 12th graders disapprove of using marijuana on a regular basis, whereas 20% do not; (d) approximately 68% of 12th graders disapprove of using marijuana on an occasional basis, whereas 32% do not; (e) approximately 54% of 12th graders disapprove of using marijuana once or twice, whereas 46% do not; and (f) since the study began in 1975, between 83% and 90% of every senior middle school class have said they could get marijuana fairly easily or very easily if they wanted some (Johnston et al. 2006).

10 Recent research by the Drug Enforcement Administration (DEA) (DEA 2006) involving government surveys that ask young people about their drug use patterns showed that about 600,000 high school seniors drive after smoking marijuana. Thirty-eight thousand seniors told surveyors that they had been involved in accidents while driving under the influence of marijuana. Other surveys conducted by MADD and the Liberty Mutual insurance company revealed that many teenagers (41%) were not concerned about driving after taking drugs. Medical data indicates a connection between drugged driving and accidents — patients in a shock-trauma unit who had been in collisions revealed that 15% of those who had been driving a car or motorcycle had been smoking marijuana and another 17% had both THC and alcohol in their blood. Another significant and notable study revealed the link between smoking marijuana and car accidents. Habitual marijuana users (used every day) were 9.5 times more likely to be involved in crashes, with 5.6% of people who had crashed having taken the drug, compared to 0.5% of the control group. This study revealed that that habitual use of marijuana is strongly associated with car crash injury.

11 Since 1996, the following twelve states have legalized medical marijuana use: Arkansas, California, Colorado, Hawaii, Maine, Montana, Nevada, New Mexico, Oregon, Rhode Island, Vermont, and Washington. Legalization of medical use of marijuana entails permitting physicians to prescribe marijuana for medical problems, with the idea that terminally ill patients could be given the option of smoking marijuana as opposed to the already-approved Marinol (dronabinol).

References

Abel, E. L. *Marijuana: The First Twelve Thousand Years*. New York: Plenum, 1989.

Abood, M., and B. Martin. "Neurobiology of Marijuana Abuse." *Trends in Pharmacological Sciences* 13 (May 1992): 201–206.

Abood, M. E., and B. R. Martin. "Molecular Neurobiology of the Cannabinoid Receptor." *International Review of Neurobiology* 39 (May 1996): 197–219.

Adams, I. B., and B. R. Martin, "Cannabis: Pharmacology and Toxicology in Animals and Humans." *Addiction* 91 (1996): 1585–1614.

American Psychiatric Association (APA). *Diagnostic and Statistical Manual of Mental Disorders*, 4th ed. [*DSM-IV*]. Washington, DC: APA, 1994.

Anslinger, H. J., and C. R. Cooper. "Marijuana: Assassin of Youth." *American Magazine* 124 (July 1937): 19–20, 150–153.

Associated Press. "Hawaii Becomes First State to Approve Medical Marijuana Bill." *The New York Times on the Web* (15 June 2000). Available http://www.nytimes.com/library/national/science/health/061500hth-hawaiimarijuana.html.

Berkowitz, A. "Following Imaginary Peers: How Norm Misperceptions Influence Student Substance Abuse." In *Project Direction*, edited by G. Lindsay and G. Rulf, 12–15 (Module No. 2). Muncie, IN: Ball State University, 1991.

Block, R. I. "Does Heavy Marijuana Use Impair Human Cognition and Brain Function?" *Journal of the American Medical Association* 275 (1996): 560–561.

Bloodworth, R. C. "Major Problems Associated with Marijuana Use." *Psychiatric Medicine* 3 (1987): 173–184.

Brown, M. W., and S. Massaro. "Attention and Memory Impaired in Heavy Users of Marijuana." Rockville, MD: NIDA, 20 February 1996.

Buff, J. "Greasers, Dopers, and Hippies: Three Responses to the Adult World." In *The White Majority*, edited by L. Howe, 60–70. New York: Random House, 1970.

Califano, J. A. "Dangerous Indifference to Drugs." *Washington Post* (23 September 1996): A-19.

Campbell, A. G., M. Evans, J. L. Thomson, and M. J. Williams. "Cerebral Atrophy in Young Cannabis Smokers." *Lancet* 19 (1971): 1219–1225.

Carter, E. *Cannabis in Costa Rica*. Philadelphia, PA: Institute for the Study of Human Issues, 1980.

Center for Substance Abuse Research (CESAR). "Marijuana Distribution Relies Primarily on Generosity of Friends and Family." *CESAR FAX*, 16 (19 March 2007). College Park, Maryland. Available http://www.cesar.umd.edu/cesar/cesarfax/vol16/16-11.pdf.

Chait, L., and J. Pierri. "Effect of Smoked Marijuana on Human Performance: A Critical Review." In *Marijuana/Cannabinoids, Neurobiology and Neurophysiology*, edited by L. Murphy and A. Bartke, 387–424. Boca Raton, FL: CRC Press, 1992.

Christina, D. *Marijuana: Personality and Behavior*. Tempe, AZ: Do It Now, 1994.

Coleman, J. S. *The Adolescent Society.* New York: Free Press of Glencoe, 1961.

Consroe, P., and R. Sandyk. "Potential Role of Cannabinoids for Therapy of Neurological Disorders." In *Marijuana/Cannabinoids, Neurobiology and Neurophysiology,* edited by L. Murphy and A. Bartke, 459–524. Boca Raton, FL: CRC Press, 1992.

Dewey, W. L. "Cannabinoid Pharmacology." *Pharmacological Reviews* 38 (1986): 48–50.

Dreher, M. C. "Working Men and Ganja: Marijuana Use in Rural Jamaica." Philadelphia, PA: Institute for the Study of Human Issues, 1982.

Eckert, P. *Jocks and Burnouts: Social Categories and Identity in the High School.* New York: Teachers College, Columbia University, 1989.

Fernandez-Ruiz, J., F. Rodriguez de Fonseca, M. Navarro, and J. Ramos. "Maternal Cannabinoid Exposure and Brain Development: Changes in the Ontogeny of Dopaminergic Neurons." In *Marijuana/Cannabinoids, Neurobiology and Neurophysiology,* edited by L. Murphy and A. Bartke, 118–164. Boca Raton, FL: CRC Press, 1992.

Gaines, G. *Teenage Wasteland: Suburbia's Dead-End Kids.* New York: Harper Perennial, 1992.

Gardner, E. "Cannabinoid Interaction with Brain Reward Systems: The Neurobiological Basis of Cannabinoid Abuse." In *Marijuana/Cannabinoids, Neurobiology and Neurophysiology,* edited by L. Murphy and A. Bartke, 275–335. Boca Raton, FL: CRC Press, 1992.

Goldstein, A. *Addiction from Biology to Drug Policy.* New York: Freeman, 1994.

Goldstein, F. "Pharmacological Aspects of Substance Abuse." *Remington's Pharmaceutical Sciences,* 19th ed. Easton, PA: Mack, 1995.

Gossop, M. *Living with Drugs,* 2nd ed. Aldershot, England: Wildwood House, 1987.

Greenblatt, J. C. *Adolescent Self-Reported Behaviors and Their Association with Marijuana Use.* Office of Applied Studies (OAS) of the Substance Abuse and Mental Health Services Administration (SAMHSA). Rockville, MD: National Clearinghouse for Alcohol and Drug Information, July 1999.

Grinspoon, L. "Marijuana." *Harvard Medical School Mental Health Letter* 4 (November 1987): 1–4.

Grinspoon, L., and J. B. Bakalar. "Commentary, Marijuana as Medicine: A Plea for Reconsideration." *Journal of the American Medical Association* 273 (1995): 1875–1876.

Hamid, A. *Drugs in America: Sociology, Economics, and Politics.* Gaithersburg, MD: Aspen Publishers Inc., 1998.

Heitzeg, N. *Deviance: Rulemakers and Rulebreakers.* St. Paul, MN: West Publishing, 1996.

Henneberger, M. "Pot Surges Back, It's Like a Whole New World." *New York Times* (6 February 1994): C19.

Hollister, L. E. "Health Aspects of Cannabis." *Pharmacological Reviews* 38 (1986): 39–42.

Hopps, J. "Tory Press Open to Reform on Cannabis." *Reuters* (30 March 2000).

Hubbard, J. R., S. E. Franco, and E. S. Onaivi. "Marijuana: Medical Implications." *American Family Physician* 283 (1999): 231–240.

Hudson, R. "Researchers Identify Gene That Triggers Marijuana's 'High.'" *Wall Street Journal* (9 August 1990): B-2.

Indiana Prevention Resource Center. *Factline on: Marijuana.* Bloomington, IN: Indiana Prevention Resource Center, 1996.

Iversen, L. "Medicinal Use of Marijuana." *Nature* 365 (1993): 12–13.

Jaffe, J. H. "Drug Addiction and Drug Abuse." In *The Pharmacological Basis of Therapeutics,* 8th ed., edited by A. Gilman, T. Rall, A. Nies, and P. Taylor. New York: Pergamon, 1990: 522–575.

Johnston, L. D., P. M. O'Malley, J. G. Bachman, and J. E. Schulenberg. *Monitoring the Future: National Results on Adolescent Drug Use.* Bethesda, MD: National Institute on Drug Abuse, 2006.

Jones, R. T. "Human Effects: An Overview." In *Marijuana Research Findings: 1980.* NIDA Research Monograph No. 31. Washington, DC: National Institute on Drug Abuse, 1980.

Julian, B. S. "alt.hemp CANNABIS/MARIJUANA FAQ." FAQ Maintainer (online publication). Amherst, MA: University of Massachusetts at Amherst, 1994. Available http://www.faqs.org/faqs/drugs/hemp-marijuana/.

Kandel, D. B., P. C. Griesler, G. Lee, M. Davies, and C. Shaffsan. *Parental Influences on Adolescent Marijuana Use and the Baby Boom Generation: Findings from the 1995–1996 National Household Surveys on Drug Abuse.* Department of Health and Human Services (DHHS). Rockville, MD: Substance Abuse and Mental Health Services Administration, 2001.

Kaplan, L. F., and R. Whitmire. "Pot — It's Potent, Prevalent and Preventable." *Salt Lake Tribune* 250 (21 May 1995): 9.

Kassirer, J. "Federal Foolishness and Marijuana" (editorial). *New England Journal of Medicine* 336 (1997): 14–32.

Kelly, T., R. Foltin, C. Enurian, and M. Fischman. "Effects of THC on Marijuana Smoking, Drug Choice and Verbal Report of Drug Liking." *Journal of Experimental Analysis of Behavior* 61 (1994): 203–211.

Kendler, K. S., C. O. Gardner, and C. A. Prescott. "Religion, Psychopathology, and Substance Use and Abuse: A Multimeasure, Genetic-Epidemiologic Study." *American Journal of Psychiatry,* 154 (1997): 322–329.

Kryger, A. H. *Preventive Medicine Clinic of Monterey: Marijuana Mental Disturbances.* Iowa City, IA: Virtual Hospital Home Page, 24 October 1995: 1–6. Available http://vh.radiology.uiowa.edu.

Liska, K. *Drugs and the Human Body,* 5th ed. Upper Saddle River, NJ: Prentice Hall, 1997.

"Marijuana Menaces Youth." *Scientific American* 154 (1936): 151.

Mathias, R. "Marijuana Impairs Driving-Related Skills and Workplace Performance." *NIDA Notes* 11 (January/February 1996): 6.

MSNBC.com. *Marijuana Sold in U.S. Stronger than Ever.* Reuters Limited (28 April 2007). Available http://www.msnbc.msn.com/id/18310976.

Murphy, L., and A. Bartke. "Effects of THC on Pregnancy, Puberty, and the Neuroendocrine System." In *Marijuana/Cannabinoids, Neurobiology and Neurophysiology*, edited by L. Murphy and A. Bartke, 539. Boca Raton, FL: CRC Press, 1992.

Musto, D. F. *The American Disease: Origins of Narcotic Control*, 3rd ed. New York: Oxford University Press, 1999.

Nahas, G., and C. Latour. "The Human Toxicity of Marijuana." *Medical Journal of Australia* 156 (1992): 495–497.

National Center on Addiction and Substance Abuse at Columbia University. *Casa Report: Spirituality and Religion Reduce Risk of Substance Abuse.* New York: Author, 2001. Available http://www.casacolumbia.org/absolutenm/templates/PressReleases.aspx?articleid=115&zoneid=48.

National Clearinghouse on Alcohol and Drug Information (NCADI). *Marijuana: Facts Parents Need to Know.* Quick Screen, At Home Drug Test. Rockville, MD: National Clearinghouse on Alcohol and Drug Information, revised November 1998.

National Institute on Drug Abuse (NIDA). *Drug Abuse and Drug Abuse Research.* DHHS Publication No. 91-1704. Washington, DC: U.S. Department of Health and Human Services, 1991.

National Institute on Drug Abuse (NIDA). *Marijuana: Facts Parents Need to Know.* NIH Publication No. 95-4037. Rockville, MD: National Clearinghouse on Alcohol and Drug Information, 1998. Available http://web.archive.org/web/20000307153943/http://www.athomedrugtest.com/drugabusemarij.html.

National Institute on Drug Abuse (NIDA) (Infofax). *Marijuana.* Bethesda, MD: U.S. Department of Health and Human Services, 29 March 2000. Available http://www.nida.nih.gov/infofax/marijuana.html.

Office of National Drug Control Policy (ONDCP). "Drug Facts: Marijuana." Washington, DC: ONDCP, 2003. Available http://whitehousedrugpolicy.gov/drugfact/marijuana/index.html.

Oliwenstein, L. "The Perils of Pot." *Discover* 9 (1988): 18.

Palfai, T., and H. Jankiewicz. *Drugs and Human Behavior.* Dubuque, IA: William C. Brown, 1991.

Pollan, M. "Medical Marijuana: Can It Help You? Should It Be Legal? A Report from California." *Herbs for Health* (March/April 1998): 38–50.

Pope, H. G., Jr., and D. Yurgulen-Todd. "The Residual Cognitive Effects of Heavy Marijuana Use in College Students." *Journal of the American Medical Association* 275 (1996): 521–527.

Rand Drug Policy Research Center. "Rand Releases Study on Marijuana 'Gateway Effect.'" Press release. Santa Monica, CA: Join Together on Line, 26 December 2002. Available http://www.jointogether.org.

Reaney, P. "Getting High May Not Be So Harmless After All." *Reuters Limited* (20 March 2000).

Robert Wood Johnson Foundation. *Substance Abuse: The Nation's Number One Health Problem.* Prepared by the Schneider Institute for Health Policy for the Robert Wood Johnson Foundation, Brandeis University, Princeton, NJ: Robert Wood Johnson Foundation, February 2001.

Roffman, R. A., and W. H. George. "Cannabis Abuse." In *Assessment of Addictive Behaviors*, edited by D. M. Donovan and G. A. Marlatt, 78–86. New York: Guilford, 1988.

Rubin, V., and L. Comitas. *Ganja in Jamaica: A Medical Anthropological Study of Chronic Marijuana Use.* Paris: Mouton, 1975.

Schultes, R. E. "Ethnopharmacological Significance of Psychotropic Drugs of Vegetal Origin." *Principles of Psychopharmacology*, 2nd ed., edited by W. G. Clark and J. del Giudice. New York: Academic Press, 1978.

Sewester, S. *Drug Facts and Comparisons.* St. Louis, MO: Kluwer, 1993: 259h–259k.

Solomon, D., ed. *The Marihuana Papers.* New York: New American Library, 1966.

Stenchever, M. A., T. J. Kunysz, and M. A. Allen. "Chromosome Breakage in Users of Marijuana." *American Journal of Obstetrics and Gynecology* 118 (January 1974): 106–113.

Substance Abuse and Mental Health Services Administration (SAMHSA). *Results from the 2005 National Survey on Drug Use and Health: National Findings.* Rockville, MD: Office of Applied Studies, 2006.

Substance Abuse and Mental Health Services Administration (SAMHSA), Office of Applied Studies. "The NHSDA Report. Religious Involvement and Substance Use among Adults." (23 March 2007a). Available http://www.oas.samhsa.gov.

Substance Abuse and Mental Health Services Administration (SAMHSA), Office of Applied Studies. "The NHSDA Report. Youth Activities, Substance Use, and Family Income." (19 April 2007b). Available http://www.oas.samhsa.gov.

Suciu-Foca, N., J. P. Armand, and A. Morishima. "Inhibition of Cellular Immunity in Marijuana Smokers." *Science* 183 (1974): 419–420.

Swan, N. "Researchers Make Pivotal Marijuana and Heroin Discoveries." *NIDA Notes* 8 (10 September 1993): 1.

Swan, N. "A Look at Marijuana's Harmful Effects." *NIDA Notes* 9 (February/March 1994): 3–4.

Swan, N. "Facts About Marijuana and Marijuana Abuse." *NIDA Notes* 11 (March/April 1996): 15.

Taylor N. *Narcotics: Nature's Dangerous Gifts.* New York: Dell, 1963.

Taylor, N. "The Pleasant Assassin: The Story of Marijuana." *The Marijuana Papers*, ed. D. Solomon. New York: Signet Books, 1966.

Teen Challenge. *Drugs: Frequently Asked Questions.* South Australia: Pragin Press, 2000.

Tudor, C. G., D. M. Petersen, and K. W. Elifson. "An Examination of the Relationships Between Peer and Parental

Influences and Adolescent Drug Use." In *Chemical Dependencies: Patterns, Costs, and Consequences*, edited by C. D. Chambers, J. A. Inciardi, D. M. Petersen, H. A. Siegal, and O. Z. White. Athens, OH: Ohio University Press, 1987.

Turner, C. E. "Chemistry and Metabolism." In *Marijuana Research Findings: 1980*. NIDA Research Monograph No. 31. Washington, DC: National Institute on Drug Abuse, 1980.

U.S. Health and Human Services (HHS). "Substance Abuse — A National Challenge" (6 May 1996). Available www.thebody.com/content/whatis/art12895.html.

Venturelli, P. J. "Drugs in Schools: Myths and Reality." In *The Annals of the American Academy of Political and Social Science*, edited by W. Hinkle and S. Henry, 72–87. Thousand Oaks, CA: Sage Publications, January 2000.

Wallace, J. M., V. L. Myers, and E. R. Osai. *Faith Matters: Race/Ethnicity, Religion and Substance Use*. Baltimore, MD: The Annie E. Casey Foundation, 2004.

Wren, C. S. "Youth Marijuana Use Rises." *Themes of the Times, New York Times* (20 February 1996): 1.

Zimmer, L., and J. P. Morgan. *Marijuana Myths, Marijuana Facts: A Review of the Scientific Evidence*. New York: Lindesmith Center, 1997.

CHAPTER 14

Inhalants

Learning ◎bjectives

On completing this chapter you will be able to:

◎ Understand that inhalant use is not harmless and that even one-time use could lead to sudden sniffing death syndrome.

◎ List the household and commercial products that are most often abused as inhalants.

◎ Describe the principal means of using household and commercial products as inhalants.

◎ Identify signs of abuse.

◎ Examine the current patterns of abuse among various groups.

◎ List the dangers of inhalant abuse.

Did You Know?

○ More than 1000 different commercial and household products are abused commonly in the United States.

○ Ordinary household products are misused as inhalants: glues/adhesives, nail polish remover, gasoline, paint thinner, spray paint, butane lighter fluid, propane gas, typewriter correction fluid, household cleaners, cooking sprays, deodorants, whipping cream aerosols, marking pens, and air conditioning coolants.

○ Inhalant abuse is typically a problem of adolescents and teenagers. By the time children reach 8th grade, 16.1% will have misused inhalants.

○ Every year, young people in this country die of inhalant abuse or suffer severe consequences, including permanent brain damage and destruction of the heart, kidney, liver, and bone marrow.

○ Inhalant abusers can die suddenly and without warning; even first-time abusers have died from sniffing inhalants.

Drugs and Society Online is a great source for additional drugs and society information for both students and instructors.
Visit **http://drugsandsociety.jbpub.com** to find a variety of useful tools for learning, thinking, and teaching.

Introduction

Inhalants are **volatile** substances that elicit psychological or physiological changes when introduced into the body via the lungs. They are rarely administered by any other route. Most cause intoxicating and/or **euphorigenic** effects. Many of these substances were never intended to be used by humans as drugs; consequently, they are not often thought of as having abuse potential. However, abuse of inhalants is a serious public health problem; according to data obtained from the National Institute on Drug Abuse (NIDA)-sponsored Monitoring the Future study, 16.1% of 8th graders have misused an inhalant at least once in their lifetime. Among 10th and 12th graders, lifetime reported use was 13.3% and 11.1%, respectively (Johnston et al. 2007). This frequency of inhalant abuse among 8th graders surpasses the frequency of abuse of such highly publicized drugs as cocaine (3.4%), amphetamines (7.3%), and marijuana (15.7%) in this age group (Johnston et al. 2007).

A widespread misconception is that inhalant abuse is a harmless phase that occurs commonly during normal childhood and teenage development and as such is not worthy of significant concern because young people will grow out of it without experiencing harm. On the contrary, hundreds of adolescents and teenagers in the United States die or are seriously injured each year as a result of inhalant abuse. Even first-time users may die from sudden sniffing death syndrome (SSDS), a condition characterized by serious cardiac **arrhythmia** occurring during or immediately after inhaling. Accurate statistics regarding the number of inhalant-associated deaths and injuries each year are unavailable, in part because medical examiners often attribute deaths from inhalant use to suicide, suffocation, or accidents. Nevertheless, every year young people in the United States die from inhalant abuse, and many more suffer severe consequences such as damage to the brain, heart, kidney, and liver (U.S. Consumer Product Safety Commission 2007).

KEY TERMS

volatile
readily evaporated at low temperatures

euphorigenic
having the ability to cause feelings of pleasure and well-being

arrhythmia
an irregular heartbeat

Most inhalants are household or commercial products composed of several different chemicals. These compounds can act alone or synergistically to exert toxic effects. The potential of these agents to cause harm is compounded by the high concentrations of these substances absorbed in the body by inhalation and the tendency for these often *lipid* (oil or fat)-rich substances to be retained in lipid-containing vital organs. Another important consideration is that the users are often developmentally immature and as such can be more susceptible to the toxic effects of inhalants. The summation of these factors makes inhalants dangerous substances of abuse.

History of Inhalants

The modern era of inhalant abuse can be traced to 1776, when British chemist Joseph Priestley synthesized nitrous oxide (Kennedy and Longnecker 1990), a colorless gas with a slightly sweet odor and no noticeable taste. Roughly 20 years later, he and Humphry Davy suggested correctly that the gas might be useful as an anesthetic, and experiments were conducted to test this possibility. Meanwhile, many people learned that inhalation of nitrous oxide produces a euphoria that lasts for minutes. Hence, during the decades between its discovery and clinical use, the inhalant was abused. Its abuse continued to be fashionable into the early 19th century because it served as a means of rapidly attaining drunkenness without consuming alcohol.

Dentists contributed greatly to the introduction of nitrous oxide as an anesthetic. At a stage show in the 1840s, Horace Wells, a dentist, noticed that one of the persons involved in the show injured himself while under the influence of nitrous oxide, and yet felt no pain. Wells was so impressed by this anesthetic effect that he subsequently allowed his own tooth to be extracted while under the influence of the gas. His experiment was a success; Wells felt no pain. He went on to attempt to demonstrate his discovery at Massachusetts General Hospital in Boston; unfortunately, the patient cried out during the operation and the experiment was deemed unsuccessful. Nevertheless, word of this demonstration and others like it spread, ultimately leading to the use of nitrous oxide and other volatile anesthetics as legitimate medical therapy (Kennedy and Longnecker 1990).

Over the years, it was discovered that many chemicals, in addition to nitrous oxide, could be inhaled so as to alter psychological function. Such abuse of inhalants came to public attention in the 1950s when the news media reported that young people were getting high from sniffing glue. The term *glue sniffing* is still used today, but it is often used to describe inhalation of many products besides glue. In fact, more than 1000 different products are currently misused as inhalants (U.S. Consumer Product Safety Commission 2007), some of which are listed in Table 14.1. These

chemicals are not regulated like other drugs of abuse; hence, they are readily available to young people. This category of drugs can be classified into three major groups: volatile substances, anesthetics, and nitrites.

Types of Inhalants

Volatile Substances

Over the past 50 years, the number of products containing volatile substances has increased substantially. This category of agents includes aerosols (e.g., spray paints, hair sprays, deodorants, air fresheners), art or office supplies (e.g., correction fluids, felt-tip marker fluids), adhesives (e.g., airplane and other glues), fuels (e.g., propane, gasoline), and industrial or household solvents (e.g., nail polish remover, paint thinners, dry-cleaning fluids). Some volatile substances exist as gases (e.g., nitrous oxide; the propellant in whipping cream cans), and others as liquids that vaporize at room temperature (e.g., gasoline). In some cases, the abuser inhales vapors directly from their original containers (called *sniffing* or *snorting*). Still others inhale volatile solvents from plastic bags (called *bagging*) or from old rags or bandannas soaked in the solvent fluid and held over the mouth (called *huffing*).

Acute effects of the volatile chemicals that are commonly abused include initial nausea with some irritation of airways causing coughing and sneezing. Low doses often bring a brief feeling of lightheadedness, mild stimulation followed by a loss of control, lack of coordination, and disorientation accompanied by dizziness and possible hallucinations. In some instances, higher doses can produce relaxation and depression leading to sleep or coma. If inhalation is continued, dangerous **hypoxia** may occur and cause brain damage or death. In other cases, SSDS can occur. Other potential toxic consequences of inhaling such substances include hypertension and damage to the cardiac muscle, peripheral nerves, brain, and kidneys. In addition, chronic users of inhalants frequently lose their appetite, are continually tired,

Table 14.1 Inhalants

VOLATILE SOLVENTS	
Adhesives	
Airplane glue	Rubber cement
Polyvinylchloride cement	
Aerosols	
Spray paint	Hair spray
Deodorant, air freshener	Analgesic spray, asthma spray
Solvents and Gases	
Nail polish remover	Paint remover
Paint thinner	Correction fluid and thinner
Fuel gas	Cigarette lighter fluid
Gasoline	
Cleaning Agents	
Dry-cleaning fluid	Spot remover
Degreaser	
Dessert Topping Sprays	
Whipped cream, whippets	
ANESTHETICS	
Gas	Liquid
Local	
NITRITES	
Nitrite room odorizers	
"Poppers" and "rush"	

Source: Adapted from National Institute on Drug Abuse (NIDA). Research Report Services — Inhalant Abuse, NIH Publication No. 94–3818. July 1999.

KEY TERMS

hypoxia
a state of oxygen deficiency

and experience nosebleeds. If use of inhalants persists, some of the damage becomes irreversible.

Aerosols

Chemicals associated with aerosol sprays are popular among young inhalant abusers. Aerosol sprays are often abused not because of the effects produced by their principal ingredients but rather because of the effects of their propellant gases. In addition, some aerosol sprays (i.e., those necessary to suspend metallic paints) are inhaled because of the psychoactive effects caused by the solvents used to dissolve the product (NIDA 1999). Inhalation of aerosol preparations can be dangerous because these devices are capable of generating very high concentrations of the inhaled chemicals, much greater than those released more slowly from liquid products.

Toluene

Aerosol preparations can contain a variety of chemicals. One such chemical is toluene. Toluene is found in some glues, paints, thinners, nail polishes, and typewriter correction fluid. It is a principal ingredient in "Texas shoe shine" (a shoe spray containing toluene). Toluene represents one of the more dangerous chemicals found in aerosols and other solvents. Because this molecule is highly lipid soluble and has a low molecular weight, it is rapidly absorbed by the lungs, brain, heart, and liver. Accordingly, toluene abuse can cause damage to the brain resulting in incoordination, impaired cognition, limb spasms, convulsions, behavioral abnormalities, and coma. In addition, chronic abuse of toluene-containing products can damage other organs, especially the liver and kidneys. Toluene inhalation can also cause heart arrhythmia.

Butane and Propane

Butane and propane are found commonly in aero-sols (e.g., spray paints, air fresheners, hair sprays) and are used as fuel gas or in lighter fluid. Use of these agents is quite common among inhalant abusers. For instance, one survey of adolescents in a Virginia correctional facility reported that butane lighter fluid was the third most frequently used inhalant among members of that population (gasoline was the most frequently used, and Freon the second most commonly used [McGarvey et al. 1999]). These chemicals constitute some of the most common sniffing death hazards among abusers. Furthermore, these chemicals are highly flammable; fires and serious burn injuries have resulted when inhalation has been combined with smoking.

Gasoline

Because of its widespread availability, gasoline is abused commonly by young people, particularly in rural settings. Gasoline is a mixture of volatile chemicals, including toluene, benzene, and tri-orthocresyl phosphate (TCP). As a mixture of chemicals, its intentional inhalation can be especially dangerous. Benzene is an organic compound that causes serious injury to bone marrow and suppresses the immune system. TCP is a fuel additive that causes degeneration of motor neurons. Lead, formerly a common constituent of gasoline, can cause lead poisoning, which leads to persistent CNS damage. Furthermore, gasoline is highly flammable; as with butane and propane, fires and serious burn injuries have resulted when gasoline inhalation has been combined with smoking of marijuana, tobacco, or other drugs.

Freons

Freons and other fluorinated hydrocarbons are used in a number of products including refrigerators, air conditioners, and airbrushes. Their inhalation can cause not only serious liver damage but also SSDS. Inhaling these agents also poses other dangers; freeze injuries can occur when individuals inhaling Freon lose consciousness, leaving unprotected skin in close proximity to cold. In one serious, but rare, case, a 16-year-old male attempted to get high by inhaling airbrush propellant. The patient lost consciousness. When he awoke, he discovered that his tongue and lips were frozen, and that he had suffered serious burns on his larynx, vocal cords, trachea, bronchi, and esophagus (Kuspis and Krenzelok 1999).

■ Anesthetics

When used properly, other forms of inhalants with abuse potential are important therapeutic agents. Included in this category are anesthetics such as ether, chloroform, halothane, and nitrous oxide. Although all the anesthetic gases work much like the central nervous system (CNS) depressants, only nitrous oxide is available enough to be a significant abuse concern.

Nitrous oxide is a colorless gas that is used frequently for minor outpatient procedures in offices

Here and Now

Chronic Solvent Abuse, Brain Abnormalities, and Cognitive Deficits

Chronic inhalant abuse has long been associated with neurological damage and cognitive abnormalities that can range from mild impairment to severe dementia. In fact, the severity of these problems can be greater than for drugs often considered by the general population as being more harmful. For example, a 2002 report published by Neil Rosenberg of the University of Colorado Health Sciences Center found that chronic solvent abusers performed worse than chronic users of other drugs (especially cocaine and alcohol) on tests of working memory and executive function. In this study, abusers inhaled primarily vapors from spray paint containing toluene, and averaged more than 10 years of abuse. More than half of the group reported near-daily inhalant intoxication.

According to Rosenberg, "the extensive neurological damage and cognitive impairments we found among chronic solvent abusers in our study could limit their ability to control their behavior and perceive problems associated with their substance abuse. ... Some of the brain damage and cognitive deficits seen in both primary inhalant and cocaine abusers in the study could stem from the heavy use of alcohol that was common among both groups. ... However, the diffuse white matter changes and abnormalities found in the thalamus have not been seen in alcohol abusers and are clearly from solvent abuse."

Sources: R. Mathias. "Chronic Solvent Abusers Have More Brain Abnormalities and Cognitive Impairments Than Cocaine Abusers." *NIDA Notes*, 17. November 2002. Available http://www.drugabuse.gov/NIDA_notes/NNVol17N4/Chronic.html; Rosenberg, N.L., et al. "Neuropsychologic Impairment and MRI Abnormalities with Chronic Solvent Abuse." *Journal of Clinical Toxicology* 40 (2002): 21–34.

of both physicians and dentists. It is often referred to as "laughing gas" because it can cause giggling and laughter in the patient receiving it. Nitrous oxide produces a unique profile of stimulant, hallucinogenic, and depressant effects. Because it is readily accessible, health professionals themselves or their staff are most likely to abuse nitrous oxide.

In addition to being found in a clinical setting, nitrous oxide is sold in large balloons from which the gas is released and inhaled for its mind-altering effects. It is also found in small cylindrical cartridges used as charges for whipped cream dispensers. These cylinders and other plastic containers filled with nitrous oxide are referred to as "whippets." Although significant abuse problems of nitrous oxide are infrequent (Dohrn et al. 1993), there are occasional reports of severe hypoxia (i.e., a lack of oxygen) or death due to acute overdoses or psychosis. For the most part,

nitrous oxide does not pose a significant abuse problem for the general public.

◼ Nitrites

Nitrites are chemicals that cause vasodilation. Owing to this property, the prototype of this group, amyl nitrite, is available by prescription to treat angina. Nitrites were first abused in the 1960s as ampules of the compound were available over the counter (OTC). The ampules were popped between the fingers (hence, the name "poppers") and held to the nostrils for inhalation. They have been abused by only a few, selective groups, such as some homosexual men, to enhance sexual pleasure (NIDA 2005). According to a recent survey, only 1.2% of 12th graders reported any nitrite use in 2006 (Johnston et al. 2007).

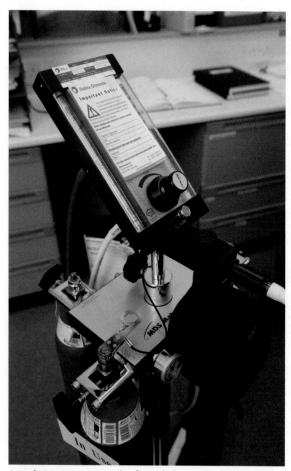

Anesthetics are an example of an inhalant.

Current Patterns and Signs of Abuse

Inhalants, particularly gases and aerosols, are often among the first drugs that young children misuse. The inhalants are popular for several reasons:

- They are legally obtained.
- They are readily available in most households and workplaces.
- They are inexpensive.
- They are easy to conceal.
- Most users are uninformed about the potential dangers.

In addition, inhalation is popular because it causes feelings of intoxication and euphoria much more rapidly than does the consumption of agents such as alcohol. Furthermore, the withdrawal (hangover) is often less severe than with alcohol.

Adolescent and Teenage Usage

Adolescents most commonly use inhalants, with usage decreasing as students grow older. For example, according to the 2006 *Monitoring the Future* study (Johnston et al. 2007), 4.1% of 8th graders reported using inhalants within the past month, whereas only 2.3% of 10th graders and 1.5% of high school seniors reported a similar pattern of use (see Table 14.2). Past-month use in college students and young adults (ages 19–28) was further decreased to 0.4% and 0.3%, respectively. One reason for this age difference is that older individuals often view use of inhalants with disdain and consider it unsophisticated and a kid's habit.

Inhalants were used by high percentages of 10th and 12th graders in 2006. Lifetime inhalant use among 12th graders in 2006 was 11.1%, compared with 13.3% among 10th graders (see Table 14.2). Use of inhalants has changed little since reaching a low point in 2002 and 2003 (Johnston et al. 2007).

Of considerable concern are reports that inhalant abuse can begin as early as the preschool years (Spiller and Krenzelok 1997). Researchers and poison information centers have described cases of 2- to 6-year-old children inhaling gasoline vapors. Imitation of older siblings or neighbors often accounts for this initial exposure. At least one study indicates that many 7- and 8-year-olds are familiar with the psychological effects of inhaling gasoline (Kaufman 1973). Hence, education efforts should be directed at very young children as well as adolescents and their parents.

Gender, Race, Socioeconomics, and Abuse

According to the 2005 National Survey on Drug Use and Health, a greater percentage of men (2.7%) than women (1.5%) ages 18 to 25 have used an inhalant during the past year. However, that gender difference is diminishing, as evidenced by recent findings that rates of past-year inhalant use were similar among females (4.9%) and males (4.2%) ages 12 to 17. Nearly 22% of American Indian or Alaskan Natives ages 12–17 have abused an inhalant at least once. White, non-Hispanic, and Hispanic individuals ages 12 to 17 were more likely than black or Asian individuals to have misused an inhalant at least once in their lifetime (10.8%, 10.2%, 9.4%, and 9.1%, respectively; Substance Abuse and Mental Health Services Administration [SAMHSA] 2006).

Table 14.2 **Inhalant Use Among 8th, 10th, and 12th Graders**

Data show the percentages of 8th, 10th, and 12th graders who used inhalants.

	8TH GRADERS			10TH GRADERS			12TH GRADERS		
	2004	2005	2006	2004	2005	2006	2004	2005	2006
Lifetime	17.3	17.1	16.1	12.4	13.1	13.3	10.9	11.4	11.1
Annual	9.6	9.5	9.1	5.9	6.0	6.5	4.2	5.0	4.5
30-Day	4.5	4.2	4.1	2.4	2.2	2.3	1.5	2.0	1.5

Source: Johnston, et al. 2007.

Chronic inhalant users frequently have a profile like that associated with other substance abusers. That is, often they live in unhappy surroundings with severe family or school problems, they have poor self-images, and sniffing gives them an accessible escape. Poverty, a history of child abuse, or poor grades are all associated with inhalant abuse (NIDA 2005). The problem of inhalant abuse is not unique to the United States. According to research data reported by the National Institute on Drug Abuse (NIDA), inhalant abuse is of worldwide concern.

■ Signs of Inhalant Abuse

Individuals under the influence of inhalants are often uncoordinated and disoriented and appear drunken as if having consumed alcohol. Red and watery eyes, slurred speech, nausea, headaches, and nosebleeds are also common. Rashes around the nose and mouth or unexplained paint on the hands and mouth can be signs of inhalant abuse. Other signs include smelling a chemical odor in the room or in unusual containers (e.g., soda cans, plastic bags), finding cans of aerosol whipped cream that will not foam, or discovering air conditioners that do not work. In addition, children who are frequent users of inhalants have the following characteristics:

- Often collect an unusual assortment of chemicals (such as glues, paints, thinners and solvents, nail polish, liquid eraser, and cleaning fluids) in bedrooms or with belongings

Signs & Symptoms Inhalants

POSSIBLE SIGNS OF MISUSE:	
Drunken behavior	Unexplained paint on the hands and mouth
Red and watery eyes	Room has a chemical odor
Slurred speech	Having the sniffles without other cold symptoms
Nausea	Vomiting
Headaches	Respiratory depression
Nosebleeds	Loss of consciousness
Rashes around the nose and mouth	Possible death

- Have breath that occasionally smells of solvents
- Often have the sniffles similar to a cold but without other symptoms of the ailment
- Appear drunk for short periods of time (15 to 60 minutes) but recover quickly
- Do not do well in school and are usually unkempt

Other signs of inhalant abuse can include the following:

- Sitting with a pen or marker near nose
- Constantly smelling clothing sleeves
- Hiding rags, clothes, or empty containers of the potentially abused products in closets, boxes, and other places
- Possessing chemical-soaked rags, bags, or socks
- Abusable household items missing

Dangers of Inhalant Abuse

The dangers of inhalant abuse stretch beyond simply the direct physical damage to the heart, lungs, liver, and brain. Other dangers include choking on vomitus, asphyxiation, and suffocation. In addition, abusers can seriously injure themselves or others while in an intoxicated state caused by the inhalant. In particular, frequent falls or accidents involving impaired driving occur in individuals under the influence of inhalants.

Other damage caused by inhalants include destruction of nerves that relay sound to the brain and thereby may cause deafness. The ability of the kidneys to control the amount of acid in the blood can be impaired. Severe rashes around the nose and mouth may also result (Office of National Drug Control Policy [ONDCP] 2003).

Use of inhalants by pregnant women can also put newborns at risk of developmental deficits. Animal studies suggest that prenatal exposure to trichlorethylene (TCE) or toluene can cause delayed neurobehavioral development, reduced birthweight, and occasional skeletal abnormalities (NIDA 2005). Although it is not yet possible to link prenatal exposure to specific inhalants with a specific birth defect, case reports have documented developmental abnormalities in offspring of mothers who chronically abuse inhalants (NIDA 2005).

According to SAMHSA (2003), early inhalant abuse has been linked to later use of illicit drugs. Definitive evidence that inhalants are a gateway drug is not available. Instead, inhalant abuse may be a marker for risk of other illicit drug use.

Discussion Questions

1. Name the three types of inhalants and list examples of each type. List the dangerous side effects associated with the misuse of each type of inhalant.

2. Why are inhalants widely abused?

3. What is sudden sniffing death syndrome?

4. What chemical properties of inhalants make these agents particularly dangerous?

5. Who is most likely to abuse inhalants?

6. List several signs of inhalant abuse.

7. List several dangers of inhalant abuse other than the direct physical damage done by the chemical itself.

Summary

1 Inhalants are volatile substances that cause intoxicating and/or euphorigenic effects. Most were never intended to be used as drugs and are not often thought of as having abuse potential. However, inhalant abuse is a serious public health problem. Hundreds of adolescents and teenagers in the United States die or are seriously injured each year as a result of inhalant abuse. Even first-time users can die from a condition referred to as sudden sniffing death syndrome (SSDS).

2 Most inhalants are household or commercial products composed of several different fat-soluble chemicals that can act alone or synergistically to exert toxic effects. These agents can be classified into three groups: volatile substances, anesthetics, and nitrites.

3 Volatile substances include aerosols, adhesives, fuels, and household solvents. Abusers inhale vapors directly from their original containers (called *sniffing* or *snorting*), from plastic bags (called *bagging*), or from old rags or bandannas soaked in the solvent fluid and held over the mouth (called *huffing*). Abuse of these agents can cause damage to the liver, brain, kidney, and immune system, as well as SSDS.

4 Anesthetics include ether, chloroform, halothane, and nitrous oxide. When used properly, these forms of inhalants are important therapeutic agents. However, their misuse can cause severe hypoxia and death.

5 Nitrites are vasodilators abused by only a few, selective groups to enhance sexual pleasure. Their use has declined since many of these chemicals were banned in 1991.

6 Inhalants are popular because they are legally obtained, readily available, inexpensive, and easy to conceal.

7 Inhalant abuse is typically a problem of adolescents and teenagers, although it can begin as early as the preschool years. Nevertheless, one in every six 8th graders has abused an inhalant.

8 Signs of inhalant abuse include a drunken appearance, watery eyes, nausea, headaches, and nosebleeds. Rashes around the nose and mouth or unexplained paint on the hands and mouth can be signs of inhalant abuse. Other signs can include smelling a chemical odor in the room or in unusual containers (e.g., soda cans, plastic bags), finding cans of aerosol whipped cream that will not foam, or discovering air conditioners that do not work.

9 Dangers of inhalant abuse beyond those caused by the chemicals per se include choking on vomitus, asphyxiation, and suffocation.

References

Dohrn, C., J. Lichtor, A. Coalson, H. Uitvlugt, H. deWit, and J. Zachny. "Reinforcing Effects of Extended Inhalation of Nitrous Oxide in Humans." *Drugs and Alcohol Dependence* 31 (1993): 265–280.

Johnston, L. D., P. M. O'Malley, J. G. Bachman, and J. E. Schulenberg. *Monitoring the Future, National Survey of Results on Drug Use 1975–2006.* Vol. I, Secondary School Students. NIH Publication No. 07-6205. Besthesda, MD: National Institute on Drug Abuse, 2007.

Kaufman, A. "Gasoline Sniffing Among Children in a Pueblo Indian Village." *Pediatrics* 51 (1973): 1060–1064.

Kennedy, S. K., and D. E. Longnecker. "History and Principles of Anesthesiology." In *The Pharmacological Basis of Therapeutics*, edited by A. G. Gilman, T. W. Rall, A. S. Nies, and P. Taylor, 269. New York: Pergamon Press, 1990.

Kuspis, D. A., and E. P. Krenzelok. "Oral Frostbite Injury from Intentional Abuse of a Fluorinated Hydrocarbon." *Journal of Toxicology and Clinical Toxicology* 37 (1999): 873–875.

McGarvey, E. L., G. J. Calvet, W. Mason, and D. Waite. "Adolescent Inhalant Abuse: Environments of Use." *American Journal of Drug and Alcohol Abuse* 25 (1999): 731–741.

National Institute on Drug Abuse (NIDA). *Research Report, Inhalant Abuse.* NIH Publication No. 94-3818, July 1999.

National Institute on Drug Abuse (NIDA). *Research Report Series — Inhalant Abuse.* NIH Publication No. 00-3818, March 2004.

National Institute on Drug Abuse (NIDA). *Research Report, Inhalant Abuse.* NIH Publication No. 05-3818. March 2005.

Office of National Drug Control Policy (ONDCP). Inhalants Fact Sheet (February 2003). Available www.streetdrugs.org/pdf/inhalants.pdf.

Spiller, H. A., and E. P. Krenzelok. "Epidemiology of Inhalant Abuse Reported to Two Regional Poison Centers" *Clinical Toxicology* 35 (1997): 167–173.

Substance Abuse and Mental Health Services Administration (SAMHSA), *Substance Abuse Treatment Advisory: Inhalants, 2003.* DHHS Publication No. (SMA) 03-3788.

U.S. Consumer Product Safety Commission. "A Parent's Guide to Preventing Inhalant Abuse, 2007." Available www.cpsc.gov/CPSCPUB/PUBS/inhpdf.html.

CHAPTER 15

Over-the-Counter (OTC), Prescription, and Herbal Drugs

Learning ◎bjectives

On completing this chapter you will be able to:

- ◎ Outline the general differences between prescription and nonprescription drugs.
- ◎ Explain why the FDA occasionally switches prescription drugs to over-the-counter (OTC) status.
- ◎ Describe potential abuse problems with OTC, herbal, and prescription drugs.
- ◎ Identify some of the drugs that have been switched to OTC.
- ◎ Discuss the potential problems of making more effective OTC drugs available to the public for self-care.
- ◎ Describe the type of information that is included on the labels of nonprescription medicines.
- ◎ Discuss the rules for safe use of nonprescription drugs.
- ◎ Determine the difference between herbal products and OTC medications.
- ◎ Explain why the FDA has removed ephedrine and ephedra from its list of approved OTC products.
- ◎ Discuss the type of information that should be communicated between doctor and patient to avoid unnecessary drug side effects.
- ◎ Explain the advantages and disadvantages of generic and proprietary drugs.
- ◎ Explain why some prescription drugs are so commonly abused.

Did You Know?

- ○ More than 700 of the current over-the-counter (OTC) drug products were available only by prescription 30 years ago.
- ○ Pharmacists can provide useful counseling in selecting appropriate OTC products.
- ○ Careless, excessive use of some OTC medications can cause addiction, physical dependence, tolerance, and withdrawal symptoms.
- ○ When used together, prescription drugs or drugs of abuse can interact with OTC or herbal drugs in a dangerous and sometimes even lethal manner.
- ○ Most herbal remedies are very popular products that, despite containing drugs, are available without a prescription and by law are excluded from routine OTC regulation by the Food and Drug Administration (FDA).
- ○ More people die in the United States from adverse reactions to legal medications than succumb to all illegal drug use.
- ○ Most generic drugs are as effective as, but substantially less expensive than, their proprietary counterparts.

Drugs and Society Online is a great source for additional drugs and society information for both students and instructors. Visit **http://drugsandsociety.jbpub.com** to find a variety of useful tools for learning, thinking, and teaching.

Introduction

More than $44 billion is spent each year in the United States on prescription and nonprescription (over-the-counter or OTC) drugs (Just the Facts 2003) and at least 1.5 million Americans are hurt or killed by errors in prescribing, dispensing, or taking these products (Kaufman 2006b). Prescription and OTC drugs have been viewed differently by the public since these classifications were formally established by the Durham-Humphrey Amendment of 1951. In general, we view OTC medications as less effective, relatively free from side effects, and rarely abused; in contrast, we often consider prescription drugs as much more potent, typically used for more serious medical conditions, and frequently dangerous. However, distinctions between prescription and non-prescription drugs, which at one time appeared to be obvious, have become blurred by changes in public demand and federal policies. Because of escalating health costs and a growing interest in self-care, people today want access to effective medications, and governmental agencies such as the Food and Drug Administration (FDA) are responding to their demands. Consequently, the FDA is actively involved in switching effective and relatively safe prescription medications to OTC status. In fact, more than 700 drug products sold OTC today were available only by prescription 30 years ago (Pal 2006). It is clear that in the future, many more drugs will be removed from behind the pharmacist's counter and made available for public access as nonprescription medications. These changes emphasize the arbitrary nature of classifying drugs as prescription and OTC and remind us that similar care should be taken with all medications to achieve maximal benefit and minimal risk.

In this chapter, we begin by discussing OTC (nonprescription) drugs. The first topic encompasses policies regarding OTC drug regulation and is followed by a discussion of safe self-care with nonprescription drug products. Explanations of some of the most common medications in this category, including herbal remedies, conclude the section on OTC drugs. The second part of this chapter gives a general overview of prescription drugs. The consequences of misusing prescription drugs, as well as ways for you to avoid such problems, are discussed. A brief presentation of some of the most commonly prescribed drugs ends the chapter.

OTC Drugs

Each year people in the United States spend more than $18 billion on drug products that are purchased OTC, at a savings of $20 billion in health-care costs annually (Pal 2006). Today, more than 300,000 different OTC products are available to treat everything from age spots to halitosis; they account for 60% of the annual drug purchases in this country (Pal 2006). An estimated three out of four people routinely self-medicate with these drug products (Pal 2006). Some of the 80 major drug classes currently approved for OTC status are shown in Table 15.1.

OTC remedies are nonprescription drugs that may be obtained and used without the supervision of a physician or other health professional. Nevertheless, for some people, certain OTC products can be dangerous when used alone or in combination with other drugs. Although some OTC drugs are very beneficial in the self-treatment of minor to moderate uncomplicated health problems, others are of questionable therapeutic value, and their usefulness is often misrepresented by manufacturers.

Abuse of OTC Drugs

A couple of high school students from Oregon became extremely ill from overdosing on multiple boxes of cold and cough OTC products that they had shoplifted while ditching school. The students were found stumbling around in an alley near their school, disoriented and lethargic. A local secondary education official implied that the practice was routine and referred to by the local kids as "popping Skittles" because the cold medicine capsules are multicolored.

Although the consequences of abusing OTC drugs can be severe, relatively speaking the occurrence rate is low, although there are some notable exceptions such as cough medicines and decongestants (Martinez 2007).

Because these drugs are usually available on demand, perceived as being exceptionally safe, and poorly understood by the general public, their abuse patterns differ somewhat from those seen with the so-called hard-core drugs of abuse; nevertheless, they can be equally harmful. Even though the OTC products generally have a greater margin of safety than their prescription counterparts, issues of abuse need to be considered. For example, many

Table 15.1 Some Major Drug Classes Approved by the FDA for OTC Status

DRUG CLASS	EFFECTS
Analgesics and anti-inflammatories	Relieve pain, fever, and inflammation
Cold remedies	Relieve cold symptoms
Antihistamines and allergy products	Relieve allergy symptoms
Stimulants	Diminish fatigue and drowsiness
Sedatives and sleep aids	Promote sleep
Antacids	Relieve indigestion from rebound acidity
Laxatives	Relieve self-limiting constipation
Antidiarrheals	Relieve minor, self-limiting diarrhea
Gastric secretion blockers	Relieve heartburn
Topical antimicrobials	Treat skin infections
Bronchodilators and antiasthmatics	Assist breathing
Dentifrices and dental products	Promote oral hygiene
Acne medications	Treat and prevent acne
Sunburn treatments and sunscreens	Treat and prevent skin damage from ultraviolet rays
Dandruff and athlete's foot medications	Treat and prevent specific skin conditions
Contraceptives and vaginal products	Prevent pregnancy and treat vaginal infections
Ophthalmics	Promote eye hygiene and treat eye infections
Vitamins and minerals	Provide diet supplements
Antiperspirants	Promote body hygiene
Hair growth stimulators	Promote hair growth

Source: Pal, S. "Self Care and Nonprescription Pharmacotherapy." *Handbook of Nonprescription Drugs*, 15th ed., edited by I. Bernardi, 3–14. Washington DC: American Pharmacists Association, 2006.

OTC drugs, when misused, can cause physical and psychological dependence. Nonprescription products that can be severely habit-forming include nasal and ophthalmic (eye) decongestants, laxatives, antihistamines, sleep aids, and antacids. Of particular abuse concern are the OTC stimulants, such as ephedrine, which either can be severely toxic by themselves or can be used as precursors to the synthesis of the extremely addicting and dangerous amphetamines. In fact, because of these concerns, the FDA ruled that ephedrine no longer can be included in OTC or herbal products, and most states require that cold products containing amphetamine precursors be safeguarded behind the counter (Leinwand 2007).

Because use of OTC products is unrestricted, the patterns of abuse are impossible to determine accurately. However, these products are more likely to be abused by members of the unsuspecting general public who inadvertently become dependent due to excessive self-medication than by hard-core drug addicts who obtain the most potent drugs of abuse by illicit means.

■ Federal Regulation of OTC Drugs

In the United States, the FDA is responsible for regulating OTC drugs. Under the direction of the FDA, the active ingredients in OTC drugs have been, and continue to be, evaluated and classified according to their effectiveness and safety (Pal 2006). At this time, the principal ingredients included in nonprescription drug products are category I (that is, they are considered safe and effective) (Bernstein and Rickert 2006).

The FDA has attempted to make even more drugs available to the general public by switching some frequently used and safe prescription medications to OTC status. This policy is in response to public demand to have access to effective drugs for self-medication and has resulted in approximately 80 successful switches leading to more than 700 new OTC products (Consumer Healthcare 2007; Pal 2006). This policy helps to cut medical costs by eliminating the need for costly visits to healthcare providers for treatment of minor, self-limiting ailments (Stolberg 2000). A few of the more notable drugs that have been switched from prescription to nonprescription status since 1985 (Consumer Healthcare 2007) are naproxen (analgesic, anti-inflammatory: Aleve); ketoprofen (analgesic: Orudis); hydrocortisone (anti-inflammatory steroid: Cortaid); loperamide (antidiarrheal: Imodium); tioconazole (vaginal antifungal: Vagistat-1); epinephrine (bronchodilator: Bronkaid Mist); miconazole (antifungal: Monistat 7); cimetidine (heartburn medication: Tagamet); increased-strength minoxidil (hair growth stimulant: Rogaine); nicotine patch (smoking cessation aid: Nicotrol); cromolyn (allergy medication: Nasalcrom); triclosan (antibacterial for gum disease: Colgate Total toothpaste); loratadine (nonsedating antihistamine: Claritin); levonorgestrel (contraceptive: Plan B); and orlistat (weight loss: Alli).

A major concern of health professionals is that reclassification of safe prescription drugs to OTC status will result in overuse or misuse of these agents. The reclassified drugs may tempt individuals to self-medicate rather than seek medical care for potentially serious health problems or encourage the use of multiple drugs at the same time, increasing the likelihood of dangerous interactions (Stolberg 2000). Clearly, the FDA has slowed down this process. Since 2002, only five ingredients have been switched, including OTC versions of Claritin and the heartburn medication Prilosec (Consumer Healthcare 2007).

It is likely that effective and safe prescription drugs will continue to be made available OTC, albeit at a slower pace. In fact, the FDA is considering other groups of drugs currently available by prescription for OTC status in the next several years.

OTC Drugs and Self-Care

Of approximately 3.5 billion health problems treated in the United States annually, almost 2 billion can be treated with an OTC drug (OTC Observations 1998). This fact demonstrates that the public frequently engages in medical self-care with OTC products. Self-care with nonprescription medications occurs because we decide that we have a health problem that can be adequately self-medicated without involving a health professional. Proper self-care assumes that the individual has made a correct diagnosis of the health problem and is informed enough to select the appropriate OTC product. If done correctly, self-care with OTC medications can provide significant relief from minor, self-limiting health problems at minimal cost. However, a lack of understanding about the nature of the OTC products — what they can and cannot do — and their potential side effects can result in harmful misuse. For this reason, it is important that those who consume OTC medications be fully aware of their proper use. This goal usually can be achieved by reading product labels carefully and asking questions of health professionals such as pharmacists and physicians.

OTC Labels

Information about proper use of OTC medications is required to be cited on the drug label and is regulated by the FDA. Required label information includes (1) approved uses of the product, (2) detailed instructions on safe and effective use, and (3) cautions or warnings to those at greatest risk when taking the medication. FDA regulations require that this information be readily intelligible to the lay public and easily read (Bernstein and Rickert 2006) (see Figure 15.1).

Many consumers experience adverse side effects because they either choose to ignore the warnings on OTC labels or simply do not bother to read them. For example, excessive or inappropriate use of some nonprescription drugs can cause drug dependence; consequently, people who are always dropping medication in the eyes "to get the red out" or popping antacids like dessert after every meal are likely dependent. They continue to use OTC products to avoid unpleasant eye redness or stomach acidity, which are likely withdrawal consequences of excessive use of these medications.

Rules for Proper OTC Drug Use

The OTC marketplace for drugs operates differently than does its prescription counterpart. The

(a) Product Label Front

Each tablet individually sealed for your protection

Product Name

Soothe

COLD TABLETS

48 Tablets

Manufactured by J&B Pharmaceuticals

Quantity   Name and Address of Manufacturer

(b) Back of Label

List of Active Ingredients

Drug Facts	
Active ingredient (in each tablet)	**Purpose**
Chlorpheniramine maleate 2 mg	Antihistamine
Uses: temporarily relieves these symptoms due to hay fever or other upper respiratory allergies: • sneezing • runny nose • itchy, watery eyes • itchy throat	
Warnings: Ask a doctor before use if you have: • glaucoma • a breathing problem such as emphysema or chronic bronchitis • trouble urinating due to an enlarged prostate gland	
Ask a doctor or pharmacist before use if you are taking tranquilizers or sedatives	
When using this product: • you may get drowsy • avoid alcoholic drinks • alcohol, sedatives, and tranquilizers may increase drowsiness • be careful when driving a motor vehicle or operating machinery • excitability may occur, especially in children	
If pregnant or breast-feeding, ask a health professional before use. *Keep out of reach of children.* In case of overdose, get medical help or contact a Poison Control Center right away.	
Directions	
adults and children 12 years and over	take 2 tablets every 4 to 6 hours; not more than 12 tablets in 24 hours
children 6 years to under 12 years	take 1 tablet every 4 to 6 hours; not more than 6 tablets in 24 hours
children under 6 years	ask a doctor
Other Information: • store at 20-25C (68-77F) • protect from excessive moisture	
Inactive Ingredients: D&C yellow no. 10, lactose, magnesium stearate, microcrystalline cellulose, pregelatinized starch	

Directions   Warnings   Indications for Use

FIGURE 15.1

OTC Label

Certain information must appear on the labels of an OTC medicinal product.

use of OTC drugs is not restricted, and consumers are responsible for making correct decisions about these products. Thus, to a large degree, the consumer sets policy and determines use patterns.

Because there are no formal controls over the use of OTC drugs, abuse often occurs. In extreme situations, the abuse of OTC medication can be very troublesome, even causing structural damage to the body and, on rare occasions, death. Proper education about the pharmacological features of these agents is necessary if consumers are to make intelligent and informed decisions about OTC drug use. To reduce the incidence of problems, the following rules should be observed when using

nonprescription products (Center for Drug Evaluation and Research [CDER] 2002):

1. Always know what you are taking. Identify the active ingredients in the product.
2. Know the effects. Be sure you know both the desired and potential undesired effects of each active ingredient.
3. Read and heed the warnings and cautions. The warnings are not intended to scare but to protect.
4. Do not use OTC drug products for more than 1 to 2 weeks. If the problem being treated persists beyond this time, consult a health professional.
5. Be particularly cautious if you are also taking prescription or herbal drugs. Serious interactions between OTC drugs and these medications frequently occur. If you have a question, be sure to find out the answer.
6. If you have questions, ask a pharmacist. Pharmacists are excellent sources of information about OTC drugs. They possess up-to-date knowledge of OTC products and can assist consumers in selecting correct medications for their health needs. Ask them to help you.
7. Most importantly: If you don't need it, don't use it!

■ Types of OTC Drugs

It is impossible to provide a detailed description of the hundreds of active ingredients approved by the FDA for OTC distribution; however, the following includes a brief discussion of the most common OTC drugs available in this country.

Internal Analgesics

We spend more than $2 billion on internal (taken by mouth) **analgesics**, the largest sales category of OTC drugs in the United States. Most of the money is for **salicylates** (aspirin products—Anacin, Bayer), acetaminophen (Tylenol, Datril, Pamprin, Panadol), ibuprofen (Advil, Nuprin), and ibuprofen-like drugs such as naproxen (Aleve) and ketoprofen (Orudis). The compositions of common OTC internal analgesics are given in Table 15.2.

KEY TERMS

analgesics
drugs that relieve pain while allowing consciousness

salicylates
aspirin-like drugs

Table 15.2 **Compositions of OTC Internal Analgesics (Dose Per Unit)**

PRODUCT	ASPIRIN (MG)	ACETAMINOPHEN (MG)	IBUPROFEN (MG)	OTHER
Bayer Aspirin	325	—	—	—
Empirin	325	—	—	—
Alka-Seltzer, Extra Strength	325	—	—	Antacid
Ecotrin	325	—	—	Coated tablet
Tylenol, Children's	—	80	—	—
Advil	—	—	200	—
Motrin IB	—	—	200	—
Motrin, Children's	—	—	100	—
Nuprin	—	—	200	—
Aleve	—	—	—	Naproxen (220 mg)
Orudis	—	—	—	Ketoprofen (12.5 mg)

Source: Remington, T. "Headache." *Handbook of Nonprescription Drugs,* 15th ed., edited by I. Bernardi, 69–90. Washington DC: American Pharmacists Association, 2006.

Therapeutic Considerations The internal analgesic products are effective in treating several common ailments.

- *Analgesic Action.* The OTC analgesics effectively relieve mild to moderate somatic pain associated with musculoskeletal structures such as bones, skin, teeth, joints, and ligaments. Pains that are relieved by the use of these drugs include headaches, toothaches, earaches, and muscle strains. In contrast, these drugs are not effective in the treatment of severe pain or pain associated with internal organs, such as the heart, stomach, and intestines (*Drug Facts and Comparisons* 2007).

- *Anti-Inflammatory Effects.* Use of high doses (two to three times the analgesic dose) of the salicylates and ibuprofen relieves the symptoms of inflammation such as those associated with arthritis (*Drug Facts and Comparisons* 2007). In contrast, even high doses of acetaminophen have little anti-inflammatory action. Because of this **anti-inflammatory** effect, these drugs are frequently compared with a group of natural, very potent anti-inflammatory compounds, the **steroids**. To distinguish drugs such as the salicylates and ibuprofen from steroids, these drugs are often called **nonsteroidal anti-inflammatory drugs (NSAIDs)**.

- *Antipyretic Effects.* The OTC analgesics, such as aspirin and acetaminophen, reduce fever but do not alter normal body temperature (*Drug Facts and Comparisons* 2007). Such drugs are called **antipyretics**. The frequent use of these drugs to eliminate fevers is very controversial. Some clinicians believe that low-grade fever may be a defense mechanism that helps destroy infecting microorganisms such as bacteria and

KEY TERMS

anti-inflammatory
relieves symptoms of inflammation

steroids
potent hormones released from the adrenal glands

nonsteroidal anti-inflammatory drugs (NSAIDs)
anti-inflammatory drugs that do not have steroid properties

antipyretics
drugs that reduce fevers

viruses; thus, interfering with fevers may hamper the body's ability to rid itself of infection-causing microorganisms. Because no serious problems are associated with fevers of 102°F or less, they are probably better left unmedicated.

- *Side Effects.* When selecting an OTC analgesic drug for relief of pain, inflammation, or fever, possible side effects should be considered. Although salicylates such as aspirin are frequently used, they can cause problems for both children and adults (see "Signs & Symptoms," Common Side Effects of OTC Nonsteroidal Anti-Inflammatory Drugs [NSAIDs]). Because of their side effects, salicylates are not recommended for (1) children, because of the potential for **Reye's syndrome**; (2) people suffering gastrointestinal problems, such as ulcers; or (3) people with bleeding problems, who are taking anticlot medication, who are scheduled for surgery, or who are near term in pregnancy, because salicylates interfere with blood clotting and prolong bleeding.

For minor aches and pains, acetaminophen substitutes adequately for salicylates, has no effect on blood clotting, and does not cause stomach irritation. In addition, acetaminophen does not influence the occurrence of Reye's syndrome, a potentially deadly complication of colds, flu, and chicken pox in children up to the age of 18 years who are using salicylates (*Drug Facts and Comparisons* 2007).

Caffeine and Other Additives A number of OTC analgesic products contain caffeine. Caffeine may relieve the aversion of pain due to its stimulant effect, which may be perceived as pleasant and energizing. The combination of caffeine with OTC analgesics may enhance pain relief (*Drug Facts and Comparisons* 2007) and be especially useful in treating vascular headaches because of the vasoconstrictive properties on cerebral blood vessels caused by this stimulant. In most OTC analgesic products — for example, Anacin or Excedrin — the amount of caffeine is less than that found in one-fourth to one-half cup of coffee (about 30 milligrams/tablet).

Other ingredients — such as antacids, antihistamines, and decongestants — sometimes included in OTC pain-relieving products have little or no analgesic action and usually add little to the therapeutic value of the medication.

A recent development for OTC analgesic products was FDA permission to advertise pain-relieving products effective in the relief of migraine headaches. Although these products have been found to provide relief from minor migraine headaches, they do not contain any new breakthrough drugs; these products contain previously available ingredients, such as aspirin, ibuprofen, and caffeine, just in higher doses (e.g., Migraine Extra Strength Excedrin).

Cold, Allergy, and Cough Remedies

One billion colds occur each year in the United States, and patients spend $300 million on OTC cold products (Scolaro 2006).

The incidence of the common cold varies with age. Children between 1 and 5 years are most susceptible; each child averages six to twelve respiratory illnesses per year, most of which are common colds. Individuals 25 to 30 years old average about six respiratory illnesses a year, and older adults average two or three. The declining incidence of colds with age is owing to the immunity that occurs after each infection with a cold virus; thus, if reinfected with the same virus, the microorganism is rapidly destroyed by the body's defense and the full-blown symptoms of a cold do not occur (Scolaro 2006).

Most colds have similar general symptoms. In the first stage, the throat and nose are dry and scratchy; in the second stage, secretions accumulate in the air passages, nose, throat, and bronchial tubes. The second stage is marked by continuous sneezing, nasal obstruction, sore throat, coughing, and nasal discharge. There may be watering and redness of the eyes and pain in the face (particularly near the sinuses) and ears. One of the most bothersome symptoms of the common cold is the congestion of the mucous membranes of the nasal passages, due in part to capillary dilation, which causes these blood vessels to enlarge and become more permeable. Such vascular changes allow fluids to escape, resulting in drainage and also inflammation due to fluid-swollen tissues (Scolaro 2006).

There has been a growing problem of young people abusing these OTC products. Recent surveys suggest that up to 7% of high school seniors have used cough medicine with dextromethorphan to get high (Johnston 2007). This practice is

KEY TERMS

Reye's syndrome
potentially fatal complication of colds, flu, or chicken pox in children

Signs & Symptoms Common Side Effects of OTC Nonsteroidal Anti-Inflammatory Drugs (NSAIDs)

DRUGS:	SYSTEM AFFECTED:	SIDE EFFECTS:
Salicylates (aspirin-like)	Gastrointestinal	Cause irritation, bleeding; aggravate ulcers
	Blood	Interfere with clotting; prolong bleeding
	Ears	Chronic high doses cause ringing (tinnitus) and hearing loss
	Pediatric	Cause Reye's syndrome
Acetaminophen	Liver	High acute doses or chronic exposure can cause severe damage
Ibuprofen (includes other, newer NSAIDs)	Gastrointestinal	Similar to salicylates but less severe
	Blood	Similar to salicylates but less severe
	Kidneys	Damage in elderly or those with existing kidney disease

sometimes referred to as "robo-tripping" or "skittling." Common side effects include confusion, dizziness, excessive sweating, stomach pain, numbness, and blurred vision (Martinez 2007).

Decongestants The cold and allergy products we use are formulated with such drugs as decongestants (sympathomimetics), antihistamines (chlorpheniramine and pheniramine), analgesics (aspirin and acetaminophen), and an assortment of other substances (vitamin C, alcohol, caffeine, and so on). Table 15.3 lists the ingredients found in many common OTC cold and allergy products.

Antihistamines reduce congestion caused by allergies, but their effectiveness in the treatment of virus-induced colds is controversial (Mackowiak 1999). In high doses, the anticholinergic action of antihistamines (see Chapter 4) also decreases mucus secretion, relieving the runny nose; however, this action is probably insignificant at the lower recommended doses of OTC preparations (Mackowiak 1999; Scolaro 2006). An anticholiner-

gic drying action may actually be harmful because it can lead to a serious coughing response. Due to anticholinergic effects, antihistamines also may cause dizziness, drowsiness, impaired judgment, constipation, and dry mouth; they sometimes are abused because of psychedelic effects resulting from high-dose consumption. Because of the limited usefulness and the side effects of antihistamine for treating colds, decongestant products without such agents are usually preferred for these viral infections. In contrast, antihistamines are very useful in relieving allergy-related congestion and symptoms.

The sympathomimetic drugs used as decongestants cause nasal membranes to shrink because of their vasoconstrictive effect, which reduces the congestion caused by both colds and allergies. Such drugs can be used in the form of sprays or drops (topical decongestants) or systemically (oral decongestants) (see Table 15.4). FDA-approved sympathomimetics include pseudoephredrine, phenylephrine (probably the most

Table 15.3 Compositions of Common OTC Cold and Allergy Products (Dose Per Tablet)

PRODUCT	SYMPATHOMIMETIC (MG)	ANTIHISTAMINE (MG)	ANALGESIC (MG)
Actifed	Pseudoephedrine (30)	Triprolidine (2.5)	—
Chlor-Trimeton Allergy	—	Chlorpheniramine (4)	—
Advil Allergy Sinus	Phenylephrine (30)	Chlorpheniramine (2)	Ibuprofen (200)
Sudafed Sinus	Pseudoephedrine (30)	—	Acetaminophen (325)

Source: Scolaro, K. "Disorders Related to Colds and Allergies." *Handbook of Nonprescription Drugs,* 15th ed., edited by I. Bernardi, 203–228. Washington DC: American Pharmacists Association, 2006.

Table 15.4 Compositions of OTC Topical Decongestants (Drug Concentrations)

PRODUCT	SYMPATHOMIMETIC
Afrin nasal spray	Oxymetazoline (0.05%)
Neo-Synephrine, 12-Hour	Oxymetazoline (0.025%)
Vicks Sinex, 12-Hour	Phenylephrine (0.5%)

Source: Scolaro, K. "Disorders Related to Colds and Allergies." *Handbook of Nonprescription Drugs,* 15th ed., edited by I. Bernardi, 203–228. Washington DC: American Pharmacists Association, 2006.

effective topical), naphazoline, and oxymetazoline (Scolaro 2006). Another substantial problem associated with the sympathomimetic decongestant ingredients in cold medicines is that they can easily be chemically converted into methamphetamine. For this reason, state and local governments have passed laws that require these decongestant products to be kept behind the counter and records to be kept of those who pur-

The common cold accounts for 20% of all acute illnesses in the United States.

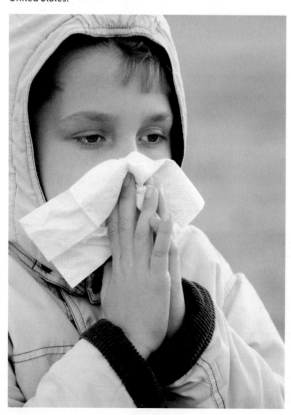

chase these medications (see "Here and Now," Fighting the "Common Cold" Pills; Baldauf 2006).

One who uses decongestant nasal sprays frequently can experience **congestion rebound** due to tissue dependence. After using a nasal spray regularly for longer than the recommended period of time, the nasal membranes adjust to the effect of the vasoconstrictor and become very congested when the drug is not present. One can become hooked and use the spray more and more with less and less relief until one's tissues no longer respond and the sinus passages become almost completely obstructed (Mackowiak 1999). Allergists frequently see new patients who are addicted to nasal decongestant sprays and are desperate for relief from congestion. This problem can be prevented by using nasal sprays sparingly and for no longer than the recommended time.

Orally ingested sympathomimetic drugs give less relief from congestion than the topical medications but are less likely to cause rebound effects. In contrast, systemic administration of these drugs is more likely to cause cardiovascular problems (that is, stimulate the heart, cause arrhythmia, increase blood pressure, and cause stroke).

Antitussives Other drugs used to relieve the common cold are intended to treat coughing. The cough reflex helps clear the lower respiratory tract of foreign matter, particularly in the later stages of a cold. There are two types of cough: productive and nonproductive. A *productive cough* removes mucus secretions and foreign matter so that breathing becomes easier and the infection clears up. A *nonproductive, or dry, cough* causes throat irritation; this type of cough is of little cleansing value. Some types of cough suppressant (antitussive) medication are useful for treating a nonproductive cough but should not be used to suppress a productive cough (Tietze 2006).

Two kinds of OTC preparations are available to treat coughing:

1. **Antitussives** — such as codeine, dextromethorphan, and diphenhydramine (an antihistamine)—

Here and Now

Fighting the "Common Cold" Pills

It is becoming harder and harder to get those pills we all buy to fight the common cold. This problem is not because drugs like Sudafed are themselves particularly addicting. Rather, the concern arises because of what they can become and is leading to the imposition of tighter controls on these popular decongestants. Because ingredients in OTC cold medicines, such as pseudo-ephedrine, can easily be converted into methampheta-mine, these products have been bought in large quantities to be used in makeshift meth labs across the country. As a result, law enforcement agencies and even Congress itself have pointed out these drugs' potential dangers. Besides requiring that these OTC products be kept be-hind the counter in pharmacies, there have been attempts to pass local and national legislation to limit purchases of these drugs to about 9 grams (roughly 300 pills) in a 30-day period. This quantity of pseudoephedrine can be turned into approximately 25 doses of methampheta-mine. It is hoped that such restrictions will make it diffi-cult for small neighborhood meth labs to cook their dangerous brew. This strategy has been very effective, causing a dramatic decline in methamphetamine labs across the country.

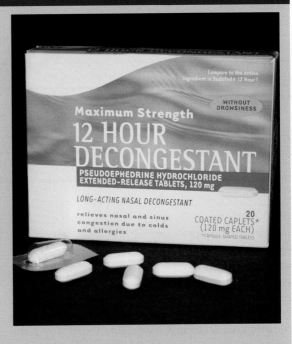

Source: "Bill Would Restrict Cold Pills to Fight 'Meth.'" *Reuters Health* (27 January 2005).

---

that act on the central nervous system (CNS) to raise the threshold of the cough-coordinating center, thereby reducing the frequency and intensity of a cough

2. **Expectorants** — such as guaifenesin and ter-pin hydrate — which theoretically (but not very effectively) increase and thin the fluids of the respiratory tract in an attempt to soothe the irritated respiratory tract mem-branes and decrease the thickness of the accumulated secretions so that coughing becomes more productive

Table 15.5 lists commonly used OTC antitus-sives and their compositions.

KEY TERMS

expectorants
substances that stimulate mucus secretion and diminish mucus viscosity

Often, the tickling sensation in the throat that triggers a cough can be eased by sucking on a cough drop or hard candy, which stimulates saliva flow to soothe the irritated membranes. Unless the cough is severe, sour hard candy often works just as well as more expensive cough lozenges.

Cough remedies, like other medications, have a psychological value. Many patients with respira-tory tract infections claim they cough less after using cough remedies, even when it is objectively demonstrated that the remedies reduce neither the frequency nor the intensity of the cough. Cough remedies work in part by reducing pa-tients' anxiety about the cough and causing them to believe that their cough is lessening. If one believes in the remedy, one often can get as much relief from a simple, inexpensive product as from the most sophisticated and costly one. If a cough does not ease in a few days, one should consult a doctor (Tietze 2006).

Table 15.5 **Compositions of Common OTC Antitussives (Dose Per Unit)**

PRODUCT	DEXTROMETHORPHAN (MG)	EXPECTORANT	OTHER
Benylin Adult	15/5mL	—	—
Hold DM Lozenges	5	—	—
Benylin	5/5mL	Guaifenesin	—
Robitussin CF	10	Guaifenesin	—
Vicks NyQuil	10	—	Sympathomimetic; antihistamine; analgesic

Source: Tietze, K. "Cough." In *Handbook of Nonprescription Drugs*, 15th ed., edited by I. Bernardi, 229–242. Washington DC: American Pharmacists Association, 2006.

Becoming more widely known, abuse of antitussive products by teenagers is a significant problem in some regions of this country. This abuse likely relates to the fact that the antitussive ingredient, dextromethorphan, in high doses can have a phencyclidine (PCP)–like effect (see "Here and Now," The Dextromethorphan Trip). In 2006 almost 10% of young people reported using antitussives to get high (Earth Times 2007).

What Really Works? With all the advances in medicine today, there is still no cure for the common cold. In most cases, the best treatment is plenty of rest, increased fluid intake to prevent dehydration and to facilitate productive coughing, humidification of the air if it is dry, gargling with diluted salt water (2 teaspoons per quart), an analgesic

to relieve the accompanying headache or muscle ache, and perhaps an occasional decongestant if nasal stuffiness is unbearable. Allergy symptoms, in contrast, are best relieved by antihistamines.

Sleep Aids

In 1995, an estimated 49% of the U.S. population experienced insomnia (the inability to fall asleep or stay asleep) at least 5 nights each month (Gill 1999). About 1% of the adult population routinely self-medicate their insomnia with OTC sleep aids that are advertised as inducing a "safe and restful sleep." Described as nonbarbiturate and non-habit forming, these low-potency products are frequently misused (Shuster 1996). For example, the parents of a young child were traveling cross country. They knew the trip would be long and the child likely

Here and Now

The Dextromethorphan Trip

Dextromethorphan is the antitussive ingredient frequently found in nonprescription cough medicine. Because of pharmacological properties that resemble those of PCP, OTC cough medicines are sometimes abused by teenagers. One such person, who had consumed almost an entire bottle of a popular anticough product, described his experience. He related that the effects of the drug hit first with lightheadedness and slight disorientation. After 1 hour, the disorientation became severe. He explained that it felt as though he were outside of himself looking in. The hallucinations were somewhat subtle with things appearing grainy

and distorted. He found that breathing was sometimes constricted as though he were wearing a tight shirt collar. Then came hot flashes, which caused him to turn on a fan to cool down. He found walking was difficult, and time became distorted. The trip lasted 1 to 2 hours for the strong effects, but it seemed to continue forever. This person was an experienced user of acid (LSD) and mushrooms, but he had never been on a trip as scary as the one with the cough medicine. Several times he thought he was going to die. He found that coming down took a while. He decided that he would never do "dex" (dextromethorphan) again.

would grow tired and cranky. To keep the child quiet and manageable, the parents used Benadryl, an allergy medication, that contained an antihistamine to cause sedation (personal communication to Hanson, 2003). Use of these products in young children is inappropriate and can be dangerous.

The drugs commonly used in OTC sleep aids are antihistamines, particularly diphenhydramine (Kirkwood and Melton 2006). Although antihistamines have been classified as OTC category I sleep aid ingredients (see Chapter 3), their usefulness in treating significant sleep disorders is highly questionable (Kirkwood and Melton 2006). At best, some people who suffer mild, temporary sleep disturbances caused by problems such as physical discomfort, short-term disruption in daily routines (such as jet lag), and extreme emotional upset might experience temporary relief. However, even for those few who initially benefit from these agents, tolerance develops within 4 days. For long-term sleep problems, OTC sleep aids are of no therapeutic value and are rarely recommended by health professionals. Actually, their placebo benefit is likely more significant than their actual pharmacological benefit. Usually counseling and psychotherapy are more effective approaches for resolving chronic insomnia than OTC or even prescription sleep aid drugs (Kirkwood and Melton 2006).

Because antihistamines are CNS depressants, in low doses they can cause sedation and antianxiety action (see Chapter 6). Although in the past, some OTC products containing antihistamines were promoted for their relaxing effects (e.g., Quietworld and Compoz), currently, no sedatives are approved for OTC marketing. The FDA decided that the earlier products relieved anxiety by causing drowsiness, so, in fact, they were not legitimate sedatives. Because of this ruling, medications that are promoted as antianxiety products are no longer available without a prescription. However, antihistamines have been added to an array of other OTC drug products marketed for the purpose of causing relaxation or promoting sleep; such products include analgesics (Excedrin P.M.) and cold medicines (Triaminic Cold and Allergy). The rationale for such combinations is questionable, and their therapeutic value unsubstantiated.

Melatonin The hormone melatonin is currently being used by millions to induce sleep or to help the body's natural clock readjust after the effects of jet lag. Melatonin was referred to as the "all-natural nightcap of the 1990s." Although most users of this hormone want assistance in falling asleep, melatonin is also claimed to slow the aging process, stimulate the immune system, and enhance the sex drive. Melatonin is a naturally occurring hormone, also found in some foods. Under the 1994 Dietary Supplement and Education Act, melatonin is considered a dietary supplement and is not regulated by the FDA. Despite the popularity of melatonin products, little is known about the benefits or the potential adverse effects of this hormone; consequently, these products should be used cautiously, if at all (van den Heuval et al. 2005).

Stimulants

Some OTC drugs are promoted as stay-awake (NōDōz) or energy-promoting (Vivarin) products (Anderson and Nykamp 2006). In general, these medications contain high doses of caffeine (100–200 milligrams per tablet). (Caffeine and its pharmacological and abuse properties are discussed at length in Chapter 10.) Although it is true that CNS stimulation by ingesting significant doses of caffeine can increase the state of alertness during periods of drowsiness, the usefulness of such an approach is highly suspect.

For example, college students sometimes rely on such products to enhance mental endurance during cramming sessions for examinations. In fact, at one western U.S. university, the back page of a quarterly class schedule, printed and distributed by the university, included a full-page advertisement for the OTC stimulant Vivarin with the caption, "Exam Survival Kit." The implications of such promotions are obvious and disturbing. Due to the objections of the faculty, the advertisement was not run again at the university.

Routine use of stay-awake or energy-promoting products to enhance performance at work or in school can lead to dependence, resulting in withdrawal when the person stops using the drug. Most health professionals agree that there are more effective and safer ways to deal with fatigue and drowsiness — for example, managing time efficiently and getting plenty of rest (Anderson and Nykamp 2006).

Sympathomimetics Mild OTC sympathomimetics have been marketed as safe stimulants and as legal alternatives to cocaine and other illicit stimulants (Associated Press 2003). The principal drugs found in the mild stimulants are drugs such as phenylephrine and caffeine. The same drugs are also found in OTC decongestants and diet aids

(Scolaro 2006). Ephedrine, a naturally occurring stimulant (i.e., in the ephedra plant), has been withdrawn from OTC use due to its potential toxicity on the cardiovascular system (FDA 2004).

Although much less potent than amphetamines, when used in high doses, the OTC stimulants can cause anxiety, restlessness, throbbing headaches, breathing problems, and tachycardia (rapid heartbeat). There have been reports of death due to heart arrhythmia, cerebral hemorrhaging, and strokes, as discussed earlier from excessive ephedrine use (see Chapter 10).

Gastrointestinal Medications

The gastrointestinal (GI) system consists principally of the esophagus, stomach, and intestines and is responsible for the absorption of nutrients and water into the body, as well as the elimination of body wastes. The function of the GI system can be altered by changes in eating habits, stress, infection, and diseases such as ulcers and cancers. Such problems may affect appetite, cause discomfort or pain, result in nausea and vomiting, and alter the formation and passage of stools from the intestines.

A variety of OTC medications are available to treat GI disorders such as indigestion (antacids), heartburn (gastric secretion blockers), constipation (laxatives), and diarrhea (antidiarrheals) (Curry and Butler 2006; Walker 2006; Zweber and Berardi 2006). However, before individuals self-medicate with nonprescription drugs, they should be certain that the cause of their GI problem is minor, is self-limiting, and does not require professional care. Because antacids are the most frequently used of the GI nonprescription drugs, they are discussed here.

Antacids and Antiheartburn Medication More than $1 billion is spent annually on antacid preparations that claim to give relief from heartburn and indigestion caused by excessive eating or drinking and to provide long-term treatment of chronic peptic ulcer disease. It is estimated that as much as 50% of the population has had one or more attacks of **gastritis**, often referred to as "acid indigestion, heartburn, upset stomach, and sour or acid stomach." These attacks are often due to acid rebound, occurring 1 to 2 hours after eating; by

More than $1 billion is spent each year on antacid products such as this in the United States.

this time, the stomach contents have passed into the small intestines, leaving the gastric acids to irritate or damage the lining of the empty stomach. Heartburn, or gastroesophageal reflux, occurs after exposure of the lower esophagus to these very irritating gastric chemicals.

Some cases of severe, chronic acid indigestion may progress to peptic ulcer disease. Peptic ulcers (open sores) most frequently affect the duodenum (first part of the intestine) and the stomach. Although this condition is serious, it can be treated effectively with antacids, which are often combined with drugs available OTC or by prescription such as cimetidine (Tagamet), ranitidine (Zantac), and famotidine (Pepcid). A person with acute, severe stomach pain; chronic gastritis; blood in the stools (common ulcer symptoms); diarrhea; or vomiting should see a physician promptly and should not attempt to self-medicate with OTC antacids (Zweber and Berardi 2006).

Most bouts of acid rebound, however, are associated with overeating or consuming irritating foods or drinks; these self-limiting cases can usually be managed safely with OTC antacids (such as sodium bicarbonate, calcium carbonate, aluminum salts, and magnesium salts). Because of their alkaline (opposite of acidic) nature, the nonprescription products neutralize gastric acids and give relief.

Generally speaking, OTC antacid preparations are safe for occasional use at low recommended doses, but excessive use can cause serious problems. In addition, all antacids can interact with other drugs; they may alter the GI absorption or renal elimination of other medications. For example, some antacids inhibit the absorption of tetracycline antibiotics; thus, these products should not be taken at the same time. Consequently, patients using prescription drugs should consult with their physicians before taking OTC antacids (Zweber and Berardi 2006).

Heartburn can be treated effectively with low doses of Tagamet, Zantac, or Pepcid. These drugs were switched to OTC status in the mid-1990s and help reduce gastric secretions (Zweber and Berardi 2006).

Diet Aids

In U.S. society, being slim and trim are prerequisites to being attractive. It is estimated that approximately 33% of the people in the United States are *obese* (body fat in excess of 20% of normal) and 50% are overweight (Crespo and Arbesman 2003). Being obese has been linked to cardiovascular disease, some cancers, diabetes, chronic fatigue, and an array of aches and pains, not to mention psychological disorders such as depression (Miller and Bartels 2006). Popular remedies for losing weight often include fad diets advertised in supermarket journals, expensive weight loss programs, or both prescription and OTC diet aids.

Approximately 25% to 30% of the people in the United States are obese and 50% are overweight.

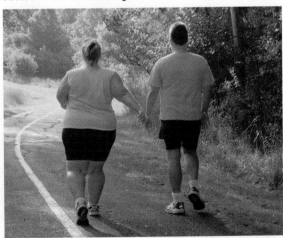

Using drugs as diet aids is highly controversial (Miller and Bartels 2006). Most experts view them as useless or even dangerous. These drugs are supposed to depress the appetite, which helps users maintain low-calorie diets. The most effective of these agents are called **anorexiants**. Potent anorexiants, such as amphetamine-like drugs (including the once-popular diet aid, Phen-fen), can cause dangerous side effects (see Chapter 10) and are available only by prescription. The appetite suppression effects of prescription anorexiants are usually temporary, after which tolerance often builds. Thus, even prescription diet aid drugs are usually effective for only a short period. There are no wonder drugs to help the obese lose weight permanently.

The most potent and most frequently used OTC diet aid ingredient used to be the sympathomimetic phenylpropanolamine. Since the FDA required that this drug be removed from all OTC products (Public Health Advisory 2000), it is not clear if any sympathomimetic will replace it in OTC diet aids (Miller and Bartels 2006). The OTC diet aids are minimally effective and of no value in the treatment of significant obesity. Despite their questionable value, frequent use of high doses of the OTC diet aid products is a common practice by weight-conscious female high school and college students. As one college sophomore who routinely carried a package of Dexatrim in her purse said, "Popping two or three of these before an important date helps me to eat like a bird and appear more petite" (from Hanson's files). Interestingly, this same woman also occasionally induced vomiting after eating because of her fear that she was gaining weight. Such weight-management practices are extremely worrisome.

Skin Products

Because the skin is so accessible and readily visible, most people are sensitive about its appearance. These cosmetic concerns are motivated by attempts to look good and preserve youth. Almost 5% of the population in the United States have a chronic skin problem while many others suffer from seasonal or acute skin disorders (Scott and Martin 2006). Only a few of the most commonly

KEY TERMS

anorexiants
drugs that suppress the activity of the brain's appetite center, causing reduced food intake

used products are mentioned here: acne medications, sun products, and basic first-aid products.

Acne Medications Acne is the most common skin disorder affecting adolescents (Foster and Coffrey 2006) and typically occurs during puberty in response to the secretion of the male hormone androgen (both males and females have this hormone) (Foster and Coffrey 2006). Acne is usually chronic inflammation caused by bacteria trapped in plugged sebaceous (oil) glands and hair follicles. This condition consists of whiteheads, pimples, nodules, and, in more severe cases, pustules, cysts, and abscesses. Moderate to severe acne can cause unsightly scarring on the face, back, chest, and arms and should be treated aggressively by a dermatologist with drugs such as antibiotics (tetracycline) and potent **keratolytics**, such as Retin A (retinoic acid) or vitamin A or Accutane (isotretinoin). Usually, minor to moderate acne does not cause scarring or permanent skin damage and often can be safely self-medicated with OTC acne medications (Foster and Coffrey 2006).

Several nonprescription approaches to treating mild acne are available, including the following:

1. *Sebum removal.* Oil and fatty chemicals (*sebum*) can accumulate on the skin and plug the sebaceous glands and hair follicles. Use of OTC products such as alcohol wipes (e.g., Stri-Dex) can help remove such accumulations.

2. *Peeling agents.* The FDA found several keratolytic agents safe and effective for treatment of minor acne: benzoyl peroxide (Oxy 5 and Oxy 10), salicylic acid (Oxy Medicated Pads), resorcinol, and sulfur (Liquimet Lotion), alone or in combination. These drugs help to prevent acne eruption by causing the **keratin layer** of the skin to peel or by killing the bacteria that cause inflammation associated with acne. If multiple concentrations of a keratolytic are available (such as Oxy 5 and Oxy 10 Advanced Formula), it is better to start with a lower concentration and move up to the higher one, allowing the skin to become accustomed to the caustic action of these products. The initial exposure may worsen the appearance of acne temporarily; however, with continual use, the acne usually improves.

Sun Products The damaging effects of sun exposure on the skin have been well publicized in recent years. It is now clear that the ultraviolet (UV) rays associated with sunlight have several adverse effects on the skin. It has been demonstrated that almost 1 million cases of skin cancer each year occur in the United States, most of which are a direct consequence of exposure to UV rays and cause cumulative skin damage throughout our lives (Carroll and Crosby 2006). Almost 10,000 deaths occur from skin cancer each year, most of which are melanomas (American Cancer Society 2005).

The majority of cases will be cancers of skin cells called basal cell or squamous cell carcinomas (Carroll and Crosby 2006). These cancers usually are easily removed by minor surgery, and patients have a good prognosis for recovery. About 0.5% of the population will suffer a much more deadly form of skin cancer called *melanoma*. Melanomas are cancers of the pigment-forming cells of the skin, called *melanocytes*, and spread rapidly from the skin throughout the body, causing death in 20% to 25% of patients (Carroll and Crosby 2006).

Another long-term concern related to UV exposure is premature aging. Skin frequently exposed to UV rays, such as during routine tanning, experiences deterioration associated with the aging process. Elastin and collagen fibers are damaged, causing a loss of pliability and elasticity in the skin and resulting in a leathery, wrinkled appearance (Carroll and Crosby 2006).

Because of these damaging effects of sun exposure, an array of protective sunscreen products are available OTC. Most sunscreens are formulated to screen out the shorter UVB rays. These products have deliberately been designed to allow passage, in varying degrees, of the UVA rays because researchers once thought that these longer rays would help skin to tan without causing damage. Now it appears scientists were mistaken. Due to their deep penetration in the skin, UVA rays likely contribute to melanoma as well as chronic skin damage, causing skin to wrinkle, sag, and lose tone (Carroll and Crosby 2006).

The protection afforded by sunscreens is designated by an **SPF (sun protection factor) number**. This designation tells users the relative length of time

KEY TERMS

keratolytics
caustic agents that cause the keratin skin layer to peel

keratin layer
outermost protective layer of the skin

SPF (sun protection factor) number
designation to indicate a product's ability to screen ultraviolet rays

This skin cancer is melanoma and is caused by excessive exposure to ultraviolet light.

they can stay in the sun before burning and includes ratings of 2 to 11 (*minimum*), 12 to 30 (*moderate*), and greater than 30 (*high*) (Carroll and Crosby 2006). For example, proper application of a product with an SPF of 10 allows users to remain in the sun without burning 10 times longer than if it was not applied. It is important to remember that the SPF designation does not indicate protection against UVA rays. Although there currently is no convenient rating system to assess UVA screening, products with SPF ratings of 15 or greater usually offer some protection against the longer UV radiation. In addition, a compound called *avobenzone* appears to offer the fullest protection against UVA rays (Carroll and Crosby 2006).

Because the natural pigment in the skin affords some UV protection, people with fair complexions (less skin pigmentation) require products with higher SPF numbers than do dark-skinned people.

People who want complete protection from UVB exposure can use OTC sunblockers, which prevent any tanning. Sunscreen ingredients in high concentrations essentially become sunblockers. In addition, an opaque zinc oxide ointment is a highly effective and inexpensive sun-blocking product and is available OTC.

Skin First-Aid Products

A variety of unrelated OTC drugs are available as first-aid products for the self-treatment of minor skin problems (Bowman 2006). Included in this category of agents are the following products:

1. Local anesthetics, such as benzocaine (e.g., Dermoplast) to relieve the discomfort and pain of burns or trauma

2. Antibiotics and antiseptics, such as bacitracin (Polysporin), neomycin (Neosporin), betadine, and tincture of iodine to treat or prevent skin infections

3. Antihistamines (Benadryl) or corticosteroids (hydrocortisone [Cortaid]) to relieve itching or inflammation associated with skin rashes, allergies, or insect bites

These first-aid skin products can be effective when used properly. In general, side effects to such topical products are few and minor when they occur.

OTC Herbal (Natural) Products

There are approximately 500 herbal medicines currently available in the United States and other countries (Tan 2001). Herbal products are a unique category of OTC remedies that account for almost $5 billion a year in U.S. sales (McQueen and Hume 2006). They are unique because, despite the presence of active ingredients, there is little or no federal regulation due to a 1994 law, supported by the dietary supplement industry, called the Dietary Supplement Health and Education Act (McQueen and Hume 2006). This law requires the government to demonstrate that substances in the herbal products are harmful before such products can be removed from the market; the burden of proof lies with the FDA, not the manufacturer (Bernstein and Rickert 2006).

This act also (1) makes the manufacturer responsible for its product's safety; (2) explains how product literature is used for product promotion; and (3) describes what can be included on labels. Due to these regulations, manufacturers cannot use terms such as *diagnose, treat, prevent,* or *cure.* Companies can, however, make claims about affecting body function. For example, manufacturers of glucosamine cannot claim their product helps cure arthritis, but they can say products with glucosamine help the joints function better (Tatro 1999). Because of the lack of regulation, these products often are not scientifically tested, and they vary considerably in both the quantity and quality of active ingredients (Frontlines 2000b; Tatro 1999). Herbal products have been viewed with considerable skepticism by many experts who argue that "assertions, speculation and testimonials do not substitute for evidence" when it comes to establishing the value of a drug (McQueen and Hume 2006).

Herbal products have become very popular and widely accepted.

In the past few years, some changes in attitude toward herbal products have occurred. More people, including health professionals, have become convinced that some herbs may be useful in the treatment of minor health problems (McQueen and Hume 2006). In fact, it has become quite common for doctors, nurses, and other formally trained health professionals to recommend herbal treatments for medical problems (*Consumer Reports* 2000). Despite greater acceptance, the fact that most people who use herbs to treat medical conditions still consider prescription drugs to be considerably more effective suggests persistent skepticism regarding these products (*Consumer Reports* 2000).

Frequent uses of herbal products include treatment of anxiety, chronic fatigue, arthritis, and digestive problems (Hume and Strong 2006). Another common use of these natural products is to elevate mood. The most popular herbs for this purpose are St. John's wort, *S*-adenosylmethionine (SAM-e), and kava kava (see "Here and Now," Herbal Options; Hume and Strong 2006; Williams et al. 2005). It is generally thought that although these products do have some effect in the treatment of minor to moderate depression, there is no evidence they elevate a normal, undisturbed mood nor are they particularly effective against severe mood disturbances (*CBS Evening News* 2001). A major risk of self-administering these remedies for mood disorders is that some of the people self-treating their depression are severely emotionally unstable. Overall, depression leads to approximately 20,000 suicides in this country each year (Frontlines 2000a). Another considerable problem of self-medicating with herbal products for mood disorders is the lack of standardization for these substances. A recent survey revealed that the actual amount of active SAM-e per pill in products claim-ing to contain 200 mg active ingredient ranged from 80 to 250 mg. For these reasons, it is almost universally recommended that patients with serious emotional disturbances, especially depression, be diagnosed by a mental health professional even though some of these professionals may find use of the natural products to be acceptable for treatment of mild emotional problems (Frontlines 2000a).

Other concerns with herbal products include the possibility of interaction with other OTC and prescription medications, especially in the elderly population (Dergal et al. 2002). This can be more problematic as the routine use of herbs becomes common, especially because unscrupulous manufacturers may deceive customers into thinking that these products are perfectly safe and do not really contain any drugs. Some interactions identified occur between products containing herbs such as garlic, ginkgo biloba, ephedra, and ginseng (Fugh-Berman 2000). A notable example of drug interactions has been reported with St. John's wort and kava, which increase the metabolism and inactivate drugs used to treat heart failure, asthma, infections, or blood clots (Fugh-Berman 2000; Hume and Strong 2006).

Finally, lack of regulation has encouraged such a lackadaisical attitude concerning herbs that their use has been trivialized to the extent that they and their associated active drugs are now being included in foods and marketed in both health-food stores and supermarkets. Recent snacks, cereals, and beverages spiked with medicinal herbs include ginseng ginger ale, kava kava corn chips, echinacea fruit drinks, and ginkgo-biloba chocolate bars (Frontlines 2000b). These products, sometimes referred to as "functional foods," are typically packaged in colorful containers with cartoon figures that are likely to appeal to kids and accompanied by subtle suggestive promotions implying that they can "support emotional and mental balance." The exact quantities of herbal substances added to such food and snack products and their actual effects (if any) are difficult to monitor. Although concerned, regulator agencies are uncertain as to how to deal with the potential problems associated with this marketing strategy (Frontlines 2000b).

Herbals and Abuse

Despite the lack of governmental control, drugs found naturally in plants or herbs can have serious side effects or can be abused (see "Here and Now," Herbs Can Make You Sick). In fact, some of the most powerful substances of abuse are extracted

Here and Now

Herbal Options

With the increasing popularity of herbal products, an array of choices have become available for dealing with many common, usually self-limiting health problems. The following is a list of some of the most popular of these medicinal herbs.

Echinacea

Common Claim: Stimulates immune system and helps fight infections.
Common Use: Reduce cold symptoms and help accelerate recovery.
Effectiveness: May shorten duration of cold, but does not prevent it; however, even this is controversial.
Concerns: Relatively well tolerated, but fatigue and sleepiness occasionally occur.

Garlic

Common Claim: Inhibits production of cholesterol and reduces blood sugar.
Common Use: Treat diabetes and prevent cardiovascular disease.
Effectiveness: Most studies do not find garlic effective against serious diseases.
Concerns: Mild stomach discomfort and possible interaction with blood-thinning (anticlotting) prescription drugs occur.

Ginkgo Biloba

Common Claim: Improves memory.
Common Use: Often promoted to enhance memory for patients with Alzheimer's disease.
Effectiveness: At best helps to prevent some mental decline in Alzheimer's patients but does not appear to reverse memory loss or help normal or age-related memory losses.
Concerns: Can interact with blood-thinning medications such as aspirin.

Glucosamine and Chondroitin

Common Claim: Contributes to joint strength.
Common Use: Relieve the discomfort of arthritis.
Effectiveness: Provides moderate relief from the pain of arthritis and may help to slow progress of the disease.

Concerns: May interact with blood thinners and adversely affect adult-onset diabetes.

Saw Palmetto

Common Claim: Relieves discomforts associated with prostate gland.
Common Use: Shrink enlarged prostate and facilitate urination.
Effectiveness: Provides relief for most men within a month of use.
Concerns: Well tolerated by most men.

SAM-e

Common Claim: Helps regulate brain transmitters such as dopamine.
Common Use: Relieve symptoms of depression.
Effectiveness: Some evidence that it relieves moderate depression.
Concerns: Side effects are typically mild, such as stomach upset, insomnia, and nervousness. Can be very expensive, ranging from $55 to $260 per month.

St. John's Wort

Common Claim: Elevates mood.
Common Use: To treat mild to moderate depression.
Effectiveness: Appears to relieve some cases of mild depression for the short term.
Concerns: Recent alert from the FDA warns about interactions with numerous medications, such as birth-control pills and other antidepressants.

Ginseng

Common Claim: Increases energy.
Common Use: Treat fatigue and enhance performance.
Effectiveness: There may be some mild stimulation, but there is no evidence of enhanced performance.
Concerns: Well tolerated for the most part, although there are some reports of minor addiction.

Source: Hume, A. and K. Strong. "Botanical Medicines." In *Handbook of Nonprescription Drugs*, 15th ed., edited by I. Bernardi, 1103–1136. Washington DC: American Pharmacists Association, 2006.

Here and Now

Herbs Can Make You Sick

Recently, a Chinese herb that is sold in the United States was linked to kidney failure and urinary cancer in a Belgian weight-loss clinic. The herb, *A. fangchi*, contains ingredients known to be potent carcinogens in laboratory animals. Illnesses related to the use of this herb have been reported in several European countries. *A. fangchi* has been used to treat asthma and has been included in weight-loss products as well. Episodes such as this strengthen the argument that the FDA should be more active in the regulation of herbal products and dietary supplements and argue against the common misconception that herbal products are always healthy and cannot hurt you because they are natural.

Source: Sternberg, S. "Herb Raises Regulatory Alarm." *USA Today Health* (8 June, 2000). Available www.usatoday.com/life/health/alternative.

from plants and include drugs such as cocaine (*Erythroxylum coca*), marijuana (*Cannabis sativa*), peyote (*Lophophora williamsii*), and tobacco (*Nicotiana tabacum*). Because these substances are reviewed elsewhere in this book, they will not be discussed further here; they are mentioned to emphasize the point that being associated with herbs and natural products does not exclude a drug from being abused. Of concern in this section are unregulated herbal products and their potential for abuse and addiction. As a general rule, if a substance (including a natural product) elevates mood, causes a feeling of energy, or brings on a feeling of relaxation and relief from stress, it likely has potential for abuse (Tinsley 1999). Based on these principles, the herbal products most likely to be abused include those containing ma huang, ginseng, kava kava, and ephedrine (Gruber and Pope 1998; Tinsley 1999). Of course, with addiction typically comes high-quantity use and a greater chance of serious side effects — for example, the anorexia, thought disturbances, insomnia, racing heart, and loss of sensation in the limbs sometimes experienced by users addicted to Herbal Ecstasy, a product containing caffeine, kava kava, and ephedrine (Yates et al. 2000). Even though serious abuse of herbal products is possible, it does not occur frequently and, when it does occur, it is generally relatively easy to treat.

Prescription Drugs

The Durham-Humphrey Amendment of 1951 established the criteria that are still used today to determine whether a drug should be used only under the direction of a licensed health professional, such as a physician. According to this piece of legislation, drugs are controlled with prescriptions if they are (1) habit-forming, (2) not safe for self-medication, (3) intended to treat ailments that require the supervision of a health professional, or (4) new and without an established safe track record. Currently more than 10,000 prescription products are sold in the United States, representing approximately 1500 different drugs, with 20 to 50 new medications approved each year by the FDA (Borgsdorf 2007).

Because of their specialized training, physicians, dentists, and, under certain conditions, podiatrists, physician assistants, nurse practitioners, pharmacists, and optometrists are granted drug-prescribing privileges. The health professionals who write prescriptions are expected to accurately diagnose medical conditions requiring therapy, consider the benefits and risks of drug treatment for the patient, and identify the best drug and safest manner of administering it. The responsibility of the health professional does not conclude with the writing of a prescription; in many ways, it only just begins. Professional monitoring to ensure proper drug use and to evaluate the patient's response is crucial for successful therapy.

■ Prescription Drug Abuse

"In what seemed like the blink of an eye, our son went from marijuana and an occasional beer to so much Xanax that one day we had to pick him up when he fell asleep on a street corner waiting for friends. He hid his drug use so well." This young man told his parents Xanax helped him deal with anxiety. He eventually received treatment after being admitted to a hospital for overdosing. (Leinwand 2006)

In many places, abuse of prescription drugs is a greater problem than use of illicit drugs (Burke 2007). According to the Substance Abuse and Mental Health Services Administration (SAMHSA), more than 15 million Americans use prescription drugs for nonmedical purposes each year (Compton and Volkow 2006). In addition, a study in 2008 found one fifth of U.S. college students were taking prescription drugs to get high (MSNBC 2008). The three classes of prescription drugs most likely to be abused are narcotic analgesics, CNS depressants, and stimulants (used to treat obesity and attention-deficit hyperactivity disorder [ADHD]) (Monitoring the Future 2007). Particularly troubling is what appears to be an exploding epidemic of abusing prescription narcotic drugs such as OxyContin and Vicodin. Headlines announcing a celebrity seeking treatment for dependence on these drugs are becoming disturbingly routine. In fact, abuse of prescription narcotics appears to be the leading problem with prescription drugs resulting in a 163% increase in emergency room visits for abusing narcotic pain killers since 1995 (Griffin 2007). Often young people abuse a combination of these prescribed drugs, and their sources include the medicine cabinets in their parents' home or the Internet from "web pharmacies" that do not require legitimate prescriptions (Johnson 2007). This is a problem with youth from all backgrounds. For example, Al Gore III (son of former Vice President Al Gore) was arrested in 2007 for driving around 100 mph on the San Diego Freeway. Besides speeding, he was also charged with illegally possessing the prescription drugs Vicodin (narcotic pain reliever), Adderall (amphetamine for ADHD), and Xanax (benzodiazepine for anxiety), not to mention marijuana (Johnson 2007).

Dealing with suspected abuse of prescription medication can pose a difficult management problem for physicians and pharmacists. It has become such a major issue that some third-party payers (that is, health insurance companies) have implemented tight monitoring procedures. Those who try to fraudulently obtain controlled substances with valid and invalid prescriptions include persons from all walks of life (CNN.com 2002). (See "Case in Point," Prescription Drugs Can Also Cause Addiction.) Illicit use of prescription drug products may be prompted by any of the following reasons (Longo et al. 2000; Wick 1995): (1) to relieve withdrawal caused by drug habits (e.g., benzodiazepines are used to relieve alcohol withdrawal); (2) to treat

►Case in Point Prescription Drugs Can Also Cause Addiction

Anne's grandmother was taken to the hospital after complaining of chest pains. When questioned, she could not recall which medications she had been taking, so the doctors instructed Anne to go to her grandmother's home to check her medicine cabinet. Anne came face to face with an emerging major problem: prescription drug use and addiction. Anne discovered a cupboard with several copies of *Physicians' Desk Reference*, a balance for weighing the pills, and shelves filled with 11 different prescription drugs, including 400 Valium tablets. In all, the street value of these drugs was estimated to approach $15,000.

To obtain the pills, Anne's grandmother would go from doctor to doctor complaining of anxiety or pain. The doctors didn't have the slightest idea they were being deceived. This tactic, known as "doctor shopping," is a common strategy used by both young and old to obtain prescription drugs that are abused and can cause dependence and addiction.

Sometimes the drug dependence can begin innocently enough, when a patient uses a drug to excess without good clinical supervision. What started for legitimate medical reasons can, however, become transformed into destructive abuse of prescription drugs with serious medical and legal consequences. Dealing with this form of drug abuse requires more finesse than force, and prevention typically can be realized through education of both patients and clinicians about the addiction potential of some prescription medications.

Source: Querna, E. "The Newest War on Drugs." *US News & World Report* (21 February 2005).

Here and Now

Pharm Parties and Russian Roulette

One expression of prescription abuse is seen with high school students who bring samples of prescription drugs from home and dump them into a common bowl. The teens then grab a handful and pop them into their mouths like trail mix and swallow. The objective is to try to produce bizarre feelings and unusual highs. The mixtures often include medications such as antidepressants, stimulants, sleeping pills, antianxiety drugs, and narcotic pain relievers. One doctor described the activity as "Russian roulette," only with pills instead of bullets. The source of the drugs are often parents' or grandparents' medicine cabinets that frequently are filled with years of drug accumulation. One girl acknowledges that many kids think it's great fun and exciting, but she admits it can also be dangerous because she lost her best friend from an overdose at one of these parties. These kids think that because the drugs they are using are prescribed that they must be safer than illegal substances. Of course, when the prescription drugs belong to someone else, are mixed, and then are taken in high quantities, the outcome can be disastrous and even deadly and very difficult to treat.

Source: WIXT/WSYR TV ABC 9. "Pharm Parties. Popping Prescriptions." Syracuse (18 May, 2007).

infections caused by drug abuse (e.g., antibiotics are used to treat injection infections); (3) to provide a source of fresh, clean needles for injecting drugs of abuse (e.g., via insulin syringes); (4) to prolong the high caused by drugs of abuse (e.g., appetite suppressants are taken to enhance the effects of stimulants of abuse); and (5) ignorance on the part of the patient and/or doctor about the process of addiction (Schuster 2006).

In the United States, young people frequently abuse prescription drugs. A recent trend is called "pharm parties," where high school students get together and try to get high on a mixture of prescription drugs followed by a chaser of alcohol (WIXT/WSYR TV 2007; see "Here and Now," Pharm Parties and Russian Roulette). However, young people rarely obtain the drugs by theft, fraud, or doctor shopping, although occasionally unscrupulous doctors will write prescriptions without questions for money (Reavy 2007). Instead, they usually obtain their prescription drugs from peers, friends, or family members or often purchase them from rogue Internet pharmacies (Krebs 2007). In some areas, the problem is so severe that high schools have implemented programs to prevent such sharing (U.S. Department of Justice 2002). Abusers of prescription drugs often have multiple addictions, including dependence on caffeine, alcohol, or nicotine. In addition, once a pharmacy is recognized as an easy target, word spreads and other abusers often begin to frequent the same store (Wick 1995). Signs of patients with drug-seeking behavior include the following:

- Use of altered or forged prescriptions
- Claims that a prescription has been lost and a physician is unavailable for confirmation
- Frequent visits to emergency rooms or clinics for poorly defined health problems
- Visits made to a pharmacy late in the day, on weekends, or just before closing
- Alteration of doses on a legitimate prescription
- Loud, abusive, and insulting behavior
- Use of several names
- Being particularly knowledgeable about drugs

■ Proper Doctor–Patient Communication

Many unnecessary side effects and delays in proper care are caused by poor communication between the health professional and the patient when a drug is prescribed. The smaller a drug's margin of safety (the difference between therapeutic and toxic doses), the greater the need for clear directions from a health professional concerning its proper use. The following is a brief overview of principles to help ensure that satisfactory communication takes place between the health professional and the patient.

Doctor–patient communication must be reciprocal. We tend to think that patients listen while doctors talk when it comes to deciding on the best medication for treatment. To ensure a proper diagnosis, precise and complete information from the patient is also essential. In fact, if a doctor is to select the best and safest drug for a patient, he or she needs to know everything possible about the medical problems to be treated. In addition, the patient should provide the doctor with a complete medical and drug history, particularly if there has been a problem with the patient's cardiovascular system, kidneys, liver, or mental functions. Other information that should be shared with the doctor includes previous drug reactions as well as a complete list of drugs routinely being used, including prescription, nonprescription, and herbal products.

The patient needs to be educated about proper drug use. If the doctor does not volunteer this information, the patient should insist on answers to the following questions:

- What is being treated? This question does not require a long, unintelligible scientific answer. It should include an easy-to-understand explanation of the medical problem.
- What is the desired outcome? The patient should know why the drug is prescribed and what the drug treatment is intended to accomplish. It is difficult for the patient to become involved in therapy if he or she is not aware of its objectives.
- What are the possible side effects of the drug? This answer does not necessitate an exhaustive list of every adverse reaction ever recorded in the medical literature; however, it is important to realize that adverse drug reactions to prescription drugs are very common. In the United States, more people die from adverse reactions to legal medications than succumb to all illegal drug use. It is estimated that approximately 20,000 people die while another 2.1 million are seriously injured in this country each year from reactions to legal medications (Whitney 2007). In general, if adverse reactions occur in more than 1% of users, this should be mentioned to the patient. In addition, the patient should be made aware of ways to minimize the occurrence of side effects (e.g., an irritating drug should not be taken on an empty stomach to minimize nausea) as well as what to do if a side effect occurs (e.g., if a rash occurs, call the doctor immediately).
- How should the drug be taken to minimize problems and maximize benefits? This answer should include details on how much, how often, and how long the drug should be taken.

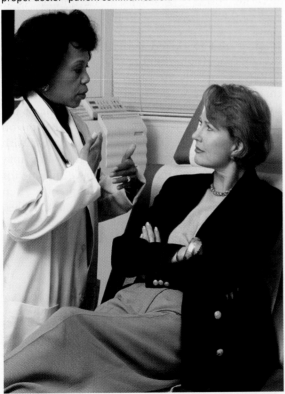

In order to maximize benefit and minimize risk, there must be proper doctor–patient communication.

Although it is a health professional's legal and professional obligation to communicate this information, patients frequently leave the doctor's office with a prescription that gives them legal permission to use a drug but without the knowledge of how to use it properly. Because of this all-too-common problem, pharmacists have been mandated by legislation referred to as the Omnibus Budget Reconciliation Act of 1990 to provide the necessary information to patients on proper drug use (Waroholak-Juarez et al. 2000; Zak 1993) (see "Here and Now," OBRA '90). Patients should be encouraged to ask questions of those who write and fill prescriptions.

Here and Now

OBRA '90: The Evolving Role of Pharmacists in Drug Management

In 1990, the U.S. Congress passed section 4401 of the Omnibus Budget Reconciliation Act (commonly referred to as OBRA '90), which substantially altered the role of pharmacists in drug management. This act designated the pharmacist as the key player in improving the quality of drug care for patients in this country. Because OBRA '90 is federal legislation, it can require drug-related services for Medicare patients only; however, most states have recognized that similar services should be made available to all patients and have enacted legislation to that end. OBRA '90 requires pharmacists to conduct a drug use review (DUR) for each prescription to improve the outcome of drug therapy and reduce adverse side effects. The DUR program describes four basic professional services that a pharmacist must render whenever a drug prescription is filled:

1. Prescriptions and patients' records must be screened to avoid problems caused by drug duplications, adverse drug–drug interactions, medical complications, incorrect drug doses, and incorrect duration of drug treatment.

2. Patients should be counseled regarding the following:
   - How to safely and effectively administer the drug
   - Common adverse effects and interactions with other drugs, food, and so forth
   - How to avoid problems with the drug
   - How to monitor the progress of drug therapy
   - How to store the drug properly
   - Whether a refill is intended
   - What to do if a dose is missed

3. Patient profiles, including information on disease, a list of medications, and the pharmacist's comments relevant to drug therapy, must be maintained. This information should be stored in computer files for future reference.

4. Documentation must record if the patient refuses consultation from the pharmacist, or if a potential drug therapy problem is identified and the patient is warned.

Source: Abood, R. "OBRA '90: Implementation and Enforcement." *NABP U.S. Pharmacists, State Boards — A Continuing Education Series.* Park Ridge, IL: National Association of Boards of Pharmacy, 1992.

▨ Drug Selection: Generic Versus Proprietary

Although it is the primary responsibility of the doctor or healthcare provider to decide which drug is most suitable for a treatment, often an inexpensive choice can be as effective and safe as a more costly option. This statement frequently is true when choosing between generic and proprietary drugs. The term **generic** is used by the public to refer to the common name of a drug that is not subject to trademark rights; in contrast, **proprietary** denotes medications marketed under specific brand names. For example, diazepam is the generic designation for the proprietary name Valium. Often, the most common proprietary name associated with a drug is the name given when it is newly released for marketing. Because such drugs are almost always covered by patent restrictions for several years when first sold to the public, they become identified with their first proprietary names. After the patent lapses, the same drug

often is also marketed by its less-known generic designation (Dighe 1999).

Because usually the pharmaceutical companies that market the generic products have not invested in the discovery or development of the drug, they often charge much less for their version of the medication. This situation contrasts with that of the original drug manufacturer, which may have invested as much as $0.5–1 billion for research and development (see Chapter 3). Even though the generic product frequently is less expensive, the quality usually is not inferior to the related proprietary drug; thus, substitution of

KEY TERMS

generic
official, nonpatented, nonproprietary name of a drug

proprietary
brand or trademark name that is registered with the U.S. Patent Office

generic for proprietary products rarely compromises therapy (CDER 2007). It should be noted that occasionally an inferior generic drug product is marketed to increase profit margins for the manufacturer and is not therapeutically equivalent to the proprietary drug product; however, physicians and pharmacists should be aware of these differences and prescribe accordingly. If a patient alerts the physician to concerns about drug costs, less expensive generic brands often can be substituted.

Because of reduced cost, generic products have become very popular. Currently, generic drugs account for more than 30% of all prescription drug sales, amounting to approximately $10 billion annually (CDER 2007). Because of the great demand, all states have laws that govern the use and substitution of generic drugs; unfortunately, the laws are not all the same. Some states have positive laws that require pharmacists to substitute a generic product unless the physician gives specific instructions not to do so. Other states have negative laws that forbid substitution without the physician's permission. Some physicians use convenient prescription forms with "May" or "May Not" substitution boxes that can be checked when the prescription is filled out.

Common Categories of Prescription Drugs

Of the approximately 10,000 different prescription drugs available in the United States, the top 50 drugs in sales account for almost 30% of all new and refilled prescriptions (RxList 2007). As an example, a list of the 25 top-selling prescription drugs in 2006 is shown in Table 15.6. The following includes a brief discussion of some drug groups represented in the 25 most frequently prescribed medications. This list is not intended to be all-inclusive, but gives only a sampling of common prescription products.

Analgesics

The prescription analgesics consist mainly of narcotic and NSAID types. The narcotic analgesics most often dispensed to patients by prescription are (1) the low-potency agents propoxyphene (Darvon) and codeine, (2) the moderate-potency agents pentazocine (Talwin) and oxycodone (Percodan), and (3) the high-potency drug meperidine (Demerol). All narcotic analgesics are scheduled drugs because of their abuse potential and are effective against most types of pain. The narcotic analgesic products are often combined with aspirin or acetaminophen (e.g., Percocet is a combination of oxycodone and acetaminophen) to enhance their pain-relieving actions. These are the most likely prescription drugs to be abused and cause severe substance dependence. For additional information about the narcotics, see Chapter 9.

The NSAIDs constitute the other major group of analgesics available by prescription. The pharmacology of these drugs is very similar to that of the OTC compound ibuprofen, discussed earlier in this chapter. These medications are used to relieve inflammatory conditions such as arthritis and are effective in relieving minor to moderate *musculoskeletal pain* (pain associated with body structures such as muscles, ligaments, bones, teeth, and skin). These drugs have no abuse potential and are not scheduled; several are also available OTC (see the discussion of OTC analgesics). Their principal adverse side effects include stomach irritation, kidney damage, tinnitus (ringing in the ears), dizziness, and swelling from fluid retention. Most prescription NSAIDs have similar pharmacological and side effects. Included in the group of prescription NSAIDs are ibuprofen (Motrin), naproxen (Anaprox), indomethacin (Indocin), sulindac (Clinoril), mefenamic acid (Ponstel), tolmetin (Tolectin), piroxicam (Feldene), and ketoprofen (Orudis) (Borgsdorf 2007).

Antibiotics

Drugs referred to by the layperson as "antibiotics" are more accurately described by the term *antibacterials*, although the more common term will be used here. For the most part, *antibiotics* are effective in treating infections caused by microorganisms classified as bacteria. Bacterial infections can occur anywhere in the body, resulting in tissue damage, loss of function, and, if untreated, ultimately death. Even though bacterial infections continue to be the most common serious diseases in the United States and throughout the world today, the vast majority of these can be cured with antibiotic treatment.

There are currently close to 100 different antibiotic drugs, which differ from one another in (1) whether they kill bacteria (*bactericidal*) or stop their growth (*bacteriostatic*), and (2) the species of bacteria that are sensitive to their antibacterial action (Chambers 2006). Antibiotics that are effective against many species of bacteria are classified

Table 15.6 The Top 25 Prescription Drugs, 2006, by U.S. Sales

RANKING	PROPRIETARY NAME	GENERIC NAME	PRINCIPAL CLINICAL USE
1	Lipitor	Atorvastin	Reduce cholesterol
2	Nexium	Esomeprazole	Relieve ulcers
3	Prevacid	Lansoprazole	Relieve ulcers
4	Advair Diskus	Corticosteroid	Treat asthma
5	Singulair	Nontelukast	Treat asthma
6	Effexor XR	Venlafaxine	Antidepressant
7	Plavix	Chlopidogrel	Reduce clots
8	Zocor	Simvastin	Reduce cholesterol
9	Norvasc	Amlodipine	Reduce hypertension
10	Lexapro	Escitalopram	Antidepressant
11	Seroquel	Quietiapine	Antipsychotic
12	Protonix	Pantoprazole	Relieve esophagitis
13	Ambien	Zolpidem	Sedative
14	Actos	Pioglitazone	Treat diabetes
15	Zoloft	Sertraline	Antidepressant
16	Wellbutrin	Bupropion	Antidepressant
17	Avandia	Rosiglitazone	Treat diabetes
18	Risperdal	Risperidone	Antipsychotic
19	Zyprexa	Olanzapine	Bipolar/schizophrenia
20	Topamax	Topiramate	Anticonvulsant
21	Toprol XL	Metoprolol	Treat heart disease
22	Vytorin	Combination	Lower cholesterol
23	Fosamax	Alendromate	Treat osteoporosis
24	Abilify	Aripiprazole	Antipsychotic
25	Levaquin	Levofloxacin	Antibiotic

Source: Top 200 Drugs for 2006 by Sales, Drugs.com. Drug Information Online (2007). Available www.drugs.com/top200.html.

as broad-spectrum types, whereas those antibiotics that are relatively selective and effective against only a few species of bacteria are considered narrow-spectrum drugs.

Although most antibiotics are well tolerated by patients, they can cause very serious side effects, especially if not used properly. For example, the penicillins have a very wide margin of safety for most patients, but 5% to 10% of the population is allergic to these drugs and life-threatening reactions can occur in sensitized patients if penicillins are used.

The most common groups of antibiotics include penicillins (e.g., amoxicillin — Amoxil, Augmentin, and Trimox), cephalosporins (e.g., cephalexin), fluoroquinolones (e.g., ciprofloxacin — Cipro), tetracyclines (e.g., minocycline — Minocin), aminoglycosides (e.g., streptomycin), sulfonamides (e.g., sulfamethoxazole — Bactrim and Septra), and macrolides (e.g., erythromycin — E-Mycin).

Antidepressants

Severe depression is characterized by diminished interest or pleasure in normal activities accompanied by feelings of fatigue, pessimism, and guilt as well as sleep and appetite disturbances and suicidal desires (American Psychiatric Association 2000). Severe depression afflicts approximately 5% to 6% of the population at any one time, and it is estimated that about 17% of the population will become severely depressed during their life (Baldessarini 2006). This high prevalence makes depression the most common psychiatric disorder (Baldessarini 2006). According to the classification of the *Diagnostic and Statistical Manual of Mental Disorders* (*DSM-IV-TR*) of the American Psychiatric Association, several types of depression exist, based on their origin:

1. *Endogenous major depression,* a genetic disorder that can occur spontaneously and is due to transmitter imbalances in the brain
2. *Depression associated with bipolar mood disorder* (that is, manic-depressive disorder)
3. *Reactive depression,* the most common form of depression, which is a response to situations of grief, personal loss, illness, or other very stressful situations

Antidepressant medication is typically used to treat endogenous major depression, although on occasion these drugs are used to treat other forms of depression if they are resistant to conventional therapy (Baldessarini 2006).

Several groups of prescription antidepressant medications are approved for use in the United States (Baldessarini 2006). The most commonly used category is the **tricyclic antidepressants.** Included in this group are drugs such as amitriptyline (Elavil), imipramine (Tofranil), and nortriptyline (Pamelor). Although usually well tolerated, the tricyclic antidepressants can cause annoying side effects due to their anticholinergic activity. These adverse reactions include drowsiness, dry mouth, blurred vision, and constipation. Tolerance to these side effects usually develops with continued use.

The second group of drugs used to treat depression is referred to as the **monoamine oxidase inhibitors (MAOIs).** Historically, these agents have been backup drugs for the tricyclic antidepressants. Because of their annoying and sometimes dangerous side effects as well as problems interacting with other drugs or even food, the MAOIs have become less popular with clinicians. These drugs can have deadly interactions with many of the stimulants of abuse such as methamphetamine, cocaine, and Ecstasy. Drugs belonging to this group include phenelzine (Nardil) and tranylcypromine (Parnate).

Agents from a third, somewhat disparate, group of antidepressants that are safer and with fewer side effects than the tricyclic or MAOI antidepressants are very popular. They include fluoxetine (Prozac), sertraline (Zoloft), paroxetine (Paxil), fluvoxamine (Luvox), bupropion (Wellbutrin), and trazodone (Desyrel). Although side effects and the margin of safety of these groups of antidepressants may differ, in general they all appear to have similar therapeutic benefits. Of this third group of antidepressants, Prozac is the best known and used to be the most frequently prescribed antidepressant; in 2003 it was the 11th most frequently prescribed drug in the United States, although by 2006 it had been replaced by other antidepressants such as Lexapro (RxList 2007) (see Table 15.6). Although most commonly used to treat depression, Prozac has also been prescribed by physicians to treat more than 30 other conditions ranging from drug addiction (although not found to be generally effective) to kleptomania. The vast majority of these uses are not proven to be effective nor are they approved by the FDA.

Antidiabetic Drugs

Diabetes mellitus afflicts approximately 20 million people in the United States and is the result of insufficient or ineffective activity of insulin, a hormone secreted from the pancreas (CDC 2007; Davis 2006). Due to the lack of insulin, untreated diabetics have severe problems with metabolism

KEY TERMS

tricyclic antidepressants
most commonly used group of drugs to treat severe depression

monoamine oxidase inhibitors (MAOIs)
drugs used to treat severe depression

diabetes mellitus
disease caused by elevated blood sugar due to insufficient insulin

Insulin is self-administered by diabetic patients in subcutaneous injections.

and elevated blood sugar (called **hyperglycemia**). The two major types of diabetes are type I (or juvenile type) and type II (or adult-onset type). **Type I diabetes** is caused by total destruction of the insulin-producing cells in the pancreas and usually begins in juveniles, but it occasionally begins during adulthood. In contrast, **type II diabetes** typically occurs after age 40 and is frequently associated with obesity. Recently, however, because severe obesity is occurring more often in younger persons, there has erupted an epidemic of type II diabetes in adolescents (Davis 2006). In type II diabetes, the pancreas is able to produce insulin, but insulin receptors no longer respond normally to this hormone (Gasbarro 1999). In both types of diabetes mellitus, drugs are administered to restore proper insulin function.

Because of the inability to produce or release insulin in the type I diabetic, these patients are universally treated with subcutaneous injections of insulin one to three times per day, depending on their needs. Usually the levels of sugar (glucose) in the blood are evaluated to determine the effectiveness of treatment. Insulin products are characterized by their onset of action and duration of effects. Two types of insulin are used: *short-acting* (regular) and *medium-acting* (NPH and lente) types.

The strategy for treating type II diabetics is somewhat different. For many of these patients, the symptoms of diabetes and problems of insufficient insulin function subside with proper diet, weight, and exercise management. If an appropriate change in lifestyle does not correct the diabetes-associated problems, drugs called **oral hypoglycemics** (meaning they are taken by mouth and lower blood sugar) are often prescribed. These drugs, which stimulate the release of additional insulin from the pancreas, include popular drugs such as rosiglitazone (Avandia). If the diabetic symptoms are not adequately controlled with the oral hypoglycemic drugs, type II diabetics are treated with insulin injections, as are type I patients. There has been substantial improvement in the treatment of diabetes in the past few years due to new, more selective and effective drugs that control glucose blood levels (Davis 2006).

Antiepileptic Drugs

Approximately 1% of the population in the United States has some form of **epilepsy**. Although appropriate medication can control the disease in 80% of these patients, many people in this country with epilepsy are inadequately treated. Epilepsy is a neurological condition characterized by recurring seizures (that is, uncontrolled hyperactivity of the brain). Seizures are classified according to the region of the brain involved and the extent to which the hyperactivity spreads. Thus, seizures are considered to be either *partial* (brain involvement stays local) or *generalized* (brain involvement is widespread) and can involve severe motor activity

KEY TERMS

hyperglycemia
elevated blood sugar

type I diabetes
disease associated with complete loss of insulin-producing cells in the pancreas

type II diabetes
disease usually associated with obesity; does not involve a loss of insulin-producing cells

oral hypoglycemics
drugs taken by mouth to treat type II diabetes

epilepsy
disease consisting of spontaneous, repetitive seizures

(e.g., grand mal seizures) or few motor symptoms (e.g., petit mal seizures). Because of the diverse nature of different types of epilepsy, several drugs are used as antiepileptics. Thus, phenytoin (Dilantin), carbamazepine (Tegretol), and phenobarbital are prescribed to control partial and grand mal seizures, whereas ethosuximide (Zarontin) and valproic acid (Depakene) are used to treat generalized and petit mal seizures (McNamara 2006). Interestingly, recent research has examined some of these antiseizure drugs as treatment for psychostimulant dependence (Zickler 2003). The value of this approach has yet to be determined.

Antiulcer Drugs

Peptic ulcers are sores that recur in the lining of the lower stomach (*gastric ulcer*) or most often in the upper portion of the small intestines (*duodenal ulcer*). It is apparent that secretions of gastric acids and digestive enzymes are necessary for ulcer development. Because gastric secretions are involved in developing peptic ulcers, several drug types are useful in ulcer treatment.

Obesity in young children has reached epidemic status and is causing type II diabetes to occur at a younger age.

Antacids help to relieve acute discomfort due to ulcers by neutralizing gastric acidity. These drugs are discussed in greater detail in the OTC section of this chapter. Prescription drugs that block gastric secretion have been the mainstay of ulcer treatment. Because the endogenous chemical histamine is important in regulating gastric secretions, drugs that selectively block the activity of gastric histamine (called H_2 *blockers*) substantially reduce secretion of gastric acids and digestive enzymes. The very popular prescription drugs cimetidine (Tagamet), ranitidine (Zantac), and famotidine (Pepcid) function in this manner. Because Tagamet, Zantac, and Pepcid are used so frequently, they have been switched to OTC status by the FDA — not to treat ulcers, but to relieve heartburn (*esophageal reflux*) (Hoogerwerf and Pasricha 2006).

Although the exact causes of peptic ulcers are not completely understood, a role for the bacteria *Helicobacter pylori* is now widely accepted. Because of the involvement of these microorganisms, most clinicians treat patients with recurring ulcers with multiple antibiotics to eliminate these bacteria (Hoogerwerf and Pasricha 2006).

Bronchodilators

Drugs that widen air passages (*bronchi*) facilitate breathing in patients with air passage constriction or obstruction. Such drugs are called **bronchodilators** and are particularly useful in relieving respiratory difficulty associated with asthma. Asthmatic patients frequently experience bouts of intense coughing, shortness of breath, tightness in the chest, and wheezing. Many of the symptoms of asthma are due to an increased sensitivity of the airways to irritating substances and can result in serious asthma attacks that are life threatening if not treated promptly. Two major categories of bronchodilators are the sympathomimetics known as **β-adrenergic stimulants** — for example, isoproterenol (Isuprel) and albuterol (Proventil and Ventolin) — and xanthines (caffeine-like drugs)

KEY TERMS

peptic ulcers
open sores that occur in the stomach or upper segment of the small intestine

bronchodilators
drugs that widen air passages

β-adrenergic stimulants
drugs that stimulate a subtype of adrenaline and nonadrenaline receptors

such as theophylline and its derivatives. These drugs relax the muscles of the air passages, cause bronchodilation, and facilitate breathing. In the early 1990s, some bronchial dilator medications were switched to OTC status, such as Bronkaid Mist and Primatene Mist.

Cardiovascular Drugs

Cardiovascular disease has been the number one cause of death in the United States for the past several decades. Consequently, of the 25 top-selling drugs in this country, 6 are medications for diseases related to the cardiovascular system (RxList 2007). The following are brief discussions of the major categories of cardiovascular drugs.

Antihypertensive Agents It is estimated that about 50% of American adults over the age of 60 require treatment for **hypertension** (persistent elevated high blood pressure) (Hoffman 2006). Because hypertension can result in serious damage to the heart, kidneys, and brain, this condition needs to be treated aggressively. Treatment should consist of changes in lifestyle, including exercise and diet, but usually also requires drug therapy. Two of the principal classes of antihypertensive agents are diuretics and direct vasodilators (Hoffman 2006):

1. *Diuretics* lower blood pressure by eliminating sodium and excess water from the body. Included in this category is hydrochlorothiazide (Dyazide).
2. *Direct vasodilators* reduce blood pressure by relaxing the muscles in the walls of blood vessels that cause vasoconstriction, thereby dilating the blood vessels and decreasing their resistance to the flow of blood. Drugs included in this category are calcium-channel blockers (diltiazem [Cardizem], verapamil [Calan], nifedipine [Procardia]); inhibitors of the enzyme that synthesizes the vasoconstricting hormone, angiotensin II (enalapril [Vasotec]); and drugs that block the vasoconstricting action of the sympathetic nervous system (clonidine [Catapre]; prazosin [Minipres]).

Antianginal Agents When the heart is deprived of sufficient blood (a condition called **ischemia**), the oxygen requirements of the cardiac muscle are not met and the breakdown of chemicals caused by the continual activity of the heart results in pain; this viselike chest pain is called **angina pectoris**. The most frequent cause of angina is obstruction of the coronary vessels (Michel 2006). Angina pectoris frequently occurs in patients with hypertension; left untreated, the underlying blockage of coronary vessels can result in heart attacks. All the drugs used to relieve or prevent angina decrease the oxygen deficit of the heart either by decreasing the amount of work required of the heart during normal functioning or by increasing the blood supply to the heart (Michel 2006). The three types of drugs prescribed for treating angina pectoris are (1) calcium-channel blockers (e.g., verapamil [Calan] and diltiazem [Cardizem]); (2) nitrates and nitrites (e.g., amylnitrite [Vaporate] and nitroglycerin [Transderm-Nitro]); and (3) blockers of the sympathetic nervous system, specifically classified as β-adrenergic blockers (e.g., atenolol [Tenormin] and propranolol [Inderal]).

Drugs to Treat Congestive Heart Failure When the cardiac muscle is unable to pump sufficient blood to satisfy the oxygen needs of the body, **congestive heart failure** occurs. This condition causes an enlarged heart, decreased ability to exercise, shortness of breath, and accumulation of fluid (**edema**) in the lungs and limbs (Rocco and Fang 2006). The principal treatment for congestive heart failure consists of drugs that improve the heart's efficiency, such as digoxin (Lanoxin).

Drugs that cause vasodilation are also sometimes used successfully to reduce the work required of the heart as it pumps blood through the body. Among the drugs causing vasodilation are those already discussed in conjunction with other heart conditions such as hypertension and angina pectoris (e.g., enalapril [Vasotec] and captopril [Capoten]).

KEY TERMS

hypertension
elevated blood pressure

ischemia
tissue deprived of sufficient blood and oxygen

angina pectoris
severe chest pain usually caused by a deficiency of blood to the heart muscle

congestive heart failure
heart is unable to pump sufficient blood for the body's needs

edema
swollen tissue due to an accumulation of fluid

Cholesterol- and Lipid-Lowering Drugs Cholesterol and some types of fatty (*lipid*) molecules can accumulate in the walls of arteries and narrow the openings of these blood vessels. Such arterial changes cause hypertension, heart attacks, strokes, and heart failure and are the leading cause of death in the United States (Mahley and Bersot 2006). These health problems can often be avoided by adopting a lifestyle that includes a low-fat and low-cholesterol diet combined with regular, appropriate exercise. However, sometimes lifestyle changes are insufficient; in such cases, cholesterol-lowering drugs can be used to prevent the damaging changes in blood vessel walls. The drugs most often used include lovastatin (Mevacor), cholestyramine (Questran), and niacin (vitamin B_3).

Hormone-Related Drugs

As explained in Chapter 4, hormones are released from endocrine (ductless) glands and are important in regulating metabolism, growth, tissue repair, reproduction, and other vital functions. When there is a deficiency or excess of specific hormones, body functions can be impaired, causing abnormal growth, imbalance in metabolism, disease, and often death. Hormones, or hormone-like substances, are sometimes administered as drugs to compensate for an endocrine deficiency and to restore normal function. This is the case for (1) insulin used to treat diabetes (see the earlier discussion for more details), (2) levothyroxine (Synthroid, an artificial thyroid hormone) to treat **hypothyroidism** (insufficient activity of the thyroid gland), and (3) conjugated estrogens (Premarin) to relieve the symptoms caused by estrogen deficiency during menopause.

Hormones can also be administered as drugs to alter normal body processes. Thus, drugs containing the female hormones, estrogen and progesterone (norethindrone, ethinyl estradiol [Ortho Novum]), can be used as contraceptives to alter the female reproductive cycles and prevent pregnancy. Another example involves drugs related to *corticosteroids* (hormones from the cortex of the adrenal glands), which are often prescribed because of their immune-suppressing effects. In high doses, the corticosteroid drugs (e.g., triamci-

nolone [Kenalog]) reduce symptoms of inflammation and are used to treat severe forms of inflammatory diseases, such as arthritis (Schimmer and Parker 2006).

Sedative-Hypnotic Agents

The sedative-hypnotics are discussed in considerable detail in Chapter 6. About 43 million prescriptions for sleeping pills were filled in the United States in 2006. This represents a 32% increase compared to 2001. The most popular sleeping medications include Ambien, Lunesta, Rozerem, and Soneta (Payne 2006). If one is not careful, these drugs can be used excessively for reducing stress and aiding sleep, leading to addictions and adverse consequences. Benzodiazepines commonly prescribed for these purposes are clonazepam (Klonopin) and lorazepam (Ativan) (Charney et al. 2006).

Stimulants

One of the most common uses for prescription stimulants is the treatment of attention-deficit hyperactivity disorder (ADHD). This neurobehavioral disorder is the most common mental health problem in children, affecting approximately 8% of all children ages 5 to 17 years (*Physician's Weekly* 2007). Of those children diagnosed with ADHD, the majority will continue to manifest associated impairment into adolescence and even adulthood (*Physician's Weekly* 2007). The most frequent treatment for ADHD includes stimulants such as Ritalin and Adderall (amphetamine), which have been proven to improve attention while controlling impulsivity and disruptive behaviors. Of some concern is a dramatic increase of stimulant prescriptions for ADHD treatment (Wallis 2006). This rise in ADHD-related medication use has corresponded with a disturbing increase in the use of these stimulants without prescriptions. It has been estimated that approximately 21 million people age 12 or older in the United States have been prescribed these stimulants, and of these 7.3 million persons abused those drugs used to treat ADHD (*Physician's Weekly* 2007).

Perhaps the most troubling issue is the trend for college students to abuse these short-acting stimulants to stay awake in order to study or party well into the night (Jaffe and Chip 2006). Another common reason for this group to abuse these drugs is to lose weight due to their appetite suppressing actions. It is likely that the increase of stimulant abuse by college students reflects an

KEY TERMS

hypothyroidism
thyroid gland does not produce sufficient hormone

assumption that these agents must be safe or they would not be prescribed by physicians. Due to this growing problem there is a major effort by scientists and drug companies to develop nonaddicting medications to treat ADHD (*Physician's Weekly* 2007).

Drugs to Treat HIV

Although not included in the top 25 list of prescription drugs (see Table 15.6), medications to treat HIV infection are of special relevance to drug abuse because of the high prevalence of infection by this deadly virus in intravenous drug addicts. The issue of AIDS and drug abuse is discussed at length in Chapter 17; of relevance to our discussion on prescription drugs are recent advances in pharmacological management of this disease. Although no cure for HIV or immunization against this virus is available yet, some drug therapies can delay the onset or slow the progression of this infection. The first drugs to be used effectively in AIDS therapy are the transcriptase inhibitors such as AZT (zidovudine) and Stavudine, which block a unique enzyme essential for HIV replication (Flexner 2006). Another group of anti-AIDS drugs called the *protease inhibitors* prevent HIV maturation; they include Saquinar. The protease inhibitors are particularly effective when used in combination with the transcriptase inhibitor drugs (Flexner 2006). This combination is referred to by the acronym HAART (highly active antiretroviral therapy) (Flexner 2006).

Common Principles of Drug Use

Probably the most effective way to teach people not to use drugs improperly is to help them understand how to use drugs correctly. This goal can be achieved by educating the drug-using public about prescription, OTC, and herbal drug products. If people can appreciate the difference between the benefits of therapeutic drug use and the negative consequences of drug misuse or abuse, they will be more likely to use medications in a cautious and thoughtful manner. To reach this level of understanding, patients must be able to communicate freely with health professionals. Before prescription or OTC drugs are purchased and used, patients should have all questions answered about the therapeutic objective, the most effective mode of administration, and side effects.

Education about proper drug use greatly diminishes drug-related problems and unnecessary health costs.

To minimize problems, before using any drug product, the patient should be able to answer the following questions:

1. Why am I using this drug?
2. How should I be taking this drug?
3. What are the active ingredients in this drug product?
4. What are the most likely side effects of this drug?
5. How long should this drug be used?

Discussion Questions

1. Why are some prescription drugs appropriate for switching to OTC status?

2. What should the FDA use as a standard of safety when evaluating OTC and prescription drugs?

3. What role should the pharmacist play in providing information about OTC and prescription drugs to patients?

4. What type of formal training should be required before a health professional is allowed to prescribe drugs?

5. What kinds of questions should be asked by a health professional to ensure that a patient has sufficient understanding concerning a drug to use it properly and safely?

6. What are the basic rules for using OTC drugs properly?

7. Why is abuse of prescription drugs such a common problem?

8. Should the FDA require that generic and proprietary versions of the same drug be exactly the same?

9. Even though some antibiotics have a wide margin of safety, currently there is no systemic antibiotic available OTC. Why is the FDA not willing to make some of these drugs available on a nonprescription basis?

10. Should herbal remedies be required to be safe and effective by the FDA like other OTC drug products?

11. What, if any, role should the FDA have in regulating herbal products?

Summary

1 Prescription drugs are available only by recommendation of an authorized health professional, such as a physician. Nonprescription (OTC) drugs are available on request and do not require approval by a health professional. In general, OTC medications are safer than their prescription counterparts but often less effective.

2 The switching policy of the FDA is an attempt to make available more effective medications to the general public on a nonprescription basis. This policy has been implemented in response to the interest in self-treatment by the public and in an attempt to reduce healthcare costs.

3 Drugs switched by the FDA to OTC status include ulcer medications, such as Tagamet and Zantac, medications for asthma and allergies, the contraceptive levonorgestral, and the weight loss drug orlistat.

4 Potential problems that come by making more effective drugs available OTC include overuse and inappropriate use, leading to dependence and other undesirable side effects. For example, these more effective drugs could encourage self-treatment of medical problems that usually require professional care.

5 Information on OTC product labels is crucial for proper use of these drugs and thus is regulated by the FDA. Product labels must list the active ingredients and their quantities in the product. Labels must also provide instructions for safe and effective treatment with the drug as well as cautions and warnings.

6 Many herbal products contain active drugs and have become very popular. The lack of regulation makes these remedies difficult to assess for either efficacy or safety.

7 Although OTC drug products can be useful for treatment of many minor to moderate, self-limiting medical problems, when used without proper precautions, they can cause problems.

8 The principal drug groups available OTC are used in the treatment of common, minor medical problems and include analgesics, cold remedies, allergy products, mild stimulants, sleep aids, antacids, laxatives, antidiarrheals, antiasthmatics, acne medications, sunscreens, contraceptives, and nutrients.

9 For drugs to be prescribed properly, patients need to provide complete and accurate information about their medical condition and medical history to their physicians. In turn, providers need to communicate to patients what is being treated, why the drug is being used, how it should be used for maximum benefit, and what potential side effects can occur.

10 Proprietary drug names can be used legally only by the drug company that has trademark rights. Often, the original proprietary name becomes the popular name associated with the drug. Because the pharmaceutical company that develops a drug is trying to recover its investment, a newly marketed proprietary drug is expensive. Once the patent rights expire, other drug companies can also market the drug but under a different name; often, the common, generic name is used because it cannot be trademarked. The generic drugs are less expensive because the manufacturers do not need to recover any significant investment. Generally, the less expensive generic drug is as effective and safe as the proprietary counterpart.

11 Of the approximately 1500 different prescription drugs currently available in the United States, the most commonly prescribed groups are analgesics, antibiotics, antidepressants, drugs used for diabetes, antiulcer drugs, antiepileptic drugs, bronchodilators, drugs used to treat cardiovascular diseases, hormone-related drugs, and sedative-hypnotics.

12 Abuse of prescription drugs is a serious problem in the United States. Some patients try to persuade clinicians or pharmacists to make prescription medications available by using deceit or intimidation. Legal drugs obtained in this manner are often used to relieve drug dependence or to reduce withdrawal symptoms from illicit substances.

References

American Cancer Society. "Skin Cancer Facts" (2005). Available www.cancer.org/docroot/PED/content/ped_7_1_what_you_need_to_know_about_skin_cancer.asp?sitearea=PED.

American Psychiatric Association (APA). *Diagnostic and Statistical Manual of Mental Disorders*, 4th ed. revised [*DSM-IV-TR*]. Washington, DC: Author, 2000.

Anderson, R., and D. Nykamp. "Drowsiness and Fatigue." In *Handbook of Nonprescription Drugs*, 15th ed., edited by

I. Bernardi, 1009–1020. Washington, DC: *American Pharmacists Association*, 2006.

Associated Press. "FDA Warns on Sales of Street Drug Alternatives." *The Washington Post* (1 April 2003): A-9.

Baldauf, S. "Vanished Behind the Counter." *U.S. News and World Report* (2 October 2006). Available http://health. usnews.com/usnews/health/articles/060924/2cold.htm.

Baldessarini, R. "Drug Therapy of Depression and Anxiety Disorders." In *The Pharmacological Basis of Therapeutics*, 11th ed., edited by L. Brunton, J. Lazo, and K. Parker, 429–459. New York: McGraw-Hill, 2006.

Bernstein, I., and E. Rickert. "Legal and Regulatory Issues in Self-Care Pharmacy Practice." In *Handbook of Nonprescription Drugs*, 15th ed., edited by I. Bernardi, 51–65. Washington, DC: *American Pharmacists Association*, 2006.

Borgsdorf, L. "Preface." In *Drug Facts and Comparison*, edited by L. Borgsdorf et al., xi. St. Louis: Wolters & Kluwar, 2007.

Bowman, J. "Minor Burns and Sunburn." In *Handbook of Nonprescription Drugs*, 15th ed., edited by I. Bernardi, 853–868. Washington, DC: *American Pharmacists Association*, 2006.

Burke, J. "Worldwide Prescription Drug Abuse." *Pharmacy Times* (19 April 2007).

Carroll, D., and K. Crosby. "Prevention of Sun-Induced Skin Disorders." In *Handbook of Nonprescription Drugs*, 15th ed., edited by I. Bernardi, 817–837. Washington, DC: *American Pharmacists Association*, 2006.

CBS Evening News. "Study: St. John's Won't Cure Big Blues." National News (17 April 2001). Available www. cbsnews.com/stories/2001/04/17/eveningnews/main28 6149.shtml?source=search_story.

Center for Drug Evaluation and Research (CDER). "Over-the-Counter Medicine: What's Right for You?" FDA (February 2002). Available www.fda.gov/cder.

Center for Drug Evaluation and Research (CDER). *Office of Generic Drugs (*2007). Available www.fda.gov/cder/ogd/ index.htm#Approvals.

Centers for Disease Control and Prevention (CDC). "National Diabetes Surveillance System." *Diabetes Public Health Resource* (2007). Available www.cdc.gov/diabetes/ statistics/incidence/index.htm.

Chambers, H. "General Principles of Antimicrobial Therapy." In *The Pharmacological Basis of Therapeutics*, 11th ed., edited by L. Brunton, J. Lazo, and K. Parker, 1095–1202. New York: McGraw-Hill, 2006.

Charney, D., S. Mihic, and R. Harris. "Hypnotics and Sedatives." In *The Pharmacological Basis of Therapeutics*, 11th ed., edited by L. Brunton, J. Lazo, and K. Parker, 401–427. New York: McGraw-Hill, 2006.

Compton, W., and N. Volkow. "Abuse of Prescription Drugs and the Risk of Addiction." *Drug and Alcohol Dependence* 835 (2006): A8.

Consumer Healthcare Products Association. "FAQS About Rx-to-OTC Switch." (2007). Available www.chpa-info. org/chpaPortal/PressRoom/FAQs/Switch.htm.

CNN.com. "Jeb Bush's Daughter Charged with Prescription Fraud." (29 January 2002). Available www.cnn. com/2002/us/01/29/jeb.bush.daughter.drugs.

Consumer Reports. "The Mainstreaming of Alternative Medicine." (May 2000): 17–24.

Crespo, C., and J. Arbesman. "Obesity in the United States." *The Physician and Sports Medicine* 31 (November 2003): 1.

Curry, C., and D. Butler, "Constipation." In *Handbook of Nonprescription Drugs*, 15th ed., edited by I. Bernardi, 299–326. Washington, DC: *American Pharmacists Association*, 2006.

Davis, S. "Insulin, Oral Hypoglycemic Agents, and the Pharmacology of the Endocrine Pancreas." In *The Pharmacological Basis of Therapeutics*, 11th ed., edited by L. Brunton, J. Lazo, and K. Parker, 1613–1645. New York: McGraw-Hill, 2006.

Dergal, J., J. Gold, D. Laxer, M. Lee, M. Binns, K. Lanctot, M. Freeman, and P. Rochon. "Potential Interactions Between Herbal Medicines and Conventional Drug Therapies Used by Older Adults Attending a Memory Clinic." *Drugs and Aging* 19 (2002): 879–886.

Dighe, S. V. "A Review of the Safety of Generic Drugs." *Transplant Proceedings* 31 (3A suppl) (1999): 23S–24S.

Drug Facts and Comparisons, St. Louis: Wolters Kluwar Health, 2007.

Drugs.com. "Top 200 Drugs for 2006 by Sales." Available www.drugs.com/top200.html.

Earth Times. "Moms Spread Word on Cough Medicine Abuse." (9 May 2007). Available www.earthtimes.org/ articles/show/61052.html.

FDA Center for Drug Evaluations. Public Health Advisory. "Phenylpropanolamine Advisory." (November 2000). Available www.fda.gov/cder/drug/infopage/ppa/advisory.htm.

Flexner, C. "Antiretroviral Agents and Treatment of HIV Infection." In *The Pharmacological Basis of Therapeutics*, 11th ed., edited by L. Brunton, J. Lazo, and K. Parker, 1273–1314. New York: McGraw-Hill, 2006.

Food and Drug Administration (FDA). "Final Rule Declaring Dietary Supplements Containing Ephedrine Alkaloids Adulterated Because They Present an Unreasonable Risk. Final Rule." *Federal Registrar* 69 (2004): 6787–6854.

Foster, K., and C. Coffrey. "Acne." In *Handbook of Nonprescription Drugs*, 15th ed., edited by I. Bernardi, 803–816. Washington, DC: *American Pharmacists Association*, 2006.

Frontlines. "Emotional 'Aspirin.'" *Consumer Reports* (December 2000a): 60–62.

Frontlines. "Herbal Supplements, What's in the Chips?" *Consumer Reports* (December 2000b): 8.

Fugh-Berman, A. "Herb–Drug Interactions." *Lancet* 355 (2000): 134–138.

Gasbarro, R. "Counseling the Patient with Diabetes." *Pharmacy Times* (October 1999): 53–66.

Gill, M. "The Pharmacist's Role in Sleep Disorders." *Pharmacy Times* (August 1999): 103–116.

Grady, D. "Chinese Herb Is Suspected in Cancer." *The New York Times on the Web* (8 June 2000). Available www. nytimes.com/library/national/science/health/060800hth-alternative-herb.html.

Griffin, M. "Back Pain: Medication and Addiction." *WebMD Health* (7 May 2007). Available www.webmd.com/back-pain/features/back-pain-medication-addiction.

Gruber, A. J., and H. G. Pope. "Ephedrine Abuse Among 36 Female Weightlifters." *American Journal of Addiction* 7 (1998): 256–261.

Hoffman, B. "Therapy of Hypertension." In *The Pharmacological Basis of Therapeutics,* 11th ed., edited by L. Brunton, J. Lazo, and K. Parker, 845–897. New York: McGraw-Hill, 2006.

Hoogerwerf, W., and P. Pasricha, "Pharmacotherapy of Gastric Acidity, Peptic Ulcers, and Gastroesophageal Reflux Disease." In *The Pharmacological Basis of Therapeutics,* 11th ed., edited by L. Brunton, J. Lazo, and K. Parker, 967–1008. New York: McGraw-Hill, 2006.

Hume, A., and K. Strong. "Botanical Medicines." In *Handbook of Nonprescription Drugs,* 15th ed., edited by I. Bernardi, 1103–1136. Washington, DC: *American Pharmacists Association,* 2006.

Jaffe, H., and A. Chip. "Got Any Smart Pills?" *Washingtonian* (January 2006): 41–45.

Johnson, C. "Gore Arrest Highlights Rx Drug Abuse." *Washington Post* (6 July 2007)" A8. Available www.washington post.com/wp-dyn/content/article/2007/07/05/AR2007 070501415.html.

Just the Facts. "Prescription and Over-the-Counter Drugs." Alcohol and Drug Abuse Program, Alcohol and Drug Abuse Association Resource Center, 1030 E. Lafayette Street, Suite 100, Tallahassee, FL (2003).

Kaufman, M. "DEA Revises Rule on Prescribing Painkillers." *The Washington Post* (7 September 2006a).

Kaufman, M. "Medication Errors Harming Millions." *The Washington Post* (21 July 2006b): A8.

Kirkwood, C., and S. Melton. "Insomnia." In *Handbook of Nonprescription Drugs,* 15th ed., edited by I. Bernardi, 995–1008. Washington, DC: *American Pharmacists Association,* 2006.

Leinwand, D. "Feds Score Against Homegrown Meth." *USA Today* (2 July 2007). Available www.mywire.com/pubs/USATODAY/2007/07/02/3879233?&pbl=86.

Longo, L. P., T. Parran, B. Johnson, and W. Kinsey. "Addiction: Part II. Identification and Management of the Drug-Seeking Patient." *American Family Physician* 61 (2000): 2401–2481.

Mackowiak, E. "The Common Cold: Prevention and Treatment." *Pharmacy Times* (November 1999): 95–106.

Mahley, R., and T. Bersot, "Drug Therapy for Hypercholesterolemia and Dyslipidemia." In *The Pharmacological Basis of Therapeutics,* 11th ed., edited by L. Brunton, J. Lazo, and K. Parker, 933–966. New York: McGraw-Hill, 2006.

Marso, S. "Optimizing the Diabetic Formulary: Beyond Aspirin and Insulin." *Journal of American College of Cardiology* 40 (2002): 652–661.

Martinez, B. "Study Shows Teens Using Prescription, OTC Drugs to Get High." *Defiance Crescent News* (16 January 2007). Available www.crescent-news.com/news/article/1486152.

McNamara, J. "Pharmacotherapy of the Epilepsies." In *The Pharmacological Basis of Therapeutics,* 11th ed., edited by L. Brunton, J. Lazo, and K. Parker, 501–525. New York: McGraw-Hill, 2006.

McQueen, C., and A. Hume. "Introduction to Botanical and Nonbotanical Natural Medicines." In *Handbook of Nonprescription Drugs,* 15th ed., edited by I. Bernardi, 1095–1101. Washington, DC: *American Pharmacists Association,* 2006.

Michel, T. "Treatment of Myocardial Ischemia." In *The Pharmacological Basis of Therapeutics,* 11th ed., edited by L. Brunton, J. Lazo, and K. Parker, 823–844. New York: McGraw-Hill, 2006.

Miller, S., and C. Bartels, "Overweight and Obesity." In *Handbook of Nonprescription Drugs,* 15th ed., edited by I. Bernardi, 553–573. Washington, DC: *American Pharmacists Association,* 2006.

Monitoring the Future. (21 December 2007). Available www.monitoringthefuture.org.

MSNBC. "College Students Abusing Prescription Drugs." (3 March 2008). Available www.msnbc.msn.com/id/23453371/.

National Institute on Drug Abuse (NIDA). "Studies Identify Factors Surrounding Rise in Abuse of Prescription Drugs by College Students." *NIDA Notes* 20, 4 (2006): 6.

OTC Observations. "Facts and Figures About OTC Medicines." *Pharmacy Times* (suppl) (September 1998): 3.

Pal, S. "Self Care and Nonprescription Pharmacotherapy." In *Handbook of Nonprescription Drugs,* 15th ed., edited by I. Bernardi, 3–14. Washington, DC: *American Pharmacists Association,* 2006.

Payne, J. "Report: Go Easy on Sleeping Pills." *Washington Post* (15 August 2006): HE03.

Physician's Weekly. "Curbing Abuse of Prescription ADHD Stimulants." (12 April 2007). Available www.physicians weekly.com/pc.asp?issueid=444&questionid=434.

Reavy, P. "Murray Doctor Arrested — Called the Drug 'Candyman.'" *Deseret News* 157 (2007): A1.

Remington, T. "Headache." In *Handbook of Nonprescription Drugs,* 15th ed., edited by I. Bernardi, 69–90. Washington, DC: *American Pharmacists Association,* 2006.

Rocco, T., and J. Fang. "Pharmacotherapy of Congestive Heart Failure." In *The Pharmacological Basis of Therapeutics,* 11th ed., edited by L. Brunton, J. Lazo, and K. Parker, 869–897. New York: McGraw-Hill, 2006.

RxList. *Top 200 Drugs* (September 2007). Available www. rxlist.com/script/main/hp.asp.

Schimmer, B., and K. Parker. "Adrenocorticotropic Steroids and Their Synthetic Analogs: Inhibitors of the Synthesis and Actions of Adrenocortical Hormones." In *The Pharmacological Basis of Therapeutics,* 11th ed., edited by L. Brunton, J. Lazo, and K. Parker, 1587–1612. New York: McGraw-Hill, 2006.

Schuster, C. "History and Current Perspectives on the Use of Drug Formulations to Decrease the Abuse of Prescription Drugs." *Drug and Alcohol Dependence* 835 (2006): S8–S14.

Scolaro, K. "Disorders Related to Colds and Allergies." In *Handbook of Nonprescription Drugs,* 15th ed., edited by I. Bernardi, 203–228. Washington, DC: *American Pharmacists Association,* 2006.

Scott, S., and R. Martin, "Atopic Dermatitis and Dry Skin." In *Handbook of Nonprescription Drugs,* 15th ed., edited by

I. Bernardi, 711–728. Washington, DC: *American Pharmacists Association,* 2006.

Shuster, J. "Insomnia: Understanding Its Pharmacological Treatment Options." *Pharmacy Times* 62 (August 1996): 67–76.

Stolberg, S. "F.D.A. Considers Switching Some Prescription Drugs to Over-the-Counter Status." *The New York Times on the Web* (28 June 2000): A1.

Tatro, D. "Drug Interactions with Natural Product." *Drug Facts and Comparison News* (May 1999): 34–38.

Tietze, K. "Cough." In *Handbook of Nonprescription Drugs,* 15th ed., edited by I. Bernardi, 229–242. Washington, DC: *American Pharmacists Association,* 2006.

Tinsley, J. A. "The Hazards of Psychotropic Herbs." *Minnesota Medicine* 82 (1999): 29–31.

U.S. Department of Justice. Information Brief. "Prescription Drug Abuse and Youth." (August 2002): Product #2002-L0424-004.

van den Heuval, C., S. Ferguson, M. Macchiand, and D. Dawson. "Melatonin as a Hypnotic: Con." *Sleep Medicine Review* 9 (2005): 71–80.

Walker, P. "Diarrhea." In *Handbook of Nonprescription Drugs,* 15th ed., edited by I. Bernardi, 326–350. Washington, DC: *American Pharmacists Association,* 2006.

Wallis, C. "Suggested Strong Warnings for Ritalin, Freaking Out Parent and Patients — And Even Doctors." *Time* (12 February 2006). Available www.time.com/time/magazine/article/0,9171,1158957,00.html.

Warholak-Juarez, T., M. Rupp, T. Salazar, and S. Foster. "Effect of Patient Information on the Quality of Pharmacists' Drug Use Review Decisions." *Journal of American Pharmaceutical Association* 40 (2000): 500–508.

Whitney, M. "Prescription Drug Deaths Skyrocket 68 Percent over Five Years as Americans Swallow More Pills." *NewsTarget.com* (14 September 2007). Available www.newstarget.com/z021635.html.

Wick, J. "Outsmarting Prescription Fraud." *Pharmacy Times* 61 (April 1995): 33–36.

Williams, A., C. Girard, D. Jui, A. Sabina, and D. Katz. "SAMe as Treatment for Depression: A Systemic Review." *Clinical Investigation of Medicine* 28 (2005): 132–139.

WIXT/WSYR TV ABC 9, "Pharm Parties. Popping Prescriptions." Syracuse. (18 May 2007).

Yates, K. M., A. O'Connor, and C. A. Horsley. "Herbal Ecstasy: A Case Series of Adverse Reactions." *New Zealand Medical Journal* 113 (2000): 315–317.

Zak, J. "OBRA '90 and DUR." *American Druggist* (October 1993): 57.

Zickler, P. "Addictive Drugs and Stress Trigger Similar Change in the Brain Cells, Animal Study Finds." *NIDA Notes* 18 (December 2003). Available www.nida.nih.gov/NIDA_notes/NNvol18N5/Addictive.html.

Zweber, A., and R. Berardi. "Heartburn and Dyspepsia." In *Handbook of Nonprescription Drugs,* 15th ed., edited by I. Bernardi, 265–282. Washington, DC: *American Pharmacists Association,* 2006.

CHAPTER 16

Drug Use Within Major Subcultures

Learning Objectives

On completing this chapter you will be able to:

◎ Know which drugs are most likely to be abused by athletes and why.

◎ Describe the use of drug testing in athletic competitions.

◎ Determine where anabolic steroids come from.

◎ Describe the purpose and goals of the Adolescents Training and Learning to Avoid Steroids (ATLAS) prevention program.

◎ Explain two major ways women's history differs from men's history with regard to drug abuse.

◎ Explain why adolescents use substances of abuse.

◎ Explain which types of parents are more likely to raise drug-abusing adolescents.

◎ List which types of drugs adolescents are most likely to abuse.

◎ List two major findings from research regarding drug use by college student subcultures.

◎ Know what club drugs are and how they are used.

◎ Explain how drug abuse contributes to the spread of AIDS.

◎ Know the key statistics regarding AIDS.

◎ List the major strategies to prevent contracting HIV infection.

◎ Know how the use of alcohol and other drugs is presented in popular movies and songs.

Did You Know?

○ Athletes are much more likely than other subcultural groups to take drugs that enhance physical attributes.

○ Approximately 500,000 teenagers use steroids and 52,000 American children (12 and younger) use anabolic steroids.

○ In general, compared with men, women are more likely to become addicted to tobacco.

○ Approximately 70% of women in drug abuse treatment report histories of physical and sexual abuse with victimization beginning before 11 years of age and occurring repeatedly.

○ Research shows that teenage gangs are major players in the drug trade.

○ Alcohol use is implicated in one third to two thirds of sexual assaults and acquaintance or date rape cases among teens and college students.

○ Among drug-using college students, 24% report using MDMA (Ecstasy) and psilocybin (mushrooms).

○ An HIV-infected individual may not manifest symptoms of AIDS for as many as 10 to 12 years after the initial infection.

Drugs and Society Online is a great source for additional drugs and society information for both students and instructors.
Visit **http://drugsandsociety.jbpub.com** to find a variety of useful tools for learning, thinking, and teaching.

Introduction

Although similarities appear in the patterns of addiction among drug users, the development of initial use and eventual abuse varies immensely from individual to individual. When attempting to understand common causes and patterns of drug use, examining subcultures often provides a semblance of group commonalities. A **subculture** is defined as a subgroup within the population whose members share similar values and patterns of related behaviors that differ from those of other subcultures and the larger population. Even though many subcultures can be so broad and diverse that not all members may be consciously aware of one another, from an **outsider's perspective** (discussed in Chapter 1) they qualify as subcultures because they share similar behavior patterns. For example, sport, gender, age, and drug subcultures are often very large across the United States, and not all members of such subcultures can be aware of one another. However, from an outsider's perspective, they have similar patterns of behavior. When we refer to an insider's perspective, we are looking at a subculture from the inside and, therefore, expect the members to be aware of one another as a distinct group. An **insider's perspective** refers to viewing the subculture from the inside, just as members experience the ongoing activity. For example, a group of adolescents using drugs from a particular locality in a city or town and divorced women meeting to discuss coping with separation and being single qualify as distinct subcultures. Both insiders' and outsiders' perspectives include similar behavior patterns, just from different perspectives — inside and outside.

KEY TERMS

subculture
subgroup within the population whose members share similar values and patterns of related behaviors that differ from other subcultures and the larger population

outsider's perspective
viewing a group or subculture from outside the group and viewing the group and its members as an observer; looking "in" at the members

insider's perspective
viewing a group or subculture from inside the group; seeing members as they perceive themselves

When defining a subculture, some sociologists refer to it as a "world within a world." Subcultures create and provide their members with lifestyle patterns that are observable, fairly consistent, and interwoven. Although it is a general perspective, viewing a group as a subculture offers a way to look at more generalized and distinctive patterns of drug use.

First, we examine why individuals within various subcultures might initially turn to drugs. The two types of forces that affect members of a subculture are internal and external forces, both of which affect these individuals' drug use behavior. *Internal subcultural forces* include:

1. Shared attitudes about drug users and nonusers
2. Compatibility with other members of the peer group (often peer members share complementary personality traits)
3. Shared attitudes favorable to drug use despite conventional society's view that such behavior is deviant
4. Addiction to drugs or, at minimum, habitual drug usage
5. A common secrecy about drug use

External subcultural forces include:

1. Preoccupation with law enforcement while procuring the drugs and while under the effects of illicit drugs
2. A desire to identify other users and sellers of illicit drugs such as verifying the dependability of the drug dealer (who best to hook up with)
3. Constant preoccupation regarding when more difficult-to-acquire-type drugs are available and seizing this opportunity
4. Preoccupation with being caught using or acting high in public, at work, at school, or at a social function at which drug use would be perceived as deviant social behavior

To further understand how similar patterns of drug use and/or abuse occur, in this chapter we look at drug users from both outsiders' and insiders' perspectives, from the vantage point of the members belonging to a distinct subculture. This chapter examines drug use and potential abuse in the following seven *drug-using* subcultures:

1. Sports/athletics
2. Women
3. Adolescents
4. College students
5. HIV and AIDS carriers

6. A certain percentage of professional actors, actresses, and entertainers who perform in movies

7. A certain percentage of Internet users who are seeking and purchasing illicit drugs

Athletes and Drug Abuse

Drug abuse has been reported since the Greeks started the Olympics in 776 BC. It was then reported that certain substances were ingested by competitors in attempts to gain some ground against fellow competitors (Lajis n.d.).

Using performance-enhancing drugs for increased athletic ability is known as **doping**. Current reports reveal that "'Doping' among world-class competitors is rampant, admit many athletes, and the governing bodies of individual sports, as well as the International Olympic Committee, turn a blind eye" (Begley et al. 1999, p. 49). Further, the reasons boil down to winning in sports, especially when millisecond differences exist between gold and silver medals. The differences between the two medals "can amount to millions in endorsement contract and appearance fees" (Begley et al. 1999, p. 49), and apparently the world of professional sports and "drugs [performance-enhancing drugs] go together like socks and sweat" (Begley et al. 1999, p. 49). Recently, Mr. Yesalis, an epidemiologist at Pennsylvania State University at University Park, stated that

> Elite athletes stay away from traditional anabolic steroids. They use testosterone creams or gels, which dramatically reduce the chance of being caught, in conjunction with insulin or insulin-like growth factor, and we don't even have a test for those. . . . The supplement industry has exploded since the passage of the Dietary Supplement Health and Education Act in 1994. . . . Anyone can buy substances like testosterone, human-growth hormone HGH, and insulin-like growth factor over the Internet. One site requires a doctor's prescription, but will sell one to any customer for $100. Or someone can just walk down to the local GNC, like Mr. Jackson's teammates at Florida State. There, one can buy muscle-building steroid "precursors" like androstenedione and creatine monohydrage. "Andro" is banned by the National Collegiate Athletic Association and other sports governing

> bodies, but it's legal to buy. They're not as effective as older anabolic steroids, but they do provide some benefits. . . . The law allows stores to sell vitamins, herbal remedies, and other supplements over-the-counter. (Suggs 2003, p. 36)

To understand why athletes are willing to risk using these drugs, it is necessary to further explore mind-set. Young athletes receive exaggerated attention and prestige in almost every university, college, high school, and junior high school in the United States. Pressure to excel or be the best is placed on athletes by parents, peers, teachers, coaches, school administrators, the media, and the surrounding community. The importance of sports is frequently distorted and even used by some to evaluate the quality of educational institutions (Lawn 1984) or the quality of living conditions in a city. Athletic success can determine the level of financial support these institutions receive from local and state governments, alumni, and other private donors; thus, winning in athletics often translates into fiscal stability and institutional prosperity.

For the athlete, success in sports means psychological rewards such as the admiration of peers, school officials, family, and the community. In addition, athletic success can mean financial rewards such as scholarships, paid living expenses in college, advertising endorsement opportunities, and, for a few, incredible salaries as professional athletes. With the rewards of winning, athletes have to deal with the added pressures of not winning: "What will people think of me if I lose?" "When I lose, I let everybody down." "Losing shows that I am not as good as everyone thinks." These pressures on young, immature athletes can result in poor coping responses. Being better than competitors, no matter the cost, becomes the driving motivation, and doing one's best is no longer sufficient. Such attitudes may lead to serious risk-taking behavior in an attempt to develop an advantage over the competition; this situation can include using drugs to improve performance.

The Canadian sprinter Ben Johnson, once known as the fastest human in history, was banned

KEY TERMS

doping
the use of performance-enhancing drugs to increase athletic ability

for life from competitive running in March 1993 (Begley et al. 1999; Hoberman and Yesalis 1995). Five years earlier, at the 1988 Seoul Olympics, Johnson was stripped of a world's record for the 100-meter dash and forfeited the gold medal when his urine tested positive for steroids. Because of the first incident, Johnson was suspended from competition for 2 years. However, in 1992, the 31-year-old sprinter was attempting a comeback, with speeds that approached his world record times. In January 1993, a routine urine test determined Johnson was again using steroids to enhance his athletic performance (Ferrente 1993). Another, more recent incident involving the use of steroids that ended in shocking tragedy was the case of wrestler Chris Benoit's double murder–suicide. Evidence proved that the pro wrestler asphyxiated his son and wife before he hanged himself in a basement weight room using a cord from one of the weight machines . . ." (ABC News 2007). "Steroids were among the prescription medications found by investigators going through . . . Benoit's house" (Donaldson-Evans 2007). "Anabolic steroids affect neurochemicals in the brain. . . . It's those neurochemical changes that cause the extreme anger . . . Officials found many different prescription medications — including prescription anabolic steroids — inside the house . . ." (Donaldson-Evans 2007). In another story, "eighty-three players have been suspended under baseball's controversial new steroids policy" (Anonymous, as told by Penn 2005, p. 292). "Guys did steroids because it was easy to get away with." Several other noteworthy and revealing quotes from this report are: "So many people were doing it that it didn't feel like cheating. If anything, it felt like leveling the field. . . . I juiced because I love playing more than anything else in the world, and I would have pretty much done anything to keep my career going" (Anonymous, as told by Penn 2005, p. 297). Widely publicized incidents such as these concerning illicit use of so-called **ergogenic** (performance-enhancing) drugs by professional and amateur athletes have created intense interest in the problems of drug abuse in sports (Begley et al. 1999; Merchant 1992). (See "Point/Counterpoint," How the "Juice" Is Flowing in Baseball.)

KEY TERMS

ergogenic
drugs that enhance athletic performance

■ Drugs Used by Athletes

Yes, the steroids I used certainly made me get bigger. I was going out for football and I had just made the team, so I kept using them and the results were phenomenal. Now, 2 years later, I won't be graduating. Several months ago, they removed a tumor on my liver, but they didn't get all the cancer. I am going home at the end of this semester. My parents want me to stay with them for the time I have left. When I go, I only have one wish — I want to die big and always be known as big Jim. *(From Venturelli's research files, interview with a 20-year-old male, December 13, 1996.)*

Studies have shown that athletes are less likely than nonathletes to use other drugs of abuse such as marijuana, alcohol, barbiturates, cocaine, and hallucinogens (Hoberman and Yesalis 1995; Substance Abuse and Mental Health Services Administration [SAMHSA] 2007). However, athletes *are* much more likely than other populations to take drugs that enhance (physically or psychologically) or are thought to enhance competitive performance; these drugs include stimulants such as amphetamines and cocaine and an array of drugs with presumed ergogenic effects, such as anabolic steroids (Bell 1987; National Institute on Drug Abuse [NIDA] 2006). Some of the major drugs abused by athletes are listed in Table 16.1, along with their desired effects. The sections that follow discuss the drugs that are most frequently self-administered by athletes in an effort to improve their competitive performance.

Anabolic Steroids

Anabolic steroids consist of a group of natural and synthetic drugs that are chemically similar to cholesterol and related to the male hormone testosterone (Guide4living.com 2005; Lukas 1993) and its artificial derivatives. Steroids are used for treatment of certain diseases such as specific types of anemia, some breast cancers, and testosterone deficiency. Although illegal when taken for nonmedical purposes, steroids have been illegally used by both athletes and nonathletes since the late 1950s to improve athletic ability and physical appearance because steroids have performance-enhancing and bodybuilding properties. Steroids are taken orally or injected into the muscles. Although males and females use steroids, males have higher rates of use (SAMHSA 1999c).

►Point/Counterpoint How the "Juice" Is Flowing in Baseball

We embrace instant gratification in the United States. We are a society that embraces "bigger, faster, stronger" and winning at all costs (in Dvorchak 2005). This concept now applies to professional sports with a devious outcome. A sampling from news sources reveals the following:

▶ Jose Canseco, a Major League Baseball player for the Oakland Athletics and Texas Rangers (among other teams), wrote a tell-all book titled *Juiced,* in which he exposed "not only the rampant use of performance-enhancing substances in baseball (with steroids replacing the amphetamines of Bouton's day) . . . A steroid devotee since the age of 20, Conseco goes beyond admitting his own usage . . . [to claiming that] . . . he often injected [Mark] McGwire while they were teammates . . . According to Canseco, steroids and human growth hormone gave McGwire and Sammy Sosa (whose own usage was 'so obvious, it was a joke') the strength, stamina, regenerative ability, and confidence they needed for [the] record setting home run duels often credited with restoring baseball's popularity after the 1994 strike" (Amazon.Com 2005).

▶ [S]everal star athletes, including New York Yankees slugger Jason Giambi, have reportedly told a federal grand jury investigating the [Balco] lab that they used illegal steroids, prompting Congress to hold hearings on the testing policies of all the major sports leagues" (Coile 2005).

▶ "Seattle Mariners minor-league outfielder Jamal Strong was suspended for 10 days . . . making him the fourth player to test positive under Major League Baseball's new policy on performance-enhancing drugs" (Associated Press 2005).

▶ "Washington — How lawmakers introduced a bill . . . that would create a national standard for steroids testing for all professional sports and require a two-year suspension for the first positive test and a lifetime ban for a second offense" (Coile 2005).

▶ "The same anti-steroid rules that apply to badminton, billiards and bridge ought to apply to baseball, basketball and football, according to U.S. lawmakers who introduced a bill on Tuesday requiring American professional sports to adopt international drug testing standards" (Health Reuters and Yahoo! News 2005).

▶ "MLB's (Major League Baseball's) drug policy was denounced as laced with loopholes and lawmakers threatened to draft legislation calling for a national testing standard" (Health Reuters and Yahoo! News 2005).

▶ "McGwire's shameful refusal to answer questions about his alleged steroid use before a congressional committee and Bonds' unbelievable claim that he did not know that substances rubbed into his body were steroids clearly suggest deceit and dishonesty" (Eilek 2005).

▶ "Robert Eilek is a teacher at Temecula Middle School. He recently removed dozens of pieces of Mark McGwire memorabilia from his classroom in protest of McGwire's refusal to answer questions at a congressional inquiry on steroid use" (Eilek 2005).

These events bring up some questions to consider.

1. Are professional sports players entitled to claim records set if they were on drugs during their successful career? If they are entitled to their accomplishments regardless of their drug usage, how would it affect non–drug-using players? Is it fair to the sport and to the fans supporting the players? If they are not entitled to their accomplishments under drugged conditions, what should the penalty be?

2. Should *all* players in professional sports be continuously tested for drugs? Should this policy extend to both high school and college sport players? If so, what should the penalties for such drug violations be? If high school and college sports players should not be tested for drugs, why not?

3. What if we find clear evidence that some currently admired major sports figures who scored big-time records in the past were using steroids or other performance-enhancing drugs while setting new and impressive records? Should anything be done about such evidence? If so, what penalties should the athletes receive? If not, why should we let them remain unblemished?

4. Are the real victims of this tragedy America's youth? Have athletes such as McGwire and Bonds betrayed the young who admire and emulate them? Do you think America's youth are affected by drug use in professional sports?

▶Point/Counterpoint *(continued)*

5. Does this scandal about professional sports and drug use suggest anything about the findings by the Centers of Disease Control and Prevention that steroid use among high school students more than doubled from 1991 to 2003?

6. As a high school teacher, is Robert Eilek being overly severe regarding his treatment of McGwire's refusal to answer questions on steroid use at a congressional inquiry on steroid use?

Sources:

Amazon.com. "Editorial Reviews." Available http://www.amazon.com/exec/obidos/asin/0060746408/ref=bxgy (accessed 1 May 2005).

Associated Press. "Strong Suspended for Performance-Enhancing Drugs." *Sports ESPN* (26 April 2005).

Coile, Z. "House Bill Seeks to Toughen Steroid Rules: Athletes in All Leagues Would Be Held to the Strict Standards Used in Olympics." *San Francisco Chronicle, Washington Bureau* (27 April 2005).

Dvorchak, R. "Former Steeler Courson Outlines Solutions for Steroid Use." *Post-Gazette.com* (27 April 2005). Available http://www.post-gazette.com/pg/05117/494862.stm.

Eilek, R. "Pro Sports Keep Heads in Sand on Steroids." *North County Times* (North San Diego and Southwest Riverside County columnists) (23 April 2005). Available http://www.nctimes.com/articles/2005/04/24/opinion/commentary/19_31_454_23_05.txt.

Health Reuters and Yahoo News. "Anti-steroid Rules Proposed for U.S. Pro Sports" (27 April 2005).

Table 16.1 **Partial List of Ergogenic Substances and Expected Effects**

DRUGS	EXPECTED RESULTS
Amino acids	Stimulate natural production of growth hormone
Amphetamines and cocaine	Increase strength, alertness, and endurance
Anabolic steroids	Increase muscle mass and strength
B-complex vitamins	Enhance body metabolism and increase energy
Caffeine	Reduce fatigue
Chromium	Enhance carbohydrate metabolism
Ephedrine	Improve breathing
Asthma medication	Improve breathing
OTC decongestants	Increase endurance
Thyroid hormone	Enhance metabolism and energy
Beta-blockers	Reduce hand tremor and stimulate growth hormone
Methylphenidate	Enhance alertness and endurance
Furosemide	Mask steroid use and enable rapid weight loss

Source: Harlan, R., and M. Garcia. "Neurobiology of Androgen Abuse." In *Drugs of Abuse,* edited by R. Watson, 185–201. Boca Raton, FL: CRC Press, 1992. Reprinted with permission. Copyright CRC Press.

Naturally occurring male hormones, or **androgens**, are produced by the testes in males. These hormones are essential for normal growth and development of male sex organs as well as secondary sex characteristics such as muscular development, male hair patterns, voice changes, and fat distribution. The androgens are also necessary for appropriate growth spurts during adolescence (*Drug Facts and Comparisons* 1994). The principal accepted therapeutic use for androgens is for hormone replacement in males with abnormally functioning testes. In such cases, the androgens are administered before puberty and for prolonged periods during puberty to stimulate proper male development (*Drug Facts and Comparisons* 1994).

Abuse of Anabolic Steroids and the Major Reasons for the Abuse of This Drug Under some conditions, androgen-like drugs can increase muscle mass and strength; for this reason, they are referred to as **anabolic** (able to stimulate the conversion of nutrients into tissue) **steroids** (because chemically, they are similar to the steroids produced in the adrenal glands). They are used by many athletes to improve performance (Burke and Davis 1992; NIDA 2006).

One of the major reasons athletes give for abusing steroids is to improve their athletic performance. Another reason for taking steroids is to increase their muscle size or to reduce their body fat (NIDA 2006). Others who abuse steroids in order to boost their muscle size have experienced physical or sexual abuse. In one series of interviews with male weightlifters, 25% who abused steroids reported memories of childhood physical or sexual abuse. Similarly, female weightlifters who had been raped were found to be twice as likely to report use of anabolic steroids or another purported muscle-building drug, compared with those women who had not been raped. Moreover, almost all of those who had been raped reported that they markedly increased their bodybuilding activities after the attack (NIDA 2006). Finally, regarding adolescent steroid abuse, it is part of a pattern of high-risk behaviors. Such steroid-abusing adolescents have been found to take risks such as drinking and driving, carrying a gun, driving a motorcycle without a helmet, and abusing other illicit drugs. In conclusion, conditions such as **muscle dysmorphia** (a behavioral syndrome that causes individuals to have a distorted image of their bodies, perceiving themselves as looking small and weak, even when they may be large and muscular), a history of physical or sexual abuse, or

FIGURE 16.1

Reasons for nonmedicinal steroid use by college students.

Source: Harlan, R., and M. Garcia. "Neurobiology of Androgen Abuse." In *Drugs of Abuse*, edited by R. Watson, 186. Boca Raton, FL: CRC Press, 1992. Reprinted with permission. Copyright CRC Press.

a history of engaging in high-risk behaviors have all been associated with an increased risk of initiating or continuing steroid abuse.

It is estimated that as many as 1 million Americans have used or are currently using these drugs to achieve a competitive edge or for other purposes (Welder and Melchert 1993; see Figure 16.1). Studies suggest that approximately 2% of college-age men and 6.7% of male high school students use anabolic steroids (Harlan and Garcia 1992). "A 2001 NCAA survey found that usage of stimulants, including ephedrine and amphetamines, and anabolic steroids had risen slightly since 1997. Between 3 and 4 percent of athletes surveyed admitted using stimulants, and 1.4 percent admitted using steroids"

KEY TERMS

androgens
naturally occurring male hormones, such as testosterone

anabolic steroids
androgen-like drugs that can increase muscle mass and strength

muscle dysmorphia
behavioral syndrome that causes men to have a distorted image of their bodies, perceiving themselves as looking small and weak, even when they may be large and muscular; women with this condition think they look fat and flabby, even though they may actually be lean and muscular

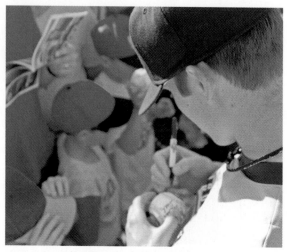

Besides risking their health, athletes who choose to dope should remember that they are role models. Seventy-three percent of youth want to be like a famous athlete; 53% of youth say it is common for famous athletes to use banned substances to get ahead.

(Suggs 2003). Also realize that these percentages are much lower than what the survey revealed because athletes are inclined to hide drug usage for fear of jeopardizing their eligibility to play sports as well as other more personal reasons having to do with image in the eyes of others. Further, approximately 500,000 adolescents use steroids, and 52,000 American *children* use anabolic steroids; "a study in the journal *Pediatrics . . .* found that 2.7% of Massachusetts middle-school athletes were using steroids" (Begley et al. 1999, p. 54). Another source indicates that males are more likely to use and abuse steroids than females (Johnston et al. 2006a). In a much larger nationwide study, in 2005, annual use rates were 1.2%, 1.8%, and 2.6% for boys in grades 8, 10, and 12, compared with 0.9%, 0.7%, and 0.4% for girls (Johnston et al. 2006a). Encouraging results indicate that steroid use among adolescents in 8th, 10th, and 12th grade is significantly lower than in previous years (Johnston et al. 2006a). Competition for scholarships and entry into professional sports are major factors that influence young athletes to use steroids (Scott et al. 1996).

Although the vast majority of anabolic steroid users are male, women involved in bodybuilding and strength and endurance sports also abuse these drugs. Among seniors in high school, 3.2% of the males reported steroid use in the past year compared with 1.1% of the females. These statistics are much lower among 19- to 32-year-olds — 0.4% — with males accounting for all steroid use (Johnston et al. 2004a).

The first report of use of anabolic steroids to improve athletic performance was in 1954

by the Russian weightlifting team. These drugs' performance-enhancing advantages were quickly recognized by other athletes, and it has been estimated that as many as 90% of the competitors in the 1960 Olympic games used some form of steroid (Toronto 1992). Because of the widespread misuse and associated problems with the use of these drugs, anabolic steroids were classified as Schedule III controlled drugs (see Chapter 3 for drug schedules) in 1991 (Merchant 1992).

Due to federal regulations, individuals convicted of a first offense of trafficking with anabolic steroids can be sentenced to a maximum prison term of 5 years and a $250,000 fine. For a second offense, the prison term can increase to 10 years with a $500,000 fine. Even possession of illicitly obtained anabolic steroids can result in a 1-year term with at least a $1000 fine (U.S. Department of Justice 1991–1992).

Patterns of Abuse Geographical factors appear to have little to do with the use of anabolic steroids among athletes. In both inner-city and suburban schools, all are equally attracted to these drugs. However, some athletes are more inclined to abuse anabolic steroids than others. For example, football players have the highest rate of abuse; 9% self-reported out of 11 National Collegiate Athletic Association (NCAA) colleges and universities — in a survey conducted by the NCAA — whereas track and field athletes have the lowest rate of abuse (4% reported) (National Institutes of Health [NIH]/ NIDA 1998). Another study using a more indirect method of interviewing found rates three times higher than the percentages just reported. In addition, the likelihood of abusing these drugs increases as the level of competition increases. Usage rates were approximately 14% in NCAA Division I athletes and 30% to 75% in professional athletes (Lukas 1993). In general, usage patterns for anabolic steroids vary considerably according to athletes' motivation, the level of competition, the type of sport, and the pressure for winning.

The pattern usually consists of self-administering doses that are 10 to 200 times greater than dosages used for legitimate medical conditions (Welder and Melchert 1993). Users take nonmedical anabolic-androgenic steroids in *cycles*, periods of use lasting 6 to 12 weeks or longer. **Stacking** these drugs means taking more than one at a time, which is common.

KEY TERMS

stacking
use of several types of steroids at the same time

The use of different steroids taken singly but in sequence is called "**cycling**." To avoid developing tolerance to a particular steroid (**plateauing**), athletes often stagger the various drugs, sometimes taking them in overlapping patterns or alternately. Users often move from a low daily dose at the beginning of a cycle to a higher dose, then reduce their use toward the end of the cycle (**pyramiding**). To combat the unwanted side effects of steroids, such as severe skin rashes and development of irreversible masculine traits in women, as well as sudden anger and explosive physical aggressiveness (known as "roid rage" in men), other drugs such as diuretics, antiestrogens, human chorionic gonadotropin, and antiacne medication are often taken concurrently. This pattern of use is referred to by users as an **array**. In general, power athletes prefer stacking, whereas bodybuilders prefer cycling.

Because steroid use has been prohibited by almost all legitimate sporting organizations, urine testing just before the athletic event has become commonplace (Lukas 1993). Steroid-using athletes attempt to avoid detection by trying to fool the tests. These highly questionable strategies include the following (Lukas 1993; Merchant 1992):

- Using the steroid only during training for the athletic events, but discontinuing its use several weeks before the competition to allow the drug to disappear from the body. Because oral steroids are cleared from the body faster than the injectable types, they are usually discontinued 2 to 4 weeks prior to competition, and the injection steroids are stopped 3 to 6 weeks before competition.
- Taking drugs, such as probenecid, that block the excretion of steroids in the urine. Probenecid inhibits the substance from reaching the urine. In addition, urine tests are all that

the International Olympic Committee (IOC) requires (Begley et al. 1999).
- Using diuretics and drinking large quantities of water to increase the urine output and dilute the steroid so that it cannot be detected by the test.
- Adding adulterant chemicals to the urine, such as Drano, Clorox, ammonia, or eye drops to invalidate the tests.

Recent Developments in Evading Detection One serious problem today, according to Prince Alexandre de Merode, who has been in charge of the IOC's Medical Commission for 31 years, is that

the newest doping agents pose the risk of serious health problems, and even death. But a larger reason is that it is ridiculously easy to dope and not be caught. Doping and detection are like an arms race. First trainers discover a performance-enhancing drug. Then, sports officials develop a test for it. Trainers retaliate by inventing a way to elude the detectors. So far, doping has stayed a lap ahead.

Other comments from the same source:

"Undetectable drugs are 90 percent of estimated doping cases," said Hein Verbruggen, head of International Cycling Union. (Begley et al. 1999, p. 50)

Chemists constantly use the 72 banned steroids to change the testosterone molecule. "All you have to do is take a steroid not on the list. Or, simply by going cold turkey a few weeks before competition, an athlete can get the muscle-bulking effects without getting caught" (Begley et al. 1999, p. 51).

Some of the most recent types of drugs that athletes use even though they are all banned by the NCAA are listed in Table 16.2. This table lists the class of performance-enhancing substances, examples, what these drugs do, who is likely to use such drugs, status regarding whether the drug is illicit or licit, and where athletes are likely to secure the drug.

Effects of Anabolic Steroids Low to moderate doses of anabolic steroids have little effect on the strength or athletic skills of the average adult. However, when high doses are used by athletes during intense training programs, these drugs cause significant gains in lean body mass (i.e., muscle) and strength while decreasing fat (Lukas 1993). Because most of these effects are transient and will disappear when steroid use is stopped, athletes feel compelled to continue using them

Table 16.2 Performance-Enhancing Substances Banned by the NCAA

The following are among the substances many athletes use even though they are banned by the National Collegiate Athletic Association, and some are illegal under federal and state laws.

CLASS	EXAMPLES	WHAT DOES IT DO?	WHO USES IT?	IS IT LEGAL?	WHERE DO ATHLETES GET IT?
Steroids	Nandrolone, stanozol	Increases testosterone levels, thus building muscle.	Any athlete in a sport that requires strength and doesn't penalize muscle bulk can benefit. In an NCAA survey, football, baseball, rifle, and water-polo athletes admitted using steroids.	Not without a prescription.	Over the Internet or from a complicit doctor.
Steroid precursors	Androstenedione, 19-norandrostenediol	Can be converted into testosterone in the body.	Same as above.	Yes, under the Dietary Supplement and Health Education Act of 1994.	In drugstores, gyms, nutritional-supplement stores, and some grocery stores.
Hormones	Human growth hormone (HGH), erythropoietin (EPO)	HGH promotes growth in children and muscle development in adults. EPO increases production of red blood cells.	HGH is used by the same kinds of athletes who use steroids, while endurance athletes benefit from EPO.	Not without a prescription.	Over the Internet.
Stimulants	Ephedrine, caffeine (in excessive amounts)	Raises metabolic rate, giving a burst of energy.	Virtually all types of athletes. Not only do strength-oriented athletes like football players use them to get pumped up for workouts, but athletes like gymnasts use them to try to lose weight.	Yes. The Food and Drug Administration has banned ephedrine and caffeine (if the concentration in urine exceeds 15 micrograms/mL) as of 2001.	Generally available in drugstores and specialty stores.

Source: Suggs, W. "Deadly Fuel: As Supplements and Steroids Tempt and Endanger More Athletes, What Are Colleges Doing?" *Chronicle of Higher Education* XLIX (14 March 2003): A37. Copyright 2006, *Chronicle of Higher Education.* Reprinted with permission.

and become psychologically hooked (Toronto 1992). The drugs are most likely to benefit athletes in contact and strength sports in which increased muscle mass provides an advantage, such as weightlifting and football; anabolic steroids are less likely to benefit athletes involved in sports requiring dexterity and agility, such as baseball or tennis.

The risks associated with anabolic steroids are not completely understood. Most certainly, the higher the doses and the longer the use, the greater the potential damage these drugs can do to the body. Some of the adverse effects thought to occur with heavy steroid use (10 to 30 times the doses used therapeutically) include the following:

- Increased bad blood cholesterol levels, which could eventually clog arteries and cause heart attacks and strokes (National Clearinghouse for Alcohol and Drug Information [NCADI] 1999)

- Increased risk of liver disorders, such as jaundice and tumors (Lukas 1993)
- Psychological side effects, including irritability, outbursts of anger, mania, psychosis, and major depression
- Possible psychological and physical dependence with continual use of high doses, resulting in withdrawal symptoms, such as steroid craving (52%), fatigue (43%), depression (41%), restlessness (29%), loss of appetite (24%), insomnia (20%), diminished sex drive (20%), and headaches (20%) (Lukas 1993)
- Alterations in reproductive systems and sex hormones, causing changes in gender-related characteristics (Burke and Davis 1992): breast enlargement in males, breast reduction and bodily hair growth in females, infertility in both genders, and changes in genitalia — atrophy (shrinkage) of the penis and testicles in males and enlargement of external genitalia in females (Street et al. 1996)
- Changes in skin and hair in both genders: increased incidence and severity of acne, male pattern baldness, and increased body hair (Burke and Davis 1992)
- Persistent unpleasant breath odor (NCADI 1999)
- Swelling of the feet or lower limbs (NCADI 1999)
- Other changes, including stunted growth in adolescents, deepening of voice in females, and water retention, causing bloating (Burke and Davis 1992; Street et al. 1996)

Sources of Steroids Where do the anabolic steroids come from? About 50% of the anabolic steroids used in the United States are prescribed by doctors; the other 50% are obtained from the black market. Black market sources of steroids include drugs diverted from legitimate channels, smuggled from foreign countries — Brazil, Italy, Mexico, Great Britain, Portugal, France, and Peru (NIDA 1996) — that are designated for veterinarian use, or inactive counterfeits (U.S. Department of Justice 1991–1992). Recently, it was discovered that the primary source for steroids in the United States is the Baja, California, area of Mexico (Yesalis and Cowart 1998). The steroids are manufactured in Mexico City and shipped to pharmacies in the Baja region. Some health food stores and mail-order firms also offer products with names similar to the prescription anabolic steroids, such as Dynabdin, Metrobolin, and Diostero. These sham steroids contain only vitamins, amino acids, or micronutrients (Merchant 1992).

Most steroids used for nonmedical purposes are obtained illegally. A major federal report indicates that sources of illicit steroids fall into three rough categories: (1) smuggled steroids manufactured licitly or illicitly abroad, (2) drugs legally manufactured in this country and diverted to illicit sales at various places in the distribution chain, and (3) drugs clandestinely produced domestically. Small minorities of users obtain their drugs by prescription. Actual doses are often difficult to estimate because the product may have been produced in an uncontrolled laboratory with unknown quality control, may have been intended for veterinary use with its human equivalent doses not known, or may be counterfeit (NIH and NIDA 1998). Another source noted that the majority of young people report that steroids are easily available through their friends and coaches (McCaffrey 1999).

Stimulant Use Among Athletes

There are often reports in the media of football, basketball, or baseball players who have tested positive in a drug-screening evaluation or who have been suspended from competition due to drug abuse. In 1986, reports of cocaine-related deaths of sports figures included basketball star Len Bias and professional football player Don Rogers. Perhaps such sports tragedies helped convince some U.S. youth of the dangers of stimulant abuse and contributed to the decline in drug abuse in the late 1980s (Johnston et al. 1993). Clearly, no one — not even an athlete — is immune from the risks of these drugs.

Amphetamines and cocaine are abused to improve athletic skills (McDonald 1995). However, it is not clear if stimulants actually enhance athletic performance or merely the athlete's perception of performance. Many athletes believe these drugs promote quickness, enhance endurance, delay fatigue, increase self-confidence and aggression, and mask pain (Hoberman and Yesalis 1995). In fact, some studies have shown that stimulants can improve some aspects of athletic performance, especially in the presence of fatigue (NIDA 1996). However, the risk of using stimulants in sports is substantial because these drugs mask extreme fatigue, increase the risk of heat exhaustion, and can have severe cardiovascular consequences, such as heart attacks and strokes (Bell 1987; see "Case in Point," When Drugs Enter the Boxing Ring).

Although some athletes would never consider using the hard stimulants, such as cocaine and

►Case in Point When Drugs Enter the Boxing Ring

When Oliver McCall entered the boxing ring to fight for the heavyweight championship on February 7, 1997, he was not alone. With him came the spectre of years of drug abuse.

Just 7 weeks before, McCall had been arrested for swinging a Christmas tree around a hotel lobby while in a drug-induced haze. A few years earlier, he was found in a crack house after having been mugged by a fellow addict, to whom he lost the $1.5 million check he had carried with him in a sock to buy drugs. These events were just two of many drug-related occurrences on his record. His most recent arrest, however, had been followed by a drug treatment program, which he attended daily.

But something went wrong the night of February 7. After having announced to a friend, "I want my title. I'm fighting for my life," McCall seemed to want to get knocked out. In the third round, in the middle of the ring, in front of a packed audience, he listlessly walked around as his opponent, Lennox Lewis, threw punches at him. McCall dodged and bobbed his head, yet refused to fight back. After the fourth round, McCall stood alone, away from his corner, sobbing uncontrollably, seemingly having a nervous breakdown in front of a worldwide cable television audience. Fifty-five seconds into the fifth round, referee Mills Lane stopped the fight. Lewis was the winner. McCall, in more ways than one, was not.

While drugs have been an unwelcome part of sports in recent years, there are few cases where the consequences became more publicly evident. Here was a great contradiction for the world to see: Lennox Lewis, the athlete who had never been knocked down, and Oliver McCall, the man floored by the pain and drugs in his life. McCall's trainer, George Benton, said, "It was hard to watch, but it could be the best thing that ever happened to the human race. Now a father can tell his kids, 'You see what you saw on T.V.? You see what happens on drugs?' It was a hell of a lesson."

Sources: Boston Globe (8 February 1997); *New York Times* (9 February 1997).

---

amphetamines, milder stimulants that are legal and available over-the-counter (OTC) may be thought to be acceptable. Such stimulants include caffeine and OTC decongestants (for example, phenylpropanolamine and phenylephrine). These drugs can be a double-edged sword for the athlete. Their use can reduce fatigue, give a sense of energy, and even mask pain. Nevertheless, in high doses, especially when combined, they can cause nervousness, tremors, and restlessness; impair concentration; accelerate dehydration; and interfere with sleep ("OTC Drugs and Athletes" 1992). Some athletic competitions limit permissible blood levels of caffeine and do not allow the use of OTC stimulants such as decongestant drugs.

Miscellaneous Ergogenic Drugs

Most athletic organizations have banned the use of anabolic steroids and stimulants and are using more effective screening procedures to detect offenders. A result of this clampdown has been the search for alternative performance-enhancing drugs by athletes who feel a need for such pharmacological assistance. The following are brief discussions of a few of these substitute ergogenic substances.

Clenbuterol At the 1992 Olympic Games in Barcelona, Spain, at least four athletes, including German world sprint champion Katrina Krabbe, were disqualified from competition for using the drug clenbuterol to enhance their athletic performance (Merchant 1992). Not available in the United States, this drug is known as "Doper's Delight" and is supposed to improve breathing and increase strength. Currently, most athletic urine examinations test for it.

Erythropoietin Clinically, erythropoietin is a drug used to treat patients with anemia. Because it stimulates the production of *red blood cells* (the oxygen-carrying cells in the blood), it is thought that this drug enhances oxygen use and produces additional energy. Erythropoietin is being used as a substitute for blood doping. *Blood doping* is when athletes attempt to increase their number of red blood cells by reinfusing some of their own blood (which has been stored) before an athletic event.

Erythropoietin is impossible to detect and has been reported to be used by athletes engaged in endurance activities such as long-distance cycling. The use of erythropoietin by athletes is extremely dangerous and is thought to be responsible for several deaths. It is also very expensive, which likely has helped to limit its abuse (Merchant 1992).

Human Growth Factor and Human Growth Hormone
Athletes have begun to abuse two types of steroids: **human growth factor (HGF)** and its designer drug synthetic version, **human growth hormone (HGH)**. HGF, also known as *somatotropin*, is a hormone naturally secreted by the pituitary gland at the base of the brain that helps to achieve normal growth potential of muscles, bones, and internal organs. Some athletes claim that release of natural HGF can be simulated by using drugs such as levodopa (used to treat Parkinson's disease), clonidine (used to treat hypertension), and amino acids. Athletes use commercially prepared HGF because it cannot be distinguished from naturally occurring HGF.

Use of this hormone by athletes is limited, however, by its high cost. The benefits of HGF to athletic performance are very controversial, although the potential side effects are substantial, including abnormal growth patterns (called *acromegaly*), diabetes, thyroid gland problems, heart disease, and loss of sex drive (Merchant 1992).

In recent years, the synthetic HGH has become available in the form of a newly structured steroid-type analog sold in vials; this product is used to build muscle tissue, with corresponding decreases in body fat, without exercise (McDonald 1995). HGH is probably the most potent anabolic agent ever discovered, but it is also one of the most expensive. In fact, HGH is so expensive that until the mid-1990s, "its use in the United States was confined to pediatric endocrinologists who used it to treat undersized children" (McDonald 1995, p. C1). To date, no tests have proved capable of detecting HGH in the blood or urine. In addition, the side effects of this drug remain largely unknown. As a result, this drug is highly vulnerable to abuse.

Beta (β)-Adrenergic Blockers The β-adrenergic blockers are drugs that affect the cardiovascular system and are frequently used to treat hypertension. They have been used in sports because they reduce heart rate and signs of nervousness, which in turn quiets hand tremors. Consequently, these drugs are most likely to be used by individuals participating in sports that require steady hands, such as competitive shooting. The use of these drugs is prohibited by most athletic organizations (Merchant 1992).

Gamma-Hydroxybutyrate The substance gamma-hydroxybutyrate (GHB) is found naturally in the brain and has been used in England to treat insomnia. Athletes and bodybuilders have used GHB to increase muscle mass and strength. Although the actual effects of the compound are not known, it has been reported to cause euphoria and increase the release of growth hormone. Acute poisoning with GHB has occurred, causing hospitalization; other adverse effects can include headaches, nausea, vomiting, muscle jerking, and even short-term coma, though full recovery has been universal ("Bodybuilding Drug" 1992; "Multistate Outbreak" 1994). Prolonged use may cause withdrawal (insomnia, anxiety, and tremor). GHB is especially dangerous when combined with central nervous system (CNS) stimulants such as amphetamines and cocaine.

■ Prevention and Treatment

If the problem of drug abuse among athletes is to be dealt with effectively, sports programs must be designed to discourage inappropriate drug use and assist athletes who have developed drug abuse problems. Coaches and administrators should make it clear to sports participants that substance abuse will never give an athlete a competitive advantage in their programs and will not be tolerated. The Adolescents Training and Learning to Avoid Steroids **(ATLAS) program**, which was developed by Dr. Linn Goldberg of Oregon Health Sciences at the University of Portland, is one of the most successful prevention programs for steroid abuse. Athletes, coaches, and team leaders are trained to educate team members about the effects of anabolic steroid abuse. Because adolescents already know that anabolic steroids build muscles and can increase athletic abilities, both desirable and adverse effects of steroid use are

KEY TERMS

human growth factor (HGF)
a hormone that stimulates normal growth

human growth hormone (HGH)
a designer drug synthetic version of HGF

ATLAS program
Adolescents Training and Learning to Avoid Steroids (ATLAS); an anabolic abuse prevention educational program that empowers student athletes to make the right choices about steroid use

taught. Research has shown that information about anabolic steroids that fails to acknowledge potential benefits creates a credibility gap that can make youths distrustful of the prevention program. The program consists of three components: classroom, weight training, and parent information components to "give the student athletes the knowledge and skills to resist steroid use and achieve their athletic goals in more effective, healthier ways" (Goldberg et al. 1996, p. 1555):

1. The classroom component consists of football coaches and student leaders conducting highly interactive sessions that explore the effects of steroids, the elements of sports nutrition, and strength training alternatives to steroid use. In this setting, while the coaches introduce topics and act as leaders, the students are exploring and learning from one another (Goldberg et al. 1996).

2. In the weight-training component, research staff members conduct seven hands-on sessions that teach the students proper weight training techniques (Goldberg et al. 1996).

3. The parent information component consists of discussions and information sessions with parents. The staff provides nutrition guidelines and seeks compliance while stressing the very best nutrition for the athletes and their families. Parents become more vigilant against steroid use and learn to enjoy well-balanced, nutritious meals (Goldberg et al. 1996).

Briefly summarized, results indicate that the students who participated in this program in comparison with the control group (a group of students not participating in the program) showed they (1) knew more about proper exercise, (2) had a clear understanding of the dangers of using steroids and had become much more sensitized to the harmful effects of such drugs, (3) held more unfavorable views of others' use of anabolic steroids, and (4) were more likely to avoid unhealthy eating (such as frequenting fast-food restaurants) (Goldberg et al. 1996).

Drug Use Among Women

Until recently, little was known about the patterns of female drug abuse. In general, most clinical drug abuse research, including treatment and rehabilitation outcomes, was either conducted in male populations and the results were extrapo-

lated to women or the research was done in general populations with little regard to gender influences (About.com 2007a; Dicker and Leighton 1994; Klee and Jackson 2002; Lin 1994; USDHHS and NIDA 1999;). Most researchers considered drug abuse to be a male problem. Today, the research focusing on women and drug use is better, but a greater amount of study is still needed. Even today, scientists performing even basic research with animals generally prefer male animal models to avoid the hormonal complexities of female animals. However, a growing concern for the importance of unique emotional, social, biochemical, and hormonal features in females has caused researchers to acknowledge the importance of gender differences.

Women More Concerned About Drug Use than Men

Women are expressing greater concerns about drug use than men. When asked whether drug abuse is a greater problem now than 5 years earlier, 51% of women and 42% of men answered "yes" (Drug Strategies 1998). When asked whether drug use is a big concern among youth, 58% of women and 48% of men answered "yes" (Drug Strategies 1998). Further, 58% of women and 50% of men thought it was wrong to reduce prevention funds while increasing prison funds (Drug Strategies 1998). One reason for this discrepancy may be that women traditionally have been primary caregivers; therefore, they feel more responsible about issues that can plague their communities and their families and often feel the need to be more vocal and be in positions that maintain harmony within the family setting. Women also generally express more concerns about safety issues than men because they are more likely to be victims of violent crimes, such as muggings or sexual assaults.

Patterns of Drug Use: Comparing Females with Males

Recent surveys comparing male and female drug use patterns confirm that differences exist among the licit and illicit drug-using populations. Table 16.3 compares annual female and male drug use among respondents ages 19 to 30. The research findings in this table indicate the following gender-related differences in drug use (Johnston et al. 2006b):

1. Overall, females consistently use fewer licit and illicit drugs (30% of females versus 34% of males use illicit drugs).
2. Males have higher annual prevalence rates for nearly all of the specific illicit drugs, with ratios greater than 2 for steroids, PCP, crystal methamphetamine (ice), LSD, and hallucino-

gens other than LSD. For example, among 19- to 30-year-olds, steroids were used by 1.0% of males versus less than 0.1% of females during the prior 12 months, and fewer females use cocaine (5.3%, compared to 8.3% for males), and hallucinogens (2.9% for females compared to 8.3% for males).

3. Other, greater gender differences among 19- to 30-year-olds are found in marijuana use (24.7% for males versus 29.7% for females),

Table 16.3 **Annual Use of Various Types of Drugs by Gender Among Respondent of Modal, Ages 19–30 (Percent of Total Population)**

	FEMALES	MALES	TOTAL
Any illicit drug	30.0	34.0	31.6
Any illicit drug other than marijuana	16.8	20.1	18.1
Alcohol	83.5	84.5	83.9
Five or more drinks in a row in last 2 weeks	28.1	47.0	35.7
Cigarettes	37.1	39.1	37.9
Marijuana	24.7	29.7	26.7
Other narcotics	7.9	9.5	8.5
Tranquilizers*	6.2	7.5	6.8
Cocaine	5.3	8.3	6.5
Amphetamines*	4.4	5.2	4.7
Other cocaine	4.7	8.1	6.0
MDMA (Ecstasy)	2.7	3.0	2.9
Hallucinogens	2.9	5.9	4.1
Sedatives (barbiturates)*	4.1	4.3	4.2
Crack	1.0	1.6	1.2
Crystal methamphetamine (ice)	1.1	2.4	1.6
Inhalants	0.9	1.8	1.3
LSD	0.5	1.1	0.8
Heroin	0.3	0.6	0.5
PCP	0.3	0.8	0.5
Steroids	<0.05	1.0	0.4

*Nonprescription use.

Source: Johnston, L. D., P. M. O'Malley, J. G. Bachman, and J. E. Schulenberg. *Monitoring the Future: National Survey Results on Drug Use, 1975–2005. Volume II: College Students and Adults.* Bethesda, MD: National Institute on Drug Abuse, 2005.

daily alcohol use (8.4% versus 3.2%; not shown in table), and occasions of drinking five or more drinks in a row in the prior 2 weeks (47% versus 28%). This gender difference in occasions of heavy drinking is even greater among young adults than among 12th graders, which is 33% for males versus 23% for females.

4. Females (62.6%) have a greater tendency to drink flavored alcoholic beverages (not shown in table) than males (48.3%). (This is the prevalence rate where females significantly outnumber males in alcohol use.)

5. MDMA (Ecstasy) use is only slightly higher among males than among females in the young adult sample overall (annual prevalence 3.0% versus 2.7%, respectively).

6. The use of narcotics other than heroin outside of medical supervision is at 9.5% annual prevalence for males versus 7.9% for females. Use of Vicodin (not shown in table), one of the most widely used drugs, differs a bit more (11.3% versus 7.5%). There is also a gender contrast for OxyContin (also not shown in the table; annual prevalence of 3.8% for males versus 2.4% for females).

7. Males are also slightly more likely to smoke cigarettes than females (39.1% for males versus 37.1% for females).

8. Steroid use among young adults (19- to 30-year-olds) is much more prevalent among males than females, as is true for 12th graders. Among 12th graders, 2.6% of males reported steroid use in the past year versus 0.4% of females.

One finding that is often hidden by *current* drug use statistics is that nationwide surveys confirm that drug use is increasing among women, often more rapidly than among men (Drug Strategies 1998). From 1990 through 1996, the number of women seeking emergency drug treatment rose more rapidly than the number of men seeking such emergency treatment. Hospital records indicate that there were more women seeking emergency drug treatment for heroin and marijuana (Drug Strategies 1998). Other gender differences are that older women (over 60) tend to abuse tranquilizers, sedatives, and antidepressants (Drug Strategies 1998) and, in some cases, girls in junior high and high school are now surpassing boys with regard to alcohol and tobacco use. Drinking rates are increasing more rapidly for girls than for boys (Drug Strategies 1998), and women in general are more likely than men to become addicted to tobacco.

Two factors that make smoking attractive to women (and girls) are that they believe it reduces stress and controls weight (Drug Strategies 1998).

Although some similarities appear between genders in drug usage rates for specific types of drugs, the general differences in the prevalence rates for females and males compel researchers to look for explanations so that we can better understand and deal with gender-related drug abuse problems.

■ Female Roles and Drug Addiction

Women are expected to take on more responsibilities than in my mother's day. Not only are we expected to work like men, but we also take care of the house, worry about the children, and get dinner on the table. If the house needs cleaning, everyone looks at the woman of the house. Men still have these expectations. I know things are changing with more equality between the sexes, but *real* equality of responsibilities has yet to occur. After everyone gets to bed on weekdays, I have a few drinks in order to calm me down before I go to bed. *(From Venturelli's research files, interview with a 43-year-old female, employed full-time, June 30, 1996.)*

Another interview revealed the following:

My boyfriend does vacuum when I ask, but not much else. Of course, if his boss is coming to visit, then he appears concerned about cleaning the house. How many times is he fast asleep and I am having some hard liquor and a few puffs from a joint after cleaning everything before we get up the next morning. I used to complain but he does not really care about the housework, so I compensate by getting buzzed before going to sleep. *(From Venturelli's research files, interview with a 29-year-old female, employed part-time.)*

To appreciate the impact of drug abuse on women, it is necessary to understand the uniqueness of female roles in our society. Relative to drug abuse problems, women today are often judged by a double standard. Women suffering from drug addictions are often perceived less tolerantly than comparably addicted men (Erickson and Murray 1989). Because of these social biases, women are afraid of being condemned and are less likely to seek professional help for their own personal drug abuse problems. In addition, family, friends, and associates are less inclined to provide drug-dependent women with important emotional support (Klee and Jackson 2002; U.S. Department of Health and Human Services [USDHHS], NIDA 1999).

The image of the alcoholic woman has always been that of one who is boisterous, flirtatious, effusive, and, sometimes, loudmouthed. This may be the person she might become on occasion, but more often she is secluded in the privacy of her apartment or home after getting the kids off to school or having just come home from the office, classroom, or business. She is shy, reclusive to a point, alienated, retrospective, and lacking in self-esteem. Later in her drinking, she may become self-pitying, resentful, and even childishly cruel because of the drug alcohol (Kirkpatrick 1999).

Due to their unique socioeconomic and family roles, women are especially vulnerable to emotional disruptions resulting from divorce, loneliness, and professional failures. Studies suggest that such stresses aggravate tendencies for women to abuse alcohol and other substances (Kirkpatrick 1999; Korolenko and Donskih 1990). More specifically, "women drink from a feeling of inadequacy and from a need for love, the kind of love not found within a sexual relationship but, rather, a love that is deeper and more primal" (Kirkpatrick 1999, p. 1).

In addition, drug addiction can occur in some women as a result of domestic adversities. Consequently, there is a high prevalence of drug dependence in women who are victims of sexual and/or physical abuse (Ladwig and Anderson 1989). "Approximately 70% of women in drug abuse treatment report histories of physical and sexual abuse, with victimization beginning before 11 years of age and occurring repeatedly" (SAMHSA 1999b, p. 1). These physical and emotional traumas result in, or are precursors to, factors leading to drug abuse, such as low self-esteem, self-condemnation, anxiety and personal conflicts, dysfunctional dependencies, and overwhelming feelings of guilt (Kirkpatrick 1999). In addition, because of the crucial nurturing roles women hold, drug abuse problems can be particularly damaging to family stability.

Another unique role for women in drug abuse situations is that of a spouse, significant other, or mother to a drug addict. Often, in both traditional and nontraditional family relationships, women are expected to be nurturing, understanding, and willing to sacrifice to preserve the family integrity. If a family member becomes afflicted by drug dependence, the wife or mother is viewed as a failure. In other words, if the woman had maintained a good home and conducted her domestic chores properly, the family member would not have been driven to drugs (Klee and Jackson 2002; USDHHS, NIDA 1999).

Despite the disruption and considerable stress caused by drug addiction in the home, women continue to bear the burden of raising children, performing domestic chores, and keeping the family together. In addition, women in such circumstances are frequently put at great physical risk. The risk is from an addicted spouse who becomes abusive to his partner or from exposure to sexually transmitted diseases, such as HIV or hepatitis, transmitted by a careless infected partner. The anxiety and frustrations resulting from these stressful circumstances can encourage women themselves to become dependent as they seek emotional relief by using drugs.

■ Women's Response to Drugs

Research continues to lag regarding how women respond to substances of abuse. Although matters are slowly changing, the trend in drug abuse studies is still to avoid female populations; the effects of the drugs in men are still extrapolated to women. Even when drug abuse research is conducted on women, frequently the woman's response is not of primary concern; the objective is to determine the effects on a fetus during pregnancy or an infant during nursing (Klee and Jackson 2002; USDHHS, NIDA 1999).

Although it generally can be assumed that the physiological and drug responses of men and women are similar, some distinctions should be recognized. For example, one study compared the risk for lung cancer in men and women after a lifetime of cigarette smoking. It was found that female smokers were twice as likely to get lung cancer as males who had smoked an identical number of cigarettes in their lifetimes ("Women Smokers" 1994). Another study indicated that women are *three* times more likely to contract lung cancer than men when smoking the same amount of cigarettes (Kirkpatrick 1999). These differences clearly indicate that cigarette smoking is far more dangerous for women than for men. Finally, women's unique response to drugs includes a finding discovered by researchers at the University of California at San Francisco that women respond to a class of painkillers called kappa-opioids, which are ineffective in men (*Science Daily* 2000).

Drug Abuse and Reproduction

A very important physiological distinction that sets women apart from men about taking drugs is their ability to bear children. Because of this unique function, men and women have different endocrine (hormone) systems, organs, and structures, and women have varied drug responses according to their reproductive state. The unique features of women have a substantial impact on the response to drug abuse in the presence and absence of pregnancy.

Drug abuse patterns can influence the outcome of pregnancy even if they occur before a woman becomes pregnant. For example, women who are addicted to heroin are more likely to have poor health, including chronic infections, poor nutrition, and sexually transmitted diseases such as HIV infection, which can damage the offspring if pregnancy occurs. If substances are abused during pregnancy, they may directly affect the fetus and adversely alter its growth and development. The incidence of substance abuse during pregnancy is not known precisely, but undoubtedly hundreds of thousands of children have been exposed to drugs in utero. The effects of individual drugs of abuse taken during pregnancy are discussed in detail in the corresponding chapters, but several specific observations merit reiteration here:

1. Cocaine is a substantial threat for both the pregnant woman and the fetus. Although a number of specific claims for the fetal effects of cocaine are controversial (see Chapter 10), several observations appear legitimate: Cocaine use increases the likelihood of miscarriage when used during pregnancy; cocaine use in the late stages of pregnancy can cause cardiovascular or CNS complications in the baby at birth and immediately thereafter; and due to its vasoconstrictor effects, cocaine may deprive the fetal brain of oxygen, resulting in strokes and permanent physical and mental damage to the child.

2. The impact of alcohol consumption during pregnancy has been well documented and publicized (Mathias 1995). When alcohol is consumed by the mother, it crosses the placenta, but the effect of this drug on the fetus is highly variable and depends on the quantity of alcohol consumed, timing of exposure, maternal drug metabolism, maternal state of health, and presence of other drugs. A particularly alarming consequence of high alcohol intake during pregnancy is an aggregate of physical and men-

tal defects called *fetal alcohol syndrome* (FAS). Characteristics of this syndrome include low birthweight, abnormal facial features, mental retardation, and retarded sensorimotor development. For additional details, see Chapters 7 and 8. In addition to its direct effects on the fetus, alcohol has played a major role in many unwanted pregnancies or has resulted in women's exposure to sexually transmitted diseases. As a CNS depressant, alcohol impairs judgment and reason and, in turn, encourages sexual risk taking that normally would not occur. The results are all too frequently tragic for women (SAMHSA 1999b).

3. Tobacco use during pregnancy is particularly rampant in the United States. Specifically, 20% of the smoking female adult population is pregnant. Some experts suggest smoking cigarettes during pregnancy may pose a greater risk to the fetus than taking cocaine. Tobacco use by pregnant women may interfere with blood flow to the fetus, deprive it of oxygen and nutrition, and disrupt development of its organs — particularly the brain. Also of significant concern is the possibility that exposure of nonsmoking pregnant women to secondhand tobacco smoke may be damaging to the fetus.

4. Other drugs of abuse that have been associated with abnormal fetal development when used during pregnancy include barbiturates, benzodiazepines, amphetamines, marijuana, lysergic acid diethylamide (LSD), and even caffeine when consumed in high doses. Clearly, women should be strongly urged to avoid all substances of abuse, especially during pregnancy.

Women and Alcohol

Alcohol is the drug most widely used and abused by women in the United States. According to the 2005 *National Household Survey on Drug Abuse* among women aged 12 and older, 45.9% used alcohol in the past month and 15.2% reported binge drinking (SAMHSA 2007). Alcohol abuse is also a major problem for women on college campuses, even though male college students are more likely than their female counterparts to use alcohol on a daily basis.

As a rule, women are less likely than men to develop severe alcohol dependence; thus, only 25% of the alcoholics in the United States are female. Women are also likely to initiate their drinking patterns later in life than men (Klee and Jackson 2002; USDHHS, NIDA 1999). Interesting ethnic patterns of alcohol consumption have been reported in females, with black and white women manifesting similar drinking patterns. Although the proportions are similar, black women are more likely to completely abstain from alcohol than white women are.

Women who are dependent on alcohol are usually judged more harshly than men with similar difficulties. Alcoholic males are more likely to be excused because their drinking problems are often perceived as being caused by frustrating work conditions, family demands, economic pressures, or so-called nagging wives and children. In contrast, women with drinking problems are often perceived as spoiled or pampered, weak, deviant, or immoral. Such stigmas, referred to as labels in Chapter 2 (see labeling theory), cause women to experience more guilt and anxiety about their alcohol dependence and discourage them from admitting their drug problems and seeking professional help (Kirkpatrick 1999).

The principal reasons for excessive alcohol consumption in women range from loneliness, boredom, and domestic stress in the housewife drinker to financial problems, sexual harassment, lack of challenge, discrimination, and powerlessness in the career woman. Depression is often associated with alcohol problems in women, although it is not clear whether this condition is a cause or an effect of the excessive use.

Women's Physiological Responses to Alcohol Health consequences for excessive alcohol consumption appear to be more severe for women than for men. For example, alcoholic women are more likely to suffer premature death than alcoholic men. In addition, liver disease is more common and occurs at a younger age in female drinkers than in male alcoholics. In general, higher morbidity rates are experienced by alcoholic women than their male counterparts.

Several explanations have been suggested for the higher rate of adverse effects seen in female alcoholics. Their higher blood alcohol concentrations may be due to a smaller blood volume and more rapid absorption into the bloodstream after drinking. Alternatively, slower alcohol metabolism in the stomach and liver might cause more alcohol to reach the brain and other organs as well as prolong exposure to the drug following consumption (Goldstein 1995). Studies have shown that for a woman of average size, one alcoholic drink has

effects equivalent to two drinks in an average-size man (see Chapter 7).

Dealing with Women's Alcohol Problems Alcoholic consumption varies considerably in women, ranging from total abstinence or an occasional drink to daily intake of large amounts of alcohol. Clearly, much is yet to be learned about the cause of some women's excessive drinking and dependence on alcohol. The role of genetic factors in predisposing women to alcohol-related problems is still unclear. The environment is certainly a major factor contributing to excessive alcohol consumption in women. It is well established that depression, stress, and trauma encourage alcohol consumption because of the antianxiety and amnesic properties of this drug. Because of unreasonable societal expectations and numerous socioeconomic disadvantages, women are especially vulnerable to the emotional upheavals that encourage excessive alcohol consumption.

As with all drug dependence problems, prevention is the preferred solution to alcohol abuse by women. Alcohol usually becomes problematic when it is no longer used occasionally to enhance social events but used daily to deal with personal problems. Such alcohol dependence can best be avoided by using constructive techniques to manage stress and frustrations. Because of unique female roles and society's expectations, women especially need to learn to be assertive with family members, associates in the workplace (including bosses), and other contacts in their daily routines. By expecting and demanding equitable treatment and consideration in personal and professional activities, stress and anxiety can often be reduced. Education, career training, and development of communication abilities can be particularly important in establishing a sense of self-worth (see also Chapter 17). With these skills and confidence, women are better able to manage problems associated with their lives and less likely to resort to drugs for an escape.

Women and Prescription Drugs

Women are more likely than men to suffer depression, anxiety, and panic attacks (About.com 2006); be unable to express anger; be victims of physical and sexual abuse; and be subject to overwhelming guilt feelings (Kirkpatrick 1999). Consequently, they are also more likely to take and become addicted to the prescription drugs used in treating these disorders. Because these drugs are used as part of psychiatric therapy and under the supervision of a physician, drug dependence frequently is not recognized and may be ignored for months or even years. This type of legitimate drug abuse occurs most often in elderly women and includes the use of sedatives, antidepressants, and antianxiety medications. A recent study found that one in four women older than age 60 takes at least one of these drugs daily and that some of them develop serious drug problems (Drug Strategies 1998). Excessive use of these drugs by older women results in side effects such as insomnia, mood fluctuations, and disruption of cognitive and motor functions that can substantially compromise the quality of life.

■ Treatment of Drug Dependency in Women

As previously discussed, women are less likely than men to seek treatment for, and rehabilitation from, drug dependence (Kirkpatrick 1999). Possible reasons for their reluctance are as follows:

1. In more traditional families, women have unique roles with high expectations. They are expected to assume demanding and ongoing responsibilities, such as motherhood, child rearing, and family maintenance that cannot be postponed and often cannot be delegated, even temporarily, to others. Consequently, many women feel that they are too essential for the well-being of other family members to leave the home and seek time-consuming treatment for drug abuse problems.

2. Drug treatment centers often are not designed to handle the unique health requirements of females — thus, women face more obstacles. These obstacles involve barriers to treatment entry, treatment engagement, and long-term recovery (NIDA 1999). Women have been shown to have greater health needs than men due to more frequent respiratory, genitourinary (associated with the sex and urinary organs), and circulatory problems. If drug treatment centers are not capable of providing the necessary physical care, women are less likely to participate in associated drug abuse programs.

3. Drug-dependent women are more inclined to be unemployed than their male counterparts and more likely to be receiving public support. The implications of this difference are twofold. First, because concerns about one's job often motivate drug-dependent workers to seek treatment, this issue is less likely to be a factor in unemployed women. Second, without the financial security of a job, unemployed women may feel that good treatment for their drug problems is unaffordable. (For more on treatment, see Chapter 18.)

The unique female requirements must be recognized and considered if women are to receive adequate treatment for drug dependence. Some considerations on how to achieve this objective include the following: (1) availability of female-sensitive services; (2) nonpunitive and noncoercive treatment that incorporates supportive behavior change approaches; and (3) treatment for a wide range of medical problems, mental disorders, and psychosocial problems (NIDA 1999). The role of motherhood needs to be used in a positive manner in drug treatment strategies. For most women, motherhood is viewed with high regard and linked to self-esteem. Approximately 90% of female drug abusers are in their childbearing years, and many have family responsibilities. Consequently, treatment approaches need to be tailored to allow women to fulfill their domestic responsibilities and satisfy their maternal obligations.

Women dependent on drugs often lack important coping skills. Because many women lead restricted, almost isolated lives that focus entirely on domestic responsibilities, they face limited alternatives for dealing with stressful situations. Under these restrictive circumstances, the use of drugs to cope with anxieties and frustrations is very appealing. To enhance their ability to cope, drug-dependent women need to develop communication and assertiveness skills. Further, they need to be encouraged to control situations rather than allowing themselves to be controlled by the situation. Specific techniques that have proven useful in coping management are exercise (particularly relaxation types), relaxing visual imagery, personal hobbies, and outside interests that require active participation. Many drug-dependent women require experiences that divert their attention from the source of their frustrations while affording them an opportunity to succeed and develop a sense of self-worth.

Finally, one research study found that the most effective treatment for women included a mutually supportive therapeutic environment that addressed the following issues: psychopathology (such as depression); a woman's role as mother; interpersonal relationships; and the need for parenting education. Another study found that cocaine-using women whose children were living with them during residential treatment remained in the treatment programs significantly longer than women whose children were not living with them at the facility. Thus, having the children in the treatment facility provides opportunities to assess and meet women's needs, which in turn affects the women's prognosis (NIDA 1999; About.com 2007b).

Prevention of Drug Dependence in Women

The best treatment for drug addiction is prevention. To help prevent drug problems in women as opposed to men, socioeconomic disadvantages need to be recognized as factors that make women more vulnerable to drug dependence, especially from prescription medication. Women need to learn that nondrug approaches are often more desirable for dealing with situational problems than prescribed medications. For example, for older women suffering loneliness, isolation, or depression, it is better to encourage participation in outside interests, such as hobbies and service activities. In addition, social support and concern should be encouraged from family, friends, and neighbors. Such nonmedicinal approaches are preferred over prescribing sedatives and hypnotics to cope with emotional distresses. Similarly, medical conditions such as obesity, constipation, or insomnia should be treated by changing lifestyle, eating, and exercise habits rather than using drug "bandage therapy."

When women are prescribed drugs, they should ask about the associated risks, especially as they relate to drug abuse potential. Frequently, drug dependency develops insidiously and is not recognized by either the patient or attending physician until it is already firmly established. If a woman taking medication is aware of the potential for becoming dependent and is instructed on how to avoid its occurrence, the problems of dependence and abuse can frequently be averted. (See Chapter 17 for more on prevention and education.)

Drug Use in Adolescent Subcultures

I love waking up in the morning and smoking a nice fat joint. I live above the garage now, and my mom lives across the yard from the garage. This is a great living arrangement! I go to my room a few hours before crashing on many school nights, get high, drink some vodka that my older brother buys for me, then finally crash. In the morning, I always wake myself up so my mom stays away from my room, and my hideaway stash box is always locked. I roll me a joint and get a little high before I greet mom in the morning for a quick breakfast. I think she gets high too, but if I ask her and she says "no," what if she then asks me and gets all suspicious and shit? Besides, my Uncle Prentice always gets high with me, so I still think my mom really does not care about smoking weed. In fact, I know she is more worried about me drinking and driving than my friend "Mary Jane" [nickname for marijuana]. That's just my private life and no one needs to know. *(From Venturelli's research files, male, age 18, residing in Chicago, July 10, 2000.)*

From ages 13 through 18, adolescents are more likely to experience heightened psychological, social, and biological changes. Often, such internal and external changes are manifested by emotional outbursts. Why do such changes and urges arise? The adolescent's body is stretching, growing, and sometimes appearing out of control due to the hormonal changes of puberty.

Adolescents are uncertain and confused about not knowing who or what they are becoming. They are often confused as to their worth to family, peers, society, and even to themselves (Kantrowitz and Wingert 1999). Adding to the frustration of growing up, the cultural status of adolescents is poorly defined. They find themselves trapped in a "no-man's land" between the acceptance, simplicity, and security of childhood, and the stress, complexities, expectations, independence, and responsibilities of adulthood. Not only do adolescents have difficulty deciding who and what they are, but adults are equally unsure as to how to deal with these transitional human beings. While the grown-up world tries to push adolescents out of the secure nest of childhood, it is not willing to bestow the full membership and rights of adulthood upon them (Johnson et al. 1996; Kantrowitz and Wingert 1999).

Because of their uniquely rapid development, several developmental issues are particularly important to evolving adolescents (Elmen and Offer 1993; Johnson et al. 1996; Kantrowitz and Wingert 1999):

- Discovering and understanding their distinctive identities
- Forming more intimate and caring relationships with others
- Establishing a sense of autonomy

- Coming to terms with the hormone-related feelings of puberty and expressing their sexuality
- Learning to become productive contributors to society
- Feeling alone and alienated

Due to all this developmental confusion, "normal" behavior for the adolescent is difficult to define precisely. Experts generally agree that persistent low self-esteem, depression, feelings of alienation, and other emotional disturbances can be troublesome for teenagers. Most adolescents are relatively well adjusted and are able to cope with **sociobiological changes**. Emotionally stable adolescents relate well to family and peers and function productively within their schools, neighborhoods, and communities. The majority of adolescents experience transient problems, which they are able to resolve, but some become deeply disturbed and are unable to grow out of their problems without counseling and therapy (see also Jayson 2007). Those adolescents who are unable or unwilling to ask for assistance often turn to destructive devices, such as drugs or violence (Kantrowitz and Wingert 1999), for relief from their emotional dilemmas.

■ Why Adolescents Use Drugs

Although there is no such thing as a typical substance-abusing adolescent, certain physiological, psychological, and sociological factors are often associated with drug problems in this subculture (Johnson et al. 1996). In looking at an array of explanations regarding why adolescents use drugs, one recent study by Columbia University's National Center on Addiction and Substance Abuse found that

> Children ages 12 to 17 who are frequently bored are 50% more likely to smoke, drink, get drunk and use illegal drugs. In addition, kids with $25 or more a week in spending money are nearly twice as likely to smoke, drink or use drugs as children with less money. Anxiety is another risk factor. The study found that

youngsters who said they're highly stressed are twice as likely as low-stress kids to smoke, drink or use drugs. (Associated Press 2003)

It is important to remember that not all drug use by adolescents means therapy is necessary or even desirable. More traditional proven and accepted explanations stress that most excessive drug use that often leads to abuse by adolescents results from the desire to experience new behaviors and sensations, a passing fancy of maturation, an attempt to relieve peer pressure, feelings of alienation, or an inclination to enhance a social setting with chemistry (Jayson 2007; Kantrowitz and Wingert 1999). Most of these adolescent users will not go on to develop problematic dependence on drugs and, for the most part, should be watched but not aggressively confronted or treated. The adolescents who usually have significant difficulty with drug use are those who turn to drugs for extended support as coping devices and become drug reliant because they are unable to find alternative, less destructive solutions to their problems. Several major factors can contribute to serious drug dependence in adolescents (Archambault 1992; Johnson et al. 1996; Walsh and Scheinkman 1992).

Research indicates that the most important factor influencing drug use among adolescents is peer drug use (Bahr et al. 1995; Jayson 2007; Kandel 1980; NIDA 1999; Swadi 1992; Winters 1997). Consequently, eventual transition to heavier substance use also directly correlates with peer use (Steinberg et al. 1994). Conversely, individuals whose peer groups do not use or abuse drugs are less likely to use drugs themselves (Venturelli 2000). Research has identified a correlation between strong family bonds and non–drug-using peer groups (NIDA 1999). "Adolescents with higher [stronger] family bonds are less likely than adolescents with lower [weaker] bonds to have close friends who use drugs" (Bahr et al. 1995, p. 466). In addition, family bonding is highly correlated with educational commitment. In essence, family bonding influences choice of friends and educational goals and aspirations (Bahr et al. 1995).

Three noteworthy differences exist between male and female adolescents: (1) Males demonstrate a stronger association between educational achievement and family bonds; (2) among females, peer drug use is negatively associated with family bonds, so peer drug use and family bonds are not likely to influence the use of licit and illicit drugs by females; and (3) the impact of age on

KEY TERMS

sociobiological changes
the belief that biological forces (largely genes) have a direct influence on the root causes of social psychological behavior

peer drug use (the younger the age, the more vulnerable to peer pressure) and on the amount of alcohol consumed can be predicted with slightly greater accuracy for males than females (Teen Challenge 2000).

Many adolescents use drugs to help cope with boredom, unpleasant feelings, emotions, and stress or to relieve depression, reduce tension, and reduce alienation (Teen Challenge 2000). Psychological differences among adolescents who are frequent drug users, experimenters, and abstainers often can be traced to early childhood, the quality of parenting in their homes, and their home environment. It has been suggested that certain types of parents are more likely to raise children at high risk for substance abuse (Archambault 1992). For example, an alcoholic adolescent usually has at least one parent of the following types:

Alcoholic. This parent serves as a negative role model for the adolescent. The child sees the parent dealing with problems by consuming drugs. Even though drinking alcohol is not illegal for adults, it sends the message that drugs can solve problems. The guilt-ridden alcoholic parent is unable to provide the child with a loving, supportive relationship. In addition, the presence of the alcoholic parent is often disruptive or abusive to the family and creates fear or embarrassment in the child.

Nonconsuming and condemning. This type of parent not only chooses to abstain from drinking but also is very judgmental about drinkers and condemns them for their behavior. Such persons, who are often referred to as *teetotalers,* have a rigid, moralistic approach to life. Their black-and-white attitudes frequently prove inadequate and unforgiving in an imperfect, gray world. Children in these families can feel inferior and guilty when they are unable to live up to parental expectations, and they may resort to drugs to cope with their frustrations.

Overly demanding. This type of parent forces unrealistic expectations on his or her children. These parents often live vicariously through their children and require sons and daughters to pursue endeavors in which the parents were unable to succeed. Particular emphasis may be placed on achievements in athletics, academics, or career selections. Even though the parents' efforts may be well intended, the children get the message that their parents are more concerned about what they are than who they are. These parents frequently encourage sibling rivalries to enhance performance, but such competitions always yield a loser.

Overly protective. These types of parents do not give their children a chance to develop a sense of self-worth and independence. Because the parents deprive their children of the opportunities to learn how to master their abilities within their surroundings, the children are not able to develop confidence and a positive self-image. Such children are frequently unsure about who they are and what they are capable of achieving. Parents who use children to satisfy their own ego needs or who are trying to convince themselves that they really do like their children tend to be overly protective.

The principal influence for learned behavior is usually the home; therefore, several other family-related variables can significantly affect adolescents' decision to start, maintain, or cease a drug habit (Kinney 2000; Lawson and Lawson 1992). For example, adolescents usually learn their attitudes about drug use from family models. In other words, what are the drug-consuming patterns of parents and siblings? Adolescents are more likely to develop drug problems if other members of the family (1) are excessive in their drug (legal or illegal) consumption, (2) approve of the use of illicit drugs, or (3) use drugs as a problem-solving strategy.

Sociological factors that damage self-image can also encourage adolescent drug use. Feelings of rejection may cause poor relationships with family members, peers, school personnel, or coworkers. Ethnic differences sometimes contribute to a poor self-image because people of minority races or cultures are frequently socially excluded and are sometimes viewed as being inferior and undesirable by the majority population. This type of negative message is very difficult for adolescents to deal with. Sometimes, to ensure acceptance, adolescents adopt the attitudes and behaviors of their affiliated groups. If a peer group, or a gang, views drug use as cool, desirable, or even necessary, members (or those desiring membership) feel compelled to conform and become involved in drugs.

■ Patterns of Drug Use in Adolescents

Growing minorities of younger teenagers are exposed to drug use within their own families. A recent study reported that "20% of . . . 600 teens in drug treatment in New York, Texas, Florida and California said they have shared drugs other than alcohol with their parents, and that about 5% of the teens actually were introduced to drugs — usually marijuana — by their moms and dads" (Leinwand 2000, p. 1). In 1999, Partnership for a Drug-Free America reported similar shocking findings (Leinwand 2000).

Jason, 17, a recovering addict from an upper-middle-class family in Simi Valley, California, says he wishes his father had been more of a parent and less of a buddy when it came to marijuana. "[Jason] made his drug purchase: a $5 bag of pot. Jason says his father walked by his room's open door as he was stashing it in a dresser drawer. [His father then] '. . . told about his marijuana use,' Jason says. 'We went into his [dad's] office, and he had a (water pipe) and we got high together.' [Jason reports that at the time, he] '. . . thought it was *sooo* cool'" (Leinwand 2000, p. 2).

In another example, La'kiesha, 15, of southern California, is the third generation of a family in which members have become addicted to drugs. La'kiesha said her grandmother smoked pot regularly and gave her a few puffs when she was 5 years old, to settle her down before bedtime (Leinwand 2000).

A more recent phenomenon especially in middle- and upper-middle class families is that teenagers are being introduced to drugs or using drugs with parents. Years ago, alcohol may have been shared between parents and their children in a low percentage of cases; however, today there are parents who either have been or are currently using illicit drugs and they appear to be influencing the use of these drugs by their children. Currently, this occurs in a small minority of families; nevertheless, it remains shocking.

Recent surveys regarding drug use patterns found that by 12th grade (seniors in high school), approximately 75.1% of the teens had used alcohol, approximately 50% had used cigarettes, 44.8% had used marijuana, and 11.4% had used inhalants in 2005 (see Table 16.4).

Table 16.4 Drug Use Among 8th, 10th, and 12th Graders

Data show the percentages of 8th, 10th, and 12th graders who used both licit and illicit types of drugs in 2002, 2003, and 2004, and 2005.

	8TH GRADERS				10TH GRADERS				12TH GRADERS			
	2002	2003	2004	2005	2002	2003	2004	2005	2002	2003	2004	2005
Any Illicit Drug												
Lifetime	24.5	22.8	21.5	21.4	44.6	41.4	39.8	38.2	53.0	51.1	51.1	50.4
Annual	17.7	16.1	15.2	15.5	34.8	32.0	31.1	29.8	41.0	39.3	38.8	38.4
30-day	10.4	9.7	8.4	8.5	20.8	19.5	18.3	17.3	25.4	24.1	23.4	23.1
Alcohol												
Lifetime	47.0	45.6	43.9	41.0	66.9	66.0	64.2	63.2	78.4	76.6	76.8	75.1
Annual	38.7	34.2	36.7	33.9	60.0	59.3	58.2	56.7	71.5	70.1	70.6	68.6
30-day	19.6	19.7	18.6	17.1	35.4	35.4	35.2	33.2	48.6	47.5	48.4	47.0
Cigarettes (Any Use)												
Lifetime	31.4	28.4	27.9	25.9	47.4	43.0	40.7	38.9	57.2	53.7	52.8	50.0
Annual*	—	—	—	—	—	—	—	—	—	—	—	—
30-day	10.7	10.2	9.2	9.3	17.7	16.7	16.0	14.9	26.7	24.4	25.0	23.2

Table 16.4 (continued)

	8TH GRADERS				10TH GRADERS				12TH GRADERS			
	2002	2003	2004	2005	2002	2003	2004	2005	2002	2003	2004	2005
Marijuana/Hashish												
Lifetime	19.2	17.5	16.3	16.5	38.7	36.4	35.1	34.1	47.8	46.1	45.7	44.8
Annual	14.6	12.8	11.8	12.2	30.3	28.2	27.5	26.6	36.2	34.9	34.4	33.6
30-day	8.3	7.5	6.4	6.6	17.8	17.0	15.9	15.2	21.5	21.2	19.9	19.8
Inhalants												
Lifetime	15.2	15.8	17.3	17.1	13.5	12.7	12.4	13.1	11.7	11.2	10.9	11.4
Annual	7.7	8.7	9.6	9.5	5.8	5.4	5.9	6.0	4.5	3.9	4.2	5.0
30-day	3.8	4.1	4.5	4.2	2.4	2.2	2.4	2.2	1.5	1.5	1.5	2.0
Amphetamines												
Lifetime	8.7	8.4	7.5	7.4	14.9	13.1	11.9	11.1	16.8	14.4	15.0	13.1
Annual	5.5	5.5	4.9	4.9	10.7	9.0	8.5	7.8	5.5	5.0	4.6	3.9
30-day	2.8	2.7	2.3	2.3	5.2	4.3	4.0	3.7	5.5	5.0	4.6	3.9
Hallucinogens												
Lifetime	3.3	3.2	3.0	3.8	6.3	5.9	5.8	5.8	9.2	9.0	8.7	8.8
Annual	2.6	2.6	2.2	2.4	4.7	4.1	4.1	4.0	6.6	5.9	6.2	5.5
30-day	1.2	1.2	1.0	1.1	1.6	1.5	1.6	1.5	2.3	1.8	1.9	1.9
Cocaine												
Lifetime	3.6	3.6	3.4	3.7	6.1	5.1	5.4	5.2	7.9	7.7	8.1	8.0
Annual	2.3	2.2	2.0	2.2	4.0	3.3	3.7	3.5	5.0	4.8	5.3	5.1
30-day	1.2	1.2	1.0	1.1	1.6	1.3	1.7	1.5	2.3	1.8	1.9	1.9
Crack Cocaine												
Lifetime	2.5	2.5	2.4	2.4	3.6	2.7	2.6	2.5	3.8	3.6	3.9	3.5
Annual	0.8	0.7	0.6	0.6	1.0	0.7	0.8	0.7	1.2	0.9	1.0	1.0
30-day	0.8	0.7	0.6	0.6	1.0	0.7	0.8	0.7	1.2	0.9	1.0	1.0
Steroids												
Lifetime	2.5	2.5	1.9	1.7	3.5	3.0	2.4	2.0	4.0	3.5	3.4	2.6
Annual	1.5	1.4	1.1	1.1	2.2	1.7	1.5	1.3	2.5	2.1	2.5	1.5
30-day	0.8	0.7	0.5	0.5	1.0	0.8	0.8	0.6	1.4	1.3	1.6	0.9
Heroin												
Lifetime	1.6	1.6	1.6	1.5	1.8	1.5	1.5	1.5	1.7	1.5	1.5	1.5
Annual	0.9	0.9	1.0	0.8	1.1	0.7	0.9	0.9	1.0	0.8	0.9	0.8
30-day	0.5	0.4	0.5	0.5	0.5	0.3	0.5	0.5	0.5	0.4	0.5	0.5

*Not available at time of printing.

Source: Johnston, L. D., P. M. O'Malley, J. G. Bachman, and J. E. Schulenberg. *Monitoring the Future: National Results on Adolescent Drug Use, Overview of Key Findings.* Bethesda, MD: National Institute on Drug Abuse, 2006.

■ Current Changes in Teen Drug Use Cause Concern

There are now more new users (12 and older) of prescription drugs than any other illegal drug — even marijuana. Teens are turning away from street drugs and the stigma that goes along with using them, and abusing prescription drugs to get the same type of high. Many young people are under the false notion that prescription and OTC drugs are medically safer, when in fact, they can be just as dangerous and addictive as street drugs (National Youth Anti-Drug Media Campaign n.d.).

In a press conference recently, White House drug czar John Walters stated "The drug dealer is us . . ." (CNN.com 2007). What the national drug policy director was alluding to was that ". . . many teenagers are obtaining drugs over the Internet, getting them free from friends, or taking them from someone's medicine cabinet . . ." and that ". . . 2.1 million teenagers abused prescription drugs in 2005" (CNN.com 2007).

This same source indicates that although teen marijuana use declined from 30.1% to 25.8% from 2002 to 2006, use of OxyContin rose among 12th graders, but not among 8th or 10th graders. Since 2002, annual prevalence has increased almost 40% among 12th graders, to 5.5% in 2005. Considering the addictive potential of this drug, this rate seems quite high for them to have attained. Annual prevalence for 8th graders is 1.8% and for 10 graders, 3.2% (Johnston et al. 2006a). Finally, "Teens are also abusing stimulants like Adderall and anti-anxiety drugs like Xanax because they are readily available and perceived as safer than street drugs" says White House drug czar Walters (CNN.com 2007). The extent of naiveté is best illustrated by the interview of one female in Indiana, as stated in the *Daily News*, Muncie, on November 6, 2006: "It's not like I'm taking cocaine or crack — it's OK, these are pharmaceutical drugs made by professionals who know what they are doing" (National Youth Anti-Drug Media Campaign n.d.).

The use of prescription-type drugs by high numbers of young people is of special concern. There is a long-term gradual increase in their use of sedatives (including barbiturates), tranquilizers, and narcotics other than heroin. If amphetamines are included, about one in four 12th graders (23.5%) report such use at some time in their life, while one in six (16.7%) report such use in just the past year. Excluding amphetamines, the numbers using any of the three classes of prescription drugs that are central nervous system depressants (sedatives/barbiturates, tranquilizers, or narcotics other than heroin) are one in five (19.5%) 12th graders using in their lifetime and one in seven (13.9%) using in the prior 12 months. These prescription-type drugs have become more important in the nation's larger drug abuse problem, largely as a result of their gradual increase in popularity over an extended period of time (Johnston et al. 2006a). Finally, another type of illicit drug use is inhalant use. Nearly a third (30%) have used inhalants as early as 8th grade, when most students are only 13 or 14 years old.

Two licit drugs plaguing early and mid-teens are cigarettes and alcohol. Half (50%) of American young people have tried cigarettes by 12th grade, and nearly a quarter (23%) of 12th graders are *current* smokers. Even as early as 8th grade, more than a quarter (26%) have tried cigarettes, and 1 in 11 (9%) already has become a current smoker. Alcohol use also remains extremely widespread among today's teenagers. Three out of every four students (75%) have consumed alcohol (more than just a few sips) by the end of high school; about two-fifths (41%) have done so by 8th grade. In fact, more than half (58%) of the 12th graders and a fifth (20%) of the 8th graders in 2005 report having been drunk at least once in their life (Johnston et al. 2006a).

■ Adolescent Versus Adult Drug Abuse

Adolescent patterns of drug abuse are very different from drug use patterns in adults (Moss et al. 1994). The uniqueness of adolescent drug abuse means that drug-dependent teenagers usually are not successfully treated with adult-directed therapy. For example, compared with adults who abuse drugs, drug-using adolescents are (1) more likely to be involved in criminal activity and at earlier ages; (2) more likely to have other members of the family who abuse drugs; (3) more likely to be associated with a dysfunctional family that engages in emotional and/or physical abuse of its members; and (4) more likely to begin drug use because of curiosity or peer pressure (Bahr et al. 1995; Daily 1992b; Hoshino 1992; Steinberg et al. 1994; Teen Challenge 2000). Such differences need to be considered when developing adolescent-targeted treatment programs.

■ Consequences and Coincidental Problems

Researchers have concluded that the problem of adolescent drug use is a symptom and not a cause of personal social maladjustment. Even so, because of the pharmacological actions of drugs, routine use can contribute to school and social failures, unintended injuries (usually automobile-related), criminal and violent behavior, sexual risk taking, depression, and suicide (Curry and Spergel 1997).

It is important to realize that, because serious drug abuse is usually the result of emotional instability, consequences of the underlying disorders may be expressed with chemical dependence, making diagnosis and treatment more difficult. The undesirable coincidental problems may include self-destruction, risk taking, abuse, or negative group behaviors. Some of these adolescent problems and their relationship to drug abuse are discussed in the following sections.

Adolescent Suicide

Current research shows that although no cause-and-effect relationship exists between use of alcohol and/or other drugs and suicide, such drugs are often contributing factors (Minnesota Institute of Public Health 1995). Adolescents are particularly vulnerable to suicide actions; in fact, white males between 14 and 20 years old are the most likely to commit suicide in the United States (Daily 1992b). Further, the teenage suicide rate has doubled since 1980 (Siegel and Senna 1997). "Suicides among young people continue to be a serious problem. Each year in the U.S., thousands of teenagers commit suicide. Suicide is the third leading cause of death for 15-to-24-year-olds, and the sixth leading cause of death for 5-to-14-year-olds" (American Academy of Child and Adolescent Psychiatry 2004). Twenty percent to 36% of suicide victims have a history of alcohol abuse or were drinking shortly before their suicide. Some experts have described severe chemical dependence as a form of slow, drug-related suicide. For clinicians, every case of serious drug addiction conceals a suicidal individual because all drug abuse inevitably constitutes a game of life and death very similar to "Russian roulette," which comes back into fashion at certain times and under certain circumstances (Bergeret 1981).

Clearly, many teenagers who abuse alcohol and other drugs possess a self-destructive attitude, as this quote from an online chat with Dr. David Shaf-fer, a teen suicide expert, demonstrates: "[T]wo-thirds of all suicides amongst boys occur in boys who are abusing alcohol or other drugs; so the link between suicide and alcohol and certain drugs, like cocaine and Ecstasy and other stimulant drugs, is a very close one" (Schaefer et al. 1993, p. 39).

According to Shaffer, adolescents who attempt suicide are more likely to (1) have disciplinary problems, then abuse alcohol and feel even more depressed; (2) be very anxious and not display any bad behavior problems; or (3) have a perfectionist attitude and never be satisfied with their outcomes. Nearly all suffer from depression before their suicide attempts. Females generally differ from males in that they are prone to even greater amounts of depression with fewer cases of alcohol or other drug abuse (ABC News 2000).

Besides posing a direct health threat because of their physiological effects, drugs of abuse can precipitate suicide attempts due to their pharmacological impact. A number of studies have found a very high correlation between acute suicidal behavior and drug use (Buckstein et al. 1993). One report noted that adolescent alcoholics have a suicide rate 58 times greater than the national average. In another study, 30% of adolescent alcoholics had made suicide attempts, although 92% admitted to a history of having suicidal thoughts (Daily 1992b).

It has been speculated that the incidence of suicide in drug-consuming adolescents is high because both types of behavior are the consequence of an inability to develop fundamental adult attributes of confidence, self-esteem, and independence. When drug use does not make up for their need for these characteristics, the resulting frustrations are intensified and ultimately played out in the suicide act.

Most adolescents experiment with drugs for reasons not related to antisocial or deviant behavior but rather due to curiosity, desire for recreation, boredom, desire to gain new insights and experiences, or urge to heighten social interactions. These adolescents are not likely to engage in self-destructive behavior. In addition, adolescents from "healthy" family environments are not likely to attempt suicide. Specifically, Daily (1992b) stated that the families least likely to have suicidal members are those that

- Express love and show mutual concern
- Are tolerant of differences and overlook failings
- Encourage the development of self-confidence and self-expression

- Have parents who assume strong leadership roles but are not autocratic
- Have interaction characterized by humor and good-natured teasing
- Are able to serve as a source of joy and happiness to their members

Suicide is more likely to be attempted by those adolescents who turn to alcohol and other drugs to help them cope with serious emotional and personality conflicts and frustrations. These susceptible teenagers represent approximately 5% of the adolescent population (Beschner and Friedman 1985; Siegel and Senna 1997). Wright (1985) found that four features significantly contribute to the likelihood of suicidal thought in high school students:

1. Parents with interpersonal conflicts who often use an adolescent child with drug problems as the scapegoat for family problems
2. Fathers who have poor, and often confrontational, relationships with their children
3. Parents who are viewed by their adolescent children as being emotionally unstable, usually suffering from perpetual anger and depression
4. A sense of frustration, desperation, and inability to resolve personal and emotional difficulties through traditional means

Clearly, it is important to identify those adolescents who are at risk for suicide and to provide immediate care and appropriate emotional support.

Sexual Violence and Drugs

Alcohol use has been closely associated with almost every type of sexual abuse in which the adolescent is victimized. "For the perpetrator, being under the influence may remove both physical and psychological inhibitors which keep people from acting out violently. They may also use alcohol or drugs as an excuse for criminal behavior" (Wisconsin Coalition Against Sexual Assault [WCASA] 1997, p. 13). For example, alcohol is by far the most significant factor in date, acquaintance, and gang rapes involving teenagers (Parrot 1988; Prendergast 1994). The evidence for alcohol involvement in incest is particularly overwhelming. Approximately 4 million children in America live in incestuous homes with alcoholic parents. In addition, 42% of drug-abusing female adolescents have been victims of sexual abuse (Daily 1992a). It is estimated that almost half of the offenders consume alcohol before molesting a child and at least one-third of the perpetrators are

chronic alcoholics. Finally, 85% of child molesters were sexually abused themselves as children, usually at the same age as their victims, and the vast majority of these molesters abused drugs as adolescents (Daily 1992a).

These very disturbing associations illustrate the relationship between drugs and violent sexual behavior both in terms of initiating the act and because of the act. The effects of such sexual violence are devastating and far-reaching. Thus, incest victims are themselves more likely than the general population to abuse drugs as adolescents and to engage in antisocial delinquency, prostitution, depression, and suicide (Daily 1992a).

Gangs and Drugs

The very disturbing involvement of adolescents in gangs and gang-related activities and violence is a social phenomenon that first became widely recognized in the 1950s and 1960s. Hollywood, for example, introduced America to the problems of adolescent gangs in the classic movies *Blackboard Jungle* and *West Side Story*. Although the basis for gang involvement has not changed over the years, the levels of violence and public concern have increased dramatically. Many communities consider gang-related problems to be their number one social issue. Access to sophisticated weaponry and greater mobility have drawn unsuspecting neighborhoods and innocent bystanders into the often-violent clashes of **intragang** and **intergang** warfare. Individuals and communities have been reacting angrily to this growing menace. To deal effectively with the threats of gang-initiated violence and crime, however, it is important to understand why gangs form, what their objectives are, how they are structured, and how to discourage adolescent involvement.

Children often join gangs because they are neglected by their parents, lack positive role models, and fail to receive adequate adult supervision. Other motivations for joining a gang include peer pressures, low self-esteem, and the perceived easy acquisition of money from gang-related drug dealing and other criminal activities.

KEY TERMS

intragang
between members of the *same* gang

intergang
between members of *different* gangs

In comparison to traditional, formal youth organizations, juvenile gangs may appear disorganized. Research shows, however, that verbal rules, policies, customs, and hierarchies of command are rigidly observed within the gang. Thus, common values and attitudes exist:

1. Gang membership is usually defined in socioeconomic, racial, and ethnic terms, and adolescents involved have similar backgrounds.
2. Gang members are distinguished by a distinctive and well-defined dress code. Violation of this code by members, or mimicking of the dress code by nongang members, can result in ostracism, ridicule, physical abuse, and violence.
3. Leadership and seniority within the gang are defined by vested time in belonging to the gang, age, loyalty, and demonstrated delinquent cleverness (often related to drug dealing and other crimes).
4. Gang members use gang slang to ensure *camaraderie* and group loyalty.

Although a stable home life does not ensure that an adolescent will not become involved with gang-related activity, a strong family environment and guidance from respected parents and guardians are clearly deterrents (Lale 1992). Many gang members are children from dysfunctional, broken, or single-parent homes. Many parents are aware of their children's gang involvement but they lack the skill, confidence, and authority to deter the gang or curtail drug involvement of their teenagers. To make matters worse, ineffective parents often discourage or even interfere with involvement by outside authorities due to misdirected loyalty to their children and/or to avoid embarrassment to their family and community.

Because troubled adolescents are often estranged from their families, they are particularly influenced by their peer groups. These teenagers are most likely to associate with groups whose members have similar backgrounds and problems and who make them feel accepted. Because of this vulnerability, adolescents may become involved with local gangs. In summary, gangs offer the following:

- Fellowship and camaraderie
- Identity and recognition
- Membership and belonging
- Family substitution and role models
- Security and protection
- Diversion and excitement
- Friendships and structure

- Money and financial gain for relatively little effort
- Ability to live the crazy life (*vida loca*) (Sanders 1994; Shelden et al. 2001) or *locura* (craziness) (Shelden et al. 2004)

In the United States, estimates of the total number of existing gangs vary widely. For example, in Chicago, estimates range from 12,000 to 120,000 gang members. Spergel (1990) provided the following percentages of those who are reportedly in gangs within a particular school population in the Chicago area: 5% of the elementary school youths, 10% of all high school youths, 20% of those in special school programs, and, more alarmingly perhaps, 35% of those between 16 and 19 years of age who have dropped out of school (Shelden et al. 2001). Keep in mind that these data are for just one city.

Research shows that teenage gangs are becoming major players in the drug trade (Siegel and Senna 1997). Two of the largest gangs in Los Angeles, the Bloods and the Crips, are examples of this trend. Estimated membership in these two gangs exceeds 20,000. In the past, organized crime families maintained a monopoly on the Asian heroin market. Today, youth gangs have entered this trade, for two reasons: (1) Recent efforts and successes in prosecuting top mob bosses by criminal justice officials have created opportunities for new players, and (2) demand has grown for cocaine and synthetic drugs that are produced locally in many U.S. cities. In Los Angeles and most major larger cities, drug-dealing gangs maintain "rock houses" or "stash houses" (where crack cocaine is used and sold) that serve as selling and distribution centers for hard drugs. The crack cocaine found in these "rock houses" is often supplied or run by gang members (Siegel and Senna 1997).

To a lesser extent, other, less violent gangs with smaller memberships are also involved in drug dealing. Recent research shows that the media may exaggerate the percentage of gangs involved in drug dealing. Citywide drug dealing by tightly organized "super" gangs appears to be on the decline and is being superseded by the activities of loosely organized, neighborhood-based groups (Siegel and Senna 1997). The main reason for this shift is that federal and state law enforcement of drug laws have forced drug dealers to become "flexible, informal organizations [rather] than rigid vertically organized gangs with . . . [leaders] . . . who are far removed from day-to-day action [on the street]" (Siegel and Senna 1997, p. 409).

Drug use and gang-related activities are often linked but the relationship is highly variable (Curry and Spergel 1997; Fagan 1990). Clearly, problems with drugs exist without gangs and gang-related activities can occur despite the absence of drugs; however, because they have common etiologies, their occurrences are often intertwined. Most adolescents who are associated with gangs are knowledgeable about drugs. Many gang members have experimented with drugs, much like other adolescents their age. However, the hard-core gang members are more likely to be engaged not only in drug use, but also in drug dealing as a source of revenue to support the gang-related activities (Lale 1992; Siegel and Senna 1997). The types of drugs used and their significance and functions vary from gang to gang (Fagan 1990; Siegel and Senna 1997). For example, many Latino gangs do not profit from drug trafficking but are primarily interested in using hard-core drugs such as heroin and phencyclidine (PCP). In contrast, African American gangs tend to be more interested in the illicit commercial value of drugs and often engage in dealing crack and other cocaine forms.

■ Prevention, Intervention, and Treatment of Adolescent Drug Problems

The most effective way to prevent adolescent gang involvement is to identify, at an early age, those children at risk and provide them with lifestyle alternatives. Important components of such strategies are as follows:

- Encourage parental awareness of gangs and teach parents how to address problems in their own families that may encourage gang involvement.
- Provide teenagers with alternative participation in organizations or groups that satisfy their needs for camaraderie, participation, and emotional security in a constructive way. These groups can be organized around athletics, school activities, career development, or service rendering.
- Help children to develop coping skills that will enable them to deal with the frustration and stress in their personal lives.
- Educate children about gang-related problems and help them understand that, like drugs, gangs are the result of problems and are not the solutions.

As with most health problems, the sooner drug abuse is identified in the adolescent, the greater the likelihood that the problem can be resolved. It can be difficult to recognize signs of drug abuse in teenagers because their behavior can be erratic and unpredictable even under the best of circumstances. In fact, many of the behavioral patterns that occur coincidentally with drug problems are also present when drugs are not a problem. However, frequent occurrence or clustering of these behaviors may indicate the presence of substance abuse. The behaviors that can be warning signs include the following (Archambault 1992):

- Abruptly changing the circle of friends
- Experiencing major mood swings
- Continually challenging rules and regulations
- Overreacting to frustrations
- Being particularly submissive to peer pressures
- Sleeping excessively
- Keeping very late hours
- Withdrawing from family involvement
- Letting personal hygiene deteriorate
- Becoming isolated
- Engaging in unusual selling of possessions
- Manipulating family members
- Becoming abusive toward other members of the family
- Frequently coming home at night high

Prevention of Adolescent Drug Abuse

Logically, the best treatment for drug abuse is to prevent the problem from starting. This approach, referred to as **primary prevention**, has been typically viewed as total abstinence from drug use (see Chapter 17). Informational scare tactics are frequently used as a component of primary prevention strategies. These messages often focus on a dangerous (although in some cases rare) potential side effect and present the warning against drug use in a graphic and frightening fashion. Although this approach may scare naive adolescents away from drugs, many adolescents today, especially if they are experienced, question the validity of the scare tactics and ignore the message.

Another form of primary prevention is to encourage adolescents to become involved in formal groups, such as structured clubs or organizations, in an effort to reduce the likelihood of substance

KEY TERMS

primary prevention
prevention of any drug use

abuse (Howard 1992). Group memberships can help adolescents develop a sense of belonging and contributing to a productive, desirable objective. This involvement can also provide the adolescent with the strength to resist undesirable peer pressures. In contrast, belonging to informal groups such as gangs — groups with loose structures and ill-defined, often antisocial objectives — can lead to participation in poorly chaperoned parties, excessive sexual involvement, and nonproductive activities. Adolescent members of such poorly defined organizations tend to drink alcohol at an earlier age and are more likely to use other substances of abuse.

Some experts claim that primary prevention against drug use is unrealistic for many adolescents. They believe that no strategy is likely to stop adolescents from experimenting with alcohol or other drugs of abuse, especially if these substances are part of their home environment (e.g., if alcohol or tobacco is routinely used) and are viewed as normal, acceptable, and even expected behaviors (Howard 1992). For these adolescents, it is important to recognize when drug use moves from experimentation or a social exercise to early stages of a problem and to prevent serious dependence from developing. This approach, referred to as **secondary prevention**, consists of (1) teaching adolescents about the early signs of abuse, (2) teaching adolescents how to assist peers and family members with drug problems, and (3) teaching adolescents how and where help is available for people with drug problems (Archambault 1992). Regardless of the prevention approach used, adolescents need to understand that drugs are never the solution for emotional difficulties, nor are they useful for long-term coping.

Treatment of Adolescent Drug Abuse

To provide appropriate treatment for adolescent drug abuse, the severity of the problem must be ascertained. The criteria for such assessments include the following:

- Differentiating between abuse and normal adolescent experimentation with drugs
- Distinguishing between minor abuse and severe dependency on drugs

- Distinguishing among behavioral problems resulting from (1) general behavioral disorders, such as juvenile delinquency; (2) mental retardation; and (3) drugs of abuse

There is no single best approach for treating adolescent substance abuse. Occasionally, the troubled adolescent is admitted to a clinic and treated on an inpatient basis. The inpatient approach is very expensive and creates a temporary artificial environment that may be of limited value in preparing adolescents for the problems to be faced in their real homes and neighborhoods. However, the advantage of an inpatient approach is that adolescents can be managed better and their behavior can be more tightly monitored and controlled (Hoshino 1992).

A more practical and routine treatment approach is to allow adolescents to remain in their natural environment and to provide the necessary life skills to be successful at home, in school, and in the community. For example, adolescents being treated for drug dependence should be helped with

- Schoolwork, so that appropriate progress toward high school graduation occurs
- Career skills, so that adolescents can become self-reliant and learn to care for themselves and others
- Family problems and learning to communicate and resolve conflicts

If therapy is to be successful, it is important to improve the environment of the drug-abusing adolescent. This aspect of treatment includes disassociation of the adolescent from groups (such as gangs) or surroundings that encourage drug use and promotes association with healthy and supportive groups (such as a nurturing family) and experiences (such as athletics and school activities). Although desirable, such separation is not always possible, especially if the family and home environment are factors that encourage abuse; the likelihood of therapeutic success is substantially diminished under these circumstances.

Often, therapeutic objectives are facilitated by positive reinforcement that encourages life changes that eliminate access to and use of drugs. This goal can frequently be achieved by association with peers who have similar drug and social problems but are motivated to make positive changes in their life. Group sessions with such peers are held under the supervision of a trained therapist and consist of members sharing problems and solutions (Hoshino 1992). Some other recent options include holistic

KEY TERMS

secondary prevention
preventing drug use from either casual or recreational to drug dependence

therapies such as acupuncture, homeotherapy, massage therapy, aromatherapy, yoga, nutrition therapy, and many more options that were once marginalized by the medical profession (Apostolides 1996).

Another useful approach is to discourage use of drugs by reducing their reinforcing effects. This result can sometimes be achieved by substituting a stronger positive or negative reinforcer. For example, if adolescents use drugs because they believe these substances cause good feelings and help them cope with emotional problems, it may be necessary to replace the drug-taking behavior with other activities that make the adolescent feel good without the drug (such as participation in sports or recreational activities). Negative reinforcers, such as parental discovery and punishment or police apprehension, may discourage drug use by teenagers who are willing to conform and respect authorities. However, negative approaches are ineffective deterrents for nonconforming, rebellious adolescents. Negative reinforcers also do not tend to discourage adolescent use of substances that are more socially acceptable, such as alcohol, tobacco, and even marijuana (Howard 1992).

Regardless of the treatment approach, adolescents must meet several basic objectives if therapy for their drug dependence is to be successful (Daily 1992b):

- Realize that drugs do not solve problems — they only make the problems worse.
- Understand why they turned to drugs in the first place.
- Be convinced that abandoning drugs grants them greater independence and control over their own lives.
- Understand that drug abuse is a symptom of underlying problems that need to be resolved.

▨ Summary of Adolescent Drug Abuse

Drug abuse by adolescents is particularly problematic in the United States. The teenage years are filled with experimentation, searching, confusion, rebellion, poor self-image, and insecurity. These attributes, if not managed properly, can cause inappropriate coping and lead to problems such as drug dependence, gang involvement, violence, criminal behavior, and suicide. Clearly, early detection of severe underlying emotional problems and application of effective early preventive therapy are important for proper management. Approaches to treatment of drug abuse problems

must be individualized because each adolescent is a unique product of physiological, psychological, and environmental factors.

Almost as important as early intervention for adolescent drug abuse problems is recognizing when treatment is *unnecessary*. We should not be too quick to label all young drug users as antisocial and emotionally unstable. In most cases, teenagers who have used drugs are merely experimenting with new emotions or exercising their newfound freedom. In such situations, nonintervention is usually better than therapeutic meddling. For the most part, if adolescents are given the opportunity, they will work through their own feelings, conflicts, and attitudes about substance abuse, and they will develop a responsible philosophy concerning the use of these drugs.

Drug Use in College Student Subcultures

Chapter 8 includes a lengthy discussion of alcohol use and abuse by college students. This section focuses on college undergraduate use of alcohol not discussed in that chapter, with additional emphasis on the use and abuse of illicit drugs by college students currently attending institutions of higher education.

Table 16.5 compares trends in the annual use of various types of licit and illicit drugs by full-time college students with others who are the same age (1 to 4 years beyond high school) but are *not* attending college. Overall, Table 16.5 shows the following noteworthy prevalence trends (Johnston et al. 2006b):

1. Full-time college students (36.6%) were slightly less likely to use any illicit drugs in 2005 than others (39.6%). A slightly larger proportional difference exists for the annual prevalence of any illicit drug other than marijuana (1.9% versus 2.9%).

2. Annual marijuana use is very similar among college students and high school graduates of the same age that are not in college (33% versus 35%). However, the rate of current daily marijuana use is lower among college students (4.0% versus 7.8% by their out-of-school counterparts).

3. Annual prevalence for all the illicit drugs is *lower* among college students; Vicodin, narcotics other than heroin, and OxyContin show the largest absolute difference in annual prevalence. For Vicodin, it is 9.6% for college stu-

Table 16.5 Annual Prevalence of Drug Use, 2005: Full-Time College Students Versus Others 1 to 4 Years Beyond High School (Entries are Percentages, Highest to Lowest)

	FULL-TIME COLLEGE STUDENTS	OTHERS
Any illicit drug*	36.6%	39.6%
Any illicit drug* other than marijuana	18.5	23.4
Alcohol	83.0	76.9
Cigarettes	36.0	45.2
Marijuana	33.3	34.6
Other narcotics†	8.4	12.7
OxyContin	2.1	6.2
Vicodin	9.6	14.0
Hallucinogens	5.0	7.3
LSD	0.7	2.1
Amphetamines†	6.7	7.2
Ritalin	4.2	4.3
Methamphetamine	1.7	4.9
Ice	1.4	3.1
Tranquilizers	6.4	9.3
Cocaine	5.7	9.0
Crack	6.8	2.9
MDMA (Ecstasy)	2.9	4.9
Sedatives† (barbiturates)	3.9	6.9
Inhalants	1.8	1.8
Rohypnol	0.1	0.6
GHBs	0.4	0.6
Heroin	0.3	1.1
Ketamine	0.5	1.5

*Use of any illicit drug includes use of marijuana, hallucinogens, cocaine, or heroin, or any use of other narcotics, amphetamines, sedatives (barbiturates), or tranquilizers not under a doctor's orders.

†Only drug use that was not under a doctor's orders is included here.

Source: Johnston, L. D., P. M. O'Malley, J. G. Bachman, and J. E. Schulenberg. *Monitoring the Future National Survey Results on Drug Use, 1975–2005. Volume II: College Students and Adults Ages 19–45.* Bethesda, MD: National Institute on Drug Abuse, 2005.

dents versus 14.0% for those not in college; for narcotics other than heroin, 8.4% versus 12.7%, and for OxyContin, 2.1% versus 6.2%.

4. Smaller absolute differences occur for cocaine, with 5.7 of the college students versus 9.0% of their noncollege age peers reporting use in the past year; methamphetamine, at 1.7% versus 4.9%; tranquilizers, at 6.4% versus 9.3%; sedatives (barbiturates), at 3.9% versus 6.9%; hallucinogens, at 5.0% versus 7.3%; crack cocaine, at 0.8% versus

2.9%; MDMA (Ecstasy), at 2.9% versus 4.9%; ice, at 1.4% versus 3.1%; and LSD, at 0.7% versus 2.1%.

5. In 2005, college students were modestly higher in their prevalence of lifetime or annual use of alcohol than the noncollege group, but were appreciably higher than their age peers in monthly use (68% versus 59%).

6. College students also had a significantly higher prevalence of occasions of heavy drinking (five or more drinks in a row in the past 2 weeks) —

40% versus 35% among their age peers — but their rates of daily drinking were not significantly different from rates of their age peers (4.6% versus 5.1%).

7. In 2005, two-thirds (67%) of college students reported using flavored alcohol beverages in the prior years versus one half (51%) of the noncollege group.

8. Finally, out of all the drugs, both licit and illicit, *cigarette use had the largest absolute difference in 30-day and daily prevalence use.* The prevalence of daily smoking for college students is only 12% versus 28% for their age-mates not enrolled full time in college. Similarly, 7% of college students versus 18% of noncollege students reported smoking at the rate of a half-pack per day. (The smoking differences would be even greater if dropouts were included in the noncollege group because they have an exceptionally high rate of smoking.)

Table 16.6 shows yearly trends in drug use among U.S. college students from 2002 through 2005 (Johnston et al., 2006b). This table details the percentages of college students who used drugs in the past 12 months before the surveys were administered. The main finding is that the overall use of any illicit drugs remained fairly constant from 2002 to 2005 — approximately 37%, when averaging the 4 years of surveying. From 2002 to 2005, some slight increases and decreases (depending on the drug) in the overall use of illicit drugs, including marijuana, MDMA, and opioids were noted. Further, the following trends show modest increases, decreases, and not much change.

Modest percentage *increased usage* from 2002 to 2005 (unless noted otherwise):

- Any illicit drug other than marijuana
- LSD (steep drop in percentage using)
- Cocaine and crack use (decrease from 2004)
- Other narcotics, Oxycontin, and Vicodin
- Tranquilizers
- Sedatives (barbiturates)

Modest percentage *decreased usage* from 2002 to 2005:

- Cigarettes
- MDMA (Ecstasy)
- Hallucinogens

Not much change (fairly stable percentages) in usage from 2002 to 2005:

- Alcohol
- Marijuana
- Amphetamines

Reasons for College Students' Drug Use

Figure 16.2 shows the primary reasons why a sample survey of 785 male and female college students used alcohol and other drugs (47% were male and 53% were female). The major reasons cited in this sample survey were (1) breaks the ice (78.1%), (2) enhances social activity (78%), (3) gives people something to do (75.3%), (4) gives people something to talk about (68%), (5) allows people to have more fun (64%), (6) facilitates contact with peers (60.6%), (7) facilitates sexual opportunities (56.8%), and (8) facilitates male bonding (56.3%). Though not shown in this figure, this same survey revealed that 34.1% consumed one to four drinks in a week, 17.7% consumed five to ten drinks, and 11.4% consumed eleven or more drinks in a week. Further, 54.7% did not binge drink, 15.6% binged once, 11.3% binged twice, and 14% binged three to five times. Five percent used marijuana six times per year and 9.7% used marijuana once per year from the time they began their college career to the date of this survey. Approximately 68% taking this survey were white, 13% Hispanic, 6% black, 9% Asian/Pacific Islander, 0.1% American Indian/Alaska Native, and 3% were classified as other ethnicity (Campus Alcohol and Drug Resource Center 2006). This survey may indicate that the use of alcohol and other drugs on a fairly typical larger state campus continues to be readily prevalent.

Additional Noteworthy Findings Regarding Drug Use by College Students

The following sections describe the most recent significant studies and findings regarding the use of drugs by college students.

Patterns of Alcohol and Other Drug Use

Recent literature reviews of undergraduates' substance use and abuse and the prevalence patterns of alcohol and other drug use found that the most popular substance used by undergraduates is alcohol, which was used by about 90% of students at least once a year. Heavy alcohol use, which includes binge drinking, ranged from 20% to 40% in this group: "while binge drinking decreased by 6% among dormitory residents between 1993 and 1999, it increased by about the same amount among those living off campus. Nearly 80% of

Table 16.6 Trends in Annual Use of Drugs Among College Students 1 to 4 Years Beyond High School (Percentage Who Used in the Past 12 Months Except as Noted)

	2002	2003	2004	2005
Approximate weighted *N*	1260	1270	1400	1360
Any illicit drug*	37.0%	36.5%	36.2%	36.6%
Any illicit drug other than marijuana*	16.6	17.9	18.6	18.5
Alcohol	82.9	81.7	81.2	83.0
Cigarettes	38.3	35.2	36.7	36.0
Marijuana	34.7	33.7	33.3	33.3
Hallucinogens	6.3	7.4	5.9	5.0
LSD	2.1	1.4	1.2	0.7
MDMA (Ecstasy)	6.8	4.4	2.2	2.9
Amphetamines†	7.0	7.1	7.0	6.7
Ritalin	5.7	4.7	4.7	4.2
Methamphetamine	1.2	2.6	2.9	1.7
Crystal methamphetamine (ice)	0.8	0.9	1.1	1.4
Cocaine	4.8	5.4	6.6	5.7
Crack	0.4	1.3	1.3	0.8
Other narcotics†	7.4	8.7	8.2	8.4
OxyContin	1.5	2.2	2.5	2.1
Vicodin	6.9	7.5	7.4	9.6
Tranquilizers	6.7	6.9	6.7	6.4
Sedatives (barbiturates)†	3.7	4.1	4.2	3.9
Inhalants	2.0	1.8	2.7	1.8
Heroin	0.1	0.2	0.4	0.3
Rohypnol	0.7	0.4	0.3	0.1
GHB	0.6	0.3	0.7	0.4
Ketamine	1.3	1.0	1.5	0.5

*Use of any illicit drug includes any use of marijuana, hallucinogens, cocaine, or heroin, or any use of other narcotics, amphetamines, sedatives (barbiturates), or tranquilizers not under a doctor's orders.

†Only drug use that was not under a doctor's orders is included here.

Source: Johnston, L. D., P. M. O'Malley, J. G. Bachman, and J. E. Schulenberg. *Monitoring the Future National Survey Results on Drug Use, 1975–2005. Volume II: College Students and Adults Ages 19–45.* Bethesda, MD: National Institute on Drug Abuse, 2005.

binge drinkers live in a fraternity or sorority house, often off campus" (Marklein 2000, p. 1). Other results showed that alcohol use was associated with serious and acute problems such as alcoholism, poor academic performance, drinking and driving, and criminalistic behavior (e.g., driving while intoxicated, vandalism, violence). From 1997 to 1998, alcohol arrests in the nation's colleges increased by 24.3%; this is reported as the largest increase in 7 years. In comparing the same 2 years, drug law violations on U.S. campuses increased by 11.1% (Nicklin 2000).

Summarized in the following list are other significant findings regarding alcohol and other drug use:

- During the 2 weeks before the survey, 39% of college students had binged on alcohol (Johnston et al. 2000b).

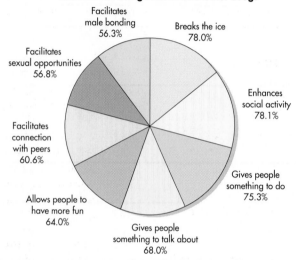

FIGURE 16.2

Sample of reasons for using alcohol and other drugs from the Campus Alcohol and Drug Resource Center at the University of Florida, 2006.

....

Source: Reprinted with permission from Campus Alcohol Drug Resource Center at the University of Florida, *Core Alcohol and Drug Survey Key Findings, 2006.* University of Florida, 2006. Available http://www.shcc.ufl.edu/gatorwell/atod/pdf/key06.pdf.

- Among college students, rates of binge drinking were highest among whites — 43.3% for males and 24.4% for females. Among African Americans, the rates were 24.8% for males and 5.4% for females. Among Asians, the rates were 32% for males and 20% for females.
- Young adults ages 18 to 25 are most likely to binge or drink heavily; 54% of the drinkers in this age group binge and about one in four are heavy drinkers.
- "College students who frequently binge drink are more likely to smoke cigarettes and use illegal drugs as well" (Hitt 2001, p. 1).
- Past-month alcohol use was reported by 63.1% of full-time college students compared with 53.3% of their counterparts who were not currently enrolled full time. Binge and heavy-use rates for college students were 42.5% and 18.2%, respectively, compared with 37.7%

and 12.1%, respectively, for other persons ages 18 to 22 (SAMHSA 2002).
- A clear relationship exists between alcohol use and grade point average (GPA) among college students: students with GPAs of a D or F equivalent drink three times as much as those who earn A equivalent GPAs.
- The National Household Survey on Drug Abuse (NHSDA) reports that youths who received grades of D or lower were more likely than those with higher grades to have used cigarettes, alcohol, or illicit drugs during the past month (NHSDA 2002).
- Almost half of college students who were victims of campus crimes said they were drinking or using other drugs when they were victimized.
- Researchers estimate that alcohol use is implicated in one to two thirds of sexual assault and acquaintance or date rape cases among teens and college students.

Predicting Drug Use for First-Year College Students

The best predictor of drug use for first-year college students was drug use during a typical month in the senior year of high school. Overall, college students responding to a questionnaire were found to use marijuana less frequently than they did in high school. Further, alcohol use increased early in the college years. Although the frequency of alcohol use increased, the number of times that college students got drunk did not rise. Most of these students found new friends in college with whom they got drunk. Alcohol and drug use depended on the choice of new college friends (Leibsohn 1994).

Dormitories for Non–Drug-Using Students

In 1988, Rutgers University was one of the first universities to create a dormitory for students who are recuperating addicts and who want to stay away from the alcohol-charged atmosphere of conventional dormitories. The dormitory at Rutgers maintains strict rules and careful management (Witham 1995). Other universities offer similar variations for on-campus living. In 1989, the University of Michigan opened a substance-free housing facility and set aside 500 dormitory spaces; 1200 students applied for these spaces (Belsie 1995). More recent findings indicate that "[N]ow that substance-free housing is commonplace, a handful of campuses, including Rutgers, have gone [even] further, offering 'recovery' housing for students who have been in treatment for addiction" (Lewin 2005). Today, substance-free housing has become a nationwide choice since it began at Rutgers University in 1988. This type of housing is found ". . . at dozens of campuses nationwide, from huge state universities like the University of Michigan to Ivy League schools like Dartmouth and small liberal arts colleges like Vassar" (Lewin 2005). For example,

> . . . a junior at Earlham College who asked that his name not be used . . . [said] "When I got to college, I didn't want to have to worry about having all that stuff in my face [in reference to having to live with drunk and drugged students in the dorm]. I've been in wellness housing my whole time here. I could handle normal housing now, but I like the people I live with, and there's a very good atmosphere. (Lewin 2005)

Further, on some campuses, substance-free living accommodations, mainly dormitories as well as other types of housing, have large numbers of entering freshmen preferring such living accommodations. "At Dartmouth, for example, about 400 of the 1,075 incoming freshmen requested it,

compared with only about 200 of the 2,200 sophomores, juniors and seniors who live on campus" (Lewin 2005).

Remaining Popularity of Certain Types of "Softer" Drugs

Marijuana and psilocybin mushrooms are two types of illicit recreational drugs whose popularity appeared to grow in the 1990s and to date remain sought after (popular) on most college campuses. Referred to as "soft drugs," these substances are commonly used on most college campuses (Ravid 1995).

> Weed and coke are great, but when the "shrooms" [referring to psilocybin mushrooms] are in town, it is a special treat. Friends on other campuses, the big state university campuses, are lucky to have more different types of drugs available. At our university, both "shrooms" and real hydroponic weed happen about one or two times a semester. *(From Venturelli's research files, male, 21 years of age, attending a smaller comprehensive university in the Midwest, June 12, 2003.)*

Nationwide surveys showed that in yearly drug use averages from 1984 through 1999, there was a steady progressive increase in the use of hallucinogens, which includes psilocybin mushrooms, Ecstasy, and LSD. In 1984 (the first year of the survey), 3.7% of college students used LSD; in 1999, 5.4% used this same drug. Similarly, in 1984, 6.2% used hallucinogens (excluding LSD) and in 1999, 7.8% used these same hallucinogenic-type drugs (Johnston et al. 2000b). Concerning college students' use of MDMA (Ecstasy) in 2000, the annual use was 9% (Johnston et al. 2001).

According to a 1990 study, with the exception of marijuana, psilocybin mushrooms and Ecstasy/MDMA were the most widely used illicit drugs among first- and second-year, full-time college students. Through studies based on self-reporting (which is not a representative nationwide sample), a fair number of universities reported that about 24% of their drug-using students use psilocybin mushrooms. Use of Ecstasy/MDMA also increased from 16% to 24%.

The occasional use of cocaine (a "harder" drug) increased from 5.9% in 1995 to 6.7% in 1996 (Bennett et al. 1999). This increase was documented in a sample of 2710 students at an undergraduate university in the Southwest. More than likely, the high cost of cocaine keeps the occasional use from becoming frequent use. Nevertheless, cocaine is another drug that appeared to be part of the drug scene on most campuses in the 1990s and in the beginning of the 21st century.

Steroid Usage Patterns

A study of 58,625 college students from 78 colleges and universities in the United States (Meilman et al. 1995) concluded the following:

- Steroid users consumed dramatically more alcohol and demonstrated higher rates of binge drinking than other students.
- A significantly higher percentage of steroid users than nonusers reported using tobacco, marijuana, cocaine, amphetamines, sedatives, hallucinogens, opiates, inhalants, and designer drugs.
- A higher percentage of steroid users than nonusers reported experiencing negative consequences because of substance abuse. Such negative consequences included arrest, public intoxication, driving under the influence, court-ordered community service, and disciplinary actions by university officials.
- A greater percentage of steroid users than nonusers reported family histories of alcohol abuse and other drugs.

Rohypnol and Date Rape

Rohypnol, also known as the "date-rape drug," is one of six drugs recently referred to as **club drugs**. The other club drugs are MDMA (Ecstasy), gamma-hydroxybutyrate (GHB), ketamine, methamphetamine, and LSD. Club drugs are used by individuals at all-night dance parties such as raves or trances, dance clubs, and bars. All of these drugs are colorless, tasteless, and odorless. They can be added unobtrusively to beverages by individuals who may want to intoxicate or sedate others (NIDA 2000). In cases of sexual assault or rape, the small white Rohypnol pills are slipped into a person's drink, causing the person to black out and have no memories of events that occurred while he or she was under the influence of the drug. A minority of undergraduates also use the drug to intensify the effects of marijuana and alcohol. One problem with identifying whether this drug has been given to an unwilling recipient is that Rohypnol can be detected only for 60 hours after ingestion (Lively 1996).

Rohypnol (flunitrazepam) belongs to a class of drugs known as benzodiazepines (such as Valium and Xanax). Although this drug is not approved for prescription use in the United States, it is approved and used in more than 60 countries as a treatment for insomnia, as a sedative, and as a presurgery anesthetic (NIDA 2000).

HIV and AIDS

AIDS came to the attention of medical authorities in the United States on June 4, 1981, in a newsletter from the Centers for Disease Control and Prevention (CDC) in Atlanta, Georgia (Zuger 2000). HIV, the virus that causes AIDS, was not discovered until 1983. More than 40 million people are living with HIV worldwide, including 5 million new cases in 2005 alone. For the United States, the latest numbers indicate that by 2004, 1 million Americans were living with HIV — and one in four of them did not know it (NIDA 2007). Another source indicates that at the end of 2003, an estimated 1,039,000 to 1,185,000 persons in the United States were living with HIV/AIDS (Glynn and Rhodes 2007). The CDC has estimated that approximately 40,000 persons in the United States become infected with HIV each year (CDC 2005). During 2005, 74% of those diagnosed with HIV/AIDS were male and 26% were female. Forty-nine percent were black, 31% white, 18% Hispanic, 1% Asian/Pacific Islander, and less than 1% American Indian/Alaska Native. The noteworthy finding is that in 2005, blacks (including African Americans), who make up approximately 13% of the U.S. population, accounted for almost half of the estimated number of HIV/AIDS cases diagnosed (CDC 2006). From 1981 through 2005, the CDC estimates that 952,629 cases of AIDS were diagnosed; of these, 530,756 died with AIDS as a major cause of death, and as of 2005, 421,873 people were living with AIDS (CDC 2006). Table 16.7 shows the estimated number of people living with HIV worldwide in 2006.

KEY TERMS

Rohypnol
the "date-rape drug," used on many college campuses

club drugs
a new class of illicit drugs used on college campuses, at bars, in night clubs, and at raves where drinking and dancing occur; club drugs include MDMA (Ecstasy), GHB, Rohypnol, ketamine, methamphetamine, and LSD

Table 16.7 Worldwide, the Estimated Number of People Living with HIV

REGION OF THE WORLD	NUMBERS	PERCENTAGE CHANGE FROM 1995
Sub-Saharan Africa	22.5 million*	+73%*
Asia	8.3 million	+295%
Latin America and Caribbean	2.1 million	+ 75%
Eastern Europe and Central Asia	1.6 million	+1,900%
North America	1.2 million	N/A
Western and Central Europe	720,000	N/A
North Africa and Middle East	510,000	-6%
Oceania	74,000	+1,831%

Source: Data from Clinton, Bill. "My Question to Improve Care." *Newsweek.* CXLVII (15 May 2006): 50–53.

*UNAIDS (United Nations AIDS). "Global HIV Prevalence Has Levelled Off; AIDS is Among the Leading Causes of Death Globally and Remains the Primary Cause of Death in Africa." Geneva, Switzerland: World Health Organization, 2007. Available http://search.unaids.org/Results.aspx?q=Global+HIV+prevalence+has+levelled+off%3A+&o=html&d=en&l=en&s=false (For example, see http://www.ccsa.ca/pdf/ccsa-004011-1993.pdf; http://www.habitsmart.com/hrmtitle.html; and http://www.druglibrary.org/schaffer/library/studies/redfern/rf5.htm).

Nature of HIV Infection and Related Symptoms

AIDS (acquired immunodeficiency syndrome) is caused by the human immunodeficiency virus (HIV).

AIDS is a disease in which the body's immune system breaks down and is unable to fight off certain infections, known as "opportunistic infections," and other illnesses that take advantage of a weakened immune system.

When a person is infected with HIV, the virus enters the body and lives and multiplies primarily in the white blood cells. These immune cells normally protect us from disease. The hallmark of HIV infection is the progressive loss of a specific type of immune cells called T-helper or CD4 cells.

As the virus grows, it damages or kills CD4 and other cells, weakening the immune system and leaving the individual vulnerable to numerous opportunistic infections and other illnesses, ranging from pneumonia to cancer. The CDC defines someone as having a clinical diagnosis of AIDS if he or she has tested positive for HIV and has one or both of these conditions:

- The person has experienced one or more AIDS-related infections or illnesses.

- The number of CD4 cells has reached or fallen below 200 per cubic millimeter of blood (a measurement known as a T-cell count) (Schernoff and Smith 2001).

As mentioned previously, the immune systems of HIV-positive individuals become severely compromised as important immune cells called CD4+ helper T lymphocytes and macrophages are destroyed (see Figure 16.3). Because these immune cells are crucial in identifying and eliminating infection-causing microorganisms such as bacteria, fungi, and viruses, their deficiency substantially increases the likelihood and severity of infectious diseases. Progression of the disease brings weight loss, infections in the throat ("thrush") and skin (shingles), and other opportunistic infections and/or cancer (e.g., Kaposi's sarcoma). Infections become increasingly difficult to control with medication, and consequently severe opportunistic infections, such as pneumonia, meningitis, hepatitis, and tuberculosis occur and eventually lead to death. The likelihood of introducing these opportunistic infections into the body increases in patients who are injection drug users because they often share injection equipment, such as needles and syringes that are contaminated with disease-causing microorganisms.

FIGURE 16.3

Disrupting the Assembly Line

HIV survives by invading white blood cells and turning them into virus factories. The process involves several steps, and each offers a potential target for therapy. This diagram shows how HIV does its work and how antiviral drugs do theirs.

....

Source: Crowley, G. "Targeting a Deadly Scrap of Genetic Code." C. Blumrich, graphic designer. *Newsweek* (2 December 1996): 69. Copyright © Newsweek, Inc. All rights reserved. Reprinted by permission.

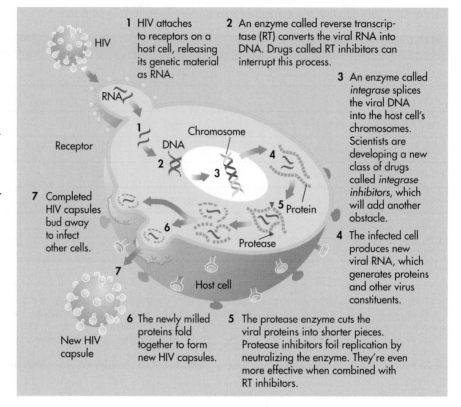

1 HIV attaches to receptors on a host cell, releasing its genetic material as RNA.

2 An enzyme called reverse transcriptase (RT) converts the viral RNA into DNA. Drugs called RT inhibitors can interrupt this process.

3 An enzyme called *integrase* splices the viral DNA into the host cell's chromosomes. Scientists are developing a new class of drugs called *integrase inhibitors*, which will add another obstacle.

4 The infected cell produces new viral RNA, which generates proteins and other virus constituents.

5 The protease enzyme cuts the viral proteins into shorter pieces. Protease inhibitors foil replication by neutralizing the enzyme. They're even more effective when combined with RT inhibitors.

6 The newly milled proteins fold together to form new HIV capsules.

7 Completed HIV capsules bud away to infect other cells.

An HIV-infected individual may not manifest symptoms of AIDS for as many as 10 to 12 years after the initial infection. Although the HIV-infected individual may experience no symptoms, he or she is highly contagious.

After an individual has become infected, he or she may have a brief flu-like illness usually within 6 to 12 weeks. It is not known what determines the length of the latency period, when symptoms are not present. The asymptomatic period eventually ends, however, and signs of immune disorder appear. Initial symptoms of this disease include night sweats, swollen lymph glands, fever, and/or headaches.

■ Diagnosis and Treatment

It is crucial that HIV-infected people be aware of their condition to avoid activities that might transmit the infection to others. Testing for the presence of infection has been available since 1985 and is done by determining whether the body is producing antibodies against HIV. Further, since 1996, newspapers, magazines, radio, and television have been advertising a take-at-home HIV anti-body test. The presence of these specific antibodies indicates HIV infection. If an individual is infected, it takes 6 to 12 weeks after the HIV exposure before the body produces enough antibodies to be detected in currently available tests. If the antibody is not present within 6 months after HIV exposure, it is likely that infection did not occur (Pietroski 1993).

Although the tests for HIV infection are reliable, false negatives (i.e., the test says no HIV is present even though the individual is infected) and false positives (i.e., the test says the individual is infected even though no HIV is present) occur in 1 out of 30,000 tests. Because testing positive for HIV is currently perceived as eventually life-threatening and is a highly emotional diagnosis, great effort is made to ensure confidentiality of the test results. The blood specimens to be tested are coded, and the personnel conducting the tests are not allowed to divulge the results to anyone but the individual who was tested. The issue of confidentiality is very controversial, however. It is often difficult to decide who has the right to know when HIV has been detected (see "Point/Counterpoint," Who Should Know the Results of Your HIV Test *If* You Test Positive?).

▶Point/Counterpoint

Most people would probably want to keep such results private, but consider the following. Would your opinion about HIV-positive people keeping their results confidential change in the following circumstances:

▶ You require first aid after a serious auto accident and the emergency medical technician assisting is HIV-positive?

▶ Your doctor is HIV-positive?

▶ Your dentist is HIV-positive?

▶ Your manicurist is HIV-positive?

▶ Your massage therapist is HIV-positive?

▶ Your severely handicapped daughter's elementary school teacher is HIV-positive?

▶ Your lover is HIV-positive?

▶ Your tattoo artist is HIV-positive?

▶ Your jeweler who is about to pierce your daughter's ears is HIV-positive?

▶ Your boxing partner is HIV-positive?

▶ Your jail cellmate is HIV-positive?

Arguments for *not* disclosing HIV-positive results to anyone other than the person undergoing HIV screening are that reporting such results to others would (1) cause many people not to take the test for fear of disclosure to others; (2) possibly cause loss of employment (if the results require mandatory reporting to supervisors or managers); (3) unnecessarily stigmatize the HIV-positive person, exposing an infected person to social ostracism and gossip and potentially creating fear and panic in others; and (4) potentially destroy a partner or marriage relationship if the significant other or spouse is notified.

Arguments *for* mandatory disclosure to others potentially affected by the results of this disease include (1) to protect domestic or marital partners, (2) to protect others from HIV-positive workers who could infect them (such as surgeons who are involved in invasive bodily care or procedures), and (3) to honor the public's right to know of the threat of contracting this terminal disease.

Currently, employers cannot legally terminate a worker for being HIV-positive. In cases of direct potential threat to the public, an HIV-positive worker can be reassigned to a different position. Also, in most cases, employers cannot legally inquire about HIV test results. An exception to this is the military and prison, where mandatory testing is required.

What is your opinion about this issue?

The sooner an HIV-positive person begins drug treatment, the more effective the treatment may be. Knowing this, should HIV-positive individuals be required to inform past sexual partners and people with whom they have shared needles so that these people can be tested (known as "partner notification" or "contact tracing")?

If an HIV-positive surgeon is going to operate on you, your mother, your father, or your child — do you have the right to know? What are the rights of the HIV-positive individual versus the rights of the public?

After a positive HIV diagnosis, the best way to lengthen one's life is to immediately begin drug treatments. The first prescription drug treatment for AIDS, AZT, was introduced in 1987. In 1996, **protease inhibitors** came on the market. When combined with AZT and other drugs, protease inhibitors resulted in miraculous remissions of desperately ill AIDS patients (Zuger 2000). Further, it appears that with such drug combinations, HIV blood levels in newly infected patients remain at exceedingly low levels (Zuger 2000). Although the drug combinations do not rid the body of infected cells, results indicate that HIV infections could become as manageable as diabetes (Crowley 1996).

Today, people in the United States and other developed countries can use a number of drugs to treat HIV infection and AIDS. Some of these are designed to treat the opportunistic infections and illnesses that affect people with HIV/AIDS. In

KEY TERMS

protease inhibitors
a major breakthrough class of drugs used to treat HIV-infected individuals

addition, several types of drugs seek to prevent HIV from reproducing and destroying the body's immune system. Reverse transcriptase inhibitors attach an HIV enzyme called reverse transcriptase. They include abacavir, delavirdine, didanosine (ddI), efavirenz, lamivudine (3TC), nevirapine, stavudine (d4T), zalcitabine (ddC), and zidovudine (AZT).

Many HIV patents are taking several of these drugs in combination — a regimen known as **highly active antiretroviral therapy (HAART)**. When successful, combinations or "cocktail" therapy can reduce the level of HIV in the bloodstream to very low — even undetectable — levels and sometimes enable the body's CD4 immune cells to rebound to normal levels (American Foundation for AIDS Research [amfAR] 2001, pp. 6–9). Less than 10 years ago the drug regimen was difficult:

> I take the famous drug "cocktail" and have to wake myself up in the middle of the night around 4 in the morning, then go back to sleep. I am used to it. I know it is a pain in the neck, but I think that despite this, the side effects can even be worse at times. I really don't want to go into it; it's depressing. The bright side: I am still alive after 9 years since diagnosed with AIDS; I am not dead yet. *(Interview with a 52-year-old male, working as a bartender in Chicago, May 18, 2000.)*

An update on HAART indicates that this therapy regimen results in dramatic reduction in the incidence of AIDS and death in individuals infected with HIV (MyDNA.com 2005). Less than 5 years ago, patients took approximately 37 pills per day, a few years later it was a 14-pill-a-day regimen, and today in the majority of cases, only three pills have to be taken each day (Scripps Howard News Service 2003). The pills must be taken regularly each day to ensure effective therapy. The cost of the cocktail was $2000 to $3000 per month. Today, the annual cost of care is about $25,200 (Associated Press 2006). More recently, there is an experimental AIDS drug that is part of a new class of medicines known as integrase inhibitors that is more efficient in controlling HIV than drugs that

are currently on the market (Chong 2006). Though only in the testing stages and not available (as of the date of this edition), "Integrase inhibitors prevent HIV, or human immunodeficiency virus, from replicating by blocking its ability to patch its DNA onto cells" (Chong 2006, p. A9). When combined with two other drugs, tenoflovir and lamivudine, it appears promising. Used as part of a drug "cocktail," "the amount of HIV in 90% of patients . . . [was reduced to] . . . undetectable levels in 24 weeks" (Chong 2006, p. A9). Unfortunately, many health insurance companies continue to actively issue restrictive amendments on their policies that cap reimbursement for such expensive drug therapies. As a result, infected individuals with extensive debt obligations and patients without health insurance are often unable to afford the latest drug therapy.

Some HIV-infected persons taking the current treatment regimens suffer side effects that are so severe they choose to stop taking some of the drugs necessary to hold off the development of AIDS. Side effects can include diarrhea, bone-marrow suppression, an inability to tolerate the drugs, and tumor-like growths on the neck and other parts of the body. However, the overall success in treating HIV-positive patients has resulted in a 23% drop in HIV-related deaths in 1996 and a 40% drop in such deaths in 1997. Because the drugs halt the progression of HIV to AIDS, the rates of new AIDS cases fell 25% by 1998 (Zuger 2000).

A successful prognosis for HIV infection and AIDS relies on three factors: (1) initiation of a drug regimen as soon as possible after an HIV-positive diagnosis, (2) strict adherence to medical advice and treatment, and (3) maintenance of a healthy diet without drug use or abuse so as to avoid taxing the immune system.

Scientists are optimistic that eventually there will be a vaccine against HIV/AIDS. Although approximately 30 types of vaccines are being studied, the development of such a vaccine after clinical trials can take more than a decade (Fischer 2000). The key is to invent "killer" T cells to shut down or destroy HIV-infected cells (Fischer 2000).

Who Is at Risk for AIDS?

Although anyone can become infected with HIV, its routes of transmission are limited to blood, semen, vaginal fluid, and possibly some other body fluids (Grinspoon 1994). Before the advent of AZT, mothers were more likely to the pass the virus to their children prenatally or through breast milk. HIV is a virus that is not likely to survive outside of the body. Consequently, it is not spread by casual contact, such as by shaking hands, touching, hugging, or kissing (although "deep" kissing with an infected person is not recommended). In addition, it is not spread through food or water, by sharing cups or glasses, by coughing and sneezing, or by using common toilets. It is not spread by mosquitoes or other insects.

The following populations are at greatest risk for contracting AIDS:

1. Men with a history of having had multiple homosexual or bisexual partners
2. Injecting drug users and their sexual partners
3. Heterosexuals with multiple partners
4. Infants born to HIV-infected women (approximately 10% of all HIV-positive mothers have HIV-positive babies)
5. People who receive contaminated blood products, such as for transfusions or treatment of blood disorders (blood banks have improved the screening of their blood supplies in the last decade)

See Figures 16.4 and 16.5 for a detailed breakdown of categories of U.S. AIDS cases by type of HIV exposure.

Figure 16.4 shows that approximately 59% of all adult/adolescent men with AIDS report sex with men, and another approximately 19% report injection drug use. An estimated 7% of cases are attributed to male-to-male sexual contact and injection drug use, 13% of male cases are attributed to heterosexual contact, and other risk exposures account for the remaining 1% of cases. Figure 16.5 shows that 72% of women with AIDS attribute their exposure to heterosexual contact, and 28% attribute their exposure to injection drug use.

Other findings regarding age at diagnosis of HIV infection and AIDS reported through 2003 follow (CDC 2004a).

- HIV is the fifth leading cause of death for all Americans between the ages of 25 and 44.
- By age group, 41% of persons living with AIDS were 35 to 44 years old.
- Among African American men and women between the ages of 25 and 44, HIV is the number one cause of death.
- In the United States, approximately 77% of all people who currently have AIDS are male and 23% are female. Worldwide, 73 women are infected for every 100 infected men.
- African Americans account for 42% of all reported AIDS patients in the United States,

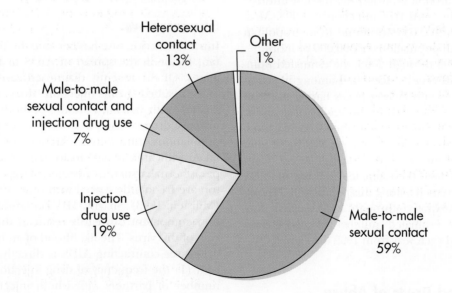

FIGURE 16.4

Approximate percentages of AIDS cases in adult/adolescent men, by risk exposure, United States, 2001–2005.

Source: Centers for Disease Control and Prevention (CDC). *HIV/AIDS Surveillance Report, 2005.* Atlanta: U.S. Department of Health and Human Services, CDC, 2005.

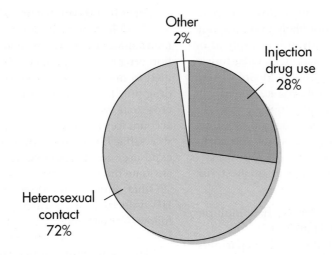

FIGURE 16.5

Approximate percentages of AIDS cases in adult/adolescent women, by risk exposure, United States, 2001–2005.

Source: Centers for Disease Control and Prevention (CDC). *HIV/AIDS Surveillance Report, 2005.* Atlanta: U.S. Department of Health and Human Services, CDC, 2005.

white Americans account for 36% of AIDS cases, and Hispanic Americans account for 20% of cases (CDC 2004a).

- By region, 39% of HIV/AIDS patients resided in the South, 29% in the Northeast, 19% in the West, 10% in the Midwest, and 3% in the U.S. territories. New York, Florida, Texas, and North Carolina reported the highest number of persons with HIV infection in 2003. Most people with AIDS are found in metropolitan areas with populations of 500,000 or more.

- From 1999 through 2003, the estimated number of AIDS cases decreased among injection drug users and among males having sex with males who were also intravenous drug users. From 1999 through 2000, the estimated number of AIDS cases decreased slightly among males having sex with males; however, from 2001 to 2003, the estimated number of AIDS cases increased among this population. Among persons exposed through heterosexual contact, the estimated number of AIDS cases increased each year from 1999 through 2003.

■ AIDS and Drugs of Abuse

During the past several years, the AIDS epidemic has become closely associated with drug abuse problems. As mentioned earlier, individuals addicted to illicit drugs are currently the second

largest risk group for contracting AIDS. AIDS in women is particularly linked to drug abuse. Nearly 70% of the female AIDS patients are infected because of injection drug use by themselves or by a sexual partner (Glave 1994). Several reasons account for the high incidence of this deadly infection in the drug-abusing population.

Intravenous Drugs

Intravenous drug use has become the most important factor in the spread of AIDS in the United States. Of the recently diagnosed cases of AIDS, 29% resulted from injection drug use (CDC 2000c), with heroin, cocaine, or both being the primary drugs injected. Among severely addicted populations, intravenous drug use is often undertaken with little regard to hygiene, and injection paraphernalia such as needles, syringes, and cotton are frequently shared with other drug addicts (Millstein 1993). Sharing HIV-contaminated injection equipment can easily result in the transmission of this virus. The likelihood of an intravenous drug user contracting AIDS is directly correlated with (1) the frequency of drug injections, (2) the number of partners with whom injection equipment is shared, (3) the frequency of needle sharing, and (4) the frequency of injections in locations where there are high AIDS infection rates, such as in shooting galleries or crack houses (Booth et al. 1993).

Crack

Use of drugs such as crack (Ciba Foundation 1992) and alcohol (Colthurst 1993) tends to compromise judgment and encourage high-risk activities such as injection drug use or sexual risk taking (Beard and Kunsman 1993; Inciardi et al. 1993). In particular, the use of crack has been associated with high rates of HIV infection. Crack addicts often exchange sex for drugs or money to purchase drugs (Inciardi et al. 1993; Mathias 1993). These dangerous activities frequently occur in populations with an already high rate of HIV infection. Once infected, almost half of crack users continue to use sex to obtain their drugs and become a source of HIV infection for others (Diaz and Chu 1993).

■ Adolescents and AIDS

Since the beginning of the HIV/AIDS epidemic, more than 2200 adolescent males ages 13 to 19 years have been reported to have AIDS. Approximately 27% of AIDS cases among adolescent males ages 13 to 19 occurred among those who had hemophilia and acquired their infection before blood products were heat treated to prevent HIV transmission. Injection drug use is more common among the 20- to 24-year-old men reported to have AIDS than among adolescents with AIDS, but less common than among men older than 24 years of age who have AIDS. Approximately 7% of AIDS cases among men ages 13 to 24 years reported heterosexual contact as their exposure category. In 2002, male adolescents between the ages of 13 and 19 who were diagnosed with AIDS contracted the disease in the following ways (CDC 2004b):

- Male-to-male sexual contact: 41%
- Hemophilia: 27%
- Injection drug use: 10%
- Heterosexual contact: 8%
- Male-to-male sexual contact and injection drug use: 6%
- Other/not identified: 6%
- Transfusion recipient: 4%

Other recent important findings include the following:

- "It is estimated that 50% of all new HIV infections are among young people (about 7,000 young people become infected every day), and that 30% of the 40 million people living with HIV/AIDS are in the 15–24 age group" (World Health Organization [WHO] 2000–2004). Equally serious is the fact that "[T]he vast majority of young people who are HIV positive do not know that they are infected, and few young people who are engaging in sex know the HIV status of their partners" (WHO 2000–2004).

- Young people in the United States use alcohol, tobacco, and other drugs at high rates. Both casual and chronic substance users are more likely to engage in high-risk behaviors, such as unprotected sex, when they are under the influence of drugs or alcohol. Runaways and other homeless people are at high risk for HIV infection if they are exchanging sex for drugs or money (CDC 2007b).

- Black and Hispanic adolescents have been disproportionately affected by the HIV/AIDS epidemic. In the United States in 2002, 15% of the adolescent population was black, yet 65% of AIDS cases reported in 13- to 19-year-olds involved African Americans. Hispanics accounted for 16% of the total adolescent population, yet 20% of AIDS cases reported in adolescents involved Hispanic patients.

- Approximately two-thirds of AIDS cases among adolescent and young adult women were attributed to heterosexual contact as the mode of exposure to HIV. Cases among 13- to 19-year-old women (19%) were less likely to be attributed to injection drug use than were cases among 20- to 24-year-old women (29%).

- Most 13- to 19-year-old females reported contracting HIV followed by AIDS through heterosexual contact (66%), injection drug use (19%), and other/not identified causes (15%) (CDC 2004c).

- A recent United Nations Aids Report (UNAIDS) estimated that throughout the world, "one-third of those living with AIDS are aged 15–24" (MSNBC 2004). Further, most of these individuals who contract HIV do not even know they have the disease.

- HIV infection is spreading rapidly among younger urban gay men who are too young to recall the beginning of the AIDS epidemic two decades ago.

- Medical journalists from the University of Massachusetts Medical School in Worcester have reported positive outcomes for infants born with HIV infection. "During the first 15 years of the epidemic, they note, 15,000 U.S. infants acquired HIV, mainly from their mothers. Today, fewer than 200 U.S. children acquire HIV in a year, and these infections occur largely because the mother did not have appropriate prenatal care to prevent transmission" (Yahoo! and Reuters 2001).

- Nearly half of the roughly 40,000 Americans who become newly infected with HIV each year are younger than the age of 25. Approximately 25% of the people now living with HIV in this country became infected when they were teenagers. More importantly, many young people also use drugs and alcohol, which can increase the likelihood that they will engage in high-risk sexual behavior.
- Adolescents who are most vulnerable to HIV infection include those who are homeless or runaways, juvenile offenders, and school dropouts.
- Worldwide, sexual intercourse is by far the most common mode of HIV transmission. In the United States, as many as half of all new HIV infections are associated either directly or indirectly with injection drug use (i.e., using HIV-contaminated needles to inject drugs or having sexual contact with an HIV-infected drug user) (amFAR 2006).

Three of the principal ways adolescents become infected with HIV are as follows: (1) high-risk sexual activity (unprotected sexual intercourse is reported by more than half of adolescents by the age of 17 years); (2) injection of substances of abuse; and (3) sex with multiple partners (CDC 2004a, 2004b; Schaefer et al. 1993). Clearly, young people must be better educated about HIV, its transmission, and potential consequences before this epidemic becomes even more disastrous in adolescents.

■ What to Do About HIV and AIDS

What can I do about being HIV-positive? I was diagnosed 3 years ago, and so far, I am basically okay. I have started taking medication to slow down the rate of infection, but one never knows when the first symptoms will suddenly pop up. My lover is clear of the infection and we are careful — usually. I am worried about my condition, but nothing can be done about it. Life is full of good luck and bad luck; so far I have been spared. Regarding tomorrow, who knows. *(From Venturelli's research files, interview with a 32-year-old male hospital administrator, October 10, 1996.)*

To date, the combination of various types of protease inhibitors and antiretroviral therapy medications is the most promising treatment for remaining relatively healthy with HIV. Although protease inhibitors do not completely rid the body of HIV antibodies, this category of drugs is usually successful in holding the virus at low levels in the bloodstream. The current lack of a permanent cure makes prevention the most important element in dealing with the AIDS problem. There are two main strategies for preventing HIV:

- People should be encouraged to adopt safer sexual behavior. Some of the steps to help achieve this include (1) avoiding multiple sex partners, especially if they are strangers or only casual acquaintances; (2) avoiding risk-taking sexual behavior that may allow HIV transmission, such as unprotected vaginal, oral, and anal intercourse; and (3) encouraging individuals who choose to continue high-risk sexual behaviors to use condoms or insist that their sexual partner use a condom.
- Drug abusers should be educated about their risk of contracting AIDS. They should be encouraged to reduce their risk by (1) abstaining from injecting drugs; (2) not sharing injection paraphernalia or always using clean needles (if available through "needle exchange programs"); (3) not sharing drugs with groups with high rates of HIV infection such as those in shooting galleries or crack houses; and (4) disinfecting the equipment (cleaning and boiling equipment for at least 15 minutes) between uses if they continue to share injection equipment.

One of the major difficulties in controlling the AIDS epidemic is identifying where preventive efforts should be focused. Because of limited resources, it is impossible to personally educate everyone in this country about HIV and AIDS. Consequently, our most intense efforts must be targeted at populations and neighborhoods with particularly high HIV infection rates. The National Research Council has declared that, although anyone can acquire AIDS, a handful of neighborhoods have been devastated by this infection, whereas most of the nation remains relatively unscathed (Kolata 1993). It has been speculated that some 35 to 45 large neighborhoods in the United States fuel the AIDS epidemic throughout the country; if HIV infection could be controlled in these areas, the national epidemic would diminish significantly. Because of this hypothesis, it has been proposed that AIDS prevention efforts particularly be focused on younger gay men and injection drug users who have multiple sex partners in the high-density AIDS neighborhoods found in many large metropolitan cities throughout the United States. Even with this focused approach, no one should be fooled into thinking that the HIV/AIDS problem will be eliminated. Everyone should approach potential sexual partners with some degree of caution, especially because the carrier of HIV may be unaware of infection or be reluctant to admit being a carrier for fear of abandonment. One thing is evident: If any doubt exists, we strongly recommend both partners being tested several times in a row before engaging in potentially life-threatening sexual contact.

The Entertainment Industry and Drug Use

Musicians sing about guzzling liquor and movie stars puff cigarettes and take drugs on the big screen. However, federal officials ask: Where is the unglamorous side of substance use — like hangovers, slurred speech, or trouble with the law (*News Tribune* 1999)? Drug use has a tendency to be displayed or fueled (depending on your perspective) by popular culture. In this section, we discuss three important genres of popular culture — movies, music, and the Internet — as one electronic subculture that depicts and promotes drug use.

At the Lollapalooza music festival held in July 1997 in an amphitheater in Massachusetts, the mostly white, suburban teen crowd cheered wildly when rap group Cypress Hill pushed a 6-foot-tall *bong*, or water pipe, onstage. The group sold 5 million copies of its first two albums, one of which included songs titled "Legalize It," "Hits from the Bong," and "I Wanna Get High" (Winters 1997).

In a research study for Columbia's Center on Addiction and Substance Abuse, 76% of 12- to 17-year-olds indicated that the entertainment industry encourages illegal drug use. One 16-year-old daily marijuana user said, "All I know is that almost every song you listen to says something about [drug use]. It puts it into your mind constantly. . . . When you see the celebrities doing it, it makes it seem okay"(Winters 1997, p. 41).

Approximately 10 years ago, the rock and rap music industries experienced a heroin epidemic.

Although many other rock stars before Kurt Cobain used and abused drugs, Cobain's struggle with heroin and his 1994 suicide appear to have glamorized the use of this drug. "The number of top alternative bands that have been linked to heroin through a member's overdose, arrest, admitted use, or recovery is staggering: Nirvana, Hole, Smashing Pumpkins, Everclear, Blind Melon, Skinny Puppy, 7 Year Bitch, Red Hot Chili Peppers, Stone Temple Pilots, Breeders, Alice in Chains, Sublime, Sex Pistols, Porno for Pyros, and Depeche Mode" (Schoemer 1996, p. 50).

Together these bands have sold more than 60 million albums — "that's a heck of a lot of white, middle-class kids in the heartland" (Schoemer 1996, p. 50). Despite some factions in the music industry attempting to curtail heroin use by rock stars, many claim that the music industry still glamorizes heroin and other drug use.

How pervasive is drug use in today's popular movies and music? Research indicates that there is much substance abuse in popular movies and

Mel Gibson consuming a drug. Do such pictures have any effect on viewers?

music. Studies revealed that 98% of movies reviewed depicted illicit drugs, alcohol, tobacco, or OTC and prescription medicines. Alcohol and tobacco appeared in more than 90% of movies, and illicit drugs appeared in 22%. About one-fourth (26%) of the movies that depicted illicit drugs contained explicit, graphic portrayals of their preparation and/or ingestion. Substance use was almost never a central theme, and very few movies ever specified motivations for use. Less than one half (49%) of the movies portrayed short-term consequences of substance use, and about 12% depicted long-term consequences. Of the 669 adult major characters featured in the 200 movies studied, 5% used illicit drugs, 25% smoked tobacco, and 65% consumed alcohol. At least two major characters used illicit drugs in 12% of the movies, tobacco in 44%, and alcohol in 85% (Office of National Drug Control Policy [ONDCP] 1999).

In summarizing main findings from a study conducted by the Office of National Drug Control Policy (1999) regarding substance use in both movies and songs, the following results were found:

- Alcohol appeared in 93% of the movies and 17% of the songs; tobacco appeared in 89% of the movies but only 3% of the songs.
- Alcohol use was associated with wealth or luxury in 34% of the movies in which it appeared, with sexual activity in 19%, and with crime or violence in 37%.
- Alcohol use was associated with wealth or luxury in 24% of the songs in which it was referenced, with sexual activity in 3%, and with crime or violence in 13%.
- Sixty-three percent of rap songs contained references to substances; only 10% of songs in other categories did.
- In movies depicting illicit drugs, marijuana appeared most frequently (51%); followed by powder cocaine (33%); hallucinogens, heroin or other opiates, and miscellaneous others (each 12%); and crack cocaine (2%).
- In songs referring to illicit drugs, marijuana appeared most frequently (63%); followed by crack cocaine (15%); powder cocaine (10%); and hallucinogens, heroin or other opiates, and miscellaneous others (4% each).

These findings clearly indicate that both movies and songs continue to reflect widespread use of alcohol and other drugs in our culture. Furthermore, their influence on the public viewing audiences continues to have an impact on values and attitudes about the use and/or abuse of drugs. One executive director of a Washington, D.C., area youth group, said, "It's becoming increasingly difficult to administer our preventive drug programs because the youth culture has changed in a manner that a lot more of popular music idolizes the use of marijuana and hallucinogens and that has a profound effect on young people" (Haywood 1996, p. 14).

Another top administrator at the Center for Substance Abuse Prevention of the Substance Abuse and Mental Health Services Administration, agreed, "Our pop culture is sending a lot of pro-drug messages" (Haywood 1996). In addition to these observations, the major findings noted earlier with regard to substance use in movies and songs support the amount of alcohol and other drugs used in these two major types of electronic and audio mediums.

■ More Recent Promoter of Drug Use: The Internet

According to the UCLA Center for Communication Policy, for those who use online technology, the Internet is considered the most important source for information — more important than TV or radio. "Some 55% of Internet users said 'most' or 'all' information in cyberspace is reliable and accurate, while only a third of non-users agreed" (Reuters and CNN.com 2000a). A survey of 55,000 Internet users performed by a market research firm called Media Matrix discovered that low-income World Wide Web users are now the fastest-growing U.S. market (Reuters and CNN.com 2000b).

There is no question that pro-drug messages and detailed information are readily available over the Internet. The Internet maintains a unique subculture of drug enthusiasts. Drug use information found online includes how to roll super joints, bake marijuana-laced brownies, grow "magic" psilocybin mushrooms, and create formulas for making amphetamine-like drugs; where to purchase the latest equipment for indoor growing of marijuana; and where to obtain catalogs that offer drug paraphernalia for sale. Similarly, magazines such as *High Times* and *Hemp Times* claim growing numbers of subscribers. Such magazines devote most of their articles, features, advice columns, hemp festival information, and advertisements to the pleasures of drug consumption. Further, chat rooms devoted to finding, growing, purchasing, and making drug substances are growing in popularity. Often, chat rooms and exchange of information on the Internet remain oblivious to nonillicit drug users.

A more recent and alarming occurrence is the boom in illicit drug sales online. Prescription drugs are being sold without a prescription over the Internet. Often solicitations are in the form of spam (unsolicited emails), including multiple offers each day. The International Narcotics Control Board (INCB) reported recently, "90% of online drugs sales take place without a medical prescription" (Join Together.Online and BBC News 2005). The INCB said, "The illicit trade over the Internet has been identified as one of the major sources for prescription medicines abused by children and adolescents in certain countries such as the United States."

> Billions of [doses of] controlled substances — some of them highly potent drugs such as oxycodone, equivalent to morphine, and fentanyl, which is many times stronger than morphine, [including Viagra, Xanex and OxyContin (to name a few)] — are being sold by unlicensed Internet pharmacies. (Join Together Online and BBC News 2005)

Recently, *USA Today* reported that ". . . more than 10 million online messages written by teens in the past year shows they regularly chat about drinking alcohol, smoking pot, partying and hooking up" (Leinwand 2007). "Many of the teens who posted messages about drugs or alcohol often traded information about using illicit substances without getting hurt or caught. Some teens debated drug legalization and the drinking age. Other teens recounted their partying experiences, including sexual liaisons while drunk or high" (Leinwand 2007).

Clearly, the Internet is becoming a source of illicit drugs for anyone having access to computers, and this audience includes younger teens and adults. Legal suppliers appear to be fueling the trade by providing their products to unlicensed Internet pharmacies that then sell these legally restricted types of drugs (Join Together Online and BBC News 2005).

Although the Internet serves as an immensely valuable medium for learning, conducting business, communicating, and making information available, it is also used by a growing number of drug users as a forum for exchanging and learning about the latest information and techniques of drug consumption.

Individuals who use the Internet for this type of information should be particularly wary because it is difficult, if not impossible, for harmful myths and fallacies posted on the web to be regulated.

Discussion Questions

1. What are two strengths and two weaknesses of studying subcultures from (1) an insider's perspective and (2) an outsider's perspective?

2. What are the principal drugs abused by athletes?

3. What are the principal effects and side effects of steroids?

4. What factors encourage drug use by athletes?

5. From the world of steroid abusers, define and give an example of the following terms: stacking, cycling, plateauing, pyramiding, and array.

6. Argue both for and against drug testing in sports.

7. What type of penalties do you think should be used against athletes who abuse drugs?

8. Review the ATLAS steroid prevention program. Can you improve its methods for lessening steroid use among adolescents? How effective do you think this program would be at your college or university?

9. List the reasons why women are more concerned about drug use and abuse than men. Can you add several additional reasons not mentioned in this chapter?

10. Do you believe that drug prevention programs should be created uniquely for males and females?

11. What factors in the unique female roles encourage the use of substances of abuse?

12. Should childbearing women who abuse drugs be punished? Why or why not?

13. Why are women who have been or are sexually abused more likely to become addicted to drugs?

14. Why are adolescents especially vulnerable to drug abuse problems?

15. List and explain three reasons why you think adolescents from upper-middle-class socioeconomic backgrounds become drug abusers.

16. What types of parents are most likely to have children who develop drug abuse problems?

17. How do adolescent drug abuse patterns differ from those in adults?

18. In what way are drugs of abuse associated with juvenile gang activity?

19. Should all adolescents who use drugs of abuse be treated for drug dependence? Explain your answer.

20. Do you think that it is realistic to expect drug abusers to change their habits to prevent the spread of AIDS? Why or why not?

21. Should prisoners who test positive for HIV be segregated from the non–HIV-positive populations? Should prisoners be given free access to condoms in prisons? Why or why not?

22. John was caught by campus or city police growing psilocybin (hallucinogenic) mushrooms in his off-campus college apartment. Should John be punished by his college or university in addition to the punishment that will be meted out by the criminal justice system? Why or why not?

23. What if you discover that your roommate is HIV positive? How would you handle this situation?

24. Do you think that the excessive use of alcohol and other drugs in movies influences viewers? Further, are people who enjoy rap or rock music affected by the lyrics that refer to drug use and/or abuse? Why or why not?

25. Do you believe that drug information over the Internet, such as chat rooms devoted to the use of certain drugs (e.g., where to purchase equipment for growing marijuana, OTC stimulant pills, and the spores of psilocybin mushrooms), promotes drug use? Why or why not?

Summary

1 The most common drugs abused by athletes are the ergogenic (performance-enhancing) substances. They include the anabolic steroids, for building muscle mass and strength, and the CNS stimulants, to achieve energy, quickness, and endurance.

2 Drug testing is conducted for most professional athletic competitions and usually includes screens for steroids and stimulants. However, some performance-enhancing drugs, such as erythropoietin and HGF, are undetectable. Yet, undetectable drugs are involved in 90% of the estimated doping cases. Athletes who use performance-enhancing drugs often go to great lengths to avoid detection by these drug tests.

3 About 50% of the anabolic steroids used in the United States are prescribed by doctors; the other 50% are obtained from the black market. Black market steroids include drugs diverted from legitimate channels smuggled from foreign countries — for example, Brazil, Italy, Mexico, Great Britain, Portugal, France, and Peru — designated for veterinarian use, or inactive counterfeits.

4 The ATLAS prevention program uses athletes, coaches, and team leaders who are trained to educate team members about the effects of anabolic steroid abuse. They emphasize both desirable and adverse effects of steroid use. Presenting a balanced perspective is stressed because adolescents know very well how anabolic steroids build muscles and can increase athletic abilities.

5 In general, women are (1) more concerned about drugs and drug use than men; (2) more likely to believe in drug prevention programs, such as needle exchange and testing reckless drivers for drug use than men; and (3) more likely to speak with their children about drug use than men (Drug Strategies 1998).

6 There is a high prevalence of drug dependence in women who are victims of sexual and/or physical abuse. Approximately 70% of women in drug abuse treatment report histories of physical abuse with victimization beginning at 11 years of age and occurring repeatedly. Further, women and men have different endocrine (hormone) systems, organs, and structures, and women's responses to drugs vary according to their reproductive states.

7 For women to receive adequate treatment for drug dependence, certain considerations must be met: (1) availability of female-sensitive services, (2) nonpunitive and noncoercive treatment that incorporates supportive behavior change approaches, and (3) treatment for a wide range of medical problems, mental disorders, and psychosocial problems.

8 Most adolescents who use substances of abuse are going through normal psychosocial development and will not develop problematic dependence on these drugs. The adolescent users who have difficulty with drugs often lack coping skills to deal with their problems, have dysfunctional families, possess poor self-images, and/or feel socially and emotionally insecure.

9 Parents who are most likely to raise drug-abusing adolescents are (1) drug abusers, (2) non–drug-using coupled with being constantly condemning, (3) overly demanding, (4) overly protective, or (5) unable to communicate effectively with their children.

10 The substances adolescents are most likely to abuse are alcohol, cigarettes, inhalants, marijuana, LSD, Ecstasy, and prescription stimulants. High-frequency use is most likely to occur with cigarettes, alcohol, and marijuana.

11 People who become gang members were often neglected by their parents, lacked positive role models, and failed to receive adequate adult supervision. Other motivations for joining a gang include peer pressures, low self-esteem, and perceived easy acquisition of money from gang-related drug dealing and other criminal activities.

12 The major reasons cited by college students for their use of drugs were: (1) breaks the ice, (2) enhances social activity, (3) gives people something to do, (4) gives people something to talk about, (5) allows people to have more fun, (6) facilitates contact with peers, (7) facilitates sexual opportunities, and (8) facilitates male bonding.

13 Two interesting findings from research regarding drug use by college student subcultures are that (1) the best predictor of drug use for first-year college students is drug use during a typical month in the senior year of high school, and (2) usually recreational drug use does not begin in college but has already been established in high school.

14 Club drugs include MDMA (Ecstasy), GHB, Rohypnol, ketamine, methamphetamine, and LSD. The phrase *club drug* is derived from the use of these drugs at all-night dance parties such as raves or trances, dance clubs, and bars. All these drugs are colorless, tasteless, and odorless. Individuals who want to intoxicate, sedate, and later sexually take advantage of others can add them unobtrusively to beverages.

15 After homosexual men, individuals who are addicted to illicit drugs are the second largest group at risk for contracting AIDS. This risk results from sharing of blood-contaminated needles and syringes and increased involvement in sexual risk taking because of the effects of drugs or in securing payment for drugs.

16 More than 40 million people are living with HIV worldwide, including 5 million new cases in 2005 alone. For the United States, the latest numbers indicate that by 2004, 1 million Americans were living with HIV — and one in four of them did not know it (NIDA 2007). Another source indicates that at the end of 2003, an estimated 1,039,000 to 1,185,000 persons in the United States were living with HIV/AIDS (Glynn and Rhodes 2005). The CDC has estimated that approximately 40,000 persons in the United States become infected with HIV each year (CDC 2005). During 2005, 74% of those diagnosed with HIV/AIDS were male and 26% were female. Forty-nine percent were black, 31% white, 18% Hispanic, 1% Asian/Pacific Islander, and less than 1% American Indian/Alaska Native. The noteworthy finding is that in 2005, blacks (including African Americans), who make up approximately 13% of the U.S. population, accounted for almost half of the estimated number of HIV/AIDS cases diagnosed (CDC 2007). From 1981 through 2005, the CDC estimates that 952,629 cases of AIDS were diagnosed; of these, 530,756 died with AIDS as a major cause of death, and as of 2005, 421,873 people were living with AIDS (CDC 2007a).

17 Major ways to prevent contracting HIV include (1) engaging in safe (protected) sexual behavior, (2) avoiding use of contaminated drug paraphernalia and especially use of intravenous drugs, (3) avoiding use of drugs in groups with high rates of HIV infection, and (4) frankly discussing past sexual histories with potential sexual partners and, if in any doubt, having potential partners be tested for HIV several times in a row.

18 The extent of alcohol and drug use in movies and songs is startling. Overall, findings of one study revealed that 98% of movies reviewed depicted illicit drugs, alcohol, and tobacco or OTC/prescription medicines. In this same detailed study, alcohol appeared in 93% of the movies and in 17% of the songs; tobacco appeared in 89% of movies but only 3% of songs. The lyrics of 63% of rap songs versus about 10% of the lyrics in other categories had substance references.

19 The music industry has been setting up drug-using celebrities as teen role models. The message conveyed by much of the music and by many bands is that drug use is acceptable. After several drug-related deaths of celebrities over the past few years, the industry is working to change such perceptions.

20 New media influences contribute to drug use. The Internet is considered to be the latest source of information where knowledge about use of illicit drugs is burgeoning.

References

About.com. "Alcoholism and Substance Abuse." Alcohol Alert from the National Institute on Alcohol Abuse and Alcoholism (NIAAA) (June 2007a). Available http://alcoholism.about.com/cs/alerts/1/blnaa10.htm.

About.com. "Alcohol and Women." Alcohol Alert from the National Institute on Alcohol Abuse and Alcoholism (NIAAA) (June 2007b). Available http://alcoholism.about.com/cs/alerts/1/binaa10.htm.

About.com. "Alcohol and Hormones." Alcohol Alert from the National Institute on Alcohol Abuse and Alcoholism (NIAAA) (2006). Available http://alcoholism.about.com/cs/alerts/1/binaa26.htm.

ABC News. "Police Paint Grisly Picture of Benoit Home." New York (26 June 2007). Available http://abcnews.go.com/print?id=3315501.

American Academy of Child and Adolescent Psychiatry. "Facts for Families: Teen Suicide." American Academy of child Adolescent Psychiatry, 2004. Available http://www.aacap.org/cs/root/facts_for_families/teen_suicide

American Foundation for AIDS Research (amfAR). *Facts About HIV/AIDS, 2001.* New York: Body Health Resources Corporation, 2001.

Amfar AIDS Research. "Facts for Life: What you and the people you care about need to know about HIV/AIDS." New York, NY, 2006. Available http://www.amfar.org/binary-data/AMFAR_PUBLICATION/download_file/3.pdf.

Anonymous, as told by Penn, N. "Confession: Why I Juiced." *Gentleman's Quarterly* (September 2005): 292–297.

Apostolides, M. "How to Quit the Holistic Way." *Psychology Today* 29 (September/ October 1996): 30–43, 75–76.

Archambault, D. "Adolescence, a Physiological, Cultural and Psychological No Man's Land." In *Adolescent Substance Abuse, Etiology, Treatment and Prevention,* edited by G. Lawson and A. Lawson, 11–28. Gaithersburg, MD: Aspen, 1992.

Associated Press. "Boredom, Stress, Money Linked to Drug Abuse." *Chesterton/Valparaiso Post Tribune* (20 August 2003): 1, A8.

Associated Press. "Surviving with AIDS Carries Big Price Tag." *Post Tribune* (11 November 2006): 7.

Bahr, S. J., A. C. Marcos, and S. L. Maughan. "Family, Educational and Peer Influences on Alcohol Use of Female and Male Adolescents." *Journal of Studies on Alcohol* 56 (1995): 457–469.

Beard, B., and V. Kunsman. "A Cause for Concern: Alcohol-Induced Risky Sex on College Campuses." *Prevention Pipeline* 6 (September–October 1993): 24.

Begley, S., and M. Brant with Dickey, C., K. Helmstaedt, R. Nordland, and T. Hayden. "The Real Scandal." *Newsweek* 133 (15 February 1999): 48–54.

Bell, J. "Athletes' Use and Abuse of Drugs." *The Physician and Sports Medicine* 15 (March 1987): 99–108.

Belsie, L. "Temperance Movement Hits College Dorms." *The Christian Science Monitor* 87 (30 August 1995): 1, 2.

Bennett, M. E., J. Miller, and W. Gill. "Drinking, Binge Drinking, and Other Drug Use Among Southwestern Undergraduates: Three-Year Trends." *American Journal of Drug and Alcohol Abuse* 25 (1999): 331–346.

Bergeret, J. "Young People, Drugs . . . and Others." Rockville, MD: United Nations Office for Drug Control Office for Drug Control and Crime Prevention (UN/ODCCP) (1 January 1981).

Beschner, G., and A. Friedman. "Treatment of Adolescent Drug Abusers." *International Journal of the Addictions* 20 (1985): 977–993.

"Bodybuilding Drug Yields 'High.'" *Pharmacy Times* (June 1992): 14.

Booth, R., J. Watters, and D. Chitwood. "HIV Risk-Related Sex Behaviors Among Injection Drug Users, Crack Smokers, and Injection Drug Users Who Smoke Crack." *American Journal of Public Health* 83 (1993): 1144–1148.

Buckstein, D., D. Brent, J. Perper, G. Moritz, M. Baugher, J. Schweers, C. Roth, and L. Balach. "Risk Factors for Completed Suicide Among Adolescents with a Lifetime History of Substance Abuse: A Case-Control Study." *Acta Psychiatry Scandinavia* 88 (1993): 403–408.

Burke, C., and S. Davis. "Anabolic Steroid Abuse." *Pharmacy Times* (June 1992): 35–40.

Campus Alcohol and Drug Resource Center at the University of Florida, "Core Alcohol and Drug Survey Long Form: Key Findings 2006." University of Florida (2006). Available http://www.shcc.ufl.edu/gatorwell/atod/pdf/key06.pdf.

Centers for Disease Control and Prevention (CDC). *Facts About Adolescents and HIV/AIDS.* Atlanta, GA: CDC, March 1998.

Centers for Disease Control and Prevention (CDC). "HIV/AIDS." *Surveillance Reports* 11 (1999): 1–3.

Centers for Disease Control and Prevention (CDC). *Age at Diagnosis of HIV Infection or AIDS, Reported Through 1999, United States.* HIV/AIDS Surveillance — General Epidemiology 178 Slide Series Through 1999, Slide 24 of 24. Atlanta, GA: National Center for HIV, STD, and TB Prevention, January 2000a.

Centers for Disease Control and Prevention (CDC). *AIDS Cases by Age and Sex Reported 1981–1999, United States.* HIV/AIDS Surveillance — General Epidemiology 178 Slide Series Through 1999, Slide 2 of 24. Atlanta, GA: National Center for HIV, STD, and TB Prevention, January 2000b.

Centers for Disease Control and Prevention (CDC). *Adult/Adolescent AIDS Cases by Exposure Category and Year of Diagnosis, 1985–June 1999, United States.* HIV/AIDS Surveillance — General Epidemiology 178 Slide Series Through 1999, Slide 8 of 24. Atlanta, GA: National Center for HIV, STD, and TB Prevention, January 2000c.

Centers for Disease Control and Prevention (CDC). *HIV/AIDS Surveillance Report, 2003 (Volume 15).* Atlanta, GA: U.S. Department of Health and Human Services, CDC, 2004a.

Centers for Disease Control and Prevention (CDC). *Estimated AIDS Cases Among Male Adolescents and Young Adults by Exposure Category, Diagnosed Through 2002, United States.* National Center for HIV, STD, and TB Prevention, Divisions of HIV/AIDS Prevention Surveillance Branch. Washington, DC: CDC, 2004b.

Centers for Disease Control and Prevention (CDC). *Estimated AIDS Cases Among Female Adolescents and Young Adults by Exposure Category, Diagnosed through 2002, United States.* National Center for HIV, STD, and TB Prevention, Divisions of HIV/AIDS Prevention Surveillance Branch. Washington, DC: CDC, 2004c.

Centers for Disease Control and Prevention (CDC). "Guidelines for National Human Immunodeficiency Virus Case Surveillance, Including Monitoring for Human Immunodeficiency Virus Infection and Acquired Immunodeficiency Syndrome." *Morbidity and Mortality Weekly Report (MMWR)*; 48(2005): 1–28.

Centers for Disease Control and Prevention (CDC). "A Glance at the HIV/AIDS Epidemic." Department of Health and Human Services. Atlanta, GA (2007a). Available http://www.cdc.gov/hiv/resources/factsheets/at-a-glance.htm.

Centers for Disease Control and Prevention (CDC). "HIV/AIDS Among Youth." The Body Health Resources Corporation (2007b). Available http://www.thebody.com/content/art17110.html.

Chong J-R. "Study Casts Positive Light on AIDS Drug." *Los Angeles Times*, reported in *Post Tribune*, Merrillville, IN (13 August 2006): A9.

Ciba Foundation. "AIDS and HIV Infection in Cocaine Users." In *Cocaine: Scientific and Social Dimensions*, edited by G. Block and J. Whelan. 181–194. New York: Wiley, 1992.

Clinton, B. "My Quest to Improve Care." *Newsweek* (15 May 2006): 50–53.

CNN.com. "Teen Prescription Drug Abuse Reportedly Holding Steady." The Associated Press. (2007). Available http://www.cnn.com/2007/HEALTH/02/14/teens.drugs.ap/index.html.

Colthurst, T. "HIV and Alcohol Impairment: Reducing Risks." *Prevention Pipeline* 6 (July–August 1993): 24.

Crowley, G. "Targeting a Deadly Scrap of Genetic Code." *Newsweek* (2 December 1996): 68–69.

Curry, D. G., and I. A. Spergel. "Gang Homicide, Delinquency, and Community." In *Gangs and Gang Behavior*, edited by G. Larry Mays, 314–336. Chicago, IL: Nelson-Hall, 1997.

Daily, S. "Alcohol, Incest, and Adolescence." In *Adolescent Substance Abuse, Etiology, Treatment and Prevention*, edited by G. Lawson and A. Lawson, 251–266. Gaithersburg, MD: Aspen, 1992a.

Daily, S. "Suicide Solution: The Relationship of Alcohol and Drug Abuse to Adolescent Suicide." In *Adolescent Substance Abuse, Etiology, Treatment and Prevention*, edited by G. Lawson and A. Lawson, 233–250. Gaithersburg, MD: Aspen, 1992b.

Diaz, T., and S. Chu. "Crack Cocaine Use and Sexual Behavior Among People with AIDS." *Journal of the American Medical Association* 269 (1993): 2845–2846.

Dicker, M., and E. A. Leighton. "Trends in the U.S. Prevalence of Drug-Using Parturient Women and Drug-Affected Newborns, 1979 Through 1990." *American Journal of Public Health* 84 (September 1994): 1433.

Donaldson-Evans, C. "Wrestler Chris Benoit Double Murder-Suicide: Was It 'Roid Rage'?" FoxNews.com. (27 June 2007) Available http://www.foxnews.com/printer_friendly_story/0,3566,286834,00.html.

Drug Facts and Comparisons, 109–109c. St. Louis, MO: Kluwer, 1994.

Drug Strategies. "Keeping Score 1998, Drug Use and Attitudes." Washington, DC, 1998. Available http://www.drugstrategies.org/ks1998/use.html.

Elmen, J., and D. Offer. "Normality, Turmoil and Adolescence." In *Handbook of Clinical Research and Practice with Adolescents*, edited by P. Tolan and B. Cohler, 5–19. New York: Wiley, 1993.

Erickson, P. G., and G. F. Murray: "Sex Differences in Cocaine Use and Experiences: A Double Standard Revived?" *American Journal of Drug and Alcohol Abuse* 15 (1989): 135–152.

Fagan, J. "Social Processes of Delinquency and Drug Use Among Urban Gangs." In *Gangs in America*, edited by C. R. Huff, 183–213. Newbury Park, CA: Sage, 1990.

Ferrente, R. "Ben Johnson Retires from Running After Positive Test." *Morning Edition* on National Public Radio (8 March 1993).

Fischer, J. S. "Searching for That Ounce of Prevention: Promising Strategies for an AIDS Vaccine." *U.S. News and World Report* (17 July 2000).

Glave, J. "Betty Ford Got Help, But Addiction Stalks Thousands of Women." *Salt Lake Tribune* 248 (3 June 1994): A-1.

Glynn M. and P. Rhodes. "A Glance at the HIV/AIDS Epidemic." CDC/HIV Fact Sheet National HIV Prevention Conference (Revised June 2007). Available http://www.cdc.gov/hiv/resources/factsheets/at-a-glance.pdf.

Goldberg, L., D. Elliot, G. N. Clarke, D. P. MacKinnon, E. Moe, L. Zoref, C. Green, S. L. Wolf, E. Greffrath, D. J. Miller, and A. Lapin. "Effects of a Multidimensional Anabolic Steroid Prevention Intervention: The Adolescents Training and Learning to Avoid Steroids (ATLAS) Program. *Journal of the American Medical Association* 276 (1996): 1555–1562.

Goldstein, F. "Pharmacological Aspects of Substance Abuse." In *Remington's Pharmaceutical Sciences*, edited by the American Journal of Pharmaceutical Education 19th ed. Easton, PA: Mack, 1995.

Grinspoon, L. "AIDS and Mental Health — Part 1." *Harvard Mental Health Letter* 10 (January 1994): 1–4.

Guide4Living.com. "Steroid Abuse and Addiction." (2005). Available http://www.guide4living.com/drugabuse/steroids.htm.

Harlan, R., and M. Garcia. "Neurobiology of Androgen Abuse." In *Drugs of Abuse*, edited by R. Watson, 185–201. Boca Raton, FL: CRC Press, 1992.

Haywood, R. L. "Why More Young People Are Using Drugs." *Jet* 90 (9 September 1996).

Hitt, E. "Binge-Drinking Students Use Other Drugs: Report." *Health — Reuters* (12 September 2001).

Hoberman, J. M., and C. E. Yesalis. "The History of Synthetic Testosterone." *Scientific American* (February 1995).

Hoshino, J. "Assessment of Adolescent Substance Abuse." In *Adolescent Substance Abuse, Etiology, Treatment and Prevention*, edited by G. Lawson and A. Lawson, 87–104. Gaithersburg, MD: Aspen, 1992.

Howard, M. "Adolescent Substance Abuse: A Social Learning Theory Perspective." In *Adolescent Substance Abuse, Etiology, Treatment and Prevention*, edited by G. Lawson and A. Lawson, 29–40. Gaithersburg, MD: Aspen, 1992.

Inciardi, James A., D. Lockwood, and A. E. Pottieger. *Woman and Crack-Cocaine*. New York: Macmillian, 1993.

Jayson, S. "Expert: Risky Teen Behavior Is All in the Brain." USA Today.com (2007). Available http://www.usatoday.com/news/health/2007-04-04-teen-brain_N.htm.

Johnson, R. A., J. P. Hoffmann, and D. R. Gerstein. *The Relationship Between Family Structure and Adolescent Substance Use*. Rockville, MD: SAMHSA, Office of Applied Studies, July 1996.

Johnston, L. D., P. M. O'Malley, and J. G. Bachman. *National Survey Results from the Monitoring the Future Study, 1975–1992*. Rockville, MD: National Institute on Drug Abuse, 1993.

Johnston, L. D., P. M. O'Malley, and J. G. Bachman. *National Survey Results from the Monitoring the Future Study, 1975–1994*. Rockville, MD: National Institute on Drug Abuse, 1996.

Johnston, L. D., P. M. O'Malley, and J. G. Bachman. *National Survey on Drug Abuse from the Monitoring the Future Study, 1975–1998; College and Young Adults*. The University of Michigan Institute for Social Research, National Institute on Drug Abuse, U.S. Department of Human Services, National Institutes of Health, 1999.

Johnston, L. D., P. O'Malley, and J. G. Bachman. *The Monitoring the Future National Results on Adolescent Drug Use: Overview of Key Findings, 1999*. The University of Michigan Institute for Social Research, National Institute on Drug Abuse, U.S. Department of Human Services, National Institutes of Health, 2000a.

Johnston, L. D., P. O'Malley, and J. G. Bachman. *National Survey Results on Drug Use from the Monitoring the Future Study, 1975–1999. Vol. 2, College Students and Young Adults*. U.S. Department of Health and Human Services (USDHHS), National Institute on Drug Abuse (NIDA). Washington, DC: U.S. Government Printing Office, 2000b.

Johnston, L. D., P. O'Malley, and J. G. Bachman. *National Survey Results on Drug Use from the Monitoring the Future Study, 1975–2000. Vol. 2, College Students and Young Adults*, U.S. Department of Health and Human Services (USDHHS), National Institute on Drug Abuse (NIDA). Washington, DC: U.S. Government Printing Office, 2001.

Johnston, L. D., P. M. O'Malley, J. G. Bachman, and J. E. Schulenberg. *Monitoring the Future: National Survey Results on Drug Use, 1975–2003. Volume I: Secondary School Students*. Bethesda, MD: National Institute on Drug Abuse, 2004a.

Johnston, L. D., P. M. O'Malley, J. G. Bachman, and J. E. Schulenberg. *Monitoring the Future National Survey Results on Drug Use, 1975–2003. Volume II: College Students and Adults Ages 19–45*. Bethesda, MD: National Institute on Drug Abuse, 2004b.

Johnston, L. D., P. M. O'Malley, J. G. Bachman, and J. E. Schulenberg. "Overall Teen Drug Use Continues Gradual Decline but Use of Inhalants Rises." *Monitoring the Future National Survey Results on Drug Use*. University of Michigan and National Institute on Drug Abuse. Bethesda, MD: National Institute on Drug Abuse, 2004c.

Johnston, L. D., P. M. O'Malley, J. G. Bachman, and J. E. Schulenberg. *Monitoring the Future: National Results on Adolescent Drug Use*. Bethesda, MD: National Institute on Drug Abuse, 2006a.

Johnston, L. D., P. M. O'Malley, J. G. Bachman, and J. E. Schulenberg. *Monitoring the Future: National Results on Adolescent Drug Use 1975–2005, Volume II College Students and Adults 19–45*. Bethesda, MD: National Institute on Drug Abuse, 2006b.

Join Together Online and BBC (British Broadcasting Company) News. "Illicit Drug Sales Booming Online." Boston, MA: Boston University School of Public Health, 2005.

Kandel, D. B. "Drug and Drinking Behavior Among Youth." *Annual Review of Sociology* 6 (1980): 235–285.

Kantrowitz, B., and P. Wingert. "Beyond Littleton: How Well Do You Know Your Kid?" *Newsweek* (10 May 1999).

Kinney, J. *Loosening the Grip*, 6th ed. Boston: McGraw Hill, 2000.

Kirkpatrick, J. *The Woman Alcoholic*. Quakertown, PA: Women for Sobriety, 1999.

Klee, H., and M. Jackson. *Drug Misuse and Motherhood*. New York: Routledge, 2002.

Kolata, G. "Targeting Urged in Attack on AIDS." *New York Times* 142 (7 March 1993): 1.

Korolenko, C. P., and T. A. Donskih. "Addictive Behavior in Women: A Theoretical Perspective." *Drugs and Society* 4 (1990): 39–65.

Ladwig, G. B., and M. D. Anderson. "Substance Abuse in Women: Relationship Between Chemical Dependency of Women and Past Reports of Physical and/or Sexual Abuse." *International Journal of the Addictions* 24 (1989): 739–754.

Lajis, R. H. *The History of Drug Abuse in Sports*. Malaysian Drug and Poison Net, PRN 8099. Professional Bulletin of the National Poison Center, Malaysia (2007). Available http://www.prn2.usm.my/mainsite/bulletin/sun/1996/sun27.html.

Lale, T. "Gangs and Drugs." In *Adolescent Substance Abuse, Etiology, Treatment and Prevention*, edited by G. Lawson and A. Lawson, 267–281. Gaithersburg, MD: Aspen, 1992.

Lawn, J. *Team Up for Drug Prevention with America's Young Athletes*. Washington, DC: Drug Enforcement Administration, U.S. Department of Justice, 1984.

Lawson, G., and A. Lawson, "Etiology." In *Adolescent Substance Abuse, Etiology, Treatment and Prevention*, edited by G. Lawson and A. Lawson, 1–10. Gaithersburg, MD: Aspen, 1992.

Leibsohn, J. "The Relationship Between Drug and Alcohol Use and Peer Group Associations of College Freshmen as They Transition from High School." *Journal of Drug Education* 24 (1994): 177–192.

Leinwand, D. "20% Say They Used Drugs with Their Mom or Dad. Among Reasons: Boomer Culture and Misguided Attempts to Bond." *USA Today* (27 August 2000). Available http://www.usatoday.com/usatonline/20000824/25790504s.htm.

Leinwand, D. "Study: Drug Chat Pervasive Online — Teens Use Internet to Share Stories, Get How-To Advice." *USA Today* (Print Edition), 2007, accessed 12 September 2007. Available http://www.usatoday.com/printedition/news/20070619/a_online19.art.htm.

Lewin, T. "Clean Living on Campus." NYtimes.com. 6 November 2005. Available at http://www.nytimes.com/2005/11/06/education/edlife/work.html?p...

Lin, A. Y. F. "Should Women Be Included in Clinical Trials?" *Pharmacy Times* 10 (November 1994): 27.

Lively, K. "The 'Date-Rape Drug': Colleges Worry about Reports of Growing Use of Rohypnol, a Sedative." *Chronicle of Higher Education* 42 (28 June 1996): A-29.

Lukas, S. "Urine Testing for Anabolic-Androgenic Steroids." *Trends in Pharmacological Sciences* 14 (1993): 61–68.

Marklein, M. B. "College Binge Drinking Heads Off Campus." *USA Today* (14 March 2000).

Mathias, R. "Sex-for-Crack Phenomenon Poses Risk for Spread of AIDS in Heterosexuals." *NIDA Notes* 8 (May/June 1993): 8–11.

Mathias, R. "NIDA Survey Provides First National Data on Drug Use During Pregnancy." *NIDA Notes* 10 (January/February 1995): 6–7.

McCaffrey, B. R. "McCaffrey Announces Strategy to Fight Drug Use in Sports." *Daily Washington File* (21 October 1999).

McDonald, M. "Fast, Strong, Dead?" *Salt Lake Tribune* 250 (22 June 1995): C1, C8.

Meilman, P. W., R. K. Grace, C. A. Presley, and R. Lyerla. "Beyond Performance Enhancement: Polypharmacy Among Collegiate Users of Steroids." *Journal of American College Health* 44 (November 1995): 98–104.

Merchant, W. "Medications and Athletes." *American Druggist* (October 1992): 6–14.

Millstein, R. *Community Alert Bulletin.* Rockville, MD: National Institute on Drug Abuse, U.S. Department of Health and Human Services, 25 March 1993.

Minnesota Institute of Public Health. *Alcohol and Other Drugs & Suicide.* Chemical Health Division, Minnesota Dept. of Human Services, Mounds View, MN: Spring 1995.

Moss, H., L. Kirisci, H. Gordon, and R. Tarter. "A Neuropsychological Profile of Adolescent Alcoholics." *Alcoholism: Clinical and Experimental Research* 18 (1994): 159–163.

MSNBC. "AIDS Outruns Efforts to Combat It, Says U.N. Report: New HIV Infections Hit Record High Last Year." *Health News* (2004). Available http://www.msnbc.msn.com/ID/5377027.

"Multistate Outbreak of Poisonings Associated with Illicit Use of GHB." *Prevention Pipeline* 7 (May–June 1994): 95, 96.

MyDNA.com. "News Center: HAART Therapy Slows Progression to AIDS." Washington, DC: American Medical Association, 2005.

National Clearinghouse for Alcohol and Drug Information (NCADI). *Drugs of Abuse.* Rockville, MD: Substance Abuse and Mental Health Services Administration, 1999.

National Household Survey on Drug Abuse. "Academic Performance and Youth Substance Use." Rockville, MD: Office of Applied Studies (OAS), Substance Abuse and Mental Health Services Administration (SAMHSA), 6 September 2002.

National Institute on Drug Abuse (NIDA). *Anabolic Steroid Abuse.* Capsule 43. Rockville, MD: NIDA, 1996.

National Institute on Drug Abuse (NIDA). *Drug Abuse and Addiction Research: The Sixth Triennial Report to Congress.* Rockville, MD: U.S. Department of Health and Human Services, 1999.

National Institute on Drug Abuse (NIDA). "Club Drugs: Community Alert Bulletin." *NIDA Notes* 14 (30 March 2000).

National Institute on Drug Abuse (NIDA). *Research Report Series — Anabolic Steroid Abuse.* Bethesda, MD: U.S. Government Printing Office, 2006.

National Institute on Drug Abuse (NIDA). *Drugs and HIV.* U.S. Department of Health and Human Services (UDHHS). Bethesda, MD: U.S. Government Printing Office, 2007.

National Institutes of Health (NIH) and National Institute on Drug Abuse (NIDA). *Drug Abuse and Drug Abuse Research: Executive Summary.* Rockville, MD: Substance Abuse and Mental Health Services Administration, 1998.

National Youth Anti-Drug Media Campaign. "The 411 on Rx Drugs." (2007). Available http://www.theantidrug.com/drug_info/prescription_411.asp.

News Tribune. "Alcohol, Tobacco or Drugs Used in 98% of Popular Movies." (29 April 1999): 7–8, 14.

Nicklin, J. L. "Arrests at Colleges Surge for Alcohol and Drug Violations." *Chronicle of Higher Education* (9 June 2000).

Office of National Drug Control Policy (ONDCP). *Substance Use in Popular Movies and Music.* Media Campaign, Campaign Publications. Rockville, MD: ONDCP Drugs and Crime Clearinghouse, 1999.

Olufs, C. "The AIDS Time Line: 20 Years, 20 Drugs, 20 Million Deaths — No Cure in Sight." *Women Alive* (Spring 2001).

"OTC Drugs and Athletes." *Pharmacy Times* (June 1992): 16.

Parrot, A. *Date Rape and Acquaintance Rape.* New York: Rosen, 1988.

Pietroski, N. "Counseling HIV/AIDS Patients." *American Druggist* (August 1993): 50–56.

Prendergast, M. L. "Substance Use and Abuse Among College Students: A Review of Recent Literature." *Journal of American College Health* 43 (1994): 99–113.

Ravid, J. "The Hard-Core Curriculum." *Rolling Stone* 719 (19 October 1995): 99.

Reuters and CNN.com. "Users See Internet as Key Information Source." *Reuters* (16 August 2000a): 2–3.

Reuters and CNN.com. "Study: Lower-Income Web Users Now Fastest-Growing U.S. Market." *Reuters* (22 August 2000b): 9.

Samples, P. "Alcoholism in Athletes: New Directions for Treatment." *The Physician and Sports Medicine* (17 April 1989): 193–202.

Sanders, W. B. *Gangbangs and Drive-bys.* New York: Aldine De Gruyter, 1994.

Schaefer, M. A., J. F. Hilton, M. Ekstrand, and J. Keogh. "Relationship Between Drug Use and Sexual Behaviors and the Occurrence of Sexually Transmitted Diseases Among High-Risk Male Youth." *Sexually Transmitted Diseases* 20 (November–December 1993): 39–47.

Schernoff M., and R. A. Smith. "HIV Treatments: A History of Scientific Advance." *Body Positive* XIV (July 2001): 1–7.

Schoemer, K. "Rockers, Models and the New Allure of Heroin." *Newsweek* (26 August 1996): 24–36.

Science Daily. "Pain Drug Reveals What Most Already Know — Men's and Women's Brains Are Simply Different." (15 March 2000). Available http://www.sciencedaily.com/releases/2000/03/000315075845.htm.

Scott, D. M., J. C. Wagner, and T. W. Barlow. "Anabolic Steroids Use Among Adolescents in Nebraska Schools." *American Journal of Health-System Pharmacy* 53 (1996): 2068–2072.

Scripps Howard News Service. "AIDS Fear: Complacency: Infection Rate Is on Rise for First Time Since 1994." Reported in *Post-Tribune* (21 August 2003): A-10.

Shelden, R. G., S. Tracy, and W. Brown. *Youth Gangs in American Society.* Belmont, CA: Wadsworth/Thomson Learning, 2001.

Shelden, R. G., S. K. Tracy, and W. B. Brown. *Youth Gangs in American Society,* 3rd ed. Belmont, CA: Wadsworth/Thomson Learning, 2004.

Siegel, L., and J. Senna. *Juvenile Delinquency,* 6th ed. St. Paul, MN: West, 1997.

Spergel, I. A. *Youth Gangs: Problem and Response.* Chicago, IL: University of Chicago, School of Social Service Administration, 1990.

Steinberg, L., A. Fletcher, and N. Darling. "Parental Monitoring and Peer Influences on Adolescent Substance Use." *Pediatrics* 93 (1994): 1060–1064.

Sternberg, S. "AIDS Apocalypse Expanding." *USA Today* (28 June 2000): 2.

Street, C., J. Antonio, and D. Cudlipp. "Androgen Use by Athletes: A Reevaluation of the Health Risks." *Canadian Journal of Applied Physiology* 2 (1996): 421–440.

Substance Abuse and Mental Health Services Administration (SAMHSA). *1999 Household Survey on Drug Abuse* (1999a).

Substance Abuse and Mental Health Services Administration (SAMHSA). *Making the Connection Between Substance Abuse and HIV/AIDS Prevention for Women of Color and Youth.* Rockville, MD: U.S. Department of Health and Human Services, 1999b.

Substance Abuse and Mental Health Services Administration (SAMHSA). *Tips for Teens: About Steroids.* Center for Substance Abuse Prevention. Rockville, MD: U.S. Department of Health and Human Services, 1999c.

Substance Abuse and Mental Health Services Administration (SAMHSA). *Results from the 2001 National Household Survey on Drug Abuse: Volume I. Summary of National Findings* (Office of Applied Studies, NHSDA Series). Rockville, MD: U.S. Department of Health and Human Services, 2002.

Substance Abuse and Mental Health Services Administration (SAMHSA), Office of Applied Studies. *National Household Survey on Drug Abuse, The NHSDA Report. Team Sports Participation and Substance Use Among Youths.* Rockville, MD: SAMHSA. (17 March 2007).

Suggs, W. "Deadly Fuel: As Supplements and Steroids Tempt and Endanger More Athletes, What Are Colleges Doing?" *Chronicle of Higher Education* XLIX (14 March 2003): A36–A38.

Swadi, H. "Relative Risk Factors in Detecting Adolescent Drug Abuse." *Drug and Alcohol Dependence* 29 (1992): 253–254.

Teen Challenge. *Drugs: Frequently Asked Questions.* South Australia: Pragin Press, 2000.

Toronto, R. "Young Athletes Who Use 'Enhancing' Steroids Risk Severe Physical Consequences." *Salt Lake Tribune* 244 (6 July 1992): C-5.

USA Today. "AIDS Likely to Devastate Teen Population." *USA Today: Health* (28 August 2000): 1.

U.S. Department of Health and Human Services (USDHHS), National Institute on Drug Abuse (NIDA). *Drug Abuse and Addiction Research: The Sixth Triennial Report to Congress. NIDA Research Priorities and Highlights, Role of Research: Women's Health and Gender Differences,* Washington, DC: U.S. Government Printing Office, 1999.

U.S. Department of Justice. "Anabolic Steroids and You." Washington, DC: Demand Reduction Section, Drug Enforcement Administration, 1991–1992.

Venturelli, P. J. "Drugs in Schools: Myths and Reality." In *The Annals of the American Academy of Political and Social Science* 567, edited by W. H. Hinkle and S. Henry, 72–87. Thousand Oaks, CA: Sage, January 2000.

Walsh, F., and M. Sheinkman. "Family Context of Adolescence." In *Adolescent Substance Abuse, Etiology, Treatment and Prevention,* edited by G. Lawson and A. Lawson, 149–171. Gaithersburg, MD: Aspen, 1992.

Welder, A., and R. Melchert. "Cardiotoxic Effects of Cocaine and Anabolic-Androgenic Steroids in the Athlete." *Journal of Pharmacological and Toxicological Methods* 29 (1993): 61–68.

Winters, P. A. *Teen Addiction.* San Diego, CA: Greenhaven Press, 1997.

Wisconsin Coalition Against Sexual Assault (WCASA). *Sexual Violence and Sexual Abuse.* Madison, WI: WCASA, 1997.

Witham, D. "Recovery in the Dorm: Rutgers University's Special Housing for Addicted Students." *Chronicle of Higher Education* 42 (10 November 1995): A-33.

"Women Smokers Run High Risk for Lung Cancer." *Prevention Pipeline* 7 (May–June 1994): 7.

World Health Organization (WHO). "HIV/AIDS: HIV/AIDS and Adolescents." Geneva, Switzerland (2000–2004). Available http://www.who.int/child-adolescent-health/HIV/HIV_adolescents.htm.

Wright, L. "Suicidal Thoughts and Their Relationship to Family Stress and Personal Problems Among High School Seniors and College Undergraduates." *Adolescence* 20 (1985): 575–580.

Yahoo! and Reuters. "HIV Drug Combinations Benefit Teens, Children Too." *Health — Reuters* (2001).

Yesalis, C. E., and J. S. Cowart. *The Steroids Game.* Champaign, IL: Human Kinetics, 1998.

Zuger, A. M. D. "Epidemic: An Overview." *New York Times* (8 August 2000). Available http://www.nytimes.com/library/national/science/aids/aids-overview.html.

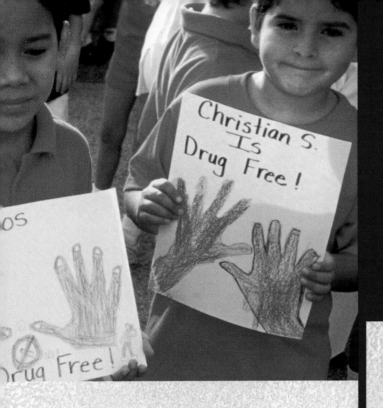

CHAPTER 17

Drug Abuse Prevention

Learning Objectives

On completing this chapter you will be able to:

◎ List the 10 most prominent factors influencing alcohol and other drug use surrounding the individual.

◎ List and briefly explain the three major types of drug prevention programs.

◎ List the five types of drug users that have to be considered *before* implementing a drug prevention program.

◎ List the four levels of comprehensive prevention programs for drug use and abuse.

◎ List the three family factors that can prevent initiation to drugs or extensive drug use.

◎ List four existing prevention programs largely found in higher education.

◎ Understand the main goals of the following large-scale drug prevention programs: The BACCHUS Network, DARE, and drug courts.

◎ Describe two other alternatives to drug use.

Did You Know?

O Comprehensive prevention programs involving the community, school, and family are more effective than single-unit programs.

O The harm reduction drug prevention model that is practiced in the Netherlands is a preventive model that meets drug users on their own turf in dealing with drug use and/or abuse.

O Drug prevention programs must distinguish among early experimenters, nonproblem drug users, nondetected committed or secret users, problem users, and former users.

O Students in drug prevention programs who do not know how to say "no" need refusal skills training or peer resistance training.

O Drug education actually began in the 1830s with the temperance movement.

O Drug courts are a newer form of drug prevention in which drug defendants are more likely to undergo treatment (rehabilitation) than incarceration (punishment).

O Other strategies for dealing with drug use include the alternatives approach and meditation.

Drugs and Society Online is a great source for additional drugs and society information for both students and instructors.
Visit **http://drugsandsociety.jbpub.com** to find a variety of useful tools for learning, thinking, and teaching.

Introduction

When someone tells another person "Just don't do drugs" and if that person is addicted to, say, cocaine like I was, that comes across as a retarded answer. You cannot just quit when you are addicted because even the idea of addiction continually blocks the possibility of casually deciding to stop using the drug. A lot has to go into the day you actually stop using the drug. First of all, the craving for the drug continually reminds you to do it maybe just a few more times. Then, your life appears to be less engaging because your body is missing the chemical properties of the drug that it became accustomed to and this affects your level of depression. So you have to sort of go through that slow abstinence period — you are without the drug and sometimes you can only deal with abstaining 1 hour at a time for the first week or so. Then slowly, ever so slowly, for me at least, the addict has to rebuild her or his daily living without the drug. It's just not easy. If it were, most people addicted to drugs would probably quit on their own. Especially when you realize that you are not controlling the drug, the drug is controlling you. Just remember, most addicts continually deceive (lie) themselves and others that they are not "really" addicted. Do you know how hard it is to become aware that these lies are part of the addiction? Before the extended therapy I had, no one could convince me that the daily cocaine I was snorting and smoking was bad. *(From Venturelli's research files, female, age 37, academic administrator in higher education, who for the past 3 years has been drug free, June 21, 2000.)*

This chapter explores and provides information on doing *something* about drug use and abuse. With so many potential causes for the unnecessary and non-medical use of psychoactive substances, it becomes increasingly important to discuss methods, programs, and strategies that prevent, delay, or at the very least, moderate the habitual use of drugs.

Figure 17.1 shows many of the potential environmental factors involved in what influences alcohol and other drug use (**AOD**). The core in

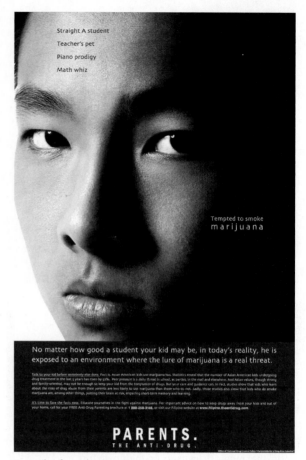

Example of an advertisement aimed at alerting parents about the dangers of early drug use.

this figure starts with the individual, and each concentric zone represents clusters of factors that influence an individual's views, attitudes, and behaviors toward drug use. With so many factors, each having an independent potential effect on the individual, you can see why comprehensive prevention programs involving the community, school, and family are more effective than single-unit programs, such as having a mandatory drug education program in elementary grades without other complementary and overlapping drug programs in the community and the family. Prevention research clearly shows that "we must attend to all factors; prevention that focuses on only one or two factors and ignores or discounts the rest is likely to fail to have a long-term, permanent impact" (Tinzmann and Hixson 1992, p. 3).

Through comprehensive prevention programs that are multifaceted and complementary, we are able to more effectively tease out which factors are most influential. The televised commercial in the early 1990s that showed two eggs frying in a pan:

AOD
alcohol and other drugs

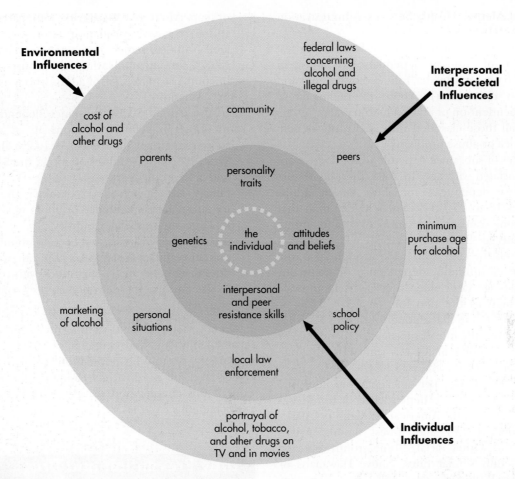

Environmental Influences

cost of alcohol and other drugs

federal laws concerning alcohol and illegal drugs

community

parents

Interpersonal and Societal Influences

peers

personality traits

genetics

the individual

attitudes and beliefs

minimum purchase age for alcohol

interpersonal and peer resistance skills

marketing of alcohol

personal situations

school policy

local law enforcement

portrayal of alcohol, tobacco, and other drugs on TV and in movies

Individual Influences

FIGURE 17.1

Potential factors that influence alcohol and other drug use.

Source: U.S. Department of Health and Human Services, Office for Substance Abuse Prevention (1989). Figure 2.1, Factors that Influence Alcohol and Other Drug Use. In *Prevention plus II: Tools for creating and sustaining drug-free communities* (p. 19). (DHHS Publication No. (ADM) 89-1649). Rockville, MD: Author. Distributed by the National Clearinghouse for Alcohol and Drug Information.

"This is your brain . . . this is your brain on drugs," sponsored by the Partnership for a Drug-Free America, was an early attempt at prevention through a disturbing analogy. Although its effect was poor on drug users, who had never felt their brains frying, it was an initial step toward innovative prevention efforts. Was it worth the airtime? Can the success of these programs be adequately measured?

In 1997, fifteen states thought prevention of alcohol and other drug abuse was important enough to maintain certified prevention specialist credentialing. Today, a bewildering variety of programs exist from coast to coast in school districts, churches, and other communities, all with the goal of preventing initial drug use or halting use before it becomes a problem ("Be Smart, Don't Start").

How Serious Is the Problem of Drug Dependence?

In looking at drug dependence, the severity of this problem can be highlighted by the following current trends:

1. In 2006, an estimated 22.6 million persons age 12 or older were classified with substance dependence or abuse in the past year (9.2%). Of these, 3.2 million were classified with dependence on or abuse of both alcohol and illicit drugs, 3.8 million were dependent on or abused illicit drugs but not alcohol, and 15.6 million were dependent on or abused alcohol but not illicit drugs (Substance Abuse

and Mental Health Services Administration [SAMHSA] 2007).

2. The specific illicit drugs that had the highest levels of past-year dependence or abuse in 2006 were marijuana, followed by cocaine and pain relievers. (In 2006, 4.2 million were dependent on or abused marijuana, or 59.4% of all those classified with illicit drug dependence or abuse problems.)

3. Rates of substance dependence or abuse were associated with age. In 2006, the rate of substance dependence or abuse among adults ages 18 to 25 (21.3%) was higher than that among youths ages 12 to 17 (8%) and among adults age 26 or older (7.2%).

4. As was the case from 2002 through 2005, the rate of substance dependence or abuse for males age 12 or older in 2006 was about twice as high as the rate for females (12.3% vs. 6.3%). (Note that among youth ages 12 to 17, however, the rate of substance dependence or abuse among males was similar to the rate among females [8% vs. 8.1%].)

5. In 2006, among persons age 12 or older, the rate of substance dependence or abuse was highest among American Indians or Alaska Natives (19%) and lowest among Asians (4.3%). Other racial/ethnic groups reported generally similar rates: Native Hawaiians or Other Pacific Islanders (12%), persons reporting two or more races (10.9%), whites (9.2%), Hispanics (10%), and blacks (9%). (These rates were all similar to the rates in 2005.)

6. Rate of substance dependence or abuse was associated with level of education. Among adults age 18 or older, those who graduated from high school but did not attend any college and those who graduated from college had lower rates of dependence or abuse (7.3% and 9.4%, respectively) than those who were not high school graduates and those with some college (10.3% and 10.8%, respectively).

7. Most adults age 18 or older with substance dependence or abuse in 2006 were employed either full or part time. Of the 20.6 million adults classified with dependence or abuse, 12.7 million (61.5%) were employed.

8. In 2006, adults age 18 or older who were on parole or a supervised release from jail during the past year were more likely to be classified with dependence on or abuse of a substance (36.9%) than those who were not on parole

or supervised release during the past year (9.1%). Similarly, probation status was associated with substance dependence or abuse (39.7% among adults who were on probation in comparison to 8.7% of adults who were not on probation).

9. In the United States, substance dependence or abuse in 2006 for persons 12 or older showed regional differences — 10.2% in the West, 10% in the Midwest, 8.5% in the South, and 8.4% in the Northeast.

10. Finally, among persons 12 or older, the rate for substance dependence or abuse was 9.4% in large metropolitan counties, 9% in small metropolitan counties, and 8.9% in nonmetropolitan counties (SAMHSA 2007). (No longer does drug dependence vary much with regard to size and type of metropolitan area as it did years ago.)

After reviewing such significant findings in terms of numbers and percentages of substance-dependent or abusing populations, we can now understand the need for discussing drug prevention in this chapter and drug treatment in the next chapter.

Drug Prevention and Drug Prevention Programs

"In the broadest sense, prevention is organized activity designed to avoid or decrease health problems" (Wilson and Kolander, 2003, p. 6). In addition to this definition of prevention, we add that in this chapter, **drug prevention** is aimed at preventing and/or decreasing not only health problems, but also social and personal problems. In previous chapters, we learned that when both licit and illicit types of drugs are used and/or abused for nonmedical purposes, they compromise psychological, social, and biological behavior. In the remaining sections of this chapter, we will review what drug prevention entails.

KEY TERMS

drug prevention
preventing or decreasing health problems, which includes social and personal problems, caused by drug dependency

Risk Factors and Protective Factors

From a broad perspective, when considering any drug prevention program, both **protective factors** and **risk factors** have to be considered. The following are the main principles that have to be considered when planning effective drug prevention programs:

1. Prevention programs should enhance protective factors and reverse or reduce risk factors.
   - The risk of becoming a drug abuser involves the relationship among the number and type of risk factors (e.g., deviant attitudes and behaviors) and protective factors (e.g., parental support).
   - The potential impact of specific risk and protective factors changes with age. For example, risk factors within the family have greater impact on a younger child while association with drug-abusing peers may be a more significant risk factor for an adolescent.
   - Early intervention with risk factors (e.g., aggressive behavior and poor self-control) often has a greater impact than later intervention by changing a child's life path (trajectory) away from problems and toward positive behaviors.
   - Although risk and protective factors can affect people of all groups, these factors can have a different effect depending on a person's age, gender, ethnicity, culture, and environment.
2. Prevention programs should address all forms of drug abuse, alone or in combination, including the underage use of legal drugs (e.g., tobacco or alcohol), the use of illegal drugs (e.g., marijuana or heroin), and the inappropriate use of legally obtained substances (e.g., inhalants), prescription medications, or over-the-counter drugs.
3. Prevention programs should address the type of drug abuse problem in the local community, target modifiable risk factors, and strengthen identified protective factors.
4. Prevention programs should be tailored to address risks specific to population or audience characteristics, such as age, gender, and ethnicity, to improve program effectiveness (quoted extensively from Robertson et al. and National Institute on Drug Abuse [NIDA] 2003, p. 7).

There are three levels of drug prevention programs, each suited to different types of drug users. **Primary drug prevention programs** are aimed at nonusers, and the goal is to inoculate potential users against drug use. Primary prevention is often targeted at at-risk youth who may live in areas where licit and illicit types of drugs are rampant, may come from problem families, or are surrounded by drug-abusing peers.

The other two major types of drug prevention programs are (1) **secondary drug prevention programs** — their aim is toward newer drug users with a limited history of use; and (2) **tertiary drug prevention programs** — their goal is to focus directly on intervention and target chemically dependent individuals who need treatment.

Usually primary, secondary, and tertiary programs are used in combination because, in most settings, all three types of drug users constitute the targeted population. Table 17.1 further illustrates these levels of drug prevention and corresponding suggested activities; what can be accomplished is listed under each of the three types of prevention (primary, secondary, and tertiary).

KEY TERMS

protective factors
factors associated with preventing the potential for drug abuse such as self control, parental monitoring, academic competence, anti-drug use policies, and strong neighborhood attachment

risk factors
drug prevention is aimed at reducing risk factors, such as early aggressive behavior, lack of parental supervision, the lure of gang membership, drug availability, and poverty

primary drug prevention programs
the very broad range of activities aimed at reducing the risk of drug use among nonusers and assuring continued nonuse

secondary drug prevention programs
targeting at-risk groups, experimenters, and early-abuse populations to reverse the progression of abusive behaviors, similar to "early intervention"

tertiary drug prevention programs
intervention at an advanced state of drug abuse; basically the same as drug abuse treatment

Table 17.1 Levels of Drug Prevention and Suggested Activities

Primary Prevention (risk reduction before abuse)	

Intrapersonal factors	Affective education (emotional literacy)
	Resilience training
	Values clarification
	Personal and social skills development
	   Assertiveness skills training
	   Refusal skills
	Drug information and education

Small group factors	Peer mentoring, counseling, outreach, modeling Conflict resolution Curriculum infusion Activities demonstrating misperception of peer norms Alternatives to use: recreational, cultural, athletic Strengthening families
Systems level	Strengthening school–family links Strengthening school–community group links Strengthening community support systems Media advocacy efforts, reducing alcohol marketing
Secondary Prevention (intervening in early abuse)	
	Assessment strategies: identification of abuse subgroups and individual diagnoses Early intervention coupled with sanctions Teacher–counselor–parent team approach Developing healthy alternative youth culture Recovering role models
Tertiary Prevention (intervening in advanced abuse)	
	Assessment and diagnosis Referral into treatment Case management Reentry

Considering the Audience and Approach

It is important to be aware that drug users vary in their exposure and past histories of substance use and/or abuse. The audience for drug prevention comprises both users and nonusers. In analyzing the population of users, categories include the following:

- Nonusers
- Early experimenters
- Nonproblem drug users — those who abuse drugs on occasion, mostly for recreation
- Nondetected, committed, or secret users — those who abuse drugs and have no interest in stopping
- Problem users
- Former users

It is important that role models, counselors, teachers, and anyone else involved in drug prevention programs take into consideration that there are different types of substance users/abusers.

Therefore, drug prevention programs must cater to the specific needs of these groups. For non-problem users, drug education programs should examine the abuse of drugs and reinforce the message that uncontrolled use leads to abuse. For committed users, drug education should aim to prevent or delay drug abuse. Former users should be given information that will reinforce their decision to stop abusing drugs.

A number of questions should be considered by a professional planning a prevention program. To what type of audience should the drug information be targeted? Youths or adults? Peers or parents? Should information focus on knowledge, attitudes, or behavior? Should the program emphasize and recommend abstinence or responsible use?

In most cases, it is appropriate for drug prevention to focus on knowledge, attitudes, and behavior; the three are clearly related. For instance, if the goal is to increase knowledge, should we assume that attitudes and behavior will change accordingly, or should knowledge about the harmful effects of drugs be kept separate from attitudes and behavior? For example, if you learn that smoking marijuana is a health hazard, equal to or more destructive than smoking cigarettes, does this knowledge limit the satisfaction you derive from smoking marijuana with friends? Some would say "yes." Unfortunately, many would say "no." In fact, knowledge about the harmful effects of certain types of drugs has very little effect on the personal attitudes and habits of most people. Most cigarette smokers are aware of the health hazards before they start smoking, but this does not always stop them from starting or becoming addicted.

Drug education programs have to direct their attention to a small range of behavioral objectives. They will not be effective if they address too many issues.

Finally, drug prevention programs must decide whether they will stress total abstinence or responsible use. Abstinence is radically different from responsible use. A program cannot advocate both. Information and scare tactics alone have no effect on drug use. Educational prevention models have been modified lately to achieve the following goals:

- Convey the message that society is inconsistent concerning drug use. For example, certain drugs that cause serious harm to a large percentage of the population are legal, whereas other drugs that have less impact are illegal.
- Convey that the reasons for drug use are complex and that drug users vary.
- Demonstrate to youth that young and old alike are affected by role models, in that attitudes regarding drug use are often patterned from family members who are role models.
- Acknowledge that other influential role models in music, sports, art, drama, business, and education who use and abuse drugs can affect attitudes toward drug use (see Chapter 16).

An Example of Drug Prevention at Central High in Elmtown

This section describes how a school-based prevention program is implemented and demonstrates that programs must be comprehensive and multifaceted to be successful.

Let us stand in the shoes of a parent and teacher committee trying to design a primary prevention program for students at Central High in Elmtown. The group has some prevention research materials that it received from the National Clearinghouse for Alcohol and Drug Information. After some thought, most members of the committee decide not to address individual, personal risk factors (discussed in Chapters 2 and 18) that may generate anxieties or conflicts or painful or threatening feelings. They have spoken with some students and ascertained that most of the 9th and 10th graders — even those who tend toward rebelliousness and avant-garde styles — are against taking drugs. Although many students feel this way, there are trends in the school that worry the committee members. Some popular 11th- and 12th-grade peer group leaders are drug users, and drug sales have been occurring on school grounds. The presence and availability of drugs and the beginning of a drug-using atmosphere make it more likely that some of the younger students will initiate use.

In brainstorming sessions, different committee members suggest ways to help these students avert initiation of drug use. Depending on their thinking, theoretical perspective, and exposure to prevention models, members come up with the following ideas:

- Students need to be grounded in good, solid knowledge about the negative effects and dangers of drugs (1) as provided in a drug education course or (2) more subtly, in a curriculum concerning drug effects and drug-using behaviors (also covered later, in the section on higher education).

- Students with low self-esteem will feel uncomfortable asserting individual choices or points of view that deviate from those held by peers or peer leaders. Bolstering a positive self-image would allow such students to refuse drugs.
- Students who have low expectations regarding their ability to refuse drugs will be least likely to actually refuse. The school might try to increase their "self-efficacy" — that is, their belief that their behaviors are powerful and will have results.
- Students just do not know how to say "no" and need refusal skills training or peer-resistance training.
- Although a clique leadership may set a pro-use tone, it is probable that the quiet antidrug students represent a silent majority. They may misperceive the amount of drug use that occurs in their school. If the antidrug students are shown that their own attitudes and beliefs are actually in the majority, they will see that the "emperor has no clothes."
- A more confrontational approach involves removing drugs from the school environment by infiltrating the student body or using informants to gather information about who is distributing drugs. Dealers and users can then be identified or counseled and their parents notified. The school could make the decision to go as far as having the student arrested or expelling him or her.

With so many options put forth, some of the committee members become frustrated and fear that a sufficient program will never be created. Some of them have experienced alcoholism in their families and fear that many of these approaches are too ineffective for helping the students who are already experimenting.

Seeing a disaster brewing, the committee chair makes a call to the Division of Substance Abuse Services in the state Department of Health to inquire about drug prevention programs. The operator refers the call to the prevention specialists at the agency, who are linked to the National Prevention Network, which is part of the National Association of State Alcohol and Drug Abuse Directors. The specialist schedules a meeting with the committee, in which she makes the following points:

1. A prevention needs assessment is helpful, and necessitates using validated survey instruments to determine the patterns of behavior and attitudes regarding drug use among the student body.

2. A combination of primary and secondary prevention would be good for the majority of the student body, and group treatment for substance abuse should be made available at an adolescent outpatient clinic. The outpatient clinic will assess some students who are well on their way to addiction and refer them into inpatient treatment. Because this intervention occurs when the student is at an advanced abuse state, this is considered tertiary prevention.

Notice how all three types of approaches (primary, secondary, and tertiary) are necessary to implement a comprehensive prevention strategy.

The specialist brought along a staff member of the Local Council on Alcoholism and Drug Dependence, an affiliate of the National Council on Alcoholism and Drug Dependence (NCADD) branch serving a three-county region of the state. Thousands of branches of NCADD exist in the United States, and their goal is to help local groups design and implement prevention programs. Many branches have developed specialized programs for teens, children, women, and the elderly. The staff member conducts preliminary sessions with the prevention committee and arranges to sign an affiliation agreement with the school administration, whereby NCADD will act as consultants to the school, aiding it in designing a prevention program to fit its particular needs. It will design a project, which will be based on a needs assessment that incorporates a survey of chemical attitudes and use and interviews with parents, teachers, and students. The project design will include the program objectives, a method and management plan, a timeline, and an evaluation component.

To help those members bewildered by the many possible factors identified by the committee in its brainstorming session (such as self-esteem, self-efficacy, and refusal skills), the staff member invites the committee to sample a number of available, attractive packages of user-friendly activities such as the following:

- Broad-brush packages, which cover a variety of personal choice and primary prevention areas (Holstein et al. 1995)

- More targeted strategies, which might include a training package to be implemented by a consultant hired by the school district to address issues such as assertiveness training

Assertiveness training skills, which include a variety of personal and social skills, enable people to communicate their needs and feelings in an open, direct, and appropriate manner, while still recognizing the needs and feelings of others. They make people feel more powerful and better about themselves (less like doormats), and they offer strategies for saying "no" without hurting, provoking, or manipulating others (Alberti and Emmons 1988). Assertive behavior contrasts with hostile or belligerent behavior, passive and helpless behavior, and passive-aggressive or indirect manipulation. The exercises included in assertiveness training are nonthreatening, concrete, direct, and enjoyable.

Many intrapersonal prevention concepts, or personal and social skills development concepts, have come and gone, with a trendy buzz word accompanying each in the year it was introduced. Many of these concepts overlap, such as life skills training, self-esteem, self-efficacy, resilience training, and assertiveness training (McIntyre et al. 1990; Norman 1994). The danger lies in employing them as gimmicks or slogans that accomplish little. Nevertheless, as Botvin and others have shown, personal and skills training that is carefully based on known cognitive and behavioral change factors, if carefully put into place, can indeed make a difference (Botvin and Wills 1985; Shiffman and Wills 1987). It is also true that almost any positive lifestyle activity is likely to act as an alternative to participating in a drug-using subculture.

Comprehensive Prevention Programs for Drug Use and Abuse

Harm Reduction Model

At the broadest level is a society-wide prevention model that would entail a much more comprehensive approach. The **harm reduction model** is an approach to drug use and addiction practiced in some cites in the Netherlands and the United Kingdom. It is described by Westermeyer as an addiction model that connects "with the addicted community, by having an 'open door policy' that welcomes addicts to take part in services, regardless of level of motivation for change, goals or personal ideology" (Westermeyer n.d.). In a sense, it is a model that meets addicts on their own level.

Westermeyer identifies three central beliefs of the harm reduction model:

1. Excessive behaviors occur along a continuum of risk ranging from minimal to extreme. Addictive behaviors are not all-or-nothing phenomena. Although a drug or alcohol abstainer has a lower risk of harm than a drug or alcohol user, a moderate drinker is causing less harm than a binge drinker is; a crystal methamphetamine smoker or sniffer is causing less harm than a crystal injector.

2. Changing addictive behavior is a stepwise process, with complete abstinence being the final step. Those who embrace the harm reduction model believe that any movement in the direction of reduced harm — no matter how small — is positive in and of itself.

3. Sobriety simply is not for everybody. This statement requires the acceptance that many people live in horrible circumstances. Some are able to cope without the use of drugs; others use drugs as a primary means of coping. Until we are in a position to offer an alternative means of survival to these individuals, we are in no position to cast moral judgment. The health and well-being of the individual are of primary concern; if individuals are unwilling or unable to change addictive behavior at this time, they should not be denied services. *Attempts should be made to reduce the harm of their habits as much as possible* (Westermeyer n.d.).

According to Westermeyer, the Dutch (who created this approach to prevention of drug use and abuse) have "an 80% connection rate with the addicted population," while in the United States we are 80% disconnected from our addicted populations. In fact, through our punitive model in dealing with drug users, the strongest connection we have with the addicted population in the United States comes when they are arrested and jailed.

KEY TERMS

harm reduction model
a society-wide approach to drug use and/or abuse that focuses on reducing the harm experienced by the drug user and/or abuser as well as the harm to society

■ Community-Based Drug Prevention

Community-based programs are very broad and take into account the community's youth, parents, businesses, media, schools, law enforcement, religious or fraternal groups, civic or volunteer groups, healthcare professionals, and government agencies with expertise in the field of substance abuse. The primary goal of community-based prevention is to provide coordinated programs among the numerous agencies and organizations involved in prevention. Prevention requires communities to conduct a structured review of current prevention programs to determine (1) whether the programs in place were examined and tested according to rigorous scientific standards during their development and (2) whether these programs incorporate the basic principles of prevention that have been identified in research. Usually, prevention programs at the community level ask the following questions (Robertson et al. and NIDA 2003; Sloboda and David 1999):

- Does the program have components for the individual, the family, the school, the media, community organizations, and healthcare providers? Are the program components well integrated in theme and content so that they reinforce rather than duplicate one another?
- Does the prevention program use media and community education strategies to increase public awareness, attracting community support, reinforcing the school-based curriculum for students and parents, and keeping the public informed of the program's progress?
- Are interventions carefully designed to reach different at-risk populations, and are they of sufficient duration to make an impact?
- Does the program follow a structured organizational plan that progresses from needs assessment through planning, implementation, and review to refinement, with feedback to and from the community at all stages?
- Are the objectives and activities specific, time-limited, feasible (in terms of available resources), and integrated so that they work together across program components and can be used to evaluate program progress and outcomes?

Often, these programs set up prevention policy boards to oversee planning and implementation. Boards should include representatives from law enforcement, juvenile justice, education, recre-ation, social services, private industry, health and mental health agencies, churches, civic organizations, and other community agencies that serve youth and families. They should also include one or several youth members. "The community can be a target group, especially when there is extensive community denial or lack of awareness, lack of clear policies, poor law enforcement, and so on. Public awareness campaigns, political action, and similar efforts are appropriate at this level of prevention" (Tinzmann and Hixson 1992, pp. 2, 3).

Community prevention programs can also direct their attention to changing the legal and social environment regarding alcohol, tobacco, and other drug supplies (**ATOD**) and toward youth (Center for Prevention Research and Development [CPRD] 2000). This effort also includes individual and environmental strategies. For example, an environmental approach to reducing underage drinking might involve training clerks to insist on proper age identification when selling alcoholic beverages. An individual approach might involve education efforts, such as a media campaign, aimed at discouraging young people from drinking (Silver Gate Group and Robert Wood Johnson Foundation 2001).

Other community-based strategies include the following:

- Strengthening the enforcement of existing legal regulations of ATOD sales and use
- Educating merchants and servers about alcohol and tobacco sales laws
- Regulating legislation regarding the sale of alcohol and tobacco to minors
- Implementing use and lose laws, which allow for the suspension of the driver's license of a person younger than 21 years of age following a conviction for any alcohol or drug violation (e.g., use, possession, or attempt to purchase with or without false identification)
- Imposing regulations on location and density of retail outlets — that is, monitoring the number of unsupervised vending machines dispensing cigarettes to minors in a given community and monitoring the number of retail establishments selling alcohol and tobacco near schools

KEY TERMS

ATOD
alcohol, tobacco, and other drugs

In conclusion, community prevention emphasizes comprehensive drug abuse prevention programs that include multiple components, such as the use of media, drug education in schools, parent education, community organizations, and formulation of drug-related health policy. In essence, community drug prevention seeks to reduce drug abuse by informing, coordinating, and decreasing the level of drug use at the community level.

School-Based Drug Prevention

Education has been used extensively in the past to control the use and abuse of drugs, especially alcohol and tobacco. Drug education actually began in the late 1800s, when most states required that the harmful effects of certain drugs be taught. An example of an early educational attempt to curb or stop drug abuse is the temperance movement in the late 19th century. The Women's Christian Temperance Union (WCTU) and the Anti-Saloon League taught that alcohol consumption was harmful and contrary to Christian morality.

Years ago, when drug prevention was first attempted, most substance abuse experts thought that schools should be responsible for educating the public about the dangerous use and eventual abuse of drugs because education is school's main objective. Schools began teaching about drug use, but in the beginning, drug prevention focused on individual factors, such as the dangers of particular types of drugs, the dangers of trusting individuals who sell drugs, and other scare tactics. One problem with this approach was that students varied enormously with regard to their drug experiences. Often, the students had already tried the dangerous drugs and had experienced only pleasurable effects with few negative consequences. Their experiences occurred *before* their exposure to drug prevention programs that relied on negative information, which is generally known as the **scare tactic approach**. Many self-reported use

surveys revealed that these programs were not successful. With such audiences of drug users, the warnings are short lived, not believed, or perceived as exaggerations. Table 17.2 summarizes the most popular, common, school-based drug prevention programs by including the premise, strategies, and effectiveness of the following approaches: (a) cognitive, (b) affective, (c) combined cognitive and affective, (d) social learning/cognitive behavioral, and (e) normative education. Table 17.2 also details the strengths (if any) and weaknesses of each approach.

Curriculum-Based Drug Education Objectives

In an effort to educate students about the dangers of drug use, school-based drug education programs and objectives have been implemented in most U.S. school curriculums. Specific educational topics have been established for elementary, junior high, and senior high and college levels:

Elementary Level

Drugs versus poisons

Effects of alcohol, tobacco, and marijuana on the body

Differences between candy and drugs

Drug overdoses

Dangers of experimentation

How to say "no" to peers offering drugs

Reasons for taking drugs: curing illness, pleasure, escape, parental use, and ceremony

Junior High Level

How peer pressure works

How to say "no" to peer pressure

How drugs affect the body, physiologically and psychologically

Where to seek help when needed

Attitudes toward drug use

How to have fun without drugs

Harmful effects of tobacco, alcohol, and marijuana on the body

Stress management and building positive self-esteem

How advertisers push drugs

Consequences of breaking drug laws

Table 17.2 **Summary of Common School-Based Drug Prevention Approaches**

APPROACH	PREMISE	STRATEGIES	EFFECTIVENESS
Cognitive	If youths understand the dangers of AOD, they will not use them.	Teach pharmacology of alcohol and other drugs, how they are used, long-range consequences of use — usually through scare tactics.	Seldom effective; sometimes detrimental — arouses curiosity and encourages experimentation. Dire facts are not credible; knowledge alone does not counteract peer pressure. Knowledge is necessary, but not sufficient; focus on more immediate physical/social consequences may work.
Affective	High self-esteem, values consistent with nonuse, and good problem-solving and decision-making skills help youth avoid AOD.	Raise self-esteem. Teach values and life skills. Typically, do not include AOD information.	Do not decrease rate of use. Some community members and parents protest teaching values and decision making. Need to include AOD information.
Combined cognitive and affective	Students need both information and life skills to avoid AOD use.	Teach problem-solving, decision-making, peer pressure resistance skills; and provide explicit information about AOD to connect life skills and AOD use and consequences.	Little consistent effect on reducing AOD use, although some successes have been reported.
Social learning/ cognitive-behavioral approach	AOD use usually begins in a social setting between grades 5 and 9, usually with peers, but sometimes adults; youth need skills for resisting these pressures. (Based on Bandura's social learning theory.)	Teach how to identify pressures from peers, media, advertising, families. Teach resistance skills, model counterarguments. Students role play pressure situations and actively practice resisting.	Sometimes effective, especially if peers are involved in instruction and when students already have other fairly well-developed social skills. Little evidence that effects last.
Normative education approach	Youth overestimate the extent of AOD use among peers and thus may use AOD to feel part of the group.	Correct misconceptions, demonstrate actual norms through discussion, develop nonuse norms.	Success with some drugs; not very effective with alcohol. Some youngsters may believe that fewer peers use AOD than actually do, and may come to feel AOD use is more acceptable than they did before entering the program.

AOD: alcohol and other drugs.

Source: U.S. Department of Health and Human Services, Office for Substance Abuse Prevention (1989). Figure 2.1, Factors that Influence Alcohol and Other Drug Use. In *Prevention plus II: Tools for creating and sustaining drug-free communities* (p. 19). (DHHS Publication No. (ADM) 89-1649). Rockville, MD: Author. Distributed by the National Clearinghouse for Alcohol and Drug Information.

Differences between wine, beer, and distilled spirits

Family drug use

Family drinking problems and family members who may have drug addiction problems

Images of violence and drug use in rock and rap music

Teenage drug abuse and associated problems

Senior High and College Level

Responsible use of medications

How drugs affect the body and the mind

Legal versus illegal drugs

Drinking and driving

Drug effects on the fetus

Recreational drug use

Ways of coping with problems: anger and stress management

How to detect problem drug users

Drug education, prevention, and treatment

Positive and negative role models

How to build positive self-esteem

Criminal sanctions for various types of drug use

Binge drinking

Drugs and driving

Date rape

Addiction to drugs and alcoholism

Principal Questions for School-Based Programs

The following questions should be asked to improve the outcomes of drug education programs:

- Do the school-based programs reach children from kindergarten through high school? If not, do they at least reach children during the critical middle school or junior high years?
- Do the programs contain multiple years of intervention (all through the middle school or junior high years)?
- Do the programs use a well-tested, standardized intervention with detailed lesson plans and student materials?
- Do the programs use age-appropriate interactive teaching methods (modeling, role playing, discussion, group feedback, reinforcement, extended practice)?

- Do the programs foster prosocial bonding to the school and community?
- Do the programs teach social competence (communication, self-efficacy, assertiveness) and drug resistance skills that are culturally and developmentally appropriate?
- Do the programs promote positive peer influence?
- Do the programs promote antidrug social norms?
- Do the programs emphasize skills-training teaching methods?
- Do the programs include an adequate "dosage" (10–15 sessions in year 1 and another 10–15 booster sessions)?
- Is there periodic evaluation to determine whether the programs are effective?

■ Family-Based Prevention Programs

Primary family risk factors that predispose youth to find drugs attractive include the following:

- Chaotic home environments, particularly in which parents abuse substances or suffer from mental illnesses
- Ineffective parenting, especially with children with difficult temperaments and conduct disorders
- Lack of mutual attachments and nurturing

"Results from longitudinal studies of children, particularly those children most at risk for problems, indicate that families can protect children and youth against drug use and abuse through effective family management practices that impart skills young people can use in resisting social pressures to use drugs" (National Institutes of Health [NIH] and NIDA 1998, p. 49).

If the just listed risk factors are the primary risk factors, *protective factors* — the factors that can insulate against drug use — include the following:

- Strong parent–child bonds
- Parental monitoring with clear rules of conduct within the family unit and involvement of parents in the lives of their children
- Open communication of values within the family
- High levels of supervision and monitoring
- No inconsistent disciplining from lackadaisical to extreme enforcement of rules, and no saying one thing and then doing another
- Consistent high levels of parental warmth, affection, and emotional support

In addition, research shows that protective family factors can moderate the effects of risk factors. The risk of associating with peers who use drugs can be offset by protective family factors, such as parent conventionality, maternal adjustment, and strong parent–child attachment.

Prevention at the family level needs to stress parent–child interaction strategies, communication skills, child management practices, and family management skills. Research has also shown that parents need to take a more active role in their children's lives. This includes talking to their children about drugs, monitoring their activities, getting to know their friends, and understanding their problems and personal concerns (NIH and NIDA 1998).

Prevention Principles for Family-Based Programs

In conclusion, family-based prevention programs need to do the following:

- Reach families of children at each stage of development.
- Train parents in behavioral skills to
  - Reduce conduct problems in children.
  - Improve parent–child relations, including positive reinforcement, listening and communication skills, and problem solving.
  - Provide consistent discipline and rule making.
  - Monitor children's activities during adolescence.
- Include an educational component for parents with drug information for them and their children.
- Focus on families whose children are in kindergarten through 12th grade to enhance protective factors.
- Provide access to counseling services for families at risk.

Drug Prevention Programs in Higher Education

The seriousness of alcohol and other drug use on college campuses is underscored by the following findings (Phoenix House 2000):

- According to the Core Institute, an organization that surveys college drinking practices, 300,000 of today's college students will eventually die of alcohol-related causes, such as drunk driving accidents, cirrhosis of the liver, various cancers, and heart disease.

- Of today's first-year college students, 159,000 will drop out of school next year because of alcohol or other drug-related reasons.
- Almost one-third of college students admit to having missed at least one class because of their alcohol or drug use.
- One night of heavy drinking can impair a person's ability to think abstractly for up to 30 days, limiting the ability to relate textbook reading to classroom discussions or to think through processes such as football plays.

As we can see, the use of alcohol and other drugs is a serious problem within the college or university environment. Major problems on college campuses resulting from such drug abuse include property damage, poor academic performance, damaged relationships, unprotected sexual activity, physical injuries, date rape, and suicide (Perkins 1997).

It is obvious that with all these negative findings regarding alcohol and other drug use on college campuses, prevention programs are vital. Next, we review the major prevention programs that currently exist in higher education.

■ Overview and Critique of Existing Prevention Programs

Information-Only or Awareness Model

One of the earliest preventive interventions, this model is based on the belief that if people are given extensive information about the harmful effects of drugs, it will change their attitudes about use and abuse. This model assumes that people are rational enough to seriously curtail or stop drug use based on information. Obviously, today we know that, at most, the majority of drug users exposed to the **information-only or awareness model** become more knowledgeable about the effects of drugs, but this approach has very little influence on the use of habitual or addictive-type drugs.

KEY TERMS

information-only or awareness model
assumes that teaching about the harmful effects of drugs will change attitudes about use and abuse

Attitude Change Model or Affective Education Model

The **attitude change model or affective education model** assumes that people use drugs because they have poor self-esteem (Gonzalez and Clement 1994). As a result, prevention focuses on strengthening self-image, building up positive self-esteem, and boosting self-confidence. A problem with this model is that attitudes often are resistant to change and fluctuate depending on such environmental influences as peer and party settings. Attitudes that were formed in an educational setting (drug and alcohol classes) are abandoned in substance use settings.

Social Influences Model

The **social influences model** assumes that substance abuse results from multiple influences. Although outside influences are perceived as major influences, inner influences are also taken into account. Inner influences such as prior socialization, a vulnerability to please others, and a need to be accepted by friends and peers are likewise taken into account. This prevention strategy emphasizes peer resistance and inoculation techniques. Techniques primarily include the following (Gonzalez and Clement 1994):

1. Offering factual information about the consequences of drug use
2. Guiding development of skills to recognize outer and inner pressures to use drugs, and methods and techniques to resist usage
3. Communicating correct information about the extent of drug use by students of similar ages
4. Modeling, rehearsing, and reinforcing skills for resisting drugs when friends or peers expect compliance
5. Persuading students to try these resistance approaches and techniques in classroom or group settings and in peer group settings away from the classroom

By far, this method has been more successful than the information-only and attitude change models. Although it works best when it begins at the junior high school level, refresher courses should be administered at least every 2 years. Some research findings indicate that although this method is least effective with alcohol consumption, it *is* effective with marijuana and cigarette smoking (Gonzalez and Clement 1994).

Ecological or Person-in-Environment Model

This model is one of the newest types of prevention programs. "Interventions based on this model have multiple components and are designed to address both individuals and the policies, practices, and social norms that affect students on campuses or in the community" (Gonzalez and Clement 1994, p. 3). Developed from human ecology, the **ecological or person-in-environment model** stresses that changes in the environment change people. Although the ecological or person-in-environment model does not ignore substance use from individual causes, such as personal beliefs and perception of risk, it does primarily focus on the causes from the social environment (Hansen 1997, p. 6). "The central tenet [belief] of social ecology is that individual behavior is mainly the result of socialization; to change the behavior, we must change the social institutions that shape it" (Hansen 1997, p. 6). Hansen also stated "the strongest predictors of alcohol and drug abuse among young people are social (p. 6)."

This perspective emphasizes that it is important to take into account all of the environments that may have an impact on drug use. Friends, acquaintances, roommates, and classmates in dorms, sororities, and fraternities, at parties, cafes, and nightspots can influence students (U.S. Dept. of Education 1994).

As a result, this model advocates the following drug prevention strategies (Gonzalez and Clement 1994):

1. Dissemination of drug information
2. Cognitive and behavioral skills training for youth, parents, and professionals
3. Mass media programming
4. Development of grassroots citizen interest groups

KEY TERMS

attitude change model or affective education model
assumes that people use drugs because of lack of self-esteem

social influences model
assumes that drug users lack resistance skills

ecological or person-in-environment model
stresses that changes in the environment change people's attitudes about drugs

5. Leadership training for key organization and community officials
6. Policy analysis and reformulation

The college campus has long served as an initiator and perpetuator for drug use and abuse. Fraternity drunkenness, for example, was decried as early as 1840 (Horowitz 1987). In 1988, an 18-year-old student attending Rutgers University died of alcohol poisoning at a fraternity party. In a television interview following the incident, then-Chancellor Edward Bloustein described fraternities as "organized conspiracies dedicated to the consumption of alcohol" (Hansen 1997, p. 5).

Chemical abuse on campus is linked to the vast majority of vandalism, fights, accidents, sexually transmitted diseases, unplanned pregnancies, racial bias incidents, date rape, and at least one-third of academic attrition (Koss et al. 1987). Although campus prevention programs and research date back several decades, such efforts remained isolated and sporadic until the late 1970s. All campuses now have medium to extensive alcohol and other drug prevention programs in effect.

Examples of Large-Scale Drug Prevention Programs

■ BACCHUS and GAMMA Peer Education Network

In 1975, an organization known as BACCHUS (Boosting Alcohol Consciousness Concerning the Health of University Students) was developed as a national student organization. Soon BACCHUS realized that many of its affiliates were members of sororities and fraternities; therefore, it renamed the organization BACCHUS and GAMMA (Greeks Advocating Mature Management of Alcohol) to **the BACCHUS Network** effective July 1, 2005. Today there are ". . . more than 32,000 student leaders and advisors impacting over 8 million peers on

more than 1,000 campuses throughout the world." The BACCHUS Network is a university and community based network focusing on comprehensive health and safety initiatives (The BACCHUS Network 2007).

The original goal of this program was to prevent alcohol abuse. Today, the program has broadened its goals to include other student health and safety issues, such as sexual responsibility, tobacco use, marijuana use, and sexual assault. The organization devotes a substantial portion of its resources and activities to the following goals on university-affiliated campuses:

- Create and foster a thriving network of institutions and young adult-led peer education groups supporting health and safety initiatives
- Empower students and administrators to voice their opinions and needs to create healthier and safer campus communities
- Develop and promote cutting edge resources and health promotion campaigns that support peer education, campus leadership, and activism on health and safety issues
- Provide exceptional conferencing and training opportunities for students, young adults and professionals to support health and safety strategies
- Encourage national forums on young adult health and safety concerns
- Promote and disseminate research and effective strategies that better help campuses and communities address health and safety issues
- Advocate for effective and sensible policies and practices for campus and community health and safety issues (The BACCHUS Network 2007)

The BACCHUS philosophy is that students can play a uniquely effective role — unmatched by professional educators — in encouraging their peers to consider, talk honestly about and develop responsible habits and attitudes toward high-risk health and safety issues. The organization now hosts four web sites to assist students in their prevention efforts. Bacchusnetwork.org contains information about the organization's activities, services, conferences, campaigns and resource materials. Smartersex.org addresses sexual health, features an "Ask the Sexpert" area, and offers complete information on STIs, HIV, abstinence and birth control. TobaccofreeU.org addresses complete information on tobacco control, prevention, and cessation. Friendsdrivesober.org is the newest edition to the network and primarily focuses

KEY TERMS

the BACCHUS Network
a national and international association of college and university peer education programs focused on alcohol abuse prevention and other related student health and safety issues

on impaired driving prevention and highway safety (The BACCHUS Network 2007).

Each campus affiliate group plans programs according to the needs of its specific campus. "Some members choose to focus on National Collegiate Awareness Week, Sexual Responsibility Week, Safe Spring Break programs, or tobacco prevention. Others use formal peer education training to present programs to the campus community."

Fund for the Improvement of Postsecondary Education Drug Prevention Programs

In 1987, a huge explosion of campus drug prevention programs began. It was spawned by a $14 billion annual budget for college drug prevention placed in the Drug-Free Schools and Communities Act of 1986 (now titled the Safe and Free Schools and Communities Act). The funding was parceled out by the Department of Education, Fund for the Improvement of Postsecondary Education (FIPSE). FIPSE Drug Prevention Programs awarded about 100 grants per year from 1987 until 1996 via a grant competition that called for colleges to mount institution-wide programs. The guiding philosophy included the following points:

- A small, isolated program was seen as making little difference, but a comprehensive program reaching into several areas of the institution could send many consistent antiuse messages that would eventually reach critical mass and change the campus environment.
- There should be well-known, top-down administrative support for prevention programming.
- There should be well-written and carefully implemented policies about chemical use on campus.

The hundreds of new programs, whose administrators met and interacted in annual grantee conferences, generated the sense that there was a national prevention movement in higher education. The Network of Colleges and Universities Dedicated to Prevention of Alcohol and Other Drug Abuse was founded, incorporating 900 institutions. The network is supported by the Higher Education Center for Alcohol and Other Drug Prevention funded by the U.S. Department of Education, which provides a range of materials and newsletters (Ryan et al. 1995).

In 1989, FIPSE initiated a grant program for regional campus prevention consortia. By joining a consortium, colleges and universities could pool scarce resources, create support networks, and train new workers. In 1994, more than 100 regional consortia were listed on a database maintained by the Higher Education Center. In 1999, more than two thirds of all 3300 institutions of higher education were affiliates of the network, belonged to a regional consortium, or had started other programs under the aegis of FIPSE.

From more than a decade of experience, several exemplary approaches emerged. These strategies might be the predominant focus of a program or one of a number of complementary components of a comprehensive effort. The strategies are addressed next.

Peer-Based Efforts

Student peers can be involved in a number of ways: as educators, mentors, counselors, or facilitators of prevention and outreach work. Such an approach multiplies manpower tremendously, reaches the students who are apt to become lost in the flow, is not perceived as an outside or authoritarian intrusion, speaks the language of students, and works to change the predominant cultural tone on campus. Peers can conduct classroom presentations, work informational tables or drop-in centers, create prevention newsletters, and establish links to community groups. It is important to carefully train and supervise peer facilitators. Many peer programs are residence hall based, taking advantage of the training of residence hall assistants and peer facilitators (BACCHUS and GAMMA 1994).

Curriculum Infusion

Infusion of a skill or topic across the curriculum has been used in conjunction with classes on writing skills, gender issues, and other areas. Curriculum infusion can be undertaken at individual institutions or as a consortium project. The advantage of curriculum infusion is that it involves faculty members, achieves open discussion of drug issues in the classroom as part of the normal educational process, and stimulates critical thinking about drug issues.

Improvisational Theater Groups

Improvisational theater groups that tackle health and wellness issues can be lively, stimulating, and provocative, often breaking through peer and institutional denial and bringing issues home to students with a dramatic emotional impact. Improvisational topics can include date rape, sexually transmitted disease, children of alcoholics on campus, and denial of chemical dependency.

Strategies to Change Misperceptions of Use

Social psychologists Alan Berkowitz and Wesley Perkins, both of Hobart and William Smith Colleges, have conducted influential research illustrating that students often have incorrect estimates (exaggerated misperceptions) of drug use by their peers (Perkins 1991 and 1997; Perkins and Berkowitz 1986). Thus, they misperceive the peer norms governing drug use, which may lead them to follow imaginary peers. This idea is a modification of the traditional understanding that peers influence peers. It follows logically that activities demonstrating the accurate use pattern to students and correcting misperceptions will indirectly affect overall use patterns. These efforts have included simply publicizing the results of alcohol and drug use surveys and awarding prizes for coming up with correct estimates.

Alternative Events

Alternative events, such as mocktail parties, alcohol-free discos, and indoor rock climbing, especially as alternatives to presporting events and holiday parties, help avoid some events that are traditionally associated with chemical abuse.

Programs That Change Marketing of Alcohol on and Near Campuses

Institutions of higher education are a major focus of alcohol marketing. Alcoholic beverage producers sponsor many campus events, and these companies buy considerable newspaper advertising. The National College Magazine *U*, for example, had a 3-year advertising contract with Anheuser-Busch (Magnum and Taylor 1990). This publicity sends many pro-use messages. Prevention programs have recruited business and advertising majors to work on curtailing such marketing projects.

Finally, it is better to embed prevention messages within an overall wellness perspective. Students are concerned about health and wellness issues, not programs that come off as dogmatic or preachy, moralizing, exaggerating, and nagging — perhaps reminding them of life at home.

■ DARE (Drug Abuse Resistance Education)

One major drug prevention program that had high hopes for success was the school-based drug education programs incorporated in approxi-

mately 70% of the nation's school districts — **DARE (Drug Abuse Resistance Education).** DARE reaches 25 million students and has been adopted in 44 foreign countries (*Law Enforcement News* 1996). Recent evaluations of this program show that, on a short-term basis, DARE improved students' views of themselves and increased their sense of personal responsibility. However, the program has *not* yielded a measurable, significant change in drug use (Rosenbaum and Hanson 1998; Vogt, 2003, p. 1). Moreover, this drug education program showed a strong inconsistency between students' self-reported attitudes about use and actual drug use (Clayton et al. 1991; Ennett et al. 1994; Vogt 2003). (See "Holding the Line" for more information on DARE and several other programs that attempt to prevent drug use.)

One major problem is that "over the past decade, a flurry of studies — by the U.S. surgeon general and the General Accounting Office, among others — found no significant difference in drug use between DARE graduates and students never exposed to the curriculum" (Vogt 2003, p. 1). Further, regarding graduates of the DARE program, one official said,

> I can't tell you how many kids told me DARE introduced them to drugs. The problem with DARE, other than that it's a multimillion dollar conglomerate in the business of selling T-shirts, is that it takes the burden off parents to raise their kids [drug free]. (Vogt 2003, p. 3)

Another major problem that has been identified is that the DARE drug education program is presented in the classroom by fully uniformed police officers. Although the officers are well intentioned and their efforts are commendable, they are hardly a mechanism for transmitting new norms that would find converts among students, except perhaps those already successfully socialized (Gopelrud 1991). More importantly, uniformed police officers used as teachers "sends the wrong message that drugs are a law enforcement issue, rather than a public health issue" (Zeese and Lewin 1998, p. 1).

KEY TERMS

DARE (Drug Abuse Resistance Education)
drug education program presented in elementary and junior high schools nationwide by police officers

Holding the Line

Frustrating Results from National Drug Prevention Campaigns and Programs

In 1995, a disturbing study published by a group of researchers at the University of Michigan and backed by the U.S. Department of Health and Human Services (DHHS) and the National Institute on Drug Abuse (NIDA) showed that the use of illicit drugs by young people had been rising steadily since 1992. The results of this study were even more perplexing because overall drug use had been declining over the same period. The increase was happening despite several seemingly successful efforts to combat drug abuse with high-powered prevention programs.

Since the 1980s, most funds allocated for drug prevention have been spent in three areas: criminal justice, major advertising campaigns, and DARE (Drug Abuse Resistance Education). Law enforcement professionals for hard-core addicts, especially in poor urban neighborhoods, have favored compulsory preventive programs. According to William N. Brownsberger, Assistant State Attorney General in the Massachusetts Narcotics and Special Investigations Division, addicts who are forced against their will to enter and remain in therapy can overcome their addiction. Roughly 90% of all addicts are arrested at least once every year, giving the criminal justice system plenty of opportunities to help them kick their habits.

One highly visible persuasive effort to end drug abuse has been the advertising campaign created by the Partnership for a Drug-Free America. The nation's advertising industry developed the partnership and funded it by collaborating with advertisers and a variety of health and educational agencies. The goal was to promote images designed to make drug use look "uncool," especially to younger people. In addition to the creative services donated by advertising agencies, media organizations donated more than $2 billion of public service and advertising space to the partnership between the late 1980s and 1990s.

In the early 1990s, the partnership commissioned surveys to measure the effect of its media campaign on students in the Los Angeles and New York City school systems. On both coasts, increased exposure to the partnership's messages appeared to dramatically change students' attitudes toward drugs. At the same time, however, the number of students who admitted using drugs actually increased.

Another high-visibility persuasive effort has been the nationwide DARE program, which was launched in Los Angeles in 1983. "DARE's curriculum reflects mainstream theories about the best way to reduce drinking, smoking, and drug use by children. . . . The program began as a collaboration between the Los Angeles Police Department and the city's school district" (Miller 2001, p. A14). Using role-playing techniques and resistance training, uniformed police officers become social workers, talking with students in their classrooms, educating them about the dangers of drugs, and giving them the tools to resist temptation or peer pressure. They generally teach 17 classroom sessions.

> Today most school-based prevention programs, including DARE, assume that adolescents need grown-ups' help in resisting social pressures to use [drugs]. Therefore, they try to correct children's exaggerated beliefs about the prevalence of drug use among their peers. They offer them information about the physical and social effects of using and they try to impart "resistance skills" for making and acting on thoughtful decisions. (Miller 2001, p. A14)

Although DARE is the most popular drug education program ever developed for children, increasing numbers of critics claim that its benefits, if any, are short-lasting. Most DARE training begins in the 5th grade. At this age, students accept most of what they hear. By middle school, however, the effectiveness of DARE begins to erode. By high school, many students resist participation in the program. According to a researcher from the Research Triangle Institute in Durham, North Carolina, which conducted a $300,000 study on the impact of DARE, "Unless there's some sort of booster session that reinforces the original curriculum, the effects of most drug use prevention programs decay rather than increase over time." The findings of numerous research studies conducted on DARE's effectiveness suggest that DARE students were no less likely to use drugs than students who had not gone through the program (Ennett et al. 1994; Vogt 2003, p. 3). Some have even claimed that the DARE program teaches kids to become curious about illicit drug use or actually motivates them to do drugs (Vogt 2003, p. 3). Further, "[a]s DARE America celebrated its 20th anniversary, the nation's most widely used school-based drug prevention program was struggling with a credibility crisis that has devastated the organization financially and threatens its survival" (Vogt 2003). Reports indicate that a number of school districts throughout the country have abandoned the program, finding DARE to be ineffective in curbing both licit and illicit drug use.

In light of the diminishing returns from various drug prevention programs, in late 1996 the Clinton administration proposed a compulsory drug test for teenagers who are applying for their driver's licenses.

Like everything else, the proposal had both supporters and critics. Although this tactic may be part of the answer, prevention programs that have measurable, *long-lasting* effects remain difficult to find.

Sources: Brownsberger, W. N. "Just Say 'Criminal Justice.'" *Boston Globe* (20 October 1996).

Ennett, S. T., N. S. Tobler, C. L. Ringwalt, and R. L. Flewelling. "How Effective Is Drug Abuse Resistance Education? A Metaanalysis of Project D.A.R.E. Outcome Evaluations." *American Journal of Public Health* 84 (1994): 1394–1401.

Gordon, P. "The Truth About D.A.R.E." *Buzz Magazine* (July 1996).

Gordon, P. "Can Madison Avenue Really Save America by Making Illegal Drugs Totally Uncool?" *Buzz Magazine* (August 1996).

Miller, D. W. "DARE Reinvents Itself — With Help from Its Social-Scientist Critics." *Chronicle of Higher Education* 48 (19 October 2001): A12–A14.

Vogt, A. "Now Many 'Just Say No' to DARE." *Chicago Tribune* (26 January 2003): 1, 3.

■ Drug Courts

Although these courts of law vary in organization, in scope, and at what point intervention occurs, the underlying premise is that drug possession and use is not only a law enforcement/criminal justice problem, but also a public health problem (Sherin and Mahoney 1996). In **drug court** programs, criminal justice agencies collaborate closely with the substance abuse treatment community and other societal institutions to design and operate the program. Thus, the key goal is to divert substance abusers into supervised community treatment centers in an attempt to eliminate the destructive behavior. A committee usually composed of a judge, the district attorney, a public defender, the probation department, and treatment center officials determines whether treatment is needed and the type and length of treatment. At the first National Drug Court Conference, one researcher reported, "These courts rely on strong collaboration among judges, prosecutors, defense lawyers, and related supporting agencies (such as case management, corrections, pretrial services, probation, etc.), on the one hand, and a partnership with treatment agencies (or providers) and other community organizations and representatives on the other" (Goldkamp 1993, p. 33).

The treatment phase generally consists of: (1) detoxification (removal of physical dependence on drugs from body), (2) stabilization (treating the psychological craving for the drug), and (3) aftercare (helping the defendant obtain education or job training, find a job, and remain drug free). (Office of Justice Programs [OJP] 2000)

A recent report stated that "A recent survey of more than 120 evaluations of drug court programs showed that they outperformed virtually all other strategies that have been attempted for drug offenders within the 1 to 2 years that courts typically monitor offenders. Offenders who graduated from drug courts had significant reductions in rearrest rates and in charges for serious crimes. Data show that within the first year of release, 43.5% of drug offenders are rearrested, whereas only 16.4% of drug court graduates are rearrested" (Office of National Drug Control Policy [ONDCP] 2007, p. 25) Figure 17.2 shows the current number of drug courts in each state as of January 2007. When drug courts were first implemented, there was one drug court in the United States in 1989 and 1990 (American University 2003). Today, we are at the point were each state has multiple drug courts, totaling 1927 drug courts in the United States (ONDCP 2007).

Overall, there have been lower rearrest rates for defendants participating in drug court sentencing and there were statistically significant differences in disposition between those assigned to drug court and the comparison groups. Those assigned to drug court were more likely not to face further prosecution and less likely to serve probation or short jail terms. Finally, using drug court and its system of administering treatment within a legal

KEY TERMS

drug court
court designed to focus on treatment programs and options in place of punishment for drug offenses

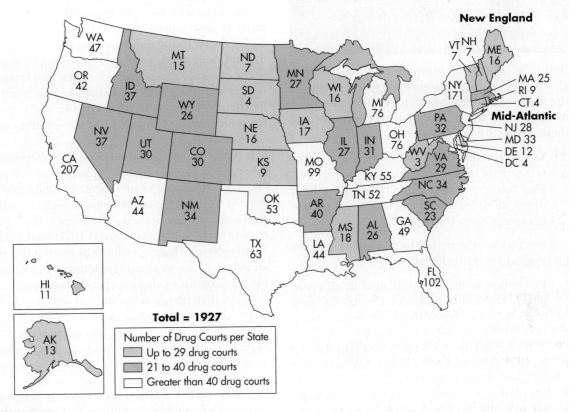

FIGURE 17.2

Drug courts by state for January 2007.

Source: Office of National Drug Control Policy (ONDCP). *National Drug Control Strategy: The White House, February 2007.* Washington, DC: U.S. Government Printing Office, 2007.

atmosphere is more cost-effective than criminal courts — between \$1200 and \$3500 per participant compared with approximately \$5000 to incarcerate the same defendant (OJP Drug Court Clearinghouse and Technical Assistance Project [DCCTAP] 1999). More recent findings show that:

> Surveys completed by treatment providers indicate that the annual cost of treatment services for drug court participants differs widely based on many factors. These factors include the target population treated in the program and the type of treatment services provided (which range widely in availability, cost, and application; i.e., intensive outpatient, medically monitored inpatient, methadone maintenance, therapeutic communities, etc.). In addition, annualized treatment costs may include ancillary services offered (i.e., job training, anger management counseling, etc.), drug testing, and case management. . . . Given these varia-

tions in services offered and services delivered, 61% of drug court treatment providers report that the annual cost of treatment services per client ranges between \$900 and \$3500 (American University 2003).

Research shows, however, that we should be cautious for two reasons: (1) The research on the effectiveness of these courts was done very early — the courts were in operation fewer than 10 months, and (2) these courts were very selective of the defendants allowed to participate — the criticism being that the courts tended to select violators who would have a better chance for rehabilitation.

It is apparent that drug courts need more time to operate, and more evaluation research needs to be conducted. The most promising aspect of these courts is the emphasis on treating drug addiction instead of simply punishing without treating as has been the case historically.

Problems with Assessing the Success of Drug Prevention Programs

Both the National Institute on Drug Abuse (NIDA) and individual researchers have evaluated the multitude of drug abuse prevention programs in the United States. The general conclusions of these studies are as follows:

- Very few programs have demonstrated clear success or have adequately evaluated themselves.
- The relationships among information about drugs, attitudes toward use, and actual use are unclear in these programs.

Some factors that are key to developing successful programs include the following:

- Prevention must be coordinated at different levels. Successful programs involve families, schools, and communities. In some cases, these efforts are not coordinated.
- The program must be integrated into the ongoing activities of schools, families, and community organizations. Superficial introduction of drug prevention strategies has limited effects. For instance, distributing literature door-to-door, making in-class presentations of the harmful effects of drugs, and posting banners and slogans warning of the consequences of drug abuse in communities are not successful methods. Instead, programs that are comprehensive and community-wide, integrated into neighborhood clubs, organizations, and church activities, are more likely to have a long-term impact on preventing drug use. A clear example is the yearly Great American Smokeout launched against tobacco use.
- Personal autobiographical and social experience accounts of former drug abusers should be included in drug information that is distributed. Recipients of drug prevention information should be given real-life accounts of use, abuse, despair, and successful drug rehabilitation. Just receiving drug information alone has little impact, either initially or over the long term.

Other Alternatives to Drug Use

It has been suggested that people have an innate need to alter their conscious state. This belief is based on the observation that, as part of their normal play, preschoolers deliberately whirl themselves dizzy and even momentarily choke each other to lose consciousness (Wilson and Wilson 1975). Some young children progress to discovering and using chemicals (such as sniffing shoe polish or gasoline) to alter consciousness and learn to be very secretive about this behavior. They learn to be circumspect or come to feel guilty and repress the desire to alter consciousness when adults catch them in these activities.

If this desire to alter the state of consciousness is inherent in human beings, then the use of psychoactive drugs, legal or illegal, in adulthood is natural. Drug abuse is, therefore, a logical continuation of a developmental sequence that goes back to early childhood (Carroll 1977; Weil 1972).

Other researchers question why, even if there is an innate desire to alter consciousness, only some people progress to abusing chemical substances. It appears that people who do not abuse psychoactive drugs have found positive alternatives to altering consciousness; they feel no need to take chemical substances for this purpose. Involvement in activities such as Boy Scouts and Girl Scouts, youth sports teams, music groups, the YMCA and YWCA, drug-free video game centers, drug-free dances, environmental and historical preservation projects, and social and service projects are viable alternatives to drug use. The rationale for these programs is that youth will find these activities engaging enough to forgo alcohol and drug use (Forman and Linney 1988).

This strategy is known as the **alternatives approach**. Workers in the drug abuse field tend to agree on its effectiveness. They note that young ex-abusers of common illicit drugs are more likely to stop when they gain satisfaction from exploring positive alternatives rather than from a fear of consequent harm. The alternatives approach assumes the following (Cohen 1971):

1. People abuse drugs voluntarily to fill a need or basic drive.
2. Most people abuse drugs for negative reasons. They may be dealing with negative feelings or

KEY TERMS

alternatives approach
an approach emphasizing the exploration of positive alternatives to drug abuse, based on replacing the pleasurable feelings gained from drug abuse with involvement in social and educational activities

situations, such as relieving boredom, anxiety, depression, tension, or other unpleasant emotional and psychological states. They may be rebelling against authority, trying to escape feelings of loneliness or inadequacy, or trying to be accepted by peers. Peer pressure is extremely important as an inducing force.

3. Some people who abuse drugs believe the experience is positive. They may feel that their sensual experiences or music enjoyment is enhanced, or that they have achieved altered states of consciousness, or they may simply experience a sense of adventure. Some people may want to explore their own consciousness and reasons for the attraction to drug use.

Whether the reasons for drug use are positive or negative, the effects sought can be achieved through alternative, nondrug means. Such means are preferable to drug use and more constructive because the person is not relying on a psychoactive substance for satisfaction; rather, he or she is finding satisfaction based on personal achievements. Ideally, this approach should lead to a lifetime of self-satisfaction.

Table 17.3 lists various types of experiences, the motives for such experiences, the probable drugs of abuse with which they are associated, and alternatives to these drugs. As shown in the table, any constructive activity can be considered an alternative to drug abuse. For example, a young person who needs an outlet for increased physical energy might respond better to dance and movement training or a project in preventive medicine than to work on ecological projects. In a large alternatives program established in Idaho, the following activities were planned during a month: arts and crafts, karate, reforestation, backpacking, Humane Society dog show, horseback riding, artwork for posters for various programs, astronomy, camping, and volunteering in a local hospital.

Meditation

Some of the most intriguing research about the brain is being done on the state of the mind during **meditation**. In certain countries, such as India, people have long histories of being able to achieve certain goals through meditation. The word *yoga* is derived from the Sanskrit word for union, or yoking, meaning the process of discipline by which a person attains union with the absolute. In a sense, it refers to the use of the mind to control itself and the body.

Meditation involves brain wave activity centered on ponderous, contemplative, and reflective thought. An individual who meditates is able to decrease oxygen consumption within a matter of minutes by as much as 20%, a level usually reached only after 4 to 5 hours of sleep. However, meditation is physiologically different from sleep, based on the electroencephalograph (EEG) pattern and rate of decline of oxygen consumption. Along with the decreased metabolic rate and changes in EEG, there is also a marked decrease in blood lactate. Lactate is produced by metabolism of skeletal muscle, and the decrease is probably due to the reduced activity of the sympathetic nervous system during meditation. Heart rate and respiration are also slowed.

The Natural Mind Approach

Some people who take drugs eventually look for other methods of maintaining the valuable parts of the drug experience. These people may learn to value the meditation high and abandon drugs. Long-term drug users sometimes credit their drug experiences with having given them a taste of their potential, even though continued use has diminished the novelty of drug use. After these individuals become established in careers, they claim to have grown out of chemically induced altered states of consciousness. As Andrew Weil (1972, p. 67) put it, "One does not see any long-time meditators give up meditation to become acid heads."

Although chemical highs are effective means of altering the state of consciousness, they interfere with the most worthwhile states of altered consciousness because they reinforce the illusion that highs come from external, material agents rather than from within your own nervous system.

Some people have difficulty using meditation as an alternative to drugs because, to be effective, meditation takes practice and concentration; in contrast, the effects of drugs are immediate. Nevertheless, it is within everyone's potential to meditate.

KEY TERMS

meditation
a state of consciousness in which there is a constant level of awareness focusing on one object; for example, yoga and Zen Buddhism

Table 17.3 Experiences, Motives, and Possible Alternatives for a Drug Abuser

EXPERIENCE	CORRESPONDING MOTIVES	DRUGS ABUSED	POSSIBLE ALTERNATIVES
Physical	Desire for physical well-being: physical relaxation, relief from sickness, desire for more energy	Alcohol, sedative-hypnotics, stimulants, marijuana	Athletics, dance, exercise, hiking, diet, carpentry, outdoor work, swimming, hatha yoga
Sensory	Desire to magnify sensorium: sound, touch, taste, need for sensual/sexual stimulation	Hallucinogens, marijuana, alcohol	Sensory awareness training, sky diving, experiencing sensory beauty of nature, scuba diving
Emotional	Relief from psychological pain: attempt to resolve personal problems, relief from bad mood, escape from anxiety, desire for emotional insight, liberation of feeling and emotional relaxation	Narcotics, alcohol, barbiturates, sedative-hypnotics	Competent individual counseling, well-run group therapy, instruction in psychology of personal development
Interpersonal	Desire to gain peer acceptance, break through interpersonal barriers, "communicate"; defiance of authority figures	Any, especially alcohol, marijuana	Expertly managed sensitivity and encounter groups, well-run group therapy, instruction in social customs, confidence training, emphasis on assisting others (e.g., YMCA or YWCA volunteers)
Social	Desire to promote social change, find identifiable subculture, tune out intolerable environmental conditions (e.g., poverty)	Marijuana, psychedelics	Social service community action in positive social change; helping the poor, aged, infirm, or young; tutoring handicapped individuals; ecology action; YMCA or YWCA Big Brother/Sister programs
Political	Desire to promote political change (out of desperation with the social-political order) and to identify with antiestablishment subgroup	Marijuana, psychedelics	Political service, lobbying for nonpartisan projects (e.g., Common Cause); field work with politicians and public officials
Intellectual	Desire to escape boredom, out of intellectual curiosity, to solve cognitive problems, gain new understanding in the world of ideas, research one's own awareness	Stimulants, sometimes psychedelics	Intellectual excitement through reading, debate, and discussion; creative games and puzzles; self-hypnosis; training in concentration
Creative-aesthetic	Desire to improve creative performance, enhance enjoyment of art already produced (e.g., music); enjoy imaginative mental productions	Marijuana, stimulants, psychedelics	Nongraded instruction in producing and/or appreciating art, music, drama, and creative hobbies
Philosophical	Desire to discover meaningful values, find meaning in life, help establish personal identity, organize a belief structure	Psychedelics, marijuana, stimulants	Discussions, seminars, courses on ethics, the nature of reality, relevant philosophical literature; explorations of value systems
Spiritual-mystical	Desire to transcend orthodox religion, develop spiritual insights, reach higher levels of consciousness, augment yogic practices, take a spiritual shortcut	Psychedelics, marijuana	Exposure to nonchemical methods of spiritual development; study of world religions, mysticism, meditation, yogic techniques

Discussion Questions

1. Figure 17.1 lists many factors that can influence drug use. Design a drug prevention program by selecting any one of the concentric circles and include all factors within that circle.

2. Look at all of the findings in the section of this chapter entitled "How Serious Is the Problem of Drug Dependence?" Which two findings regarding dependence were the most interesting and why were they the most interesting?

3. Comment on the harm reduction model as presented here and in other literature you may have. (For example, see http://www.ccsa.ca/pdf/ccsa-004011-1993.pdf; http://www.habitsmart.com/hrmtitle.html; and http://www.druglibrary.org/schaffer/library/studies/redfern/rf5.htm.) What are the major strengths and weaknesses of this model in comparison to the way the United States views drug users and/or abusers? Why do you think the U.S. government remains opposed to this approach? Speculate on how the United States would change if it were to adopt the harm reduction model.

4. What would you emphasize in a primary prevention program for junior high school students? High school students? College students?

5. How would you design a drug prevention program for nondetected committed or secret users? What would you emphasize?

6. What do you think is more likely to work today in drug prevention programs for America's youth: teaching moderate use or total abstinence? Why?

7. Your boss says, "We received a much smaller amount of money from the federal government to create a drug prevention program. I want you to focus on a community-based approach, school-based approach, or family-based prevention program." Which would you select and why?

8. How effective has the BACCHUS Network been on your campus? Can you give examples?

9. List and explain two potential strengths and two potential weaknesses of drug courts in comparison with traditional criminal courts in the United States.

10. Evaluate the DARE drug prevention program. What problems has this program encountered with regard to its effectiveness?

11. What is your assessment of using the alternatives approach and meditation for preventing drug use? Do you think it works? Why or why not?

Summary

1. The ten most prominent factors affecting an individual's use of drugs are as follows: (1) genetics, (2) personality traits, (3) attitudes and beliefs, (4) interpersonal and peer resistance skills, (5) community, (6) peers, (7) school policy, (8) local law enforcement, (9) personal situations, and (10) parents.

2. The seriousness of the problem with regard to drug dependence is highlighted by the fact that in 2006, an estimated 22.6 million persons age 12 or older were classified with substance dependence or abuse in the past year (9.2%). Of these, 3.2 million were classified with dependence on or abuse of both alcohol and illicit drugs, 3.8 million were dependent on or abused illicit drugs but not alcohol, and 15.6 million were dependent on or abused alcohol but not illicit drugs. Further, the specific illicit drugs that had the highest levels of past-year dependence or abuse in 2006 were marijuana, followed by cocaine and pain relievers.

3. Three major types of prevention programs are (1) primary, (2) secondary, and (3) tertiary prevention.

4. Five major types of drug users that drug prevention programs have to recognize before assembling a program are (1) early experimenters, (2) nonproblem drug users/recreational users, (3) nondetected committed or secret users, (4) problem users, and (5) former users.

5. The four levels of comprehensive prevention programs for drug use and abuse are (1) the harm reduction model, (2) community-based prevention, (3) school-based prevention, and (4) family-based prevention.

6. Proactive family factors can moderate the effects of drug risk factors. The risk of associating with peers who use drugs can be offset by

protective family factors, such as parent conventionality, maternal adjustment, and strong parent–child attachment.

7 Four primary prevention programs that exist in higher education are the (1) information-only or awareness model, (2) attitude change model or affective education model, (3) social influences model, and (4) ecological or person-in-environment model.

8 The main goals of three of today's large-scale prevention programs include (1) BACCHUS and GAMMA Peer Education Network — a national and international association of college and university peer-education programs focused on alcohol abuse prevention and other related student health and safety issues; (2) DARE — a once-popular nationwide drug prevention program presented in junior high schools by police officers; and (3) drug courts — a newer nationwide approach to prevention in which the primary purpose is to focus on treatment programs and options instead of punishment for drug offenses.

9 Two additional possibilities for lessening or eliminating drug use are the alternatives approach and meditation. Alternatives to drug abuse are based on replacing the euphoria and pleasure gained by being high with involvement in social, recreational, and educational activities. Meditation is producing a state of consciousness in which there is a constant level of very satisfying awareness that is rewarding in itself without artificial inducements (drugs). Yoga and Zen Buddhism are examples.

References

Alberti, R. E., and M. L. Emmons. *Your Perfect Right.* San Luis Obispo, CA: Impact Publishers, 1988.

American University. *Drug Court Clearinghouse and Technical Assistance Project: Summary of Drug Court Activity by State and County.* Washington, DC: Author, 7 November 2003. Available http://www.ndci.org/courtfacts_benefits.html.

The Bacchus Network. *Mission Statement.* Denver, CO: The BACCHUS Network National Office, 2007a. Available http://www.bacchusgamma.org/mission.asp.

BACCHUS and GAMMA. *What Is BACCHUS and GAMMA Network?* Denver, CO: The BACCHUS and GAMMA Peer Education Network, 2000b. Available http://www.bacchusgamma.org/tour_2.asp.

Botvin, G. J., and T. A. Wills. "Personal and Social Skills Training: Cognitive-Behavioral Approaches to Substance Abuse Prevention." In *Prevention Research: Deter-*

ring Drug Abuse Among Children and Adolescents. NIDA Research Monograph 64. Rockville, MD: NIDA (U.S. DHHS, PHS, ADAMHA), 1985.

Carroll, E. "Notes on the Epidemiology of Inhalants." In *Review of Inhalants*, edited by C. W. Sharp and M. L. Brehm. NIDA Research Monograph No. 15. Washington, DC: National Institute on Drug Abuse, 1977.

Center for Prevention Research and Development (CPRD). *Research Based Approaches in the Community Domain.* Champaign, IL: University of Illinois Urbana Champaign, 2000.

Clayton, R. R., R. Cattarello, L. E. Cay, and K. P. Walden. "Persuasive Communication and Drug Prevention: An Evaluation of the D.A.R.E. Program." In *Persuasive Communication and Drug Abuse Prevention*, edited by L. Donohew, H. Sypepher, and W. Bukowski, 83–107. Hillsdale, NJ: Erlbaum, 1991.

Cohen, A. Y. "The Journey Beyond Trips: Alternatives to Drugs." *Journal of Psychedelic Drugs* 3 (Spring 1971): 7–14.

Ennett, S. T., N. S. Tobler, C. L. Ringwalt, and R. L. Flewelling. "How Effective Is Drug Abuse Resistance Education? A Meta-analysis of Project D.A.R.E. Outcome Evaluations." *American Journal of Public Health* 84 (1994): 1394–1401.

Forman, S. G., and J. A. Linney. "School-Based Prevention of Adolescent Substance Abuse: Programs, Implementation and Future Direction." *School Psychology Review* 17 (1988): 550–558.

Goldkamp, J. *Justice and Treatment Innovation: The Drug Court Movement.* Washington, DC: National Institute of Justice and the State Justice Institute, 1993.

Gonzalez, G. M., and V. V. Clement, eds. *Preventing Substance Abuse.* U.S. Department of Education. Washington, DC: U.S. Government Printing Office, 1994.

Gopelrud E. N., ed. *Preventing Adolescent Drug Use: From Theory to Practice.* OSAP Monograph #8, DHHS Publication No. (ADM) 91–1725. Rockville, MD: Office of Substance Abuse Prevention, 1991.

Hansen, W. B. "A Social Ecology Theory of Alcohol and Drug Use Prevention Among College and University Students." In *Designing Alcohol and Other Drug Prevention Programs in Higher Education.* Newton, MA: Higher Education Center for Alcohol and Other Drug Prevention, U.S. Department of Education, 1997. Available http://www.edc.org/hec/pubs/theorybook/Hansen.html.

Holstein, M. E., W. E. Cohen, and P. Steinbroner. *A Matter of Balance: Personal Strategies for Alcohol and Other Drugs.* Ashland, OR: CNS Productions, 1995.

Horowitz, H. L. *Campus Life.* New York: Knopf, 1987.

Koss, M. P., C. A. Gidycz, and R. Wisniewski. "The Scope of Rape: Incidence and Prevalence of Sexual Aggression and Victimization in a National Sample of Higher Education Students." *Journal of Consulting and Clinical Psychology* 34 (1987): 186–196.

Law Enforcement News. "When It Comes to the Young, Anti-drug Efforts Are Going to Pot." 22 (1996): 441–447.

Magnum, A., and P. Taylor. "Peddling Booze on Campus: How to Spot It, How to Fight It." *Eta Sigma Gamman* 22 (1990): 1.

McIntyre, K., D. White, and R. Yoast. *Resilience Among High–Risk Youth.* Madison, WI: University of Wisconsin, 1990.

National Institutes of Health (NIH) and National Institute on Drug Abuse (NIDA). *Drug Abuse and Drug Abuse Research.* Washington, DC: U.S. Government Printing Office, 1998.

Norman, E. "Personal Factors Related to Substance Misuse: Risk Abatement and/or Resiliency Enhancement." In *Substance Abuse in Adolescence,* edited by T. P. Gulotta, G. R. Adams, and R. Montemayor, 47–56. Thousand Oaks, CA: Sage Publications, 1994.

Office of Justice Programs (OJP). *OJP Drug Court Clearinghouse and Technical Assistance Project: Summary of Drug Court Activity by State and County.* Washington, DC: U.S. Government Printing Office, 10 January 2000.

Office of Justice Programs (OJP) Drug Court Clearinghouse and Technical Assistance Project (DCCTAP). *Looking at a Decade of Drug Courts.* Washington, DC: Drug Court Clearinghouse and Technical Assistance Project, 1999.

Office of National Drug Control Policy (ONDCP). *National Drug Control Strategy: The White House, February 2007.* Washington, DC: U.S. Government Printing Office, 2007.

Perkins, H. W. "Confronting Misperceptions of Peer Use Norms Among College Students: An Alternative Approach for Alcohol and Other Drug Education Programs." In *The Higher Education Leaders/Peers Network Peer Prevention Program Resource Manual.* Washington, DC: Texas Christian University, U.S. Department of Education (FIPSE), 1991: 18–32.

Perkins, H. W. "College Student Misperceptions of Alcohol and Other Drug Norms Among Peers: Exploring Causes, Consequences, and Implications for Prevention Programs." In *Designing Alcohol and Other Drug Prevention Programs in Higher Education.* Newton, MA: U.S. Department of Education, Higher Education Center for Alcohol and Other Drug Prevention, 1997. Available http://www.edc.org/hec/pubs/theorybook/perkins.html.

Perkins, H. W., and A. D. Berkowitz. "Perceiving the Community Norms of Alcohol Use Among Students: Some Research Implications for Campus Alcohol Education Programming." *International Journal of the Addictions* 21, (1986): 861–976.

Phoenix House. *School Daze?* (2000). Available http://www.factsontap.org/factsontap/alcohol_and_student_life/school_daze.htm.

Robertson, E. B., S. L. David, S. A. Rao, and National Institute on Drug Abuse (NIDA). *Preventing Drug Use Among Children and Adolescents, 2nd Ed.* U.S. Department of Health and Human Services (USDHHS), Bethesda, MD, 2003.

Rosenbaum, D. P., and S. Hanson. "Assessing the Effects of School-Based Drug Education; A Six-Year Multi-level Analysis of Project DARE." Department of Criminal Justice and Center for Research in Law and Justice. Chicago, IL: University of Illinois at Chicago, 6 April 1998.

Ryan, B. E., T. Colthurst, and L. Segars. *College Alcohol Risk Assessment Guide.* San Diego: UCSD Extension, University of California at San Diego, 1995.

Sherin, K. M., and B. Mahoney. *Treatment Drug Courts: Integrating Substance Abuse Treatment with Legal Case Processing.* Rockville, MD: U.S. Department of Health and Human Services, 1996.

Shiffman, S., and T. A. Wills, eds. *Coping and Substance Abuse.* New York: Academic Press, 1987.

Silver Gate Group and Robert Wood Johnson Foundation. *Prevention 2000: Moving Effective Prevention Programs into Practice.* Princeton, NJ: Robert Wood Johnson Foundation, 2001.

Sloboda, Z., and S. L. David. *Preventing Drug Use Among Children and Adolescents: A Research-Based Guide.* Washington, DC: National Institute on Drug Abuse and National Institutes of Health, April 1999.

Substance Abuse and Mental Health Services Administration (SAMHSA). *Results from the 2006 National Survey on Drug Use and Health: National Findings.* Rockville, MD: Office of Applied Studies, 2007.

Tinzmann, M. B., and J. Hixson. *What Does Research Say About Prevention?* Oak Brook, IL: North Central Regional Educational Laboratory, 1992.

U.S. Department of Education. *Archived Information: Current Knowledge in Prevention of Alcohol and Other Drug Abuse.* G. M. Gonzalez and V. V. Clement, eds. Washington, DC: Government Printing Office, 1994. Available at http://www.ed.gov/pubs/preventingsubstanceabuse/current.html

Vogt, A. "Now Many 'Just Say No' to DARE." *Chicago Tribune* (26 January 2003), 1, 3.

Weil, A. *The Natural Mind.* Boston, MA: Houghton Mifflin, 1972.

Westermeyer, R. W. "Reducing Harm: A Very Good Idea" (no date). Available http://www.habitsmart.com/harm.html.

Wilson, M., and S. Wilson, eds. *Drugs in American Life, Vol. 1.* New York: Wilson, 1975.

Wilson, R., and C. Kolander. *Drug Abuse Prevention: A School and Community Partnership,* 2nd Ed. Sudbury, MA: Jones and Bartlett Publishers, Inc., 2003.

Zeese, K. B., and P. M. Lewin. *The Effective Drug Control Strategy.* Washington, DC: Network of Reform Group and the National Coalition for Effective Drug Policies, 1998. Available http://www.csdp.org/edcs/edc.htm.

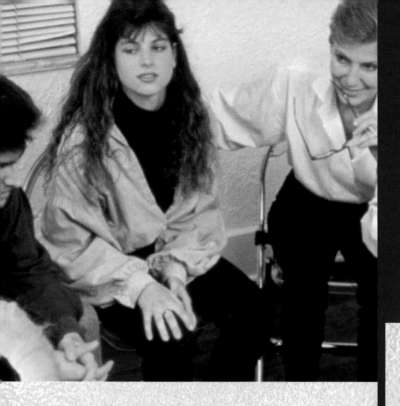

CHAPTER 18

Treating Drug Dependence

Learning ◎bjectives

On completing this chapter you will be able to:

◎ Discuss assessment of addiction severity and readiness to change.

◎ List several principles that characterize effective drug treatment.

◎ List the advantages and disadvantages of several strategies to treat addiction.

◎ Discuss pharmacological strategies to treat addiction.

Did You Know?

○ A variety of approaches to drug addiction treatment exist, including behavioral and pharmacological therapies.

○ No single treatment approach is appropriate for all individuals.

○ Medical detoxification is not a treatment, but rather a precursor to treatment.

○ The most successful treatment programs provide a combination of therapies and other services to meet the needs of the individual abuser.

Drugs and Society Online is a great source for additional drugs and society information for both students and instructors. Visit **http://drugsandsociety.jbpub.com** to find a variety of useful tools for learning, thinking, and teaching.

Treatment of Addiction

Individuals who are addicted to drugs come from all walks of life. Many suffer from occupational, social, psychiatric or other medical problems that can make their addictions difficult to treat. Even in the absence of such complicating issues, the severity of addictions varies widely. It is essential to match treatment with the needs of the client. Further, it is valuable to intervene at the earliest possible stage of addiction with the least restrictive form of appropriate treatment. To accomplish this, it is important that treatment providers determine the severity of addiction as well as the readiness of an individual to change his or her behavior.

Assessing Addiction Severity and Readiness to Change

The process of determining addiction severity can be accomplished in many ways, including the administration of standardized questionnaires. Of these, the Addiction Severity Index (ASI) is among the most widely used assessment instruments in the field of addiction (McLellan et al. 1980, 1985, 1992). First released in the late 1970s, it is now in its fifth version with a sixth in development. The ASI is one of the most reliable and valid measurements of the magnitude and characteristics of client problems. It focuses on possible problems in six areas: medical status, employment and support, alcohol and drug use, legal status, family and social relationships, and psychiatric status. The ASI provides information that can be used to identify and prioritize which problem areas are most significant and require prompt attention.

Treatment facilities provide a variety of services to people dealing with substance abuse.

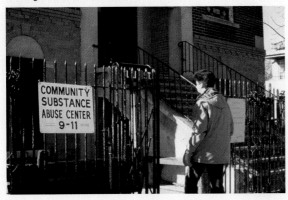

When assessing and prioritizing problems, one model of individual development that is often considered is Maslow's hierarchy of needs. This theory postulates that individuals are motivated by unsatisfied needs, and that lower fundamental needs must be satisfied before higher needs can be satisfied. These primary needs include food, drink, warmth, sleep, and shelter. These can be extended in the case of substance abusers to problems including: (1) unidentified or inappropriately managed health problems, (2) medication adherence issues (particularly in the presence of co-occurring mental or physical health disorders), and (3) physical alterations due to drug and/or alcohol dependence (Stilen et al. 2007). Once these fundamental needs are addressed, a second level of needs involving security and safety can be addressed. Simplistically, these include such issues as stability, order, law, and limits. Examples of common problem areas reflecting this level include inability for self-care, management of mental health issues, personal/public safety issues, and legal issues. If these needs are not met, individuals receiving substance abuse treatment cannot move to higher levels wherein love and belonging, self-esteem, and self-actualization (i.e., fulfilling personal potential) can be attained (Stilen et al. 2007).

As important as assessing addiction severity and prioritizing problem areas on which to focus is consideration of a person's readiness to change his or her abuse behavior. Pioneering work by DiClemente and Prochaska (1998) revealed that behavioral change is a many-stage process, rather than a singular event. The stages described by DiClemente and Prochaska include:

- *Precontemplation:* An individual does not want to change or is not considering changing his or her behavior. The latter may be because he or she does not see a need for change.
- *Contemplation:* A person is considering changing his or her behavior.
- *Preparation:* A person is committed to a strategy for change.
- *Action:* A person is actively attempting to change.
- *Maintenance:* A person has changed his or her behavior. In order to complete the process of change, this behavior must become a part of his or her lifestyle.

Determining the state of change at which an individual finds him- or herself can help providers select the best treatment plan to address a client's needs. This may help prevent the individual from refusing to accept all or parts of the treatment plan.

Principles of Treatment

A variety of approaches to drug addiction treatment exist. Some include behavioral therapy, such as counseling, psychotherapy, or cognitive therapy. Others include medications ranging from treatment medications (e.g., methadone, buprenorphine, nicotine patches, and nicotine gum) to those intended to treat co-occurring mental disorders (e.g., antidepressants or mood stabilizers). The most successful drug abuse treatment programs typically provide a combination of therapies and other services to meet the needs of the individual abuser. They incorporate adequate assessment of treatment needs required not only as a direct consequence of the physiological and psychological effects of the drug, but also from indirect problems, such as the need for housing, legal, and financial services, educational and vocational assistance, and family/child-care services. Such needs are often shaped by the gender, age, race, culture, and sexual orientation of the abuser.

In the United States, thousands of specialized treatment facilities provide rehabilitation, counseling, behavioral therapy, medication, case management, and other types of services to people dealing with substance abuse. Treatment can take various lengths of time and can occur in many different forms in a variety of settings. Because drug addiction is generally a chronic disorder characterized by occasional relapses, a one-time, short-term treatment is often inadequate. Research has shown that good outcomes are contingent on adequate duration of treatment. Generally, for residential or outpatient treatment, participation for fewer than 90 days is of limited or no effectiveness; treatments lasting significantly longer are needed (National Institute on Drug Abuse [NIDA] 1999). For methadone maintenance, 12 months of treatment is often the minimum needed, and some individuals who are addicted to opiates require extended treatment lasting several years (NIDA 1999). Many individuals who enter treatment drop out before receiving all of its benefits; hence, successful treatment often requires more than one treatment experience.

To best target treatment for an individual, the type and goals of treatment must be determined. Consideration must be given to the fact that both the type and the goals of treatment largely depend on the view one holds of addiction. For example, if the disease model is applied to addiction, total abstinence is required because this model views drug abuse as a biological condition that is largely uncontrollable. The user is perceived as ill and thus irrational about continued drug use. On the other hand, if responsible drug use is the goal, then occasional and moderate drug use can be the intended end result.

Effective treatment allows addicts to stop abusing drugs, returns them to a drug-free state of existence, and transforms them into employable and productive members of society. Measures of effectiveness typically include assessing levels of family functioning, employability, criminal behavior, and medical condition. Overall, treatment of addiction is as successful as treatment of other chronic diseases such as diabetes, hypertension, and asthma (NIDA 1999).

Studies clearly show that treatment is much less expensive than continuing addiction. Treatment is also less expensive than simply incarcerating addicts. For example, the average cost for 1 full year of methadone maintenance treatment is approximately $4700 per patient, whereas 1 full year of imprisonment costs approximately $18,400 per person (NIDA 1999, 2006c) or more. It has been estimated conservatively that every $1 invested in addiction treatment programs yields a return of between $4 and $7 in reduced drug-related crime, theft, and criminal justice costs (NIDA 1999, 2006a, c). With health care saving included, total savings can exceed costs by a ratio of 12:1 (NIDA 1999, 2006a). Major savings to the individual and society also come from significantly fewer interpersonal conflicts, improvements in workplace productivity, and reductions in drug-related incidents (NIDA 1999).

Successful outcomes depend on retaining the person in treatment long enough to gain the full benefit. Several factors influence retention, including individual motivation to change drug-using behavior and degree of support from family and friends. Pressure from employers, the criminal justice system, or extensions of the court (i.e., child protective services) can also be important. Because individual problems such as mental illness or criminal involvement decrease the likelihood of retaining patients in treatment, broad-ranging programs (i.e., with medical and legal services) are important. It is also important for providers to ensure a transition to continuing care or aftercare following a patient's completion of formal treatment (NIDA 1999).

NIDA has delineated thirteen overarching principles that characterize effective addiction treatment (NIDA 1999). These tenets, similar to those described by the majority of treatment researchers and providers, include the following:

1. *No single treatment is appropriate for all individuals.* Treatment settings, interventions, and services must be matched to each individual's particular problems and needs.

2. *Treatment needs to be readily available.* Individuals who are addicted to drugs are often uncertain about whether to seek treatment. Hence, it is crucial that services be available as soon as an individual makes the decision to seek help for his or her addiction. Opportunities for treatment can be lost if it is not immediately available or is not readily accessible.

3. *Effective treatment attends to multiple needs of the individual, not just his or her drug use.* To be effective, treatment must address the individual's drug use and any associated medical, psychological, social, vocational, and legal problems.

4. *An individual's treatment and services plan must be assessed continually and modified as necessary to ensure that the plan meets his or her changing needs.* A person undergoing treatment may require varying combinations of services and treatment components during the course of treatment and recovery. In addition to counseling or psychotherapy, medication, other medical services, family therapy, parenting instruction, vocational rehabilitation, and social and legal services may be required. Hence, continual monitoring is important.

5. *Remaining in treatment for an adequate period is critical for treatment effectiveness.* The appropriate duration for an individual depends on his or her problems and needs. As noted earlier, research indicates that for most patients, the threshold of significant improvement is reached at about 3 months in treatment.

6. *Counseling (individual and/or group) and other behavioral therapies are critical components of effective treatment for addiction.* In behavioral therapy, patients address issues of motivation, build skills to resist drug use, replace drug-using activities with constructive and rewarding non–drug-using activities, and improve problem-solving abilities.

7. *Medications are an important element of treatment for many patients, especially when combined with counseling and other behavioral therapies.* Methadone, naltrexone, and nicotine patches are just some examples of medications that can be effective treatments. For patients with mental disorders, medications (i.e., antidepressants, anxiolytics) can be especially important.

8. *Addicted or drug-abusing individuals with coexisting mental disorders should have both disorders treated in an integrated way.* Because addictive and mental disorders often occur in the same individual, patients presenting for either condition should be assessed and treated for the co-occurrence of the other.

9. *Medical detoxification is only the first stage of addiction treatment and by itself does little to change long-term drug use.* Medical detoxification (that is, the process of safely managing the acute physical symptoms of withdrawal associated with stopping drug use) can be an important first step toward abstinence. However, detoxification alone is rarely sufficient to help addicts achieve long-term abstinence.

10. *Treatment does not need to be voluntary to be effective.* Strong motivation can facilitate the treatment process. Sanctions or enticements in the family, criminal justice system, or employment setting can facilitate treatment entry and increase both retention rates and success of drug treatment interventions.

11. *Possible drug use during treatment must be monitored continuously.* Backsliding into drug use often occurs during addiction treatment. The objective of monitoring a patient's drug and alcohol use during treatment is that it can help the patient withstand urges to use drugs. Such monitoring also can provide early evidence of drug use so that the individual's treatment plan can be adjusted. Feedback to patients who test positive for illicit drug use is an important element of monitoring.

12. *Treatment programs should provide assessment for HIV/AIDS, hepatitis B and C, tuberculosis, and other infectious diseases and counseling to help patients modify or stop behaviors that place them or others at risk of infection.*

13. *Recovery from drug addiction can be a long-term process and frequently requires multiple episodes of treatment.* As with other chronic illnesses, relapses to drug use can occur during or after successful treatment episodes. Addicted individuals may require prolonged and multiple episodes of treatment to achieve long-term abstinence and fully restored functioning. Participation in self-help support programs during and following treatment often is helpful in maintaining abstinence.

Many treatment programs apply one or more of these listed principles as part of their therapeutic strategy.

Drug Addiction Treatment in the United States

■ Therapeutic Strategies

There is a wide array of general therapeutic strategies for treatment. Some involve pharmacological interventions, such as methadone maintenance or narcotic antagonist treatment. Other programs apply a drug-free approach. Programs can be short or long term and can be individualized or involve group participation. The following is an overview of various treatment approaches. It is important to realize that many treatment programs blend one or more of these approaches as part of their therapeutic strategy.

■ Historical Approaches

Considerable effort has been expended to find treatments for substance abuse. Several approaches, or at least components of them, continue to be utilized today. These include:

Alcoholics Anonymous

Founded in the mid-1930s, Alcoholics Anonymous (AA) is now an international organization. The desire to stop drinking is the sole criterion required to join. The original founders of AA were strongly influenced by a religious movement known as the "Oxford Group." AA outlines twelve successive measures referred to as steps that alcoholics should accomplish during the recovery process. These steps include admitting that the person addicted to alcohol has no power over the drug. He or she must also believe in a greater power who can help him or her overcome shortcomings. Individuals must make initial and ongoing assessments of their life, and admit to others the character of their wrongs. In addition, individuals must make amends to those whom they have adversely affected, except in situations where such actions could harm others (Alcoholics Anonymous 2007).

It is difficult to assess the success of AA for four reasons:

1. AA insists on anonymity; it does not reveal names of members.
2. Membership is strictly voluntary. Those who want to join become members when they vow to give up drinking.
3. Members are often a homogeneous group.

4. Some addiction researchers are of the opinion that the more severe, hard-core alcoholics who refuse to seek help generally do not go to AA, whereas a smaller percentage of problem drinkers who come to view themselves as addicted to alcohol take this path (see Rudy 1994 for further discussion of this and other related findings). In part, this self-selection may be responsible for the group's relatively high success rate.

Regardless, AA has been, and continues to be, a very important method for treating many recovering alcoholics.

AA has two types of meetings: open and closed. **Open meetings** are open to anyone who has an interest in attending and witnessing these meetings, and they last approximately 45 minutes to 1 hour. **Closed meetings** are for alcoholics who have a serious desire to completely stop drinking. These meetings are not open to viewers or "shoppers." At closed meetings, recovering alcoholics address, through testimonials, how alcohol has diminished their quality of life.

Some outgrowths of AA include Al-Anon, Adult Children of Alcoholics, and Alateen. These are parallel organizations supporting AA. Al-Anon is for spouses and other close relatives of alcoholics, and Alateen is exclusively for teenagers whose lives have been affected by someone else's alcoholism. Both relatives and teen members of alcoholic families learn means and methods for coping with destructive behaviors exhibited by alcoholic members.

Rehabilitation Programs

The first rehabilitation programs grew out of the work that AA members did with other active alcoholics. Known as "Twelfth stepping," this program involves reaching out to others in need and attempting to draw them in. The movement began in the early days of AA when the organization's founder, Bill W., had alcoholics trying to

KEY TERMS

open meetings
meetings to which anyone having an interest in attending and witnessing is invited

closed meetings
meetings to which only alcoholics having a serious desire to completely stop drinking are invited

stop drinking or "dry out" living at his house in Brooklyn. At that time, "[his] home was stuffed, from cellar to attic, with alcoholics in all stages of recovery" (Al-Anon 1970). It was a natural transition to opening up "drying out houses" in the 1940s and 1950s.

Also during the 1950s, the **Minnesota model**, an inpatient rehabilitation model, was developed. It combined the AA philosophy with a multidisciplinary treatment team. A treatment plan was used, based on assessment of the individual and prioritization of goals. This model, which borrows from social work practice, is still used in treatment programs. Due to the vagaries of insurance reimbursement in Minnesota, the program lasted 28 days because that was the length covered by insurance; therefore, alcoholism programs traditionally were roughly 1 month long.

Common alcohol abuse–related problems are shared at AA meetings.

General Therapeutic Strategies

In addition to the approaches mentioned previously, there are numerous strategies to drug addiction treatment. Although not all treatment programs fit perfectly into any one of these categories, the following provides an overview of the general types of services available (NIDA 1999).

Medical Detoxification

Medical detoxification is a process whereby individuals are systematically withdrawn from drugs, typically under the care of a physician. Medications are available for detoxification from benzodiazepines, alcohol, barbiturates, opiates, nicotine, and other sedatives. Detoxification can be medically necessary, as untreated withdrawal from some agents (that is, alcohol and barbiturates) can be fatal. Although detox is sometimes referred to as a distinct treatment modality, it is more appropriately considered a precursor to treatment because it is designed to treat the acute

physiological effects of stopping drug use. It is not designed to address the psychological, social, and behavioral problems associated with addiction and, therefore, does not typically produce lasting behavioral changes. Detoxification is most useful when it incorporates formal processes of assessment and referral to subsequent drug addiction treatment (NIDA 1999).

Outpatient Drug-Free Treatment

The outpatient strategy varies in the intensity and forms of services offered. Such treatment often is more suitable for individuals who are employed or who have extensive family and/or community support. Low-intensity programs may offer little more than drug education, warnings, and advice. Other outpatient models, such as intensive day treatment, can be comparable to residential programs in effectiveness and services. Group counseling is often emphasized (NIDA 1999).

Short-Term Residential Programs

Short-term residential programs provide relatively brief treatment based on a modified twelve-step approach. These programs were originally designed to treat alcoholism, but have been used to treat other forms of addiction. The original residential treatment model consisted of a 3- to 6-week hospital-based, inpatient treatment phase, followed by extended outpatient therapy and participation in a self-help group, such as AA. Reduced healthcare insurance coverage for substance abuse treatment has resulted in a diminished number of these programs, and the average length of stay under managed care review is much shorter than in early programs (NIDA 1999).

Long-Term Residential Treatment Programs

Long-term residential programs provide care 24 hours per day, generally in nonhospital settings. The best-known residential treatment model is the **therapeutic community** (TC), but residential treatment may also employ other models, such as cognitive-behavioral therapy. In general, TCs are drug-free residential settings that use a hierarchical model with treatment stages that reflect increased levels of responsibility.

The typical TC resident has more severe problems compared with patients in other forms of drug treatment — sometimes with more co-occurring mental health problems and criminal involvement. His or her addiction is viewed in the context of his or her social and psychological deficits, and treatment focuses on developing personal accountability and responsibility. Research shows that TCs can be modified to treat individuals with special needs, including adolescents, women, those with severe mental disorders, and individuals in the criminal justice system (NIDA 1999).

Participation in a TC involves planned lengths of stay of 6 to 12 months. Treatment is highly structured and can at times be confrontational. Activities are designed to help residents examine damaging self-concepts, beliefs, and patterns of behavior and to find constructive ways to interact with others. The TC focuses on the resocialization of the individual and uses the other residents, staff, and social context as active components of treatment. Many TCs also provide employment training and other support services on-site.

Treating Criminal Justice–Involved Drug Abusers and Addicts

Research has shown that combining drug treatment with criminal justice sanctions can decrease drug use and related crime. Treatment may be delivered prior to, during, after, or in lieu of incarceration. Individuals under legal coercion tend to stay in treatment for a longer period of time and do as well as or better than individuals who are not under legal pressure (NIDA 1999).

KEY TERMS

therapeutic community
drug-free residential settings that use a hierarchical model with treatment stages that reflect increased levels of responsibility

■ Specific Therapeutic Strategies

NIDA (1999) has described several scientifically based approaches to drug addiction treatment that are not described in detail in the previous sections. Some are designed to address the consequences of addiction for the individual, family, or society. All, according to NIDA, should supplement or enhance — but not replace — existing treatment programs.

Relapse Prevention

This approach is a cognitive-behavioral therapy based on the theory that learning processes play a critical role in the development of maladaptive behavioral patterns. Thus, patients learn to identify and correct problematic behaviors. They learn strategies intended to enhance self-control so as to facilitate abstinence. Specific techniques include exploring the positive and negative consequences of continued use, self-monitoring to recognize drug

A patient receives individual counseling in an alcoholism treatment center.

cravings early on and identifying high-risk situations for use, and developing strategies for coping with and avoiding high-risk situations and the desire to use. An important element of treatment is anticipating the problems patients are likely to meet and helping them develop effective coping strategies (NIDA 1999).

The Matrix Model

The matrix model provides a framework for engaging stimulant abusers in treatment with the goal of achieving abstinence. Patients learn about issues critical to addiction and relapse, receive assistance from a trained therapist, become familiar with self-help programs, and are monitored for drug use by urine testing. The model includes education for family members affected by the addiction. Other components include early recovery skills groups, relapse prevention groups, twelve-step programs, relapse analysis, and social support groups.

The therapist functions simultaneously as teacher and coach, fostering a positive, encouraging relationship with the patient and using that relationship to reinforce positive behavior change. The interaction between the therapist and the patient is realistic and direct but not confrontational or parental. Therapists are trained to conduct treatment sessions in a way that promotes the patient's self-esteem (NIDA 1999).

Supportive-Expressive Psychotherapy

This approach is a time-limited, focused psychotherapy that has been adapted for heroin- and cocaine-addicted individuals. Its two main components are (1) supportive techniques to help patients feel comfortable in discussing their personal experiences and (2) expressive techniques to help patients identify and work through interpersonal relationship issues. Particular attention is paid to the relationship between drugs and problem feelings and behaviors, and how problems may be solved without the use of drugs (NIDA 1999).

Individualized Drug Counseling

Individualized counseling focuses on stopping or reducing an individual's illicit drug use. Through weekly or biweekly sessions, the counselor helps the patient develop coping strategies and tools for abstaining from drug use and then maintaining abstinence. The addiction counselor often encourages twelve-step participation and makes referrals for needed supplemental medical, psychiatric, and employment services (NIDA 1999).

Motivational Enhancement Therapy

Motivational enhancement therapy (MET) is a patient-centered counseling approach for initiating behavior change by helping clients to resolve ambivalence about engaging in treatment and discontinuing drug use. Instead of guiding the patient through the recovery process, MET employs strategies to evoke rapid and internally motivated change in the client. Therapy consists of an initial assessment battery session, followed by two to four individual treatment sessions with a therapist. Feedback generated from the initial assessment battery is provided to the patient to stimulate discussion regarding personal substance abuse and to elicit self-motivational statements. Coping strategies for high-risk situations are discussed. In subsequent sessions, the therapist monitors change, reviews cessation strategies being used, and continues to encourage commitment to change or sustained abstinence (NIDA 1999).

Community Reinforcement Approach Plus Vouchers

This intensive, 24-week outpatient therapy has been used for treatment of cocaine addiction. The treatment goals are (1) to achieve cocaine abstinence long enough for patients to learn new life skills that will help sustain abstinence and (2) to reduce alcohol consumption for patients whose drinking is associated with cocaine use. Patients attend weekly or biweekly individual counseling sessions in which they learn a variety of skills to minimize drug use. Patients also submit urine samples and receive vouchers for cocaine-negative samples. The value of the vouchers increases with consecutive drug-free samples. Patients may exchange vouchers for retail goods that are consistent with a cocaine-free lifestyle. Voucher-based reinforcement has also been employed in conjunction with methadone maintenance therapy (NIDA 1999).

■ Pharmacological Strategies

Some treatment strategies employ pharmacological approaches to help patients with their addiction(s). These strategies are based on the properties of the drug to which they are addicted. Examples of these strategies are discussed in the following sections.

Opioid Agonist Maintenance Therapy

Treatment for opiate addicts is often conducted in outpatient settings using methadone. Methadone is an opioid **agonist** (that is, a drug that activates opioid receptors). It is a long-acting synthetic opiate medication administered orally for a sustained period at a dosage sufficient to prevent opiate withdrawal and decrease craving. Patients stabilized on adequate, sustained dosages of methadone can function normally. They can hold jobs, avoid the crime and violence of the street culture, and reduce their exposure to HIV by stopping or decreasing injection drug use and drug-related, high-risk sexual behavior.

Patients stabilized on opiate agonists can engage more readily in counseling and other behavioral interventions essential to recovery and rehabilitation. The best, most effective opiate agonist maintenance programs include individual and/or group counseling as well as provision of or referral to other needed medical, psychological, and social services (NIDA 1999).

Although many criticisms have been levied against the use of methadone, other research findings contradict this skepticism. According to NIDA (2006b), research indicates that methadone maintenance treatment is an effective treatment for heroin and prescription narcotic addiction as assessed by several outcome factors, including:

- Reduction in illicit drug use
- Reduction in criminal activity
- Reduction in HIV infection rates
- Reduction in needle sharing
- Improvements in social health and productivity
- Improvements in health conditions
- Cost-effectiveness
- Reduction in suicide and lethal overdose

Nicotine Replacement Therapy

Nicotine was the first pharmacological agent approved by the FDA for use in smoking cessation therapy. As discussed in Chapter 11, nicotine replacement therapies, such as nicotine gum, transdermal patches, nasal sprays, and inhalers, are used to relieve withdrawal symptoms. An added benefit is that these forms of nicotine have little abuse potential because they do not produce the pleasurable effects of tobacco products.

Antagonist Therapy

An **antagonist** is a compound that suppresses the actions of a drug. Narcotic antagonists have properties that make them important tools in the clinical treatment of narcotic drug dependence. For instance, they counteract the central nervous system depressant effects in opioid drug overdoses.

Opiate antagonists are often used in the emergency treatment of opiate poisoning (overdose). Some physicians claim to perform instant detoxification with the use of an opiate antagonist during sedation. The opiate antagonist naltrexone blocks heroin from having an effect on the heroin addict. Further, naloxone (Narcan) is often used as an antidote for opioid overdose (commonly known as "narcotic poisoning"). It is also used as a component of a treatment for opioid dependence that was FDA-approved in 2000 (see "Holding the Line").

Antagonists were developed as a by-product of research in analgesics. Scientists were interested in dissociating the dependence-producing and necessary pain-relieving properties of substances that could replace morphine. This research led to the development of nalorphine, the first specific opiate antagonist. Although its short duration of action and frequent unpleasant side effects limited its clinical usefulness, its properties stimulated further research into this class of drugs (Archer 1981; Palfai and Jankiewicz 1991).

Other Pharmacological Therapies

Clonidine is useful in treating several substance abuse disorders, including treatment of opiate-dependent people during the difficult withdrawal stages (Substance Abuse and Mental Health Services Administration [SAMHSA] 2006). Clonidine is not addictive and does not cause euphoria, but it does block cravings for drugs. In contrast to some treatments, no special licensing is required to dispense this medication.

Antabuse, whose generic name is disulfiram, is a drug used for treating alcoholics. This drug causes nausea, vomiting, flushing, and anxiety if an individual consumes alcohol while taking the drug (SAMHSA 2007). Thus, this drug is perceived as a deterrent drug.

Acamprosate is another medication used to treat individuals who are alcohol dependent. Approved in 2004 by the FDA, the drug reduces the symptoms of withdrawal, including anxiety and insomnia (SAMHSA 2005).

KEY TERMS

agonist
a type of substance that activates a receptor

antagonist
a drug that blocks another drug from producing its effects

▌Holding the Line Expanded Options for Treatment of Heroin Addiction

Until 2000, opiate dependence treatments such as methadone could be dispensed only in a very limited number of clinics that specialize in addiction treatment. As a consequence of the Drug Addiction Treatment Act of 2000 (see Chapter 3), the FDA announced approval of Subutex and Suboxone tablets for the treatment of opiate dependence by specially trained physicians. Accordingly, the drugs can be prescribed in an office setting and, therefore, can provide greater access to patients needing treatment.

Subutex and Suboxone treat opiate addiction by preventing symptoms of withdrawal from heroin and other opiates. Subutex contains only buprenorphine (a partial opioid agonist) and is intended for use at the beginning of treatment for drug abuse after medical detoxification. Suboxone contains both buprenorphine and the opiate antagonist naloxone, and is intended to be used in maintenance treatment of opiate addiction. Naloxone has limited effects if administered sublingually, but is effective as an antagonist if administered intravenously. It has been added to Suboxone to guard against intravenous abuse of buprenorphine by individuals who are physically dependent on opiates.

Discussion Questions

1. Discuss the need to assess addiction severity and readiness to change.

2. List several principles that characterize effective addiction treatment.

3. Describe Alcoholics Anonymous and its approach to assisting individuals addicted to alcohol.

4. Describe several therapeutic strategies to treat addiction.

5. Describe the therapeutic community approach to treating substance abuse.

6. Describe three pharmacological strategies to treat opioid dependence.

Summary

1 Individuals who are addicted to drugs come from all walks of life. It is important that treatment providers determine the severity of their addiction as well as the readiness of an individual to change his or her behavior.

2 The process of determining addiction severity can be accomplished in many ways, including the administration of standardized questionnaires such as the Addiction Severity Index (ASI). The ASI provides information that can be used to identify and prioritize which problem domains are the most critical and require immediate attention.

3 It is important to assess a person's readiness to change his or her abuse behavior, as this can help providers select the best treatment plan to address a client's needs. This may help prevent the individual who is receiving treatment from rejecting all or parts of the treatment plan.

4 One of the earliest real alcoholism recovery efforts was Alcoholics Anonymous (AA). Programs modeled on AA, known as twelve-step fellowships, are major routes to recovery.

5 There are numerous approaches to drug addiction treatment, including outpatient and residential treatment. Medical detoxification is not a treatment per se, but rather a precursor to treatment.

6 Relapse prevention is a cognitive-behavioral approach based on the theory that learning processes play a critical role in the development of maladaptive behavioral patterns. According to this approach, to overcome addiction, patients must learn to identify and correct problematic behaviors.

7 Motivational enhancement therapy is a client-centered counseling approach for initiating behavior change by helping clients to resolve ambivalence about engaging in treatment and discontinuing drug use.

8 A major approach to heroin and other opiate addiction has involved the provision of methadone, a synthetic opiate.

References

Al-Anon. *Al-Anon's Favorite Forum Editorials.* New York: Al-Anon Family Group Headquarters, 1970.

Alcoholics Anonymous. "The Twelve Steps of Alcoholics Anonymous" (2007). Available http://www.aa.org/en_services_for_members.cfm?PageID=98&SubPage=117.

Archer, S. "Historical Perspective on the Chemistry and Development of Naltrexone." In *Narcotic Antagonists: Naltrexone Pharmaco-Chemistry and Sustained-Release Preparations*, edited by R. E. Willette and G. Barnett. NIDA Research Monograph 28. Washington, DC: National Institute on Drug Abuse, 1981.

DiClemente, C. C., and J. O. Prochaska. "Toward a Comprehensive, Transtheoretical Model of Change." In *Treating Addictive Behaviors: Processes of Change*, edited by W. R. Miller and N. Heather. New York: Plenum Press, 1998.

McLellan, A. T., H. Kushner D. Metzger, R. Peters, I. Smith, G. Grissom, et al. "The Fifth Edition of the Addiction Severity Index." *Journal of Substance Abuse Treatment* 9 (1992): 199–213.

McLellan, A. T., L. Luborsky, G. E. Woody, and C. P. O'Brien. "An Improved Diagnostic Evaluation Instrument for Substance Abuse Patients. The Addiction Severity Index." *Journal of Nervous and Mental Disease* 168 (1980): 26–33.

McLellan, A. T., L. Luborsky, J. Cacciola, J. Griffith, F. Evans, H. L. Barr, et al. "New Data from the Addiction Severity Index. Reliability and Validity in Three Centers." *Journal of Nervous and Mental Disease* 173 (1985), 412–423.

National Institute on Drug Abuse (NIDA). *Principles of Drug Addiction Treatment.* National Institutes of Health Publication No. 99-4180, October 1999.

National Institute on Drug Abuse (NIDA). Research Report — Therapeutic Community, 2002. Available www.drugabuse.gov/ResearchReports/Therapeutic/default.html.

National Institute on Drug Addiction (NIDA). "InfoFacts: Treatment Approaches for Drug Addiction" (2006a). Available http://www.drugabuse.gov/infofacts/treatmeth.html.

National Institute on Drug Addiction (NIDA). "International Program, Methadone Research Web Guide," (December 2006b). Available http://international.drugabuse.gov/methadone/methadone_webguide/toc.html.

National Institute on Drug Addiction (NIDA). "Understanding Drug Abuse and Addiction: What Science Says" (2006c). Available http://www.drugabuse.gov/pubs/teaching/Teaching3/Teaching5.html.

Palfai, T., and H. Jankiewicz. *Drugs and Human Behavior.* Dubuque, IA: William C. Brown, 1991.

Rudy, D. "Perspectives on Alcoholism: Lessons from Alcoholics and Alcohologists." In *Drug Use in America: Social, Cultural, and Political Perspectives*, edited by P. J. Venturelli, 23–29. Boston, MA: Jones and Bartlett, 1994.

Substance Abuse and Mental Health Services Administration (SAMHSA). *Quick Click for Clinicians, Detoxification and Substance Abuse Treatment.* DHHS Publication No. (SMA) 06-4225, 2006.

Substance Abuse and Mental Health Services Administration (SAMHSA). What Is Substance Abuse Treatment? DHHS Publication No. (SMA) 07-4126. 2007.

Substance Abuse and Mental Health Services Administration (SAMHSA). *Substance Abuse Treatment Advisory, Acamprosate: A New Medication of Alcohol Use Disorders.* DHHS Publication No. (SMA) 05-4114. 2005.

Stilen, P., D. Carise, N. Roget, and A. Wendler. *Treatment Planning M.A.T.R.S. Utilizing the Addiction Severity Index (ASI) to Make Required Data Collection Useful.* Kansas City, MO: Mid-America Addiction Technology Transfer Center in residence at the University of Missouri-Kansas City, 2007.

APPENDIX A

Federal Agencies with Drug Abuse Missions

Drug Enforcement Administration (DEA)

Because of the unique problems of drug abuse in 1930, Congress authorized the establishment of the Bureau of Narcotics in the Treasury Department to administer the relevant laws. This agency remained in the Treasury Department until 1968, when it became part of a new group in the Justice Department, the Bureau of Narcotics and Dangerous Drugs. Harry Anslinger served as head of the bureau for over 30 years, from its creation until his retirement in 1962. Anslinger was an agent during Prohibition, and later, as head of the bureau, he played an important role in getting marijuana outlawed by the federal government. In 1973, the Bureau of Narcotics and Dangerous Drugs became the Drug Enforcement Administration (DEA). Today, the DEA has the responsibility of infiltrating and breaking up illegal drug traffic in the United States, as well as controlling the use of scheduled substances.

The Substance Abuse and Mental Health Services Administration (SAMHSA)

With passage of the ADAMHA Reorganization Act of 1992, the services programs of NIDA, NIAAA, and NIMH were incorporated into the newly created SAMHSA. This agency was given the lead responsibility for prevention and treatment of addictive and mental health problems and disorders. Its overall mission is to reduce the incidence and prevalence of substance abuse and mental disorders by ensuring the best thera-peutic use of scientific knowledge and improving access to high-quality, effective programs (Bush 1992).

State Regulations

There have always been questions regarding the relative responsibilities of state versus federal laws and their respective regulatory agencies. In general, the U.S. form of government has allowed local control to take precedence over national control. Because of this historic attitude, states were the first to pass laws to regulate the abuse or misuse of drugs. Federal laws developed later, after the federal government gained greater jurisdiction over the well-being and lives of the citizens and it became apparent that, due to interstate trafficking, national drug abuse problems could not be effectively dealt with on a state-by-state basis. Some early state laws banned the use of smoking opium, regulated the sale of various psychoactive drug substances, and, in a few instances, set up treatment programs. However, these early legislative actions made no effort to *prevent* drug abuse. Drug abuse was controlled to a great extent by social pressure rather than by law. It was considered morally wrong to be an alcoholic or an addict to opium or some other drug.

The drug laws varied considerably from state to state in 1932, so the National Conference of Commissioners on Uniform State Laws set up the Uniform Narcotic Drug Act (UNDA), which was later adopted by nearly all states. The UNDA provided for the control of possession, use, and distribution of opiates and cocaine. In 1942, marijuana was included under this act because it was classified as a narcotic.

In 1967, the Food and Drug Administration proposed the Model Drug Abuse Control Act and urged the states to adopt it on a uniform basis. This law extended controls over depressant, stimulant, and hallucinogenic drugs, similar to the 1965 federal law. Many states set up laws based on this model.

The federal Controlled Substances Act of 1970 stimulated the National Conference of Commissioners to propose a new Uniform Controlled Substances Act (UCSA). The UCSA permits enactment of a single state law regulating the illicit possession, use, manufacture, and dispensing of controlled psychoactive substances. At this time, most states have enacted the UCSA or modifications of it.

Today, state law enforcement of drug statutes does not always reflect federal regulations, although for the most part, the two statutory levels are harmonious. For example, marijuana has tentatively been approved for medicinal use in California and Arizona but is considered a Schedule I substance by federal regulatory agencies (as of this writing).

Reference

Bush, G. "Statement on Signing the ADAMHA Reorganization Act," 1992. Available www.presidency.ucsb.edu/ws/index.php?pid=21218.

APPENDIX B

Drugs of Use and Abuse

The table that follows provides detailed information about the drugs listed. Note that the heading *CSA Schedules* refers to categorization under the Controlled Substances Act (CSA).

The roman numeral(s) to the right of each drug name specifies each as a Schedule I, II, III, IV, or V drug. See Chapter 3 for more information on scheduling.

DRUGS	CSA SCHEDULES	TRADE OR OTHER NAMES	MEDICAL USES	DEPENDENCE	
				PHYSICAL	PSYCHOLOGICAL
Narcotics					
Heroin	Substance I	Diamorphine, horse, smack, black tar, chiva, negra, H. stuff, junk, Al Capone, antifreeze, brown sugar, hard candy	None in U.S., analgesic, antitussive	High	High
Morphine	Substance II	MS-Contin, Roxanol, Oramorph SR, MSIR, God's drug, Mister Blue, morpho, unkie	Analgesic	High	High
Hydrocodone	Substance II, Product III, V	Hydrocodone w/ acetaminophen, Vicodin, Vicoprofen, Tussionex, Lortab,	Analgesic, antitussive	High	High
Hydromorphone	Substance II	Dilaudid, little D, lords	Analgesic	High	High
Oxycodone	Substance II	Roxicet, oxycodone w/acetaminophen, OxyContin, Endocet, Percocet, Percodan	Analgesic	High	High
Codeine	Substance II, Product III, V	Acetaminophen, guaifenesin, or promethazine w/ codeine; Fiorinal, Fioricet, or Tylenol w/ codeine, coties, school boy	Analgesic, antitussive	Moderate	Moderate
Other narcotics	Substance II, III, IV	Fentanyl, Demerol, methadone, Darvon, Stadol, Talwin, Paregoric, Buprenex, T. and Blue's, designer drugs (fentanyl derivatives), China white, gravy	Analgesic, antidiarrheal, antitussive	High-low	High-low
Depressants					
Gamma hydroxybutyric acid	Substance I, Product III	GHB, liquid Ecstasy, liquid X, sodium oxybate, Xytem	None in U.S., anesthetic	Moderate	Moderate

TOLERANCE	DURATION (HOURS)	USUAL METHOD	POSSIBLE EFFECTS	EFFECTS OF OVERDOSE	WITHDRAWAL SYNDROME
Yes	3–4	Injected, snorted, smoked	Euphoria, drowsiness, respiratory depression, constricted pupils, nausea	Slow and shallow breathing, clammy skin, convulsions, coma, possible death	Watery eyes, runny nose, yawning, loss of appetite, irritability, tremors, panic, cramps, nausea, chills, sweating
Yes	3–12	Oral, injected			
Yes	3–6	Oral			
Yes	3–4	Oral, injected			
Yes	3–12	Oral			
Yes	3–4	Oral, injected			
Yes	Variable	Oral, injected, snorted, smoked			
Yes	3–6	Oral	Slurred speech, disorientation, drunken behavior without odor of alcohol, impaired memory of events, interacts with alcohol	Shallow respiration, clammy skin, dilated pupils, weak and rapid pulse, coma, possible death	Anxiety, insomnia, tremors, delirium, convulsions, possible death

(continued)

DRUGS	CSA SCHEDULES	TRADE OR OTHER NAMES	MEDICAL USES	DEPENDENCE	
				PHYSICAL	PSYCHOLOGICAL
Depressants (continued)					
Benzodiazepines	Substance IV	Valium, Xanax, Halcion, Ativan, Restoril, Rohypnol, (roofies, R-2), Klonopin, downers, goof balls, sleeping pills, candy	Antianxiety, sedative, anticonvulsant, hypnotic, muscle relaxant	Moderate	Moderate
Other depressants	Substance I, II, III, IV	Ambien, Sonata, Meprobamate, chloral hydrate, barbiturates, methaqualone (Quaalude), tranquilizers, muscle relaxants, sleeping pills	Antianxiety, sedative, hypnotic	Moderate	Moderate
Stimulants					
Cocaine	Substance II	Coke, flake, snow, crack, coca, blanca, perico, nieve, soda, bump, toot, C, candy, nose candy	Local anesthetic	Possible	High
Amphetamine/ methamphetamine	Substance II	Crank, ice, cristal, krystal meth, speed, Adderall, Dexedrine, Desoxyn, pep pills, bennies, uppers, truck drivers, dexies, black beauties, sparklers, beens	Attention deficit/ hyperactivity disorder, narcolepsy, weight control	Possible	High
Methylphenidate	Substance II	Ritalin (illy's), Concerta, Focalin, Metadate, speed, meth, crystal, crank, go fast	Attention deficit/ hyperactivity disorder	Possible	High
Other stimulants	Substance III, IV	Adipex P, Ionamin, Prelu-2, Didrex, Provigil	Vasoconstriction	Possible	Moderate
Hallinogens					
MDMA and analogs	Substance I	Ecstasy, XTC, Adam, MDA (love drug), MDEA (Eve), MBDB	None	None	Moderate
LSD	Substance I	Acid, microdot, sunshine, boomers, blue chairs, Loony Toons, pane, cubes	None	None	Unknown

TOLERANCE	DURATION (HOURS)	USUAL METHOD	POSSIBLE EFFECTS	EFFECTS OF OVERDOSE	WITHDRAWAL SYNDROME
Yes	1–8	Oral, injected			
Yes	2–6	Oral			
Yes	1–2	Snorted, smoked injected	Increased alertness, excitation, euphoria. increased pulse rate and blood pressure, insomnia, loss of appetite	Agitation, increased body temperature, hallucinations, convulsions, possible death	Apathy, long periods of sleep, irritability, depression, disorientation
Yes	2–4	Oral, injected, smoked			
Yes	2–4	Oral, injected, snorted, smoked			
Yes	2–4	Oral			
Yes	4–6	Oral snorted smoked	Heightened senses, teeth grinding, dehydration	Increased body temperature, electrolyte imbalance, cardiac arrest	Muscle aches, drowsiness, depression, acne
Yes	8–12	Oral	Illusions and hallucinations, altered perception of time and distance	(LSD) Longer, more intense trip episodes	None

(continued)

DRUGS	CSA SCHEDULES	TRADE OR OTHER NAMES	MEDICAL USES	DEPENDENCE PHYSICAL	PSYCHOLOGICAL
Hallucinogens (continued)					
Phencyclidine and analogs	Substance I, II, III	PCP, angel dust, hog, loveboat, ketamine (special K), PCE, PCPy, TCP, peace pill	Anesthetic (ketamine)	Possible	High
Other hallucinogens	Substance I	Psilocybe mushrooms, mescaline, peyote cactus, ayahausca, DMT, dextromethorphan* (DXM), sacred mushrooms, magic mushrooms, mushrooms, ying yang, strawberry fields	None	None	None
Cannabis					
Marijuana	Substance I	Pot, grass, sinsemilla, blunts, mota, yerba, grifa, 420, airhead (marijuana user), bud, catnip, reefer, roach, joint, weed, loco weed, Mary Jane	None	Unknown	Moderate
Tetrahydro-cannabinol	Substance I, Product III	THC, Marinol	Antinauseant, appetite stimulant	Yes	Moderate
Hashish and hashish oil	Substance I	Hash, hash oil	None	Unknown	Moderate
Anabolic Steroids					
Testosterone	Substance III	Depo Testosterone, Sustanon, sten, cypt	Hypogonadism	Unknown	Unknown
Other anabolic steroids	Substance III	Parabolan, Winstrol, Equipose, Anadrol, Dianabol, Primabolin-Depo, D-Ball	Anemia, breast cancer	Unknown	Yes
Inhalants					
Amyl and butyl nitrate		Pearls, poppers, rush locker room	Angina (amyl)	Unknown	Unknown

TOLERANCE	DURATION (HOURS)	USUAL METHOD	POSSIBLE EFFECTS	EFFECTS OF OVERDOSE	WITHDRAWAL SYNDROME
Yes	1–12	Smoked, oral, injected, snorted		Unable to direct movement, feel pain, or remember	Drug-seeking behavior *Not regulated
Possible	4–8	Oral			
Yes	2–4	Smoked, oral	Euphoria, relaxed inhibitions, increased appetite, disorientation	Fatigue, paranoia, possible psychosis	Occasional reports of insomnia, hyperactivity, decreased appetite
Yes	2–4	Smoked, oral			
Yes	2–4	Smoked oral			
Unknown	14–28 days	Injected	Virilization, edema, testicular atrophy, gynecomastia, acne, aggressive behavior	Unknown	Possible depression
Unknown	Variable	Oral, injected			
No	1	Inhaled	Flushing, hypotension, headache	Methemoglobinemia	Agitation

(continued)

DRUGS	CSA SCHEDULES	TRADE OR OTHER NAMES	MEDICAL USES	DEPENDENCE PHYSICAL	PSYCHOLOGICAL
Inhalants (continued)					
Nitrous oxide		Laughing gas, balloons, whippets	Anesthetic	Unknown	Low
Other inhalants		Adhesives, spray paint, hair spray, dry cleaning fluid, spot remover, lighter fluid, air blast, moon gas, sniffing, glue sniffing	None	Unknown	High
Alcohol		Beer, wine, liquor	None	High	High

*Not designated as a narcotic under Controlled Substances Act

Source: Adapted from Drug Enforcement Administration, U.S. Department of Justice. *Drugs of Abuse* (2004). Available http://www.usdoj.gov/dea/pubs/abuse/chart.htm.

TOLERANCE	DURATION (HOURS)	USUAL METHOD	POSSIBLE EFFECTS	EFFECTS OF OVERDOSE	WITHDRAWAL SYNDROME
No	0.5	Inhaled	Impaired memory, slurred speech, drunken behavior, slow onset vitamin deficiency, organ damage	Vomiting, respiratory depression, loss of consciousness, possible death	Trembling, anxiety, insomnia, vitamin deficiency, confusion, hallucinations, convulsions
No	0.5–2	Inhaled			
Yes	1–3	Oral			

GLOSSARY

β-adrenergic stimulants
drugs that stimulate a subtype of adrenaline and noradrenaline receptors

acquaintance and date rape
unplanned and unwanted forced sexual attack from a friend or a date partner

acute
immediate or short-term effects after taking a single drug dose

acute alcohol withdrawal syndrome
symptoms that occur when an individual who is addicted to alcohol does not maintain his or her usual blood alcohol level

addiction
generally refers to the psychological attachment to a drug(s); addiction to "harder" drugs such as heroin results in both psychological and physical attachment to the chemical properties of the drug, with the resulting satisfaction (reward) derived from using the drug in question

"addiction to pleasure" theory
the theory assuming that it is biologically normal to continue a pleasure stimulus once begun

additive interactions
effects created when drugs are similar and actions are added together

adulterated
contaminating substances are mixed in to dilute the drugs

agonist
a type of substance that activates a receptor

agonistic
a type of substance that activates a receptor

alcohol abuse
uncontrollable drinking that leads to alcohol craving, loss of control, and physical dependence but with less prominent characteristics than found in alcoholism

alcohol dehydrogenase
principal enzyme that metabolizes ethanol

alcoholic cardiomyopathy
congestive heart failure due to the replacement of heart muscle with fat and fiber

alcoholic hepatitis
the second stage of alcohol-induced liver disease in which chronic inflammation occurs; reversible if alcoholic consumption ceases

alcoholism
a state of physical and psychological addiction to ethanol, a psychoactive substance

altered perceptions
changes in the interpretation of stimuli resulting from marijuana

alternatives approach
an approach emphasizing the exploration of positive alternatives to drug abuse, based on replacing the pleasurable feelings gained from drug abuse with involvement in social and educational activities

amnesiac
causing the loss of memory

amotivational syndrome
the assertion by some drug researchers that heavy use of marijuana causes a lack of motivation in achieving goal-directed behavior; a belief that heavy use of marijuana causes a lack of motivation and reduced productivity

anabolic steroids
compounds chemically like the steroids that stimulate production of tissue mass; androgen-like drugs that can increase muscle mass and strength

analgesics
drugs that relieve pain without affecting consciousness; drugs that relieve pain while allowing consciousness

analogs
drugs with similar structures

anandamide
possible neurotransmitter acting at the marijuana (cannabinoid) receptor

androgens
male sex hormones; naturally occurring male hormones, such as testosterone

anesthesia
a state characterized by loss of sensation or consciousness

anesthetic
a drug that blocks sensitivity to pain

angina pectoris
severe chest pain usually caused by a deficiency of blood to the heart muscle

anorexiants
drugs that suppress appetite for food; drugs that suppress the activity of the brain's appetite center, causing reduced food intake

ANS
the autonomic nervous system; controls the unconscious functions of the body

antagonist
a drug that blocks another drug from producing its effects

antagonistic
a type of substance that blocks a receptor

antagonistic interactions
effects created when drugs cancel one another

anticholinergic
agents that antagonize the effects of acetylcholine

antihistamines
drugs that often cause CNS depression, are used to treat allergies, and are often included in over-the-counter sleep aids

anti-inflammatory
relieves symptoms of inflammation

antipyretics
drugs that reduce fevers

antitussive
drug that blocks coughing

anxiolytic
drug that relieves anxiety

AOD
alcohol and other drugs

aphrodisiac
a compound that is believed to be the cause of sexual arousal

array
use of other drugs while taking anabolic steroids to avoid possible side effects

arrhythmia
an irregular heartbeat

ATLAS program
Adolescents Training and Learning to Avoid Steroids (ATLAS) is an anabolic abuse prevention educational program that empowers student athletes to make the right choices about steroid use

ATOD
alcohol, tobacco, and other drugs

attitude change model or affective education model
assumes that people use drugs because of lack of self-esteem

axons
an extension of the neuronal cell body along which electrochemical signals travel

the BACCHUS Network
a national and international association of college and university peer education programs focused on alcohol abuse prevention and other related student health and safety issues

barbiturates
potent CNS depressants, usually not preferred because of their narrow margin of safety

behavioral stereotypy
meaningless repetition of a single activity

behavioral tolerance
compensation for motor impairments through behavioral pattern modification by chronic alcohol users

benzodiazepines
the most popular and safest CNS depressants in use today

binge
similar to a run, but usually of shorter duration

binge use (binge drinking)
five or more drinks on the same occasion (i.e., at the same time or within a couple of hours of each other) on at least 1 day in the past 30 days; includes heavy use

biotransformation
process of changing the chemical properties of a drug, usually by metabolism

blood alcohol concentration (BAC)
concentration of alcohol found in the blood, often expressed as a percentage

blood–brain barrier
selective filtering between the cerebral blood vessels and the brain

bootlegging
making, distributing, and selling alcoholic beverages during the Prohibition era

bronchodilators
drugs that widen air passages

caffeinism
symptoms caused by taking high chronic doses of caffeine

Cannabis sativa
biological species name for the variety of hemp plant known as *marijuana*

catatonia
a condition of physical rigidity, excitement, and stupor

catecholamines
a class of biochemical compounds including the transmitters norepinephrine, epinephrine, and dopamine

central nervous system
one of the major divisions of the nervous system, composed of the brain and the spinal cord

characterological or personality predisposition model
the view of chemical dependency as a symptom of problems in the development or operation of the system of needs, motives, and attitudes within the individual

chewing tobacco
tobacco leaves shredded and twisted into strands for chewing purposes

chronic
long-term effects, usually after taking multiple drug doses

cirrhosis
scarring of the liver and formation of fibrous tissues; results from alcohol abuse; irreversible

closed meetings
meetings to which only alcoholics having a serious desire to completely stop drinking are invited

club drug
drug used at all-night raves, parties, dance clubs, and bars to enhance sensory experiences; drugs used by young adults at dance parties such as raves; a new class of illicit drugs used on college campuses, at bars, in night clubs, and at raves where drinking and dancing occur; club drugs include MDMA (Ecstasy), GHB, Rohypnol, ketamine, methamphetamine, and LSD

CNS
the central nervous system, including the brain and spinal cord

cocaine babies
infants born to women who used cocaine during their pregnancy

codependency
behavior displayed by either addicted or nonaddicted family members (codependents) who identify with the alcohol addict and cover-up the excessive drinking behavior, allowing it to continue and letting it affect the codependent's life

compulsive users
second category of drug use, typified by an insatiable attraction followed by a psychological dependence onto drugs

congestion rebound
withdrawal from excessive use of a decongestant, resulting in congestion

congestive heart failure
heart is unable to pump sufficient blood for the body's needs

control theory
theory that emphasizes when people are left without bonds to other groups (peers, family, social groups), they generally have a tendency to deviate from upheld values and attitudes

conventional behavior
behavior largely dictated by custom and tradition, which is often disrupted by the forces of rapid technological change

crack
already processed and inexpensive "freebased" cocaine, ready for smoking

crack babies
infants born to women who use crack cocaine during pregnancy

cross-dependence
dependence on a drug can be relieved by other similar drugs

cross-tolerance
development of tolerance to one drug causes tolerance to related drugs

cumulative effect
buildup of a drug in the body after multiple doses taken at short intervals

current alcohol use (current drinkers)
at least one drink in the past 30 days; can include binge and heavy use

cycling
use of different types of steroids singly, but in sequence

DARE (Drug Abuse Resistance Education)
drug education program presented in elementary and junior high schools nationwide by police officers

DEA
Drug Enforcement Administration, the principal federal agency responsible for enforcing U.S. drug laws

delirium tremens
the DTs; the most severe, even life-threatening form of alcohol withdrawal, involving hallucinations, delirium, and fever

demand reduction
attempts to decrease individuals' tendencies to use drugs, often aimed at youth, with emphasis on reformulating values and behaviors

dendrites
short branches of neurons that receive transmitter signals

dependence
physiological and psychological changes or adaptations that occur in response to the frequent administration of a drug

dependency phase
synonym for addiction

designer drugs/synthetic drugs or synthetic opioids
new drugs that are developed by people intending to circumvent the illegality of a drug by modifying a drug into a new compound; Ecstasy is an example

detoxification
elimination of a toxic substance, such as a drug, and its effects from the body

diabetes mellitus
disease caused by elevated blood sugar due to insufficient insulin

differential association
process by which individuals become socialized into the perceptions and values of a group

differential reinforcement
ratio between reinforcers, both favorable and disfavorable, for sustaining drug use behavior

disease model
the belief that people abuse alcohol because of some biologically caused condition

disinhibition
loss of conditioned reflexes due to depression of inhibitory centers of the brain

disinhibitor
a psychoactive chemical that depresses thought and judgment functions in the cerebral cortex, which has the effect of allowing relatively unrestrained behavior (as in alcohol inebriation)

distillation
heating fermented mixtures of cereal grains or fruits in a still to evaporate and be trapped as purified alcohol

diuretic
a drug or substance that increases the production of urine

dopamine
the brain transmitter believed to mediate the rewarding aspects of most drugs of abuse

doping
the use of performance-enhancing drugs to increase athletic ability

dose-response
correlation between the amount of a drug given and its effects

"double wall" of encapsulation
an adaption to pain and avoidance of reality, in which the individual withdraws emotionally and further anesthetizes himself or herself by chemical means

drug courts
a process that integrates substance abuse treatment, incentives, and sanctions and places nonviolent, drug-involved defendants in judicially supervised rehabilitation programs; court designed to focus on treatment programs and options in place of punishment for drug offenses

drug interaction
presence of one drug alters the action of another drug

drug prevention
preventing or decreasing health problems, which includes social and personal problems caused by drug dependency

drug testing
urine, blood screening, or hair analysis used to identify those who may be using drugs

drug(s)
any substance that modifies (either by enhancing, inhibiting, or distorting) mind and/or body functioning

drunken comportment
behavior exhibited while under the direct influence of alcohol; determined by the norms and expectations of a particular culture

dysphoric
characterized by unpleasant mental effects; the opposite of euphoric

ecological or person-in-environment model
stresses that changes in the environment change people's attitudes about drugs

edema
swollen tissue due to an accumulation of fluid

employee assistance programs (EAPs)
drug assistance programs for drug-dependent employees

enablers
those close to the alcohol addict who deny or make excuses for enabling the excessive drinking

endocrine system
relating to hormones, their functions, and sources

endorphins
neurotransmitters that have narcotic-like effects

entactogens
drugs that enhance the sensation and pleasure of touching

environmental tobacco smoke
the mixture of predominantly sidestream smoke and exhaled mainstream smoke that is inhaled by the passive smoker

epilepsy
disease consisting of spontaneous, repetitive seizures

equal-opportunity affliction
refers to the use of drugs, stressing that drug use cuts across all members of society regardless of income, education, occupation, social class, and age

ergogenic

drugs that enhance athletic performance

ergotism

poisoning by toxic substances from the ergot fungus *Claviceps purpurea*

ethanol

the pharmacological term for alcohol; consumable type of alcohol that is the psychoactive ingredient in alcoholic beverages; often called *grain alcohol*

ethylene glycol

alcohol used as antifreeze

euphorigenic

having the ability to cause feelings of pleasure and well-being

expectorants

substances that stimulate mucus secretion and diminish mucous viscosity

experimenters

first category of drug use, typified as being in the initial stages of drug use; these people often use drugs for recreational purposes

fermentation

biochemical process through which yeast converts sugar to alcohol

fetal alcohol syndrome (FAS)

a condition affecting children born to alcohol-consuming mothers that is characterized by facial deformities, growth deficiency, and mental retardation

flashbacks

recurrences of earlier drug-induced sensory experiences in the absence of the drug

floaters or chippers

third category of drug use; these users vacillate between the need for pleasure seeking and the desire to relieve moderate to serious psychological problems. This category of drug use have two major characteristics: (1) a general focus mostly on using other people's drugs (often without maintaining a personal supply of the drug) and (2) vacillation between the characteristics of chronic drug users and experimenter types

freebasing

conversion of cocaine into its alkaline form for smoking

gastritis

inflammation or irritation of the gut

gateway drugs

alcohol, tobacco, and marijuana—types of drugs that, when used excessively, may lead to using other and often more addictive drugs such as hallucinogens, cocaine, heroin, or crack; drug whose use leads to the use of other drugs; alcohol, cigarettes, and marijuana are considered gateway drugs

generic

official, nonpatented, nonproprietary name of a drug

genetic and biophysiological theories

explanations of addiction in terms of genetic brain dysfunction and biochemical patterns

genogram

a family therapy technique that records information about behavior and relationships on a type of family tree to elucidate persistent patterns of dysfunctional behavior

glaucoma

potentially blinding eye disease causing continual and increasing intraocular pressure

habituation

repeating certain patterns of behavior until they become established or habitual

half-life

time required for the body to eliminate and/or metabolize half of a drug dose

hallucinogens

substances that alter sensory processing in the brain, causing perceptual disturbances, changes in thought processing, and depersonalization

harm reduction model

a society-wide approach to drug use and/or abuse that focuses on reducing the harm experienced by the drug user and/or abuser as well as the harm to society

Harrison Act of 1914

the first legitimate effort by the U.S. government to regulate addicting substances

hashish

sticky resin from the female marijuana plant flowers, which has an average THC level of 3.6% but can contain as much as 28%

heavy use (heavy drinkers)

five or more drinks on the same occasion for each of 5 or more days in the past 30 days

hepatotoxic effect

a situation in which liver cells increase the production of fat, resulting in an enlarged liver

high

4 to 16 hours after drug use; includes feelings of energy and power

highly active antiretroviral therapy (HAART)

more recent types of medications used to treat HIV/AIDS-infected individuals

high-risk drug choices

developing values and attitudes that lead to using drugs both habitually and addictively

holistic self-awareness approach
emphasizes that nonmedical and often recreational drug use interferes with the healthy balance among the mind, the body, and the spirit

homeostasis
maintenance of internal stability; often biochemical in nature

hormones
chemical messengers released into the blood by glands; regulatory chemicals released by endocrine systems

human growth factor (HGF)
a hormone that stimulates normal growth

human growth hormone (HGH)
a "designer drug" synthetic version of HGF

hyperglycemia
elevated blood sugar

hyperpyrexia
elevated body temperature

hypertension
elevated blood pressure

hypnotics
CNS depressants used to induce drowsiness and encourage sleep

hypothyroidism
thyroid gland does not produce sufficient hormone

hypoxia
a state of oxygen deficiency

ice
a smokable form of methamphetamine

illicit drugs
illegal drugs such as marijuana, cocaine, and LSD

increased use phase
taking increasing quantities of the drug

information-only or awareness model
assumes that teaching about the harmful effects of drugs will change attitudes about use and abuse

inoculation
a method of abuse prevention that protects drug users by teaching them responsibility

insiders
people on the inside; those who either approve of and/or use drugs

insider's perspective
viewing a group or subculture from inside the group; seeing members as they perceive themselves

interdiction
the policy of cutting off or destroying supplies of illicit drugs

intergang
between members of *different* gangs

intragang
between members of the *same* gang

intramuscular (IM)
drug injection into a muscle

intravenous (IV)
drug injection into a vein

ischemia
tissue deprived of sufficient blood and oxygen

isopropyl alcohol
rubbing alcohol, sometimes used as an antiseptic

jimsonweed
a potent hallucinogenic plant

keratin layer
outermost protective layer of the skin

keratolytics
caustic agents that cause the keratin skin layer to peel

labeling theory
the theory emphasizing that other people's perceptions directly influence one's self-image

licit drugs
legalized drugs such as coffee, alcohol, and tobacco

low-risk drug choices
developing values and attitudes that lead to controlling the use of alcohol and drugs

mainline
to inject a drug of abuse intravenously

mainstream smoke
smoke drawn directly through the mouthpiece of a cigarette

margin of safety
range in dose between the amount of drug necessary to cause a therapeutic effect and that needed to create a toxic effect

Marinol
FDA-approved THC in capsule form (dronabinol)

master status
major status position in the eyes of others that clearly identifies an individual—for example, doctor, professor, alcoholic, heroin addict

MDMA
a type of illicit drug known as "Ecstasy" or "Adam" and having stimulant and hallucinogenic properties

mead
fermented honey often made into an alcoholic beverage

medical marijuana use
use of the THC in cannabis as a drug to calm or to relieve symptoms of an illness

meditation
a state of consciousness in which there is a constant level of awareness focusing on one object; for example, yoga and Zen Buddhism

mental set
the collection of psychological and environmental factors that influence an individual's response to drugs

metabolism
chemical alteration of drugs by body processes

metabolites
chemical products of metabolism

methyl alcohol
wood alcohol

Minnesota model
a major model in the treatment of alcohol and drug abuse, involving a month-long stay in an inpatient rehabilitation facility, a multidisciplinary treatment team, systematic assessment, and a formal treatment plan with long- and short-term goals

monoamine oxidase inhibitors (MAOIs)
drugs used to treat severe depression

moral model
the belief that people abuse alcohol because they choose to do so

munchies
hunger experienced while under the effects of marijuana

muscarinic
a receptor type activated by ACh; usually inhibitory

muscle dysmorphia
behavioral syndrome that causes men to have a distorted image of themselves, perceiving themselves as looking small and weak, even when they may be large and muscular; women with this condition think they look fat and flabby, even though they may actually be lean and muscular

mydriasis
pupil dilation

narcolepsy
a condition causing spontaneous and uncontrolled sleeping episodes

needle-exchange programs
publically funded programs that distribute new, uncontaminated needles to drug addicts in exchange for used injection needles in order to prevent the spread of HIV and hepatitis B and C.

neurons
specialized nerve cells that make up the nervous system and release neuron transmitters

neurotransmitters
the chemical messengers released by nervous (nerve) cells for communication with other cells; chemical messengers released by neurons

nicotine
a colorless, highly volatile liquid alkaloid

nicotinic
a receptor type activated by ACh; usually excitatory

NIDA
National Institute on Drug Abuse, the principal federal agency responsible for directing drug use–and abuse–related research

nonsteroidal anti-inflammatory drugs (NSAIDs)
anti-inflammatory drugs that do not have steroid properties

open meetings
meetings to which anyone having an interest in attending and witnessing is invited

opiate receptors
receptors activated by opioid narcotic drugs such as heroin and morphine

opioid
relating to the drugs that are derived from opium

oral hypoglycemics
drugs taken by mouth to treat type II diabetes

outsiders
people on the outside; those who do not approve of and/or use drugs

outsider's perspective
viewing a group or subculture from outside the group and viewing the group and its members as an observer; looking "in" at the members

over-the-counter (OTC)
drugs sold without a prescription

paradoxical effects
unexpected effects

passive smoking
nonsmoker's inhalation of tobacco smoke

patent medicines
the ingredients in these uncontrolled "medicines" were secret, often consisting of large amounts of colored water, alcohol, cocaine, or opiates

peptic ulcers
open sores that occur in the stomach or upper segment of the small intestine

personality disorders
a broad category of psychiatric disorders, formerly called "character disorders," that includes the antisocial personality disorder, borderline personality disorder, schizoid personality disorder, and others; these serious, ongoing impairments are difficult to treat

pharmacokinetics
the study of factors that influence the distribution and concentration of drugs in the body

phocomelia
a birth defect; impaired development of the arms, legs, or both

placebo effects
effects caused by suggestion and psychological factors independent of the pharmacological activity of a drug

plateau effect
maximum drug effect, regardless of dose

plateauing
developing tolerance to the effects of anabolic steroids

PNS
the peripheral nervous system, including neurons outside the CNS

polydrug use
the concurrent use of multiple drugs

posttraumatic stress disorder
a psychiatric syndrome in which an individual who has been exposed to a traumatic event or situation experiences persistent psychological stress that may manifest itself in a wide range of symptoms, including reexperiencing the trauma, numbing of general responsiveness, and hyperarousal

potency
amount of drug necessary to cause an effect

precursor chemicals
chemicals used to produce a drug

preoccupation phase
constant concern with the supply of the drug

primary deviance
any type of initial deviant behavior in which the perpetrator does not identify with the deviance

primary drug prevention programs
the very broad range of activities aimed at reducing the risk of drug use among nonusers and assuring continued nonuse

primary prevention
prevention of any drug use

proprietary
brand or trademark name that is registered with the U.S. Patent Office

protease inhibitors
a major breakthrough class of drugs used to treat HIV-infected individuals

protective factors
factors associated with potential for drug abuse such as preventing the self control, parental monitoring, academic competence, anti-drug use policies, and strong neighborhood attachment

pseudointoxicated
acting drunk even before alcohol has had a chance to cause its effects

psychedelics
substances that expand or heighten perception and consciousness

psychoactive
drugs that affect mood or alter the state of consciousness

psychoactive drugs (substances)
drug compounds (substances) that affect the central nervous system and alter consciousness and/or perceptions

psychoactive effects
how drug substances alter and affect the brain's mental functions

psychoanalysis
a theory of personality and method of psychotherapy originated by Sigmund Freud, focused on unconscious forces and conflicts and a series of psychosexual stages

psychodrama
a family therapy system developed by Jacques Moreno in which significant interpersonal and intrapersonal issues are enacted in a focused setting using dramatic techniques

psychological dependence
dependence that results because a drug produces pleasant mental effects

psychotogenic
substances that initiate psychotic behavior

psychotomimetic
substances that cause psychosis-like symptoms

pyramiding
moving from a low daily dose at the beginning of the cycle to a higher dose, then reducing use toward the end of the cycle

rebound effect
form of withdrawal; paradoxical effects that occur when a drug has been eliminated from the body

receptors
special proteins in a membrane that are activated by natural substances or drugs to alter cell function

relapsing syndrome
returning to the use of alcohol after quitting

relief phase
satisfaction derived from escaping negative feelings in using the drug

REM sleep
the restive phase of sleep associated with dreaming

retrospective interpretation
social psychological process of redefining a person in light of a major status position—for example, homosexual, physician, professor, alcoholic, convicted felon, or mental patient

reverse tolerance
enhanced response to a given drug dose; opposite of tolerance

Reye's syndrome
potentially fatal complication of colds, flu, or chicken pox in children

risk factors
drug prevention is aimed at reducing risk factors, such as early aggressive behavior, lack of parental supervision, the lure of gang membership, drug availability, and poverty

Rohypnol
the "date rape drug," used on many college campuses

role playing
a therapeutic technique in which group members play assigned parts to elicit emotional reactions

run
intense use of a stimulant, consisting of multiple administrations over a period of days

rush
initial pleasure after amphetamine use that includes racing heartbeat and elevated blood pressure

salicylates
aspirin-like drugs

scare tactic approach
drug prevention information based on emphasizing the extreme negative effects of drug use—scaring the audience of potential and current drug users/abusers into not using drugs

secondary deviance
any type of deviant behavior in which the perpetrator identifies with the deviance

secondary drug prevention programs
targeting at-risk groups, experimenters, and early abuse populations to reverse the progression of abusive behaviors, similar to "early intervention"

secondary prevention
preventing drug use from either casual or recreational to drug dependence

secondhand smoke
smoke released into the air from a lighted cigarette, cigar, or pipe tip and exhaled mainstream smoke

sedatives
CNS depressants used to relieve anxiety, fear, and apprehension

sensation-seeking individuals
types of people who characteristically are continually seeking new or novel thrills in their experiences

set and setting
set refers to the individual's expectation of what a drug will do to his or her personality; *setting* is the physical and social environments where the drug is consumed

side effects
unintended drug responses

sinsemilla
meaning without seeds, this marijuana is made from the buds and flowering tops of female plants and is one of the most potent types

snuff
finely ground smokeless tobacco that can be moist or dry

snuff dippers
placing a pinch of tobacco between the gums and the cheek

social influence theories
social psychological theories that view a person's day-to-day social relations as a primary cause for drug use

social influences model
assumes that drug users lack resistance skills

social learning theory
the theory that places emphasis on how an individual learns patterns of behavior from the attitudes of others, society, and peers

social lubricant
belief that drinking (misconceived as safe) represses inhibitions, strengthens extroversion, and leads to increased sociability

socialization
the growth and development process responsible for learning how to become a responsible, functioning human being

sociobiological changes
the belief that biological forces (largely genes) have a direct influence on the root causes of social psychological behavior

speakeasies
places where alcoholic beverages were illegally sold during the Prohibition era

speed
an injectable methamphetamine used by drug addicts

speedballing
combining heroin and cocaine

speedballs
combinations of amphetamine or cocaine with an opioid narcotic, often heroin

SPF (sun protection factor) number
designation to indicate a product's ability to screen ultraviolet rays

stacking
use of several types of steroids at the same time

steroids
hormones related to the corticosteroids released from the adrenal cortex; potent hormones released from the adrenal glands

structural analogs
modifying the basic molecular skeleton of a compound to form a new molecular species; structural analogs are structurally related to the parent compound

structural influence theories
theories that view the structural organization of a society, peer group, or subculture as directly responsible for drug use

subculture
subgroup within the population whose members share similar values and patterns of related behaviors that differ from other subcultures and the larger population

subculture theory
explains drug use as a peer-generated activity

subcutaneous (SC)
drug injection beneath the skin

subjective euphoric effects
ongoing social and psychological experiences incurred while intoxicated with marijuana

sudden infant death syndrome (SIDS)
unexpected and unexplainable death that occurs while infants are sleeping

supply reduction
a drug reduction policy aimed at reducing the supply of illegal drugs and controlling other therapeutic drugs

switching policy
an FDA policy allowing the change of suitable prescription drugs to over-the-counter status

sympathomimetic
agents that mimic the effects of norepinephrine or epinephrine

synapse
site of communication between a message-sending neuron and its message-receiving target cell

synaptic cleft
a minute gap between the neuron and target cell, across which neurotransmitters travel

synergism
ability of one drug to enhance the effect of another; also called *potentiation*

synesthesia
a subjective sensation or image of a sense other than the one being stimulated, such as an auditory sensation caused by a visual stimulus

teetotalers
individuals who drink no alcoholic beverages whatsoever; a term in common usage in decades past

teratogenic
something that causes physical defects in the fetus

tertiary drug prevention programs
intervention at an advanced state of drug abuse; basically the same as drug abuse treatment

thalidomide
a sedative drug that, when used during pregnancy, can cause severe developmental damage to a fetus

therapeutic community
drug-free residential settings that use a hierarchical model with treatment stages that reflect increased levels of responsibility

threshold dose
minimum drug dose necessary to cause an effect

tobacco chewing
the absorption of nicotine through the mucous lining of the mouth

tolerance
changes in the body that decrease response to a drug even though the dose remains the same

toxicity
capacity of one drug to damage or cause adverse effects in the body

tricyclic antidepressants
most commonly used group of drugs to treat severe depression

tweaking
repeated administration of methamphetamine to maintain the high

type I diabetes
disease associated with complete loss of insulin-producing cells in the pancreas

type II diabetes
disease usually associated with obesity; does not involve a loss of insulin-producing cells

uppers
CNS stimulants

volatile
readily evaporated at low temperatures

Wernicke-Korsakoff's syndrome
psychotic condition connected with heavy alcohol use and associated vitamin deficiencies

withdrawal
unpleasant effects that occur when use of a drug is stopped

withdrawal phase
physical and/or psychological effects derived from not using the drug

withdrawal symptoms
psychological and physical symptoms that result when a drug is absent from the body; physical symptoms are generally present in cases of drug dependence to more addictive drugs such as heroin; physical and psychological symptoms of withdrawal include perspiration, nausea, boredom, anxiety, and muscle spasms

xanthines
the family of drugs that includes caffeine

INDEX

PHOTO CREDITS